Directions for accessing your
eBook and Digital Course Materials

Of the People
A History of the United States

VOLUME II: SINCE 1865, WITH SOURCES
FIFTH EDITION

Michael McGerr, Camilla Townsend,
Karen M. Dunak, Mark Summers,
Jan Ellen Lewis

Carefully scratch off the silver
coating to see your personal
redemption code.

D0761244   nk

61500621-CVNR3J7Y

Visit **www.oup.com/he/mcgerr5e**

Select the edition you are using and
the student resources for that edition.

Click the link to upgrade your access
to the student resources.

Follow the on-screen instructions.

Enter your personal
redemption code when prompted.

**This code can be used only
once and cannot be shared!**

If the code has been scratched
off when you receive it, the
code may not be valid. Once
the code has been scratched
off, this access card cannot be
returned to the publisher. You
may buy access at
www.oup.com/he/mcgerr5e

The code on this card is valid for
2 years from the date of first
purchase. Complete terms
and conditions are available at
learninglink.oup.com.

Access length: 6 months from
redemption of the code.

VIA YOUR SCHOOL'S LEARNING MANAGEMENT SYSTEM

Log in to your instructor's course.

When you click a link to a protected resource,
you will be prompted to register for access.

Follow the on-screen instructions.

Enter your personal
redemption code when prompted.

For assistance with code redemption
or registration, please contact customer
support at **learninglink.support@oup.com**.

OXFORD
UNIVERSITY PRESS

About the Cover

A self-described propagandist for civil rights, photojournalist Matt Herron (1931–2020) moved south with his family in the early 1960s and assembled a team of photographers to document the freedom struggle. In 1965, he captured an iconic image of the voting rights protests in Selma, Alabama. Against a gray, cloudy sky, a mostly male, African American column of marchers carries two American flags—at once a proclamation of loyalty and a demand for full US citizenship.

OF THE PEOPLE

OF THE PEOPLE

A History of the United States

WITH SOURCES

FIFTH EDITION

VOLUME II
Since 1865

Michael McGerr
Camilla Townsend
Karen M. Dunak
Mark Summers
Jan Ellen Lewis

New York | Oxford
Oxford Unviersity Press

Oxford University Press is a department of the University of Oxford.
It furthers the University's objective of excellence in research, scholarship,
and education by publishing worldwide. Oxford is a registered trademark of
Oxford University Press in the UK and certain other countries.

Published in the United States of America by Oxford University Press
198 Madison Avenue, New York, NY 10016, United States of America.

Library of Congress Cataloging-in-Publication Data

Names: McGerr, Michael E., author. | Townsend, Camilla, 1965- author. |
    Dunak, Karen M., author. | Summers, Mark (History professor), author. |
    Lewis, Jan, 1949-2018, author.
Title: Of the people : a history of the United States with sources /
    Michael McGerr, Camilla Townsend, Karen M. Dunak, Mark Summers, Jan
    Ellen Lewis.
Other titles: History of the United States with sources
Description: Fifth edition. | New York : Oxford University Press, [2022] |
    Includes bibliographical references and index. | Contents: Volume 1. To
    1877—Volume 2. Since 1865. | Summary: "A higher education history
    text for United States history courses"— Provided by publisher.
Identifiers: LCCN 2021006879 (print) | LCCN 2021006880 (ebook) | ISBN
    9780197585955 (v. 1 ; paperback) | ISBN 9780197585962 | ISBN
    9780197586150 (v. 2 ; paperback) | ISBN 9780197586167 | ISBN
    9780197585986 (v. 1 ; epub) | ISBN 9780197585979 (v. 1 ; pdf) | ISBN
    9780197586181 (v. 2 ; epub) | ISBN 9780197586174 (v. 2 ; pdf)
Subjects: LCSH: United States—History—Textbooks. | United
    States—History—Sources.
Classification: LCC E178.1 .M455 2022 (print) | LCC E178.1 (ebook) | DDC
    973—dc23
LC record available at https://lccn.loc.gov/2021006879
LC ebook record available at https://lccn.loc.gov/2021006880

9 8 7 6 5 4 3 2 1
Printed in Mexico by Quad/Mexico

Jan Ellen Lewis
1949–2018
Historian, Teacher, Friend

Brief Contents

Contents

CHAPTER 16

The Triumph of Industrial Capitalism,
1850–1890   522

CHAPTER 17

The Culture and Politics of Industrial America, 1870–1892   554

CHAPTER 18

Industry and Empire, 1890–1900   588

CHAPTER 19

A United Body of Action, 1900–1916   622

CHAPTER 20

A Global Power, 1914–1919   654

CHAPTER 21

The Modern Nation, 1919–1928   684

CHAPTER 22

A Great Depression and a New Deal,
1929–1940 716

CHAPTER 23
The Second World War, 1941–1945   746

CHAPTER 24
The Cold War, 1945–1954   780

CHAPTER 25

The Consumer Society, 1945–1961   812

CHAPTER 27

Living with Less, 1968–1980   880

CHAPTER 28
The Triumph of Conservatism,
1980–1991   914

CHAPTER 29
The Globalized, Information Society,
1989–2008   950

CHAPTER 30

"The American Dream," 2008–2021 986

Maps

Features

AMERICAN PORTRAIT

AMERICAN LANDSCAPE

AMERICA IN THE WORLD

STRUGGLES FOR DEMOCRACY

Preface

At Gettysburg, Pennsylvania, on November 19, 1863, President Abraham Lincoln dedicated a memorial to the more than 3,000 Union soldiers who had died turning back a Confederate invasion in the first days of July. There were at least a few ways that the president could have justified the sad loss of life in the third year of a brutal war dividing North and South. He could have said it was necessary to destroy the Confederacy's cherished institution of slavery, to punish southerners for seceding from the United States, or to preserve the nation intact. Instead, at this crucial moment in American history, Lincoln gave a short, stunning speech about democracy. The president did not use the word, but he offered its essence. The term *democracy* came from the ancient Greek word *demos*—for "the people." To honor the dead of Gettysburg, Lincoln called on northerners to ensure "that government of the people, by the people, for the people, shall not perish from the earth."

With these words, Lincoln put democracy at the center of the Civil War and at the center of American history. The authors of this book share his belief in the centrality of democracy; his words, "of the people," give our book its title and its main theme. We see American history as a story "of the people," of their struggles to shape their lives and their land.

Our choice of theme does not mean we believe that America has always been a democracy. Clearly, it has not. As Lincoln gave the Gettysburg Address, most African Americans still lived in slavery. American women, North and South, lacked rights that many men enjoyed; for all their disagreements, white southerners and northerners viewed Native Americans as enemies. Neither do we believe that there is only a single definition of democracy, either in the narrow sense of a particular form of government or in the larger one of a society whose members participate equally in its creation. Although Lincoln defined the northern cause as a struggle for democracy, southerners believed it was anything but democratic to force them to remain in the Union at gunpoint. As bloody draft riots in New York City in July 1863 made clear, many northern men thought it was anything but democratic to force them to fight in Lincoln's armies. Such disagreements have been typical of American history. For more than 500 years, people have struggled over whose vision of life in the New World would prevail.

That reality has been especially clear as we completed revising the book for this new edition. The tumultuous presidential campaign of 2020, one of the most divisive in American history, took place in the midst of a deadly pandemic and culminated in the extraordinary storming of the federal Capitol building in Washington, DC in January 2021. With the nation arguably more divided than at any time since the Civil War, we have carried our coverage down to the events of January. Recent history is always a challenge and always subject to revision, but we have wanted to show how contemporary struggles over democracy are rooted in the past. As always, we feel that our balanced, inclusive approach makes it more possible for teachers and students to deal with the most controversial events.

It is precisely such struggles as those of the 2020s and the 1860s that offer the best angle of vision for seeing and understanding the most important developments in the nation's history. In particular, the democratic theme concentrates attention on the most fundamental concerns of history: people and power.

Lincoln's words serve as a reminder of the basic truth that history is about people. Across the 30 chapters of this book, we write extensively about complex events. But we also write in the awareness that these developments are only abstractions unless they are grounded in the lives of people. The test of a historical narrative, we believe, is whether its characters are fully rounded, believable human beings.

The choice of Lincoln's words also reflects our belief that history is about power. To ask whether America was democratic at some point in the past is to ask how much power various groups of people had to make their lives and their nation. Such questions of power necessarily take us to political processes, to the ways in which people work separately and collectively to enforce their will. We define politics quite broadly in this book. With the feminists of the 1960s, we believe that "the personal is the political," that power relations shape people's lives in private as well as in public. *Of the People* looks for democracy in the living room as well as the legislature, and in the bedroom as well as the business office.

Focusing on democracy, people, and power, we have necessarily written as wide-ranging a history as possible. In the features and in the main text, *Of the People* conveys both the unity and the great diversity of the American people across time and place. We chronicle the racial and ethnic groups who have shaped America, differences of religious and regional identity, the changing nature of social classes, and the different ways that gender identities have been constructed over the centuries.

While treating different groups in their distinctiveness, we have integrated them into the broader narrative as much as possible. A true history "of the people" means not only acknowledging their individuality and diversity but also showing their interrelationships and their roles in the larger narrative. More integrated coverage of Native Americans, African Americans, Latinos, and other minority groups appears throughout the fourth edition.

Of the People also offers comprehensive coverage of the different spheres of human life—cultural as well as governmental, social as well as economic, environmental as well as military. This commitment to comprehensiveness is a reflection of our belief that all aspects of human existence are the stuff of history. It is also an expression of the fundamental theme of the book: the focus on democracy leads naturally to the study of people's struggles for power in every dimension of their lives. Moreover, the democratic approach emphasizes the interconnections between the different aspects of Americans' lives; we cannot understand politics and government without tracing their connection to economics, religion, culture, art, sexuality, and so on.

The economic connection is especially important. *Of the People* devotes much attention to economic life, to the ways in which Americans have worked and saved and spent. Economic power, the authors believe, is basic to democracy. Americans' power to shape their lives and their country has been greatly affected by whether they were farmers or hunters, plantation owners or enslaved people, wage workers or capitalists, domestic servants or bureaucrats. The authors do not see economics as an impersonal, all-conquering force; instead, we try to show how the values and actions of ordinary people, as well as the laws and regulations of government, have made economic life.

We have also tried especially to place America in a global context. The history of America, or any nation, cannot be adequately explained without understanding its relationship to transnational events and global developments. That is true for the first chapter of the book, which shows how America began to emerge from the collision of Native Americans, West Africans, and Europeans in the fifteenth and sixteenth centuries. It is just as true for the last chapters of the book, which demonstrate how globalization and the war on terror transformed the United States at the turn of the twenty-first century. In the chapters in between, we detail how the world has changed America and how America has changed the world. Reflecting the concerns of the rest of the book, we focus particularly on the movement of people, the evolution of power, and the attempt to spread democracy abroad.

Abraham Lincoln wanted to sell a war, of course. But he also truly believed that his audience would see democracy as quintessentially American. Whether he was right is the burden of this book.

HALLMARK FEATURES

- Each chapter opens with an **American Portrait** feature, a story of someone whose life in one way or another embodies the basic theme of the pages to follow.
- Select chapters include an **American Landscape** feature, a particular place in time where issues of power appeared in especially sharp relief. The new American Landscape features in the fifth edition more explicitly look at American places from an environmental perspective.
- To underscore the fundamental importance of global relationships, select chapters include a feature on **America in the World**. Formerly called "America and the World," the subtle change to the name of this feature reflects the greater attention it now gives to topics related to immigration.
- Each chapter includes a **Struggles for Democracy** feature, focusing on moments of debate and public conversation surrounding events that have contributed to the changing ideas of democracy, as well as the sometimes constricting but overall gradually widening opportunities that evolved for the American people as a result.
- **Common Threads**, located at the beginning of each chapter, offer focus questions that ask the student to consider the main problems examined in the discussions that follow.
- **Timelines** provide dates for all the key events discussed in the chapters.
- A list of chapter-ending key terms, **Who, What, Where**, helps students recall the important people, events, and places of that chapter.
- All chapters end with both **Review Questions**, which test students' memory and understanding of chapter content, and **Critical-Thinking Questions**, which ask students to analyze and interpret chapter content.

NEW TO THE FIFTH EDITION

We are grateful that the first four editions of *Of the People* have been welcomed by instructors and students as a useful instructional aid. In preparing the fifth edition, our primary goal has been to maintain the text's overarching focus on the evolution of American democracy, people, and power; its strong portrayal of political and social history; and its clear, compelling narrative voice. Throughout, we have continued to intensify the focus on the environment, diversity, and immigration and to offer coverage of events such as the devastation of Tenochtitlan in the face of smallpox in the sixteenth century, the influenza pandemic of 1918, and the Tulsa Race massacre of 1921 that speak to the contemporary challenges of the United States. Acknowledging the upheavals of recent history, we have reorganized and rewritten chapters 29 and 30 to give full coverage to the twenty-first century. One of the text's strengths is its critical-thinking pedagogy because the study of history entails careful analysis, not mere memorization of names and dates.

Strengthened Learning Aids

We have significantly revised the Who, What, Where glossary terms so that the most essential and fundamental ideas, people, and places are consistently highlighted, and the terms are now boldfaced in the text. Many chapters now include new "Common Thread" focus questions, and new maps have been added to Chapters 25 and 27.

New American Portrait, American Landscape, America in the World, and Struggles for Democracy Features

These popular features have been updated with three new American Portraits, seven new American Landscapes, five new America and in the World features, and three new Struggles for Democracy:

American Portrait
Chapter 12: Joe, an Enslaved Man at the Alamo
Chapter 29: David Rockefeller
Chapter 30: Maria "Bambi" Roaquin

Struggles for Democracy
Chapter 25: "SOS'"—SMOG!
Chapter 27: The Pollster
Chapter 30: #BlackLivesMatter, "Black Twitter," and Smartphones

American Landscape
Chapter 1: Tenochtitlan
Chapter 9: American Indians Watch Home Slip Away
Chapter 16: Pioneers' Paradise Lost
Chapter 22: The 1937 Ohio River Flood
Chapter 25: West Texas
Chapter 28: Times Beach, Missouri
Chapter 30: The Winter Strawberry Capital of the World

America in the World

Chapter 2: Squanto Comes Back to America
Chapter 11: Harriet Forten Purvis Invites the World's Ideas Home
Chapter 13: The Nativist Attack on Immigration
Chapter 20: The 1918 Influenza Pandemic
Chapter 23: Martial Law in Hawaii

New Primary Sources

All versions of the text now include end-of-chapter primary source documents, both textual and visual, designed to reinforce students' understanding of the material by drawing connections among topics and thinking critically. Nearly all chapters in the fifth edition include at least one new source document:

Source 1.1 Aztec Songs
Source 2.3 A Smallpox Epidemic in Canada (1639–1640)
Source 4.1: The Dutch Lose Power in America: A Meeting with Indians on the Delaware (1670)
Source 5.4: George Whitefield, Account of a Visit to South Carolina (1740)
Source 6.1 Letters between Sir Jeffrey Amherst and Henry Bouquet (1763)
Source 7.5 The Federalists and the Anti-Federalists (1787–1788)
Source 8.4 Charles Brockden Brown's Defense of Education for Women (1798)
Source 9.2 Tecumseh's Speech to Governor Harrison, August 20, 1810
Source 10.3 Theodore Frelinghuysen's Argument Against the Removal Act (1830)
Source 11.3 William Apess, "An Indian-Looking Glass for the White Man" (1833)
Source 13.2 The Fugitive Slave Law Claims a Victim (1852)
Source 13.3 Letter from Edward Bridgman about Kansas Warfare (1856)
Source 14.3 Louisa May Alcott Nurses the Wounded (1863)
Source 15.2 A Black Tenant Farmer Describes Working Conditions (1904)
Source 16.1 Stephen Crane visits the "breaker" at a coal mine (1894)
Source 16.6 William A. Peffer Pleads the Farmer's Cause, 1891
Source 17.4 Jacob Riis, Visual Document "Nomads of the Street" (ca. 1890)
Source 18.4 Platform of the American Anti-Imperialist League (1899)
Source 19.1 Daniel Hudson Burnham and Edward H. Bennett, *Plan of Chicago.* Commercial Club of Chicago (1909)
Source 20.1 Eugene V. Debs, Excerpts from Canton, Ohio, Speech (1918)
Source 21.2 Marie Prevost on "The Flapper" (1923)
Source 22.3 Ballad for Americans, Federal Theater Project, *Sing for Your Supper* (1939)
Source 23.4 "Italy to Chicago," *Yank: The Army Weekly* (March 1945)
Source 24.1 President Harry S. Truman (1947)
Source 25.3 Malvina Lindsay, "Science Alone No Answer to Sputnik" (1957)
Source 26.4 Diane Carlson Evans, Oral History Interview on Her Service as an Army Nurse in Vietnam (2012)
Source 27.5 Clyde Warrior, "Statement" (1967)
Source 28.3 The Debate Over the Defense Build-Up (1983)
Source 28.4 Equal Pay for Women (1982)
Source 30.5 Children and Immigration Policy (2018)

DIGITAL LEARNING RESOURCES FOR
OF THE PEOPLE

Oxford University Press offers instructors and students digital learning resources that increase student engagement and optimize the classroom teaching experience

Oxford Insight

Developed with a foundation in learning science, Oxford Insight courseware enables instructors to deliver a personalized and engaging learning experience that empowers students by actively engaging them in course content. Oxford Insight delivers high quality content within powerful, data-driven courseware designed to optimize student success. To learn more, and to book a demo of Oxford Insight Courseware, go to https://pages.oup.com/he/us/oxfordinsight.

Oxford Learning Link (OLL) and Oxford Learning Link Direct (OLLD)

This online resource center https://learninglink.oup.com/ is available to adopters of *Of the People*, offers a wealth of teaching resources, including a test-item file, a computerized test bank, quizzes, PowerPoint slides, videos, and primary sources. Oxford Learning Link Direct (OLLD) makes OUP's digital learning resources for *Of the People* available to adopters within their institution's own LMS via a one-time course integration.

Sources for *Of the People*

Edited by Maxwell Johnson, this two-volume sourcebook includes five to six primary sources per chapter, both textual and visual. Chapter introductions, document headnotes, and study questions provide learning support. The sourcebooks are also available as eBooks.

Mapping and Coloring Book of US History

This two-volume workbook includes approximately 80 outline maps that provide opportunities for students to deepen their understanding of geography through quizzes, coloring exercises, and other activities. *The Mapping and Coloring Book of US History* is free when bundled with *Of the People*.

E-Books

Digital versions of *Of the People* are available at many popular distributors, including Chegg, RedShelf, and VitalSource.

Other Oxford Titles of Interest for the US History Classroom

Oxford University Press publishes a vast array of titles in American history. The following list is just a small selection of books that pair particularly well with *Of the People: A History of the United States*, Fourth Edition. Any of these books can be packaged with *Of the People* at a significant discount to students. Please contact your Oxford University Press sales representative for specific pricing information or for additional packaging suggestions. Please visit www.oup.com/us for a full listing of Oxford titles.

***Writing History: A Guide for Students,* Sixth Edition, by William Kelleher Storey**
Bringing together practical methods from both history and composition, *Writing History* provides a wealth of tips and advice to help students research and write essays for history classes.

***The Information-Literate Historian: A Guide to Research for History Students,* Third Edition, by Jenny Presnell**
This is the only book specifically designed to teach today's history student how to most successfully select and use sources—primary, secondary, and electronic—to carry out and present their research. Written by a college librarian, *The Information-Literate Historian* is an indispensable reference for historians, students, and other readers doing history research.

ACKNOWLEDGMENTS

We are grateful to our families, friends, and colleagues who encouraged us during the planning and writing of this book. We would like once again to thank Bruce Nichols for helping launch this book years ago. We are grateful to the editors and staff at Oxford University Press, especially our acquisitions editor, Charles Cavaliere. Charles's commitment made this book possible. Thanks also to our talented production team, Theresa Stockton, senior production editor, and Michele Laseau, art director, who helped to fulfill the book's vision. And special thanks go to Anne Sanow, our copyeditor; to Danica Donovan, assistant editor; and to the many other people behind the scenes at Oxford for helping this complex project happen.

The authors and editors would also like to thank the following people, whose time and insights have contributed to the first, second, third, fourth, and fifth editions.

Expert Reviewers of the Fifth Edition

Cara Shelly
Oakland University

Mervyn Roberts
Central Texas College

Ian Hartman
University of Alaska Anchorage

Brian Peterson
Shasta College

MayaLisa Holzman
Oregon State University—Cascades

Michael Holm
Boston University

Leslie S. Leighton
Georgia State University

Kevin Butler
University of Arkansas at Pine Bluff

Judith Ridner
Mississippi State University

Sandy Moats
University of Wisconsin Parkside

James Mills
University of Texas Rio Grande Valley

Damon Bach
Texas A&M University

Robert Genter
Nassau Community College

Christopher Childers
Pittsburgh State University

Jennifer Lawrence
Tarrant County College

Jennifer Grohol
Bakersfield College

Jeffrey Gonda
Syracuse University

Mary Lyons-Carmona
University of Nebraska Omaha

Ana Fodor
Danville Community College

Kenneth Heineman
Angelo State University

Richard Mowrer
Folsom Lake College

William Wantland
Mount Vernon Nazarene University

John Varga
College of the Canyons

Joshua Farrington
Eastern Kentucky University

Mark Freshwater
Snead State Community College

Jeff Ewen
Ivy Tech Community College

Brady L. Holley
Middle Tennessee State University

Evan Turiano
CUNY Grad Center

John Ryder
Radford University

Colt Chaney
Murray Sate College

Leslie Leighton
Georgia State University

Michael J. Stout
University of Texas Arlington

Expert Reviewers of the Fourth Edition

Daniel Anderson
Cincinnati State University

Sakina M. Hughes
University of Southern Indiana

Tramaine Anderson
Tarrant County College

Katrina Lacher
University of Central Oklahoma

Matthew Campbell
Lone Star College–Cypress Fairbanks

Robert Lee
St. Louis Community College–Meramec

Gregg S. Clemmer
Carroll Community College

Matthew Oyos
Radford University

John Patrick Daly
*College at Brockport, State University
of New York*

Stephen Todd Pfeffer
Columbus State Community College

Brenden Rensink
Brigham Young University

Maureen Elgersman Lee
Hampton University

Marie Stango
California State University, Bakersfield

Michael Frawley
University of Texas of the Permian Basin

Robert Genter
Nassau Community College

Expert Reviewers of the Third Edition

Greg Hall
Western Illinois University

Ross A. Kennedy
Illinois State University

Randall M. Miller
Saint Joseph's University

David W. Morris
Santa Barbara City College

Adam Pratt
University of Scranton

Judith Ridner
Mississippi State University

Robert A. Smith
Pittsburg State University

Timothy B. Smith
University of Tennessee at Martin

Linda D. Tomlinson
Fayetteville State University

Gerald Wilson
Eastern Washington University

Expert Reviewers of the Second Edition

Marjorie Berman
Red Rocks Community College–Lakewood

Will Carter
South Texas Community College

Jonathan Chu
University of Massachusetts, Boston

Sara Combs
Virginia Highlands Community College

Mark Elliott
University of North Carolina–Greensboro

David Hamilton
University of Kentucky

James Harvey
Houston Community College

Courtney Joiner
East Georgia College

Timothy Mahoney
University of Nebraska–Lincoln

Abigail Markwyn
Carroll University

Brian Maxson
Eastern Tennessee State University

Matthew Oyos
Radford University

John Pinheiro
Aquinas College

James Pula
Purdue University–North Central

John Rosinbum
Arizona State University

Christopher Thrasher
Texas Tech University

Jeffrey Trask
University of Massachusetts–Amherst

Michael Ward
California State University–Northridge

Bridgette Williams-Searle
The College of Saint Rose

Expert Reviewers of the First Edition

Thomas L. Altherr
Metropolitan State College of Denver

Luis Alvarez
University of California–San Diego

Adam Arenson
University of Texas–El Paso

Melissa Estes Blair
University of Georgia

Lawrence Bowdish
Ohio State University

Susan Roth Breitzer
Fayetteville State University

Margaret Lynn Brown
Brevard College

W. Fitzhugh Brundage
University of North Carolina–Chapel Hill

Gregory Bush
University of Miami

Brian Casserly
University of Washington

Ann Chirhart
Indiana State University

Bradley R. Clampitt
East Central University

William W. Cobb Jr.
Utah Valley University

Cheryll Ann Cody
Houston Community College

Sondra Cosgrove
College of Southern Nevada

Thomas H. Cox
Sam Houston State University

Carl Creasman
Valencia Community College

Christine Daniels
Michigan State University

Brian J. Daugherity
Virginia Commonwealth University

Mark Elliott
University of North Carolina–Greensboro

Katherine Carté Enge
Texas A&M University

Michael Faubion
University of Texas–Pan American

John Fea
Messiah College

Anne L. Foster
Indiana State University

Matthew Garrett
Arizona State University

Tim Garvin
California State University–Long Beach

Suzanne Cooper Guasco
Queens University of Charlotte

Lloyd Ray Gunn
University of Utah

Richard Hall
Columbus State University

Marsha Hamilton
University of South Alabama

Mark Hanna
University of California–San Diego

Joseph M. Hawes
University of Memphis

Melissa Hovsepian
University of Houston–Downtown

Jorge Iber
Texas Tech University

David K. Johnson
University of South Florida

Lloyd Johnson
Campbell University

Catherine O'Donnell Kaplan
Arizona State University

Rebecca M. Kluchin
California State University–Sacramento

Michael Kramer
Northwestern University

Louis M. Kyriakoudes
University of Southern Mississippi

Jason S. Lantzer
Butler University

Shelly Lemons
St. Louis Community College

Charlie Levine
Mesa Community College

Denise Lynn
University of Southern Indiana

Lillian Marrujo-Duck
City College of San Francisco

Michael McCoy
Orange County Community College

Noeleen McIlvenna
Wright State University

Elizabeth Brand Monroe
Indiana University–Purdue University Indianapolis

Kevin C. Motl
Ouachita Baptist University

Todd Moye
University of North Texas

Charlotte Negrete
Mt. San Antonio College

Julie Nicoletta
University of Washington–Tacoma

David M. Parker
California State University–Northridge

Jason Parker
Texas A&M University

Herbert Sloan
Barnard College, Columbia University

Burton W. Peretti
Western Connecticut State University

Vincent L. Toscano
Nova Southeastern University

Jim Piecuch
Kennesaw State University

William E. Weeks
San Diego State University

John Putman
San Diego State University

Timothy L. Wood
Southwest Baptist University

R. J. Rockefeller
Loyola College of Maryland

Jason Young
SUNY–Buffalo

Expert Reviewers of the Concise Second Edition

Hedrick Alixopulos
Santa Rosa Junior College

Daniel K. Lewis
California State Polytechnic University

Guy Alain Aronoff
Humboldt State University

Scott P. Marler
University of Memphis

Melissa Estes Blair
Warren Wilson College

Laura McCall
Metropolitan State College of Denver

Amanda Bruce
Nassau Community College

Stephen P. McGrath
Central Connecticut State University

Jonathan Chu
University of Massachusetts–Boston

Vincent P. Mikkelsen
Florida State University

Paul G. E. Clemens
Rutgers University

Julie Nicoletta
University of Washington–Tacoma

Martha Anne Fielder
Cedar Valley College

Caitlin Stewart
Eastern Connecticut State University

Tim Hacsi
University of Massachusetts–Boston

Thomas Summerhill
Michigan State University

Matthew Isham
Pennsylvania State University

David Tegeder
Santa Fe College

Ross A. Kennedy
Illinois State University

Eric H. Walther
University of Houston

Eve Kornfeld
San Diego State University

William E. Weeks
University of San Diego

Peggy Lambert
Lone Star College–Kingwood

Kenneth B. White
Modesto Junior College

Shelly L. Lemons
St. Louis Community College

Julie Winch
University of Massachusetts–Boston

Carolyn Herbst Lewis
Louisiana State University

Mary Montgomery Wolf
University of Georgia

Catherine M. Lewis
Kennesaw State University

Kyle F. Zelner
University of Southern Mississippi

Expert Reviewers of the Concise First Edition

Hedrick Alixopulos
Santa Rosa Junior College

Guy Alain Aronoff
Humboldt State University

Melissa Estes Blair
Warren Wilson College

Amanda Bruce
Nassau Community College

Jonathan Chu
University of Massachusetts–Boston

Paul G. E. Clemens
Rutgers University

Martha Anne Fielder
Cedar Valley College

Tim Hacsi
University of Massachusetts–Boston

Matthew Isham
Pennsylvania State University

Ross A. Kennedy
Illinois State University

Eve Kornfeld
San Diego State University

Peggy Lambert
Lone Star College–Kingwood

Shelly L. Lemons
St. Louis Community College

Carolyn Herbst Lewis
Louisiana State University

Catherine M. Lewis
Kennesaw State University

Daniel K. Lewis
California State Polytechnic University

Scott P. Marler
University of Memphis

Laura McCall
Metropolitan State College of Denver

Stephen P. McGrath
Central Connecticut State University

Vincent P. Mikkelsen
Florida State University

Julie Nicoletta
University of Washington–Tacoma

Caitlin Stewart
Eastern Connecticut State University

Thomas Summerhill
Michigan State University

David Tegeder
Santa Fe College

Eric H. Walther
University of Houston

William E. Weeks
University of San Diego

Kenneth B. White
Modesto Junior College

Julie Winch
University of Massachusetts–Boston

Mary Montgomery Wolf
University of Georgia

Kyle F. Zelner
University of Southern Mississippi

About the Authors

Michael McGerr is the Paul V. McNutt Professor of History and Chair of the Department of History at Indiana University–Bloomington. He is the author of *The Decline of Popular Politics: The American North, 1865–1928* (1986) and *A Fierce Discontent: The Rise and Fall of the Progressive Movement, 1870–1920* (2003), both from Oxford University Press. He is writing *"The Public Be Damned": The Kingdom and the Dream of the Vanderbilts.* The recipient of a fellowship from the National Endowment for the Humanities, Professor McGerr has won numerous teaching awards at Indiana, where his courses include the US Survey; War in Modern American History; Rock, Hip Hop, and Revolution; The Rich; The Sixties; and American Pleasure. He has previously taught at Yale University and the Massachusetts Institute of Technology. He received his BA, MA, and PhD from Yale.

Camilla Townsend is Distinguished Professor of History at Rutgers University—New Brunswick. She is the author of six books, among them *Fifth Sun: A New History of the Aztecs* (2019), *Annals of Native America* (2016), *Malintzin's Choices: An Indian Woman in the Conquest of Mexico* (2006), and *Pocahontas and the Powhatan Dilemma* (2004). She is also the editor of *American Indian History: A Documentary Reader* (2010). Her books have won numerous prizes, including the 2020 Cundill Prize for *Fifth Sun.* The recipient of fellowships from the National Endowment for the Humanities and the John Simon Guggenheim Memorial Foundation, she has also won awards at Rutgers and at Colgate, where she used to teach. Her courses cover the colonial history of the Americas as well as Native American history, early and modern. She received her BA from Bryn Mawr and her PhD from Rutgers.

Karen M. Dunak is Associate Professor of History and Chair of the Department of History at Muskingum University in New Concord, Ohio. She is the author of *As Long as We Both Shall Love: The White Wedding in Postwar America* (2013), published by New York University Press. She currently is working on a book about media representations of and responses to Jacqueline Kennedy Onassis. Her courses include the US Survey, Women in US History, Gender and Sexuality in US History, and various topics related to modern US history. She earned her BA from American University and her PhD from Indiana University.

Mark Summers is the Thomas D. Clark Professor of History at the University of Kentucky–Lexington. In addition to various articles, he has written *Railroads, Reconstruction, and the Gospel of Prosperity* (1984), *The Plundering Generation* (1988), *The Era of Good Stealings* (1993), *The Press Gang* (1994), *The Gilded Age; or, The Hazard of New Functions* (1997), *Rum, Romanism and Rebellion* (2000), *Party Games* (2004), and *A Dangerous Stir* (2009). At present, he has just completed a book about a Tammany politician, *Big Tim and the Tiger.* He is now writing a survey of Reconstruction and a book about 1868. He teaches the American history survey (both halves), the Gilded Age, the Progressive Era, the Age of Jackson, Civil War and Reconstruction, the British Empire (both halves), the Old West (both halves), a history of political cartooning, and various graduate courses. He earned his BA from Yale and his PhD from the University of California–Berkeley.

Jan Ellen Lewis was Professor of History and Dean of the Faculty of Arts and Sciences, Rutgers University–Newark. She also taught in the history PhD program at Rutgers, New Brunswick, and was a visiting professor of history at Princeton. A specialist in colonial and early national history, she wrote *The Pursuit of Happiness: Family and Values in Jefferson's Virginia* (1983) as well as numerous articles and reviews. She coedited *An Emotional History of the United States* (1998), *Sally Hemings and Thomas Jefferson: History, Memory, and Civic Culture* (1999), and *The Revolution of 1800: Democracy, Race, and the New Republic* (2002). She served as president of the Society of Historians of the Early American Republic, as chair of the New Jersey Historical Commission, and on the editorial board of the *American Historical Review*. An elected member of the Society of American Historians and the American Antiquarian Society, she received her AB from Bryn Mawr College and MAs and PhD from the University of Michigan.

OF THE PEOPLE

Reconstructing a Nation

1865–1877

< White supremacists fire upon Black men, women, and children, Choctaw County, Alabama, 1874

John Dennett Visits a Freedmen's Bureau Court

John Richard Dennett arrived in Liberty, Virginia, on August 17, 1865, on a tour of the South reporting for the magazine *The Nation*. The editors wanted accurate weekly accounts of conditions in the recently defeated Confederate states, and Dennett was the kind of man they could trust: a Harvard graduate, a firm believer in the sanctity of the Union, and a member of the class of elite Yankees who thought of themselves as the "best men" the country had to offer.

At Liberty, Dennett was accompanied by a Freedmen's Bureau agent. The **Freedmen's Bureau** was a branch of the US Army established by Congress to assist the freedpeople, as the formerly enslaved were known. Dennett and the agent went to the courthouse because one of the Freedmen's Bureau's functions was to adjudicate disputes between the freedpeople and southern whites.

The first case was that of an old white farmer who complained that two Black people who worked on his farm were "roamin' about and refusin' to work." He wanted the agent to help find the men and bring them back. Both men had wives and children living on his farm and eating his corn, the old man complained. "Have you been paying any wages?" the Freedmen's Bureau agent asked. "Well, they get what the other niggers get," the farmer answered. "I a'n't payin' great wages this year." There was not much the agent could do, but one of his soldiers volunteered to go and tell the men that "they ought to be at home supporting their wives and children."

A well-to-do planter came in to see if he could fire the Black people who had been working on his plantation since the beginning of the year. Warned not to beat his workers the way he would enslaved people, the planter complained that they were unmanageable without what he considered proper punishment. Under the circumstances, the planter wondered, "Will the Government take them off our hands?" The agent suspected that the planter was looking for a way to dismiss his workforce unpaid at the end of the growing season. "If they've worked on your crops all the year so far," the agent told the planter, "I guess they've got a claim on you to keep them a while longer."

Next came a "good-looking mulatto man" representing a number of African Americans worried that they would be forced into five-year contracts with their employers. "No, it a'n't true," the agent said. Could they rent or buy land to work themselves? "Yes, rent or buy," the agent said. But with no horses, mules, or plows, the formerly enslaved people wanted to see "if the Government would help us out after we get the land." All that the agent could offer was a note from the bureau authorizing them to acquire farms of their own.

The last case involved a field hand whose master had beaten him with a stick. The agent sent the field hand back to work. "Don't be sassy, don't be lazy when you've got work to do; and I guess he won't trouble you." A minute later, the worker returned to procure a letter to his master "enjoining him to keep the peace, as he feared the man would shoot him, he having on two or three occasions threatened to do so."

Most of the cases Dennett witnessed centered on labor relations, which often spilled over into other matters, including the family lives of the formerly enslaved, their civil rights, and their ability to buy land. The freedpeople preferred to work their own land but lacked the resources to rent or buy farms. Black workers and white owners who negotiated wage contracts had trouble figuring out each other's rights and responsibilities. The former masters clung to all their old authority that they could. Freedpeople wanted as free a hand as possible.

The Freedmen's Bureau was in the middle of these conflicts. Generally, agents tried to see to it that freedpeople had written contracts guaranteeing their essential right to work as free laborers, uncoerced by whip, club, or gun. Southern whites resented any intrusion with people they still saw as essentially property, and they let civil authorities know it. The Freedmen's Bureau became a lightning rod for the political conflicts of the Reconstruction period.

Conditions in the South elicited sharply different responses from lawmakers in Washington. At one extreme was President Andrew Johnson, who believed in small government and a speedy readmission of the southern states and looked on the Freedmen's Bureau with suspicion. At the other extreme were radical Republicans calling on the federal government to redistribute confiscated land to former enslaved people, give African American men the vote, and take it away from whites who were not loyal to the United States during the war. In between, there were moderate Republicans who at first tried to work with the president and were content simply to guarantee African Americans' basic civil rights. But as reports of violence and the abusive treatment of the freedpeople reached Washington, Republicans shifted in more radical directions.

Back and forth it went: events in the South triggered policy decisions in Washington, which in turn shaped events in the South. What John Dennett saw in Liberty, Virginia, was a good example of this. Policies set in Washington shaped what the Freedmen's Bureau agent could do for former masters and enslaved people. However, those policies shifted when the Bureau's reports and those of journalists, like Dennett, exposed just how troubled southern conditions were. From this interaction the politics of Reconstruction, and with it a "New South," slowly emerged.

WARTIME RECONSTRUCTION

Even as emancipation began, the US government began experimenting with reconstructing the Union. The two goals merged: by creating new, loyal southern states and making their abolition of slavery a condition for reunion, Lincoln could enact emancipation there without court challenge. Through a generous policy of pardons, he could encourage Confederates to make their peace with the Union, speeding the war's end.

Despite the chorus of cries for hanging Jefferson Davis from a sour-apple tree, few northerners wanted to pursue bloody punishments for the million Confederate soldiers who were technically guilty of treason. In the end, Confederate generals went home unharmed to become lawyers, businessmen, and planters; General Robert E. Lee became a college president. No civil leader was hanged for treason, not even Jefferson Davis. Two years after his arrest, he walked out of prison, thanks to bail put up by northerners like editor Horace Greeley. In later years, former Confederates became senators, governors, and federal judges. Months before the war ended, northerners were raising money to rebuild the southern economy and feed its destitute people. What the North wanted was not vengeance, but guarantees of lasting loyalty and a meaningful freedom. Questions arose with no easy answers: What did it take to reunite America? Should it be restored, or reconstructed, and if the latter, how drastically? How far could yesterday's enemies be trusted? What did freedom mean, and what rights should the "freedpeople" enjoy? In reconstructing society, how far did the government's power go?

Lincoln's Ten Percent Plan Versus the Wade-Davis Bill

Lincoln moved to shape a postwar South based on free labor and to replace military control, Banks's included, with new civil governments. However, wartime Reconstruction had to take Confederate resistance into account. Any terms the president set would need to draw as much white southern support as it could and hold out an inducement to those at war with the United States to return to their old loyalties. In December 1863, Lincoln issued a Proclamation of Amnesty and Reconstruction, offering a full pardon and the restoration of civil rights to all those who swore loyalty to the Union, excluding only a few high-ranking Confederate military and political leaders. When the number of loyal whites in a former Confederate state reached 10 percent of the 1860 voting population, they could organize a new state constitution and government. But Lincoln's "**Ten Per Cent Plan**" also required that the state abolish slavery, just as Congress had demanded before admitting West Virginia earlier that year. Attempts to coax Confederate states back to loyalty foundered, but circumstances in Union-occupied bits of Louisiana proved more promising. Under General Nathaniel Banks's guidance, Free State whites met in New Orleans in 1864 and produced a new state constitution abolishing slavery.

By that time, however, radical Unionists were expecting more. Propertied and well educated, the free Black community in New Orleans pleaded that without equal rights to education and the vote, mere freedom would not be enough. Impressed by their argument, Lincoln hinted to Louisiana authorities that he would welcome steps opening the vote for at least some Blacks. The hints were ignored.

Black spokesmen found a friendlier audience among radical Republicans in Congress, among them Thaddeus Stevens of Pennsylvania and Charles Sumner of Massachusetts. Believing that justice required lowering the color bar for suffrage and setting a more rigorous standard of loyalty for white southerners than Lincoln's plan offered, they shared a much wider concern that any new government must rest on statutory law, not presidential proclamations and military commanders' decrees. They agreed that secession had thrown the political character of the states so far out of kilter that they could not reconstruct themselves unaided—that the federal government must decide what it would take to restore them to proper functioning (a judgment that the Supreme Court would confirm in *Texas v. White* later). But they were not at all prepared to treat Lincoln's "loyal" states as fit to return to Congress—not when so much of Louisiana and Arkansas remained in Confederate hands and was barred from the new constitution-making—not when a speckling of enclaves pretended to speak for the state of Virginia.

As doubts grew about Louisiana's Reconstruction, Congress edged away from Lincoln's program. In mid-1864, Senator Benjamin F. Wade of Ohio and Congressman Henry Winter Davis of Maryland advanced a different plan, requiring a majority of a state's white voters to swear allegiance to the Union before Reconstruction could begin. Slavery must also be abolished and African Americans given full equality before the law. Lincoln pocket-vetoed the Wade-Davis bill to protect the governments that were already under way toward reform. However, he could not make Congress admit a single one of his newly reconstructed states.

The Meaning of Freedom

"We was glad to be set free," a former enslaved person remembered years afterward. "I didn't know what it would be like. It was just like opening the door and lettin' the bird fly out. He might starve, or freeze, or be killed pretty soon but he just felt good because he was free." Blacks' departure came as a terrible shock to masters lulled into believing that their "servants" appreciated their treatment. Some former slave owners persuaded themselves that they were the real gainers of slavery's abolition. "I was glad and thankful—on my own account—when slavery ended and I ceased to belong, body and soul, to my negroes," a Virginia woman later insisted. Forced to do their own cooking or washing, other mistresses fumed at Blacks' ingratitude. In fact, many African Americans left, not out of unkindness, but simply to prove that they could get along on their own. White fears that Blacks, once free, would murder their masters proved groundless.

Leaving the plantation was the first step in a long journey for African Americans. Many took to the roads, some of them returning to their old homes near the coasts, from which masters had evacuated as Union armies approached. Others went searching for family members, parted from them during slavery. For 20 years, Black newspapers carried advertisements, begging for news of a husband or wife long since lost. Those who had not been separated went out of their way to have their marriages secured by law. That way, their children could be made legitimate and their vows made permanent. Once married, men sought work contracts that allowed their families to live with them on plantations. Because Black women across the South had become what the law called "domestic dependents," husbands could refuse employers their wives' services and keep them home. In fact, freedwomen were likelier to work outside the home than white women. They tended the family garden, raised children, hired out as domestics, and, as cotton prices fell, shared the work of hoeing and picking in the fields just so the family could make ends meet.

The end of slavery meant many things to freedpeople. It meant that they could move about their neighborhoods without passes, and that they did not have to step aside to let whites pass them on the street. They could own dogs or carry canes, both among the master's exclusive privileges. They could dress as they pleased or choose their own names, including, for the first time, a surname.

Freedom liberated African Americans from the white minister's take on Christianity. No longer were large portions of the Bible closed off to them. Most southern Blacks withdrew from white churches and established their own congregations, particularly in the Methodist and Baptist faith. In time, the church emerged as a central institution in the southern Black community, the meeting place, social center, and source of comfort that larger society denied them. A dozen years after the war, South Carolina had a thousand ministers of the African Methodist Episcopal Church alone.

To read the Gospel, however, freedpeople needed schooling. One former enslaved man remembered his master's parting words on this matter: "Charles, you is a free man they say, but Ah tells you now, you is still a slave and if you lives to be a hundred you'll STILL be a slave, 'cause you got no education, and education is what makes a man free!" Even before the war ended, northern teachers poured into the South to set up schools. When the fighting stopped, the US Army helped recruit and organize thousands of northern women as teachers, but they could never send enough. Old and young spared what time they had from work, paying teachers in eggs or produce when coin was scarce. Black classes met wherever they could: in mule stables and cotton houses, even the slave pen in New Orleans, where the old auction block became a globe stand. Due to a lack of schoolbooks, they read dictionaries and almanacs. On meager resources, hundreds of thousands of southern Blacks learned to read and write over the next generation. The first Black colleges would be founded in the postwar years, including Hampton Institute in Virginia and Howard University in Washington, DC. The American Missionary Association established seven, Atlanta and Fisk Universities among them.

Finally, freedom allowed freedpeople to congregate, to celebrate the Fourth of July or Emancipation Day, or to petition for equal rights before the law. Memorial Day may have begun with Blacks gathering to honor the Union dead whose sacrifices had helped make them free.

Experiments with Free Labor

Many whites insisted that Blacks would never work in freedom and foresaw a South ruined forever. Freedpeople proved just the opposite. When Union troops landed on the Sea Islands off South Carolina in November 1861, the landlords fled, leaving behind between 5,000 and 10,000 enslaved people. Within months the abandoned plantations of the Sea Islands were being reorganized. Eventually Black families were given small plots of their own to till. In return for their labor they received a "share" of the year's crop. When the masters returned after the war to reclaim their lands, the labor system had already proven itself. Much modified, it would form the basis for the arrangement known as **sharecropping**.

The sugar and cotton plantations around New Orleans provided another opportunity to shape the future of free labor. When the Union army came to occupy New Orleans in 1862, the tens of thousands of field hands on these plantations were no longer enslaved, but the landowners still held possession of the land. Unlike the Sea Islands, these plantations could not be broken up. And sugar plantations could not be effectively organized into small sharecropping units.

Hoping to stem the flow of Black refugees to Union lines and cut the loss of Black lives in the contraband camps, Union general Nathaniel Banks issued stringent regulations to put the freedpeople back to work quickly in Louisiana. At the time, Banks was the commander of the Department of the Gulf during the occupation of New Orleans and his policy, known as the Banks Plan, required freedpeople to sign yearlong contracts to work on their former plantations. Workers would be paid either 5 percent of the proceeds of the crop or three dollars per month. The former masters would provide food and shelter, and African American workers were forbidden to leave the plantations without permission. Established planters welcomed the plan, but many critics protested that Banks had simply replaced one form of slavery with another; however, most freedpeople knew the difference and accepted the work conditions. The Banks Plan became the model for plantations throughout the lower Mississippi Valley.

Understandably, freedpeople wanted land of their own. Only then could they avoid working for their old masters on any terms. "The labor of these people had for two hundred years cleared away the forests and produced crops that brought millions of dollars annually," H. C. Bruce explained. "It does seem to me that a Christian Nation would, at least, have given them one year's support, 40 acres of land and a mule each." As the war ended, many African Americans expected the government's help in becoming landowners. Union general William Tecumseh Sherman heard an appeal from freedpeople on the Sea Islands. "The way we can best take care of ourselves is to have land," they argued, "and turn it out and till it by our own labor." Convinced, Sherman issued Special Field Order No. 15 granting them captured land. By June, 400,000 acres had been distributed to 40,000 former enslaved people.

Congress did not leave matters there. In March 1865, the Republicans established the Bureau of Refugees, Freedmen, and Abandoned Lands, commonly known as the Freedmen's Bureau. In the area of labor relations, the Bureau sometimes sided with landowners against the interests of the freedpeople. But it also provided immediate relief for thousands of people of both races. Indeed, of more than 18 million rations distributed over three years, more than 5 million went to whites in need. The Bureau joined with northern religious groups in creating some 4,000 Black schools. It ran charity hospitals and provided medical services. Freedpeople came to Bureau agents for justice when white-dominated courts denied it and took counsel when labor contracts were to be negotiated. Some agents sided instinctively with the former masters. Most courted white hostility by protecting freedpeople from violence, settling their complaints, advising them on labor contracts, and seeing that employers paid as promised.

The Freedmen's Bureau also became involved in the politics of land redistribution and controlled the disposition of 850,000 acres of confiscated and abandoned Confederate lands. In July 1865, General Oliver Otis Howard, the head of the Bureau, directed his agents to rent the land to the freedpeople in 40-acre plots that they could eventually buy. Many agents believed that to reeducate them in the values of thrift and hard work, the freedpeople should be encouraged to save money and acquire land for themselves. A Freedman's Savings Bank helped many do just that.

Moderate and radical Republicans alike were resolved to press for more than a nominal freedom for Blacks. Equally important, Congress made it clear that it would insist on being consulted in any Reconstruction policy.

PRESIDENTIAL RECONSTRUCTION, 1865–1867

Andrew Johnson took office in April 1865 as a great unknown. Born in a log cabin and too poor to attend school, he began his career on a tailor's bench where he had shown grit and enterprise. In time he had risen to moderate wealth in the eastern Tennessee hill country, enough to own enslaved people, but he never forgot his humble beginnings. Before the war, he had defended slavery and the common man, called for taxpayer-supported public schools, and free homesteads. A courageous Union Democrat in wartime, he had run roughshod over Tennessee Confederates as military governor. He hated treason and the rich planters that he blamed for the war. Johnson deserved much of the credit for Tennessee abolishing slavery; however, he alarmed some radicals along the way who found more pardons than penalties in his policies. Convinced that a lasting reunion of the states could only come by earning white southerners' good will and determined to see the Thirteenth Amendment ratified quickly, the president started Reconstruction six months before Congress convened and left it wholly in white hands. In doing so, he offended not only the radicals favoring a color-blind suffrage but also the moderates who felt that Reconstruction must be done by law and not executive order.

The Political Economy of Contract Labor

Presidential Reconstruction began in late May 1865, when President Johnson offered amnesty and the restoration of property to white southerners who swore loyalty to the Union, excluding only high-ranking Confederate military and political leaders and very rich planters. He named provisional governors in seven seceded states and told them to summon constitutional conventions. For readmission to the Union and restoration of their full privileges, conventions must adopt the Thirteenth Amendment, void their secession ordinances, and repudiate their Confederate war debt. Most of the constitutional conventions met those conditions, though with grumbling and legal quibbling. Many made clear that they still thought the South had been right all along and only bowed to military force. "We have for breakfast salt-fish, fried potatoes, and treason," a lodger at a Virginia boarding house wrote. "Fried potatoes, treason, and salt-fish for dinner. At supper the fare is slightly varied, and we have treason, salt-fish, fried potatoes, and a little more treason."

Elections under these new constitutions would then choose civil governments to replace provisional authority. Only white men covered by the amnesty proclamation or subsequent pardons could vote, but by September Johnson was signing pardons wholesale. Secessionists flocked to the polls. Freshly pardoned Confederates won some of the top offices, former Confederate Vice President Alexander Stephens among them.

White southerners welcomed Johnson's leniency. Once pardoned, they petitioned for restoration of their confiscated or abandoned properties. In September 1865, Johnson ordered the lands returned to their former owners. By late 1865, former enslaved people were being forced off the 40-acre plots that the government agency had given them.

No sooner did conservative legislatures meet than they fashioned **Black Codes** defining, or rather confining, Blacks' new freedom. Some states ordered different punishments: fines for whites and whipping or sale for Black offenders. Elsewhere, lawmakers forbade freedpeople from renting land, owning guns, or buying liquor. Vagrancy laws gave police wide discretion to collar any Black and subject him or her to forced labor, sometimes for an old master. Apprenticeship statutes let the courts take away Black children without parents' consent and bind them out to years of unpaid labor. Blacks were allowed to testify only in certain cases. They were taxed to pay for white schools; the Johnsonian state governments provided them with none of their own.

Landowners gave their Black employees as little as they could. With the legal machinery backing them up, they forced them into labor contracts that stipulated what they could do with their private time. One planter required his Black workers to "go by his direction the same as in slavery time." Other landowners denied them the right to leave the plantation without their "master's" consent. Some arrangements allotted as little as a tenth of the crop in wages, and many employers found an excuse to turn their field hands off unpaid as soon as the crop was in. No wonder many freedmen saw contract labor as slavery under a new name, or that thousands refused to sign any terms at the year's end.

Resistance to Presidential Reconstruction

An undercurrent of violence underlay conservative control. In North Carolina, a resident wrote, the Negro was "sneered at by all and informed daily yes hourly that he is incompetent to care for himself—that his race is now doomed to perish from off the face of the Earth—that he will not work—that he is a thief by nature[,] that he lies more easily and naturally than an honest man breathes." Blacks were assaulted for not showing proper deference to whites, for disputing the terms of labor contracts, or for failing to meet the standards that white employers demanded. Black churches were burned, rebuilt, and burned again. A Bureau agent in Kentucky classified the incidents in just a few counties: twenty-three "cases of severe and inhuman beating and whipping of men; four of beating and shooting; two of robbing and shooting; three of robbing; five men shot and killed; two shot and wounded; four beaten to death; one beaten and roasted; three women assaulted and ravished; four women beaten, two women tied up and whipped until insensible; two men and their families beaten and driven from their homes, and their property destroyed; two instances of burning of dwellings and one of the inmates shot." White witnesses refused to acknowledge what they knew to be true, white judges dismissed cases involving Black defendants, and white juries invariably acquitted offenders. If Johnson expressed content with the speedy restoration of loyalty in the South, a growing chorus of complaints from freedpeople and Unionists down South told a different story.

Congress Clashes with the President

Troubled by presidential Reconstruction's failings, a Republican Congress refused to readmit former Confederate states without investigation. A Joint Committee on Reconstruction was formed to examine their loyalty and the safety of white and Black Unionists' rights. At the same time, moderate Republicans also wanted to design a program for readmission that Johnson would support. By expanding the power of the Freedmen's Bureau and proposing a Civil Rights bill, they thought they had the makings of a compromise.

The first extended the Bureau's life, strengthened its powers, and let it set up courts that allowed Black testimony. The second overturned the Dred Scott decision, by granting United States citizenship to American men regardless of race. This marked the first time that the federal government intervened in states' rights to guarantee due process and basic civil rights.

To Republicans' amazement, Johnson vetoed both bills and in terms that made no compromise possible. Hinting that Congress had no right to reconstruct until the southern states were readmitted and doubting Blacks' fitness to enjoy the same civil rights as whites, the president declared Reconstruction completed. Unable to override the Freedmen's Bureau bill veto, Congress did pass the Civil Rights bill, which served as the foundation for section one of the Fourteenth Amendment, and later carried a new Freedmen's Bureau bill.

Origins of the Fourteenth Amendment

During the spring of 1866, the Joint Committee on Reconstruction proposed a Fourteenth Amendment to the Constitution, outlining the conditions that Republicans thought were essential for a just and lasting peace. Provisions guaranteed payment of the national debt and prevented payment of the Confederate one. Confederates who had held public office before the war were barred from office until Congress removed their disabilities. Replacing the Constitution's three-fifths clause, which counted enslaved people as three-fifths of a person for the purpose of taxation and representation, representation in Congress would now be based on a state's voting population. If freed Blacks entitled southern states to additional House seats, that representation entitled Blacks to the right to vote (see Table 15–1). "Happy will our disappointment be if this dry stalk shall bud and blossom into Impartial Suffrage," one radical wrote, doubtfully. Even if it did not, the South would return to Congress weaker in strength than it had left. But the crucial provision wrote civil rights guarantees into fundamental law, guaranteeing citizenship to all American-born males. Few of its authors could foresee how, over the century to come, its promise would expand the national commitment to furthering equality, not just for men but for women and other disadvantaged groups; nor could they see how far it could be used to expand the government's authority to set things right.

Deserted by the party that had elected him, Johnson fought on. He launched the National Union movement, a bipartisan coalition of conservatives whose goal was to defeat Republicans at the midterm elections. A railroad tour to Chicago and back to Washington allowed him to make his case to the American people. However, the National Union movement fizzled; hardly any Republican thought the proposed Amendment presented unfair terms for a defeated South. Johnson's "Swing Around the Circle" tour ended in crowds trading insults with the president.

X **Anti-Freedmen's Bureau Poster** Led by President Andrew Johnson, attacks on the Freedmen's Bureau became more and more openly racist in late 1865 and 1866. This Democratic Party broadside was circulated during the 1866 election.

Two incidents confirmed northern fears that presidential Reconstruction had left southern Unionists defenseless. On May 1, 1866, after two drivers—one Black, one white—had a traffic accident, Memphis police arrested the Black one. A group of Black veterans tried to prevent the arrest, and as a result, a white crowd gathered. A riot broke out. Over the next three days, white mobs burned hundreds of homes, destroyed churches, and attacked Black schools. Five Black women were raped; nearly fifty people, all but two of them Black, were killed.

Three months later, violence of an explicitly political dimension broke out in New Orleans. Alarmed at former Confederates' return to power in Louisiana, "Free Staters" sought to recall the state's 1864 constitutional convention. They may have meant to open voting rights to some Blacks or cut "rebels" out, but they never got the chance. On July 30, 1866, when a few dozen delegates assembled at Mechanics' Institute, white mobs set on the convention's supporters, who were mostly Black. Led by police and firemen, many of them Confederate veterans, rioters opened fire on a Black parade and broke into the convention hall. "The floor was covered with blood," one victim remembered, "and in walking downstairs the blood splashed under the soles of my boots." Blacks trying to surrender were gunned down. By the time the attackers dispersed, 34 Blacks and 3 white supporters had been killed, and another 100 had been injured.

Table 15–1 Reconstruction Amendments, 1865–1870

Amendment	Main Provisions	Congressional Passage (two-thirds majority in each house required)	Ratification Process (three-quarters of all states including ex-Confederate states required)
13	Slavery prohibited in the United States	January 1865	December 1865 (27 states, including 8 southern states)
14	1. National citizenship for all men and women born in the United States	June 1866	Rejected by 12 southern and border states, February 1867
	2. State representation in Congress reduced proportionally to number of voters disfranchised		Radicals make readmission of southern states hinge on ratification
	3. Former high-ranking Confederates denied right to hold office until Congress removes disabilities		Ratified July 1868
	4. Confederate debt repudiated		
15	Denial of franchise because of race, color, or past servitude explicitly prohibited	February 1869	Ratification required for readmission of Virginia, Texas, Mississippi, and Georgia; ratified March 1870

CONGRESSIONAL RECONSTRUCTION

The elections of 1866 became a referendum on whether Johnson's policies had gone far enough to assure the permanent safety of the Union. But they also posed competing visions of what American democracy should mean. For President Johnson, "democracy" meant government by local majorities, which often meant white supremacy. For African Americans and a growing number of Republicans in Congress, genuine democracy demanded a firm foundation of equal civil and political rights. The sweep that followed brought in an even more solidly Republican Congress than before and doomed presidential Reconstruction. Congressional Reconstruction would be far different. It was an extraordinary series of events, second only to emancipation in its impact on the history of the United States.

The South Remade

Republicans had agreed on the Fourteenth Amendment's provisions as a final settlement of the war's issues. Southern states that ratified it would be readmitted, whether they enfranchised Blacks or not. Tennessee ratified the amendment and was readmitted to Congress immediately. But in the remaining southern states, conservatives rejected the amendment by wide margins, and with the president's encouragement. As unpunished assaults on Unionists and freedpeople continued, Congress lost patience. In the short run, the army could keep order, but a long-term solution was needed. Moderate Republicans came to agree with radicals: only by putting loyal men, regardless of race, in charge could a loyal, just South come into being. The only other alternative would be an open-ended national commitment to rule the South by force.

Although they were far from what radical Republicans had hoped for, in March 1867, Congress passed two Reconstruction Acts. Leaving the Johnsonian state governments in office, the acts declared them provisional and their officeholders subject to removal if they hamstrung the Reconstruction process. Ten ex-Confederate states were divided into five military districts and placed under army supervision (see Map 15–1). The army would register voters, both white and Black, except for the comparatively small number disqualified by the not-yet-ratified Fourteenth Amendment. To regain congressional representation, each state must call a constitutional convention and draw up a new constitution providing for equal civil and political rights. Voters then must ratify it, and the newly elected governments must adopt the Fourteenth Amendment. Military oversight would end as civil authority replaced it. Thus, most white southern men had a say in constructing the new political order, and when those states were readmitted, they were granted the same rights as others. For all the laws' limits, remaking state governments and requiring a broader male suffrage promised a Radical Reconstruction indeed.

The Impeachment and Trial of Andrew Johnson

Johnson could not stop congressional Reconstruction. But he could temper it. Battling now to protect the executive's powers, Johnson shared Democrats' fears that Congress had veered far from the Constitution, placing military authority above civil authority and overturning what he saw as the natural order of society, where Blacks were kept in subordination.

In vain, radical Republicans called for Johnson's impeachment. Instead, Congress tried to restrain him by law. The **Tenure of Office Act** kept the president from removing officials who had been appointed in his administration with Senate confirmation. Another law required that every presidential order to the military pass through General **Ulysses S. Grant**. Johnson could still dismiss district commanders (and did when they interpreted their powers differently than he did), but as long as Grant headed the army and Edwin M. Stanton the War Department, Republicans felt that they had safeguarded the Reconstruction Acts against a potential coup.

Provoked by these challenges to his authority, Johnson issued interpretations of the Reconstruction Acts to permit wider conservative registration, forcing Congress into special session to revise the law with a Third Reconstruction Act. He issued broader amnesty proclamations for former Confederates, forced the dismissal of Republican officers, and, abiding by the Tenure of Office Act, suspended Stanton in August 1867. When the Senate reinstated him the following winter, Johnson ordered him ejected. "What good did your moderation do you?" radical Republican Thaddeus Stevens taunted moderates. "If you don't kill the beast, he will kill you." With the law seemingly broken, the House impeached Johnson.

**Map 15–1
Reconstruction and
Redemption** By
1870, Congress had
readmitted every
southern state to the
Union. In most cases
the Republican Party
retained control of
the "reconstructed"
state governments for
only a few years.

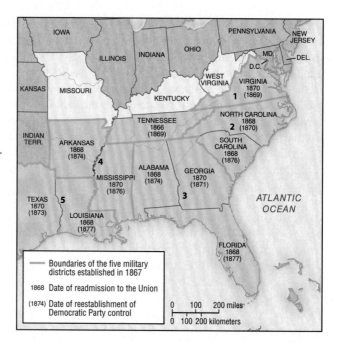

Boundaries of the five military districts established in 1867

1868 Date of readmission to the Union

(1874) Date of reestablishment of Democratic Party control

0   100   200 miles
0 100 200 kilometers

The expected removal never happened. Rejecting Stevens's argument that presidential obstruction was enough for conviction, senators required an intentional violation of law. The Tenure of Office Act's wording was so unclear that it may not have applied to Stanton. When the president promised to restrain himself and chose a successor to Stanton that moderates trusted, the impeachment process lost momentum. In May, the Senate fell one vote short of the two-thirds needed to convict. Within a month, Congress had readmitted seven southern states, thus limiting Johnson's power to stymie Reconstruction in those states; with Grant's election to the presidency that fall, the new governments had whatever backing the army could afford them.

Radical Reconstruction in the South

With the help of Union Leagues, auxiliaries of the Republican Party whose goal was to mobilize and educate Black voters, and with military protection against conservative violence in place, Radical Reconstruction transformed the Cotton South dramatically. Within six months, 735,000 Blacks and 635,000 whites had registered to vote. Blacks formed electoral majorities in South Carolina, Florida, Mississippi, Alabama, and Louisiana. In most states they found white support in the so-called scalawags, white Southerners who supported Reconstruction and Republican policies. Wartime Unionists, hill farmers neglected by planter-dominated governments, debtors seeking relief, development-minded businessmen seeking a new, more diversified South, and even some Confederate leaders and planters all welcomed Radical Reconstruction. Carpetbaggers, northerners who had come south to farm, invest, preach, or teach, were few in numbers, but they took a front rank among the leaders in Black-majority states.

Starting in the fall of 1867, ten states called constitutional conventions, heavily Republican and predominantly, but not exclusively, white. The results of these conventions' so-called Black and Tan constitutions guaranteed a color-blind right to suffrage, mandated public school systems, and overhauled the tax structure. They also included a right to bear arms in their bills of rights. Only a few states shut any Confederates out of the vote, and most of those that did removed the electoral disabilities before a year was out.

Achievements and Failures of Radical Government

Later caricatured as a dire era of "bayonet" and "negro rule," Radical Reconstruction was neither. The Republican governments won in fairer elections and with greater turnouts than any that the South had known up until that time. Republican leadership remained overwhelmingly white and southern born. While some 700 Blacks served in state legislatures, only in South Carolina and possibly Louisiana did they ever outnumber whites. No state elected a Black governor, while only 16 Blacks served in Congress, 2 of whom were senators. Still, the contrast between what had been and what would follow was revolutionary. These Reconstruction legislatures were more representative of their constituents than most legislatures in nineteenth-century America (see Figure 15–1). While some African American officeholders were indeed illiterate, former enslaved people who did not own land, a disproportionate number came from the tiny prewar free African American elite of ministers, teachers, and small business owners. Freedpeople also filled hundreds of county offices. They served as sheriffs, bailiffs, judges, and jurors, offering the promise, at least, of a fair hearing in court for Black defendants and litigants. Sharing power locally meant a greater chance for Black communities to share in the benefits of public expenditures.

Republican rule delivered on its promises. The whipping post and debtor's prison vanished. The new governments funded insane asylums, roads, and prisons.

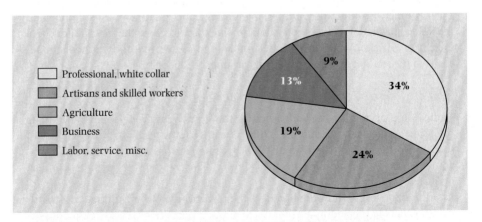

Figure 15–1 Occupations of Black Officeholders During Reconstruction
Although former enslaved people were underrepresented among Black officeholders, the Reconstruction governments were among the most broadly representative legislatures in US history.

Radical Members
One of the greatest achievements of congressional Reconstruction was the election of a significant number of African Americans to public office.

Homestead exemptions protected debtors' real estate, and lien laws gave tenant farmers more control over the crops they grew and awarded artisans a first right to their employer's assets. The right of married women to hold property in their own name was expanded. Across the Deep South, laws took on racial discrimination on streetcars and railroad lines, mandating equal treatment. Most important, most Reconstruction governments built or extended access to the free public school system to African Americans. Underfunded and segregated, those schools nonetheless boosted literacy rates, especially among freedpeople.

The Political Economy of Sharecropping

Radical Reconstruction made it easier for the former enslaved people to negotiate the terms of their labor contracts. Workers with grievances had a better chance of securing justice, as southern Republicans became sheriffs, justices of the peace, and county clerks, and as southern courts allowed Blacks to serve as witnesses and sit on juries.

The strongest card in the hands of the freedpeople was a shortage of agricultural workers in the South. After emancipation, thousands of Blacks sought opportunities in towns and cities or in the North. Though most Blacks remained in the South as farmers, they reduced their working hours in several ways. Black women still worked the fields but spent more time nursing their infants and caring for their children. The children went to school when they were able. The resulting labor shortage forced white landlords to renegotiate their labor arrangements with the freedpeople.

The contract labor system that had developed during the war and under presidential Reconstruction was replaced with a variety of regional arrangements. On the Louisiana sugar plantations, the freedpeople became wage laborers. But in tobacco and cotton regions, where most freedpeople lived, a new system of labor, sharecropping, developed. Under this system, an agricultural worker and his family typically agreed to work for one year on a particular plot of land, with the landowner providing the tools, seed, and work animals. At the end of the year, the crop was split, perhaps one-third going to the sharecropper and two-thirds to the owner.

Sharecropping shaped the economy of the postwar South by transforming the production and marketing of cash crops. Landowners broke up their plantations into family-sized plots, worked by sharecroppers in family units with no direct supervision. Each sharecropping family established its own relationship with local merchants to sell crops and buy supplies. Merchants became crucial to the southern credit system, because most southern banks could not meet the banking standards established by Congress during the Civil War. Storekeepers, usually the only people who could extend credit to sharecroppers, provided sharecroppers with food, fertilizer, animal feed, and other provisions during the year until the crop was harvested.

These developments had important consequences for white small farmers. More merchants fanned out into up-country areas inhabited mostly by ordinary whites, areas now served by railroads sponsored by the Reconstruction legislatures. With merchants offering credit and railroads offering transportation, small farmers started to produce cash crops. Thus, Reconstruction sped the process by which southern yeomen abandoned self-sufficient farming for cash crops.

Sharecropping spread quickly among Black farmers in the Cotton South. By 1880, 80 percent of cotton farms had fewer than 50 acres, and the majority of those farms were operated by sharecroppers (see Maps 15–2 and 15–3). Sharecropping had special advantages for landlords. It reduced their risk when cotton prices were low and encouraged workers to increase production without costly supervision. Further, if sharecroppers changed jobs before the crop was harvested, they lost a whole year's pay. But there were at least a few compensating factors for workers—at least, when the crops sold for high prices, as they did, briefly, in the postwar decade. For freedpeople with no hope of owning their own farms, sharecropping held out the promise of rewarding the hardest workers with the greatest gains. The bigger the crop, the more they earned. It gave them more independence than contract labor.

Sharecropping also let freedpeople work in families rather than in gangs. Freedom alone had rearranged the powers of men, women, and children within the families of former enslaved people. Parents gained new control over their children. They could send sons and daughters to school or put them to work. Successful families could give their children an important head start in life. Similarly, African American husbands gained new powers.

The marriage laws of the mid-nineteenth century that defined the husband as the head of the household were irrelevant to enslaved people, because their

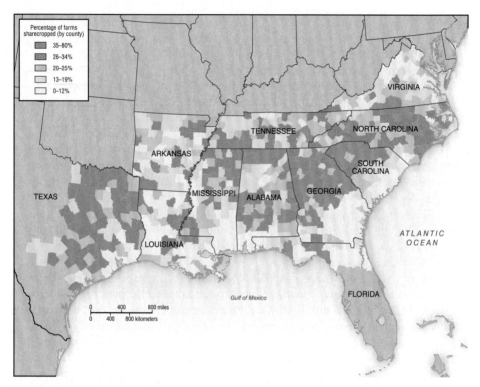

Map 15-2 Sharecropping By 1880, the sharecropping system had spread across the South. It was most common in the inland areas, where primarily cotton and tobacco plantations existed before the Civil War.

marriages had no legal standing. With emancipation, these patriarchal assumptions of American family law shaped the lives of freed men and women. Once married, women often found that their property belonged to their husbands. The sharecropping system further assumed that as head of the household the husband made the economic decisions for the entire family. Men signed most labor contracts, and most contracts assumed that the husband would take his family to work with him.

Sharecropping shaped the social system of the postwar South. It influenced the balance of power between men and women. It established the balance of power between landowners and sharecroppers. It tied the southern economy to agriculture, in particular to cotton production, impeding the region's overall economic development.

The Gospel of Prosperity

Only a diversified economy could break the planters' hold over a Black labor force; railroads could lower farmers' shipping costs and tap the South's coal and iron resources. Economic development might even give the South an independence worth having: it was no longer required to look north for its investment capital or finished goods. A program that made all classes prosper seemed ready-made to recruit more whites for a party and push racial issues into the background. Republicans

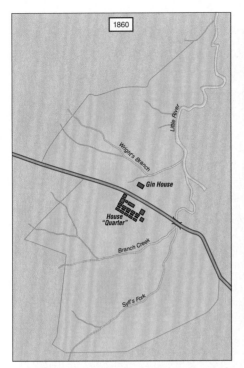
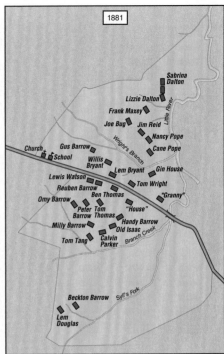

Map 15–3   The Effect of Sharecropping in the South: The Barrow Plantation in Oglethorpe County, Georgia   Sharecropping cut large estates into small landholdings worked by sharecroppers and tenants, changing the landscape of the South.

preached a "gospel of prosperity" that would use government aid to build a richer South and benefit ordinary white southerners. Reconstruction governments committed the states' credit and funds to building its industrial base.

The strategy had big drawbacks. Diverting scarce resources to railroads and corporations left less for Black constituencies' needs, especially school systems. Investors hesitated to invest in bonds issued by governments at risk of violent overthrow. Hungry corporations hounded the legislature for favors and made bribery their clinching argument. State-owned railroads were sold to private firms for a song—and a payoff. States already spending heavily to repair the damage of the war and to build new state services on a much-reduced tax base obligated themselves for millions more. As taxes soared, white farmers became increasingly receptive to Democratic claims that they were being robbed, their money wasted by swag-grabbing outsiders and ignorant Black upstarts in office. The passage of civil rights bills, ending discrimination in public transportation, only alienated former scalawags further and stirred conservatives to bring the stay-at-homes to the polls. Everywhere, Republicans split over how far to trust former Confederates. That division cost Virginia and Tennessee to the "Redeemers," conservative white Democrats, in 1869. In Arkansas, two Republicans claimed the governorship in 1872. Two years later they raised armies to fight it out. The "Brooks-Baxter war" ended with the Democrat-backed contestant winning and a new constitution that put both Republicans out for good.

"A COMPANY OF WHITES LAY IN AMBUSH FOR A PARTY OF NEGROES RETURNING FROM CHURCH, KILLED TEN, AND WOUNDED THIRTEEN."

Reconstruction Violence Terrorism against Republican governments targeted churches, schools, and Black landowners, not just the politically active. In this engraving, a band of white supremacists fire upon a group of Black people returning from church services in Choctaw County, Alabama, August 1, 1874.

A Counterrevolution of Terrorism and Economic Pressure

Republicans' policy failures alone did not destroy them. Terrorism and economic pressure did. Everywhere planters used their power to keep Black tenants from voting. White radicals found themselves shunned by society. They were denied credit or employment unless they left politics. As early as 1867, secret organizations were arising, bent on Reconstruction's overthrow and the restoration of white dominance, which, effectively, meant bringing Democrats into power by threats, beatings, and killings. From the Carolinas to Texas, the Ku-Klux Klan and similar organizations shot Republican lawmakers and burned Black schools and

America In The World
Reconstructing America's Foreign Policy

As the Civil War approached, slavery's expansionists tainted manifest destiny for everyone but Democrats. Republicans had no intention of spreading an empire of the unfree—nor of letting any European power do so. In Mexico, the French emperor had installed a puppet state headed by Maximilian, the Austrian archduke. The Johnson administration helped force France to withdraw its troops. Unbacked, Maximilian's regime collapsed. Spreading the republic's bounds would only spread liberty. It might even give Black southerners a place free of race prejudice where they could fulfill their potential. Secretary of State William Seward dreamed of all North America, perhaps even most of the Caribbean, as one vast federation; Senator Charles Sumner suggested that the United States ease Canada into the Union.

Nothing of the kind happened. Seward's biggest success came in 1867, in purchasing Alaska from Russia. A few months later, however, the Senate rejected a treaty buying the Virgin Islands from Denmark and held off on leasing a naval base in Santo Domingo. A treaty with Colombia giving the United States exclusive rights to build a canal across the Isthmus of Panama came to nothing. Canadians showed no interest in joining the Union and instead forged a union of their own separate provinces.

Not all the wealth of the West Indies could carry the United States beyond trade to the taking of territory. Slavery's end killed most of the zest for annexing Cuba; the fact that its people were Catholics and racially diverse alarmed even some Republicans. When a rebellion broke out there in 1868, Congress did nothing about it. Similar inhibitions thwarted Grant's plan to annex Santo Domingo in 1870. As head of the Senate Foreign Relations Committee, Sumner's opposition doomed the treaty and, ironically, himself; as a result, Grant and Fish forced the Senate to depose him from his chairmanship.

churches, often in broad daylight. Black landowners and renters were targeted. African American employees or tenants who complained about being cheated faced flogging or death for "insolence." Teachers, party organizers, and white wartime Unionists all fell victim. Politically active Blacks were threatened, driven from their homes, whipped, or shot. Their wives were raped and their homes plundered while Democratic newspapers defamed the victims. In a single year, authorities counted well over 500 killings in Georgia alone—and just about no arrests, much less indictments. Witnesses refused to testify, cowed juries dared not convict, and sheriffs dared not arrest. In Arkansas, Texas, and Tennessee, Republican governors mustered a white militia that broke the terrorist movement. Elsewhere they found themselves powerless or outgunned. Terrorism carried North Carolina, Alabama, and Georgia for the Democrats in 1870, crippling Reconstruction in the first state and effectively ending it in the other two. By 1872, Redeemers had regained the whole upper and border South. After that, they rigged the election laws to curb the Black vote and put any Republican comeback out of reach.

Reconstruction had not been meant to work that way. Instead of being able to defend themselves, Reconstruction governments found themselves desperately dependent on national support. But that support had been dissipating ever since the passage of the Reconstruction Acts.

As terrorism mounted, Congress legislated to protect a free, fair vote. The most important, the 1871 "Ku-Klux" Act, gave the US government the power to suppress the Klan, even suspending the writ of habeas corpus. President Grant moved cautiously, however, because the newly created Justice Department lacked both funds and personnel. When the time limit on the law's most effective provisions expired, Congress did not renew them. It did nothing to expand the government's ability to cope with violence when it broke out again a few years later. Still, thousands of arrests and hundreds of convictions ended the Klan, restoring peace in time for the 1872 presidential elections.

A RECONSTRUCTED WEST

Events out west may have contributed to the nation's declining interest in southern affairs. The lands beyond the Missouri River were being reconstructed just as dramatically, and when it came to their original inhabitants, far more brutally. In the West, most troops occupied states and territories and kept the peace. Here, too, the Gospel of Prosperity promised a new civilization, based on outsiders settling and bringing their eastern values and eastern capital with them. Passed during the Civil War, the Homestead Act was meant to populate the West with independent small farmers. Millions came in the 40 years that followed and continued to take out titles until 1934; millions more bought land at nominal prices under supplementary laws. Their movement has become the stuff of legend. But these hardy individuals did not settle an empty prairie. Native people held it already.

The Overland Trail

In popular images, the West was a haven for rugged men who struck out on their own, but most migrants went in family groups, and the families were mostly middle class. Few poor people could afford the journey and still hope to buy land and set up a farm.

The journey across the Overland Trail (see Map 15–4) had become safer over the years. The US government built forts to supply migrants and protect the trails from (rare) Indian attacks. Mormon settlers in Utah had built Salt Lake City into a major stopping point and the heart of a thriving economy. On May 10, 1869, two railroads, the Central Pacific, building from California, and the Union Pacific, building from the Missouri River, joined at Promontory Point, Utah. This first transcontinental railroad line effectively replaced the five-month journey of covered wagons with a trip of a little less than a week. Four more transcontinentals would reach the Pacific over the next generation. Out from them radiated branch lines and side spurs, to tie the West into eastern markets. Where the companies set down depots, towns sprang up, unlike in the East, where the towns came first and the railroads afterward. Irresponsibly and sometimes crookedly financed, subsidized by all levels of government, their construction almost guaranteeing an eventual wreck (actual and financial),

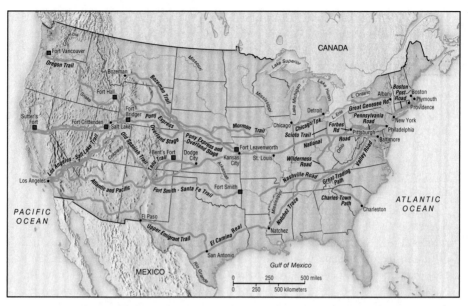

Map 15-4   The Overland Trails No transcontinental railroad existed until 1869. Even thereafter, most settlers moved west on a series of well-developed overland trails.

railroads became the symbol for the age. They represented to many Americans the enterprising spirit, the intrepid nature, and the arrogance of industrial capitalism. They turned Minnesota's Red River valley into a sea of wheat and dominated California's government. They also gave the army an unprecedented mobility that it would very much need. By the time the railroad presidents drove the golden spike at Promontory Point, the government had become occupied by the growing problem of Native American–white relations in the West.

The Origins of Indian Reservations

In 1851, more than 10,000 Native Americans from across the Great Plains converged on Fort Laramie in Wyoming Territory. All the major Indian peoples were represented: Sioux, Cheyenne, Arapaho, Crow, and many others. They came to meet with government officials who hoped to develop a lasting means of avoiding Indian–white conflict. Since the discovery of gold a few years earlier, white migrants had been crossing through Indian territory on their way to California, most of them already prejudiced against the Indians. US officials wanted to prevent outbreaks of violence between whites and Indians as well as between Indian nations. They proposed creating a separate territory for each Indian tribe, with government subsidies to entice the Indians to stay within their territories. This was the beginning of the reservation system, and for the rest of the century the US government struggled to force the Indians to accept it.

The government had good reason to advocate for reservations. At their worst, both whites and Indians behaved ferociously. Civilians in one territory raised $5,000 for Indian scalps, promising $25 for any "with ears on." At Sand Creek,

Colorado, militia slaughtered and scalped over 100 friendly Indians, two-thirds of them women and children. Fingers were cut off for the rings, body parts for souvenirs. In the northern Rockies, warriors led by the Northern Plains Indian leader Red Cloud lured forces from Fort Phil Kearny, killed them all, and stripped and mutilated the bodies. But Red Cloud could also say truthfully, "When the white man comes in my country, he leaves a trail of blood behind him." The reservation system was corrupt and badly handled. Agents for the Bureau of Indian Affairs cheated Indians and the government alike, sometimes reaping huge profits. But the reservations failed mostly because not all Indians agreed to stay within their designated territories, leading to armed confrontations and reprisals. "The more we can kill this year, the less will have to be killed the next war," General William Tecumseh Sherman declared.

Instead of extermination, the government opted for a more comprehensive reservation policy. Two treaties divided the Great Plains into two vast Indian territories. The Medicine Lodge Treaty, signed in Kansas in 1867, organized thousands of Indians across the southern plains. In return for government supplies, most of the southern plains peoples agreed to restrict themselves to the reservation. The Northern Plains Indians did not agree so readily. Inspired by Red Cloud, some insisted that the United States abandon forts along the Bozeman Trail. When the government agreed, Red Cloud signed the Fort Laramie Treaty in 1868. (It was one of the last. Starting in 1871, the government stopped treating the tribes as separate nations. They were subject peoples, nothing more.)

Red Cloud abided by the treaties for the rest of his life. They failed all the same. Not all the tribes approved of the treaties, and on the southern plains, raiding parties gave the army all the excuse it needed for payback. On Thanksgiving Day, 1868, the Seventh Cavalry, led by Lieutenant-Colonel George Armstrong Custer, massacred Cheyennes at Washita River, Oklahoma. Among the fallen was Black Kettle, who had survived the Sand Creek massacre in Colorado and whose influence had brought other tribes to make peace at Medicine Lodge. President Grant's "Peace Policy" had replaced selfish politicians with high-minded ministers as its go-betweens to the tribes and emphasized negotiation and assimilation over war and expulsion. However, there was no peace out West; not for the Comanches, Navajos, Modocs, or Lakota Sioux. And those last, in one general's opinion, were the greatest light cavalry in history.

The Lakota had a chance to prove their skill in battle. In Dakota Territory the discovery of gold in the Black Hills in 1874 brought thousands of whites onto Indian territory. When the Lakota refused to cede their lands to the miners, the government sent in the army, led by the charismatic, headstrong Lieutenant-Colonel Custer. In June 1876, Custer made two critical mistakes: he split his forces, and he failed to keep them in communication with each other. He and hundreds of his men were slaughtered at Little Bighorn, Montana, by 2,000 Indian warriors led by Crazy Horse.

"Custer's Last Stand" was the stuff of legends, but the real story came afterward. The Lakota could win battles, but not the war. Significantly, Crow warriors died with Custer. As in most other struggles, Native Americans served as US scouts, adjuncts, and allies. There was never a united Indian resistance; as far as Native Americans were concerned, there were no such things as Indians. There

Chinese Laborers Building Railroad This 1877 picture of a Southern Pacific Railroad trestle shows the crude construction methods used to build the first line across the Sierra Nevada.

were Blackfoots, Nez Percés, Arapahoes, and Comanches. They could be broken and beaten one by one, or turned against one another—and they were. The longer a war went on, the more tribes gave up or switched sides. The army had learned to adapt to a different kind of fighting. It hit the enemy in winter, when its forces were pinned down as they had been at Washita River. It destroyed not only Indian soldiers but also villages and crops to starve them into submission. In the Southwest, it used Apaches to hunt down other Apaches and adopted mule trains in place of slow, cumbersome supply wagons.

In the Northwest in 1877, the Nez Percés, fleeing from Union troops, began a dramatic trek across the mountains in an attempt to reach Canada. The Nez Percés eluded the troops and nearly made it over the Canadian border. However, hunger and the elements forced Chief Joseph and his exhausted people to agree to go to their reservations.

Pursued and deprived of allies one by one, Chief Sitting Bull and his last few warriors gave up in 1881. By then, most Indian wars were like jail breakouts: small,

Charles Russell, *Buffalo Hunt* More devastating to Plains nations than military attacks were the slaughter of the buffalo herds that fed and clothed them and were used in every aspect of their culture.

sporadic, and ugly. The ugliest came at Wounded Knee, South Dakota, in 1890. Fearing that the Ghost Dance religious revival movement would stir up rebellion, soldiers gunned down over 200 Native American men, women, and children. Sitting Bull did not live to see it. He had been shot resisting arrest days before.

Reforming Native American Tribes out of Existence

Sharing none of the settlers' fear of and less of their contempt for Indians, reformers hoped that reservations would function not just as holding pens, but as schools and civilizers. Lincoln's commissioner of Indian Affairs, William P. Dole, believed that "Indians are capable of attaining a high degree of civilization." Like other reformers, Dole equated civilization with a belief in individual property rather than communal holdings, Christian values rather than native religions, and the discipline of the regular hours that farmers and workers, rather than hunters, observed. Accordingly, reformers set out, as one of them put it, to destroy the Indian and save the person. They introduced government schools on reservations to teach the virtues of private property, individual achievement, and social mobility.

The reformers' influence peaked in 1887 when Congress passed the Dawes Severalty Act, the most important Indian legislation of the century, and the very kind of confiscation never done on freedpeoples' behalf. Reservation land was broken up into separate plots and distributed among individual families. The goal was to force Indians to live like white farmers, or as one reformer would put it later, killing the Indian and saving the man. But the lands allotted were generally so poor, and the plots so small, that their owners quickly sold them. Large tracts were kept in trust by the government and gradually sold off, purportedly to pay for uplifting and assimilating the Indians. By the early twentieth century only a few, sharply diminished reservations remained outside the desert Southwest. Native American cultures endured, but many Native Americans did not. Poverty, overcrowding, and epidemic disease brought their population to its lowest point. For many eastern on-lookers, those conditions only proved how unworthy the race was to compete in the struggle for life—a conclusion all too many had drawn about African Americans from Reconstruction's downfall.

THE RETREAT FROM REPUBLICAN RADICALISM

A series of makeshift laws and improvisations, congressional Reconstruction had stirred misgivings among moderate Republicans who were fearful of stretching the Constitution too far and uneasy with using the expanded authority that war had given them in peacetime. New steps, such as confiscating planters' property, say, or a nationally funded school system, were out of the question. Even the Freedmen's Bureau was cut back, and except for education, closed down completely when reconstructed states were readmitted to Congress. Public backlash against radicalism gave Democrats heavy gains in the 1867 elections. In order to survive, Reconstruction had to consolidate its gains and leave the new state governments to meet its promises.

Republicans Become the Party of Moderation

By then, the 1868 presidential campaign was under way. Running the war hero General Ulysses S. Grant for president, Republicans could offer a candidate above politics. His slogan, "Let us have peace," emphasized that the party meant to restore the Union, rather than advance radicalism. The platform endorsed congressional Reconstruction and defended Black voting in the South, but it left states not covered by Reconstruction to decide the issue of suffrage for themselves. Positioning themselves as protectors of the war's accomplishments came all the more easily after Democrats nominated former New York governor Horatio Seymour on a platform declaring the Reconstruction Acts as illegal, null, and void. Their fiercest spokesmen swore that if Democrats won, they would overturn the newly elected southern governments and install white conservative ones. Voiding those governments would invalidate the Fourteenth Amendment, ratified by southern legislatures; some partisans even argued that every measure passed since southern congressmen walked out in 1861 had no legal force. Bondholders, fearful that Democrats would turn their national securities into waste paper or pay them in depreciated "greenbacks," thought Grant the safer choice, even without Republicans' shouting that Seymour's election would reward traitors and bring on civil war again.

Northern voters got a taste of what Democratic rule would mean in an epidemic of violence across the South. Riots and massacres in Louisiana and Georgia kept Republicans from voting and carried both states for Seymour. For Northern voters, those outrages may have been decisive in electing Grant. Carrying the electoral college by a huge margin, he won the popular vote more narrowly with just 53 percent, and then only because of a heavy Black turnout in his favor.

RECONSTRUCTING THE NORTH

Although Reconstruction was aimed primarily at the South, the North was affected as well, especially by the struggle over the Black vote. The transformation of the North was an important chapter in the history of Reconstruction.

The Fifteenth Amendment and Nationwide African American Suffrage

Segregated into separate facilities or excluded entirely, denied the right to vote in nearly every state outside of New England, Blacks in wartime fought to end discrimination in the North. Biracial efforts chipped away at many states' discriminatory Black Laws and the Fourteenth Amendment eliminated the rest nationwide. Streetcar lines in some cities stopped running separate cars, Black testimony was admitted on the same terms as white, and in a few northern communities, Black children began attending white schools. Ending the color bar on voting and jury service proved to be more difficult: when impartial suffrage went on the ballot, most northern states voted against it (though most Republicans favored it and Congress mandated it in the territories and the District of Columbia).

The shocking electoral violence of 1868 persuaded Republicans that equal suffrage in the South needed permanent protection. In 1869, Congress added a **Fifteenth Amendment** to the Constitution forbidding the use of "race, color, or previous condition of servitude" as a bar to suffrage in the North as well as the South. For those states not yet readmitted to the Union (Virginia, Mississippi, and Texas), it made ratification of the amendment an additional condition. On March 30, 1870, the Fifteenth Amendment became part of the Constitution.

Revolutionary as it was, the Fifteenth Amendment had serious limitations that would weaken its impact later. As the Supreme Court would note, it conferred no right to vote on anybody. It simply limited the grounds on which it could be denied. States could impose property or taxpaying qualifications or a literacy test if they pleased, as long as the restrictions made no distinction on the basis of race. They could set up residency requirements or limit the vote to naturalized citizens, or to men.

Women and Suffrage

The issue of Black voting added to tensions among northern radicals. Feminists and abolitionists had worked together in the struggle for emancipation, but signs of trouble appeared as early as May 1863 at the convention of the Woman's National Loyal League in New York City. The League had been organized to assist in defeating the slave South. One of the convention's resolutions declared that "there never can be a true peace in this Republic until the civil and political rights of all citizens of African descent and all women are practically established." For some delegates, this went too far. They argued that it was inappropriate to inject the issue of women's rights into the struggle to restore the Union.

With the war's end, the radical crusade for Black suffrage intensified debate among reformers. **Elizabeth Cady Stanton** and others pointed out the injustice of letting "Patrick and Sambo and Hans and Yung Tung" vote while propertied, educated women were denied suffrage. The Fourteenth Amendment, by privileging male inhabitants' right to vote explicitly, appalled Stanton, and the Fifteenth Amendment's failure to address gender discrimination at the polls only confirmed her suspicion that what one abolitionist called "the Negro's hour" would never give way to one for women. Friendly to women's suffrage though they were, abolitionists like Frederick Douglass and suffragists like Lucy Stone argued that the critical issue was the protection of the freedpeople. "When women, because they are women, are dragged from their homes and hung upon lamp-posts," Douglass reminded an audience, "when their children are torn from their arms and their brains dashed to the pavement; when they are the objects of insult and outrage at every turn; when they are in danger of having their homes burnt down over their heads; when their children are not allowed to enter schools; then they will have an urgency to obtain the ballot." In 1869, radical and abolitionist allies parted ways. The women's suffrage movement divided into rival organizations, Stanton's National Woman Suffrage Association and Stone's American Woman Suffrage Association.

Some radicals, Charles Sumner among them, favored women's suffrage. Most Republicans did not. The territories of Wyoming and Utah enfranchised women. Elsewhere, lawmakers let women participate in school-board elections, but voting reform went no further. Most states refused even to put the issue on the ballot. When they did so, it was voted down. Denying women's appeal that as citizens they were entitled to vote, the Supreme Court declared that the Fourteenth Amendment's right of citizenship carried no such right with it.

THE END OF RECONSTRUCTION

Events outside the South helped speed Reconstruction's collapse. Reform-oriented Republicans felt alarm at the spread of political corruption after the war. Convinced, too, that full reconciliation must come, now that the war's goals had been met, they broke with the party and abandoned their support for federal intervention in southern affairs. Additionally, a depression took voters' minds off Reconstruction issues. By 1876, Redemption had carried white Democrats to power in all but a few southern states. Yet a hotly disputed presidential election and divided power would doom even those.

Corruption Is the Fashion

Never before had corruption loomed so large in the United States. With more money to spend, more favors to give, and more functions to perform, both state and federal governments found themselves besieged by supplicants, and office-holders found opportunities to turn a dishonest penny where none had existed before. In New York City, infamous state senator William M. Tweed used the Tammany Hall political machine to steal tens of millions of dollars. Senators bought their seats in Kansas and South Carolina, while Tennessee congressmen sold appointments to West Point. The Standard Oil Company did everything with the Pennsylvania legislature except refine it. As Henry Clay Warmoth, the governor of Louisiana put it, corruption was "the fashion." He, incidentally, was very fashionable himself.

President Grant as a Strong Man Despite solid accomplishments and his own honesty, Ulysses S. Grant would be remembered for scandals in just about every department. Here he upholds various corrupt "rings" and the thieves and hacks that mulcted the War and Navy Departments, the government of the District of Columbia, and the custom-house service.

With an honest but credulous chief executive, Grant's administration became notoriously corrupt. Customs collectors shook down merchants and used their employees to manage party conventions. With help from administration insiders, the notorious speculators Jay Gould and Jim Fisk tried to corner the nation's gold supply and brought on a brief, ruinous panic on Wall Street. Grant's private secretary was even exposed as a member of the "Whiskey Ring," a group of distillers and revenue agents who cheated the government out of millions of dollars in taxes. Charges of making money by swindling the Indians forced the Secretary of Interior out of office. Months later, the Secretary of War quit when investigators traced kickbacks to his wife. Having overcharged the government for supplies while building the Union Pacific Railroad, the fraudulent Credit Mobilier contracting firm shared mammoth profits with nearly a dozen top congressmen. The Republican platform, one critic snarled, was just a conjugation of the verb "to steal."

Southern corruption reflected national patterns. In the worst states, both parties stole, bribed, and profited. But in the South, Democrats blamed such action on ignorant Black voters and nonlandowning white Republicans. Shifting the issue from equal rights to honest government, they insisted that clean, cheap government, run by society's natural leaders (white and well-heeled), would benefit all races. Every scandal discredited Republican rule further, including the many upright and talented leaders, both Black and white, that fought against corruption. This helped galvanize the opposition, destroying Republican hopes of attracting white voters and weakening support for Reconstruction. By 1875, northerners assumed the worst of any carpetbagger, even one fighting to cut taxes and block cheats.

Liberal Republicans Revolt

Voicing widely held concerns, a small, potent group of northern Republican intellectuals, editors, and activists challenged a political system that, in their view, rested on greed, selfishness, partisanship, and politicians' keeping war hatreds alive. Known as **liberal Republicans**, they viewed bosses and political machines, which were out to loot the Treasury, and special interests as detrimental to good government. They were weary of railroads receiving land grants, of steamship lines receiving subsidies, and government clerkships given to cronies. Decrying corruption and disenchanted with Reconstruction, they called for reform: a lower tariff, a stable currency system based on gold, a merit-based civil service system for appointments to office, and full, universal amnesty for former Confederates.

When Democrats announced a "New Departure," accepting the three constitutional amendments, liberal Republicans took them at their word. Despairing of preventing Grant's renomination, they nominated the eccentric, reform-minded editor **Horace Greeley** for president in 1872. The platform promised to remove all political disabilities and reconcile North and South, in essence by ending all federal intervention on Black southerners' behalf. Desperate to win, Democrats endorsed the editor, their lifelong enemy, but thousands stayed home on Election Day rather than vote for him. Having cut the tariff and restored the office-holding rights of all but a handful of ex-Confederates, Republicans won many reformers back. Greeley lost in a landslide and died in a sanitarium less than a month later.

Grant's reelection bought Reconstruction time; it could not do more than that. Northerners, even Republican ones, became increasingly alarmed every time the national government used its power to act on behalf of Reconstruction governments and deal with issues that should be handled by local authorities. As a result, the president found it increasingly hard to justify intervening on the behalf of Black voters.

"Redeeming" the South

In September 1873, America's premier financial institution, Jay Cooke & Company, went bankrupt after overextending itself on investments in the Northern Pacific Railroad. Within weeks, hundreds of banks and thousands of businesses failed. The country sank into a depression that lasted five years. Unemployment rose to 14 percent as corporations slashed wages. Bitter strikes in textile plants, coal fields, and on the railroad lines ended in failure and violence. As America turned its attention to issues of corruption, labor unrest, and economic depression, Reconstruction took a backseat.

Between the corruption scandals buffeting the Grant administration and the economic crisis, northern voters' interest in Reconstruction plummeted. Those who had favored government intervention to keep "Rebels" from coming to power no longer saw the need. Former Confederates stood by the flag as earnestly as Unionists. In the 1874 elections, Democrats made a dramatic comeback. For the first time since 1859, they carried the House, guaranteeing a deadlocked Congress. Outgoing Republicans made one last advance, passing Charles Sumner's civil rights bill, which outlawed discrimination in public places. The law left segregated schools and cemeteries alone, and most southern establishments ignored even those provisions that did pass. But with Congress's adjournment in March 1875, Republicans no longer had any chance of bolstering Reconstruction with legislation, or even funding an army big enough to protect a fair vote at the polls.

Supreme Court rulings made implementing Reconstruction legislation harder still. In the 1873 *Slaughterhouse* cases, a majority decided that the Fourteenth Amendment's protection of equal rights under the law covered only those rights associated with national citizenship. Rights affiliated with state citizenship—for

Struggles For Democracy

An Incident at Coushatta, August 1874

If biracial democracy had a chance anywhere in Reconstruction Louisiana, it was upstate in Red River parish. With African Americans outnumbering whites more than two to one, majority rule meant Republican government. As in so many other Black counties, whites held the choicest offices: sheriff, tax collector, and mayor of the parish seat in Coushatta. A Vermont-born Union veteran, Marshall Harvey Twitchell, represented Red River in the state senate. Most of the wealth and nearly all the property stayed in native white hands, just as it had before the war. Blacks continued to raise and harvest the cotton on other people's land.

Nevertheless, Reconstruction made a difference for African Americans. They elected members of their own race to the police jury that did most of the parish's day-to-day governing. Several justices of the peace who handled minor civil cases were Black. Farmers, field hands, and day laborers performed jury duty. What freedpeople wanted most, however, was what white conservatives had long denied them: a functioning public school system. Twitchell saw that they got one, with separate schools for whites and Blacks. So prosperous was

Red River under "Negro rule," Twitchell bragged, that it was evident to "the most perfect stranger."

Having the most votes was not enough, however. All the influential newspapers and nearly all the property and firepower in Red River parish remained with the Democrats. When hard times hit, Republicans' enemies organized rifle clubs and a White League, which acted as the military arm of the Democratic Party. Unlike the Ku Klux Klan, it operated in the open and without disguises. By mid-1874, death threats against Republican officials were being posted on the streets of Coushatta. "Your fate is sealed," one letter warned judges. "Nothing but your blood will appease us." Alarmed, the police jury resigned and white Republicans left the parish.

That August, White Leaguers pretended to have uncovered a Black plot to slaughter white residents. On that excuse, they arrested several dozen Black Republican leaders and all the white parish officers. To save their lives, the officials resigned. The vigilantes promised them an armed escort out of the parish, but instead, it led them into an ambush. Mounted gunmen from the neighboring parish killed six prisoners. Later they rode

example, the right to butcher cattle when a Louisiana state law gave a monopoly to one particular firm—could only be upheld by the state. In 1876, the justices whittled down the national government's power to protect Black voters from intimidation and violence or even their right to bear arms and hold public meetings. In *United States v. Cruikshank*, the Court took up a horrific massacre of some 150 Black state militiamen at Colfax, Louisiana, on Easter Sunday, 1873; it decided that the equal protection clause applied only to state governments' actions, not that of the paramilitaries responsible. In *Hall v. DeCuir* (1878), the Supreme Court invalidated a Louisiana law prohibiting racial segregation on public transportation. In the Civil

Terror in the South Thomas Nast's 1874 cartoon depicts a White League member and a Klan member joining hands over a terrorized Black family. Nast's point was not that emancipation had been a mistake, but that without national protection, freedpeople's fate was worse than slavery.

into Coushatta and hanged two of the captured Blacks as well. Absent on political business, Twitchell alone survived. When he returned in 1876, an unknown gunman shot him, costing him both arms. From then on, Republican majorities counted for nothing. Democrats did the voting and governing, and thus radical Reconstruction's gains melted away.

Coushatta's fate was Louisiana's. White Leaguers overthrew the governor in September 1874. Federal intervention restored him, but it could not save local Republican governments like Red River's. "The State government has no power outside of the United States Army ... no power at all," an officer confessed. "The White League is the only power in the State."

Rights Cases of 1883, the Supreme Court declared that the Fourteenth Amendment did not cover discriminatory practices by private persons.

Even before the 1874 elections, southern Reconstruction was collapsing. As the number of white Republicans fell, the number of Black Republicans holding office in the South increased. But the persistence of Black officeholders only reinforced the Democrats' determination to "redeem" their states from Republican rule. Blaming hard times on "carpetbagger" corruption and high taxes, conservatives formed taxpayers' leagues and armed themselves in White Leagues, paramilitary groups whose goal was to remove Republicans from office and prevent freedmen from voting. Crude appeals to white supremacy and harsh economic pressure forced most scalawags to drop out of politics, making it easier to draw a sharp color line. Paramilitaries then applied violence and intimidation to keep Blacks from the polls. By the fall of 1874, they were overthrowing local governments in Mississippi and Louisiana. White Leagues took over the streets in New Orleans and briefly ousted the governor. Terrorism helped "redeem" Alabama that November, among other places.

That left two securely Republican states, both with considerable Black majorities: South Carolina and Mississippi. In 1875, Democrats in the latter mounted the most flagrant show of force yet. Governor Adelbert Ames begged for federal help and was told to look to his own resources first. The election that followed was as quiet as White League shotguns could make it. In the end, enough Blacks were disfranchised and enough scalawags voted their racial prejudices to hand power to the Democrats. Within months they forced Ames's resignation. In 1876, South Carolina whites adopted the "Mississippi Plan" with an even more open commitment to violent overthrow of the Republican majority. Mounted, armed men broke up Republican rallies. In Hamburg, white paramilitaries besieged local Black militiamen and, after their surrender, killed seven of them. "We write to tell you that our people are being shot down like dogs, and no matter what democrats may say," one South Carolinian wrote the president, "unless you help us our folks will not dare go to the polls." In Louisiana, Redeemer violence may have been worse still.

The Twice-Stolen Election of 1876

Amid a serious economic depression, and with an electorate tired of Reconstruction, the Democrats stood a good chance of winning the presidency in 1876. The Democratic candidate, New York governor Samuel J. Tilden, had won a reputation for fighting thieves in his own party. On election night, Tilden won 250,000 more votes than his equally reform-minded Republican opponent, Ohio governor Rutherford B. Hayes (see Map 15–5). But Republican "returning boards" in three southern states—Florida, South Carolina, and Louisiana—counted Hayes in to a one-electoral vote victory.

Democrats swore that they had been cheated out of the presidency, though even without white violence and vote-rigging, Hayes probably would have won not just in the three disputed states but elsewhere in the South. As Congress deadlocked on the electoral count, cries of "Tilden or Blood" rang in the air. In the end, both sides compromised by choosing a special electoral commission to settle the matter. In an eight-to-seven vote, it awarded Hayes every disputed state. House Democrats could not stop "His Fraudulency" from being sworn in, but their southern members, cutting the best deal they could, agreed to drop their obstruction in return for assurances that Hayes would not prop up the last two Reconstruction governments. A month after taking office, Hayes withdrew the regiments guarding Republican statehouses in South Carolina and Louisiana; by then Redeemer Democrats had full control of the states anyway. So Reconstruction met its symbolic end. Hereafter, the president would emphasize goodwill between the North and South and trust Redeemers' promises to protect Black rights—a trust speedily betrayed, and nowhere more so than on the farms where most freedpeople worked for a white landowner.

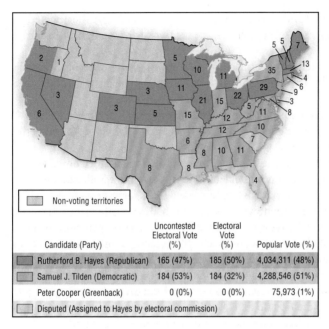

Map 15-5 The Presidential Election, 1876 In 1876, the Democratic presidential candidate, Samuel Tilden, won what popular vote white southern Democrats permitted to be cast, but he was denied the presidency because Republicans claimed that a fair count gave Louisiana, South Carolina, Oregon, and Florida to their candidate, Rutherford B. Hayes.

	Uncontested Electoral Vote (%)	Electoral Vote (%)	Popular Vote (%)
Candidate (Party)			
Rutherford B. Hayes (Republican)	165 (47%)	185 (50%)	4,034,311 (48%)
Samuel J. Tilden (Democratic)	184 (53%)	184 (32%)	4,288,546 (51%)
Peter Cooper (Greenback)	0 (0%)	0 (0%)	75,973 (1%)
Disputed (Assigned to Hayes by electoral commission)			

Non-voting territories

Sharecropping Becomes Wage Labor

As the southern economy recovered from the devastation of the Civil War, many observers predicted a bright future for the region. Optimists saw a wealth of opportunities from untapped natural and human resources, a South freed from the inefficient slave labor system and ripe for investment.

Americans were building railroads at an exuberant clip, but southerners built them faster—with northern money. By 1890, steel mills lit the night skies of Birmingham, Alabama. Textile mills dotted the Piedmont Plateau (along the eastern foothills of the Appalachian Mountains from Virginia to Georgia). Southerners were migrating from the countryside to the towns, expanding cotton production into new areas, like the rich Mississippi delta soil. Yet ordinary southerners, especially African Americans, did not share in the New South's prosperity.

Redemption shifted the terms of the new labor relationship between landlords and sharecroppers in landowners' direction. The most important question was who owned the cotton crop at the end of the year: the sharecropper who raised it, the landlord who owned the farm, or the merchant who lent the supplies to bring the crop in.

Legal resolution in favor of the landlord came by the middle of the 1880s. The courts defined a sharecropper as a wage laborer. The landlord owned the crop and paid his workers a share of it as a wage. Landlords also won a stronger claim on the crop than the merchant creditors. Under the circumstances, merchants were reluctant to advance money to sharecroppers. Many left plantation districts and moved up-country, doing business with white yeomen farmers. Trapped in a cycle of debt, white farmers in the 1880s began losing their land and falling into tenancy. Meanwhile, in the "Black belt" (where most African Americans lived and most of the cotton was produced), successful landlords became merchants while successful merchants purchased land and hired sharecroppers of their own. By the mid-1880s, Black sharecroppers worked as wage laborers for the landlord-merchant class across much of the South.

Sharecropping differed in two critical ways from the wage work of industrial America. First, sharecropping was family labor, depending on a husband and father who signed the contract and delivered the labor of his wife and children to the landlord. Second, because sharecropping contracts were yearlong, the labor market was restricted to a few weeks at the end of each year. If croppers left before the end of the year, they risked losing everything.

The political economy of sharecropping impoverished the South by binding the region to cotton, a crop that steadily depleted the soil even as prices fell. Yet most southern Blacks found few alternatives. In time a few Black farmers purchased their own land, but their farms were generally tiny and the soil poor. The skilled Black artisans who had worked on plantations before the Civil War moved to southern cities, where they took unskilled, low-paying jobs. Northern factories were segregated, as were the steel mills of Birmingham, Alabama, and the Piedmont textile mills. Black women worked as domestic servants to supplement their husbands' meager incomes. Wage labor transformed southern Blacks' lives, but it brought no prosperity.

The New South of industry and diversified agriculture opened southern forests to northern timber companies and dotted southern rivers with textile mills, but it did not break the stranglehold that cash crops and plantations had over the economy. It made the region more dependent on northern capital and finished goods

TIME LINE

▼**1851**
Fort Laramie Treaty
  establishes Indian
  reservations

▼**1862**
Passage of Homestead Act

▼**1863**
Lincoln's Proclamation
  of Amnesty and
  Reconstruction

▼**1864**
Wade-Davis Bill

▼**1865**
Thirteenth Amendment
  adopted and ratified

Freedmen's Bureau
  established
Confederate armies
  surrender
Lincoln assassinated;
  Andrew Johnson
  becomes president
Johnson creates provisional
  governments in
  the South; new civil
  governments begin
Joint Committee on
  Reconstruction
  established by Congress

▼**1866**
Congress renews
  Freedmen's Bureau;
  Johnson vetoes it

Civil Rights Act vetoed
  by Johnson; Congress
  overrides veto
Congress passes
  Fourteenth Amendment
New Orleans and Memphis
  massacres
Republicans sweep
  midterm elections

▼**1867**
First, Second, and Third
  Reconstruction Acts
  passed
Tenure of Office Act
Medicine Lodge Treaty

than ever. Most of all, for the freedpeople outside a few large cities, it did not prove new at all. They found themselves excluded from juries and unprotected from white harassment and attack. White judges, white police, and white sheriffs guaranteed a white justice that treated every Black witness's testimony as suspect and turned petty larceny into an excuse for jail time and permanent disfranchisement. Black convicts stood more chance of serving on the chain gang, often hired out as cheap labor to employers who paid the state pennies a day for the work done. In the Deep South, lynchings became almost an everyday occurrence, and, to judge from the souvenir sellers and excursion trains bringing in viewers, a kind of obscene spectator sport. Prejudice closed the door to Blacks seeking to become professionals or craftsmen and guaranteed the skimpiest of funding for their schools. In a few states, the whipping post made a comeback. With the laws and the lawless working together to keep most Blacks from voting, freedom meant much less than it had in Reconstruction days. But now, there were few northerners willing to listen when Black southerners appealed for help.

Hoping to escape poverty and discrimination, some former enslaved people moved west. One group, the **Exodusters,** moved to the Kansas prairie during the mid-1870s. By 1880, more than 6,000 Blacks had joined them, searching for cheap land for independent farms. Like white farmers, the Exodusters fought with cattlemen. Blacks who settled in cow towns such as Dodge City and Topeka found the same discrimination they had known in the South. Still, some of the Exodusters did buy land and build farms.

▼**1868**
Second Fort Laramie Treaty
Washita River Massacre
Johnson fires Secretary of
  War Stanton
House of Representatives
  impeaches Johnson
Senate trial of Johnson
  ends in acquittal
Fourteenth Amendment
  ratified
Waves of Klan violence
  sweep Cotton South
Ulysses S. Grant elected
  president

▼**1869**
Congress passes Fifteenth
  Amendment

▼**1870**
Fifteenth Amendment
  ratified

▼**1872**
Liberal Republican revolt
Grant reelected

▼**1873**
Financial panic sets off
  depression

▼**1875**
Mississippi Plan succeeds
Civil Rights Act enacted

▼**1876**
Disputed presidential
  election of Rutherford

B. Hayes and Samuel J.
  Tilden
Custer's Last Stand at Little
  Bighorn

▼**1877**
Electoral commission
  counts in Rutherford B.
  Hayes as president
Last Reconstruction
  governments collapse

▼**1887**
Dawes Severalty Act

CONCLUSION

Inspired by a vision of society based on equal rights and free labor, Republicans expected emancipation to transform the South. Freed from the shackles of the slave power, the region might yet become a shining example of democracy and prosperity. Twenty years later, events seemed to mock that promise. The South was scarcely more industrial than before the war and, as far as former enslaved people were concerned, far from completely free. Cotton, sugar, rice, and tobacco still defined the South's economy far more than the hoped-for mines and mills. Only a small fraction of freedpeople had become landowners, and most of them would never escape poverty and dependence on propertied whites. After the Panic of 1873, sharecropping eliminated most Blacks' hope of real economic independence. As fears of a new rebellion dimmed, Republicans lost their zeal for federal intervention in the South. Republican state authorities could not save themselves, much less their Black constituents. Chastened by Reconstruction's defects, Americans began to turn their attention to the new problems of urban, industrial America and to the epic success story, as they saw it, of the "winning of the West."

Even so, the achievements of Reconstruction were monumental. In the West, it settled vast multitudes of people—and unsettled multitudes more. Over two generations, it created as many states as had gone into rebellion in 1861. Across the South, African Americans carved out a space in which their families could live more freely than before. Black and white men elected to office some of the most democratic state legislatures of the nineteenth century. Thousands of Black workers had escaped a stifling contract-labor system for the comparatively wider autonomy of sharecropping. Hundreds of thousands of former enslaved people learned to read and write and were able to worship in churches of their own making. Most important, Reconstruction added three important amendments to the Constitution that transformed civil rights and electoral laws throughout the nation. For the first time, the protections in the Bill of Rights would apply not just against national encroachment but that of the states as well. As a result of those changes in fundamental law, Reconstruction, then, was not so much a promise broken as one waiting to be fulfilled.

WHO, WHAT, WHERE

✶ REVIEW QUESTIONS

1. What made congressional Reconstruction radical?
2. How did conditions for the readmission of states into the Union change over time?
3. How did Reconstruction change the South?
4. How did western Indians respond to westward expansion?
5. How did Reconstruction change the North?
6. What were the major factors that brought Reconstruction to an end?

CRITICAL-THINKING QUESTIONS

1. Compare and contrast wartime Reconstruction, presidential Reconstruction, and congressional (radical) Reconstruction. What were the key differences between the three phases?
2. How critical was the failure of land redistribution for Blacks? Was sharecropping an acceptable substitute for achieving economic freedom? Why or why not?
3. How did terrorism and economic pressure both hinder and help the Reconstruction of the South?

SUGGESTED READINGS

Foner, Eric. *Reconstruction: America's Unfinished Revolution, 1863–1877.* New York: Harper-Collins, 2014.

Hahn, Steven. *A Nation Under Our Feet: Black Political Struggles in the Rural South from Slavery to the Great Migration.* Cambridge, MA: Harvard University Press, 2003.

Litwack, Leon. *Been in the Storm So Long: The Aftermath of Slavery.* New York: Oxford University Press, 1979.

Summers, Mark Wahlgren. *The Ordeal of the Reunion: A New History of Reconstruction.* Chapel Hill: University of North Carolina Press, 2014.

For further review materials and resource information, please visit www.oup.com/us/ofthepeople

Study Guide

CHAPTER 15: Reconstructing a Nation, 1865–1877
Primary Sources

15.1 PETROLEUM V. NASBY [DAVID ROSS LOCKE], *A PLATFORM FOR NORTHERN DEMOCRATS (1865)*

David Ross Locke, the editor of the *Toledo Blade*, made his fortune under another name: Petroleum V. Nasby, a fictional postmaster and sometimes pastor, whose letters gave a Republican spoof of what Copperhead Democrats believed. Bad spelling was a common way of signaling to readers that a piece was meant to be humorous, though Locke also meant to show that Nasby's ideas were not only vicious and absurd but founded on a virtually illiterate ignorance.

Saint's Rest (wich is in the Stait uv Noo Jersey), June the 23d, 1865

These is the dark days uv the dimokrasy. The misforchoons that befell our armies in front uv Richmond, the fall uv our capital, follered by the surrender uv our armies to Grant and Sherman, hez hurt us. Our leaders are either pinin in loathsome dunguns, incarseratid by the hevin-defyin, man-destroyin, tyrannical edix uv our late lamented President, or are baskin in the free air uv Italy and Canady. We hev no way uv keepin our voters together. Opposin the war won't do no good, for before the next elecshun the heft uv our voters will hev diskiverd that the war is over. The fear uv drafts may do suthin in some parts uv Pennsylvany and suthern Illinoy, for sum time yuit, but that can't be depended on.

But we hev wun resource for a ishoo—ther will alluz be a dimokrasy so long as ther's a nigger.

Ther is a uncompromising dislike to the nigger in the mind uv a ginooine dimekrat. The Spanish bullfighter, when he wants to inflame the bull to extra cavortin, waves a red flag afore him. When yoo desire a dimekrat to froth at the mouth, yoo will find a Black face will anser the purpose. Therefore, the nigger is, today, our best and only holt. Let us use him.

For the guidance uv the faithful, I shel lay down a few plain rools to be observed, in order to make the most uv the capital we hev:

1. Alluz assert that the nigger will never be able to take care uv hisself, but will alluz be a public burden. He may, possibly, give us the lie by goin to work. In such a emergency, the dooty uv every dimekrat is plane. He must not be allowed to work. Assosiashens must be organized, pledged to neither give him employment, to work with him, to work for anyone who will give him work, or patronize any wun who duz. (I wood sejest that sich uv us ez hev bin forchoonit enuff to git credit, pay a trifle on account, so ez to make our patronage worth suthin.) This course, rigidly and persistently follered, will drive the best uv em to stealin, and the balance to the poorhouses, provin wat we hev alluz claimed, that they are a idle and vishus race. Think, my brethren, wat a inspirin effeck our poorhouses and jails full uv niggers wood hev on the people! My sole expands ez I contemplate the deliteful vision.

2. Likewise assert that the nigger will come North, and take all the good places, throwin all our skilled mechanics out uv work by underbiddin uv em. This mite be open to two objecshuns, to-wit: It crosses slitely rool the 1, and white men mite say, ef there's jist enuff labor for wat's here, why not perhibit furriners from comin?

I anser: It's the biznis uv the voter to reconcile the contraicshun—he may believe either or both. Ez to the second objeckshun, wher is the Dimekrat who coodent be underbid, and stand it even to starvashen, ef the underbiddin wux dun by a man uv the proud Caukashen race? And wher is the Dimekrat so lost to manhjood ez not to drink blood, ef the same underbiddin is dun by a nigger? The starving for work ain't the question—it's the color uv the cause uv the starvashen that makes the difference.

Nigger equality may be worked agin to advantage. All men, without distincshun uv sex, are fond uv flatrin theirselves that somebody's lower down in the scale uv humanity than they is. Ef 'twan't for niggers, what wood the dimokrasy do for sumbody to look down upon? It's also shoor to enlist wun style uv wimmen on our sides. In times gone by, I've notist gushin virgins uv forty-five, full sixteen hands high and tough ez wire, holdin aloft banners onto which wuz inscribd—"Save us from Nigger Equality." Yoo see it soothed em to hev a chase uv advertising, 1st, That they wuz frail, helplis critters; and, 2d, That, anshent and tough ez they wuz, some wun wuz still goin for em.

Ef ther ain't no niggers, central commities must furnish em. A half dozen will do for a ordinary county, ef they're hustled along with energy. Ef they won't steal, the central commities must do it theirselves. Show yer niggers in a township in the morning, an the same nite rob the clothes-lines and hen-roosts. Ever willin to sacrifice myself for the cause, I volunteer to do this latter dooty in six populous counties.

These ijees, ef follered, will, no doubt, keep us together until our enemies split, when we will reap the reward uv our constancy and fidelity. May the Lord hasten the day.

Petroleum V. Nasby

Lait Paster uv the Church uv the Noo Dispensashun

Source: David Ross Locke/Petroleum V. Nasby, *A Platform for Northern Democrats*, from Locke, *The Struggles, Social, Financial and Political of Petroleum V. Nasby* (Boston, 1888), quoted in William Benton, publ., *The Annals of America. Volume 9, 1858–1865: The Crisis of the Union* (Chicago: Encyclopedia Britannica, Inc., 1968), pp. 597–598.

15.2 A BLACK TENANT FARMER DESCRIBES WORKING CONDITIONS

Landless African Americans found few options in the late-nineteenth-century southern countryside. Their exploitation came in varying degrees of injustice, the worst of them a peonage not far from slavery. White society was rarely interested in their condition, and those who spoke out did so at their own physical peril. This account from a Black who chose to remain anonymous appeared in a religious periodical early in the twentieth century.

I am a negro and was born some time during the war in Elbert County, Ga., and I reckon by this time I must be a little over forty years old. My mother was not married when I was born, and I never knew who my father was or anything about him. Shortly after the war my mother died, and I was left to the care of my uncle. All this happened before I was eight years old, and so I can't remember very much about it. When I was about ten years old, my uncle hired me out to Captain—. I had already learned how to plow, and was also a good hand at picking cotton. I was told that the Captain wanted me for his house-boy, and that later on he was going to train me to be his coachman. To be a coachman in those days was considered a post of honor, and, young as I was, I was glad of the chance. But I had not been at the Captain's a month before I was put to work on the farm, with some twenty or thirty other negroes—men, women and children. From the beginning the boys had the same tasks as the men and women. There was no difference. We all worked hard during the week, and would frolic on Saturday nights and often on Sundays. And everybody was happy. The men got $3 a week and the women $2. I don't know what the children got. Every week my uncle collected my money for me, but it was very little of it that I ever saw. My uncle fed and clothed me, gave me a place to sleep, and allowed me ten or fifteen cents a week for "spending change," as he called it. I must have been seventeen or eighteen years old before I got tired of that arrangement, and felt that I was man enough to be working for myself and handling my own wages. The other boys about my age and size were "drawing" their own pay, and they used to laugh at me and call me "Baby" because my old uncle was always on hand to "draw" my pay. Worked up by these things, I made a break for liberty. Unknown to my uncle or the Captain I went off to a neighboring plantation and hired myself out to another man. The new landlord agreed to give me forty cents a day and furnish me one meal. I thought that was doing fine. Bright and early one Monday morning I started for work, still not letting the others know anything about it. But they found out before sundown. The Captain came over to the new place and brought some kind of officer of the law. The officer pulled out a long piece of paper from his pocket and read it to my new employer. When this was done I heard my boss say:

"I beg your pardon, Captain. I didn't know this nigger was bound out to you, or I wouldn't have hired him."

"He certainly is bound out to me," said the Captain. "He belongs to me until he is twenty-one, and I'm going to make him know his place."

So I was carried back to the Captain's. That night he made me strip off my clothing down to my waist, had me tied to a tree in his backyard, ordered his foreman to give me thirty lashes with a buggy whip across my bare back, and stood by until it was done. After that experience the Captain made me stay on his place night and day,—but my uncle still continued to "draw" my money.

I was a man nearly grown before I knew how to count from one to one hundred. I was a man nearly grown before I ever saw a colored school teacher. I never went to school a day in my life. To-day I can't write my own name, tho I can read a little. I was a man nearly grown before I ever rode on a railroad train, and then I went on an excursion from Elberton to Athens. What was true of me was true of hundreds of other negroes around me—'way off there in the country, fifteen or twenty miles from the nearest town.

When I reached twenty-one the Captain told me I was a free man, but he urged me to stay with him. He said he would treat me right, and pay me as much as anybody else would. The Captain's son and I were about the same age, and the Captain said that, as he had owned my mother and uncle during slavery, and as his son didn't want me to leave them (since I had been with them so long), he wanted me to stay with the old family. And I stayed. I signed a contract—that is, I made my mark—for one year. The Captain was to give me $3.50 a week, and furnish me a little house on the plantation—a one-room log cabin similar to those used by his other laborers.

During that year I married Mandy. For several years Mandy had been the house-servant for the Captain, his wife, his son and his three daughters, and they all seemed to think a good deal of her. As an evidence of their regard they gave us a suit of furniture, which cost about $25, and we set up housekeeping in one of the Captain's two-room shanties. I thought I was the biggest man in Georgia. Mandy still kept her place in the "Big House" after our marriage. We did so well for the first year that I renewed my contract for the second year, and for the third, fourth and fifth year I did the same thing. Before the end of the fifth year the Captain had died, and his son, who had married some two or three years before, took charge of the plantation. Also, for two or three years, this son had been serving in Atlanta in some big office to which he had been elected. I think it was in the Legislature or something of that sort—anyhow, the people called him Senator. At the end of the fifth year the Senator suggested that I sign up a contract for ten years; then, he said, we wouldn't have to fix up papers every year. I asked my wife about it; she consented; and so I made a ten-year contract.

Not long afterward the Senator had a long, low shanty built on his place. A great big chimney, with a wide, open fireplace, was built at one end of it, and on each side of the house, running lengthwise, there was a row of frames or stalls just large enough to hold a single mattress. The places for these were fixed one above the other; so that there was a double row of these stalls or pens on each side. They looked for all the world like stalls for horses. Since then I have seen cabooses similarly arranged as sleeping quarters for railroad laborers. Nobody seemed to know what the Senator was fixing for. All doubts were put aside one bright day when about forty able-bodied negroes, bound in iron chains, and some of them handcuffed, were brought out to the Senator's farm in three big wagons. They were quartered in the long, low shanty, and it was afterward called to stockade. This was the beginning of the Senator's convict camp. These men were prisoners who had been leased by the Senator from the State of Georgia at about $200 each per year, the State agreeing to pay for guards and physicians, for necessary inspection, for inquests, all rewards for escaped convicts, the costs of litigation and all other incidental camp expenses. When I saw these men in shackled, and the guards with their guns, I was scared nearly to death. I felt like running away, but I didn't know where to go. And if there had been any place to go to, I would have had to leave my wife and child behind. We free laborers held a meeting. We all wanted to quit. We sent a man to tell the Senator about it. Word came back that we were all under contract for ten years and that the Senator would hold us to the letter of the contract, or put us in chains and lock us up—the same as the other prisoners. It was made plain to us by some white people that in the contracts we had signed we had all agreed to be locked up in a stockade at night or at any other time that our employer saw fit; further, we learned that we could not lawfully break our contract for any reason and go and hire ourselves to somebody else without the consent of our employer; and, more than that, if we got mad and ran away, we could be run down by bloodhounds, arrested without process of law, and be returned to our employer, who, according to the contract, might beat us brutally or administer any other kind of punishment that he though proper. In other words, we had sold ourselves into slavery—and what could we do about it? The white folks had all the courts, all the guns, all the hounds, all the railroads, all the telegraph wires, all the newspapers, all the money, and nearly all the land—and we had only our ignorance, our poverty and our empty hands. We decided that the best thing to do was to shut our mouths, say nothing, and go back to work. And most of us worked side by side with those convicts during the remainder of the ten years.

But this first batch of convicts was only the beginning. Within six months another stockade was built, and twenty or thirty other convicts were brought to the plantation, among them six or eight women! The Senator had bought an additional thousand acres of land, and to his already large cotton plantation he added two great big saw-mills and went into the lumber business. Within two years the Senator had in all nearly 200 negroes working on his plantation—about his half of them free laborers, so-called, and about half of them convicts. The only difference between the free laborers and the others was that the free laborers could come and go as they pleased, at night—that is, they were not locked up at night, and were not, as a general thing, whipped for slight offenses. The troubles of the free laborers began at the close of the ten-year period. To a man, they all wanted to quit when the time was up. To a man, they all refused to sign new contracts—even for one year, not to say anything of ten years. And just when we thought that our bondage was at an end we found that it had really just begun. Two or three years before, or about a year and a half after the Senator had started his camp, he had established a large store, which was called the commissary. All of us free laborers were compelled to buy our supplies—food, clothing, etc.—from that store. We never used any money in our dealings with the commissary, only tickets or orders, and we had a general settlement once each year, in October. In this store we were charged all sorts of high prices for goods, because every year we would come out in debt to our employer. If not that, we seldom had more than $5 or $10 coming to us—and that for a whole year's work. Well, at the close of the tenth year, when we kicked and meant to leave the Senator, he said to some of us with a smile (and I never will forget that smile—I can see it now):

"Boys, I'm sorry you're going to leave me. I hope you will do well in your new places—so well that you will be able to pay me the little balances which most of you owe me."

Word was sent out for all of us to meet him at the commissary at 2 o'clock. There he told us that, after we had signed what he called a written acknowledgment of our debts, we might go and look for new places. The storekeeper took us one by one and read to us statements of our accounts. According to the books there was no man of us who owed the Senator less than $100; some of us were put down for as much as $200. I owed $165, according to the bookkeeper. These debts were not accumulated during one year, but ran back for three and four years, so we were told—in spite of the fact that we understood that we had had a full settlement at the end of each year. But no one of us would have dared to dispute a white man's word—oh, no; not in those days. Besides, we fellows didn't care anything about the amounts—we were after getting away; and we had been told that we might go, if we signed the acknowledgments. We would have signed anything, just to get away. So we stepped up, we did, and made our marks. That same night we were rounded up by a constable and ten or twelve white men, who aided him, and we were locked up, every one of us, in one of the Senator's stockades. The next morning it was explained to us by the two guards appointed to watch us that, in the papers we had signed the day before, we had not only made acknowledgment of our indebtedness, but that we had also agreed to work for the Senator until the debts were paid off by hard labor. And from that day forward we were treated just like convicts. Really we had made ourselves lifetime slaves, or peons, as the law called us. But, call it slavery, peonage, or what not, the truth is we lived in a hell on earth what time we spent in the Senator's peon camp.

Source: "A Georgia Negro Peon," "The New Slavery in the South – an Autobiography." *Independent*, February 25, 1904.

15.3   SHARECROPPING CONTRACT BETWEEN ALONZO T. MIAL AND FENNER POWELL (1886)

For Republicans, the essence of "free labor" was the *contract*, the notion that either a governing figure and his people, or a wealthy man and those who labored for him, both had to subscribe voluntarily to an explicit agreement outlining their mutual responsibilities in order for their relationship to be binding. Unfortunately, after the war, southern Blacks freed from slavery but without land sometimes had little choice but to sign stringent labor contracts with landlords, who were often former slave owners. A system emerged known as sharecropping. The tenant, or "cropper," would sign an annual contract to work a plot of land in return for a share of the crop. The following is a sharecropping contract from 1886, between a landlord named A. T. Mial and a sharecropper named Fenner Powell.

This contract made and entered into between A. T. Mial of one part and Fenner Powell of the other part both of the County of Wake and state of North Carolina—

Witnesseth—That the Said Fenner Powell hath barganed and agreed with the Said Mial to work as a cropper for the year 1886 on Said Mial's land on the land now occupied by Said Powell on the west Side of Poplar Creek and a point on the east Side of Said Creek and both South and North of the Mial road, leading to Raleigh, That the said Fenner Powell agrees to work faithfully and diligently without any unnecessary loss of time, to do all manner of work on Said farm as may be directed by Said Mial, And to be respectful in manners and deportment to Said Mial. And the Said Mial agrees on his part to furnish mule and feed for the same and all plantation tools and Seed to plant the crop free of charge, and to give the said Powell One half of all crops raised and housed by Said Powell on Said land except the cotton seed. The Said Mial agrees to advance as provisions to Said Powell fifty pound of bacon and two sacks of meal per month and occasionally some flour to be paid out of his the Said Powell's part of the crop or from any other advance that may be made to Said Powell by Said Mial. As witness our hands and seals this the 16th day of January AD. 1886.

Source: Contract between Alonzo T. Mial and Fenner Powell, January 1886, in Roger Ransom and Richard Sutch, *One Kind of Freedom: The Economic Consequences of Emancipation* (New York: Cambridge University Press, 1977), p. 91.

15.4   JOSEPH FARLEY, AN ACCOUNT OF RECONSTRUCTION

Joseph Farley, born in 1843 in Virginia, ran away and joined the Union army. Later he was given a pension. "At that time I never thought about dying," he remembers. "I never thought about anybody shooting me; I just thought about shooting them." Interviewed in 1930 by a Black student from Fisk University, he gave a rambling account, from which the postwar material has been excerpted. As with all distant recollections, Farley's may have been affected by the lapse of time and the person conducting the interview.

It was a long, long time before everything got quiet after the war. On Franklin Street here I saw once 100 Ku Klux Klans, with long robes and faces covered. You don't know anything of them. They were going down here a piece to hang a man. There were about 600 of us soldiers, so we followed them to protect the man. The Klan knew this, and passed on by the house and went on back to town and never did bother the man.

One time a colored soldier married a white woman over here at Fort Bruce. The man belonged to my company. His name was Sergeant Cook. About twenty of the soldiers went to the wedding, and they had about five or six white men who said he couldn't marry this woman. Old Dr. Taylor … came over to marry them. He stood near me and I told him to go on and marry this couple or else someone here would die. He looked around and saw all these soldiers and he knew about us and that we meant for him to do as he had been told. He married them and we guarded our hack over to the war boat on the Cumberland. They went over to Nashville and lived there. They had a daughter whose name was Mrs. Gnatt. When they married was in 1866. Mrs. Gnatt could tell you her father was named Cyrus Cook. Guess you know you can't do that now, no sir; you just can't do that now. At one time a colored man could ride anywhere he wanted to, but now he can't do it. I am one of the first voters of Montgomery County. They told me at one time that I was not to come to the polls or I would be met by 600 men on horses. So about six or eight hundred of us armed and went to the polls with our bayonets. That man that had told me that did not show up. So we voted, and voted for whom we wanted. At that time the Rebels who rebelled against this country could not vote and they said that these Negroes shouldn't vote but we showed them. Of course, they came down and stood and looked at us but they didn't bother us. We went there armed and prepared for fighting so that if they started anything, there would be trouble. When they mustered me out from the army, I brought my gun from Nashville right here to Clarksville and kept it twenty-five years. Finally I let an old soldier have it.

When I first came here we had no teachers here but white teachers. They would call the roll same as calling the roll for soldiers. They taught school in the churches before they had school houses. They used to go to school at night and work all day. Clarence C. White's father, Will White, was the first teacher or principal of the school here in Clarksville.

…

When the War was over some of the colored returned to their white folks, but I didn't want to be under the white folks again. I was glad to get out. Once, for fifteen years here, I run a saloon and livery stable. One time I worked on a boat. When I was on my first boat, one time I went to vote. A white man told me that if I voted Republican he would fire me, so I told him to fire me then. I just told him he could fire me right now for I didn't want to work anyway. I went on and voted the Republican ticket, and they told me they liked my principle and I could go on and go to work.

I still got my discharge from way back in 1866. I keeps it and I mean to keep it as long as I live. I am proud of it.

Source: George P. Rawick, ed. *The American Slave: A Composite Autobiography. Volume 18. Unwritten History of Slavery* (Fisk University) (Westport, CT: Greenwood, 1972), pp. 121–128.

15.5   A SOUTHERN UNIONIST JUDGE'S DAUGHTER WRITES THE PRESIDENT FOR HELP (1874)

Mrs. S. A. Wayne was the daughter of an Alabama Unionist, Judge James A. Abrahams. As the 1874 political campaign grew more violent, she wrote begging President Grant to send protection to Republicans like herself. Soon after the letter was sent, Abrahams was shot by persons unknown. Shortly after that, Grant sent troops to Livingston County. It was not enough to give Black and white voters the security they needed; Democratic Redeemers swept the election.

I feel more like addressing you as my dear Father & Friend for such you have proven to me & mine—but—Oh, my God! you have no conception of the trouble we are in—War is declared in our midst and though the U. S. troops are here the Ku Klux are worse than before they came—And who are they fighting? The poor defenseless negroes—Why? For voting or rather expressing their determination to vote the Republican ticket—This evening the lives of my husband—father & brother were threatened—with the intention of making them renounce their principles—God only knows what the end will be—I have seen the Capt & Lt stationed at this place—& they say the only hope is Martial law—& that is the only remedy—Since I last wrote you some four or five negroes have been killed in this County—& the Ku Klux are now at Belmont 16 miles from this place in force & will probably murder as many more—They are exasperated against the three white Republicans in this place because they refused to go with them on one of their raids last weeks—hence the threats against their lives—My Father left this evening & I pray God he may not return until Martial law is declared—Oh my dear Sir *you can save* the country—oh protect the Union loving men against those who despise it & are doing all to overthrow it—I write you this not thinking my enlisting in the cause will help it, but because I feel it my duty to let you know how great our trouble is—No excuse can be given by these murderers—for since the assassination of Mr Billings not one single Republican meeting has been held in this county—And this is what the Democrats are fighting for—Unless Martial law is declared hundreds of the poor negroes will be killed—even now they do not sleep in their houses & are hunted down like wild beasts by the Democracy because they will not vote their ticket—Oh! My dear Sir act & be our friends. God knows the innocent only suffer—& the blush of shame mantles my cheek when I read the pitiable excuses in the Democratic papers—apologizing for their cowardly deeds—No brave man is afraid of a few of them in open daylight but a hundred or two banded together; making night hideous with their demoniac yells is enough to make the stoutest heart quail—I have written you hurriedly— There is no security in the mails & I send this by a U.S. Paymaster who arrived here this afternoon & leaves to night—Again I beg you to help us in this dreadful emergency—No U.S. Marshall has been here & if they were to come they could not punish these murderers immediately—& they ought to be dealt with severely & immediately—This is private & I write as to my own dear Father & confide to you our troubles—We have lived in the midst of it since the war & it is more terrible now than ever—Every Union man will be killed if active steps are not taken by the Government to stop it—I am ever your true & loving Union woman.

Source: S. A. Wayne to Ulysses S. Grant, September 18, 1874, quoted in John Y. Simon, ed., *The Papers of Ulysses S. Grant: Volume 25: 1874* (Carbondale: Southern Illinois University Press, 2003), pp. 195–196.

15.6 RED CLOUD PLEADS THE PLAINS INDIANS' POINT OF VIEW AT COOPER UNION (1870)

As one of the foremost leaders of the Teton Sioux, Red Cloud had kept the US Army at bay for several years. The war, as his speech pointed out, had never been his own doing. He, like many other Indians, sought a fair peace; like them, he found that all the power to define what peace meant and how it would be enforced lay in the hands of the indifferent, the ill-informed, and the insatiable.

My brethren and my friends who are here before me this day, God Almighty has made us all, and He is here to bless what I have to say to you today. The Good Spirit made us both. He gave you lands and He gave us lands; He gave us these lands; you came in here, and we respected you as brothers. God Almighty made you but made you all white and clothed you; when He made us He made us with red skins and poor; now you have come.

When you first came we were very many, and you were few; now you are many, and we are getting very few, and we are poor. You do not know who appears before you today to speak. I am a representative of the original American race, the first people of this continent. We are good and not bad. The reports that you hear concerning us are all on one side. We are always well-disposed to them. You are here told that we are traders and thieves, and it is not so. We have given you nearly all our lands, and if we had any more land to give we would be very glad to give it. We have nothing more. We are driven into a very little land, and we want you now, as our dear friends, to help us with the government of the United States.

The Great Father made us poor and ignorant—made you rich and wise and more skillful in these things that we know nothing about. The Great Father, the Good Father in Heaven, made you all to eat tame food—made us to eat wild food—gives us the wild food. You ask anybody who has gone through our country to California; ask those who have settled there and in Utah, and you will find that we have treated them always well. You have children; we have children. You want to raise your children and make them happy and prosperous; we want to raise and make them happy and prosperous. We ask you to help us to do it.

At the mouth of the Horse Creek, in 1852, the Great Father made a treaty with us by which we agreed to let all that country open for fifty-five years for the transit of those who were going through. We kept this treaty; we never treated any man wrong; we never committed any murder or depredation until afterward the troops were sent into that country, and the troops killed our people and ill-treated them, and thus war and trouble arose; but before the troops were sent there we were quiet and peaceable, and there was no disturbance. Since that time there have been various goods sent from time to time to us, the only ones that ever reached us, and then after they reached us (very soon after) the government took them away. You, as good men, ought to help us to these goods.

Colonel Fitzpatrick of the government said we must all go to farm, and some of the people went to Fort Laramie and were badly treated. I only want to do that which is peaceful, and the Great Fathers know it, and also the Great Father who made us both. I came to Washington to see the Great Father in order to have peace and in order to have peace continue. That is all we want, and that is the reason why we are here now.

In 1868 men came out and brought papers. We are ignorant and do not read papers, and they did not tell us right what was in these papers. We wanted them to take away their forts, leave our country, would not make war, and give our traders something. They said we had bound ourselves to trade on the Missouri, and we said, no, we did not want that. The interpreters deceived us. When I went to Washington I saw the Great Father. The Great Father showed me what the treaties were; he showed me all these points and showed me that the interpreters had deceived me and did not let me know what the right side of the treaty was. All I want is right and justice. ... I represent the Sioux Nation; they will be governed by what I say and what I represent. ...

Look at me. I am poor and naked, but I am the Chief of the Nation. We do not want riches, we do not ask for riches, but we want our children properly trained and brought up. We look to you for your sympathy. Our riches will ... do us no good; we cannot take away into the other world anything we have—we want to have love and peace. ... We would like to know why commissioners are sent out there to do nothing but rob [us] and get the riches of this world away from us?

I was brought up among the traders and those who came out there in those early times. I had a good time for they treated us nicely and well. They taught me how to wear clothes and use tobacco, and to use firearms and ammunition, and all went on very well until the Great Father sent out another kind of men—men who drank whisky. He sent out whisky-men, men who drank and quarreled, men who were so bad that he could not keep them at home, and so he sent them out there. I have sent a great many words to the Great Father, but I don't know that they ever reach the Great Father. They were drowned on the way, therefore I was a little offended with it. The words I told the Great Father lately would never come to him, so I thought I would come and tell you myself.

And I am going to leave you today, and I am going back to my home. I want to tell the people that we cannot trust his agents and superintendents. I don't want strange people that we know nothing about. I am very glad that you belong to us. I am very glad that we have come here and found you and that we can understand one another. I don't want any more such men sent out there, who are so poor that when they come out there their first thoughts are how they can fill their own pockets.

We want preserves in our reserves. We want honest men, and we want you to help to keep us in the lands that belong to us so that we may not be a prey to those who are viciously disposed. I am going back home. I am very glad that you have listened to me, and I wish you good-bye and give you an affectionate farewell.

Source: New York Times, July 17, 1870, cited in William Benton, publ., *Annals of America, Volume 10: Reconstruction and Industrialization* (Chicago: Encyclopedia Britannica, Inc., 1968), 242–244.

16

The Triumph of Industrial Capitalism
1850–1890

< Packingtown, 1880

Rosa Cassettari

In 1884, **Rosa Cassettari** left an Italian village near Milan and joined the stream of migrants from all across Europe bound for America. Others went full of dreams. "The country where everyone would find work! Where wages were so high that no one had to go hungry! Where all men were free and equal and where even the poor could own land!" But Rosa left behind her son to rejoin her brutal, abusive husband, Santino, an iron miner in Missouri. Unable to read or write, she expected the worst, and rightly. "All us poor people had to go down through a hole to the bottom of the ship," she remembered. Crowded in darkness, sleeping on wooden shelves, feeding from tin plates, Rosa felt no relief to see land. Cheated in New York and forced to make her way to Missouri with nothing to eat, she arrived in a shabby cluster of tents and shanties, where she added to Santino's wages by cooking for a dozen miners. With no doctors or midwives available, Rosa gave birth to a premature child alone on the floor of her cabin. The last straw came when Santino used his savings to open a house of prostitution. Rosa fled for her life, and friends helped her move to Chicago. Was this the Promised Land?

Rosa thought so. She worked hard all her life, knew hunger in bad times, and just got by in good ones. But she always found friends to help her and religious faith to comfort her. In time she found work at Chicago Commons, a settlement house founded to help immigrants get by in a strange, often bewildering city. She discovered a strength and courage she had never known at home. When she went back to Italy to bring over her son, villagers gaped. She was wearing a hat and new shoes, and "they thought I was something wonderful." When she told them that poor people in America ate meat every day, they could not believe it. And she lived to see her children doing better than she had—not rich, but not in want.

Rosa was one of millions of people uprooting themselves worldwide in the late nineteenth century. They moved from the countryside to the city or from town to town. They shifted from less developed regions to places where industrialization was well under way. The magnet for most of the movement was a core of industrial capitalist societies, and the United States was just one destination among many.

Common laborers moved from place to place because jobs were unsteady, or they moved when work was finished. Hired hands plodded the roads in autumn following the harvest, spent winters working in Washington's lumber camps, and toiled by summer along the Erie Canal. African American **sharecroppers** in the South moved at year's end, eventually into cotton-growing districts, into towns and cities, or out of the South. White tenant farmers found new homes and better living conditions in company-owned coal- and textile-mill towns. Native Americans, their domains already in flux for centuries, now lost most of their lands to white settlement and were herded onto reservations. And all across America, the children of farmers traded the charm and endless labor of rural life for the bright-lit, squalid metropolises of the East.

They went seeking work, and that meant working for somebody else, on terms that the employer set. It meant working with new, complicated machines, with foul air, dirty rivers, or ravaged land. Working people had been freed from the things that once tied them to the land, such as feudal dues and slavery. But wage labor often compelled men and women to shift from country to country, and finally from continent to continent. To watch Rosa Cassettari as she traveled from Italy to Chicago is to witness one small part of a process set in motion by global needs and once-unimaginable aspirations.

THE POLITICAL ECONOMY OF GLOBAL CAPITALISM

The economic history of the late nineteenth century was sandwiched between two great financial panics in 1873 and 1893. Both were followed by prolonged periods of high joblessness and labor strife. Between the two panics, prices dropped. Farmers with crops selling for less felt the crushing weight of money borrowed when prices were high. Manufacturers cut costs by increasing production, by replacing skilled labor with technology, and by drawing on the international labor market for a cheaper workforce. Still, amid bouts of hard times, the American economy transformed dramatically and, for consumers and many workers, for the better.

The "Great Depression" of the Late Nineteenth Century

On July 16, 1877, workers for the Baltimore and Ohio Railroad struck at Martinsburg, West Virginia, over one wage cut too many. Within days, the strike spread to the Pennsylvania Railroad, the New York Central, the Great Western, and the Texas Pacific. Governors ordered the strikers to disperse. They asked for federal troops and got them. Soldiers fired on protestors in Pittsburgh, and for a while, confrontations between workers and armed forces fanned the flames of insurrection. "Other workingmen followed the example of the railroad employees," explained Henry Demarest Lloyd, a prominent social critic. "At Zanesville, Ohio, fifty manufactories stopped work. Baltimore ceased to export petroleum. The rolling mills, foundries, and refineries of Cleveland were closed. . . . Merchants could not sell, manufacturers could not work, banks could not lend. The country went to the verge of a panic." The strike was broken, though a hundred lives were lost by that time. Alarmed state authorities went on an armory-building binge and recruited a National Guard to keep order or break strikes in the future. Between 1875 and 1910, state troops were called out nearly 500 times.

The **Great Railroad Strike of 1877** was fueled by an economic depression that began with the Panic of 1873 (see Chapter 15) and spread throughout the developed world. Immigrant arrivals in New York—200,000 every year between 1865 and 1873—fell to less than 65,000 in 1877. Although employment (and immigration) recovered in the 1880s, prices and wages continued to fall. Then, in 1893, another panic struck. Major railroads went bankrupt, including four of the five transcontinentals. Over 500 banks and 15,000 businesses shut down.

The world was shrinking. In 1866, Cyrus Field's telegraph cable was laid under the Atlantic Ocean. Now Americans could read Europe's latest news the next morning. They could cluster at the depot to hear the latest box score, sent by telegraph even as the game went on. Railroads carried Pillsbury's flour from Minneapolis mills to Massachusetts; refrigerated cars carried Chicago's "dressed beef" carcasses to California; and the catalog brought the goods of a nation to every farm on the high plains so efficiently that consumers swore "by God, the Ten Commandments, and Sears, Roebuck." Thanks to the steamship, midwestern wheat fed customers in Russia, and boards cut from the forests of the Cascades turned into flooring for plantations in Malaya. In Pittsburgh's steel mills, Slavic languages and Hungarian were as common as German and Russian in **Lower East Side** New York's needle trades. Capitalism, not just transportation, had mingled peoples together.

An industrializing and liberalizing Europe had cut families free from their traditional ties to the land. Many migrated to better themselves: some within Europe, some to South America or Canada, and many to America (see Map 16–1). In many Irish families, sending sons and daughters abroad meant money packets sent home to allow the rest to stay behind. Italians and eastern Europeans, known as "birds of passage," often came west only to earn money and return. But their cheap labor and that of millions who came to stay built the railroads and forged the steel. They slaughtered sheep and cattle in Chicago's stockyard district, "Packingtown," for Philip Armour and Gustavus Swift. Others worked as domestic servants, served behind store sales counters, or ran the sewing machines that met a national demand for ready-made clothing.

THE ECONOMIC TRANSFORMATION OF THE WEST

For novelists, the West seemed like a separate world from the industrial transformation of the East: a land where the old-fashioned manly virtues of the cowboy, the trapper, the prospector, and the homesteader carved a destiny out of the wilderness. In fact, the economic revolution may have changed the West more than anywhere else. Lawless violence and wild speculation were part of the western experience, but so were the struggling families, start-up companies, and hard-working immigrants that remade Cleveland and Chicago. By 1900, thanks to the revolution that eastern-run railroads made, the West provided Americans with the meat and bread for their dinner tables, the wood that built their homes, and the gold and silver that backed up their currency. The West was being drawn into the **political economy** of global capitalism. As much as any eastern city, it had become diverse and ethnically and economically complex well before the director of the US Census declared the

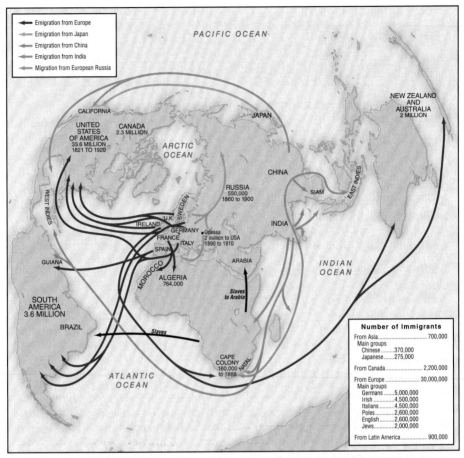

Map 16–1   Patterns of Global Migration, 1840–1900 Emigration was a global process by the late nineteenth century. But more immigrants went to the United States than to all other nations combined.
Source: London Times Atlas.

frontier "closed" in 1890. And when it came to savage labor strife, there was nothing Pittsburgh's victims could have told the miners in Cripple Creek or Leadville, Colorado.

Cattlemen: From Drovers to Ranchers

The cowboy is the mythic figure of the American West: a rugged loner who scorned society for the freedom of the trail. In fact, cowboys were usually single men. They worked hard and played harder, spending their earnings on a shave, a new suit of clothes, and a few good nights in town. Civil War veterans, former enslaved people, displaced Indians, and Mexicans all became cowboys. Their pay was low, their work dangerous and unsteady, and their chances of reaching real independence were slim.

America In The World
The Global Migration of Labor

Nineteenth-century migrants tended to leave areas already in the grip of social and economic change. Rosa Cassettari, for example, had worked in a silk-weaving factory in Italy. At first, the largest numbers emigrated from the most developed nations, such as Great Britain and Germany. Later in the century, as industrial or agricultural revolution spread, growing numbers of immigrants came from Scandinavia, Russia, Italy, and Hungary (see Map 16–1). As capitalism developed in these areas, small farmers were forced to produce for a highly competitive international market. The resulting upheaval sent millions of rural people into the worldwide migratory stream.

Improvements in transportation and communication made migration easier. In 1856, more than 95 percent of immigrants came to America aboard sailing vessels. By the end of the century, more than 95 percent came in steamships. The Atlantic crossing took one to three months under sail, but only 10 days by steam. Beginning in the 1880s, fierce competition among steamship lines lowered the cost of a transatlantic ticket. But the great migrations were also related to economic and political turmoil. After 1890, immigration from northern and western Europe fell off sharply, as industrial growth soaked up surplus labor. At the same time, agrarian crises drove out peasants from eastern and southern Europe. Southern Italy could barely compete with Florida and California's lemons and oranges and found the American protective tariff closing off its biggest overseas wine market. Straitened Italian farmers started coming to the United States.

Jewish immigration was propelled by different impulses. In the Russian empire, pogroms, anti-Jewish riots, erupted in 1881–1882, 1891, and 1905–1906. Many Jews were killed. Anti-Semitic laws confined Russian Jews to the so-called Pale of Settlement along the empire's western and southern borders. The May Laws of 1882 severely restricted their religious and economic life. Starting in the 1880s, anti-Semitic riots brought fire and murder into the Jewish ghettoes. Sometimes the police looked on; sometimes they joined the rioters. The government not only encouraged the persecution; at times, it provoked it. By 1890, Russian Jews were making new homes for themselves in America. Swanky hotels snubbed them, clubs blackballed them, but here they could publish newspapers in Yiddish or Hebrew, worship freely, hope for schooling, even a college education, for their children, and make a living. A few went to Congress. One later became the prime minister of Israel.

Most immigrants, though, just came to America looking for work. Many planned to make money and then return home, as thousands of Italians and Slovaks did. (Some, discovering to their surprise that they had become more American than they expected, came back to stay.) Some came with education and skills, most with little more than their ability to work. They usually found their jobs through families, friends, and fellow immigrants. Letters from America told of high wages and steady employment. Communities of immigrant workers provided the support that newcomers like Rosa Cassettari needed. Some immigrants settled directly on farms, but the overwhelming mass lived in cities.

Longhorn cattle were as much a part of western legend as the cowboys who drove them. With the westward spread of the railroads, Texas ranchers began driving huge herds of Texas longhorns up the Chisholm Trail north onto the Great Plains. They brought the herds to railroad towns from which the cattle could be shipped, such as Abilene, Wichita, or Dodge City, Kansas. Cattlemen sold half of their stock to eastern markets and the other half in the West, some to the government for feeding soldiers and reservation Indians.

But the Texas longhorn had several drawbacks: it was tough and rangy, it produced more bone and sinew than meat, it carried a tick that devastated many of the other grazing animals, and it took a long time to fatten up. Investors began to breed hybrid cattle that were less hardy but beefier and of higher quality. By the early 1880s, investors were pouring capital into mammoth cattle-herding companies. The Great Plains became seriously overstocked. Long drives became increasingly difficult as farmers fenced in the plains, but they also became less necessary because railroads could pick up cattle just about everywhere. By the 1890s, huge cattle companies were giving way to smaller ranches that raised hybrid cattle. Cowboys became ranch hands with regular wages, like miners and factory workers.

In the mid-1880s, more than 7 million head of cattle roamed the Great Plains, but as their numbers declined, sheep replaced them. Although sheep proved even more ecologically destructive than cattle, by 1900 sheepherding had largely taken the place of the cattle industry in Wyoming and Montana and was spreading to Nevada. Sheepherding had the advantage of not interfering with small farmers as much as cattle driving did.

Commercial Farmers Remake the Plains

Between 1860 and 1900, the number of farms in America nearly tripled, thanks largely to the economic development of the West. On the Great Plains and in the desert Southwest, farmers took up former Indian lands. In California, white settlers poached on the estates of Spanish-speaking landlords, stripping them of their natural resources and undermining their profitability. Over time, Hispanic ranchers gave way to European American farmers. The Hispanic population of Los Angeles fell from 82 percent in 1850 to 19 percent in 1880. A similar pattern occurred in New Mexico and Texas.

This ethnic shift signaled profound changes in the ecology and political economy of the West, driven by the exploding global demand for western products. Cattle ranchers were feeding eastern cities. Lumber from the Pacific Northwest found its way to Asia and South America; the United States led the world in copper production. By 1890, western farmers produced half of the wheat grown in the United States, and they shipped it across the globe.

But farming in the arid West was unlike eastern farming. The 160-acre homesteads that lawmakers proposed in the original **Homestead Act** proved too small for guaranteeing a viable living on the parched prairies, though hundreds of thousands staked claims—and kept on doing so until 1934. Farmers needed costly equipment and extensive irrigation to produce wheat and corn for international markets. To make these capital investments, they mortgaged their lands. For mechanized, commercial agriculture to succeed on mortgaged land, western farms had to be much bigger than 160 acres.

Government homesteads made up only a fraction of all the lands sold. Speculators may have bought up as much as 350 million acres from state or federal governments or from Indian reservations. Railroads were granted another 200 million acres by the federal government. They sold much of it at bargain rates. The more farmers the railroads could settle on their lands, the more customers they would have, and the more farm produce there would be to ship. Railroads set up immigration bureaus and offered settlers cheap transportation, credit, and agricultural aid. The Great Plains filled with settlers from the East Coast and from Ireland, Germany, and Scandinavia.

Changes in the Land

No Garden of Eden welcomed prairie farmers. "All Montana needs is rain," a promoter was said to have told one settler—who agreed: but that was also all that Hell needed. Rain fell rarely and in sparse amounts on the Great Plains and the desert Southwest. Howling blizzards, blistering summers that warped railroad track out of alignment, sky-blackening clouds of locusts, and loneliness meant ruin for some, despair for others. Yet settlers came, worked, endured, and improvised. With little wood or stone available, many farmers built sod houses—even sod schoolhouses. Joseph Glidden's invention, barbed wire, provided them fencing. Strong steel plows cut a sod so knotted with grass roots that hoes bounced off it like paving. Windmills rose from the prairie to pump water from hundreds of feet below ground and over time drain much of it dry. Mennonite settlers from Russia brought durum wheat, ideal for the harsh climate. Everywhere, families built schools, churches, and communities alongside the now-ubiquitous railroad stations.

The West as a Treasure-House

Rosa Cassettari's mining camp experience had none of the glamour that mythology lends those farther West. Findings in California actually peaked years after the Forty-Niners' gold rush. New discoveries pulled prospectors eastward, into Colorado in 1859, Idaho in 1862, and Montana in 1864. In Nevada, prospectors hit the largest vein of all, the Comstock Lode. It would yield $350 million worth of gold and silver over 20 years.

Western mining camps were raw, violent, male-dominated, and diverse. New England Yankees mingled with Australians, Mexicans, Chinese, and African Americans. Alone or in small groups, they panned for gold, squatting in icy stream beds. Once the surface gold had been captured, miners shoveled dirt into boxes or sluices to capture ore by running water over it. A few miners struck it rich. The biggest winners may have been the storekeepers who sold blasting powder, shovels, and groceries. Four became partners and built the western half of America's first transcontinental railroad. They had such a stranglehold on California's transit system that locals called their company "the Octopus."

Penniless Irish-born Marcus Daly did even better. Pooling resources, he and some San Francisco investors dug for silver in Montana and hit one of the world's largest veins of copper. High-grade found a worldwide demand wherever cities and industries needed copper wire to harness electricity's power and the Anaconda Company made Daly fabulously rich.

Chinese and Anglo Miners near Sacramento, California, 1852 Digging for gold paid off mostly in aches, misery, and loneliness. The so-called Forty-Niners included immigrants from across the Pacific and from Latin America, but just about no women.

Daly's venture represented the future. By the 1870s, gold veins ran too deep for lone prospectors to reach; heavy, costly machines were needed. Minerals like zinc and copper required a heavier initial investment that would take much longer to be repaid. Mine shafts needed timber supports in a treeless land, as well as blowers to cool the 130-degree temperatures deep underground. Deep mines needed constant pumping: 2 million gallons of water seeped into the Comstock every day. Copper or silver took smelting. Thus, corporations alone could tap most of the West's mineral wealth. Engineers and wage laborers, managed from boardrooms miles away, extracted, smelted, and shipped the ore. Even Comstock's 750 miles of tunnels 3,000 feet underground were corporation run. Companies built the railroads to carry ore to market and to the towns where miners lived. These were shabby, utilitarian places without libraries, parks, schools—or the chance to strike it rich on one's own. The Comstocks had given way to the Cassettaris.

By the turn of the century, states and reservations stood where the Cheyenne, Dakota, and Comanche nations had commanded vast domains. Settlers of many ethnicities—Swedish, Finnish, Hispanic, and others—experienced the bounty and hardship of what had once been Indian land. Corporate enterprises and mechanized farms now shared the West with the homesteaders and storekeepers. Farmers had connected to world markets. They were clothed and supplied by cities' industries. They owed eastern railroad corporations their access to the world, and they owed nearly everything else to eastern mortgage holders. Mining and lumber corporations employed tens of thousands of wage laborers. Thanks to the gold rush, San Francisco rose from 5,000 inhabitants mid-century to 150,000 twenty years later. Denver was incorporated in 1861 with a population just below 5,000. By 1870, it had grown twentyfold.

America Moves to the City

Between 1850 and 1900, the map of the United States was redrawn, thanks to the appearance of dozens of new cities (see Figure 16–1). In 1850, the largest city in the United States was New York, with a population of just over half a million.

American Landscape
Pioneers' Paradise Lost

"Nature only served an apprenticeship when she made the East," a newcomer wrote from California. "A master hand fashioned the charm of the Sierra Nevada." That wonder did not last, not when making a living (or a killing) stood in the way. Never had so vast a landscape been changed so quickly to suit miners, farmers, ranchers, and lumberjacks.

Much of the western environment endured. As early as 1864, the US government put the wonders of Yosemite Valley out of land-grabbers' reach. Yellowstone with its geysers and hot springs became the first national park in 1872, and within a generation, Congress had created national forests, where exploitation at least could be controlled. But the more usable the soil was, the quicker emigrants changed it from grassland to cropland. California oranges found a market in New England, and Washington apple orchards filled the stalls in eastern markets. The price, though, came in a wholly new mix of plant and animal life, as alien to what had thrived there before as the manicured lawns in Anglo-remade Tucson.

PUCK.

PRESERVE YOUR FORESTS FROM DESTRUCTION, AND PROTECT YOUR COUNTRY FROM FLOODS AND DROUGHT.

Deforestation Already by the 1880s, clear-cutting in the Upper Midwest and in the Far West had brought flood and drought to farmers downriver and sparked uncontrollable forest fires. What the cartoonist missed in this 1884 lithograph was the timber companies' technological revolution. "Donkey engines," band saws, and narrow-gauge railroads had dramatically increased their reach into remoter areas inaccessible and their ability to harvest trees of monumental size.

Wolves, elk, and bears were exterminated as farmers brought in pigs, cattle, and sheep. At the same time as the discovery of gold in the Black Hills, the demand for hides brought a different kind of gold rush to the plains: the mass slaughter of buffalo herds. Profit and sport drove the hunt, but cattlemen had no objection to opening up the range for their own stock. The army saw a bonus in anything wiping out subsistence for Indians off the reservation. "Kill every buffalo you can," a colonel urged one hunter. "Every buffalo dead is an Indian gone." Railroads joined in, sponsoring mass kills from slow-moving trains on the prairies. Some 13 million bison in 1850 dwindled by 1880 to a few hundred. The only buffalo a westerner was likely to see by 1920 was the one on the back of the nickel.

Whoever saw the West as a bottomless treasure-chest fooled themselves. When timber companies stripped the hillsides bare, precious watersheds vanished. Treeless slopes could not hold rainfall. Streams that ran all year turned into raging torrents after a cloudburst and dry gullies the rest of the time. Tulare Lake, covering hundreds of square miles of California's Central Valley, was sucked dry by 1900. Irrigation systems leached salt into the soil. Mines sent tons of earth and rock down the rivers of the Sierra Nevada, threatening entire cities with flooding. The skies above Butte, Montana, turned gray from pollutants released by copper-smelting plants. The depleted grazing lands left the cattle weak from malnutrition, and in the late 1880s several devastating winters wiped out whole herds. It was said that a person could walk across Kansas and never touch ground, just stepping from carcass to carcass. Open-range herding became so environmentally destructive that it was no longer economically feasible. Sheepherding destroyed the vegetation on the eastern slopes of the Rocky Mountains and the Sierra Nevada.

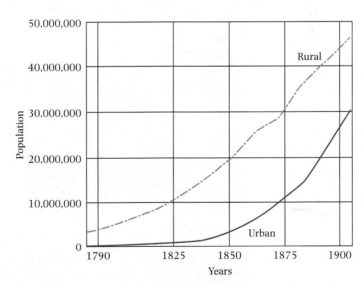

Figure 16–1   Proportion of Population Living in Cities, 1790–1900 While a growing proportion of Americans lived in cities, city dwellers would outnumber rural Americans only in the twentieth century.

By 1900, New York, Philadelphia, and Chicago each had more than a million residents.

The industrial city was different from its predecessors. By the middle of the nineteenth century the modern "downtown" was born, a place where people shopped and worked but did not necessarily live. Residential neighborhoods separated city dwellers from the downtown districts and separated the classes from one another. Streetcars and commuter railroads brought middle-class clerks and professionals from their homes to their jobs and back, but the fares were beyond the means of the working class. The rich built their mansions uptown, but workers had to stay within walking distance of their jobs.

Cities became more crowded, unsanitary, and unsafe. Yellow fever and cholera epidemics were frequent. Fires periodically wiped out entire neighborhoods. In October 1871, much of Chicago went up in flames. Immigrant slums sprang up in most major cities of America, as well as in mill towns and mining camps. In 1890, **Jacob Riis** published *How the Other Half Lives*, exposing conditions in downtown New York, the breeding grounds of vice, crime, and despair. He described a dark three-room apartment that six people shared. The two bedrooms were tiny, the beds nothing more than boxes filled with "foul straw." Such conditions were a common feature of urban poverty in the late nineteenth century.

Yet during these same years urban reformers and technology made city life less dangerous and more

Wanamaker's Grand Depot Department Store, 1876 "Big business" in the late nineteenth century not only mass-produced goods but also sold them in large quantities at low prices. John Wanamaker's Philadelphia department store was among the most famous of these large, new retailers and funded Wanamaker's political activity against corrupt city officials.

comfortable. Professional fire and police departments protected cities from fire outbreaks and violence. Boards of health and quarantine laws brought epidemics under control. By the century's end, city dwellers could count on clean drinking water, efficient transportation, great museums, public libraries, parks, and a variety of entertainment unimaginable in the countryside.

By 1900, travelers walking down New York City's Bowery at midnight could feel safer, basking in the blaze of electric lights. Thomas Alva Edison's invention of the commercially viable incandescent light bulb in 1879 was only one invention among many to dispel that darkness. He and other inventors created the dynamo to generate electricity, as well as alternating current to transmit power more efficiently. City dwellers would be the first to light their homes with electricity, the first to install telephones, and those most likely to receive mail every day, Sundays included. They would also be the ones most likely to eat fruits and vegetables out of season. Thanks to mass production, Gilded Age manufacturers would introduce canned foods into American diets. For those with money to spare, nothing could compare with the new, gigantic department stores, able to sell an endless variety of goods at the lowest prices because they dealt in such tremendous volume. Where else but Philadelphia would have Wanamaker's, with three acres of selling area and 129 counters, stretching two-thirds of a mile? Where else but New York would have a Heinz food sign six stories high, requiring 1,200 light bulbs? Cities showed off industrial capitalism's riches at their best, as well as its victims at their worst.

Nobody represented both sides of capitalism as well as a young Scots immigrant who came with his parents to Pittsburgh and started out in a textile mill for $1.20 a week. Fifty years later, Andrew Carnegie sold his steel mills to J. Pierpont Morgan for $480 million.

THE RISE OF BIG BUSINESS

Before the Civil War the only enterprises in the United States that could be called "big businesses" were the railroads (see Map 16–2). Indeed, railroads became the model for a new kind of business—big business—that emerged during the 1880s. Big businesses had massive bureaucracies managed by professionals rather than owners and were financed through a national banking system centered on Wall Street. They marketed their goods and services across the world and generated wealth in staggering concentrations, giving rise to a class of men whose names—Carnegie, Rockefeller, Morgan, and Vanderbilt—became synonymous with American capitalism.

The Rise of Andrew Carnegie

Andrew Carnegie was an immigrant, whereas most businessmen were native born. His childhood in Scotland was marked by poverty, whereas most of America's leading men of business were raised in comfort. Nevertheless, Andrew Carnegie was the perfect reflection of the rise of big business. In the course of his career, Carnegie mastered the telegraph, railroad, petroleum, iron, and steel industries and set the example for modern management techniques and strict accounting procedures in manufacturing. Other great industrialists and financiers made their mark in the

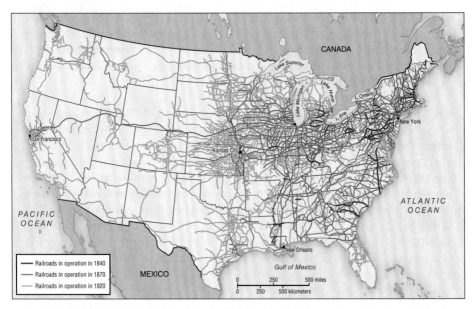

Map 16–2 The Growth of Railroads, 1850–1890 Railroads were more than a means of transportation; they were also America's first "big business." They set the model for running huge industrial corporations, and the growth of railroads fostered the iron and steel industries.

last half of the nineteenth century. Canadian-born James J. Hill's railroad empire filled the grain elevators with wheat that made Minneapolis the country's great flour-making center; his money built copper smelters in Montana and an apple-growing industry in Washington. German-born Friederich Weyerhäuser's timber company logged the West and furnished the boards that homesteaders on the tree-less prairie needed so desperately. However, none had lives that took on the mythic proportions of that of the Scottish lad who came to America at the age of 12 and ended up the world's richest man.

Not content with his job at a textile mill, Carnegie enrolled in a night course to study accounting, and a year later he got a job as a messenger boy in a telegraph office. So astute and hard-working was Andrew that by 1851 he was promoted to telegraph operator. There he displayed a rare talent for leadership. He recruited bright, hard-working men and organized them with such stunning efficiency that the Pennsylvania Railroad offered Carnegie a job, first as a private secretary and later in management.

Carnegie came to the firm at a time when rail construction was soaring. Petro-leum refiners shipped their kerosene by rail. Mining corporations needed railroads to ship their coal and iron. By the mid-1850s, the largest factory in the country, the Pepperell Mills in Biddeford, Maine, employed 800 workers, whereas the Pennsyl-vania Railroad then had more than 4,000 employees. If an engineer arrived late, or if a fireman came to work drunk, trains were wrecked, lives were lost, and busi-ness failed. The railroads thus borrowed the disciplinary methods and bureaucratic structure of the military to ensure that the trains ran safely and on time. J. Edgar Thomson, the Pennsylvania's president, established an elaborate bookkeeping system providing detailed knowledge of every aspect of the Pennsylvania's operations. Based on that data, the company could reward managers who improved the company's profits and eliminate those who failed.

Carnegie succeeded. As superintendent of the western division, he helped make the Pennsylvania a model of efficiency. By 1865, with 30,000 employees and lines stretching east to New York City and west to Chicago, it was the largest private company in the world. It was also necessarily one of the most financially intricate. Railroads dwarfed all previous business enterprises in the amount of investment capital they required and in the complexity of their financial arrangements. A major line might require over a hundred separate kinds of account books. Railroads were the first corporations to issue stocks through sophisticated trading mechanisms that attracted investors from around the world. To organize the market in such vast numbers of securities, the modern investment house was developed.

Carnegie Dominates the Steel Industry

By 1872, Carnegie had taken on other interests as well. His Keystone Bridge Company built the first steel arch bridge over the Mississippi. Acquiring a controlling interest in the Union Iron Company, Carnegie had overhauled it, adapting the Pennsylvania's managerial techniques and accounting practices. He also integrated operations: unlike other firms, his would not just melt iron ore into pig iron, but make bars of it, and turn those bars into beams and plates. Eliminating middlemen meant savings, and savings let him sell for less. As Carnegie put it, "Watch the costs and the profits will take care of themselves."

More important, his railroad experience taught him that steel, not iron, was the future. Under the loads of larger, heavier trains, iron rails simply could not hold up for long. Though prohibitively expensive at first, steel rails lasted 20 years, whereas iron ones needed replacement at 5. Steel also proved better for making locomotives, boilers, and railroad cars. In the 1860s, two developments cleared the path for the transition from iron to steel. First, Henry **Bessemer's patented process** for turning iron into steel became available to American manufacturers. Second, iron ore began flowing from deposits in northern Michigan. With access to investment capital and Thomson for his partner, Carnegie opened a steel plant in 1873. Despite a worldwide depression, it turned a profit immediately.

Big Business Consolidates

In the late nineteenth century, every great industry conjured up the name of a magnate: Carnegie in steel, Gustavus Swift or Philip Armour in meatpacking, John D. Rockefeller in oil refining, James J. Hill or Collis P. Huntington in railroads, and J. P. Morgan in financing (see Map 16–3). Actually, no single individual or family could own most big businesses because they required too much capital (financial resources). They were run by professionally trained managers. The highest profits went to companies with the most efficient bureaucracies. Because the businesses were so big and their equipment so expensive, they had to operate continuously. In

The Eads Bridge The steel arches of the Eads Bridge across the Mississippi River at St. Louis were both an engineering marvel and a triumph of Andrew Carnegie's entrepreneurial skills.

an economic slowdown, an average factory could close its doors for a while, but big businesses could not.

With railroads and telegraph lines opening up national markets and new technology allowing mass production at lower costs, industries faced unprecedented competition. They met this challenge of competition and the need for a regular source of supply by adopting **vertical integration**. This was the attempt to control as many aspects of a business as possible, from the production of raw materials to the sale of the finished product. Carnegie did not just manufacture steel; he owned the iron mines and handled the marketing of finished steel. He also grasped two profit-making strategies that other firms, from breweries to makers of canned goods, had learned: economies of scale and *continuous flow*. Bigger furnaces could produce steel more cheaply. Running them 24 hours a day, seven days a week, made every minute count. And with the help of the Jones Mixer, a container keeping pig iron molten, the biggest component in steel would be ready for immediate use. Rails poured into molds did not even wait in the plant to cool. Flatcars carried them outside, while others lined up to be filled. By such means over 15 years, Carnegie cut steel prices in half. Without these innovations, the gridwork of steel railroad lines would never have been—nor that new, lighter superstructure of girders that allowed the first skyscrapers to tower above Chicago and New York.

The same commitment to continuous flow made Philip D. Armour and Gustavus Swift into the nation's premier meatpackers. Instead of the local slaughterhouse, firms in Chicago's **Packingtown** had assembly lines carrying a steady stream of carcasses, with each employee assigned one task in the disassembling of pigs and cattle. To save on freight rates for live cattle, the packers built refrigerator cars to carry the "dressed beef" alone to distant markets. Armour also realized that by making money off the rest of the animal, he could lower the price for which he sold

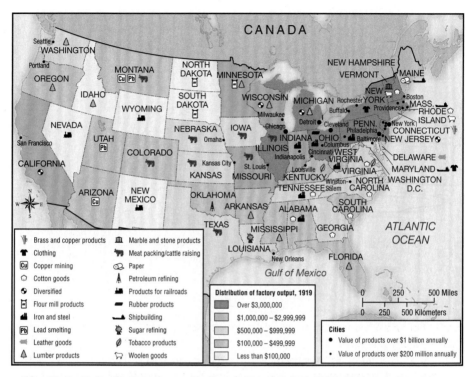

Map 16-3   States' Industries and Industrial Production, 1890-1919 An industrial map of late nineteenth-century America shows regions increasingly defined not only by what they grew but by what they made—or relied on the Northeast to make.

his meat. By 1900, the fat, bones, blood, and bristles were turned into hairbrushes, fertilizer, soap, and even the stuffing for automobile cushions—and Armour could sell his beef at four cents a pound.

John D. Rockefeller tried the other solution to cutthroat competition, **horizontal consolidation**: control of one step in the industrial process. Rockefeller had founded Standard Oil in 1867 in Cleveland, Ohio. Like Carnegie, Rockefeller hired the best managers and financiers to build and run the most efficient modern refineries and cut his dependence on railroad transport by investing in pipelines to carry the oil. However, he was also more willing than Carnegie to wipe out his competitors by any means available. Rockefeller squeezed from the railroads preferential shipping rates and rebates, the return of part of the standard price charged to other refiners—a critical advantage in a savagely competitive business. As president of the National Refiners' Association, he formed cartels, alliances with the major operators in other states. But the cartels were too weak to eliminate independent refiners.

Rockefeller found his solution in merging all the major companies under Standard Oil leadership. In 1882, the Standard Oil combine was formalized as a **trust**, an elaborate legal device by which different producers came together under the

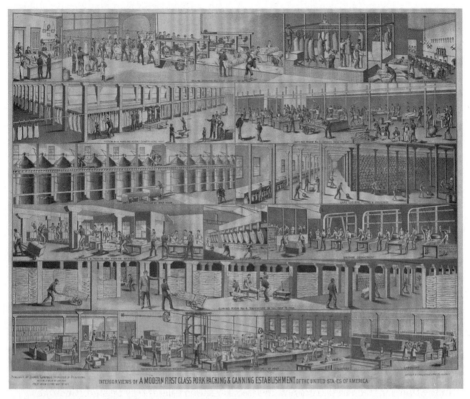

Packingtown, 1880 Large scale meat-packing, like any other big business, required a division of labor, with workers assigned different, discrete tasks, and carving the carcass done on the assembly line.

umbrella of a single company that could police competition internally. In 1889, the New Jersey legislature passed a law allowing corporations based in that state to form "holding companies" that controlled companies in other states. Thus, the trust gave way to the holding company, with Standard Oil of New Jersey its most prominent example. Within a decade, holding companies dominated some of America's largest industries.

Standard Oil became a notorious example of how big business had changed the American economy—and, some thought, for the worse. Rockefeller's many charities never buried his reputation as a "robber baron," a term thrown at the titans of industry, transport, and finance. Exceptional in an age when most firms remained small and most industries stayed competitive (railroads mercilessly so), these "captains of industry" were admired and feared in equal measure.

A NEW SOCIAL ORDER

Americans took pride in having no such rigid class system as in Europe. Anyone could rise, and, as Rosa Cassettari noticed, the poor need not doff their caps before the rich. But class divisions ran deep all the same. One could see that clearly, just by comparing Carnegie's Scottish castle with Painters' Row, where his unskilled workers lived in unventilated wooden houses without running water and with privies for all perched up the hill.

Lifestyles of the Very Rich

Between 1850 and 1890, the proportion of the nation's wealth owned by the 4,000 richest families nearly tripled. At the top of the social pyramid clustered some 200 families worth more than $20 million each. Concentrated in the Northeast, New York especially, these families flaunted their opulence. Spread more evenly across America were the several thousand millionaires made rich by cattle ranching, agricultural equipment, mining, commerce, and real estate. Most of America's millionaires traced their ancestry to Great Britain. Usually they were Protestant, mostly Episcopalians, Presbyterians, or Congregationalists. By the standards of their day they were unusually well educated, and more often than not, voted Republican. (Southerners remained firmly Democratic.)

The upper classes lived in mammoth houses. Some addresses became celebrated for their wealth: Fifth Avenue in Manhattan, Nob Hill in San Francisco, and Boston's Back Bay. Wealthy suburbs (Brooklyn Heights, Philadelphia's Main Line, and Brookline, Massachusetts) became privileged retreats. The richest families also built country estates that rivaled the stately homes of England and the chateaus of France, such as the palace-sized "cottages" along the Newport, Rhode Island, shoreline. The leading figures in New York's high society competed to stage the most lavish balls and dinner parties, in one case with hundred-dollar bills as party favors. It was left to the new middle class to display the traditional virtues of thrift and self-denial.

The Consolidation of the New Middle Class

In 1889, the *Century Dictionary* introduced the phrase "middle class" in the United States. The new term reflected a fresh awareness that American society had distinct gradations. Professionals were the backbone of the new middle class of the nineteenth century. All professions organized themselves into associations—some 200 between 1870 and 1890 alone—that set educational and ethical standards for admission and practice. Corporations needed professional managers, not swashbuckling gamblers. Business schools arose, teaching the science of accounting and the art of management. By 1920, 1,700 schools trained nurses, nearly all of them women. (At the same time, doctors' associations used their power over licensing to get rid of midwives; Rosa Cassettari was not the only one to do without.) Educators even gave a professional veneer to housekeeping by inventing "home economics" courses. States had a vested interest in professionalism, too. By 1900, most required association-drafted bar exams for lawyers and medical exams for doctors.

Behind the new professional managers marched an expanding white-collar army of cashiers, clerks, and government employees, mostly men. Their annual incomes far outpaced independent craftsmen and factory workers. They also had a better chance to rise. A beginning clerk might make only $100 a year, but within five years his salary could approach $1,000. At a time when a skilled Philadelphia factory hand made under $600, over 80 percent of the male clerks in the Treasury Department earned twice that.

Improved roads and mass-transit systems allowed middle-class families to escape the city's clamor and crowdedness, though suburbs, like city neighborhoods, were made for every income. The invention of oil-based house paints in the 1870s allowed owners to give the outside any color they pleased. Thanks to the mass-produced "Excelsior" mower and romantic associations with the Old South, the normal middle-class residence had a front porch and a lawn; but the crabgrass got blamed on eastern European immigrants, who supposedly brought it with them.

Only the most successful craftsmen matched the incomes and suburban life-styles of white-collar clerks. Butchers might earn more than $1,600 annually, for example, but shoemakers averaged little more than $500. But while a shoemaker earned little more than a skilled factory worker, if he owned his own shop, he enjoyed an independence that middle-class Americans cherished. A cigar maker working on high-priced "seed and Havanas" had skills that gave him far more say in his work than the unskilled employees making two-cent "stogies" with a cigar mold. Pride and power, not just pay, defined job satisfaction. In carpentry and in the coal mines, specialized skills made workers hard to replace. But around them, labor-saving machinery was increasing a far more dependent industrial working class made up of people like Rosa Cassettari.

The Industrial Working Class Comes of Age

"When I first went to learn the trade," John Morrison told a congressional committee in 1883, "a machinist considered himself more than the average working-man; in fact, he did not like to be called a workingman. He liked to be called a mechanic." Morrison identified one of the great changes in nineteenth-century America. "Today," Morrison lamented, the mechanic "is simply a laborer." Technological innovations replaced artisans with semiskilled or unskilled factory laborers. For traditional mechanics, this felt like downward mobility.

Because most factory workers and common laborers were migrants (or children of migrants) from small towns, farms, or abroad, few experienced factory work as a degradation of their traditional skills, as Morrison did. They had a chance to move upward from unskilled to skilled positions. Shop foremen might become storekeepers. Working-class families took comfort that their children had a still better chance of moving into the middle class. But industrial labor was a harsh existence for all factory operatives, who toiled long hours in difficult conditions performing repetitious tasks with little job security. Most luckless and hardest pressed were the common laborers, earning their keep by physical exertion. Their numbers grew throughout the century until by 1900 unskilled labor made up a third of the industrial workforce.

In 1900, women accounted for nearly one of every five Americans gainfully employed, mostly in unskilled or semiskilled labor. In northern middle-class homes, young Irish women worked as domestics, jobs held in the South by African American women. Jewish women sewed garments for as little as three dollars for a six-day week, and Italians worked on lace and paper flowers in their **tenements**. A smaller proportion of women held white-collar jobs, as teachers, nurses, or low-paid clerical workers and salesclerks behind department store counters.

The same hierarchy that favored men in the white-collar and professional labor force existed in the factories and sweatshops. In the clothing industry, for example, units dominated by male workers were higher up the chain of command than those dominated by women. Indeed, as the textile industry became a big business, the proportion of women working in textile mills steadily declined. The reverse trend affected white-collar workers. As department stores expanded in the 1870s and 1880s, they hired women, often Irish immigrants, for jobs with low wages and none of the prospects for promotion men still had. White-collar work did not confer middle-class status upon women as it did upon men in the late nineteenth century.

Few working-class wives and mothers took jobs outside the home, but many took in boarders or did laundry. The poorer working-class families survived by sending their children to work. The rich sent their daughters to finishing schools and their sons to boarding schools; middle-class parents sent their children to public schools; anything beyond grade school ranked as a luxury among those less well off than that. Ten-year-olds could be found tending the cotton spindles or picking shale off the conveyor belts coming up from the coal mines. They ran barefoot through New York's streets hawking newspapers and lugged red-hot, newly cast bottles from the furnaces in glass factories. Only in Horatio Alger novels did "Mark the Match-Boy" strike it rich.

Division of labor allowed more goods to be made for much lower per-unit labor costs. The introduction of the sewing machine in the 1850s, for example, gave rise to sweatshops where work was subdivided into simple, repetitive tasks. One group produced collars for men's shirts, another produced sleeves, and another stitched the parts together. Division of labor saved employers on training, and in industries where turnover was high, it kept the machinery running. Factory work was at best insecure, subject to swings in the business cycle. But unskilled workers also lacked the leverage to improve their own conditions. If Carnegie's workers, blinded or crippled on the job, got nothing more than the privilege of begging at the mill gates—if lung diseases were as common in textile factories as the "mill child's cough" and gangrene of the jaw among boys making matches—workers had no options beyond leaving and being fired.

Workmen's compensation was rare, and retirement pensions were unknown. Helplessness and the pool of surplus labor made organizing unions a challenge among the unskilled. Men laying railroad track or digging subway tunnels were always moving on, with common labor often seasonal and factory turnover high. In some meatpacking houses, turnover came close to 100 percent annually. A strike depleted workers' savings quickly. Exceptionally mobile and easily replaceable, immigrants increasingly came from places unfamiliar with the idea of organized labor and from cultures where religion defined identity more than class. Employers knew that by using them or, better still, Black Americans as strikebreakers, they could turn race against race, native against foreigner. **Scabs**, as those taking strikers' places were called, faced insult and threat. Some were beaten, others killed. Some firms built private armies to enforce control, but they could usually count on the police and state militia to help them win a strike.

Social Darwinism and the Growth of Scientific Racism

As ethnicity identification developed in the late nineteenth century, class divisions were increasingly difficult to isolate from cultural distinctions. The middle class, for example, was overwhelmingly native born, white, Anglo-Saxon, and Protestant. By contrast, the working class came largely from racial and religious minorities,

Cannery in Sunnyvale, California The mass production of food involved a large female labor force, as this picture shows. Quite possibly, employers hired so readily not just because they could pay women less, but because anything involving the preparation of food fit in with the stereotype of "woman's work."

many of them foreign born (see Figure 16–2). By 1900, 75 percent of manufacturing workers were immigrants or their children, and in large cities, nearer 85 percent. The South's laborers were overwhelmingly Black sharecroppers. As educated elites defined high culture, they drew on traditions and tastes formed by the propertied classes of a less culturally diverse America, one increasingly under challenge.

Pundits and professors argued that this form of society, stratified by class, race, ethnicity, and gender, was not only how things had to be, but how natural law required them to be. In 1859, Charles Darwin published his masterpiece of evolutionary theory, *On the Origin of Species*. Several scientists had already suggested that life had evolved over a long period of time, but Darwin offered the first persuasive explanation of how this had taken place. He argued that a process of "natural selection" favored those biological changes that were most suited to the surrounding environment. American scientists took readily to Darwinism. Asa Gray at Harvard and Joseph LeConte at the University of California spread the evolutionary word in their influential textbooks on botany and geology. By 1900, virtually all American high school science textbooks embraced evolution.

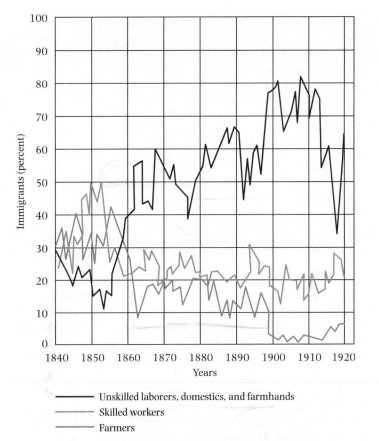

Figure 16–2   Working-Class Immigration, 1840–1920
Source: US Bureau of Census.

Darwin's influence did not stop with the natural sciences. Social scientists applied the theory of natural selection to social evolution. To Social Darwinists, inequality was the natural order of things, the outcome of a struggle for survival in which the fittest rose to the top. That premise made the rich seem more deserving than the poor and blamed the disadvantages of most immigrants as **Social Darwinism**'s judgment on their own unworthiness, compared to white males from the British Isles and northern Europe."Before the tribunal of nature," Yale University's Professor William Graham Sumner asserted, "a man has no more right to life than a rattlesnake." Any government intervention to help the unfortunate interfered with natural selection. It would be useless in the long run and a harmful interference with the rigid economic laws of supply and demand in the short run. In this way, Darwin's concepts were hijacked to defend the new social order of industrial capitalism.

Natural selection was also invoked to show an inherent African racial inferiority (and that of Indians as well). Racists had argued that without slavery, freed Blacks could not compete—or even survive. After the war, newspapers predicted the disappearance of African Americans by century's end and of Indians within a generation or two more. The 1890 census seemed to show a declining African

Struggles For Democracy

"The Chinese Must Go"

For the Chinese, immigrating to America proved a disastrous success. With no other group did the promise of a new beginning suffer so badly in the translation.

In the mid-nineteenth century, the Chinese fled the convulsions of the Taiping Rebellion, a massive civil war that left 20 million dead. Some immigrants found work in the California gold fields; others dug the mines or laid track on the transcontinental railroad. Contractors swore by them: they did the hardest work at the lowest wage and never complained. Mines in Idaho and Montana imported Chinese labor. In California's inland valley, they earned a dollar a day digging the irrigation ditches for the great farms. As tourist hotels opened in southern California, they welcomed the Chinese as cooks and help. Along the Pacific coast, their vessels hauled in shoals of fish, ready to be dried, salted, and barreled for sale in China. Others dove for abalone; well-polished, the shells sold by the hundreds of thousands in Europe. They planted the vineyards north of San Francisco Bay and harvested the orchards south of it. The Bing cherry was developed by a Chinese horticulturist in Oregon, the frost-resistant orange by a Chinese immigrant in Florida. Saving their money, the thriftier Chinese opened up laundries and retail shops. Every major city had its "Chinatown," colorful, congested, and overwhelmingly male: the first generations of Chinese were sojourners, meaning to prosper and return home. They rented rather than bought homes and left their families behind. Those who died in America, if they could afford it, had their remains shipped back to their native soil for burial.

Hard-working, resourceful, sober, willing, and almost obsessive about paying what they owed, the Chinese were the very personification of the Horatio Alger ideal for success. That, however, was just the problem. White workers resented their cheap labor and the corporations that used them as strikebreakers. Keeping apart and failing to assimilate, Chinese immigrants remained alien, closed off by differences in language and religion from their neighbors. It was widely believed that the Chinese ate birds' nests, rats, squirrels, and, worst of all, abalone. Ignorance only kindled fantasies among whites, of a Chinatown crowded with opium dens, racketeers, and prostitution rings—all of which did exist—and not much else. Alarmist writers forecast a race war, where the "Celestials" conquered the world for their emperor.

Even as other immigrants became voters, the Chinese found themselves isolated and imperiled. Courts refused Chinese testimony because of the race's supposed habit of lying. Trade unions refused to admit them. Rioters in Los Angeles tore through the Asian community, beating up and killing whomever they could find and looting every store; a city councilman led the mob, and the chief of police sealed Chinatown off so that the victims could not escape. Vigilantes burned down Chinatowns across the West. Farmers employing Chinese laborers had their barns and fields torched. By 1877, anger against the Chinese and railroad barons had become a political uprising, with the cry, "The Chinese must go!" California's new constitution barred them from public schools and taxed them out of the mining and fishing

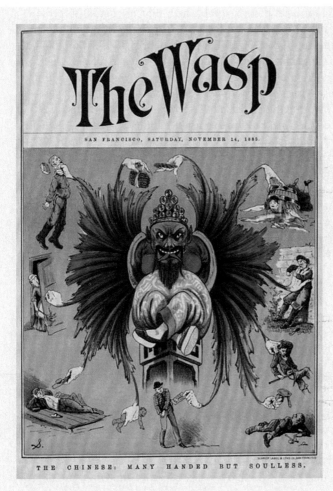

THE CHINESE: MANY HANDED BUT SOULLESS.

Anti-Chinese stereotypes from *The Wasp*, 1885 Encapsuling all white society's nightmare images of Chinese immigration, this San Francisco humor magazine emphasized the economic threat it posed to the working class rather than the boost it gave to the West's economy as a whole.

industries. National laws over the next 20 years would close the doors to new immigration and make it harder for residents to visit home and return to the United States.

Closing the doors to their home country had an unexpected effect. Cut off from their Old World communities, forced to make a lifetime commitment to their new homeland, the survivors learned English, brought their families over, and remade themselves as Chinese Americans. They adopted Western clothing; their sons and daughters went to Sunday school, joined the Boy Scouts, and organized chapters of the YMCA and YWCA. All the same, full assimilation would not come in their lifetimes, nor their grandchildren's. In more than a mere physical sense, the Statue of Liberty faced away from the newcomers of the Pacific Rim.

American population, and racial theorists published influential studies "proving" that competition with whites was killing Blacks off. Their only salvation, biologist Joseph LeConte argued, would come through permanent subordination. Statistician Frederick L. Hoffman's treatise *Race Traits and Tendencies of the American Negro* went further. Using tables and figures to clinch his conclusions, Hoffman insisted that ever since leaving the shelter of slavery, Blacks had been degenerating morally. Evolutionary theory doomed them to poverty and social inferiority.

But the Sumners of the world found themselves under increasing challenge well before the century ended. Ministers, who saw man as a moral, rather than an economic, animal, rejected the concept of a natural selection process based on selfishness and scramble. Economist Richard T. Ely argued that even in economic decisions, self-interest did not play the all-controlling role that Social Darwinism presumed. Success, a younger generation of economists and social scientists argued, depended not just on a person's natural gifts but also on the surrounding conditions. Change the conditions—replace a slum with clean and healthy apartments, an alley with a playground or a park, a pittance with a living wage—and the man or woman with abilities might have the chance to use them to rise.

In that sense, the modern university reflected the inequalities of the age—and the promise. Leading scholars in the new "social sciences" of sociology, anthropology, and political science gave authority to Social Darwinism's conjectures, by dividing the world into great and inferior nations. At the top were the so-called Teutonic nations of Western Europe and North America. This hierarchy, far from reflecting the biases of its creators, was grounded in the objective methods of pure science—or so anthropologists, sociologists, and professional economists claimed. However, a vocal minority, just as well trained abroad, came back to apply objective standards to Social Darwinism and expose its fallacies.

Colleges thus helped reinforce elite power while opening the door a crack to those wanting to enter that elite realm. Only a tiny fraction of Americans attended college, mostly native-born and well-to-do males. Nevertheless, it was a larger fraction than ever before. One reason was that the first Morrill Land Grant Act of 1862

TIME LINE

▼**1848**
Andrew Carnegie emigrates to the United States

▼**1857**
Henry Bessemer develops process for making steel

▼**1859**
Oil discovered in western Pennsylvania and the petroleum boom begins

▼**1862**
Homestead Act

▼**1866**
First successful transatlantic telegraph cable begins operation

▼**1869**
Opening of the first transcontinental railroad

▼**1871**
Great Chicago Fire

▼**1872**
Andrew Carnegie organizes construction of steelworks near Pittsburgh

▼**1873**
Financial panic, followed by depression

had endowed the states with great tracts to fund institutions teaching "agriculture and the mechanic arts." Seventy "land grant" institutions were founded, including the major state university systems of New York, Illinois, Michigan, and California. Those in the Midwest admitted women as well as men. Women's colleges also opened their doors: six of the "Seven Sisters" began after the Civil War. By 1910, two in five college students were women. If Blacks found themselves largely shut out of the elite schools (which also set quotas limiting Jewish admissions), they, too, had new opportunities in land grant institutions as well as in Black colleges like Fisk University in Tennessee or Booker T. Washington's Tuskegee Institute in Alabama.

Social scientists such as Ely and Hoffman prided themselves on their commitment to the truth as facts and statistics revealed it. Like advocates of high culture, sociologists and anthropologists claimed to have isolated the definitive truths of human society. But not all "realists" sought solace in statistics. Some of America's best artists responded to the realities of a diverse, urban, industrial America. They could see what it took no advanced degree to grasp: that a many-cultured society was being enriched and reshaped by those very people that Social Darwinists had dismissed as the losers in humankind's struggle to advance.

The Knights of Labor and the Haymarket Disaster

Workers had known that all along, their share fell far behind what their labor deserved. Between 1860 and 1890, wages overall grew by 50 percent, but elite skilled and semiskilled workers in a handful of industries, such as printing and metalworking, got the lion's share of the gains. The vast majority of workers suffered directly from deflation and economic instability. By 1880, 40 percent of industrial workers lived at or below the poverty line, and the average worker was unemployed for 15 to 20 percent of the year. To relieve their plight, American workers sought political solutions to economic problems.

Inspired by the radicalism of the Civil War and Reconstruction, industrial workers across the North organized dozens of craft unions, Eight-Hour Leagues, and workingmen's associations, all designed to protect northern workers who were

▼**1877**
The "Great Railroad Strike"

▼**1882**
John D. Rockefeller forms Standard Oil trust
Thomas Edison develops the first commercially

viable incandescent electric light

▼**1886**
Nationwide strike for eight-hour day
Riot at Haymarket Square in Chicago

▼**1890**
Jacob Riis publishes *How the Other Half Lives*
Director of US Census declares frontier "closed"

▼**1893**
Financial panic, followed by depression

overworked and underpaid. They called strikes, initiated consumer boycotts, and formed consumer cooperatives. In 1867 and 1868, workers in New York and Massachusetts campaigned for laws restricting the workday to eight hours. Soon, workers began electing their own candidates to state legislatures.

Before the **Gilded Age**, labor organizations had never drawn many workers. The tradition of individuals lifting themselves up bred a distrust of collective solutions. Founded in 1866, the **National Labor Union** (NLU) was the first significant postwar effort to organize all "working people" into a national union. William Sylvis, an iron molder, founded the NLU and became its president in 1868. He denied any "harmony of interests" between workers and capitalists. On the contrary, every wage earner was at war with every capitalist, whose "profits" robbed working people of the fruits of their labor.

Under Sylvis's direction, the NLU advocated a wide range of political reforms, not just bread-and-butter issues. Sylvis believed that through organization American workers could take the "first step toward competence and independence." He argued for a doubling of the average worker's wages. He supported voting rights for Blacks and women. Nevertheless, after a miserable showing in the elections of 1872, the NLU fell apart.

Despite the collapse of the NLU, a more successful alternative had already begun. In 1869, some Philadelphia garment makers formed the Noble and Holy Order of the Knights of Labor. The Knights were inspired by the producers' ideology and admitted everyone from self-employed farmers to unskilled factory workers. Stressing the need for uplift and temperance, the Knights advocated a host of reforms, including the eight-hour day, equal pay for men and women, the abolition of child and prison labor, inflation of the currency to counteract the deflationary spiral, and a national income tax.

Only a strong national organization able to hold various locals together and provide necessary funds would give the Knights credibility among potential recruits. In the late 1870s, a new constitution required all members to pay dues and let the national organization support local boycotts. Open to women as well as men, skilled and unskilled, Black and white (but not Chinese), the Knights grew rapidly, from 19,000 members in 1881 to nearly a quarter million in 1886. Terence Powderly, leader of this largely working-class movement, believed in neither socialism nor the notion that there was any necessary conflict between labor and capital. Wage earners were "producers," and he meant to overthrow "wage slavery," not capitalism itself. Powderly favored arbitration and conciliation over confrontation, and the consumer boycott over the strike. Local assemblies struck anyhow. They even forced a settlement out of the railroads of the Southwest, including those of the notorious Jay Gould, who had bragged that he "could hire one half of the working class to kill the other half." The Knights' lobbying helped put through the Chinese Exclusion Act in 1882 and a federal law against imported contract labor three years later. Labor parties elected mayors and city councilmen; only vote fraud kept them from making Henry George mayor of New York. They even talked of fielding a presidential ticket.

But the more the **Knights of Labor** grew, the more the strains among its members showed. Shopkeepers and small-factory owners had very different interests from wage laborers, especially when it came to strikes. By 1886, work stoppages were twice what they had been the year before. The "Great Upheaval" had begun. The more

Haymarket Riot The Haymarket "riot," as it was misnamed, set off a wave of middle-class hysteria against foreigners, radicals, and labor unions. This image correctly shows police firing into the crowd. Inaccurately, it shows members of the crowd firing back, the orator apparently urging them on. It also leaves out the women and children who attended.

Knights there were, the more militant they sounded. The culmination came when trade unions called for a nationwide strike for the eight-hour day. On May 1, 1886, workers across the country walked off their jobs in one of the largest labor walkouts in American history. In Chicago 80,000 workers went out on strike. The Chicago strike was largely peaceful until May 4, when, at an anarchist rally at **Haymarket Square**, someone from the crowd tossed a bomb into a line of police. Eight policemen were killed. Police shot into the crowd. Four people died. Many more were wounded.

Anarchists—who questioned the legitimacy of all government power—had little influence on the labor movement, but their fiery rhetoric invoking the use of violence made them conspicuous. In a blatantly unfair trial with perjured testimony, eight of them were found guilty of inciting the "Haymarket riot." Four were hanged, one committed suicide, and the others went to prison. (In 1893, Governor John Peter Altgeld pardoned the survivors. He knew it would doom him politically; it did.) Haymarket was a turning point in American labor politics. A wave of revulsion against labor agitation swept the country, and state antilabor laws sprinkled the statute books. The Knights never recovered from the Haymarket disaster. Instead, the labor movement found its new leadership in Samuel Gompers's American Federation of Labor, which concentrated on organizing skilled workers and making demands that could be met immediately, without waiting for political reforms: "bread-and-butter unionism," as some called it.

CONCLUSION

Rosa Cassettari and Andrew Carnegie—two immigrants whom the new global economy of industrial capitalism helped draw overseas—met wholly different destinies. Not just their origins, but gender roles, opportunity, and good luck explained how they ended up. Yet both shared the same striving spirit that held out at least the chance for them to better themselves (as Cassettari did, however modestly) and their adopted country. Cassettari's experience with failure impelled her to search for something better. Carnegie's success made him yearn for more than money. By 1900, having thrown his energies into getting, Carnegie threw them all into giving. He set up endowments, funded universities, and founded an institute for peace. He had helped create an industrial nation. Now he set out to re-create American culture. Ironically, the Rosa Cassettaris of the world had beaten him to it.

WHO, WHAT, WHERE

Bessemer process   537

Carnegie, Andrew   535

Cassettari, Rosa   524

Gilded Age   550

Great Railroad Strike of 1877   526

Haymarket Square   551

Homestead Act   529

horizontal consolidation   539

Knights of Labor   550

Longhorn cattle   529

Lower East Side   526

National Labor Union   550

Packingtown   538

political economy   526

Riis, Jacob   534

Rockefeller, John D.   539

scabs   543

sharecropping   524

Social Darwinism   545

tenement   542

trust   539

vertical integration   538

REVIEW QUESTIONS

1. Define industrial capitalism. How was industrial capitalism a global phenomenon in the late nineteenth century?

2. What were the differences in lifestyle and in opportunities for those in America's upper, middle, and lower classes, and how did those differences widen or narrow during the late nineteenth century?

3. How was the West absorbed into the national and international markets?

CRITICAL-THINKING QUESTIONS

1. How and why did the effects of industrial capitalism differ in the South, West, and North?

2. Historians often refer to this period as the Gilded Age. "Gilded" refers to something of base or common substance coated with a thin layer of gold, so that it seems far brighter and more valuable than it is. In view of America's industrial development at this time, do you think the term "Gilded Age" is appropriate? Why or why not?

3. Aside from the expansion of industrial capitalism, what factors affected American development during this period? How important are those factors in comparison to capitalism's growth?

SUGGESTED READINGS

Chandler, Alfred D. *The Visible Hand: The Managerial Revolution in American Business*. Cambridge, MA: Harvard University Press, 1977.

Cronon, William. *Nature's Metropolis: Chicago and the Great West*. New York: Norton, 1991.

White, Richard. *The Republic for Which It Stands: The United States During Reconstruction and the Gilded Age, 1865–1896*. New York: Oxford University Press, 2016.

For further review materials and resource information, please visit www.oup.com/us/ofthepeople

CHAPTER 16: The Triumph of Industrial Capitalism, 1850–1890
Primary Sources

16.1 STEPHEN CRANE VISITS THE "BREAKER" AT A COAL MINE

Success came hard to the novelist and poet Stephen Crane. His first book, *Maggie: A Girl of the Streets*, sold so poorly that he found himself nearly destitute. To pay the bills, he free-lanced as a reporter. This account of one aspect of coal mining came out a few months before his *Red Badge of Courage* won his recognition as one of the finest writers of his day.

The "breakers" squatted upon the hillsides and in the valley like enormous preying monsters, eating of the sunshine, the grass, the green leaves. The smoke from their nostrils had ravaged the air of coolness and fragrance. All that remained of vegetation looked dark, miserable, half-strangled. Along the summit line of the mountain a few unhappy trees were etched upon the clouds. Overhead stretched a sky of imperial blue, incredibly far away from the somber land.

We approached the colliery over paths of coal dust that wound among the switches. A "breaker" loomed aboe us, a huge and towering frame of blackened wood. It ended in a little curious peak, and upon its sides there was a profusion of windows appearing at strange and unexpected points. Through occasional doors one could see the flash of whirring machinery. Men with wondrously blackened faces and garments came forth from it. The sole glitter upon their persons was at their hats, where the little tin lamps were carried. They went stolidly along, some swinging lunch-pails carelessly; but the marks upon them of their forbidding and mystic calling fascinated our new eyes until they passed from sight. They were symbols of a grim, strange war that was being waged in the sunless depths of the earth.

Around a huge central building clustered other and lower ones, sheds, engine-houses, machine-shops, office. Railroad tracks extended in web-like ways. Upon them stood files of begrimed coal cars. Other huge structures similar to the one near us, upreared their uncouth heads upon the hills of the surrounding country. From each a mighty hill of culm extended. Upon these tremendous heaps of waste from the mines, mules and cars appeared like toys. Down in the valley, upon the railroads, long trains crawled painfully southward, where a low-hanging gray cloud, with a few projecting spires and chimneys, indicated a town.

Car after car came from a shed beneath which lay hidden the mouth of the shaft.

They were dragged, creaking, up an inclined cable road to the top of the "breaker."

At the top of the "breaker," laborers were dumping the coal into chutes. The huge lumps slid slowly on their journey down through the building, from which they were to emerge in classified fragments. Great teeth on revolving cylinders caught them and chewed them. At places there were grates that bid each size go into its proper chute. The dust lay inches deep on every motionless thing, and clouds of it made the air dark as from a violent tempest. A mighty gnashing sound filled the ears. With terrible appetite this huge and hideous monster sat imperturbably munching coal, grinding its mammoth jaws with unearthly and monotonous uproar.

In a large room sat the little slate-pickers. The floor slanted at an angle of forty-five degrees, and the coal, having been masticated by the great teeth, was streaming sluggishly in long iron troughs. The boys sat straddling these troughs, and as the mass moved slowly, they grabbed deftly at the pieces of slate therein. There were five or si of them, one above another, over each trough. The coal is expected to be fairly pure after it passes the final boy. The howling machinery was above them. High up, dim figures moved about in the dust clouds.

These little men were a terrifically dirty band. They resembled the New York gamins in some ways, but they laughed more, and when they laughed their faces were a wonder and a terror. They had an air of supreme independence, and seemed proud of their kind of villainy. They swore long oaths with skill.

Through their ragged shirts we could get occasional glimpses of shoulders black as stoves. They looked precisely like imps as they scrambled to get a view of us. Work ceased while they tried to ascertain if we were willing to give away any tobacco. The man who perhaps believes that he controls them came and harangued the crowd. He talked to the air.

The slate-pickers all through this region are yet at the spanking period. One continually wonders about their mothers, and if there are any schoolhouses. But as for them, they are not concerned. When they get time off, they go out on the culm heap and play baseball, or fight with boys from other "breakers" or among themselves, according to the opportunities. And before them always is the hope of one day getting to be door-boys down in the mines; and, later, mule-boys; and yet later, laborers and helpers. Finally, when they have grown to be great big men, they may become miners, real miners, and go down and get "squeezed," or perhaps escape to a shattered old man's estate with a mere "miner's asthma." They are very ambitious.

Meanwhile they live in a place of infernal dins. The crash and thunder of the machinery is like the roar of an immense cataract. The room shrieks and blames and bellows. Clouds of dust blur the air until the windows shine pallidly afar off. All the structure is a-tremble from the heavy sweep and circle of the ponderous mechanism. Down in the midst of it sit these tiny urchins, where they earn fifty-five cents a day each. They breathe this atmosphere until heir lungs grow heavy and sick with it. They have this clamor in their ears until it is wonderful that they have any hoodlum valor remaining. But they are uncowed; they continue to swagger. And at the top of the "breaker" laborers can always bee= seen dumping the roaring coal down the wide, voracious maw of the creature.

Source: Stephen Crane, "In the Depths of a Coal Mine." McClure's Magazine, 3 (August 1894)

16.2   VISUAL DOCUMENT: ALFRED R. WAUD, "BESSEMER STEEL MANUFACTURE" (1876)

The manufacture of steel began in the Middle Ages in Europe and Asia, but industrialization enabled the manufacture of high-quality steel in massive quantities. The transformation of iron ore into steel was an intensive process. The arrival of huge converters in enormous steel mills caused some observers to consider both the wondrousness of the new technology and the hell-like conditions that employed it. While the United States benefited from large quantities of steel for railroads, construction, and equipment, steel workers labored under harsh conditions. The forges poured liquid hot metal; workers were exposed to air pollution; and wages provided little to no income for long hours and an extensive workweek with no substantial breaks.

Source: Alfred R. Waud, 1828–1891, artist. "Bessemer Steel Manufacture" (1876). Library of Congress Prints and Photographs Division, Washington, DC.

16.3   GEORGE STEEVENS, EXCERPT FROM *THE LAND OF THE DOLLAR* (1897)

George Steevens, a British journalist, came across the Atlantic in 1896 to collect material for *The Land of the Dollar*. While visiting Philadelphia, he went to one of the most celebrated department stores in the country, Wanamaker's. His guess that the owner had been a "rattling good" Cabinet officer was half right. In terms of efficiency, Wanamaker proved excellent; as a partisan Republican, he willingly saw to the discharge of as many Democratic postmasters as he could manage, and his readiness to forbid mailing materials that he considered indecent stirred outrage among authors.

In Philadelphia everybody goes to Wanamaker's. Mr. [John] Wanamaker was once Post-master-General of the Republic, and I should think he was a rattling good one. His store was already the largest retail drapery and hosiery and haberdashery, and all that sort of business, in the world, when by the recent purchase of a giant establishment in New York he made it more largest still. Now the working of Wanamaker's, as I am informed, is this. It is no use going there to get what you want. You must go to get what Mr. Wanamaker wants to sell. He tells you each morning in the newspapers what he has got today, and if you want it you had better go and get it; the chances are it will be gone tomorrow. The head of each department is entrusted with a certain amount of capital, and buys his goods at his own discretion. But woe unto him if he does not turn over his capital quickly. There is a rule that no stock may be in the house more than, I think, three months; after that off it must go at any sacrifice.

"You can always tell when Mr. Wanamaker's in town," said a shopwalker, "because there's always some change being made." And then he added, in a half-voice of awestricken worship, "I believe Mr. Wanamaker loves change for its own sake." For the sake of custom, I should say; for this formula of change for change's sake is one of the master-keys of American character. Mr. Wanamaker keeps a picture-gallery, with some really fine modern paintings, to beguile his patrons. To-day he will have an orchestrion playing, tomorrow a costume exhibition of spinning—girls from all the lands of the earth,—every day something new. One day, by moving a table six feet, so that people had to walk round it instead of past it, he increased the sales of an article from three shillings to hundreds of pounds. If that is not genius, tell me what is.

But the really Napoleonic—I was going to say daemonic—feature of the Wanamaker system is the unerring skill with which it reaps its profits out of the necessities of others. Fixing his price according to the economic doctrine of final utility—taking no account, that is, of the cost of production, but only of the price at which most people will find it worth their while to buy—Mr. Wanamaker realizes 10 percent for himself, and an enormous saving for the consumers. A cargo of rose-trees had been consigned from Holland to a firm of florists, which failed while the plants were in mid-ocean. They went a-begging till Mr. Wanamaker bought them up and put them on the market at about half the rate current in Philadelphia. In ten days not one of the twenty thousand was left. A firm which manufactured hundred-dollar bicycles found itself without cash to meet its liabilities. Mr. Wanamaker bought up the stock and altered the maker's label as well as one peculiarity of the gear. Then he broke the price to sixty-six dollars, and subsequently to thirty-three. They all went off in a week or so. He bought the plates of a huge edition of the hundred-dollar Century Dictionary, altered the title-page, bound them for himself, and put the article on the market at fifty-one dollars and a half. In six weeks he had sold two thousand. A firm in California, which manufactures an excellent kind of blanket, was in difficulties. Mr. Wanamaker bought up the stock, and sold it at a third of the normal price in three days.

All this is magnificent for the customer, and apparently not unprofitable to Mr. Wanamaker. But plainly somebody has to pay, and who? The small trader. After the rose-tree deal nobody wanted to buy roses of the florists of Philadelphia. The city is stocked with bicycles and Century Dictionaries, and nobody within a radius of miles will want to buy a pair of blankets for a generation. Mr. Wanamaker sends out three hundred and sixty-five thousand parcels to his customers in the slackest month of the year, and turns over thirteen million dollars annually. The small people, it is presumed, are ground to powder against the wall.

Source: George Steevens, *The Land of the Dollar* (New York, 1897), quoted in David Colbert, ed., *Eyewitness to America: 500 Years of America in the Words of Those Who Saw It Happen* (New York: Pantheon Books, 1997), pp. 305–306.

16.4   JAMES BAIRD WEAVER, *A CALL TO ACTION* (1892)

A Union officer and later an insurgent Iowa Republican, James B. Weaver moved first into the Greenback Party and then joined the Populists. As their presidential candidate in 1892, he issued *A Call to Action*, exposing the gap between the life-styles of the rich and the conditions of the underprivileged.

If the master builders of our civilization one hundred years ago had been told that at the end of a single century, American society would present such melancholy contrasts of wealth and poverty, of individual happiness and widespread infelicity as are to be found to-day throughout the Republic, the person making the unwelcome prediction would have been looked upon as a misanthropist, and his loyalty to Democratic institutions would have been seriously called in question. Our federal machine, with its delicate inter-lace work of National, State and municipal supervision, each intended to secure perfect individual equality, was expected to captivate the world by its operation and insure domestic contentment and personal security to a degree never before realized by mankind.

But there is a vast difference between the generation which made the heroic struggle for Self-government in colonial days, and the third generation which is now engaged in a mad rush for wealth. The first took its stand upon the inalienable rights of man and made a fight which shook the world. But the leading spirits of the latter are entrenched behind class laws and revel in special privileges. It will require another revolution to overthrow them. That revolution is upon us even now.

Two representative characters—Dives and Lazarus—always make their appearance side by side in disturbing contrast just before the tragic stage of revolution is reached. They were present at the overthrow of ancient civilizations; the hungry multitude stood outside the gates when Belshazzar's impious feast was spread; they were both at the cave of Adullam when the scepter was about to depart from the tyrant Saul to the hands of the youthful David; they stood side by side when Alaric thundered at the gates of Rome; they confronted one another in the fiery tempest of the French revolution and they are sullenly face to face in our own country to-day.…

THE BANKER'S BANQUET

The following editorial appeared in the *Kansas City Times*, August 30, 1889:

"The contract for serving the banquet for the convention of the American Bankers' Association was yesterday awarded to C.M. Hill, of the Midland Hotel. There were sixty competitors. The price is such as to insure one of the finest banquets ever served in this country. No expense will be spared to make the affair a grand success, even aside from the menu. The banquet will be given in the Priests of Pallas' Temple, at Seventh and Lydia. It will be necessary to build and furnish an annex, where the cooking can be done for 1,500 covers. The preparations seem to take into contemplation a great flow of wine, as there will be six thousand wine glasses and about forty wine servers. There will be in all nearly three hundred waiters. It is estimated that the entire cost of the banquet will be from $15,000 to $20,000. Mr. Hill anticipates some difficulty in securing efficient waiters, and with this particular object in view, will make a trip to New York and Chicago."

This impious feast which took place in the very heart of the mortgage-ridden and debt-cursed West, was the most shocking and brazen exhibition of wanton extravagance and bad morals combined, which the laboring millions of America were ever called upon to behold. What a travesty upon common sense and the ordinary instinct of self-preservation to intrust the finances of a great Nation and the welfare of labor to the hands of such men.

This carousal was but history repeating itself. It is not necessary in our day that an armless hand shall come out of the darkness and write the decree of Heaven upon the wall of the palace while the drunken carousal is being held, as in the time of Belshazzar; nor does it now require an expert Hebrew prophet, like Daniel, to disclose to the King that the sword is about to enter, and that a greater than Darius is thundering at the gates of Babylon, commissioned from on high to restore the stolen treasures of the temple, and to transfer the kingdom to another."

AT THE RICH MAN'S GATE

About the time these princely entertainments were given, and in the same year with some of them, one of the metropolitan journals caused a careful canvass to be made of the unemployed of that city. The number was found to be one hundred and fifty thousand persons who were daily unsuccessfully seeking work within the city limits of New York. Another one hundred and fifty thousand earn less than sixty cents per day. Thousands of these are poor girls who work from eleven to sixteen hours per day.

In the year 1890, over twenty-three thousand families, numbering about one hundred thousand people, were forcibly evicted in New York City owing to their inability to pay rent, and one-tenth, of all who died in that city during the year were buried in the Potters Field.

In the *Arena* for June, 1891, will be found a description of tenement house horrors, by Mr. B.O. Flower. He has done a valuable service to humanity by laying before the world the result of his investigations. After describing a family whose head was unable to find work, Mr. Flower says:

"This poor woman supports her husband, her two children and herself, by making pants at twelve cents a pair. No rest, no surcease, a perpetual grind from early dawn, often till far into the night; and what is more appalling, outraged nature has rebelled; the long months of semi-starvation and lack of sleep have brought on rheumatism, which has settled in the joints of her fingers, so that every stitch means a throb of pain. The afternoon we called she was completing an enormous pair of custom-made pants of very fine blue cloth, for one of the largest clothing houses in the city. The suit would probably bring sixty or sixty-five dollars, yet her employer graciously informed his poor white slave that as the garment was so large he would give her an extra cent. Thirteen cents for fine custom-made pants, manufactured for a wealthy firm, which repeatedly asserts that its clothing is not made in tenement houses! Thus with one of the most painful diseases enthroned in that part of the body which must move incessantly from dawn till midnight, with two small dependent children and a husband powerless to help her, this poor woman struggles bravely, confronted ever by a nameless dread of impending misfortune. Eviction, sickness, starvation—such are the ever present spectres, while every year marks the steady encroachment of disease and the lowering of the register of vitality. Moreover, from the window of her soul falls the light of no star athwart the pathway of life.

"In another tenement Mr. Flower found a poor widow with three children, making pants at twelve cents a pair. One of the children had been engaged, since she was two and one-half years old in overcasting the long seams of the garments, made by her mother! In the attic of another tenement a widow was found weeping and working by the side of a cradle where lay a sick child, whose large luminous eyes shone with almost phosphorescent brilliancy from great cavernous sockets, as they wandered from one to another, with a wistful, soul-querying gaze. Its forehead was large and prominent, so much so that looking at the upper part of the head one would little imagine the terrible emaciation of the body, which was little more than skin and hones, and the sight of which spoke more eloquently than words of the ravages of slow starvation and wasting disease. The woman was weeping because she had been notified that if one week's rent was not paid on Saturday she would be evicted, which meant death to her child who was suffering from a rupture, and for whom she was unable to purchase a truss.

"The making at home of clothing, cigars, etc., in New York and Brooklyn is paid at prices on which no women could live were there not other workers in the family. Some of their occupations involved great risks to girls, such as the loss of joints, of fingers, of the hand, or sometimes of the whole arm."

Source: James Baird Weaver, *A Call to Action: An Interpretation of the Great Uprising, Its Sources and Causes* (Des Moines: Iowa Printing Company, 1892), 362–363, 367–370.

16.5 VISUAL DOCUMENTS: "GIFT FOR THE GRANGERS" (1873) AND THE JORNS FAMILY OF DRY VALLEY, CUSTER COUNTY, NEBRASKA (1886)

The image of the self-sufficient "yeoman farmer" in close communion with nature always had been more fantasy than real; but on the bare prairies, where it took a family working full time just to keep body and soul together, the harsh reality made the old myths feel like bitter mockery. These contrasting documents depict two versions of farm life: the ideal and the real.

Source: "Gift for the Grangers," J. Hale Powers & Co. Fraternity & Fine Art Publishers, Cincinnati; Strobridge & Co. Lith.

Source: Photograph by Solomon D. Butcher, Library of Congress American Memory Historical Collections.

16.6 WILLIAM A. PEFFER PLEADS THE FARMER'S CAUSE, 1891

Elected Senator from Kansas in 1891, William A. Peffer had a long history of reform politics, from the labor movement through Prohibition. Long-bearded and scholarly, he made an easy mark for cartoonists' ridicule—undeservedly, as his summing-up of prairie farmers' plight shows.

Farmers are passing through the "valley and shadow of death"; farming as a business is profitless; values of farm products have fallen 50 percent since the great war, and farm values have depreciated 25 to 50 percent during the last ten years; farmers are overwhelmed with debts secured by mortgages on their homes, unable in many instances to pay even the interest as it falls due, and unable to renew the loans because securities are weakening by reason of the general depression; many farmers losing their homes under this dreadful blight, and the mortgage mill still grinds. We are in the hands of a merciless power; the people's homes are at stake. . . .

The American farmer of today is altogether a different sort of a man from his ancestor of fifty or a hundred years ago. . . . All over the West, . . . the farmer thrashes his wheat all at one time, he disposes of it all at one time, and in a great many instances the straw is wasted. He sells his hogs, and buys bacon and pork; he sells his cattle, and buys fresh beef and canned beef or corned beef, as the case may be; he sells his fruit, and buys it back in cans. . . . Not more than one farmer in fifty now keeps sheep at all; he relies upon the large sheep farmer for the wool, which is put into cloth or clothing ready for his use. Instead of having clothing made up on the farm in his own house or by a neighbor woman or country tailor a mile away, he either purchases his clothing ready made at the nearest town, or he buys the cloth and has a city tailor make it up for him. Instead of making implements which he uses about the farm—forks, rakes, etc., he goes to town to purchase even a handle for his axe or his mallet; . . . indeed, he buys nearly everything now that he produced at one time himself, and these things all cost money.

Besides all this, and what seems stranger than anything else, whereas in the earlier time the American home was a free home, unencumbered, . . . and whereas but a small amount of money was then needed for actual use in conducting the business of farming, there was always enough of it among the farmers to supply the demand, now, when at least ten times as much is needed, there is little or none to be obtained. . . .

The railroad builder, the banker, the money changer, and the manufacturer under-mined the farmer. . . . The manufacturer came with his woolen mill, his carding mill, his broom factory, his rope factory, his wooden-ware factory, his cotton factory, his pork-packing establishment, his canning factory and fruit-preserving houses; the little shop on the farm has given place to the large shop in town; the wagon-maker's shop in the neighborhood has given way to the large establishment in the city where men by the thousand work and where a hundred or two hundred wagons are made in a week; the shoemaker's shop has given way to large establishments in the cities where most of the work is done by machines; the old smoke house has given way to the packing house, and the fruit cellars have been displaced by preserving factories. The farmer now is compelled to go to town for nearly everything that he wants. . . . And what is worse than all, if he needs a little more money than he has about him, he is compelled to go to town to borrow it. But he does not find the money there; in place of it he finds an agent who will "negotiate" a loan for him. The money is in the East . . . five thousand miles away. He pays the agent his commission, pays all the expenses of looking through the records and furnishing abstracts, pays for every postage stamp used in the transaction, and finally receives a draft for the amount of money required, minus these expenses. In this way the farmers of the country today are maintaining an army of middlemen, loan agents, bankers, and others, who are absolutely worthless for all good purposes in the community. . . .

These things, however, are on only the mechanical side of the farmer. His domain has been invaded by men of his own calling, who have taken up large tracts of land and farmed upon the plan of the manufacturers who employ a great many persons to perform the work under one management. This is "bonanza" farming. . . . The aim of some of the great "bonanza farms" of Dakota has been to apply machinery so effectually that the cultivation of one full section, or six hundred and forty acres, shall represent one year's work of only one man. This has not yet been reached, but so far as the production of the grain of wheat is concerned, one man's work will now give to each of one thousand persons enough for a barrel of flour a year, which is the average ration. . . .

The manufacture of oleomargarine came into active competition with farm butter. And about the same time a process was discovered by which a substitute for lard was produced—an article so very like the genuine lard taken from the fat of swine that the farmer himself was deceived by it. . . .

From this array of testimony the reader need have no difficulty in determining for himself "how we got here." The hand of the money changer is upon us. Money dictates our financial policy; money controls the business of the country; money is despoiling the people. . . . These men of Wall Street . . . hold the bonds of nearly every state, county, city and township in the Union; every railroad owes them more than it is worth. Corners in grain and other products of toil are the legitimate fruits of Wall Street methods. Every trust and combine made to rob the people had its origin in the example of Wall Street dealers. . . . This dangerous power which money gives is fast undermining the liberties of the people. It now has control of nearly half their homes, and is reaching out its clutching hands for the rest. This is the power we have to deal with.

Source: William A. Peffer, *The Farmer's Side* (New York, 1891).

The Culture and Politics of Industrial America

1870–1892

COMMON THREADS

How did the social construction of gender impact men's and women's lives in the late nineteenth century?

How did both culture and politics reflect sharp distinctions between men and women?

How did culture and politics break those distinctions down?

What was the overriding issue of American politics in the late nineteenth century?

Was American politics headed for a crisis in the 1890s?

< Anti-immigration cartoon, 1891

555

Luna Kellie and the Farmers' Alliance

As a girl, Luna Kellie dreamed of raising a family on her own farm. Her father, a railroad worker on the Northern Pacific line, did try to make a go of farming in Minnesota but when the farm failed, he moved the family to St. Louis, Missouri. There Luna met and married James T. Kellie. At the age of 18, Luna moved with her husband and their infant to a homestead near Hastings, Nebraska.

Life on the prairie fell far short of her dreams. The Kellies lived in an 8-by-12-foot sod house dug into a hillside. She gave birth to 12 children. Two died. Weakened by the strain of childbirth and constant toil, Luna dreamed of a brighter future, a holiday to Yellowstone's geysers. "Our trip never materialized," she recalled years later, "but we put in some happiest hours of life planning it."

The life of sturdy independence that farmers supposedly enjoyed turned out to be a pinched, isolated existence. Luna tried to connect with friends and neighbors, but there was not much choice. Her family attended a Methodist church until James quarreled with the pastor. Schools were even scarcer than churches, but Luna went out of her way to become active in the school district, where she took part in discussions over whether women should have the right to vote.

Like many rural women, Luna shared the responsibility for managing the farm. She kept a garden, which helped feed the family and brought in extra income from the sale of chickens and eggs. Luna also learned how to tend livestock and grow fruit trees. Her husband tried to grow spring wheat, but between falling prices and high interest rates, their work never freed them from debt. After seven years, the Kellies lost the farm. They struggled to survive by raising chickens, sheep, and livestock.

Like so many prairie farmers just barely scraping by, Luna Kellie turned to the Farmers' Alliance the largest and most powerful association that coped with agricultural woes. She was not alone: 250,000 women joined the Alliance, making it the largest women's organization in the United States.

For Kellie, the Alliance held out the hope of realizing the dreams of her youth. Its program could break down the isolation of rural life, bringing farmers together in cooperative enterprises while giving them the advantages that the "money power" had taken away. In 1892, when the Nebraska Farmers' Alliance affiliated with the National Farmers' Alliance and Industrial Union, Kellie was elected state secretary. She worked as tirelessly on Alliance business as she had on her own farm, writing countless letters. She edited and set the type for articles for the Alliance newspaper.

Without setting foot outside her home, Luna Kellie found herself at the center of a vast network of farmers who learned from each other by discussing key issues. Starting in efforts to improve rural Americans' lives, the movement quickly advanced into broader questions of political reform. By 1892, the Farmers' Alliance had fostered the most important political insurgency of the late nineteenth century, the Populist Party.

THE ELUSIVE BOUNDARIES OF MALE AND FEMALE

Luna Kellie's involvement in politics was a sign that the old assumptions about a "woman's place" in society were shifting, along with notions of how to preserve the independence, opportunity, and equal voice that the republic once had promised to ordinary people. In fact, the political economy of industrial capitalism and the triumph of wage labor helped men and women rethink traditional concepts of masculinity and femininity. As they did so, new cities and newfound leisure time offered unprecedented opportunities to test the conventional boundaries of sexual identity.

The Victorian Construction of Male and Female

Until the mid-1700s, most European doctors believed that there was only one sex: females were simply inferior, insufficiently developed males. Sometime after 1750, however, scientists and intellectuals began to argue that males and females were fundamentally different, that they were "opposite" sexes. For the first time it was possible to argue that women were naturally less interested in sex than men or that men were "active" whereas women were "passive." Nature itself seemed to justify the infamous double standard that condoned sexual activity by men but punished it in women.

Nineteenth-century society drew even more extreme differences between men and women. Taking its name from the long reign of Britain's Queen Victoria, the Victorian era is often stereotyped as an age of sexual repression and cultural conservatism. So it was, up to a point. Boys reading moralistic stories of heroes who overcame their fears prepared for the competitive worlds of business and politics, both largely male preserves. To be a "man" in industrial America was to work in the rough-and-tumble world of the capitalist market. Men proved themselves by their success at making a living and thereby at taking care of a wife and children.

Victorian men defined themselves as rational creatures threatened by insistent sexual drives. Physical exertion was an important device for controlling a man's powerful sexual urges, just as masturbation was deemed an unacceptable outlet for these drives. Men were urged to channel their sexual energies into strenuous activities such as sports and, conveniently enough, wage labor.

Where masculinity became a more rigid concept, femininity became less certain. Women's schools established their own sports programs. Affluent women took up bicycling, tennis, swimming, and croquet. Yet the stereotype persisted that women were too frail for the hurly-burly of business and enterprise. Lacking the competitive instinct of the male, the female was best fitted to become a wife and mother within the protective confines of the home. Just as men joined social clubs and sports teams, a "female world of love and ritual" developed. Middle-class women often displayed among themselves a passionate affection that was often expressed in nearly erotic terms. But genuinely passionate female sexuality disturbed genteel taste-makers. Evidence of sexual passion among women was increasingly diagnosed, mostly by male doctors, as a symptom of a new disorder called "neurasthenia."

Over time, the differences between men and women were defined in increasingly medical terms. Late nineteenth-century doctors redefined homosexuality as a medical abnormality, a perversion, and urged the passage of laws outlawing homosexual relations. The new science of gynecology powerfully reinforced popular assumptions about gender differences. Leading male physicians argued that the energy women expended in reproduction left them unable to withstand the rigors of higher education. In extreme cases, physicians would excise a woman's clitoris to thwart masturbation or remove her ovaries to cure neurasthenia.

On the assumption that motherhood was a female's natural destiny, doctors pressed to restrict women's access to contraception and to prohibit abortion. Before the Civil War, many Americans tolerated abortion in the first three months of pregnancy, though they did not necessarily approve of it. This began to change as the medical profession laid claim to the regulation of female reproduction. The American Medical Association (AMA, founded in 1847) campaigned to suppress abortionists and criminalize abortion. The AMA also supported passage of the Comstock Law, which in addition to being the first federal law to ban the production, distribution, and public display of obscenity, outlawed the sale of contraceptive devices. "Our Heavenly Father never sends more mouths than He can feed," one doctor explained. To hear an advocate of the law tell it, the only naysayers were "long-haired men and short-haired women"—the unmanly and unfeminine.

To bolster traditional marriage, states passed laws raising the age of consent, forbidding common-law and interracial marriage, punishing polygamists, and tightening restrictions on divorce. Only in the West did authorities allow incompatibility grounds for ending a marriage. Many places set up family courts to handle desertion and juvenile delinquency. Congress passed several antipolygamy laws to protect Mormon wives and, as a fringe benefit, to take the vote away from a religious group known to lean Democratic.

The Moralists' Crusade for Virtue and Self-Control

Nineteenth-century genteel reformers saw the city as a place where traditional morality broke down, particularly standards of sexual propriety. With corrupt police lackadaisical about enforcing morality, reformers established private organizations to smite smut with prosecutions and citizens' arrests. Moral crusader Anthony Comstock's New York Society for the Suppression of Vice inspired many others. It deputized itself to enforce laws "for the suppression of the trade in, and circulation of, obscene literature and illustrations, advertisements, and articles of indecent or immoral use." Comstock's chief concern was the protection of children. In his book *Traps for the Young* (1883), he warned that obscenity was luring American youngsters into deviant ways by stoking youthful wants and passions until they had "a well-nigh irresistible mastery over their victim." As head of the society, Comstock acted as a special post office agent. "You must hunt these men as you hunt rats," Comstock declared, "without mercy." In many cases, that meant without respecting the rights of due process. Reformers entrapped perpetrators by enticing and then arresting them. Comstock caught America's most notorious abortionist that way. He felt no remorse when she cut her throat rather than go to trial.

Such efforts, however, could not reverse the underlying trends. Illegal contraceptive devices were widely known and used. In major cities, abortionists charged $10 for their services. As for the divorce rate, it increased 15 times over. By 1915, the United States had the highest divorce rate in the world, affecting one marriage in seven. In a new economy based on wage labor, single young men found the city ideal for cutting loose at comparatively little risk. Workers had more leisure and white-collar employees more still. Those looking for prostitutes found them readily available (see Map 17–1). In many towns, they had their own neighborhood, the "red-light district," and sometimes the "sporting trade" published guidebooks detailing different houses' specialties. The relative anonymity of urban life and the cash value set

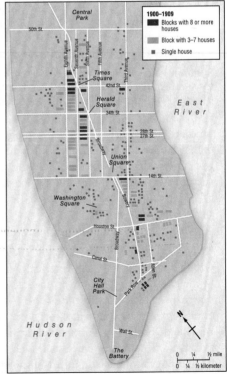

Map 17–1   Houses of Prostitution, 1850–1859 and 1900–1909 One measure of the sexual freedom characteristic of city life was the explosive increase in prostitution. As the demand for prostitution rose, so did attempts to suppress it.
Source: Timothy J. *Gilfoyle, City of Eros* (New York: Norton, 1992), p. 33.

Summer Resort Piety By the 1880s, big-city magazines were taking jabs at the prudery that Protestant reformers had imposed and that foreign immigrants like the artist found of a piece with bone-dry Prohibition and Sunday shutdowns.

on everything made sin pay better than ever before and perpetrators less fearful of being shamed for it. With prostitutes renting their bodies for as little as 50 cents a trick and with saloon keepers doubling as brothel keepers (or tripling as aldermen), the Society for the Suppression of Vice might win battles, but never the war.

Urban Culture

Cities reflected the diversity and vitality of a changing America, far from the rhythms of Luna Kellie's world and the cherished ideal of the self-sufficient farmer. Urban centers crystallized Americans' larger ambivalence about the social changes of the era. Boasting of how up-to-date their country was, Americans longed for a reassuring past. Tenement kids cheered Buffalo Bill Cody's romanticized re-creations of the plains wars and loved the chance to see Sitting Bull himself. (Sitting Bull liked "Buffalo Bill" more than he liked white civilization. He puzzled at how a society so rich could leave homeless children begging in the streets.) Yankees paid good money for tickets to minstrel shows about happy plantation life down South, and everybody read Joel Chandler Harris's "Uncle Remus" stories, recasting Afri-can folk tales with a kindly old enslaved person as their narrator.

At the same time, city culture took on a life all its own. From the 1880s on, it meant bright lights: electricity, in place of dimmer gaslight, and a vigorous "night life." Electric trolleys and suburban rail networks drew tens of thousands downtown

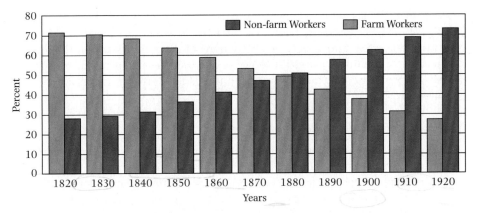

Figure 17–1   Growth of the Nonfarm Sector Underpinning the rise of urban culture was the emergence of a wage-earning labor force. Concentrated in cities, wage earners had cash at their disposal to spend on the amusements cities had to offer.

(see Figure 17–1), to department stores, firms, and factories by day and to theaters, music halls, and concert saloons by night.

One did not have to venture far in the biggest cities to find shows flouting traditional middle-class standards of propriety by using sexual titillation to entertain audiences. Can-can girls, off-color jokes, and comedy skits focusing on the war of the sexes played well in working-class districts. Even among the "respectable classes," both men's and women's clothing became simpler, looser, and more comfortable. Within limits, popular culture idealized the sensuous human body, while for the first time male sports heroes were openly admired for their physiques. Police cracked down on homosexual conduct more severely than before, but the old rules still applied: private and consensual behavior involved relatively little risk.

While reformers like Comstock saw the cities' vice and corruption, linking both to immigrant slums, some of America's best artists created art that reflected the gritty truths of everyday life and celebrated the cities' vitality. If Comstock's admirers defined "culture" as limited to only the great works in the Western European tradition (even suppressing some, such as those by Voltaire, Walt Whitman, Aristophanes, and Ovid), city dwellers embraced a wider array of influences. Out of "Storyville," the red-light district in New Orleans, came the beginnings of jazz; out of the honky-tonks came the first great composers of ragtime. And a canny publicity agent knew how to sell a faintly risqué painting, *September Morn*: he got Comstock to arrest the gallery owner for indecency. Firms running off copies of it could not keep up with the demand.

A NEW CULTURAL ORDER: NEW AMERICANS STIR OLD FEARS

When novelist Henry James returned to the United States in 1907 after a quarter of a century in Europe, he was appalled by the pervasive presence of immigrants in New York City. On the streetcars, he confronted "a row of faces, up and down, testifying, without exception, to alienism unmistakable, alienism undisguised and unashamed." James was one of the many native-born Americans who assumed that their culture was Protestant, democratic, and English-speaking. They saw a threat in vast numbers of immigrants who were none of those things and in the roots that ethnic subcultures were setting down in the cities. Yet among immigrants and their children, an ethnic identity was often traded for a broader assimilation into American culture.

Josiah Strong Attacks Immigration

"Every race which has deeply impressed itself on the human family has been the representative of some great idea," clergyman Josiah Strong wrote in *Our Country*. Greek civilization was famed for its beauty, he explained; the Romans for their law; and the Hebrews for their purity. The Anglo-Saxons claimed two great ideas: the love of liberty and "pure spiritual Christianity." Strong was optimistic that as representatives of "the largest liberty, the purest Christianity, the highest civilization," the Anglo-Saxon race would "spread itself over the earth." Published in 1885, Strong's best-selling book went through many editions and was serialized in newspapers across America. Like him, many native-born Americans saw themselves as the defenders of Anglo-Saxon culture.

But there was a problem. Strong and his followers saw the arrival of millions of immigrants as a challenge to Anglo-Saxon America. By 1900, more than 10 million Americans were foreign born. The typical immigrant, he warned, was not a freedom-loving Anglo-Saxon Protestant but a narrow-minded "European peasant" whose "moral and religious training has been meager or false." Immigrants brought crime to America's cities and, voting in blocs, undermined the nation's politics. "There is no more serious menace to our civilization," Strong warned, "than our rabble-ruled cities."

For Strong, the problem was that immigrants were coming in such huge numbers that assimilation was becoming impossible (see Map 17–2). Worst of all—in Strong's view—the Catholic Church held millions of immigrants in its grip, filling their heads with superstition rather than "pure Christianity." Through its parochial schools, the Catholic Church was training new generations to love tyranny rather than liberty.

Strong and his readers need not have worried (and to be fair, Strong himself saw the real solution in what came to be called the Social Gospel, the active involvement of Protestants in helping those less well off than themselves). Indeed, they misread their own evidence. By cultivating the German vote or the Irish vote, for example, politicians brought immigrants into American culture. Nor were immigrants as slavishly subservient to the Catholic Church as Strong thought.

From Immigrants to Ethnic Americans

In the middle of the nineteenth century, most immigrants came with loyalties to their regions and villages, not to a nationality. German-speaking immigrants thought of themselves primarily as Bavarian or Prussian rather than German, just as Rosa Cassettari thought of herself as Tuscanese and did not count Sicilians as Italians at all. For many Slavs, identification went no further than the parish whose church bells they heard on Sunday morning.

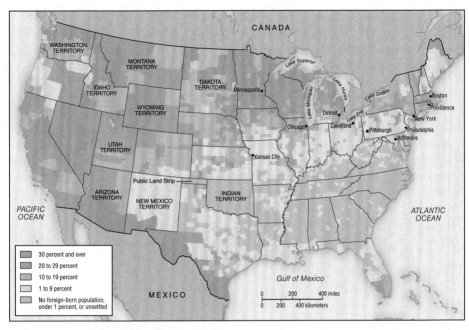

Map 17–2   Population of Foreign Birth by Region, 1880
Source: Clifford L. Lord and Elizabeth H. Lord, *Historical Atlas of the United States* (New York: Holt, 1953).

Regional differences faded, an ocean away from home, but they would have done so anyhow. Nationalism as a self-identifying concept was spreading throughout the Western world. It was reflected in a unifying Italy, a consolidated German Reich, the czar's "Russification" program that laid the whip on Jewish backs and made Russian, not French, the language of the St. Petersburg elite. The patriotic fervor that the Civil War unleashed in the United States, liberal revolutions did in Paris and Berlin. Immigrants brought an increasingly robust sense of their ethnic identities with them. At the same time, in the United States secular fraternal organizations and mutual aid societies, designed to help newcomers find jobs and housing, forged wider ethnic identities. In 1893, mine workers formed the Pennsylvania Slovak Catholic Union to help cover burial expenses for those killed in the mines. Most often, however, middle-class immigrants or local priests took the lead in forming fraternal organizations, which eventually counted about half of all immigrants as members.

Some immigrant businessmen led the drive toward larger ethnic definitions. Because regional loyalties among his workers hindered efficiency, Marco Fontana, who ran the Del Monte Company in California, encouraged the growth of an "Italian" identity.

The Catholic Church and Its Limits in Immigrant Culture

The Roman Catholic Church played a complicated role in the development of ethnic immigrant cultures. Many ethnic communities collected donations to build churches to preserve their Old World traditions. But the church also eased the transition into American life. Polish churches in Chicago and German parishes in Milwaukee used their women's groups and youth clubs as mutual aid societies for newcomers.

The church sometimes unintentionally sped the development of ethnic identities. The Irish became more devout in America as they came to rely on the church for help resisting an overwhelmingly Protestant culture. Through the church, Germans also overcame their regional differences. But the more they came to equate their German identity with Catholicism, the more they resented Irish domination of the church hierarchy. German Catholics worked to establish their own churches, with sermons preached in German. By contrast, the Italians distrusted and distanced themselves from the official church. Ethnic diversity made it all the more important for Catholic leaders to find some middle ground. Bishops across North America worked on standardizing Catholic rituals and ceremonies into a uniquely American blend. They published uniform catechisms, established powerful bureaucracies, and discouraged the folk rituals that Italians, Irish, and Slavs had carried with them.

Unlike in Europe, the church had to struggle just to share in the education of immigrant children; controlling it lay wholly beyond their power. Public schools were heavily Protestant. Shifting the focus away from the classics and toward "practical" education and language training, reformers hoped to shape reliable workers and patriotic citizens. But immigrants balked at "Americanization" efforts beyond providing them with skills they could use to get ahead, and the bulwark of their resistance was the church.

During the second half of the nineteenth century, both the Catholic and Lutheran Churches established parochial school systems to give immigrant children an alternative to the biases of public education. In most states and cities, tax revenues went for public schools only, and Germans set up their own parish schools. Even so, parochial education did its part toward eventual assimilation to the New World. Schools in Irish Catholic or German Lutheran parishes fostered distinctly American ethnic identities, as well as a Catholicism and Lutheranism that diverged from Old World norms.

Immigrant Cultures

Newcomers adjusted to American culture on their own terms. Some changed their names to English equivalents: Piccolo became Little, Wahlgren became Green, and Schmidt became Smith. Even those who did not set out to assimilate found that the longer they stayed, the more their customs diverged from those of the Old World. Irish Americans fused together songs from various parts of Ireland and added piano accompaniment. Polish immigrant bands expanded beyond the traditional violin by adding accordions, clarinets, and trumpets. Hundreds of immigrant theaters offered productions that adjusted traditional plot lines to the New World. Jewish plays told of humble peddlers who outwitted their prosperous patrons. Italian folktales celebrated the importance of the family. In these ways, distinctive ethnic identities adapted to urban and industrial America.

At a time when middle-class families had only two or three children, immigrant families remained large. At the turn of the century, Italian mothers in Buffalo, New York, had an average of 11 children. Among Polish wives, the average was closer to 8. In Pennsylvania's coal-mining district, working-class immigrant women

Immigrants Immigrants often crowded into tenements, a new form of apartment build-ing that actually improved living conditions for many of America's poor city dwellers.

had 45 percent more children than native-born women. They had sound economic reasons: families often needed children's income to get by. However, the death rate among immigrant children was also high. In 1900, one out of three Polish and Italian mothers had seen one of their children die before his or her first birthday.

The Enemy at the Gates

Culture was contested ground, as much a part of urbanization as class conflict and political upheaval. Rural Americans were drawn by urban culture's freedom but troubled by its licentiousness. Native-born Protestants, often truly concerned with helping immigrants, were also suspicious of immigrant folkways. Genteel moralists assailed the collapse of traditional gender distinctions. All these struggles reflected the efforts of Americans to cope with dramatic social transformations. There were no clear winners—unless diversity and a wide array of choices made everyone a winner.

Big-city life stirred images of an alarming diversity: "Chinatowns" in San Francisco and Los Angeles, Polish athletics clubs and German *schutzenvereine* (shooting clubs), pushcart peddlers haggling in Yiddish, Irish Americans demanding that New York's City Hall fly the Irish flag on St. Patrick's Day, Catholics expecting a day off from school on Good Friday. Native-born Protestants fretted that "E Pluribus Unum" might no longer apply: How could we become one, out of so many?

Political opposition to immigration, known as nativism, had enjoyed a brief success in the 1850s. Even foreign-born workers resented low-paid Chinese labor, and in 1882, Congress passed the first Chinese exclusion act. Not the least of the

As the Number of Immigrants to America Swelled, So Did Opposition to Them This 1891 cartoon blames immigration for causing a host of social and political evils.

Tammany Hall political machine's sins, in New York reformers' eyes, was how Irish it was, and how public funds endowed Catholic schools there. Especially in the Midwest, anti-Catholicism drew on Protestant nightmares of the Inquisition and beliefs that the church's leaders combined religious intolerance with a hatred of free government. In the 1890s, the American Protective Association (APA) threw its weight behind candidates favoring Protestant interests.

As immigration increased, nativist rhetoric grew more racist and drew on the dubious sociology of Social Darwinism (see Chapter 16). The threat was no longer merely from radicals and Catholics but also from darker-skinned peoples from Italy, Russia, and eastern Europe. Experts proclaimed the inherent intellectual inferiority of such peoples, giving the imprimatur of science to the most vicious stereotypes. Italians were said to be genetically predisposed to organized violence, Jews to thievery and manipulation. Anti-immigrant societies appeared across America. Mob violence sacked Chinese neighborhoods in Los Angeles in 1871, and 11 Italians were lynched by a New Orleans mob, on charges of having murdered the police chief.

But Protestant cultural politics failed to shut out immigration from southern and eastern Europe; the United States would not even require immigrants to pass a literacy test until 1917. The APA died quickly when politicians recognized that they did better by appealing to immigrant voters. They passed resolutions favoring Irish "home rule" (rather than English occupation), denounced the Russian czar's persecution of Jews, and made Columbus Day a holiday. The real cultural fights came at the state level over issues like outlawing boxing, charging prohibitively high licenses on working-class saloons, making Jewish stores close on the Protestant Sabbath, requiring Protestant Bible reading in public schools, and forcing parochial schools to use Protestant state-mandated textbooks.

TWO POLITICAL STYLES

In a multicultural America, politics did more to assimilate newcomers than to make them feel unwelcome. With only two major parties vying for power, neither could afford to alienate all immigrant groups; however, some Republicans scapegoated the Catholic and Irish ones. Each organization welcomed the foreign-born into its ranks and adjusted its policies at the state and local level to keep their loyalty.

Politics came in two flavors in the Gilded Age: the male-dominated partisan-ship of voters, political operatives, and officeholders; and the voluntarism of those who put cause above party, from reform societies and women's organizations to labor unions and farmers' groups. The politicians had every advantage on their side. Because the "spoils system" let them appoint every official down to janitor when they took power, they could extort a share of government employees' wages to fund a campaign. They chose the candidates and counted the returns. In close elections, they had "soap" (payoffs to voters) to buy a winning margin. Most of the newspapers framed the news in one party's way. Political organizations became more sophisticated and much more centralized. In this age, people began to speak of "bosses" and "political machines" in which, supposedly, the leader rallied his party followers like an army to carry every election and fill every office: the Democratic hordes in New York City that the Tammany Hall machine mobilized, for example. But time and again, politicians—even Tammany's—found themselves forced to accommodate outside pressures, and by the 1890s, those pressures had remade the very basis of the political game.

The Triumph of Party Politics

Ever since Lincoln's day, most Americans had voted the straight party line every time. Political parties printed and passed out their own ballots for loyalists to drop in the right box. Nobody needed to be literate to make his choice (no state gave women the vote until Wyoming's admission in 1890). Partisans could remove candidates' names from these ballots, and organizers often bribed voters. Intimidation also played a role. In much of the South, passing out Republican ballots was nearly as fatal as yellow fever. "Resurrectionists" voted in dead men's names, "colonizers" crossed state lines to vote in crucial elections, and political agents might even march their purchased public to vote in "blocks of five," as one Indiana Republican advised in 1888. But most voters cast honest ballots and cared so strongly that if they could have voted a dozen times they would have—as, in big cities, some did!

From the 1840s through the 1860s, an average of 69 percent of those eligible voted in presidential elections. During the final quarter of the century, the average rose to 77 percent (see Figure 17–2). Southern figures lagged slightly: between 1876 and 1892, nearly two out of three southern men voted in presidential elections, compared with 82 percent of northern ones. The gap would widen as Democrats perfected the tools for keeping African Americans from casting a ballot or southern Republicans from having the least hope of a free vote and a fair count.

Newspapers played a critical role in maintaining this level of political participation. Much of the press acted as cheerleaders and opinion makers. Most papers survived with the help of party and government advertisements as well as contracts

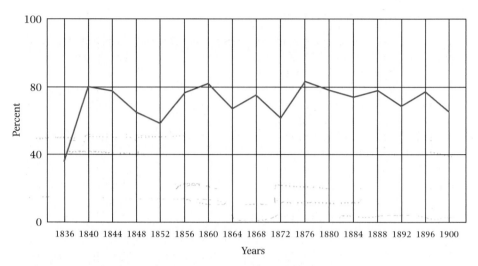

Figure 17-2   Percent of Eligible Voters Casting Ballots Between 1840 and 1896, a huge proportion—often 80 percent—of those eligible to vote did so in presidential elections. In the twentieth century, turnout dropped substantially.

to print ballots and campaign documents. Papers slanted stories their party's way, and proudly. "Republican in everything, independent in nothing," the *Chicago Inter Ocean* boasted.

Campaign hoopla offered voters unrivaled spectacle. Political clubs and military companies paraded. Marchers rang bells, flew banners, and escorted floats with pretty girls representing Liberty, Columbia, or the various states. A good mass meeting combined barbecue, rousing oratory, band music, and fireworks. Together, they made politics America's most popular participatory sport.

However, politics was more than sport. Civil War veterans were reminded, "Vote as you shot!" Roused by the Union veterans' organization, the Grand Army of the Republic (four hundred thousand members' strong), and speeches that used the memory of the war to inflame sectional grievances, Union veterans typically backed the Republican Party. Black Americans also usually supported the party that had ended slavery. Confederates mostly voted Democratic. Democrats spoke for states' rights, small government, and white supremacy. In their eyes, Republicanism meant state and local laws telling people what to drink and how to use their Sundays. As Democrats saw it, "the party of moral ideas" protected the national banker, the railroad tycoon, and the upstart Negro. To Republicans, Democrats were the party of "rum, Romanism, and rebellion," of Catholics, saloon keepers, violence, and vice. They themselves spoke for the northern middle class, especially the better-educated ones. Government, local and national, had a duty to make Americans better off. As the Republicans told it, their party's symbol was the schoolhouse, while the Democrats' was the whipping post of slavery. And each side knew that the republic's fate depended on its winning. If the Apocalypse came "under Democratic auspices," one man joked, Republican leaders "would object to the Resurrection and move to postpone the Millennium."

Masculine Partisanship and Feminine Voluntarism

The public sphere of campaigns and voting was a man's world; the private sphere of home and family was widely celebrated as a woman's. In practice, though, women shared in popular politics. They decorated the meeting halls, prepared the food, watched and sometimes joined the parades. By the end of the 1880s, both parties pitched part of their appeals to wives and families. Nevertheless, politically active women opted for a different style of politics.

A stereotype that had previously limited female political activity now gave women their chance to enter public debate. Seen as the special protectors of the family's values, women found that their views on marriage, morality, and the need to protect America's children would get a respectful hearing from lawmakers. "Man looks upon himself as the head of the church," a reporter wrote, "but woman is the hand, and, nine times out of ten, head and hand both." Women's supposed superior virtue gave them a privileged position in moral reform movements. These included antialcohol temperance societies and campaigns for laws to keep the Christian Sabbath holy—by keeping barbershops, museums, and baseball parks closed on Sunday. To protect the private sphere, many women claimed the right to enter the public one.

Women could pursue politics only as representatives of voluntary associations dedicated to specific reforms. Voluntarism mostly recruited members from the educated middle class, who brought their class biases with them.

Sometimes women's associations copied the style of partisan politics, staging mass marches and rallies. But the marching, chanting, military flavor of mass politics did not sit well with society's image of women's traditional role. So activists were likely to concentrate less on rousing voters than on educating them and lobbying elected officials. Men also joined voluntary associations, but they were dismissed by mainstream politicians as "namby-pamby, goody-goody gentlemen." In the late nineteenth century, voluntarism was associated with feminine politics, and party politics was associated with masculinity.

The Women's Christian Temperance Union

Still, voluntarism could do wonders, and over time, the boundaries of the women's sphere became increasingly unclear. One of the most prominent female-backed political movements, the Women's Christian Temperance Union (WCTU), emerged in 1874 to battle the ravages of alcohol. Led by Frances Willard from 1879 until her death in 1898, the WCTU built itself on women's calling as protectors of the home. A decentralized structure allowed groups to tailor their activities to local needs. Women found in the WCTU a source of camaraderie as well as political activism. They made it among the largest women's political organizations in the late nineteenth century, with 150,000 adult members. (The National American Woman Suffrage Association had only 13,000.) The WCTU convened huge rallies with none of the masculine rowdiness of party conventions. Willard and her associates gave speeches, wrote articles, published books and newspaper columns on the evils of drink, organized petition campaigns, and lobbied officeholders.

Under Willard, the crusade against alcohol broadened to tackle the problems of a new industrial society. The WCTU endorsed women's suffrage and formed an alliance with the country's largest labor union. Willard supported laws restricting the workday to eight hours and prohibiting child labor. By the 1890s Willard was treating drunkenness as a public health issue rather than a personal sin, a social problem rather than an individual failure. Temperance advocates supported reforms designed to relieve poverty, improve public health, raise literacy, alleviate the conditions of workers, reform prisons, suppress public immorality, and preserve peace.

In the cities, especially up north, temperance remained a middle-class reform movement, with little appeal in immigrant neighborhoods. The WCTU's strongly evangelical Protestant identity and its association of saloons with aliens and Catholics spoke louder than its official policy of religious toleration. Irish Catholics and German Lutherans resented a campaign aimed to replace altar wine with grape juice in Christian services.

The Critics of Popular Politics

The mix of partisanship and voluntarism made American politics more "popular" than ever before, drawing women and men, Blacks and whites, immigrants and the native born, working class and middle class. But some Americans saw behind the spectacle to the games professional politicians played. After the Civil War, a small but influential group known as Liberals (and later as **Mugwumps**) challenged the party-run state. Alarmed at its selfishness, corruption, and incompetence, they called for government by professionals and independent agencies. Though some agreed with Charles Francis Adams that "universal suffrage can only mean in plain English the government of ignorance and vice," most believed that with a cleaner politics and "campaigns of education," the people would see where their true interests lay. A merit system must reward ability in the public service; a government-issued official (Australian) ballot distributed only at polling places must give every voter the chance to choose, in privacy, among all the possibilities. Tasks like setting a fair railroad rate or tariff duty, running a park system, or policing a great city should no longer be left to vote-getters. Education and expertise, not political pull, must drive policy.

Thanks to Liberals, the nonpartisan secret ballot was adopted everywhere. In 1881, supporters of good government organized the National Civil Service Reform League to prevent political parties from filling government positions. Victory came two years later with the establishment of a Civil Service Commission that would assign federal jobs on the basis of merit rather than **patronage**. Some states followed suit. But regarding the problems of rapid industrialization, Liberals' solutions fell short.

Most Americans approached their politics looking backward to the issues of the Civil War and Reconstruction. Every president but one between 1869 and 1901 had served in the Civil War (and the one exception, Grover Cleveland, sent a substitute). But many Americans also came to feel deep concerns about a society becoming more diverse, urban, and industrial. Such issues would dominate public life by the close of the century.

Joseph Keppler, "The Army-Worm" (1880) The cartoonist's point was that a Union war record led straight to the top in politics; he could have said the same for Confederate service. At the front of the horde are the two major party presidential candidates that year, Generals Winfield Scott Hancock and James A. Garfield. In the upper left, former General Rutherford Hayes heads homeward; on the far right, former General Ulysses S. Grant enjoys some "Republican rye."

ECONOMIC ISSUES DOMINATE NATIONAL POLITICS

By the late nineteenth century, Americans were used to the idea that government should oversee the distribution of the nation's natural resources. After the Civil War, federal officials distributed public lands to homesteaders and railroads and granted rights to mining, ranching, and timber companies. During those same decades, the rise of big business led many Americans to believe that the government should regulate the currency. Many others saw salvation in trade barriers to protect American commerce and workers from ruinous foreign competition. Because the two major parties commanded nearly even support at the national level, the outcome was that no issue could be finally settled. Shaped by clusters of special interests until they covered over 4,000 items, tariffs rose, fell, and rose again. Congresses tinkered with the currency, even while gold continued to hold a privileged place as backing for paper money. The bolder a policy initiative, the likelier it was to founder.

Greenbacks and Greenbackers

The money question demonstrated the inability of Gilded Age politicians to act decisively on major issues. To support the Union effort during the Civil War, the US government printed $450 million worth of "greenbacks," paper bills backed by the

Struggles For Democracy

The "Crusade" Against Alcohol

Just before Christmas in 1873, Dr. Diocletian Lewis arrived in Hillsboro, Ohio, to speak on the evils of alcohol. He had given the speech many times before, but this time the women who came proved unusually responsive. The next morning a group of Hillsboro women met for prayer and then marched through the town urging local merchants to stop selling liquor. Inspired by their success, the women kept up the pressure through the winter of 1873–1874. Neither jail nor a rain of curses, eggs, and sour beer could dampen their spirits.

The Crusade, as it came to be called, spread quickly into 31 states and territories. Druggists and hotel keepers promised to quit selling alcohol. Nearly 70 breweries closed. The women's fervor inspired crusaders to establish a permanent organization, the WCTU. In years to come, like-minded reformers set up "temperance saloons" that served ice cream or coffee. They opened YMCA chapters with reading rooms and employment agencies to co-opt services that bars had provided. Sunday schools recruited children to break from their parents' habits and to parade, chanting, "Tremble, King Alcohol! We shall grow up!"

But Americans' drinking habits hardly changed at all. Saloons throve. People went there not just to drink but to find companionship and release. Italians went there to read newspapers in their own language. Workers went there to find jobs listings, and foremen to do hiring. Bartenders knew everybody, which was one reason that saloons were tied closely to party machines. The fastest way to empty a Chicago council meeting, residents joked, was to shout, "Your saloon's on fire!"

In the end, lasting change took political action, first by creating local or statewide majorities for prohibiting alcohol, and then by forcing the minority to give way. So across the West, states and territories outlawed the sale of

government's word but not by the traditional reserves of specie, meaning gold or silver. When the war ended, most Americans agreed that the greenbacks should be withdrawn from circulation until any paper dollar could be exchanged for a dollar in specie at the bank. But with the onset of the 1870s, wage cuts and tight money led to a debate. Resumptionists, those who wanted to return to the gold standard, found themselves battling debtors and industrialists who thought that a shrinking money supply would worsen the economy. Greenbackers went further. They called for issuing even more greenbacks, without any requirement that precious metals back the notes up. In the middle were many Republicans and Democrats who favored inflation, but by backing dollars in silver as well as gold. The currency had been backed in this way before Congress legislated silver out of its privileged place with the "Crime of 1873," as the Coinage Act of 1873 came to be called. Later reformers blamed a bankers' plot for the change: gold, in shorter supply, meant a smaller money supply, big enough for eastern needs and small enough to make every dollar more valuable. A dollar that could buy three times as much forced a farmer to work

Protestors Outside an Ohio Saloon The WCTU's fight against alcohol could never have succeeded without the active support of many men. They felt as deep a concern at the moral and social consequences of too much tippling.

alcohol, with the "dry" countryside imposing its will on the "wet" cities. Because women took leading roles in the cause, prohibitionists became the foremost advocates of woman suffrage. For good reason, Frances Willard was the first woman honored with a statue in the US Capitol; for good reason, saloon keepers fought for a males-only suffrage to the last.

three times as hard to pay off debts contracted before the "Crime of '73." Holders of mortgages and bonds, agrarians shouted, had legislated themselves a bonanza.

To gold's defenders, any shift back to silver—the "dollar of the Daddies"—or to paper meant national dishonor. "Honest money," they cried, was morality itself. A flood of silver into Treasury vaults meant a flood of paper, with wild speculation, inflation out of control, and debts paid off in such depreciated currency that creditors would face ruinous losses. The Greenback-Labor Party peaked in 1878, when it garnered over a million votes and elected 14 congressmen. However, as economic skies brightened, its appeal dwindled. In 1879, resumption took place, with the $300 million in circulating greenbacks made convertible into gold. Support for silver did not die away, and every time the economy contracted, calls for limited silver coinage rose across the West and South. Farmers there found loans hardest to get, except at interest rates that (to their thinking) verged on extortion. Until times improved all over, neither side could win a final victory. They could take only half steps in one direction or the other.

Table 17–1 Razor-Thin Electoral Margins in the Gilded Age

Year	Popular Vote	% of Popular Vote	Electoral Vote
1876	4,036,572	48.0	185
	4,284,020	51.0	184
1880	4,453,295	48.5	214
	4,414,082	48.1	155
	308,578	3.4	—
1884	4,879,507	48.5	219
	4,850,293	48.2	182
1888	5,477,129	47.9	233
	5,537,857	48.6	168

Weak Presidents Oversee a Stronger Federal Government

Starting in the mid-1870s, the Democrats and Republicans had nearly equal electoral strength (see Table 17–1). From 1876 through 1896, no president took office with an overwhelming electoral mandate. The results of the 1880 election were typical of the era. Republican James A. Garfield won by a tiny margin. He received 48.5 percent of the votes, and Democrat Winfield Scott Hancock received 48.1 percent. Grover Cleveland won a plurality in 1888, but he lost the Electoral College. In both cases, the losers accused vote-buying Republicans of making the difference. But Republicans could reply that in the South, Republican votes never received a fair count. No president enjoyed a full term during which his own party controlled both houses of Congress. Reelected in 1872, Grant was the last president in the century to serve two consecutive terms.

In some cases, a president took office already discredited by the electoral process, as did Rutherford B. Hayes in 1877 (see Chapter 15). Furious that their presidential candidate had been "counted out," Democrats threatened "His Fraudulency" with impeachment. Hayes's fellow Republicans protested his overtures to win over southern conservatives at the expense of protection for Black voters. Guests resented his ban on liquor at state dinners (though a grateful WCTU dedicated a drinking-fountain to his wife). The party bosses raged at his steps toward a professional civil service. Hayes forbade his party to exact tribute from Republican officeholders. He fought Roscoe Conkling, New York's ruthless Republican boss, for control of the New York Customs House—the most lucrative source of spoils in America. When the English writer Samuel Johnson defined patriotism as the last refuge of a scoundrel, Conkling snarled, he little anticipated the possibilities of the word "reform." With cabinet officers controlling civil service appointments, improvements were patchier than Hayes would have liked, and civil service reformers were crestfallen.

By sending federal troops to suppress the 1877 railroad strike (see Chapter 16), Hayes set an important precedent for federal intervention in industrial disputes. He vetoed the Chinese immigration exclusion legislation passed by Congress in 1879. A modest, thoughtful man, troubled by widespread suffering, Hayes had no cure for the economic slump of the 1870s. To protect the public credit, he opposed any steps to end the deflation of currency that had forced wages and prices down so sharply and brought ruin to farmers and industrial workers. In 1878, he vetoed the Bland-Allison Act, hailed as a way to modestly inflate the currency by coining silver in amounts tied to the amount of gold being minted. (It passed anyway, with little effect on the money supply.) Though prosperity returned soon after, Republicans felt as much relief to see his term end as he did. They did not protest his decision not to stand for reelection.

Economic, rather than racial, issues dominated the 1880 campaign, although Democratic state governments were rolling back the gains Blacks had made during Reconstruction. Both parties relied on the spoils system too much to press civil service reform. Democrats favored lower tariffs than the Republicans, though both parties had strong protectionist blocs (supporting high tariffs to protect American producers) as well as members who favored lower tariff rates. Neither party wanted free trade; the government needed the revenue from tariff duties. So Garfield's victory in 1880 did not foreshadow any major shifts in government policy. It took a national tragedy to bring that about.

On July 2, 1881, after four months consumed in Republican brawling over patronage appointments, a neglected office seeker shot the president as he stood waiting for the train taking him to his college reunion. Garfield died two agonizing months later, and Chester A. Arthur, the dapper product of Conkling's patronage machine, became president. The assassination made it dangerous for the new president to resist the swell of popular support for civil service reform. The Republicans in control of Congress did resist, however, and Democrats swept into office on a tide of resentment against Republican corruption and favoritism. The following year Congress passed, and President Arthur signed, the landmark **Pendleton Civil Service Act.** The Pendleton Act prohibited patronage officeholders from contributing to the party machine that gave them their jobs. More important, the law authorized the president to empower a Civil Service Commission to administer competitive examinations for federal jobs. Before the century ended, the majority of federal jobs were removed from the reach of the patronage machines. The Pendleton Act was a major turning point in the creation of a stable and professional civil service.

Dying of a kidney disease, Arthur could not win renomination. The irresistibly charming, corrupt Republican candidate, James G. Blaine, offended Liberals and gave Democrats a chance. They nominated New York's reforming governor Grover Cleveland, who was elected after a mud-spattered campaign, complete with anti-Catholic slurs and a scandal about Cleveland's illegitimate child. His slogan, "Public office is a public trust," expressed the Liberals' ideal. However, Blaine would have won had he not alienated prohibitionists and had the Black vote not been suppressed in the South.

Cleveland was upright, downright, and forthright, a workaholic who took a perverse pleasure in turning down backers come to collect their political i.o.u.'s. One politician urged him to advance the party's principles more aggressively. "Ah," the president snapped, "I suppose you mean that I should appoint two horse-thieves a day, instead of one!" He carried out the Pendleton Act to the letter, though not much beyond it, and harried railroad interests that exploited public land, including some of his campaign contributors. Special veterans' pension bills met ringing vetoes. So did a bill to relieve drought victims on the plains. Union veterans shouted when he tried to return captured Confederate flags to the southern states, and for once Cleveland backed down. Believing in a cheap, limited national government, he offered no great programs, but neither did he thwart congressional moves to broaden government's scope. He signed legislation raising the Agriculture Department to cabinet status and the Dawes Severalty Act (see Chapter 16). Equally important, he approved the Interstate Commerce Act, creating an Interstate Commerce Commission (ICC) with power to regulate the railroads. Ever since the 1860s, states had been creating similar commissions, some of them setting railroad rates and all of them able to investigate and publicize abuses. Although weak and sometimes captive to the interests they regulated, they represented a growing state role overseeing many activities. Like the state agencies, the ICC promised more in the way of controlling rates and unfair practices than it could deliver, especially with court decisions hobbling the regulators.

With few accomplishments beyond a White House wedding to Frances Folsom and ominous political rumblings at the midterm elections, Cleveland needed a stirring issue. He found it in the high protective tariff. The tariff had worked too well. Government surpluses had been growing, tightening credit as Treasury vaults locked away more and more of the nation's money, and tempting politicians to spend the revenue for pensions and subsidies. Critics saw it as filching money from consumers' pockets to fill those of monopolists, who, safe from foreign competition, could keep their prices high. Cautious presidents had left the tariff alone, but Cleveland devoted his annual message to Congress in December 1887 to tariff reform. Favoring free trade would be political suicide, but adjustments downward, especially for raw materials, might make American exports more competitive and drive prices down.

It might drive wages down, too; so Republicans warned. Shouting that rate reductions would shutter factories and flood America in cheaper British goods, they had the Senate votes to block any bill that the House passed. Even one less skewed to serve southern interests than the House-begotten Mills bill would have had no chance. Better in pointing the way than in working out the details of an actual measure, Cleveland did not push for the Mills bill or even for a strong endorsement of tariff reform in the 1888 Democratic platform. All the same, the issue dominated the campaign, with Republicans charging that free-trading England wanted a Cleveland victory. He won a plurality of the popular vote but lost the Electoral College to Benjamin Harrison (see Map 17–3).

Having won House, Senate, and presidency on a protectionist platform, Republicans had two years to deliver. Under the forceful leadership of "Czar" Thomas Brackett Reed and with influence from President Harrison, the "Billion Dollar Congress" put through the new, higher McKinley Tariff, named for Congressman William McKinley of Ohio. At the same time, Congress gave the president the authority to lower tariffs with nations opening their markets to American goods, granting him important new power in the conduct of foreign affairs. Congress also passed a lavish Dependents' Pension Law, subsidies to encourage shipping, and a silver-purchase act that westerners hoped would inject more coinage into the money supply. The Sherman Anti-Trust Act of 1890 outlawed "combinations" in "restraint of trade," though what precisely that covered was uncertain. Five years later the Supreme Court even ruled out most manufacturing. Republicans also introduced—but failed to pass—both a federal enforcement bill that

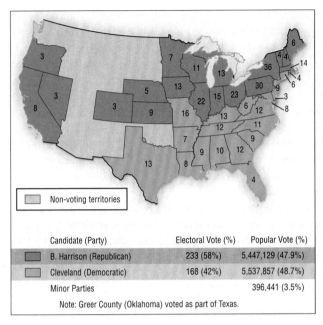

Map 17–3   The Election of 1888 With the Solid South locked up, Democrats only needed two of the biggest northern states to win. They failed this year—just barely. But for Republicans, it was a wake-up call: either they must admit enough new states to pack the Electoral College their way or they must pass a law protecting a free, fair vote down South.

Candidate (Party)	Electoral Vote (%)	Popular Vote (%)
B. Harrison (Republican)	233 (58%)	5,447,129 (47.9%)
Cleveland (Democratic)	168 (42%)	5,537,857 (48.7%)
Minor Parties		396,441 (3.5%)

Non-voting territories

Note: Greer County (Oklahoma) voted as part of Texas.

might have protected Black southern voters and the Blair Education Bill, which might have provided federal money to guarantee Black southerners an adequate education.

Nothing offends like success. Derided as a "human iceberg" whose "'yes' was as uninspiring as another man's 'no,'" Harrison lacked the common touch. But he was not the real problem. Democrats blamed higher prices on the tariff. White southerners rose in alarm at the threat of a full and fair Black vote. Reformers considered the pensions a steal, and in the Midwest, Republicans ran into trouble when they tried to regulate parochial and German-language schools—the first step, immigrants cried, to foisting their own values on Catholic children. In 1890 voters put the Democrats back in control of the House of Representatives. Two years later, Cleveland won the presidency, this time with an outright majority.

GOVERNMENT ACTIVISM AND ITS LIMITS

Two themes dominate the traditional impression of late nineteenth-century political history: first, brazen corruption, and second, limited government that left the new industrial economy to develop as it pleased. The real heroes, according to this view, were those outside the party system, the Liberals and Populists, the moral crusaders and insurgents. While corruption was a problem, the foregoing view falls short as a true picture of the age.

Only by later standards was the national government limited. When peace came, Congress cut taxes, trimmed the army to a mere 25,000 men, and virtually abandoned any oceangoing navy. Yet it never returned to its proportions or role in 1861. Civilian federal employees rose from 53,000 in 1871 to 256,000 30

America In The World

Foreign Policy: The Limited Significance of Commercial Expansion

Money was not everything—neither in domestic politics nor in foreign policy. In the 1860s, Secretary of State William Henry Seward shifted the emphasis of American foreign policy from the acquisition of territory to the expansion of American commerce. Working to open markets in the Americas and across the Pacific, Seward saw the nation's influence following its trade. He still dreamed of a nation extending beyond the water's edge. What he discovered was that, however adventurous American empire builders had been, the war had made them stingy in paying for new domains, either in money or in lives.

Expansionism in the Gilded Age, then, meant expanding markets, and even then not always through government action. Between 1860 and 1897, American exports tripled, surpassing $1 billion per year. In 1874, for the first time, Americans sold more than they bought. Nearly 85 percent of those exports were farm goods, but the share of industrial exports grew prodigiously as the century closed. Between 1889 and 1898, iron and steel exports jumped by 230 percent.

Mexico provided a different example of commercial expansion: investment abroad. Political instability had hindered investment, but Porfirio Díaz's seizure of power in 1876 brought decades of reassuring autocracy—at least for investors. They rushed south to build railroads, dig oil wells, sell life insurance, and invest in commercial farming. By 1910, Americans owned 43 percent of all the property in Mexico; Mexicans owned rather less.

Secretaries of state reaffirmed Seward's commitment to commercial expansion. Treaties with Japan and Korea opened new Asian markets. A treaty with King Kalakaua of Hawaii gave the islands' sugar favored treatment on the American market, prompting a huge influx into the United States (along with a backlash by sugar producers on the mainland). Worried that European nations would divert Latin American commerce from the United States, Secretary of State James G. Blaine became the champion

years later. Congress created a Department of Justice in 1870 and a Department of Agriculture in 1889. The postal service tripled in size over a quarter of a century, delivering 7 billion pieces of mail in 1900. More than a quarter of the national budget in 1900 went for veterans' pensions, awarded to over a million veterans and their dependents.

By the turn of the century, the rudiments of a modern federal government were in place. The Interstate Commerce Commission was able to compel safety machinery like automatic brakes and coupling devices on trains, but it lacked the power to enforce its own rulings, especially where unfair rates were concerned. It had to rely on courts friendly to government action protecting health, safety, and morals, but distrustful of any interference in the marketplace. Crippled by a damaging of "reciprocity," breaking down American trade barriers in return for special access to foreign markets. In 1889, he convened the first Pan-American conference. Concern for access to foreign markets pushed successive administrations to assert America's exclusive right to build a canal across Central America. But that motive never stood alone—not in a world that every year Americans could see being devoured by European empires, and where Britain's and Germany's flags (and artillery) so often followed where their loans and exporters had ventured first.

Beyond that, America steered clear of foreign entanglements. In the 1880s, the United States, Germany, and England rattled sabers over disputed claims in Samoa; a riot in Valparaiso led to threats of naval force against Chile; and "jingoes," as friends of an aggressive foreign policy were called, complained about English mistreatment of Irish patriots and British claims in Latin America. If they had gotten their way, America would have gone to war to punish Spanish "insolence" in stopping American gunrunners to Cuba and to punish Canadian claims to sovereignty over the offshore fisheries and seal islands. They got no war.

Still, by the 1890s there were inklings of a new American assertiveness, mixing economic interest and a sense of America's mission to spread democracy. That showed itself most clearly in Hawaii. By 1886, two-thirds of the islands' sugar was produced on American-owned plantations. American power in Hawaii grew so great that it provoked a backlash among native Hawaiians. Queen Liliuokalani's ascension to the throne in 1891 spelt trouble for sugar growers. Two years later, they helped Hawaiians dethrone the queen and appealed for the United States to annex the islands. Undeceived by white planters pretending to speak for a Polynesian people, the Cleveland administration refused, but McKinley's carried annexation through. Nobody dreamed of statehood for so dark-skinned and foreign an electorate.

Only in the late 1880s did America's hemispheric interests begin to shape military policy. In 1890, Congress authorizing the building of the first modern warships, and the Supreme Court extended the president's control over "our international relations." The growing links between commercial and diplomatic interests were reviving the powers of the American presidency. But as the story of domestic politics has made clear, those links were never the whole story—nor did the scramble for markets make America forge a steel navy in a world grown different and more dangerous.

Supreme Court ruling in 1895, the weak Sherman Anti-Trust Act threatened few monopolies. In both cases, government action had not yet lived up to its potential. By comparison, state and municipal governments responded more aggressively to the problems of a transforming society.

States Discover Activism

Americans continued to clamor for state constitutions restricting government powers. They resented tax hikes and objected to bureaucrats. They had good reasons to distrust their officials. Lobbyists swarmed the capitols. Standard Oil did everything to the Pennsylvania legislators except refine them, a critic complained. Railroad tycoons, silver-mine owners, and copper kings bought themselves Senate seats, and the insurance lobby in New York spent tens of thousands of dollars making friends in Albany every year.

But lawmakers kept doing more every year—and that, contradictory as it might seem, was what Americans also seem to have wanted. In spite of lobbyists, corporation taxes went up. So did spending. Public school systems expanded. School years lengthened. In 20 years, spending per pupil doubled, and in almost every state outside the South, attendance became compulsory. "Tramp laws" jailed jobless workers for bad reputations or "criminal idleness." Upset that customers might buy "butterine," made from animal or vegetable fats, dairy farmers got legislatures to require the new name "oleomargarine" and, in some places, unappetizing colors like pink. Unions put through laws establishing Labor Day and setting up fact-finding bureaus of labor statistics. Hundreds of laws went through to protect women workers or keep children out of the coal mines, to forbid employers from paying their workers in company-issued paper money, "scrip," and even to set up arbitration machinery, so that industrial disputes could be settled by negotiation rather than confrontation. The laws promised more than they performed: enforcement was sometimes spotty or nonexistent—much less stringent than for laws forbidding boycotting of shop owners and picketing by strikers. The courts weakened or killed many statutes, especially the ones that regulated workers' hours.

Cities: Boss Rule and New Responsibilities

States also intervened to help govern the swelling municipalities. One reason for that was the cities' reputation for boss rule and control by party machines such as New York City's Tammany Hall. With urban services expanding so fast, the city government had more than enough jobs to do, and every job bought the machine a friend. Trading services for votes, the ward and precinct captains working for the "boss" made government matter in the most personal way. But as reformers pointed out, the money to do that had to come from somewhere: shakedowns and graft, perhaps; protection money from gamblers and saloon keepers; and forced donations from storekeepers afraid to have an enemy in city hall. Government by two-bit politicians out to line their own pockets meant rotten government, and in many ways poorer neighborhoods suffered most. Boss rule meant garbage-choked streets, tenements that were firetraps, and police and fire chiefs turning their services into party armies.

Scandals and abuses gave legislatures the excuse to shift authority away from partisan elected officials to experts and specialists on unelected boards. Mayors, city council members, and aldermen lost much of their authority over budgets, schools, health, transportation, police, and parks to commissions generally staffed by middle-class professionals. The commissioners found help among city reformers, and in many cases, the bosses did not put up much of a fight. With competing private fire companies no longer rushing to a fire and beating each other up, and with patrolmen no longer paying a kickback for their appointment and expected to take it out of saloons, prostitutes, and shopkeepers, the quality of the fire and police departments could only improve.

Bosses were never the uncrowned emperors reformers made them out to be. Nowhere, not even in Tammany's New York, did they have total power. They had to accommodate interest groups, including labor and reform organizations. That was one reason why, in the late nineteenth century, city governments provided broader social services than anywhere else and produced some of the century's great urban achievements: New York's Central Park, San Francisco's Golden Gate Park, and the Brooklyn Bridge. Chicagoans literally reversed the flow of the Chicago River.

CHALLENGING THE NEW INDUSTRIAL ORDER

In the late nineteenth century, disparate voices rose, arguing that something had gone wrong in a new, industrialized America where technology had made a few millionaires, living off the toil of unpropertied millions. Middle-class radicals argued that economic development had undermined individual liberty and equality. Yet although their attacks on capitalism were severe, their assumptions were traditional. They often worried that without substantial reforms, a discontented working class would threaten private property and social order. On the other hand, radicalized workers questioned one of the premises of producers' ideology—that American democracy was secured by a unique harmony between capital and labor. The Knights of Labor had called for a workers' party and carried their tickets in many local elections. In the mills and mines, labor agitation often became violent and was replied to with violence, as happened most notoriously in Haymarket Square in 1886. But even if the harmony of capital and labor had been destroyed, advocates of the producers' ideology continued to hold faith in political solutions to the labor problem.

Henry George and the Limits of Producers' Ideology

Henry George was born in Philadelphia in 1839 to middle-class parents. Although his formal education was limited, George traveled and read widely. Shocked that as the nation grew richer its number of poor people grew as well, he published his conclusions in 1879 in a best-selling book called *Progress and Poverty*.

George's explanation rested on what historians have called producers' ideology. He assumed that only human labor could create legitimate wealth and that anything of value, such as food, clothing, or steel rails, came from the world's producing classes. By contrast, stockbrokers, bankers, and speculators made money from money rather than from the goods they produced. Their wealth was therefore illegitimate. From these premises, George divided the world into two classes: producers and predators.

The harmony of capital and labor was a central theme of producers' ideology. Henry George dreamed of a world in which working people owned their own farms and shops, making them both capitalists and laborers, a vision that recalled Thomas Jefferson's ideal society of small farmers and independent shopkeepers. America used to be that way, George believed, but as society "progressed," the land was monopolized by a wealthy few. Producers were forced to work for wealthy landholders. Employers invested in technology that increased the productivity of their workers but kept the added wealth for themselves. George's solution was a so-called single tax on rents. Because all wealth derived from labor applied to land, he reasoned, rents were an unnatural transfer of wealth from the producers to the landlords. To discourage the landowning class from accumulating land, George suggested pro-hibitively high taxes on rents and improvements on land. All other taxes would be abolished, including the tariffs protecting big business.

George was no socialist. He presented his single tax as an alternative to the dangerous radical doctrines he thought were spreading among the working class. But his work challenged the Social Darwinists' idea that those who were poor owed it to their own inadequacies, and that the rich owed their place to their superiority. George depicted a world in which the system itself had made a cluster of winners and a host of losers, and in which government policy could right the balance.

Edward Bellamy and the Nationalist Clubs

In 1888, Edward Bellamy, a Massachusetts editor, published a best-selling critique of capitalism even more powerful than Henry George's. Bellamy's *Looking Backward* was a utopian novel set in the future, where technology had raised the standard of living for all. Industrial civilization's problems had been solved by overcoming the "excessive individualism" of Bellamy's day. Progress came, not through Social Darwinism's competition, but through its opposite: cooperation. Whereas *Progress and Poverty* proposed the restoration of the simple virtues of Jeffersonian society, *Looking Backward* imagined a high-tech future filled with consumer goods. In Bellamy's ideal world, production and consumption would no longer be subject to the whims of the market; instead, they would be harmonized by "nationalism," an obscure pro-cess of centralized planning. *Looking Backward* catered to a middle-class craving for order amid the chaos of industrial society. Decisions about what to produce were made collectively, and society as a whole owned the means of production. Whereas Henry George reasserted the values of hard work and self-restraint, Edward Bel-lamy embraced the modern cult of leisure and looked to the day when there would be little need for government. This vision inspired thousands of middle-class Amer-icans to form "Bellamy Clubs" or Nationalist Clubs, particularly in New England.

Agrarian Revolt

The late nineteenth century was a desperate time for American farmers in the grain and cotton belts of the West and South. To compete, they had to buy costly agricul-tural equipment, often from manufacturers who benefited from tariff protection. Then they had to ship their goods on railroads that charged higher rates to small farmers than to big industrialists. At the market, they faced steadily declining prices.

A global economy put southern cotton in competition with cotton from India and Egypt. Western wheat competed with Russian and eastern European wheat. To keep up, farmers increasingly went into debt, and in a deflationary spiral the money they borrowed to plant their crops was worth more when it came time to pay it back, whereas their crops were worth less. The proportion of owner-occupied farms declined, and the number of tenants rose. A few years of drought meant ruin on the plains. "In God we trusted, in Kansas we busted," one departing farmer wrote on his wagon.

Scattered over large sections of the country, farmers were committed to an ide-ology of economic independence and cool to government intervention. The indus-trial transformation of the late nineteenth century taught many of them that they could no longer stand alone. One of the first attempts to organize farmers was the Patrons of Husbandry, generally called the Grange. The Grange claimed 1.5 million members by 1874. Consistent with producers' ideology, the Grange organized co-operatives to eliminate the role of merchants and creditors. By storing grain collectively, farmers held their products back from the market in the hope of gaining control over commodity prices. But inexperience made the Grange cooperatives difficult to organize and sustain. After 1875, their membership dwindled.

The National Farmers' Alliance and Industrial Union, known simply as the Farmers' Alliance, was much more effective than the Grange. Founded in Texas in 1877, the Alliance spread rapidly across the South and West. Its goal was not to restore rural Jeffersonian simplicity but to bring American farmers into the modern world of industry and prosperity. The Alliance focused above all on education, broadly conceived. That meant public schools and the spread of scientific agriculture and sound business practices. The Alliance also built its own network of newspapers and lecturers to free farmers from their isolation. For rural men and women alike, the Farmers' Alliance offered the chance to share in the progress and prosperity of American life.

At its core the Alliance was a reform organization calling for a specific set of economic policies. Above all, the farmers wanted to inflate the currency, whether by the circulation of more silver currency or of more paper currency ("greenbacks") or a combination of the two. Inspired by the successes of highly organized corporations, especially railroads, the Alliance also supported a system of cooperative "subtreasuries" that would provide low-interest loans, backed by farmers' crops, held until the best prices were available.

By the late 1880s, the Farmers' Alliance had drawn millions of members, concentrated in the southern, western, and plains states. Created at a huge meeting at Ocala, Florida, in 1890, the Ocala Platform supported a host of new policies that joined economic progress to democratic reform. The platform called for the free coinage of silver, lower tariffs, government subtreasuries, and a constitutional amendment providing for direct election of senators. Finally, the Alliance called for strict government regulation, and if necessary direct government ownership, of the railroad and telegraph industries.

The Farmers' Alliance steered clear of politics and instead judged political candidates by their support of the Ocala Platform reforms. They elected shoals of congressmen and even a few senators by cooperating with Democrats in the West and, where neither party gave satisfaction, by running independent candidates. Out of these efforts came the most significant third party of the late nineteenth century, the People's Party, otherwise known as the Populists.

The Rise of the Populists

On February 22, 1892, a coalition of reform organizations met in St. Louis, including representatives of the Knights of Labor and the Farmers' Alliance. Together they founded the People's Party. At Omaha on July 4, they nominated General James B. Weaver of Iowa for president and drew up the Omaha Platform, demanding an inflationary currency policy and a subtreasury system. The Populists also called for a graduated income tax, direct government ownership of railroads and telegraph lines, and the confiscation of railroad land grants. But they also spoke for a government restored to the people by a secret ballot, popularly elected senators, and the power of voters to make laws for themselves by initiative and referendum.

Kansas Farm Families on the Road to a People's Party Gathering In a state usually locked up for the GOP, the farmer's revolt revived political competition and an evangelical passion about issues absent since the Civil War.

TIME LINE

▼**1867**
Patrons of Husbandry (the Grange) founded

▼**1869**
Noble and Holy Order of the Knights of Labor founded

▼**1870**
Department of Justice created

▼**1872**
Grant reelected

▼**1873**
"Crusade" against alcohol begins in Hillsboro, Ohio

▼**1874**
Women's Christian Temperance Union (WCTU) is formed

▼**1876**
Rutherford B. Hayes elected president

▼**1877**
Farmers' Alliance founded

▼**1878**
Bland-Allison Act

▼**1879**
Henry George publishes *Progress and Poverty*

▼**1880**
James Garfield elected president

▼**1881**
Garfield assassinated; Chester Arthur becomes president
WCTU endorses women's suffrage

▼**1883**
Pendleton Civil Service Act

▼**1884**
Grover Cleveland elected president

Populism took in more than wheat and cotton farmers. Small ranchers joined to fight the politically privileged cattle kings. Townspeople joined to oppose the railroads. Prohibitionists, woman suffragists, and the dwindling membership of the Knights of Labor found friends aplenty in the People's Party. Rallies took on the spirit of a revival, with speakers promising a return to the lost promise of the Revolution. In the 1892 elections, Weaver won about 1 million votes, and the Populists elected several senators, representatives, governors, and state legislators. But wage earners in the industrial North and East still held back. The Populist platform, for all its talk of the unity of the toiling masses, offered industrial workers little. They depended on the protective tariff to shield them from cheap foreign labor. Higher prices for the farmer meant price hikes in the stores, when most workers had no hope of raising their wages to keep up. They knew how paper money worked: many were paid in company-issued "scrip," redeemable only at the company store at a steep discount. Conversely, farmers who hired workers had no zeal for an eight-hour day or laws restricting child labor. Wherever the Populists were strong, mainstream parties adopted their most popular causes.

Southern Populists faced a particularly difficult challenge. To win, they needed help from the largest class of impoverished farmers, Black sharecroppers. Only by downplaying racial differences could they make such a coalition work. Not all whites could overcome their prejudices. The Farmers' Alliance had always been strictly segregated, with a separate Colored Farmers' Alliance. And in fact the economic interests of the two groups were not always compatible. Black leaders appreciated the limits of any alliance with white reformers, and most Black southerners kept voting Republican. Coalitions between Republicans and Populists sometimes came about. But any multiracial alliance inspired the ugliest race-baiting that Democrats could devise, to break the partners apart and restore the color line. It

▼**1887**
Interstate Commerce Act
Dawes Severalty Act

▼**1888**
Benjamin Harrison elected
   president
Edward Bellamy publishes
   Looking Backward

▼**1889**
United States convenes
   first Pan-American
   Conference
Department of Agriculture
   created

▼**1890**
McKinley Tariff
Sherman Anti-Trust Act
Ocala Platform

▼**1891**
Queen Liliuokalani as-
   sumes the Hawaiian
   throne

▼**1892**
Omaha Platform of the
   People's Party
Grover Cleveland reelected

▼**1893**
Queen Liliuokalani
   overthrown

▼**1898**
Frances Willard dies

gave them all the excuse they needed to stuff ballot boxes, count votes creatively, and remake the laws to cut as many Populists, white and Black, out of the suffrage as possible—always in the name of reform.

CONCLUSION

Luna Kellie was not alone in seeing a nation on the edge of catastrophe by the early 1890s. Americans still went to the polls in record numbers, but the political system was showing serious strains. Strident voices rose, against Catholics, foreigners, Negroes, and Jews. Farmers cried out against the "money power." Bloody strikes convulsed the coalfields and Carnegie's mills. Culture wars disrupted politics in the Midwest, while southern Democrats fended off political challengers by invoking white supremacy in its rawest form. In big cities, reformers cried that boss rule had replaced government by the people. But Gilded Age politics offered more hope than it appeared. In its tumultuous variety, it showed a country bursting with reform impulses, and with the energy to regenerate a nation in crisis.

WHO, WHAT, WHERE

REVIEW QUESTIONS

1. Discuss how constructions of gender defined what men and women could do and be.

2. How did urbanization and immigration challenge cultural norms in the late nineteenth century?

3. Describe the two major styles of politics in the late nineteenth century.

4. Describe the changes in the roles of national, state, and local government during this period.

5. What did Henry George, Edward Bellamy, and Frances Willard have in common? What did the Farmers' Alliance stand for?

CRITICAL-THINKING QUESTIONS

1. Why did elite attitudes on gender and morality break down in this period?

2. What was the case that guardians of traditional culture made against a multicultural society?

3. Why did so many people participate in politics in the late nineteenth century? What did they expect to get out of it?

4. To what extent did the industrial revolution described in Chapter 16 affect politics and the issues politicians discussed in this period?

5. What were the major challenges to politics-as-usual in this age, and where did those challenges come from? Why did they arise, and how successful were they in remaking American society?

SUGGESTED READINGS

Burrows, Edwin G., and Mike Wallace. *Gotham: A History of New York to 1898.* New York: Oxford University Press, 1999.

Goodwyn, Lawrence. *The Populist Moment: A Short History of the Agrarian Revolt in America.* New York: Oxford University Press, 1978.

Morgan, H. Wayne. *From Hayes to McKinley: National Party Politics, 1877–1896.* Syracuse, NY: Syracuse University Press, 1969.

For further review materials and resource information, please visit www.oup.com/us/ofthepeople

CHAPTER 17: The Culture and Politics of Industrial America, 1870–1892
Primary Sources

17.1 EMMA LAZARUS, "THE NEW COLOSSUS" (1883)

Emma Lazarus became a prominent writer against anti-Semitism, particularly the Russian empire's pogroms against Jewish people. As an organizer of relief agencies, she was deeply involved in the struggle to keep America's doors open to immigration. Her sonnet, titled "The New Colossus," was inscribed on the pedestal of the Statue of Liberty, which was dedicated in late 1886.

Not like the brazen giant of Greek fame,
With conquering limbs astride from land to land;
Here at our sea-washed, sunset gates shall stand
A mighty woman with a torch, whose flame
Is the imprisoned lightning, and her name
Mother of Exiles. From her beacon-hand
Glows world-wide welcome; her mild eyes command
The air-bridged harbor that twin cities frame.
"Keep, ancient lands, your storied pomp!" cries she
With silent lips. "Give me your tired, your poor,
Your huddled masses yearning to breathe free,
The wretched refuse of your teeming shore.
Send these, the homeless, tempest-tost to me,
I lift my lamp beside the golden door!"

Source: Emma Lazarus, "The New Colossus," quoted in William Benton, publ., *The Annals of America. Volume 11, 1884–1894: Agrarianism and Urbanization* (Chicago: Encyclopedia Britannica, Inc., 1968), p. 107.

17.2 JOSIAH STRONG, EXCERPTS FROM "THE SUPERIORITY OF THE ANGLO-SAXON RACE" (1885)

As the new secretary to the Congregational Home Missionary Society, Josiah Strong began with a revision of the society's manual and ended up publishing a book, combining his notions of social Darwinism and his fears that a white America stood imperiled by what he felt were inferior races: not just African Americans and Chinese immigrants, but the Irish, the Italians, the Slavs, and those of the Jewish faith. Strong's *Our Country* was first published in 1885.

It is not necessary to argue to those for whom I write that the two great needs of mankind, that all men may be lifted up into the light of the highest Christian civilization, are, first, a pure, spiritual Christianity, and second, civil liberty. Without controversy, these are the forces which, in the past, have contributed most to the elevation of the human race, and they must continue to be, in the future, the most efficient ministers to its progress.

It follows, then, that the Anglo-Saxon, as the great representative of these two ideas, the despositary of these two greatest blessings, sustains peculiar relations to the world's future, is divinely commissioned to be, in a peculiar sense, his brother's keeper. Add to this the fact of his rapidly increasing strength in modern times, and we have well-nigh a demonstration of his destiny.... In one century the United States has increased its territory ten-fold, while the enormous acquisition of foreign territory by Great Britain—and chiefly within the last hundred years—is wholly unparalleled in history. This mighty Anglo-Saxon race, though comprising only one-thirteenth part of mankind, now rules more than one-third of the earth's surface, and more than one-fourth of its people. And if this race, while growing from 6,000,000 to 120,000,000, thus gained possession of a third portion of the earth, is it to be supposed that when it numbers 1,000,000,000, it will lose the disposition, or lack the power to extend its sway?...

America is to have the great preponderance of numbers and of wealth, and by the logic of events will follow the scepter of controlling influence. This will be but the consummation of a movement as old as civilization—a result to which men have looked forward for centuries. John Adams records that nothing was "more ancient in his memory than the observation that arts, sciences and empire had traveled westward; and in conversation it was always added that their next leap would be over the Atlantic into America." He recalled a couplet that had been inscribed or rather drilled, into a rock on the shore of Monument Bay in our old colony of Plymouth:
The Eastern nations sink, their glory ends,
And empire rises where the sun descends...

... Looking at the distant future, I do not think that the Rev. Mr. Zincke takes an exaggerated view when he says: 'All other series of events—as that which resulted in the culture of mind in Greece, and that which resulted in the Empire of Rome—only appear to have purpose and value when viewed in connection with, or rather as subsidiary to, the great stream of Anglo-Saxon emigration to the West.'"

There is abundant reason to believe that the Anglo-Saxon race is to be, is, indeed, already becoming, more effective here than in the mother country. The marked superiority of this race is due, in large measure, to its highly mixed origin. Says Rawlinson: "It is a general rule, now almost universally admitted by ethnologists, that the mixed races of mankind are superior to the pure ones"; and adds: "Even the Jews, who are so often cited as an example of a race at once pure and strong, may, with more reason, be adduced on the opposite side of the argument." The ancient Egyptians, the Greeks, and the Romans, were all mixed races. Among modern races, the most conspicuous example is afforded by the Anglo Saxons.... There is here a new commingling of races; and, while the largest injections of foreign blood are substantially the same elements that constituted the original Anglo-Saxon admixture, so that we may infer the general type will be preserved, there are strains of other bloods being added, which, if Mr. Emerson's remark is true, that "the best nations are those most widely related," may be expected to improve the stock, and aid it to a higher destiny. If the dangers of immigration, which have been pointed out, can be successfully met for the next few years, until it has passed its climax, it may be expected to add value to the amalgam which will constitute the new Anglo-Saxon race of the New World....

It may be easily shown, and is of no small significance, that the two great ideas of which the Anglo-Saxon is the exponent are having a fuller development in the United States than in Great Britain. There the union of Church and State tends strongly to paralyze some of the members of the body of Christ. Here there is no such influence to destroy spiritual life and power. Here, also, has been evolved the form of government consistent with the largest possible civil liberty. Furthermore, it is significant that the marked characteristics of this race are being here emphasized most. Among the most striking features of the Anglo-Saxon is his moneymaking power—a power of increasing importance in the widening commerce of the world's future. We have seen... that, although England is by far the richest nation of Europe, we have already outstripped her in the race after wealth, and we have only begun the development of our vast resources.

Again, another marked characteristic of the Anglo-Saxon is what may be called an instinct or genius for colonizing. His unequaled energy, his indomitable perseverance, and his personal independence, made him a pioneer. He excels all others in pushing his way into new countries. It was those in whom this tendency was strongest that came to America, and this inherited tendency has been further developed by the westward sweep of successive generations across the continent. So noticeable has this characteristic become that English visitors remark it. Charles Dickens once said that the typical American would hesitate to enter heaven unless assured that he could go farther west.

What is the significance of such facts? These tendencies infold the future; they are the mighty alphabet with which God writes his prophecies. May we not, by a careful laying together of the letters, spell out something of his meaning? It seems to me that God, with infinite wisdom and skill, is training the Anglo-Saxon race for an hour sure to come in the world's future. Heretofore there has always been in the history of the world a comparatively unoccupied land westward, into which the crowded countries of the East have poured their surplus populations. But the widening waves of migration, which millenniums ago rolled east and west from the valley of the Euphrates, meet today on our Pacific coast. There are no more new worlds. The unoccupied arable lands of the earth are limited, and will soon be taken. The time is coming when the pressure of population on the means of subsistence will be felt here as it is now felt in Europe and Asia. Then will the world enter upon a new stage of its history—the *final competition of races, for which the Anglo-Saxon is being schooled.* Long before the thousand millions are here, the mighty *centrifugal* tendency, inherent in this stock and strengthened in the United States, will assert itself. Then this race of unequaled energy, with all the majesty of numbers and the might of wealth behind it—the representative, let us hope, of the largest liberty, the purest Christianity, the highest civilization—having developed peculiarly aggressive traits calculated to impress its institutions upon mankind, will spread itself over the earth. If I read not amiss, this powerful race will move down upon Mexico, down upon Central and South America, out upon the islands of the sea, over upon Africa and beyond. And can any one doubt that the results of this competition of races will be the "survival of the fittest?" "Any people," says Dr. Bushnell, "that is physiologically advanced in culture, though it be only in a degree beyond another which is mingled with it on strictly equal terms, is sure to live down and finally live out its inferior. Nothing can save the inferior race but a ready and pliant assimilation. Whether the feebler and more abject races are going to be regenerated and raised up, is already, very much of a question. What if it should be God's plan to people the world with better and finer material?"

Source: Josiah Strong, "The Superiority of the Anglo-Saxon Race," quoted in William Benton, publ., *The Annals of America. Volume 11, 1884–1894: Agrarianism and Urbanization* (Chicago: Encyclopedia Britannica, Inc., 1968), pp. 72–76.

17.3   HENRY GEORGE, EXCERPTS FROM "THAT WE MIGHT ALL BE RICH" (1883)

As the author of *Progress and Poverty*, Henry George became a celebrated authority on class conflict and social injustice in industrializing America. Socialists agreed with his diagnosis of society, though not with his solutions, among which were a single tax falling on landed property and an end to protective tariffs. Nearly winning the New York City mayoral race in 1886 and at the forefront of efforts to create a workers' party, George campaigned on distrust of government and detestation of privilege. Many of his essays were gathered together in the book *Social Problems*, published in 1883.

The terms rich and poor are of course frequently used in a relative sense. Among Irish peasants, kept on the verge of starvation by the tribute wrung from them to maintain the luxury of absentee landlords in London or Paris, "the woman of three cows" will be looked on as rich, while in the society of millionaires a man with only $500,000 will be regarded as poor. Now, we cannot, of course, all be rich in the sense of having more than others; but when people say, as they so often do, that we cannot all be rich, or when they say that we must always have the poor with us, they do not use the words in this comparative sense. They mean by the rich those who have enough, or more than enough, wealth to gratify all reasonable wants, and by the poor those who have not.

Now, using the words in this sense, I join issue with those who say that we cannot all be rich; with those who declare that in human society the poor must always exist. I do not, of course, mean that we all might have an array of servants; that we all might outshine each other in dress, in equipage, in the lavishness of our balls or dinners, in the magnificence of our houses. That would be a contradiction in terms. What I mean is, that we all might have leisure, comfort and abundance, not merely of the necessaries, but even of what are now esteemed the elegancies and luxuries of life. I do not mean to say that absolute equality could be had, or would be desirable. I do not mean to say that we could all have, or would want, the same quantity of all the different forms of wealth. But I do mean to say that we might all have enough wealth to satisfy reasonable desires; that we might all have so much of the material things we now struggle for, that no one would want to rob or swindle his neighbor; that no one would worry all day, or lie awake at nights, fearing he might be brought to poverty, or thinking how he might acquire wealth.

Does this seem an utopian dream? What would people of fifty years ago have thought of one who would have told them that it was possible to sew by steam-power; to cross the Atlantic in six days, or the continent in three; to have a message sent from London at noon delivered in Boston three hours before noon; to hear in New York the voice of a man talking in Chicago?

Did you ever see a pail of swill given to a pen of hungry hogs? That is human society as it is.

Did you ever see a company of well-bred men and women sitting down to a good dinner, without scrambling, or jostling, or gluttony, each, knowing that his own appetite will be satisfied, deferring to and helping the others? That is human society as it might be.

"Devil catch the hindmost" is the motto of our so-called civilized society today. We learn early to "take care of No. 1," lest No.1 should suffer; we learn early to grasp from others that we may not want ourselves. The fear of poverty makes us admire great wealth; and so habits of greed are formed, and we behold the pitiable spectacle of men who have already more than they can by any possibility use, toiling, striving, grasping to add to their store up to the very verge of the grave—that grave which, whatever else it may mean, does certainly mean the parting with all earthly possessions however great they be.

In vain, in gorgeous churches, on the appointed Sunday, is the parable of Dives and Lazarus read. What can it mean in churches where Dives would be welcomed and Lazarus shown the door? In vain may the preacher preach of the vanity of riches, while poverty engulfs the hindmost. But the mad struggle would cease when the fear of poverty had vanished. Then, and not till then, will a truly Christian civilization become possible.

And may not this be?

. . .

The passenger who leaves New York on a trans-Atlantic steamer does not fear that the provisions will give out. The men who run these steamers do not send them to sea without provisions enough for all they carry. Did He who made this whirling planet for our sojourn lack the forethought of man? Not so. In soil and sunshine, in vegetable and animal life, in veins of minerals, and in pulsing forces which we are only beginning to use, are capabilities which we cannot exhaust—materials and powers from which human effort, guided by intelligence, may gratify every material want of every human creature. There is in nature no reason for poverty—not even for the poverty of the crippled or the decrepit. For man is by nature a social animal, and the family affections and the social sympathies would, where chronic poverty did not distort and embrute, amply provide for those who could not provide for themselves.

But if we will not use the intelligence with which we have been gifted to adapt social organization to natural laws—if we allow dogs in the manger to monopolize what they cannot use; if we allow strength and cunning to rob honest labor, we must have chronic poverty, and all the social evils it inevitably brings. Under such conditions there would be poverty in paradise.

"The poor ye have always with you." If ever a scripture has been wrested to the devil's service, this is that scripture. How often have these words been distorted from their obvious meaning to soothe conscience into acquiescence in human misery and degradation—to bolster that blasphemy, the very negation and denial of Christ's teachings, that the All-Wise and Most Merciful, the Infinite Father, has decreed that so many of his creatures must be poor in order that others of his creatures to whom he wills the good things of life should enjoy the pleasure and virtue of doling out alms! "The poor ye have always with you," said Christ; but all his teachings supply the limitation, "until the coming of the Kingdom." In that kingdom of God on earth, that kingdom of justice and love for which he taught his followers to strive and pray, there will be no poor. But though the faith and the hope and the striving for this kingdom are of the very essence of Christ's teaching, the staunchest disbelievers and revilers of its possibility are found among those who call themselves Christians. Queer ideas of the Divinity have some of these Christians who hold themselves orthodox and contribute to the conversion of the heathen. A very rich orthodox Christian said to a newspaper reporter, a while ago, on the completion of a large work out of which he is said to have made millions: "We have been peculiarly favored by Divine Providence; iron never was so cheap before, and labor has been a drug in the market."

. . .

The wealth-producing powers that would be evoked in a social state based on justice, where wealth went to the producers of wealth, and the banishment of poverty had banished the fear and greed and lusts that spring from it, we now can only faintly imagine. Wonderful as have been the discoveries and inventions of this century, it is evident that we have only begun to grasp that dominion which it is given to mind to obtain over matter. Discovery and invention are born of leisure, of material comfort, of freedom. These secured to all, and who shall say to what command over nature man may not attain?

It is not necessary that any one should be condemned to monotonous toil; it is not necessary that any one should lack the wealth and the leisure which permit the development of the faculties that raise man above the animal. Mind, not muscle, is the motor of progress, the force which compels nature and produces wealth. In turning men into machines we are wasting the highest powers. Already in our society there is a favored class who need take no thought for the morrow—what they shall eat, or what they shall drink, or wherewithal they shall be clothed. And may it not be that Christ was more than a dreamer when he told his disciples that in that kingdom of justice for which he taught them to work and pray this might be the condition of all?

Source: Henry George, "That We All Might Be Rich," from *Social Problems* (Chicago: 1883) quoted in William Benton, publ., *The Annals of America. Volume 10, 1866–1883: Reconstruction and Industrialization.*

17.4 JACOB RIIS, EXCERPT FROM *HOW THE OTHER HALF LIVES* (1890) AND VISUAL DOCUMENT: JACOB RIIS, "NOMADS OF THE STREET" (CA. 1890)

In 1890, the Danish American police reporter Jacob Riis published a book about the slums of New York City entitled *How the Other Half Lives*. Its stark text, excerpted in the following, was accompanied by Riis's haunting photographs. In addition to being a pioneer in photojournalism, Riis contributed to the record that reformers used to advocate for public health programs, government policing of housing, and other public measures to relieve poverty and its accompanying ills.

The "Rock of Ages" is the name over the door of a low saloon that blocks the entrance to another alley, if possible more forlorn and dreary than the rest, as we pass out of the Alderman's court. It sounds like a jeer from the days, happily past, when the "wickedest man in New York" lived around the corner a little way and boasted of his title. One cannot take many steps in Cherry Street without encountering some relic of past or present prominence in the ways of crime, scarce one that does not turn up specimen bricks of the coming thief. The Cherry Street tough is all-pervading. Ask Superintendent Murray, who, as captain of the Oak Street squad, in seven months secured convictions for theft, robbery, and murder aggregating no less than five hundred and thirty years of penal servitude, and he will tell you his opinion that the Fourth Ward, even in the last twenty years, has turned out more criminals than all the rest of the city together.

But though the "Swamp Angels" have gone to their reward, their successors carry on business at the old stand as successfully, if not as boldly. There goes one who was once a shining light in thiefdom. He has reformed since, they say. The policeman on the corner, who is addicted to a professional unbelief in reform of any kind, will tell you that while on the Island once he sailed away on a shutter, paddling along until he was picked up in Hell Gate by a schooner's crew, whom he persuaded that he was a fanatic performing some sort of religious penance by his singular expedition.

....

We have crossed the boundary of the Seventh Ward. Penitentiary Row, suggestive name for a block of Cherry Street tenements, is behind us. Within recent days it has become peopled wholly with Hebrews, the overflow from Jewtown adjoining, pedlars and tailors, all of them. It is odd to read this legend from other days over the door: "No pedlars allowed in this house." These thrifty people are not only crowding into the tenements of this once exclusive district—they are buying them. The Jew runs to real estate as soon as he can save up enough for a deposit to clinch the bargain. As fast as the old houses are torn down, towering structures go up in their place, and Hebrews are found to be the builders. Here is a whole alley nicknamed after the intruder, Jews' Alley. But abuse and ridicule are not weapons to fight the Israelite with. He pockets them quietly with the rent and bides his time. He knows from experience, both sweet and bitter, that all things come to those who wait, including the houses and lands of their persecutors.

Here comes a pleasure party, as gay as any on the avenue, though the carry-all is an ash-cart. The father is the driver and he has taken his brown-legged boy for a ride. How proud and happy they both look up there on their perch! The queer old building they have halted in front of is "The Ship," famous for fifty years as a ramshackle tenement filled with the oddest crowd. No one knows why it is called "The Ship," though there is a tradition that once the river came clear up here to Hamilton Street, and boats were moored along-side

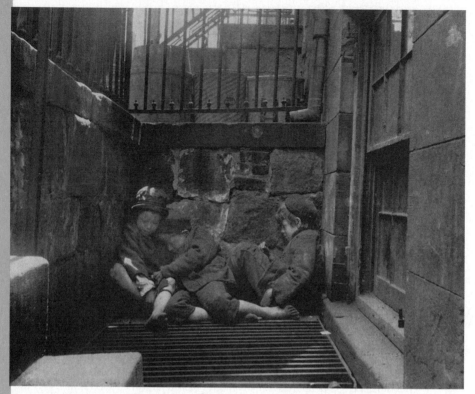

Jacob Riis's powerful exposures of the links between poverty, grime, crime, and exploitation were strengthened by the pictures he took in the slums of downtown New York. Danish-born, the reformer was one of the pioneers in what came to be called photojournalism.
Source: "Nomads of the Street," Photograph by Jacob Riis, *How the Other Half Lives* (1890)

it. More likely it is because it is as bewildering inside as a crazy old ship, with its ups and downs of ladders parading as stairs, and its unexpected pitfalls. But Hamilton Street, like Water Street, is not what it was. The missions drove from the latter the worst of its dives. A sailors' mission has lately made its appearance in Hamilton Street, but there are no dives there, nothing worse than the ubiquitous saloon and tough tenements.

Enough of them everywhere. Suppose we look into one? No.—Cherry Street. Be a little careful, please! The hall is dark and you might stumble over the children pitching pennies back there. Not that it would hurt them; kicks and cuffs are their daily diet. They have little else. Here where the hall turns and dives into utter darkness is a step, and an-other, another. A flight of stairs. You can feel your way, if you cannot see it. Close? Yes! What would you have? All the fresh air that ever enters these stairs comes from the hall-door that is forever slamming, and from the windows of dark bedrooms that in turn receive from the stairs their sole supply of the elements God meant to be free, but man deals out with such niggardly hand. That was a woman filling her pail by the hydrant you just bumped against. The sinks are in the hallway, that all the tenants may have access—and all be poisoned alike by their summer stenches. Hear the pump squeak! It is the lullaby of tenement-house babes. In summer, when a thousand thirsty throats pant for a cooling drink in this block, it is worked in vain. But the saloon, whose open door you passed in the hall, is always there. The smell of it has followed you up. Here is a door. Listen! That short hacking cough, that tiny, helpless wail—what do they mean? They mean that the soiled bow of white you saw on the door downstairs will have another story to tell—Oh! a sadly familiar story—before the day is at an end. The child is dying with measles. With half a chance it might have lived; but it had none. That dark bedroom killed it.

"It was took all of a suddint," says the mother, smoothing the throbbing little body with trembling hands. There is no unkindness in the rough voice of the man in the jumper, who sits by the window grimly smoking a clay pipe, with the little life ebbing out in his sight, bitter as his words sound: "Hush, Mary! If we cannot keep the baby, need we complain—such as we?"

Such as we! What if the words ring in your ears as we grope our way up the stairs and down from floor to floor, listening to the sounds behind the closed doors—some of quarrelling, some of coarse songs, more of profanity. They are true. When the summer heats come with their suffering they have meaning more terrible than words can tell. Come over here. Step carefully over this baby—it is a baby, spite of its rags and dirt—under these iron bridges called fire-escapes, but loaded down, despite the incessant watchfulness of the firemen, with broken household goods, with wash-tubs and barrels, over which no man could climb from a fire. This gap between dingy brick-walls is the yard. That strip of smoke-colored sky up there is the heaven of these people. Do you wonder the name does not attract them to the churches? That baby's parents live in the rear tenement here. She is at least as clean as the steps we are now climbing. There are plenty of houses with half a hundred such in. The tenement is much like the one in front we just left, only fouler, closer, darker—we will not say more cheerless. The word is a mockery. A hundred thousand people lived in rear tenements in New York last year. Here is a room neater than the rest. The woman, a stout matron with hard lines of care in her face, is at the wash-tub. "I try to keep the childer clean," she says, apologetically, but with a hopeless glance around. The spice of hot soap-suds is added to the air already tainted with the smell of boiling cabbage, of rags and uncleanliness all about. It makes an overpowering compound. It is Thursday, but patched linen is hung upon the pulley-line from the window. There is no Monday cleaning in the tenements. It is washday all the week round, for a change of clothing is scarce among the poor. They are poverty's honest badge, these perennial lines of rags hung out to dry, those that are not the washerwoman's professional shingle. The true line to be drawn between pauperism and honest poverty is the clothes-line. With it begins the effort to be clean that is the first and the best evidence of a desire to be honest.

What sort of an answer, think you, would come from these tenements to the question "Is life worth living?" were they heard at all in the discussion?

Source: Jacob A. Riis, *How the Other Half Lives: Studies Among the Tenements of New York* (New York: Charles Scribner's Sons, 1890), pp. 39–47.

17.5 *NEW YORK WORLD*, "HOW TIM GOT THE VOTES" (1892)

New York City's Tammany Hall machine was nationally infamous, but no critic could deny that the Democratic organization knew how to bring every supporter to the polls. Local election-district leaders took pride in getting a full turnout, and those with political ambitions spared no effort on Election Day. One of the hardest working politicians was "Big Tim" Sullivan, a state assemblyman and rising star in downtown Manhattan. Helped by his cousins "Big Florry" and "Boston Tim" Sullivan, he demonstrated his skills during the 1892 Cleveland-Harrison presidential election, when he set the goal of carrying every man on the voter rolls.

"Now here comes a duck," whispered Tim, to his cousin Florry, "who's been gettin' drunk on Denny Shea. Watch me fix him."

"Say, young feller," demanded Tim with a frown, surrounded by eight fierce-looking Sullivans, "how are y' goin' to vote?"

"I'm fer Cleevelan' an' th' hull ticket," replied the fellow, with apparent enthusiasm.

"You're lyin' an' y' know it," said Tim, with painful frankness. "Do y' see this paster?" He did.

"Well, jes' take it, an' slap it on a ballot. An' I want y' to slap it on so I can hear it, too. See?"

"All right," was the reply, "but you've gotto do dis fer me. You gotta promise to look out fer me if de cops take me in fer hittin' de bowl."

The agreement was made on the spot.

This was followed by sixty Tammany ballots which were above suspicion. Then the Republican district captain cast his vote.

"That's one fer Harrison," commented Tim, sadly.

Just then a woman came up to Tim and called him aside, confidentially.

"My husband's so drunk, begorra, he can't walk," she said. "Pfhat are yez goin' to do?"

"How many times have I told that duck," said Tim indignantly, "not to getta jag until after he voted. Here, Florry, get ten cents' worth o' ammonia and straighten 'im out."

Five minutes later the fellow came, supported by two Sullivans.

"You don't needa think I've been drinkin', Mr. Sullivan," he apologized. "I was workin' all night, an' I felt so tired I fell asleep. Hooray for Tim Sullivan an' Cleveland!"

Then there was a lull of five minutes. It was broken by the Republican Supervisor.

"That's two," said Tim, mournfully, "but I'll see that duck don't sling ink around here next year. The bloke who was here last year was a square feller."

There were twenty-eight votes still out by three o'clock, and among them were several who were under suspicion.

"Go hunt up Lake," he instructed his nephew, Tim, Jr: "He's another one o' Denny Shea's gang."

When Lake came he admitted frankly that he was going to vote for Harrison, but he promised to vote for the Tammany ticket.

"Do you wantta ruin my chances to get to th' Senate?" demanded Tim. "Are you goin' to be the only man in the district who's goin' back on me? What do you think Grover Cleveland'll say to me when he sees I let Gilroy have an extra vote? You'll be wantin' a favor, but when I got to Cleveland he'll fire me out."

Much as he loved Harrison, Jake would not have Tim put on the black list if he could help it. So he voted for Cleveland.

"But don't tell Denny," he enjoined Tim.

Next the Republican poll clerk voted. How aggravating it was to see him, with his cynical smile hand over a Republican ballot!

"That duck thinks he's smart," growled Tim, "but I know how to get even with 'im."

There were still half a dozen Baxter street clothiers who had not voted. Tim, Jr., reported they were busy selling clothing. Tim concluded to go around himself.

"Now here, Jake," he said to Jacob Harris, who keeps a store near Walker Street, "you gotta go out an' vote now."

"How can I, Mr. Sullivan," was protested. "I'm waitin' on a customer."

"Yes," responded Dry Dollar, "an' you've been waitin' on him fer two hours. How much are yer dickering over?"

"The gentleman wants it for two dollars less," was explained.

"Well, hully gee!" ejaculated Tim, "is that all? I'll pay the difference."

The Republican inspector had not yet voted. Tim looked in at him wistfully. Then he whistled to him and made a frantic endeavor to coax him out into the street, but the inspector was not in the market. A few minutes later he cast his ballot for Harrison and the agony was over.

"Now look here, Tim," consoled Florry, "wot's the use o' gettin' huffy over four votes? Those ducks couldn't get out of it. They had to vote for Harrison."

"I know," admitted Tim; "but it's pretty tough to come so near carryin' th' distric' unanimous, an' have four stubborn ducks hold out like that."

Judge Patrick Divver, when seen by a *World* reporter, said:

"Yes, Tim did first rate. He did all that could be expected of him. That boy's a good politician, and when he gets older he'll be a wonder."

Source: "How Tim Got the Votes," *New York World*, November 10, 1892.

17.6   *TAMMANY TIMES,* "AND REFORM MOVES ON" (1895)

In 1894, New York City reformers drove Tammany Hall from power and installed a Republican coalition. It only lasted a single term. When the new police commissioner, Theodore Roosevelt, began enforcing the state law forbidding the sale of alcohol on Sunday, his actions split working-class and immigrant voters from middle-class and native-born ones. The man with the "growler"—the bucket in which workers collected beer to consume on the job—narrowed all reform down to the narrow-mindedness of the prohibitionists. Tammany Hall had a winning issue and knew it, as these lyrics show, set to the tune of a popular favorite, "And the Band Played On."

New York on Sunday is awfully dry,
And Reform moves on,
Can't open the side-door, police standing by,
And Reform moves on.
The growler gets rusty, our throats are so dusty—
Oh dear, when will this end?—
When Roosevelt's dead or tucked snugly in bed,
As Reform moves on.
One Sunday our Roosevelt rode all over town,
When Reform moved on,
For side doors wide open he looked up and down,
As Reform moved on.
They say he was looking to have them closed up, but I'll give you a tip,
He simply was dry and he'd drink on the sly,
As Reform moves on.

Source: Tammany Times, November 18, 1895.

Industry and Empire
1890–1900

< The Rough Riders

J. P. Morgan

It was a short distance from the Arlington Hotel to the White House, and although it was icy and dark, J. Pierpont Morgan chose to walk. He pulled his scarf up around a scowling face known to millions of newspaper readers. He had not wanted to come to Washington. There were "large interests" that depended on keeping the currency of the United States sound, he told a Treasury official, and those interests were now in jeopardy. The commander in chief of the nation's bankers was going to meet the president to keep the United States from going bankrupt.

The events leading up to this meeting stretched back five years to 1890, when business failures toppled London's Baring Brothers investment house and triggered a collapse in European stock prices. Depression spread through Britain, Germany, and France. Anxious European investors began selling off their large American holdings. In early 1893, the panic reached the United States. The Philadelphia and Reading Railroad folded in February. Fourteen thousand businesses soon followed, along with more than 600 banks.

Summer brought more bad news from abroad. The government of India stopped minting silver, causing US silver dollars to lose one-sixth of their value. Wall Street went into another tailspin. In New York, 55,000 men, women, and girls in the clothing industry were thrown out of work. Banks refused to cash checks, and coins vanished from circulation. Tens of thousands of homeless poor people filled the roads. Breadlines formed. "The world surely cannot remain as mad as it is," the historian Henry Adams observed.

For Grover Cleveland the madness was only starting. The anger of workers and farmers, simmering for decades, was boiling over. The president pledged to keep the dollar on the **gold standard**, but it was not enough. A wave of strikes swept the country. Unemployed workers battled police on the Capitol grounds. By January 1895 so many panicky investors were cashing government bonds that the Treasury's gold reserve was half gone, and it looked as if the remainder might last only two weeks. Reluctantly, Cleveland agreed to open negotiations with Morgan.

Admired and reviled, Morgan was known as the leading financial manipulator of the late nineteenth century. Born to wealth in Hartford, Connecticut, he had been a Wall Street fixture since before the Civil War. Like two of his contemporaries, steelmaker Andrew Carnegie and oil magnate John D. Rockefeller, Morgan's skill lay in organization. He restructured railroads, rooting out corruption, waste, and competition and driving down wages. Instead of taking risks, he eliminated them. He convinced leaders of warring firms to strike bargains and share the profits. Cleveland was about to place the Treasury in this man's hands.

The president opened the meeting by suggesting that things might not be so bad; a new bond issue might stabilize the dollar. No, Morgan replied flatly, the run on gold would continue until European investors regained confidence.

If the president agreed, Morgan would arrange a private loan and personally guarantee the solvency of the US Treasury. After a stunned silence, the two men shook hands. News of the deal instantly calmed the bond markets. The crisis was over. The *New York Sun* reported that the deal "revived a confidence in the wealth and resources of this country," but Populist newspapers denounced it as a conspiracy and a "great bunco game."

Culminating two decades of turbulence, the Panic of 1893 permanently transformed the American political economy. Businessmen such as Morgan created even larger corporate combinations and placed them under professional managers. They used technology and "scientific management" to control the workplace and push laborers to work faster and harder. Workers resisted, and the 1890s saw brutal clashes between capital and labor. Looking for jobs and schools, country people moved to the city and found both promise and danger. Social mobility among African Americans aroused fears in whites, and southerners created a system of formal segregation, enforced by law and terror. Amid growing violence, industrial workers, Native Americans, and African Americans debated how best to deal with the overwhelming forces ranged against them.

The 1890s were also a turning point in American political history. After the 1896 election, many Americans walked away from the electoral process. Others were removed from the voter rolls through a process known as "disfranchisement." African American leaders and union organizers urged their followers to turn away from politics in favor of "bread-and-butter" economic issues. The masculine, public spectacle of nineteenth-century politics with its parades and flag raisings died out. Patriotism, once synonymous with partisanship, now stood for America's global military and economic ambitions. Civic events featured army bands and cannon salutes. Newspapers conjured up foreign threats. As Americans became more conscious of their military power, they watched the horizon for threats to their well-being.

Americans began to feel that their economy's links to the world—and the changes wrought by manufacturing and rapid communications—separated their times from all that had happened before. Morgan's rescue required transactions on two continents, instantaneously coordinated by telegraph. The speed of industry, trade, and information and the way carbon technologies spanned distance and time created a sense that the environment and the future could be controlled. Many felt that those who possessed this newfound control—citizens of modern countries—stood apart from those in other lands whose lives were not guided by science and information.

Between 1890 and 1900 Americans made their country recognizably modern. Those with the means to do so enlarged and refashioned many aspects of work and daily life. Financiers and giant corporations assumed control of the economy. Huge cities grew. The significance of voting declined, and a decade that opened with a global economic catastrophe ended with a dramatic display of the global reach of US power.

THE CRISIS OF THE 1890s

Financial convulsions, strikes, and the powerlessness of government against wealth rudely reminded Americans of how much their country had changed since the Civil War. When Illinois sent Abraham Lincoln to Congress, Chicago's population was less than 5,000; in 1890, it exceeded 1 million. Gone was the America of myth and memory, in which class tensions were slight and upward (or at least westward) and mobility seemed easy. Many Americans foresaw the collapse of civilization. Others, however, felt that the United States was passing into a new phase of history that would lead to still greater trials and achievements.

Hard Times and Demands for Help

Chicago in 1893 captured the hopes and fears of the new age. To celebrate the 400th anniversary of Columbus's discovery of America, the city staged the World's Columbian Exposition, transforming a lakefront bog into a gleaming vision of the past and the future. Just outside the exposition's gates was the city of the present. In December 1893, Chicago had 75,000 unemployed, and the head of a local relief committee declared that "famine is in our midst." In the nation's second-largest city, thousands lived in shacks or high-rise tenements with only a single bathroom on each densely packed floor. Jobs were scarce, and when men gathered at the exposition's gates to beg for work, the police drove them away.

As the depression deepened, the Cleveland administration ordered troops to guard Treasury branches in New York and Chicago. Jobless people banded together into "industrial armies," many with decidedly revolutionary aims. Hundreds heeded the call of Jacob Coxey, an Ohio landowner and Populist. In 1894, Coxey urged the unemployed to march on Washington and demand free silver and a public road-building program that would hire a half-million workers. When Coxey set out with 100 followers, reporters predicted the ragged band would disintegrate as soon as food ran out, but well-wishers turned out by the thousands to greet the Coxeyites with supplies for the trip.

Industrial armies set out from Boston, St. Louis, Chicago, Portland, Seattle, and Los Angeles. When Coxey arrived in Washington on May 1 with 500 marchers, Cleveland put the US Army on alert. The march ended ignominiously. In front of the Capitol, police arrested Coxey, and his disillusioned army dispersed. Still, no one could deny that something was seriously wrong and that, as Ray Stannard Baker, a reporter for the *Chicago Record*, noted, "the conditions in the country warranted some such explosion."

The Overseas Frontier

At noon on September 16, 1893, thousands of settlers massed along the borders of the Cherokee Strip, a 6-million-acre tract in northwestern Oklahoma. In the next six hours the last great land rush came to an end, and the line of settlement long marked on census maps ceased to exist.

Frederick Jackson Turner, a historian at the University of Wisconsin, described the implications of this event. Steady westward movement had placed Americans in "touch with the simplicity of primitive life," he explained, and helped renew the process of social development. The frontier furnished "the forces dominating the American character," and without its rejuvenating influence, democracy itself might be in danger. Turner's thesis resonated with Americans' fears that modernity had robbed their country of its unique strengths and that the end of free lands would put free institutions at risk. "There is no unexplored part of the world left suitable for men to inhabit," Populist writer William "Coin" Harvey claimed.

That assertion turned out to be premature. More homesteaders claimed more western lands after 1890 than before, and well into the next century new "resource frontiers"—oil fields, timber ranges, Alaskan ore strikes—were explored. Irrigation technology and markets for new crops created a boom for dry-land farmers. Nonetheless, the upheavals of the 1890s seemed to confirm Turner's contention that new frontiers lay overseas.

Whereas farmers had always needed to sell a large portion of their output abroad, until the 1890s the market for manufactured goods was almost exclusively domestic. As the volume of manufactured goods increased, the composition of exports changed. Oil, steel, textiles, typewriters, and sewing machines made up a larger portion of overseas trade. Americans still bought nine-tenths of domestic manufactures, but by 1898 the extra tenth was worth more than $1 billion (see Figure 18–1).

As American firms entered foreign markets, they discovered that other nations and empires also used restrictive tariffs to guard their markets and promote domestic manufacturing. Government and business leaders saw that the United States might have to use political or military leverage to open foreign markets to gain a larger share of world trade. Their social Darwinist view of the world—as a jungle in which only the fittest nations would survive—justified the global competition for trade and economic survival.

Recognizing that a strong navy could extend America's economic reach, Congress authorized the construction of three large battleships in 1890. Four years later, an official commission investigated the feasibility of a canal across Central America. A newly organized National Association of Manufacturers urged the government to open foreign markets. The administration created a Bureau of Foreign Commerce and urged US consuls to seize opportunities to extend sales of American industrial products abroad.

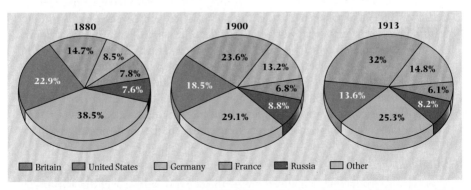

Figure 18–1 Relative Shares of World Manufacturing The United States was a significant industrial power by 1880, and by the turn of the century it moved into a position of dominance.

Congress also knew that tariff rates could influence the expansion of trade. Before 1890, taxes on imports had been set high to raise revenue and to help domestic manufacturers by making foreign goods unaffordable. The Harrison-McKinley Tariff of 1890 did something different. It allowed the president to use the tariff to punish countries that closed their markets to US goods or to reward them for lifting customs barriers. This "bargaining tariff" used the weight of the US economy to open markets around the world.

The United States began reorganizing to compete in a global marketplace. The struggle required the executive branch to enlarge the military and take on additional authority. It also meant that domestic industries had to produce higher quality goods at reduced cost to match those from Germany or Japan. Employers and workers had to gear up for the global contest for profits.

The Drive for Efficiency

In mines, factories, and mills, production relied on the knowledge of skilled workers. Laborers used their knowledge to set work routines, assure their own safety, and bargain with managers who wanted to change the nature of work. As profits stagnated and competition intensified, employers tried to prevent labor from sharing control over production. Employers relied on three allies: technology, scientific management, and federal power. Workers resisted, organizing themselves and enlisting the support of their communities.

Advances in management techniques enabled employers to dictate new methods. Frederick Winslow Taylor, the first "efficiency expert," reduced each occupation to a series of simple, precise movements that could be easily taught and endlessly repeated. To manage time and motion scientifically, Taylor explained, employers should convert traditional workplace skills and knowledge into "rules, laws, and formulae."

Taylor's stopwatch studies determined everything from how much pig iron a man should load into a boxcar in a day (75 tons) to how he should be paid (3.75 cents per ton). Even office work could be separated into simple, unvaried tasks. "Taylorism" created a new layer of college-educated "middle managers" who supervised production in offices and factories.

Although Taylorism accelerated production, it also increased absenteeism and worker dissatisfaction. Another new technique, "personnel management," promised to solve this problem with tests to select suitable employees, team sports to ward off boredom, and social workers to regulate the activities of workers at home.

As the nineteenth century ended, management was establishing a monopoly on expertise and using it to set the rhythms of work and play, but workers did not easily relinquish control. In the 1890s, the labor struggle entered a new phase. New unions confronted corporations in bloody struggles that forced the federal government to decide whether communities or property had more rights. Skilled workers rallied the labor movement to the cause of retaining control of the conditions of work.

The Struggle Between Management and Labor

To accelerate production, employers aimed to seize full control over the workplace. They had private detective agencies, the courts, and federal troops on their side and were ready to act. In Pennsylvania and Chicago, this antagonism led to bloody confrontations.

The most modern steelworks in the world, Andrew Carnegie's mill at Homestead, Pennsylvania made armor plating for American warships and steel rails for shipment abroad. In June 1892, Carnegie's partner, Henry Clay Frick, broke off talks with the plant's American Federation of Labor–affiliated union and announced that the plant would close on July 2 and reopen a week later with a nonunion workforce. The union contended that Frick's actions were an assault on the community, and the town agreed. On the morning of July 6, townspeople equipped with a cannon confronted 300 armed company guards and forced them to surrender.

The victory was short-lived. A week later the governor of Pennsylvania sent in the state militia, and under martial law strikebreakers reignited the furnaces. The battle at Homestead broke the union and showed that corporations, backed by government, would defend their prerogatives at any cost.

The **Pullman strike,** centered in Chicago, paralyzed the railroads for two weeks in the summer of 1894. It pitted the American Railway Union (ARU) against 24 railroads and the powerful Pullman Company over the company's decision to cut pay by 30 percent, an action taken in response to the economic crisis of 1893. Eugene V. Debs, the charismatic president of the ARU, urged strikers to obey the law, avoid violence, and respect strikebreakers. When Cleveland sent in the army over the governor's protests, enraged crowds blocked tracks and burned railroad cars. Police arrested hundreds of strikers. Debs went to jail for six months and came

Pullman Strike After President Cleveland sent troops to end the Pullman Strike and restore rail travel, American Railway Union workers destroyed hundreds of railcars in Chicago.

out a socialist. Pullman and Homestead showed that the law was now on the side of the proprietors.

Newspapers, magazines, and novels portrayed Pullman and Homestead as two more battles in an unending war against the savage opponents of progress, with the forces of government rescuing civilization from the unions.

The business elite's cultural influence allowed it to define the terms of this contest, to label its enemies as enemies of progress. Workers did not object to efficiency or modernization, but they wanted a share of its benefits and some control over the process of change. With state and corporate power stacked against them, their goals appeared beyond reach.

Just as the massacre at Wounded Knee in 1890 had ended the armed resistance of Native Americans, the violence at Homestead and Chicago marked a new phase in the struggle of industrial workers.

Corporate Consolidation

In a wave of mergers between 1897 and 1904, investment bankers consolidated leading industries under the control of a few corporate giants, and J. P. Morgan led the movement. His goal was to take industry away from the industrialists and give it to the bankers. Bankers, he felt, had better information about the true worth of an industry and so could make better decisions about its future. They could create the larger, leaner firms needed to take on foreign competitors.

Morgan's greatest triumph was the merger of eight huge steel companies, their ore ranges, rolling mills, railroads, and shipping lines into the colossal US Steel. The 1901 merger created the world's largest corporation. Its capital amounted to 7 percent of the total wealth of the United States (by comparison, the largest US firm in 2008, Exxon Mobil, had assets valued at only six-tenths of 1 percent of gross domestic product). US Steel's investors (Morgan especially) earned profits "greatly in excess of reasonable compensation," according to one government report.

Bankers outnumbered steelmakers on US Steel's board, and they controlled the company. *McClure's* magazine reported that the new company was "planning the first really systematic effort ever made by Americans to capture the foreign steel trade."

A MODERN ECONOMY

Grover Cleveland's bargain with Morgan revived the industrial economy, but farm prices, wages, and the president's popularity remained flat. Cash-strapped farmers in the West and South disliked the president's hard-money policies and cozy relationships with plutocrats such as Morgan. Calling out troops to crush the Pullman strike cost Cleveland the support of northern workers. The escalating cycle of economic and political crises, farmer and labor insurgencies, middle-class radicalism, and upper-class conservatism fractured political parties. Democrats, Republicans, and Populists all called for stronger government action, but each party split over what action to take. In 1896, the "currency question" dominated a watershed election that transformed the two major parties and destroyed the third.

The year 1896 was the last time presidential candidates openly debated great economic questions in terms that had been familiar to voters since Thomas Jefferson ran for president in 1800; 1896 was also the first recognizably modern presidential election, the first time a successful candidate used the advertising and fund-raising techniques of twentieth-century campaigns.

Currency: Gold Versus Silver

The soundness of the dollar, which Morgan and Cleveland worked so hard to preserve, was a mixed blessing for Americans. Based on gold, the dollar helped sell American goods in foreign markets, especially in Europe, where currencies were also based on gold. The United States traded on a much smaller scale with countries—such as Mexico and China—that used silver. Gold, however, was valuable because it was scarce, and many Americans suffered from that scarcity. The low prices and high interest rates Populists complained of were a result of the gold standard.

Increasing the money supply would reduce interest rates and make credit more available. There were two ways to put more money in circulation: the government could print paper greenbacks, or it could coin silver. "Free silver" advocates generally favored coining a ratio of 16 ounces of silver for each ounce of gold. Both Populists and western mining interests pushed silver. The Republican and Democratic Parties officially endorsed the gold standard, but by 1896 each party had a renegade faction of silverites. In the 1890s, the crucial political issues—jobs, foreign trade, the survival of small farms, and the prosperity of big corporations—boiled down to one question: Would the dollar be backed by gold or silver? The election of 1896 was "the battle of the standards."

The Cross of Gold

A dark mood hung over Chicago as delegates arrived at the Democratic convention in July 1896. They had come to bury Cleveland and the party's commitment to the gold standard along with him. The draft platform denounced Cleveland for imposing "government by injunction" during the Pullman strike. When the platform came before the full convention, delegates had to decide whether the party would stand for silver or gold and who would replace Cleveland as the candidate for president.

Both questions were decided when a former congressman from Nebraska, William Jennings Bryan, mounted the stage. He was an electrifying speaker. "You come and tell us that the great cities are in favor of the gold standard," he said. "Destroy our farms, and the grass will grow in the streets of every city in the country!" Bryan spoke in the rhythmic cadence of a camp preacher. "We will answer their demand for a gold standard by saying to them"—he paused, stretching out his arms in an attitude of crucifixion—"You shall not press down upon the brow of labor this crown of thorns. You shall not crucify mankind upon a cross of gold!" The hall exploded with cheers. Bryan won the nomination handily.

Two weeks later the Populists, meeting in St. Louis, also nominated Bryan. The Ocala and Omaha platforms, which imagined comprehensive changes in the money system and American institutions, had been reduced to a single panacea: silver. Republicans overwhelmingly adopted a pro-gold plank, drafted with the approval of J. P. Morgan, and nominated William McKinley, the governor of Ohio and a supporter of industry. The parties could hardly have offered two more different candidates or two more different visions of the future.

The Battle of the Standards

In one of the most exciting electoral contests since the Civil War, the candidates employed new techniques in radically different ways. McKinley ran like an incumbent: he never left his home. Instead, delegations came to him. Some 750,000 people from 30 states trampled McKinley's grass and listened to speeches affirming his commitment to high tariffs and sound money. The speeches were distributed as newspaper columns, fliers, and pamphlets across the country. The campaign used public relations techniques to educate the electorate on the virtues of the gold standard. Posters reduced the campaign's themes to pithy slogans like "Prosperity or Poverty" and "Vote for Free Silver and Be Prosperous Like Guatemala."

The genius behind the campaign was a Cleveland coal-and-oil millionaire named Marcus Hanna who bankrolled his publicity blitz with between $3 million and $7 million raised from industrialists. The combination of big money and advertising revolutionized presidential politics.

With only $300,000 to spend, Bryan ran like a challenger, even though his party occupied the White House. He logged 29,000 miles by rail and buggy and made more than 500 speeches in 29 states. Oratorical ability had won Bryan the nomination, but audiences were unaccustomed to hearing a candidate speak for himself, and many considered it undignified. "The Boy Orator has one speech," wrote an unsympathetic Republican, John Hay. "He simply reiterates the unquestioned truths that gold is vile, that silver is lovely and holy."

Despite the scorn of eastern newspapers, industrialists feared the prospect of a Bryan presidency. Factory owners threatened to close shop if Bryan won. Just before Election Day, the global markets that McKinley praised returned the favor. Crop failures abroad doubled the price of wheat in the Midwest, raising farm incomes and alleviating the anxieties that drove farmers to Bryan. Bryan won the South and West decisively, but McKinley won the populous industrial Northeast and several farm states in the upper Midwest, capturing the Electoral College by 271 to 176 (see Map 18–1).

The election of 1896 changed the style of campaigns and shifted the political positions of both major parties. By pushing currency policies to improve the lives of workers and farmers, Bryan's Democrats abandoned their traditional Jacksonian commitment to minimal government. The Republicans recognized that voters would judge the president on his ability to bring them prosperity. Electoral democracy now had a distinctly economic cast. As president, McKinley asserted his leadership over economic policy, calling Congress into special session to pass the Dingley Tariff Act, which levied the highest taxes on imports in American history. He extended presidential power even more dramatically through an expansionist foreign and military policy.

In the election of 1896, basic economic questions—Who is the economy supposed to serve? What is the nature of money?—were at stake in a closely matched campaign. No wonder voter turnout hit an all-time high. Administrative agencies took over those issues after the turn of the century, but Americans long

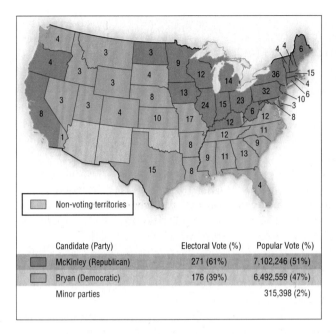

Map 18–1 The Election of 1896
William McKinley's "front-porch campaign" carried the northern industrial states, along with the key farm states of Iowa and Minnesota, securing a narrow victory over Bryan.

Candidate (Party)	Electoral Vote (%)	Popular Vote (%)
McKinley (Republican)	271 (61%)	7,102,246 (51%)
Bryan (Democratic)	176 (39%)	6,492,559 (47%)
Minor parties		315,398 (2%)

remembered that raucous campaign when the nation's economic future was up for grabs. As late as the 1960s, schoolchildren still recited the Cross of Gold speech.

THE RETREAT FROM POLITICS

The economy improved steadily after 1895, but this latest business panic left lasting marks on corporate and political culture. Industrial workers made a tactical retreat in the face of a new political and legal climate. In the South, depression, urbanization, and the modernizing influence of railroads accelerated the spread of legalized racial segregation and disfranchisement. What was happening in the South and the nation was part of a nationwide decline of participatory politics. With the slackening of both agrarian unrest and resistance to corporate capitalism, politics lost some of its value. Voter participation declined, and Americans felt less of a personal stake in elections. Disaffected groups—such as labor and African Americans—had to devise new ways to build community and express resistance.

The Lure of the Cities

In the South as in the North, people left the countryside and moved to towns and cities. By 1900, one out of six southerners lived in town. Except for Birmingham, Alabama, southern cities were not devoted to manufacturing but to commerce and services. Doctors' offices, clothing and dry goods stores, and groceries could be

American Landscape

Galveston, Texas, 1900

Looking back, many survivors would remember warning signs: an unusual stillness in the Gulf of Mexico, lightning flashes in a clear sky. But when the winds began to pick up early in the morning on September 8, 1900, the residents of Galveston believed their solid slate-roofed homes would protect them from what turned out to be the deadliest storm in American history.

Galveston was a Gilded Age boomtown, the "New York of the Gulf." Sited like Manhattan on an island at the mouth of a deep-water bay, it was Texas's principal port. Railroads brought cotton and cattle from San Antonio, Dallas, and Fort Worth to the wharves, where they met steamships from Hamburg, Cartagena, and Marseille. Galveston was a major arrival point for immigrants, who had their papers and throats checked at Pelican Island before setting foot in a land advertised as exuberantly fertile. Alongside hotels, offices, boutiques, and the Grand Opera House on the Strand were the consulates of 16 countries, including Russia and Japan.

Like many American cities, Galveston was ostensibly governed by a mayor and a council, comprised of aldermen elected by each of the 12 wards, but an elite of wealthy brokers and merchants maintained the city's dominance through private monopolies. The Galveston Wharf Company charged outrageous port fees and steered trade into the hands of favored clients. The Cotton Exchange set prices for the region's principal crop. Economics and politics were a kind of competition; for boosters it was not enough for Galveston to be prosperous; it also had to trounce its rival, Houston. Traders on the powerful (and unelected) Deepwater Port Commission used their connections to get federal money to dredge the shipping canals, removing protective sandbars and sealing Galveston's lead. Even the weather bureau joined in, playing up the tornado threat to inland cities while dismissing the danger from hurricanes as "an absurd delusion."

Galveston shared the confidence of the country at the dawn of a new century. Leaving the doldrums of the early 1890s, the national economy forged ahead. American armies were victorious in Cuba and Asia, and scientific advances—telecommunications, medicine, steam propulsion, and weather prediction—strengthened a sense that distance, disease, and nature itself could be tamed. Galveston was at the forefront of these changes, the first city in Texas with electric lights and telephones. Its streetcar line defied geography, traveling on elevated trestles over the Gulf itself. The city grew by 30 percent in the previous decade, the Galveston *News* reported on September 7, and "the prospects are bright even to surpass it."

found near warehouses in which cotton was stored, ginned, and pressed and near the railway station, from which it was shipped to textile mills.

The growth of villages and towns in the South was the product of rural decay. Crop liens, which gave bankers ownership of a crop before it was planted, and debt

The 1900 storm was not unprecedented. In 1886, the coastal town of Indianola was wiped out by a hurricane. Still, when the red and black storm flags went up, Galvestonians and the thousands of tourists in town for a weekend at the beach sought shelter in the city rather than escaping to the mainland. It was a fatal choice. The storm surge pulverized the commercial district. The streetcar trestle, lifted by the flood, bulldozed through neighborhoods, smashing houses in its path. Thousands were swept out to sea, while thousands more drowned in the wreckage. The clouds cleared over a ruined city. From one end to the other along the high-water mark stretched a ridge of broken timbers, masonry, furniture, and human and animal corpses.

With hospitals, churches, and city hall destroyed, the victims organized their own relief. Middle- and upper-class women distributed thousands of pounds of supplies from the Red Cross. An ad hoc Women's Health Protective Committee (WHPC) rallied survivors to care for the injured, clear debris, and set up tent cities. Meanwhile, the Deep Water Commission struggled to clear wrecked ships and reopen the port. Together, WHPC and port officials petitioned the legislature to replace the city's elected government with a board of appointed commissioners who would head departments of finance, fire, police, water, sewage, and streets. Democratic institutions were not up to the challenge, they agreed; this emergency required experts.

The commissioner system unmasked the control that brokers and merchants had always had over Galveston's politics, but it also revealed the new power of educated women (who still lacked the vote) and reform groups. The commissioners launched an ambitious reconstruction scheme, beginning with data collection. They carefully mapped currents, wave patterns, and the debris wall, using it to mark the outer limits of new construction. Instead of relocating to the mainland, they laid plans for raising the city 17 feet and placing it behind a three-mile-long concrete seawall to hold back any future storm surge. The WHPC laid out lots for new houses separated by wide, well-drained streets and barriers of vegetation to disrupt flood currents.

Galveston lost the competition to become the state's largest city. The discovery of oil at Spindletop Dome a year later made Houston the next boomtown. But the commissioner system became a model of progressive reform imitated by over 500 cities, mostly in the Midwest. The "Galveston Plan" offered a cure for the corruption of urban machines. Commissioners agreed that "economy and business methods, not politics" should be the ruling principle. While efficient, it was also undemocratic. Only two members of the board were elected; the rest were appointed by the legislature. None were African American, despite Black majorities in two of the wards. Residents were grateful for the speedy action, but uneasy about the new order. "Commission government is far from a perfect plan," wrote a journalist who survived the disaster; "it only marks a transition toward better things."

drove people from farms. The young and the ambitious left first, while older and poorer residents stayed behind.

While white newcomers settled on the outskirts, African Americans moved into industrial districts along the railroad tracks. Still, towns offered things that were missing in the country, such as schools. A Little Rock, Arkansas, resident noted that newly arrived African American parents were "very anxious to send their children to school." Jobs were often available, too, although more frequently for women than for men. Men looked for seasonal labor at farms or lumber camps outside towns. This meant families faced a tough choice between poverty and separation.

Despite setbacks, newcomers gained a place for themselves in urban life. By 1890, every southern city had an African American business district with churches, insurance companies, lawyers, doctors, undertakers, and usually a weekly newspaper. Benevolent and reform organizations, sewing circles, and book clubs enriched community life. African American professionals such as lawyers, doctors, and nurses were limited to working within their community. Jobs on the bottom rung of the corporate ladder—clerk, salesman, telephone operator, stenographer, railroad conductor—were reserved for whites.

Inventing Jim Crow

In June 1892, **Homer Plessy** boarded the East Louisiana Railway in New Orleans for a trip to Covington, Louisiana. Having purchased a first-class ticket, he attempted to board the whites-only car and was arrested under a Louisiana law that required African Americans and whites to ride in "equal but separate accommodations." Before Judge John H. Ferguson could try the case, Plessy's lawyer appealed on the grounds that the separate-car law violated the Constitution's Fourteenth Amendment.

When *Plessy v. Ferguson* came before the Supreme Court in April 1896, the State of Louisiana argued that the law was necessary to avoid the "danger of friction from too intimate contact" between the races. In separate cars, all citizens enjoyed equal privileges. Plessy's lawyer, Albion Tourgée, replied that the question was not "the equality of the privileges enjoyed, but the right of the state to label one citizen as white and another as colored." In doing so, the government gave unearned advantages to some citizens and not to others. The issue for Tourgée was not racial conflict or even prejudice, but whether the government should be allowed to divide people arbitrarily. The court upheld the "**separate but equal**" doctrine, and the decision provided legal justification for the system of official inequality that expanded in the twentieth century. Informal **segregation** had existed since the Civil War, and unwritten local customs usually governed the public interaction of whites and African Americans—at work, in business, or when traveling. By the 1890s those informal customs were being codified in law. Railroads, as symbols of progress, were a chief point of contention.

The political and economic tensions created by the depression helped turn racist customs into a rigid caste division. Competition for jobs fed racial antagonisms, as did the migration into cities and towns of a new generation of African Americans, born since the Civil War, who showed less deference to whites. New notions of "scientific" racism led intellectuals and churchmen to regard racial hostility as natural. Angry southern voters deposed the governing coalitions of landowners and New South industrialists and replaced them with Populist "demagogues."

Lynchings Were Public Spectacles When 17-year-old Jesse Washington was killed in Waco, Texas, in 1916, a crowd of several thousand, including the mayor, police chief, and students from Waco High, attended the event on the lawn of city hall. Afterward, the murderers posed for a photograph and sold their victim's teeth for $5 apiece.

Between 1887 and 1891, nine states in the South passed railroad segregation laws. Trains included separate cars for African Americans, called "Jim Crow" cars after the name of a character in a minstrel show. Soon Jim Crow laws were extended to waiting rooms, drinking fountains, and other places where African Americans and whites might meet.

Segregation was also enforced by terror. The threat of lynching poisoned relations between the races, and African Americans learned that they could be tortured and killed for committing a crime, talking back, or simply looking the wrong way at a white woman. Between 1882 and 1903, nearly 2,000 African American southerners were killed by mobs. Victims were routinely tortured, flayed, castrated, gouged, and burned alive, and members of the mob often took home grisly souvenirs such as a piece of bone or a severed thumb.

Many African American southerners fought segregation with boycotts, lawsuits, and disobedience. Ida Wells-Barnett, a Nashville journalist, organized an international antilynching campaign (see Chapter 19). Segregation was constantly negotiated and challenged, but after 1896 it was backed by the US Supreme Court.

The Atlanta Compromise

When Atlanta invited African American educator Booker T. Washington to address the Cotton States Exposition in 1895, northern newspapers proclaimed a new era of racial progress. The speech made Washington the most recognized African American in the United States. Starting with 40 students and an abandoned shack, Washington had built Tuskegee Institute into the preeminent technical school for African Americans. Washington was a guest in the stately homes of Newport and at Andrew Carnegie's castle in Scotland. When Atlanta staged an exposition to showcase the region's industrial and social progress, the organizers asked Washington to speak.

Washington's address stressed racial accommodation. It had been a mistake, he argued, to try to attain equality by asserting civil and political rights, and he stated that progress "must be the result of severe and constant struggle rather than artificial forcing." He urged white businessmen to employ African American

Struggles For Democracy

The Wilmington Race Riot

In 1894, the Populist-Republican "Fusion" ticket won both houses of the North Carolina General Assembly, the powerful state legislature. Fusion officials, anxious to overturn the machine style politics the Democratic Party had established since Reconstruction, set to restoring direct power to the people of North Carolina. Eliminating policies that benefited the white elite at the expense of the farming poor, unskilled labor, and Black southerners, Fusionists terminated official appointments and made all positions subject to local election. They enacted new electoral laws and registration practices to encourage Black voting. By 1896, the Fusionists, with their focus on class rather than racial solidarity, won every statewide race in North Carolina, and Daniel L. Russell, a Republican, was elected governor. A new brand of truly democratic politics seemed to be on the horizon.

Wilmington, the largest city in North Carolina, had a majority Black population and had long been known for the political and economic opportunities it afforded African Americans. But in 1897, when city elections resulted in a Fusionist mayor and several Fusionist aldermen, the tide turned. Anxious at the results achieved by the Populist-Republican pairing, Democratic Party leaders were determined to redeem themselves politically. Embracing the language of "Negro rule" to frighten white voters and "white supremacy" to encourage racial solidarity, Democrats drew a sharp color line among voters, a strategy that coincided with the Jim Crow system of segregation that was rapidly spreading throughout the South.

A public exchange over the question of lynching and interracial relations galvanized the Democratic Party. In August 1897, Rebecca Felton, a Georgia feminist and white supremacist, declared the Black rapist to be among the greatest threats faced by southern white farm women. She demanded that white men use vigilante justice to protect the virtue of their women. If necessary, men should be prepared to "lynch a thousand times a week." Alexander Manly, a Black Wilmingtonian and editor of the only Black-owned daily newspaper in the nation, the *Daily Record*, responded with an editorial in August 1898 in which he defended Black men and attempted to dismantle the myth of the Black sexual aggressor. He argued that rape claims against Black men were exaggerated and that the majority of sexual relations between Black men and white women were consensual.

This enraged white southerners. In the aftermath of the Manly editorial, a radical white supremacist faction of the Democratic Party, the Red Shirts, began a campaign of fear and coercion. In October 1898, the Red Shirts terrorized interracial political alliances across eastern North Carolina

southerners "who have, without strikes and labor wars, tilled your fields, cleared your forests, builded your railroads and cities." Stretching out his fingers and then closing them into a fist, he summarized his approach to race relations: "In all things that are purely social, we can be as separate as the fingers, yet one as

Wilmington White citizens stand before the destroyed *Daily Record* office, 1898.

by breaking up political meetings, destroying property, and committing violent acts. Their goal: keep Republican and Populist voters—especially Black voters—from going to the polls. The night before the election, Wilmington Democratic Party leader Colonel Alfred Moor Waddell instructed a mass meeting of white citizens "Go to the polls tomorrow, and if you find the negro out voting, tell him to leave the polls, and if he refuses, kill him."

Democrats' tactics (including stuffed ballots and voter fraud) succeeded, and their candidates secured offices throughout the state. But many of those who had reclaimed Democratic seats in Wilmington were unwilling to accept Fusionists as their peers and colleagues. On November 9, the day after Election Day, a mass meeting of white Wilmingtonians adopted a Wilmington Declaration of Independence, which claimed white supremacy as a right, called for an end to Black political participation and interracial politics, and demanded the expulsion of Manly from Wilmington (he had already left).

When Black Wilmingtonians responded too slowly to the demands of the Declaration, the white citizenry was all too ready to strike. On November 10, armed, anxious white men filled the Wilmington armory; an early procession of about 500 men grew to 2,000. The first target was Manly's *Daily Record*. A mob ransacked the offices and torched the building. As the crowd marched into one of Wilmington's Black neighborhoods, they used repeating rifles to outgun the Black men who attempted to defend their property. Hundreds of Black citizens escaped Wilmington, hoping to wait out the riot. The number of Black deaths remains unknown; most estimates range from 7 to 20.

Those leading the insurrection demanded the resignation of Fusionist officials and then took power for themselves. Political opponents of the rioters were run out of the city. Over the course of the next month, 1,400 African Americans fled Wilmington. No one in Wilmington spoke out against the rioters and no outside forces came to the aid of Black citizens. The tactics used in Wilmington spread a clear message throughout the Jim Crow South: those challenging a political system based on white supremacy and elite rule would suffer the consequences.

the hand in all things essential to mutual progress." The largely white audience erupted into applause.

Washington's "**Atlanta Compromise**" stressed the mutual obligations of African Americans and whites. African Americans would give up the vote and stop insisting on social equality if white leaders would keep violence in check and allow African Americans to succeed in agriculture and business. White industrialists welcomed this arrangement, and African American leaders felt that for the moment it might be the best that could be achieved.

Disfranchisement and the Decline of Popular Politics

After the feverish campaign of 1896, elections began to lose some of their appeal. Attendance fell off at the polls, from 79 percent of voters in 1888 down to 65 percent in 1896. The public events surrounding campaigns also drew thinner crowds, and apathy seemed to have become a national epidemic.

In the South, the disappearance of voters was easy to explain. As Jim Crow laws multiplied, southern states disfranchised African Americans (and one out of four whites) by requiring voters to demonstrate literacy, property ownership, or knowledge of the Constitution in order to register. Louisiana added the notorious grandfather clause, which denied the vote to men whose grandfathers had been prohibited from voting (see Table 18–1).

Whites saw **disfranchisement** and segregation as modern, managed race relations. Demonizing African Americans enforced solidarity among white voters otherwise divided by local or class interests.

No new legal restrictions hampered voting in the North and West, but participation fell there, too. This withdrawal from politics reflected the declining importance of political pageantry and the disappearance of intense partisanship. A developing economy with new patterns of social and cultural life undermined partisanship, but so did the new style of campaigns. For American men, the cliffhanger contests of the late nineteenth century had provided a sense of identity that strengthened ethnic, religious, and neighborhood identities.

Table 18–1 The Spread of Disfranchisement

Year	State	Strategies
1889	Florida	Poll tax
1889	Tennessee	Poll tax
1890	Mississippi	Poll tax, literacy test, understanding clause
1891	Arkansas	Poll tax
1893, 1901	Alabama	Poll tax, literacy test, grandfather clause
1894, 1895	South Carolina	Poll tax, literacy test, understanding clause
1894, 1902	Virginia	Poll tax, literacy test, understanding clause
1897, 1898	Louisiana	Poll tax, literacy test, grandfather clause
1899, 1900	North Carolina	Poll tax, literacy test, grandfather clause
1902	Texas	Poll tax
1908	Georgia	Poll tax, literacy test, understanding clause, grandfather clause

The new emphasis on advertising, education, and fund-raising reduced the personal stakes for voters. Educated middle- and upper-class voters liked the new style, feeling that raucous campaigns were no way to decide important issues. They sought to influence policy more directly, through interest groups rather than parties. Unintentionally, they discarded traditions that unified communities and connected voters to their country and its leaders.

Organized Labor Retreats from Politics

Workers followed organized labor as it turned away from political activity and redefined objectives in economic terms. As traditional crafts came under attack, skilled workers created new organizations that addressed immediate issues: wages, hours, and the conditions of work. The American Federation of Labor (AFL), founded in 1886, built a base around skilled trades and grew from 150,000 members to more than 2 million by 1904. The AFL focused on immediate goals to improve the working lives of its members. Its founder, **Samuel Gompers**, was born in London's East End and apprenticed as a cigar maker at the age of 10. After his family moved to New York, Gompers joined the Cigar Makers' International Union.

Although affiliated with the Knights of Labor, the cigar makers were more interested in shortening work hours and increasing wages than in remaking the economy. High dues and centralized control allowed the union to offer insurance and death benefits to members while maintaining a strike fund. Gompers applied the same practices to the AFL. His "pure and simple unionism" made modest demands, but it still encountered fierce resistance from corporations, which were backed by the courts.

In the 1895 case of *In re Debs*, the Supreme Court allowed the use of injunctions to criminalize strikes. The court then disarmed one of labor's last weapons, the boycott. In *Loewe v. Lawlor* (1908), known as the Danbury Hatters case, the court ruled that advertising a consumer boycott was illegal under the Sherman Anti-Trust Act.

Gompers believed that industrial unions, which drew members from all occupations within an industry, lacked the discipline and shared values needed to face down corporations and government, whereas unions organized around a single trade or craft would be stronger. However, because the AFL was organized by skill, it often ignored unskilled workers, such as women or recent immigrants. Because employers used unskilled newcomers to break strikes or to run machinery that replaced expert hands, Gompers excluded a large part of the labor force. Organizers recruited Irish and German workers while ignoring Italian, African American, Jewish, and Slavic workers. The union attacked female workers for "stealing" jobs that once belonged to men.

Other unions were built to represent the immediate interests of their members. Under Eugene V. Debs, railroad workers merged the old railroad brotherhoods into the ARU in 1893. The United Mine Workers (UMW), founded in 1890, unionized coal mines in Pennsylvania, Ohio, Indiana, and Michigan. The ARU and the UMW were industrial unions that tried to organize all of the workers in an industry. Able to disrupt the energy and transport systems on which the whole economy depended, these new unions had immense potential power. They faced determined opposition from business and its allies in government. "Our government cannot stand, nor its free institutions endure," the National Association of Manufacturers declared, "if the Gompers-Debs ideals of liberty and freedom of speech and press are allowed to dominate."

AMERICAN DIPLOMACY ENTERS THE MODERN WORLD

The Republican victory in 1896 gave heart to proponents of prosperity through foreign trade. Before the turn of the century, the new president announced, the United States would control the world's markets. "We will establish trading posts throughout the world as distributing points for American products," Senator Albert Beveridge forecast. "Great colonies, governing themselves, flying our flag and trading with us, will grow about our posts of trade." McKinley sought neither war nor colonies, but many in his party wanted both. These jingoes included Assistant Secretary of the Navy Theodore Roosevelt; John Hay, the ambassador to London; and Senators Beveridge and Henry Cabot Lodge. Britain, France, and Germany were seizing territory around the world, and jingoes believed the United States needed to do the same for strategic, religious, and economic reasons. Spain was the most likely target, clinging feebly to the remnants of its once-vast empire in Cuba, the Philippines, Guam, and Puerto Rico. Under Cleveland, the United States had moved away from confrontation with Spain, but McKinley pushed for the creation of an American empire that stretched to the far shores of the Pacific.

Sea Power and the Imperial Urge

Few men better exemplified the jingoes' combination of religiosity, martial spirit, and fascination with the laws of history than Alfred Thayer Mahan. A naval officer and strategist, he argued that since the Roman Empire, world leadership had belonged to the nation that controlled the sea. Published in 1890, his book *The Influence of Sea Power upon History, 1660–1783* became an instant classic.

Mahan connected naval expansion and empire to the problem of overproduction that the United States faced. A great industrial country needed trade; trade required a merchant fleet; and merchant shipping needed naval protection and overseas bases. Colonies could provide markets for goods and congregations for Christian missionaries, but, more important, they allowed naval forces to protect sea lanes and project power in Asia, Latin America, and Africa.

Mahan urged the United States to build a canal across Central America for better access to Asian markets. He urged the building of naval bases along routes to Latin America and the Far East. Congress and the Navy Department began implementing these recommendations even before McKinley took office (see Figure 18–2).

Mahan was not the only prophet who recalled the Roman Empire. Brooks Adams's *The Law of Civilization and Decay* (1895) detailed the effects of the closed frontier: greater concentration of wealth, social inequality, and eventual collapse.

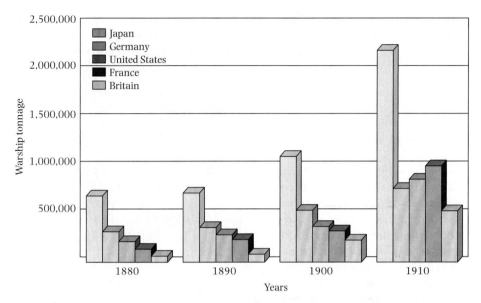

Figure 18–2   Warship Tonnage of the World's Navies Naval strength was the primary index of power before World War I. The United States held onto third place in the naval arms race, while Germany and Japan made significant gains.
Source: Paul Kennedy, *Rise and Fall of the Great Powers* (New York: Random House, 1987), p. 203.

To repeal this "law," the United States needed a new frontier in Asia where it could regenerate itself through combat. Sharing the social Darwinist belief that nations and races were locked in a savage struggle for survival, Mahan and Adams expected the United States to win the approaching conflict.

If subduing continents with the cross, Constitution, and Gatling gun appealed to anyone, it was Theodore Roosevelt. Roosevelt paid keen attention to the forces that were magnifying the power of some nations and diminishing others. Imperialism seemed to him the essential characteristic of modernizing countries. A frontiersman, writer, soldier, and politician, Roosevelt was acutely conscious of how modern forces—globalized trade, instant communications, modern navies, and imperialism—had altered the rules of domestic and international politics. He sought to position the United States at the center of these modernizing currents, a place that would have to be earned, he felt, both on foreign battlefields and at home, where the gains of the nineteenth century had not yet been translated into the social and moral advancement that marked a true civilization.

The Scramble for Empire

For jingoes, China was the ultimate prize in the global contest for trade and mastery. It had more people than any other country, hence more customers and more souls for Christ. The number of American missionaries in China doubled in the 1890s, many of them from the Student Volunteer movement, which had chapters

Pears' Soap Advertisements emphasized the celebrated civilizing capacities of imperialism, as shown in this advertisement for Pears' Soap, 1899.

The first step towards lightening

The White Man's Burden

is through teaching the virtues of cleanliness.

Pears' Soap

is a potent factor in brightening the dark corners of the earth as civilization advances, while amongst the cultured of all nations it holds the highest place—it is the ideal toilet soap.

on nearly every college campus. Even though no more than 1 or 2 percent of US exports had ever gone to China, manufacturers believed that China could absorb the output of America's overproductive factories. James B. Duke founded the British-American Tobacco Company based on "China's population of 450 million people, and assuming that in the future they might average a cigarette a day." In 1890, Standard Oil began selling kerosene in Shanghai. Fifteen years later, China was the largest overseas market for American oil. Mahan had predicted that China would be the arena for the coming struggle for industrial and military supremacy, and by 1897 he seemed to be right.

In 1894, Japan declared war on China and soon occupied Korea, Manchuria, and China's coastal cities. When the fighting was over, Western powers seized slices of Chinese territory. In 1897, German troops captured the port of Qingdao on the Shandong Peninsula. An industrial area, Shandong was the center of American missionary activity, investment, and trade. To Americans, the invasion of Shandong presaged an imperial grab for territory and influence. In the 1880s, European powers had carved up Africa. Now it appeared that the same thing was about to happen in China. The McKinley administration watched events in China carefully, but in the winter of 1897–1898 it had more pressing concerns closer to home.

War with Spain

While other European powers were expanding their empires, Spain was barely hanging on to the one it had. Since the 1860s, its two largest colonies, Cuba and the Philippines, had been torn by revolution. Between 1868 and 1878, Cuban nationalists fought for independence. Spain ended the war by promising autonomy but not independence. US officials wanted an end to Spanish rule, but the McKinley Tariff and the Panic of 1893 ruined Cuba's chief export industry, sugar. Under a crushing debt, Spain reneged on its promise, and in 1895 the rebellion resumed. The rebels practiced a scorched-earth policy, dynamiting trains and burning plantations in an attempt to force Spain out.

Spain retaliated with a brutal campaign of pacification, killing nearly 100,000 civilians, but it was no use. The Spanish army was disintegrating. Cuban rebels, in control of the countryside, prepared a final assault on the cities. US officials, many of whom wanted to annex the island, now worried that Cuba would gain full independence. McKinley explored the options of either purchasing it from Spain or intervening on the pretext of ending the strife. William Randolph Hearst's *New York Journal* and other newspapers favored the latter, inciting readers with lurid stories of Spanish atrocities and Cuban rioting. Cuba sold newspapers. McKinley moved quickly toward confrontation. When riots erupted in the Cuban capital, he ordered a warship to Havana. Theodore Roosevelt sent one of the newest battleships, the USS *Maine*. The arrival of the *Maine* reduced tensions for a while, but on February 15 an explosion ripped through the ship, killing 266 of a crew that had numbered 350. Navy investigators later concluded that boilers had exploded accidentally, but the newspapers blamed both Spanish and Cuban treachery. Hearst printed a full-page diagram of the ship being destroyed by a "sunken torpedo."

McKinley hesitated, mindful of the budget and events in China, but Roosevelt ordered Commodore George Dewey's Asiatic Squadron to ready an attack on the Philippines. Congress appropriated $50 million for arms. Spanish emissaries tried to gain support from other European countries, but they were rebuffed.

In March, the economic picture brightened, and McKinley sent Spain an ultimatum demanding independence for Cuba. On April 11, he asked Congress for authorization to use force, and Congress passed a declaration of war. Expansionists such as Roosevelt, Mahan, and Adams would not have succeeded if war had been less popular. Corporate interests favored it, immigrants and southerners saw it as a way to assert their patriotism, and newspapers found it made good copy. "We are all jingoes now," declared the *New York Sun*.

Neither side had many illusions about the outcome. Fighting Spain, novelist Sherwood Anderson wrote, was "like robbing an old gypsy woman in a vacant lot at night after the fair," but the war opened with a cliffhanger that even Hearst could not have invented. On May 1, news arrived that Dewey's forces were fighting the Spanish fleet in Manila Bay in the Philippines. The war had begun, not in Cuba, but instead half a world away. There the information stopped. The telegraph cable from Manila had been cut. Official Spanish reports alleged that the Americans had suffered a "considerable loss of life." Dewey's squadron contained only two modern cruisers, but in contrast to Spain's wooden vessels, all of its ships were steel hulled. For six anxious days Americans awaited word from the far edge of the Pacific.

It arrived early on May 7. The *New York Herald*'s Hong Kong correspondent had been at the battle. Dewey destroyed Spain's entire fleet of 12 warships without a single serious casualty. The country went wild with relief and triumph. New York staged a parade on Fifth Avenue. A Dewey-for-president movement began. In Washington, McKinley consulted a map to see where the Philippines were. Roosevelt quit his job and ordered up a uniform.

The war in Cuba unfolded more modestly. The navy bottled up Spain's ships in the Bay of Santiago de Cuba, and American warships cut the fleet to pieces as it attempted to escape. "Don't cheer, men," an officer ordered the gun crews. "Those poor devils are dying."

The Rough Riders Theodore Roosevelt's regiment, with its blend of educated men from the east and rough-and-tumble western frontiersmen, represented his idealized blend of American military manhood.

In the years before the war, Congress had poured money into the navy but not the army, and it took some time before soldiers could be trained and equipped. Recruits were herded into camps in Florida without tents, proper clothing, or latrines. There were few medical supplies or doctors. In these unsanitary camps, soldiers died of dysentery and malaria. Of the 5,462 US soldiers who died in the war with Spain, 5,083 succumbed to disease, a scandal that forced the government to elevate the status of the surgeon general and to improve sanitation and disease prevention in the military.

The army landed on the Cuban coast and marched inland to engage Spanish defenders. Roosevelt came ashore with the First Volunteer Cavalry, known as the "Rough Riders." He recruited, trained, and publicized the regiment and wrote its history. An assortment of outlaws, cowboys, Ivy League athletes, New York City policemen, a novelist, and a Harvard Medical School graduate, its membership combined frontier heroism with eastern elite leadership. The regiment traveled with its own film crew and a correspondent from the *New York Herald*.

Spanish forces stubbornly resisted around the city of Santiago. At San Juan Hill, 500 defenders forced a regiment of the New York National Guard to retreat.

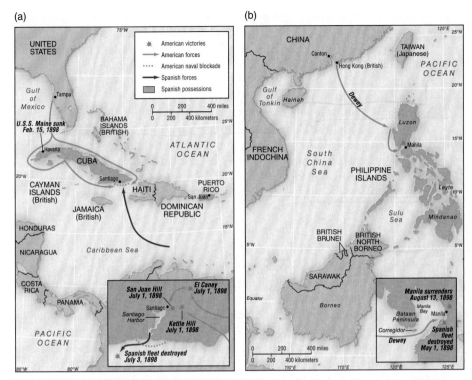

Map 18-2   The Spanish-American War: (a) Caribbean Theater; (b) Pacific Theater

The all–African American 9th and 10th Cavalry fought alongside the Rough Riders. "The negroes saved that fight," a white soldier reported. The capture of Santiago effectively ended Spanish resistance. When fighting ended in August, US troops occupied Cuba, Guam, Puerto Rico, and the city of Manila. The war had lasted only four months.

As American and Spanish diplomats met in Paris to conclude a peace treaty, McKinley had to decide which occupied territories to keep as colonies. Congress, not wanting to inherit the island's $400 million in debt, had already resolved not to annex Cuba. McKinley decided that Guam and Puerto Rico would make ideal naval bases (see Map 18-2).

The president also seized the opportunity to annex the island nation of Hawaii. In 1893, American sugar planters, led by Sanford Dole, overthrew the islands' last queen, Liliuokalani, and petitioned for annexation. They were motivated by the Harrison-McKinley Tariff, which would ruin the planters unless they could reconnect Hawaii's trade to the United States. Annexation was their best chance, and they had a powerful ally in the US Navy. Mahan had identified Pearl Harbor, on Oahu, as a vital base. McKinley decided to take up Dole's annexation offer.

The Philippines were more of a problem. The 7,000 islands were far from the United States and had a population of several million. The United States needed a naval base and supply station close to the China coast, but holding just one island would be impossible if another power controlled the others. Shortly after Dewey's victory, British and German warships anchored in Manila Bay, clearly intending to divide up the territory the United States did not claim. McKinley felt trapped.

Spain recognized Cuban independence and surrendered most of its empire to the United States for free, but it gave up the Philippines only after the United States agreed to pay $20 million, or, as an American satirist calculated, $1.25 for every Filipino. The treaty was signed December 10, 1898.

McKinley did not take into account the fact that the Philippines had already declared independence. With Dewey's encouragement, rebels under the command of Emilio Aguinaldo had liberated the countryside surrounding Manila and laid siege to the city. At Malolos, north of Manila, a national assembly, including lawyers, doctors, professors, and landowners, issued a constitution. By the time the US Army arrived in 1899, Filipinos had overthrown the Spanish and rallied to their new government.

The Anti-Imperialists

Many prominent Americans opposed both the annexation of new colonies and the approaching war with the Philippines. During the treaty fight in Congress in January 1899, they tried to mobilize opinion against the treaty. The movement included ex-presidents Grover Cleveland and Benjamin Harrison; William Jennings Bryan; labor unionists, including Samuel Gompers and Eugene Debs; writers such as Mark Twain and Ambrose Bierce; and industrialists, including Andrew Carnegie. The anti-imperialists advanced an array of moral, economic, and strategic arguments. Filipinos and Hawaiians, they said, had sought American help in good faith and were capable of governing themselves. The islands could not be defended, and US forces would be exposed to attack at Pearl Harbor or Manila. Carnegie argued that imperialism took tax dollars and attention away from domestic problems. White supremacists asked whether Filipinos would become citizens or be allowed to vote and emigrate to the mainland.

The most moving objections came from those who believed imperialism betrayed America's fundamental principles. To Mark Twain, imperialism was only the newest form of greed: "There is more money in it, more territory, more sovereignty, and other kinds of emolument, than there is in any other game that is played." Opponents of annexation organized an Anti-Imperialist League and lobbied for the rejection of the Paris Treaty.

Congress responded to anti-imperialist objections, banning Philippine immigration, placing the colonies outside the tariff walls, and promising eventual self-government. Jingoes had a military victory on their side. Anti-imperialists could not offer a vision comparable to naval supremacy, the evangelization of the world, or the China market. On February 6, 1899, the US Senate ratified the Paris Treaty and annexed the Philippines. A day earlier, on the other side of the world, the Philippine-American War began.

The Philippine-American War

McKinley believed he had annexed islands full of near savages "unfit for self-rule," but the Philippines by 1899 had an old civilization with a long tradition of resistance to colonialism. When Magellan discovered the islands in 1521, he found a literate population linked by trade ties to India, Japan, and China. The Spanish converted most Filipinos to Catholicism and established schools and a centralized government. Manila's oldest university was older than Harvard. By 1898, much of the upper class, the *illustrados*, had been educated in Europe.

Dewey gave Aguinaldo his word that America desired no colonies. Aguinaldo continued to trust the Americans despite the arrival of fresh US troops. On February 4, an argument between American and Filipino sentries ended in gunfire. Aguinaldo was despondent: "No one can deplore more than I this rupture. I have a clear conscience that I endeavored to avoid it at all costs."

Kansas volunteers drove the Filipino armies into the mountains. Aguinaldo adopted a guerilla strategy, which proved effective. Some 4,000 Americans were killed during the war and another 3,000 wounded out of a total force of 70,000. Frustrated by guerilla conflict, American soldiers customarily executed prisoners, looted villages, and raped Filipino women. An American general on the island of Samar ordered his soldiers to kill everyone over the age of 10. "No cruelty is too severe for these brainless monkeys," a soldier wrote home. "I am in my glory when I can sight some dark skin and pull the trigger."

The army's preferred mode of torture was "the water cure," in which a soldier forced water down a prisoner's throat until the abdomen swelled, and then kicked the prisoner's stomach to force the water out again. Military officials argued that Filipinos were "half-civilized" and that force was the best language for dealing with them.

Newspaper accounts of torture and massacres fueled American opposition to the war, just as US forces scored some victories. Recognizing that they were fighting a political war, US officers took pains to win over dissidents and ethnic minorities. In 1901, this strategy began to pay off. When American troops intercepted a messenger bound for Aguinaldo's secret headquarters, Brigadier General Frederick Funston devised a bold (and, under the rules of war, illegal) plan. He dressed a group of Filipinos loyal to the American side in the uniforms of captured Filipinos, and, posing as a prisoner, Funston entered Aguinaldo's camp and kidnapped the president.

After three weeks in a Manila prison, Aguinaldo issued a proclamation of surrender. When resistance continued in Batangas Province for another year, the US Army responded by herding people into concentration camps, a practice the United States had condemned in Cuba. It had the same tragic result. Perhaps a third of the province's population died of disease and starvation. On July 4, 1902, President Theodore Roosevelt declared the war over.

The American flag flew over the Philippines until 1942, but the colony never lived up to its imperial promise. Instead of defending American trade interests, US troops were pinned down in garrisons, guarding against uprisings and the threat of Japanese invasion. The costs of occupation far exceeded the profits generated by Philippine trade. The colony chiefly attracted American reformers and missionaries, who built schools, churches, and agricultural colleges. Some colonists sought statehood, but Americans liked their colonial experiment less and less. Labor unions feared a flood of immigration from the islands, and farmers resented competition from Philippine producers; in 1933, Congress voted to phase out American rule.

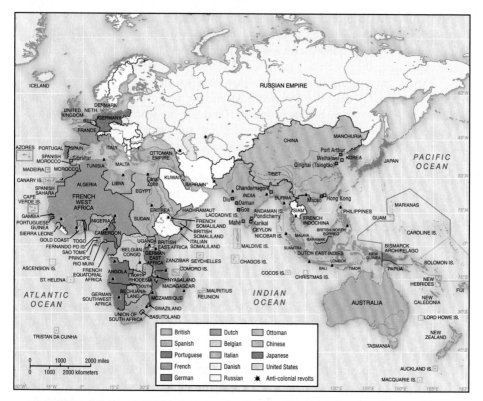

Map 18–3a   The Imperial World: Asia, Africa, and the Middle East Modern imperialism reached its apex between 1880 and 1945. Most of Africa, the Middle East, and Asia, a third of the world's population, was absorbed into global empires linked by telegraph and steamship to centers of government and commerce in London, Paris, Tokyo, and Washington, DC.

The Open Door

As Americans celebrated their victories, European powers continued to divide China into quasi-colonial "concessions." An alarmed imperial court in Beijing began a crash program of modernization, but reactionaries overthrew the emperor and installed the conservative "dowager empress" Cixi. In the countryside, Western missionaries and traders came under attack from local residents led by martial artists known as Boxers. Many Americans feared that the approaching disintegration of China would mean the exclusion of US trade.

Secretary of State John Hay watched events in China carefully. "The inherent weakness of our position is this," he wrote McKinley. "We do not want to rob China ourselves, and our public opinion will not allow us to interfere, with an army, to prevent others from robbing her. Besides, we have no army." Seeking some way to keep China's markets open, McKinley turned to William Rockhill, a legendary foreign service officer who had lived in China and had been the first westerner to visit Tibet. He, in turn, consulted his friend Alfred Hippisley,

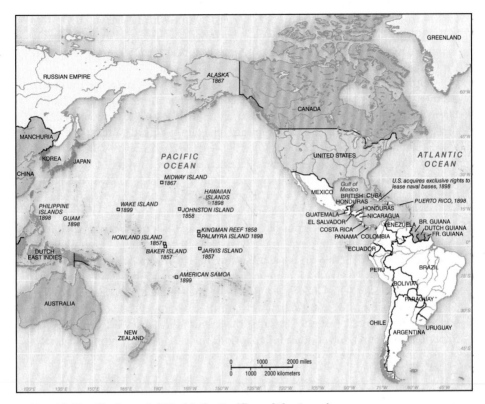

Map 18–3b   The Imperial World: the Pacific and the Americas

an Englishman returning from service with the British-run Chinese imperial customs.

Rockhill, Hippisley, and Hay drafted an official letter known as the Open Door Note. Sent to each of the imperial powers, it acknowledged the partitioning of China into spheres and observed that none of the powers had yet closed its areas to the trade of other countries. The note urged the powers to declare publicly their intention to continue this policy. The Open Door was mostly bluff. The United States had no authority to ask for such a pledge and no military power to enforce one. The foreign ministers of Germany, Japan, Russia, Britain, and France replied cautiously at first, but Hay adroitly played one power off another, starting with Britain and Japan. Once the two strongest powers in China had agreed, France and then Russia and Germany followed. The United States had secured access to China without war or partition, but the limits of Hay's success soon became apparent.

In early 1900, the antiforeign Boxer movement swept through Shandong Province. Armed Chinese attacked missions and foreign businesses, destroyed railroads, and massacred Chinese Christians. Empress Cixi recruited 30,000 Boxers into her army and declared war on all foreign countries. The Western powers rushed troops to China, but before they arrived, Chinese armies attacked Western embassies in Beijing. A British, Russian, Japanese, and French force gathered at Tianjin to march to the rescue. European powers appeared all too eager to capture the Chinese capital.

Without consulting Congress, McKinley ordered American troops into battle on the Asian mainland. Five thousand soldiers rushed from Manila to Tianjin. Hay issued a second Open Door Note, asking the allies to pledge to protect China's independence. Again, the imperial powers reluctantly agreed rather than admit their secret plans to carve up China. On August 15, 1900, US cavalry units reached Beijing, along with Russian Cossacks, French Zouaves, British-Indian sepoys, German hussars, and Japanese dragoons. After freeing the captive diplomats, the armies of the civilized world looted the city. The United States was unable to maintain the Open Door in China for long. Russia and Japan established separate military zones in northeast China, but the principle of the Open Door, of encouraging free trade and open markets, guided American foreign policy throughout the twentieth century. It rested on the assumption that, in an equal contest, American firms would prevail, spreading manufactured goods around the world and American influence with them. Under the Open Door, the United States was better off in a world without empires, a world in which consumers in independent nations could buy what they wanted. Just one year after the Spanish-American War, Hay rejected imperial expansion in favor of trade expansion. This new strategy promised greater gains, but it placed the United States on a collision course with the empires of the world (see Map 18–3).

TIME LINE

▼**1890**
Global depression begins
United Mine Workers founded
Battle of Wounded Knee ends Indian wars
Harrison-McKinley Tariff passed
Alfred T. Mahan publishes *The Influence of Sea Power upon History, 1660–1783*
Standard Oil markets kerosene in China

▼**1892**
Homestead strike

▼**1893**
Financial crisis leads to business failures and mass unemployment

World's Columbian Exposition, Chicago
Cherokee Strip land rush
American sugar planters overthrow Queen Liliuokalani of Hawaii

▼**1894**
Coxey's Army marches on Washington
Pullman strike
US commission charts canal route across Nicaragua

▼**1895**
Morgan agrees to Treasury bailout
National Association of Manufacturers founded

Brooks Adams publishes *The Law of Civilization and Decay*
Booker T. Washington gives "Atlanta Compromise" address
Revolution begins in Cuba
Japan annexes Korea and Taiwan

▼**1896**
Plessy v. Ferguson declares "separate but equal" facilities constitutional
William McKinley elected president

CONCLUSION

In the turbulent 1890s, the social and economic divisions among Americans widened. The hope that a solution to these divisions could be found outside the United States was short-lived. Imperialism promised new markets and an end to the cycle of depression and labor strife. The United States conquered an overseas empire and challenged other empires to open their ports to free trade, but the goal of prosperity and peace at home proved elusive.

In many ways social Darwinism became a self-fulfilling prophecy, as competition rather than compromise prevailed. Workers and businessmen, farmers and bankers, middle-class radicals and conservatives, whites and African Americans saw each other as enemies. Racial segregation showed that middle ground, on which whites and African Americans could meet on equal terms, had disappeared. Americans now had to decide what was politically possible and devise new bargaining strategies.

Economic recovery and military victory closed the decade on an optimistic note. Prosperity, power, and technology seemed to have rewritten the rules of human affairs to America's advantage. In the American exhibit at the Paris Exposition of 1900, Henry Adams contemplated a 40-foot dynamo—a "huge wheel, revolving within arm's length"—and felt as if he had crossed a "historical chasm." The machine's mysterious silent force, emanating from "a dirty engine house carefully kept out of sight," seemed a metaphor for the modern age.

▼**1897**
Germany captures Qingdao, on China's Shandong Peninsula
McKinley issues formal protest to Spain

▼**1898**
USS *Maine* explodes in Havana's harbor
United States declares war on Spain
Dewey defeats Spanish fleet at Manila Bay
In the Treaty of Paris, Spain grants Cuba independence and cedes Guam, Puerto Rico, and the Philippines to the United States
Aguinaldo proclaims Philippine independence

▼**1899**
Senate votes to annex Puerto Rico, Hawaii, and the Philippines
Philippine-American War begins
Hay issues first Open Door Note

▼**1900**
Hay issues second Open Door Note
US Army joins British, French, Russian, German, and Japanese forces in capture of Beijing
Great Exposition of Paris showcases American technology
William McKinley reelected

▼**1901**
Aguinaldo captured
McKinley assassinated; Theodore Roosevelt becomes president

▼**1902**
Roosevelt declares Philippine-American War over

WHO, WHAT, WHERE *25*

Atlanta Compromise   605

Bryan, William Jennings   597

crop liens   600

disfranchisement   606

gold standard   580

Gompers, Samuel   607

Hearst, William Randolph   611

Homestead, Pennsylvania   595

Jim Crow laws   603

jingoes   608

lynching   603

Mahan, Alfred Thayer   608

Morgan, J. P.   596

Open Door   617

the Philippines   608

Plessy, Homer   602

Pullman strike   595

Roosevelt, Theodore   609

segregation   602

separate but equal   602

scientific management   594

Taylorism   594

Washington, Booker T.   603

Wilmington   604

World's Columbian Exposition   592

REVIEW QUESTIONS

1. What new techniques and practices made US industries more efficient?

2. What motivated Americans to seek an empire?

3. Why did the weather bureau discount the hurricane threat to Galveston?

4. Which cities were the main centers of industry and culture in the 1890s?

CRITICAL-THINKING QUESTIONS

1. How did the concept of individual rights evolve in reaction to new economic conditions? Name key figures who articulated a concept of democratic rights, and describe their ideas.

2. Contrast the arguments for empire with the rhetoric of the anti-imperialists. Which dangers to the nation and democracy did each side stress?

3. Why was the issue of currency so important to Americans in 1896? What was at stake?

SUGGESTED READINGS

Brewer, Susan A. *Why America Fights: Patriotism and War Propaganda from the Philippines to Iraq*. New York: Oxford University Press, 2009.

Edwards, Rebecca, and DeFeo, Sarah. The Presidential Campaign: Cartoons and Commentary. 2000. http://projects.vassar.edu/1896/1896home.html

Immerwahr, Daniel. *How to Hide an Empire: A History of the Greater United States*. New York: Farrar, Straus and Giroux, 2019.

Lears, Jackson. *Rebirth of a Nation: The Making of Modern America, 1877–1920*. New York: Harper Perennial, 2010.

Young, Jeremy C. *The Age of Charisma: Leaders, Followers, and Emotions in American Society, 1870–1940*. New York: Cambridge University Press, 2016.

For further review materials and resource information, please visit www.oup.com/us/ofthepeople

CHAPTER 18:   Industry and Empire, 1890–1900
Primary Sources

18.1   FREDERICK WINSLOW TAYLOR, EXCERPTS FROM *THE PRINCIPLES OF SCIENTIFIC MANAGEMENT* (1911)

Frederick Winslow Taylor aimed to identify the most basic movements of workplace skills to provide management with the means to train workers to complete tasks with the highest levels of efficiency. With managerial oversight and the cooperation of labor, industry could produce at higher levels, thereby benefiting owners, consumers, and through Taylor's imagined wage increases, workers.

> Under the old type of management success depends almost entirely upon getting the "initiative" of the workmen, and it is indeed a rare case in which this initiative is really attained. Under scientific management the "initiative" of the workmen (that is, their hard work, their good-will, and their ingenuity) is obtained with absolute uniformity and to a greater extent than is possible under the old system; and in addition to this improvement on the part of the men, the managers assume new burdens, new duties, and responsibilities never dreamed of in the past. The managers assume, for instance, the burden of gathering together all of the traditional knowledge which in the past has been possessed by the workmen and then of classifying, tabulating, and reducing this knowledge to rules, laws, and formulæ which are immensely helpful to the workmen in doing their daily work. In addition to developing a science in this way, the management take on three other types of duties which involve new and heavy burdens for themselves.
>
> These new duties are grouped under four heads:
>
> First. They develop a science for each element of a man's work, which replaces the old rule-of-thumb method.
>
> Second. They scientifically select and then train, teach, and develop the workman, whereas in the past he chose his own work and trained himself as best he could.
>
> Third. They heartily cooperate with the men so as to insure all of the work being done in accordance with the principles of the science which has been developed.
>
> Fourth. There is an almost equal division of the work and the responsibility between the management and the workmen. The management take over all work for which they are better fitted than the workmen, while in the past almost all of the work and the greater part of the responsibility were thrown upon the men.
>
> It is this combination of the initiative of the workmen, coupled with the new types of work done by the management, that makes scientific management so much more efficient than the old plan.
>
> Perhaps the most prominent single element in modern scientific management is the task idea. The work of every workman is fully planned out by the management at least one day in advance, and each man receives in most cases complete written instructions, describing in detail the task which he is to accomplish, as well as the means to be used in doing the work. And the work planned in advance in this way constitutes a task which is to be solved, as explained above, not by the workman alone, but in almost all cases by the joint effort of the workman and the management. This task specifies not only what is to be

done but how it is to be done and the exact time allowed for doing it. And whenever the workman succeeds in doing his task right, and within the time limit specified, he receives an addition of from 30 percent to 100 percent to his ordinary wages. These tasks are carefully planned, so that both good and careful work are called for in their performance, but it should be distinctly understood that in no case is the workman called upon to work at a pace which would be injurious to his health. The task is always so regulated that the man who is well suited to his job will thrive while working at this rate during a long term of years and grow happier and more prosperous, instead of being over-worked. Scientific management consists very largely in preparing for and carrying out these tasks.

Doubtless some of those who are especially interested in working men will complain because under scientific management the workman, when he is shown how to do twice as much work as he formerly did, is not paid twice his former wages, while others who are more interested in the dividends than the workmen will complain that under this system the men receive much higher wages than they did before.

It is not fair, however, to form any final judgment until all of the elements in the case have been considered. At the first glance we see only two parties to the transaction, the workmen and their employers. We overlook the third great party, the whole people—the consumers, who buy the product of the first two and who ultimately pay both the wages of the workmen and the profits of the employers.

[A] glance at industrial history shows that in the end the whole people receive the greater part of the benefit coming from industrial improvements. In the past hundred years, for example, the greatest factor tending toward increasing the output, and thereby the prosperity of the civilized world, has been the introduction of machinery to replace hand labor. And without doubt the greatest gain through this change has come to the whole people—the consumer.

It is no single element, but rather this whole combination, that constitutes scientific management, which may be summarized as:

Science, not rule of thumb.

Harmony, not discord.

Cooperation, not individualism.

Maximum output, in place of restricted output.

The development of each man to his greatest efficiency and prosperity.

The writer wishes to again state that: "The time is fast going by for the great personal or individual achievement of any one man standing alone and without the help of those around him. And the time is coming when all great things will be done by that type of cooperation in which each man performs the function for which he is best suited, each man preserves his own individuality and is supreme in his particular function, and each man at the same time loses none of his originality and proper personal initiative, and yet is controlled by and must work harmoniously with many other men."

Source: Frederick Winslow Taylor, *The Principles of Scientific Management* (New York: Harper & Brothers, 1911), chapter 2.

18.2 BOOKER T. WASHINGTON, "THE ATLANTA COMPROMISE" (1895)

On September 18, 1895, noted Black leader Booker T. Washington addressed a predominantly white audience at the Cotton States and International Exposition in Atlanta. The "Atlanta Compromise," as it came to be known, much like the curriculum of Washington's Tuskegee Institute, advocated hard work and morality as the path to upward mobility for the Black population. As the South moved increasingly in the direction of Jim Crow segregation, white southerners celebrated the speech, pleased by Washington's emphasis on economic cooperation rather than social integration.

One-third of the population of the South is of the Negro race. No enterprise seeking the material, civil, or moral welfare of this section can disregard this element of our population and reach the highest success. I but convey to you, Mr. President and Directors, the sentiment of the masses of my race when I say that in no way have the value and manhood of the American Negro been more fittingly and generously recognized than by the managers of this magnificent Exposition at every stage of its progress. It is a recognition that will do more to cement the friendship of the two races than any occurrence since the dawn of our freedom.

Not only this, but the opportunity here afforded will awaken among us a new era of industrial progress. Ignorant and inexperienced, it is not strange that in the first years of our new life we began at the top instead of at the bottom; that a seat in Congress or the state legislature was more sought than real estate or industrial skill; that the political convention or stump speaking had more attractions than starting a dairy farm or truck garden.

A ship lost at sea for many days suddenly sighted a friendly vessel. From the mast of the unfortunate vessel was seen a signal, "Water, water; we die of thirst!" The answer from the friendly vessel at once came back, "Cast down your bucket where you are." A second time the signal, "Water, water; send us water!" ran up from the distressed vessel, and was answered, "Cast down your bucket where you are." And a third and fourth signal for water was answered, "Cast down your bucket where you are." The captain of the distressed vessel, at last heeding the injunction, cast down his bucket, and it came up full of fresh, sparkling water from the mouth of the Amazon River. To those of my race who depend on bettering their condition in a foreign land or who underestimate the importance of cultivating friendly relations with the Southern white man, who is their next-door neighbor, I would say: "Cast down your bucket where you are"—cast it down in making friends in every manly way of the people of all races by whom we are surrounded.

Cast it down in agriculture, mechanics, in commerce, in domestic service, and in the professions. And in this connection it is well to bear in mind that whatever other sins the South may be called to bear, when it comes to business, pure and simple, it is in the South that the Negro is given a man's chance in the commercial world, and in nothing is this Exposition more eloquent than in emphasizing this chance. Our greatest danger is that in the great leap from slavery to freedom we may overlook the fact that the masses of us are to live by the productions of our hands, and fail to keep in mind that we shall prosper in proportion as we learn to dignify and glorify common labour, and put brains and skill into the common occupations of life; shall prosper in proportion as we learn to draw the line between the superficial and the substantial, the ornamental gewgaws of life and the useful. No race can prosper till it learns that there is as much dignity in tilling a field as in writing a poem. It is at the bottom of life we must begin, and not at the top. Nor should we permit our grievances to overshadow our opportunities.

To those of the white race who look to the incoming of those of foreign birth and strange tongue and habits for the prosperity of the South, were I permitted I would repeat what I say to my own race, "Cast down your bucket where you are." Cast it down among the eight millions of Negroes whose habits you know, whose fidelity and love you have tested in days when to have proved treacherous meant the ruin of your firesides. Cast down your bucket among these people who have, without strikes and labour wars, tilled your fields, cleared your forests, builded your railroads and cities, and brought forth treasures from the bowels of the earth, and helped make possible this magnificent representation of the progress of the South. Casting down your bucket among my people, helping and encouraging them as you are doing on these grounds, and to education of head, hand, and heart, you will find that they will buy your surplus land, make blossom the waste places in your fields, and run your factories. While doing this, you can be sure in the future, as in the past, that you and your families will be surrounded by the most patient, faithful, law-abiding, and unresentful people that the world has seen. As we have proved our loyalty to you in the past, in nursing your children, watching by the sick-bed of your mothers and fathers, and often following them with tear-dimmed eyes to their graves, so in the future, in our humble way, we shall stand by you with a devotion that no foreigner can approach, ready to lay down our lives, if need be, in defense of yours, interlacing our industrial, commercial, civil, and religious life with yours in a way that shall make the interests of both races one. In all things that are purely social we can be as separate as the fingers, yet one as the hand in all things essential to mutual progress.

Nearly sixteen millions of hands will aid you in pulling the load upward, or they will pull against you the load downward. We shall constitute one-third and more of the ignorance and crime of the South, or one-third [of] its intelligence and progress; we shall contribute one-third to the business and industrial prosperity of the South, or we shall prove a veritable body of death, stagnating, depressing, retarding every effort to advance the body politic.

Gentlemen of the Exposition, as we present to you our humble effort at an exhibition of our progress, you must not expect overmuch. Starting thirty years ago with ownership here and there in a few quilts and pumpkins and chickens (gathered from miscellaneous sources), remember the path that has led from these to the inventions and production of agricultural implements, buggies, steam-engines, newspapers, books, statuary, carving, paintings, the management of drug stores and banks, has not been trodden without contact with thorns and thistles. While we take pride in what we exhibit as a result of our independent efforts, we do not for a moment forget that our part in this exhibition would fall far short of your expectations but for the constant help that has come to our educational life, not only from the Southern states, but especially from Northern philanthropists, who have made their gifts a constant stream of blessing and encouragement.

The wisest among my race understand that the agitation of questions of social equality is the extremest folly, and that progress in the enjoyment of all the privileges that will come to us must be the result of severe and constant struggle rather than of artificial forcing. No race that has anything to contribute to the markets of the world is long in any degree ostracized. It is important and right that all privileges of the law be ours, but it is vastly more important that we be prepared for the exercise of these privileges. The opportunity to earn a dollar in a factory just now is worth infinitely more than the opportunity to spend a dollar in an opera-house.

In conclusion, may I repeat that nothing in thirty years has given us more hope and encouragement, and drawn us so near to you of the white race, as this opportunity offered by the Exposition; and here bending, as it were, over the altar that represents the results of the struggles of your race and mine, both starting practically empty-handed three decades ago, I pledge that in your effort to work out the great and intricate problem which God has laid at the doors of the South, you shall have at all times the patient, sympathetic help of my race; only let this be constantly in mind, that, while from representations in these buildings of the product of field, of forest, of mine, of factory, letters, and art, much good will come, yet far above and beyond material benefits will be that higher good, that, let us pray God, will come, in a blotting out of sectional differences and racial animosities and suspicions, in a determination to administer absolute justice, in a willing obedience among all classes to the mandates of law. This, coupled with our material prosperity, will bring into our beloved South a new heaven and a new earth.

Source: Louis R. Harlan, ed., *The Booker T. Washington Papers*, vol. 3 (Urbana: University of Illinois Press, 1974), pp. 583–587.

18.3 THEODORE ROOSEVELT, EXCERPTS FROM "THE STRENUOUS LIFE" (1899)

Drawing upon a national history that celebrated the rugged individual and the conquest of the frontier, Theodore Roosevelt saw an imperial future for the United States as the nineteenth century concluded. In Chicago in April 1899, he addressed an audience of wealthy businessmen at the Hamilton Club and called for bravery and decisive action from public leaders. Roosevelt believed those who wished to lead had a responsibility to uplift both white civilization and the American nation. Manliness was a fundamental part of national leadership, and Roosevelt believed manly, martial action was the only way for the United States to compete in the modern world.

We of this generation do not have to face a task such as that our fathers faced, but we have our tasks, and woe to us if we fail to perform them! We cannot, if we would, play the part of China, and be content to rot by inches in ignoble ease within our borders, taking no interest in what goes on beyond them, sunk in a scrambling commercialism; heedless of the higher life, the life of aspiration, of toil and risk, busying ourselves only with the wants of our bodies for the day, until suddenly we should find, beyond a shadow of question, what China has already found, that in this world the nation that has trained itself to a career of unwarlike and isolated ease is bound, in the end, to go down before other nations which have not lost the manly and adventurous qualities. If we are to be a really great people, we must strive in good faith to play a great part in the world. We cannot avoid meeting great issues. All that we can determine for ourselves is whether we shall meet them well or ill. Last year we could not help being brought face to face with the problem of war with Spain. All we could decide was whether we should shrink like cowards from the contest, or enter into it as beseemed a brave and high-spirited people; and, once in, whether failure or success should crown our banners. So it is now. We cannot avoid the responsibilities that confront us in Hawaii, Cuba, Porto Rico, and the Philippines. All we can decide is whether we shall meet them in a way that will redound to the national credit, or whether we shall make of our dealings with these new problems a dark and shameful page in our history. To refuse to deal with them at all merely amounts to dealing with them badly. We have a given problem to solve. If we undertake the solution, there is, of course, always danger that we may not solve it aright; but to refuse to undertake the solution simply renders it certain that we cannot possibly solve it aright.

The timid man, the lazy man, the man who distrusts his country, the over-civilized man, who has lost the great fighting, masterful virtues, the ignorant man, and the man of dull mind, whose soul is incapable of feeling the mighty lift that thrills "stern men with empires in their brains"—all these, of course, shrink from seeing the nation undertake its new duties; shrink from seeing us build a navy and an army adequate to our needs; shrink from seeing us do our share of the world's work, by bringing order out of chaos in the great, fair tropic islands from which the valor of our soldiers and sailors has driven the Spanish flag. These are the men who fear the strenuous life, who fear the only national life which is really worth leading. They believe in that cloistered life which saps the hardy virtues in a nation, as it saps them in the individual; or else they are wedded to that base spirit of gain and greed which recognizes in commercialism the be-all and end-all of national life, instead of realizing that, though an indispensable element, it is, after all, but one of the many elements that go to make up true national greatness. No country can long endure if its foundations are not laid deep in the material prosperity which comes from thrift, from business energy and enterprise, from hard, unsparing effort in the fields of industrial activity; but neither was any nation ever yet truly great if it relied upon material prosperity alone. All honor must be paid to the architects of our material prosperity, to the great captains of industry who have built our factories and our railroads, to the strong men who toil for wealth with brain or hand; for great is the debt of the nation to these and their kind. But our debt is yet greater to the men whose highest type is to be found in a statesman like Lincoln, a soldier like Grant. They showed by their lives that they recognized the law of work, the law of strife; they toiled to win a competence for themselves and those dependent upon them; but they recognized that there were yet other and even loftier duties—duties to the nation and duties to the race.

We cannot sit huddled within our own borders and avow ourselves merely an assemblage of well-to-do hucksters who care nothing for what happens beyond. Such a policy would defeat even its own end; for as the nations grow to have ever wider and wider interests, and are brought into closer and closer contact, if we are to hold our own in the struggle for naval and commercial supremacy, we must build up our power without our own borders. We must build the isthmian canal, and we must grasp the points of vantage which will enable us to have our say in deciding the destiny of the oceans of the East and the West.

So much for the commercial side. From the standpoint of international honor the argument is even stronger. The guns that thundered off Manila and Santiago, left us echoes of glory, but they also left us a legacy of duty. If we drove out a medieval tyranny only to make room for savage anarchy, we had better not have begun the task at all. It is worse than idle to say that we have no duty to perform, and can leave to their fates the islands we have conquered. Such a course would be the course of infamy. It would be followed at once by utter chaos in the wretched islands themselves. Some stronger, manlier power would have to step in and do the work, and we would have shown ourselves weaklings, unable to carry to successful completion the labors that great and high-spirited nations are eager to undertake.

The work must be done; we cannot escape our responsibility; and if we are worth our salt, we shall be glad of the chance to do the work—glad of the chance to show ourselves equal to one of the great tasks set modern civilization. But let us not deceive ourselves as to the importance of the task. Let us not be misled by vainglory into underestimating the strain it will put on our powers. Above all, let us, as we value our own self-respect, face the responsibilities with proper seriousness, courage, and high resolve. We must demand the highest order of integrity and ability in our public men who are to grapple with these new problems. We must hold to a rigid accountability those public servants who show unfaithfulness to the interests of the nation or inability to rise to the high level of the new demands upon our strength and our resources.

Our army needs complete reorganization—not merely enlarging—and the reorganization can only come as the result of legislation. A proper general staff should be established, and the positions of ordnance, commissary, and quartermaster officers should be filled by detail from the line. Above all, the army must be given the chance to exercise in large bodies. Never again should we see, as we saw in the Spanish war, major-generals in command of divisions who had never before commanded three companies together in the field. Yet, incredible to relate, the recent Congress has shown a queer inability to learn some of the lessons of the war. There were large bodies, of men in both branches who opposed the declaration of war, who opposed the ratification of peace, who opposed the upbuilding of the army, and who even opposed the purchase of: armor at a reasonable price for the battle-ships and cruisers, thereby putting an absolute stop to the building of any new fighting-ships for the navy. If, during the years to come, any disaster should befall our arms, afloat or ashore, and thereby any shame come to the United States, remember that the blame will lie upon the men whose names appear upon the roll-calls of Congress on the wrong side of these great questions. On them will lie the burden of any loss of our soldiers and sailors, of any dishonor to the flag; and upon you and the people of this country will lie the blame if you do not repudiate, in no unmistakable way, what these men have done. The blame will not rest upon the untrained commander of untried troops, upon the civil officers of a department the organization of which has been left utterly inadequate, or upon the admiral with an insufficient number of ships; but upon the public men who have so lamentably failed in forethought as to refuse to remedy these evils long in advance, and upon the nation that stands behind those public men.

When once we have put down armed resistance, when once our rule is acknowledged, then an even more difficult task will begin, for then we must see to it that the islands are administered with absolute honesty and with good judgment. If we let the public service of the islands be turned into the prey of the spoils politician, we shall have begun to tread the path which Spain trod to her own destruction. We must send out there only good and able men, chosen for their fitness, and not because of their partisan service, and these men must not only administer impartial justice to the natives and serve their own government with honesty and fidelity, but must show the utmost tact and firmness, remembering that, with such people as those with whom we are to deal, weakness is the greatest of crimes, and that next to weakness comes lack of consideration for their principles and prejudices.

I preach to you, then, my countrymen, that our country calls not for the life of ease but for the life of strenuous endeavor. The twentieth century looms before us big with the fate of many nations. If we stand idly by, if we seek merely swollen, slothful ease and ignoble peace, if we shrink from the hard contests where men must win at hazard of their lives and at the risk of all they hold dear, then the bolder and stronger peoples will pass us by, and will win for themselves the domination of the world. Let us therefore boldly face the life of strife, resolute to do our duty well and manfully; resolute to uphold righteousness by deed and by word; resolute to be both honest and brave, to serve high ideals, yet to use practical methods. Above all, let us shrink from no strife, moral or physical, within or without the nation, provided we are certain that the strife is justified, for it is only through strife, through hard and dangerous endeavor, that we shall ultimately win the goal of true national greatness.

Source: Theodore Roosevelt, "The Strenuous Life" (April 10, 1899), accessed at https://www.gutenberg. org/files/58821/58821-h/58821-h.htm.

18.4 PLATFORM FOR THE ANTI-IMPERIALIST LEAGUE (1899)

Anti-imperialists rejected the United States' move toward global expansion at the turn of the century, arguing it was against the nation's founding principles and core beliefs. Continuing to espouse the value of self-government, the Anti-Imperialist League opposed efforts to extend American rule across the globe.

We hold that the policy known as imperialism is hostile to liberty and tends toward militarism, an evil from which it has been our glory to be free. We regret that it has become necessary in the land of Washington and Lincoln *to* reaffirm that all men, of whatever race or color, are entitled to life, liberty and the pursuit of happiness. We maintain that governments derive their just powers from the consent of the governed. We insist that the subjugation of any people is "criminal aggression" and open disloyalty to the distinctive principles of our Government.

We earnestly condemn the policy of the present National Administration in the Philippines. It seeks to extinguish the spirit of 1776 in those islands. We deplore the sacrifice of our soldiers and sailors, whose bravery deserves admiration even in an unjust war.

We denounce the slaughter of the Filipinos as a needless horror. We protest against the extension of American sovereignty by Spanish methods.

We demand the immediate cessation of the war against liberty, begun by Spain and continued by us. We urge that Congress be promptly convened to announce to the Filipinos our purpose to concede to them the independence for which they have so long fought and which of right is theirs.

The United States have always protested against the doctrine of international law which permits the subjugation of the weak by the strong. A self-governing state cannot accept sovereignty over an unwilling people. The United States cannot act upon the ancient heresy that might makes right.

Imperialists assume that with the destruction of self-government in the Philippines by American hands, all opposition here will cease. This is a grievous error. Much as we abhor the war of "criminal aggression" in the Philippines, greatly as we regret that the blood of the Filipinos is on American hands, we more deeply resent the betrayal of American institutions at home. The real firing line is not in the suburbs of Manila. The foe is of our own household. The attempt of 1861 was to divide the country. That of 1899 is to destroy its fundamental principles and noblest ideals.

Whether the ruthless slaughter of the Filipinos shall end next month or next year is but an incident in a contest that must go on until the Declaration of Independence and the Constitution of the United States are rescued from the hands of their betrayers. Those who dispute about standards of value while the foundation of the Republic is undermined will be listened to as little as those who would wrangle about the small economies of the household while the house is on fire. The training of a great people for a century, the aspiration for liberty of a vast immigration are forces that will hurl aside those who in the delirium of conquest seek to destroy the character of our institutions.

We deny that the obligation of all citizens to support their Government in times of grave National peril applies to the present situation. If an Administration may with impunity ignore the issues upon which it was chosen, deliberately create a condition of war anywhere on the face of the globe, debauch the civil service for spoils to promote the adventure, organize a truth-suppressing censorship and demand of all citizens a suspension of judgment and their unanimous support while it chooses to continue the fighting, representative government itself is imperiled.

We propose to contribute to the defeat of any person or party that stands for the forcible subjugation of any people. We shall oppose for reelection all who in the White House or in Congress betray American liberty in pursuit of un-American ends. We still hope that both of our great political parties will support and defend the Declaration of Independence in the closing campaign of the century.

We hold, with Abraham Lincoln, that "no man is good enough to govern another man without that other's consent. When the white man governs himself, that is self-government, but when he governs himself and also governs another man, that is more than self-government—that is despotism." "Our reliance is in the love of liberty which God has planted in us. Our defense is in the spirit which prizes liberty as the heritage of all men in all lands. Those who deny freedom to others deserve it not for themselves, and under a just God cannot long retain it."

We cordially invite the cooperation of all men and women who remain loyal to the Declaration of Independence and the Constitution of the United States.

Source: https://sourcebooks.fordham.edu/mod/1899antiimp.asp

A United Body of Action
1900–1916

< NAACP Silent Protest Parade, 1917

Helen Keller

Like many women of her generation, Helen Keller, born in 1880 to a wealthy family in Tuscumbia, Alabama, attended college. Of her first day, she later wrote, "It was a day full of interest for me. I had looked forward to it for years." In 1904, she graduated cum laude from Radcliffe College, the all-women sister institution to Harvard College. Diploma in hand, Keller joined many turn-of-the-century middle-class Americans as they assessed an America in need of change and dedicated themselves to improving it.

Keller, though, was unlike her peers. Blind and deaf since she had been stricken by "brain fever" when she was 19 months old, Keller had completed her university education with the assistance of her long-time friend and teacher, Anne Sullivan, who signed for Helen all the lectures and readings that were not available in Braille. As the first deaf and blind person to earn a college degree, Helen was an object of public fascination, something of a celebrity. The public celebrated her as an example of the triumph of the individual against the most difficult of circumstances. With hard work and dedication, she had overcome unimaginable hurdles.

But Keller, like so many activists at the turn of the century, rejected this model of individualism. An ongoing commitment to the rights of the disabled, coupled with continued reading on society and philosophy by radical authors such as Karl Marx, H. G. Wells, and **Eugene Debs**, led Keller, in 1908, to join the American Socialist Party, which assessed modern problems as economic in nature and advocated on behalf of (ideally, nonviolent) revolution.

The leading causes of disability in the United States, Keller determined, were related to accidents occurring and diseases acquired in the industrial workplace. These accidents and health issues arose as a result of employer greed and negligence, a refusal to make worker safety a priority. Once disabled, people were dismissed, Keller argued, and constituted a class that, as a rule, were poor. They joined the ranks of the impoverished as they were cut off from educational and employment opportunities, condemned to live in overcrowded slums, and received often limited and insufficient medical care.

While Keller claimed the necessity of a full-scale revolution, she echoed the views of those who believed in the need to reform the existing social structure. In her conception of disability rights, the issue was not that disabled people did not fit into society as it was. The issue was that society was constructed in such a way that it failed to fit all of its existing members. She extended this view to a class analysis, believing that capitalism inevitably subjugated the working class and resulted in tremendous inequality. In a 1913 lecture, she made clear the limits of individualism and the need to change society: "No one of us can do anything alone. . . we are bound together. I do not like this world as it is. I am trying to make it a little more as I would like to have it."

Many of Keller's contemporaries likewise believed in the necessity of co-operation and similarly wished to make the world more as they would like to have it. The majority of American reformers—known as progressives—did not, however, share her political radicalism. The possibility of a violent conflict between rich and poor seemed a very real threat. As a whole, progressive reformers—social workers, journalists, lawyers—optimistically believed in people's ability to improve society and each other (a radicalism of its own kind). They believed in the need for the establishment of and adherence to a moral, distinctly middle-class model, cultivated and spread by new institutions and enforced by new laws. Progressives employed science and religion to justify their beliefs and, upon that basis, advocated for the supervision of human affairs by qualified experts. Critical of the rich and the poor, progressives believed in the necessity of an activist government to oversee the actions and behaviors of both. The radicalism espoused by socialists like Keller pushed conservatives who had long supported a laissez-faire style of government to respond to progressive calls for reform rather than face the possibility of a full-scale political uprising.

TOWARD A NEW POLITICS

Progressivism displaced the intensely partisan politics of the late nineteenth century. The political and economic crises of the 1890s left Americans disillusioned with traditional parties. A growing socialist movement threatened more radical action if moderate reform failed. Protestant churches spoke out against capitalism's abuses, and new interpretations of Christian ethics lent a moral urgency to reform. The dangers of urban life gave educated, affluent Americans a sense that civic problems needed to be dealt with immediately. Women took leading roles, using pressure groups to extend their influence while also seeking the vote.

Egged on by the press, progressives organized to solve the problems of the new industrial world. Although they sometimes idealized smaller towns and bygone eras, progressives recognized that large-scale industrial capitalism was here to stay. They worked as troubleshooters to make an erratic and brutal system more predictable, efficient, and humane. In pushing for reform, they were willing to enlarge the power of the state and to use it to tell people what was good for them. As reform gained momentum, mayors, governors, and presidential candidates identified themselves and their agendas as progressive.

The Insecurity of Modern Life

Most people who lived in cities at the turn of the century had grown up in the country (see Figure 19–1). They remembered living in communities where people knew each other, where much of what they ate and wore was made locally. In the modern

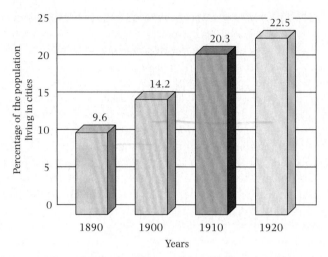

Figure 19-1 Percentage of the Population Living in Cities, 1890–1920 Cities and towns underwent dramatic growth around the turn of the century. Offices, department stores, and new forms of mass entertainment—from vaudeville to professional sports— drew people to the city center. Railroads and trolleys allowed cities to spread outward, segregating residents by class.
Source: Paul Kennedy, *Rise and Fall of the Great Powers* (New York: Random House, 1987), p. 200.

city, water, fuel, and transportation were all supplied by large, anonymous corporations. Unknown executives made decisions that affected the livelihoods, savings, and safety of thousands of people. City dwellers felt more sophisticated than their parents but also less secure.

City living carried risks. Inspecting a Chicago market, journalist Upton Sinclair found milk laced with formaldehyde, peas colored green with copper salts, and sausage doctored with toxic chemicals. Dozens of patent medicines—including aspirin, cocaine, and heroin—were sold as remedies for everything from hay fever to cancer.

Tenement blocks housing hundreds of people often had no fire escapes or plumbing. Tragedy reminded New Yorkers of these dangers on March 25, 1911, when fire engulfed the Triangle Shirtwaist Company on the top three floors of a 10-story building. Five hundred Jewish and Italian seamstresses were trapped; many jumped from ledges in groups, holding hands. In all, 146 died. Such episodes demonstrated that an unregulated economy could be both productive and deadly.

Government added to the problem. Regulation often created kickbacks and bribery. In 1904 and 1905, journalist Lincoln Steffens uncovered corruption in state after state. In New York, insurance companies paid off elected officials in return for favorable legislation. In San Francisco, boss Abraham Ruef ruled the city with a slush fund from public utilities. The Minneapolis police, along with the mayor's office, protected brothels and gambling dens in return for bribes. Elections made the system less accountable, not more. By creating a demand for campaign funds and jobs, elections became invitations to graft.

The rising middle class found public and corporate irresponsibility infuriating. In stately Victorian "streetcar suburbs," business managers, accountants, engineers,

Triangle Shirtwaist Fire
Disasters often galvanized support for new laws. After the March 25, 1911, fire at the Triangle Shirtwaist Company in Greenwich Village killed 146 young workers, many of whom jumped from the seventh, eighth, and ninth stories of the building to escape flames, New York finally enacted legislation on factory safety.

lawyers, and doctors became aware of themselves as a class, but one trapped between two groups, the rich and the masses of wage laborers. Because of education and experience, members of the middle class had their own ideas on how organizations, such as utility companies, cities, and states, should run. Modern corporations needed clear lines of authority, an emphasis on efficiency, and reliable sources of information. Yet these virtues were frustratingly absent from civic life.

The Decline of Partisan Politics

Participation in elections declined by choice and coercion. Nationally, 79 percent of the electorate voted in 1896, but four years later only 73 percent voted, and by 1904 the total fell to 65 percent (see Figure 19–2). Literacy tests accounted for much of the decline in the South, but in all regions the old spectacular style of electioneering, with parades and rallies, gave way to campaigns that were more educational and less participatory. Worse for the parties, the voters split their tickets. The ethnic and sectional loyalties that led to straight party ballots in the late nineteenth century seemed to be weakening.

Increasingly, Americans participated in politics through associations. Voluntary and professional societies took over functions that once belonged to the parties: educating voters and even making policy. These "interest groups" worked outside the system to gather support for a cause or proposal. Many were patterned after corporations, with a board of directors and state and local chapters. Built on the idea that reform was a continuous process, they strove for permanence. Some, such as the **National Association for the Advancement of Colored People (NAACP),** the Salvation Army, and the Sierra Club, are still prominent.

Social Housekeeping

The mounting clamor for change aroused political strength in unexpected places. Women's social clubs had been nonpolitical before the turn of the century. Dedicated to developing public talents such as art, speaking, reading, and conversation, they were highly organized, with local, state, and national chapters. A General Federation of Women's Clubs was formed in 1890. Within 10 years, the urgency of

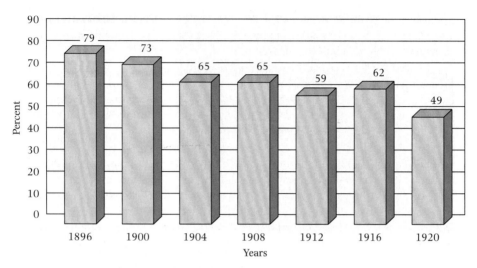

Figure 19-2 Voter Participation, 1896–1920 After the intense partisanship and high-stakes elections of the 1890s, campaigns became more "educational" and voters lost interest.

social problems led many clubs to campaign for free kindergartens, civil service reform, and public health.

A growing cohort of professional women energized reform. The first generation of graduates from the new women's colleges had reached adulthood, and some, like **Helen Keller**, had attained advanced degrees at a time when few men went to college. These "new women," as historians have called them, had ambitions and values different from those of their mothers' generation. About half did not marry. With career paths closed to them, educated women found careers by finding problems that needed solving. Florence Kelley, trained as a lawyer, became Illinois's first state factory inspector and later directed the National Consumers League. Margaret Sanger, a New York public health nurse, distributed literature on birth control and sex education when it was illegal to do so. Sophonisba Breckinridge, with a doctorate from the University of Chicago, led the struggle against child labor. Female activists discovered problems, publicized them, lobbied for new laws, and then staffed the bureaus and agencies administering the solutions.

Women's professional associations, unions, business clubs, ethnic and patriotic societies, and foundations changed the practice of democracy. What was once considered charity or volunteer work became political. Some groups, such as the Young Women's Christian Association (YWCA, 1894) and the International Council of Nurses (1899), had a global reach. The experiences of women's groups taught activists the importance of cooperation, organization, and expertise. When women's clubs built a playground and donated it to the city, they increased their stake in the political system. Likewise, advocating on behalf of women's political role was the National Association of Colored Women's Clubs (NACWC, 1896), which launched campaigns against lynching and Jim Crow laws. All of these organizations gave women new reasons to demand full citizenship.

The **women's suffrage movement** grew quietly in the early years of the century. Women had gained the vote in four states—Colorado, Wyoming, Utah, and

Idaho—but between 1896 and 1910 no other states adopted a women's suffrage amendment. The movement was stubbornly opposed by the Catholic Church, machine politicians, and business interests.

Competing suffrage organizations joined forces under the National American Woman Suffrage Association (NAWSA). Led by Carrie Chapman Catt and Anna Howard Shaw, NAWSA developed a strategy based on professional lobbying and publicity. Suffragists appealed to clubwomen and middle-class reformers by cultivating an image of Victorian respectability and linking suffrage to moderate social causes, such as temperance and education. At first, NAWSA's strategy paid off. After 1910, five states adopted suffrage amendments, but the opposition rallied and defeated referenda in three states.

Frustrated with the glacial pace of progress, Alice Paul's National Woman's Party adopted more radical tactics, picketing the White House and staging hunger strikes. Despite setbacks, women led the transformation of politics through voluntary organizations and interest groups and were on the threshold of even greater gains.

Evolution or Revolution?

Founded in 1901, the Socialist Party's swelling membership seemed to confirm its claims that the future would be revolutionary rather than progressive. In 1912, **Eugene V. Debs,** the party's candidate for president, won almost a million votes, or 6 percent of the total. "Gas and water" Socialists, who demanded public ownership of utilities, captured offices in many smaller cities. In the plains states, socialism drew strength from primitive Baptist and Holiness churches and held revival-style tent meetings. In Oklahoma, almost one-quarter of the electorate voted Socialist in 1914.

Although tinged with religion, Socialists' analysis of modern problems was economic. They maintained that the profit motive distorted human behavior, forcing people to compete for survival as individuals instead of joining to promote the common good. Driven by profits, corporations could not be trusted with the welfare of consumers or workers. Socialists demanded the collective ownership of industries, starting with ones that most directly affected people's lives: railroads and city utilities. Socialists had faith that America could make the transition without violence and that socialism was surely "coming like a prairie fire," a Socialist newspaperman told his readers. "Social Gospel" clergymen preached this coming millennium. Washington Gladden, a Congregationalist pastor from Ohio; Walter Rauschenbusch, a Baptist minister from New York; William Dwight Porter Bliss, who founded the Society for Christian Socialists; and George Herron, an Iowa Congregationalist, were among the prominent ministers who interpreted the Bible as a call to social action. Their visions of the Christian commonwealth ranged from reform to revolution, but they all believed that corporate capitalism was organized sin and that the church had an obligation to stand against it.

When the Industrial Workers of the World (IWW) talked about revolution, they meant class war, not elections. Founded in 1905, the IWW (known as the "Wobblies") unionized some of the most rugged individuals in the West: miners, loggers, and even rodeo cowboys (under the Bronco Busters and Range Riders Union). Gathering unskilled workers into "one big union," the Wobblies challenged the AFL's elite unionism and the Socialists' gradualism. With fewer than 100,000 members, the union and its leader, William "Big Bill" Haywood, had a reputation

for radicalism. In Lawrence, Massachusetts, and Paterson, New Jersey, IWW strikers clashed with police and paraded under red flags with thousands of marchers.
To an anxious middle class, these activities looked like signs of an approaching
conflict between rich and poor.

Conservatives and reformers alike felt the hot breath of revolution on their
necks, and socialism's greatest influence may have been the push it gave conservatives to support moderate reform. **Theodore Roosevelt** warned that without
reform the United States would divide into two parties, one representing workers,
the other capital.

The failure of the two parties to deal with urgent problems created a chance to
redefine democracy. As the new century began, Americans were testing their political ideals, scrapping old rules, and getting ready to fashion new institutions and
laws to deal with the challenges of modern society.

THE PROGRESSIVES

Historians have found it difficult to define the **progressives**. They addressed a
wide variety of social problems with many different tactics but appealed to a
broad audience. A rally to end child labor, for instance, might draw out young
lawyers, teachers, labor unionists, woman suffragists, professors, and politicians.
A series of overlapping movements, campaigns, and crusades defined the era from
1890 to 1920.

Progressivism was a political style, a way of approaching problems. Progressives had no illusions that wage labor or industrialism could be eliminated or
that it was possible to re-create a rural commonwealth. Big cities and big corporations, they believed, were permanent features of modern life, but progressives
were convinced that modern institutions could be made humane, responsive,
and moral.

In choosing solutions, progressives relied on scientific expertise as a way to
avoid the clash of interests. Those raised during the Civil War knew democracy
was no guarantee against mass violence. Rival points of view could be reconciled
more easily by impartial authority. Like the salaried managers many of them were,
progressives valued efficiency and organization. No problem could be solved in a
single stroke, but only by persistent action.

Sure that science and God were on their side, progressives did not balk at imposing their views on other people, even if democracy got in the way. Such measures
as naming "born criminals" to be put on probation before committing a crime were
called "progressive." To southern progressives, "scientific" principles justified racial
segregation. Progressives demanded more democracy when it led to "good government," but if the majority was wrong, in their view, progressives handed power to
unelected managers. The basic structure of American society, they felt, should not
be open to political debate.

Above all, progressives shared an urgency. "There are two kinds of people,"
reformer and occupational health expert Alice Hamilton learned from her mother,
"the ones who say, 'Someone ought to do something about it but why should it be
I?' and the ones who say, 'Somebody must do something about it, then why not I?'"
Hamilton and other progressives never doubted which kind they were.

Social Workers and Muckrakers

Among the first to hear the call to service were the young women and men who volunteered to live among the urban poor in "settlement houses." Stanton Coit established the first on New York's Lower East Side in 1886, but the most famous was **Hull House**, which opened in Chicago three years later. Its founders, **Jane Addams** and Ellen Starr, bought a rundown mansion at the center of an inner-city ward thick with sweatshops, factories, and overcrowded tenements. The women of Hull House opened a kindergarten and a clinic, took sweatshop bosses to court, investigated corrupt landlords, criticized the ward's powerful alderman, and built the city's first public playground.

Addams drew together at Hull House a remarkable group of women with similar backgrounds. Florence Kelley organized a movement for occupational safety laws. Julia Lathrop headed the state's Children's Bureau. All three women were raised in affluent Quaker homes during or shortly after the Civil War, and their parents were all abolitionists. Like Helen Keller, all three attended college and traveled or studied in Europe.

As the fame of Hull House spread, women (and some men) organized settlement houses in cities across the country. By the turn of the century there were more than 100, and by 1910 more than 400. Reformers often began by using social science techniques to survey the surrounding neighborhoods, gathering information on the national origins, income, housing conditions, and occupations of residents.

The Hull House Choir in Recital, 1910 Chicago, according to Lincoln Steffens, was "loud, lawless, unlovely, ill-smelling, new; an overgrown gawk of a village." Addams and other settlement workers sought to tame this urban wilderness through culture and activism.

Struggles For Democracy
Public Response to *The Jungle*

Like other reform-minded journalists of the Progressive Era, **Upton Sinclair** believed in the power of the pen to bring attention to various social troubles and inspire demands for social, economic, and political reform. In 1904, Sinclair began an investigation of Chicago's Packingtown during which he learned firsthand of workers' challenges as they attempted to make a living doing the foul work available in Chicago's stockyards. The result of his investigation was the 1906 novel *The Jungle.* The title reflected Sinclair's critique of the United States' capitalist economy—a cut-throat system, he believed, that robbed people of their humanity as they struggled to survive. Chronicling the travails of the working poor and revealing the horrors of the American meatpacking enterprise through the struggles of Lithuanian immigrant Jurgis Rudkus and his family, the book revealed the limits to the rugged individualism so celebrated by Gilded Age leaders and those who touted the virtues of social Darwinism. Sinclair hoped readers would empathize with workers who toiled under atrocious work conditions, lived in squalor, and suffered from political corruption, all while struggling to achieve the upward mobility they had imagined American life would provide. Socialism, the book concludes, with its focus on equity and cooperation, could lead the American people to a more humane existence.

The novel was an immediate sensation. In the first month and a half after publication, the book sold 25,000 copies. Audiences read Sinclair's fictional account as though it were fact and were outraged by what they read. But the outrage—and calls for reform—differed from what Sinclair had intended. Rather than creating cross-class consciousness or fostering a sense of solidarity with the working-class immigrants described in the text, the novel succeeded in outraging middle-class citizens in their identification as consumers, horrified by descriptions of diseased meat and chemical preservatives in products they might have purchased.

Addams released *Hull-House Maps and Papers*, a survey of the 19th Ward, in 1895. One of the most ambitious research projects was the Pittsburgh Survey, a massive investigation of city living and working conditions published between 1909 and 1914. Its data confirmed that the causes of poverty were social, not personal, contradicting a common belief that the poor had only themselves to blame. Settlements did "social work" rather than charity.

Surveys also used maps, photographs, and even three-dimensional models. In 1900, housing reformers exhibited a scale cutaway model of a New York tenement block, showing how airless, overcrowded rooms contributed to disease and crime. Shelby Harrison, director of surveys for the Russell Sage Foundation, explained that the survey itself was reform, stimulating popular action with "the correcting power of facts."

Meat Inspectors Hogs receive a final inspection at Swift & Co., Chicago, 1906.

President Theodore Roosevelt, no fan of **muckrakers,** was persuaded by Sinclair's indictment of the meatpacking industry. A self-identified progressive, Roosevelt was inclined to regulate food and drugs to prevent misbranding and adulteration. Direct response from readers pushed him to act. When angry letters from those who had read *The Jungle* began to arrive at the White House, Roosevelt authorized the Department of Agriculture to investigate meatpacking in Chicago. Their claim that conditions were fine came as no surprise to Sinclair, who told the president that sending those officials was tantamount to sending a criminal to investigate a crime. When the two men met in the aftermath of this first investigation, Roosevelt resolved to send the US labor commissioner Charles P. Neill and Assistant Treasury Secretary James Bronson Reynolds, assisted by Socialist activist and political organizer Ella Reeve Bloor, to conduct an independent investigation. Their June 1906 report matched descriptions from Sinclair's text. They described "a humid atmosphere heavy with the odors of rotten wood, decayed meats, stinking offal, and entrails" and "dirty, blood-soaked, rotting wood floors, fruitful culture beds for the disease germs of men and animals."

This statistical outlook motivated settlement workers to attack urban problems across a broad front. Social workers labored to ensure food safety, repair housing, and sponsor festivals and pageants. Working conditions, especially for women and children, drew special attention, but employers, landlords, and city bosses were not the only targets: those involved in working-class vices—in gambling establishments, saloons, and brothels—were also attacked. The loudest voice of progressivism came from a new type of journalism introduced in 1902. In successive issues, *McClure's* magazine published Lincoln Steffens's investigation of graft in St. Louis and Ida Tarbell's "History of the Standard Oil Company," sensational exposés of the crimes of the nation's political and economic elite. As periodicals competed for readers, the old partisan style of journalism gave way to crusades, celebrities, and "sob sister" features. The new 10-cent magazines, such as *Everybody's*, *Cosmopolitan*, and *McClure's*, had audiences and budgets big enough to pay for in-depth investigations. The result was a type of reporting Theodore Roosevelt disdainfully called "muckraking." Readers loved it, and an article exposing some new corporate or public villainy could easily sell half a million copies.

In the aftermath of the report—and as a result of the efforts of other muckrakers like Samuel Hopkins Adams, who called attention to the patent medicine industry's false claims and peddling of often dangerous products—President Roosevelt endorsed the Pure Food and Drug Act of 1906 as well as the Federal Meat Inspection Act of the same year. The laws created sanitary standards for the meatpacking industry and federal inspections of animals to be slaughtered, and made criminal the misbranding of food and drugs. Demonstrating the progressive commitment to research, problem solving, and government oversight, the legislation also represented the power of the public voice in effecting real change.

Muckrakers named names. Upton Sinclair described the grisly business of canning beef. Ray Stannard Baker investigated railroads and segregation. Samuel Hopkins Adams catalogued the damage done by narcotics in popular medicines. Tarbell exposed Standard Oil's camouflaged companies, espionage, sweetheart deals, and predatory pricing. Her series shattered the notion that industrial giants competed in a free market and pushed the Justice Department to sue Standard Oil in 1906 for conspiracy to restrain trade.

The 10-cent magazines projected local problems onto a national canvas. Newspapers had covered municipal corruption before, but Steffens's series in *McClure's* revealed that bribery, influence peddling, and protection rackets operated in nearly every major city. Magazines also reported on progressive victories, allowing solutions adopted in Toledo or Milwaukee to spread quickly. Muckraking declined after 1912, the victim of corporate advertising boycotts and declining readership, but while it lasted, "public opinion" became a force that could shake the powerful.

Dictatorship of the Experts

For doctors, lawyers, and engineers, reform offered a chance to apply their skills to urgent problems, and the Progressive Era coincided with the rise in influence of the social sciences and the professions. Experts could mediate potentially violent conflicts and eliminate the uncertainties of democracy. Scientific advances seemed to justify this faith. In just a generation, antiseptic techniques, X-rays, and new drugs created a new understanding of disease. Electric light, recorded sound, motion pictures, radio, and flight confirmed science's ability to shape the future.

Social workers copied doctors, diagnosing each case with clinical impartiality. Newly professionalized police forces applied the techniques of fingerprinting, handwriting analysis, and psychology to law enforcement. Dietitians installed bland but nutritionally balanced meals in school cafeterias. Reformers tried (but failed) to simplify spelling and bring "efficiency" to the English language.

Trust in science sometimes led to extreme measures. One was the practice of **eugenics**, an attempt to rid society of alcoholism, poverty, and crime through selective breeding. "If the knowledge [of eugenics] were applied, the defective classes would disappear within a generation," the president of the University of Wisconsin predicted. Persuaded that genetics could save the state money, the Indiana legislature passed a law in 1907 authorizing the forced sterilization of "criminals, idiots, rapists, and imbeciles." Patients with epilepsy, psychiatric disorders, or mental handicaps who sought help at state hospitals were surgically sterilized. Criminals received the same treatment. Seven other states also adopted the "Indiana Plan."

The emphasis on expertise hid a thinly veiled distrust of democracy. Professional educators, for example, took control of the schools away from local boards and gave it to expert administrators and superintendents. They certified teachers and classified students based on "scientific" intelligence tests. To reformers, education was too important to be left to amateurs, such as teachers, parents, or voters.

Progressivism created new social sciences and made universities centers of advocacy. Sociology was a product of the progressive impulse. The study of government became political science, and "scientific" historians searched the past for answers to modern problems. John R. Commons, Richard Ely, and Thorstein Veblen used economics to study how modern institutions developed and functioned. Legal scholars such as Louis Brandeis and Roscoe Pound called for revising the law to reflect social realities.

This stress on expertise made Progressive Era reforms different from those of earlier periods. Instead of trying to succeed at a single stroke—by passing a law or trouncing a corrupt politician—progressives believed in process and established organizations and procedures that would keep the pressure on and make progress a habit.

Progressives on the Color Line

In her international crusade against lynching, **Ida B. Wells-Barnett** pioneered some of the progressive tactics of research, exposure, and organization. A schoolteacher in Memphis, Wells-Barnett documented mob violence against African Americans and mobilized opinion in the United States and Britain. Cities that condoned extralegal executions soon faced a barrage of condemnation from church groups and women's clubs. As her Afro-American Council grew, Wells-Barnett joined forces with white suffragists, social workers, and journalists, but her cause was not fully embraced. Many reform groups sympathized with white southerners or wanted to avoid dividing their membership over race.

Reformers debated how much progress non-Anglo-Saxons were capable of, but they were inclined to be pessimistic. Eugenics gave white supremacy the endorsement of science. A new technology, the motion picture, showed its power to rewrite history from a racial viewpoint in D. W. Griffith's classic *Birth of a Nation* (1915), which romanticized the Klan's campaign of terror during Reconstruction. Policy was often based on racial assumptions. Trade schools, not universities, were deemed appropriate for educating Filipinos and Hawaiians. Progressives took Native American children from their families and placed them in boarding schools. Electoral reform in Texas meant disfranchising Spanish-speaking voters.

Wells-Barnett was not alone in finding doors through this wall of racial ideology. **William Edward Burghardt DuBois** documented the costs of racism in *The Philadelphia Negro* (1898). The survey spoke the progressives' language, insisting that discrimination was not just morally wrong but inefficient, because it took away work and encouraged alcoholism and crime. DuBois transformed the politics of race as profoundly as Addams transformed the politics of cities.

Silent Protest Parade Organized by the NAACP, church, and community leadership, nearly 10,000 African Americans marched along Fifth Avenue in New York City in July 1917. Inspired by the racial violence that had recently transpired in East St. Louis, Illinois, the parade more broadly served as a protest against racial discrimination and oppression in the United States and around the world.

Raised in Massachusetts, DuBois learned Latin and Greek in public schools. At 17, he went to Fisk University in Tennessee, where he "came in contact for the first time with a sort of violence that [he] had never realized in New England." He also had his first encounter with African American religion and gospel music, which was "full of the voices of the past." DuBois later studied at Harvard and Berlin.

DuBois and Booker T. Washington espoused opposing visions of African Americans' place in the United States. Both emphasized the importance of thrift and hard work. DuBois, however, rejected Washington's willingness to accept legal inequality. DuBois came to believe that the Atlanta Compromise (see Chapter 18) led only to disfranchisement and segregation. He disliked the way Washington's influence with white philanthropists silenced other voices. Five years after the Atlanta speech he opened a sustained attack on Washington's "Tuskegee Machine."

In *The Souls of Black Folk* (1903), DuBois argued that the strategy of accommodation contained a "triple paradox": Washington had urged African Americans to seek industrial training, build self-respect, and become successful in business, while asking them to stop striving for higher education, civil rights, or political power. How could a people train themselves without higher education or gain self-respect without having any of the rights other Americans enjoyed—or succeed in business without the power to protect themselves or their property? Economic, political, and educational progress had to move together. Like other progressives, DuBois insisted on the importance of process and organization. African Americans could not stop demanding the vote, equality, or education.

In July 1905, DuBois and 28 African American leaders met on the Canadian side of Niagara Falls (no hotel on the US side would admit them) to organize a campaign against racial violence, segregation, and disfranchisement. The Niagara Movement was one of several such organizations. In 1909, Wells-Barnett, Addams, and other reformers created the **National Association for the Advancement of Colored People** to carry on the fight in the courts. In 1915, the NAACP won a Supreme Court decision outlawing the grandfather clause, which denied the vote to descendants of enslaved people; but another 40 years passed before it succeeded in overturning *Plessy v. Ferguson.*

PROGRESSIVES IN STATE AND LOCAL POLITICS

Progressives were of two minds about the public. Walter Lippmann, a journalist and reformer, could write fondly of "the voiceless multitudes" and contemptuously of the "great dull mass of people who just don't care." Progressives' tactics betrayed this split vision. Their reforms made city government less democratic and more "businesslike." Reforms at the state level, however, expanded voters' power to initiate legislation and remove officeholders. In both cases, the changes enlarged the influence of small-town and urban-middle-class reformers while reducing that of immigrants and the working class.

Redesigning the City

The machine politicians who ran American cities adapted well to change. To immigrants and factory workers, the local boss was one of the few people looking out for the average person. He rushed to fire scenes to aid homeless victims. He distributed turkeys in poor neighborhoods at Christmas. He could be counted on to post bail or find someone a job. Jane Addams acknowledged that she could not compete with Johnny Powers, the popular local ward boss, this "big manifestation of human friendliness, this stalking survival of village kindness."

Powers and other aldermen sheltered the brothels, saloons, and gambling dens that, in Addams's view, exploited honest workers. Hull House organized to beat Powers in 1895, and in defeat the reformers revealed their frustrations with democracy. The reformers nominated an Irish bricklayer, William Gleeson, whom they thought would appeal to the 19th Ward's working-class voters. But voters said they wanted someone grander to represent them, such as Powers, with his big house and diamond buttons. Gleeson was trounced. Addams was "puzzled, then astounded and indignant" at the outcome.

With officials like Powers in charge, corporations could do what they liked if they padded the right wallets. "If you want to get anything out of the council," the head of the Chicago Chamber of Commerce advised, "the quickest way is to pay for it—not to the city, but to the aldermen." City machines lost their appeal by providing not too few services but too many. As tax burdens grew, wealthier voters clamored for reform. Progressives set out to replace paternalism with efficient, scientific administration.

After the depression of 1893, many groups sprang up to criticize municipal government, which often resembled the federal system in miniature. A mayor, elected by the whole city, presided over a council of representatives from each neighborhood, or ward. This system diluted the influence of the "better classes" and allowed a few powerful wards to rule the city. In 1899, Louisville's Conference for Good City Government proposed a new model, later known as the "strong mayor" system. It gave more power to the mayor and required each council member to represent the whole city. Two years later, after the hurricane and tidal wave destroyed Galveston, Texas, the devastated city tried an even bolder plan (see Chapter 18). The recovery would be run by a commission of five unelected officials, each managing a city department. Des Moines, Iowa, improved on Galveston's design, and by 1911 some 160 cities had commission governments.

The commission resembled a corporate board of directors. Professionalism and accountability, the keys to business success, could make a city run, too. This philosophy led Detroit voters to elect Ford Motor Company's chief efficiency expert, James Couzens, as mayor. Other cities, led by Dayton, Ohio, tried to improve on the **city-commission plan** by placing local government in the hands of an unelected "city manager."

Middle- and upper-class professionals led this revolution in city government, and they gained the most from it. The new officials could explain where tax money was spent, but there were no turkeys at Christmas. Getting a job from the city meant filling out the proper forms. Reform administrations targeted urban "vice," which included most working-class recreations. Voters also learned that efficiency did not lower taxes. Budgets grew along with the public's demand for services.

Reform Mayors and City Services

While commissioners rewrote the rules, a new breed of reform mayors cleaned up their cities. Samuel "Golden Rule" Jones, a Welsh immigrant who earned a fortune in the oil fields, won election three times as independent mayor of Toledo. He enacted the eight-hour day for city employees, pushed for public ownership of city utilities, and staged free concerts in the parks. Like Tom Johnson in Cleveland and Hazen Pingree in Detroit, Jones worried less about saloons and more about utilities. Milwaukee, Schenectady, and other cities bought or regulated the private monopolies that supplied lighting, garbage removal, water, and streetcars.

The reform mayors' efforts to humanize the city were supported by architects and engineers who looked to improve urban life through the arrangement of public space. The City Beautiful movement sought to soften the urban landscape with vistas, open spaces, and greenery. The District of Columbia, with its commission government, broad avenues, and parks, furnished a model of city planning, and Congress sought to make it a model of municipal reform as well by introducing a model child-labor law, slum-clearance plan, and school system. The new urban spaces performed social and educational functions as well, especially to

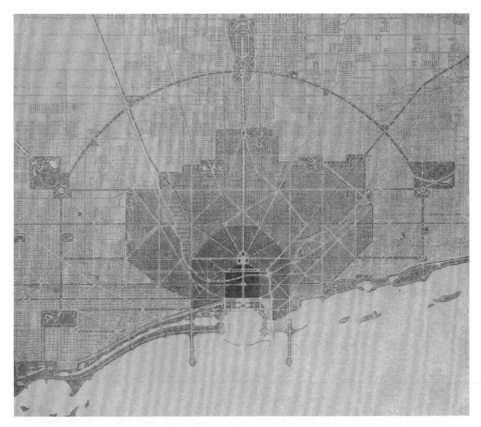

Daniel Burnham's City Plan for Chicago, 1909 Through comprehensive planning, Burnham sought to save cities from "the chaos incident to rapid growth." He drafted designs for Washington, DC as well as Cleveland, San Francisco, and Manila.

Americanize and uplift immigrant city dwellers. New York enacted zoning laws in 1916, and "city planners" joined the ranks of specialists by organizing themselves as a profession.

Progressives and the States

State reform varied by region. The East mimicked the agenda of urban reform. New York's progressive governor, Charles Evans Hughes, passed laws that prohibited gambling and created a state commission to regulate utilities. In southern states, progressivism often meant refining the techniques of segregation and disfranchisement. Lynching and mob assaults on African Americans were weekly occurrences in the Progressive Era. White leaders justified segregation and violence in terms used to justify urban reform in the North: the "better classes" had an obligation to rein in the excesses of democracy.

States in the West and Midwest produced the boldest experiments. Oregon introduced the secret ballot, voter registration, and three measures originally proposed by the Populists: the **initiative, recall, and referendum.** The initiative allowed voters to place legislation on the ballot by petition; the referendum let the legislature put proposals on the ballot; and the recall gave voters the chance to remove officials from office before the end of their terms. Other states soon adopted all or part of the "Oregon system."

The best known of the progressive governors was **Robert M. "Fighting Bob" La Follette,** whose model of state government came to be known as the "Wisconsin Idea." Elected in 1900, La Follette pushed through a comprehensive program of social legislation. Railways and public utilities were placed under public control. One commission designed a "scientific" distribution of the tax burden, including an income tax, whereas others regulated hours and working conditions and protected the environment. Wisconsin also implemented the direct primary, which allowed party nominees to be chosen directly by voters rather than by party caucuses.

Few machine politicians had as much personal power as the reform governors did. Wisconsin papers would call La Follette a "demagogue," but the reform governors brought policy making out of the "smoke-filled rooms." By shaking up city halls and statehouses, progressives made the public less cynical and government more responsive to reform. They knew, however, that social problems did not respect political boundaries: national corporations and nationwide problems had to be attacked at the federal level, and that meant capturing the White House.

A PUSH FOR "GENUINE DEMOCRACY" AND A "MORAL AWAKENING"

If Theodore Roosevelt stood at the center of the two great movements of his age, imperialism and progressivism, it was because he prepared himself for the part. The Roosevelt family was wealthy and one of the oldest in New York, but Theodore embarked instead on pursuits that were unusual for a man of his class. After graduating from Harvard in 1880, he married, started law school, wrote a history of the War of 1812, bought a cattle ranch in the Dakota Territory, and, most surprisingly, ran for the state legislature.

For Roosevelt's family and friends, government was no place for gentlemen. Roosevelt himself described his colleagues as "a stupid, sodden, vicious lot, most of them being equally deficient in brains and virtue." Avoiding the "rough and tumble," he argued, only conceded high offices to those less fit to lead. Roosevelt's flair for publicity got him noticed, and in 1886 the Republican Party nominated him for mayor of New York. He finished third, behind the Tammany nominee and the Socialist candidate.

A turn as head of New York's board of police commissioners from 1895 to 1897 deepened Roosevelt's commitment to reform. The commission supervised an army of 38,000 policemen. Roosevelt's crackdown on saloons and corruption in the police department earned him a reputation as a man who would not be intimidated, even by his own party's bosses, and when McKinley won the presidency, he named Roosevelt assistant secretary of the navy. The Spanish-American War catapulted him to national fame, and in quick succession he became governor of New York, vice president, and then president of the United States.

Roosevelt believed that to restore democracy—"genuine democracy"—America needed a mission, "a genuine and permanent moral awakening." In the White House, he sought great tasks—duties to be carried out, principles to be upheld, isthmuses to be cut, and lands to be conserved—to inspire a common purpose and test the national will. In the process, he rewrote the president's job description, seizing new powers for the executive branch and turning the presidency into "the administration."

The Executive Branch Against the Trusts

Roosevelt approached politics the way Jane Addams approached poverty: studying it, living in its midst, and carefully choosing his battles. His fear of radicalism was borne out in September 1901. President William McKinley was shaking hands at the Pan American Exposition in Buffalo, New York, when a man thrust a pistol into his chest and fired twice. The assassin, Leon Czolgosz, came from the Cleveland slums and claimed to seek vengeance for the poor.

At age 42, Roosevelt was the youngest man to attain the presidency. He was the first president to call himself a progressive, and the first, according to Lippmann, "who realized clearly that national stability and social justice had to be sought deliberately and had consciously to be maintained." Unsatisfied merely to lead his party, he set out to remake the executive as the preeminent branch of government, initiating legislation, shaping public opinion, and protecting the national interest at home and abroad. "I believe in power," he explained. Instead of asking Congress for legislation, he drafted bills and lobbied for them personally. He believed government should intervene in the economy to protect citizens or to save business from itself. McKinley had already planned against the trusts, but his plans were not as bold as his successor's.

Challenging the corporations would not be easy. Roosevelt took office less than a decade after J. P. Morgan rescued the federal Treasury. In 1895, the Supreme Court gutted the Sherman Act, one of the few laws allowing federal action against monopolies. The underfunded Interstate Commerce Commission possessed few powers. Roosevelt told Congress "publicity is the only sure remedy which we can now invoke." He used it to the limit, putting Wall Street on notice in his first inaugural when he asserted that trusts "are creatures of the State, and the State not only has the right to control them, but it is duty bound to control them." In 1903, Roosevelt established a Department of Commerce and Labor that required annual reports, making corporate activities transparent.

The Justice Department revitalized the Sherman Act with vigorous prosecutions, and Roosevelt selected cases for maximum publicity value. Attorney General Philander Knox filed suit against J. P. Morgan's holding company, Northern Securities. Morgan expected the matter to be settled in the usual way, and his attorney asked how they might "fix it up." "We don't want to fix it up," Knox replied. "We want to stop it." When the Court handed Roosevelt a victory in 1904, Americans cheered.

With this case, Roosevelt gained an undeserved reputation as a "trust buster." He did oppose serious abuses, but he distinguished between good and bad trusts and believed that government should encourage responsible corporations to grow. He agreed with such progressive writers as Herbert Croly, editor of the *New Republic*, who imagined a central government staffed by nonpartisan experts who would monitor big corporations to assure efficiency and head off destructive actions.

Not all progressives agreed. Louis Brandeis and **Woodrow Wilson** envisioned a political economy of small, highly competitive firms kept in line by regular use of the Sherman Act. To Roosevelt, there was no future in a small-business economy. Only large combinations could compete on a world scale, and government's obligation was not to break them up but to regulate them. He secured passage of the Hepburn Act (1906), which allowed the commission to set freight rates and banned "sweetheart" deals (of the kind Standard Oil enjoyed) with favored clients. The Mann-Elkins Act (1910) regulated telephone, telegraph, and cable communications. The Pure Food and Drug Act (1906) responded to Upton Sinclair's exposé of the meatpacking industry by making it a crime to ship or sell contaminated or fraudulently labeled food and drugs. Under Roosevelt, the federal government gained the tools to counterbalance the power of business. It grew to match its responsibilities. The number of federal employees almost doubled between 1900 and 1916.

The Square Deal

Roosevelt's exasperation with big business reached a peak during the coal strike of 1902. The United Mine Workers represented 150,000 miners in the coalfields of eastern Pennsylvania. The miners, mostly Polish, Hungarian, and Italian immigrants, earned less than $6 a week, and more than 400 died yearly to supply the coal to run railroads and heat homes. Seventy percent of the mines were owned by six railroads, which in turn were controlled by the usual financiers, including Morgan and Rockefeller. The owners refused to deal with the union, declaring it a band of outlaws. When the miners struck in May, they had the public's sympathy. Editorials, even in Republican newspapers, urged the president to take the mines away from the owners.

The "gross blindness of the operators" infuriated Roosevelt. Coal was the only fuel for heating, and a strike might cause hundreds to freeze. After failing to get the sides to negotiate, he invited union officials and the operators to Washington so that he could personally arbitrate. John Mitchell, head of the mine workers, eagerly accepted the offer, but the owners refused.

For Roosevelt this was the final straw. He prepared the army to move into the coalfields and put the mines under government control. The owners capitulated, agreeing to submit the dispute to a federal commission. The result was a compromise: miners received a 10 percent increase in pay and a nine-hour workday, but owners did not have to recognize the union.

Roosevelt's direct action made the federal government a third force in labor disputes. For the first time a strike was settled by federal arbitration, and for the first time a union had struck a strategic industry without being denounced as a radical conspiracy. The government would no longer automatically side with the corporations. "We demand that big business give the people a square deal," Roosevelt explained. "In return, we must insist that when anyone engaged in big business honestly endeavors to do right, he shall be given a square deal."

Conserving Water, Land, and Forests

When Roosevelt felt important issues were at stake, he pushed the limits of his office. He enraged Congress by stretching the definitions of presidential power, especially in the area of **conservation** (see Map 19–1). When Congress sent him a

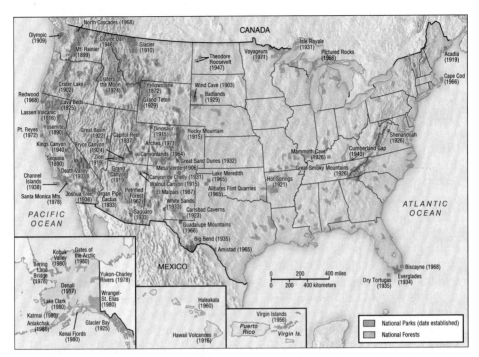

Map 19–1 Growth of Public Lands Responding to a national conservation movement, Roosevelt set aside public lands for use as parks and managed-yield forests. The National Park Service was founded in 1916.

bill to halt the creation of new national forests in the West, Roosevelt first created or enlarged 32 national forests and then signed the bill. To stop private companies from damming rivers, he reserved 2,500 of the best hydropower sites by declaring them "ranger stations." Behind his program was Gifford Pinchot, the chief forester of the United States, who saw conservation as a new frontier. Unsettled, undeveloped lands were growing scarce, and Pinchot convinced the president of the value in managing resources more efficiently. Forests, deserts, and ore ranges were to be used wisely, scientifically, and in the national interest.

One of Roosevelt's first victories was the Newlands Reclamation Act (1902), which gave the Agriculture Department authority to build reservoirs and irrigation systems in the West. In the next four years, 3 million acres were "reclaimed" from the desert and turned into farms. To prevent waste, Roosevelt put tighter controls on prospecting, grazing, and logging. Big lumber and mining companies accepted rationalized resource administration, but small-scale prospectors and ranchers were shut out of federal lands. Naturalists like John Muir also resisted, pointing out that nature was to be appreciated, not used.

By 1909, conservation had become a national issue and created a new constituency of hikers, sightseers, and tourism entrepreneurs. By quadrupling the acreage in federal reserves, professionalizing the Forest Service, and using his "bully pulpit" to build support for conservation, Roosevelt helped create the modern environmental movement.

Theodore Roosevelt and Big Stick Diplomacy

Imperial and commercial expansion put new strains on foreign and military policy after the turn of the century. US investors wanted Washington to protect their overseas factories and railroads against civil wars and hostile governments. Diplomatic and military budgets grew to meet these demands. Diplomats were no longer political cronies but trained professionals, and diplomacy was no longer a matter of weathering "incidents" but of making policy.

Roosevelt's view of world affairs flowed from his understanding of the past and the future. Global trade and communications, he believed, united "civilized" nations. His foreign policy aimed to keep the United States in the mainstream of commerce, imperialism, and military (particularly naval) modernization. He felt a duty to interfere with "barbarian" governments in Asia, Latin America, or Africa that blocked progress. The United States was obliged, he felt, to overthrow governments and even to seize territory when it was acting in the interests of the world as a whole.

Building an interoceanic canal topped Roosevelt's list of foreign policy priorities. A canal would be a hub of world trade and naval power in the Atlantic and Pacific, and Roosevelt aimed to prevent France or Britain from building it. He negotiated a deal to buy out a failed French venture in the Colombian province of Panama.

A civil war in Colombia complicated his plans. In 1902, American diplomats brokered a peace between modernizers led by José Marroquín and traditionalists who fiercely opposed the canal. Marroquín favored it but knew war would erupt again unless the Americans gave Bogotá full control over the canal. For Roosevelt, control was not negotiable.

In the spring of 1903, Panamanian senators, upset by the rejection of the US offer, began planning to secede. Panama had had revolutions before, but the United States had always stepped in to preserve Colombia's sovereignty. Together with Philippe Bunau-Varilla, who represented the French company, the Panamanians lobbied US officials to support their plot. Bunau-Varilla predicted a revolution for November 3, thereby ensuring that the rebels, the Colombian army (which had been bribed into surrendering), and US warships would all be on hand.

The revolution went off without a hitch, and Roosevelt presented the new Panamanian government with a treaty that gave less and took more than the one offered to Colombia. Congress launched an investigation. "I took the canal and let Congress debate," Roosevelt said, "and while the debate goes on the canal does also." The **Panama Canal**, a 50-mile cut built under the direction of George W. Goethals at a cost of $352 million and more than 5,600 lives, opened in 1914.

With construction under way, Roosevelt acted to protect the canal from other powers. Poverty in the region created opportunities for imperial governments to establish bases on Panama's doorstep. In 1902, Germany almost invaded Venezuela over an unpaid loan, but Roosevelt stepped in to mediate. When the Dominican Republic later reneged on its loans, four European nations laid plans for a debt-collecting expedition.

Roosevelt went before Congress in December 1904 and announced a policy later known as the Roosevelt Corollary. It stipulated that when chronic "wrongdoing or impotence" in a Latin American country required "intervention by some civilized nation," the United States would do the intervening. In Roosevelt's view, white "civilized" nations acted; nonwhite "impotent" nations were acted on. The next month, the United States took over the Dominican Republic's customs offices and began repaying creditors. The economic intervention turned military in 1916, when the United States landed marines to protect the customs from Dominican rebels. US troops stayed in the Dominican Republic until the early 1920s.

By enforcing order and efficiency in the Caribbean, Roosevelt extended progressivism beyond the borders of the United States. The movement spread to the Far East, too. In 1906, a US federal court was created in Shanghai, China, to control prostitution in the American community there.

Taft and Dollar Diplomacy

Enormously popular at the end of his second term, Roosevelt chose his friend William H. Taft to succeed him. Taft gained national attention as a circuit judge whose decisions enlarged federal power to regulate trusts. As governor general of the Philippines, he brought reform to Manila. Taft easily defeated William Jennings Bryan in the 1908 election, and as president he began consolidating Roosevelt's gains. He sent to the states constitutional amendments for the direct election of senators and for the income tax. He increased antitrust enforcement and levied the first tax on corporations. Satisfied that his legacy would continue, Roosevelt left for a tour of Africa.

In the Caribbean, Taft put the Roosevelt Corollary into action (see Map 19–2). The United States bought up the debts of Honduras and Nicaragua. Taft persuaded New York banks to refinance Haiti's debt to prevent German intervention there. Taft intended "**dollar diplomacy**" to replace force as an instrument of policy, but in most cases, dollars preceded bullets. For Caribbean nations, American protection

American Landscape
The Hetch Hetchy Valley

When landscape painter Albert Bierstadt visited in 1875, he saw a panorama of waterfalls. The canyon walls towered 2,500 feet above a wide, forested meadow populated by herds of elk. Twenty-five years later, San Francisco's mayor James Phelan beheld the cliffs and the pure glacier water pouring into the Tuolumne River and saw his city's answer to the problems of "monopoly and microbes."

The **Hetch Hetchy Valley** hypnotized naturalists and engineers equally because of its magnificence and its location. It was only 152 miles from San Francisco, close enough both to lure visitors and to channel its waters to the city. A village of less than a thousand in 1848, the City by the Bay was, by 1900, the nation's ninth largest, with 340,000

people. Only water kept it from growing larger.

Hemmed in by ocean on three sides, San Francisco faced a chronic scarcity of fresh water. As the Gold Rush swelled the population, entrepreneurs bought up all available water supplies and formed the Spring Valley Water Company, which monopolized the city's water for 60 years. Water tycoons supported the political machine, led by "Boss" Abe Ruef. The company's water was neither cheap nor safe, causing occasional outbreaks of cholera and typhus.

When voters elected Phelan and a reform ticket in 1897, they expected something to be done about water. The Republican mayor proposed to dam the Hetch Hetchy and build an aqueduct across the Central Valley,

continued

American Landscape continued

breaking the monopoly and making water an abundant, safe public utility.

Many obstacles stood in the way. The city's board of superintendents, controlled by Ruef, sided with Spring Valley and blocked plans for a city reservoir. But it was even harder to get permission from the federal government. Hetch Hetchy was located in Yosemite National Park, one of the first nature preserves, created in 1890 to save its peaks and waterfalls. The parks system was new, and the philosophy of conservation—how to preserve natural resources, and for what purposes—was evolving rapidly. Phelan found an ally in Gifford Pinchot, who filled the newly created office of chief forester.

Pinchot's father had made millions in the lumber trade. Gifford argued that the job of forestry was "to grow trees as a crop." He and Phelan agreed that the two main threats to any resource were inefficient use and monopoly control. The few hikers who might enjoy Hetch Hetchy's magnificence were less important than the need "to supply pure water to a great center of population."

Natural and political disasters worked to Phelan's advantage. After the 1906 San Francisco earthquake and fire vividly demonstrated the need for a water supply, Congress allowed the city to apply to use part of Yosemite's land. The following year, a lurid scandal led to a bribery conviction for Ruef and disgrace for his followers. But just as the way seemed clear, a public outcry urged the secretary of the interior to save the Hetch Hetchy.

Behind the campaign were the 1,000-member Sierra Club and its ascetic founder, John Muir. A wilderness explorer and naturalist, Muir was popular for his writings on the transcendent, spiritual aspects of the natural world. "Dam Hetch Hetchy!" he remonstrated. "As well dam for water tanks the people's cathedrals and churches." Historians have characterized the debate between Muir and Pinchot as a contest between rival concepts of environmentalism—conservation for use versus preservation for nature's sake—but the two men also represented opposing interpretations of democracy and the dangers it faced.

"Conservation is the most democratic movement this country has known for generations," Pinchot believed. The Hetch Hetchy project would replace unbridled corporate power with management of natural resources for the public good.

Democratic values were scientific values: efficiency, expertise, and "the greatest good, for the greatest number, for the longest time." For Muir, nature was a refuge where democratic values could survive amid the culture of self-interest and scientific progress. The valley had to be preserved, not just to save the trees but also to "save humans for the wilderness." Only there could people share the nonmaterial values in which democracy took root.

The Sierra Club did not advocate leaving the area pristine. They imagined making Hetch Hetchy a retreat for harried city dwellers, managed by the park service. The public outcry surprised dam advocates, but they managed to cast the "nature lovers" as unwitting tools of the water and power monopolies.

The Roosevelt administration wavered, but in 1913, Phelan got his dam. Muir died a year later. Today the Hetch Hetchy aqueduct delivers 300 million gallons of water a day to San Francisco. But the battle for the valley gave birth to a modern environmental movement. When municipal and mining interests encroached on the Yosemite and Yellowstone preserves in the following decades, they were opposed by a national constituency that saw both activism and wilderness as part of America's heritage.

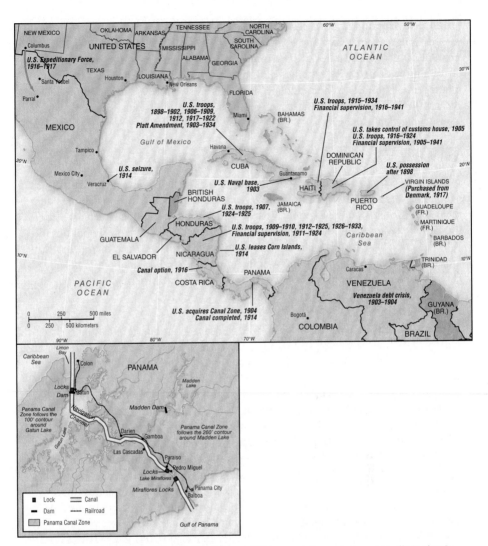

Map 19-2   United States in the Caribbean US troops intervened repeatedly in the Caribbean and Central America to protect investments and guard against perceived threats to order. Panama, Nicaragua, Haiti, and the Dominican Republic were under nearly constant US occupation until the mid-1920s.
Source: Thomas Paterson et al., *American Foreign Relations* (Lexington, MA: D.C. Heath, 1995), vol. 2, pp. 55, 40.

meant high import taxes. A revolt usually followed. Marines went into Honduras and Nicaragua in 1912 and stayed until 1933.

Dollar diplomacy also aimed to harness economic power for diplomatic purposes. Taft mobilized a consortium to finance China's Chinchow-Aigun railway. Railroads were instruments of power in North China, and Taft felt he could drive a wedge between the imperial powers—Britain, Russia, and Japan—and compel them to resume open-door trade. Instead, they joined forces against the United States and the Open Door. Despite the setback, Taft still believed that economic power, not military force, was what mattered.

Taft disappointed both conservatives and progressives in his party. He first urged Congress to reduce the tariff, but then he signed the Payne-Aldrich Tariff in 1909, which raised rates on key imports. Taft's secretary of the interior, Richard Ballinger, sided with ranchers and miners who opposed Roosevelt's resource-management policies. When Pinchot, the chief forester, fought back, Taft fired him. When the Ballinger-Pinchot affair revealed the party's divisions, Roosevelt felt his country needed him back.

RIVAL VISIONS OF THE INDUSTRIAL FUTURE

After Roosevelt returned from Africa in 1910, Pinchot, La Follette, Croly, and others trooped to his home at Sagamore Hill to complain about Taft. The former president denied any interest in the Republican nomination, but he could not keep his pledge. Roosevelt reentered politics because his views had evolved and because politics was what he knew best. Just 54 years old, his energy undiminished, he took more radical positions on corporations, public welfare, and labor than he had while president. The election of 1912 would define the future of industrial America.

The New Nationalism

At a sun-baked junction in Osawatomie, Kansas, in August 1910, Roosevelt declared that "the essence of any struggle for liberty... is to destroy privilege and give the life of every individual the highest possible value." He laid out a program he called the New Nationalism. It included the elimination of corporate campaign contributions, the regulation of industrial combinations, an expert commission to set tariffs, a graduated income tax, banking reorganization, and a national workers' compensation program. "This New Nationalism regards the executive power as the steward of the public welfare." The message drew cheers.

Roosevelt had the newspapers, whereas Taft had the delegates. The nomination fight tested the new system of direct primaries. Taft's control of the party machinery helped him in states that chose delegates by convention, but in key states Roosevelt could take his campaign to the voters. At the convention in Chicago in June 1912, Taft's slim but decisive majority allowed him to control the platform and win over undecided delegates. Grumbling that he had been robbed, Roosevelt walked out.

Roosevelt returned to Chicago in August to accept the nomination of the newly formed Progressive Party. The delegates were a mixed group. They included Hiram Johnson, the reform governor of California; muckraking publisher Frank Munsey; imperialist senator Albert Beveridge; and J. P. Morgan's business partner George W. Perkins. The party platform endorsed the New Nationalism, along with popular election of senators, popular review of judicial decisions, and women's suffrage. Women were delegates, and Jane Addams seconded Roosevelt's nomination. The gathering had an evangelical spirit. "Our cause is based on the eternal principles of righteousness," Roosevelt said. "We stand at Armageddon and we battle for the Lord."

The 1912 Election

In Baltimore the Democrats nominated a former college professor and governor of New Jersey. Like Roosevelt, the young Woodrow Wilson defied his family's expectations by pursuing a political career. He took an unusual route. While studying for a doctorate in government at Johns Hopkins University in 1886, he published his first book, *Congressional Government*, at the age of 28. It advocated enlarging the power of the executive branch. As a professor and later president of Princeton University, he became a well-known lecturer and commentator for new national political magazines such as *Harper's* and the *Atlantic Monthly*. In 1910, he was elected governor of New Jersey and enacted sweeping progressive reforms. For Democrats, smarting from losses under Bryan's leadership, Wilson offered a new image and the ability to unite the South and the East under a progressive program.

With Roosevelt in the race, Wilson had to stake his own claim to the progressive constituency. With the help of Louis Brandeis, Wilson devised a program called the New Freedom. It challenged Roosevelt on his approaches to the economy and politics. Simply regulating the trusts, Wilson argued, would not help consumers, workers, or small entrepreneurs. Instead, it would create a paternalistic bureaucracy. Wilson wanted a lean, strong government and antitrust laws to encourage a return to competition and economic mobility. Both agreed on the importance of a strong executive, but they had different economic formulas. Roosevelt appealed to a collective, national interest, whereas Wilson stressed the needs of individual consumers and investors. The New Nationalism was evangelical, aiming to inspire people to work for the common good. Wilson appealed to reason and self-interest.

On Election Day, the split in the Republican Party gave Wilson a plurality. He won 42 percent of the popular vote, compared with 27 for Roosevelt, 23 for Taft, and 6 for Debs (see Map 19–3). Although his margin was thin, Wilson could interpret

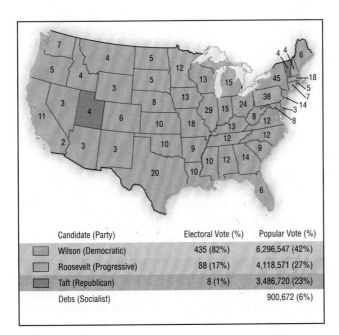

Candidate (Party)	Electoral Vote (%)	Popular Vote (%)
Wilson (Democratic)	435 (82%)	6,296,547 (42%)
Roosevelt (Progressive)	88 (17%)	4,118,571 (27%)
Taft (Republican)	8 (1%)	3,486,720 (23%)
Debs (Socialist)		900,672 (6%)

Map 19–3 The Election of 1912
The election pitted rival visions of progressivism against each other. The decentralized regulation of Wilson's "New Freedom" had more appeal than Roosevelt's far-reaching "New Nationalism."

Taft's loss and the large combined vote for the progressive candidates as a mandate for change. "What the Democratic Party proposes," he told his followers, is "to do the things the Republican Party has been talking about doing for sixteen years."

The New Freedom

Within a year and a half of his inauguration, Wilson produced one of the most coherent and far-reaching legislative programs ever devised by a president. Drawing on his long study of congressional politics, he seized the advantage of his party's majority and exercised an unprecedented degree of personal control through the majority leaders in both houses. The New Freedom advocated lower tariffs, increased competition, and vigorous antitrust enforcement. Three monumental bills passed through Congress in rapid succession.

The first bill was the Underwood-Simmons Tariff (1913), which made the first deep cuts in tariff rates since before the Civil War. The bill overturned a cornerstone of Republican economic policy, the protectionist tariff. It helped farmers and consumers by lowering prices and increasing competition, but Wilson argued that its real beneficiaries would be manufacturers. Lower tariffs would help persuade other countries to reduce taxes on imports from the United States, opening new markets for American-made goods. Wilson created an expert Tariff Commission in 1916 to improve tariff bargaining. The most-favored-nation policies it implemented (and which remain in place) induced European powers to open their empires to

TIME LINE

▼**1889**
Hull House founded

▼**1890**
General Federation of Women's Clubs founded

▼**1893**
Illinois passes eight-hour day for women

▼**1900**
Robert La Follette elected governor of Wisconsin

▼**1901**
Socialist Party of America founded
Galveston introduces commission government

McKinley assassinated; Theodore Roosevelt inaugurated president

▼**1902**
Newlands Reclamation Act funds construction of dams and irrigation systems
McClure's publishes first episodes of Ida Tarbell's "History of the Standard Oil Company" and Lincoln Steffens's "The Shame of the Cities"
Roosevelt settles anthracite strike

▼**1903**
Roosevelt establishes Department of Commerce and Labor

Panama declares independence from Colombia
W. E. B. DuBois publishes *The Souls of Black Folk*

▼**1904**
Justice Department sues Standard Oil under the Sherman Anti-Trust Act
US Supreme Court orders Northern Securities Company dissolved as an illegal combination
Roosevelt elected president
The Roosevelt Corollary announced

▼**1905**
United States takes over Dominican customs
Industrial Workers of the World founded

American goods. The Singer, Ford, and Camel brand names began appearing in markets from Caracas to Mandalay.

Wilson next targeted the banking system. When Steffens and Lippmann investigated banking for *Everybody's* magazine in 1908, they found that its structure was "strikingly like that of Tammany Hall," with a similar concentration of power, lack of accountability, and extralegal maneuvering. The Federal Reserve Act of 1913 set up a national board to supervise the system and created 12 regional reserve banks throughout the country. Banks were now watched to ensure that their reserves matched their deposits. The system's real advantage was the flexibility it gave the currency. The board could put more dollars into circulation when demand was high and retire them when it subsided. Regional banks could adjust the money supply to meet local needs. The system broke Wall Street's stranglehold on credit and opened new opportunities for entrepreneurship and competition.

Finally, Wilson attacked the trusts. He established the Federal Trade Commission (FTC), an independent regulatory commission assigned to enforce free and fair competition. It absorbed the functions of Roosevelt's Bureau of Corporations, but with more authority, including the right to subpoena corporate records and issue cease-and-desist orders. The Clayton Antitrust Act (1914) prohibited price fixing, outlawed interlocking directorates, and made it illegal for a company to own the stock of competitors. To enforce these provisions, citizens were entitled to sue for triple the amount of the actual damages they suffered. In 1916, Wilson produced more reform legislation, including the first national workers' compensation and

▼**1906**
Hepburn Act passed, allowing the Interstate Commerce Commission to set freight rates
Pure Food and Drug Act requires accurate labeling

▼**1907**
Indiana passes forcible sterilization law

▼**1908**
William H. Taft elected president
Helen Keller joins the American Socialist Party

▼**1909**
Payne-Aldrich Tariff goes into effect
NAACP founded

▼**1910**
Taft fires chief forester Gifford Pinchot
Elkins Act authorizes Interstate Commerce Commission to regulate electronic communications
Roosevelt announces the New Nationalism

▼**1911**
Triangle Shirtwaist Company fire

▼**1912**
US troops occupy Nicaragua
Woodrow Wilson elected president

▼**1913**
Federal Reserve Act reorganizes banking system
Underwood-Simmons Tariff

▼**1914**
Panama Canal completed
Clayton Antitrust Act strengthens antitrust enforcement

▼**1916**
New York City enacts zoning laws
Federal workers' compensation, child-labor, and eight-hour-day laws passed

child-labor laws, the eight-hour day for railroad workers, and the Warehouse Act, which extended credit to cash-strapped farmers.

These programs furthered Wilson's goal of "releasing the energies" of consumers and entrepreneurs, but they also helped business. Businessmen headed many of the regulatory boards, and the FTC and Federal Reserve Board helped stabilize unruly markets. The New Freedom brought reform without the elaborate state machinery of the New Nationalism or European industrial nations. The New Freedom linked liberal reform to individual initiative and free markets.

CONCLUSION

By 1900, America's political economy had outgrown the social relationships and laws that served the rural republic for most of the nineteenth century. Squeezed between corporate elites and the large, transient immigrant communities that controlled urban politics, middle-class reformers created a new style of political participation. They experimented with new forms of political decision making and vested the state with responsibility for the quality of life of its citizens. Progressives challenged but never upset the system. Science and the pressure of informed opinion, they believed, could produce managed, orderly change without open conflict.

The progressive presidents took this movement to the national stage. Roosevelt and Wilson touted their programs as attacks on privilege, but both presidents helped position the federal government as a broker among business, consumer, and labor interests. In less than two decades, the federal government overcame its reputation for corruption and impotence and moved to the center of economic and social life. The concept of a "national interest" greater than individual and property rights was now firmly ingrained; so, too, was the need to protect it. The president's leadership now extended beyond the administration to Congress and public opinion. These achievements created a modern central government just as military, diplomatic, and economic victories made the United States a global power. War and its aftermath would curtail the progressive movement, as support for a strong central government would be tested by events unfolding in Europe.

WHO, WHAT, WHERE

REVIEW QUESTIONS

1. Why did reformers feel that privately owned utilities caused corruption?

2. What were the Oregon system and the Wisconsin Idea?

3. Choose one level of government—local, state, or federal—and describe three key progressive reforms.

CRITICAL-THINKING QUESTIONS

1. Were the progressives' goals conservative or radical? What about their strategies? Explain your answers.

2. Theodore Roosevelt has been called the first modern president. In what ways did he change the presidency?

3. Did the progressives' emphasis on research and documentation indicate their respect for public opinion or not? Explain your answer.

SUGGESTED READINGS

Library of Congress. Progressive Era to New Era. http://www.loc.gov/teachers/classroommaterials/presentationsandactivities/presentations/timeline/progress/

Lindsey, Treva B. *Colored No More: Reinventing Black Womanhood in Washington, D.C.* Champaign: University of Illinois Press, 2017.

Marten, James, ed. *Children and Youth During the Gilded Age and Progressive Era*. New York: New York University Press, 2014.

McGerr, Michael. *A Fierce Discontent: The Rise and Fall of the Progressive Movement in America, 1870–1920*. New York: Free Press, 2003.

Painter, Nell Irvin. *Standing at Armageddon: The United States, 1877–1919*. New York: Norton, 1987.

For further review materials and resource information, please visit www.oup.com/us/ofthepeople

CHAPTER 19:   A United Body of Action, 1900–1916

Primary Sources

19.1   DANIEL BURNHAM AND EDWARD H. BENNET, *PLAN OF CHICAGO* (1909)

Following his creation of the "White City," so celebrated during the 1893 Chicago World's Fair, Daniel Burnham, along with Edward H. Bennet, drew up a plan for Chicago. Their plan expressed a commitment to the promise of urban life and their confidence that cities were the way of the future. As a work in progress, the American city might serve a host of interests and, with sustained attention, investment, and innovation, benefit all of those living and working in the nation's urban areas.

The tendency of mankind to congregate in cities is a marked characteristic of modern times. This movement is confined to no one country, but is world-wide. Each year Rome, and the cities of the Orient, as well as Berlin, New York, and Chicago, are adding to their population at an unprecedented rate. Coincident with this urban development there has been a widespread increase in wealth, and also an enlarged participation on the part of the people in the work of government. As a natural result of these causes has come the desire to better the conditions of living. Men are becoming convinced that the formless growth of the city is neither economical nor satisfactory; and that overcrowding and congestion of traffic paralyze the vital functions of the city. The complicated problems which the great city develops are now seen not to be beyond the control of aroused public sentiment; and practical men of affairs are turning their attention to working out the means whereby the city may be made an efficient instrument for providing all its people with the best possible conditions of living.

Chicago, in common with other great cities, realizes that the time has come to bring order out of the chaos incident to rapid growth, and especially to the influx of people of many nationalities without common traditions or habits of life. Among the various instrumentalities designed to accomplish this result, a plan for a well-ordered and convenient city is seen to be indispensable; and to the task of producing such a plan the Commercial Club has devoted its energies for the past three years.

It is not to be expected that any plan devised while as yet few civic problems have received final solution will be perfect in all its details. It is claimed for the plan herein presented, that it is the result of extended and careful study of the needs of Chicago, made by disinterested men of wide experience, amid the very conditions which it is sought to remedy; and that during the years devoted to its preparation the plan has had the benefit of varied and competent criticism.

The real test of this plan will be found in its application; for, such is the determination of the people to secure more perfect conditions, it is certain that if the plan is really good it will commend itself to the progressive spirit of the times, and sooner or later it will be carried out.

It should be understood, however, that such radical changes as are proposed herein cannot possibly be realized immediately. Indeed, the aim has been to anticipate the needs of the future as well as to provide for the necessities of the present: in short, to direct the development of the city towards an end that must seem ideal, but is practical. Therefore it is quite possible that when particular portions of the plan shall be taken up for execution, wider knowledge, longer experience, or a change in local conditions may suggest a better solution; but, on the other hand, before any departure shall be determined upon, it should be made clear that such a change is justified.

If many elements of the proposed plan shall seem familiar, it should be remembered that the purpose has not been to invent novel problems for solution, but to take up the pressing needs of today, and to find the best methods of meeting those requirements, carrying each particular problem to its ultimate conclusion as a component part of a great entity, a well-ordered, convenient, and unified city.

This conception of the task is the justification of a comprehensive plan of Chicago. To many who have given little consideration to the subject, a plan seems to call for large expenditures and a consequent increase in taxation. The reverse is the case. It is certain that civic improvement will go on at an accelerated rate; and if those improvements shall be marshaled according to a well-ordered plan great saving must result. Good order and convenience are not expensive; but haphazard and ill-considered projects invariably result in extravagance and wastefulness. A plan insures that whenever any public or semi-public work shall be undertaken, it will fall into its proper and predetermined place in the general scheme, and thus contribute to the unity and dignity of the city.

The plan frankly takes into consideration the fact that the American city, and Chicago preeminently, is a center of industry and traffic. Therefore attention is given to the betterment of commercial facilities; to methods of transportation for persons and for goods; to removing the obstacles which prevent or obstruct circulation; and to the increase of convenience. It is realized, also, that good workmanship requires a large degree of comfort on the part of the workers in their homes and their surroundings, and ample opportunity for that rest and recreation with-out which all work becomes drudgery. Then, too, the city has a dignity to be maintained; and good order is essential to material advancement. Consequently, the plan provides for impressive groupings of public buildings, and reciprocal relations among such groups. Moreover, consideration is given to the fact that in all probability Chicago, within the lifetime of persons now living, will become a greater city than any existing at the present time; and that therefore the most comprehensive plans of to-day will need to be supplemented in a not remote future.

Opportunity for such expansion is provided for.

The origin of the plan of Chicago can be traced directly to the World's Columbian Exposition. The World's Fair of 1893 was the beginning, in our day and in this country, of the orderly arrangement of extensive public grounds and buildings. The result came about quite naturally. Chicago had become a commercial community wherein men were accustomed to get together to plan for the general good. Moreover, those at the head of affairs were, many of them, the same individuals who had taken part in every movement since the city had emerged from the condition of a mere village. They were so accustomed to results even beyond their most sanguine predictions, that it was easy for them to believe that their Fair might surpass all fairs that had preceded it.

Then, too, the men of Chicago, trained in intense commercial activity, had learned the lesson that great success cannot be attained unless the special work in hand shall be entrusted to those best fitted to undertake it. It had become the habit of our businessmen to select some one to take the responsibility in every important enterprise; and to give to that person earnest, loyal, and steadfast support. Thus the design and arrangement of the buildings of the World's Columbian Exposition, which have never been surpassed, were due primarily to the feeling of loyalty to the city and to its undertakings; and secondly, to the habit of entrusting great works to men trained in the practice of such undertakings.

The results of the World's Fair of 1893 were many and far-reaching. To the people of Chicago the dignity, beauty, and convenience of the transitory city in Jackson Park seemed to call for the improvement of the water front of the city. With this idea in mind, the South Park Commissioners, during the year following the Fair, proposed the improvement of the Lake front from Jackson Park to Grant Park. Following out this suggestion, a plan for a connection between the two parks was drawn to a large scale, and the project was presented at a meeting of the West and South Park Commissioners. Later this design was exhibited at a dinner given by the Commercial Club; and many businessmen were emphatic in express-ing their conviction that the proposed scheme would be of enormous value to Chicago, and that it should be adopted and carried into execution. This was the inception of the project for a park out in the Lake, having a lagoon between it and the shore.

During the next three or four years more careful studies of the Lake front scheme were made, and very large drawings were prepared for a meeting at the Women's Club and the Art Institute, and for a Merchants Club dinner at the Auditorium. The newspapers and magazines, both at home and throughout the country, united in commenting on and com-mending the undertaking; and during the decade that has elapsed since the plans were first presented, the proposed improvement has never been forgotten, but has ever been looked upon as something sure to be accomplished. This was the beginning of a general plan for the city. . . .

In presenting this report, the Commercial Club realizes that from time to time sup-plementary reports will be necessary to emphasize one feature or another which may come prominently before the public for adoption. At the same time, it is confidently believed that this presentation of the entire subject accomplishes the task which has been recognized from the outset, namely: First, to make the careful study of the physical conditions of Chi-cago as they now exist; Second, to discover how those conditions may be improved; Third, to record such conclusions in the shape of drawings and texts which shall become a guide for the future development of Chicago.

In creating the ideal arrangement, everyone who lives here is better accommodated in his business and his social activities. In bringing about better freight and passenger facilities, every merchant and manufacturer is helped. In establishing a complete park and parkway system, the life of the wage-earner and of his family is made healthier and pleas-anter; while the greater attractiveness thus produced keeps at home the people of means and taste, and acts as a magnet to draw those who seek to live amid pleasing surroundings. The very beauty that attracts him who has money makes pleasant the life of those among whom he lives, while anchoring him and his wealth to the city. The prosperity aimed at is for all Chicago.

This same spirit which carried out the Exposition in such a manner as to make it a lasting credit to the city is still the soul of Chicago, vital and dominant; and even now, although many new men are at the front, it still controls and is doing a greater work than it was in 1893. It finds the men; it makes the occasion; it attracts the sincere and unself-ish; it vitalizes the organization, and impels it to reach heights not believed possible of attainment. This spirit still exists. It is present to-day among us. Indeed, it seems to gather force with the years and the opportunities. It is even now impelling us to larger and better achievements for the public good. It conceals no private purpose, no hidden ends. This spirit the spirit of Chicago is our greatest asset. It is not merely civic pride: it is rather the constant, steady determination to bring about the very best conditions of city life for all the people, with full knowledge that what we as a people decide to do in the public interest we can and surely will bring to pass.

Source: Daniel Hudson Burnham and Edward H. Bennett, *Plan of Chicago* (Chicago: Commercial Club of Chicago, 1909), Chapter 1.

19.2 UPTON SINCLAIR, EXCERPTS FROM *THE JUNGLE* (1906)

Muckraking journalist Upton Sinclair used the power of his pen to expose the cor-rupt conditions of Packingtown, Chicago's meatpacking district in the early 1900s. In 1906, after spending weeks interviewing and living among workers, Sinclair wrote *The Jungle*, the story of Jurgis Rudkus and his family, which chronicles working-class poverty and the immigrant experience. In the novel, Sinclair detailed the ways packing houses "doctored" the meat sold to the American public. Outrage at the conditions exposed by Sinclair led to nationwide reform.

The people of Chicago saw the government inspectors in Packingtown, and they all took that to mean that they were protected from diseased meat; they did not understand that these hundred and sixty-three inspectors had been appointed at the request of the packers, and that they were paid by the United States government to certify that all the diseased meat was kept in the state. They had no authority beyond that; for the inspection of meat to be sold in the city and state the whole force in Packingtown consisted of three henchmen of the local political machine!

And shortly afterward one of these, a physician, made the discovery that the carcasses of steers which had been condemned as tubercular by the government inspectors, and which therefore contained ptomaines, which are deadly poisons, were left upon an open platform and carted away to be sold in the city; and so he insisted that these carcasses be treated with an injection of kerosene—and was ordered to resign the same week! So indignant were the packers that they went farther, and compelled the mayor to abolish the whole bureau of inspection; so that since then there has not been even a pretense of any interference with the graft. There was said to be two thousand dollars a week hush money from the tubercular steers alone; and as much again from the hogs which had died of cholera on the trains, and which you might see any day being loaded into boxcars and hauled away to a place called Globe, in Indiana, where they made a fancy grade of lard.

Jurgis heard of these things little by little, in the gossip of those who were obliged to perpetrate them. It seemed as if every time you met a person from a new department, you heard of new swindles and new crimes. There was, for instance, a Lithuanian who was a cattle butcher for the plant where Marija had worked, which killed meat for canning only; and to hear this man describe the animals which came to his place would have been worthwhile for a Dante or a Zola. It seemed that they must have agencies all over the country, to hunt out old and crippled and diseased cattle to be canned. There were cattle which had been fed on "whisky-malt," the refuse of the breweries, and had become what the men called "steerly"—which means covered with boils. It was a nasty job killing these, for when you plunged your knife into them they would burst and splash foul-smelling stuff into your face; and when a man's sleeves were smeared with blood, and his hands steeped in it, how was he ever to wipe his face, or to clear his eyes so that he could see? It was stuff such as this that made the "embalmed beef" that had killed several times as many United States soldiers as all the bullets of the Spaniards; only the army beef, besides, was not fresh canned, it was old stuff that had been lying for years in the cellars.

Then one Sunday evening, Jurgis sat puffing his pipe by the kitchen stove, and talking with an old fellow whom Jonas had introduced, and who worked in the canning rooms at Durham's; and so Jurgis learned a few things about the great and only Durham canned goods, which had become a national institution. They were regular alchemists at Durham's; they advertised a mushroom-catsup, and the men who made it did not know what a mushroom looked like. They advertised "potted chicken,"—and it was like the boardinghouse soup of the comic papers, through which a chicken had walked with rubbers on. Perhaps they had a secret process for making chickens chemically—who knows? said Jurgis' friend; the things that went into the mixture were tripe, and the fat of pork, and beef suet, and hearts of beef, and finally the waste ends of veal, when they had any. They put these up in several grades, and sold them at several prices; but the contents of the cans all came out of the same hopper. And then there was "potted game" and "potted grouse," "potted ham," and "deviled ham"—de-vyled, as the men called it. "De-vyled" ham was made out of the waste ends of smoked beef that were too small to be sliced by the machines; and also tripe, dyed with chemicals so that it would not show white; and trimmings of hams and corned beef; and potatoes, skins and all; and finally the hard cartilaginous gullets of beef, after the tongues had been cut out. All this ingenious mixture was ground up and flavored with spices to make it taste like something. Anybody who could invent a new imitation had been sure of a fortune from old Durham, said Jurgis' informant; but it was hard to think of anything new in a place where so many sharp wits had been at work for so long; where men welcomed tuberculosis in the cattle they were feeding, because it made them fatten more quickly; and where they bought up all the old rancid butter left over in the grocery stores of a continent, and "oxidized" it by a forced-air process, to take away the odor, rechurned it with skim milk, and sold it in bricks in the cities! Up to a year or two ago it had been the custom to kill horses in the yards—ostensibly for fertilizer; but after long agitation the newspapers had been able to make the public realize that the horses were being canned. Now it was against the law to kill horses in Packingtown, and the law was really complied with—for the present, at any rate. Any day, however, one might see sharp-horned and shaggy-haired creatures running with the sheep and yet what a job you would have to get the public to believe that a good part of what it buys for lamb and mutton is really goat's flesh!

Upton Sinclair wrote about the hazardous working conditions immigrant and American workers endured as they took up employment in Chicago's meatpacking industry. But while Sinclair hoped to outrage readers about the plight of workers, such as those pictured here, readers generally focused more on the potential health risks they faced as consumers of the meat processed in Chicago's stockyards.
Source: Copyright 1909, by Kelley & Chadwick. Library of Congress Prints and Photographs Division Washington, DC.

There was another interesting set of statistics that a person might have gathered in Packingtown—those of the various afflictions of the workers. When Jurgis had first inspected the packing plants with Szedvilas, he had marveled while he listened to the tale of all the things that were made out of the carcasses of animals, and of all the lesser industries that were maintained there; now he found that each one of these lesser industries was a separate little inferno, in its way as horrible as the killing beds, the source and fountain of them all. The workers in each of them had their own peculiar diseases. And the wandering visitor might be skeptical about all the swindles, but he could not be skeptical about these, for the worker bore the evidence of them about on his own person—generally he had only to hold out his hand.

There were the men in the pickle rooms, for instance, where old Antanas had gotten his death; scarce a one of these that had not some spot of horror on his person. Let a man so much as scrape his finger pushing a truck in the pickle rooms, and he might have a sore that would put him out of the world; all the joints in his fingers might be eaten by the acid, one by one. Of the butchers and floorsmen, the beef-boners and trimmers, and all those who used knives, you could scarcely find a person who had the use of his thumb; time and time again the base of it had been slashed, till it was a mere lump of flesh against which the man pressed the knife to hold it. The hands of these men would be criss-crossed with cuts, until you could no longer pretend to count them or to trace them. They would have no nails,—they had worn them off pulling hides; their knuckles were swollen so that their fingers spread out like a fan. There were men who worked in the cooking rooms, in the midst of steam and sickening odors, by artificial light; in these rooms the germs of tuberculosis might live for two years, but the supply was renewed every hour. There were the beef-luggers, who carried two-hundred-pound quarters into the refrigerator-cars; a fearful kind of work, that began at four o'clock in the morning, and that wore out the most powerful men in a few years. There were those who worked in the chilling rooms, and whose special disease was rheumatism; the time limit that a man could work in the chilling rooms was said to be five years. There were the wool-pluckers, whose hands went to pieces even sooner than the hands of the pickle men; for the pelts of the sheep had to be painted with acid to loosen the wool, and then the pluckers had to pull out this wool with their bare hands, till the acid had eaten their fingers off. There were those who made the tins for the canned meat; and their hands, too, were a maze of cuts, and each cut represented a chance for blood poisoning. Some worked at the stamping machines, and it was very seldom that one could work long there at the pace that was set, and not give out and forget himself and have a part of his hand chopped off. There were the "hoisters," as they were called, whose task it was to press the lever which lifted the dead cattle off the floor. They ran along upon a rafter, peering down through the damp and the steam; and as old Durham's architects had not built the killing room for the convenience of the hoisters, at every few feet they would have to stoop under a beam, say four feet above the one they ran on; which got them into the habit of stooping, so that in a few years they would be walking like chimpanzees. Worst of any, however, were the fertilizer men, and those who served in the cooking rooms. These people could not be shown to the visitor,—for the odor of a fertilizer man would scare any ordinary visitor at a hundred yards, and as for the other men, who worked in tank rooms full of steam, and in some of which there were open vats near the level of the floor, their peculiar trouble was that they fell into the vats; and when they were fished out, there was never enough of them left to be worth exhibiting,—sometimes they would be overlooked for days, till all but the bones of them had gone out to the world as Durham's Pure Leaf Lard!

Source: Upton Sinclair, *The Jungle* (1906; Project Gutenberg EBook, 2006), http://www.gutenberg.org/files/140/140-h/140-h.htm#link2HCH0009.

19.3   VISUAL DOCUMENTS: LEWIS WICKES HINE, NATIONAL CHILD LABOR COMMITTEE PHOTO-GRAPHS (EARLY 1900s)

Lewis Hine worked as an investigative photographer for the National Child Labor Committee, an organization dedicated to child labor reform, between 1908 and 1924. Through his photography, Hine chronicled labor conditions in sites such as coal mines, textile mills, and family farms. Hine's images brought public attention to the conditions under which children labored and effectively underscored the difference between the idealized vision of American childhood and the reality in which many children lived.

Three adults and six children from seven years to twelve years hard at work on a sugar beet farm near Greeley, Colorado. July 1915.

A 14-year-old spinner in a Brazos Valley Cotton Mill in West, Texas. November 1913.

Young drivers and trapper boy, Brown Mine, Brown, West Virginia. September 1908. Source: Lewis Wickes Hine, 1874–1940, photographer. National Child Labor Committee Collection. Library of Congress Prints and Photographs Division, Washington, DC.

19.4   HELEN KELLER, EXCERPTS FROM "BLIND LEADERS" (1913)

When she expressed politically and economically radical views, Helen Keller often faced charges that her disabilities made her unfit for social commentary, that her ailments impeded her ability to think rationally. Keller continued to advocate a Socialist position and charged that those who saw the horrors of unfettered industrial capitalism and the inequalities it created, yet allowed the system to continue, were the truly and willfully blind members of American society.

I do not doubt that many persons who read what I am going to write will say to themselves: "She is indeed blind. She is so blind she imagines everybody else to be blind." As a matter of fact, I have been thinking for a long time that most of us are afflicted with spiritual blindness. Certainly, very few people open fresh, fearless eyes upon the world they live in. They do not look at anything straight. They have not learned to use their eyes, except in the most rudimentary ways. They will usually see a lamp-post—if it is a large one—and sometimes they are able to read the danger signal on a railway crossing, but not always. Most of the time they expect some one else to see for them. They often pay fabulous sums to lawyers, doctors, ministers, and other "experts" to do their seeing for them; but, unfortunately, it frequently happens that those hired guides and leaders are also blind. Of course they deny that their sight is imperfect. They claim to have extraordinary powers of vision and many people believe them. Consequently, they are permitted to lead their fellows. But how often do they steer them to their destruction!

When we look about us with seeing eyes, what do we behold? Men and women at our very doors wrung with hard labor, want or the dread of want, needing help and receiving none, toiling for less than a living wage! If we had had penetrating vision, I know that we could not, we would not, have endured what we saw—cruelty, ignorance, poverty, disease—almost all preventable, unnecessary. Our blind leaders whom we have sent away told us that the poverty and misery of mankind were divinely ordained. They taught us that the words, "Ye have the poor always with you," mean that Christ sanctioned poverty as necessary and irremediable. Now we read the Gospel with our own eyes, and we see that Christ meant no such thing.

Much poverty is abominable, unnecessary, a disgrace to our civilization, or rather a denial that we are civilized. Let us try to understand poverty. What is the cause of it? Simply this: that the land, the machinery, the means of life, belong to the few, while the many are born and live with nothing that they can call their own except their hands and their brains. They live by selling their hands and their brains to the few; and all the work they do makes the rich more rich, and gains for the workers a mere livelihood, or less than a livelihood. The ownership of the world by a small class is the main cause of poverty. Strange that we could not see it before, and that when we did see it we accepted it in blind contentment! Our blind guides consoled us by saying that there was much charity, and that the rich were generous and gave to the poor. We now see that what the rich give is only a small part of the money which is made for them by the labor of the poor! They never stop to think that if the workers received an equitable share of their product, there would be no rich, there would be little need of philanthropy. Charity covers a multitude of sins. It does something worse than that. It covers the fact so that they cannot be seen. It covers the fact that the property of the few is made by the labor of the many. The rich are willing to do everything for the poor but to get off their backs. . . .

When we inquire why things are as they are, the answer is: The foundation of society is laid upon a basis of individualism, conquest, and exploitation, with a total disregard of the good of the whole. The structure of society built upon such wrong basic principles is bound to retard the development of all men, even the most successful ones, because it tends to divert man's energies into useless channels and to degrade his character. The result is a false standard of values. Trade and material prosperity are held to the be the main objects of pursuit, and consequently the lowest instincts in human natures—love of gain, cunning, and selfishness—are fostered. The output of a cotton mill or a coal mine is considered of greater importance than the production of healthy, happy-hearted, free human beings.

This unmoral state of society will continue as long as we live under a system of universal competition for the means of existence. The workers cannot lift up their heads so long as a small favored class in each generation is allowed to inherit the accumulated labor of all preceding generations, and many who produce the wealth inherit nothing. (We often forget what wealth is. It is the stored-up labor of men, women, and little children. Money does not create anything. Money is about as productive as a wheel revolving in a void. It has value only in proportion to the toil and sweat of human hands that went into the getting of it.)

During the past century man has gained greater mastery over the forces of nature than he ever had before. Consequently the wealth produced in the world has increased a hundredfold. With the help of the machines he has invented, man can produce enough to provide necessaries, comforts, and even some luxuries for every human being. But in spite of this enormously greater productive power the condition of the workers has not essentially improved. Because the industrial system under which we live denies them the fruits of their labor, they have not received their fair share in the products of civilization.

As a matter of fact, machinery has widened the gulf between those who own and those who toil. It has become a means of perpetuating man's slavery, because it may be run by unskilled laborers who receive low wages, which of course increase the profits of employers and stock holders. So the worker become part of the machine they manipulate; but the machine is expensive, while human life is cheap. When the workers can no longer live, they go on strike, and what happens? The masters evict them from the hovels that they call home; the police and militia break up their protest-meetings, imprison their leaders, and when they can, drive them out of town. This appalling condition of things exists in many different parts of our country at this moment. For even the Constitution does not safeguard the liberties of the workers when their interests are opposed to those of the capitalist. Our administration of justice, which blind leaders used to tell us was a splendid inheritance from our fathers, is grossly unequal and unjust. It is based on a system of money fees. It is so encumbered at every step with technicalities that it is necessary to employ experts at great cost to explain and interpret the law. Then, too, all the petty offenses are punishable by fine or imprisonment. This means the poor will always be punished, while the rich are usually allowed to go free.

We cannot longer shut our eyes to these glaring evils. They divide the world into economic classes antagonistic to each other it is because of all these undeniable evils that I am the determined foe of the capitalist system, which denies the workers the rights of human beings. I consider it fundamentally wrong, radically unjust and cruel. It inflicts purposeless misery upon millions of my fellow men and women. It robs little children of the joy of life, embitters motherhood, breaks the bodies of men and degrades their manhood. It must, therefore, be changed, it must be destroyed, and a better, saner, kinder social order established. Competition must give place to cooperation, and class antagonism to brotherhood. "Each for all" is a far more stimulating and effective doctrine than "each for himself." Private ownership of land and the means of production and distribution of the necessaries of life must be replaced by public ownership and democratic management.

Oh, no, it is not human nature that we have to change. Our task is not so difficult as that. All that is necessary to make this world a comfortable abode for man is to abolish the capitalist system. In the words of Sir Oliver Lodge, "we have entered upon the period of conscious evolution, and have begun the adaptation of environment to organism." In other words, we have learned to curb and utilize the forces of nature. The time of blind struggle is drawing to a close. The forces governing the law of the survival of the fittest will continue to operate; but they will be under the conscious, intelligent control of man.

Source: Helen Keller, "Blind Leaders," *Outlook* 105 (September 27, 1913), 231–236.

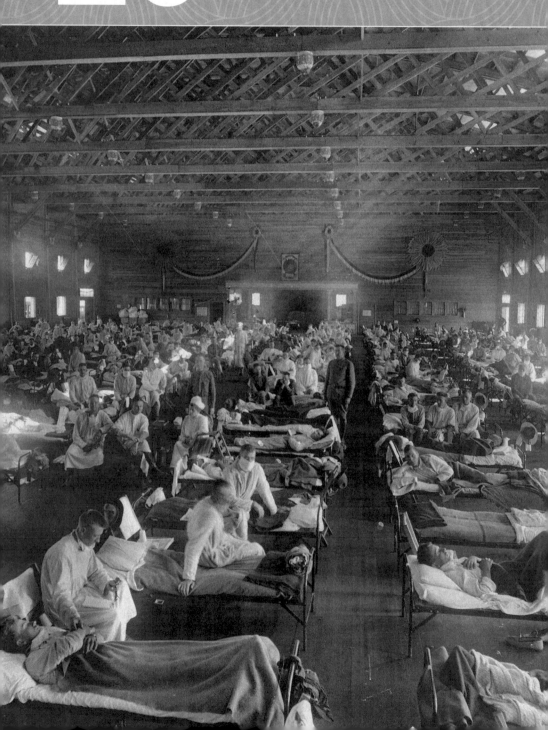

A Global Power

1914–1919

COMMON THREADS

As a progressive, Wilson was committed to order, efficiency, and gradual reform. How did his policies toward Mexico and Europe reflect this commitment?

Both the Philippine-American War of 1899 and US involvement in World War I in 1917 provoked dissent at home. Why did the government tolerate opposition in the first case but suppress it in the second?

How did the repression of the war years set the stage for the Red Scare?

< Emergency hospital for influenza patients, Camp Funston, Kansas, 1918

Walter Lippmann

Walter Lippmann had just landed in Brussels in July 1914 when the trains stopped running. At the station, "crowds of angry, jostling people" were struggling to leave the city. This looked, he confided to his diary, like the beginning of a war. Four weeks earlier, Austria-Hungary's crown prince, Archduke Ferdinand, had been shot in the Serbian city of Sarajevo. Austria threatened to attack unless Serbia punished the terrorists. Russia mobilized to come to Serbia's defense. As stock markets tumbled and banks collapsed, Lippmann found himself caught in a conflict between the world's most powerful states: Austria and Germany on one side, Russia, France, and Britain on the other. As land borders closed, he escaped across the channel to England.

In the twilight of August 4, he stood with an anxious crowd outside the House of Commons, as Parliament passed a war resolution. In Berlin, the Reichstag declared war on France. "We sit and stare at each other and make idiotically cheerful remarks," Lippmann wrote, "and in the meantime, so far as anyone can see, nothing can stop the awful disintegration now."

Twenty-four years old, Lippmann had come of age in the Progressive Era. As a student at Harvard, he came to believe that reason and science would allow his generation to "treat life not as something given but as something to be shaped." After graduation, he set out to become a journalist, studying under the legendary investigator Lincoln Steffens and helping to start a magazine called the *New Republic*. "It was a happy time, those last few years before the First World War," he later remembered; "the air was soft, and it was easy for a young man to believe in the inevitability of progress, in the perfectibility of man and of society, and in the sublimation of evil."

The European war crushed those hopes. Just days after Lippmann left Belgium, German armies slashed through the neutral nation in a great maneuver designed to encircle the French army, but before the ring could be closed, reserve troops from Paris, many of them rushed to the front in taxicabs, stopped the German advance at the Marne River. By November, the **Western Front** had stabilized into the bloody stalemate that would last the next four years, taking between 5,000 and 50,000 lives a day. Two inventions first used in the American West, barbed wire and the machine gun, defeated all attempts to break through the enemy's trench lines. Colossal artillery, poison gas, submarine warfare, aerial bombardment, and suicide charges would each be used in desperate bids to break the deadlock, and all would fail.

The carnage horrified Americans. German soldiers terrorized Belgian civilians in retaliation for guerilla attacks, killing over 5,000 hostages and burning the medieval city of Louvain. The gruesome tragedy of modern war made Americans feel both fortunate and guilty to be so uninvolved. "We Americans have been witnessing supreme drama, clenching our fists, talking, yet unable to fasten any reaction to realities," Lippmann told his readers. For three years, Americans watched a civilization they had admired sink into barbarism. They recoiled from the war's violence and the motives behind it, and they debated what, if anything, they could do to stop it.

When the United States entered the fight in 1917, it mobilized its economy and society to send an army of a million to Europe. The war disrupted and culminated the progressive movement. In the name of efficiency, the state stepped in to manage the economy as never before, placing corporations under federal supervision but allowing them profits and some autonomy. The war transformed controversial items on the progressive agenda—women's suffrage, prohibition of alcohol, restrictions on prostitution—into matters of national urgency. The federal government punished political dissenters. On the battlefield, American forces brought swift triumph, but not the permanent peace Wilson sought. Defeated powers collapsed into revolution and anarchy. New ideologies threatened American ideals. The experience of war brought home the dangers of a modern, interdependent world, but it also revealed the United States' power to shape the global future.

THE CHALLENGE OF REVOLUTION

Like other progressives, Wilson saw threats to democracy arising from rapid change in industrial society. Revolution, militarism, and imperial rivalries threatened global stability just as surely as labor wars, reckless corporations, and corrupt officials endangered the republic. Wilson opposed radicalism at home and abroad, and he tried to foster orderly change. Stability, like reform, was a process, not a goal, but Wilson believed it had to be forced on those who resisted.

Imposing order, the president believed, was both a duty and an opportunity. An expanding commercial power such as the United States had talent, technology, and capital to share. "Prosperity in one part of the world ministers to prosperity everywhere," he declared, but only in safe markets. Imperialism and revolution endangered the trade necessary for peace in the world and growth at home. It was the government's duty to safeguard goods and investments in order to secure American prosperity and its benefits for the world.

This combination of idealism and self-interest, humanitarianism and force, produced a seemingly contradictory policy. Wilson renounced "dollar diplomacy" only to use Taft's tactics himself in China. He atoned for US imperialism but intervened repeatedly in Central America. Secretary of State William Jennings Bryan negotiated a series of "cooling-off" treaties that required arbitration before resorting to war, but Wilson seldom submitted his own policies to arbitration. He believed the United States had a mission to promote democracy, yet he considered many peoples—including Filipinos—unready to govern themselves.

These contradictions arose from Wilson's view of history. As he saw it, modern commerce and communications were creating a global society with new rules of international conduct. Meanwhile, relics of the past—militarism and revolution—threatened to "throw the world back three or four centuries." Resolving the struggle between the past and the future would require "a new international psychology," new norms and institutions to regulate conflict. Wilson's sympathies lay with Britain and France, but with Europe aflame, the United States, the sole voice of reason, had to remain aloof. "Somebody must keep the great economic processes of the world of business alive," he protested. He was also preoccupied with matters closer at hand. In April 1914, American troops invaded Mexico in an attempt to overthrow its revolutionary government.

The Mexican Revolution

In May 1911, rebels took control of Mexico City, ending over three decades of enforced order and rapid industrialization under the dictatorship of **Porfirio Díaz**. Díaz and a clique of intellectuals and planners known as the *científicos* had made Mexico one of the world's leading oil exporters. They confiscated communal lands, forcing Indians to farm as tenants on commercial haciendas. Foreign investment poured in, and by 1911 Americans owned 40 percent of the property in the country. Mexicans grew to resent foreign business and the regime's taxes. When Francisco Madero's revolt broke out, the army folded, Díaz fled to Spain, and power changed hands in a nearly bloodless coup.

The fall of Díaz hardly troubled the United States: Madero held an election to confirm his presidency. But in February 1913, two weeks before Wilson's inauguration, General Victoriano Huerta seized power and had Madero shot. Mexican states raised armies and revolted against Huerta's regime, beginning one of the twentieth century's longest and bloodiest civil wars. In the mountains south of Mexico City, Emiliano Zapata led a guerilla resistance. Meanwhile, along Mexico's northern border, Venustiano Carranza organized a constitutionalist army.

Wilson denounced Huerta, gave arms to Carranza's soldiers, and sent 7,000 marines to occupy Mexico's largest port, Veracruz, in April 1914. The invasion radicalized the revolution, unifying all sides against the United States. When Carranza deposed Huerta a few months later, he promised to nationalize US oil fields. Wilson pressured Carranza to resign while providing arms to his enemy, Francisco "Pancho" Villa. Villa briefly seized the capital at the end of 1914, but Carranza drove Villa's army north toward the border. Reluctantly, Wilson recognized the Carranza government and cut ties to Villa. Stung by Wilson's betrayal, Villa crossed the border and attacked the 13th Cavalry outpost at Columbus, New Mexico, killing 17 Americans and stealing horses and guns.

Furious, Wilson sent 10,000 troops under General **John J. Pershing** into Mexico (see Map 20–1). Pershing never found Villa, but the invasion again unified Mexicans against the United States. Rather than declare war, Wilson ordered Pershing home. After three years of trying to bring democracy and stability to Mexico, Wilson had nothing to show for his efforts. He failed to tame nationalism and revolution in Mexico. The civil war still raged, and American property was more in danger than ever.

Map 20–1   The US Invasions of Mexico, 1914, 1917 General John Pershing led 10,000 troops together with observation aircraft and a convoy of trucks 419 miles into Mexico on a fruitless hunt for Francisco Villa's band. Federal forces loyal to Carranza confronted Pershing near Parral, bringing the US advance to a halt.

Bringing Order to the Caribbean

In principle, Wilson opposed imperialism, but his desire to bring order to neighboring countries led him to use force again and again. He sent the marines into more countries in Latin America than any other president. Marines quashed a revolution in Haiti in 1915 and then occupied the country. They landed in the Dominican Republic the following year to supervise an election and stayed to fight a guerilla war until 1924. Wilson kept marines in Honduras, Panama, and Nicaragua and briefly sent troops into Cuba.

Progressive senators wondered why Wilson busted trusts and reorganized banks at home but put the marines at their service abroad. Senators Robert La Follette and George Norris argued that revolutions might be necessary in some countries to protect the many against the few. On August 29, 1914, some 1,500 women, dressed in black, marched down Fifth Avenue in New York City to oppose wars in the Caribbean and Europe. Peace advocates, such as Jane Addams, saw signs of a country being drawn toward war.

A One-Sided Neutrality

As German armies crossed Belgium in August 1914, Wilson declared a policy of strict neutrality. The war took him by surprise, and like Addams he found it "incredible" that civilized nations could display such savagery. His first worry was that America's immigrant communities would take sides. Shortly after the crisis began, 450 steel-workers from Gary, Indiana, enlisted in the Serbian army. Irish Americans, who wanted independence for their homeland, sided with Germany against England. The Allies (Britain, France, Italy, and Russia) and the Central powers (Germany, Austria-Hungary, and Turkey) each used **propaganda** to manipulate US opinion.

Wilson sent his closest aide, Colonel Edward House, to Europe with offers to broker a peace agreement. Privately the president believed that a German victory would be a catastrophe. Protected by Britain's control of the seas, the United States had expanded its influence during the previous century. In an Allied defeat, he said, "the United States, itself, will have to become a military nation, for Germany will push her conquests into South America." With Europe and possibly Asia controlled by a single power, the United States would be vulnerable and alone.

Modern warfare and commerce made true neutrality difficult. The belligerent powers desperately needed everything the United States had to export. As purchasing agent for France and Britain, J. P. Morgan's firm soon became the world's largest customer, buying more than $3 billion worth of armaments, food, textiles, steel, chemicals, and fuel. US loans to the Allies grew to $2.5 billion by 1917, but the Central powers received only $127 million in credit. Trade with the Central powers meanwhile sank from $170 million to less than $1 million by 1916. An Allied victory would make the United States the world's leading creditor, whereas defeat might mean financial collapse. The United States had not formally taken sides, but the American economy was already in the war on the side of the Allies.

Wilson's response to the British and German naval blockades reinforced the tilt toward the Allies. Both sides violated the "freedom of the seas," Britain with mines and warships, Germany with submarines. Wilson considered Britain's violation justifiable, but not Germany's. Britain's surface fleet was able to capture civilian ships as required by international law, but a German *Unterseeboot*, or U-boat—a small, fragile submarine—could not do that without giving up the stealth and surprise that were its only weapons.

The *Lusitania*'s Last Voyage

Germany used advertisements in American newspapers to warn against travel on ships bound for the war zone. The State Department was divided. Robert Lansing, the department's counselor, condemned submarine attacks as an offense against law and morality, but Bryan wanted to bar Americans from traveling on belligerent ships. Wilson sided with Lansing and declared that Germany would be held to "strict accountability" for American lives or property.

On the afternoon of May 7, 1915, submarine U-20 sighted the luxury liner *Lusitania* off the coast of Ireland and fired a torpedo that detonated against the starboard side. In 18 minutes, the *Lusitania* broke apart and sank. Of almost 2,000 passengers aboard, 1,198 drowned, including 94 children and 124 Americans. The newspapers reacted with rage and horror, but Wilson's advisers again disagreed on how to respond. Bryan wanted to balance a protest with a denunciation of Britain's violation of neutral rights. Wilson ignored him and demanded that submarine warfare stop altogether. He hinted that unless his demands were met, the United States would break relations.

Public opinion was equally divided. Lippmann told a friend in England that "the feeling against war in this country is a great deal deeper than you would imagine by reading editorials." When Germany promised not to attack passenger liners without warning, Wilson accepted this pledge as a diplomatic triumph. It momentarily restored calm, but official and public opinion had turned against Germany. The *Lusitania* crisis, Lippmann predicted, "united Englishmen and Americans in a common grief and a common indignation" and might "unite them in a common war."

THE DRIFT TO WAR

The *Lusitania* disaster divided progressives on the issue of the war. Peace advocates such as Addams, Bryan, and La Follette urged a stricter neutrality. Others believed war, or preparations for war, were justified. Theodore Roosevelt clamored for it. He endorsed the preparedness campaign mounted by organizations such as the National Security League and the American Defense Society. Thousands marched down New York's Fifth Avenue under an electric sign declaring "Absolute and Unqualified Loyalty to Our Country."

Preparedness leagues, headed by businessmen and conservative political figures, called attention to the state of the armed forces, equipped only for tropical wars and lacking trucks, planes, and modern arms. The preparedness campaign appropriated patriotic rituals once reserved for elections. Wilson himself led the parade in Washington in 1916, wearing a red tie, white trousers, and a blue blazer. Hundreds of young Americans, positive that a German victory would mean the defeat of civilization, went to Paris to enlist. The French army soon had an American Volunteer Corps and a squadron of American fliers, the Lafayette Escadrille, whose exploits filled American newspapers. Magazines featured the poems of Alan Seeger, a Harvard graduate who joined the foreign legion. While Americans slept "pillowed in silk and scented down," Seeger wrote, "I've a rendezvous with death/At midnight in some flaming town." Wilson felt that to shape the world after the war, Americans would have to meet that rendezvous.

The Election of 1916

Although Wilson believed the United States would need to enter the fight, he campaigned for reelection under the slogan "He kept us out of war." The preparedness issue reunited Theodore Roosevelt and the Republicans behind Supreme Court Justice Charles Evans Hughes, who attacked Wilson for failing to defend American honor in Mexico and Europe. Woman suffragists campaigned against Wilson and picketed the White House with signs asking, "Mr. President? How long must women wait for liberty?" Although the Republicans remained dominant, Hughes was an inept campaigner. He won New York, Pennsylvania, and Illinois but lost in the South and West. Wilson won narrowly, whereas Republicans controlled the House and the Senate. Still, reelection freed Wilson to pursue a more vigorous foreign policy. As Lippmann realized, "What we're electing is a war president—not the man who kept us out of war."

The Last Attempts at Peace

After the election, Wilson launched a new peace initiative. Looking for an opening after years of stalemate, he asked each of the belligerent powers to state its war aims. Each insisted on punishing the other and enlarging its own territories.

Before Congress in January 1917, the president called for a "peace without victory," based on the self-determination of all nations and the creation of an international organization to enforce peace.

Germany toyed with accepting Wilson's proposals but decided to wait. With the defeat of Russia in 1917, it could shift armies from the eastern front to France. U-boats again torpedoed British passenger liners and American merchant ships. In late February, British intelligence officers showed the US ambassador in London a telegram from the German foreign minister, Arthur Zimmermann, plotting an alliance with Mexico. With the Zimmermann Telegram revealed, if Wilson did not declare war now, Roosevelt declared, he would "skin him alive."

Americans disagreed then, as historians do today, on why the United States went to war. Critics pointed to the corporate interests that stood to gain. Publicly and in private, Wilson stressed two considerations: the attacks on American ships and the peace settlement. The treaty conference would settle scores of issues affecting American interests. Unless it went to war, Wilson told Jane Addams, the United States would have to shout "through a crack in the door."

War Aims

Rain was falling on the evening of April 2, 1917, as Wilson went to ask Congress for war. Some on Pennsylvania Avenue cheered and waved flags, whereas others stared silently at the president's limousine. The war, Wilson told the assembly, was in its last stages. American armies could bring it to a merciful end. The United States had tried to stand apart, but it had failed. Neutrality had provided no safety for travelers or trade. The only hope for avoiding even more dangerous future wars was for the United States to dictate the peace, to establish a "concert of free peoples." This would be a war to end all wars, to make the world safe for democracy.

In urging the vote for war, the president explicitly rejected the aims of the Allies. "We have no quarrel with the German people," he said, but with the kaiser and all other emperors and autocrats who blocked his road to a new world order. Wilson realized, however, that imperial France and Britain did not stand for democracy or self-determination, either. The United States would fight with Britain and France as an "associated power."

Edward House assembled a secret committee, known as the Inquiry, to draft a peace proposal both generous enough to show "sympathy and friendship" to the German people and harsh enough to punish their leaders. Made up of economists, historians, geographers, and legal experts, with Lippmann as its secretary, the Inquiry produced a set of 14 recommendations that redrew the boundaries of Europe, created a league of nations, and based peace on the principles of freedom of the seas, open-door trade, and ethnic self-determination.

The Fight in Congress

During the ovation after Wilson's speech to Congress, one senator stood silently, his arms folded. La Follette told his colleagues that if this was a war for democracy, it should be declared democratically. The country had voted for the peace candidate for president, and there were strong reasons to suspect a declaration would fail a national vote. Representatives found that voters opposed American entry, often by two to one. Midwestern farmers, William Allen White reported from Iowa, "don't seem to get the war."

Prowar representatives blocked La Follette's move for a referendum and brought the declaration to a vote on April 6, when it passed 82 to 6 in the Senate and 373 to 50 in the House. Divisions resurfaced over questions of how to pay for the war and who would fight in it. Wilson wanted universal conscription, the first draft since the Civil War. The 1917 draft law deputized 4,000 local boards to induct men between 18 and 45. Both supporters and opponents believed the draft would mold citizens. It would "break down distinctions of race and class," said one representative, turning immigrants into "new Americans." La Follette countered that the new Americans would be like the new Germans, indoctrinated by the army.

Newspapers and politicians denounced the antiwar progressives as traitors. They had too few votes to stop conscription, but they did create an exemption for conscientious objectors and reduced some taxes used to pay for the war. Opposition voices were soon silenced by patriotic calls for unity. "I pray God," Wilson avowed, "that some day historians will remember these momentous years as the years which made a single people of the great body of those who call themselves Americans."

MOBILIZING THE NATION AND THE ECONOMY

News of the war declaration, carried in banner headlines on Easter Sunday, 1917, set the nation abuzz with activity. Wilson recognized that he was asking for an unprecedented effort. Raising an army of over 3 million, supplying it with modern equipment, and transporting it across submarine-infested waters were herculean feats. By midsummer, there were more men at work building barracks than had been in both armies at Gettysburg. Americans would send to Europe 1.8 million tons of meat, 8.8 million tons of grain, and 1.5 million tons of sugar. Factories that produced sewing machines and automobiles would retool to make howitzers and tanks.

The strain war placed on the American people and economy was severe. Wilson and others feared that it could widen political divisions and destroy 15 years of progressive achievements. Others felt that sharing the sacrifices of war would consolidate the gains. "We shall exchange our material thinking for something quite different," the General Federation of Women's Clubs predicted. "We shall all be enfranchised, prohibition will prevail, many wrongs will be righted." Lippmann hoped war would bring a new American revolution.

Enforcing Patriotism

Authorities dealt severely with dissent. Suspicions about the loyalties of ethnic communities and rumors of German saboteurs fed the hysteria. On July 30, 1916, across the river from New York City, the largest arms storage facility in the country blew up. The explosion destroyed thousands of pounds of shells and guns bound for Russia and tore away parts of the Statue of Liberty. Federal agents responded by rounding up aliens. However, domestic opinion posed a greater danger to the war effort than enemy agents. While initial enthusiasm ran high, the skepticism

Wake Up, America! After a prolonged effort at neutrality, the United States faced the challenge of preparedness upon entering World War I. Propaganda posters encouraged Americans to support the war effort.

La Follette expressed was just beneath the surface. Victories might not come quickly, and if the public should start to turn against the war, consent would have to be manufactured by propaganda or the police.

Congress gave the president sweeping powers to suppress dissent. The Espionage Act (1917) and the Sedition Act (1918) effectively outlawed opposition to the war and used the postal service to catch offenders. Although there was no link between the labor movement and

Struggles For Democracy

Eugene V. Debs Speaks Out Against the War

When the United States declared war on Germany in April 1917, the Socialist Party convened to draft a response to the war. The party committed to an ongoing, active opposition to the war, the draft, and all funding of the war effort. This public stance, combined with steadily increasing membership due to antiwar sentiments from both farm and urban working-class communities, made the Socialist Party a target for those dedicated to promoting "Americanism," unquestioning loyalty, and total support for the war effort. Those who failed to demonstrate their patriotism sufficiently

were subject to harassment, violence, or worse. Legislation such as the Sedition Act and Espionage Act made dissent not only unpopular, but illegal.

Eugene V. Debs, a long-time Socialist leader, watched much of this occur from his home in Indiana. After a lifetime of advocating on behalf of the American worker and attempting to spread the party's message, the 63-year-old Debs suffered from poor health and was confined to his bed. But as he saw his friends and associates beaten and jailed, and as he read Socialist views misrepresented in the press, he felt compelled to defend the party to which he had dedicated so much of his life.

Debs traveled to Canton, Ohio, where three local party leaders had been imprisoned under the Espionage Act for publicly opposing the war. After visiting with these men, Debs addressed a crowd of more than 1,000 people in nearby Nimisilla Park. He angrily asserted that his comrades had been persecuted merely for exercising their "constitutional right of free speech." Debs critiqued the American government for failing to live up to its promise as a free republic. He lamented the power of the business elite, who claimed to set the standard for American patriotism even as they made handsome profits from the war effort. These men, Debs proclaimed, "shout their claim from the housetops that they are the only patriots, and who have their magnifying glasses in hand, scanning the country for evidence of disloyalty, eager to apply the brand of treason to the men who dare to even whisper their opposition." The wealthy, he asserted, fervently promoted the war as they happily allowed other men to fight it. To that end, Debs told the crowd, "You are fit for something better than slavery and cannon fodder. You need to know that you were not created to work and produce and impoverish yourself to enrich an idle exploiter. You need to know that you have a mind to improve, a soul to develop, and a manhood to sustain."

In his speech, Debs said nothing he had not said before, but his supporters were not the only ones in the crowd. Also present were stenographers hired by the US Attorney for Northern Ohio, E. S. Wertz. Although the Justice Department in Washington, DC was not enthusiastic about the possibility of prosecution, Wertz obtained an indictment, charging Debs with 10 violations of the Espionage Act.

When Debs went to trial, he instructed his lawyers not to contest the charges, which had been reduced to two violations. He had given the speech and would stand by it. In his estimation, he had been well within his rights of free speech. As Debs addressed the jury, he invoked great American patriots like George Washington and Thomas Paine, men who had spoken out against injustice, just as he had. Those men were heroes, but contemporaries who followed their examples were subject to persecution. His defense mattered not. The jury found Debs guilty, and he was sentenced to 10 years in jail.

Debs's speech and sentencing initially electrified American Socialists, but optimism on the left was short-lived. Debs appealed the decision, but in March 1919, the US Supreme Court upheld his conviction. Ohio Senator Atlee Pomerene feared leniency for Debs would suggest national weakness against the perceived growing threat from radicals and revolutionaries inspired by the Bolshevik Revolution in Russia. Attorney General A. Mitchell Palmer, who would go on to lead raids against political radicals as part of the post–World War I Red Scare, rejected the possibility of clemency altogether.

Debs ultimately served less than three years of his sentence. While in prison, he ran as the Socialist candidate for president of the United States and received nearly a million votes. When he emerged from prison in December 1921, however, he was hobbled by poor health and his party was hampered by an increasingly conservative political climate that would limit radical activism for much of the decade ahead. The rights and freedoms advocated by Debs would be restricted for the foreseeable future.

sabotage, unions were the prime target. The Justice Department raided the Chicago offices of the Industrial Workers of the World and sent 96 leaders to prison on charges of sedition. William D. "Big Bill" Haywood was sentenced to 20 years. Eugene V. Debs, leader of the Socialist Party, received 10 years for telling Ohioans they were "fit for something better than slavery and cannon fodder."

States also passed laws criminalizing "unpatriotic" activity. Indiana's Council for Defense licensed citizens to raid German homes, prevent church services in German, and make sure German Americans bought war bonds. Towns, schools, and clubs with German-sounding names changed them. East Germantown, Indiana, became Pershing. Hamburgers became "liberty sandwiches." Schools in the Midwest stopped teaching German altogether. Americans who had once proudly displayed their ethnicity now took pains to disguise it.

Pacifist faiths had their own ordeals. Some sects had come to America to avoid conscription in Germany or Russia. Many could not comply with the conscientious objector statute, which required submission to military control. Fifteen hundred Mennonites fled to Canada to avoid being placed in camps. Thirty-four Russian Pentecostals were arrested in Arizona, turned over to the army, court-martialed, and sent to Leavenworth.

The government's propaganda effort was managed by the Committee on Public Information (CPI) under former muckraker **George Creel**. It made films, staged pageants, and churned out ads, billboards, and press releases. The CPI sold the war by telling Americans they were fighting to save their own homes. One poster showed German bombers over a shattered, headless Statue of Liberty. Like Wilson, propaganda distinguished between Germany and the German people. CPI leaflets in German offered "Friendly Words to the Foreign Born." It cast immigrants as potential patriots and women as symbols of progress and sacrifice. Creel drafted Charles Dana Gibson, whose "Gibson Girl" ads personified glamour, to depict women as mothers, nurses, and patriotic consumers. As advertising mobilized American thought for the war effort, it also advanced progressive agendas.

Regimenting the Economy

The first prolonged conflict between industrial nations, World War I introduced the term "**total war**." By 1917, all of the resources, manpower, and productive capacities of the combatants had been mobilized. It soon became clear that the economy of the United States would have to be organized in new ways.

The navy planned a vast shipyard on **Hog Island**, near Philadelphia, with 250 buildings, 80 miles of railroad track, and 34,000 workers. It would be larger than Britain's seven largest shipyards combined, but in April 1917, Hog Island was 847 acres of swamp. Steelmaker Charles M. Schwab, in charge of the project, signed contracts for machinery, cement, steel, and timber. Materials were loaded on trains headed east. The result was the Great Pile Up, the biggest traffic jam in railroad history. Without enough workers to unload, cars began to back up on sidings in Philadelphia and then all the way back to Pittsburgh and Buffalo, their loads dumped on the outskirts of cities. Schwab begged the railroads to cooperate, to no avail. The voluntary system had failed, and on January 1, 1918, Wilson nationalized the railroads.

The Hog Island fiasco demonstrated the need for supervision of the economy. Wilson created a War Industries Board (WIB) to regulate prices, manufacturing, and transport. The job was enormous, and Wilson found the overseer he needed in Bernard Baruch, a Wall Street financier, who believed in regulation by "socially responsible" businessmen. Baruch recruited corporate executives for top positions and paid them a dollar a year. The president of the Aluminum Company of America became chairman of the WIB's aluminum committee, and a former top executive of John Deere headed the agricultural implements section.

The dollar-a-year men regimented the economy and put business to work for government, but they also guaranteed profits and looked after their own interests. One of their innovations, the "**cost-plus" contract**, assured contractors the recovery of costs plus a percentage for profit. Under these arrangements, the Black and Decker Company made gun sights, Akron Tire made army cots, and the Evinrude Company stopped making outboard motors and turned out grenades. Each company built up revenues to launch new product lines after the war. Standardization also helped industry. The WIB set standard designs and sizes for everything from

Hog Island Shipyard Building the massive shipyard at Hog Island was a major feat. The railroad network broke down under the strain, leading Wilson to nationalize the railroads.

shirts to lug nuts. One steel executive observed, "We are all making more money out of this war than the average human being ought to."

Not all businesses submitted willingly to "war socialism." The Ford Motor Company had just set up a national dealer network, and it refused to stop delivering cars. When other automakers followed suit, the board threatened to cut off the industry's supply of coal and steel. After long negotiations, the automakers agreed to cut production by three-fourths. The delay hurt. When American troops went into battle, they had a grand total of two tanks.

The war economy was a culmination of two movements: Wall Street's drive for corporate consolidation and the progressives' push for federal regulation. Businessmen saw that the WIB could rationalize the economy. These "New Capitalists" wanted to end cutthroat competition and make business predictable. They encouraged workers to identify with the company through stock sharing and bonus plans. The WIB's example of government-industry cooperation would serve as a model in national crises to come.

The Great Migration

The war economy gave Americans new choices and opportunities. As factories geared up, they faced a shortage of labor. The draft took eligible employees from the cities, and the usual source of new workers—Europe—was sealed off by a screen of U-boats. Employers found eager workers in the South. In small towns and rural junctions, labor recruiters arrived offering free rides to the North and well-paid employment on arrival. Manufacturers came to rely on the labor of former sharecroppers. Westinghouse employed 25 African Americans in 1916; by 1918, it employed 1,500. The Pennsylvania Railroad recruited 10,000 workers from Florida and Georgia. Veterans saw no reason to go back to sharecropping after the war. In some northern cities, a thousand migrants were arriving each week. This massive movement from the rural South to the urban North and West came to be called the **Great Migration.**

Lynchings, intimidation, and a declining southern economy encouraged migration. Almost half a million people came north during the war years—so many that some counties emptied out, creating panic among whites left behind. Mississippi alone lost 75,000 workers. "We must have the Negro in the South," the Macon, Georgia, *Telegraph* pined. "It is the only labor we have. . . . If we lose it, we go bankrupt." Southern states banned recruiters. In some places violence provoked migration. "Every time a lynching takes place in a community down south," one observer noted, "you can depend on it that colored people will arrive in Chicago within two weeks."

African American workers moved into jobs at the bottom of the pay scale: janitors, domestics, and factory hands. Rent, groceries, and other necessities were substantially more expensive in the cities. Still, African American workers could earn wages 70 percent higher than what they were used to at home. Almost no one went back, and the new arrivals adapted to the rhythms of city life. "South State Street was in its glory then, a teeming Negro street with crowded theaters, restaurants, and cabarets," **Langston Hughes** wrote of Chicago in 1918. Housing was scarce, and African American renters were limited to overcrowded districts wedged between industrial zones and hostile white neighborhoods. W. E. B. DuBois noted that African Americans had lived in many neighborhoods of Philadelphia before the war, but by the end of the war they were concentrated in just one ward. Ghetto neighborhoods were both expensive and decrepit. On Chicago's South Side, rents were 15 to

20 percent higher than in white neighborhoods, and the death rate was comparable to that of Bombay, India. White property owners and real estate agents worked to create the ghettos, enforce their boundaries, and "Make Hyde Park White." A real estate agent said that African American homeowners "hurt our values." When discrimination failed, there was dynamite. From 1917 to 1919, whites bombed 26 African American residences in Chicago. On July 2, 1917, in East St. Louis, an arms manufacturing center in southern Illinois, competition for housing and political offices led a mob of white workers to attack "Black Valley," an African American neighborhood along the Southern Railroad track. Forty-seven people were killed and six thousand left homeless.

After East St. Louis, white mobs found Black neighborhoods less easy to attack. When a mob invaded a Washington, DC ghetto three years later, residents fought back with guns. The novelist Alden Bland wrote that the mood in Chicago's Black Belt, under attack in the hot summer of 1919, was "get them before they get you." An African American newspaper explained drily that "New Negroes are determined to make their dying a costly investment for all concerned." The New Negro, urban, defiant, often a war veteran who demanded rather than asked for rights, became the subject of admiring and apprehensive reports. Police kept files on suspected militants, but the mobility and anonymity of northern cities translated into freedom.

Reforms Become "War Measures"

On August 3, 1917, thousands of protestors marched in New York under signs demanding "Why not make America safe for democracy?" In the wake of the East St. Louis outrage, the NAACP urged Congress to outlaw lynching as a "war measure." African Americans were not alone in using the president's language to justify reform. Carrie Chapman Catt told Wilson that he could enact women's suffrage as a "war measure." Advocates of progressive change demanded that the United States practice at home the ideals it fought for abroad.

Suffragists hitched their cause to the national struggle. Catt's National American Woman Suffrage Association (NAWSA) abandoned its state-by-state lobbying to identify women with the national cause. Members sold liberty bonds and knitted socks for the Red Cross, making it clear they expected a constitutional amendment in return. Alice Paul's National Woman's Party (NWP) picketed the White House with signs quoting Wilson's demand for all peoples to "have a voice in their own governments." When Wilson announced his support in 1918, he cited women's war service as the reason. The Nineteenth Amendment was finally ratified in 1920, "so soon after the war," according to Jane Addams, "that it must be accounted as the direct result of war psychology."

As it had for African Americans, the labor shortage increased opportunities for women. Although most women workers were already in the labor force, many took jobs previously considered "inappropriate" for their sex. Women replaced men as bank tellers, streetcar operators, mail carriers, and steelworkers. Many of these opportunities vanished when the war ended, but in expanding sectors such as finance, communications, and office work, women made permanent gains. By 1920, more than 25 percent worked in offices or as telephone operators, and 13 percent were in professions such as teaching, nursing, and social work. The new opportunities gave women a source of prestige and enjoyment. Alice Hamilton remarked on the "strange spirit of exaltation among the men and women who thronged to

Washington, engaged in all sorts of 'war work' and loving it." Army General Order 13 set standards for women's work, including an eight-hour day, prohibitions on working at night or in dangerous conditions, and provisions for rest periods, lunchrooms, and bathrooms. The government also empowered women consumers, encouraging them to report on shopkeepers who charged above the official price.

Wilson authorized a National War Labor Board to intervene in essential industries. The board set an unofficial minimum wage. For the first time, the federal government recognized workers' rights to organize, bargain collectively, and join unions. Unskilled workers earned higher real wages than ever before. When the Smith and Wesson Company refused to acknowledge its workers' right to bargain collectively, the army seized the factory and recognized the union. There were limits, however, for the administration. When skilled machinists at the Remington Arms plant made demands the board considered excessive, Baruch threatened to have them drafted and sent to France.

Prohibition did not please workers, either, but beer, wine, and spirits were early casualties of war. The Anti-Saloon League and the Woman's Christian Temperance Union had built a powerful antiliquor coalition by 1916. Congress would have passed Prohibition without war, but temperance became a patriotic crusade. Military regulations prohibited liquor near army camps. Finally, in 1919 the states ratified the Eighteenth Amendment, banning the "manufacture, sale, or transportation of intoxicating liquors." The Anti-Saloon League celebrated the dawn of "an era of clear thinking and clean living." America was "so dry it couldn't spit," according to Billy Sunday. He overstated the case. By some estimates, after the ban illegal speakeasies in New York outnumbered the saloons they replaced. Bootleggers and smugglers slaked American thirsts, but liquor prices rose and consumption declined. Americans never again drank anything like the average two and a half gallons of pure alcohol per person annually imbibed before Prohibition.

The war also lent patriotic zeal to antivice crusaders. During the Progressive Era, muckrakers exposed the police-protection rackets that allowed gambling dens and brothels to thrive. Within days of the declaration of war, reformers identified prostitutes as enemies of the health of American troops. Gonorrhea afflicted a quarter of the Allied forces in France, and middle-class Americans were appalled. Before 1917, reformers targeted commercial vice as a source of political and social corruption, but afterward they directed their efforts at women as carriers of disease.

The army acted against liquor and prostitution to protect the welfare of soldiers, but it did not challenge racial injustice, even when lives were at stake. At camps in the South, it was often unclear who had more authority, uniformed African American soldiers or white local officials. Clashes could easily turn violent. A riot in Houston in August 1917 began when soldiers from nearby Camp Logan rushed to the aid of an African American woman being beaten by police. Twenty policemen and soldiers were killed, and 54 soldiers received life sentences in the largest court-martial in US history.

After the Houston riot, African American units were dispersed across the country, and the army remained segregated. Worse, many southern communities used military discipline to strengthen their own Jim Crow laws. Encouraged by the army's "work or fight" order, which required draft-age men to either enlist or get a job, states and localities passed compulsory work laws that applied to women and older men. The laws were intended to keep laborers in the fields and servants in the kitchens at prewar wages.

In this "war welfare state," the government mediated among labor, industry, and other organized interests. Social activism became a matter of lobbying federal agencies that could either dictate sweeping changes or use wartime powers to maintain the status quo. Success required organization and an ability to tie one's goals to the government's ambitions.

OVER THERE

When the Senate took up the enormous war budget Wilson submitted in April 1917, the finance committee questioned Major Palmer E. Pierce about what would be done with the money. "Clothing, cots, camps, food, pay," he replied, "and we may have to have an army in France." "Good Lord!" exclaimed Senator Thomas Martin of Virginia. "You're not going to send soldiers over there, are you?" After the horrors of the Somme and Verdun, where men were fed to machine guns by the tens of thousands, it hardly seemed reasonable to send Americans to such a place. "One would think that, after almost four years of war, after the most detailed and realistic accounts of murderous fighting,. . . it would have been all but impossible to get anyone to serve," one veteran later recalled. "But it was not so; we and many thousands of others volunteered."

Americans went to France optimistically believing they could change the war and the peace. Trench warfare was not for them. They planned to fight a war of movement, sweeping in formations across open fields, like those at Antietam and Gettysburg. To a remarkable degree, they got the war they wanted. Europeans watched their civilization destroy itself in the Great War, but Americans saw theirs rising. Soldiers, "doughboys," said so in their letters, echoing the words of their leaders, their newspapers, and the volumes of poetry they carried with them into battle.

Citizens into Soldiers

Enlisting, training, and transporting soldiers began in a rush. Camps housing 400,000 recruits went up in the first 30 days. Conscription went smoothly, and soon 32 camps were housing 1.3 million men. Commander John J. Pershing arrived in France in June with 40,000 men and the first of some 16,000 women who would serve in the American Expeditionary Force (AEF).

Neither the Wilson administration nor the Allies initially anticipated that soldiers would be the United States' main contribution to the war effort. Britain urgently needed financial support, and Wilson advanced $200 million immediately, the first of an eventual $10 billion in loans to the Allies. Funds, food, and ammunition were needed more urgently than men, but that changed in October 1917, when German and Austrian forces smashed through the Italian lines at Caporetto, capturing 275,000 men and finishing the war on that front. When the Bolshevik Revolution curtailed Russian resistance in the East in November, Britain and France saw that by the next spring Germany would be able to mass its armies on the line from Belgium to Switzerland and break through to Paris. The war became a race to the Western Front between the United States and Germany.

Getting troops to the war required ships, but the American merchant fleet was smaller in 1917 than it was during the Civil War. For a time the United States had to cut back draft calls because it lacked ships to transport soldiers. The navy, meanwhile, cured the U-boat problem. The American destroyer fleet drove submarines from the sea lanes with depth charges, allowing the Allies to convoy effectively for the first time. By July 18, some 10,000 troops a day boarded the "Atlantic Ferry" for the ride to France.

The Fourteen Points

In December 1917, the Inquiry sent the president a memorandum titled "The War Aims and the Peace Terms It Suggests." Wilson redrafted it and presented it to Congress on January 8, 1918. The **Fourteen Points** outlined US objectives, but more fundamentally they offered an entirely new basis for peace. Unlike nineteenth-century wars waged for limited territorial or political objectives, the Great War was a total war, fought for unlimited aims. The principal belligerents—Britain, France, Russia, Germany, and Austria-Hungary—were global empires. Germany hoped both to defeat Britain and to take its empire. France wanted to destroy Germany's future as a great power, economically and militarily. Wilson replaced these imperial visions of total victory with a peace based on limited gains for nations, not empires.

The Fourteen Points addressed four themes: national self-determination; freedom of the seas; enforcement of peace by a league of nations; and open diplomacy. The Inquiry's memorandum included maps marked with new European boundaries based on national, ethnic identities. The new state of Poland, for instance, should govern only territories with "indisputably Polish populations." Point three restated the Open Door, urging international free trade, reflecting Wilson's hope of eliminating what he saw as the two leading causes of war, imperial ambition and commercial rivalry. By calling for an end to secret diplomacy, he appealed directly to the people of Europe. The expectation was that the hope of a just peace would weaken the enemy nations' will and inspire the Allies to fight harder. Creel printed 60 million copies and had them distributed around the world. Planes dropped copies over Germany and Austria.

Wilson hoped the Fourteen Points would dispel both the old dream of empire and the new one of socialist revolution. On November 7, two months before Wilson presented the points to Congress, Russian workers overthrew the Provisional Government of Alexander Kerensky. The one-party regime of the Bolsheviks, led by Vladimir Lenin, summoned workers everywhere to rise against their governments and to make peace without indemnities or annexations. "The crimes of the ruling, exploiting classes in this war have been countless. These crimes cry out for revolutionary revenge." In December, Lenin revealed the contents of the secret treaties, unmasking the imperial ambitions of the Allies. He sued for peace based on the principle of self-determination. The Council of People's Commissars allocated 2 million rubles to encourage revolutions around the world and called "upon the working classes of all countries to revolt."

Two world leaders—Lenin and Wilson—now offered radically different visions of the new world order, and Lenin was putting his into effect. The Bolsheviks' contempt for democracy angered Wilson, but he hoped that Russia would stay in the war. Those hopes ended with the Treaty of Brest-Litovsk, signed by Russia and Germany in March 1918. The treaty showed the fearful price of defeat in modern war. Russia lost the Ukraine, Poland, and Finland, most of its iron, steel, and best farmland, and one-quarter of its population. Those assets went into the German war machine, which began transferring 10 divisions a month to the West, its eastern front now secure.

Wilson was the first, but not the last, American president to be haunted by the specter of a German-Russian alliance, uniting the immense war-making resources of Europe and Asia. In Wilson's strategic vision, the great land powers of Eurasia, not Alfred Thayer Mahan's sea powers, most threatened US security. He refused to recognize the Bolshevik government and sent 7,000 American troops to Russia to support anti-Bolshevik forces on the eastern front. US and Japanese forces invaded Siberia from the east. The Bolshevik government now counted the United States among its enemies. Meanwhile, the battle for the control of Europe was about to begin.

The Final Offensive

The German high command knew the spring offensive would be the last. Their exhausted economy no longer could supply food or ammunition for a sustained effort. Breadlines, strikes, and industrial breakdowns foreshadowed the chaos

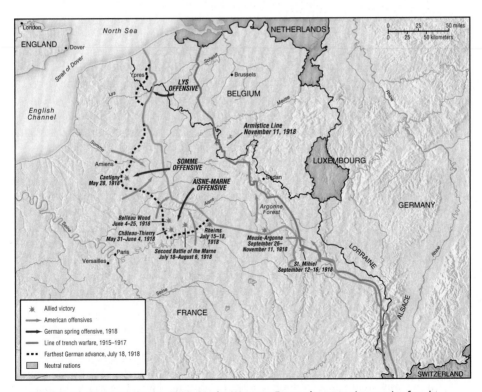

Map 20–2 Western Front, 1918 On the Western Front, the opposing armies fought from trenches fortified with earthworks and barbed wire. The parallel trench lines stretched thousands of miles from the North Sea to Switzerland.

that would follow defeat. Risking everything, the German commander Erich Ludendorff launched his offensive on March 21, 1918 (see Map 20–2). Shock troops hurled the British Fifth Army back to Amiens. In May they penetrated French lines as far as Soissons, 37 miles from Paris. As gaps split the lines, French general Ferdinand Foch and General Douglas Haig of Britain appealed urgently to Pershing to put American troops under British and French command. Pershing opposed the idea. He wanted the American army to play its own part in the war.

Pershing criticized European commanders for remaining on the defensive instead of "driving the enemy out into the open and engaging him in a war of movement." Trained at West Point in Civil War tactics, he imagined himself a General Grant replacing European McClellans and saw trenches as symbols of inertia. Pershing favored massed assaults in which the sheer numbers of American troops would overwhelm the Germans, rifles against machine guns. In seeing Europe's war as a replay of the US Civil War, Pershing revealed a habit of mind that would typify American geopolitical thinking for the next century: the belief that Americans could understand the world through the prism of their own experience. He was not alone in wanting a decisive alternative to trench warfare. Billy Mitchell, head of the army's aviation section, noted that "we could cross the lines of these contending armies in a few minutes in our aeroplanes."

On May 27, German divisions pierced French lines at Château-Thierry and began advancing on Paris at a rate of 10 miles a day. The French government considered whether to abandon the capital or surrender. Bowing to urgent requests, Pershing threw the AEF into the breach. Column upon column of fresh American troops filled the roads from Paris to the front. "We are real soldiers now and not afread [*sic*] of Germans," John F. Dixon, an African American infantryman from New York, wrote home. "Our boys went on the battlefield last night singing." Ahead lay five German divisions, poison gas, minefields, rolling artillery barrages, and machine guns in interlocking fields of fire. The Germans were stopped, but at a fearful cost. The marine brigade that took Belleau Wood suffered 4,600 casualties, half the force. Without artillery or tanks, they assaulted machine gun nests head-on, with rifles.

By mid-July, the initiative passed to the Allies. On September 12, Foch allowed Pershing to try his tactics against the St. Mihiel salient, a bulge in the French lines which, unknown to the Allies, the Germans had already begun to evacuate. The doughboys raced behind the retreating enemy past their planned objectives. Pershing was delighted. St. Mihiel had vindicated his strategy, and he yearned for another chance. It came two weeks later, at the battle of the Meuse-Argonne.

Ten miles northwest of Verdun, the Argonne Forest contained some of the most formidable natural and man-made defenses on the Western Front. Atop parallel ridges lay three fortified trench lines, *Stellungen*—barriers of concrete pillboxes, barbed wire, artillery, and observation posts. Half a million German troops had defended these fortifications for four years. Against this force, Pershing arrayed the American First Army, 1,031,000 men. The average doughboy at the Meuse-Argonne had a total of four months of training, and some had as little as 10 days. Pershing's battle plan called for overwhelming the German defenses with

The Western Front From 1914 to 1918 the Western Front was the largest metropolis on earth, in Robert Cowley's phrase, an "unreal city" whose inhabitants—8,000 of whom died each day—worked in an industry of destruction. Here, Australian soldiers tread through the wasteland near Ypres, Belgium, in October 1917.

speed and numbers, reaching the second trench line, 10 miles inside the German front, the first day.

"Moving slowly forward, never heeding the bursting shells, nor gas, we followed a road forking to the left... into no man's land. It was soon noticed that we were in the bracket of a German barrage," a soldier wrote from the battlefield. They broke through the first line of German trenches after a day and a half; then the battle turned into a deadly crawl. In two weeks of fighting, 26,277 Americans died. French soldiers reported seeing the American dead lying in rows, cut down by machine guns as they marched in formation. Finally, on November 10, American troops reached their objective and dynamited the rail line connecting the cities of Metz and Sedan. Meanwhile, Germany announced that it would accept the Fourteen Points as the basis for an armistice and negotiations. At 11:00 a.m. on November 11, 1918, the guns fell silent.

American intervention had been decisive. The American economy, two and a half times the size of Germany's, lent its industrial and agricultural strength to the Allies at a crucial moment. American military power also tipped the balance. Pershing failed to transform strategy—it remained a mechanized war of attrition until the end—but by striking the final blow, Americans had the illusion that their way of war had been triumphant. American losses, 116,516 dead, were smaller than those of the British (908,371), the French (1.4 million), or the Germans (1.8 million), but they still show the colossal destructiveness of industrial war. In just six months, the United States suffered twice as many combat deaths as it would in the Vietnam War and almost a third as many as in World War II.

Americans and Europeans fought two vastly different wars on the same battlefields. The Americans' war was swift and victorious, but the Europeans experienced a catastrophe that consumed an entire generation. For Europeans, their faith in modernity and in the ability of science and democracy to create a better future vanished forever. Confidence in the inevitability of progress became a distinctive feature of US culture in the postwar era. In much of the world, "American" became almost synonymous with "modern," but not everywhere. In the East, another political and economic system shouted its claim to the future.

REVOLUTIONARY ANXIETIES

Americans celebrated the armistice with bonfires, church bells, automobile horns, and uplifted voices. Wilson told Congress that "everything for which America fought has been accomplished," but he observed that the situation in Russia cast doubt on the durability of peace. Even before the armistice, German revolutionaries took power in Bavaria. Over the next months, revolutions broke out throughout eastern Europe. From the trenches of Flanders to the Sea of Japan, not a single government remained intact, and in Moscow the new Soviet state towered above the ruins of the old regimes.

Wilson in Paris

For Wilson, the moment he had planned for in 1917 had arrived—the United States could help set the terms of peace—but war had exhausted the president. Confident that the public would view the nation's victory as his victory, he committed mistakes. Had he remained in Washington, some historians argue, he could have taken credit for the peace while keeping a close eye on his critics. Instead, he went to Paris, staking the treaty's success on his own popularity. He passed up a chance to include in the delegation a prominent Republican, such as Henry Cabot Lodge, who could guide the treaty through Congress.

Wilson in Paris Woodrow Wilson received a hero's welcome on the Rue Royale when he arrived in France to join the other Allied Powers in crafting the postwar world. His triumph was short-lived, however, as many of his Fourteen Points fell to the wayside during treaty talks at the Palace of Versailles.

In December 1918, Walter Lippmann, now an army captain, watched Wilson's triumphal entry into Paris. Crowds lined the streets, and as the procession crossed the Pont du Concorde, a great cheer echoed off the walls of the Chamber of Deputies. "Never has a king, never has an emperor received such a welcome," *L'Europe Nouvelle* declared. For the next month, Wilson toured France, Italy, and Britain to cries of "Viva Veelson." "They say he thinks of us, the poor people," a workingman remarked, "that he wants us all to have a fair chance; that he is going to do something when he gets here that will make it impossible for our government to send us to war again. If he had only come sooner!"

By the time Wilson arrived for treaty talks at the Palace of Versailles, two of the Fourteen Points had already been compromised. Britain refused to accept the point on freedom of the seas, which would thwart the use of the Royal Navy in a future conflict. Wilson also undercut his own position on point six, respect for Russia's sovereignty, as American troops were occupying Russian Siberia. Wilson was unable to prevent Britain, France, and Japan from dividing Germany's colonies among themselves and imposing harsh peace terms. Germany had to sign a humiliating "war guilt" clause and pay $33 billion in reparations, enough to cripple its economy for decades. Wilson concentrated on the **League of Nations,** which might make up for the treaty's other weaknesses and provide some safety against the rising tide of revolution. He took the lead in drafting the League Covenant, which committed each member to submit disputes to arbitration and pledged them to take action against "any war or threat of war."

The Senate Rejects the League

To many observers in the United States the Treaty of Versailles betrayed the goals Americans had fought to attain. "This Is Not Peace," declared the *New Republic*. Congress saw the League of Nations less as a way to prevent wars than as a guarantee that the United States would be involved. Americans were "far more afraid of Lenin than they ever were of the Kaiser," Lippmann wrote. To Republican leaders such as Henry Cabot Lodge, the United States' best bet was to look to its own security, keep its options open, and work out its international relations independently rather than as part of an alliance or league.

In March 1919, before the treaty was concluded, Lodge and 38 other senators—more than enough to defeat the treaty—signed a petition opposing the League of Nations. James A. Reed of Missouri said the covenant would turn American foreign policy over to foreigners. Editorials feared that American troops would be summoned to settle blood feuds in the Balkans. Wilson expected to fight, but he believed that the Senate would not reject the treaty.

In September, Wilson went "over the heads" of Congress and stumped for the treaty on a nationwide tour. He assured listeners in Sioux Falls that "the peace of the world cannot be established without America." He promised the citizens of Salt Lake City that China's independence would be respected. Traveling more than 8,000 miles and speaking before large audiences without loudspeakers took a toll on his health. After a speech in Pueblo, Colorado, he became so ill that he was rushed back to Washington, where he suffered a stroke that left him partially paralyzed and unable to concentrate for more than a few minutes a day.

Mrs. Wilson and the president's physician kept his condition a secret and refused to allow anyone to see him.

With Wilson secluded in the White House, the Senate voted against ratification. To the end, Wilson refused to allow Senate Democrats to accept any modifications. Even Lippmann's *New Republic*, a mouthpiece for Wilson throughout the war, called the treaty's demise "desirable and wholesome." Lodge and the Republicans were not ready for isolation, but they preferred diplomatic strategies based on economic strength rather than a relatively weak military. They also saw Latin America as more critical than Europe to US security. Meanwhile, European governments organized the League of Nations without delegations from the United States or the Soviet Union.

Over the next decade, US influence abroad grew enormously. American automobiles, radios, and movies could be seen in far corners of the globe. The United States still practiced cautious diplomacy in Europe and Asia, to avoid being drawn into what the *New York Tribune* called the "vast seething mass of anarchy extending from the Rhine to the Siberian wastes."

Red Scare

On May 1, 1919, a dozen or more mail bombs were sent to prominent Americans: J. P. Morgan, John D. Rockefeller, senators, cabinet officials, and Supreme Court Justice Oliver Wendell Holmes. None of the packages reached its intended target, but one injured a maid in the home of Senator Thomas Hardwick and another exploded at the residence of Attorney General A. Mitchell Palmer in Washington, nearly injuring Franklin and Eleanor Roosevelt, who lived next door. Investigations later showed that the bombings were the work of lone lunatics, but many people quickly concluded that the United States was under attack. Since the Russian Revolution, newspapers, evangelists, and government officials had fed fears of Bolshevism. Revolution, Palmer alleged, was "licking at the altars of the churches, leaping into the belfry of the school bell, crawling into the sacred corners of American homes."

Revolutions in Europe terrified conservatives in the United States and led them to look for Soviet terrorists, particularly among immigrants and unionized workers. They drew no distinctions among Socialists, anarchists, Communists, and labor unionists; they were all "red." Seattle's mayor called in the army to break a dockworkers' strike. When steelworkers in Gary, Indiana, struck for higher wages and shorter hours in September 1919, Judge Elbert Gary, president of US Steel, denounced them as followers of Russian "anarchy and Bolshevism." During the war they had worked 12 hours a day, 7 days a week, for an average wage of $28 a week. With the help of local loyalty leagues, Gary broke the strike.

Using the patriotic rhetoric of the war, industry leaders labeled strikers as dangerous aliens. They persuaded allies in the courts to take action, and a series of Supreme Court decisions made union activity virtually illegal. In 1919, the Court allowed antitrust suits to be filed against unions and later outlawed boycotts and picketing. Then, in January 1920, a series of crackdowns known as the Palmer raids rounded up and deported 250 members of the Union of Russian Workers. In one night, 4,000 suspected Communists were arrested in raids across the country.

America In The World
The 1918 Influenza Epidemic

In the Spring of 1918, **influenza** spread across the many militaries mobilized across the globe. In Haskell County, Kansas, where the flu originated, its reach was widespread and its impact severe. Influenza traveled from Haskell County to nearby Camp Funston, and then from Funston, to the other army camps around the United States, surrounding towns and cities, and then to Europe and beyond. Through the spring and summer of 1918, influenza impeded militaries' abilities to wage war, but widespread as it was, the virus did not replicate the severity seen in Haskell. Troops ultimately regarded it as a "three-day fever," generally recovering relatively quickly and returning to the front lines. On August 20, 1918, a British medical journal concluded that the influenza epidemic "has completely disappeared."

But that was not the case. A second wave of the virus, one that had adapted itself to human life and grown more efficient in its attack on the human body, emerged just as British experts suggested the worst had passed.

In late August and into early September, thousands of American troops in transit awaited orders at Commonwealth Pier in Boston. In Boston, and at nearby Camp Devens, the evolved strain of influenza swept through barracks. No longer a three-day fever, this virus attacked the human body with a ferocity that staggered even the most seasoned medical professionals. Devens, with a hospital meant to hold twelve hundred soldiers, served an excess of six thousand men at a time. Colonel Victor Vaughan, head of the army's Division of Communicable Disease and dean of the University of Michigan Medical School, wrote, "hundreds of young stalwart men in the uniform of their country coming into the wards of the hospital in groups of ten or more. They are placed on the cots until every bed is full and yet others crowd in. The faces wear a bluish cast; a distressing cough brings up the blood-stained sputum."

The virus was not contained to Massachusetts. Wartime required mobilization. And symptoms of influenza appeared after several days. As men began falling ill in Boston, three hundred sailors left Boston for the Philadelphia Navy Yard. Within days of the sailors' arrival, nineteen suffered from symptoms of influenza. Lieutenant Commander R. W. Plummer, a doctor and chief health officer for the Philadelphia naval district, aware of the virus's spread through Massachusetts, ordered immediate quarantine and disinfection of all areas and items with which the men had had contact. But by that point, more than 300 sailors already were headed for the Puget Sound.

In Philadelphia, the situation worsened. With the naval hospital full, medical personnel sent patients to the civilian Pennsylvania Hospital. And yet despite this outbreak, despite knowledge of events transpiring in Massachusetts, despite knowledge also of an outbreak at the Great Lakes Naval Training Station in Illinois, Wilmer Krusen, Philadelphia public health director, determined no municipal action was necessary. He publicly denied the very real threat influenza posed to the residents of Philadelphia, justified, he claimed, by a desire to maintain public calm and avoid disruption to the American war effort.

Indeed, so great was Krusen's desire to maintain wartime morale, he chose not to cancel or reschedule a massive Liberty Loan parade scheduled for September 28. Inspired at least in part by the nation's total war effort, Krusen privileged wartime morale and fundraising over public health and safety.

continued

America In The World continued

Influenza As influenza spread across the United States, public officials created makeshift hospitals, such as this one at Camp Funston, Kansas, to serve the vast populations afflicted by the epidemic.

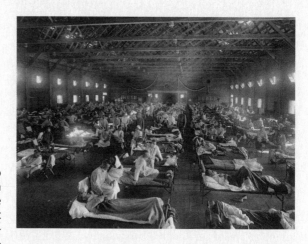

He ignored doctors who encouraged cancellation of the parade. When those doctors attempted to get local media to print a warning about the parade, Philadelphia newspapers, hesitant to print anything that might be categorized as disloyal to the war effort, refused.

With 1400 sailors in the Philadelphia Navy Yard hospitalized, with the next scheduled draft call postponed due to the influenza outbreak, the September 28 Liberty Loan parade in Philadelphia commenced. Spanning two miles, featuring bands, Boy Scouts, women's auxiliaries, American troops, cheered by several thousand city residents, the parade was the spectacle its organizers intended.

Two days after the parade, Krusen stated, "The epidemic is now present in the civilian population and is assuming the type found in naval stations and cantonments." Within seventy-two hours of the parade, every bed in every one of Philadelphia's thirty-one hospitals was occupied. In the weeks to come, daily death totals resulting from influenza surpassed typical weekly totals for deaths from all causes combined. As the Great War continued abroad, the United States' populations—military and civilian—waged war against a virus that would replicate its Philadelphia spread in other locations, foreign and domestic, ultimately claiming somewhere between fifty and one hundred million lives around the world.

TIME LINE

▼1911
Mexican Revolution begins

▼1914
US troops occupy Veracruz, Mexico
World War I begins

▼1915
US troops occupy Haiti (until 1934)
Lusitania sunk

▼1916
US forces invade Mexico in search of Pancho Villa
US forces enter the Dominican Republic
Woodrow Wilson reelected

▼1917
Russian czar abdicates; parliamentary regime takes power

United States declares war on Germany
East St. Louis riot
Houston riot
October Revolution overthrows Russian government; Lenin takes power

▼1918
Wilson announces US war aims: the Fourteen Points

Wall Street Bombing On September 16, 1920, Mario Buda detonated a horse-drawn wagon filled with dynamite and scrap metal in front of the J. P. Morgan offices on Wall Street. It was the first use of a new technology of terror, the car bomb. Sending shock waves through an America already anxious about revolutionaries, the blast intensified the hunt for radicals and "reds."

The most notorious case associated with the **Red Scare** began in May 1920 when Nicola Sacco and Bartolomeo Vanzetti, a shoemaker and a fish peddler, were arrested for robbing a shoe company in South Braintree, Massachusetts. Two men died of gunshot wounds during the robbery, and ballistics experts claimed the bullets came from Sacco's gun. The trial, however, focused less on the evidence than on the fact that the defendants were Italian and anarchists. The state doctored evidence and witnesses changed testimony, but the judge favored the prosecution. The appeals lasted six years, as protests for their release mounted. With the execution approaching, labor parties organized worldwide boycotts of American products. Riots in Paris took 20 lives. Uruguayan workers called a general strike. Governments called on the president to intervene, but on August 23, 1927, Sacco and Vanzetti died in the electric chair.

Americans who had talked in 1917 about making the world safe for democracy now seemed ready to restrict their own freedoms out of fear. Lippmann found it "incredible that an administration announcing the most spacious ideals in our history should have done more to endanger fundamental American liberties than

	▼1919	▼1920
Wilson nationalizes railroads	Eighteenth Amendment outlaws manufacture, sale, and transport of alcoholic beverages	Nineteenth Amendment secures the vote for women
Sedition Act outlaws criticism of the US government		
US troops stop German advance	Versailles Treaty signed in Paris	Palmer raids arrest thousands of suspected Communists
Wilson sends troops to Siberia	Mail bombs target prominent government and business figures	Sacco and Vanzetti arrested on charges of robbery and murder
Armistice ends fighting on the Western Front	Gary, Indiana, steel strike	
Influenza pandemic peaks in September	US Senate rejects Versailles Treaty	

any group of men for a hundred years." By the end of 1920, the terror subsided, but labor unions and social radicals would have to fight the charge of communism for decades to come.

CONCLUSION

Wilson tried to lead America toward what he called a new world order, in which nations and international law would count more than empires and in which the United States could light the way toward progress, stability, and peace. He failed to recognize that for many Americans this future was filled with terrors, as well as promise. The strains of war had introduced new divisions into American society. Progressivism, which had given coherence and direction to social change, was a spent force. The growth of federal administration, the new powers of big business, internal migrations, and new social movements and values added up to what Lippmann called a "revolutionary world." Many of the changes that began during the war had not fully played out, nor were their consequences apparent, but Americans entered the 1920s with a sense of uneasiness. They knew that their nation was now the world's strongest, but they were unsure about what that might mean for their lives.

WHO, WHAT, WHERE 16

cost-plus contract 667	League of Nations 677
Creel, George 666	pacifist 666
Díaz, Porfirio 658	Pershing, John J. 658
Fourteen Points 672	Prohibition 670
Great Migration 668	propaganda 660
Hog Island 666	Red Scare 681
Hughes, Langston 668	total war 666
influenza 679	Western Front 656

REVIEW QUESTIONS

1. Wilson encouraged Americans to fight a war for democracy, but what other goals did US intervention serve?

2. How did mobilization for war advance the progressive agenda? In what ways did it set progressives back?

3. Where were the main battles in which US troops fought?

CRITICAL-THINKING QUESTIONS

1. Allied commanders wanted to use American troops as a reserve, but Pershing wanted his soldiers to enter the battle as an army. Why was that so important to him?

2. Why did Senate Republicans reject the League of Nations? Did they want the United States to withdraw from the world, or did they want to deal with the world in a different way?

3. Managing the pace of change posed a tricky problem for leaders in the early twentieth century. How did Wilson try to control the dynamic of social and political change? What methods of change was he unwilling to accept?

4. Why were American leaders so much more concerned about sedition and dissent during World War I than they were during the Civil War or World War II?

SUGGESTED READINGS

Barry, John. *The Great Influenza: The Story of the Deadliest Pandemic in History*. New York: Viking Press, 2004.

Capozzola, Christopher. *Uncle Sam Wants You: World War I and the Making of the Modern American Citizen*. New York: Oxford University Press, 2008.

National Archives. World War I Centennial. https://www.archives.gov/topics/wwi#event-/timeline/item/archduke-assassination

Neiberg, Michael S. *The Path to War: How the First World War Created Modern America*. New York: Oxford University Press, 2016.

For further review materials and resource information, please visit www.oup.com/us/ofthepeople

CHAPTER 20:   A Global Power, 1914–1919
Primary Sources

20.1   EUGENE V. DEBS, EXCERPTS FROM CANTON, OHIO, SPEECH (1918)

Eugene V. Debs, a leader of the Socialist Party of America, vehemently opposed American involvement in World War I. In June 1918, after visiting several local Socialist leaders who had been jailed for their opposition to the war, Debs spoke in Canton, Ohio. During his speech, he criticized the war as a capitalist undertaking and charged that those who led the patriotic charge did so for purely financial purposes. He called for the working classes to join the Socialist Party and fight for a socialist republic in America. In the aftermath of his speech, Debs was convicted for sedition under the Espionage Act of 1917 and sentenced to 10 years in prison. President Warren Harding commuted his sentence in 1921.

I hate, I loathe, I despise junkers and junkerdom. I have no earthly use for the junkers of Germany, and not one particle more use for the junkers in the United States. They tell us that we live in a great free republic; that our institutions are democratic; that we are a free and self-governing people. This is too much, even for a joke. But it is not a subject for levity; it is an exceedingly serious matter.

To whom do the Wall Street junkers in our country marry their daughters? After they have wrung their countless millions from your sweat, your agony and your life's blood, in a time of war as in a time of peace, they invest these untold millions in the purchase of titles of broken-down aristocrats, such as princes, dukes, counts and other parasites and no-accounts. Would they be satisfied to wed their daughters to honest workingmen? To real democrats? Oh, no!

They scour the markets of Europe for vampires who are titled and nothing else. And they swap their millions for the titles, so that matrimony with them becomes literally a matter of money. These are the gentry who are today wrapped up in the American flag, who shout their claim from the housetops that they are the only patriots, and who have their magnifying glasses in hand, scanning the country for evidence of disloyalty, eager to apply the brand of treason to the men who dare to even whisper their opposition to junker rule in the United States. No wonder Sam Johnson declared that "patriotism is the last refuge of the scoundrel." He must have had this Wall Street gentry in mind, or at least their prototypes, for in every age it has been the tyrant, the oppressor and the exploiter who has wrapped himself in the cloak of patriotism, or religion, or both to deceive and overawe the people.

They would have you believe that the Socialist Party consists in the main of disloyalists and traitors. It is true in a sense not at all to their discredit. We frankly admit that we *are* disloyalists and traitors to the real traitors of this nation. . . .

Every solitary one of these aristocratic conspirators and would-be murderers claims to be an arch-patriot; every one of them insists that the war is being waged to make the world safe for democracy. What humbug! What rot! What false pretense! These autocrats, these tyrants, these red-handed robbers and murderers, the "patriots," while the men who have the courage to stand face to face with them, speak the truth, and fight for their exploited victims—they are the disloyalists and traitors. If this be true, I want to take my place side by side with the traitors in this fight. . . .

Socialism is a growing idea; an expanding philosophy. It is spreading over the entire face of the earth: It is as vain to resist it as it would be to arrest the sunrise on the morrow.

It is coming, coming, coming all along the line. Can you not see it?... It is the mightiest movement in the history of mankind. What a privilege to serve it!...

Our hearts are with the Bolsheviki of Russia. Those heroic men and women, those unconquerable comrades have by their incomparable valor and sacrifice added fresh luster to the fame of the international movement. Those Russian comrades of ours have made greater sacrifices, have suffered more, and have shed more heroic blood than any like number of men and women anywhere on earth; they have laid the foundation of the first real democracy that ever drew the breath of life in this world. And the very first act of the triumphant Russian revolution was to proclaim a state of peace with all mankind, coupled with a fervent moral appeal, not to kings, not to emperors, rulers or diplomats but to *the people* of all nations. Here we have the very breath of democracy, the quintessence of the dawning freedom. The Russian revolution proclaimed its glorious triumph in its ringing and inspiring appeal to *the peoples* of all the earth. In a humane and fraternal spirit new Russia, emancipated at last from the curse of the centuries, called upon all nations engaged in the frightful war, the Central Powers as well as the Allies, to send representatives to a conference to lay down terms of peace that should be just and lasting. Here was the supreme opportunity to strike the blow to make the world safe for democracy. Was there any response to that noble appeal that in some day to come will be written in letters of gold in the history of the world? Was there any response whatever to that appeal for universal peace? [*From the crowd, "No!"*] No, not the slightest attention was paid to it by the Christian nations engaged in the terrible slaughter....

Wars throughout history have been waged for conquest and plunder. In the Middle Ages when the feudal lords who inhabited the castles whose towers may still be seen along the Rhine concluded to enlarge their domains, to increase their power, their prestige and their wealth they declared war upon one another. But they themselves did not go to war any more than the modern feudal lords, the barons of Wall Street go to war. The feudal barons of the Middle Ages, the economic predecessors of the capitalists of our day, declared all wars. And their miserable serfs fought all the battles. The poor, ignorant serfs had been taught to revere their masters; to believe that when their masters declared war upon one another, it was their patriotic duty to fall upon one another and to cut one another's throats for the profit and glory of the lords and barons who held them in contempt. And that is war in a nutshell. The master class has always declared the wars; the subject class has always fought the battles. The master class has had all to gain and nothing to lose, while the subject class has had nothing to gain and all to lose—especially their lives.

They have always taught and trained you to believe it to be your patriotic duty to go to war and to have yourselves slaughtered at their command. But in all the history of the world you, the people, have never had a voice in declaring war, and strange as it certainly appears, no war by any nation in any age has ever been declared by the people.

And here let me emphasize the fact—and it cannot be repeated too often—that the working class who fight all the battles, the working class who make the supreme sacrifices, the working class who freely shed their blood and furnish the corpses, have never yet had a voice in either declaring war or making peace. It is the ruling class that invariably does both. They alone declare war and they alone make peace.

What a compliment it is to the Socialist movement to be thus persecuted for the sake of the truth! The truth alone will make the people free. And for this reason the truth must not be permitted to reach the people. The truth has always been dangerous to the rule of the rogue, the exploiter, the robber. So the truth must be ruthlessly suppressed. That is why they are trying to destroy the Socialist movement; and every time they strike a blow they add a thousand new voices to the hosts proclaiming that socialism is the hope of humanity and has come to emancipate the people from their final form of servitude....

[Socialists] are pressing forward, here, there and everywhere, in all the zones that girdle the globe. Everywhere these awakening workers, these class-conscious proletarians, these hardy sons and daughters of honest toil are proclaiming the glad tidings of the coming emancipation; everywhere their hearts are attuned to the most sacred cause that ever challenged men and women to action in all the history of the world. Everywhere they are moving toward democracy and the dawn; marching toward the sunrise, their faces all aglow with the light of the coming day. These are the Socialists, the most zealous and enthusiastic crusaders the world has ever known. They are making history that will light up the horizon of coming generations, for their mission is the emancipation of the human race. They have been reviled; they have been ridiculed, persecuted, imprisoned and have suffered death, but they have been sufficient to themselves and their cause, and their final triumph is but a question of time.

Do you wish to hasten the day of victory? Join the Socialist Party! Don't wait for the morrow. Join now! Enroll your name without fear and take your place where you belong. You cannot do your duty by proxy. You have got to do it yourself and do it squarely and then as you look yourself in the face you will have no occasion to blush. You will know what it is to be a real *man* or *woman*. You will lose nothing; you will gain everything....

Source: Jean Y. Tussey, ed., *Eugene V. Debs Speaks* (New York: Pathfinder Press, 1970), pp. 243–279.

20.2   GEORGE CREEL, EXCERPTS FROM *HOW WE ADVERTISED AMERICA* (1920)

In April 1917, after the United States entered World War I, President Woodrow Wilson created the Committee on Public Information (CPI) headed by George Creel (1876–1953), a former muckraking journalist, newspaper editor, and politician. The CPI managed the nation's propaganda effort, creating films, staging pageants, and turning out advertisements, billboards, and press releases intended to educate the American public and build support for war efforts such as bond drives and rationing. In this memoir of his years at the CPI, published in 1920, Creel defended the work of the CPI against those who saw the agency as engaging in promotion of the war effort in any way other than an "open" and "positive" manner.

As Secretary Baker points out, the war was not fought in France alone. Back of the firing-line, back of armies and navies, back of the great supply-depots, another struggle waged with the same intensity and with almost equal significance attaching to its victories and defeats. It was the fight for the *minds* of men, for the "conquest of their convictions," and the battle-line ran through every home in every country.

It was in this recognition of Public Opinion as a major force that the Great War differed most essentially from all previous conflicts. The trial of strength was not only between massed bodies of armed men, but between opposed ideals, and moral verdicts took on all the value of military decisions. Other wars went no deeper than the physical aspects, but German *Kultur* raised issues that had to be fought out in the hearts and minds of people as well as on the actual firing-line. The approval of the world meant the steady flow of inspiration into the trenches; it meant the strengthened resolve and the renewed determination of the civilian population that is a nation's second line. The condemnation of the world meant the destruction of morale and the surrender of that conviction of justice which is the very heart of courage. The Committee on Public Information was called into existence to make this fight for the "verdict of mankind," the voice created to plead the justice of America's cause before the jury of Public Opinion....

In no degree was the Committee an agency of censorship, a machinery of concealment or repression. Its emphasis throughout was on the open and the positive. At no point did it seek or exercise authorities under those war laws that limited the freedom of speech and press.

In all things, from first to last, without halt or change, it was a plain publicity proposition, a vast enterprise in salesmanship, the world's greatest adventure in advertising.

Under the pressure of tremendous necessities an organization grew that not only reached deep into every American community, but that carried to every corner of the civilized globe the full message of America's idealism, unselfishness, and indomitable purpose. We fought prejudice, indifference, and disaffection at home and we fought ignorance and falsehood abroad. We strove for the maintenance of our own morale and the Allied morale by every process of stimulation; every possible expedient was employed to break through the barrage of lies that kept the people of the Central Powers in darkness and delusion; we sought the friendship and support of the neutral nations by continuous presentation of facts. We did not call it propaganda, for that word, in German hands, had come to be associated with deceit and corruption. Our effort was educational and informative throughout, for we had such confidence in our case as to feel that no other argument was needed than the simple, straightforward presentation of facts.

There was no part of the great war machinery that we did not touch, no medium of appeal that we did not employ. The printed word, the spoken word, the motion picture, the telegraph, the cable, the wireless, the poster, the sign-board—all these were used in our campaign to make our own people and all other peoples understand the causes that compelled America to take arms. All that was fine and ardent in the civilian population came at our call until more than one hundred and fifty thousand men and women were devoting highly specialized abilities to the work of the Committee, as faithful and devoted in their service as though they wore the khaki. While America's summons was answered without question by the citizenship as a whole, it is to be remembered that during the three and a half years of our neutrality the land had been torn by a thousand divisive prejudices, stunned by the voices of anger and confusion, and muddled by the pull and haul of opposed interests. These were conditions that could not be permitted to endure. What we had to have was no mere surface unity, but a passionate belief in the justice of America's cause that should weld the people of the United States into one white-hot mass instinct with fraternity, devotion, courage, and deathless determination. The *war-will*, the will-to-win, of a democracy depends upon the degree to which each one of all the people of that democracy can concentrate and consecrate body and soul and spirit in the supreme effort of service and sacrifice. What had to be driven home was that all business was the nation's business, and every task a common task for a single purpose. . . .

As swiftly as might be, there were put into pamphlet form America's reasons for entering the war, the meaning of America, the nature of our free institutions, our war aims, likewise analyses of the Prussian system, the purposes of the imperial German government, and full exposure of the enemy's misrepresentations, aggressions, and barbarities. Written by the country's foremost publicists, scholars, and historians, and distinguished for their conciseness, accuracy, and simplicity, these pamphlets blew as a great wind against the clouds of confusion and misrepresentation. Money could not have purchased the volunteer aid that was given freely, the various universities lending their best men and the National Board of Historical Service placing its three thousand members at the complete disposal of the Committee. Some thirty-odd booklets, covering every phase of America's ideals, purposes, and aims, were printed in many languages other than English. Seventy-five million reached the people of America, and other millions went to every corner of the world, carrying our defense and our attack.

The importance of the spoken word was not underestimated. A speaking division toured great groups like the Blue Devils, Pershing's Veterans, and the Belgians, arranged mass-meetings in the communities, conducted forty-five war conferences from coast to coast, coordinated the entire speaking activities of the nation, and assured consideration to the crossroads hamlet as well as to the city.

The Four Minute Men, an organization that will live in history by reason of its originality and effectiveness, commanded the volunteer services of 75,000 speakers, operating in 5,200 communities, and making a total of 755,190 speeches, every one having the carry of shrapnel.

With the aid of a volunteer staff of several hundred translators, the Committee kept in direct touch with the foreign-language press, supplying selected articles designed to combat ignorance and disaffection. It organized and directed twenty-three societies and leagues designed to appeal to certain classes and particular foreign-language groups, each body carrying a specific message of unity and enthusiasm to its section of America's adopted peoples.

It planned war exhibits for the state fairs of the United States, also a great series of interallied war expositions that brought home to our millions the exact nature of the struggle that was being waged in France. In Chicago alone two million people attended in two weeks, and in nineteen cities the receipts aggregated $1,432,261.36. The Committee mobilized the advertising forces of the country—press, periodical, car, and outdoor—for the patriotic campaign that gave millions of dollars' worth of free space to the national service.

It assembled the artists of America on a volunteer basis for the production of posters, window cards, and similar material of pictorial publicity for the use of various government departments and patriotic societies. A total of 1,438 drawings was used....

It organized a bureau of information for all persons who sought direction in volunteer war-work, in acquiring knowledge of any administrative activities, or in approaching business dealings with the government. In the ten months of its existence it gave answers to eighty-six thousand requests for specific information.

It gathered together the leading novelists, essayists, and publicists of the land, and these men and women, without payment, worked faithfully in the production of brilliant, comprehensive articles that went to the press as syndicate features. One division paid particular attention to the rural press and the plate-matter service. Others looked after the specialized needs of the labor press, the religious press, and the periodical press. The Division of Women's War Work prepared and issued the information of peculiar interest to the women of the United States, also aiding in the task of organizing and directing. Through the medium of the motion picture, America's war progress, as well as the meanings and purposes of democracy, were carried to every community in the United States and to every corner of the world. "Pershing's Crusaders," "America's Answer," and "Under Four Flags" were types of feature films by which we drove home America's resources and determinations, while other pictures, showing our social and industrial life, made our free institutions vivid to foreign peoples.

Turning away from the United States to the world beyond our borders, a triple task confronted us. First, there were the peoples of the Allied nations that had to be fired by the magnitude of the American effort and the certainty of speedy and effective aid, in order to relieve the war weariness of the civilian population and also to fan the enthusiasm of the firing-line to new flame. Second, we had to carry the truth to the neutral nations, poisoned by German lies; and third, we had to get the ideals of America, the determination of America, and the invincibility of America into the Central Powers....

Source: George Creel, *How We Advertised America* (New York: Harper and Brothers, 1920), pp. 3–8.

20.3 WOODROW WILSON, "FOURTEEN POINTS" SPEECH (1918)

As Woodrow Wilson addressed Congress on January 8, 1918, he attempted to link American involvement in World War I to a moral cause, much as he had when he asked for a declaration of war in order to "make the world safe for democracy." As he outlined his goals for peace, he attempted to address many of the issues that had led to the outbreak of the war. By eliminating the main causes of the war— imperial desire and commercial competition—and establishing a just peace, he hoped to avoid such conflicts in the future.

It will be our wish and purpose that the processes of peace, when they are begun, shall be absolutely open and that they shall involve and permit henceforth no secret understandings of any kind. The day of conquest and aggrandizement is gone by; so is also the day of secret covenants entered into in the interest of particular governments and likely at some unlooked-for moment to upset the peace of the world. It is this happy fact, now clear to the view of every public man whose thoughts do not still linger in an age that is dead and gone, which makes it possible for every nation whose purposes are consistent with justice and the peace of the world to avow now or at any other time the objects it has in view.

We entered this war because violations of right had occurred which touched us to the quick and made the life of our own people impossible unless they were corrected and the world secured once and for all against their recurrence. What we demand in this war, therefore, is nothing peculiar to ourselves. It is that the world be made fit and safe to live in; and particularly that it be made safe for every peace-loving nation which, like our own, wishes to live its own life, determine its own institutions, be assured of justice and fair dealing by the other peoples of the world as against force and selfish aggression. All the peoples of the world are in effect partners in this interest, and for our own part we see very clearly that unless justice be done to others it will not be done to us. The programme of the world's peace, therefore, is our programme; and that programme, the only possible programme, as we see it, is this:

I.   Open covenants of peace, openly arrived at, after which there shall be no private international understandings of any kind but diplomacy shall proceed always frankly and in the public view.

II. Absolute freedom of navigation upon the seas, outside territorial waters, alike in peace and in war, except as the seas may be closed in whole or in part by international action for the enforcement of international covenants.

III. The removal, so far as possible, of all economic barriers and the establishment of an equality of trade conditions among all the nations consenting to the peace and associating themselves for its maintenance.

IV. Adequate guarantees given and taken that national armaments will be reduced to the lowest point consistent with domestic safety.

V.   A free, open-minded, and absolutely impartial adjustment of all colonial claims, based upon a strict observance of the principle that in determining all such questions of sovereignty the interests of the populations concerned must have equal weight with the equitable claims of the government whose title is to be determined.

VI. The evacuation of all Russian territory and such a settlement of all questions affecting Russia as will secure the best and freest cooperation of the other nations of the world in obtaining for her an unhampered and unembarrassed opportunity for the independent determination of her own political development and national policy and assure her of a sincere welcome into the society of free nations under institutions of her own choosing; and, more than a welcome, assistance also of every kind that she may need and may herself desire. The treatment accorded Russia by her sister nations in the months to come will be the acid test of their good will, of their comprehension of her needs as distinguished from their own interests, and of their intelligent and unselfish sympathy.

VII. Belgium, the whole world will agree, must be evacuated and restored, without any attempt to limit the sovereignty which she enjoys in common with all other free nations. No other single act will serve as this will serve to restore confidence among the nations in the laws which they have themselves set and determined for the government of their relations with one another. Without this healing act the whole structure and validity of international law is forever impaired.

VIII. All French territory should be freed and the invaded portions restored, and the wrong done to France by Prussia in 1871 in the matter of Alsace-Lorraine, which has unsettled the peace of the world for nearly fifty years, should be righted, in order that peace may once more be made secure in the interest of all.

IX. A readjustment of the frontiers of Italy should be effected along clearly recognizable lines of nationality.

X. The peoples of Austria-Hungary, whose place among the nations we wish to see safeguarded and assured, should be accorded the freest opportunity of autonomous development.

XI. Rumania, Serbia, and Montenegro should be evacuated; occupied territories restored; Serbia accorded free and secure access to the sea; and the relations of the several Balkan states to one another determined by friendly counsel along historically established lines of allegiance and nationality; and international guarantees of the political and economic independence and territorial integrity of the several Balkan states should be entered into.

XII. The Turkish portions of the present Ottoman Empire should be assured a secure sovereignty, but the other nationalities which are now under Turkish rule should be assured an undoubted security of life and an absolutely unmolested opportunity of autonomous development, and the Dardanelles should be permanently opened as a free passage to the ships and commerce of all nations under international guarantees.

XIII. An independent Polish state should be erected which should include the territories inhabited by indisputably Polish populations, which should be assured a free and secure access to the sea, and whose political and economic independence and territorial integrity should be guaranteed by international covenant.

XIV. A general association of nations must be formed under specific covenants for the purpose of affording mutual guarantees of political independence and territorial integrity to great and small states alike.

In regard to these essential rectifications of wrong and assertions of right we feel ourselves to be intimate partners of all the governments and peoples associated together against the Imperialists. We cannot be separated in interest or divided in purpose. We stand together until the end.

For such arrangements and covenants we are willing to fight and to continue to fight until they are achieved; but only because we wish the right to prevail and desire a just and stable peace such as can be secured only by removing the chief provocations to war, which this programme does remove. We have no jealousy of German greatness, and there is nothing in this programme that impairs it. We grudge her no achievement or distinction of learning or of pacific enterprise such as have made her record very bright and very enviable. We do not wish to injure her or to block in any way her legitimate influence or power. We do not wish to fight her either with arms or with hostile arrangements of trade if she is willing to associate herself with us and the other peace-loving nations of the world in covenants of justice and law and fair dealing. We wish her only to accept a place of equality among the peoples of the world,—the new world in which we now live,—instead of a place of mastery.

Neither do we presume to suggest to her any alteration or modification of her institutions. But it is necessary, we must frankly say, and necessary as a preliminary to any intelligent dealings with her on our part, that we should know whom her spokesmen speak for when they speak to us, whether for the Reichstag majority or for the military party and the men whose creed is imperial domination.

We have spoken now, surely, in terms too concrete to admit of any further doubt or question. An evident principle runs through the whole programme I have outlined. It is the principle of justice to all peoples and nationalities, and their right to live on equal terms of liberty and safety with one another, whether they be strong or weak. Unless this principle be made its foundation no part of the structure of international justice can stand. The people of the United States could act upon no other principle; and to the vindication of this principle they are ready to devote their lives, their honor, and everything that they possess. The moral climax of this the culminating and final war for human liberty has come, and they are ready to put their own strength, their own highest purpose, their own integrity and devotion to the test.

Source: Woodrow Wilson, Address on the Fourteen Points for Peace, January 8, 1918. https://miller-center.org/the-presidency/presidential-speeches/january-8-1918-wilsons-fourteen-points.

(20.4) *MARYSVILLE EVENING TRIBUNE*, INFLUENZA, AND THE AMERICAN MILITARY (1918)

As the Influenza Pandemic spread across the United States, it disrupted not only civilian life but also the nation's ability to raise the necessary manpower to sustain its desired war effort. National and local media chronicled the effect of the flu as it undermined conscription efforts and wreaked havoc on American military camps.

Marysville Evening Tribune (OHIO), September 27, 1918, 1.

CROWDER HALTS OCTOBER CALL

Influenza in the Army Camps Prompts the Action.

142,000 DRAFTEES AFFECTED

More Than 6000 New Cases of the Plague Reported to the Office of the Surgeon General, With 700 New Cases of Pneumonia—Registrants Not to Entrain Until the Epidemic Is Checked.

Washington. Sept. 27.—Provost Marshal General Crowder, because of the epidemic of Spanish Influenza in army camps, canceled calls for the entrainment between Oil. 7 and 11 of 142,00 draft registrants.

More than 6,000 new cases of influenza in army camps have been reported to the office of the surgeon general of the army. One hundred and seventy deaths, resulting chiefly from pneumonia following influenza, and 723 new cases of pneumonia, also were reported.

Two camps, Kearney, California, and Eustis, Virginia, were added to the list of those where influenza has made its appearance, leaving only 13 camps free from the disease. The total number of cases of influenza in all camps was placed at 23,146, with 3,036 cases of pneumonia. One out of every four men at Camp Devens. Mass., has contracted influenza, it was announced, and 10 percent of the cases have developed into pneumonia.

In canceling the call for the entrainment of the draft registrants early next month General Crowder acted upon instructions from General March, chief of staff. Every state and the District of Columbia had been assigned quotas and the men were to have gone to practically all of the camps in the country. The men probably will not be entrained until after the Influenza epidemic has been checked.

It was said at the office of the surgeon general of the army that every possible precaution is being taken in all camps to check the spread of the disease, but that despite all measures it is believed the disease will run its course and probably spread to still other camps. Additional physicians and nurses have been sent to camps where the epidemic is most severe.

The greatest number of new influenza cases, 1,007, was reported, from Camp Dix. While Camp Devens reported fewer new cases, pneumonia showed an increase there, 309 new cases and 83 deaths being reported. Influenza also is bn the increase among the civilian population, particularly in New England.

Source: "Crowder halts October Call," *Marysville Evening Tribune* (OHIO), September 27, 1918, 1.

The Modern Nation

1919–1928

< A Hollywood film premiere at Grauman's Chinese Theater

"America's Sweetheart"

By the end of World War I, 26-year-old Mary Pickford had become "America's sweetheart." After a decade in Hollywood, the diminutive, long-haired actress was one of the first and greatest stars of the movies. Fans flocked to her films, eagerly read news about her, and mobbed her in public. The actress, earning hundreds of thousands of dollars a year, was one of the richest women in the United States.

Mary Pickford's phenomenal success was certainly a product of her talent and good luck. But her career was also a product of increasingly important trends after World War I. A dynamic industrial economy, drawing on such rapidly developing technologies as motion pictures, seemed effortlessly to produce plenty of prosperity, leisure, and consumer goods. More than ever before, Americans had both the money and time to enjoy themselves, to consume a host of pleasures.

Pickford exemplified the new national culture that emerged from the needs of the booming consumer economy. Breaking with the past, this modern culture celebrated innovation, modernity, and the future. "One should always go forward," Pickford declared. "It isn't good to go back to anything, not even to the old home farm, or one's old loves." The new culture welcomed leisure, including moviegoing, spectator sports, and other diversions. Pickford worked hard, but she entertained lavishly and took highly publicized vacations, too. The new culture also glorified conspicuous consumption. Living well, Pickford bought such indulgences as a miniature, glass-enclosed, two-seater Rolls-Royce automobile, one of only three in the world.

The movie star embodied still other aspects of the new culture—its fascination with youth and its infatuation with independent, nontraditional women. Well into her 20s, "Little Mary" still portrayed plucky, playful young girls. Although married, Pickford focused on her career and increasingly took control of the production of her films. Like the new culture, Pickford broke free from old restraints. Americans, as she wrote, had seen divorce as a "dreadful disease," but even so, in March 1920, she divorced her first husband and married the star Douglas Fairbanks Sr. Her popularity did not decrease.

Going her own way so often, Pickford also exemplified a resurgent individualism that shaped the Republican-dominated politics of the 1920s. In the movies and real life, she seemed to prove that individuals, even immigrants and the poor, could still find opportunity and achieve great things in an increasingly corporatized and bureaucratized society. Born to poverty in Canada, Pickford had found success in America. Remaking her identity, she changed her name from Gladys Smith. In 1919, she escaped the control of the big movie studios by joining with Douglas Fairbanks Sr., comic actor Charlie

Chaplin, and director D. W. Griffith to create their own distribution company, United Artists.

The new culture helped redefine the United States in the eyes of the world. Pickford's films were popular around the globe. When she and Fairbanks traveled to Europe in the 1920s, they met huge crowds and near riots. Even citizens of the communist Union of Soviet Socialist Republics lionized the visiting "Little Mary."

Amid all the trappings of Mary Pickford's popularity, it was easy to conclude that Americans loved the emerging cultural and political order as much as they loved America's sweetheart. In fact, many people were troubled by the changes of the 1920s. The modern order did not reflect the values of millions of Americans. For all the celebration of the individual, many Americans felt they did not have enough power over their lives. American democracy seemed too limited. As a result, the new cultural and political order faced a powerful backlash as the decade went on.

A DYNAMIC ECONOMY

By and large, the 1920s were a prosperous time for America. After a recession during 1920 to 1921, the economy continued to grow. Consumer prices remained steady throughout the decade, and jobs were plentiful; the unemployment rate dropped as low as 1.8 percent in 1926. Wages jumped: the nation's net income—the value of its earnings from labor and property—leapt from $64 billion in 1921 to $86.8 billion in 1929. This prosperity was driven by a dynamically evolving industrial economy featuring new technologies, increased efficiency, a maturing automobile industry, and new businesses.

Despite general prosperity, the transformation of the economy involved defeats for organized labor and decline for many farmers. The relative weakness of agriculture and the strength of industry helped to turn the United States into a predominantly urban nation. In the prosperous 1920s, as always, industrial capitalism was a transforming force.

The Development of Industry

Several long-term factors shaped the development of American industry in the 1920s. Searching for more efficient production, businessmen used a flood of new technologies, other innovations, and new technical expertise. More patents were issued for new inventions—421,000 of them—than in any preceding decade. During the 1920s, the number of engineers in the country nearly doubled.

The switch from coal to electricity, under way since the 1910s, was a critical innovation. By the end of the 1920s, electricity powered more than two-thirds of American manufacturing plants. **Henry Ford's** car company pioneered another crucial innovation, the system that became known as Fordism, or mass production. By the 1910s, Ford, like other American manufacturers, used interchangeable parts, simple and accurate machine tools, and electric power to speed output at its Highland Park plant in Detroit. But traditional manufacturing practice slowed production. Frames, transmissions, and other key subassemblies waited on stands while teams of workers moved from one stand to another. Eager to meet the rising demand for the popular Model T car, Ford's managers reversed the process by "moving the work to the men." Beginning in 1913, conveyor belts and chains sent subassemblies past groups of stationary workers. Instead of making an entire engine, a worker might tighten a few bolts or install a single part. The results were astonishing: in 1914, Ford produced 300,000 Model Ts; in 1923, more than 2 million. Other manufacturers raced to copy Ford's techniques.

Mass production, electrification, and other innovations spurred an extraordinary increase in productivity for American industry. Output per worker skyrocketed 72 percent from 1919 to 1929.

Along with increased productivity, the rise of several industries drove the economy. Auto production now dominated as textiles, railroads, iron, and steel had earlier. In 1921, there were 9.3 million cars on American roads; by 1929, there were 23 million. The manufacture of all those cars stimulated demand for plate glass, oil, gasoline, and rubber.

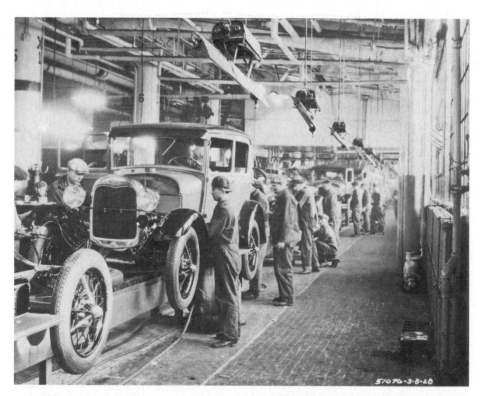

Ford Assembly Line Mass production at work: the assembly line at the Ford Motor Company plant in Dearborn, Michigan, 1928.

Other sectors of the economy also grew rapidly. The demand for processed foods, household appliances, office machinery, and chemicals increased dramatically. Emerging industries such as aircraft demonstrated their potential importance.

Arguably the first powered, fixed-wing flight had occurred in December 1903, when Wilbur and Orville Wright's "Flyer" flew 120 feet in 12 seconds over the beach at Kitty Hawk, North Carolina. But the civilian airplane industry did not take off until the 1920s. Aircraft production rose from fewer than 300 in 1922 to more than 6,000 in 1929. By then, fledgling airlines were flying passengers on scheduled flights.

The Trend Toward Large-Scale Organization

The development of industry reinforced the trend toward large-scale organization that was basic to US capitalism. Only giant corporations, with thousands of employees and hundreds of millions of dollars in capitalization, had the financial resources to pay for mass production. A wave of mergers meant that these big businesses controlled more factories and assets than ever. By 1929, corporations produced 92 percent of the nation's manufactured goods.

The largest firms also benefited from more efficient organization. When the recession of 1920 to 1921 left them with too many unsold goods, companies reorganized. Top managers, aided by financial, legal, and other experts, now oversaw semiautonomous divisions that supplied different markets. At General Motors, the Chevrolet division produced huge numbers of relatively inexpensive cars, while the Cadillac division turned out a smaller number of expensive cars. The new system made corporations more flexible, efficient, and responsive to consumer demand.

Corporate growth was not confined to industry. Chains such as A. & P. grocers and F. W. Woolworth variety stores increased their share of retail sales from 4 percent to 20 percent. One percent of the nation's banks managed nearly half of the country's financial assets. By 1929, just 200 corporations held about one-fifth of national wealth.

Giant firms and their leaders had often been targets of hostility and reform during the Progressive Era, but the decade's prosperity led many Americans to soften their attitude toward business. There were fewer calls to break up or regulate giant corporations. Big businessmen had seemed to be selfless patriots during World War I. Now their companies were apparently creating a new period of economic well-being. To ensure a better image, businessmen paid for public relations campaigns that stressed their commitment to ethical behavior and social service. Basking in the glow of public approval, big business was confident about its role in the nation's destiny.

The Transformation of Work and the Workforce

The quest for productivity had dramatic consequences for American workers. Industrial efficiency was not just a matter of electricity and machines. To speed up production, the managers at Ford and other factories had to change the nature of work.

Accordingly, the spirit of scientific management continued to sweep across the factory floor. Under ever-tighter supervision, workers were pushed to work faster and harder. In textile mills, the "stretch-out" required workers to tend more looms than before. Ford's system of mass production shared Frederick Winslow Taylor's determination to simplify and regiment labor. The result was less-satisfying work. Instead of making a whole engine, a Ford assembly-line worker might spend his day turning a few nuts on one engine after another. In 1913, Ford's labor turnover rate soared to 380 percent as unhappy workers quit their jobs.

As production grew more efficient, about a million workers lost manufacturing, mining, and railroading jobs. The growth of other kinds of employment more than compensated for this decrease, however. The ranks of white-collar workers increased 80 percent from 1910 to 1930, or nearly one worker in three. The nation had already begun to evolve from an industrial economy based on manual labor to a postindustrial economy based on sales and service.

Economic development also encouraged the gradual movement of women into the paid workforce. By the end of the 1920s, women, most of them unmarried, made up a majority of clerical workers. In 1900, 22 percent of women had worked for pay; by the 1940s, the percentage would reach 27.

Despite these changes, women still faced discrimination. Mary Pickford was exceptional. Overwhelmingly concentrated in low-wage occupations such as domestic service, factory work, and agriculture, they were paid less than men who did comparable work. Female sales workers earned between 42 and 63 percent of the wages paid to their male counterparts. Few women held high-level managerial jobs. Moreover, most people continued to believe that a woman's place was in the home, especially if she had children, and many men feared that paid labor would make women too independent. Only economic necessities reconciled American society to women's employment in the 1920s.

The Defeat of Organized Labor

The American labor movement did not respond effectively to the transformation of work and the workforce. In an age of increasing economic organization, workers became less organized. In 1920 nearly 1 nonagricultural worker in 5 belonged to a union. By 1929, little more than 1 in 10 did. The labor movement was especially weak in such developing mass-production industries as automobiles and steel and barely addressed the growing ranks of clerks and other white-collar workers.

Prosperity also weakened organized labor. Earning relatively good wages, many workers were less interested in joining unions. To show that unions were unnecessary, corporations promoted welfare capitalism, highly publicized programs ranging from lunch-hour movies to sports teams to profit-sharing plans. Many firms created company unions, but when it became clear that they did not give employees a real voice in management, their membership dwindled.

Although some firms tried to win over their workers with baseball teams and company unions, many others used tougher tactics to battle the labor movement. Management crusaded for the "open shop"—a workplace free of labor organization—and found an ally in the judicial system. Rulings by the US Supreme Court, such as *Duplex Printing Press Co. v. Deering* (1921) and *Bedford Cut Stone Co. v. Journeymen Stone Cutters' Assn.* (1927), made it easier for state and federal courts to grant injunctions to stop unions from striking and exercising their rights. Businesses could sue unions for damages. They also demanded that workers sign "yellow-dog contracts" promising not to join a union.

The labor movement also hurt its own cause. The leadership of the major national organization, the **American Federation of Labor**, was increasingly conservative and timid. The heads of the AFL, mostly white males of western European extraction who represented skilled crafts, had little interest in organizing women workers and wanted nothing to do with Socialists, radical unionists, or African American workers. The AFL was slow to acknowledge the Brotherhood of Sleeping Car Porters, the assertive union of African American workers organized in 1925 under Socialist A. Philip Randolph. Despite pleas from Randolph and others, the AFL failed to organize unskilled workers, many of whom were African Americans or white immigrants from eastern and southern Europe.

Weakened by internal divisions, welfare capitalism, the open-shop crusade, and the courts, the labor movement did not effectively challenge the transformation of industrial labor. Nationwide, the number of strikes and lockouts dropped from 3,411 in 1920 to 604 in 1928. These labor actions often ended in defeat for workers.

The Decline of Agriculture

Despite national prosperity, American agriculture continued its long decline. Prices for basic crops such as cotton and wheat fell, and the number of farms dropped.

The larger story of decline obscured important signs of growth and health. Some agricultural sectors were as dynamic as industry and for the same reasons—increased efficiency promoted by new technologies and large-scale organization. Mechanization, including the introduction of powerful tractors, made farm labor more efficient. So did the development of irrigation systems. By the 1920s, the irrigated farms of the Southwest were producing bumper crops of cotton, fruits, and vegetables. The Southwest also witnessed the rise of huge, mechanized farms with hundreds and even thousands of irrigated acres. These "factories in the fields" depended not only on size and technology but also on the old-fashioned exploitation of farm labor. In California's Imperial Valley and elsewhere, migrant workers labored in harsh conditions for low pay on modern farms.

Ironically, the dynamic agricultural economy created a problem for many farmers. Midsize farms, too big to be run by their owners alone and too small for mechanization, could not compete with the vast factories in the fields. Increased efficiency, meanwhile, led to bumper crops that did not always find a good market price. Farmers were hurt by a changing American diet, with declining consumption of bread and potatoes, and by the rise of competitors overseas. Productive American farmers could no longer export enough of their surplus. The resulting glut reduced the price of farm products. As their incomes lagged behind those of urban workers, farmers yearned for the return of high pre–World War I agricultural prices to restore parity between city and country. As a Georgia farmer observed, "The hand that is feeding the world is being spit upon."

The Urban Nation

The woes of agriculture contributed to a long-term shift in the American population. For the first time, according to the census of 1920, a majority of Americans—54 million out of 105 million—lived in urban territory. The census defined "urban territory" as places with as few as 2,500 people, many of them small towns close to country life. Still, the population of the United States was no longer predominantly rural.

The decline of farming spurred this shift. As agricultural prices fell, millions of Americans fled the nation's farms. The total US population increased by 17 million during the 1920s, but the farm population declined by more than 1.5 million.

At the same time, the growth of the industrial economy swelled the population of towns and cities. In the 1920s, factory production was still centered in urban areas and gave many cities their identity. Detroit was becoming the "Motor City." Akron was the home of rubber production. Pittsburgh and Birmingham symbolized the steel industry. Most of the new white-collar jobs were located in cities. Corporations also put their headquarters in cities, especially the two largest, Chicago and New York.

The rise of the automobile further contributed to the emergence of the urban nation. The car made it practical for Americans to live in suburbs and drive into the city to work and shop. In the 1920s, the suburban lifestyle was still reserved mostly for the well-to-do. Elite suburbs, such as Grosse Pointe and Ferndale outside Detroit and Beverly Hills and Glendale outside Los Angeles, grew explosively. The transformation of farms into suburbs symbolized the new urban nation.

A MODERN CULTURE

The 1920s saw the full emergence of a modern culture that had been taking shape for decades and that now surrounded Americans with something fundamentally new. Symbolized by **Mary Pickford**, the new culture extolled the virtues of modernity and pleasure. Rooted in the nation's economic development, the new culture reflected both the needs of businessmen with goods to sell and the desires of Americans with more money and free time than ever. Supported by advertising and installment buying, the culture of leisure and consumption offered movies, spectator sports, popular music, radio, and sex. It also offered new views of gender, family life, and youth and renewed old values of individualism in an increasingly organized society.

The Spread of Consumerism

Encouraged by big business, many Americans now defined life as the pursuit of pleasure and found happiness in leisure and consumption rather than in work. This philosophy of **consumerism** saturated society by the end of the decade.

Increased efficiency and profitability enabled American employers to allow their workers higher wages and more leisure hours. Some employers, notably Ford, also raised wages in order to hold on to workers alienated by the drudgery of mass production. And Ford himself increased workers' pay to enable them to buy the products of modern factories. The incomes of workers and other employees reached a new high in the 1920s. Factory workers' real wages rose 19 percent from 1914 to 1923.

Many workers had more time to enjoy their wages. For salaried, middle-class workers, the annual vacation had become a tradition by the 1910s. Although blue-collar workers seldom enjoyed a vacation, they spent less time on the job. Some employers, including Henry Ford, instituted a five-day workweek during the 1920s. More businesses shortened their workdays, and the average workweek fell from

47.4 hours in 1920 to 44.2 in 1929. "The shorter work day brought me my first idea of there being such a thing as pleasure," said one young female worker. "Before this time it was just sleep and eat and hurry off to work."

A change in attitude accompanied these changes in wages and workdays. The work ethic seemed less necessary in a prospering economy. Thanks to Fordism and Taylorism, work was also less satisfying, and people justified pleasure as an essential antidote to labor.

The advertising industry encouraged the new attitude toward pleasure. Although advertising agencies had first appeared in the 1850s and 1860s, the business did not mature until the 1920s. Now, ads appeared everywhere—in newspapers and magazines, on billboards and big electric signs. Major advertising agencies such as J. Walter Thompson and Batten, Barton, Durstine, and Osborn concentrated in New York City, home to so many corporations. Impressed by successful ad campaigns for Listerine mouthwash and Fleischmann's yeast, big business hired ad agencies to sell goods and services. Expenditures for advertising leapt from $682 million in 1914 to nearly $3 billion by 1929.

Advertising, like the new culture, optimistically embraced change and trumpeted the new. In advertisements, purchasing the right products solved problems, made up for the drudgery of work, and brought fulfillment. To enthusiastic ad men, advertising was as important as the products it sold. In his best-selling book *The Man Nobody Knows* (1925), ad pioneer Bruce Barton portrayed Jesus Christ as a great advertiser, whose disciples "conquered the world" by selling a new product, Christianity. Along with advertising, business used installment loans to encourage Americans to buy goods and services "on time." Credit buying spread so rapidly that total consumer debt more than doubled from 1922 to 1929. The sales of such consumer goods as pianos, washing machines, and automobiles boomed. Americans bought 181,000 automobiles in 1910; they bought 4,455,000 in 1929. Thanks to the availability of another kind of loan, the mortgage, more Americans were able to invest in a home of their own. Spending on new private housing jumped from $2 billion in 1920 to $5 billion by 1924. Loan-driven spending helped power the economic prosperity of the 1920s.

New Pleasures for a Mass Audience

The culture of the 1920s offered many escapes, especially sports, movies, popular music, and radio. Although people still played games themselves, they also watched other people's games more than ever before. Tennis, boxing, and auto racing flourished as spectator sports during the decade. The American Professional Football Association, which became the National Football League, played its first season in 1920. Although crowds packed college football stadiums, baseball remained the most popular American sport. Minor-league baseball covered the nation. Meanwhile, the popularity of major-league baseball surged, thanks in part to the exploits of home run–hitting Babe Ruth and his New York Yankees.

Spectator sports enthralled millions, but another passive enjoyment, the movies, was the most popular consumer attraction of the 1920s (see Table 21–1). A novelty in the mid-1890s, silent films had become a big business. In city neighborhoods in the 1900s, crowds packed into stuffy "nickelodeons"—storefront theaters showing short, silent one-reel films for the price of a nickel. The movies became

Table 21-1 Spending for Recreational Services, 1909–1929

Year	Total (millions of dollars)	Motion Picture Theaters (millions of dollars)	Spectator Sports (millions of dollars)
1909	377	###	###
1914	434	###	###
1919	806	###	###
1921	911	301	30
1923	1,082	336	46
1927	1,405	526	48
1929	1,670	720	66

Source: Historical Statistics of the United States, Millennial Online Edition (Cambridge: Cambridge University Press, 2008), Table Dh309–318.

Note: ### = no data.

longer and more sophisticated, and theaters became larger and more lavish. Nationwide, weekly attendance doubled from 40 million in 1922 to 80 million in 1929.

Booming attendance fueled the growth of a handful of corporate movie studios, including Warner Brothers and RKO, that dominated the film industry. By the 1920s, the center of movie production had shifted from New York to **Hollywood**, California. Now called "Hollywood," the film industry grew still bigger toward the end of the decade, when studios learned to synchronize sound and moving images in such films as *The Jazz Singer* of 1927.

It was fitting that one of the first "talking pictures" was about **jazz**. Popular music in general and jazz in particular played an important role in the new consumer culture. Created by African Americans in the 1910s, jazz was a rhythmically and harmonically innovative music that featured improvised solos and a hot beat. The new music emerged around the country, but its first great center was the streets, brothels, and dives of New Orleans. The Louisiana city was home to the first major jazz composer, Jelly Roll Morton, and to the first jazz superstar, trumpeter and singer Louis Armstrong. As jazz became nationally popular, Morton, Armstrong, and the focus of jazz moved on, as did so many African Americans, to Chicago and New York City (see Chapter 20).

The new music quickly attracted white Americans, especially the young, who yearned for something more daring than the relatively sedate popular music of the day. Even its name—a reference perhaps to speed or sexual intercourse—conjured up pleasure and liberation. Soon white musicians were contributing to the music. For many whites, jazz summed up a period marked by the pursuit of liberating pleasures. The 1920s became known as the "Jazz Age," after the title of a 1922 book of short stories by F. Scott Fitzgerald.

The great popularity of jazz and other musical genres was made possible by the phonograph, originated by Thomas Edison in the 1870s and modified by other inventors. In the 1920s, the electrical recording microphone dramatically improved sound quality and made the new music accessible to millions of Americans.

A Hollywood Film Premiere A premiere at Grauman's Chinese Theater, which opened in 1927, reflected both the growing influence of California on the film industry and the growing popularity of film as a form of modern entertainment.

A newer technological innovation, the radio, also allowed Americans to hear popular music. In 1895, Italian inventor Guglielmo Marconi transmitted the first radio waves; by 1920, commercial radio broadcasting began in the United States. The federal government started licensing radio stations the next year.

Like the movies, radio quickly became corporatized big business. By 1923, there were more than 500 stations, and by 1926, the first permanent radio network, the National Broadcasting Company (NBC). Americans tuned in to broadcasts of live music, news, sports, and soap operas. By 1925, manufacturers turned out more than 2 million radios a year. Radio, like the movies, disseminated the values of consumerism, as corporations rushed to advertise their products by sponsoring radio programs.

A Sexual Revolution

Along with such new pleasures as radio and movies, the modern culture offered a new attitude toward an old pleasure, sex. By the 1920s, Americans' sexual attitudes and behavior were changing. People openly discussed sex and placed a new emphasis on the importance of sexual satisfaction, primarily in marriage. And there were signs of greater sexual exploration among unmarried young people.

In the nineteenth century, Americans, especially middle-class Victorians, had largely kept a discreet silence about sex. That silence gave way in the twentieth century. Progressive-Era reformers had forced public discussion of issues such as prostitution and venereal disease. The reformers, anxious to control extramarital sexual behavior, hardly wanted to glorify sexual pleasure. But they helped pave the way for an approving depiction of sexuality.

Popular amusements of the 1910s and 1920s were filled with sexual images. The movies explored sexual topics in such films as *The Anatomy of a Kiss* and *A Bedroom Blunder.* Popular music featured suggestive songs about sex, such as "It's Tight Like That" and "I Need a Little Sugar in My Bowl." Popular dances such as the grizzly bear and the turkey trot promoted close physical contact or sexually suggestive steps. As early as 1913, a magazine concluded that "Sex O'Clock" had struck in the United States.

The increased openness about sex reflected the growing belief that sexual pleasure was necessary and desirable, particularly within marriage. Married couples increasingly considered intercourse an opportunity for pleasure, as well as procreation. Experts insisted that healthy marriages required sexual satisfaction for both partners.

The new view of marital sexuality helped change attitudes toward contraception. By the 1910s, a grassroots movement, led by Socialists and other radicals, promoted sex education and contraceptives, which were largely illegal. The crusade's best-known figure was the fiery former nurse and Socialist organizer **Margaret Sanger**, who coined the term "birth control." Although Sanger once had to flee the country to avoid prosecution, birth control became respectable—and widely practiced—in the 1920s.

At the same time, most adult Americans still condemned premarital sex. Nevertheless, premarital intercourse apparently became more common. Many couples believed that intercourse was acceptable if they were "in love" and intended to marry. There was also an apparent increase in "petting"—sexual contact short of intercourse.

While changing some of their attitudes about sexual behavior, most heterosexual Americans still condemned homosexuality. Nevertheless, a sexual revolution was under way.

Changing Gender Ideals

Shifting sexual attitudes were tied to new gender ideals. By the 1920s, Americans' sense of what it meant to be female was changing. Since the late nineteenth century, Americans had been talking about the independent, assertive "**New Woman**" who claimed the right to attend school, vote, and have a career. The New Woman of the 1920s, exemplified by Mary Pickford, was now a sexual being, too, a fun-loving individual with desires of her own.

The sexual nature of women was central to a new movement, known as feminism, that had emerged in the 1910s. The feminists, like earlier female reformers, were generally white, well-educated, Protestant, urban women. Concentrated in New York's **Greenwich Village,** feminists broke with older reformers by insisting on sharing the sexual opportunities that men had presumably long enjoyed. Unlike the older generation of activist women, feminists were unwilling to give up marriage and

Struggles For Democracy

Flappers and Feminists

CHRONICLING THE EXCITEMENT of 1920s New York City nightlife, the *New Yorker* column "Table for Two" allowed readers to live vicariously through the exploits of the author known as "Lipstick." Lois Long, the woman behind "Lipstick," spent her nights traveling from one nightclub to the next, often ending her evenings at one of the famed mixed-race clubs of Harlem. With her smoking, drinking, and dancing, she embraced all that the Roaring Twenties had to offer.

Long embodied the **flapper** figure that captured American imaginations during the 1920s with her devil-may-care attitude, bobbed hair, rouged cheeks, and fashionable dress. Reveling in the freedom enjoyed by the New Woman of the decade, Long described her life with verve and wit and apologized for nothing, delighting in the adventure modern life afforded. Typical of her column was her description of a raid on a New York City bar. She wrote, a "big Irish cop regarded me with a sad eye and remarked, 'Kid, you're too good for this dump,' and politely opened a window leading to the fire escape. I made a graceful exit." After such a night, it was not uncommon for Long to stroll into the *New Yorker* offices, sometimes at 3 or 4 a.m., and type up a column in time to meet a deadline.

While many readers idolized Lipstick and women across the country embraced the flapper style, others were scandalized by this kind of behavior. Those unnerved by the power of the urban center to shape American values, Victorians unwilling to cede their visions of men and women's appropriate roles, and Christian moralists abhorred the flapper's influence. But some of the harshest critics of women like Long were the suffragettes who had advocated on behalf of women's right to vote in the years leading up to the 1920 passage of the Nineteenth Amendment. Lillian Symes, a veteran of the suffrage cause and feminist journalist, lamented how little her generation had in common with "the post-war, spike-heeled, over-rouged flapper," a figure she saw as completely devoid of political engagement. Educated women like Long, a Vassar College graduate, should be doing more with her life than hopping from one mindless entertainment to the next.

Imagining a new political landscape in which women wielded greater power and influence, veteran feminists were disappointed by the world of the 1920s. But the younger generation's embrace of the flapper image, with a focus on leisure rather than political action, was only part of the problem for a movement that had begun to splinter. Having achieved their objective—the right to vote—the conflicting identities and allegiances of women across race, class, ethnicity, region, age, and ideology prevented the creation of a powerful women's political bloc. Feminists were divided in their beliefs about the relationship between men and women—were they fundamentally different or did the pursuit of sexual equality rest on the premise that men and women were the same? How would this debate shape goals of the future? Furthermore, the political tide had shifted. In the aftermath of the activism and reform of the Progressive Era, the 1920s bore witness to a far more conservative political culture, one characterized by a focus on individualism and a largely disinterested electorate. The flapper, then, was only part of the problem, but her visibility, her direct rejection of causes

continued

Struggles For Democracy continued

greater than herself, and her mishandling of the freedom feminists had fought so hard to achieve made her a direct target for criticism.

Dorothy Dunbar Bromley, a prominent writer on women's issues, defended the New Women of the 1920s with the celebrated language of individualism. She imagined these women as a new kind of feminist: she "knows that it is her American, her twentieth-century birthright to emerge from a creature of instinct into a full-fledged *individual* who is capable of molding her own life. And in this respect she holds that she is becoming man's equal." Flappers embraced the gains made by feminists who had come before them, but they embraced those gains in unexpected ways and with little recognition of feminists' efforts. In a culture increasingly shaped by the influences of the consumer marketplace and mass media, for some women, equality had little to do with the traditional style of politics and much more to do with the opportunity to inhabit public space and enjoy entertainments previously off limits. This was not the style of politics imagined by suffragettes or their Progressive-Era contemporaries, but as Americans living in this new modern age were coming to learn, times had changed.

children for careers outside the home. Feminism insisted on women's right to pleasure and satisfaction in all phases of life, from the most public to the most intimate.

Small in number, the feminists commanded a great deal of attention. Several of their ideas and practices were too radical for many American men and women, such as some feminists' decision to retain their maiden names in married life or to explore sexual relationships outside of marriage. Most fundamentally, many Americans were unwilling to accept the feminist insistence on full equality with men.

American culture proved rather open to a more liberated view of female sexuality. The most popular image of the American woman of the 1920s was the vivacious "flapper," with her short skirt, bound breasts, and bobbed hair. The flapper was likely to wear cosmetics and to smoke cigarettes—practices once associated only with prostitutes.

Notions of masculinity were also changing. With the growing emphasis on female needs and desires, men were urged to be attentive and responsive and to focus on the home. As the world of work became less satisfying, experts told men to look for fulfillment in family life. The family man of the 1920s was no longer to be a distant, stern patriarch but a companion to his wife and a doting friend to his children.

In practice, many men still defined themselves in terms of their work rather than their domestic life, and society still regarded women as the primary caretakers of children. Despite the change in domestic values, many men were still relative outsiders in the home.

The Family and Youth

Changing gender ideals were directly related to a reconsideration of family life and youth. Although whole families still labored together in fields and mills, most Americans no longer regarded the family as a group of productive workers. Child-labor laws

American Landscape
The Tulsa Race Massacre

Oil brought people to Tulsa. From a sparsely populated outpost struggling to establish itself alongside the banks of a seemingly untamable Arkansas River, by 1920, Tulsa emerged as a thriving mid-continent metropolis of 72,075 thanks to citizens' initiative, hard work, and not insignificant boosterism.

The city's appeal extended across racial lines. African Americans in the South heard about a place where they could start fresh, beyond the confines of an increasingly re-established Confederacy. But White Southerners also saw the possibility of Tulsa, and brought with them a commitment to the Jim Crow laws shaping southern life. While the 1907 state Constitution did not mention segregation, the segregation of public facilities was the first state law legislators passed. Thus, segregation marked Tulsa's development. African Americans created Greenwood, a flourishing Black community, on the north end of the city, home to a high school, hotel, hospital, churches, and other businesses operated by and intended to serve Tulsa's African American population. For its residents, Greenwood embodied the prosperity that was so much a focus of the 1920s and further claimed that prosperity for Black Americans.

But when oil prices sunk in 1921, economic instability enhanced existing racial resentments. For white Tulsans, Black achievement was an affront—evidence that a race they believed inferior could achieve not only above the expected station of African Americans, but even more challenging, above their white counterparts.

These resentments came to a head on May 31, 1921, when African American shoeshine Dick Rowland shared an elevator with the white operator, Sarah Page. When the shaky elevator likely threw Rowland into Page, she yelped and Rowland rapidly left the scene. Before a proper investigation could take place, the *Tulsa Tribune* stoked white fears of interracial sexual impropriety and African American men's alleged insatiable desire for white women with the headline "Negro assaults a white girl!" Whether to serve white Tulsans' desires or to protect him from vigilante efforts, the police took Rowland into custody.

Sheriff Willard McCullough refused to turn Rowland over to angry white people who gathered at the courthouse. Black Tulsans, hearing of Rowland's arrest, were determined that one of their own would not become another African American victim, lynched by white mob. When a group of armed Black men approached the courthouse, African American Deputy Sheriff Barney Cleaver guaranteed Rowland's safety. The crowd dispersed.

As the night continued, rumors about groups of armed Tulsans, Black and white, stimulated fears on either side. When armed groups of both races returned to the courthouse later in the evening, a member of the crowd—intentionally or not—fired a shot. From there, Sheriff McCullough recalled, "all hell broke loose."

Gunfire originated at the courthouse, but whites quickly took the fight to Greenwood. While African Americans "fought like tigers," as one local Guardsman noted, their efforts to defend their neighborhood were overwhelmed not only by the numbers of the white mob but by the mob's willingness to use fire with impunity. Deputized by Tulsa police and the National Guard, white citizens terrorized Black

continued

American Landscape continued

Tulsa A man surveys the damage of the 1921 Tulsa Race Massacre after a white mob invaded the African American district of Tulsa, Oklahoma and burned it to the ground.

"Everything has been destroyed except the earth on which the town was built. I guess if there had been any way to set fire to the soil, it would be gone too." African Americans who had worked hard to accumulate wealth and property and possessions over a lifetime were left with nothing.

residents, looting homes and businesses, burning buildings, and brutalizing African Americans at will. Tulsa police, rather than protecting the city's Black residents, contributed to the violence and destruction.

Many African Americans escaped Greenwood and walked miles to nearby towns where they took refuge. Some left Oklahoma forever. Others, removed from their homes at gunpoint, were made to march down Greenwood's streets, hands raised, as they were directed to the city jail, and eventually the city's fairgrounds. Their homes destroyed, many would live in makeshift tents for months to come.

Greenwood lay in shambles. The Red Cross calculated that white mobs had burned 1256 buildings in a thirty-six-square block area, with a loss in property valued at approximately $1.5 million. As one observer noted,

Following the race massacre, Tulsa's mayor organized a committee to evaluate Tulsa's legal standing in the attacks on Greenwood. The committee determined Tulsa was not liable for "an unlawful uprising of Negroes," thereby setting grounds to deny residents' claims to compensation and framing the event in a manner that limited white responsibility, individual or institutional. Insurance companies denied claims filed by Greenwood residents. Race relations in Tulsa only worsened as the Ku Klux Klan, emboldened by the riot's outcome, gained a foothold in the city. As Black Tulsans rebuilt their lives and their neighborhood and aimed to protect their community, they were left to rely on themselves.

increasingly made sure that boys and girls went to school rather than to work. The family became primarily a unit of leisure and consumption. The home was where men, women, and children, gathered around the radio, found pleasure and fulfillment.

Reflecting modern cultural values, parents became more likely to indulge their children, who enjoyed more toys, possessions, and spending money than had earlier generations. The automobile gave young people more mobility, too. With their new freedom, they began to create their own separate culture. One sign was the dramatic spread of petting among high school youth, newly free from parental control.

Most adults accepted this situation partly because they admired and envied youthfulness. The modern culture, unsatisfied with work and anxious for fun, glorified sexually adventurous, fast-living young people. The title of the 1923 novel *Flaming Youth* became a catchphrase for the youth culture of the 1920s.

The Celebration of the Individual

The emphasis on the individual, so evident in changing views of sex, gender, family, and youth, was fundamental to the modern culture. In addition to Babe Ruth, Americans admired a host of sports heroes and heroines, and the movie industry increasingly showcased the distinctive personalities of such stars as Mary Pickford and Douglas Fairbanks Sr. Individualism was basic to the New Woman, too.

The resurgence of individualism was not surprising. The belief in the importance of the individual was deeply ingrained in American culture. Paradoxically, the development of industrial capitalism intensified the importance of both individuals and organizations. As corporations grew larger and produced more, they needed to stimulate consumerism, the gratification of individual needs and desires.

There were serious obstacles to true individualism in the 1920s. Powerful organizations, including corporations, controlled individual life. Even the most famous individual exploit of the decade depended on organization. On May 20–21, 1927, Charles A. Lindbergh flew the *Spirit of St. Louis* from New York City to Paris. This first nonstop solo crossing of the Atlantic made Lindbergh an international symbol of individual achievement, but his feat relied on businessmen who put up the money and a corporation that built the plane. So, too, Mary Pickford's individual success culminated in the creation of a corporation, United Artists. Organization and individualism, the new and the old, were interdependent in the 1920s.

THE LIMITS OF THE MODERN CULTURE

The modern culture had clear limits in the 1920s. For millions of Americans, much of the consumer lifestyle was out of reach. Many Americans, including artists and intellectuals, chose not to define themselves by the pursuit of pleasure, leisure, and consumption. For them, modern society—with its emphasis on the new, including the "**New Negro**," the New Woman, and the "**New Era**"—represented an unwelcome abandonment of old values. In different ways, fundamentalist Christians, immigration restrictionists, and the Ku Klux Klan demanded a return to an earlier United States. Mexican Americans, African Americans, and others found that the new culture, like the old, treated them like second-class citizens.

The Limits of Prosperity

Despite the aura of prosperity, low incomes and poverty persisted in the 1920s. As late as 1928, 6 out of 10 families made less than the $2,000 a year required for the "basic needs of life." Despite the housing boom, most American household heads did not own their own homes.

The towns and cities of the increasingly urban nation were still divided by social class. In *Middletown* (1929), their pioneering study of a small midwestern city in the 1920s, Helen and Staughton Lynd discovered that the "division into the working class and business class. . . constitutes the outstanding cleavage." The working class of "Middletown"—Muncie, Indiana—had less money and leisure to enjoy the new culture. About a third of the city still did not own automobiles.

The "Lost Generation" of Intellectuals

Many artists and intellectuals felt alienated from the United States in the 1920s. For white, mostly male writers and artists who came of age during World War I, the conflict represented a failure of civilization, a pointless exercise in destruction. Its aftermath left them angry, alienated, and rootless. In a nation supposedly devoted to **individualism**, they did not feel free. They were, as the writer Gertrude Stein described them, a "**Lost Generation**." Some of them, such as Stein and her fellow writer Ernest Hemingway, left the United States for Paris and other places in Europe.

However prosperous and peaceful, the postwar years did not reassure the Lost Generation that American life had changed much. In such works as *Winesburg, Ohio* (1919), novelist Sherwood Anderson portrayed a still-repressive society that denied people real freedom and individuality. The acid-tongued H. L. Mencken, editor of the *American Mercury*, condemned a provincial culture still dominated by the "booboisie" and its rural values.

Still other American artists and intellectuals feared their country had changed too much. Although excited by the potential of the machine, they criticized the routinized work and superficial pleasures of modern life. In his 1922 novel *Babbitt*, Sinclair Lewis satirized a midwestern Republican businessman whose consumerism made him a conformist, not an individualist. F. Scott Fitzgerald, in such fiction as *This Side of Paradise* (1920) and *The Great Gatsby* (1925), conveyed the sense of loss and emptiness in the lives of fashionable "flaming youth" in the "Jazz Age."

From a different angle, 12 southern intellectuals, including Allen Tate, Robert Penn Warren, Donald Davidson, and John Crowe Ransom, attacked the modern culture in *I'll Take My Stand: The South and the Agrarian Tradition* (1930). Their essays offered a defense of rural culture and a critique of a consumer society that demeaned work and exalted individualism.

Artists and intellectuals did not set off a mass rebellion against modern culture, but they did express a widespread ambivalence and uneasiness. In different and contradictory ways, they laid out an agenda for Americans as they came to terms with modern, consumer society.

Fundamentalist Christians and "Old-Time Religion"

For many Americans of faith, the modern culture promoted a sense of deep, unsettling change. "The world has been convulsed," declared *Presbyterian Magazine*. "The most settled principles and laws of society have been attacked." The new culture was troubling because it was so secular and seemed to define life in terms of material satisfaction rather than spiritual commitment. Many Protestants, feeling betrayed by their own churches, resented the influence of liberal Protestants who had tried to accommodate religion to science and scholarship.

Fundamentalists, the opponents of liberalism, took their name from *The Fundamentals*, a series of essays by conservative Protestant theologians that began to appear in 1909. Emerging across the continent, fundamentalists were strongest in the countryside and in the South and West. By the end of World War I, they dominated the Southern Baptist Convention and were fighting liberals for control of northern churches.

Fundamentalists rejected liberalism above all for its willingness to question the historical truth of the Bible. The fundamentalist movement urged a return to biblical, patriarchal, and denominational authority, to what came to be called "old-time religion."

The high point in the fundamentalist-liberal battle came in a Tennessee courtroom in 1925. That year, a high school biology teacher, **John Scopes**, defied a new state law banning the teaching of "any theory that denies the story of the divine creation of man as taught in the Bible, and that teaches instead that man has descended from a lower order of animals." Scopes's trial became a national media event. The chief lawyer for the prosecution was William Jennings Bryan, the former Democratic presidential candidate and now a leading crusader for **fundamentalism**. While Bryan was a champion of rural America, Scopes's attorneys—Clarence Darrow and Dudley Field Malone—represented the city and modern culture. In a dramatic confrontation, Darrow called Bryan to the stand and forced him to concede that the Bible might not be literally accurate. Although Scopes was convicted and fined, the fundamentalists lost some credibility. Other southern and western states later passed antievolution laws, but similar measures failed in the more urbanized Northeast.

The Scopes trial did not end the war between fundamentalism and liberalism. Fundamentalists were numerous. Their hostility to liberal Protestantism and modern culture would affect American life for decades to come.

Nativists and Immigration Restriction

While fundamentalist Christianity sought a return to old-time religion, a resurgent nativist movement wanted to go back to a supposedly more homogeneous America. As mass migration from Europe resumed after World War I, nativist feeling revived among Americans from western European backgrounds. Thanks to the Russian Revolution and the domestic Red Scare, they associated immigrants with anarchism and radicalism and derided Asians and southern and eastern Europeans as inferior races that would weaken the nation.

In response, Congress overwhelmingly passed the Immigration Act of 1921, which limited annual immigration from any European country to 3 percent of the number of its immigrants living in the United States in 1910. This quota sharply reduced the number of new immigrants from southern and eastern Europe, but nativists wanted tougher action. Congress responded with the **Immigration Act of 1924**, which reduced the annual intake from a European country to 2 percent of the number of its immigrants living in the United States in 1890, when there were far fewer southern and eastern Europeans in America. The act also effectively excluded Asian immigrants altogether. The legislation worked: immigration fell from 805,000 arrivals in 1921 to 280,000 in 1929 (see Table 21–2).

The Rebirth of the Ku Klux Klan

Nativism and fundamentalism helped spur another challenge to the new order of the 1920s. In 1915, the Ku Klux Klan, the vigilante group that had terrorized African Americans in the South during Reconstruction, was reborn in a ceremony on Stone Mountain, Georgia. It enjoyed explosive growth after World War I, inspired, in part, by D. W. Griffith's film *The Birth of a Nation* (1915), which depicted African

Table 21-2 The Impact of Nativism: Immigration, 1921–1929

	Arrivals (in thousands)		
Origin	1921	1925	1929
Eastern Europe and Poland	138	10	14
Southern Europe	299	8	22
Asia	25	4	4
Mexico	31	33	40
Total	805	294	280

Source: Historical Statistics of the United States (Cambridge: Cambridge University Press), vol. I, p. 401.

Note: Itemized groups do not add up to totals.

Americans as sexual aggressors and the Klan of the 1860s as a heroic and necessary force. The "Invisible Empire" borrowed the rituals of the nineteenth-century Klan, including its white robes and hoods. The twentieth-century KKK adopted cross burnings based upon popular remembrances of its predecessor. The new Klan was still driven by a racist hatred of African Americans, but it took on new targets, including Jews, Roman Catholics, immigrants, religious liberalism, and change in general.

The Invisible Empire condemned big business and modern culture for valuing "money above manhood." The Klan condemned pleasure, "the god of the young people of America," and was hostile to the new gender ideals, birth control, freer sexuality, and the independence of youth. Klansmen and Klanswomen yearned for an earlier America in which white Protestant males controlled women, youth, and other groups and had nothing to fear from big business.

The Klan's tactics blended old and new. Seeing themselves as a secret army of vigilantes, some Klan members supported the age-old tactics of moral regulation—intimidation, flogging, and sometimes lynching—to scare people into good behavior. At the same time, much of the Invisible Empire repudiated violence and used the latest advertising techniques and modern technology to boost its membership.

For several years, the Klan proved extraordinarily successful. Despite its extremist views, the Invisible Empire had a mainstream membership in every region, in cities and the countryside. At its peak, there were perhaps 3 to 5 million secret members. Because so many politicians and newspaper editors feared or sympathized with it, the Klan had considerable political influence. It helped to elect governors, senators, and other officials from both major parties.

The Klan collapsed, however, when its leaders were revealed to be caught up in financial scandal, alcohol, pornography, adultery, kidnapping, and murder. Most people realized they had nothing to fear from such Klan targets as Communists, unions, and Jews. Millions of Americans, however uneasy about the new culture, had no desire to support prejudice, lawbreaking, and violence in a futile attempt to go back to the past. The Klan's membership dropped precipitously in the late 1920s.

Mexican Americans

Despite the efforts of immigration restrictionists and the Klan, the United States became more diverse than ever. Up to a million and a half Mexicans entered the United States legally or surreptitiously between 1890 and 1929. Many left to avoid the upheaval of the Mexican Revolution of 1910 (see Chapter 20) and to escape the agricultural changes driving the rural poor from the land. The dynamic US economy created opportunities for impoverished Mexican immigrants, as did, ironically, the restrictionist immigration legislation of the 1920s. Unable to get enough European or Asian workers, employers turned eagerly to Mexico as a source of cheap seasonal labor. The Southwest's rapidly developing economy particularly needed Mexican workers for mines, railroads, construction gangs, and, above all, farms.

Like many immigrants from Europe, many Mexican migrants did not plan to stay in the United States. They traveled back and forth to their homeland or returned permanently. Gradually, many chose to stay as they developed economic and family ties in the United States. The National Origins Act, which made it costly, time-consuming, and often humiliating for Mexicans to cross the border, also encouraged migrants to remain in the United States. As a result, the official Mexican population of the United States rose from 103,000 in 1900 to 478,000 by 1920. At the turn of the century, the majority of immigrants lived in Texas and Arizona, but California, with its booming agriculture, rapidly became the center of the Mexican population. Los Angeles, growing phenomenally in the early twentieth century, attracted perhaps 190,000 Mexicans by 1930.

Mexican immigrants, like so many other ethnic groups in the United States, wrestled with questions about their national identity. Were they still Mexicans, or had they become Americans or some unique combination of the two nationalities? In varying degrees, the migrants clung to old identities and adapted to their new home. Mexican Americans, eager to hold on to the advantages they had won by birth and residence in the United States, feared that newcomers would compete for jobs and cause native-born whites to denigrate all Mexicans alike. The immigrants, in turn, often derided Mexican Americans as *pochos*—bleached or faded people— who had lost their true Mexican identity.

Nevertheless, ethnic Mexicans created a distinctive culture in the United States. For all their differences, they shared a sense of common origins and common challenges. In a white-dominated society, they saw themselves as *La Raza*—The Race— set apart by heritage and skin color.

Poverty and discrimination also contributed to a sense of common identity. In many towns and cities, ethnic Mexicans were effectively segregated in certain neighborhoods—*barrios*—in poor conditions. Largely ignored by national corporations, Mexican Americans supported their own businesses and listened to their own Spanish-language radio programs. Anglo-American prejudice also drove Mexicans together. Many whites stereotyped them as a lazy and shiftless race that would take jobs from native-born workers but could not be assimilated into American life. Still other white Americans, drawing on the reform agenda of the Progressive Era, wanted to "Americanize" ethnic Mexicans by teaching them English and middle-class values.

Their sense of shared identity encouraged Mexican Americans to struggle for economic progress and equal rights. In 1928, farm workers in California created La Unión de Trabajadores del Valle Imperial (Imperial Valley Workers Union) in a successful fight for higher wages. A year later, Mexican American businessmen and professionals formed the League of United Latin American Citizens (LULAC) in Texas.

African Americans and the New Negro

Like Mexican Americans, African Americans found the new cultural terrain of the United States appealing but unsatisfying. They enjoyed and helped to create the new culture, but it did little to affect racial discrimination. South and North, African Americans still lived with economic and political inequality.

Although discrimination had not changed, many African Americans insisted that they had. It was the decade of both the New Woman and the New Negro. In 1900, Booker T. Washington titled one of his books *A New Negro for a New Century*. By the 1920s, the increased use of New Negro reflected a fresh sense of freedom as African Americans left the rural South for cities. It was also the product of frustration as African Americans encountered inequality along with opportunity. The New Negro was assertive in the face of mistreatment. "The time for cringing is over," said an African American newspaper.

The New Negro was also defined by a deep sense of racial difference and pride. Applauding their distinctive life and culture, African Americans spurred the **Harlem Renaissance**. Harlem, the section of upper Manhattan in New York where many African Americans had moved, became a center of artistic and intellectual creativity. Novelists such as Zora Neale Hurston, Jessie Fauset, Claude McKay, Jean Toomer, and Dorothy West; poets such as Langston Hughes, Sterling Brown, and Countee Cullen; and artists such as Aaron Douglas and Augusta Savage produced a new birth of African American creativity. In different ways, these women and men explored and honored the nature of American Blackness in 1920s America and its origins in Africa. The consideration of these African origins reflected a more international celebration of Blackness occurring during the 1920s.

The militancy of the New Negro was reflected in the development of the NAACP, which turned increasingly to African American leadership. Its key figure, W. E. B. DuBois, became more critical of whites and more determined that white colonizers return Africa to Africans. The NAACP also pushed the cause of African American civil rights more aggressively and attacked the white primary system that denied African Americans any say in the southern Democratic Party. The NAACP continued a longtime antilynching campaign, which bore fruit in the 1920s, as southern whites were increasingly embarrassed by vigilante justice.

For a time, the NAACP's efforts were overshadowed by the crusades of **Marcus Garvey**. A Jamaican immigrant to New York City, Garvey founded the Universal Negro Improvement Association (UNIA), which became the largest African American activist organization of the 1920s. Less interested in political rights and integration, Garvey focused on African American pride and self-help and on Africa. He exalted "a new Negro who stands erect, conscious of his manhood rights and fully determined to preserve them at all times." Garvey urged African Americans to develop their own businesses and become economically self-sufficient. Like DuBois, he insisted that the imperial powers give up their control of Africa. Sure that Blacks could never find equality in a white-dominated nation, Garvey believed African Americans should return to Africa.

Unlike the mostly middle-class NAACP, Garvey's UNIA developed a vast following among the African American working class. In 1919, he launched an economic self-help project, the Black Star Line, which, he promised, would buy ships and transport passengers and cargo from the United States to the West Indies, Central America, and Africa. Many of his followers invested in the venture, but it collapsed

UNIA Parade A parade organized by the United Negro Improvement Association in Harlem, 1920.

due to mismanagement. Garvey was indicted for mail fraud in connection with the project. In 1927, he was deported to Jamaica, and the UNIA lost its mass following.

As the fate of the UNIA suggested, militancy could be costly for African Americans. The NAACP also saw its membership drop dramatically during the decade. Nevertheless, African Americans' struggles laid the groundwork for more successful struggles in the future.

A "NEW ERA" IN POLITICS AND GOVERNMENT

The economic and cultural transformations of the 1920s shaped American democracy in important but contradictory ways. Modern culture helped empower ordinary people and transform the style of politics. But organized groups—big business above all—affected public life more decisively while a succession of conservative Republican presidents monopolized the White House during the decade. In a society fascinated by all things "new," the Republicans claimed to represent a "New Era" in politics and government. But the Republican ascendancy of the 1920s mostly meant the return of an older vision of minimalist government, individualism, and a less internationalist foreign policy. The mix of old ideology and new political styles failed to galvanize the democratic system: the prosperous 1920s became an age of apathy and low voter turnout.

The Modern Political System

In some ways, the cultural changes of the 1920s stimulated equality and reinforced the idea that the individual could make a difference in politics, too. The emphasis on female freedom and empowerment encouraged women to exercise their newly won right to vote.

The modern culture also hastened the emergence of a political style taking shape since the late nineteenth century. Copying big business, politicians used advertising to appeal to the electorate. In the Gilded Age, voters had been active participants in political campaigns. Now, citizens were political consumers choosing candidates just as they chose mouthwash or automobiles.

The shift to advertising was necessary, too, because the major parties' control over the media had dramatically decreased. Once partisan, many newspapers now took a more independent stand. The new radio stations and movie theaters had no political affiliations at all. With the decline of partisanship, political ad campaigns focused more on individual candidates than on their parties.

Economic and cultural change also benefited big business and other organized groups. Congress was besieged by lobbyists from corporations, business groups, professional organizations, and single-issue pressure groups such as the Anti-Saloon League. Organizations employed a political style that used supposedly objective facts to educate legislators and voters. Unorganized Americans had less chance of influencing the political process.

The new, less partisan politics did a poor job of mobilizing voters. Nationwide, voter turnout fell from 79 percent in the presidential election of 1896 to just 49 percent in 1920 and 1924 (Figure 21–1). A number of factors accounted for this drop-off: African Americans in the South had been effectively disfranchised, and newly enfranchised women were less likely to vote than men; but white male turnout dropped dramatically, too.

The Republican Ascendancy

The chief beneficiaries of the new politics were the Republicans. Determined to regain the White House in 1920, the Republican Party chose an uncontroversial, conservative ticket. Presidential nominee Warren G. Harding of Ohio, handsome and charismatic, had accomplished little during a term in the Senate. His running mate, Governor **Calvin Coolidge** of Massachusetts, was best known for his firm stance against a strike by the Boston police.

The Republican ticket was not imposing, but neither was the opposition. The Democratic presidential nominee, Governor James M. Cox of Ohio, was saddled with the unpopularity of the Wilson administration. His running mate, Franklin Roosevelt of New York, was a little-known cousin of former president Theodore Roosevelt who had served as assistant secretary of the navy. While the Democrats ran an ineffective campaign, the Republicans made excellent use of advertising. Harding cleverly appealed to the reaction against Wilson's activist government, offering a return to "normalcy" after years of unsettling progressive innovations. Harding won a huge victory with 60.3 percent of the popular vote, a new record; he won 37 states for a total of 404 electoral votes. The Republican Party substantially increased its majorities in Congress.

The Harding administration was plagued by revelations of fraud and corruption, some involving the so-called Ohio Gang of cronies from Harding's home state. The director of the Veterans' Bureau, caught making fraudulent deals with federal property, went to prison. One of the Ohio Gang, fearing exposure of the group's influence-peddling schemes, committed suicide.

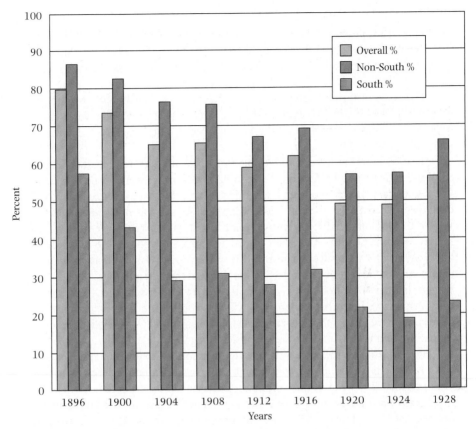

Figure 21-1   Declining Voter Turnout, 1896–1928 Why was turnout so much lower in the South?

A shaken Harding died suddenly of a misdiagnosed heart attack in August 1923, but the troubles continued. Congressional hearings revealed that former secretary of the interior Albert B. Fall had apparently accepted bribes in return for leasing US Navy oil reserves at Teapot Dome, Wyoming, and Elk Hills, California. Teapot Dome, as the scandal came to be called, earned Fall a fine and a jail term. In 1924, Harding's attorney general resigned because of his role in the Ohio Gang.

The scandals damaged Harding's reputation but did not seriously harm his party or his successor, Calvin Coolidge. The former vice president—so reserved in public that he was called "Silent Cal"—was well suited to the political moment. The picture of rectitude, Coolidge restored public confidence in the presidency.

In 1924, Coolidge easily won the presidency against the Democrat John W. Davis, a colorless, conservative corporate lawyer from West Virginia, and Wisconsin's senator Robert M. La Follette, the standard-bearer of the new Progressive Party. The choice, insisted Republicans, was either "Coolidge or Chaos." Holding on to the White House and to their majorities in Congress, the Republicans continued their ascendancy.

The Politics of Individualism

The Republicans practiced the politics of individualism. Eager to serve big business, they denounced the activist, progressive state and called for less government and more individual freedom. Coolidge declared, "The chief business of the American people is business."

Despite such slogans, Republicans sometimes used government power to spur economic development. The Federal Highway Act of 1921 provided federal matching grants to improve roads, and the Fordney-McCumber Tariff of 1922 restored high protective taxes on imports.

These measures were exceptions, however. Above all, the Harding and Coolidge administrations called for "economy"—reduced government spending and lower taxes. The Republicans also condemned budget deficits and pledged to reduce the national debt; they succeeded on all counts. Federal expenditures dropped from $6.4 billion in 1920 to $3.1 billion in 1924. Congress repeatedly cut income and other taxes, but the federal government still produced annual budget surpluses and reduced its debt.

Republicans' commitment to minimal government was obvious in their lax enforcement of Progressive-Era legislation. Under Harding and Coolidge, the federal government made only weak attempts to carry out Prohibition. The Republicans also allowed regulatory commissions to atrophy. The Interstate Commerce Commission (ICC) and the Federal Trade Commission (FTC) were effectively controlled by the businesses they were supposed to regulate.

Herbert Hoover, the secretary of commerce for both Harding and Coolidge, had a more activist view of the government's role in the economy. Sensitive to business interests, Hoover used the Commerce Department to promote "associationalism"—organized cooperation among business trade groups. However, businessmen did not trust one another enough to make voluntary cooperation effective, and Hoover did not advocate federal action to force cooperation. Afraid of too much government, Hoover believed above all in what he called "American individualism."

Republican Foreign Policy

After America's intense involvement in international affairs during World War I, the 1920s were a period of relative withdrawal. But even without a foreign policy crisis, the United States, the world's greatest economic power, played an active role around the globe.

In the aftermath of World War I, Americans were eager to reduce the size of the military and to avoid new conflict. Horrified by the "Great War," women's groups and religious organizations joined a surging international peace movement. Activists' calls for disarmament helped push the Harding administration to organize the Washington Naval Conference of 1921–1922. In the first international arms-reduction accord, the United States, Great Britain, and Japan agreed to scrap some of their largest warships and, along with France and Italy, promised to limit the tonnage of their existing large ships, abandon gas warfare, and restrict submarine warfare.

The peace movement was less successful in its second goal, outlawing war. In 1928, the United States and 14 other countries signed the Kellogg-Briand Pact forswearing war as an instrument of national policy. Enthusiastically received, the measure lacked an effective mechanism to stop a nation from going to war. US membership in a world court, the third major goal of the peace movement, was not achieved in the 1920s. Too many Americans believed that the court, like the League of Nations, would undermine US sovereignty.

Meanwhile, the United States became an increasingly active member of the world economy. During the 1920s, Americans made investments and loans around the world. American corporations, including movie studios and automobile companies, exported their products. More US corporations became multinational firms by building plants overseas.

The growth of American economic activity abroad complicated the priorities of the Harding and Coolidge administrations. In the 1920s, the United States had more interests than ever to protect overseas, but Americans were wary of policies that might lead to war. Many were also uneasy about imperialism, the nation's military role in its own possessions and in supposedly sovereign nations.

The Harding and Coolidge administrations tried to pull back from some of the imperial commitments made by presidents Taft and Wilson in the 1910s. US Marines withdrew from the Dominican Republic in 1924. They also withdrew from Nicaragua in 1925 but returned the next year when the country became politically unstable.

The Harding and Coolidge administrations also attempted to promote a stable world for American business. During the 1920s, the United States helped negotiate an increase in Chinese sovereignty to reduce the chances of conflict in Asia. The United States also tried to stabilize Europe after World War I. With the quiet approval of Republican presidents, American businessmen intervened to help resolve the controversial issue of how much Germany should pay in reparation to the Allies.

Extending the New Era

With their cautious foreign and domestic policies so popular, Republicans faced no serious challenge as the decade came to a close. The Democrats were also hurt by the backlash against modern culture. The Democratic Party depended on support not only from nativists, fundamentalists, and Klansmen but also from their frequent targets—urban Catholics and Jews. The antagonism among these constituencies helped doom the Democrats' chances in the 1924 and 1928 elections.

In 1928, the Democrats nominated Al Smith, the governor of New York, for president. The first Irish Catholic presidential nominee of a major party, Smith displeased fundamentalists and nativists. Moreover, his brassy, urban style—his campaign theme song was "The Sidewalks of New York"—alienated many rural Americans. Smith represented a new generation of urban, ethnic Democrats ready to use activist government to deal with social and economic problems. Their brand of urban liberalism would be influential in later years, but Smith could not galvanize a majority of voters in 1928.

Meanwhile, Herbert Hoover, the Republican nominee, joined by vice-presidential candidate Charles Curtis, a member of the Kaw Nation and the first person of Native American ancestry to run for the office, polled 58.2 percent of the popular vote and carried 40 states for a total of 444 electoral votes—the Republicans' largest electoral triumph of the decade (see Map 21–1). Republicans also increased their majorities in the House and Senate. The New Era would continue.

America In The World

J. Walter Thompson and International Markets

Even without an activist foreign policy, the United States played an important global role throughout the 1920s. As American manufacturers mastered the science of mass production, their goods saturated the American domestic market. In the United States, many businesses began relying on the services of expanding advertising agencies to enhance the consumer appeal of their products at home and overseas.

At the forefront of American advertising's overseas expansion was the top firm of J. Walter Thompson (JWT). The agency had opened a London branch in 1899, closed it during World War I, and, with its reopening, saw substantial growth during the first half of the 1920s. In 1927, JWT acquired the international business of automobile manufacturer General Motors (GM) and agreed to open a branch office wherever GM had a manufacturing plant. By the early 1930s, JWT had thirty-four branch offices across Europe, the Middle East, Australia, South America, South Africa, and India. While the branches aimed to solicit local accounts, they also enhanced the reach of American products to a global consumer population.

In addition to making GM a recognizable global name, JWT also established modern and professional American advertising practices throughout the world. With its unprecedented number of branches and its international agents' dedication to research and reports (in the first year and a half abroad, the agency produced 222 research reports, based on 44,086 interviews), JWT outpaced its competitors on the international market and positioned itself to be the leading international agency for

TIME LINE

▼**1913**
Introduction of the assembly line at Ford Motor Company

▼**1919**
Black Star Line founded by Marcus Garvey

Original Dixieland Jazz Band and Will Marion Cook's Southern Syncopated Orchestra bring jazz to England

▼**1920**
Commercial radio broadcasting

Warren G. Harding elected president

▼**1922**
Fordney-McCumber Tariff
Sinclair Lewis, *Babbitt*

decades to come. Its methods became *the* methods of modern advertising, at home and abroad.

Yet even as the various JWT branches compiled data that spoke to the cultural specificity of their individual locations, the advertisements produced for GM differed little from country to country. At the New York office, the international department generated "pattern" copy and illustrations, largely standardizing GM advertising worldwide. Part of the reason for this was practical: stock images and text cut down on creative work. International branches could devote themselves instead to signing new clients. Additionally, a standard image of GM lines, recognized globally, was believed to enhance the power of the brand.

Advertisements generally featured art more prominently than text. Depictions of people suggested where they stood in the larger social structure, a practice that situated consumers within the anticipated class structure of the various GM lines, from the affordable Chevrolet to the highest end vehicle, the Cadillac. JWT primarily emphasized relationships between men, women, and automobile selection and the differences in the appeal of automobiles across class lines. While automobile advertisements in the United States were far more likely to foreground the significance of the nuclear family, there was some commonality in international consumer appeals. Many of JWT's international advertisements continued to echo familiar American themes, especially those intended to appeal to an upper-class clientele: luxury, style, and leisure.

With the onset of the Great Depression and a decline in sales, GM severed its relationship with JWT. While the agency closed many of its international branches, its global business sustained and potentially strengthened JWT during the 1930s, as domestic billings declined 25 percent and international business increased 43 percent. The worldwide presence of JWT had far-reaching cultural and economic consequences in promoting American goods, ideals, and business practices. The agency's expansion in the aftermath of the Great Depression and World War II would lead *Fortune* magazine in 1947 to liken the firm to the British Empire at its height, noting "the sun never sets on J. Walter Thompson."

▼**1923**
Teapot Dome scandal
Calvin Coolidge succeeds
   Harding as president

▼**1924**
National Origins Act

▼**1925**
Founding of the Brother-
   hood of Sleeping Car
   Porters
Bruce Barton, *The Man
   Nobody Knows*
Scopes trial

▼**1927**
Charles Lindbergh's solo
   transatlantic flight

▼**1928**
Kellogg-Briand Pact
Herbert Hoover elected
   president

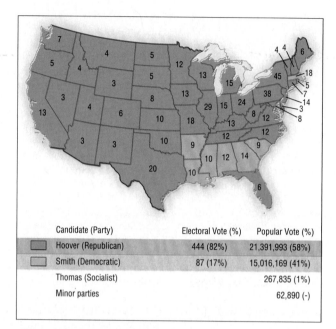

Candidate (Party)	Electoral Vote (%)	Popular Vote (%)
Hoover (Republican)	444 (82%)	21,391,993 (58%)
Smith (Democratic)	87 (17%)	15,016,169 (41%)
Thomas (Socialist)		267,835 (1%)
Minor parties		62,890 (-)

Map 21–1   The Election of 1928 Herbert Hoover's landslide victory extended the Republican "New Era."

CONCLUSION

The Republicans' victory in 1928 underscored the triumph of modern culture. The New Era had swept past the challenges of nativists, fundamentalists, and Klansmen. As Hoover prepared to take office, the appeal of the modern culture, rooted in the industrial economy, appeared undeniable. It offered a renewed sense of individual worth and possibility. It promised new freedom to women and youth. It held out an alluring vision of material pleasures—a life devoted to leisure and consumption—to all Americans. Mary Pickford still embodied the promise of the new culture and the New Era. In 1929, moving with the times, she made her first "talking picture," *Coquette*. Her performance won her an Oscar, an award for the best performance by a female actor, from the American Academy of Motion Picture Arts and Sciences, which she had helped found.

Nevertheless, Pickford, the modern culture, and its Republican defenders were vulnerable. The political New Era of the 1920s was especially dependent on the state of the economy. Perhaps more than ever before in their history, Americans equated happiness with the capacity to pay for pleasures. What would happen if Americans lost their jobs and their purchasing power? What would happen when they began to wonder whether their country was really so democratic after all? The new culture and the New Era had survived the dissent of alienated and excluded Americans in the 1920s. It would not survive the sudden end of prosperity.

WHO, WHAT, WHERE

REVIEW QUESTIONS

1. What factors created the dynamic industrial economy of the 1920s?

2. What were the main values of the modern culture that emerged after World War I?

3. What groups opposed or resisted the modern culture?

CRITICAL-THINKING QUESTIONS

1. Why was individualism such a powerful force in America despite the growing power of corporations? Did individuals really influence American life?

2. Why did the Republican Party dominate the emerging political system of the 1920s?

3. Did the United States become more or less democratic in the 1920s?

4. How would the emergence of consumer culture shape the United States beyond the 1920s?

SUGGESTED READINGS

Baldwin, Davarian L. *Chicago's New Negroes: Modernity, the Great Migration, and Black Urban Life*. Chapel Hill: University of North Carolina Press, 2007.

Duke University. Ad Access. https://repository.duke.edu/dc/adaccess

Dumenil, Lynn. *The Modern Temper: American Culture and Society in the 1920s*. New York: Hill and Wang, 1995.

McGirr, Lisa. *The War on Alcohol: Prohibition and the Rise of the American State*. New York: Norton, 2016.

Murphy, Paul V. *The New Era: American Thought and Culture in the 1920s*. Lanham, MD: Rowman and Littlefield, 2012.

For further review materials and resource information, please visit www.oup.com/us/ofthepeople

CHAPTER 21:   The Modern Nation, 1919–1928
Primary Sources

21.1   HIRAM WESLEY EVANS, EXCERPTS FROM "THE KLAN: DEFENDER OF AMERICANISM" (1925)

While many Americans eagerly embraced the modernity and excitement of the "Roaring Twenties," others rejected the cultural changes under way. Hiram Wesley Evans, the Imperial Wizard of the Ku Klux Klan from 1922 to 1939, made clear the organization's rejection of diversity and inclusivity in the body politic. Members of the Ku Klux Klan regarded differences in race, ethnicity, and religion as threats to what they imagined to be the "true" American character, possessed by the white, the Protestant, and the native born.

We believe that the pioneers who built America bequeathed to their own children a priority right to it, the control of it and of its future, and that no one on earth can claim any part of this inheritance except through our generosity. We believe, too, that the mission of America under Almighty God is to perpetuate and develop just the kind of nation and just the kind of civilization which our forefathers created. This is said without offense to other civilizations, but we do believe that ours, through all possible growth and expansion, should remain *the same kind* that was "brought forth upon this continent." Also, we believe that races of men are as distinct as breeds of animals; that any mixture between races of any great divergence is evil; that the American stock, which was bred under highly selective surroundings, has proved its value and should not be mongrelized; that it has automatically and instinctively developed the kind of civilization which is best suited to its own healthy life and growth; and that this cannot safely be changed except by ourselves and along the lines of our own character. Finally, we believe that all foreigners were admitted with the idea, and on the basis of at least an implied understanding, that they would become a part of us, adopt our ideas and ideals, and help in fulfilling our destiny along those lines, but never that they should be permitted to force us to change into anything else.

That is the basic idea of the Klan. There is, perhaps, much to be said for the liberal idea of making America a mongrel nation, but that involves the two points which, as I have pointed out, the Klan will not debate. We hold firmly that America belongs to Americans, and should be kept American. All who believe this have much in common with us, and . . . belong with us in spirit if not in actual membership. The whole purpose of the Klan is to bring this belief to fulfilment. We make many mistakes, but we are doing this one thing, and no one else is even trying to do it. Within a few years the America of our fathers will either be saved or lost, and unless some other way is found, all who wish to see it saved must work with us. If they think our methods wrong, or the details of our ideas, we will be glad of correction.

There can be no doubt about the traditional American spirit, the Americanism of the pioneers, which we are trying to save. It is to be seen in the character and spirit of those pioneers, far more than in formal political documents. Americanism is not wholly lovely, perhaps. It is certainly neither soft nor lax, neither easily ductile nor imitative, neither silken nor oily. It is a thing of rugged steel, tempered and forged in the terrific stress of the task of wresting a continent from savages and from the wilderness. It is welded of convictions, independence, self-reliance, freedom, justice, achievement, courage, acceptance of responsibility, and the guidance of his own conscience by each man personally. If inheritance counts for anything, it is to be found in the children of the pioneers far more than in any other group on earth, for only those who had this spirit survived. . . .

We are drifting away from national unity: in fact, we are being carefully and deliberately driven away from it by alien ideas and excessive liberalism toward them. The Klan, knowing this, believes the whole tendency must be stopped, and that control of the nation should return to, and remain in, the hands of men of the character and spirit of the pioneers who made the nation, a spirit most often found in the descendants of those pioneers.

We believe, also, that all who foment this disruption through alienism threaten the very foundations of all the things that have made America great. It is because of this that the Klan is intolerant—prejudiced. It is intolerant of this attack; intolerant of the people who are trying to destroy our traditional Americanism. We do not admit that we are more intolerant than our opponents; it seems to us as intolerant to condemn the Klan's attempts to save Americanism as it is for us to condemn the attempts to subvert it. But, if that is intolerance, we are proud of it.

And in our intolerance, as in other things, we are true to the American tradition; for this is our intolerance: We will not endure attempts to tear down the fundamentals on which the whole structure of our nation and our civilization is based. So long as these are not threatened, tolerance should be unlimited; we of the Klan do not wish or try to limit it. But the ideas upon which the nation rests, and which set us apart from other nations, are in a way like a corral fence. While the fence is undamaged there is no need to worry, no matter how much the animals inside may kick up and mill around. But when the fence is weakened or threatened, then it is time for action. So, in the nation, toleration becomes a vice when fundamentals are in danger. That time has come, and we who are the heirs of the American tradition are called upon to act. . . .

To sum up: The Klan speaks for the plain people of America, who believe in an American nation, built on that unity of mind and spirit which is possible only to an homogeneous people, and growing out of the purposes, spirit, and instincts of our pioneer ancestors. We know that the melting pot has failed; the reasons are unimportant now. We believe that definite steps must now be taken to prevent ours from becoming a mongrel nation, or a milling and distraught mass of opposed groups, in which the mental and spiritual qualities that made America great will be lost forever. Therefore, we oppose all alienism in any form and the excessive liberalism that supports it. We grant to all the right to their own ideas, but we claim the same right for ourselves, and a prior right to control America.

Source: Hiram Wesley Evans, "The Klan: Defender of Americanism," *The Forum* (December 1925), 801–814.

(21.2) MARIE PREVOST ON "THE FLAPPER" (1923)

The fiction of F. Scott Fitzgerald helped to popularize knowledge of the flapper, the model of womanhood that has become so linked with the Roaring Twenties. Actor Marie Prevost played Gloria Gilbert in the film version of Fitzgerald's *The*

Beautiful and the Damned. Prevost defended the flapper and highlighted the benefits this style of womanhood brought to American culture and celebrated its contrast to "traditional" understandings of women's expected roles, behaviors, and appearances.

Des Moines Capital, Feb. 18, 1923, p. 33

Marie Prevost Believes Flappers are Adorable and Loveable Creatures

A FLAPPER—just what is she and why?

Some say she represents a style in drew—very short skirt of flaming hue, loud sweater, bobbed hair, rakish hat and manly appearance.

Others claim the flapper is nothing more than a state of being, an attitude of life, the reign of the ingenue, the desire for perpetual youth, gayety, fun and dancing.

Marie Prevost, when asked the question, answered that whatever she may be, the flapper is an altogether adorable creature, feminine to her finger tips, vivaciously alive, supremely likeable.

"If there's anything in the world I love," she says, "it's the modern flapper. The world makes fun of them, calls them foolish and rattle-brained, but it would be mighty lonesome without them just the same. They have more pep in a minute than the others have in a hundred years and they're the best little gloom dispellers ever created. What if some of them are rattle-brained? Give them time and Old Experience will soon make them serious enough. The folks who criticize them the most are just jealous, that's all—they'd probably give their eyes to be a flapper themselves."

Marie is quick to come to the defense, for she has lately been acting in a flapper role, and knows the ins and outs of the type.

"People think the modern girl of today—the flapper in other words—is going to the bow wows, disgracing the traditions of womanhood. This is pure nonsense. It reminds me of the Oscar Wilde saying that as soon as a person is old enough to know better, he doesn't know anything at all.

"Instead of criticism being hurled against the flapper, it is high time to take a sensible view of things. We must begin lo consider her a result of her environment, one of the inimitable types produced by the twentieth century."

The piquant little actress who a few years ago was a bathing beauty comedienne, and who has quickly climbed to stardom, believes that everything the flapper has done is commendable, from discarding corsets and French heels lo adopting a mannish cut of coat and comfort in dress.

Other reasons given by her in defense—(if it can be called such) of the flapper, are as follows:

1—During their "flapper" fling, young girls acquire independence of spirit and knowledge of life, which is useful to them later.

2—They develop good, robust bodies by exercising out-of-doors. No other generation has produced so many girls who love sports, tennis, swimming, rowing, horseback riding, etc.

3—They dress comfortably and thus insure physical health, without having their bodies restricted and confined.

4—They are thoroughly feminine, although they sometimes glory in concealing it under a veneer of sophistication.

5—They will make better mothers than their sisters of a decade ago, since they understand life much better.

. . .

"There's something really fine about the flapper. She is independent. She knows where she stands in the world. She isn't a timid sensitive plant that used to be so much in vogue. ... The old type was carefully sheltered. Everything was a mystery, and she was taught to be incurious and content."

Miss Prevost thinks the flapper has come to stay: "You know you can't make a person enjoy chains after he has enjoyed liberty. Neither can you convince a blind man who has recovered his sight that blindness is preferable to sight. In the same way you cannot convince the flapper that her admirable freedom of dress and manner is worse than the constraint and cramped manner of the girls of past decades. So I'm all for the flapper. She has come to stay like all good things, and it would be a pity to see her go."

Source: "Marie Prevost Believes Flappers are Adorable and Loveable Creatures," *Des Moines Capital,* Feb. 18, 1923, p. 33.

21.3   VISUAL DOCUMENT: COLGATE & CO. ADVERTISEMENT (1925)

As American culture underwent a transformation whereby workers found satisfaction not in their work but in their leisure time, the advertising industry encouraged the pursuit of pleasure. As new products flooded the market, advertisements—in magazines, on billboards, in trolley cars—educated American consumers about products they had once lived without but would now absolutely need in order to compete in the modern world.

Source: Literary Digest/Courtesy Duke University Libraries. John W. Hartman Center for Sales, Advertising & Marketing History. https://repository .duke.edu/dc/adaccess/BH0714.

21.4   ROBERT LYND AND HELEN LYND, EXCERPT FROM "REMAKING LEISURE IN MIDDLETOWN" (1929)

Just as Henry Ford's moving assembly line and system of mass production changed business forever, so too did the product coming off his factory lines: the automobile. Robert and Helen Lynd's pioneering 1929 study of social and economic life in Muncie, Indiana, revealed the influence of new goods and entertainments and the resulting changes to patterns of modern American life. The car, in particular, took people away from the traditional influences of home and church and revealed the new power of media and peer culture.

Although lectures, reading, music, and art are strongly intrenched in Middletown's traditions, it is none of these that would first attract the attention of a newcomer watching Middletown at play.

"Why on earth do you need to study what's changing this country?" said a lifelong resident and shrewd observer of the Middle West. "I can tell you what's happening in just four letters: A-U-T-O!"

The first real automobile appeared in Middletown in 1900. About 1906 it was estimated that "there are probably 200 in the city and county." At the close of 1923 there were 6,221 passenger cars in the city, one for every 6.1 persons, or roughly two for every three families. Of these 6,221 cars, 41 percent were Fords; 54 percent of the total were cars of models of 1920 or later, and 17 percent models earlier than 1917. These cars average a bit over 5,000 miles a year. For some of the workers and some of the business class, use of the automobile is a seasonal matter, but the increase in surfaced roads and in closed cars is rapidly making the car a year-round tool for leisure-time as well as getting-a-living activities. As, at the turn of the century, business class people began to feel apologetic if they did not have a telephone, so ownership of an automobile has now reached the point of being an accepted essential of normal living.

Into the equilibrium of habits which constitutes for each individual some integration in living has come this new habit, upsetting old adjustments, and blasting its way through such accustomed and unquestioned dicta as "Rain or shine, I never miss a Sunday morning at church"; "A high school boy does not need much spending money"; "I don't need exercise, walking to the office keeps me fit"; "I wouldn't think of moving out of town and being so far from my friends"; "Parents ought always to know where their children are." The newcomer is most quickly and amicably incorporated into those regions of behavior in which men are engaged in doing impersonal, matter-of-fact things; much more contested is its advent where emotionally charged sanctions and taboos are concerned. No one questions the use of the auto for transporting groceries, getting to one's place of work or to the golf course, or in place of the porch for "cooling off after supper" on a hot summer evening; however much the activities concerned with getting a living may be altered by the fact that a factory can draw from workmen within a radius of forty-five miles, or however much old labor union men resent the intrusion of this new alternate way of spending an evening, these things are hardly major issues. But when auto riding tends to replace the traditional call in the family parlor as a way of approach between the unmarried, "the home is endangered," and all-day Sunday motor trips are a "threat against the church"; it is in the activities concerned with the home and religion that the automobile occasions the greatest emotional conflicts.

Group-sanctioned values are disturbed by the inroads of the automobile upon the family budget. A case in point is the not uncommon practice of mortgaging a home to buy an automobile. Data on automobile ownership were secured from 123 working class families. Of these, sixty have cars. Forty-one of the sixty own their homes. Twenty-six of these forty-one families have mortgages on their homes. Forty of the sixty-three families who do not own a car own their homes. Twenty-nine of these have mortgages on their homes. Obviously other factors are involved in many of Middletown's mortgages. That the automobile does represent a real choice in the minds of some at least is suggested by the acid retort of one citizen to the question about car ownership: "No, sir, we've *not* got a car. *That's* why we've got a home." According to an officer of a Middletown automobile financing company, 75 to 90 percent of the cars purchased locally are bought on time payment, and a working man earning $35.00 a week frequently plans to use one week's pay each month as payment for his car.

The automobile has apparently unsettled the habit of careful saving for some families. "Part of the money we spend on the car would go to the bank, I suppose," said more than one working class wife. A business man explained his recent inviting of social oblivion by selling his car by saying: "My car, counting depreciation and everything, was costing mighty nearly $100.00 a month, and my wife and I sat down together the other night and just figured that we're getting along, and if we're to have anything later on, we've just got to begin to save." The "moral" aspect of the competition between the automobile and certain accepted expenditures appears in the remark of another business man, "An automobile is a luxury, and no one has a right to one if he can't afford it. I haven't the slightest sympathy for any one who is out of work if he owns a car."

... Many families feel that an automobile is justified as an agency holding the family group together. "I never feel as close to my family as when we are all together in the car," said one business class mother, and one or two spoke of giving up Country Club membership or other recreations to get a car for this reason. "We don't spend anything on recreation except for the car. We save every place we can and put the money into the car. It keeps the family together," was an opinion voiced more than once. Sixty-one percent of 337 boys and 60 percent of 423 girls in the three upper years of the high school say that they motor more often with their parents than without them.

But this centralizing tendency of the automobile may be only a passing phase; sets in the other direction are almost equally prominent. "Our daughters [eighteen and fifteen] don't use our car much because they are always with somebody else in their car when we go out motoring," lamented one business class mother. And another said, "The two older children [eighteen and sixteen] never go out when the family motors. They always have something else on." "In the nineties we were all much more together," said another wife. "People brought chairs and cushions out of the house and sat on the lawn evenings. We rolled out a strip of carpet and put cushions on the porch step to take care of the unlimited overflow of neighbors that dropped by. We'd sit out so all evening. The younger couples perhaps would wander off for half an hour to get a soda but come back to join in the informal singing or listen while somebody strummed a mandolin or guitar." "What on earth *do* you want me to do? Just sit around home all evening!" retorted a popular high school girl of today when her father discouraged her going out motoring for the evening with a young blade in a rakish car waiting at the curb. The fact that 348 boys and 382 girls in the three upper years of the high school placed "use of the automobile" fifth and fourth respectively in a list of twelve possible sources of disagreement between them and their parents suggests that this may be an increasing decentralizing agent.

An earnest teacher in a Sunday School class of working class boys and girls in their late teens was winding up the lesson on the temptations of Jesus: "These three temptations summarize all the temptations we encounter today: physical comfort, fame, and wealth. Can you think of any temptation we have today that Jesus didn't have?" "Speed!" rejoined one boy. The unwanted interruption was quickly passed over. But the boy had mentioned a tendency underlying one of the four chief infringements of group laws in Middletown today, and the manifestations of Speed are not confined to "speeding." "Auto Polo next Sunday!!" shouts the display advertisement of an amusement park near the city. "It's motor insanity—too fast for the movies!" The boys who have cars "step on the gas," and those who haven't cars sometimes steal them: "The desire of youth to step on the gas when it has no machine of its own," said the local press, "is considered responsible for the theft of the greater part of the [154] automobiles stolen from [Middletown] during the past year."

The threat which the automobile presents to some anxious parents is suggested by the fact that of thirty girls brought before the juvenile court in the twelve months preceding September 1, 1924, charged with "sex crimes," for whom the place where the offense occurred was given in the records, nineteen were listed as having committed the offense in an automobile. Here again the automobile appears to some as an "enemy" of the home and society.

Sharp, also, is the resentment aroused by this elbowing new device when it interferes with old established religious habits. The minister trying to change people's behavior in desired directions through the spoken word must compete against the strong pull of the open road strengthened by endless printed "copy" inciting to travel. Preaching to 200 people on a hot, sunny Sunday in midsummer on "The Supreme Need of Today," a leading Middletown minister denounced "automobilitis—the thing those people have who go off motoring on Sunday instead of going to church. If you want to use your car on Sunday, take it out Sunday morning and bring some shut-ins to church and Sunday School; then in the afternoon, if you choose, go out and worship God in the beauty of nature—but don't neglect to worship Him indoors too." This same month there appeared in the *Saturday Evening Post*, reaching approximately one family in six in Middletown, a two-page spread on the automobile as an "enricher of life," quoting "a bank president in a Mid-Western city" as saying, "A man who works six days a week and spends the seventh on his own doorstep certainly will not pick up the extra dimes in the great thorough-fares of life." "Some sunny Sunday very soon," said another two page spread in the *Post*, "just drive an Overland up to your door—tell the family to hurry the packing and get aboard—and be off with smiles down the nearest road—free, loose, and happy—bound for green wonderlands." Another such advertisement urged Middletown to "Increase Your Week-End Touring Radius."

. . . "We had a fine day yesterday," exclaimed an elderly pillar of a prominent church, by way of Monday morning greeting. . . . "dinner. It's a fine thing for people to get out that way on Sundays. No question about it. They see different things and get a larger outlook."

"Did you miss church?" he was asked.

"Yes, I did, but you can't do both. I never missed church or Sunday School for thirteen years and I kind of feel as if I'd done my share. The ministers ought not to rail against people's driving on Sunday. They ought just to realize that they won't be there every Sunday during the summer, and make church interesting enough so they'll want to come."

Source: Robert Lynd and Helen Lynd, *Middletown: A Study in Contemporary American Culture*, foreword by Clark Wissler (1929; New York: Harcourt, Brace & World, Inc., 1956), pp. 251–261.

22

A Great Depression and a New Deal

1929–1940

< FDR giving a fireside chat, 1936

Dorothea Lange

The city she loved had changed and Dorothea Lange resolved to capture that change on film. In the spring of 1932, Lange descended from her fashionable second-story portrait studio and began to document the effects of the Great Depression on the streets of San Francisco. Noting the throng of men standing outside the White Angel soup kitchen, Lange recalled that she took three shots and "then I got out of there." Those three shots marked the beginning of a tremendous change in the life and career of Dorothea Lange and would forever influence the way Americans, present and future, would visualize the Great Depression.

One of San Francisco's most celebrated portrait photographers, Lange had long catered to an upscale clientele who loved the intimacy and emotion she evoked from her subjects. But as the nation fell deeper into the Depression, Lange felt a desire to move beyond photographing the city's elite. The desperation of the Depression propelled Lange in a more political, more public direction.

Lange's early 1930s images focused on urban scenes of the Depression: a woman waiting on a food distribution line; an unemployed man leaning against a wall; a 1934 strike by the city's longshoremen. When Paul Taylor, an economics professor at the University of California at Berkeley, contacted Lange about using some of her images to accompany his article on the strike, Lange became even more politicized. Through a professional and personal partnership with Taylor, Lange left San Francisco and became one of the preeminent photographers of the rural Depression experience.

Lange accompanied Taylor on travels throughout California, where she photographed the work and living conditions of migrant laborers and "Okies" who had fled the **Dust Bowl** hoping to find employment and opportunity in California. Pushing the Farm Security Administration (FSA), a **New Deal** agency intended to aid agricultural laborers and combat rural poverty, for government-built camps to house migratory workers, Taylor provided economic and sociological evidence while Lange documented the desperate living conditions of these workers and the grueling labor that men, women, and children completed in order to survive. With her images and accompanying captions, which often outlined the background and experiences of her subjects, Lange successfully depicted farmworkers as hardworking and capable—people who did not deserve their poverty, but had come to it through a range of circumstances, many of them rooted in the inequity of the American economy.

Hoping to hold off conservative critics by demonstrating the value of its efforts, the FSA adopted a photography project that ultimately became its most influential activity. By documenting the Depression and sharing the images with journalists and popular media, the FSA drew national attention to the plight of the rural poor. Lange, with her skilled portrait style, was essential in depicting this population with dignity and grace. Her images communicated a New Deal view of American citizens during the Depression. Like Progressives, New Dealers refused to believe that immoral character led to poverty. It was the structure of the American economy, not the character of the American people, that needed correction.

With great intent, Lange used her photographs to communicate that the people she photographed were better than their current circumstances. She depicted efforts to keep an orderly pantry in a lean-to shelter as a means of maintaining some measure of domesticity. She showed families gathered by their cars, loaded down with possessions, taking to the road to look for work. She captured the back-breaking nature of farm labor migrant workers were willing to endure. And most famously, in "Migrant Mother," she showed the resolve of a maternal figure, worrying over her children, determined to continue on. These people deserved more, Lange believed, and in the spirit of the New Deal, Americans were coming to believe that the government had a responsibility to see that they got it.

THE GREAT DEPRESSION

In the fall of 1929, declining confidence in the stock market shook the economy. By Thursday, October 24, panic had set in as brokers rushed to unload their stocks. Prices rallied briefly, but on October 29, "Black Tuesday," stock values lost over $14 billion, and within the month the market stood at only half its precrash worth. Hundreds of corporations and thousands of individuals were wiped out. On Wall Street, the symbol of prosperity in the 1920s, mounted police had to keep angry mobs away from the stock exchange. Although the crash did not cause the Depression, it did expose underlying weaknesses and shatter the confidence President Herbert Hoover relied on for recovery. His optimistic speeches would ring false over the years of unemployment, hunger, and homelessness.

Causes

No single factor explains the **Great Depression.** Politicians, bureaucrats, and business leaders had no clear idea why things had gone so wrong. Economists and historians still debate the issue today. Yet even without a definitive account, it is clear that structural flaws in the national and international economies and ill-conceived government policies were at fault.

In the 1920s, the base of the economy had begun to shift. No longer was it driven by steel, coal, textiles, railroads, and other heavy industries. New industries that sold complex consumer goods such as automobiles became the driving force. In addition to cars, sales of radios, clothing, processed foods, and a whole range of consumer products grew dramatically. This shift toward a new consumer-oriented economy was fueled by favorable business conditions, job growth, and plentiful consumer credit. The limits of this market had, however, been reached even before the great crash. When the stock market fell, the collapse of purchasing power caused by mass unemployment and the loss of savings slowed the transition to the new economy.

A rickety credit and financial system added to the problems of the late 1920s. Even in good times, banks failed by the hundreds. For rural banks these failures could be traced to low farm prices, but financial institutions everywhere suffered from inept and even criminal management. Banks were virtually unregulated, and in the booming 1920s many bet depositors' money on stocks or large, risky loans. Bank failures magnified the impact of the crash; many thousands lost money they thought was safe.

Like banks, corporate finance was free from regulation and given to misrepresentation, manipulation, and corrupt insider deals. Few could be sure whether investments were going into sound companies or worthless paper.

Government missteps and poor policies also had a role. The Republican administrations of the 1920s reduced government interference in the economy, lowered taxes on the wealthy, and reduced spending. They failed to address the banking mess, the problems of farmers, or the growing reliance on credit. The Federal Reserve could have dampened speculation in stocks or, after the Depression began, expanded the currency to promote growth. Concerned more about a strong dollar than about stable employment, the Harding and Coolidge administrations cut spending and the money supply, worsening the eventual collapse.

The Depression was magnified by an international economy still reeling from the effects of World War I. Under the peace terms, Germany owed $33 billion in reparations to Britain and France, who in turn owed billions in debts to the United States. Only US bank loans to Germany made these huge payments possible, so throughout the 1920s, funds that could have created jobs and industries went instead into this financial merry-go-round. The cycle was broken by the depression in the United States. European nations tried to protect themselves by devaluing their currencies and raising trade barriers. The result was a steady economic decline that made payments on reparations or loans impossible. The cycle reached a breaking point in 1931, and the international financial system came crashing down, bringing with it many more American banks and further deepening the crisis.

Descending into Depression

The statistics describing the Great Depression were alarming. Between 1929 and 1933, every index of economic activity steadily worsened. The gross national product shrank from $104.4 billion in 1929 to $74.2 billion in 1933. The combined incomes of American workers fell by more than 40 percent. Bank failures increased, from 640 in 1928 to 2,294 in 1931. A *New York Times* index of business activity dropped from 114.8 in June of 1929 to 63.7 in March of 1933. Both exports and imports fell by more than two-thirds.

As business activity collapsed, joblessness skyrocketed. Periods of unemployment had always been a feature of capitalist economies, even in good times. What distinguished the Great Depression was the extent and duration of unemployment.

At the lowest point of the slump, in the early 1930s, between 20 and 30 percent of wage earners were out of work (see Table 22-1). In some cities the jobless rate was much higher, with Chicago and Detroit near 50 percent, Akron 60 percent, and Toledo a crushing 80 percent. In 1933, the Bureau of Labor Statistics estimated that as many as one in three workers, more than 12,600,000 Americans, were unemployed.

Behind the grim statistics lay terrible human costs. In the spring of 1930, as the first Depression winter came to an end, breadlines appeared in major cities. The unemployed could be seen in the thousands, Sherwood Anderson wrote, "creeping through the streets of American cities, eating from garbage cans." Unemployed men and women stood outside factory gates desperately seeking work, at soup kitchens hoping for a meal, and at homeless shelters that were already overflowing.

Food, clothing, and shelter were suddenly hard to get. Schoolteachers reported that growing numbers of students were listless from hunger. Hospitals began receiving patients suffering from nutritional disorders, including children with rickets, a disease caused by a lack of vitamin D. *Fortune* magazine ran an article on Americans who had starved to death. Embarrassed mothers sent children to school in rags. Men wrapped newspapers beneath their shirts as protection from the cold. Desperate families, unable to pay the rent, "doubled up" with relatives. More and more tenants were evicted; more and more banks foreclosed on mortgages. Apartments stood vacant and homes went unsold, yet by 1932 more than a million homeless men, women, and children occupied shantytowns or slept in doorways and alleys. Hoboes were everywhere, searching for something to eat, somewhere to live, someplace to work.

Farmers faced both economic and environmental disaster. Farmers in the plains states and the West aggressively increased production in the 1920s and then

Table 22-1 Labor Force and Unemployment, 1929–1941
(numbers in millions)

Year	Labor Force	Number	% of Labor Force
1929	49.2	1.6	3.2
1930	49.8	4.3	8.7
1931	50.4	8.0	15.9
1932	51.0	12.1	23.6
1933	51.6	12.8	24.9
1934	52.2	11.3	21.7
1935	52.9	10.6	20.1
1936	53.4	9.0	16.9
1937	54.0	7.7	14.3
1938	54.6	10.4	19.0
1939	55.2	9.5	17.2
1940	55.6	8.1	14.6
1941	55.9	5.6	9.9

Source: United States Department of Commerce, *Historical Statistics of the United States* (1960), p. 70.

saw the markets for corn, wheat, beef, and pork collapse. Between 1929 and 1932, farmers' income dropped by two-thirds. Then drought struck. Between 1930 and 1936, rains all but stopped in much of the South, the Southwest, and the Great Plains (see Map 22–1). Exposed by decades of wasteful farming practices and a more recent propensity to plow fields immediately following the previous harvest, the earth dried up and blew away. Spectacular dust storms carried topsoil hundreds of miles through the air, giving a new name—the Dust Bowl—to much of the southern plains. Dust and depression ripped thousands of farm families from the land in Texas, Kansas, Oklahoma, and Arkansas, sending these "Okies," "Arkies," and "Texies" off to California in search of work.

The Great Depression affected nearly everyone in America, but it was most severe for those already disadvantaged. Although the shock of the Dust Bowl affected many poor white farmers, the larger agricultural depression was even more devastating for sharecroppers on the southern cotton lands, workers in the wheat fields of the Midwest, and the vast migrant labor pools that traveled the East and West Coasts picking fruits and vegetables. In cities, African Americans, who held the least-secure jobs, found themselves pushed from menial service tasks and unskilled work by desperate white workers.

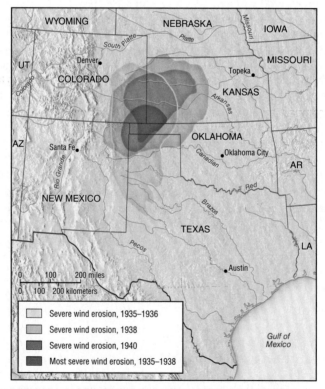

Map 22–1   Extent of the Dust Bowl The Dust Bowl of the 1930s eventually spread across thousands of square miles of the southern plains.

Dust Storm Drought and modern agriculture churned the Great Plains into silica powder that was carried by windstorms. Over half the patients in Kansas hospitals in 1935 suffered from dust pneumonia.

By 1932, private charities, the major social safety net, failed to meet the needs of desperate citizens. Ethnic organizations such as the Bohemian Charitable Association or Jewish Charities in Chicago found themselves overwhelmed. Arthur T. Burns, the president of the Association of Community Chests and Councils, flatly declared, "The funds we have are altogether inadequate to meet the situation."

Public monies were also scarce. Only eight states provided any form of unemployment insurance; most of it was meager. The few state welfare agencies were poorly funded and now stretched beyond their limits. Cities faced insolvency as their tax bases dwindled. Many states were forbidden by their constitutions to borrow for social welfare expenditures. Frustrated Americans looked to the federal government for a solution, but there was little help beyond pensions for veterans. There was no social security for the elderly and disabled, no federal unemployment insurance for those who lost their jobs, and no food stamp program to relieve hunger.

The federal government was under unprecedented pressure to do something, anything, to relieve the Depression. Even bankers and businessmen abandoned their resistance to a strong central government. The president of Columbia University suggested that a dictatorship might provide more effective leadership. Others warned of social revolution. Most of the pleas for action were aimed at the administration, and Herbert Hoover himself came to symbolize the failures of government. The newspapers that jobless men wrapped themselves in were called "Hoover shirts"; shantytowns were "**Hoovervilles**." In the popular imagination, Hoover and the Great Depression became inseparable.

Hoover Responds

In many ways, Hoover was ideally qualified to handle this emergency. He had experience with natural and human catastrophes. Orphaned at a young age, Hoover worked hard to educate himself. Trained as an engineer at Stanford University, he roamed the world building and managing mining operations and was a millionaire by his mid-20s. Like other young progressives, Hoover sought to use business skills to solve social problems. He won fame as an administrator of emergency relief, saving Belgium from starvation during World War I and overseeing rescue efforts during the Great Mississippi Flood of 1927.

He brought to the presidency a well-developed theory of the role of government in a modern economy. Hoover believed that complex societies required accurate economic information, careful planning, and large-scale coordination. His political philosophy, associationalism, envisioned a federal government that gathered information and encouraged voluntary cooperation among businesses but did not intervene further. He feared that an overbearing government would crush the creativity essential to a capitalist economy. This voluntarist dream fit well with America's dominant ideology, and Hoover easily won the presidency in 1928.

Hoover acted quickly. One of his first achievements was the Agricultural Marketing Act of 1929, designed to raise farm incomes and rationalize production. Since the turn of the century, farmers had been plagued by a "paradox of plenty." They produced more food and fiber than Americans could consume, so the more farmers grew, the less they earned. The bill established a Federal Farm Board to create cooperatives for purchasing and distributing surplus crops. It issued $500 million in loans to stabilize prices but did not limit production or dictate prices.

When the market crashed, Hoover's initial response reflected his overall vision. His goal was to get business to promise to cooperate to maintain wages and

A Hooverville in Seattle, Washington As the Depression deepened, the homeless settled in "Hoovervilles" on the edge of city centers.

investment. In 1931, as 25 banks a week were failing, he encouraged formation of the National Credit Corporation, in which banks were urged to pool resources to stave off collapse. Rather than distribute unemployment insurance or poor relief, he tried to persuade companies not to lay off workers and to contribute to charities for the homeless and unemployed. But the breadth and depth of the Depression overwhelmed Hoover's schemes. Crop prices fell so low that farmers blockaded cities and demanded compensation for their crops.

Hoover had never failed before, and he worked tirelessly to fight the Depression. By 1932, he reluctantly agreed to more aggressive government action, even at the risk of deficit spending. He proposed a Reconstruction Finance Corporation (RFC) authorized to loan $2 billion to revive large corporations. Plans to increase government revenues and distribute farm surpluses to the needy were also enacted. But it was too little, too late. The Depression was three years old and showed no signs of lifting.

Hoover's policies increased the Depression's severity. Unable to control his own party, Hoover watched Congress pass the Hawley-Smoot Tariff in 1930. The tariff raised import duties to record levels, stifling hopes that international trade might help the economy and damaging the weak nations of Europe. Despite misgivings, he signed the bill into law. At the same time, Hoover opposed other measures that might have relieved poverty or stimulated recovery. He vetoed massive public works bills sponsored by congressional Democrats. Finally, Hoover's commitment to the gold standard and a balanced budget also prevented a potential turnaround.

Hoover, whose popularity had plummeted as the Depression deepened, reinforced his reputation as a protector of the privileged by his response to the Bonus Marchers in 1932. In 1924, Congress had issued the veterans of World War I a "bonus" to be paid in 1945. But as the Depression threw millions out of work, veterans asked to have their bonuses paid early. In the summer of 1932, veterans formed a "Bonus Expeditionary Force" to march on Washington. Arriving on freight cars and buses, over 20,000 Bonus Marchers and their families encamped on Capitol grounds. Hoover ordered the army to remove the marchers. Against orders, General Douglas MacArthur attacked with tanks and mounted cavalry. Major George S. Patton, saber drawn, galloped through the encampment, setting fire to its miserable tents and shacks. Among those he attacked was Joseph T. Angelino, who won the Distinguished Service Cross in 1918 for saving Patton's life. Photographs of government brutality shocked Americans. Hoover's silence solidified his reputation for callousness.

As Congress struggled to relieve unemployment and suffering, Hoover dismissed the "futile attempt to cure poverty by the enactment of law." He questioned the motives of everyone who disagreed with his policies. By the end of his term the "Great Humanitarian" had become sullen and withdrawn. It was a dispirited Republican Convention that met in Chicago to nominate Hoover for reelection in 1932.

THE FIRST NEW DEAL

When the Democratic Convention chose a presidential candidate in 1932, **Franklin Delano Roosevelt** flew from Albany, New York, to Chicago to accept the nomination in person, a dramatic gesture in an age new to air travel and personal politics.

"I pledge myself," he told the enthusiastic crowd, "to a new deal for the American people." The phrase stuck, and the reforms enacted between 1933 and 1938 have come to be known as the New Deal. The programs came in two great waves, the "first" and "second" New Deals. The first New Deal began with the Hundred Days, a burst of executive and legislative activity following FDR's inauguration, and continued through 1934.

The Election of 1932

The Depression reached its lowest depths as the 1932 election approached, and the Republicans seemed headed for disaster. Their inability to develop a legislative program to attack the Depression had already cost them control of the House. But to take advantage of the situation, Democrats had to overcome internal divisions.

Throughout the 1920s the Democratic Party had been split between the ethnically diverse, wet (anti-Prohibition), urban wing concentrated in the North and the East and the Anglo-Saxon Protestant, rural southern and western wings. Ideological divisions on many issues separated northeastern business Democrats from western populists and urban progressives from southern conservatives.

The leading candidate for the Democratic nomination, New York's governor Franklin D. Roosevelt, had the background to overcome many of these divisions. He came from an upstate rural district, and his interest in conservation endeared him to many westerners. He had built ties to southern Democrats while serving as Wilson's assistant secretary of the navy and as a sometime resident of Warm Springs, Georgia. As governor of New York, his strong record of support for progressive social reforms appealed to urban liberals.

Roosevelt turned out to be the ideal candidate. As a distant cousin of Theodore Roosevelt, he had a recognizable name. FDR also had immense personal charm. Despite having been crippled by polio since 1921, he was a tireless campaigner and would become one of the most visible of modern presidents. Raised in wealth and educated at Groton and Harvard, he spoke in clear, direct language that ordinary Americans found reassuring.

During the campaign, Roosevelt simultaneously embraced old orthodoxies and enticed reformers with hints of radical changes. He promised to cut government spending and provide relief for the poor. FDR did not say how he would do both, but it hardly mattered. In November 1932, the Republicans were swept out of office in a tide of popular repudiation (see Map 22–2). FDR and the Democrats took control of the government with the promise of "a new deal" for the American people.

Roosevelt worked hard to develop a program to fight the Depression. While governor of New York, FDR had recruited intellectuals who provided him with an influential diagnosis of the Great Depression. Known as the "Brains Trust," they attempted to convince Roosevelt that the Depression was caused by the economy's fundamental defects. The core issue was the maldistribution of wealth. Because the rich held on to too large a share of the profits of American industry, the economy was producing much more than Americans could consume.

Roosevelt never fully bought the ideas of the Brains Trust nor allowed any one group to dominate his thinking. FDR's comfort with experimentation and chaos would hold his administration together and enable it to confront the complexities of

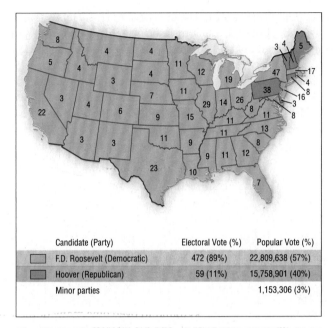

Candidate (Party)	Electoral Vote (%)	Popular Vote (%)
F.D. Roosevelt (Democratic)	472 (89%)	22,809,638 (57%)
Hoover (Republican)	59 (11%)	15,758,901 (40%)
Minor parties		1,153,306 (3%)

Map 22–2   The Presidential Election of 1932 By November 1932, most American voters blamed the Depression on Hoover and the Republicans. The Democrats, led by FDR, swept into office by huge electoral margins.

the Depression. Where Hoover had retreated into dogmatism, FDR endorsed "bold, persistent experimentation." Above all, he ordered his officials, "try something." And rather than trying to unite his followers behind a single idea or policy, Roosevelt seemed to enjoy watching his advisers feud while he orchestrated their final compromises. The president, an adviser said, was "the boss, the dynamo, the works."

FDR Takes Command

In the weeks before the inauguration, the ailing American banking system took a sharp turn for the worse. In mid-February, the governor of Michigan declared an eight-day bank holiday. In one of the most important manufacturing states, nearly a million depositors could not get their money. Stock prices dropped when the news came, and the rich began shipping their gold to safer countries. Panic struck, and funds flew out of bank tellers' windows. On the morning of the inauguration, New York and Illinois joined most of the other states in calling a bank holiday. The New York Stock Exchange and Illinois Board of Trade also closed. To many, it seemed like the end of the American economy.

With commerce at a standstill, the nation turned to the new president, and Roosevelt did not disappoint. "First of all," he declared, "let me assert my firm belief that the only thing we have to fear is fear itself—nameless, unreasoning, unjustified terror." In the midst of a frightening financial collapse, these words revitalized the nation almost overnight.

Roosevelt knew words alone would not end the crisis. On his first day in office, he declared a national bank holiday to last through the end of the week. He instructed his new secretary of the Treasury to draft emergency legislation and called Congress into special session. When Congress convened on March 9, the drafting team had barely finished the bill, but Congress was ready to act. Breaking all precedent, the House unanimously shouted its approval of the bill after less than a half hour of debate; the Senate voted to do the same with only seven dissents, and the president signed it into law that night. The Emergency Banking Act was a modest reform. It gave the Treasury secretary the power to determine which banks could safely reopen and which had to be reorganized. It also enabled the RFC to strengthen sound banks by buying their stocks.

On Sunday night, a week after taking office, FDR went on national radio to deliver the first of his many "fireside chats." Sixty million people tuned in to hear Roosevelt explain, in his resonant, fatherly voice, his response to the banking crisis. He assured Americans that their money would be "safer in a reopened bank than under the mattress." The government was not fully sure how solid most banks were, but the gamble worked. The next day, 12,756 banks reopened, the run stopped, and deposits started flowing into the system. The immediate crisis was over.

Once the banking crisis had been resolved in March 1933, Roosevelt wanted to ensure that the financial system would remain sound for the long run. He moved to restrict banks' speculations while guaranteeing their profitability. The Glass-Steagall Banking Act of 1933 imposed conservative banking practices nationwide. Chancy loans, stock investments, and shady business practices were outlawed, and close federal oversight guaranteed bank stability until Glass-Steagall was repealed in 1999. In addition, the new Federal Deposit Insurance Corporation protected deposits. The Banking Act of 1935 reorganized the Federal Reserve under more centralized and democratic control. Together, these laws established the credibility of the US banking system. One reason the banking system had become so vulnerable was its ties to the unregulated securities markets. So in 1933 the administration sponsored a Truth in Securities Act that required all companies issuing stock to

FDR During One of His Fireside Chats Hoover broadcast his speeches on radio, but Roosevelt's fireside chats took advantage of the intimacy of the new medium.

disclose accurate information to all prospective buyers. In 1934, Congress passed the Securities and Exchange Act. Whereas the 1933 law regulated companies, the 1934 legislation regulated the markets, prohibiting insider trading and other forms of manipulation. It gave the Federal Reserve Board the power to control the supply of credit and established the Securities and Exchange Commission, which quickly became one of the largest and most effective regulatory agencies in the country.

Federal Relief

Roosevelt's unemployment programs departed sharply from Hoover's relief strategies. In May, Congress passed a bill providing a half-billion dollars for relief and creating the Federal Emergency Relief Administration (FERA) to oversee it. Local and state agencies dispensed the funds. Headed by Harry Hopkins, a shrewd social worker and Roosevelt confidant, FERA distributed money at a rapid rate. As winter came on, Hopkins convinced Roosevelt that only a massive new federal program could avert disaster. At FDR's request, Congress created the Civil Works Administration (CWA), which employed 4 million men and women. During the winter, the CWA built or renovated over half a million miles of road and tens of thousands of schools and other public buildings. The CWA was eliminated in the spring—Roosevelt did not want the nation to get used to a federal welfare program—but FERA continued to run programs on a smaller scale.

Of all the relief programs, Roosevelt was most enthusiastic about one, the **Civilian Conservation Corps (CCC).** FDR believed that life in the countryside and service to the nation would have a positive moral impact on the young men of the cities and on those Depression "wild boys" roaming the nation. For the CCC, these young men built roads and trails in the national parks. By the time the program ended in 1942, it had transformed America's public lands and employed over 3 million teenagers and young adults.

The Farm Crisis

"I don't want on the relief if I can help it," a Louisiana farm woman wrote to the first lady, **Eleanor Roosevelt**, in the fall of 1935. "I want to work for my livin'." But she was desperate. She asked Mrs. Roosevelt to send money to save the family cow "for my little children to have milk." The doctor was no longer able to give her sick child medicine "unless we pay him some for he is in debt for it." The landlord was threatening to evict them. She had turned to the first lady because of Mrs. Roosevelt's reputation for caring about the poor, but political realities would limit what the first lady, or her husband, could do to help.

By the spring of 1933, farmers were desperate. Prices of commodities such as corn, cotton, wheat, and tobacco had fallen so low that it was not even worth the cost of harvesting. The banking crisis left farmers without access to necessary credit, and millions faced foreclosure, homelessness, or dust storms.

FDR saw a stark "imbalance" between city and country as a root cause of the Depression. While the land remained the only real source of wealth, modern cities absorbed all of the countryside's water, produce, talent, and people. The Dust Bowl was a result of this ecological distortion. His aim was to restore a more even pattern of development, with small manufacturing towns, suburbs, and farms linked to centers of culture and commerce. The New Deal program that came closest to fulfilling these goals was the **Tennessee Valley Authority (TVA).** In his campaign, Roosevelt had endorsed a proposal to develop the Muscle Shoals property along the Tennessee River. Congress created the TVA within the first Hundred Days. The TVA was a "corporation clothed with the power of government but possessed of the flexibility and initiative of a private enterprise." According to its administrator, it aimed to change the environment, the economy, the way of life, and the "habits, social, economic, and personal" of a region that spanned nine states.

One of the most ambitious projects of the entire New Deal, the TVA was also astonishingly successful. The dams built by the TVA controlled flooding, created reservoirs for irrigation, and provided cheap hydroelectric power (see Map 22–3). Electricity improved life for millions of farm families and made it possible for industry to move into new areas, bringing jobs to some of the poorest parts of the country. The TVA took responsibility for soil conservation, reforestation, improved navigation, and the manufacture of fertilizer and aluminum. During the Roosevelt administration, the poor Tennessee–North Carolina border region went from growing cotton to manufacturing aircraft and components for nuclear weapons. Average incomes in the area increased tenfold. As a comprehensive, centrally planned development scheme, the TVA came closest to the Brains Trusters' vision of how a modern "democracy on the march" should work.

Headed by Henry Wallace, founder of the Pioneer Hi-Bred Corn Company, the Agriculture Department was an idea factory in the first Hundred Days. An emergency farm bill gave Wallace powers to control production, buy up surpluses, regulate marketing, and levy taxes. Conservation and reclamation projects drained swamps, irrigated deserts, and sheltered the Great Plains from windstorms. The Agricultural Adjustment Act (AAA) turned agriculture into a regulated industry.

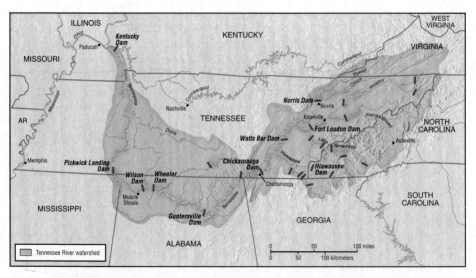

Map 22–3   TVA Projects The Tennessee Valley Authority (TVA) was one of the most ambitious of all New Deal projects. A network of dams provided electricity, irrigation, and flood control to many of the poorest regions of the South.

Struggles For Democracy

The Civilian Conservation Corps and a New Brand of Environmentalism

As Franklin Roosevelt delivered his inaugural address on March 4, 1933, he proclaimed "Our greatest primary task is to put people to work." Upon his arrival in the White House, FDR immediately proposed legislation that would do just that. On March 31, Congress passed the bill establishing the Civilian Conservation Corps (CCC), a program designed to employ young men in the conservation of national forests, the prevention of soil erosion, and the creation and maintenance of state parks. Beyond putting people to work, the program changed the shape of the American landscape and the way citizens viewed both their natural environment and the federal government. Directly rejecting the small government views of the recent past, programs like the CCC highlighted the benefits of extensive government programs and an active government role in citizens' lives.

The CCC demonstrated the government's commitment not only to creating employment opportunities but also to the broader goal of responsible land use and conservation, expanding views about the nature of federal power. From 1933 to 1942, the CCC employed 3 million men who planted 2 billion trees; worked to slow soil erosion on 40 million acres of farmland; and developed 800 new state parks nationwide. The nation's terrain was forever changed by the physical labor of CCC volunteers, as was the nature of American environmentalism. From a fairly small group of progressive conservationists at the turn of the twentieth century, the movement grew in size and scope during the Great Depression,

thanks to the work and education received by CCC volunteers, the benefits enjoyed by those in the communities surrounding the more than 5,000 CCC camps, and the regular media coverage—much of it positive—the general public received about this popular New Deal program. The CCC began the process by which environmental politics shifted from a purview of the elite to a concern shared by a broader segment of the American population. Those politicized by the program advocated on behalf of environmental protection and conservation long after the CCC ceased to exist.

Building on conservationist views developed during the early part of the twentieth century, CCC labor created outdoor spaces intended for leisure, recreation, and renewal. Travelers could visit state parks to escape the hustle and bustle of urban life and restore themselves both mentally and physically. During the lean years of the Depression, a camping trip to a state park provided an affordable alternative to an expensive vacation at an elite hotel or resort. According to the South Carolina Forestry Commission (SCFC), parks would provide "areas where families can find rest and relaxation... where they can absorb the principles of forest conservation." Parks were prized for the leisure they afforded as well as for the appreciation of the natural landscape they instilled in visitors.

South Carolina was one state tremendously influenced by the CCC. Demonstrating the possibility of cooperation between national and local programs, the CCC joined forces with the SCFC to create and maintain a

continued

Struggles For Democracy continued

state park system. When the Depression began, the state had no parks. By 1942, laborers had constructed 16 state parks and 6 wayside parks along state roadways. Unlike other state parks, particularly those in the West, South Carolina parks were not created based on an area's scenic value or natural beauty. Rather, the state used land that had been overworked and stripped of agricultural value. Through the work of the CCC, land was repurposed and value was restored toward an alternative use: recreation. CCC volunteers cleared overgrowth, planted seedling trees, and built structures or facilities, from roads and bridges to lodges and campsites, to dams and lakes. In an effort to preserve and enhance the existing landscape and history of a region, volunteers often used natural materials and local architectural styles to create continuity with the surrounding area.

Like so many New Deal programs, the CCC fundamentally changed national views. The federal government made clear its dedication to preserving the natural environment and providing public access to nature. In return, Americans became more accepting and even expectant of an active government and the possibility that they, as citizens, might play a more active role. Many of those who had volunteered in the CCC continued their conservation efforts well beyond the Depression era, taking jobs in the federal government and with conservation agencies, joining environmental groups, and advocating on behalf of similar conservation programs in the postwar years. Through New Deal programs, people came to believe not only that they had the right to respond to and benefit from public policy but also that they had the right to a voice in its creation.

After 1933, farmers, once fiercely independent, essentially worked for the federal government. The New Deal farm system permanently altered the American diet by making processed grains, grain-fed meat, sugar, and dairy products cheap and plentiful relative to unsubsidized fresh vegetables, fruits, and fish.

In many respects, however, the New Deal did little for the rural poor. Price supports and production controls helped farmers who owned their own land, whereas soil conservation, irrigation, and rural electrification tended to benefit independent commercial farmers. Subsistence farmers and the landless poor—Mexican migrant workers in the Far West and tenants and sharecroppers, Black and white, in the cotton South—gained little. An unintended consequence of New Deal production limits was to take work away from the poorest Americans, pushing them to migrate from the country to industrial cities.

Native Americans suffered an especially severe form of rural poverty. Shunted onto reservations in the late nineteenth century, most American Indians by 1930 were landless, miserably poor, and subjected to the corrupt paternalism of the Bureau of Indian Affairs. Alcoholism, crime, and infant mortality plagued reservations. John Collier, FDR's commissioner of Indian affairs, was determined to correct the situation, and the Indian Reorganization Act of 1934 gave him the power to try. Collier reversed decades of federal attempts to assimilate Native Americans into the mainstream. Under the New Deal, forced land sales ended, and reservations were enlarged. Tribal democracy replaced bureaucratic authority. But congressional opponents, even western liberals, resented attempts to preserve traditional culture. Indians themselves were divided over policies and goals, and what suited Pueblo communities might not work for the Navajo. As a result, although the New Deal relieved some poverty among Native Americans, it did not develop a satisfactory long-term solution.

The Blue Eagle

FDR had no fixed plan for industrial recovery and preferred to wait for business interests to agree on one before acting. Congress, however, moved independently to pass a bill aimed at spreading employment by limiting the workweek to 30 hours. Heading off what he thought an ill-conceived plan, Roosevelt offered his last proposal to become law in the first Hundred Days: the National Industrial Recovery Act. It mandated that business, labor, and government officials negotiate a "code" restructuring each industry into a national cartel. The code would set trade practices, wages, hours, and production quotas. The hope was to raise prices by limiting production while protecting the purchasing power of workers. The NIRA reversed decades of antitrust law. The act protected organized labor by guaranteeing unions the right of collective bargaining. Finally, $3.3 billion was earmarked for jobs creation through a Public Works Administration.

The NIRA was a bold idea, but it suffered from many of the same problems as Hoover's earlier schemes. It brought together hundreds of industries to draw up their codes, but the process tended to be dominated by business. Few strong unions existed, and smaller businesses were shut out, leaving the largest corporations to write the codes in their interest. For a time in 1933 and 1934, the Blue Eagle banner, the symbol of compliance with the codes, flew proudly in the windows of shops and factories. Dissatisfaction with the program soon dampened enthusiasm, and by 1935 the eagle had come to roost atop a shaky and unpopular agency.

THE SECOND NEW DEAL

The first Hundred Days had been extraordinary by any standard. Congress had given the president unprecedented power to regulate the economy. The financial system had been saved from collapse. Federal relief reached the unemployed. The agricultural economy was given direct federal support. The TVA had created a yardstick for public utilities. A bold experiment in industrial planning had been attempted. Almost everyone was dazzled, but not everyone was pleased. Critics noted that much of this legislation was poorly drafted, overly conservative, or just self-contradictory. If Hoover had been too rigid, FDR struck even his admirers as hopelessly flexible. By 1935, the New Deal was besieged by critics from all directions. But Roosevelt responded to political criticism and judicial setbacks by keeping Congress in session throughout the hot summer of 1935. The result was another dramatic wave of reforms known as the second New Deal.

Critics Attack from All Sides

In May 1935, one of William Randolph Hearst's emissaries traveled to Washington to warn Roosevelt that the New Deal was becoming too radical. Hearst was one of the most powerful newspaper publishers in America and, like many businessmen, had "no confidence" in Roosevelt's advisers. But by 1935 Roosevelt was losing patience with the business community. Saving capitalism was always one of Roosevelt's goals, but shortsighted capitalists never appreciated his efforts. They had their own reasons for detesting the New Deal, and they proved more potent critics than all of Roosevelt's radical opponents combined.

The fate of the Communist Party illustrates the difficulties radicals faced during the New Deal. On the one hand, the 1930s were the "heyday of American Communism," as perhaps a quarter of a million disillusioned Americans joined the Communist Party (CPUSA). The Communists organized labor unions and took the lead in defending the Scottsboro Boys, nine young African American men falsely accused of raping two white women in Alabama. On the other hand, the party's appeal was greatest after 1935, when, on orders from the Soviet Union, it adopted a "popular front" strategy in support of the New Deal. The Communists were most popular when they surrendered their revolutionary aims. Most of those who joined had left the party by the end of the decade.

Populist radicals gave Roosevelt more trouble. Father Charles Coughlin was a Catholic priest in Detroit who attracted listeners to his weekly radio show by blaming the Depression on international bankers and Wall Street. His solution was to nationalize the banking system and inflate the currency. At first the radio priest defended Roosevelt and blamed the New Deal on Communist and Jewish influence. But by 1935 Coughlin turned on the president. He formed his own organization, the National Union for Social Justice, to pressure Congress for further reforms.

A California physician, Dr. Francis Townsend, offered an agenda appealing to older Americans devastated by the Depression. Through a transaction tax of 2 percent, the government would fund retirement pensions of $200 per month. By requiring elderly retirees to spend all of their pensions each month, the program was supposed to pump money into the economy and stimulate a recovery. **Huey Long**'s "Share Our Wealth" program was more comprehensive than Townsend's and more popular than Coughlin's. As governor of Louisiana, Long slapped steep taxes on the oil industry that he used for roads, schools, hospitals, and Louisiana State University. In the process, he amassed nearly dictatorial powers, controlling the legislature and the state police. At first, Long was a loyal but critical supporter of FDR, but by 1934 he was proposing his own alternative to the New Deal.

Long believed the Depression was caused by the maldistribution of income. His program for recovery called for the radical redistribution of wealth through confiscatory taxes on the rich and a guaranteed minimum income of $2,500 per year. Townsend's, Coughlin's, and Long's plans all contained truths about the American economy. The currency did need to be inflated. Elderly Americans were indeed desperate, and wealth was unequally distributed. Roosevelt eventually defused these movements by adopting parts of their programs.

The business community's rising hostility concerned FDR as he prepared for his 1936 campaign. It would be years before bankers admitted that the New Deal had saved the financial system. Wall Street never admitted it. And most industrialists became vocal critics of the NIRA. As criticism grew, a conservative US Supreme Court moved to strike down many of the key laws of the first **Hundred Days**. On May 27, 1935, in *Schechter Poultry Corporation v. United States*, the Court invalidated the NIRA. The case had been brought by a small poultry company but was financed by larger companies out to kill the Blue Eagle. The justices ruled the NIRA unconstitutional in a way that made it difficult for Congress to regulate the national economy to any significant degree. Roosevelt feared the setback would undo most of his achievements, and his fears were borne out in January 1936, when the Court overturned the Agricultural Adjustment Act.

The Second Hundred Days

FDR loved a good fight. No longer concerned about attracting support from business, he welcomed criticism and shot right back. After 1935 the rhetoric became noticeably more radical. When the Supreme Court invalidated the NIRA, Roosevelt kept Congress in session through a sweltering summer and forced through a raft of legislation in a "second Hundred Days," which began the second New Deal.

A few of the new proposals were meant to salvage pieces of the NIRA and AAA or to silence radical critics. Hoping to undermine the "crackpot ideas" of Huey Long, Roosevelt proposed a Revenue Act to encourage a "wider distribution of the wealth." It raised estate and corporate taxes and pushed personal income taxes in the top bracket up to 79 percent. Despite the political motives behind the bill, it made economic sense. Before the 1935 Revenue Act, most New Deal programs had been financed by regressive sales and excise taxes. Thereafter, programs were funded with progressive income taxes that fell most heavily on those best able to pay.

The first New Deal had been preoccupied with the emergency of 1933. The second New Deal left a more enduring legacy. The administration finished its program to ensure the long-term security of the financial system and extend the relief programs that had helped so many to survive. It created a **Social Security** system that anchored the American welfare state for the rest of the century. With organized labor it created a new and powerful Democratic Party coalition. By the time Congress adjourned in late August 1935, the most important achievements of the New Deal were in place.

Social Security for Some

Bolstered by big Democratic gains in the 1934 elections, FDR pursued a massive effort to fund work relief by sponsoring the Emergency Relief Appropriations Bill. Providing nearly $5 billion, more than the entire 1932 federal budget, the bill rejuvenated the relief programs of the first New Deal and created a new **Works Progress Administration (WPA)**, headed by Harry Hopkins. The WPA lasted for eight years, employing as many as 3.3 million Americans. WPA workers built bridges, schools, libraries, sewer systems, the Blue Ridge Parkway, and more than 800 airports. The WPA commissioned artists to decorate post offices and historians to collect the stories of mill workers and former enslaved people. At Indiana University, the WPA paid undergraduates to build a student union. WPA lexicographers wrote a Hebrew-English dictionary. The program was hugely popular.

Critics of the WPA complained with some justice about meaningless "make-work" jobs and unqualified workers. Political corruption was a more serious problem. WPA officials, especially at the local level, often used the agency as a patronage machine, favoring loyal party regulars with contracts and jobs. In many states, particularly in the South, officials openly discriminated against African Americans. The WPA was never able to employ all those who needed work, but for millions of Americans it provided immediate relief from the very real prospect of hunger and misery.

The New Deal also created a permanent system of long-term economic security. In 1932, there were no national programs of unemployment insurance, workers' compensation, old-age pensions, or aid to needy children, and the states were only slightly more able to care for citizens. Most Americans had little or no protection from economic calamity.

The Social Security Act of 1935 took a critical first step toward providing such protection. It established matching grants to states that set up their own systems of workers' compensation, unemployment insurance, and aid to families with dependent children. More important, the federal government itself created a huge social security system that guaranteed pensions to millions of elderly Americans. FDR insisted that it be funded as an insurance plan, with payroll taxes paid by employees and employers. He hoped that this would protect the system from the political attacks that welfare programs typically encountered.

Most New Dealers hoped to go much further. Secretary of Labor Frances Perkins wanted to include agricultural laborers and domestic servants, mostly women and African Americans, in the new social security system. But that would have provoked enough opposition from southern conservatives to kill the entire program. The administration also preferred federal- rather than state-run programs. There was, however, no federal bureaucracy in place to run such programs, and there was fierce opposition to the idea of taking such programs away from the states.

Local and factional opposition limited the New Deal's plans for nationalized social welfare and economic security. Welfare and insurance programs were weaker

WPA Mural Japanese artist Eitaro Ishigaki painted this mural showing American Revolutionary War figures at the Harlem Courthouse in New York City in 1938.

in the South than in the North and weaker for women and African Americans than for white men. Despite such strong opposition, the New Deal accomplished many of its goals. By 1939 every state had a program of unemployment insurance and assistance to the elderly. Almost overnight the social security system became the federal government's first huge social welfare bureaucracy. More Americans than ever before were now protected from the ravages of unemployment, disability, poverty, and old age.

Labor and the New Deal

During the 1930s, unions took a new role in America's political and economic life. The number of Americans organized in unions leaped by the millions, and by 1940 nearly one in four non–farm workers was unionized. Labor organizations were able to enroll workers in core industries, including steel, rubber, electronics, and automobiles. Unions also became key players in the Democratic Party. None of the leading New Dealers, Roosevelt included, had anticipated this in 1932, but in critical ways the New Deal fostered the growth of organized labor and its inclusion in the Democratic electoral coalition.

Unlike past administrations, Roosevelt's had never demonstrated outright hostility toward unions. Rather, through the 1930s FDR moved from grudging acceptance to open support for organized labor. Across the country, workers responded to the change. Unions were now allowed to run organizing drives, and labor began to flex its muscle with a spontaneous wave of strikes. Mill workers in the South launched brave, but doomed, strikes against textile manufacturers. Dockworkers in San Francisco organized a successful general strike throughout the city. At the same time, the NIRA inspired a talented group of national leaders, in particular John L. Lewis of the United Mine Workers, Sidney Hillman of the Amalgamated Clothing Workers, and David Dubinsky of the International Ladies' Garment Workers.

Employers fought back against this new militancy. They used all the methods to intimidate workers—espionage, blacklisting, and armed assault—that had once worked so well. But when it became clear that the federal government would now protect workers seeking to organize and bargain collectively, employers formed company unions to thwart workers' independent action. By 1935, the employers seemed to be winning, particularly when the Supreme Court declared the NIRA, and its protection of union rights, unconstitutional. In 1935, worker militancy declined, and the unionization drive seemed stalled. But the hopes of organized labor were kept alive by an influential and imaginative liberal senator from New York named Robert Wagner.

Wagner took the lead in expanding the NIRA's limited labor protections into the National Labor Relations Act, also known as the Wagner Act. Although he had few ties to organized labor, Wagner believed workers had a basic right to join unions. He also hoped that effective unions would stimulate the economy by raising wages, thereby building consumer purchasing power. Like the NIRA provisions, the Wagner Act guaranteed workers the right to bargain collectively with their employers, but it also outlawed company unions, prohibited employers from firing workers after a strike, and restricted many other antiunion tactics. Most important, the Wagner Act created the National Labor Relations Board (NLRB) to enforce these provisions. In the summer of 1935, FDR declared the Wagner Act "must" legislation, and the bill became law.

While Wagner and his colleagues moved in Congress, John L. Lewis and Sidney Hillman took another course. In 1935, they pressed the conservative leadership of the American Federation of Labor to accept the principle of industrial unions, which would organize workers in an entire sector of the economy, such as steel. AFL traditionalists rejected the idea and held fast to the notion that workers should be organized by their crafts, not by whole industries. Thwarted by AFL leadership, Lewis, Hillman, and their allies formed a rival organization that eventually became the Congress of Industrial Organizations (CIO).

The CIO began organizing some of the most powerful and prosperous industries in the country. The government's new attitude toward organized labor played an important role in the CIO's initial success. For example, when the United Automobile Workers initiated a series of sit-down strikes against General Motors, neither Roosevelt nor the Democratic governor of Michigan sent in troops to remove workers from the factories they were occupying. This clear message to the leaders of industry helped to win the strike against America's most powerful corporation. The NLRB also protected the new unions from an employer counterattack during the recession of 1937.

By the late 1930s, a crucial political alliance had formed. A newly vigorous labor movement had become linked to a reinvigorated national Democratic Party. Thanks to this alliance, American industrial workers entered a new era. Having won the ability to organize with the help of the government, industrial workers used their power to increase wages, enhance job security, improve working conditions, and secure their retirements. Organized labor now had a stake in preserving the system from collapse. As much as the banking and financial reforms of the first New Deal, the successful unionization of industrial workers helped stabilize American capitalism.

The New Deal Coalition

Roosevelt believed that to overcome his varied opposition and win reelection he needed to create a coalition far broader than that of 1932. By 1936, the Democratic Party was transformed in fundamental ways. For the first time since the Civil War, a majority of voters identified themselves as Democrats, and the Democrats remained the majority party for decades to come. FDR achieved this feat by forging a powerful coalition between the competing wings of the party. In the end, however, the same coalition that made the New Deal possible also limited its progressivism.

The rural South had been overwhelmingly Democratic for a century, but urban voters in the North became the party's new base. This shift was well under way during the 1920s, when Al Smith's two presidential bids attracted ethnic blue-collar voters. FDR offered prominent ethnic Americans an unprecedented number of federal appointments. Jews and Catholics (Italian, as well as Irish) served Roosevelt as advisers, judges, and cabinet officers. More important, thousands of working-class city dwellers found jobs with the CWA, the WPA, or the CCC. Those New Deal programs generated a flood of patronage appointments that endeared Roosevelt to local Democratic machines. Finally, the unions reciprocated FDR's support for labor. The CIO alone poured $600,000 into Roosevelt's campaign, replacing the money no longer forthcoming from wealthy donors, and its members formed an army of campaign volunteers. By 1940, the Democratic Party became the party of the urban working class.

The New Deal's programs also explain a dramatic shift of allegiance among African American voters. Since Reconstruction, southern Blacks had supported the party of Lincoln, but as they migrated to the urban North they gained voting strength and abandoned the Republican Party. By 1936, northern Blacks voted overwhelmingly for FDR, even though the Democrats were weak on the issue of civil rights. The New Deal included no legislation against discrimination, and FDR silently allowed Congress to reject antilynching laws. New Deal agencies did offer more assistance to poor, unemployed African Americans than previous federal programs, and some leading New Dealers supported equal rights. **Mary McLeod Bethune**, a prominent African American educator and close friend of Eleanor Roosevelt, served the New Deal as director of the National Youth Administration's Office of Negro Affairs, which gave jobs and training to some 300,000 young African Americans. Besides controlling her own Special Negro Fund, Bethune convinced other New Deal administrators to open their programs to Blacks. With perhaps a million African American families depending on the WPA by 1939, Black voters had solid reasons for joining the New Deal coalition.

A similar logic explains why women reformers threw their support to the Democrats in the 1930s. Once again, FDR had no feminist agenda, and New Deal programs discriminated against women by offering lower pay and restricting jobs by sex. But women also benefited in unprecedented numbers from New Deal welfare and jobs programs. For the first time in American history, a woman, Frances Perkins, was appointed to the cabinet.

The most prominent female reformer associated with the New Deal was Eleanor Roosevelt. She was in many ways the last great representative of a woman's reform tradition that flourished in the Progressive Era. She had worked in a settlement house and campaigned for suffrage and progressive causes. Eleanor and Franklin made a remarkable political couple. Millions of Americans read Eleanor's opinions in her weekly newspaper column, "My Day." She became for many the conscience of the New Deal, the person closest to the president who spoke most forcefully for the downtrodden. Her well-deserved reputation for compassion also protected her husband. Liberals who might have been more critical of the New Deal instead relied on Eleanor Roosevelt to push the president toward more progressive reform. At the same time, conservatives who were charmed by FDR's personality blamed the faults of the New Deal on his wife. "It was very simple," one southern journalist explained. "Credit Franklin, better known as He, for all the things you like, and blame Eleanor, better known as She, or 'that woman,' for all the things you don't like."

Although four years of the New Deal had not lifted the Depression, the economy was making headway. Jobs programs had put millions of Americans to work; the banking crisis was over; the rural economy had been stabilized. Based on this record and the backing of his powerful coalition of southern whites, northern urban voters, the labor movement, and many other Americans, FDR won reelection by a landslide in 1936. He captured over 60 percent of the popular vote and, in the Electoral College, defeated his Republican opponent Alf Landon in every state but Maine and Vermont. Landon, the governor of Kansas, even lost his home state. The new Democratic coalition also won sweeping command of the Congress, and Roosevelt now stood at the peak of his power.

CRISIS OF THE NEW DEAL

In 1937, it seemed as if Roosevelt was unbeatable, but within a year the New Deal was all but paralyzed. A politically costly fight to "pack" the Supreme Court at last gave FDR's conservative opponents a winning issue. A sharp recession encouraged the New Deal's enemies and provoked an intellectual crisis within the administration. In 1938, when the Republicans regained much of their congressional strength, the reform energies of the New Deal were largely spent. Within a year the nation turned its attention to rising threats from overseas.

Conservatives Counterattack

With conservative opponents vanquished, it seemed as if New Dealers could finish the job begun in 1933. Administration progressives such as Frances Perkins hoped that existing legislation could now be strengthened.

FDR seemed poised to launch the next great wave of New Deal reforms, but one apparently immovable barrier stood in the way: the US Supreme Court. The Court had already struck down the NIRA and the AAA, and recent rulings made it seem that neither Social Security nor the Wagner Act was safe from the Court's nine "old men." Roosevelt wanted to change the Court. He had not yet had the opportunity to appoint any new justices, and pundits joked that the elderly judges refused to die. Sure that a constitutional amendment supporting his program would take too long or fail, FDR launched a reckless and unpopular effort to "reform" the Court. He proposed legislation that would allow the president to appoint a new justice for every sitting member of the Court over 70 years of age. This "court packing" plan, as opponents labeled it, would have given the president as many as six new appointments.

Conservatives had long complained of FDR's "dictatorial" powers, and the court plan seemed to confirm their warnings. They skillfully cultivated congressional allies, giving Democrats the lead in opposing the court reform. Even his allies refused to campaign for the president's bill, and it took all of FDR's political power and prestige to keep it before a hostile Congress. By the end of the summer of 1937, the bill was defeated.

Ironically, Roosevelt won his point. Several justices soon retired, giving FDR the critical appointments he needed, and the Supreme Court backed away from its narrow conception of the role of the federal government. Nevertheless, FDR's court plan proved a costly mistake, and its defeat emboldened his opponents. In November 1937, the administration's critics issued a Conservative Manifesto calling for balanced budgets, states' rights, lower taxes, and the defense of private property and the capitalist system, themes that would rally conservatives for the remainder of the century. Behind the manifesto lay some hard political realities that drove the conservatives into opposition.

American Landscape
The 1937 Ohio River Flood

On January 20, 1937, just as Franklin Roosevelt was inaugurated to serve his second term in office, the Ohio River began to flood in a manner the likes of which those in towns and cities along its flow had never seen. The federal government and local governments had long neglected river stewardship and flood prevention , and even with conservation efforts generated as part of Roosevelt's New Deal, the timing and magnitude of the 1937 flood taxed local governments, federal programs, and relief agencies as they responded to the crisis.

By the time the flood concluded, it had devastated communities from Pittsburgh, Pennsylvania to Cairo, Illinois, one million Americans who lived along the Ohio River were homeless, and property losses reached $500 million. Devastation could have been greater, however, without relatively recent developments in federal infrastructure and media technology.

Local governments, national organizations like the American Red Cross, those working for New Deal projects such as the Civilian Conservation Corps and the Works Progress Administration, and, when necessary, Coast Guard and National Guard troops shored up levees and restored power lines; evacuated people and their possession; and provided medical care, food, and supplies. In Louisville, Kentucky, as important as any of the relief and rescue organizations was local radio station WHAS.

On January 21, the station acknowledged not only rising waters and the likelihood of continued rainfall, but warned listeners that "the Ohio Valley is facing the most alarming flood we have ever had on the Ohio River." The advisory urged listeners to be prepared for a "move to higher ground at a moment's notice."

The Ohio River climbed six feet on the day of WHAS's report and then continued above the 46.7 foot crest it had reached during the epic flood of 1884, eventually hitting 57 feet. WHAS provided Louisville residents with eye witness testimony from the first. Announcers traveled around the city in hip boots, rain coats, and hats to interview those caught in the flood and report what they saw. When the station received a deluge of calls from confused city residents, unsure of the extent of the flood or how to respond, station agents decided to forgo normal programming—interviews, local news, live performances of "hill billy music"— in favor of an all-flood schedule.

WHAS employees spent the night at the station and read continuous bulletins and calls for rescue. Announcers continued to venture into the city and report back. When it looked as though the station would lose power and access to their transmitter, they asked for and were granted access to Nashville station WSM's transmitter. Powered by generators, even as Louisville went dark on January 24, widely known as Black Sunday, WHAS remained on air. Moving the story beyond Louisville, CBS broadcast the WHAS feed to their network, and the BBC received permission from Washington, DC to share the station's broadcast in the United Kingdom.

The station provided a platform for Mayor Neville Miller, whose leadership guided the city through the crisis. Sounding upbeat but never naïve, Miller maintained contact with city residents and offered guidance and reassurance. With three quarters of the city underwater but tens of thousands still

continued

American Landscape continued

Ohio River Flood Residents of Louisville, Kentucky cross a temporary bridge erected over the rising flood waters of the Ohio River.

remaining in the municipality, Mayor Miller feared the spread of communicable disease and asked for state support to evacuate holdouts. With the arrival of National Guard troops and a sustained evacuation effort, WHAS shifted its function, no longer airing rescue or supply requests but sharing bulletins about residents' whereabouts in hopes of reuniting separated families.

WHAS allowed not only for sustained communication but also cooperation among the various parties offering Louisville citizens flood rescue and relief. The station served a vital communication function and acted as a kind of logistical command center for the various enterprises responding to the flood in tandem. It shared vital information not only with residents but also among and between the local, military, and volunteer agencies navigating the city.

At 2:30 a.m., on February 1, WHAS went off air, concluding 187 hours and 30 minutes of continuous broadcast, during which announcers shared 115,000 flood-related bulletins. Announcer Barry Bingham signed off by saying, "WHAS is now preparing to sign off with a final word of gratitude to all who have helped us in this crisis through which we have passed. From our hearts we say, 'thank you and good night.'"

The Liberal Crisis of Confidence

During the 1936 campaign, Roosevelt was stung by conservative criticism of his failure to balance the budget. He had leveled the same charge against Hoover four years earlier, but the demands of the Depression made it difficult and dangerous to reduce government spending. Deficit spending seemed to help resuscitate the economy.

Hoping to silence conservative critics, Roosevelt ordered a sharp cutback in relief expenditures in 1937. On top of an ill-timed contraction of the money supply and the removal of $2 billion from the economy by the new Social Security taxes, the measure had a disastrous effect. Once again, the stock market crashed and industrial production plummeted. Even the relatively healthy automobile, rubber, and electrical industries were seriously hurt. Opponents carped about the "Roosevelt Recession" and accused the administration of destroying business confidence.

Among the president's advisers, the competition between the budget balancers and the deficit spenders intensified. This was an important turning point in the New Deal and in twentieth-century American politics. Until 1938, the orthodoxy that associated economic health with balanced budgets was entrenched in government and the business community. The recession of 1937–1938 converted young New Dealers to the newer economic theories associated with John Maynard Keynes, the great English economist. During periods of economic stagnation, Keynes argued, the government needs to stimulate recovery through deficit spending. The goal of fiscal policy was no longer to encourage production, but rather to increase the purchasing power of ordinary consumers. Roosevelt never fully embraced these theories, but more and more members of his administration did. Moreover, the breathtaking economic revival created by massive government expenditures in World War II seemed to validate Keynesian economics. Until the 1980s, presidents of both parties subscribed to Keynesian theory, although they differed on what kind of government programs federal spending should buy.

CONCLUSION

The New Deal did not bring an end to the Depression, and this was undoubtedly its greatest failure. Nevertheless, FDR achieved other important goals. "I want to save our system," he said in 1935, "the capitalistic system." By this standard, the New Deal was a smashing success. By allowing Americans to survive the worst collapse in the history of capitalism while preserving core freedoms, the New Deal reaffirmed democracy at a time when most of the industrialized world chose dictatorship. Through the expansion of the federal government, the New Deal also created a system of security for the vast majority of Americans. National systems of unemployment compensation, old-age pensions, and welfare programs were born during the 1930s, and the nature of Americans' relationship to the government changed fundamentally. With the creation of the federal system of security, the government accepted at least some responsibility for citizens' economic security. Farm owners received new protections, as did the very soil of the nation. Workers were granted the right to organize, hours of labor were limited, child labor ended, and wages were held above the bare minimum. The financial system was stabilized and strengthened. America was a safer place at the end of the 1930s, but the world had become more dangerous. After 1938 the Roosevelt administration was increasingly preoccupied with the threatening behavior of nations that had responded poorly to the challenge of the Great Depression.

WHO, WHAT, WHERE /3

Bethune, Mary McCleod   739

Civilian Conservation Corps
    (CCC)   729

Dust Bowl   718

Great Depression   719

Hoovervilles   723

Hundred Days   735

Long, Huey   734

New Deal   718

Roosevelt, Eleanor   729

Roosevelt, Franklin D.   725

Social Security   735

Tennessee Valley Authority
    (TVA)   730

Works Progress Administration
    (WPA)   735

REVIEW QUESTIONS

1. Did the stock market crash cause the Great Depression?

2. How did Roosevelt's philosophy of government differ from Hoover's?

3. What setbacks caused FDR to launch a second New Deal?

TIME LINE

▼**1929**
Stock market crash

▼**1930**
Hawley-Smoot Tariff
    enacted

▼**1931**
National Credit Corporation
    authorized

▼**1932**
Franklin D. Roosevelt
    elected president

▼**1933**
FDR declares a bank
    holiday
First Hundred Days
Emergency Banking Act
    passed
Civilian Conservation Corps
    (CCC)
United States goes off the
    gold standard
Agricultural Adjustment Act
    (AAA)
Tennessee Valley Authority
    (TVA)

Truth in Securities Act
National Industrial Recovery Act (NIRA)
Glass-Steagall Banking Act
Farm Credit Act

▼**1935**
Second Hundred Days
NIRA declared
    unconstitutional
National Labor Relations
    (Wagner) Act
Social Security Act

CRITICAL-THINKING QUESTIONS

1. Compare the American response to the Depression with that of Britain, Germany, and Japan. Why did other industrial countries choose different paths?

2. What were Roosevelt's attributes as a leader? What aspects of his style inspired confidence or animosity?

3. Histories of the Depression focus on national statistics and large-scale programs. How could you retell the story of the 1930s from a local, personal perspective?

SUGGESTED READINGS

Brinkley, Alan. *The End of Reform: New Deal Liberalism in Depression and War*. New York: Knopf, 1995.

Cohen, Lizabeth. *Making a New Deal: Industrial Workers in Chicago, 1919–1939*. New York: Cambridge University Press, 1990.

Dickstein, Morris. *Dancing in the Dark: A Cultural History of the Great Depression*. New York: Norton, 2009.

George Washington University. The Eleanor Roosevelt Papers. https://erpapers.columbian. gwu.edu/

Wall, Wendy. *Inventing the "American Way": The Politics of Consensus from the New Deal to the Civil Rights Movement*. New York: Oxford University Press, 2008.

For further review materials and resource information, please visit www.oup.com/us/ofthepeople

▼**1936**
Agricultural Adjustment Act
  (AAA) overturned
FDR reelected

▼**1937**
FDR announces "court
  packing" plan
Economy goes into
  recession

▼**1938**
Second Agricultural Adjust-
  ment Act
Fair Labor Standards Act
New Deal opponents win
  big in Congress

▼**1939**
Administrative Reorganization Act

CHAPTER 22: A Great Depression and a New Deal, 1929–1940
Primary Sources

22.1 FRANKLIN D. ROOSEVELT, FIRST INAUGURAL ADDRESS (1933)

As he faced the nation on March 4, 1933, the newly elected President Franklin Delano Roosevelt spoke candidly, but optimistically, to the American people. While admitting the terrible realities of the Depression, he also reassured the American public that they had not failed, that the nation could—and would—be restored. He called upon citizens to trust in his leadership and articulated a plan for government action as a means of solving the economic crisis.

I am certain that my fellow Americans expect that on my induction into the Presidency I will address them with a candor and a decision which the present situation of our Nation impels. This is preeminently the time to speak the truth, the whole truth, frankly and boldly. Nor need we shrink from honestly facing conditions in our country today. This great Nation will endure as it has endured, will revive and will prosper. So, first of all, let me assert my firm belief that the only thing we have to fear is fear itself—nameless, unreasoning, unjustified terror which paralyzes needed efforts to convert retreat into advance. In every dark hour of our national life a leadership of frankness and vigor has met with that understanding and support of the people themselves which is essential to victory. I am convinced that you will again give that support to leadership in these critical days.

In such a spirit on my part and on yours we face our common difficulties. They concern, thank God, only material things. Values have shrunken to fantastic levels; taxes have risen; our ability to pay has fallen; government of all kinds is faced by serious curtailment of income; the means of exchange are frozen in the currents of trade; the withered leaves of industrial enterprise lie on every side; farmers find no markets for their produce; the savings of many years in thousands of families are gone. More important, a host of unemployed citizens face the grim problem of existence, and an equally great number toil with little return. Only a foolish optimist can deny the dark realities of the moment.

Yet our distress comes from no failure of substance. We are stricken by no plague of locusts. Compared with the perils which our forefathers conquered because they believed and were not afraid, we have still much to be thankful for. Nature still offers her bounty and human efforts have multiplied it. Plenty is at our doorstep, but a generous use of it languishes in the very sight of the supply. Primarily this is because rulers of the exchange of mankind's goods have failed through their own stubbornness and their own incompetence, have admitted their failure, and have abdicated. Practices of the unscrupulous money changers stand indicted in the court of public opinion, rejected by the hearts and minds of men.

True they have tried, but their efforts have been cast in the pattern of an outworn tradition. Faced by failure of credit they have proposed only the lending of more money. Stripped of the lure of profit by which to induce our people to follow their false leadership, they have resorted to exhortations, pleading tearfully for restored confidence. They know only the rules of a generation of self-seekers. They have no vision, and when there is no vision the people perish.

The money changers have fled from their high seats in the temple of our civilization. We may now restore that temple to the ancient truths. The measure of the restoration lies in the extent to which we apply social values more noble than mere monetary profit. Happiness lies not in the mere possession of money; it lies in the joy of achievement, in the thrill of creative effort. The joy and moral stimulation of work no longer must be forgotten in the mad chase of evanescent profits. These dark days will be worth all they cost us if they teach us that our true destiny is not to be ministered unto but to minister to ourselves and to our fellow men.

Recognition of the falsity of material wealth as the standard of success goes hand in hand with the abandonment of the false belief that public office and high political position are to be valued only by the standards of pride of place and personal profit; and there must be an end to a conduct in banking and in business which too often has given to a sacred trust the likeness of callous and selfish wrongdoing. Small wonder that confidence languishes, for it thrives only on honesty, on honor, on the sacredness of obligations, on faithful protection, on unselfish performance; without them it cannot live.

Restoration calls, however, not for changes in ethics alone. This Nation asks for action, and action now.

Our greatest primary task is to put people to work. This is no unsolvable problem if we face it wisely and courageously. It can be accomplished in part by direct recruiting by the Government itself, treating the task as we would treat the emergency of a war, but at the same time, through this employment, accomplishing greatly needed projects to stimulate and reorganize the use of our natural resources.

Hand in hand with this we must frankly recognize the overbalance of population in our industrial centers and, by engaging on a national scale in a redistribution, endeavor to provide a better use of the land for those best fitted for the land. The task can be helped by definite efforts to raise the values of agricultural products and with this the power to purchase the output of our cities. It can be helped by preventing realistically the tragedy of the growing loss through foreclosure of our small homes and our farms. It can be helped by insistence that the Federal, State, and local governments act forthwith on the demand that their cost be drastically reduced. It can be helped by the unifying of relief activities which today are often scattered, uneconomical, and unequal. It can be helped by national planning for and supervision of all forms of transportation and of communications and other utilities which have a definitely public character. There are many ways in which it can be helped, but it can never be helped merely by talking about it. We must act and act quickly.

Finally, in our progress toward a resumption of work we require two safeguards against a return of the evils of the old order: there must be a strict supervision of all banking and credits and investments, so that there will be an end to speculation with other people's money; and there must be provision for an adequate but sound currency.

These are the lines of attack. I shall presently urge upon a new Congress, in special session, detailed measures for their fulfillment, and I shall seek the immediate assistance of the several States.

Through this program of action we address ourselves to putting our own national house in order and making income balance outgo. Our international trade relations, though vastly important, are in point of time and necessity secondary to the establishment of a sound national economy. I favor as a practical policy the putting of first things first. I shall spare no effort to restore world trade by international economic readjustment, but the emergency at home cannot wait on that accomplishment.

The basic thought that guides these specific means of national recovery is not narrowly nationalistic. It is the insistence, as a first consideration, upon the interdependence of the various elements in and parts of the United States—a recognition of the old and permanently important manifestation of the American spirit of the pioneer. It is the way to recovery. It is the immediate way. It is the strongest assurance that the recovery will endure. In the field of world policy I would dedicate this Nation to the policy of the good neighbor—the neighbor who resolutely respects himself and, because he does so, respects the rights of others—the neighbor who respects his obligations and respects the sanctity of his agreements in and with a world of neighbors.

If I read the temper of our people correctly, we now realize as we have never realized before our interdependence on each other; that we cannot merely take but we must give as well; that if we are to go forward, we must move as a trained and loyal army willing to sacrifice for the good of a common discipline, because without such discipline no progress is made, no leadership becomes effective. We are, I know, ready and willing to submit our lives and property to such discipline, because it makes possible a leadership which aims at a larger good. This I propose to offer, pledging that the larger purposes will bind upon us all as a First Inaugural Address sacred obligation with a unity of duty hitherto evoked only in time of armed strife.

With this pledge taken, I assume unhesitatingly the leadership of this great army of our people dedicated to a disciplined attack upon our common problems. Action in this image and to this end is feasible under the form of government which we have inherited from our ancestors. Our Constitution is so simple and practical that it is possible always to meet extraordinary needs by changes in emphasis and arrangement without loss of essential form. That is why our constitutional system has proved itself the most superbly enduring political mechanism the modern world has produced. It has met every stress of vast expansion of territory, of foreign wars, of bitter internal strife, of world relations. It is to be hoped that the normal balance of Executive and legislative authority may be wholly adequate to meet the unprecedented task before us. But it may be that an unprecedented demand and need for undelayed action may call for temporary departure from that normal balance of public procedure.

I am prepared under my constitutional duty to recommend the measures that a stricken Nation in the midst of a stricken world may require. These measures, or such other measures as the Congress may build out of its experience and wisdom, I shall seek, within my constitutional authority, to bring to speedy adoption.

But in the event that the Congress shall fail to take one of these two courses, and in the event that the national emergency is still critical, I shall not evade the clear course of duty that will then confront me. I shall ask the Congress for the one remaining instrument to meet the crisis—broad Executive power to wage a war against the emergency, as great as the power that would be given to me if we were in fact invaded by a foreign foe. For the trust reposed in me I will return the courage and the devotion that befit the time. I can do no less.

We face the arduous days that lie before us in the warm courage of national unity; with the clear consciousness of seeking old and precious moral values; with the clean satisfaction that comes from the stern performance of duty by old and young alike. We aim at the assurance of a rounded and permanent national life. We do not distrust the future of essential democracy. The people of the United States have not failed. In their need they have registered a mandate that they want direct, vigorous action. They have asked for discipline and direction under leadership. They have made me the present instrument of their wishes. In the spirit of the gift I take it.

In this dedication of a Nation we humbly ask the blessing of God. May He protect each and every one of us. May He guide me in the days to come.

Source: *The Public Papers and Addresses of Franklin D. Roosevelt with a Special Introduction and Explanatory Notes by President Roosevelt, Volume 2: The Year of Crisis, 1933* (New York: Random House, 1938), pp. 11–16.

22.2 VISUAL DOCUMENTS: DOROTHEA LANGE, FARM SECURITY ADMINISTRATION PHOTOGRAPHS (1930s)

Dorothea Lange photographed men and women as part of the Farm Security Administration's photography project. Through her work she portrayed the challenges people faced as they attempted to make a living during the harsh economic circumstances of the Great Depression. Images of families traveling in cars tightly packed with possessions as they searched for employment, living in makeshift tents as they moved from one work site to the next, and attempting to maintain some element of normalcy in the midst of financial struggle revealed the toll the Depression took on the American people.

Drought refugees from Oklahoma looking for work in the pea fields of California, near San Jose Mission. March 1935.

Florence Owens Thompson, age 32, mother of seven children. Nipomo, California. February or March 1936.

Wife and child of migrant worker encamped near Winters, California. November 1936.

Source: Dorothea Lange, photographer. US Farm Security Administration, Office of War Information Photograph Collection. Library of Congress Prints and Photographs Division, Washington, DC.

22.3 "BALLAD FOR AMERICANS," FEDERAL THEATER PROJECT, *SING FOR YOUR SUPPER* (1939)

Part of the Works Progress Administration, the Federal Theater Project was a relief program intended to employ artists, writers, and performers and provide Americans with the opportunity to see live, original theater. Critics, however, deemed it an unnecessary expenditure (despite being only 0.5 percent of the WPA budget) and claimed it a breeding ground for communist sympathies and potential revolution. While the FTP cast a critical eye on inequality, the project was hardly anti-American. "Ballad for Americans," originally called "Ballad of Uncle Sam" acknowledged the problems of the American present, but ultimately celebrated the values of the country's past and what it saw as the promise of the whole of its population, reflecting President Roosevelt's attention to and faith in the common man (and woman) of the nation.

Soloist:
In seventy-six the sky was red
Thunder rumbling overhead
Bad King George couldn't sleep in his bed
And on that stormy morn, old Uncle Sam was born.

Ensemble:
Some birthday!
S: Ol' Sam put on a three-cornered hat
And in a Richmond church he sat

And Patrick Henry told him that
While America drew breath
All: It was "Liberty or Death."
Ens: What kind of hat is a three-cornered hat?

A Woman: Did they all believe in liberty in those days?
Solo: Nobody who was anybody believed it.
Ev'rybody who was anybody they doubted it.

Nobody had faith, nobody.
Nobody but Washington, Tom Paine, Benjamin Franklin,
Chaim Solomon, Crispus Attucks, Lafayette.
Nobodies.

A Man: The nobodies ran a tea party at Boston.
A Woman: Betsy Ross organized a sewing circle.
A Man: Paul Revere had a horse race.
Solo: And a little ragged group believed it.

And some gentlemen and ladies believed it.
And some wise men and some fools,
And I believed it too.
And you know who I am.

A Man: No. Who are you, Mister?
A Woman: Yeah, how come all this?
Solo: Well, I'll tell you. Now let me—
Ens: No, let us tell you.

Then Mister Tom Jefferson, a mighty fine man.
He wrote it down in a mighty fine plan.
And the rest all signed it with a mighty fine han'
As they crossed their "t"s and dotted their "i"s

A bran' new country did arise.
Solo: And a mighty fine idea.
A Man: Adopted unanimously in Congress July 4, 1776.
Solo: We hold these truths to be self-evident,

That all men are created equal.
All: That they are endowed by their creator
With certain inalienable rights.
Ens: That among these rights are Life!

Solo: Yes sir!
Ens: Liberty!
Solo: That's right!
Ens: And the pursuit of happiness!

A Woman: Is that what they said?
Solo: The very words.
A Woman: That does sound mighty fine.
Ens: Building a nation is awful tough.

The people found the going rough.
And thirteen states weren't large enough.
So they started to expand —
Into the western lands!
Solo: Still nobody who was anybody believed it.

Everybody who was anybody they stayed at home.
But Lewis and Clark and the pioneers,
Driven by hunger, haunted by fears,
The Klondike miners and the Forty-Niners,

Some wanted freedom and some wanted riches,
Some liked to loaf while others dug ditches.
Ens: But they believed in it.
Solo: And I believed it too.

And you know who I am.
A Man: No, who are you anyway, Mister?
Solo: Well, I started to tell you
A Woman: Yes, Mister, tell us who you are.
Solo: You see, I represent the whole . . .

[Ensemble hums]
Solo: That's it!
Ens: Let my people go.
Solo: That's the idea!

All: Old Abe Lincoln was thin and long,
His heart was high and his faith was strong.
But he hated oppression, he hated wrong,
And he went down to his grave to free the slave.

Ens: Man in white skin can never be free
While his black brother is in slavery,
"And we here highly resolve that these dead
Shall not have died in vain.

And government of the people, by the people and for the people
All: Shall not perish from the Earth."
A Man: Abraham Lincoln said that on November 19, 1863 at Gettysburg,
Pennsylvania.

Solo: And he was right. I believe that too.
A Man: Say, we still don't know who you are, Mister.
Solo: Well, I started to tell you . . .
Ens: The machine age came with a great big roar,

As America grew in peace and war.
And a million wheels went around and 'round.
The cities reached into the sky
And dug down deep into the ground.

And some got rich and some got poor.
But the people carried through,
So our country grew.
Solo: Still nobody who was anybody believed it.

Everybody who was anybody they doubted it.
And they are doubting still,
And I guess they always will,
But who cares what they say

When I am on my way—
Ens: Say, will you please tell us who you are?
A Man: What's your name, Buddy?
A Man: Where you goin'?

A Man: Who are you?
Solo: Well, I'm everybody who's nobody,
I'm the nobody who's everybody.
A Man: What's your racket?

What do you do for a living?
Solo: Well, I'm an
Engineer, musician, street cleaner, carpenter, teacher,
A Man: How about a farmer?
Solo: Also.

A Woman: Office clerk?
Solo: Yes, ma'am.
A Man: Mechanic?
Solo: That's right.

A Woman: Housewife?
Solo: Certainly!
A Man: Factory worker?
Solo: You said it.

A Woman: Stenographer?
Solo: Uh huh.

A Woman: Beauty Specialist?
Solo: Absotively!

A Man: Bartender?
Solo: Posolutely!
A Man: Truck driver?
Solo: Definitely!

Ens: Miner, seamstress, ditchdigger,
Solo: All of them.
I am the "etceteras" and the "and so forths" that do the work.
A Man: Now hold on here, what are you trying to give us?

A Woman: Are you an American?
Solo: Am I an American?
I'm just an Irish, Negro, Jewish, Italian,
French and English, Spanish, Russian,

Chinese, Polish, Scotch, Hungarian,
Litvak, Swedish, Finnish, Canadian,
Greek and Turk and Czech
And double check American.

And that ain't all.
I was baptized Baptist, Methodist, Congregationalist, Lutheran,
Atheist, Roman Catholic, Orthodox Jewish, Presbyterian,
Seventh Day Adventist, Mormon, Quaker, Christian Scientist and lots more.

Ens: You sure are something.
All: Our country's strong, our country's young,
And her greatest songs are still unsung.
From her plains and mountains we have sprung

To keep the faith with those who went before.
Ens: We nobodies who are anybody believe it.
We anybodies who are everybody have no doubts.
Solo: Out of the cheating, out of the shouting.

Out of the murders and lynching
All: Out of the windbags, the patriotic spouting,
Out of uncertainty and doubting,
Out of the carpetbag and the brass spittoon
It will come again.

Our marching song will come again!
Ens: Simple as a hit tune,
Deep as our valleys,
High as our mountains,

Strong as the people who made it.
Solo: For I have always believed it,
And I believe it now.
And you know who I am.

Ens: Who are you?
Solo: America!
All: America!

Source: "Ballad for Americans" (1939) Music by Earl Robinson; lyric by John Latouche. http://blog.
nyfos.org/earl-robinson-john-latouche-ballad-americans.

22.4 REMEMBERING THE GREAT DEPRESSION, EXCERPTS FROM STUDS TERKEL'S *HARD TIMES* (1970)

Americans experienced the Great Depression in different ways, and those experiences evolved as the economic crisis continued. One constant, however, seemed to be a sense that the nation had changed and was continuing to change in fundamental ways. During the 1960s, famed radio host and oral historian Studs Terkel interviewed Americans to gain a sense of how they had endured the crisis and how they remembered the Great Depression and FDR's New Deal.

James Ward: James lost his job at a publishing house in 1935; he was out of work for six months until he began work as part of the Illinois Writers' Project.

I was out of work six months. I was losing my contacts as well as my energy. I kept going from one publishing house to another. I never got past the telephone operator. It was just wasted time. One of the worst things was occupying your time, sensibly. You'd go to the library.

You took a magazine to the room and sat and read. I didn't have a radio. I tried to do some writing and found I couldn't concentrate. The day was long. There was nothing to do evenings. I was going around in circles, it was terrifying. So I just vegetated.

With some people I knew, there was a coldness, shunning: I'd rather not see you just now. Maybe *I'll* lose my job next week. On the other hand, I made some very close friends, who were merely acquaintances before. If I needed $5 for room rent or something, it was available. . . .

I went to apply for unemployment insurance, which had just been put into effect. I went three weeks in succession. It still hadn't come through. Then I discovered the catch. At that time, anybody who earned more than $3,000 a year was not paid unemployment insurance unless his employer had O.K.'d it. It could be withheld. My employer exercised his option of not O.K.'ing it. He exercised his vindictive privilege. I don't think that's the law anymore.

I finally went on relief. It's an experience I don't want anybody to go through. It comes as close to crucifixion as. . . . You sit in an auditorium and are given a number. The interview was utterly ridiculous and mortifying. In the middle of mine, a more dramatic guy than I dived from the second floor stairway, head first, to demonstrate he was gonna get on relief even if he had to go to the hospital to do it.

There were questions like: Who are your friends? Where have you been living? Where's your family? I had sent my wife and child to her folks in Ohio, where they could live more simply. Why should anybody give you money? Why should anybody give you a place to sleep? What sort of friends? That went on for half an hour. I got angry and said, "Do you happen to know what a friend is?" He changed his attitude very shortly. I did get certified some time later. I think they paid $9 a month.

I came away feeling I didn't have any business living any more. I was imposing on somebody, a great society or something like that.

Joe Marcus: an economist who graduated from college in 1935 and went to work as part of the New Deal in 1936.

The New Deal was a young man's world. Young people, if they showed any ability, got an opportunity. I was a kid, twenty-two or twenty-three. In a few months, I was made head of the department. We had a meeting with hot shots: What's to be done? I pointed out some problems: let's define what we're looking for. They immediately had me take over. I had to set up the organization and hire seventy-five people. Given a chance as a youngster to try out ideas, I learned a fantastic amount. The challenge itself was great.

It was the idea of being asked big questions. The technical problems were small. These you had to solve by yourself. But the context was broad: Where was society going? Your statistical questions became questions of full employment. You were not prepared for it in school. If you wanted new answers, you needed a new kind of people. This is what was exciting.

Ordinarily, I might have had a job at the university, marking papers or helping a professor. All of a sudden, I'm doing original research and asking basic questions about how our society works. What makes a Depression? What makes for pulling out of it? Once you start thinking in these terms, you're in a different ball game.

The climate was exciting. You were part of a society that was on the move. You were involved in something that could make a difference. Laws could be changed. So could the conditions of people.

The idea of being involved close to the center of political life was unthinkable, just two or three years before all this happened. Unthinkable for someone like me, of lower middle-class, close to ghetto, Jewish life. Suddenly you were a significant member of society. It was not the kind of closed society you lived in before. . . .

You were really part of something, changes could be made. Bringing *immediate* results to people who were starving. You could do something about it: that was the most important thing. This you felt.

A feeling that if you had something to say, it would get to the top. As I look back now, memoranda I had written reached the White House, one way or another. The biggest thrill of my life was hearing a speech of Roosevelt's, using a selection from a memorandum I had written.

Everybody was searching for ideas. . . . there was a search, a sense of values. . . that would make a difference in the lives of people.

We weren't thinking of remaking society. That wasn't it. I didn't buy this dream stuff. What was happening was a complete change in social attitudes at the central government level. The questions was: How can you do it within this system? People working in all the New Deal agencies were dominated by this spirit. . . .

At one stage Harry Hopkins met with his staff, a lot of people, in a huge auditorium. He explained they'd have to work day and night to get this particular job done. He asked for volunteers, who would start off tonight and work straight through. Practically everybody in the auditorium raised their hands. Youth and fervor.

Normally, administrative people were much older. But even the young of the old bureaucracy were stodgy. They came to work, left their jobs when the day was over, went out for their lunches. . . . Frankly, they didn't work very hard and knocked off whenever they could. What right-wingers say about Government employees was very true in many cases.

The New Dealers were different. I'm not only talking about policy people. I'm talking about the clerks, who felt what they were doing was important. You didn't take time out for lunch because of a job that had to be done. You had a sandwich on the desk. Their jobs made sense. . . .

Source: Studs Terkel, *Hard Times: An Oral History of the Great Depression* (New York: Pantheon Books, 1970), 421–422, 265–267.

The Second World War
1941–1945

< The Black Eagles

A. Philip Randolph

"Who is this guy Randolph," Joseph Rauh wondered, and "what the hell has he got on the President of the U.S.?" It was June 1941, and Rauh, a government attorney, had just been instructed to draft a presidential order prohibiting discrimination on grounds of "race, color, creed, or national origin" in defense industries. It was a radical departure from decades of official support for legalized racism. It would use the economic muscle of the federal government to overturn job segregation and, in the process, make enemies for President Franklin Roosevelt. Rauh was enthusiastic, but he couldn't understand why FDR, with his reliance on southern votes, would even consider it. The president was bending to pressure, Rauh learned, from African Americans led by a charismatic organizer named A. Philip Randolph.

Raised in Florida and educated at New York's City College, Randolph had founded the largest African American labor union, the Brotherhood of Sleeping Car Porters, in 1925. Porters traveled the railroads as baggage handlers and valets, and during the Depression Randolph's influence extended into every station and depot reached by the Brotherhood's magazine, the *Messenger*.

In 1941, it looked to Randolph like only a matter of months before the United States entered the war raging in Europe and Asia. He believed, according to FBI informants, "that Negroes make most fundamental gains in periods of great social upheaval." War would create a chance to achieve equality, but only if African Americans demanded it. "The Negro sat by idly during the First World War thinking conditions would get better," he told an audience in Oklahoma City. "That won't be the procedure during the duration of this conflict."

In January 1941, Randolph called for African Americans to march to Washington to demand an end to job discrimination. Only 3 percent of workers in war industries were people of color. "The administration leaders in Washington will never give the Negro justice," he declared, "until they see masses, ten, twenty, fifty thousand Negroes on the White House lawn." The March on Washington movement was largely bluff, but Roosevelt and the FBI believed it enough to try to head it off.

A protest march would embarrass the government, and Roosevelt had the power to accept Randolph's demands. Leveraging federal defense contracts, the president could desegregate a large portion of the economy without even asking Congress. He opened negotiations with Randolph through Eleanor Roosevelt. The organizers agreed to cancel the march in return for a presidential directive—Executive Order 8802—establishing a Fair Employment Practices Committee to assure fairness in hiring.

It was a victory for civil rights and for Randolph personally. If the Emancipation Proclamation had ended physical slavery, the New York *Amsterdam News* declared, E.O. 8802 ended "economic slavery." Within a year, thousands of

African Americans would be working at high-tech jobs in aircraft factories and arms plants. Randolph had recognized that war created an opening for changing the economic and political rules of the game. War touched all Americans. Millions were sent to serve and fight everywhere from the Arctic to the tropics. Millions of others left home to work in plants producing war materiel. Government stepped in to run the economy and created new relationships with corporations, labor, the states, and universities. The war stimulated revolutionary advances in science, industry, and agriculture. The United States itself became the foremost military and economic power in a world destroyed by war.

These changes enlarged the discretionary powers of the presidency and the federal government. Americans willingly accepted personal sacrifices and greater federal authority as part of the price of victory. As the March on Washington movement proved, the president's enhanced powers could enlarge freedom and opportunity—but they could also restrict individual liberties. Many Japanese Americans spent the war imprisoned in "relocation centers," and the FBI placed Randolph's name on a list of persons to be placed in "custodial detention" in the event of a national emergency. The war unsettled the economy and society, enlisting all Americans in a global crusade and arousing both idealism and fear.

ISLAND IN A TOTALITARIAN SEA

Randolph's movement capitalized on a world crisis that reached back to the treaty that ended World War I. The Depression heightened international tensions, turning regional conflicts in Africa, Europe, and Asia into tests of ideology and power. In 1937, Japan attacked China. Two years later, when Germany invaded Poland, France and Britain declared war, beginning World War II in Europe. As with the previous war, Americans had time to reflect on the world crisis. Most blamed it on the failures of the Versailles Treaty and the desperation caused by the global Depression. Nations and empires were solving economic problems with military force.

Americans were divided, however, on how their country ought to respond, on its role in the world and its responsibilities at home. **Isolationists** wanted to stay out of war and secure the Western Hemisphere against attack. But Roosevelt and other **internationalists** believed the United States had to support the nations fighting Germany and Japan. Internationalists saw a free-trading, open-door world economy as a solution to international conflict. Isolationists worried about growing federal power and the ambitions of Britain and the Soviet Union. The threat of fascism forced Americans to ask whether their economy and government could compete in the world.

Both camps knew war would change American society. The future of world politics and the world economy would be shaped by America's choice of allies and aims. In 1940, most Americans feared involvement and opposed aid to the enemies of fascism. When France's defeat left Britain to fight alone, more Americans saw aid to Britain as an alternative to US involvement. Japan's attack on **Pearl Harbor** ended a debate that divided the nation.

A World of Hostile Blocs

The Depression destroyed the liberal international order based on free trade. For a century, governments had favored policies that increased the movement of goods, people, and investment across borders. The steamship and telegraph accelerated that trend. Movement toward an open-door world slowed during World War I and the 1920s, and then stopped completely with the Depression. World trade shrank from almost $3 billion a year in 1929 to less than $1 billion in 1933. Empires and nations began to restrict the movement of goods, capital, and people and to regiment their societies for self-sufficiency. Everywhere, it seemed, governments became more ruthless and less free.

Dictators offered visions of imperial conquest and racial supremacy. Mussolini promised a new Roman Empire in Africa and the Mediterranean. Japanese schoolchildren learned they belonged to a "Yamato race," purer and more virtuous than the inferior peoples they would one day rule. Hitler urged Germans to defend themselves against the *Untermenschen*, subhumans, in their midst—Jews, Gypsies, homosexuals. He built a state based on racism, total control, and brutality, where secret police, the Gestapo, hunted down enemies of the regime, and a Nazi army, the SS, enforced party rule.

Jews were the main target of Nazi terror. In 1935, the Nuremberg Laws stripped Jews of citizenship and outlawed intermarriage with members of the "Aryan race." On the night of November 9, 1938, Nazi stormtroopers and ordinary citizens rampaged throughout Germany, burning synagogues and destroying Jewish shops, homes, and hospitals, killing 100 Jews and arresting 30,000 more. Until *Kristallnacht*, this "night of the broken glass," FDR thought international opinion would restrain Hitler. Now he was no longer sure.

Roosevelt grew apprehensive as Germany, Italy, and Japan, the Axis powers, sought to solve their economic problems through military conquest. Italy invaded Ethiopia in 1935. In July 1937, Japan attacked China. In 1938, Hitler's troops marched into Austria. Roosevelt worried that the Axis would soon control most of Europe and Asia, but American leaders had an even darker fear, one they scarcely breathed: that **totalitarianism** would outcompete democracy. America's free markets and free labor might be no match for the ruthless efficiency of the fascist states. The United States would have to regiment its own citizens just to keep up, and to enlist industry, labor, and agriculture into a "state system," *Fortune* magazine predicted, "which, in its own defense, would have to take on the character of Hitler's system."

The Good Neighbor

Some believed the United States ought to retreat into its own sphere. The Hawley-Smoot Tariff of 1930 blocked most imports, but within a year, FDR reversed course and began pushing trade as the answer to America's economic problems. He reacted mainly to the vision of his single-minded secretary of state, Cordell Hull.

A conservative former senator from Tennessee, Hull believed that equal access for all to the world's markets was the cure for dictatorship and depression and the best way to ensure peace. In a world of empires and blocs, Hull turned an old foreign policy tradition, the Open Door, into a bold plan for peace and prosperity.

Roosevelt and Hull slowly began to reopen markets in Latin America. FDR expanded Hoover's "**Good Neighbor**" policy, encouraging trade and renouncing the use of force. A new Export-Import Bank financed transactions, and tariffs were lowered. Hull surprised the 1933 Pan-American Conference by approving a declaration that no nation had the right to intervene in the affairs of another. Good Neighbor policies undermined German and Japanese economic ventures, and Latin American governments invited the FBI to track down Axis agents on their soil.

In 1938, after absorbing Austria, Hitler demanded part of Czechoslovakia's territory. Fearing that a small war over the territory would escalate into a larger war, Czechoslovakia's allies, Britain and France, agreed to negotiations. In a meeting at Munich in September, they yielded to Hitler's demands. FDR cabled Hitler a last-minute appeal for restraint but accepted the final decision. After World War II, the term "Munich" came to symbolize the failed attempts to appease aggressors, but in 1938 Americans were unsure how best to guard their freedoms in a hostile world.

America First?

As the Axis threat grew, Roosevelt pushed for a buildup of US forces, but Congress and the public disagreed. Disillusioned by the last war, the public wanted to stay out of the conflicts in Europe and Asia. Polls indicated that more than 70 percent believed the United States had been tricked into World War I. Half a million students pledged their refusal to serve in another war. Senator Gerald P. Nye charged that the munitions industry was lobbying for war. Pacifists, economic nationalists, and veterans groups, backed by the *Chicago Tribune* and the Hearst newspapers, composed a powerful isolationist constituency.

From 1935 to 1937, Congress passed annual Neutrality Acts prohibiting loans and credits to nations engaged in war. The action took place against the backdrop of the Spanish Civil War, in which Fascist forces, aided by Germany and Italy, fought against democratic Loyalist forces aided by the Soviet Union. Some 3,000 Americans volunteered to fight with the Loyalists. For that reason, Congress decided to stay out of the conflict; the Neutrality Acts also restricted the president's ability to aid the enemies of fascism.

In late 1939, Roosevelt's worst nightmare came true, as the United States became an island in a world dominated by force. The Soviet Union signed a nonaggression treaty with Germany. The full terms of the Nazi-Soviet pact were secret, leading diplomats to fear the worst, a totalitarian alliance stretching from the Rhine to the Pacific. In September, German armies struck Poland, using tanks and dive-bombers in a *Blitzkrieg*, or "lightning war." Hitler and Soviet leader Josef Stalin split Poland between them. Britain and France declared war on Germany.

The following April, Nazi armies invaded Denmark and Norway. On May 10, 1940, Hitler launched an all-out offensive in the West. Tank columns pierced French lines in the Ardennes Forest and headed toward the English Channel. France, Belgium, and the Netherlands were defeated; Britain faced the German onslaught alone. Roosevelt now had to consider the possibility of a British surrender, placing the Royal Navy, control of the Atlantic, and possibly even Canada in Hitler's hands. The German air force, the *Luftwaffe*, was already dueling for control of the skies over England.

Determined to shore up this last line of defense, Roosevelt used his powers as commander in chief to bypass the Neutrality Acts. In June 1940, he submitted a bill to create the first peacetime draft in American history. He declared army weapons and supplies "surplus" so they could be donated to Britain. In September 1940, he traded Britain 50 destroyers for leases to naval bases in Canada, Bermuda, and the Caribbean.

The isolationists were now isolated. Sympathy for Britain grew as radio audiences heard the sounds of air attacks on London. Two-thirds of the public favored the draft, but isolationists were not finished. In September 1940, the America First Committee launched a new campaign that urged Americans to turn from Europe and prepare for their own defense. Charles A. Lindbergh and Senator Burton Wheeler headlined America First rallies. The only reason for United States involvement, Lindbergh argued, "is because there are powerful elements in America who desire us to take part. They represent a small minority… but they control much of the machinery of influence and propaganda."

Roosevelt worried that the 1940 election would become a referendum on intervention. Isolationist senator Robert Taft was a leading contender for the nomination, but the Republicans chose Wendell L. Willkie, an anti–New Deal internationalist who endorsed the draft and expressed sympathy for Britain. With defense and foreign policy off the table, FDR won an unprecedented third term by a 5-million-vote margin.

Means Short of War

British Prime Minister Winston Churchill could now broach the delicate but urgent issue of war finances. Britain had been buying arms on a "cash and carry" basis but was now out of funds. The Neutrality Act prohibited new loans, but without arms Britain would have to surrender. FDR gave his cabinet a weekend to devise a plan, and the following Monday he produced the answer himself. Instead of loaning money, the United States would lend arms and equipment. Roosevelt compared the idea to lending a garden hose to a neighbor whose house was on fire. "There would be a gentleman's obligation to repay," but because there would be no loans, it would not violate the Neutrality Act. Lend-Lease, as the program was called, put the US "arsenal of democracy" on Britain's side and granted FDR unprecedented powers to arm allies. The Lend-Lease bill, H.R. 1776, passed the Senate by a two-to-one margin in 1941.

Repayment took the form of economic concessions. Hull saw Lend-Lease as a chance to crack one of the largest autarkic blocs, the British Empire. He insisted that in return for aid, Britain had to discard the Ottawa Accords and open its empire's door to American trade. Churchill's economic adviser, John Maynard Keynes, reluctantly agreed. Later that year, Churchill and Roosevelt met aboard the cruiser *Augusta* to issue a declaration of war aims, the Atlantic Charter. It ensured all nations, "victor and vanquished," equal access to the trade and raw materials of the world.

In June 1941, Hitler stunned the world again with a lightning invasion of the Soviet Union. Three million men and 3,000 tanks slashed through Soviet defenses toward Moscow and Leningrad. Secretary of War Henry Stimson predicted that in three months the Axis would control Europe and Asia, but George C. Marshall, the army's chief of staff, saw that this might be a turning point. If the Soviet army could hold the area between Moscow and the Black Sea, the Germans would have a long winter. Roosevelt shared his optimism. The eastern front took pressure off Britain and gave the Allies a real chance to defeat Hitler. Roosevelt extended Lend-Lease aid to Moscow. The German columns advanced steadily, but they were no longer moving through Poland or France. "Even when encircled, the Russians stood their ground and fought," a Nazi general reported.

German U-boats worked to cut Britain's lifelines, sinking half a million tons of shipping a month. To help the British, Roosevelt fought an undeclared naval war against Germany in the western Atlantic. The US Navy convoyed merchant ships as far as Iceland, where British destroyers took over. FDR said he was offering "all aid short of war," but it was not far short. In September a U-boat fired torpedoes at the USS *Greer*, and the destroyer threw back depth charges. When Roosevelt ordered patrols to expel German and Italian vessels from the western Atlantic, he had crossed the line from neutrality to belligerency and seemed to be seeking an incident that would make it official.

Japan, meanwhile, moved into Southeast Asia. In 1939, the Japanese adopted a "go south" strategy to capture oil fields in the Dutch East Indies and encircle China. Because the Philippines, a US territory, blocked the invasion route, the question for the Japanese was not whether to declare war on the United States, but when. In July 1941, Japan established bases in French Indochina. Roosevelt saw this as a threat, but, preoccupied with Europe, he wanted to forestall war in the Pacific. US diplomats opened talks with Japan while Marshall dispatched a fleet of B-17s in an attempt to deter an attack. When Japanese troop convoys moved into the South China Sea, Hull ended negotiations and placed an embargo on oil exports to Japan, denying the nation its primary source of fuel. On November 27, Marshall warned commanders in Hawaii and the Philippines to expect "an aggressive move by Japan" in the next few days. The Philippines, Thailand, and Malaya were the likely targets.

On Sunday afternoon, December 7, Americans listening to the radio heard that aircraft "believed to be from Japan" had attacked US bases at Pearl Harbor in Hawaii. At 7:40 a.m. Hawaii time, 181 planes had bombed and strafed airfields on Oahu, destroying or damaging more than 200 planes on the ground. Bombers then attacked the 96 ships of the US Pacific Fleet anchored next to each other. Three torpedoes struck the battleship *Oklahoma*, capsizing it with 400 crew members aboard. Alongside her the *Maryland* went down. A bomb exploded in the *Arizona*'s forward magazine, breaking the ship in half and killing over a thousand men. In the Philippines, Japanese bombers also caught American planes on the ground. The following day, President Roosevelt appeared before Congress to ask for a declaration of war against Japan. Only one representative, Montana's Jeannette Rankin, voted no. On December 11, Germany honored its alliance with Japan and declared war on the United States.

Pearl Harbor Japan's attack on the US Navy's principal Pacific base at Pearl Harbor brought the United States into World War II. For Japan, it was the opening phase of a campaign to capture European and American colonies in Asia.

Some historians have argued that Roosevelt knew of the approaching attack but withheld warnings in order to draw the United States into war. In fact, naval authorities at Pearl Harbor anticipated an attack but doubted that Japan could project air and sea power across the Pacific in secrecy. When Japanese planes destroyed American aircraft on the ground in the Philippines nine hours after the Pearl Harbor attack, Douglas MacArthur said Germans must have flown the bombers. Such preconceptions blinded commanders to the warning signs.

TURNING THE TIDE

For the Allies there was only bad news in the first half of 1942. Japanese invaders walked over the larger British and Dutch armies in Southeast Asia and captured the American islands of Guam and Wake. In February, the "impregnable" fortress of Singapore surrendered with most of the Australian and Indian armies still inside. Japan's Combined Fleet ruled the seas between Hawaii and India, striking at will. MacArthur abandoned Manila and staged an Alamo-style defense of the Bataan Peninsula and the fortress island of Corregidor.

But the tide was beginning to turn. The Soviets stopped the German advance outside Moscow. On April 18, Colonel James Doolittle's B-25 bombers raided Tokyo. Roosevelt wanted to hold the line in the Pacific while coming to the aid of Britain and the Soviet Union as soon as possible. This meant stopping Japan, creating an American army, and sending it to the other side of the Atlantic. None of those jobs would be easy.

Midway and Coral Sea

"We can run wild for six months or a year," Admiral Isoroku Yamamoto prophesied before the victorious attack on Pearl Harbor, "but after that I have utterly no confidence." Panic-stricken Americans imagined enemy landings in California, but Japan was never so ambitious. It called for fortifying a defensive screen of islands in the western Pacific (see Map 23–1) and holding the Allies at bay until they sued for peace. "The fact that the Japanese did not return to Pearl Harbor and complete the job was the greatest help for us," Chester W. Nimitz, the US Pacific commander, later remembered.

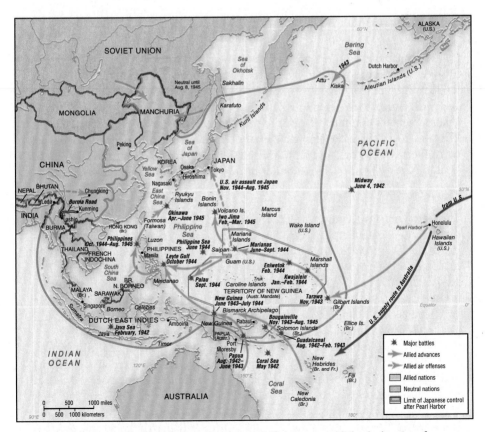

Map 23-1   World War II in the Pacific, 1942–1945 Japan established a barrier of fortified islands across the western Pacific. US forces penetrated it westward from Hawaii and from Australia northward through the Solomon Islands to the Philippines.

After the Doolittle raid, the Japanese realized their error and laid plans to lure the US Pacific Fleet into battle. The increase in radio traffic helped Commander Joseph Rochefort, who had already partly broken the Japanese codes. In late April, he was able to tell Nimitz that Japan was planning an attack on Port Moresby on the island of New Guinea. Nimitz dispatched two carriers, *Lexington* and *Yorktown*, to intercept the Japanese carrier force. The Battle of Coral Sea was the first between carrier task forces, an entirely new type of sea battle. Sailors never saw the enemy's ships, only their aircraft, which struck with devastating speed. Planes from *Yorktown* turned back the Japanese transports while Lexington's torpedo- and dive-bombers sunk the carrier *Shoho*. The Japanese fatally crippled *Lexington* and tore a hole in *Yorktown*'s deck. The two sides pulled back after fighting to a draw.

Yamamoto next chose to attack the US fleet directly. Sending a diversionary force toward the Aleutians, he aimed his attack at **Midway**, the westernmost island of the Hawaiian chain. Yamamoto gambled that Nimitz would divide his forces, allowing the Combined Fleet to crush the remnant guarding Hawaii. But trusting Rochefort's code breakers, Nimitz knew the real target was Midway. He also learned from Coral Sea that aircraft, not battleships, were the winning weapons. He hastily assembled task forces around the carriers *Hornet* and *Enterprise* and reinforced airfields on Midway and Oahu. Crews worked night and day to repair *Yorktown*. The American fleet was still outnumbered, but surprise was now on its side.

When Japanese aircraft met stiff resistance from Midway's guns on the morning of June 4, they returned to their carriers and prepared for an unplanned second attack. With bombers, bombs, and fuel littering their decks, Japan's four carriers were vulnerable, their defending Zeros busy intercepting US torpedo bombers. At that moment dive-bombers from *Yorktown* and *Enterprise* burst out of the clouds. They destroyed three carriers in a matter of minutes. The mighty Combined Fleet was almost entirely destroyed. Midway put Japan on the defensive and allowed the United States to concentrate on building an army and winning the war in Europe.

Gone with the Draft

The German army that overran France in May 1940 consisted of 136 mechanized divisions of 17,000 men each. The United States had only five divisions and was still using horse cavalry. "Against Europe's total war," *Time* observed, "the U.S. Army looked like a few nice boys with BB guns." Military officials drew up plans for a 10-million-man force. As in World War I, the United States had to find ways to house, equip, and transport the army, but this time it would be five times larger. By December 1941, 2 million men and 80,000 women had enlisted. A year later the total exceeded 5 million.

Buses rolled into the new boot camps and unloaded recruits, called selectees, in front of drill instructors. Basic training aimed to erase the civilian personality and replace it with an instinct for obedience and action. Eugene Sledge left college to join the marines and found himself at a camp in San Diego. "Your soul may belong to Jesus," his drill instructor bellowed, "but your ass belongs to the Marines." After 13 weeks of calisthenics, close-order drill, marches, and rifle practice, Sledge was assigned to the infantry.

Recruits hungered for a weekend pass, but in the South and West, where many bases were located, there was little to do. The War Department joined several charities in creating the United Services Organization (USO) to provide a "home away from home" with meals, dances, and wholesome entertainment. Still, wherever they were on leave, soldiers often fought with each other and with the locals. Distinctions of apparel and race could stimulate violence. Southerners lynched African American soldiers for wearing their uniforms. In 1943, riots erupted in Harlem after police arrested an African American soldier in uniform. The same year, sailors in Los Angeles attacked Mexican American shipyard workers who wore distinctive "zoot suits." In both cases the clothes signified a disruption of the established social order, a process accelerated by the war.

Army leadership struggled to preserve racial traditions amid wartime changes. Like the multiethnic armies of Britain and France, the US Army consisted of segregated units, some with special functions. The Japanese American 442nd Regimental Combat Team and the marines' Navajo "code talkers" became well known. African Americans served in the army in segregated units, and, until 1942, were excluded from the Marine Corps altogether. Roosevelt ordered the services to admit African Americans and appointed an African American brigadier general, Benjamin O. Davis, but injustices remained. Even blood plasma was segregated in military hospitals.

Two issues aroused the most anger among African Americans: exclusion from combat and the treatment of soldiers at southern bases. Many GIs in uniform experienced the indignity of being refused service at restaurants where German prisoners of war were allowed to eat. Mutinies and race riots erupted at bases in Florida, Alabama, and Louisiana, where African American soldiers were housed separately and denied furlough privileges. The army responded by sending African American GIs to the war theaters.

Though desperately short of infantrymen, the army kept African Americans out of front-line units and assigned them to menial chores. Combat symbolized full citizenship, and the NAACP pressed Roosevelt to create African American fighting units. An African American infantry division, the 92nd, fought in Italy; three air units—among them the 99th Pursuit Squadron, known as the **Tuskegee Airmen**—flew against the Luftwaffe; and one mechanized battalion, the 761st Tanks, received a commendation for action in the Ardennes. Most African Americans went into the line individually as replacements, and racially mixed units aroused few complaints in the field. Resistance to desegregation came mainly from Washington.

With manpower in short supply, the armed forces reluctantly enlisted women. The Women's Army Corps (the WACs) was created in 1942, while the navy signaled its reluctance in the title of its auxiliary, the Women Accepted for Volunteer Emergency Service (WAVES). Eventually more than 100,000 women served as mechanics, typists, pilots, cooks, and nurses, an unusually low rate of mobilization. Nearly every other warring country enlisted women for industry and combat, leaving the state to perform traditionally female jobs: caring for children, the sick, and the elderly. This government role came to be accepted in Europe, Canada, and Australia, but in the United States "welfare" continued to be associated with poor relief.

America In The World
Martial Law in Hawaii

Immediately following the December 7, 1941 attack on Pearl Harbor, Territorial Governor Joseph Poindexter placed Hawaii, at that time an American territory, under martial law. With the American military fully aware of the Hawaiian Islands' strategic location and import to national security, the outline for a military government already existed. Lt. Colonel Thomas H. Green, the Army's chief legal officer in Hawaii had, in the year preceding the Pearl Harbor attack, created a plan in which a military government replaced the territory's civilian authority at the executive, legislative, and judicial levels. While many civilians anticipated that such a system of government would last only a number of weeks until the Islands were secure, the military government put into place following Pearl Harbor continued, with some amendment, until October 1944, a duration of time permitted in part by the territory's geographic distance from the contiguous United States and, according to those advocating the continuation of martial law, justified by its unique demographic makeup.

Those of Japanese descent, both alien residents and Hawaiian citizens, faced the possibility of evacuation and internment much like West Coast residents of Japanese origin. Orders from Washington, DC pushed the military government to begin this process, even as that government's detainment of approximately 1,500 residents of Japanese descent—mainly Shinto and Buddhist priests, teachers at Japanese language schools, community leaders, and off-shore fishermen suspected of disloyalty—yielded no evidence of espionage. President Roosevelt, nevertheless, was convinced of the threat Japanese residents posed to national security. Citing Executive Order 9066, which provided for the declaration of military zones and further declaration of populations to be excluded from those zones, FDR declared "I do not worry about the constitutional question." Those overseeing the military government in Hawaii, however, while not particularly concerned about constitutionality, balked at the president's directives. Residents of Japanese origin comprised roughly one-third the Hawaiian population. Not only would evacuation and internment be a tremendous expense and complicated logistical undertaking, but this population was fundamental to the Hawaiian economy and wartime industries. Ultimately, using a series of delay tactics, the military government sufficiently stalled the process of Japanese **internment** until the president no longer advocated it as a priority.

Those of Japanese descent who *had* been taken from their homes were denied access to the specific charges against them. They were not allowed to confront their accusers, nor were they provided counsel. The provost court system established for the whole of the territorial population similarly denied all citizens of the protections offered in civilian court. Those arrested for violating the rules of martial law—ranging from breaking curfew to skipping work to disobeying wartime traffic ordinances—received no trial by jury. Sometimes no written charge existed. Defendants could not cross-examine witnesses brought against them and were denied the right to call witnesses on their own behalf. Many provost judges had no legal training, and it was not uncommon for judges to discourage defendants from exercising their right to counsel. Arrests were plentiful, as were convictions. In 1942–1943, of the more than 22,000 trials conducted in Honolulu's provost court, 99 percent resulted in convictions. The average trial in provost courts took less than five minutes. Sentences generally

Martial Law in Hawaii Those who violated the rules of martial law implemented in Hawaii during World War II faced trial in designated provost courts, like Wahiawa District Court, where judges quickly handed out verdicts and sentencing.

exceeded the severity meted out in civilian court, although for more minor offenses, it was not uncommon that an offender was directed to buy war bonds in lieu of paying a fine, or could choose between giving blood or serving time.

Hawaii, part of the United States and yet still distinctly apart *from* the United States, in its experience with martial law, reflected a long conflicted national sense of what role American territories played and what citizenship rights inhabitants enjoyed. The racial makeup of the Hawaiian population contributed to the extended life of martial law, a practice the Supreme Court eventually ruled unconstitutional (but not until 1946, after the war). Months following Pearl Harbor, when it was clear residents of Japanese origin presented little danger, authorities continued to detain and sometimes evacuate those arrested, both to satisfy Washington's sustained demands that the military government

demonstrate security and to justify the continuation of martial law. As noted by the Army's chief security and intelligence officer in Hawaii, evacuation of selected internees "is merely a matter of relieving pressure. ... [Detainees] really aren't dangerous and not bad at all." Despite the limited present danger, military leadership justified the continuation of martial law and provost courts by the fact that restoration of the right to trial by jury in civilian courts would require juries that reflected the demographic reality of the territory—in which white citizens made up only a third of the population. General Green, with no degree of self-consciousness, in considering the role the islands' residents of Chinese, Korean, Philippine, and Japanese origins would play, declared, "all the racial hatred, and there is plenty of it here under cover, will come to the fore, and justice, whether it be criminal or civil, is simply out of the window."

The 99th Pursuit Squadron, Known as the Black Eagles The Black Eagles trained at the Tuskegee Institute and engaged the Luftwaffe in the skies over North Africa.

The Winning Weapons

During World War II, weapons technology advanced with blinding speed. Entering the war late, the United States gained a technological edge. American factories produced models using the latest innovations, but many of these would not see combat until 1943 or later.

Until then, troops had to make do with inferior weapons. Marines landed on Guadalcanal wearing World War I–era helmets and carrying the 1903 Springfield rifle. Japan's Zero was faster and lighter than any American fighter. After 1943, the advantage began to pass to the Americans. The M1 rifle was the finest infantry weapon in the war. Artillery was precise and lethal, and American crews were skilled in the devastating "time-on-target" technique, which delivered shells from several directions simultaneously. The elegant P-51 Mustang, a high-speed ultra-long-range fighter, could escort bombers from Britain to Berlin. It dominated the skies after D-Day. American four-engine bombers—the B-17 Flying Fortress and the B-24 Liberator—were superior to German or Japanese counterparts. In 1944, the B-29 Superfortress, with its 10-ton bomb load and unrivalled range, took to the skies over the Pacific and incinerated one Japanese city after another. American tanks, however, remained inferior to their German counterparts throughout the war, owing to the flawed logistical decisions of American forces.

Quantity often trumped quality, however, and the results were impressive. When Allied troops landed in France in 1944, they enjoyed a superiority of 20 to 1 in tanks and 25 to 1 in aircraft. When Roosevelt set a production target of 50,000 aircraft in 1940, the Germans considered it a bluff, but American factories turned out almost 300,000 planes during the war (see Figure 23–1). Sometimes sheer American numbers defeated Axis skill. An American soldier in Salerno asked a captured German lieutenant why he had surrendered. "The Americans kept sending tanks down the road," the German replied. "Every time they sent a tank, we knocked it out. Finally, we ran out of ammunition, and the Americans didn't run out of tanks."

Americans also developed secret weapons. The War Department funded defense laboratories at Johns Hopkins, MIT, Harvard, and other universities, forging a permanent link between government, science, and the military. American and British scientists invented one of the first "smart" bombs, the proximity fuse. American and British scientific collaboration also produced improvements in sonar and radar, penicillin, and the **atomic bomb.**

The **Manhattan Project** that produced the atomic bomb was the war's largest military-scientific-industrial enterprise. In 1939, Albert Einstein warned Roosevelt that the Germans might invent a nuclear weapon. The National Academy of Sciences concluded that a weapon of "superlatively destructive power" could be built, and General Leslie R. Groves was put in charge of the project, which eventually employed 600,000 people and cost $2 billion. World War II's marriage of technology and war changed warfare, and it also changed science. Researchers and inventors had once worked alone on their own problems. Now they worked in teams at government-funded laboratories on problems assigned by Washington.

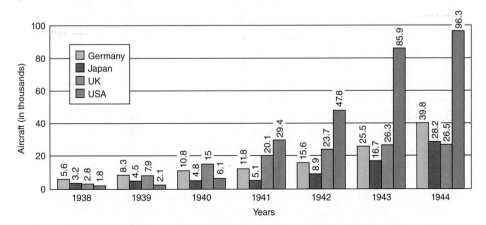

Figure 23–1   Number of Military Aircraft Produced US production of military equipment lagged at first, but once in high gear it dwarfed that of the rest of the world.
Source: I. C. B. Dear and M. R. D. Foot, eds., *The Oxford Companion to World War II* (New York: Oxford University Press, 1995), p. 22.

The Second Front

To reassure Britain and the Soviet Union, FDR adopted a "Europe First" strategy, holding the line against Japan while directing the main effort at Nazi Germany. The Allies had little in common except that Hitler had chosen them as enemies. Britain was struggling to preserve its empire. The Soviet Union had once been allied with Germany and had a nonaggression pact with Japan. Roosevelt needed to keep this shaky coalition together long enough to defeat Hitler. His greatest fear was that one or both of the Allies would make a separate peace or be knocked out of the war. Stalin and Churchill each had their own opinions about how to use American power, and their conflicting aims produced bitter disputes over strategy.

As the Nazis closed in on the Soviet oil fields during 1942, Stalin pleaded with Britain and the United States to launch an invasion of France. Roosevelt and Marshall also wanted a second front against Germany in northern Europe. But to the British, the idea of a western front evoked the horrors of the trench warfare of World War I and the losses it could no longer sustain. Instead, Churchill wanted to encircle the Nazis and attack the "soft underbelly" of the Axis from the Mediterranean.

Concerned about U-boats and the inexperience of American troops, FDR reluctantly accepted Churchill's plan (see Map 23–2). A month after Pearl Harbor he had promised Stalin a second front "this year." In late 1942, he postponed it to the spring of 1943. Finally, in June 1943, he told Stalin it would not take place until 1944. The delays reinforced Stalin's suspicions that the capitalist powers were waiting for the USSR's defeat.

Instead of invading Europe, the Americans chose a softer target, North Africa, where troops under Lieutenant General **Dwight D. Eisenhower** landed in Algeria and Morocco on November 8, 1942. As they moved east to link up with British forces attacking into Tunisia, German tank divisions under General Erwin Rommel burst through the Kasserine Pass and trapped American columns in high, rocky terrain. Panicky troops fled, blowing up their ammunition stores. Once through the pass, Rommel had a chance to encircle and defeat the Allied forces, but his Italian commanders ordered him to advance in another direction. The Americans and British regrouped for a counterattack.

Ernie Pyle, the popular war correspondent, reassured readers that despite the rout, "there was never at any time any question about the American bravery." Eisenhower was not so sure. He sacked the commander responsible for Kasserine and replaced him with Major General George S. Patton. The army increased basic training from 13 to 17 weeks and reviewed its doctrine and weapons. For Patton, Kasserine showed that firepower delivered by air, tanks, and artillery was more reliable than infantry. His preference for technology over bravery became ingrained in American strategy.

On May 7, Allied forces captured Tunis and Bizerte and took 238,000 German and Italian prisoners. Rommel escaped to fight again in France a year later. There he would encounter a different American army, larger, more experienced, and equipped with the newest weapons. As it mobilized, the United States was changing, too.

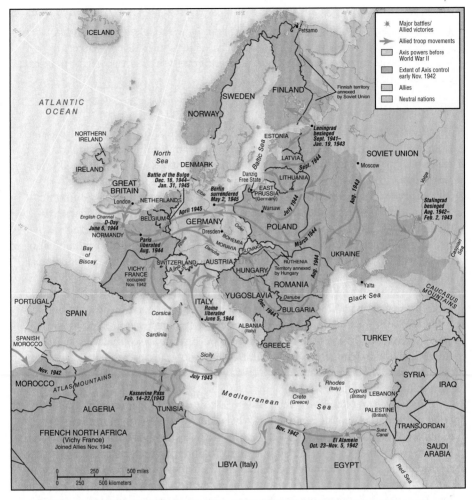

Map 23–2   World War II in Europe, 1942–1945 While the Soviets reduced the main German force along the eastern front, the British and American Allies advanced through Italy and France.

ORGANIZING FOR PRODUCTION

To defeat totalitarian regimes, Americans had to gear their economy for war. Big government and corporations made possible the "miracle of production" that was winning the war and raising living standards. During the height of the Depression, FDR did not use deficit spending to stir the economy (a technique economists call a "Keynesian stimulus"), but during the war, half the money the federal government spent was borrowed, and nobody complained. The economy boomed. War contracts created 17 million new jobs. Industrial production doubled. The employment dial reached "full" in 1942 and stayed there until Japan surrendered.

War industries worked by a new set of rules. Contractors depended on the government for financing, materials, and labor. New war plants, built at taxpayer expense, went up in towns with little industry. As industry moved, workers moved with it into the new boomtowns, organizing themselves into a powerful political and economic force.

A Mixed Economy

The Roosevelt administration added new war agencies to control prices, assign labor, and gear up industry. It dusted off methods from World War I—dollar-a-year men and "cost-plus" contracts—and added new incentives, such as tax breaks, federal loans, and subsidies. "You have to let business make money out of the process," Secretary of War Henry Stimson explained, "or business won't work." Sometimes it didn't, and the government seized at various times the steel industry, the railroads, the coal mines, and a department store chain.

Output soared. A Ford plant at Willow Run, Michigan, turned out a fleet of B-24s larger than the whole Luftwaffe. Cargo ships, which took more than a year to build in 1941, were coming out of the Kaiser Shipyards in an average of 56 days. Entirely new industries such as synthetic rubber and Lucite (a clear, hard plastic used for aircraft windshields) appeared overnight. Industrial techniques applied to agriculture—mechanization and chemical herbicides and pesticides—raised output with fewer farmers. Corporations patriotically increased their market share. Coca-Cola's mobile bottling plants followed the front lines, creating a global thirst for their product. Wrigley added a stick of gum to each K ration and made chewing gum a national habit.

Business leaders regained the prestige lost during the Depression. Major corporations such as General Electric, Allis-Chalmers, and Westinghouse ran parts of the super-secret Manhattan Project. Edwin Witte, a member of the National War Labor Board, called this partnership "a mixed economy, which is not accurately described as either capitalism or socialism." Most business was still small; 97 percent of manufacturing came from firms with just a few hundred employees. During the war, Congress and the administration drew a line between large high-tech firms, its partners in defense, and "small business" that needed tax breaks and loans. Small business acquired its own federal agency and lobbying groups, while major corporations such as Boeing and General Electric negotiated long-term contracts with the federal government. World War II permanently divided the economy into separate "government" and "market" sectors, each with its own rules and ways of dealing with Washington.

Industry Moves South and West

Although Detroit got its share, the bulk of war contracts went to states in the South and Southwest and on the Pacific coast, shifting industry's center of gravity. Airplanes flown in World War I came from Dayton and Buffalo, but the B-29 Superfortress was made in Seattle, Washington; Omaha, Nebraska; Wichita, Kansas; and Marietta, Georgia. The Manhattan Project's largest facilities at Oak Ridge, Tennessee; Hanford, Washington; and Los Alamos, New Mexico, also broke the historic concentration of industry in the Northeast and Midwest (see Map 23–3).

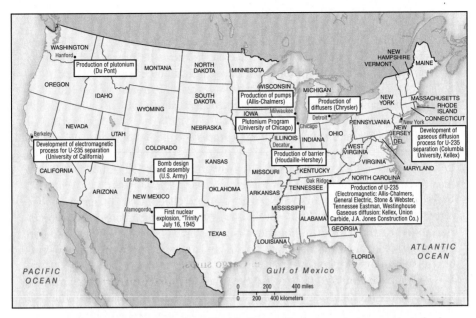

Map 23–3   The Manhattan Project The Manhattan Project created a new kind of collaboration between industry, government, and science. In a pattern of federal spending that would continue after the war, much of the new infrastructure was located in the South and West.

There were several reasons for this shift. Like other industries moving to the huge hydroelectric grids created by the New Deal, aluminum plants went up along the Tennessee and Columbia Rivers to tap abundant power from federal dams. The government also encouraged construction in the middle of the country to lessen the danger of enemy attacks. Corporations moved south and west to find low-wage nonunion workers. Powerful southern and western senators, who controlled military appropriations, steered new development into their states.

The results were visible. The population of the West increased by 40 percent. San Diego doubled in size in 1942. Los Angeles, Houston, Denver, Portland, and Seattle became boomtowns. Whereas "old" industries such as automobiles and steel remained strong above the Mason-Dixon Line, the Sunbelt states became home to the gleaming industries of the future: plastics, aluminum, aircraft, and nuclear power.

Few objected to government direction of the economy when it meant new jobs and industry in poor regions. A 1942 Gallup poll showed that two-thirds of Americans wanted the government to register all adults and assign them to war work as needed. The Office of Price Administration enlisted women consumers to enforce price ceilings by informing on their local grocers. Citizens started scrap drives, bond drives, blood drives, and victory gardens. The war effort was so popular that the administration did not worry much about propaganda. Roosevelt and other leaders—many of them former progressives—had learned a lesson from World War I: in gaining public support, inducements worked better than coercion.

New Jobs in New Places

As it had during World War I, the need for workers pushed up wages, added new employees to the workforce, and set people on the move. It also swelled the ranks of organized labor from 10 million to almost 15 million between 1941 and 1945. Enlisted as a partner in the war effort, unions grew because of a federally mandated "maintenance of membership" policy, by which new employees automatically joined the union. Through the National Defense Mediation Board (NDMB), the administration encouraged cooperation, a process begun by the New Deal. When wildcat locals of the United Auto Workers struck North American Aviation plants in Los Angeles in 1941, Stimson sent the army to break the strike, but the NDMB then forced management to accept the union's wage demands. Using carrots and sticks, federal administrators encouraged a more collaborative, managerial style of union leadership. Unions did not have to struggle for membership or recognition; in return, they curbed militant locals and accepted federal oversight. Decision making moved from one-story brick "locals" in factory towns to the marble headquarters of national unions in Washington, DC.

People moved to jobs, rather than the other way around, and some 4 million workers, and with them another 5 million family members, migrated to the new sites of war production. Some 200,000 Mexican **braceros** crossed the border to harvest crops. San Francisco's African American population doubled in a year. In Los Angeles, African Americans were arriving at a rate of 300 to 400 a day. By leaving Mississippi to take a factory job in California, a sharecropper could increase his salary six- or sevenfold.

Workers were generally happy with higher wages, but many lacked a decent place to live. New York, with plenty of housing, suffered from unemployment while new factories were located in places with no housing. There were no rooms to rent within miles of Willow Run. In many towns, workers "hot bedded"—slept in shifts in boardinghouses—or lived in cars. Frustrations over the housing shortage sometimes boiled over into racial conflict. In 1943, two days of mob violence erupted in Detroit over who would take possession of 1,000 new units of federal housing. Housing remained a chronic problem during the war and for several years afterward.

Women in Industry

"**Rosie the Riveter**," the image of the glamorous machinist laboring to bring her man home sooner, was largely a creation of the Office of War Information. Some 36 percent of the wartime labor force was female, but that was only slightly higher than the peacetime figure (see Figure 23–2). Few women left housework to take a job in a factory solely for patriotic reasons. Instead, the war economy shifted women workers into new roles, some from service jobs into industry and others from factory jobs to better-paid positions.

The number of manufacturing jobs for women grew from 12 million to 16.5 million, with many women moving into heavy industry as metalworkers, shipwrights, and assemblers of tanks and aircraft, jobs that had been off-limits before. Women worked coke ovens, blast furnaces, and rolling mills. For many women, the war and its demands offered the first real chance for mobility.

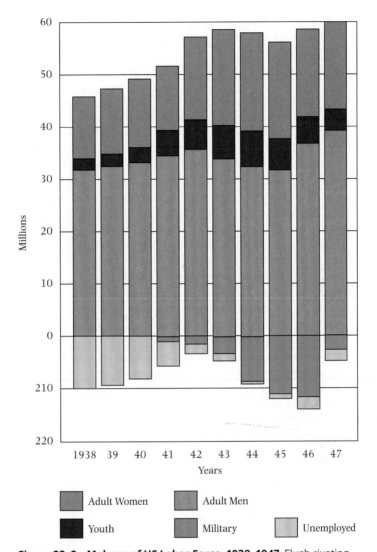

Figure 23-2   Makeup of US Labor Force, 1938–1947 Flush riveting of aluminum wing panels required a steady hand. War industries employed thousands of women.
Source: I. C. B. Dear and M. R. D. Foot, eds., *Oxford Companion to World War II* (Oxford: Oxford University Press, 2001), p. 1182.

Even so, employers did not offer equal pay or help to women trying to juggle job and family. Unions either refused women membership or expelled them when the war ended. The Lanham Act provided the first federal support for day care, but the 2,800 government centers were not nearly enough. "Latchkey children," left home alone while their mothers worked, were said to be a major problem. Experts saw female labor as necessary during the war but dangerous in the long run. "Many of them are rejecting their feminine roles," a social worker complained. After the war, women were expected to yield their jobs to returning servicemen. They were also blamed for neglecting their domestic duties and encouraging juvenile delinquency.

BETWEEN IDEALISM AND FEAR

In the movies, Americans marched to war (and war plants) singing patriotic tunes by George M. Cohan, but in real life this war was noticeably free of high-minded idealism. Americans had already fought once to end all wars and to keep the world safe for democracy. They were not ready to buy that bill of goods again. Journalist John Hersey asked marines on Guadalcanal what they were fighting for. "Scotch whiskey. Dames. A piece of blueberry pie. Music," they replied. Things were no clearer at home, where to writer Dwight Macdonald the war seemed to represent "the maximum of physical devastation accompanied by the minimum of human meaning."

If Americans weren't sure what they were fighting for, they knew what they were fighting against: totalitarianism, gestapos, and master races. Throughout the war and after, totalitarianism was a powerful symbol of what America and Americans ought to oppose. The president of the US Chamber of Commerce denounced the New Deal as "fascist" and "totalitarian." Labor unions and civil rights groups used the same words against their enemies, but wartime rhetoric also held Americans to a higher standard of tolerance. "All races and religions; that's America to me," sang Frank Sinatra in *The House I Live In* (1945).

Wartime leaders struggled to fill the inspirational vacuum with some of the century's most stirring restatements of the democratic creed. Winston Churchill spoke of protecting the liberty and culture of the "English-speaking peoples." In his State of the Union address in January 1941, Franklin Roosevelt aspired to a world based on the "**Four Freedoms**": freedom of speech, freedom of worship, freedom from want, and freedom from fear. A month later, *Life* magazine published an essay by its founder, Henry Luce, entitled "The American Century." It was a powerfully optimistic vision of globalized democracy and abundance, "a sharing with all people of our Bill of Rights, our Declaration of Independence, our Constitution, our magnificent industrial products, our technical skills." In response, Vice President Henry Wallace proclaimed that in the "Century of the Common Man," nations would "measure freedom by standards of nutrition, education and self-government." He equated democracy—as American leaders would do after the war—with schools, jobs, food, and a New Deal for the world.

African Americans sought their four freedoms in an atmosphere of increasing racial hostility. Detroit was just one city in which rapid growth touched off racial conflict. In Maryland, Michigan, New York, and Ohio, white workers engaged in "hate strikes" to prevent the hiring of African American workers. Over 3,000 white employees of a naval shipyard burned African American neighborhoods in Beaumont, Texas, in June 1943. Curfews, rumors of riots, and white citizens' committees kept many other cities on edge.

African Americans responded by linking their struggle for rights at home to the global war against fascism. Thurgood Marshall, chief counsel for the NAACP, compared the Detroit rioters to "the Nazi Gestapo." In 1942, the *Pittsburgh Courier* launched the "Double V" campaign to connect the fight against racism to the one against fascism. "Defeat Hitler, Mussolini, and Hirohito," it urged, "by Enforcing the Constitution and Abolishing Jim Crow." NAACP membership grew tenfold during the war. In Chicago, students and activists inspired by the nonviolent tactics of Mohandas Gandhi organized the Congress of Racial Equality (CORE), which desegregated restaurants and public facilities in the North. The NAACP won a legal victory in the Supreme Court case of *Smith v. Allwright* (1944), which invalidated all-white primary elections.

The experience of war may have been the greatest catalyst to change. Many African Americans returned from combat determined not to accept discrimination any longer. Amzie Moore came home to Cleveland, Mississippi, after serving in the army and was elected head of the local NAACP chapter. "Here I am being shipped overseas," he said of his service in the Pacific, "and I been segregated from this man who I might have to save or he save my life. I didn't fail to tell it." The war prepared Moore and his generation for the struggle ahead.

Japanese Internment

Idealism was no match for fear, and in the days after Pearl Harbor, panicky journalists, politicians, and military authorities perpetrated an injustice on American citizens of Japanese descent. Ominous signs reading "Civilian Exclusion Order" went up in California and the Pacific Northwest in February 1942. They instructed "Japanese aliens and non-aliens" to report to relocation centers for removal from the Pacific coast "war zone." The Western Defense Command of Lieutenant General John L. DeWitt and the *Los Angeles Times*, believing the Japanese planned to invade the West Coast, aroused the public against the Japanese "menace." FBI investigators found no suspicious plots and told the president so, but the press continued to print rumors. Responding to the press, DeWitt, and the California congressional delegation, Roosevelt ordered the relocation.

Internees and lawyers challenged the legality of confining American citizens without charge or trial. Fred Korematsu, a welder from San Leandro, California, took a new name and had his face surgically altered in a futile attempt to stay out of the camps. When he was arrested, the American Civil Liberties Union used his case to challenge the evacuation order. Supreme Court Justice Hugo Black upheld the policy as justified by "military necessity." In January 1947, the Western Defense Command praised the evacuation program and suggested that it could be used as a model for the treatment of suspect populations during the next national emergency.

No Shelter from the Holocaust

The United States might have saved more of the victims of Hitler's "final solution" had it chosen to do so. A combination of fear, anti-Semitism, and a desire to avoid unwanted burdens led American leaders to dismiss the **Holocaust** as someone else's problem. The State Department, worried that spies and saboteurs would sneak in with the refugees, erected a paper wall of bureaucratic restrictions. Refugees found it easier to get a visa from China than from the United States. In 1939, the *St. Louis* steamed from Hamburg with 930 Jewish refugees aboard. American immigration officials refused to let the refugees ashore because they lacked proper papers—papers that only their Nazi persecutors could have furnished. The ship and its passengers returned to Germany.

Nazi Germany's systematic extermination of the Jews made news in the United States. Stories in the *New York Times* as early as 1942 described the deportations

Struggles For Democracy

The Zoot Suit Riots

On May 31, 1943, a group of servicemen stationed in Los Angeles engaged in a violent confrontation with a group of young Mexican American men, all members of a vibrant pachuco street culture identified by the oversized coats and wide-legged pants of the men's zoot suits and their distinct long, greased-back, "ducktail" hairstyle. Ostensibly a fight over the servicemen's approaching a group of pachucas, the female counterpart to the pachuco, the violent interaction reflected broader hostilities against Mexican Americans that long had simmered throughout Los Angeles's white community.

Concern about pachuco "gangs" and their "hoodlumism" was rampant in Los Angeles throughout the 1940s. Authorities interpreted the young men's defiance, expressed both by their behavior and their flamboyant dress, as an assault on American sensibilities, especially during wartime. In 1942, the War Production Board outlawed the production of zoot suits, claiming the need to ration fabric for soldiers' uniforms. Pachucos, typically American born and often straining against a traditional Mexican upbringing, resented the fact that they were expected to show loyalty, submit to the draft, and fight for a country that treated them as second-class citizens. Authorities' attempts to curtail their signature style gave rise to a bootleg market of zoot suits, which more than ever, reflected Mexican American youths' resistance and rebellion.

Apprehension about Mexican American youth escalated following the August 1942 murder of a young man named José Diaz at a reservoir in Southeast Los Angeles known as Sleepy Lagoon. Local media depicted Diaz's death as the result of a Mexican American gang war. In the aftermath of what became known as the "Sleepy Lagoon Murder," the Los Angeles Police Department raided Mexican American neighborhoods and brought in more than 600 men and women for questioning. Twenty-two men were tried en masse in *The People v. Zammora*. They were made to sit separately from their lawyers and given no opportunity to seek counsel until the day's proceedings had concluded. They were not allowed to change out of their zoot suits or cut their long hair. "Scientific" evidence submitted by the sheriff's department claimed they were like wild cats, with a predisposition to violence. In January 1943, an all-white jury found three defendants guilty of first-degree murder, and they were sentenced to life in prison; nine were convicted of second-degree murder and received sentences of five years to life.

and concluded that "the greatest mass slaughter in history" was under way. At **Auschwitz**, Poland, in the most efficient death camp, 2,000 people an hour could be killed with Zyklon-B gas. Jewish leaders begged the War Department to bomb the camp or the rail lines leading to it. The city of Auschwitz was bombed twice in 1944, but John J. McCloy, the assistant secretary of war, refused to target the camp, dismissing it as a humanitarian matter of no concern to the army. Roosevelt knew

Zoot Suit Riots American servicemen walked the streets of Los Angeles in search of zoot-suited Mexican American pachucos they wished to defrock.

From the conclusion of the Sleepy Lagoon case until May of 1943, more than 50 confrontations between servicemen and zoot-suited pachucos took place. Servicemen took particular affront to the zoot suit: their uniforms, they believed, represented American service and patriotism, and the zoot suit revealed the pachucos' disregard for both the nation and soldiers' and sailors' service. When Seaman Second Class Joseph Coleman sustained a serious head injury and a broken jaw during a clash, servicemen stationed in Los Angeles undertook a full-scale attack on Mexican American youth, their targets easily identified by the pachucos' hallmark zoot suit. The ensuing "Zoot Suit Riots" raged for the better part of a week as sailors and soldiers hunted down pachucos. The servicemen feared neither interruption nor consequence from the Los Angeles Police Department.

Whites raided bars, dancehalls, movie theaters, and other public amusements. When they found someone wearing a zoot suit, they beat the individual, stripped him of his clothes, lit the zoot suit on fire, and cut his long hair. In some instances, they followed up on their assault by depositing the individual in a garbage can. In the aftermath of an attack, the Los Angeles Police Department often would place the beaten and humiliated Mexican American (although sometimes Filipino or African American) under arrest. The attackers, depicted in local Los Angeles newspapers as white knights, restoring the city to law and order, went free.

Manuel Reyes, serving his sentence in the aftermath of the Sleepy Lagoon trial, observed the Zoot Suit Riots from behind the walls of San Quentin Prison. As he listened to the radio, read articles, and saw images of the assaults, he wrote, "It sure is terrible what's going on in L.A. I never dream[ed] that things like that would happen in the U.S.A., a land of freedom. I thought it only happens in Germany and Japan."

of the Holocaust, but his inaction, according to historian David Wyman, was "the worst failure of his presidency."

When American soldiers entered Germany in 1945, they saw clearly why they were fighting. On April 15, Patton's Third Army liberated the Buchenwald death camp. Correspondent Edward R. Murrow described the scene to radio listeners in the United States: the skeletonlike survivors, the piles of the dead, the ovens.

"I pray you to believe what I have said about Buchenwald," he said. "I have reported what I saw." Eisenhower had photographs and films taken, and he brought German civilians from nearby communities to witness the mass burial, by bulldozer, of the corpses. Many GIs doubted anyone would believe what they had witnessed. "We got to talk about it, see?" one soldier told reporter Martha Gellhorn. "We got to talk about it if anyone believes us or not."

Americans entered the World War I flushed with idealism and became disillusioned in victory's aftermath. World War II reversed this trajectory. Americans slowly came to see the power of their shopworn ideals against the hatred and bigotry that afflicted all nations, including their own. Rose McClain wrote her husband in the Pacific to promise "that our children will learn kindness, patience, and the depth of love… that they shall never know hate, selfishness and death from such [a war] as this has been."

CLOSING WITH THE ENEMY

"The Americans are so helpless," Joseph Goebbels, Hitler's propaganda minister, said in 1942, "that they must fall back again and again upon boasting about their matériel." After the North Africa campaign, the United States made good on its boasts. The American army was small—only 5 million compared with Germany's 9 million—but it was amply supplied and agile, emphasizing speed and firepower. In 1944 and 1945, the United States carried the war to Japan and into the heart of Europe with a singular destructiveness. As the war drew to a close, Americans began to anticipate the difficulties of reconstructing the postwar world and to create institutions to structure a global economy at peace.

Taking the War to Europe

Using North Africa as a base, the Anglo-American Allies next attacked northward into Italy, knocking one of the Axis powers out of the war. In Sicily, where the Allies landed in July 1943, Patton applied the mobile, aggressive tactics he had advocated since 1940. Slicing the island in half and trapping a large part of the Italian army, he arrived at Messina too late to block the Germans' escape. The defeat shook Italy. Parliament deposed Mussolini and ordered his arrest. German troops took control and fiercely resisted the Allied landings at Salerno in September, and winter rains stopped the Anglo-American offensive south of Rome. American troops finally broke through to Rome on June 5, 1944.

The next day, **D-Day**, finally began the second front the Soviets had asked for. Early on the morning of June 6, 1944, the massive Allied invasion armada assembled off England's Channel coast and launched the assault on France's Normandy coast on beaches designated Juno, Gold, Sword, Utah, and Omaha. Hitler had fortified the beaches with an "Atlantic Wall" of mines, obstacles, heavy guns, and cement forts. Americans waded ashore on the lightly held Utah Beach without much difficulty, but on Omaha the small boats headed straight into concentrated fire. The boats unloaded too soon, and men with full packs plunged into deep water. Floating tanks overturned and sank with crews inside. Commanders briefly considered calling off the attack, but soldiers in small groups began moving inland to outflank German batteries. By the end of the day, they held the beach.

Invasion of Normandy The failure to seize an intact port nearly foiled the Normandy invasion plans, but low-ranking boat pilots saved the Allies from disaster. They invented the technique of driving large landing ships onto shore at high tide and unloading directly onto the beach. When the tide came in, the now-empty ships would float off and return to England for more cargo.

Eisenhower's greatest fear was another Italy. The hedgerow country behind the beaches contained the most defensible terrain between the Channel and Germany. Each field and pasture was protected by earthen mounds topped with shrubs, natural walls that isolated troops. When GIs crossed a hedgerow, "the Germans could knock off the first one or two, cause the others to duck down behind the bank and then call for his own mortar support," according to one infantryman. "The German mortars were very, very efficient." However, just as had happened on Omaha Beach, the defects of the generals' strategy were compensated for by the initiative of ordinary soldiers. On their own, tankers hand-built devices to help their tanks cut through the thick hedgerows. By the end of the month, the US advance broke through German defenses and captured the critical port city of Cherbourg.

Once in open country, highly mobile American infantry chased the retreating enemy across France to the fortified German border. There, in the Ardennes Forest, Hitler's armies rallied for a final desperate counterattack. Thirty divisions, supported by 1,000 aircraft, hit a lightly held sector of the American lines, broke through, and opened a "bulge" 40 miles wide and 60 miles deep in the Allied front. Two regiments were forced to surrender, but the 101st Airborne, encircled and besieged at Bastogne, held on to a critical road junction, slowing the German advance until Allies brought in reinforcements. The Battle of the Bulge lasted a month and cost more than 10,000 American dead and 47,000 wounded, but the German army had lost the ability to resist.

Island Hopping in the Pacific

To get close enough for a knockout blow at Japan, the United States had to pierce the barrier of fortified islands stretching across the western Pacific. The army and the navy each had a strategy and bickered over supplies and the shortest route to Tokyo. MacArthur favored a thrust from Australia through the Solomon Islands and New Guinea to retake the Philippines. Nimitz, in keeping with the US Navy's prewar plans, preferred a thrust across the central Pacific to seize islands as staging areas for an air and land assault on Japan.

By November 1943, MacArthur's American and Australian forces had advanced to Bougainville, the largest of the Solomon Islands and the nearest to the Japanese air and naval complex at Rabaul. Jungle fighting on these islands was especially vicious. Each side treated the other without mercy, killing prisoners, mutilating the dead, and fighting with "a brutish, primitive hatred," according to Eugene Sledge, whose marine comrades kept gold teeth and skulls as trophies. Air attacks pulverized Rabaul in early 1944, opening the way for an advance into the southern Philippines.

Meanwhile, Nimitz launched a naval attack on Japan's island bases. With 11 new aircraft carriers, the Fifth Fleet attacked Tarawa, a tiny atoll with 4,500 Japanese troops protected by bunkers and hidden guns. Coral reefs snagged landing craft, forcing troops to wade ashore under heavy fire. Americans were shocked by the losses, more than 3,000 dead and wounded, for such a small piece of territory, but it was only one of many island battles. "Island hopping" from Tarawa to the Marshall Islands and the Marianas, American forces bypassed strongly held islands and moved the battle closer to Japan.

The Allied capture of Saipan, Tinian, and Guam in July 1944 brought Japan within range of B-29 bombers. General Curtis LeMay landed his 21st Bomber Command on Saipan in January 1945 and began a new kind of air offensive, known as "city busting," against Japanese cities. LeMay experimented with low-level attacks using high explosives (to shatter houses) and incendiaries (to set fire to the debris). The proper mix could create a "firestorm," a flaming tornado hundreds of feet high. On the night of March 9, 1945, 334 bombers lit a fire in Tokyo that destroyed 267,000 buildings. The heat was so intense that the canals boiled and 83,000 people died from flames and suffocation. LeMay went on to burn more than 60 percent of Japan's cities. Americans felt the attacks justified, but, as historian Ronald Spector has written, bomber crews "realized that this was something new, something more terrible than even the normal awfulness of war."

Building a New World

As the war progressed across Europe and the Pacific, Allied leaders met to discuss their visions of the world after victory. In Casablanca in 1943, Roosevelt and Churchill agreed to demand the unconditional surrender of the Axis powers to give the Allies a free hand to set the terms of peace. No country planned for peace as thoroughly as the United States. The State, War, and Navy Departments undertook a comprehensive survey of the world, examining each country and territory to determine its importance to the United States. Planners had only sketchy ideas about future threats, but based on experience they believed that American security would depend on having a functioning international organization, a global system of free trade, and a worldwide network of American military bases.

The weak League of Nations stood little chance of maintaining the peace in the 1930s. Roosevelt envisioned a stronger organization led by regional powers acting as "policemen" within designated spheres of influence. The new organization would disband empires, placing "trusteeships" over colonial territories preparing for self-government. The world after victory would be a world of nations, not empires or blocs. In September 1944, delegates from 39 nations met at the Dumbarton Oaks estate in Washington, DC, and sketched out a plan for a **United Nations** (UN) organization comprising a general assembly, in which all nations would be represented, and an executive council made up of the United States, China, the Soviet Union, Britain, and France.

To American leaders, the lesson of the 1930s had been that without prosperity there could be no peace. They wanted to remove the economic conditions that caused desperate people to follow dictators into war. A true victory, they imagined, would create an open-door world, in which goods and money could move freely, eliminating the need or justification for conquest. In 1943, before the UN existed as an organization, the United States created the United Nations Relief and Rehabilitation Administration (UNRRA) to provide food and medicine to areas retaken by the Allies. The next year, the Bretton Woods Conference set conditions for a postwar expansion of trade with new institutions, the International Monetary Fund and the World Bank, to manage the flow of money in a global economy. The army established schools at universities, where officers studied languages and discussed strategies for instilling a democratic culture in enemy nations. The invasion of Italy provided a first test of these techniques, and the United States drew on its resources as an immigrant nation to staff units with Italian-speaking officers.

Military planners were not ready to stake America's future security entirely on trade or international organizations. Pearl Harbor had shown that oceans offered no protection against aggression. Military leaders could imagine aircraft and rockets striking deep into the American heartland without warning. Beginning in 1943, they laid plans for a global system of military bases from the Azores to Calcutta to Manila, encircling the vast Eurasian land mass. Planners could not say who the next enemy would be, but with such an extensive base network, the United States could act against any challenger before it could strike. Britain and the Soviet Union looked upon this plan warily, suspecting that they might be its targets, but American leaders were willing to take diplomatic risks to attain the security they felt they required.

The Fruits of Victory

Despite rumors of his failing health, Americans elected Franklin Roosevelt to a fourth term in 1944 by a margin of 53.5 percent to 46 percent for the challenger Thomas E. Dewey. On April 12, 1945, less than three months after his inauguration,

Roosevelt died suddenly of a cerebral hemorrhage at Warm Springs, Georgia. "Mr. Roosevelt's body was brought back to Washington today for the last time," reporter I. F. Stone wrote on April 21, 1945. "The marching men, the solemn bands, the armored cars, the regiment of Negro soldiers, the uniformed women's detachments. ... In that one quick look thousands of us said goodbye to a great and good man, and to an era." In Paris, French men and women offered condolences to American GIs. Flags flew at half-staff on Guadalcanal, Kwajalein, and Tarawa. Roosevelt died just days before Allied troops in Europe achieved the great victory for which he had struggled. On April 25, American and Soviet troops shook hands at Torgau in eastern Germany. On April 30, with Soviet soldiers just a few hundred yards away, Hitler committed suicide in his Berlin bunker. On May 8, all German forces surrendered unconditionally.

Harry S. Truman, the new vice president and former senator from Missouri, was now commander in chief. Shortly after he took office, aides informed him that the Manhattan Project would soon test a weapon that might end the war in Asia. The first atomic explosion took place in the desert near Alamogordo, New Mexico, on July 16, 1945. Truman, meeting with Churchill and Stalin at Potsdam, Germany, was elated by the news. He informed Stalin while Churchill looked on, watching the expression of the Soviet leader. The bomb had been developed to be used against the Axis enemy, but by the time Truman learned about it, American leaders already saw it as a powerful instrument of postwar diplomacy.

As American forces neared the Japanese home islands, defenders fought with suicidal ferocity. On Okinawa, soldiers and civilians retreated into caves and battled to the death. GIs feared the invasion of Japan's home islands, where resistance could only be worse. Then, on August 6, a B-29 dropped an atomic bomb on **Hiroshima**. Two days later, the Soviet Union declared war on Japan, and Soviet armies attacked

TIME LINE

Hiroshima The Museum of Science and Technology following the blast of the nuclear bomb.

▼**1942**
Philippines fall to Japan
Internment of Japanese
    Americans begins
Battles of Coral Sea and
    Midway turn the tide in
    the Pacific
Allies land in North Africa

▼**1943**
Allies land in Sicily
Churchill and Roosevelt
    meet at Casablanca

US troops advance to
    Bougainville
Marines capture Tarawa

▼**1944**
US troops capture Rome
Allied landings in
    Normandy
US troops capture Saipan
Bretton Woods Conference
Roosevelt reelected for
    fourth term

▼**1945**
Roosevelt dies
Harry S. Truman becomes
    president
Germany surrenders
Truman meets Churchill
    and Stalin at Potsdam
Atomic bombs dropped on
    Hiroshima and Nagasaki
Japan surrenders

deep into Manchuria. On August 9, the United States dropped a second atomic bomb, this time on Nagasaki. It detonated 1,900 feet above Shima Hospital. In a fraction of a second, the hospital and nearly a square mile of the city ignited. Bricks and granite melted in the nuclear fire. People were vaporized, some leaving shadows on the pavement. In the ruins of Hiroshima, a French Red Cross worker saw "not a bird or an animal. ... On what remained of the station facade the hands of the clock had been stopped by the fire at 8:15. It was perhaps the first time in the history of humanity that the birth of a new era was recorded on the face of a clock."

CONCLUSION

Emperor Hirohito announced Japan's unconditional surrender on August 14. In New York, crowds celebrated, but everywhere there was silence and reflection. Thirty million people had been killed; great cities lay in ruins. At the end of the war, the United States' economic, scientific, and military mastery reached a pinnacle never attained by any of the great empires of history. Two-thirds of the world's gold was in American treasuries; half of the world's manufactured goods were made in the United States. At its height, imperial Britain controlled 25 percent of the world's wealth. In 1945, the United States controlled 40 percent. America's air force, almost 80,000 planes, dominated the skies; its fleet had more ships than the navies of all its enemies and allies combined. Then there was the atomic bomb. The rest of the world looked to see how the United States would use its formidable wealth and power.

The war's sudden end meant Americans had to reconvert to a peacetime economy, preferably one more stable and prosperous than the depression economy of the 1930s. A. Philip Randolph predicted government would have to take a larger role in raising wages and stimulating key industries, such as housing, if returning soldiers were to find jobs and goods to buy. The postwar future looked tenuous. America could either succumb to "a native variety of fascism" or open an era of expanding rights, democracy, and material abundance.

WHO, WHAT, WHERE

atomic bomb   761

Auschwitz   770

braceros   766

D-Day   772

Eisenhower, Dwight D.   762

"Four Freedoms"   768

"Good Neighbor"   751

Hiroshima   776

Holocaust   769

Internationalists   749

internment   758

isolationists   749

Manhattan Project   761

Midway   756

Pearl Harbor   750

Rosie the Riveter   766

totalitarianism   750

Tuskegee Airmen   757

United Nations   775

REVIEW QUESTIONS

1. Which was more important to victory at Midway, planning or luck?
2. Why did the population of the West grow so rapidly during the war?
3. According to American leaders, what caused World War II? How did their answers to that question affect their plans for the postwar world?
4. Thurgood Marshall worried about the emergence of "gestapos" in America. What did he mean?

CRITICAL-THINKING QUESTIONS

1. Contrast isolationist and internationalist viewpoints. How did they imagine different futures for the United States?
2. The government used propaganda and repressive laws to control domestic opinion during World War I. Why was there no repeat of those policies in World War II?
3. Some historians blame Roosevelt for luring the United States into war. How might that historical view be rooted in the isolationist/internationalist debate?

SUGGESTED READINGS

Blum, John Morton. *V Was for Victory: Politics and American Culture During World War II.* New York: Harcourt Brace Jovanovich, 1976.

Borgwardt, Elizabeth. *A New Deal for the World: America's Vision for Human Rights* Cambridge, MA: Belknap, 2005.

Kersten, Andrew E. *Labor's Home Front: The American Federation of Labor During World War II.* New York: New York University Press, 2009.

Kruse, Kevin, and Stephen Tuck, eds. *Fog of War: The Second World War and the Civil Rights Movement.* New York: Oxford University Press, 2012.

The National World War II Museum. https://www.nationalww2museum.org/

For further review materials and resource information, please visit www.oup.com/us/ofthepeople

23.1   FRANKLIN D. ROOSEVELT, "FOUR FREEDOMS" SPEECH (1941)

Before American entry into World War II, in his annual State of the Union address, Franklin D. Roosevelt spoke candidly about the likelihood that the nation would face war. Even as he outlined the steps the nation and its citizens should take toward preparedness, he continued to highlight the goals of his New Deal programs. Additionally, Roosevelt outlined the "Four Freedoms," values upon which he hoped the postwar world could be based. Importantly, Roosevelt envisioned these freedoms not only for Americans but also for people all around the world.

As your President, performing my constitutional duty to "give to the Congress information of the state of the Union," I find it, unhappily, necessary to report that the future and the safety of our country and of our democracy are overwhelmingly involved in events far beyond our borders.

Armed defense of democratic existence is now being gallantly waged in four continents. If that defense fails, all the population and all the resources of Europe, Asia, Africa and Australasia will be dominated by the conquerors. Let us remember that the total of those populations and their resources in those four continents greatly exceeds the sum total of the population and the resources of the whole of the Western Hemisphere—many times over.

In times like these it is immature—and incidentally, untrue—for anybody to brag that an unprepared America, single-handed, and with one hand tied behind its back, can hold off the whole world.

No realistic American can expect from a dictator's peace international generosity, or return of true independence, or world disarmament, or freedom of expression, or freedom of religion—or even good business.

Such a peace would bring no security for us or for our neighbors. "Those, who would give up essential liberty to purchase a little temporary safety, deserve neither liberty nor safety."

As a nation, we may take pride in the fact that we are soft-hearted; but we cannot afford to be soft-headed.

We must always be wary of those who with sounding brass and a tinkling cymbal preach the "ism" of appeasement.

We must especially beware of that small group of selfish men who would clip the wings of the American eagle in order to feather their own nests.

I have recently pointed out how quickly the tempo of modern warfare could bring into our very midst the physical attack which we must eventually expect if the dictator nations win this war.

There is much loose talk of our immunity from immediate and direct invasion from across the seas. Obviously, as long as the British Navy retains its power, no such danger exists. Even if there were no British Navy, it is not probable that any enemy would be stupid enough to attack us by landing troops in the United States from across thousands of miles of ocean, until it had acquired strategic bases from which to operate.

But we learn much from the lessons of the past years in Europe—particularly the lesson of Norway, whose essential seaports were captured by treachery and surprise built up over a series of years.

The first phase of the invasion of this Hemisphere would not be the landing of regular troops. The necessary strategic points would be occupied by secret agents and their dupes—and great numbers of them are already here, and in Latin America.

As long as the aggressor nations maintain the offensive, they—not we—will choose the time and the place and the method of their attack.

That is why the future of all the American Republics is today in serious danger.

That is why this Annual Message to the Congress is unique in our history.

That is why every member of the Executive Branch of the Government and every member of the Congress faces great responsibility and great accountability.

The need of the moment is that our actions and our policy should be devoted primarily—almost exclusively—to meeting this foreign peril. For all our domestic problems are now a part of the great emergency.

Just as our national policy in internal affairs has been based upon a decent respect for the rights and the dignity of all our fellow men within our gates, so our national policy in foreign affairs has been based on a decent respect for the rights and dignity of all nations, large and small. And the justice of morality must and will win in the end.

Our national policy is this:

First, by an impressive expression of the public will and without regard to partisanship, we are committed to all-inclusive national defense.

Second, by an impressive expression of the public will and without regard to partisanship, we are committed to full support of all those resolute peoples, everywhere, who are resisting aggression and are thereby keeping war away from our Hemisphere. By this support, we express our determination that the democratic cause shall prevail; and we strengthen the defense and the security of our own nation.

Third, by an impressive expression of the public will and without regard to partisanship, we are committed to the proposition that principles of morality and considerations for our own security will never permit us to acquiesce in a peace dictated by aggressors and sponsored by appeasers. We know that enduring peace cannot be bought at the cost of other people's freedom.

In the recent national election there was no substantial difference between the two great parties in respect to that national policy. No issue was fought out on this line before the American electorate. Today it is abundantly evident that American citizens everywhere are demanding and supporting speedy and complete action in recognition of obvious danger.

Therefore, the immediate need is a swift and driving increase in our armament production.

Leaders of industry and labor have responded to our summons. Goals of speed have been set. In some cases these goals are being reached ahead of time; in some cases we are on schedule; in other cases there are slight but not serious delays; and in some cases—and I am sorry to say very important cases—we are all concerned by the slowness of the accomplishment of our plans.

The Army and Navy, however, have made substantial progress during the past year. Actual experience is improving and speeding up our methods of production with every passing day. And today's best is not good enough for tomorrow.

I am not satisfied with the progress thus far made. The men in charge of the program represent the best in training, in ability, and in patriotism. They are not satisfied with the progress thus far made. None of us will be satisfied until the job is done.

No matter whether the original goal was set too high or too low, our objective is quicker and better results. To give you two illustrations:

We are behind schedule in turning out finished airplanes; we are working day and night to solve the innumerable problems and to catch up.

We are ahead of schedule in building warships but we are working to get even further ahead of that schedule.

To change a whole nation from a basis of peacetime production of implements of peace to a basis of wartime production of implements of war is no small task. And the greatest difficulty comes at the beginning of the program, when new tools, new plant facilities, new assembly lines, and new ship ways must first be constructed before the actual materiel begins to flow steadily and speedily from them.

The Congress, of course, must rightly keep itself informed at all times of the progress of the program. However, there is certain information, as the Congress itself will readily recognize, which, in the interests of our own security and those of the nations that we are supporting, must of needs be kept in confidence.

New circumstances are constantly begetting new needs for our safety. I shall ask this Congress for greatly increased new appropriations and authorizations to carry on what we have begun.

I also ask this Congress for authority and for funds sufficient to manufacture additional munitions and war supplies of many kinds, to be turned over to those nations which are now in actual war with aggressor nations.

Our most useful and immediate role is to act as an arsenal for them as well as for ourselves. They do not need man power, but they do need billions of dollars worth of the weapons of defense.

The time is near when they will not be able to pay for them all in ready cash. We cannot, and we will not, tell them that they must surrender, merely because of present inability to pay for the weapons which we know they must have.

I do not recommend that we make them a loan of dollars with which to pay for these weapons—a loan to be repaid in dollars.

I recommend that we make it possible for those nations to continue to obtain war materials in the United States, fitting their orders into our own program. Nearly all their materiel would, if the time ever came, be useful for our own defense.

Taking counsel of expert military and naval authorities, considering what is best for our own security, we are free to decide how much should be kept here and how much should be sent abroad to our friends who by their determined and heroic resistance are giving us time in which to make ready our own defense.

For what we send abroad, we shall be repaid within a reasonable time following the close of hostilities, in similar materials, or, at our option, in other goods of many kinds, which they can produce and which we need.

Let us say to the democracies: "We Americans are vitally concerned in your defense of freedom. We are putting forth our energies, our resources and our organizing powers to give you the strength to regain and maintain a free world. We shall send you, in ever-increasing numbers, ships, planes, tanks, guns. This is our purpose and our pledge."

In fulfillment of this purpose we will not be intimidated by the threats of dictators that they will regard as a breach of international law or as an act of war our aid to the democracies which dare to resist their aggression. Such aid is not an act of war, even if a dictator should unilaterally proclaim it so to be.

When the dictators, if the dictators, are ready to make war upon us, they will not wait for an act of war on our part. They did not wait for Norway or Belgium or the Netherlands to commit an act of war.

Their only interest is in a new one-way international law, which lacks mutuality in its observance, and, therefore, becomes an instrument of oppression.

The happiness of future generations of Americans may well depend upon how effective and how immediate we can make our aid felt. No one can tell the exact character of the emergency situations that we may be called upon to meet. The Nation's hands must not be tied when the Nation's life is in danger.

We must all prepare to make the sacrifices that the emergency—almost as serious as war itself—demands. Whatever stands in the way of speed and efficiency in defense preparations must give way to the national need.

A free nation has the right to expect full cooperation from all groups. A free nation has the right to look to the leaders of business, of labor, and of agriculture to take the lead in stimulating effort, not among other groups but within their own groups.

The best way of dealing with the few slackers or trouble makers in our midst is, first, to shame them by patriotic example, and, if that fails, to use the sovereignty of Government to save Government.

As men do not live by bread alone, they do not fight by armaments alone. Those who man our defenses, and those behind them who build our defenses, must have the stamina and the courage which come from unshakable belief in the manner of life which they are defending. The mighty action that we are calling for cannot be based on a disregard of all things worth fighting for.

The Nation takes great satisfaction and much strength from the things which have been done to make its people conscious of their individual stake in the preservation of democratic life in America. Those things have toughened the fibre of our people, have renewed their faith and strengthened their devotion to the institutions we make ready to protect.

Certainly this is no time for any of us to stop thinking about the social and economic problems which are the root cause of the social revolution which is today a supreme factor in the world.

For there is nothing mysterious about the foundations of a healthy and strong democracy.

The basic things expected by our people of their political and economic systems are simple. They are:

Equality of opportunity for youth and for others.

Jobs for those who can work.

Security for those who need it.

The ending of special privilege for the few.

The preservation of civil liberties for all.

The enjoyment of the fruits of scientific progress in a wider and constantly rising standard of living.

These are the simple, basic things that must never be lost sight of in the turmoil and unbelievable complexity of our modern world. The inner and abiding strength of our economic and political systems is dependent upon the degree to which they fulfill these expectations.

Many subjects connected with our social economy call for immediate improvement.

As examples:

We should bring more citizens under the coverage of old-age pensions and unemployment insurance.

We should widen the opportunities for adequate medical care.

We should plan a better system by which persons deserving or needing gainful employment may obtain it.

I have called for personal sacrifice. I am assured of the willingness of almost all Americans to respond to that call.

A part of the sacrifice means the payment of more money in taxes. In my Budget Message I shall recommend that a greater portion of this great defense program be paid for from taxation than we are paying today. No person should try, or be allowed, to get rich out of this program; and the principle of tax payments in accordance with ability to pay should be constantly before our eyes to guide our legislation.

If the Congress maintains these principles, the voters, putting patriotism ahead of pocketbooks, will give you their applause.

In the future days, which we seek to make secure, we look forward to a world founded upon four essential human freedoms.

The first is freedom of speech and expression—everywhere in the world.

The second is freedom of every person to worship God in his own way—everywhere in the world.

The third is freedom from want—which, translated into world terms, means economic understandings which will secure to every nation a healthy peacetime life for its inhabitants—everywhere in the world.

The fourth is freedom from fear—which, translated into world terms, means a world-wide reduction of armaments to such a point and in such a thorough fashion that no nation will be in a position to commit an act of physical aggression against any neighbor—anywhere in the world.

That is no vision of a distant millennium. It is a definite basis for a kind of world attainable in our own time and generation. That kind of world is the very antithesis of the so-called new order of tyranny which the dictators seek to create with the crash of a bomb.

To that new order we oppose the greater conception—the moral order. A good society is able to face schemes of world domination and foreign revolutions alike without fear.

Since the beginning of our American history, we have been engaged in change—in a perpetual peaceful revolution—a revolution which goes on steadily, quietly adjusting itself to changing conditions—without the concentration camp or the quick-lime in the ditch. The world order which we seek is the cooperation of free countries, working together in a friendly, civilized society.

This nation has placed its destiny in the hands and heads and hearts of its millions of free men and women; and its faith in freedom under the guidance of God. Freedom means the supremacy of human rights everywhere. Our support goes to those who struggle to gain those rights or keep them. Our strength is our unity of purpose. To that high concept there can be no end save victory.

Source: Franklin D. Roosevelt, "Four Freedoms," Annual Message to Congress on the State of the Union, January 6, 1941. https://www.ourdocuments.gov/doc.php?flash=false&doc=70&page=t ranscript

23.2   CHARLES LINDBERGH, AMERICA FIRST COMMITTEE ADDRESS (1941)

Anxious at the prospect of American involvement in another world war, many Americans expressed a desire that the United States remain outside the conflict taking place overseas. Those who joined the organization America First were especially vocal about the need for the United States to maintain its independence from the conflict while developing its military capabilities for its own defense rather than the defense of its allies.

In time of war, truth is always replaced by propaganda. I do not believe we should be too quick to criticize the actions of a belligerent nation. There is always the question whether we, ourselves, would do better under similar circumstances. But we in this country have a right to think of the welfare of America first, just as the people in England thought first of their own country when they encouraged the smaller nations of Europe to fight against hopeless odds. When England asks us to enter this war, she is considering her own future, and that of her Empire. In making our reply, I believe we should consider the future of the United States and that of the Western Hemisphere. …

There are many… interventionists in America, but there are more people among us of a different type. That is why you and I are assembled here tonight. There is a policy open to this nation that will lead to success—a policy that leaves us free to follow our own way of life, and to develop our own civilization. It is not a new and untried idea. It was advocated by Washington. It was incorporated in the Monroe Doctrine. Under its guidance, the United States became the greatest nation in the world. It is based upon the belief that the security of a nation lies in the strength and character of its own people. It recommends the maintenance of armed forces sufficient to defend this hemisphere from attack by any combination of foreign powers. It demands faith in an independent American destiny. This is the policy of the America First Committee today. It is a policy not of isolation, but of independence; not of defeat, but of courage. It is a policy that led this nation to success during the most trying years of our history, and it is a policy that will lead us to success again. …

War is not inevitable for this country. Such a claim is defeatism in the true sense. No one can make us fight abroad unless we ourselves are willing to do so. No one will attempt to fight us here if we arm ourselves as a great nation should be armed. Over a hundred million people in this nation are opposed to entering the war. If the principles of Democracy mean anything at all, that is reason enough for us to stay out. If we are forced into a war against the wishes of an overwhelming majority of our people, we will have proved Democracy such a failure at home that there will be little use fighting for it abroad.

The time has come when those of us who believe in an independent American destiny must band together, and organize for strength. We have been led toward war by a minority of our people. This minority has power. It has influence. It has a loud voice. But it does not represent the American people. During the last several years, I have travelled over this country, from one end to the other. I have talked to many hundreds of men and women, and I have had letters from tens of thousands more, who feel the same way as you and I. Most of these people have no influence or power. Most of them have no means of expressing their convictions, except by their vote which has always been against this war. They are the citizens who have had to work too hard at their daily jobs to organize political meetings. Hitherto, they have relied upon their vote to express their feelings; but now they find that it is hardly remembered except in the oratory of a political campaign. These people—the majority of hard-working American citizens are with us. They are the true strength of our country. And they are beginning to realize, as you and I, that there are times when we must sacrifice our normal interests in life in order to insure the safety and the welfare of our nation.

Such a time has come. Such a crisis is here. That is why the America First Committee has been formed—to give voice to the people who have no newspaper, or news reel, or radio station at their command; to the people who must do the paying, and the fighting, and the dying, if this country enters the war.

Whether or not we do enter the war, rests upon the shoulders of you in this audience, upon us here on this platform, upon meetings of this kind that are being held by Americans in every section of the United States today. It depends upon the action we take, and the courage we show at this time. If you believe in an independent destiny for America, if you believe that this country should not enter the war in Europe, we ask you to join the America First Committee in its stand. We ask you to share our faith in the ability of this nation to defend itself, to develop its own civilization, and to contribute to the progress of mankind in a more constructive and intelligent way than has yet been found by the warring nations of Europe. We need your support, and we need it now. The time to act is here.

Source: Charles Lindbergh, speech delivered at America First Committee Meeting, April 23, 1941, http://www.charleslindbergh.com/americanfirst/speech2.asp.

23.3   LETTER FROM JAMES G. THOMPSON TO THE EDITOR OF THE *PITTSBURGH COURIER* (1942)

Black Americans served in every theater of World War II. By 1945, over 1.2 million Black soldiers were in uniform at home in the United States, in Europe, and in the Pacific. Despite their bravery and commitment to American war aims, Black servicemen and women continued to face discrimination, both at home and abroad. Hoping that the United States would honor its claims to ensure the Four Freedoms for everyone "everywhere in the world," African Americans embraced a "Double Victory" campaign, intended to conquer fascism overseas and Jim Crow at home.

Letter to the Editor, *Pittsburgh Courier*, January 31, 1942

Dear Editor:

Like all true Americans, my greatest desire at this time, this crucial point of our history, is a desire for a complete victory over the forces of evil, which threaten our existence today. Behind that desire is also a desire to serve, this, my country, in the most advantageous way. Most of our leaders are suggesting that we sacrifice every other ambition to the paramount one, victory. With this I agree; but I also wonder if another victory could not be achieved at the same time.

After all, the things that beset the world now are basically the same things which upset the equilibrium of nations internally, states, counties, cities, homes and even the individual.

Being an American of dark complexion and some 26 years, these questions flash through my mind: "Should I sacrifice my life to live half American?" "Will things be better for the next generation in the peace to follow?" "Would it be demanding too much to demand full citizenship rights in exchange for the sacrificing of my life?" "Is the kind of America I know worth defending?" "Will America be a true and pure democracy after this war?" "Will colored Americans suffer still the indignities that have been heaped upon them in the past?"

These and other questions need answering; I want to know, and I believe every colored American, who is thinking, wants to know.

This may be the wrong time to broach such subjects, but haven't all good things obtained by men been secured through sacrifice during just such times of strife?

I suggest that while we keep defense and victory in the forefront that we don't lose sight of our fight for true democracy at home.

The "V for Victory" sign is being displayed prominently in all so-called democratic countries which are fighting for victory over aggression, slavery and tyranny. If this V sign means that to those now engaged in this great conflict then let colored Americans adopt the double VV for a double victory. The first V for victory over our enemies from without, the second V for victory over our enemies within. For surely those who perpetrate these ugly prejudices here are seeing to destroy our democratic form of government just as surely as the Axis forces.

This should not and would not lessen our efforts to bring this conflict to a successful conclusion; but should and would make us stronger to resist these evil forces which threaten us. America could become united as never before and become truly the home of democracy.

In way of an answer to the foregoing questions in a preceding paragraph, I might say that there is no doubt that this country is worth defending; things will be different for the next generation; colored Americans will come into their own, and America will eventually become the true democracy it was designed to be. These things will become a reality in time; but not through any relaxation of the efforts to secure them.

In conclusion let me say that though these questions often permeate my mind, I love America and am willing to die for the America I know will someday become a reality.

James G. Thompson

Source: James G. Thompson, letter to the editor, *Pittsburgh Courier*, originally printed January 31, 1942; reprinted April 11, 1942, p. 5.

23.4 FROM ITALY TO CHICAGO, PFC. RAY LATAL COMES HOME (1945)

Yank magazine served as the weekly publication for the United States Army, featuring articles about life overseas, artwork and letters from active military, and pictures of "pin-up girls" intended to boost soldiers' morale. In 1945, the magazine featured an article about veterans returning home and encountering the changes that had occurred on the home front since they had been away, foreshadowing the larger social and cultural shifts veterans would encounter once the Second World War came to a close.

"Italy to Chicago," *Yank: The Army Weekly,* Vol. 3, No. 40, March 23, 1945

CHICAGO—Pfc. Ray Latal is back in his old Czech-Polish neighborhood on Chicago's West Side. About a year ago he was wounded by shrapnel in half a dozen places in both legs and in the left shoulder during the crossing of the Rapido River in Italy. He drew a CDD[1] after seven months in the hospital.

"Legs," as the lanky veteran is known in his section, is okay now to all appearances, but he has a silver plug in the shoulder to keep the marrow in one of the shattered bones from drying out. His legs tire if he stands too long and, although he is only 21, he can predict changes in the weather from the aches in his bones. "They tell me I talk a lot in my sleep," Legs says, "And I still get excited when I hear an airplane." But he no longer jumps up nervously, as he did at first, when a plane comes in for a landing on the nearby Chicago Municipal Airport.

After 28 months of service, mostly as a rifleman in the 36th Division, Legs received his discharge late in 1944. He did not go back to his old job of running a drill press in the small machine shop of the Wittek Manufacturing Company, though the people there offered it to him. He went instead to the huge Dodge war plant in South Chicago, where wages are twice as high. At Dodge Chicago, as they call the mile-square plant, Latal makes $62 a week minus $10 in taxes. He operates a turret lathe, cutting sleeves for the oil system of B-29 engine propeller shafts.

Unmarried, he lives at home with his parents and his sister Violet in a four-room basement apartment in a two-story red-brick house on Kedzie Avenue. To those who have not been away, the neighborhood seems the same as ever. Kaplan's dry-goods store has the familiar sales signs, and Homan's Theater still proclaims on its marquee that ladies get dishes plus two big features on Wednesdays and Thursdays. But for Legs it has been almost a matter of adjusting to a strange environment. Take the West End Bowling Alley.

---

[1] Certificate of disability for discharge.

Legs still bowls as he did before he went into the Army, and he is pleased to discover that something, possibly the marksmanship training, has boosted his score from 165 to 181. But the bowling alley seems much less fun to him now than it was, "There's a different class of people up there," Latal complains. "What we used to call 'little kids.' They're grown up now—17 and 18." The alleys swarm with women, Legs remarks, and he has to shake his head sometimes when he hears the girl bowlers scream for a strike, and scream again for a near-miss.

The Tytans, an all-sports team of local youngsters with whom Legs used to bowl at West End and play baseball in the parks, are scattered now to the four corners of the earth. Once in a while, however, Legs gets together with other stray Tytans who have also come back, such as William Navarital, who was discharged from the Marines for heart murmur, and Ted Juzynski, whose feet froze on Attu. They were privates.

The rest of the bunch are away, and some will not be back. Ray Sefcik, second-baseman for the Tytans, was killed near Aachen. He was a buck sergeant. Pvt. George (Beaner) Root, Tytan shortstop, has a cluster for his Purple Heart, after being wounded in Italy and in France. He is still overseas. Pfc, Andrew (Sausage) Sosko, Tytan catcher, is in New Guinea, but is all right according to the latest word received at Jim's candy store, the traditional Tytan meeting place. Legs, recalling that Sosko was also known as "Mr.Craps," points out that nobody rolls dice any more under the crap-shooting tree by the main doors of Cyrus McCormick Grammar School, across the street from Jim's candy store.

Jim's is still on Legs' list of stopping points at night, but going there only makes him more lonesome. In many ways, the place is unaltered. The hot-blast stove is still there.The glass case is full of penny and nickel candies, although odd new kinds like "P-38 Bubble Gum" have replaced many of the known brands as a result of various confectionery shortages. The shelves are still piled high with notebooks, Hedy Lamarr looseleaf paper, cheap fountain pens and greeting cards for all occasions. The biggest physical change was the disappearance of the two-cents-a-record juke box on which Legs used to play "Elmer's Tune." The company that owns the machines moved them all to Cicero when Chicago put a $50 license charge on juke boxes.

It's Jim's changed clientele that bothers Legs. The store's service honor roll of patrons lists 100 names, and nowadays the names heard around the place are those of the same younger element that has taken over the West Side Bowling Alley. The scarred wooden card table on which the Tytans used to deal the pasteboards has been shoved from the center of the room to a corner. The younger generation irreverently uses the table as an extra bench. ...

In paying as much attention as he does to the little changes at home and in the neighborhood. Legs knows he is not exceptional among returning veterans. Men like former T/Sgt. Leroy Huber, who lives a few blocks from Legs, say they have had the same reaction. Huber was astonished when he had his first look at the corner of Wabansia and Bosworth where his local sports team, the King Coles, had hung out.

"For a minute there," said Huber, "it looked like I was on the wrong street. Nering's, the grocery store that was near the corner, sold out and wasn't there any more. The building was torn down. King Cole's tavern had a different coat of paint, a green color. Before, I think it was white. The name of Tobacci's tavern was changed to Braumeister's. They even took the old mailbox off the corner. You have to walk two more blocks now to mail a letter — to North and Ashland. No one had told me anything at all."

Huber, by the way, says that the huddled gray houses of his part of northwest Chicago never seemed so "cooped together" as they do now that he has come from two years of outdoor living. He is taking welding at Greer's, a trade school, and plans to start a farm in Missouri after the war boom dies down. A native Chicagoan, he intends to hire out for a while on some one else's acres to learn the ropes. He figures the welding knowledge will enable him to repair his own gear. The Government is paying his expenses at Greer's under the education provisions of the GI Bill of Rights.

In working at Dodge Chicago one of Legs Latal's first difficulties was to get accustomed to the thousands of women working in the factory with him. They wear slacks and turbans and many use a terrific kind of lipstick and nail polish known as pink lightning. There is a severe shortage of eligible males, but Legs notices that the girls are a bit unenthusiastic about CDD men as if the women were worrying about what caused the man's discharge.

Latal has been an absentee from his war job a total 3 1/2 days so far in his first month's work. Aches from his wounds kept him home. Some other ex-GIs at the plant have better records, some worse. Ex-Pfc. Joe Brenner, who received a CDD for malaria and arthritis developed while he was in combat with the Americal Division on Guadalcanal, is among those with a stronger record. Brenner is hot on the subject of getting the B-29s into the air, and his face flushes when he talks about how the men on his line went on strike once because the management would not provide stools for them to sit on at lunchtime.

On the other hand, there's another Americal pfc a few aisles over from Legs' lathe who hasn't done so well. He trims bushings inside B-29 engine motorheads. Some weeks his machine is idle 40 percent of the time. He says that because of wounds from Guadalcanal and Bougainville he often has to stay home from work. The same goes for his brother who has had 18 attacks of malaria since he was a corporal in the South Pacific. It seems to work out like taking turns—on days when one is sick, the other is well and working.

The absenteeing former pfc admits that some mornings hangovers have also influenced his decision to stay home. Calvert's and coke look mighty attractive to him, he says, after some of the stuff that substituted for liquor on Guadalcanal. He particularly mentions "torpedo juice"—alcohol drained from the submarine tin fish and cooked up with glycerine, sugar and three-parts water.

Legs scarcely touched a drop before he went into the Army, but now he likes a couple of beers, or even six or seven on occasion. Before he was inducted he was not inside Buck's Tavern (now Kedzie's Cafe), the corner bar, more than three or four times. He drops in there several times a week now. "My mother still wonders why I go to the tavern," Legs says.

Latal did not go out with girls much when the Tytans were functioning. He calls on one now but does not like to say much on the subject.

Legs hears that the B-29-engine lines will be turned over to automobile manufacturing after the war, so he considers himself all set so far as a permanent job is concerned. Even so, Latal feels that he is marking time.

"Nobody's around, there's nothing to do—I believe I'd rather be back in the Army," he says moodily sometimes. Other times, as he studies the small fry at Jim's and the women at the bowling alley, he thinks of the Tytans and predicts that "things'll get back in shape when they get back." When he says that, though, his tone is more hopeful than confident.

Source: "Italy to Chicago," *Yank: The Army Weekly,* Vol. 3, No. 40, March 23, 1945.

24

IS THIS TOMORROW

The Cold War
1945–1954

< 1947 comic book cover

John Turchinetz

In January 1946, John Turchinetz finally headed home to Boston, Massachusetts, from World War II. Just out of high school, this son of a Romanian-born father and Ukrainian-born mother had joined the Navy three years earlier at the age of 18. Serving as a seaman aboard the cruiser named for his home city, John had manned an antiaircraft gun, suffered a disabling injury, and won medals in the Pacific. After the Japanese surrender, he and some of his shipmates from the *Boston* toured the city of Hiroshima, devastated by the first atomic bomb. "It was unbelievable," the seaman recalled. Like other Americans, John and his shipmates had had enough of war. "We were glad that it was over," he said. "We wanted peace."

At first, they found it. Back in Boston, John had a joyful reunion with his family. The mayor threw a big party for the crew of the *Boston*. Living with his parents again, John went to work at the federal Navy Yard in the harbor. The government needed the veteran, but not his beloved ship, in the new era of peace: the *Boston* was taken out of service—"mothballed," they called it. Although John, like many veterans, "felt a little different," his neighborhood and his country seemed the same. After the experience of war, people were friendly and united. "We were trying to help each other," John remembered. "We were trying to be normal."

The sense of normality—the feeling of friendliness, unity, and peace—did not last long at all. Before the end of 1946, the Cold War, a tense confrontation with the Soviet Union, began to disrupt American life. Soviet influence quickly spread in Eastern Europe. The USSR absorbed Ukraine, the homeland of John Turchinetz's father, and took territory from Romania, his mother's homeland, which then became a Soviet ally. Convinced the Soviets would keep trying to expand their power and spread communism across Europe, US leaders challenged their former allies. While the Cold War developed, Americans also faced the task of maintaining prosperity in peacetime. Laborers, women, and African Americans struggled to preserve and extend their rights and opportunities. President Harry Truman and the Democratic Party struggled as well to preserve their power and implement a liberal agenda.

The Cold War quickly became the dominant fact of national life in the late 1940s. To contain Soviet and communist expansion, the US government took unprecedented peacetime actions. But massive foreign aid, new alliances, and a military buildup did not prevent the Cold War from widening and intensifying. By 1950, the nation was fighting a hot war on the other side of the world in Korea. By then, too, Americans knew that the Soviet Union had nuclear weapons that could conceivably devastate the United States. In turn, the Truman administration stepped up military spending and developed more powerful nuclear weapons. As the Cold War seemed to spiral out of control, fear gripped American society. Emigres from Eastern Europe—people like John Turchinetz's parents—could be suspect. A frenzied search for communist subversives at home threatened civil liberties. In one way or another, the Cold War unsettled the lives of all Americans for years to come.

John Turchinetz was not completely surprised by what happened. "I was hoping that... there would be no more war," he said, "but people being what they are... it didn't happen." Mostly he blamed the Soviet Union, dominated by communist Russians. "Even at that time, I knew about Russia," John declared many years later. "I still don't trust them."

ORIGINS OF THE COLD WAR

In a span of two years, the United States and the Soviet Union went from a wartime alliance to the protracted rivalry known as the Cold War. The sweeping, long-term consequences of the Cold War made it particularly important for Americans to understand the origins of the conflict. From the outset, the United States and the Soviet Union tried to pin the blame for the Cold War on each other. For a long time, Americans, like John Turchinetz, wanted to believe that the Soviet Union, authoritarian and expansionist, was solely responsible. However, historians have gradually offered a more critical perspective, and they generally agree that actions by both countries caused the Cold War.

Ideological Competition

There is less agreement about the precise sources of the conflict. Ideological, political, military, and economic factors all clearly played a role. Ever since the founding of the Soviet Union toward the end of World War I, Soviets and Americans were ideological adversaries with different political systems. The Soviet Union was committed to communism and socialism, and the United States was committed to democracy and capitalism. Despite their differences, the two countries fought as allies in World War II. Wartime decisions, especially about the postwar world, laid the groundwork for animosity after 1945. In peacetime, the Soviet Union and the United States were the only countries strong enough to threaten each other, and World War II showed that with modern arms both sides could strike with devastating suddenness. Moreover, they had different political, military, and economic ambitions. By 1947, those different goals produced open antagonism. With the United States' vow to combat the spread of communism, the Cold War was under way.

The Union of Soviet Socialist Republics (USSR) emerged from the Russian Revolution of 1917 and the civil war that followed. Vladimir Lenin's Bolshevik Party introduced a socialist economy in which the state—the government—owned factories and farms. At home, the Soviet Union practiced forms of economic and social regimentation Americans recognized from Nazi Germany and imperial Japan, limiting individual rights, including freedom of speech and religion, and achieving a self-contained **autarkic** economy. Abroad, the new nation endorsed the revolutionary overthrow of capitalism.

The Soviets' ~~Marxist~~ ideology obviously set them at odds with American ideals. The vast majority of Americans favored a capitalist economy, in which private citizens owned property. They celebrated individualism, freedom of speech, freedom of religion, and democratic government based on free elections. Communists believed all modern societies would eventually eliminate religion and private property and set the collective good over the rights of the individual.

Nevertheless, open conflict was not inevitable. Although American leaders hated communism, the USSR was weak and hemmed in by powerful neighbors, Germany in the West and Japan in the East. It posed no military threat to the United States in the 1920s and 1930s and could even be helpful to American interests. President Franklin Roosevelt, eager to promote trade and restrain Japanese expansion, officially recognized the Soviet Union in 1933.

Uneasy Allies

World War II demonstrated that, despite their differences, the United States and the Soviet Union could become allies. After the German invasion of the USSR and the Japanese attack on Pearl Harbor, the United States and the Soviets were thrown together in the war against fascism. They were uneasy allies at best. For many Americans, the lesson of the war was that the United States could not tolerate aggression. No new dictator should ever be able to take over other European countries unopposed, as Hitler did, nor should any single power be allowed to dominate Eurasia. By 1945, some Americans already equated the Soviets with the Nazis by denouncing "Red Fascism."

Different experiences drove each country to protect itself from future disasters. American leaders believed autarkic trade blocs had caused both the Great Depression and the war that followed, and they resolved to rebuild the world economy as a single system, with reduced trade barriers and uniform rules. Soviet leaders feared a repeat of the last two wars, when Poland and Eastern Europe had been staging areas for invasions that claimed millions of Russian lives. But the lessons they drew from war led to opposite solutions: American leaders favored an interdependent system, with open borders allowing goods, information, and people to move freely; Soviet leaders felt only a closed system and tight controls would give it real protection.

Wartime decisions also aggravated tensions. In 1943, the American government created ill feeling by excluding the Soviets from the surrender of Italy. The delay of the Allied invasion of France until 1944 embittered the Soviets, who were desperately resisting the Germans at the cost of millions of lives. The American government further strained relations by sharing news of its secret atomic bomb project with the British but not with the Soviets.

Decisions about the postwar world led to trouble as well. At a conference in Yalta in the Soviet Union in February 1945, Franklin Roosevelt, Josef Stalin, and British Prime Minister Winston Churchill proposed a self-contradictory vision of the postwar world. The "Big Three" supported national self-determination, the idea that countries should decide their own futures. They agreed that countries should act collectively to deal with world problems and laid plans for the United Nations, which would encourage states to cooperate for security. But they also believed powerful nations should dominate other nations within a "sphere of influence." In these areas—Latin America and the Pacific for the United States; Africa and the Middle East for Britain; and Eastern Europe for the Soviet Union—each power could act independently and limit the self-determination of smaller states. Clearly, spheres of influence and unilateral action conflicted with democracy, self-determination, and collective action.

The conflict was made apparent when the three leaders dealt with the future of Poland, the Soviets' neighbor to the west. Despite talk of self-determination and democracy, Stalin wanted to install a loyal Polish government that would not become a gateway for another invasion. Churchill and Roosevelt favored a self-governing Poland under its prewar leaders. Stalin agreed to elections but believed that Roosevelt had given him a free hand in Poland. This lack of clarity set the stage for future misunderstandings.

From Allies to Enemies

The United States' ambitions for global security appeared threatening to the Soviet Union. To prevent a future Pearl Harbor, the Pentagon erected a circle of air and naval bases around Europe and Asia. Thanks to the Bretton Woods agreement, the United States led a global economy that worked to the disadvantage of controlled, socialist economies. To Roosevelt these steps were not antagonistic, but to Stalin their effect was to block his ambitions with bombers and dollars.

Disagreements over Germany sharpened these suspicions. The United States wanted defeated Germany to rejoin the world economy. The Soviets wanted the country that attacked them twice in 50 years divided and weakened forever. In the end, the Big Three agreed to split it into four zones of occupation. The United States, the USSR, Great Britain, and France would each administer a zone. Although **Berlin** lay within the Soviet zone, the four powers would each control a section of the capital. The Big Three also agreed that eventually Germany would be reunified but did not indicate when or how.

The uncertainties and contradictions of Yalta led to disagreements even before the war ended. When Vice President Harry Truman succeeded Roosevelt in April 1945, he objected to the Soviets' attempt to take tight control of Poland. Promising to "stand up to the Russians," the new president met in Washington with the Soviet foreign minister, V. M. Molotov. Truman "gave it to him straight 'one-two to the jaw.'" "I have never been talked to like that in my life," Molotov answered. "Carry out your agreements," snapped Truman, "and you won't get talked to like that."

When Truman met with Stalin and the British prime minister in Potsdam in July, relations were more cordial. Because Soviet troops occupied most of Eastern Europe and much of Germany, Truman could do little about Stalin's actions there. There was no progress on planning the future reunification of Germany. But Truman learned during the meeting of the successful test of the atomic bomb in New Mexico. The new weapon would increase US influence everywhere in the world.

NATIONAL SECURITY

After the war, relations between the United States and the Soviet Union deteriorated. Although Stalin was still committed to overthrowing capitalism, his immediate concerns were in Eastern Europe and along the southern border with Turkey and Iran. The Soviet leader also wanted to keep Germany and Japan from menacing his country again. As an added measure of security, the USSR built a completely self-reliant economy. The United States, by contrast, did not have to worry about securing its borders or supplies. Armed with nuclear weapons, it was stronger than any rival. But American leaders feared that impoverished and vulnerable states would voluntarily align themselves with Soviet power. Every election in Europe, coup in the Middle East, or uprising in Asia had the potential to build a Communist war machine. Recalling the collapse of empires and alliances in the late 1930s, they could imagine the United States suddenly alone and vulnerable.

The Truman Doctrine

To avoid this scenario, American leaders favored the quick reconstruction of nations, including Germany and Japan, within a world economy based on free trade. They also needed military bases to keep future aggressors far from American shores. The opposing interests of the Soviet and US systems soon translated into combative rhetoric. In February 1946, Stalin declared capitalism and communism incompatible. A month later, Winston Churchill, the former British prime minister, spoke at Fulton, Missouri. Introduced by Truman, Churchill ominously declared that "an Iron Curtain has descended across the Continent" of Europe. Central and Eastern Europe, he warned, "lie in the Soviet sphere." Churchill called for an alliance against this menace.

In February 1946, George Kennan, an American consul in Moscow, sent the State Department a long telegram. The Soviet leadership, he wrote, believed "there can be no permanent peaceful coexistence" between capitalism and socialism. Stalin's regime was sure that capitalist nations, beset by internal problems, would attack socialist nations. Acting on this fear, the USSR would, Kennan insisted, try to destabilize other nations and align them with the Communist bloc. The Communist system had to expand to survive.

More concerned than ever, Truman took aggressive steps to counter apparent Soviet expansion in the Mediterranean. The USSR had been pressing Turkey for control of the Dardanelles, a key waterway. Meanwhile, in Greece, a civil war pitted Communist guerillas against a monarchist government backed by Britain. By 1947, the British could no longer afford the war and wanted to pass the burden to the Americans. Truman told Congress on March 12, 1947, that the world faced a choice between freedom and totalitarianism. He announced what became known as the "**Truman Doctrine.**" The United States must "support free peoples who are resisting attempted subjugation by armed minorities or by outside pressures." The speech, said *Life* magazine, was "a bolt of lightning." Congress voted overwhelmingly to send aid to Greece and Turkey.

The crisis marked a turning point. In 1947, Walter Lippmann coined the term "Cold War" to describe the American-Soviet confrontation. There was no formal

Iron Curtain In Winston Churchill's image, an "iron curtain" divided Europe, but soon similar barriers would mark the frontiers of containment in Asia and the Middle East.

declaration of war, but with the Truman Doctrine, confrontation had certainly begun. Dividing the world into good and evil, the United States would support "free peoples" and oppose Communism. Former allies were now bitter antagonists.

Was the confrontation inevitable? There is no way for historians to prove it was, but the United States and the Soviet Union realistically could not have avoided friction. They had a history of hostility, and both possessed great military power. It is also not clear that the form the confrontation took—the Cold War—was inevitable. It was the product of choices, such as Truman's decision to aid Greece, and perceptions, such as Kennan's judgment about Soviet expansion. Those choices and judgments were not the only ones that could have been made, and Americans, with good reason, would wonder for decades whether the Cold War could have been different.

Containment

As the United States implemented diplomatic, economic, and military strategies for containing Soviet expansion, the scope of the confrontation widened to include the entire world. In 1949 China's civil war ended in a Communist victory. In 1950, five years after the end of World War II, the United States went to war again, this time to save a non-Communist regime in South Korea. The Cold War spread and became more dangerous. When the Soviets exploded their atomic bomb, the United States also increased military spending and built a hydrogen bomb. As the arms race spiraled, the Cold War seemed out of control.

Committed to opposing Soviet and Communist expansion, the Truman administration had to learn just how to fight the Cold War. It would be, in George Kennan's words, "a long-term, patient but firm and vigilant containment of Russian expansive tendencies."

The term **containment** aptly described American policy for the Cold War. The United States worked to hold back the Soviets for the next 40 years, but containment, as Kennan described it in 1947, was still a vague concept. Truman and his successors had to decide where and when to contain the Soviet Union and what combination of diplomatic, economic, and military programs to use.

Containment would not, however, rely primarily on the United Nations. Like the United States, the Soviet Union had a veto over actions by the United Nations Security Council and used it to frustrate American efforts. The United Nations would become another arena for rivalry, not an instrument of American policy.

Truman and his advisers revolutionized American policies on foreign aid, overseas alliances, and national defense. Fearing that a ruined and impoverished Europe would embrace Communism, they were determined to help Europe rebuild. In June 1947, Truman's new secretary of state, General George C. Marshall, proposed a "European Recovery Plan" to combat "hunger, poverty, desperation and chaos" and to promote "political and social conditions in which free institutions can exist." The Soviets declined to join and refused to allow Eastern European countries to participate, but 16 nations eagerly supported what became known as the **Marshall Plan**.

"The Marshall Plan saved Europe," Truman boasted. From 1948 to 1952, $13 billion went to boost agricultural and industrial output, increase exports, and promote economic cooperation. Whole cities were rebuilt. By 1950, participating countries had already exceeded prewar production. Prosperity helped stabilize Western European governments, bind them to the United States, and weaken Communist parties. Containment required more than aid. It also demanded the kind of military alliances that the United States had historically avoided as dangerous entanglements. But, challenged by the Cold War, leaders now saw alliances as a way of preventing, rather than provoking, armed conflict. In 1949, the United States joined 10 Western European nations and Canada to form the **North Atlantic Treaty Organization (NATO)** (see Map 24–1). Under NATO, an attack on any member nation would be treated as an attack on all. To strengthen the American commitment to Western Europe, Congress appropriated $1.3 billion in military aid for NATO countries, and Truman ordered American troops to the Continent. General Dwight D. Eisenhower, the commander of the Allied invasion of France in World War II, became the supreme commander of NATO forces.

Containment also required vigilance. In 1947, Congress passed the National Security Act, creating a Central Intelligence Agency (CIA) to gather and assess information for the president and a National Security Council (NSC) to advise him on military and political threats. The act placed the army, navy, and air force under a single command, the Joint Chiefs of Staff, and a single cabinet secretary, the secretary of defense. The term "national security" provided a blanket justification for responses to all kinds of threats—for actions such as election rigging, proxy wars, and other "covert operations." Congress passed a new Selective Service Act creating a draft for men between 19 and 25 years old.

Taking Risks

Containment entailed risks. There was always the chance that simmering conflict could boil over into world war. One particularly dangerous hot spot was Berlin. In 1948, the Americans, British, and French began to unify their zones of occupation in Germany into a single unit under a new currency, the deutschmark. Faced with

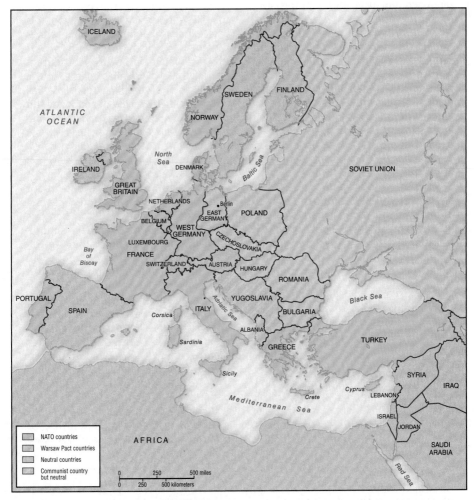

Map 24–1   Cold War in Europe, 1950 Five years after World War II, the Cold War had divided Europe into hostile camps, with NATO members allied with the United States and Warsaw Pact signers tied to the Soviet Union.

American Landscape
The Nevada Test Site

Near the southern tip of Nevada, between the Great Basin and Mojave deserts, the land was tough and unpromising. With temperatures as high as 120 degrees Fahrenheit and very little rain, places such as Frenchman Flat, Yucca Flat, and Skull Mountain remained hot and dry. Springs sustained sagebrush and creosote bushes, along with coyotes, deer, rabbits, and rattlesnakes, but over time few people settled there. Sparsely populated, the land seemed perfect when the federal government needed vast space for the Army Air Forces to practice bombing just before World War II. And it seemed perfect again in 1950 when the government needed space for the Atomic Energy Commission (AEC) to test nuclear weapons in the midst of the Cold War.

At 5:44 a.m. on January 27, 1951, an Air Force B-50D bomber dropped a small atomic bomb that exploded in the light of dawn above the new Nevada Test Site. It was the first of 928 controlled nuclear explosions that would occur over the next four decades. In addition to testing the weapons themselves, the AEC measured their effects on land, structures, animals, and people.

The government did not intentionally use human beings as test subjects in obviously lethal situations. In March 1953, for instance, Operation Annie assessed the impact of an atomic blast on "Doom Town," a collection of houses, bomb shelters, automobiles, a school bus, and department-store mannequins dressed as people. But in order to understand the effect of atomic warfare on soldiers, the AEC did have US troops observe the tests from hundreds and thousands of yards away and then had them move quickly into the blast zone.

By 1955, the Nevada Test Site grew to 1,350 square miles. Yet even this vast expanse could not contain either the spectacle of nuclear explosions or the radioactive fallout they produced. Approximately 70 miles to the south, people in the gambling resort of Las Vegas got a clear view of the flash and clouds from the tests. Thanks to wind patterns, Las Vegas did not experience much fallout. But the winds did send radioactive clouds east over Utah and on to the East Coast.

Federal officials, concerned about the public reaction to atomic testing on US soil, downplayed the dangers of nuclear fallout. "Your best action," a government pamphlet told Americans, "is not to be worried about fallout." In 1958, a leading physicist even publicly suggested that fallout "might be slightly beneficial or have no effect at all." When it became clear that fallout did have ill effects, the government tried to cover them up. After fallout from the tests killed thousands of sheep in Utah in 1953, AEC officials lied and claimed that there was no evidence of radiation found in the sheep.

Reassured by the government, most Americans accepted atomic testing at the Nevada Test Site as a necessary

an anti-Communist western Germany, Stalin sealed off his own German zone of occupation. On June 24, the Soviets cut road and rail transport into Berlin, the jointly occupied German capital. "We stay in Berlin, period," Truman snapped, calling what he felt was Stalin's bluff. But 2.5 million Berliners were at risk of

Nevada Nuclear Tests
Unprotected members of a secret federal unit film an atomic bomb explosion at the test site in Nevada, 1957. A number of the group's filmmakers would die of cancer.

part of fighting the Cold War. Atomic-inspired consumer goods such as Starburst-pattern dinnerware and Santas with eyes like the nucleus of an atom became popular.

In Nevada, politicians saw the site as a welcome boost to the state's economy. "We had long ago written off that terrain as wasteland," Governor Charles Russell insisted, "and today it's blooming with atoms." Las Vegas, home to workers from the site and host to tourists eager to see the explosions, eagerly celebrated testing. "Heck," ran a local newspaper headline, "We're Not Scared!" A casino show girl, "radiating loveliness instead of deadly atomic particles," was crowned Miss Atomic Blast.

Despite such reassurances, people in Utah were concerned about the radioactive fallout that descended on their state. "Utahns may be accumulating small doses of atomic radiation, which would some day mean the difference between life and death," a newspaper suggested. This raised the question as to whether or not people should trust the government and its scientists. "There are still many things which even our top scientists do not yet know—specifically the long-range effects of radiation," a paper in Salt Lake City worried.

There was reason to worry. Soldiers who participated in the tests lost their teeth, developed cancers, and suffered declining health. Communities in Utah, especially the town of St. George, had abnormal rates of leukemia and other cancers. Nevertheless, the government continued to avoid the issue and people did not protest against the testing. "Our state was so stupid, they wouldn't even admit the damage it was doing," lamented Jackie Maxwell, a hospital worker, who suffered miscarriages. "We were hyper-trusting because we are taught to trust authority figures."

Complying with international treaties, the US government stopped above-ground nuclear testing in the 1960s and underground testing in the 1990s. In the twenty-first century, the Nevada Test Site, pockmarked with craters from underground tests, remains a lonely expanse, hot and dry, home to sagebrush, animals, and stored nuclear waste.

running out of food and coal. Sending an armed supply convoy through the Soviet blockade could provoke a shooting war.

Instead, Berlin was supplied by air. American transport planes carried 2,500 tons of food and fuel a day. Along with this massive airlift, the Truman administration sent to Britain two squadrons of B-29 bombers, the kind that dropped the atomic bombs on Japan. In May 1949, the Soviets ended the blockade. Tested, the strategy of containment had worked: Soviet expansion had seemingly been deterred. But the risks were clear.

Those risks became even clearer later that year. In early September, American planes found radioactivity in the air over the Pacific, evidence that the Soviet Union had exploded an atomic bomb. The US nuclear weapon monopoly was over. Suddenly, confrontation with the Soviets had potentially lethal consequences. It was now, a Republican senator somberly observed, "a different world."

Global Revolutions

The Cold War soon spread from Europe to shape the politics of the world. Civil and postcolonial strife in Asia, Africa, the Middle East, and Latin America came to be seen as part of the conflict between the nuclear superpowers.

In China, the nationalist government of Jiang Jieshi had waged a civil war against Mao Zedong's Communist rebels since the 1920s. Both sides joined forces to fight the Japanese in World War II, but whereas combat strengthened the Communists, it weakened Jiang's corrupt and unpopular regime. When Japan surrendered, US forces helped Jiang regain control of Chinese cities. Truman urged a permanent settlement, but the civil war resumed. Congressional Republicans saw China as a key Cold War battleground, but Truman doubted the United States could influence the outcome. He sent the nationalists $2 billion in aid but refused to send troops. In December 1949, the defeated nationalists fled the Chinese mainland for the island of Taiwan, and Republicans angrily blamed the administration for the "loss" of China.

With most of Asia now in Communist hands, American strategists began to rethink containment. Before 1949, the danger zones were in the world's industrial heartlands, Europe and Japan. Now it seemed brushfire wars could spread nearly anywhere. Peasants had manned Mao's armies, and the rural "third world" seemed especially vulnerable. To contain Latin America, Truman organized the Rio Pact, through which the United States would provide training, weapons, and advisers for Latin American militaries. The Organization of American States (OAS), created in 1948, promoted stability and economic development from its headquarters in Washington.

Territories formerly of little strategic interest, such as Southeast Asia and Africa, became vital to security. Although the Truman administration favored self-determination, it tolerated Latin American dictatorships, European colonial dominion, and South Africa's white supremacist rule because these undemocratic regimes opposed Communism.

Korea

Working to hold off Communism at so many points, it was probably not surprising that the United States was eventually drawn into war. Nevertheless, the news that US troops were fighting in Korea startled Americans in 1950, because the conflict was so far from areas considered strategically important. But the Korean War was firmly rooted in the logic of the Cold War.

Korea, a peninsula bordering China and the Soviet Union, had been liberated from the Japanese in 1945. American and Soviet troops jointly occupied the territory, splitting it into two zones at the 38th parallel. The United States opposed the popular nationalist Kim Il Sung, a Communist, and acted unilaterally to install a regime in the South under Syngman Rhee, an anti-Communist. By 1948, Korea had two governments, each claiming jurisdiction over the whole. In June 1950, after incidents along the 38th parallel, Kim's army, led by Soviet-made tanks, invaded the South (see Map 24–2).

Truman responded boldly. By itself, South Korea was not important, but the administration believed the Soviet Union was behind the North Korean attack.

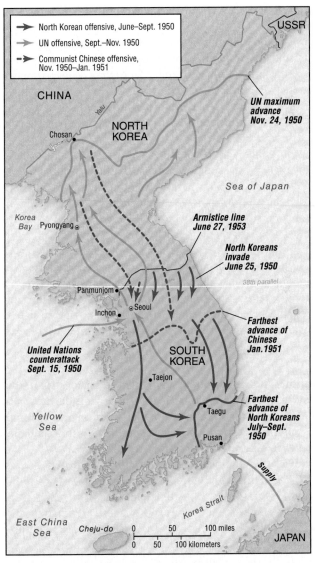

Map 24–2   The Korean War, 1950–1953 The shifting lines of advance mark the back-and-forth struggle that would end with stalemate and the division of Korea.

After the "loss" of China, Truman could not afford another Communist victory in Asia. He secured United Nations approval for international action. Troops from 15 countries eventually fought in the UN force, but nine-tenths came from the United States. Was America at war, then? Claiming the conflict was only a "police action," Truman never asked Congress for a declaration of war. For the first time, but not the last, a president sent troops to battle in the Cold War without regard for the Constitution.

At first, the fighting did not go well. Ill-prepared US troops fell back toward the coast. But in the summer, General Douglas MacArthur used the US Navy's control of the seas to put troops ashore at Inchon, deep behind enemy lines. North Korea's main armies were cut off and destroyed. Within weeks, the South had been reclaimed.

Then Truman and his advisers made a fateful decision. Rather than just contain Communism, they wanted to roll it back. Truman gave the order to invade North Korea and reunify the peninsula. MacArthur, who privately wanted war with the Chinese Communists, pushed ever closer to China. Fearing an invasion, the Chinese issued warnings, sent their forces into North Korea, and, on November 25, unleashed a massive attack on UN troops. MacArthur's shattered army pulled back to defend South Korea.

The Korean "police action" became a stalemate. A frustrated MacArthur wanted to fight aggressively, but the chastened Truman administration gave up reunification and accepted the 38th-parallel division. That was too much for MacArthur, who broke the military's unwritten rule against public criticism of civilian leaders. "There is no substitute for victory," MacArthur lectured in 1951. Fed up, Truman fired his popular general in April as the war dragged on.

The Korean stalemate underscored hard truths of the Cold War. Containment could mean sacrificing American lives in minor, nondecisive wars. As nuclear war was not an option, US troops had to be prepared, as the saying went, to "die for a tie"—to fight for something less than victory. In this kind of conflict, leaders had to convince allies, undecided nations, and citizens at home that, despite setbacks, the West would eventually win. Psychology was more important than territory.

NSC-68

Before Korea, the Truman administration tried to balance its international and domestic agendas. But by the 1950s, containment became the first priority. The administration escalated efforts against revolutionary movements even in peripheral areas, such as Southeast Asia. Colonial struggles, such as the Vietnamese rebellion against their French overlords, were seen as critical challenges.

In April 1950, the National Security Council approved a secret guideline known as **NSC-68**. Citing a growing list of threats and the "possibility of annihilation," it called for the United States to triple defense spending, impose order in postcolonial areas, and seek more powerful weapons. Truman worried about the cost, but the Korean War convinced him. By 1952, defense expenditures had nearly quadrupled, to $44 billion. Meanwhile, the armed forces grew—to 3.6 million by 1952—along with the list of combat theaters, now including Vietnam. Truman ordered the building of "the so-called hydrogen or superbomb." Successfully tested in

November 1952, the thermonuclear bomb was far more powerful than the atomic bomb, but it did not stop the arms race. Less than a year later, the USSR had its own "H-bomb."

Although it remained top secret until the 1970s, NSC-68 profoundly changed the US economy and political system. The military buildup was paid for with deficit financing, and federal borrowing generated jobs and growth, particularly in the South and West. To fight the Cold War, Americans accepted things they had long feared: secrecy, debt, alliances, a massive standing army, and centralized direction of the economy. Each of these magnified the role of the federal government.

THE RECONVERSION OF AMERICAN SOCIETY

While the Cold War intensified, domestic policy focused on restoring the economy and society to a peacetime footing. "Reconversion" was welcomed by a nation tired of war, but it was also a cause for worry. Americans feared a return to the desperate conditions of the 1930s. Labor, women, and African Americans, especially, wanted to hold on to and extend wartime gains.

The Postwar Economy

As World War II ended, the economy threatened to slide back into depression. Millions of unemployed servicemen came home at a time when government was cutting spending. The disaster never happened. Unemployment did rise in 1946 but never approached the double-digit rates of the 1930s. Despite brief downturns, the economy was vibrant. Its resilience reflected several factors, including veterans' choices, the federal role, the transformation of industry, and US economic dominance. Returning veterans did not strain the economy, partly because half of them went to school rather than work. Under the **GI Bill** of 1944, the federal government paid for up to three years of college tuition for veterans. Federal spending also helped prevent a return to the economic troubles of the 1930s. With World War II over, federal expenditures decreased dramatically, but spending was still far greater than it was during the 1930s. The GI Bill showed how spending stimulated the economy. Pumping nearly $14.5 billion into education, the bill encouraged colleges and universities to expand. As veterans swelled enrollments, institutions hired new faculty, and entire new systems, such as the State University of New York, were created.

Reconversion accelerated the economic change started by World War II. In the late 1940s, industrial production was still concentrated in the Northeast and Midwest, but new military spending was helping to shift factories and population south and west. In the 1940s, the population of the western states grew by 50 percent, compared with 10 percent in the East. The nature of the economy was changing, too. Oil and natural gas replaced coal as the chief source of power. New industries, such as plastics, electronics, and aviation, were growing rapidly.

Finally, the dominance of the United States in the world economy helped reconversion. At the end of World War II, the US economy was roughly the size of

The GI Bill in Action
William Oskay Jr. lived in a trailer with his wife and daughter while attending Pennsylvania State College (now University) under the GI Bill in 1946.

the European and Soviet economies combined. As late as 1950, America, with only 6 percent of the world's population, accounted for 40 percent of the value of all the goods and services produced in the world. Demand for American exports created jobs but also stoked inflation. Production caught up, and in the late 1940s, the economy began a prolonged peacetime boom.

The Challenge of Organized Labor

Organized labor had never been more powerful than at the end of World War II. One-third of nonagricultural civilian workers belonged to unions. The Democratic Party paid attention to influential unions, such as the Congress of Industrial Organizations (CIO), and after pledging not to strike during World War II, organized labor was eager to test its clout. Workers wanted wage increases to cope with inflation and as a reward for their contribution to wartime profits. In Europe and Japan, unions were gaining control over the way corporations did business, and some American unions also wanted a role in management. Not surprisingly, corporations were reluctant to give up any of their power or profits. Along with conservatives in Congress, they branded the unions as agents of Communism.

The result was a huge wave of strikes as soon as the war ended in August 1945. In 1946, 2 million machinists, longshoremen, and other workers around the country called a record 4,985 strikes. "Labor has gone crazy," an anxious Truman told his mother.

Significant work stoppages hit automobile factories, coal mines, and railroad yards. Late in 1945, the United Auto Workers (UAW) struck General Motors (GM) for a 30 percent raise in hourly wages, access to the company's books, and more say in company decisions. GM rejected union interference in management decisions. When the strike finally ended after 113 days, the UAW won only some of its wage demands. It marked a turning point for labor. Unions never again demanded to participate in management, but instead focused on pay and benefits.

The coal and railroad strikes were even more contentious. Members of the United Mine Workers (UMW) and the railway unions refused to accept federal arbitration. As the coal supply dwindled, power systems suffered "brownouts," and railroad passengers were stranded. The situation tested the strong relationship, forged in the New Deal, between the Democratic Party and organized labor. Truman ordered federal takeovers of the mines and the railroads. "Let Truman dig coal with his bayonets," snarled John L. Lewis, leader of the UMW. But the strikes ended in May. Many Americans applauded the president's action and believed that Lewis and other union leaders had become too powerful and demanding.

Counting on this unhappiness with unions, probusiness Republicans in Congress soon moved to limit the power of organized labor. In 1947, a coalition of Republicans and conservative, mostly southern Democrats passed the **Taft-Hartley Act**, a sweeping modification of federal labor law. The bill made it easier for employers to hire nonunion workers and to oppose the formation of unions. It also limited unions' right to organize and engage in political activity. Most humiliating, it compelled union leaders to swear that they did not belong to the Communist Party.

Despite these setbacks, workers and unions prospered. Landmark contract negotiations between the UAW and GM offered a model of labor relations. In 1948, the UAW won guaranteed cost-of-living adjustments, known as COLAs, and an annual wage increase tied to rises in worker productivity. In the so-called Treaty of Detroit, signed in 1950, the UAW won other increases and a pension plan in a long five-year contract. In return for pensions and protection against inflation, autoworkers gave management stable, predictable labor relations over the long term.

The Treaty of Detroit ended a difficult period for organized labor. Thanks to lucrative contracts, many workers were more secure than ever before, but reconversion also limited the power of organized labor and the support of the Democratic Party. Aggressive strikes produced mixed results, public hostility, and government interference. With the end of the strike wave, unions effectively abandoned their demand to participate in management.

Opportunities for Women

Reconversion also posed special challenges to the status of American women. During World War II, the shortage of male labor had expanded women's opportunities for employment. Working women prized the income and the sense of satisfaction they gained from performing jobs traditionally monopolized by men. But employers and government officials encouraged the belief that women should surrender jobs to returning veterans. The number of women in the labor force dropped 13 percent from 1945 to 1946, but reconversion did not send female workers home for good. Three-quarters of the women who wanted to stay at work after the war managed to find jobs.

Most women, of course, needed to earn a living for themselves or their families. By 1953, the number of women in the workforce matched the level of 1945. The number in nontraditional jobs increased, too. More women than ever before were skilled craftspersons, forepersons, physicians, and surgeons.

The number of married women in the postwar labor force was especially notable, as economic necessity overcame cultural prejudice against working mothers and married women. By 1947, there were more married women than single women in the wage labor force.

The armed forces, like civilian employers, initially cut back the number of women in the ranks when the war ended, but Congress granted women permanent status in the armed forces and merged the separate women's military organizations, such as the Women's Army Corps, into the regular armed services.

Despite these gains, women still faced discrimination. The majority had to settle for traditionally female, low-paying jobs in offices, stores, and factories. Women's hourly pay rose only half as much as men's pay in the first years after the war. In the military, women were largely confined to noncombatant roles such as nursing. There were no women generals.

In the larger society there was little interest in women's rights. After a meeting with female activists, Truman dismissed a constitutional amendment guaranteeing equal rights for women as a "lot of hooey."

Despite the lack of support for women's rights, women's opportunities were gradually expanding in the postwar years; the combination of women's desires and the economy's needs was slowly promoting the feminization of the labor force.

Civil Rights for African Americans

Like women, African Americans had made significant gains during World War II. They filled new roles in the military and higher-paying jobs in the civilian economy and pushed their demand for civil rights. Like women, African Americans sought to preserve and extend these rights and opportunities in the face of substantial resistance.

Several factors, including economic change, legal rulings, and wartime experiences, stimulated the postwar drive for equal rights and opportunities. By the end of the war, the transformation of the southern economy was undermining the system that segregated African Americans and denied them the right to vote. As mechanization reduced the need for field hands, African Americans left for the region's growing cities and for the North and West. One of the basic rationales for segregation—the need for an inexpensive, submissive labor force in the fields—was disappearing. The developing southern economy also attracted whites from other regions who were less committed to segregation and disfranchisement. Meanwhile, by migrating to northern and western cities, African Americans increased their votes and political influence.

In fighting the Nazis during the war and the Communists afterward, the United States dedicated itself to universal freedoms. The United Nations Declaration on Human Rights committed member states to guarantee rights to education, free movement, assembly, and personal safety. African Americans appealed to the UN, the courts, and the press to have the United States recognize these commitments.

During the 1940s, a series of US Supreme Court decisions struck at racial discrimination and encouraged African Americans to challenge inequality. In *Smith v. Allwright* in 1944, the Court had banned whites-only primary elections. In *Morgan v. Virginia* in 1946, the Court ruled that interstate bus companies could not segregate passengers. In *Shelley v. Kraemer* in 1948, the court banned restrictive covenants, the private agreements between property owners not to sell houses to African Americans and other minorities. These and other court decisions

Jackie Robinson Steals Home for the Brooklyn Dodgers His daring, speed, and power helped force the integration of Major League Baseball.

weakened discriminatory practices and suggested that African Americans might have a judicial ally in the struggle for justice.

African Americans' war experiences also encouraged them to demand more and to expect justice from the country they fought for. "Our people are not coming back with the idea of just taking up where they left off," an African American private wrote. "We are going to have the things that are rightfully due us or else."

That kind of determination spurred civil rights activism after the war. In the South, African Americans increasingly demanded the right to vote after *Smith v. Allwright*. The National Association for the Advancement of Colored People (NAACP) set up citizenship schools in the South to show African American voters how to register. The campaign was driven, too, by individual actions. In July 1946, Medgar Evers, a combat veteran who had just reached his 21st birthday, decided to try to vote in the Democratic Party's primary election in Decatur, Mississippi.

Such activism was resisted by whites deeply committed to disfranchisement and segregation. A white mob kept Evers from voting in 1946. In Georgia, whites killed an African American voter. More often, they manipulated registration laws to disqualify voters. A voter seeking to register might have to answer such questions as "How many bubbles are there in a bar of soap?" Still, African American voter registration in the South, only 2 percent in 1940, rose to 12 percent by 1947. The result was the election of a few African American officials and improved service from local government.

Alongside the campaign for voting rights, civil rights activists fought segregation across the country. The interracial **Congress of Racial Equality** (CORE) took the lead in protesting public discrimination. To test the Supreme Court's decision in *Morgan*, CORE sent an integrated team on a bus trip through the upper South, where they met with violence and arrests. Activists hardly dented segregation in the South in the 1940s but had more success promoting antidiscrimination laws in the North. By 1953, fair employment laws had been adopted in 30 cities and 12 states.

Activists also pressured Truman to support civil rights. In the spring and summer of 1946, picketers marched outside the White House with signs that read, "SPEAK, SPEAK, MR. PRESIDENT." Racial discrimination was an embarrassment for a nation claiming to represent freedom and democracy in the world, but support for civil rights was a risk for a politician dependent on white support. Nevertheless, Truman took significant steps.

In the fall of 1946, Truman supported a presidential committee report, *To Secure These Rights*, that called for strong federal action against lynching, vote suppression, job discrimination, and civil rights violations, including segregation in the armed forces. Furious white southern politicians and newspapers said Truman was "stabbing the South in the back."

African Americans, meanwhile, kept the heat on Truman. To protest discrimination in the military, A. Philip Randolph, the head of the Brotherhood of Sleeping Car Porters, proposed a boycott of the draft. In July 1948, Truman responded with Executive Order 9981, creating a committee to phase out discrimination in the military. He also established the Fair Employment Board, which moved more slowly against discrimination in federal hiring.

During the Truman years, the most publicized blow to racial inequality came not from the White House but the baseball diamond. When the Brooklyn Dodgers called up infielder **Jackie Robinson** from the minor leagues in 1947, he became the first African American to play in the major leagues since the late nineteenth century. A strong, self-disciplined former soldier, Robinson took taunts and beanballs on the field and death threats in the mail. Fast, powerful, and exciting, he finished the season as the National League's Rookie of the Year. Robinson's success paved the way for increasing numbers of African American players in the majors over the next several years.

Robinson's success also spelled the end of the Negro Leagues, created when African Americans were banned from the major leagues. Integration would sometimes undermine distinctly African American institutions. Nonetheless, the achievements of Robinson, Larry Doby, and other pioneering African American players sent a powerful message for civil rights and underscored the limits of reconversion. On the whole, African Americans preserved and sometimes expanded their wartime gains while still encountering injustice and inequality. In one respect, African Americans, women, and organized labor shared a common experience in the first years after World War II. For each of these groups, struggling for rights and opportunities, reconversion turned out to be better than feared and worse than hoped. They all confronted the limits of their power to change the society around them.

THE FRUSTRATIONS OF LIBERALISM

During the Great Depression, New Deal **liberalism** had reshaped American democracy, thrusting the federal government more deeply than ever into economic and social life. But the liberal Democratic agenda of federal activism, which stalled during World War II, met more frustration afterward. Liberals and the Democratic Party strained to provide answers for a nation no longer facing an economic or military emergency. Harry Truman struggled to prove that he was a worthy successor to Franklin Roosevelt.

The Democrats' Troubles

Many Americans were skeptical about their accidental president. Liberals who wondered whether Truman shared their ideals were incensed when he fired FDR's trusted aide Henry Wallace after Wallace criticized Truman's policy toward the

USSR. Conservatives and moderates also had their doubts. During the Depression, Americans had been willing to endorse government interventions in the economy, but they felt less need for government and more need for individual freedom in a prosperous peacetime.

The president was more liberal than the liberals expected. Shortly after he took office in 1945, he presented a legislative program that included proposals on education, employment, insurance, social security, and civil rights. Yet a full-employment bill, giving the federal government responsibility for securing jobs and prosperity, met overwhelming conservative and moderate opposition. Watered down by Congress, the resulting Employment Act of 1946 created a presidential Council of Economic Advisors but did nothing to increase the economic role of the federal government.

Truman and the liberals suffered an even sharper defeat over the president's sweeping proposal for a national health insurance system that would guarantee medical care to all Americans. Under the plan, the federal government would manage the insurance system and set doctors' and hospitals' fees. Conservatives and the medical profession promptly condemned the proposal as socialism. The bill failed, and so did most of Truman's domestic proposals.

Nevertheless, the federal role in national life continued to grow. Medical care offered a notable example. The Veterans Administration established a vast network of federal hospitals to care for returning soldiers. In 1946, the Hill-Burton Act appropriated federal money for new hospitals. That same year, Congress created a research lab in Atlanta, later called the Centers for Disease Control, to monitor infectious diseases. Congress also established the National Institute of Mental Health in 1949.

As Truman struggled with domestic and foreign policy, he became increasingly unpopular. "To err is Truman," went the joke. "Had enough?" asked Republicans. Many had. In the 1946 congressional elections, the voters gave the Republicans a majority in the House of Representatives and the Senate for the first time in 16 years.

Truman's Comeback

The 1946 elections seemed to presage a defeat for Truman in two years, but the president managed a stunning comeback. It began with the Republican majority that took control in Congress in 1947. Led by Senator Robert Taft of Ohio, Republicans hoped to replace New Deal liberalism with a different understanding of American democracy. Refuting "the corrupting idea" that prosperity, equality, or opportunity can be legislated, Taft wanted "free Americans freely working out their destiny." The Taft-Hartley Act was a blow to liberals and the administration, but Republicans found themselves trapped by Americans' ambivalence about liberalism. Only a minority was enthusiastic about such innovations as national health insurance, but there was little sentiment to roll back the New Deal and its benefits. Besides Taft-Hartley, the Eightieth Congress did not accomplish much, and soon Truman was campaigning against a "do-nothing Congress."

Still, things looked bad for Truman. By March 1948 his approval rating was 35 percent. His party was also splitting apart. On the left, his former secretary of

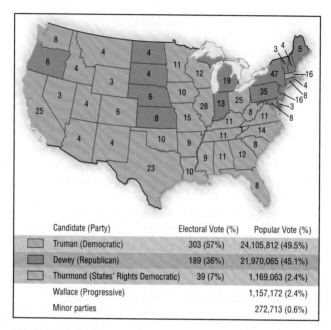

Candidate (Party)	Electoral Vote (%)	Popular Vote (%)
Truman (Democratic)	303 (57%)	24,105,812 (49.5%)
Dewey (Republican)	189 (36%)	21,970,065 (45.1%)
Thurmond (States' Rights Democratic)	39 (7%)	1,169,063 (2.4%)
Wallace (Progressive)		1,157,172 (2.4%)
Minor parties		272,713 (0.6%)

Map 24–3   The 1948 Presidential Election Segregation-ist and progressive candidacies were expected to undermine the Democratic majority, but the Roosevelt coalition returned Truman to the White House for a second term.

commerce Henry Wallace was running for president as a "Progressive." On the right, Democratic governor Strom Thurmond of South Carolina was running as a "Dixiecrat," appealing to white supporters of segregation. Truman seemed certain to lose in November. Or so his Republican opponent, Governor Thomas E. Dewey of New York, thought. Dewey believed an uncontroversial campaign would do the trick, but Truman pulled the New Deal majority back together. The president reached out to African Americans, labor, farmers, senior citizens, and other beneficiaries of New Deal liberalism. "Give 'em hell, Harry," the crowds shouted, and he did, driving home his vision. "The Democratic Party puts human rights and human welfare first," he declared. "These Republican gluttons of privilege... want a return of the Wall Street economic dictatorship."

On Election Day, Wallace and Thurmond received only a million votes each. Dewey attracted fewer votes than he had four years before. Leading Roosevelt's coalition, Truman won the presidency with only 49.5 percent of the vote (see Map 24–3). The Democrats recaptured the House and the Senate, but the triumph did not last long. Like Taft two years before, Truman soon discovered that a victory did not mean a mandate. In his State of the Union address in January 1949, Truman declared that "every individual has a right to expect from our Government a fair deal." But his "Fair Deal" legislation stalled in Congress. Despite Truman's comeback, the liberal vision could not dominate the politics of Cold War America.

FIGHTING THE COLD WAR AT HOME

Beyond the battles over domestic policy, the Cold War increasingly intruded into every aspect of life. Billions of dollars in defense expenditures stimulated economic growth and kept John Turchinetz employed at the Boston Navy Yard, but fear, doubt, and insecurity pervaded the late 1940s. Americans added a new fear of nuclear weapons to their old fear of immigrants, and society succumbed to a largely irrational dread of hidden traitors in Hollywood, Washington, the universities, and the public library. To fight the Cold War at home, anti-Communist crusaders such as Joseph McCarthy hunted for disloyal Americans. By the 1950s, McCarthyism was capable of destroying the lives of thousands of Americans.

Doubts and Fears in the Atomic Age

Despite triumph in World War II, American culture was dark and pessimistic in the late 1940s. The rise of fascism, the Holocaust, and the bombings of Hiroshima and Nagasaki raised questions about the direction of progress and the goodness of humankind. The Cold War did nothing to calm those concerns. Even the welcome prosperity of the reconversion period did not soothe this sense of doubt. People felt small and powerless in an age of big corporations, big unions, big government, and superbombs.

Americans revealed their unease in a variety of ways. Not long after the announcement of the Truman Doctrine in 1947, people began seeing lights in the sky, and "flying saucers" were reported over 35 states and Canada. In a nuclear-armed world, columnist Joseph Alsop observed, the saucer scare was a reminder that "man-made horrors are quite real, quite imminent possibilities."

Meanwhile, Hollywood films explored popular fears. In 1946, *The Best Years of Our Lives* traced the difficult, sometimes humiliating readjustment of three returning veterans. The same year, *It's a Wonderful Life* told the story of a small-town banker forced to accept the disappointment of his unfulfilled dreams. Both films expressed reservations about the morality of capitalism and the chances of achieving happiness in the modern world. A new genre, film noir, offered an even darker view. Such films as *Fear in the Night* (1947) and *Kiss Me Deadly* (1955) told the harrowing stories of individuals trapped in a confusing, immoral world.

As the greatest source of fear, nuclear weapons dominated the popular imagination. Many Americans dealt with their anxiety about the Atomic Age in a variety of ways, including dark attempts at humor. Americans drank "atomic cocktails" and danced the "atomic polka." American women wore the new "bikini," the explosively scanty bathing suit named for the Pacific atoll where the United States tested the H-bomb. The Soviets' development of the atomic bomb and the hydrogen bomb was impossible to laugh away.

Americans' fear was also reflected in the hardening of attitudes toward foreigners. In 1945, the nation welcomed the foreign wives of American servicemen by passing the War Brides Act, but as the Cold War intensified, other potential migrants met a hostile reception. The Immigration and Nationality Act of 1952 tightly restricted immigration, particularly from Asia. It kept out Communists and gays and allowed the deportation of American citizens suspected of disloyalty.

The Anti-Communist Crusade

Americans may have feared disloyalty most of all. Many believed the real Communist threat came from within. Historians debate the origins of this second "Red Scare." Some trace the anti-Communist crusade to a conservative reaction against the rise of labor, African Americans, women, and other disempowered groups. Others blame the Truman administration for using fear to justify unprecedented military activity and spending. Although anti-Communism had deep roots in American culture, politicians in both parties gave domestic anti-Communism its particularly dangerous form.

The crusaders had to search hard for local Communists. The Communist Party of the United States of America (CPUSA), a legal political party, was tiny and losing followers. Infiltrated by FBI and police informants, it never received more than 0.3 percent of the popular vote. Just to be sure, the Truman administration charged 12 party leaders with violating the Smith Act, which criminalized membership in "a group advocating . . . the overthrow of the government by force." In 1949, 11 were convicted and sent to jail.

Open Communists seemed to pose less of a threat than secret ones. In the late 1940s, self-professed former Communists and spies eagerly turned informant to reveal America's presumed hidden network of traitors. The hunt for these "subversives" was led by the House of Representatives' Un-American Activities Committee (HUAC). In 1947, HUAC held hearings on supposed Communist plots in Hollywood. The film industry cooperated, but eight screenwriters, a producer, and a director cited their First Amendment rights and declined to testify. The "Hollywood Ten" were convicted of contempt of Congress and sent to jail for up to a year. Film studios got the message and "blacklisted"—refused to hire—writers, directors, and actors even remotely suspected of Communist ties. Avoiding controversial subjects, studios put out overwrought anti-Communist movies such as *The Red Menace* and *I Was a Communist for the FBI*.

Afraid of looking "soft" on Communism, the Truman administration declared there was a real problem with domestic Communism. "Communists," said Truman's attorney general, Tom Clark, "are everywhere... and each carries with him the germs of death for society." In 1947, the president created an "employee loyalty" program. Any civil servant could lose his or her job by belonging to any of the "totalitarian, Fascist, Communist or subversive" groups listed by the attorney general. The program had little regard for due process. People accused of disloyalty could not challenge evidence or confront their accusers and were presumed guilty until they proved their innocence. Although only about 300 employees were discharged, the loyalty program helped create the impression of a serious problem in Washington.

The Hunt for Spies

There was, in fact, spying going on inside the government. The Soviet Union, like the United States, carried out espionage abroad. The Canadian government found evidence of a spy ring that had passed American atomic secrets to the Soviets during World War II. Through interceptions of Soviet communications, the CIA knew about the spy ring but chose not to share this information with Congress, prosecutors, or even the president.

Is This Tomorrow? The cover of this 1947 comic book, published by a Roman Catholic group, conveys the intensifying fear of communism after World War II.

Thanks to the Canadian evidence, the FBI began to suspect that **Alger Hiss**, an aide to the secretary of state, was a Soviet agent. Hiss was quietly eased out of his job. Then, in 1948, HUAC took testimony from Whittaker Chambers, a *Time* magazine editor who claimed to have been a Soviet agent in the 1930s. Chambers accused Hiss of passing secret documents. The patrician Hiss denied the charges and said he had never even met Chambers. He seemed more credible than the rumpled Chambers, an admitted perjurer, but Congressman Richard Nixon of California, a Republican member of HUAC, forced him to admit that he had known Chambers under an alias. With help from the FBI, Chambers charged that Hiss had given him secret information in the 1930s. When Chambers produced microfilmed photographs of the secret documents, Hiss could not explain them. Under the statute of limitations, it was too late to try Hiss for spying, but not too late to indict him for lying to Congress. Hiss's perjury trial ended in a hung jury in 1949, but a second

Struggles For Democracy

The Hollywood Ten

With the passage of time, the enormity of the anti-Communist crusade becomes harder to understand. In the midst of a violent century that saw two world wars, the search for Communist subversives seems fairly tame. Little blood was shed. Relatively few people went to jail. Yet the anti-Communist crusade damaged American democracy. As the case of the Hollywood Ten illustrates, the Red Scare harmed the careers and lives of Americans who were not traitors. In turn, the fate of these victims intimidated the American public, as well as the leaders of powerful institutions, into silence and acquiescence. Democracy, dependent on the right to free speech and dissent, suffered.

The crusade against Communism rested on the authority of the US government. The case of the Hollywood Ten began in 1947 when the House Committee on Un-American Activities (HUAC), as part of its longtime search for disloyalty, investigated "alleged Communist influence and infiltration in the motion-picture industry." Using its subpoena power, the committee compelled director Edward Dmytryk,

writers Dalton Trumbo and Ring Lardner Jr., and seven other suspected Communists to testify as so-called unfriendly witnesses at hearings in Washington, DC. The chair of the committee, J. Parnell Thomas of New Jersey, allowed only one of the Ten to read a prepared statement; the rest were not given this customary right. Badgering the witnesses, Thomas did not let them respond to accusations against them and he had three of them forcibly removed from the hearing room. Thomas also insisted that each of the Ten answer what he called the "$64 question": "Are you now, or have you ever been a member of the Communist Party of the United States?" When the witnesses declined to answer directly, HUAC had all of them cited for contempt of Congress.

In conjunction with the legal power of government, the anti-Communist crusade depended on the willing cooperation of individual Americans. Film stars such as Gary Cooper and Robert Montgomery appeared at the HUAC hearings as "friendly witnesses" to reveal the names of alleged Communists.

jury convicted him in 1950, and he served almost four years in federal prison. The case was a triumph for Republicans and conservatives and a blow to Democrats and liberals.

As the Hiss case ended, another scandal stoked Americans' fears. In early 1950, British authorities arrested Klaus Fuchs, a physicist who had worked at the US nuclear research facility in Los Alamos, New Mexico. The investigation led to David Greenglass, who worked on the atomic bomb project, and his brother-in-law, Julius Rosenberg. Julius, a former member of the CPUSA, and his wife, Ethel, were convicted of conspiring to steal atomic information in a trial controversial for its

The Red Scare also depended on the help of powerful institutions. The Screen Actors Guild, a union led by actor and future president of the United States, Ronald Reagan, gave the names of suspected Communist sympathizers. Faced with damaging publicity about Communism in Hollywood, the major movie studios ostentatiously joined the anti-Communist crusade. In November 1947, studio heads issued a statement vowing not to rehire "any of the ten until such time as he is acquitted or has purged himself of contempt and declares under oath that he is not a Communist." The studios proceeded to discriminate against suspected Communists and to make safe films that could not possibly be considered pro-Communist. In this way, HUAC managed to reshape a powerful national institution without passing a law.

The anti-Communist crusade flourished because many Americans did not speak out against it for fear of persecution. The Hollywood Ten had some famous defenders in the film industry, including actors Lauren Bacall and Humphrey Bogart. But few people were willing to risk accusations of Communism and disloyalty by supporting the "unfriendly witnesses."

Help from the judicial system was also essential to fueling the Red Scare. The courts were willing to endorse or at least ignore the often unconstitutional treatment of suspected Communists. In the spring of 1948, the US District Court in Washington, DC speedily convicted two of the Hollywood Ten, screenwriters John Howard Lawson and Dalton Trumbo, for contempt of Congress. When the US Supreme Court refused to review their cases, the rest of the Ten were convicted in 1950. As author E. B. White observed, "Ten men have been convicted, not of wrongdoing but of wrong thinking; that is... bad news."

The combination of government power, "friendly witnesses," discriminatory studios, intimidated supporters, and complaisant courts defeated the Hollywood Ten. In addition to their fines and jail sentences, they faced being blacklisted. Only one of them, director Edward Dmytryk, immediately denounced communism and went back to work in Hollywood. Some of the rest wrote screenplays under pseudonyms. But they could not work openly in Hollywood again until the 1960s, when the hysteria of the Red Scare had died down. In the meantime, HUAC had successfully used the Hollywood Ten to intimidate the film industry and send a powerful message to the rest of American society not to interfere in the search for supposed Communists. Basic rights and freedoms disappeared amid the persecution of a minority and the silence of the majority.

anti-Semitic overtones and because the act protecting atomic secrets became law after the spying allegedly took place. Though they had two young sons, both Rosenbergs were sentenced to death. Ignoring appeals for clemency, the federal government electrocuted the Rosenbergs in 1953.

There now seems little doubt that the USSR obtained American nuclear secrets, but the impact was probably not as great as conservatives feared or as small as liberals insisted. Most likely, espionage sped up work on an atomic bomb the Soviets would have eventually produced anyway.

The Rise of McCarthyism

Two weeks after Hiss's conviction, one week after Truman's announcement of the decision to build the hydrogen bomb, and days after the arrest of Klaus Fuchs, Senator Joseph McCarthy of Wisconsin spectacularly took command of the anti-Communist crusade. Speaking to the Republican Women's Club of Wheeling, West Virginia, the previously obscure senator claimed to have names of 205 Communists working in the State Department. In fact, McCarthy had no new information, only a handful of old accusations.

Nevertheless, McCarthy was instantly popular and powerful. Frightened by new dangers, many people wanted to believe in a senator bold enough to fight back. Some shared McCarthy's resentment of privileged elites—New Dealers, diplomats, scientists—whom he derided as "egg-sucking phony liberals" and "bright young men… born with silver spoons in their mouths." For some Americans—immigrants, Midwesterners, Catholics, and fundamentalists—support for McCarthy was a way to prove their patriotism. Even Democratic legislators voted for the Internal Security Act of 1950, which forced the registration of Communist and Communist-front groups, provided for the deportation of allegedly subversive aliens, barred Communists from defense jobs, made picketing a federal court house to affect a case a felony, and granted the president emergency powers to detain individuals who might engage in espionage. Refusing to "put the Government of the United States in the thought control business," Truman vetoed the bill, but Congress overrode his veto.

Eventually, McCarthy went too far. Angry that one of his aides, David Schine, had not received a draft deferment, he launched an investigation of the army. The secretary of the army, Robert T. Stevens, refused to cooperate and claimed McCarthy had tried to get preferential treatment for Schine. In April 1954, before a television audience of 20 million people, McCarthy failed to come up with evidence of treason in the army. When he tried to smear a young army lawyer as a Communist,

TIME LINE

▼**1945**
Yalta conference
Harry S. Truman inaugurated
Potsdam Conference
Industrial strikes break out

▼**1946**
Winston Churchill's "Iron Curtain" speech
George Kennan's "long telegram" on Soviet expansionism
Employment Act of 1946

Morgan v. Virginia
Election of Republican majorities in House and Senate

▼**1947**
Announcement of Truman Doctrine
Beginning of Federal Employee Loyalty Program
Integration of Major League Baseball by Jackie Robinson
HUAC Hollywood hearings
Rio Pact

Taft-Hartley Act
National Security Act
Presidential commission reports on civil rights

▼**1948**
Shelley v. Kraemer
Congressional approval of Marshall Plan
Truman's Executive Order 9981
Beginning of Berlin crisis
Selective Service Act
Truman elected president

the senator was exposed. "Have you no sense of decency, sir, at long last?" asked the army's chief counsel, Joseph Welch. It was an electric moment. The Senate hearings came to no judgment, but Americans did. McCarthy's popularity plummeted. By year's end, the Senate condemned him for "unbecoming conduct."

The fall of McCarthy did not end **McCarthyism**. Schools forced teachers to sign loyalty oaths. Faculty members at several universities lost their jobs, and deans gave the names of suspect students to the FBI. Communism had become a useful charge to hurl at anything that anybody might oppose—labor unions, civil rights, even modern art. To protect themselves, groups policed their own membership. Labor unions drove out Communist leaders and unions. The Cincinnati Reds renamed their team the "Redlegs."

Americans became more careful about what they said out loud. Many had come to believe, along with McCarthy, that the civility of democracy, the attention to rights and fairness, exposed America to a ruthless adversary not bound by similar codes of conduct. Even as the Senate was censuring McCarthy, James Doolittle, the heroic World War II aviator, handed the CIA a report on counterespionage and countersubversion. It explained that the goal of America's enemy is "world domination by whatever means and at whatever cost." "If the United States is to survive," it concluded, "long-standing American concepts of 'fair play' must be reconsidered."

CONCLUSION

To contain Communism, the United States had transformed its economy. American society dealt with the unfinished business of reconversion, including the role of government and the rights and opportunities of labor, women, and African Americans. Despite these changes, the Cold War had widened and intensified. Just seven years after dropping the first atomic bomb on Japan, Americans were again at war

▼**1949**
Formation of North Atlantic Treaty Organization
Communist takeover of mainland China

▼**1950**
NSC-68
Alger Hiss's conviction for perjury
Joseph McCarthy's speech in Wheeling, West Virginia

Treaty of Detroit
Beginning of Korean War
Internal Security Act of 1950

▼**1951**
Truman fires General Douglas MacArthur

▼**1952**
Immigration and Nationality Act
Test of hydrogen bomb

▼**1953**
Execution of Ethel and Julius Rosenberg

▼**1954**
Army-McCarthy hearings

in the Far East and were forced to live with the threat of nuclear annihilation. They lived, too, with the frenzied search for subversives. America seemed to be out of control.

As McCarthyism flourished, most Americans longed for peace. They wanted the fighting in Korea to end. Anxious to avoid a nuclear holocaust, they wanted the confrontation with the Soviets to stabilize. Meanwhile, American society, adjusting to the postwar economy, sorted out the roles that government, labor, race, and gender would play in the Cold War order. In the midst of upheaval, Americans went on with their lives. John Turchinetz, still working at the Boston Navy Yard, went to night school and got married. A disabled veteran, he wasn't needed on the frontlines of the Cold War. But in 1952, the US government took his old ship, the *Boston*, out of mothballs and began to equip it with state-of-the-art missiles for duty around the Cold War world.

WHO, WHAT, WHERE

autarkic   784

Berlin   785

Congress of Racial Equality
  (CORE)   799

containment   788

GI Bill   795

Hiss, Alger   805

liberalism   800

Marshall Plan   788

Marxist   784

McCarthyism   809

North Atlantic Treaty Organization
  (NATO)   788

NSC-68   794

Robinson, Jackie   800

Taft-Hartley Act   797

Truman Doctrine   786

REVIEW QUESTIONS

1. How did the National Security Act change the executive branch?

2. Why did Truman see Korea as important enough to defend?

3. Why were struggles in the workplace more intense in the late 1940s than during the Depression or World War II?

CRITICAL-THINKING QUESTIONS

1. McCarthyism attacked government, science, education, theater, and Hollywood. What does this pattern reveal about the nature of American anxiety in the 1950s?

2. Two-thirds of the world's peoples gained their independence between 1945 and 1961. How did the Cold War affect this movement toward nationhood?

3. In the 1950s and 1960s, historians debated the question of who started the Cold War. In the 1990s, it became more interesting to ask when it started. Why the change, and what questions might today's historians ask?

SUGGESTED READINGS

Harry S. Truman Presidential Library and Museum. Online Documents. https://www.tru-manlibrary.gov/library/online-collections

Storrs, Landon R. Y. *The Second New Deal and the Unmaking of the American Left*. Princeton, NJ: Princeton University Press, 2012.

Westad, Odd Arne. *The Cold War: A World History*. New York: Basic Books, 2017.

For further review materials and resource information, please visit www.oup.com/us/ofthepeople

CHAPTER 24: The Cold War, 1945–1954
Primary Sources

24.1 HARRY S. TRUMAN, EXCERPTS FROM SPECIAL MESSAGE TO THE CONGRESS ON GREECE AND TURKEY (1947)

When he appeared before Congress on March 12, 1947, President Harry Truman laid out not only the case for US aid to Greece and Turkey, but also the principles underlying American foreign policy for decades to come. His "Truman Doctrine," citing the example of US involvement in World War II, demanded active intervention in the rapidly developing Cold War.

The gravity of the situation which confronts the world today necessitates my appearance before a joint session of the Congress. The foreign policy and the national security of this country are involved. One aspect of the present situation ... concerns Greece and Turkey. The United States has received from the Greek Government an urgent appeal for financial and economic assistance. Preliminary reports ... corroborate the statement of the Greek Government that assistance is imperative if Greece is to survive as a free nation.

Since 1940, this industrious, peace loving country has suffered invasion, four years of cruel enemy occupation, and bitter internal strife ...

Greece is in desperate need of financial and economic assistance to enable it to resume purchases of food, clothing, fuel, and seeds. These are indispensable for the subsistence of its people and are obtainable only from abroad. Greece must have help to import the goods necessary to restore internal order and security, so essential for economic and political recovery....

The very existence of the Greek state is today threatened by the terrorist activities of several thousand armed men, led by Communists, who defy the government's authority at a number of points, particularly along the northern boundaries....

Greece must have assistance if it is to become a self-supporting and self-respecting democracy. The United States must supply this assistance ... There is no other country to which democratic Greece can turn. No other nation is willing and able to provide the necessary support for a democratic Greek government....

It is of the utmost importance that ... each dollar spent will count toward making Greece self-supporting, and will help to build an economy in which a healthy democracy can flourish....

The future of Turkey, as an independent and economically sound state, is clearly no less important to the freedom-loving peoples of the world than the future of Greece....

As in the case of Greece, if Turkey is to have the assistance it needs, the United States must supply it. We are the only country able to provide that help.

I am fully aware of the broad implications involved if the United States extends assistance to Greece and Turkey.... One of the primary objectives of the foreign policy of the United States is the creation of conditions in which we and other nations will be able to work out a way of life free from coercion. This was a fundamental issue in the war with Germany and Japan. Our victory was won over countries which sought to impose their will, and their way of life, upon other nations....

We shall not realize our objectives unless we are willing to help free peoples to maintain their free institutions and their national integrity against aggressive movements that seek to impose upon them totalitarian regimes. This is no more than a frank recognition that totalitarian regimes imposed upon free peoples, by direct or indirect aggression, undermine the foundations of international peace, and hence the security of the United States.

The peoples of a number of countries of the world have recently had totalitarian regimes forced upon them against their will. The Government of the United States has made frequent protests against coercion and intimidation in violation of the Yalta agreement in Poland, Rumania, and Bulgaria. I must also state that in a number of other countries there have been similar developments.

At the present moment in world history nearly every nation must choose between alternative ways of life. The choice is too often not a free one. One way of life is based upon the will of the majority, and is distinguished by free institutions, representative government, free elections, guarantees of individual liberty, freedom of speech and religion, and freedom from political oppression. The second way of life is based upon the will of a minority forcibly imposed upon the majority. It relies upon terror and oppression, a controlled press and radio, fixed elections, and the suppression of personal freedoms.

I believe that it must be the policy of the United States to support free peoples who are resisting attempted subjugation by armed minorities or by outside pressures.

I believe that we must assist free peoples to work out their own destinies in their own way.

I believe that our help should be primarily through economic and financial aid which is essential to economic stability and orderly political processes. . . .

It is necessary only to glance at a map to realize that the survival and integrity of the Greek nation are of grave importance in a much wider situation. If Greece should fall under the control of an armed minority, the effect upon its neighbor, Turkey, would be immediate and serious. Confusion and disorder might well spread throughout the entire Middle East. Moreover, the disappearance of Greece as an independent state would have a profound effect upon those countries in Europe whose peoples are struggling against great difficulties to maintain their freedoms and their independence while they repair the damages of war. . . .

Should we fail to aid Greece and Turkey in this fateful hour, the effect will be far reaching to the West as well as to the East.

We must take immediate and resolute action. I therefore ask the Congress to provide authority for assistance to Greece and Turkey in the amount of $400,000,000 for the period ending June 30, 1948 . . .

In addition to funds, I ask the Congress to authorize the detail of American civilian and military personnel to Greece and Turkey, at the request of those countries, to assist in the tasks of reconstruction, and for the purpose of supervising the use of such financial and material assistance as may be furnished. I recommend that authority also be provided for the instruction and training of selected Greek and Turkish personnel. . . .

The United States contributed $341,000,000,000 toward winning World War II. This is an investment in world freedom and world peace. The assistance that I am recommending for Greece and Turkey amounts to little more than 1 tenth of 1 percent of this investment. It is only common sense that we should safeguard this investment and make sure that it was not in vain. The seeds of totalitarian regimes are nurtured by misery and want. They spread and grow in the evil soil of poverty and strife. They reach their full growth when the hope of a people for a better life has died.

We must keep that hope alive.

The free peoples of the world look to us for support in maintaining their freedoms. If we falter in our leadership, we may endanger the peace of the world. And we shall surely endanger the welfare of this nation.

Great responsibilities have been placed upon us by the swift movement of events.

Source: President Harry S. Truman, *Special Message to the Congress on Greece and Turkey*, March 12, 1947. https://www.presidency.ucsb.edu/documents/special-message-the-congress-greece-and-turkey-the-truman-doctrine

24.2   HIGH SCHOOL AND COLLEGE GRADUATES IN THE COLD WAR (1948–1950)

In the first years of the Cold War, graduates from high school and college entered an uncertain, fearful adult world. Here, two newspaper editors and a columnist offer advice to young people graduating from 1948 to 1950 amid the intensifying international nuclear arms race and the domestic Red Scare. Are these pieces optimistic or pessimistic? What challenges do these graduates face? Is the advice sincere and realistic?

Editorial, *Binghamton Press and Sun Bulletin*, June 14, 1948: June graduates of high school and college are hearing the same old commencement orations. They are being told that they should concentrate on improving the world. The world, of course, could stand improvement. . . . Some day a starry-eyed youngster is going to ask a commencement speaker how it happened that his generation got the world into such shape. . . .

No one really should feel too much concern about the future of today's boys and girls. They're a little weak in the three R's, in spelling and grammar. But they look out on horizons that are wider than those of their parents. Today's youngsters in the main know what it is all about. Yes, they're smart. They have to be, considering the burdens the older generation so unfairly has thrust upon their shoulders. They'll probably do better than the older generation. They couldn't do much worse.

Editorial, *Iowa City Press-Citizen*, June 10, 1949: Graduates are being told these are troublesome times, that the threat of war hangs over us, that freedom is in peril from communism, that population is outrunning world resources, that our health, security and education need new safeguards, that a hundred other dire circumstances prevail. Most of this may well be true. Certainly there have been more restful moments in history. . . .

For long years every graduating class has been told to stick out its chin and face down the world. . . . We voice the fervent wish, however, that this time the speakers cut through the welter of the world's dilemmas and talk in simple, human terms that may serve as real guide approach we have found that we would like to repeat:

"You students are leaving the college world, where truth is the great, single, unifying goal. You are entering the outside world, where truth competes openly and violently with falsehood, half-truth, and propaganda. You will bump into baffling mixtures of these elements. If you are ever to play any useful part in bettering the world, learn quickly to recognize these cheap alloys that corrupt truth. Resist their intrusion into your own thinking. . . . Distortions of truth are a prized weapon in the battle of ideas raging today. But truth is stronger and will blunt that weapon, however lethal it sometimes is. You will need courage to combat the users of falsehood and propaganda. They will too seldom be your avowed enemies. They may be in positions of power. They may even be, on occasion, your friends.

But if you flinch from fighting, you will go down in the struggle to bring peace and order and justice to this complex world.

Hal Boyle, 1950: An open letter to Joe College, class of 1950:

Dear Joe:

Welcome to the brave new world, kid. . . . There is one word of advice I'd like to give you. It's this: "Relax."

These are jittery times, perhaps the most jittery ever known. A census might even show there are more ulcers alive in the world today than there are people. There's a growing habit to be afraid of shadows, which are usually larger than the things that cast them.

So, relax, Joe. Show the older people the example they need: That courage doesn't die in rompers, but also wears long pants.

What really is there to be afraid of? War today is only the threat of a needless possibility. There is more mass security in the United States today than there was when young Thomas Jefferson wrote the Declaration of Independence, and he lived to be an old, old man. More people live a wider, freer life than at previous periods of our national story. The good old days are a legend. The good present time is here to be enjoyed.

There's a job waiting for you to find, Joe. There's a girl for you to marry, and you'll want to bring up some kids. And the prospect for bringing them up in a happy world was never really better. But you don't find happiness by being tense. Relax, Joe.... Good luck.

Hal Boyle

Sources: "Same Old Graduation Speeches," *Binghamton Press and Sun Bulletin*, June 14, 1948, p. 6; "Advice to Graduates," *Iowa City Press-Citizen*, June 10, 1949, p. 4; Hal Boyle, "Word of Advice to Graduates Entering Jittery World—Relax," *Marshfield News Herald*, June 2, 1950.

24.3 STATEMENTS BY THE UNITED AUTO WORKERS AND GENERAL MOTORS (1945)

The United Auto Workers' (UAW) strike against General Motors in 1945–1946 laid bare basic differences over the past and future of labor relations in the United States. As President Truman appointed a fact-finding board to make recommendations on a settlement, the union and the corporation disagreed over the proper roles of the federal government, unions, and corporations. As this statement by UAW official Walter Reuther makes clear, the union wanted the government to help force corporations into supporting the buying power of all Americans. In response, General Motors flatly rejected giving up any of its power. The UAW and General Motors also had different understandings of just how good things had been before World War II.

Reuther: The President's fact-finding board will shortly report its findings and recommendations in the UAW-CIO-General Motors wage dispute to President Truman. If those findings and recommendations are based upon the arithmetic of the case, and if the President and the American people will insist that the Wall Street managers of General Motors Corporation honestly negotiate an agreement based on the economic facts of the case, General Motors workers and the American people will be spared a winter of industrial war that may spread to all of American industry.... The General Motors workers, who have already sacrificed so much in this strike, will not accept less than the 30 percent increase in wage rates needed to maintain take-home pay, except and to the extent that the economic facts may show that General Motors cannot pay that increase without increasing prices to the consumers.

... The Wall Street lawyers who have been substituted for the operating management raise the motheaten battle flags that the forces of special privilege have carried for the past hundred and fifty years. Theirs are the voices and the slogans of the past. America is going forward to a better future, of full employment, full production and full consumption.

We believe that the American people will not be frightened by hysterical screams of "revolution." We are through with blind acceptance of the bad old days of boom and bust, of chronic mass unemployment....

The workers' demands to maintain take-home pay, keep prices down and thereby maintain and increase purchasing power are geared to the welfare of the whole community, the needs of the whole nation. We refuse to operate as an economic pressure group attempting to make progress at the expense of the community. We want to make progress with the community....

Free enterprise is killing itself when it refuses to recognize that the maintenance and increase of purchasing power to keep pace with technological progress is its own life blood.

Free enterprise, to survive, must learn that it has more and greater responsibilities than merely producing a cash return for its investors. It must make its contribution to the welfare of the community as a whole; it must meet and help solve the problem of unemployment and recurrent depressions....

The GM strikers walking the picket lines in Detroit and Flint and Janesville, Wis., and all the other cities where GM plants are on strike, are fighting the fight of the majority of Americans in city and farm alike.... They are fighting to give economic substance to ideals for which the war was fought.... This fight is for keeps. Upon its outcome hangs the future of America. If we win, we and those from whom we buy our food and clothes and fuel and other necessities and comforts of life will win ground on which to build an America of new economic and political freedom. Should we lose, it would be 1919 and the Twenties all over again. We are right and we will win.

General Motors: America is at the crossroads. It must preserve the freedom of each unit of American business to determine its own destinies. Or it must transfer to some governmental bureaucracy or agency, or to a union, the responsibility of management that has been the very keystone of American business. Shall this responsibility be surrendered? That is the decision the American people face. America must choose!

General Motors has made its choice. It refuses to subscribe to what it believes will ultimately become, through the process of evolution, the death of the American system of competitive enterprise. It will not participate voluntarily in what stands out crystal clear as the end of the road—a regimented economy. If this is what the American people want, they must make that choice through their accredited representatives in Congress. General Motors declines for itself to take such a great responsibility.

It may be said that this is an exaggeration. It is not. All business questions are interrelated. Costs, prices, wages, profits, schedules, investments must be the responsibility of management. Political determination of such relationships means regimentation.

The idea of ability to pay, whatever its validity may be, is not applicable to an individual business within an industry as a basis for raising its wages beyond the going rate.

Consider the implications of such a principle. Who would risk money to develop or expand a business under such circumstances?

... The President of the United States has appointed a fact-finding board to inquire into the circumstances involved in the demands of the UAW-CIO upon General Motors and to make recommendations related thereto.... The board has ruled that General Motors' ability to pay will be considered as a factor in determining an increase in wages.... Thus the board would assume the most vital functions of management....

Source: "Statements by GM and UAW on Issues," New York Times, December 30, 1945, p. 2.

24.4 HARRY S. TRUMAN, EXCERPTS FROM SPECIAL MESSAGE TO THE CONGRESS RECOMMENDING A COMPREHENSIVE HEALTH PROGRAM (1945)

The campaign for federally supported national health insurance summed up the frustrations of liberals who hoped to expand the New Deal after World War II. In this message to Congress in November 1945, President Truman proposed a system of compulsory medical insurance that would stand with the Social Security pension plan enacted in the 1930s. With the help of new taxes, a federally supervised system would ensure that all Americans had access to both health care and benefits if illness kept them from working. Truman knew that increased taxes and federal power would provoke opposition: note his careful effort to insist that his plan did not add up to "socialized medicine."

... Millions of our citizens do not now have a full measure of opportunity to achieve and enjoy good health. Millions do not now have protection or security against the economic effects of sickness. The time has arrived for action to help them attain that opportunity and that protection....

In the past, the benefits of modern medical science have not been enjoyed by our citizens with any degree of equality. Nor are they today. Nor will they be in the future—unless government is bold enough to do something about it.

People with low or moderate incomes do not get the same medical attention as those with high incomes. The poor have more sickness, but they get less medical care. People who live in rural areas do not get the same amount or quality of medical attention as those who live in our cities....

We should resolve now that the health of this Nation is a national concern; that financial barriers in the way of attaining health shall be removed; that the health of all its citizens deserves the help of all the Nation....

The principal reason why people do not receive the care they need is that they cannot afford to pay for it on an individual basis at the time they need it. This is true not only for needy persons. It is also true for a large proportion of normally self-supporting persons.

In the aggregate, all health services—from public health agencies, physicians, hospitals, dentists, nurses and laboratories—absorb only about 4 percent of the national income. We can afford to spend more for health.

But 4 percent is only an average. It is cold comfort in individual cases. Individual families pay their individual costs, and not average costs. They may be hit by sickness that calls for many times the average cost—in extreme cases for more than their annual income. When this happens they may come face to face with economic disaster. Many families, fearful of expense, delay calling the doctor long beyond the time when medical care would do the most good....

I recommend solving the basic problem by distributing the costs through expansion of our existing compulsory social insurance system. This is not socialized medicine.

Everyone who carries fire insurance knows how the law of averages is made to work so as to spread the risk, and to benefit the insured who actually suffers the loss. If instead of the costs of sickness being paid only by those who get sick, all the people—sick and well—were required to pay premiums into an insurance fund, the pool of funds thus created would enable all who do fall sick to be adequately served without overburdening anyone. That is the principle upon which all forms of insurance are based....

Socialized medicine means that all doctors work as employees of government. The American people want no such system. No such system is here proposed.

Under the plan I suggest, our people would continue to get medical and hospital services just as they do now—on the basis of their own voluntary decisions and choices. Our doctors and hospitals would continue to deal with disease with the same professional freedom as now. There would, however, be this all-important difference: whether or not patients get the services they need would not depend on how much they can afford to pay at the time.

I am in favor of the broadest possible coverage for this insurance system. I believe that all persons who work for a living and their dependents should be covered under such an insurance plan.... In addition, needy persons and other groups should be covered through appropriate premiums paid for them by public agencies. Increased Federal funds should also be made available by the Congress under the public assistance programs to reimburse the States for part of such premiums, as well as for direct expenditures made by the States in paying for medical services provided by doctors, hospitals and other agencies to needy persons. . . .

But no matter what we do, sickness will of course come to many. Sickness brings with it loss of wages.

Therefore… the workers of the Nation and their families should be protected against loss of earnings because of illness. A comprehensive health program must include the payment of benefits to replace at least part of the earnings that are lost during the period of sickness and long-term disability. This protection can be readily and conveniently provided through expansion of our present social insurance system, with appropriate adjustment of premiums. . . .

Source: Harry S. Truman, Special Message to the Congress Recommending a Comprehensive Health Program, November 19, 1945. https://www.presidency.ucsb.edu/documents/special-message-the-congress-recommending-comprehensive-health-program https://www.presidency.ucsb.edu/documents/special-message-the-congress-recommending-comprehensive-health-program

24.5 JOSEPH MCCARTHY, EXCERPTS FROM WHEELING, WEST VIRGINIA SPEECH (1950)

At Wheeling, West Virginia, in February 1950, Republican Senator Joseph McCarthy of Wisconsin gave a speech that summed up the fervent anti-Communist worldview that had gripped the United States. Rather than trace the Cold War to differences over economic or national security interests, he blamed the conflict on religion. Rather than trace the Soviets' success to their own efforts, he blamed the disloyalty of privileged men in the US government. In particular, he accused Dean Acheson, then secretary of state, of condoning the treason of Alger Hiss, an aide to the secretary accused of being a Soviet agent. McCarthy also claimed to have the names of 57 Communists or Communist sympathizers in the State Department—a claim that was never substantiated. To some observers, such claims epitomized McCarthyism.

Five years after a world war has been won, men's hearts should anticipate a long peace, and men's minds should be free from the heavy weight that comes with war. But this is not such a period—for this is not a period of peace. This is a time of the "cold war." This is a time when all the world is split into two vast, increasingly hostile armed camps—a time of a great armaments race. . . .

We are now engaged in a show-down fight—not the usual war between nations for land areas or other material gains, but a war between two diametrically opposed ideologies.

The great difference between our western Christian world and the atheistic Communist world is not political, ladies and gentlemen, it is moral. . . .

The real, basic difference… lies in the religion of immoralism—invented by Marx, preached feverishly by Lenin, and carried to unimaginable extremes by Stalin. This religion of immoralism, if the Red half of the world wins—and well it may—this religion of immoralism will more deeply wound and damage mankind than any conceivable economic or political system. . . .

As one of our outstanding historical figures once said, "When a great democracy is destroyed, it will not be because of enemies from without, but rather because of enemies from within."

The truth of this statement is becoming terrifyingly clear as we see this country each day losing on every front....

The reason why we find ourselves in a position of impotency is not because our only powerful potential enemy has sent men to invade our shores, but rather because of the traitorous actions of those who have been treated so well by this Nation. It has not been the less fortunate or members of minority groups who have been selling this Nation out, but rather those who have had all the benefits that the wealthiest nation on earth has had to offer—the finest homes, the finest college education, and the finest jobs in Government we can give.

This is glaringly true in the State Department. There the bright young men who are born with silver spoons in their mouths are the ones who have been worst....

In my opinion the State Department, which is one of the most important government departments, is thoroughly infested with Communists.

I have in my hand 57 cases of individuals who would appear to be either card carrying members or certainly loyal to the Communist Party, but who nevertheless are still helping to shape our foreign policy.

One thing to remember in discussing the Communists in our Government is that we are not dealing with spies who get 30 pieces of silver to steal the blueprints of a new weapon. We are dealing with a far more sinister type of activity because it permits the enemy to guide and shape our policy....

This brings us down to the case of one Alger Hiss who is more important not as an individual any more, but rather because he is so representative of a group in the State Department....

As you hear this story of high treason, I know that you are saying to yourself, "Well, why doesn't the Congress do something about it?" Actually, ladies and gentlemen, one of the important reasons for the graft, the corruption, the dishonesty, the disloyalty, the treason in high Government positions—one of the most important reasons why this continues is a lack of moral uprising on the part of the 140,000,000 American people. In the light of history, however, this is not hard to explain.

It is the result of an emotional hang-over and a temporary moral lapse which follows every war. It is the apathy to evil which people who have been subjected to the tremendous evils of war feel. As the people of the world see mass murder, the destruction of defenseless and innocent people, and all of the crime and lack of morals which go with war, they become numb and apathetic....

However, the morals of our people have not been destroyed. They still exist. This cloak of numbness and apathy has only needed a spark to rekindle them. Happily, this spark has finally been supplied.

As you know, very recently the Secretary of State proclaimed his loyalty to a man guilty of what has always been considered as the most abominable of all crimes—of being a traitor to the people who gave him a position of great trust. The Secretary of State in attempting to justify his continued devotion to the man who sold out the Christian world to the atheistic world, referred to Christ's Sermon on the Mount as a justification and reason therefor....

When this pompous diplomat in striped pants, with a phony British accent, proclaimed to the American people that Christ on the Mount endorsed communism, high treason, and betrayal of a sacred trust, the blasphemy was so great that it awakened the dormant indignation of the American people.

He has lighted the spark which is resulting in a moral uprising and will end only when the whole sorry mess of twisted, warped thinkers are swept from the national scene so that we may have a new birth of national honesty and decency in Government.

Source: *Major Speeches and Debates of Senator Joe McCarthy Delivered in the United States Senate, 1950–1951* (Washington, DC: United States Government Printing Office, 1953), pp. 7–14.

25

The Consumer Society

1945–1961

< Southdale Center, the first enclosed shopping mall in the United States, opened in 1956

The Ricardos

On the evening of October 15, 1951, millions of Americans turned the channel knob and adjusted the antenna on their television sets to watch the first episode of a new comedy about bandleader and club owner Ricky Ricardo and his madcap wife, Lucy. Broadcast in black and white, *I Love Lucy* quickly became one of television's biggest hits. The show aired until 1957 and over the course of 181 half-hour long episodes, viewers laughed as homemaker Lucy schemed endlessly to get a job or buy a fur coat, while Cuban-born Ricky responded to Lucy's antics with comic exasperation. During the show's run, the couple had a baby and moved from the city to the suburbs.

Part of the fun for the audience was the relationship between the fictional *I Love Lucy* and the characters' real lives. The show's stars, Lucille Ball and Desi Arnaz, were married. *I Love Lucy* attracted an especially large audience for the groundbreaking episode about the birth of the Ricardos' son, "Little Ricky," which aired on the same day as the birth of the Arnazes' own son, Desi Jr.

I Love Lucy's reflection of real American life was another reason for the show's success. Leaving behind the economic limits and constraints of the Depression and World War II, the 1950s marked the full emergence of the consumer society foreshadowed in the 1920s. *I Love Lucy* reassured Americans that television, suburban houses, and other consumer pleasures were acceptable. The show also let people laugh away the tensions generated by a renewed emphasis on women as stay-at-home mothers in the midst of a huge baby boom. As a full-time actress and businesswoman, Lucille Ball had to reassure her audience that she was a devoted mother—"a typical woman" and "a homebody."

I Love Lucy, like other pleasures of consumerism, helped Americans forget about the Cold War. The Red Scare search for American communists was never a topic addressed by the fictional Ricardos, but it was an issue for the real-life Arnazes. In 1953, Americans learned that Lucille Ball had signed a pledge to vote for Communist Party candidates in the 1930s. With her career and her show in jeopardy, Ball testified that she had only signed the pledge as a young woman to please her dictatorial grandfather. Lucille's red hair, Desi laughed, was "the only thing red about her." Despite conservative attacks, most Americans accepted her explanation—a sign that there were limits to the Red Scare.

In later years, American culture would look back nostalgically at the 1950s as a prosperous golden age. But the consumer society did not benefit every group, end racial inequality, or win the Cold War. Underneath the prosperity and good times of the decade, there were developing tensions over race, gender, generation, the confrontation with communism, and consumerism itself. Despite their image as "America's best-loved couple," Lucille and Desi were beset by his alcoholism and adultery. The fictional Ricardos stayed married; the real-life Arnazes would divorce in 1960. By then, Americans worried about the limits of the consumer society, even as they enjoyed its benefits.

LIVING THE GOOD LIFE

Much of the consumer lifestyle was in place by the 1920s (see Chapter 21), but only in the 1950s did consumer values and habits finally dominate the American economy and culture. Never before had so many Americans had the chance to live the good life.

They tended to define that "good life" in economic terms. A dynamic, evolving economy offered more leisure and income. Sure of prosperity, Americans confidently spent more of their time and money in the pursuit of pleasure. Millions lived the dream of a home in new suburbs, bought flashy automobiles, purchased their first televisions, and enjoyed a new openness about sex.

Economic Prosperity

Consumerism could not have flourished without prosperity. Despite short recessions, the 1950s was a period of economic boom. The gross national product—the value of all the country's output of goods and services—grew solidly at an average of 3.2 percent a year.

Several major factors spurred this economic growth. Because of the Cold War, federal spending for defense and foreign aid stimulated demand for American goods and services. The shortage of consumer goods during and just after World War II left Americans with money to spend. Robust capital spending by businesses helped ensure economic growth. The industrial economy was also evolving. Traditional heavy manufacturing—steel and automobiles—was still crucial to prosperity, but newer industries, such as electronics, chemicals, plastics, aviation, and computers, became increasingly important.

The emergence of computing was especially significant for the long run. In 1946, two engineers at the University of Pennsylvania, J. Presper Eckert Jr. and John William Mauchly, completed the first fully electronic digital computer. The Electronic Numerical Integrator and Computer (ENIAC) weighed over 30 tons and filled a large room. Then Eckert and Mauchly produced the more advanced UNIVAC 1 (Universal Automatic Computer), which counted census data in 1951 and presidential election returns in 1952.

As tiny solid-state transistors replaced bulky vacuum tubes, computers became smaller, more powerful, and more common. By 1958, American companies were producing $1 billion worth of computers annually. Still large and expensive, computers were used mostly by universities, corporations, and the federal government. With about 10,000 computers in use by 1961, the nation was on the brink of the digital age.

As industry evolved, the nation's distribution and service sectors played a larger role than ever. While the number of manufacturing jobs barely changed, employment in stores increased 19 percent. Jobs in the service sector, such as restaurants, hotels, repair shops, hospitals, and universities, jumped 32 percent. The nation had begun to develop a postindustrial economy, less dependent on production and more dependent on service and consumption.

Economic prosperity greatly benefited big business. New corporations emerged and grew. Thanks to a wave of mergers, established corporations became still larger. By 1960, corporations earned 18 times as much income as the rest of the nation's businesses combined.

American Landscape
West Texas

In the summer of 1948, 26-year-old George Herbert Walker Bush, his 23-year-old wife Barbara, and two-year-old son Georgie drove from Connecticut to a new life in the oil-rich Permian Basin region of West Texas. The Bushes were privileged Northeasterners. George, the son and grandson of Wall Street bankers, had gone to elite private schools; Barbara, the daughter of a corporation president, had enjoyed elite schooling, too. Newly graduated from Yale College, George, a Navy combat pilot in World War II, wanted more excitement and independence than he could find on Wall Street. So, thanks to family connections, he and his family headed to a new job with an oil supply company in Odessa, Texas.

Nearly 2,000 miles from Wall Street, Odessa, the self-proclaimed "monarch of the petroleum industry," was a hot, flat, sandy, booming city of more than 40,000. "As far as my mother was concerned," Barbara said, "we could have been living in Russia." At first, the Bushes rented a plain duplex apartment and shared a bathroom with neighboring prostitutes, while George learned the basics of the oil business in the surrounding fields of the basin. It was hard, physical work, but Odessa, a working-class community of "roughnecks and roustabouts," was an optimistic place. The frontier days were long gone, but "this typical western community" retained a dynamic,

adventurous spirit. Odessa was a southern town, too: the local community college refused to admit any Black students. Despite heat and cramped quarters, the privileged, Northeastern Bushes loved it. "At Odessa," George recalled, "we became Texans—and proud of it."

After a year, George's company sent him to California. But in 1950, he and his family eagerly returned to the Permian Basin. "This West Texas is a fabulous place," George declared. "Fortunes can be made ... and of course can be lost." This time, the Bushes, now including a baby girl, Robin, settled down in Midland, twenty miles northeast of Odessa. Just as flat, hot, and sandy as Odessa, Midland was a smaller, more affluent community, a rapidly growing city where bankers, corporate executives, and other white-collar workers labored in tall, air-conditioned office towers, lived in new ranch houses, and wore jeans, cowboy boots, and ten-gallon hats. George and Barbara bought their first, small house on a street known as "Easter Egg Row" for its varied pastel colors.

In Midland, the Bushes continued their transformation into Texans. Friendly, outgoing, and ambitious, the family fit right in with the many middle-class migrants looking to succeed in what a magazine dubbed this "New Land." Little George happily adapted, too. "Georgie has grown to be a near-man, talks dirty once in a

Prosperity boosted corporations' confidence and popularity. Even liberals, once critical of corporate power, now celebrated the benefits of large-scale enterprise. "What is good for the country is good for General Motors, and vice versa," Charles Wilson, the head of GM, supposedly declared.

Oil! A drill in West Texas sends oil gushing into the air.

while and occasionally swears, aged 4½," his proud father observed. "He lives in his cowboy clothes." The eldest Bush, clothed in the risk-taking ethos of the basin, moved up the corporate ladder and soon started his own oil companies. Of course, the Bushes didn't shed all of their Northeastern, privileged identity. "They were just ordinary people," a friend remembered. "We knew they were from rich families, though." But rich oil families, with elite education and expensive tastes, were very much a part of post-war Texas. In 1956, 32-year-old George H. W. Bush won recognition as one of the year's "Five Outstanding Young Texans."

George was a good businessman, not a great one. He didn't make a storied oil strike in West Texas, but he did find a compelling blended identity in the "New Land" that enabled him to become the 43rd president of the United States. The same held true for his little cowboy, George Walker Bush, who went to Yale and became the 45th president.

American workers enjoyed high employment, low inflation, and rising incomes. Less than 5 percent of the workforce was unemployed at any one time. Factory workers' average hourly pay more than doubled between 1945 and 1960, while consumer prices rose less than 2 percent per year. The percentage of Americans living in poverty fell from as much as 30 in the late 1940s to 18 in 1959.

Americans also had more leisure time. By the 1950s, the 40-hour workweek was commonplace. Many workers now looked forward to two- or three-week paid vacations. As life expectancy increased and the economy boomed, more Americans expected to retire at age 65 and live off pensions and Social Security.

Workers' well-being produced labor peace, which in turn stimulated prosperity. After the contentious 1940s, workers and employers were more likely to resolve differences without strikes and lockouts. When the relatively aggressive Congress of Industrial Organizations (CIO) merged with the American Federation of Labor (AFL) to become the gigantic AFL-CIO in 1955, the union movement became more bureaucratic and complacent. "American labor never had it so good," crowed a union leader.

The Suburban Dream

For growing numbers of people, the good life meant a house in the suburbs. Most Americans had never owned their own homes. Suburbs had been mainly for the well-to-do. But entrepreneurship, new construction methods, cheap land, and federal aid made possible affordable housing outside the nation's cities. Much of America moved to the suburbs in the 1950s.

William J. Levitt's pioneering development, **Levittown**, illustrated the suburban housing boom. Back from World War II, Levitt optimistically believed he could make houses affordable for middle- and working-class people. Drawing on his military experience and Henry Ford's assembly-line techniques, Levitt intended to build houses so efficiently that they could sell at remarkably low prices. He put up simple houses, with prefabricated parts, no basements, and low price tags, on 1,000 acres of cheap farmland on New York's Long Island. Levitt's original Cape Cod–style house cost $7,990, ideal for young couples financing their first home.

Levittown quickly became a huge success. Buyers contracted for 1,400 houses on one day in 1949. The development grew to 17,500 dwellings housing 82,000 people. Levitt soon built more Levittowns, as did imitators all around the country.

The federal government made those suburbs more affordable by allowing buyers to deduct mortgage interest payments from their federal income taxes and by guaranteeing loans to military veterans. To make commuting practical, the Federal-Aid Highway Act of 1956 encouraged the construction of interstate freeways connecting cities and suburbs.

Under such favorable conditions, the United States quickly became a nation of suburban homeowners. As home ownership increased 20 percent between 1945 and 1960, nearly one-third of Americans lived in places like Levittown. The suburban dream had become an everyday reality.

The Pursuit of Pleasure

The consumer society depended on Americans' eagerness to pursue pleasure. Businesses made sure that nothing prevented people from buying. If their wages and salaries were not enough, consumers could borrow. In 1950, the Diners Club introduced the credit card for New Yorkers. By 1960, Sears Roebuck credit cards allowed

Icons of the Consumer Society The first enclosed mall in the United States—Southdale, outside Minneapolis, Minnesota.

more than 10 million Americans to spend borrowed money. In 1945, Americans owed only $5.7 billion for consumer goods other than houses. By 1960, they owed $56.1 billion.

In the 1950s, discount stores such as E.J. Korvettes made shopping simpler and more attractive. So did another new creation, the shopping mall. In 1956, Southdale, the first enclosed suburban mall, opened outside Minneapolis. Consumers ate more easily, too. The first McDonald's fast-food restaurant opened in San Bernardino, California, in 1948. Taken over by Ray Kroc, McDonald's began to grow into a national chain in the mid-1950s.

To get to McDonald's, Southdale, or Levittown, Americans needed cars. In the 1950s, automobiles reflected a new sense of affluence and self-indulgence. Big, high-compression engines burning high-octane gasoline powered ever-bigger cars stuffed with new accessories—power steering, power brakes, power windows, and air conditioning. Unlike the drab sedans of the Depression, the new models featured "Passion Pink" and "Horizon Blue" interiors and two- and even three-tone exteriors studded with shiny chrome.

Automakers used that chrome to solve one of the problems of a consumer society—getting people who already had plenty to buy even more. How could Detroit persuade Americans to trade in cars that were running just fine for new ones? The answer was what General Motors' chief designer called "**dynamic obsolescence**," the feeling that last year's model was somehow inadequate. So automakers changed chrome, colors, and tailfins from year to year (see Table 25–1).

The cars of the 1950s reflected a driver's identity and affluence. General Motors' line rose up the socioeconomic ladder, from the ordinary Chevrolet to the more

Table 25-1 Automobiles and Highways, 1945–1960

Year	Factory Sales (in 1,000s)	Registrations (in 1,000s)	Miles of Highway Completed (in 1,000s)
1945	69.5	25,796.9	3,035
1946	2,148.6	28,217.0	5,057
1947	3,558.1	30,849.3	15,473
1948	3,909.2	33,355.2	21,725
1949	5,119.4	36,457.9	19,876
1950	6,665.8	40,339.0	19,876
1951	5,338.4	42,688.3	17,060
1952	4,320.7	43,823.0	22,147
1953	6,116.9	46,429.2	21,136
1954	5,558.8	48,468.4	20,548
1955	7,920.1	52,144.7	22,571
1956	5,816.1	54,210.9	23,609
1957	6,113.3	55,917.8	22,424
1958	4,257.8	56,890.5	28,137
1959*	5,591.2	59,453.9	32,633
1960	6,674.7	61,682.3	20,969

Source: Historical Statistics of the United States, Millennial Online Edition (Cambridge: Cambridge University Press, 2008), Table Df347–352 and Table Df213–217.

* Denotes first year for which figures include Alaska and Hawaii.

prosperous Pontiac, Oldsmobile, and Buick, and up to the sumptuous success symbol Cadillac.

Automobiles also spoke to gender identities. To appeal to women, car interiors seemed like living rooms. The exterior offered men power and sexuality. While the back of a 1950s car could look like a jet's afterburner, the front might evoke the female body. A car, as a Buick ad promised, "makes you feel like the man you are."

In the 1950s, television became central to the consumer society. As TV sets became less expensive and sales boomed, broadcasters seized opportunity. By 1950, the Federal Communications Commission (FCC) had licensed 104 TV stations, mostly in cities. As television undermined the popularity of radio and movie theaters, the three major broadcasting companies quickly created TV networks and dominated the new industry. By 1960, 90 percent of the nation's households had a television (see Table 25–2). In 15 years, TV had become part of everyday life.

From its early days, television reinforced the consumer society's values. Advertisements for consumer products paid for programming. There were operas, documentaries, and live dramas in what critics consider television's golden age, but variety shows, sports, westerns, and situation comedies, such as *I Love Lucy*, filled most of the broadcast day. Nightly national news broadcasts lasted only 15 minutes.

Sexual openness also defined consumer society. Dr. **Alfred C. Kinsey** commanded enormous public attention with two pioneering academic studies—*Sexual Behavior in the Human Male* (1948) and *Sexual Behavior in the Human Female* (1953).

Table 25-2 Television, 1941–1960

Year	Television Stations	Households with Television Sets (in 1,000s)
1941	2	—
1945	9	—
1950	104	3,875
1955	458	30,700
1960	579	45,750

Source: George Thomas Kurian, *Datapedia* (Lanham, MD: Bernan Press, 1994), pp. 299–300.

Kinsey surprised Americans by reporting more sexual activity outside of marriage than had been thought. The Supreme Court contributed to sexual openness by overturning a ban on a film version of D. H. Lawrence's often erotic novel, *Lady Chatterley's Lover*, in 1959. *Playboy* magazine, first published by Hugh Hefner in December 1953, epitomized the new sexual candor. Featuring bare-breasted women, *Playboy* blended sex into a hedonistic lifestyle of flashy cars, expensive stereos, and fine liquor.

A HOMOGENEOUS SOCIETY?

The spread of consumerism reinforced a sense of sameness in America. The United States seemed a homogeneous society whose people bought the same products, watched the same TV shows, worked for the same corporations, and dreamed the same dreams. Critics worried that Americans had sacrificed individuality for **conformity.** Declining class differences and renewed emphasis on religion and family strengthened the feeling that people were becoming more alike.

Nevertheless, the United States remained a heterogeneous society. Although class and ethnic differences among whites decreased, race remained a powerful divider. Despite fears of conformity, the nation still encouraged difference and individuality.

The Discovery of Conformity

After World War II, sociologists and other writers discovered an increasing uniformity in American society for a variety of reasons. During the frenzied search for domestic Communists, people did not want to risk accusations by appearing different or unusual. As corporations merged and small businesses disappeared, more Americans worked for the same giant companies. Levittown and the other new suburbs intensified the sense of sameness. In 1957, one writer described suburbanites as "people whose age, income, number of children, problems, habits, conversations, dress, possessions, perhaps even blood types are almost precisely like yours."

The Decline of Class and Ethnicity

The apparent decline of social class differences reinforced the sense of homogeneity. By the 1950s, the old upper class—the families of the Gilded Age—no longer ran American industry and finance. Thanks to taxes and the Depression, the largest

American fortunes were smaller than at the beginning of the twentieth century. The corporate leaders of the 1950s did not have the swagger, the palaces, or the dynastic ambitions of the Gilded Age robber barons.

Meanwhile, the ranks of American farmers continued to shrink. As agriculture became more efficient and corporatized, the number of farms fell from over 6 million in 1944 to 3.7 million in 1959. Although manual and service workers remained the largest occupational group, they seemed a less distinctive social class. In an era of labor peace, well-paid blue-collar workers appeared content with American society. Labor leaders endorsed consumerism and anti-Communism. Some observers argued that American workers had become middle class in their habits and values. The middle class itself was burgeoning. By 1960, the white-collar sector made up 40 percent of the workforce.

Even ethnic differences no longer seemed significant. Whites from different national and religious backgrounds mixed together in the new suburbs. The rate of intermarriage between ethnic groups increased. Anxious to prove their loyalty during the Cold War, newer Americans avoided emphasizing their origins. Ethnicity apparently disappeared in the consumer society's melting pot.

Many Americans, especially powerful ones, had long wanted to believe theirs was a unified society devoted to middle-class values. In the 1950s, there was more basis for this belief than ever before.

The Resurgence of Religion and Family

A renewed emphasis on religion and family contributed to social homogeneity. Political leaders, fighting the Cold War, encouraged religiosity. Freedom of religion, they insisted, set the United States apart from allegedly godless Communist nations. To underscore this commitment to religion, the federal government put the words "In God We Trust" on all currency. Meanwhile, religion adapted to the consumer society. Charismatic preachers such as Roman Catholic bishop Fulton J. Sheen and Protestant evangelist Billy Graham now brought religion to Americans by television.

People participated more in organized religion. In 1945, 45 percent of Americans belonged to a religious denomination; by 1960, that figure had reached 61 percent. Weekly church attendance increased to a peak of 49 percent in 1958. By 1960, there were 64 million Protestants, 42 million Roman Catholics, and fewer than 6 million Jews (see Table 25–3).

American culture also celebrated what *McCall's* magazine christened family "togetherness." Manufacturers promoted TV viewing as a way of holding families together. Detroit called its big automobiles "family" cars.

"Togetherness" meant the nuclear family, with a mother, a father, and plenty of children. After decades of decline, the birthrate rose in the 1940s. Beginning in 1954, Americans had more than 4 million babies a year. Thanks to new drugs, nearly all these infants survived. Antibiotics reduced the risk of diphtheria, typhoid fever, and other infections. The Salk and Sabin vaccines virtually wiped out polio. As a result, the average number of children per family went from 2.4 in 1945 up to 3.2 in 1957, and the population grew by a record 29 million people to 179 million.

Like the religious revival, the **baby boom is** somewhat difficult to explain. For over a century, Americans had reduced the size of their families to ease financial

Table 25-3 Religious Revival and Baby Boom, 1945–1960

Year	Membership of Religious Bodies (in 1,000s)	Live Births (in 1,000s)
1945	71,700	2,858
1946	73,673	3,411
1947	77,386	3,817
1948	79,436	3,637
1949	81,862	3,649
1950	86,830	3,632
1951	88,673	3,823
1952	92,277	3,913
1953	94,843	3,965
1954	97,483	4,078
1955	100,163	4,104
1956	103,225	4,218
1957	104,190	4,308
1958*	109,558	4,255
1959**	112,227	4,245
1960	114,449	4,258

Source: George Thomas Kurian, *Datapedia* (Lanham, MD: Bernan Press, 1994), pp. 37, 146.

* Includes Alaska.

** Denotes first year for which figures include Alaska and Hawaii.

and personal burdens. Prosperity may have persuaded couples that they could afford more children. But affluence alone did not explain why American culture became more child centered in the 1950s. In his *Common Sense Book of Baby and Child Care* (1946), pediatrician Benjamin Spock urged parents to raise their children with less severity and more attention, warmth, tenderness, and fun. It outsold every other book in the 1950s except the Bible.

Maintaining Gender Roles

As many social differences decreased, American culture nevertheless reemphasized the distinctions between the sexes. During the baby boom, women were expected to be helpful wives and devoted mothers. Men were encouraged to define themselves primarily as family providers.

The 1950s underscored the differences between genders in a variety of ways. Blue became the color for boys and pink the color for girls. Standards of beauty highlighted physiological differences between women and men. Voluptuous actresses such as Jayne Mansfield and Marilyn Monroe defined femininity.

Nevertheless, gender roles grew more similar during the 1950s. Society stressed a man's domestic role more than before. Husbands were urged to do housework and spend more time nurturing their children, although few men lived up to the new ideal.

Female roles evolved more dramatically. To help pay for the consumer lifestyle, many wives had to find jobs. In 1940, 15.6 percent of married women participated in the paid workforce. By 1960, that percentage had nearly doubled to 31.0, and women made up more than one-third of the labor force, mostly in clerical and sales positions. In the Cold War competition with the Soviets, Americans celebrated the supposedly greater freedom and opportunity for women in the United States. Nevertheless, women had little help coping with their jobs and bigger families. Congress voted an income tax deduction for child-care costs in 1954, but little first-class child care was available. At work, women were expected to watch men get ahead of them. Women's income was only 60 percent of men's in 1960.

American culture strongly condemned women and men who strayed outside conventional gender norms. *Modern Woman: The Lost Sex*, a 1947 bestseller by Marynia Farnham and Ferdinand Lundberg, censured feminism as the "deep illness" of "neurotically disturbed women" with "penis envy." Psychologists and other experts demonized lesbians and gay men. As police cracked down on gay bars, unmarried men risked accusations of homosexuality. In 1950, a small group of gay men formed the Mattachine Society to work for homosexual rights. Five years later, a group of lesbians formed a counterpart organization, the Daughters of Bilitis. But there were no large protests against the treatment of gays and lesbians. The dominant culture expected males to be heterosexual husbands and fathers and women to be heterosexual wives and mothers.

Persisting Racial Differences

Despite pressures toward conformity, American society remained heterogeneous. As whites left for the suburbs, African Americans took their place in cities. By 1960, more than half of the Black population lived in cities, where they were typically barred from white neighborhoods. Although suburbanization broke down ethnic differences among whites, it intensified the racial divide. The suburbs were 95 percent white in 1950. That was no accident: the first Levittowns, for instance, refused to sell houses to African Americans.

Living on reservations, Native Americans were also set apart. In 1953, Congress tried to "Americanize" the Indians by terminating their special legal status as sovereign groups, and with it, the traditional rights and reservations of more than 11,000 Native Americans. Termination was intended to turn them into members of the consumer society.

It did not turn out that way. As reservations became counties in the 1950s and early 1960s, Indians had to sell valuable mineral rights and lands to pay taxes. Tribes still faced poverty, unemployment, and social problems. Encouraged by the federal government's new Voluntary Relocation Program, about one in five Native Americans moved to the city. Some tribes, including the Catawba, the Coquille, and the Klamath, began legal fights to reclaim tribal status. But whether they lived on reservations or on crowded city blocks, a quarter of a million Indians remained largely separate and ignored.

The increasing migration of Puerto Ricans reinforced the nation's multiracial character. Beginning in the 1940s, a large number of Puerto Ricans, who were US citizens, left their island for more economic opportunity. By 1960, 887,000 Puerto Ricans lived on the mainland, two-thirds of them in the East Harlem section of

New York City. They found opportunities but also separation and discrimination in their new homes.

Mexican immigration also added to racial diversity. After 1945, increasing numbers of Mexicans left their impoverished country for the United States, particularly the booming Southwest. Congress, bowing to southwestern employers, continued the Bracero Program, the supposedly temporary agreement that had brought hundreds of thousands of laborers, or *braceros*, to the wartime United States. Meanwhile, illegal Mexican migration increased dramatically.

Like other Mexican migrants before them, the newly arrived met a mixed reception. As in the years before World War II, Mexicans already living in the United States worried that the new migrants would compete for jobs, drive down wages, and feed American prejudice. Many white Americans indeed derided them as *mojados*, or "wetbacks," because so many had supposedly swum the Rio Grande River to enter the country illegally. Mexican Americans feared that the federal government would use the Internal Security Act of 1950 and the Immigration and Nationality Act of 1952 to deport Mexicans and break up families. The government's intention became clear in 1954 with Operation Wetback, which sent more than 1 million immigrants back to Mexico in that year alone.

The Plight of Mexican "Wetbacks" Illegal immigrants taken off freight trains in Los Angeles, after two days without food or water, in 1953. They were probably sent back to Mexico.

About 3.5 million Mexican Americans were living in the United States by 1960. The great majority worked for low wages in the cities and on the farms of the Southwest. Many lived in *barrios* apart from whites. Because of Operation Wetback and other instances of prejudice, some Mexican Americans became more vocal about their rights. The League of United Latin American Citizens denounced the impact of the Immigration and Nationality Act. More outspoken was the American GI Forum, an organization of Mexican American veterans formed when a Texas funeral parlor would not bury a deceased comrade. Such assertiveness made it harder to ignore the presence of Mexican Americans in the consumer society.

The experiences of Hispanics, Mexican Americans, Native Americans, and African Americans underscored the continuing importance of race in the United States. Mostly living apart, whites and nonwhites faced different conditions and different futures. Prosperity and consumerism did not change that reality. As long as race was so potent a factor, the United States would never be a homogeneous society.

The Survival of Diversity

Along with race, other forces ensured the survival of diversity, especially regional differences. As in the past, internal migration and the expansion of national boundaries promoted change. During the 1950s, more than 1.6 million people, many of them retired, moved to Florida. As a result, the state increasingly played a distinctive national role as a center for leisure and entertainment.

Other Americans headed westward. During the 1950s, over 3 million people moved to California, which earned a reputation as the pioneer state of the consumer society, home of the first Disney amusement park and the first McDonald's.

The admission of two new states highlighted the nation's continuing diversity. In 1959, Alaska and Hawaii became, respectively, the 49th and 50th states in the Union. Racially and

"160 Acres of Happiness" This ad for the opening of Disneyland in 1955 embodies the promise of pleasure for Americans in the consumer society.

culturally diverse, climatically and topographically distinctive, they demonstrated that America was not simply a land of corporations and Levittowns.

Popular music also exemplified this continuing diversity. Big swing bands gave way to such popular singers as Frank Sinatra and Patti Page. Jazz split into different camps—traditional, mainstream, and modern. Country music featured cowboy songs, western swing, honky-tonk, bluegrass, and the suburbanized "Nashville sound." A range of African American musical forms, including blues, jazz, and vocal groups, became known as "rhythm and blues" (R & B). Gospel music thrilled white and Black audiences. Mexican Americans made Tejano music in Texas, and Polish Americans danced to polka bands in Illinois.

R & B collided with country music to create rock and roll. By 1952, white disc jockey Alan Freed was playing R & B on his Cleveland radio show, "Moondog's Rock 'n' Roll Party." In 1954, a white country group, Bill Haley and the Comets, recorded the first rock-and-roll hit, "Rock Around the Clock." Early rock and roll produced both African American and white heroes—Chuck Berry, Fats Domino, Jerry Lee Lewis, and Buddy Holly, among others.

The biggest rock-and-roll sensation was a young white singer and guitar player, Elvis Presley. Born in Mississippi and raised in near poverty in Memphis, Presley drew on a variety of genres to create a distinctive personal style. "Who do you sound like?" he was asked. "I don't sound like nobody," he said.

Because of Presley and other musicians, the sound of America was anything but homogeneous. Because of Florida, California, Alaska, Hawaii, and other states, the United States hardly looked monolithic. In these ways, American society avoided uniformity after World War II.

THE EISENHOWER ERA AT HOME AND ABROAD

Prosperity subtly changed Americans' understanding of democracy. On one hand, they expected more from politics and government. Along with guarantees of national security and civil rights, people wanted government to assure their opportunity to consume. The good life became the test of democracy. On the other hand, people expected less from politics and government in the 1950s. Since the country was so prosperous and middle class, democracy must be working. As long as the federal government maintained the economy and national security, Americans did not demand dramatic, new liberal programs. The politics of the decade were dominated by President Dwight D. Eisenhower, whose middle-of-the-road domestic program, **Modern Republicanism**, appealed to a prosperous electorate wary of government innovation. But Eisenhower's anti-Communist foreign policy did little to diminish popular anxieties about the Cold War and laid the groundwork for future trouble in the Middle East and Southeast Asia.

"Ike" and 1950s America

Eisenhower, a charismatic military hero with a bright, infectious grin, would have been an ideal public figure in almost any era of American history, but the man known as "Ike" was especially suited to the 1950s. The last president born in the nineteenth century, he had successfully accommodated the changes of the twentieth. Raised on the individualism of the rural Midwest, Eisenhower adopted the bureaucratic style of modern organizations. He succeeded in the military not because he was a great fighter but because he was a great manager, a classic "organization man." As a commander in World War II, Eisenhower worked to keep fractious allies together. After the war, he deepened his organizational experience as president of Columbia University and as the first commander of NATO armed forces. Just as he adapted to big organizations, Eisenhower accommodated America's expanding commitment abroad. Raised among people who often feared American involvement in the world's problems, Ike had made his career in the world.

Eisenhower easily fit the dominant culture of the 1950s. He was an involved, loving husband and father. In a society pursuing pleasures, he was famous for his hours on the golf course. His wife, Mamie, wore the "New Look" fashions inspired by designer Christian Dior and avidly watched television soap operas.

Nominated for president by the Republicans in 1952, Eisenhower ran against Adlai Stevenson, the liberal Democratic governor of Illinois. Running a moderate campaign, Eisenhower avoided attacks on the New Deal and promised to work for an end to the Korean War. Meanwhile, his tough-talking running mate, Senator **Richard Nixon** of California, accused Stevenson of being soft on Communism. Eisenhower handily won 55 percent of the popular vote and 442 electoral votes. The Republicans took control of the White House and both houses of Congress for the first time in 20 years.

Modern Republicanism

Eisenhower's Modern Republicanism steered a middle course between traditional Republican conservatism and Democratic liberalism. With a conservative's faith in individual freedom, the president favored limited government and balanced budgets, but Eisenhower the organization man believed that Washington had an important role in protecting individuals. He also knew that most Americans wanted to keep such liberal programs as Social Security and farm subsidies.

Accordingly, his administration limited government by decreasing regulation of business and cutting taxes for the wealthy. The Submerged Lands Act of 1953 turned over offshore oil resources to the states for private exploitation. The Atomic Energy Act of 1954 allowed private firms to sell power produced by nuclear reactors.

Nevertheless, the administration left the legacy of the New Deal and the Fair Deal intact. Eisenhower accepted increases in Social Security benefits and farm subsidies. In some cases, the president wanted the government to take a more active role. The expansion of the interstate system was largely his initiative, which he justified as a matter of national defense. Despite his belief in balanced budgets, Eisenhower's administration produced several budget deficits. Federal spending helped fuel the consumer economy.

Modern Republicanism frustrated liberals, as well as conservative "Old Guard" Republicans, but "the public loves Ike," a journalist observed. "The less he does the more they love him."

Eisenhower's popularity was confirmed at the polls in 1956. Repeating 1952, Eisenhower and Nixon again defeated Stevenson, this time with a bigger victory—58 percent of the popular vote and 457 electoral votes.

An Aggressive Cold War Strategy

Like Truman, Eisenhower opposed Communism at home and around the world. The president helped the crusade against alleged Communist subversives and tolerated its excesses. He refused to criticize publicly Senator Joseph R. McCarthy and declined to stop the execution of the convicted spies, Julius and Ethel Rosenberg, in 1953. Eisenhower denied the security clearance that J. Robert Oppenheimer, the former director of the Manhattan Project, needed to work on federal nuclear projects. Thousands of others allegedly deemed security risks also lost their federal jobs during the Eisenhower era.

Whereas Truman had pledged only to contain Communist expansion, Eisenhower and his advisers talked of rolling back Soviet power in Europe and freeing "captive peoples" from Communism. Secretary of State John Foster Dulles threatened "instant, massive retaliation" with nuclear weapons in response to any Soviet aggression. To support this threat, the US military adopted the New Look strategy, named after Mamie Eisenhower's favorite fashions, that de-emphasized conventional armies and increased the nuclear arsenal with long-range bombers, missiles, and nuclear-powered submarines.

The president also used the CIA to counter Communism by stealthier means. At his direction, the CIA carried out secret activities once considered unacceptable. At home, the agency explored possible uses of lysergic acid diethylamide—the dangerous hallucinogenic drug known as LSD—by testing it on hundreds of unwitting Americans. Abroad, the agency secretly aided pro-American regimes and ran programs against uncooperative governments.

Three Communist Leaders This 1959 meeting of Soviet Premier Nikita Khrushchev, Chinese Communist Party Chairman Mao Zedong, and North Vietnamese President Ho Chi Minh embodied Americans' fears of an international Communist alliance that would lead the United States to intervene in Vietnam.

In August 1953, a covert CIA operation, code-named Ajax, orchestrated a coup that removed Mohammad Mossadeq, the nationalist prime minister of oil-rich Iran. Eisenhower and Dulles feared that this "madman," who had nationalized Iran's oil fields, would shut out US business in favor of Communism and the Soviet Union. Mossadeq's successor, the young monarch, Shah Mohammad Reza Pahlavi, accepted $45 million in US aid, turned his back on the Soviets, and made low-priced oil available to American companies.

In 1954, PBSUCCESS, a secret CIA operation modeled on Ajax, overthrew another foreign leader. Eisenhower and Dulles worried that a "Communist infection" in the Central American nation of Guatemala could spread to the United States–controlled Panama Canal and to Mexico. In fact, the Soviet Union had made no effort to help Guatemala's new president, Jacobo Arbenz Guzmán, who supported redistribution of land and threatened the interests of a powerful American corporation, United Fruit. In June, PBSUCCESS used misleading "disinformation," a force of Guatemalan exiles, and CIA-piloted bombing raids to persuade Arbenz Guzmán to resign.

More openly, Eisenhower intensified efforts to shape perceptions of American culture and values abroad. In 1953, the administration created the United States Information Agency (USIA), overseen by the State Department. Active in 76 countries by 1960, the agency published pamphlets, promoted the exchange of visitors with other nations, broadcast Voice of America radio around the world, and worked with the CIA on propaganda and psychological warfare.

Avoiding War with the Communist Powers

Despite its tough talk, the Eisenhower administration avoided direct confrontation with the two major Communist powers, the People's Republic of China and the Soviet Union. Eisenhower knew he had to end the Korean conflict. As he promised in his 1952 campaign, Eisenhower traveled to Korea to end the military stalemate that ultimately killed 33,629 Americans. A cease-fire agreement in July 1953 left North and South Korea divided and the United States without a victory. It was, Eisenhower declared, "an acceptable solution." In October 1956, Hungarians, spurred on by American broadcasts, rose up against their pro-Soviet government. The Soviet Union sent troops to break the rebellion, but Eisenhower did not intervene with **massive retaliation**, after all.

Fundamentally, Eisenhower maintained Truman's policy of containment. Cautious about military confrontation with the Soviets and the Chinese, Eisenhower declined to unleash nuclear weapons that would "destroy civilization." Although he sent CIA agents to conduct covert operations, the president was more reluctant than Truman to send American soldiers into open battle.

At the same time, Eisenhower, like Truman, knew the Cold War was an economic, political, and cultural war, waged by foreign aid and propaganda. The Eisenhower administration took modest steps to improve relations with the Soviets. Responding to the Soviets' interest in "peaceful coexistence," Eisenhower told the United Nations that he wanted disarmament and the peaceful use of atomic power. He proposed the "Atoms for Peace" plan in which an international agency would explore nonmilitary uses for nuclear materials. The Soviets dragged their feet.

In 1955, Eisenhower took another step when he joined Khrushchev in Geneva for the first meeting between an American president and a Soviet leader since World War II. Eisenhower's proposal for "Open Skies"—a plan to allow each side to fly over the other's territory—sparked optimism about better relations. In 1958, the United States and the Soviets also agreed to a program of cultural exchanges. But in May 1960, optimism plummeted when the Soviets downed an American U-2 spy plane over the USSR. After the United States denied the affair, Khrushchev triumphantly produced the captured pilot, Francis Gary Powers, along with pieces of the plane. The rivalry would continue.

Crises in the Third World

Although Eisenhower worried most about Western Europe, his administration increasingly focused on the threat of Communist expansion in Africa, Asia, Latin America, and the Middle East. These relatively rural, unindustrialized regions, which made up the "third world," were enmeshed in the confrontation between the "first world" of industrialized non-Communist nations and the "second world" of industrialized Communist countries. Plagued by poverty, violence, and civil war, many third-world societies struggled against imperial domination.

Under Khrushchev, the Soviet Union tried to exploit third-world discontent and conflict. Anxious to preserve America's influence and access to natural resources, the Eisenhower administration countered Soviet moves with the tools of containment—aid, trade, and alliances. Eisenhower offered increased foreign aid and trade opportunities to third-world countries. He pursued closer military ties, including defense pacts with the Philippines, South Korea, and Taiwan.

This approach was sorely tested in Southeast Asia. When Eisenhower took office in 1953, the United States supported France's war to hold on to Vietnam and its other Southeast Asian colonies. Despite vast American aid, the French could not defeat the nationalist forces of the Viet Minh, led by the Communist **Ho Chi Minh** and helped by the mainland Chinese. By 1954, the Viet Minh had surrounded French troops at Dien Bien Phu. Unwilling to fight another land war in Asia, Eisenhower refused to send American troops and rejected the use of atomic bombs. France surrendered in May.

In 1954, peace talks at Geneva produced an agreement to cut Vietnam, like Korea, in half. Ho Chi Minh's forces would stay north of the 17th parallel; his pro-French Vietnamese enemies would stay to the south. The agreement called for a popular election to unite Vietnam in 1956. Certain that Ho Chi Minh and the Communists would win the election, the United States refused to sign the agreement. The president feared that a Communist Vietnam would deprive the West of raw materials and encourage Communism elsewhere. Comparing the nations of Asia and the Pacific to "a row of dominoes," Eisenhower explained his theory that that the fall of the first **domino**—Vietnam—would lead to the fall of the rest, including Japan and Australia.

Instead, the Eisenhower administration worked to create an anti-Communist nation south of the 17th parallel. To protect South Vietnam, the United States joined with seven nations to create the Southeast Asia Treaty Organization (SEATO) in 1954 (see Map 25–1). To ensure South Vietnam's loyalty, the Eisenhower administration

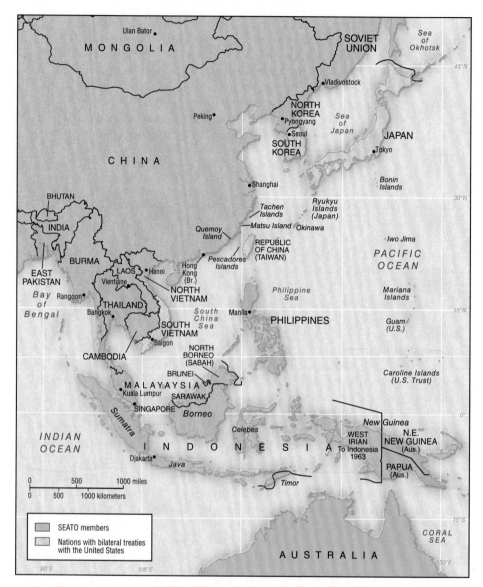

Map 25–1   America's Cold War Alliances in Asia Members of SEATO (the Southeast Asia Treaty Organization) and signers of other treaties with the United States. Through these pacts, the Eisenhower administration hoped to hold back the threat posed by Communist mainland China.

backed Ngo Dinh Diem, an anti-Communist who established a corrupt, repressive government, with military advisers and hundreds of millions of dollars.

By thwarting the Geneva Accords and installing an unpopular regime in the South, Eisenhower ensured that Vietnam would be torn by civil war. In the short run, however, he had avoided war and seemingly stopped the Asian dominoes from falling.

Eisenhower soon confronted another crisis in the Middle East. Gamal Abdel Nasser, who had seized power in Egypt in 1954, emerged as a forceful spokesman for Arab unity and nationalism. Fearing that Nasser would open the way for Soviet power in the region, **John Foster Dulles** withdrew an offer to aid the Egyptians. Nasser struck back by taking over the British- and French-owned Suez Canal in 1956. In retaliation, Britain and France, with Israel's cooperation, moved against Nasser. As Israeli troops entered Egypt in October, Britain and France prepared to take back the Suez Canal. Eisenhower, fearing the invasion would give the Soviets an excuse to move into the Middle East, threatened the British, French, and Israelis—US allies—with economic sanctions. They soon withdrew.

The **Suez crisis** was a pivotal moment. Before a joint session of Congress in January 1957, Eisenhower promised that the United States would intervene to protect any Middle Eastern nation threatened by "power-hungry Communists." He implemented this "Eisenhower Doctrine" by sending troops to Lebanon the next year. In 1959, the United States joined with Turkey and Iran to create a Middle Eastern defense alliance known as the Central Treaty Organization (CENTO) for its geographical position between NATO and SEATO (see Map 25–2). Eisenhower had helped to stabilize the Middle East and Southeast Asia temporarily, but he had also drawn the United States more deeply into these crisis-prone regions and increased the odds of future trouble. In the 1960s and 1970s, the United States would have to deal with this legacy.

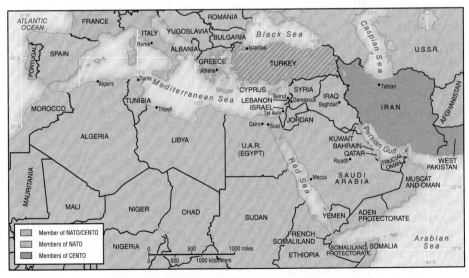

Map 25–2 America's Cold War Alliances in the Middle East Located between the members of NATO and SEATO, the members of CENTO (the Central Treaty Organization) joined with the United States to deter the threat of international Communism sponsored by the Soviet Union to the north.

America In The World
American Tourists in Cold War Europe

American Airlines Advertisement

"This is your year for Europe," an American Airlines magazine ad proclaimed in 1948. "Anyone with only a week or two—or even a few days—can enjoy a fascinating trip to the 'Old World,' traveling by time-saving American Flagship. Don't put off that dreamed-of-journey abroad. Make this your year—your family's year—for Europe!"

Hundreds of thousands of Americans were eager to follow the airline's advice. The Great Depression and then World War II had reduced overseas tourism to almost nothing. But now, Americans were prosperous again and war-torn Europe was at peace and eager for dollars. Technological advances made steam-powered ships and propeller-driven airplanes, such as American Airlines' Flagship, faster and more affordable than ever. In 1949, over half a million Americans traveled overseas; in 1955, that number soared past a million. With the advent of jet-powered air travel, that figure would reach over 2 million by 1961.

Various impulses spurred American tourists. Americans wanted to relax, enjoy themselves, and explore exotic places. A nation of immigrants, Americans wanted to see where their families originated. The consumerism and conformity of the 1950s drove tourism, too. As another American Airlines ad explained, a trip to Europe was "How to Keep up with the Joneses."

For the US government, American tourism represented something else altogether: a weapon in the Cold War. In a letter to recipients of new passports, President Eisenhower explained that "you represent us all in bringing assurance to the people you meet that the United States is a friendly nation and one dedicated to the promotion of the well-being and security of the community of nations." Echoing that sentiment, Americans and foreigners alike spoke of US tourists as "unofficial ambassadors" abroad.

Those ambassadors did a mixed job. In Europe, an unflattering stereotype of the American tourist emerged. "He is a mobile human armed with cameras and broad-rimmed sunglasses, dressed-up in many-colored shirts and multi-colored neckties, who chewing-gums his way across an old and alien continent," wrote a European tour guide. American travelers were stereotyped as too loud, too critical, too unsophisticated, and too demanding: they actually wanted cold beer and private bathrooms!

Americans pushed back. Some of the criticism, they suggested, was the product of envy and insecurity: Europeans, their nations' wealth and power diminished, resented the triumphant rise of the United States. Admitting that too many Americans favored loud clothing, a New Yorker complained that "any slight misdemeanor committed by one of us on such a trip becomes magnified and is finally blamed on the United States as a whole."

American travelers developed another image, one rooted in the 1950s ideal of a democratic United States without social classes. "What the Italians like most about Americans is their free and easy manner," a journalist reported in 1957. "They consider Americans truly democratic, since they show not the slightest trace of class consciousness, and deal considerately and politely with one and all." Despite the reputation of some, the mass of travelers seemed to promote a positive understanding of their country, as US officials hoped. "Americans who are traveling abroad this Summer," said a Swiss teen in 1948, "are good ambassadors."

Travel also helped Americans get past some of their own stereotypes and prejudices. For instance, Americans who travelled to Moscow were in for a surprise. "Many American tourists here profess astonishment... that the Russians are people, that they smile and laugh and talk like people, that there are automobiles here," a writer noted in 1959. "Almost invariably, the Russians a tourist bumps into and talks with are friendly, helpful, deeply curious about the United States."

The encounters appeared to ease some of the Cold War tensions and fears of the Soviets, too. "Some Russians who have met Americans," the writer added, "have adjusted some of their propaganda concepts of them as warmongers and imperialist exploiters scheming to blow up the Kremlin and enforce capitalism here."

CHALLENGES TO THE CONSUMER SOCIETY

Along with crises abroad, American society confronted challenges at home. In different ways, a rebellious youth culture, the alienated beat movement, a nascent environmental movement, and the divisive civil rights struggle upset the stability of the Eisenhower era. Consumerism had not solved all the nation's problems or won over all of its citizens. Moreover, despite prosperity, Americans worried about a crisis of power in the nation.

Rebellious Youth

"Never in our 180-year history," declared *Collier's* magazine in 1957, "has the United States been so aware of—or confused about—its teenagers." In the 1950s, the emergence of a distinct youth culture, built around rock and roll, cars, comic books, and premarital sex, troubled many adults. The youth culture culminated a trend apparent since the 1920s and 1930s. As more and more teenagers attended high school, they were segregated in their own world and developed their own values and practices. In the 1950s, young people claimed rock and roll as their music. They wore blue jeans; they read comic books and teen magazines. Expressing their individuality, boys modified cars into customized "hot rods." Teens were attracted to alienated and rebellious movie characters, such as the troubled son played by James Dean in *Rebel Without a Cause* (1955) and the motorcycle-gang leader played by Marlon Brando in *The Wild One* (1953). Adults worried about teenage defiance and juvenile delinquency.

Many young people were rebellious, but not nearly as much as adults feared. Juvenile delinquency did not actually increase after World War II, and neither did rates of sexual intercourse among teenagers. Girls never played a strongly visible role in male-dominated youth culture. Most young people never questioned the political system, and youth culture exaggerated rather than rejected the values of the adult consumer society.

The early career of **Elvis Presley** illustrated the boundaries of youthful rebellion. Presley's appeal rested on an unsettling combination of rock-and-roll music and open sexuality. Presley's style—his sensual mouth, disheveled "duck's ass" haircut, and gyrating hips—amplified the music's sexuality.

Despite his appeal to teenagers, Presley was always polite, soft spoken, and devoted to his parents. Buying a pink Cadillac and other luxury cars, he was caught up in the consumer culture. Like millions of other Americans, Presley joined the suburban migration when he bought his house, Graceland, on the outskirts of Memphis. He was a new version of the old American dream of upward mobility.

Still, many adults blamed Presley, rock and roll, and mass media for the spread of violence, lust, and degeneration among young Americans. One popular television program showed Presley only from the waist up. To get rid of blue jeans and other teenage fashions, high schools imposed dress codes. There was a crusade against comic books, teen magazines, and movies. In well-publicized hearings from 1954 to 1956, the Senate's Subcommittee to Investigate Juvenile Delinquency focused attention on the corrupting power of the mass media.

The campaign against youth culture had little impact in a society of free speech and consumerism. Mass culture did not stop catering to teenagers with spending money. Many adults found youth culture appealing.

The Beat Movement

A smaller and older second group of rebels was much more critical of American society. The **beat movement**, which emerged in New York City in the 1940s, expressed a sense of both alienation and hope. The term "beat" referred to a feeling of exhaustion and also to a state of transcendence, the "beatific." Worn down by contemporary culture, the beats searched for a way beyond it.

Uptown at Columbia University and downtown in Greenwich Village, Allen Ginsberg, Jack Kerouac, John Clellon Holmes, William Burroughs, and others wanted, as one of them put it, "to emote, to soak up the world." Beats explored their sexuality, sampled mind-altering drugs, and pursued Eastern religions. In a society of bright colors, "beatniks" declared their alienation from consumerism by wearing black. Kerouac captured their spirit in his novel about a trip across America, *On the Road* (1957). In San Francisco, another center of beat culture, Allen Ginsberg published his long poem "Howl" (1956), which gave voice to alienation: "I saw the best minds of my generation destroyed by madness, starving hysterical naked. ..."

Though few in number, the beats attracted a great deal of attention. Their movement signaled a new dissatisfaction with consumer society, conventional sexual mores, and politics as usual.

The Rebirth of Environmentalism

A rebirth of environmental consciousness was also evidence of concern about consumerism. By the late 1950s, Americans were more concerned about the environment than at any time since the beginning of the twentieth century. The environmental threat was obvious in the cities. A well-publicized pall of smog seemed to hang perpetually over car-choked Los Angeles. Americans could no longer ignore the fact that their automobiles, the symbol of the consumer society, were polluting the air.

The environmental threat was obvious in the countryside, too. Even as they filled new suburban developments built on old farms, some Americans lamented the disappearance of open land. They began to criticize society's attitude toward the natural world. In the mid-1950s, environmentalists, led by the Sierra Club and the Wilderness Society, blocked construction of the Echo Park Dam in the upper Colorado River because it would have flooded a national park, the Dinosaur National Monument. A new environmental movement to protect wilderness lands emerged from the battle.

The Struggle for Civil Rights

The African American struggle for civil rights also challenged the Eisenhower era. By the 1950s, segregation was under increasingly effective attack in the courts and on the streets. Focusing on public schools (see Map 25-3), the NAACP assaulted the discriminatory legacy of the Supreme Court's *Plessy v. Ferguson* ruling of 1896 (see Chapter 18). In 1951, the NAACP's special counsel, Thurgood Marshall, combined five school lawsuits, including Oliver Brown's challenge to the constitutionality of a Kansas state law that allowed cities to segregate their schools. Because of the law, Brown's eight-year-old daughter, Linda, had to ride a bus 21 blocks to a "colored-only" school, even though there was a "white-only" school just three blocks from home. When the Brown case reached the Supreme Court in December 1952, Marshall attacked the *Plessy* argument that justified "separate but equal" facilities for whites and African Americans. Because of segregation, Marshall argued, Linda Brown and other African Americans received both an inferior education and a feeling of inferiority. He concluded that segregation violated the citizenship rights guaranteed by the Fourteenth Amendment.

Struggles For Democracy

"SOS"—SMOG!

For decades, boosters of Los Angeles, California, trumpeted the beautiful weather of their "City of Sunshine." Yet after World War II, Los Angelenos often had a hard time finding the sun in the daytime. The problem was a dense combination of smoke and fog, known as "smog." One day, an anxious driver, lost in the haze, had to pull over so his wife could give birth. Afterwards, he realized the car was right in front of the hospital. Along with causing such mishaps, smog endangered tourism, agriculture, and, above all, public health.

Smog presented complex scientific challenges. The phenomenon sprang from the interaction of the city's longtime weather patterns and its relatively new industrial economy. But there the certainty ended. What caused increasing amounts of smoke? Oil refineries, factory smokestacks, incinerators, trash fires, and, observers increasingly realized in the late 1940s and 1950s, gas-powered motor vehicles. Scientists worked through the 1950s to determine just why and how much various factors contributed to the persistent problem of Smog. Then there was the equally complex question of just how to stop smog. Could smog-ridden air be treated? Or could smog be stopped in the first place? Los Angelenos, so dependent on trucks and automobiles, desperately needed some way to limit the air pollution from motor vehicles.

The political challenges were equally complex. The city of Los Angeles wasn't an island; it was surrounded by other communities with their own smog problems. Action against the myriad causes of smog required ordinances, laws, and enforcement from numerous cities, from Los Angeles county, from the state of California, and from the federal government. This reality meant that any campaign for change required many smaller initiatives from a broad range of activists, scientists, officials, and politicians. In turn, they faced opposition from some local businesses and from nation-spanning corporations, such as the automobile industry.

Women played a key role in what the press dubbed the "Smog War." Despite the post-war cultural emphasis on their domestic role as wives and mothers, women remained politically engaged. As in the past, they used their work in the home as a justification for political action. Calling themselves "Smog-atears," housewives and children wearing gas masks paraded through Pasadena, northeast of Los Angeles, in protest in 1954. Four years later, after her two-year-old daughter suffered an asthma attack, Marge Levee, the wife of a Hollywood talent agent, decided to fight rather than flee to another city. With other well-to-do, well-connected women, she founded "Stamp Out Smog"—"SOS." Forging

In May 1954, the Court, led by new Chief Justice Earl Warren, handed down its ruling in *Brown v. Board of Education, Topeka, Kansas.* Overturning *Plessy*, the justices ruled unanimously that public school segregation was unconstitutional under the Fourteenth Amendment. "Separate but equal has no place," Warren announced. African Americans and white liberals were jubilant over what an African

Struggles for Democracy Middle-class SMOG protesters in Los Angeles, 1954.

connections with a host of civic groups and women's organizations, SOS members wrote letters, made phone calls, lobbied legislators, publicized scientific findings, and staged photo-opportunities, such as a test drive of diesel-powered taxis.

"SOS probably packs the most concentrated and potent feminine determination ever directed towards achievement of a common goal in the history of our Golden State," declared a newspaper. "Woe betide the hapless politician or industrialist who fails to show complete cooperation." The organization wasn't quite that powerful. But in 1959, the California legislature enacted the first bill in any state to control air pollution from automobiles. The following year, Marge Levee was the only woman named to California's new thirteen-member anti-pollution committee. Like the Smog War, SOS would continue into the 1960s, a model for middle-class, mostly white women's participation in the complex political struggle over air pollution and in democratic struggles more generally.

American newspaper called "a second emancipation proclamation." Marshall foresaw the end of school segregation before the close of the decade.

It did not work out that way. When the Supreme Court ruled on the enforcement of its decision in 1955, the justices turned to local school boards, dominated by whites, to carry out integration. Federal district courts were to oversee the process,

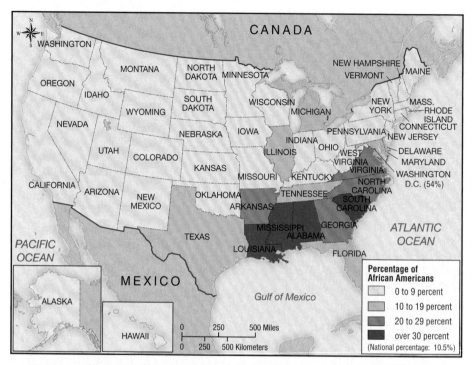

Map 25-3 African American Percentage of Population by State, 1960 Despite migration to other regions, Black Americans remained largely concentrated in the South.

which should occur with "all deliberate speed." School segregation would have to end, but not right away.

Taking heart from the enforcement ruling, many whites refused to give up Jim Crow. As one white southerner put it, a "reasonable time" for the end of segregation would be "one or two hundred years." In 1956, 101 congressmen signed a "Southern Manifesto" calling on their home states to reject the *Brown* ruling. Amid calls for massive resistance to desegregation, White Citizens' Councils formed to resist desegregation in southern states, some of which passed laws intended to stop school integration. There was violence, too. In October 1955, white Mississippians brutally killed Emmett Till, a 14-year-old Black from Chicago, who had supposedly whistled at a white woman.

African Americans were ready to fight even harder against segregation. In **Montgomery, Alabama,** the NAACP wanted to test the state law that segregated the city's buses. On December 1, 1955, **Rosa Parks,** a 42-year-old African American tailor's assistant and NAACP official, boarded a bus. Local custom required her to give her seat to a white passenger and move to the back of the bus, but when the bus driver told her to move, Parks refused. As she said, "my feet hurt." More than that, she wanted to find out "once and for all what rights I had as a human being and a citizen." The angry driver thought she had none; he had Parks arrested.

Seizing on Parks's arrest, African Americans began to boycott the bus system. Twenty-six-year-old Martin Luther King Jr., pastor of the Dexter Avenue Baptist Church, agreed to lead the boycott. The son of a noted Atlanta preacher, King was already developing a brilliant oratorical style and a philosophy of nonviolent protest against segregation.

The boycott met immediate resistance. The city indicted the leaders, and African American homes and churches were bombed. In November 1956, however, the US Supreme Court ruled Alabama's bus-segregation law unconstitutional. By then, the boycott had cost the city dearly, and the white community had lost the will to resist. The city settled with the boycotters and agreed to integrate the buses. "We just rejoiced together," one of the boycotters remembered. "We had won self-respect."

Montgomery showed that a combination of local activism and federal intervention could overcome Jim Crow. It established a charismatic new leader with a powerful message and brought forward a new civil rights organization, the Southern Christian Leadership Conference. To one journalist, Montgomery "was the beginning of a flame that would go across America."

The flame did not travel easily. In 1957, the school board of **Little Rock**, Arkansas, accepted a federal court order to integrate Central High School, but in September the state's segregationist governor, Orval Faubus, called out National Guard troops to stop Black students from enrolling. Even after meeting with Eisenhower, Faubus would not remove the troops. When he finally did, an angry mob of whites made it impossible for the African American students to stay. "Two, four, six, eight," cried the mob, "we ain't going to integrate."

Little Rock created a dilemma for the president. Not a believer in racial equality, Eisenhower wanted to avoid the divisive issue of civil rights. He privately opposed the *Brown* ruling and gave only mild support to the weak Civil Rights Act

Jubilation A packed crowd at First Baptist Church in Montgomery, Alabama, sings hymns and applauds the bus boycott in February 1956.

of 1957, which did not protect African Americans' right to vote. The president knew, however, that his government was being defied in Little Rock and humiliated around the world. So Eisenhower sent in troops of the army's 101st Airborne. With that protection, nine African American students went to Central High.

Like Montgomery, Little Rock demonstrated that a combination of federal action, however reluctant, and African American courage could triumph. The Central High crisis showed, too, how the Cold War helped tip the balance against segregation. Competing with the Soviets for support from the multiracial third world, no president could afford the embarrassment of racial inequality at home. Segregation and discrimination were, the president concluded, "troublesome beyond imagination."

The Crisis of "Misplaced Power"

Youth culture, the beat movement, the environmental movement, and the civil rights struggle contributed to an uneasy mood by the end of the 1950s. Many people, worrying that the consumer society was flawed, blamed the nature of power in post–World War II America.

To some observers, corporations had become too powerful. In his bestseller *The Hidden Persuaders* (1957), Vance Packard argued that advertisers manipulated Americans into buying corporate products. In 1958, the public got two object lessons in apparent corporate manipulation. That year, Americans learned about "payola," record companies' practice of paying disc jockeys to play particular records on the radio. Americans were shocked, too, by revelations that contestants on popular TV quiz shows had secretly been given the answers to questions in advance.

Other observers believed that not only corporations, but large institutions generally, had too much power. Conservatives such as Republican senator Barry Goldwater of Arizona decried what they saw as the excessive activism of the federal government. Sociologist C. Wright Mills argued in *The Power Elite* (1956) that an

TIME LINE

▼1947
Levittown suburban development
Announcement of Truman Doctrine

▼1948
First McDonald's fast-food restaurant
Alfred Kinsey, *Sexual Behavior in the Human Male*

▼1950
Diners Club credit card

▼1951
UNIVAC 1 computer
Television premiere of *I Love Lucy*

▼1952
Dwight D. Eisenhower elected president

▼1953
Korean cease-fire

▼1954
Baby boom birthrate over 4 million per year
Supreme Court school desegregation decision, *Brown v. Board of Education, Topeka, Kansas*
Creation of divided Vietnam in Geneva peace talks

▼1955
Formation of AFL-CIO
Disneyland opening

interlocking group of military, political, and economic managers ran the nation's institutions. In the age of nuclear weapons, still other Americans feared that scientists had too much power. Such movies as *The Day the Earth Stood Still* (1951) and *It Came from Beneath the Sea* (1955) exploited fears that scientific innovations would lead to disaster.

At the same time, Americans feared, too, that the nation might not be powerful enough. Such films as *The Deadly Mantis* (1957) and *Invasion of the Saucer Men* (1957) showed American science and technology unable to stop the destruction of the earth. There was also a sense in

"The Helicopter Era" Cartoonist Herblock lampoons President Dwight Eisenhower's apparent lack of involvement in the nation's problems.

the age of conformity that ordinary Americans lacked the willpower to face the challenges of the twentieth century.

In October 1957, worries about American power went from science fiction fantasy to Cold War reality. That month, the Soviet Union launched Sputnik, the world's first satellite, into orbit. The result was a wave of fear in the United States. If the Soviets could send up a satellite, they could be ahead in nuclear weapons and economic growth, too. Americans felt suddenly vulnerable.

Sputnik intensified concerns about American education. A diverse and growing student population and rising parental demands had strained the nation's schools. Now Americans worried that the schools were not preparing children to compete with the Soviets in science and technology. In 1958, Congress passed the National Defense Education Act. The measure promoted instruction in science, math, and foreign languages; supported construction of new schools; and offered loans and fellowships to students.

Sputnik forced Washington to accelerate the space program. The first US satellite launch collapsed in flames—Flopnik, the press called it. In January 1958, the government successfully launched its first satellite, Explorer 1. Later that year, Congress created the National Aeronautics and Space Administration (NASA) to coordinate space exploration. These initiatives did not completely wipe away Americans' worry that, as one magazine railed, "the whole kit and caboodle of our American way of life—missiles and toasters, our freedoms, fun, and foolishness—is about to go down the drain."

Eisenhower did little to calm the anxiety about American power. Slowed by poor health, he seemed old and out of ideas. In 1960, the president even created a Commission on National Goals to help figure out what the country should do. At the end of his term in January 1961, Eisenhower fed anxiety with a somber farewell address about the problem of "misplaced power" in the nation. Noting that Cold War spending had built up the military and the defense industry, he warned against allowing this "military-industrial complex" to gain too much power or "endanger our liberties or democratic processes." Eisenhower also warned that universities, fueled by federal money for research, might become too powerful. The president's farewell was a stunning admission that the Cold War could destroy rather than save democracy in America. The speech contributed to the sense of uncertainty: Was America too powerful, or not powerful enough?

CONCLUSION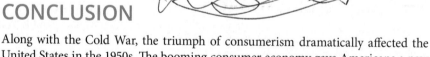

Along with the Cold War, the triumph of consumerism dramatically affected the United States in the 1950s. The booming consumer economy gave Americans a new sense of security and affluence during the unsettling confrontation with Communism. Breaking with the past, they moved to the suburbs, had record numbers of children, bought televisions, watched *I Love Lucy*, and defined life as the pursuit of material pleasures. Consumerism helped promote homogeneity and conformity and spurred the victory of Dwight Eisenhower and his moderate approach to government. For a moment, it seemed as if America had achieved stability and harmony in a dangerous world, but that feeling did not last. By the close of the 1950s, many Americans wanted more for themselves and their country. They worried that power was "misplaced." They questioned whether consumer society could provide prosperity, democracy, and security for all its citizens. The next decade would offer a dramatic answer.

WHO, WHAT, WHERE

REVIEW QUESTIONS

1. What were the basic components of "the good life" in the 1950s?

2. What factors made American society more homogeneous in the 1950s? What factors kept the nation diverse?

3. What was Eisenhower and Dulles's strategy for fighting the Cold War?

CRITICAL-THINKING QUESTIONS

1. How did the emergence of consumer society affect democracy in the United States? Did the nation become more or less democratic during the 1950s?

2. Why did so many Americans believe there was a crisis of power by the end of the 1950s? Had the nation, in fact, become less powerful?

3. Was the United States winning the Cold War in the 1950s?

SUGGESTED READINGS

Galambos, Louis. *Eisenhower: Becoming the Leader of the Free World.* Baltimore: Johns Hopkins University Press, 2017.

Klarman, Michael J. *Brown v. Board of Education and the Civil Rights Movement.* New York: Oxford University Press, 2007.

Packard, Vance. *The Hidden Persuaders.* New York: IG Publishing, 1957/2007.

For further review materials and resource information, please visit www.oup.com/us/ofthepeople

CHAPTER 25: The Consumer Society, 1945–1961

Primary Sources

25.1 GAEL GREENE, "THE BATTLE OF LEVITTOWN" (1957)

Largely because William J. Levitt sold only to whites, his second Levittown, northeast of Philadelphia, Pennsylvania, had no African American homeowners from its start in 1952. Then, in August 1957, a resident sold a ranch house at 43 Deepgreen Lane to a Black refrigeration technician, William Myers, and his wife, Daisy. Some local residents tried to drive out the Myers family by marching in protest, crowding the street outside their house, and throwing rocks at the house's windows. As local police struggled to avert violence, Pennsylvania's governor, George Leader, sent in the state police. The *New York Post* sent in young reporter Gael Greene to write about the upheaval in suburbia. The Myerses won what the *Post* called "The Battle of Levittown": the Black family stayed in the suburb until William got a new job in another city four years later.

Aug. 17. They look like folks gathered for a backyard barbecue. Housewives in Bermuda shorts. Shirt-sleeved men slapping each other on the back in greeting, Youngsters running under foot. Teenagers slouching self-consciously. ... "*We don't want no mob violence.*" That is the rumbling, southern drawl of Jim Newell, 35, an electrician who came to Levittown from North Carolina because: "I understood this was a white settlement." Newell is chairman of the Levittown Betterment Committee, formed hurriedly Thursday night in honor of Myers" impending arrival. "We don't want no mob violence." He repeats his exhortation for the TV cameras as his audience applauds. "We want you all to respect the protection officers.".... Voices in the crowd:

"*Tell Gov. Leader to get his Gestapo out of here.*".... "*Ask Gov. Leader how it feels to live next door to a Negro.*".... "The highest tribunal—the Supreme Court in Washington—has already spoken," Newell replies, using a rolled-up poster as a megaphone.

"*Well, what are we going to do?*" a dozen voices asked. "Ever hear of the old boycott trick?" Newell grinned. The crowd, 350 strong, claps and cheers. A man leaps to the platform. "Now I'm sure Jim didn't mean what he just said," he begins.

The crowd boos. "*Boycotts aren't legal. Jim wouldn't want to tell you to do anything illegal.*" "*I must have had the wrong phrase or wrong terminology,*" Jim agrees. He winks. ... "*The jigs did it in [Montgomery],*" says a voice in the crowd. "*They stayed off the buses.*"

Joining Newell on the platform is Robert Camarote in a print sports shirt. "We have lost a happy home and a nice community," Camarote mourns. "Why, it's hard to get a decent meal because our wives are so upset. But we don't want a person's home blowed up. We must demonstrate peaceably."

A voice: "They shouldn't stone him. They should string him up."

Now Newell takes over. He thrusts a massive arm into the air and quiets the restless crowd. "Let's go to church and pray to the good Lord that he carries us through the right way."

"*If the good Lord wanted us to live together he would have made us all one color,*" says a voice in the crowd.

Camarote again: "I hope the good Lord will help Myers make his decision. We are not radicals. We are God-fearing men."...

Voices: "I think the Communists are all behind this." "Me, too." "Why don't they stay with their own kind? You don't find whites trying to crash a n----- neighborhood."... "When Myers sees how many people don't want him we'll see if his heart is white enough to move out," Newell suggests. ...

"Myers drives a '57 Mercury. It really makes you wonder where he's getting all this money."

"Do you people want to keep coming every night?" Newell asks the crowd. They answer with loud applause. ...

"We don't want to set up him up as a martyr, this Mr. Myers," says Camarote. "Everything must be done peacefully." The meeting grinds to a close.

The state troopers reach instinctively to see if riot sticks are ready as the mob drifts toward the dusty-pink ranch-type home of Levittown's first Negro family.

The crowd decides to picket the house. Troopers head them off as they reach the sidewalk. They retreat, marching in a circle on the street. ... They are the residents of what has been touted as a model town. ...

Aug. 19. The homeowners of Deepgreen Lane spend long afternoons stationed on their lawn chairs—taking it all in, discussing their problem with neighbors, the egg salesman, the paper boy, and the out-of-town reporters who have flocked here.

"They ought to have a NAAWP," says a chubby youngster, parroting his parents. "A National Association for the Advancement of White People." *"It's true," said Mrs. Ruth Hughes of Deepgreen Lane. "The colored people get more protection than we do."*

A man stops his car in front of Mrs. Hughes' home. "Got any idea where the meeting is?" he asks. He says he lives in another section of Levittown, refuses to give his name, but offers some advice. *"What we got to do is make them uncomfortable," he says. "That Myers has got a lot of guts. It won't be easy."*

"I came here to get away from them," he explains. "I'm tired of running away. This time I'm making my stand. We'll freeze them out of here. Nobody sells out. Forbid your children to play with them. Sooner or later you'll get on their nerves and they'll leave."

"I won't deliver papers to them, even if it means losing my job," chimes in Mrs. Hughes' son, Dave.

The wife of a neighbor who befriended Myers drives by. "N-----lover, n------lover," kids chant after her.

"It makes me sick," [says] Mrs. John Trakimas. "It just makes me sick. If it had happened on another street I could go and sympathize with everybody and come home to sleep. But it's our own street, and we don't sleep at night anymore. It would be different if we had sons, but we have a daughter. Just think how my husband would feel if she brought one home and said this is my spouse."

"For God's sake!" cries a dissenter. "They don't want to be kissed by white people, they just want to be left alone."

***

Aug. 19. [Greene interviews with William Myers] "I want a good home for my children—that home is in Levittown. I won't give it up." The handsome, soft-spoken man spoke—not in stubborn defiance—but with calm matter-of-factness. "Nothing will make us leave Levittown. ... It is difficult to explain why we are so determined to stick this out... Yes, it is partly the principle involved. But, I guess, it is something inside that drives a man to hold fast for that principle. ... A few years ago we moved into a mixed neighborhood, in York, Pa.," Myers said. "Our home was only three blocks from my father's house, but it was on an all-white street… So you see, we have gone through something similar to this before—though in a mixed, rather than an all-white, neighborhood. We know what to expect.

"Having so many friends to support us will make it easier," he said with a glance toward the Levittown citizens seated at a long luncheon table waiting for Myers to join them. Many were members of the Friends Service Assn. which has dedicated its staff to the job of making Myers' entrance into the community of a peaceful one.

***

Aug. 23. The actions of the crowd have served only to stir new underdog sympathy for the Myerses. Hundreds have been sympathetic from the beginning. Some, being non-Levittowners, can only write—like former Dodger Jackie Robinson… "We've been hearing from people as far away as California who think there is blood running in the streets," Mrs. Myers said. "We'd like them to know how many good things have been done for us."

In a soft, tired voice, Mrs. Myers spoke of neighbors bringing groceries, friends bearing preserves and fresh fruit, the hundreds of phone calls and the mound of sympathetic mail. … Some excerpts: "We are 100 per cent behind you in your fight to live like free Americans…" "Don't judge all of this town by a few showoffs…" "Many of us are pleased we won't be a white island any longer…"…

"Neighbors have helped to mow the lawn," Mrs. Myers continued. "We've received many dinner invitations. Some local school teachers are hanging the curtains. Someone filled the refrigerator with six quarts of milk one morning. And we want to commend the police for the wonderful cooperation and protection they have given us."

… Many townspeople have tried to assuage their own guilt by blaming teen-agers for being the real trouble makers. Bristol Township Police Chief John R. Stewart told the Post: "Juveniles have been the least of these mobs. The teen-agers are not to blame. They wouldn't have come here in the first place if their parents had not set an example."

Sources: "The Lawns of Levittown," *New York Post*, August 18, 1957, pp. 5 and 27; "The Battle of Levittown," *New York Post*, August 19, 1957, pp. 3 and 33; "Levittown: Dawn of Reason and Hope?" *New York Post*, August 23, 1957, pp. 3 and 41.

25.2 H. H. REMMERS AND D. H. RADLER, EXCERPTS FROM "TEENAGE ATTITUDES" (1958)

Despite alarms about rebellious beatniks, juvenile delinquents, and rock and rollers, adults worried that young Americans were actually conformists. The extent of adult concern became clear in this 1957 article by two social scientists reporting on their annual surveys of teenagers in high schools. According to H. H. Remmers and D. H. Radler, American teenagers wanted too much to be liked, failed to think independently, and did not appreciate scientists enough. Teens' abandonment of traditional American individualism, the social scientists concluded, threatened the future of democracy in the United States.

What is today's younger generation really like? What is its prevailing attitude; what is it thinking; how is it likely to handle its own and the world's problems when it grows up? … On a statistical basis we can paint something like a portrait of "the typical teenager." Scientific surveys of the nation's young people have made clear that their problems, beliefs and desires follow a characteristic pattern. …

Our samples of the younger generation have been drawn from the nation's high schools, which since the early 1940s have enrolled virtually all of the country's teenagers. Each sample consists of about 3,000 students, chosen to represent accurately all the high-school grades, the various sections of the country, rural and city dwellers and roughly the various family backgrounds. Aside from giving the correct statistical representation to these groupings, the samples are completely random. ... The subjects' responses are recorded anonymously. ...

The most significant place to start our examination of the results of these polls is to look at what U. S. teenagers list as their most common problems. ... At the head of the list is the wistful plea: "Want people to like me more." And most of the things that 25 percent or more of the teenagers list as problems express, in one form or another, the same sentiment. A majority of teenagers want to gain or lose weight or otherwise improve their appearance; they want more dates, more friends, more popularity; they get stage fright before a group, worry about their lack of self-confidence. Their overriding concern emerges again when they are asked direct questions about their feelings with respect to approval by others. More than half admit that they try very hard to do everything that will please their friends; 38 percent declare that the worst of all calamities is to be considered an "oddball."

Naturally these feelings carry over into behavior. Nearly all the teenagers say they disapprove of high-school students drinking—but a quarter of them admit that they drink. More than three quarters disapprove of smoking—but 38 percent smoke. The whole matter is summed up in the comment of a teenage girl: "It's hard for a teenager to say 'I don't care to' when all the rest of the gang are saying, 'Ah, come on.'"

... What should concern us much more is how the passion for popularity translates itself into an almost universal tendency to conformity among our younger generation. It runs through all social classes. American teenagers show substantial class differences in many aspects of their behavior, problems and aspirations, but in their desire for popularity and their conformist attitude they are as one: low-income or high-income, their highest concern is to be liked.

This is the most striking and most consistent fact that has emerged from our polls through the 17 years. Poll after poll among our youngsters has given statistical confirmation of the phenomenon of American life which David Riesman, in his book *The Lonely Crowd*, named "other-direction"—extreme sensitivity to the opinions of others, with a concomitant conformity. As a nation we seem to have a syndrome characterized by atrophy of the will, hypertrophy of the ego and dystrophy of the intellectual musculature.

This rather unpleasant portrait is an inescapable conclusion from the mass of data on the attitudes of the younger generation. More than half of our teenagers believe that censorship of books, magazines, newspapers, radio and television is all right. More than half believe that the Federal Bureau of Investigation and local police should be allowed to use wiretapping at will, that the police should be permitted to use the "third degree," that people who refuse to testify against themselves should be forced to do so. About half of our teenagers assert that most people aren't capable of deciding what's best for themselves; fully 75 percent declare that obedience and respect for authority are the most important habits for children to learn. On practically all questions of social policy the youngsters lean strongly to stereotyped views.

Such answers may represent either unthinking responses or convinced and deliberate acceptance of an authoritarian point of view. In either case the picture is equally unhappy. The road to totalitarianism is the same length whether we walk down it consciously or merely drift down it. Unthinking conformity provides a setting which makes it possible for a demagogue to lead a nation into slavery.

As individuals our nation's young people consistently value others' opinions above their own. Fewer than half claim that they think things out for themselves and act on their own decisions. Only one fourth report that they often disagree with the group's opinion. No more than 18 percent are willing to say that their tastes are quite different from those of their friends. Yet in spite of these admissions most teenagers declare that their freedom is not too limited.

Such soundings of the younger generation's attitudes uncover some of the roots of anti-intellectualism in the U.S. Almost three quarters of the high-school students believe that the most important thing they can learn in school is "how to get along with people." Only 14 percent place academic learning first. In a recent poll of a representative sample of college students we found that the same attitude prevails at the university level: 60 percent would rather be popular than brilliant; 51 percent believe that students with low grades are more likely to be popular than those who get good marks; 72 percent believe that development of a well-rounded personality is the main purpose of education; 71 percent feel that personality counts more than grades when it comes to looking for a job.

The disdain for learning shows up most sharply and most dismayingly in the attitude of teenagers toward science and scientists. ... More than a third find scientific work boring; 25 percent think scientists as a group are "more than a little bit odd"; about 30 percent believe that a scientist cannot enjoy life or raise a normal family. In a poll in October, 1957—the month of Sputnik 1—68 percent of the teenagers said they would not like to be scientists. A majority asserted that scientists are likely to be radical, that they take no thought of the consequences of their work, that science should be restricted to physics and chemistry, that it is impossible to formulate scientific laws of human behavior. Most disquieting is the fact that views of this kind are just as common among students of high scientific aptitude as among those who have no interest in science. The climate of popular opinion among the nation's youth undoubtedly is keeping many able boys and girls out of science. ...

A need and craving to be liked, drifting with the crowd, conformity, a kind of passive anti-intellectualism—these seem to be outstanding characteristics of the present-day younger generation as it has expressed itself in our polls. ...

The present conformist spirit—demonstrably not confined to the younger generation—seems to us something new in American life. It reverses our history and the American ideal, which has been, above all, individualistic. The American tradition suggests that we have not been in the past a people who passively accepted dictation by the crowd or surrendered the exercise of our freedoms.

[Teenagers'] attitude derives in large part, of course, from their parents. ... In recent decades we have seen the individual steadily depreciated even in intellectual pursuits. There is a rising admiration for "the power of the group mind." We have team research in science and "brainstorming" in industry. In every sphere group decision is replacing individual initiative.

In this light we must take a serious view of the tendency to conformity exhibited by the younger generation. In any circumstances it is always difficult for an adolescent to find himself. The teens are a time of transition, demanding adjustments to profound biological, emotional and social changes. Probably most parents today would testify from personal experience that the teenagers of our day are having an extraordinarily difficult time of growing up and finding themselves.

Ralph Waldo Emerson pointed out that the price of group agreement is descent to the least common denominator. As T. V. Smith and Eduard C. Lindeman remarked in their book *The Democratic Way of Life*, a democracy cannot afford to devalue "the finality of the individual," from whom "all things flow." In our view, the future of our democracy is not promising unless we restore a social climate which will reward independent thinking, personal morality and truly enlightened cooperation in place of going along with the crowd.

Source: H. H. Remmers and D. H. Radler, "Teenage Attitudes," *Scientific American* 198, no. 6 (June 1958): 25–29.

25.3   MALVINA LINDSAY, "SCIENCE ALONE NO ANSWER TO SPUTNIK" (1957)

American leaders' response to the Soviets' launch of the first Sputnik satellite in 1957 focused on the need to improve education and produce more scientists and engineers. But journalist Malvina Lindsay argued that the U.S. failure to get into space first reflected broader problems, inkling the failures of American leaders themselves.

In characteristic fashion we Americans have reacted to Sputnik with cries for more and better machines and the men to make them. Most inquests into our failure to get first into outer space with a satellite end with demands for rush orders of inventors and technologists. But what about some better administrators, intelligence experts, legislators, psychologists?

It was not so much lack of scientific knowledge as lack of administration of it that has caused this Nation to appear to lag in the conquest of outer space: It was not so much lack of knowledge of technology as failure to apply knowledge of psychology, especially at high governmental levels, that caused us to let the Russians score a political and propaganda victory with a space satellite.

These failures have their roots in grass-roots attitudes. We all of us share some blame for this country's weakened psychological strength before the world. Before we try to turn every boy and girl into a technician, we might do well to consider how effectively we are going to use the brain power we develop. One reason we lagged on a satellite was that scientific talent available was not mobilized and coordinated. Efforts in the armed forces have been divided, leading to costly competition. We and our allies have failed to pool our scientific efforts. A pinch-penny policy has been necessary in some fields of research because we seem to have lacked administrators and legislators able to explain to taxpayers the pressures the Nation faced.

Some appraisers of the current state of the cold war think that psychological ignorance and insensitivity constitute the chief American handicap. These have caused both officials and citizens here to develop a stereotype of the Russians that underrates their ability. It has caused Americans to build up a stereotype of themselves (largely founded on material success) as invincible in science and invention.

Another phase of American psychological frailty is lack of respect for learning, including basic research in science. The general tendency to deride and suspect the intellectual, the dreamer, the experimenter, found its echo in governmental administrators who regarded basic scientific research that did not lead to quick concrete results as boondoggling.

The overwhelming portion of the budget for scientific research in the defense field now goes into military applied work or manufacturing development, with a relatively small amount going into pure science.

An equally serious psychological lag here is the seeming inability of Government officials, of statesmen and legislators to sense in advance emotional reactions of foreign peoples to American policies, programs, statements. One evidence was neglect of the satellite program, caused by lack of foresight as to its psychological effects. This psychological obtuseness also leads constantly to foot-in-mouth utterance in high places that frighten or offend this country's allies, or cause misunderstanding and ill will on the part of neutrals. Surely there is qualified advice in this field available.

When Congress convenes there will probably be demands for all sorts of "crash" programs to turn out scientists en masse. We will hear again and again that the Soviet Union will have graduated one million technicians by 1960, that it is graduating 66.000 engineers yearly as against the 22,000 of the United States.

Many educators are beginning to fear the country will go on a binge of technical education, train hordes of specialists, and neglect the broad general education that is needed to develop not only good administrators and politicians but also good scientists.

The Tax Education and School Finance Committee of the National Education Association has called for a broadening and deepening of the entire fiscal structure of education. Its chairman, Arvid J. Burke, points out that the "base of any successful military or technical program is a broad high quality education," and that "any nation that pays its teachers an annual average salary of $4200 cannot expect to be first in putting an earth satellite into space."

Source: Malvina Lindsay, "Science Alone No Answer to Sputnik," *Washington Post and Times Herald*, October 24, 1957, p. 12.

25.4   UNITED STATES OFFICE OF CIVIL AND DEFENSE MOBILIZATION, EXCERPTS FROM "SURVIVE NUCLEAR ATTACK" (1960)

As the United States and the Soviet Union rapidly built up their arsenals of nuclear weapons, Americans fearfully imagined what World War III would be like. A thermonuclear conflict was a frightening prospect—so frightening that the US government tried hard to persuade Americans that they could survive one. In this excerpt from a 1960 pamphlet, the federal Office of Civil and Defense Mobilization (OCDM) detailed the likely effects of a nuclear strike on the United States and listed the steps the American people could take to protect themselves. Would these recommendations, including building bomb shelters and stockpiling food, have worked in the event of a nuclear attack?

AXIOM OF SURVIVAL

If this country is attacked with nuclear weapons you can protect yourself. But, first, you must know what to do and how to do it.

FACE THESE FACTS

A 20-megaton explosion on the surface of the earth can kill most people and destroy most buildings within a 5-mile radius of ground zero, a total of about 80 square miles. The most likely targets are big cities—industrial areas—military centers.

However, you are not safe merely because you live far away from likely targets.

Distance protects you against heat and blast, but not against radioactive fallout which goes anywhere and can kill or injure the unprotected and the unprepared.

Without protection from fallout, millions would die who otherwise would survive. Put more positively, millions of Americans could save their lives by learning what to do—and doing it.

KNOWLEDGE IS YOUR KEY TO SURVIVAL

To protect yourself at the time of a nuclear explosion, you must understand NOW the hazards you would face.

You probably will be warned in advance by siren or radio that attack is coming. The Air Force, with its far-flung detection network, and the Office of Civil and Defense Mobilization are working together to do everything possible to warn you.

But surprise attack could come. You must know what to do if it does.

YOU SHOULD KNOW THE THREE MAIN DESTRUCTIVE EFFECTS OF A NUCLEAR EXPLOSION

Heat, Blast, Fallout

Heat

Dangers facing you: The bomb produces heat of several million degrees—a good deal hotter than the temperature on the surface of the sun. This heat travels at the speed of light. A megaton explosion could kill an unshielded man 8 miles from ground zero. A 20-megaton explosion could kill an unshielded man 20 miles away. It could blister and cripple the bodies of unsheltered people well beyond that.

What you should do: Beyond the 5-mile radius of total destruction, but still within range of the immediate killing power of the bomb, you would have split seconds to save your life.

You would have to act with instinctive speed to take cover behind whatever was at hand.

Blast

Dangers facing you: The shock waves of blast from a nuclear explosion travel about 900 miles an hour—nine times the force of a major hurricane!

Blast could destroy a brick building 9½ miles from ground zero.

What you should do: If caught unprotected beyond the 5-mile circle of total destruction you could save your life with an instantaneous dive for cover.

Cover is the same for both heat and blast.

In open country it might be a ditch or culvert. Lie face down and stay there until the heat and blast waves have passed.

In the city it might be a wall, a building, or even a truck.

Indoors it would be the floor (behind furniture or as close to an inside wall as possible).

The Main Idea—Get Behind Something

Fallout

Dangers facing you: The millions of tons of pulverized earth and debris sucked up as high as 15 miles by the fireball of a large nuclear explosion become a deadly radioactive fallout cloud. It spreads its lethal radioactivity over wide areas, hundreds of miles downwind from ground zero. Fallout radioactivity cannot be detected by taste or touch. Sometimes, but not always, the fine ash or dust carrying the radioactivity is visible. It fills the atmosphere, the air you breathe, and attacks the vital organs of your body with invisible radiation.

Protection from Fallout

The best protection against fallout radiation is a fallout shelter. Every family should have one. It can be an area in a building of such heavy construction as to afford the required shielding or a shelter designed to be a unit of a family dwelling. OCDM has designed several types of family fallout shelters which are described and illustrated in a new booklet entitled "The Family Fallout Shelter," MP-15. Copies may be obtained from your local civil defense director or from OCDM Operational Headquarters, Battle Creek, Mich.

Basement Concrete Block Shelter, designed as a do-it-yourself project. Solid concrete
    blocks are used to build it.

Preshaped Metal Shelter, built by placing preshaped corrugated metal sections on or close
    to the surface of the ground and mounding them over with earth.

Aboveground Double-Wall Shelter, which is a double-walled, concrete block structure with
    the walls built nearly 2 feet apart. The space between the walls is filled with earth. A
    roof is built of either poured concrete or wood and covered with earth.

How Will You Know If You Are in a Fallout Area?

Radiation from fallout cannot be detected by sight, taste, smell, hearing, or touch. If an unusual amount of dust is accumulating outside your house following a nuclear explosion you should assume it is radioactive. However, you should not depend on such an uncertain method of detection.

CONELRAD [short for Control of Electromagnetic Radiation] will be your main source of information on fallout and protective measures you might take. This is the national system of emergency broadcasting that goes into effect when the Commander of the North American Air Defense Command determines an air attack is imminent or under way. ...

This is why you should have a battery-powered portable radio in your shelter. ...

In rural sections or other localities where CONELRAD may not be operative, local officials may use different methods of communication. ...

A family in their fallout shelter.
Source: Photo by Dmitri Kessel/The LIFE Picture Collection/
Getty Images.

How Long Will You Have to Stay in Shelter?

It is not possible to know in advance what the amount of fallout or dose rate would be in any given place. Therefore, the time you would have to remain in shelter can only be determined accurately by measuring the dose-rate of the fallout in your immediate vicinity. To this end local civil defense officials are required under the National Plan to be prepared to measure radiation levels and inform the public. The National Plan also calls on individual householders to store food for a minimum of 2 weeks.

… Where widespread and heavy fallout occurs local officials might decide to evacuate people to safer areas. You should keep tuned to CONELRAD for advice and guidance. …

Prepare Now for Living in a Shelter

The National Plan calls on everyone to have a 14-day supply of food and water. Except for very brief departures from your shelter you could be pinned down longer than 2 weeks.

Two weeks after an attack State and local governments are responsible for supplying food for the next 4 weeks.

However, as in all planning for emergency, it is best to plan against the worst. It is possible that in instances local officials could not supply all of the people in their jurisdictions. There also might be instances of severe fallout from recurring attack that would keep people in their shelters for an extended period. A good plan would be to have 2 weeks' or more supply of food on hand at all times. …

BEFORE DISASTER STRIKES YOU SHOULD HAVE ON HAND

1. Flashlight and extra batteries.
2. Battery-powered portable radio and extra batteries.
3. First-aid kits.
4. Stored water or other liquid—7 gallons per person for 2 weeks. Water in hot water tanks, in toilet tanks, and ice cubes in a refrigerator can be used as an additional source.
5. A 14-day supply of food, paper plates, and napkins.
6. Cooking and eating utensils, measuring cup, can and bottle openers, pocket knife, and matches.
7. Special foods for babies and invalids.
8. Large garbage can (20 gallons).
9. Smaller can for human wastes (10 gallons).
10. Covered pail for bathroom purposes.
11. Toilet tissue, paper towels, personal sanitary supplies, disposable diapers, and soap.
12. One blanket per person, rubber sheeting, and special equipment for the sick.
13. Grocery bags, and a week's accumulation of newspapers for wrapping garbage.
14. Two pints of household chlorine, and 1 quart of 5 percent DDT.
15. Wrench, screwdriver, and shovel; axe and crowbar to free yourself from debris, if necessary, or to help others to do so.
16. Waterproof gloves.

Source: United States Office of Civil and Defense Mobilization, excerpts, *Survive Nuclear Attack* (Washington, DC: US Government Printing Office, 1960).

"The Table of Democracy"

1960–1968

< A summer flower child, 1967

The A&T Four

Franklin McCain and Joseph McNeill were scared. On the afternoon of February 1, 1960, the two African American college students had done the unthinkable at the Woolworth's in Greensboro, North Carolina: they had sat down at the lunch counter and asked for donuts and coffee. When the white waitress refused to serve them, they persisted. By arrangement, two friends from North Carolina Agricultural and Technical College, Ezell Blair and David Richmond, joined them at the counter. All four waited to see what would happen to them for challenging segregation, the policy of the Woolworth's lunch counter and the basic principle of the twentieth-century South.

Some white customers insulted the four students; but other whites even encouraged them. A white policeman stood behind them, McCain recalled, "with his club in his hand, just sort of knocking it in his hand, and just looking mean and red and a little bit upset and a little bit disgusted." Were the four students about to get beaten? Then McCain realized with surprise that the policeman "didn't know what the hell to do." The four African Americans had effectively disarmed this representative of white authority. "You had the feeling that this is the first time that this big bad man with the gun and the club has been pushed in a corner, and he's got absolutely no defense, and the thing that's killing him more than anything else—he doesn't know what he can or what he cannot do," McCain observed. "He's defenseless."

McCain and his friends stayed at the lunch counter until closing time. They did not get service. But they did get something important. For months they had talked about the frustration and humiliation of segregation; for months they had debated what to do. Now, they had confronted injustice. "I felt," McCain admitted, "as though I had gained my manhood."

The **A&T Four**, as they became known, also made a critical discovery: they had power. A group of unarmed African Americans, polite and persistent, could challenge authority and get away with it. Their nonviolent protest, inspired mainly by Christianity and the example of the Indian activist Mohandas Gandhi, actually empowered them. "To me," Blair said, "we were sitting down at the table of democracy."

That night, back on campus, the discovery of the A&T Four inspired fellow students. The next day, Blair, McCain, McNeill, and Richmond returned to the Woolworth's. This time, more than 20 other Black students went with them to contest segregation and to test the power of ordinary people.

The story of the A&T Four both inspired and reflected the experience of their country in the 1960s. In different ways, the crisis of "misplaced power" came to an end as many people, like the A&T Four, discovered that they and their society could confront the problems that plagued the nation. In the 1960s, Americans demanded to sit at "the table of democracy" and offer new solutions for the problems of consumerism, civil rights, and the Cold War. In the process, the nation turned to a new form of liberalism that pledged to confront Communism abroad and reform life at home. The result was a decade of remarkable change and conflict, both at home and abroad.

NEW APPROACHES TO POWER

The discontents at the close of the 1950s created an opportunity for new ideas and new strategies at the start of the 1960s. In a nation worried by insufficient or "misplaced power," four groups, in particular, became energized and empowered. Across the political spectrum, civil rights activists, new liberals, new conservatives, and the New Left offered fresh approaches to domestic and international problems. All these groups were driven by the participation of young people. But the four had different and often conflicting views of power and democracy in America.

Grassroots Activism for Civil Rights

The A&T Four were part of a new generation of African Americans impatient with the slow "deliberate speed" of the desegregation ordered by the Supreme Court in *Brown v. Board of Education* (see Chapter 25). Young Blacks were ready to go beyond court cases and boycotts to try new tactics. As the Greensboro protests continued, hundreds of African American students, along with some white students, besieged lunch counters. Under pressure, Woolworth's and other large stores agreed to serve African Americans.

The Greensboro sit-in, as it was called, quickly inspired grassroots civil rights activism in other communities in both the South and the North and the formation of a new national civil rights organization. There were wade-ins at whites-only beaches, kneel-ins at whites-only churches, and even paint-ins at whites-only art galleries. The demonstrations forced whites to open up facilities to Black patrons and spawned the Student Nonviolent Coordinating Committee (SNCC). The SNCC (pronounced "Snick") brought together white and African American young people. Demonstrating that ordinary people could confront the powerful, the **sit-ins** energized the civil rights movement and inspired Americans to confront other problems.

The New Liberalism

Defeated by Eisenhower and the Republicans in the 1950s, liberal intellectuals and politicians, mostly Democrats, had been forced to reconsider their ideas and plans. By the 1960s, the liberals were offering a fresh agenda in response to the civil rights movement, consumerism, and the Cold War confrontation with Communism.

Faith in economic growth drove the new liberalism. To meet its domestic and international challenges, the United States, liberals believed, had to expand its economy more rapidly. By manipulating its budget, the federal government could keep the economy growing. The right amount of taxes and expenditures would ensure full employment, strong consumer demand, and a rising gross national product.

Growth alone would not make America great, liberals cautioned. A society devoted mainly to piling up personal wealth and spending it on consumer goods was fundamentally flawed. As the liberal historian Arthur M. Schlesinger Jr. argued, the nation needed now to focus on the "quality" of life and on the broader "public interest." Economic growth should create a better life for all Americans. Because the private sector could not solve pressing problems, the federal government had to deal actively with poverty, racial inequality, pollution, housing, education, world Communism, and other problems. Unimpressed with warnings about the excessive power of big institutions, the new liberals believed that the solution to the nation's woes was a still more powerful federal government.

In this respect, 1960s liberalism was much like the New Deal liberalism of the 1930s and the Fair Deal liberalism of the 1940s (see Chapters 22 and 24), both of which argued that government could and should correct problems created or ignored by the private sector. Nevertheless, the new liberalism differed from the old in important ways. New Dealers had worried most of all about restoring prosperity in the Great Depression; the new liberals almost took prosperity for granted. The old liberals had feared big business and class conflict. Their successors generally saw racial divisions and civil rights as the country's greatest domestic problems.

The New Conservatism

As in the past, conservatives differed fundamentally with liberals over power: the conservatives believed the federal government was already too big and active. But the conservatives, like the liberals, had been unhappily out of power for quite a while. In the 1930s, Herbert Hoover's failure to halt the Great Depression had discredited the conservative faith in minimalist government; then Hitler's aggression had undercut the conservative belief in isolationism.

By 1950, conservative ideas had already begun a quiet resurgence. In 1951, conservative intellectual William F. Buckley's book *God and Man at Yale* attacked his alma mater for its liberalism and denial of individualism. Two years later, Russell Kirk published *The Conservative Mind* to prove that there was a living conservative tradition in America. In 1955, Buckley and Kirk founded the magazine *National Review* as a forum for conservative ideas, especially vigorous anti-Communism.

The leading conservative political hero was outspoken Republican senator Barry Goldwater of Arizona. With a Western belief in individual freedom and hostility to federal power, Goldwater was a blunt opponent of liberalism. A major general in the Air Force Reserve, he also advocated a more aggressive stance toward Communism.

By 1960, the growing **conservative movement** had its own younger generation of activists. That year, the Young Americans for Freedom gathered at Buckley's estate in Sharon, Connecticut, to adopt a manifesto. The Sharon Statement called for government to protect individual liberty by preserving economic freedom and maintaining a strong national defense.

The New Left

At the opposite end of the political spectrum, another young group, inspired by civil rights activism and troubled by life on campus, rejected both conservatism and liberalism. By the early 1960s, many students felt confined and oppressed in overcrowded and impersonal colleges and universities, where their lives were regulated by rules that governed eating in dining halls, drinking alcohol, keeping cars on campus, and socializing in dorm rooms. Female students were subject to particularly strict rules, including curfews.

Some of these youth formed the **New Left**, a radical movement that attempted to create a more democratic nation. The key organization of the New Left was Students for a Democratic Society (SDS), which emerged in 1960 to produce "radical alternatives to the inadequate society of today." During its national convention at Port Huron, Michigan, in 1962, SDS approved an "Agenda for a New Generation." An answer to the Sharon Statement, the Port Huron Statement argued that American society denied people real choice and real power in their lives. The answer, SDS claimed, was "**participatory democracy**." The members of SDS did not believe that liberalism would promote real democracy in America. SDS did not expect much help from the old Left of socialists and Communists, with their Marxist faith in the revolutionary power of the working class. Instead, students would lead the way by fighting for control of their schools. The message began to resonate: SDS membership rose from 2,500 to 10,000 in late 1965.

The Presidential Election of 1960

As so often in American politics, new ideas did not immediately transform mainstream politics. The presidential election of 1960 offered a choice between a vaguely liberal Democratic future and a moderate Republican status quo. The Democratic nominee, Senator **John F. Kennedy** of Massachusetts, was open to the liberals' agenda and shared their optimism. Only 42 when he announced his candidacy, Kennedy was energetic and charismatic. Although he had an undistinguished record in Congress, he exuded an enormous sense of promise.

Kennedy gave voice to that promise during the campaign. Americans, he explained, stood "on the edge of a **New Frontier**—the frontier of the 1960s—a frontier of unknown opportunities and paths, a frontier of unfulfilled hopes and threats." The United States needed to foster economic growth, rebuild slums, end poverty, improve education, and enhance retirement.

In contrast, Kennedy's Republican opponent, Vice President **Richard Nixon** of California, favored balanced budgets, limited government, and the qualified acceptance of New Deal programs that marked the Eisenhower administration's "Modern Republicanism." Nixon embraced neither the bold programs and dynamic economic growth of the new liberalism nor the soaring individualism and strident anti-Communism of the new conservatives.

Despite Kennedy's stirring rhetoric and apparent triumph in televised debates, the election was the closest in history. Kennedy managed to keep much of the Democratic New Deal coalition of liberals, workers, and African Americans together, but he won by fewer than 120,000 votes (see Map 26–1). However narrowly, the voters had turned to a Democrat, influenced by liberal ideas, who was eager to explore the New Frontier.

THE NEW FRONTIER

As president, John F. Kennedy eloquently expressed the values of the New Frontier in his speeches and in his space program. But Kennedy's weak electoral mandate made him cautious about pursuing liberal policies too aggressively when it came to most domestic issues. It took sustained pressure from African American activists before he fully embraced the cause of civil rights. A committed Cold Warrior, the president did not need any pressure to support the containment of Communism. Putting in place a new defense strategy, the president faced crises around the world that decreased the chances for nuclear war but increased the odds of US military involvement in Vietnam.

Style and Substance

Kennedy voiced the confident liberal faith in America's unlimited power and responsibility. "Let every nation know," he declared in his inaugural address in January 1961, "that we shall pay any price, bear any burden, meet any hardship, support any friend, oppose any foe to assure the survival and the success of liberty. This much we pledge—and more." He perfectly captured the optimistic spirit of the early 1960s.

So did the president's space program. The exploration of space, the ultimate frontier, seemed like an ideal occupation for confident Americans in the 1960s. Moreover, the space race allowed Kennedy to reject cautious Eisenhower policies and confront the Soviet challenge. In April 1961, the Soviet Union sent up the first astronaut to orbit Earth. The next month, NASA managed only to launch astronaut Alan Shepard for a brief, suborbital flight. Once again Americans feared "that the wave of the future is Russian."

Insistent on "beating the Soviets," the president boldly pledged to land "a man on the moon before the decade is out." Apollo, the moon project, got under way with 60,000 workers and billions of dollars. Meanwhile, in February 1962, astronaut John Glenn became the first American to orbit Earth. That year the United States launched Telstar, the first sophisticated communications satellite. The space

Map 26–1 The Presidential Election, 1960 Democrat John F. Kennedy's clear margin in the electoral vote belies just how narrowly he outpolled Republican Richard M. Nixon in the popular vote.

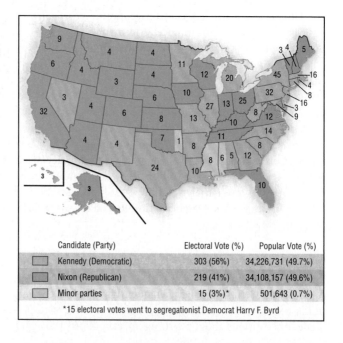

Candidate (Party)	Electoral Vote (%)	Popular Vote (%)
Kennedy (Democratic)	303 (56%)	34,226,731 (49.7%)
Nixon (Republican)	219 (41%)	34,108,157 (49.6%)
Minor parties	15 (3%)*	501,643 (0.7%)

*15 electoral votes went to segregationist Democrat Harry F. Byrd

program mixed practical achievements such as Telstar with more symbolic gestures such as manned space flights.

That mixture of style and substance epitomized the administration. The president maintained a dynamic image, but his administration, hampered by a weak mandate, did not venture too far out onto the liberal New Frontier.

For liberals, the persistence of poverty amid prosperity was a chief failure of the consumer society. Liberals argued that the government had to help the poor become productive workers; they contended that the battle against poverty should include improved housing, education, health, and job opportunities, as well as job training.

Kennedy supported some modest antipoverty measures. In 1961, he signed into law the Area Redevelopment Act to help revive depressed areas. He also signed the Omnibus Housing Act to clear slum housing and renew inner cities. But these measures were not enough to wipe out poverty.

Civil Rights

Grassroots activism for civil rights posed a critical challenge for the Kennedy administration. In one place after another, attempts to break down segregation and promote African American voting met with resistance.

After the Supreme Court outlawed the segregation of interstate bus terminals, a small group of African American and white "**Freedom Riders**" traveled south on buses to test the decision in the spring of 1961. The Freedom Riders met with beatings from white citizens and harassment from local authorities. Only then did the Kennedy administration send federal marshals to protect them.

In 1961, when SNCC started a voter-registration drive in Mississippi, white people struck back. SNCC workers were beaten and shot. When SNCC tried to register Black voters in Albany, Georgia, members of this Albany Movement were beaten and arrested. **Martin Luther King Jr.**, leader of the Southern Christian Leadership Conference (SCLC), came to Albany and was arrested, too, but segregation still ruled in the city.

SNCC activists resented the lack of presidential support. Kennedy understood that racial inequality damaged the United States' image abroad, but he also knew that the civil rights issue could split the Democratic Party.

The defiance of southern whites gradually pushed Kennedy toward action. In 1962, the governor of Mississippi, Ross Barnett, disregarded a federal court order by preventing a Black student from enrolling at the University of Mississippi. When federal marshals escorted the student, James Meredith, to school, white students pelted them with rocks and Molotov cocktails. After the rioting killed two people and wounded more than 100 marshals, Kennedy called in federal troops to stop the violence and allow Meredith to enroll.

Two confrontations in Alabama forced the president's hand in 1963. In April, Martin Luther King Jr. and the SCLC tried to end segregation in Birmingham, perhaps the most segregated city in America. The city's public safety commissioner, Eugene "Bull" Connor, was a stereotypical racist white southern law enforcement officer. King and local allies planned to boycott department stores and overwhelm the jails with arrested protestors. In the next days, Connor's officers arrested demonstrators by the hundreds. Ignoring a judge's injunction against further protests,

American Landscape
"Spaceport USA"

There was no more famous place in the United States in the 1960s than a swath of Brevard County, Florida, along the Atlantic Ocean. No community so perfectly encapsulated Americans' hopes for the future as Cape Canaveral, home of US space launches. There, in what reporters called "Spaceport USA," the United States Air Force and the National Aeronautics and Space Administration (NASA) reached for both the glowing moon and the gleaming vision of a prosperous, peaceful, high-technology future.

For centuries, the cape lived in obscurity. It was, said a visitor, "a desolate arrowhead of land jutting into the ocean," a flat terrain of scrub brush and palmettos, full of alligators, snakes, armadillos, deer, and eagles. In the sixteenth century, the Spanish named this peninsula "Canaveral" after the sugar cane cultivated by Native Americans.

In 1949, the Air Force decided the temperate, sunny cape was ideal for shooting Snark, Vanguard, Atlas, Titan, and Thor missiles thousands of miles into the South Atlantic. The new military installation, cloaked in secrecy, was a product of the Cold War; its purpose was to perfect these intermediate- and long-range weapons of mass destruction.

The development of the manned space program under President Eisenhower and then President Kennedy changed the cape's image. As NASA, a civilian agency, began testing rockets in preparation for space flights by astronauts, Cape Canaveral became a spaceport to a peaceful future of spirited, but not deadly, competition. Casting off Cold War hypersecrecy, NASA welcomed visitors to its facility.

The cape also became a prime symbol of Kennedy's New Frontier. Outgrowing the original Air Force base, NASA took over more land on Cape Canaveral and Merritt Island, west of the Banana River. More and more missile gantries, launch pads, huge cranes, tall antennas, explosion-proof storage tanks, and igloo-shaped buildings overwhelmed beaches and orange groves.

"Spaceport USA" featured seemingly new people as well as new technologies. The more than 20,000 workers, a writer insisted, "have grown accustomed to living with one foot in the stars and one on earth." Despite the intensity of the competition with

King ended up in solitary confinement. In a powerful statement, "**Letter from Birmingham Jail**," he rejected further patience: "We must come to see. . . that 'justice too long delayed is justice denied.'" Once King was out on bail, the SCLC pushed harder, with demonstrations by thousands of African American students.

Goaded by the new protests, Connor turned fire hoses on demonstrators, set dogs on them, and hit them with clubs. Shocking pictures of the scenes increased the pressure on the white leadership of Birmingham and on President Kennedy. The Justice Department arranged for a deal in which the SCLC gave up the demonstrations and local businesses gave up segregation and promised to hire African

Aerial View of "Missile Row" on Cape Canaveral

for the tourists. Broward became the fastest growing county in the nation.

The conflicts and tragedies of the 1960s also left their mark on Cape Canaveral. In booming Cocoa, east of Merritt Island, African American space workers could not buy or rent the new houses. The assassination of President Kennedy, the space program's greatest booster, inspired Lyndon Johnson to rename the space installation "Cape Kennedy." In a characteristically sweeping expansion of federal power, Johnson also renamed the land itself "Cape Kennedy," even though he had no legal authority to do so.

In 1964, construction began on the Vehicle Assembly Building (VAB) that would house up to four of the huge Saturn rockets used to launch astronauts to the moon. More than 125 million cubic feet, the VAB would be the largest structure by volume in the world—bigger than the Great Pyramid of Cheops in Egypt and the Pentagon. The "atmosphere," said a reporter, "seems to be straight out of the twenty-first century."

the Soviet Union, Cape Canaveral's scientists, engineers, technicians, and astronauts supposedly subdued human emotion "under a bland blanket of professionalism." NASA seemingly subdued the emotions of racially divided America as well. Anticipating the integrated nation of the future, the space agency hired African Americans to work alongside whites in this corner of the segregated South.

Epitomizing the economic promise of the 1960s, the development of Cape Canaveral spurred the growth of surrounding Broward County. Houses went up for NASA employees and their families; the Astrocraft, the Sea Missile, and the Satellite motels went up

Americans. However, soon thereafter the Ku Klux Klan marched outside the city, and bombs went off at the home of King's brother and at SCLC headquarters. After African Americans rioted in the streets, Kennedy was forced to send federal troops to keep the peace.

A second confrontation in Alabama drew the president still deeper into the civil rights struggle. The segregationist governor, **George Wallace**, defied federal officials and tried to stop two Black students from enrolling at the University of Alabama. In an eloquent televised address, Kennedy finally admitted that there was "a moral crisis" and called for sweeping civil rights legislation.

"I Have a Dream" Martin Luther King Jr. addresses the crowd at the Lincoln Memorial, Washington, DC, August 28, 1963.

On August 28, the **March on Washington** brought together a crowd of nearly 200,000 people, including 50,000 whites, at the Lincoln Memorial to commemorate the 100th anniversary of the Emancipation Proclamation and to demand "jobs and freedom." Demonstrators joined hands to sing the stirring civil rights anthem, "We Shall Overcome." Martin Luther King Jr. moved the nation with his vision of racial harmony. "I have a dream," he said, "that one day. . . little black boys and black girls will be able to join with little white boys and white girls as sisters and brothers." King looked forward to "that day when. . . black men and white men, Jews and Gentiles, Protestants and Catholics, will be able to join hands and sing. . . 'Free at last! Free at last! Thank God Almighty, we are free at last!'"

Kennedy's address and the March on Washington marked a turning point. The surging grassroots movement for racial equality had created broad-based support for civil rights and finally forced the federal government to act.

Flexible Response and the Third World

Like Eisenhower, Kennedy supported the containment of Communism. The new president believed the nation could afford to increase military spending. He also abandoned the doctrine of massive retaliation, Eisenhower's threat to use nuclear weapons against any Soviet aggression. Kennedy preferred the strategy of flexible response—the threat of different military options, not just nuclear weapons, to counter the Soviets. While spending generously on nuclear weapons, the Kennedy administration also built up conventional ground forces and Special Forces—the highly trained troops, known as Green Berets, who could fight in guerilla wars.

Kennedy was more willing than Eisenhower to intervene in the third world. This was partly a reflection of Kennedy's confidence about American power and partly a response to Soviet actions. In January 1961, Nikita Khrushchev announced Soviet support for "wars of national liberation," insurgencies against established governments in Asia, Africa, and Latin America.

To counter the appeal of Communism, Kennedy supported modernization for Africa, Asia, and Latin America; that is, the development of capitalist, democratic, independent, and anti-Communist regimes along the lines of the United States. In 1961, his administration created the **Peace Corps** to send young volunteers to promote literacy, public health, and agriculture around the world. The Peace Corps reflected not only the importance of the young in the new movements of the 1960s but also the idealism, anti-Communism, and arrogant sense of superiority of the Kennedy years. Not surprisingly, the organization was not always welcomed by the people it was supposed to help. To promote the modernization of Latin America, Kennedy announced the formation of the Alliance for Progress in 1961. Over the next eight years, this venture provided $20 billion for housing, health, education, and economic development in the Western Hemisphere.

The Kennedy administration sometimes helped to thwart third-world independence and democracy in the name of anti-Communism by intervening in the domestic affairs of supposedly independent countries. In the Republic of the Congo, the CIA engineered the election of an anti-Communist leader, and it secretly tried to manipulate elections in Chile as well. The United States also backed antidemocratic, but anti-Communist, regimes in Argentina, Guatemala, Haiti, and Honduras.

Similarly, Kennedy wanted to bring down Fidel Castro, whose Cuban revolution was an example for the rest of Latin America. The president inherited a plan from the Eisenhower administration for a CIA-directed invasion of the island by anti-Communist Cuban exiles. To conceal US responsibility, Kennedy canceled air cover to protect the invaders. As a result, nearly all 1,500 exiles who landed at the Bay of Pigs in April 1961 were killed or captured. Embarrassed, Kennedy turned to the CIA, which launched "Operation Mongoose," an unsuccessful secret campaign to kill or depose Castro. The Cuban leader, aware of the plot, declared himself a Communist and turned to the Soviets for help.

Two Confrontations with the Soviets

Kennedy faced two direct confrontations with the Soviet Union. In 1961, Khrushchev threatened to stop Western traffic into West Berlin, which was surrounded by Soviet-dominated East Germany. In response, Kennedy called up reserve troops, asked Congress to increase defense spending, and hinted at a preemptive nuclear strike against the Soviets. Khrushchev backed down, but the East German government built a barbed-wire and concrete fence between East Berlin and West Berlin. By halting the embarrassing flight of East Germans to freedom in West Berlin, the **Berlin Wall** defused the crisis and became a symbol of Cold War Europe, a visible "iron curtain" that separated Communists and non-Communists.

In 1962, Kennedy entered a more dangerous confrontation with the Soviet Union. On October 15, photos from a spy plane showed that the Soviets were building launch sites in Cuba for nuclear missiles that could strike the United States.

Trying to Laugh About Nuclear War President Kennedy and Soviet premier Khrushchev arm wrestle and threaten to push the buttons unleashing hydrogen bombs during the Cuban Missile Crisis, October 1962.

On October 22, after tense secret meetings, Kennedy put ships in place to intercept Soviet vessels bound for Cuba. That night, a somber Kennedy told a television audience about the missiles and demanded their removal. Fearing a nuclear war, Americans waited for the Soviets' response. Khrushchev, unable to confront the United States in its own hemisphere, backed down. The Soviets withdrew the missiles in exchange for the removal of obsolete American missiles from Turkey.

The **Cuban Missile Crisis** both eased and intensified the Cold War. Faced with a nuclear conflict, neither side found the prospect appealing. To ensure communication in a crisis, a teletype hotline was installed between the White House and the Kremlin. In 1963, the two powers also approved a Limited Test Ban Treaty halting aboveground tests of nuclear weapons, even as the Soviets and the Americans remained more determined to stand firm against each other.

Kennedy and Vietnam

Kennedy inherited a deteriorating situation in South Vietnam in 1961. Ngo Dinh Diem's anti-Communist government faced increasing attacks from the Viet Cong guerillas determined to overthrow his regime. Diem also faced the Viet Cong's new political organization, the National Liberation Front, which was trying to mobilize his Communist and non-Communist opponents. In addition, he faced the continuing hostility of Ho Chi Minh's Communist government in North Vietnam, which was secretly sending soldiers and supplies into South Vietnam.

Like Eisenhower, Kennedy tried to shore up the Diem government with financial aid and advisers. This included sending the Special Forces to train the South Vietnamese army. Before Kennedy took office, there were 900 American troops filling noncombat roles in South Vietnam. By late 1963, there were more than 16,000. Despite this support, Diem's regime spiraled downward. His army could not stop the Viet Cong. A cold, unpopular ruler, he alienated his people. Losing confidence in Diem, the Kennedy administration did nothing to stop a military coup that resulted in his murder in November.

What Kennedy would have done next will never be known. On a trip to Dallas, Texas, on November 22, 1963, the president was shot while riding in an open limousine at 12:33 p.m. Two bullets tore through Kennedy's throat and skull, and doctors pronounced him dead half an hour later. That afternoon, police arrested Lee Harvey Oswald for the shooting. A quiet former Marine, Oswald had spent time in the Soviet Union. Two days later, as police transferred him from a jail, Oswald was shot and killed by Jack Ruby, the troubled owner of a local nightclub.

Americans were shocked and numbed. Some could only believe the assassination was the product of a dark conspiracy, but there was never proof of such a plot. The presidency of John Kennedy, little more than 1,000 days long, left a sad sense of unfulfilled promise. To many Americans, Kennedy's White House seemed like "Camelot," the seat of the mythical English King Arthur. The reality was less magical. Kennedy gave voice to the new liberalism, but he seldom translated liberal ideas into action. Some wanted to believe that Kennedy, if he had lived, would not have escalated the Vietnam War. Yet there was no compelling evidence that he intended to withdraw American troops.

THE GREAT SOCIETY

After Kennedy's death, Lyndon B. Johnson and the Democratic-controlled Congress carried out most of the liberal agenda. A flood of new laws addressed poverty, race relations, consumer and environmental protection, education, and health care. At the same time, the liberal majority on the Supreme Court afforded new protections for individual rights. By the mid-1960s, the principles of the new liberalism, turned into law, were transforming American government and society.

Lyndon Johnson's Mandate

The new president, **Lyndon Johnson**, seemed far different from his slain predecessor. Born to modest circumstances in rural Texas, he had made his fortune largely through political connections. Never an eloquent public speaker or a charismatic figure, he was an especially effective legislator who knew how to bully and cajole Senate colleagues into a deal.

Still, there were fundamental similarities between Johnson and Kennedy. Both were products of the Democratic Party that had engineered the New Deal, won World War II, and fought the Cold War. Both shared the liberals' expansive sense of American might. "Hell, we're the richest country in the world, the most powerful," Johnson declared. "We can do it all."

Johnson stressed continuity with his predecessor. Yet the situation had changed: Kennedy's death left Americans more willing to accept innovation. The presidential election of 1964 strengthened Johnson's mandate. The contest offered voters a clear choice between competing visions. Embracing the new liberalism, Johnson stood for activist government, growth economics, and civil rights. His

Republican opponent, Barry Goldwater, stood unequivocally for the **new conservatism**. "We have gotten where we are," he declared, "not because of government, but in spite of government."

It was no contest. Democrats painted Goldwater as a dangerous radical who would gut popular programs and perhaps start a war. Appearing as a statesman and man of peace, Johnson won 61.1 percent of the popular vote, 44 states, and 486 electoral votes. Moreover, the Democrats increased their majorities in the House and Senate. It was a greater victory than Johnson's hero, Franklin Roosevelt, had ever enjoyed.

"Success Without Squalor"

With his mandate, Johnson moved to enact a legislative program that rivaled Roosevelt's New Deal. In May 1964, he had called for the creation of the "**Great Society**"—"a society of success without squalor, beauty without barrenness, works of genius without the wretchedness of poverty." To create that society, his administration pushed through liberal laws to wipe out poverty, end segregation, and enhance the quality of life for all Americans.

Johnson, like many Americans, was disturbed by the persistence of poverty: nearly one in five Americans was poor. Declaring an "unconditional **war on poverty**," the administration won congressional approval in 1964 of the Economic Opportunity Act, which created an independent federal agency, the Office of Economic Opportunity (OEO), to spend nearly $1 billion on antipoverty programs. The OEO managed Volunteers in Service to America (VISTA), whose workers taught literacy and other skills in impoverished areas. It ran the Job Corps, which taught job skills to poor youth, and implemented Community Action Programs (CAPs), which encouraged the urban poor to organize themselves. By supporting the "maximum feasible participation" of the poor, the CAPs, unlike other poverty programs, had the potential to redistribute power away from local officials.

In 1965 and 1966, Congress continued the war on several fronts. It established an expanded food stamp program and created Head Start, which provided early schooling, meals, and medical exams for impoverished preschool-aged children. To protect the rights of the poor, the Legal Services Program brought lawyers into slums. To improve urban life, the Model Cities Program targeted 63 cities for slum clearance and redevelopment. Congress also created the Department of Housing and Urban Development in 1965 and the Transportation Department in 1966 partly to help manage antipoverty programs.

To improve the quality of life, the Great Society took a major step toward national health insurance when Congress created Medicare in 1965. This program provided the elderly with coverage for doctors' bills, surgery, and hospitalization. Congress also created Medicaid to help the states provide medical care to the nonworking poor.

The Johnson administration confronted the growing issue of consumer protection. In 1965, Ralph Nader published a disturbing book, *Unsafe at Any Speed*, charging that car manufacturers cared more about style and sales than about safety and that executives at General Motors had ignored safety defects in the Chevrolet Corvair. General Motors attempted to discredit Nader rather than promise to improve the Corvair. In response, Congress passed the National Traffic and Motor

Vehicle Safety Act of 1966, which set the first federal safety standards for automobiles, and the Highway Safety Act, which required states to establish highway safety programs.

The president and Congress adopted the liberals' belief in using the federal government to support education. The Elementary and Secondary School Act of 1965 channeled $1.3 billion into school districts. The Higher Education Act of 1965 offered federally insured student loans.

The Great Society included programs for cultural enrichment. In 1965, Congress established the National Endowment for the Arts to fund the visual and performing arts and the National Endowment for the Humanities to support scholarly research. The Public Broadcasting Act of 1967 established the nonprofit Corporation for Public Broadcasting, which would support such commercial-free cultural and educational television shows as *Sesame Street.*

Protection of the environment was a natural issue for liberals. In 1962, the best-selling book *Silent Spring* sensitized Americans to the ecological threat posed by the consumer economy. The author, marine biologist Rachel Carson, warned that, like nuclear weapons, environmental contamination from pesticides threatened human survival.

During Johnson's presidency, more than 300 pieces of legislation led to the expenditure of more than $12 billion on environmental programs. In 1963, the Clean Air Act encouraged state and local governments to set up pollution control programs. Two years later, amendments established the first pollution emission standards for automobiles. The Air Quality Act of 1967 further strengthened federal authority to deal with air pollution. Meanwhile, the Water Quality Act of 1965 and the Clean Waters Restoration Act of 1966 enabled governments to fight water pollution. The Wilderness Act of 1964 created a system of lands protected from development.

Preserving Personal Freedom

The new liberalism contained a paradox: liberals wanted both to enhance the power of the federal government and to expand individual rights. Their concern for individual rights was apparent in their support for civil rights for African Americans and in a series of decisions by the Supreme Court, led by Chief Justice Earl Warren.

In *New York Times v. Sullivan* in 1964, the Supreme Court encouraged free speech by making it more difficult for public figures to sue news media for libel. In addition, two decisions protected the rights of people accused of crimes. In 1963, the court ruled in *Gideon v. Wainwright* that governments had to provide lawyers to poor felony defendants. Three years later, *Miranda v. Arizona* required police to inform individuals of their rights when they were arrested, including the right to remain silent and the right to an attorney.

The Warren Court also protected sexual and religious freedom. Throwing out a state law that banned the use of contraceptives in *Griswold v. Connecticut* in 1965, the court affirmed individuals' right to privacy and in effect kept government out of the bedroom. In *School District of Abington Township v. Schempp* (1963), the court prohibited state and local governments from requiring public school students to say the Lord's Prayer or read the Bible.

Table 26–1 The Growth of the Federal Government

Year	Pages
1936	2,355
1946	14,736
1956	10,528
1966	16,850
1969	20,464
1976	57,072
1986	47,418
1996	69,368
2006	78,724

There are many ways to measure the changing size and reach of the US government. One is to count the number of pages in the Federal Register, the official daily publication of new laws and proposed and new regulations.

Source: Vital Statistics on Congress, Table 6-5 Pages in the Federal Register, 1936–2013 https://www.brookings.edu/wp-content/uploads/2016/06/Vital-Statistics-Chapter-6-Legislative-Productivity-in-Congress-and-Workload_UPDATE.pdf

The Supreme Court's rulings were controversial. Some people charged that the Court was "driving God out" of the classroom. Others believed that the Court had gone too far to protect the rights of alleged criminals. Some conservatives demanded the impeachment of Chief Justice Warren. Through its rulings, the liberal majority on the court substantially increased individual freedom, but few people had yet thought much about the tension caused by expanding both individual rights and government power.

By 1967 the Great Society's programs added up to a major change in American democracy. Government claimed more authority than ever to manage many Americans' daily lives. The Great Society brought a massive expansion of the size, cost, and power of the federal government (see Table 26–1).

That expansion would be controversial for years to come. Some measures—Medicare in particular—proved to be enormously expensive. Conservatives did not welcome an enlarged federal government, and some corporations resented the regulation of business in the name of consumer protection. Despite these concerns, the attempts to improve the quality of life represented some of the major accomplishments of the new liberalism. The war on poverty was at least a partial success. Mainly because of an economic boom, the percentage of people living in poverty decreased to 13 percent by 1970. But 25 million Americans were still poor. Moreover, poverty was unevenly distributed. About a third of African Americans and a quarter of Americans of Hispanic origin were impoverished as the 1970s began.

The Death of Jim Crow

Meanwhile, the battle for civil rights had become still more intense. In the 10 weeks after the Birmingham confrontation in 1963, 758 demonstrations led to 14,733 arrests across the United States. When a bomb killed four African American girls in a

Baptist church in Birmingham in September, some African Americans rioted, and the police killed two more children.

The violence continued in 1964: CORE, SNCC, SCLC, and the NAACP had created the Council of Federated Organizations (COFO) to press for African American voting rights in Mississippi. Robert Moses, an African American schoolteacher, led the COFO crusade uniting young African American and white activists to register Black voters and start "Freedom Schools" for African American children. The effort, known as **Freedom Summer**, met hostility from whites. Two white activists, Michael Schwerner and Andrew Goodman, and one African American activist, James Chaney, were found shot to death near Philadelphia, Mississippi. Eventually, a white deputy sheriff, a local Klan leader, and five other whites were convicted of "violating the rights" of Chaney, Goodman, and Schwerner. The violence continued in Mississippi throughout Freedom Summer. Homes and churches were burned, and three more COFO workers were killed.

Lyndon Johnson could not escape the events in Mississippi. In the summer of 1964, the Mississippi Freedom Democratic Party (MFDP) sent a full delegation to the Democratic National Convention in Atlantic City, New Jersey. The MFDP delegates, including the eloquent Fannie Lou Hamer, hoped at least to share Mississippi's convention seats with the whites-only delegation. Hamer, the daughter of sharecroppers, had been jailed and beaten for trying to register African American voters. Afraid of alienating white southerners, Johnson offered the delegates two seats in the convention. "We didn't come all this way for no two seats," Hamer retorted. The MFDP delegation went away empty-handed.

Johnson and the Democratic Party were clearly not ready to share power with African American activists, but they were ready to end legalized segregation. In July, Congress adopted the **Civil Rights Act**, which outlawed racial discrimination in public places and also set up an Equal Employment Opportunity Commission (EEOC) to stop discrimination in hiring and promotion. Even the schools gradually became integrated. In 1964, hardly any African American students attended integrated schools; by 1972, nearly half of African American children did.

However, across the South, most African Americans still could not vote. In January 1965, the SCLC and SNCC tried to force the voting rights issue with protests in Selma, Alabama. Predictably, the demonstrations produced violent opposition and helpful publicity. The sight of state troopers using tear gas, cattle prods, and clubs on peaceful marchers built support for voting rights.

Seizing the moment, Johnson called for the end of disfranchisement, and Congress passed the **Voting Rights Act** of 1965. This powerful measure forced southern states to give up literacy tests used to disfranchise Black voters and empowered federal officials to make sure that African Americans could register to vote. In three years, Mississippi saw African American registration increase from 6 percent to 44 percent of eligible voters.

Together with the Civil Rights Act of 1964, the Voting Rights Act transformed the South. These twin achievements of the civil rights movement and the Great Society effectively doomed Jim Crow and laid a foundation for African American political power. However, the struggle for racial equality was far from over.

THE AMERICAN WAR IN VIETNAM

The war in Vietnam was the decisive event for the new liberalism and the nation in the 1960s. American participation in the conflict reflected the liberals' determined anti-Communism and their boundless sense of power and responsibility. Driven by these beliefs, Johnson made the fateful decision to send American troops into battle in 1965. When the war did not go according to plan, Americans divided passionately over the conflict, and the economy faltered. By the end of 1967, the war was destroying the Great Society.

Johnson's Decision for War

Like Kennedy, Johnson was a committed Cold Warrior with an optimistic view of American power. He kept flexible response in place and was equally willing to undermine the independence of third-world countries. In 1965, Johnson sent 22,000 troops to the Dominican Republic to stop an increasingly violent struggle for political power. He violated the sovereignty of this Caribbean nation without obtaining evidence of a Communist threat and without consulting Latin American countries as required by treaty.

At first, Johnson followed Kennedy's policy in Vietnam. The new president believed in the domino theory, the idea that the fall of one country to Communism would lead to the fall of others. The president also felt he could not turn his back on commitments made by Kennedy, Eisenhower, and Truman. As one weak government followed another, Johnson sent more aid and advisers to South Vietnam and stepped up covert action against the North.

This secret activity helped Johnson get congressional approval to act more aggressively. On August 2, 1964, a US destroyer, the *Maddox*, was cruising a few miles off the coast of North Vietnam in the **Gulf of Tonkin**. When three North Vietnamese torpedo boats unsuccessfully attacked the *Maddox*, the American ship sank two of the boats and damaged a third. Two days later, the *Maddox*, along with a second US destroyer, fired at a nonexistent North Vietnamese attack. Johnson ordered retaliatory air strikes and asked Congress for the power to protect American military personnel. With only two dissenting votes, Congress approved what became known as the Tonkin Gulf Resolution, which gave the president the authority, without a declaration of war, to use military force to safeguard South Vietnam. Even though Johnson knew there had been no real threat to the United States, he had misled Congress to obtain a "blank check" to fight in Southeast Asia.

He soon cashed it. After American soldiers were killed in a Viet Cong attack on a US base in February 1965, Johnson authorized air strikes against North Vietnam itself. In March, the United States began Operation Rolling Thunder, a series of bombing raids on military targets in North Vietnam.

When the raids failed, Johnson had a disagreeable but clear choice. If he wanted to save both South Vietnam and his reputation, he had to commit ground troops to battle; otherwise, he would be blamed for the loss of South Vietnam to Communism. In July 1965, Johnson gave the order to send 180,000 soldiers to fight in South Vietnam without a declaration of war.

Johnson's decision was the ultimate expression of the new liberalism. The president went to war not only because he opposed Communism but also because he had faith that American wealth and wisdom could transform a weak, divided South Vietnam into a strong, united, modern nation. Although cautious about going to war, Johnson believed that the United States could afford to fight, and win, a war abroad and still build the Great Society at home. It was a fateful choice.

Fighting a Limited War

Johnson and his advisers believed the United States did not need all its power to save South Vietnam (see Map 26–2). Instead of another total war like World War II, Vietnam was to be a **limited war** in which the US forces, led by General William Westmoreland, would use conventional weapons against military targets. The goal was not to take over territory through "unconditional surrender" but rather to kill enough enemy soldiers that the "body count" would persuade the North Vietnamese and the Viet Cong to give up. Relying on superior technology, Westmoreland expected the United States to prevail by the end of 1967.

Westmoreland's strategy turned out to be poorly suited to the realities of Vietnam. As the United States discovered, the North Vietnamese and the Viet Cong usually escaped by hiding in tunnels, fleeing through the jungle, fighting mainly at night, or retreating into Cambodia, Laos, and North Vietnam. Their strategy was to live long enough for a frustrated US military to leave South Vietnam.

American troops fought well. Yet at the close of 1967, too many North Vietnamese and Viet Cong were still alive and committed to the overthrow of South Vietnam. Meanwhile, 9,000 US troops died in 1967 alone. Even with half a million troops in his command, Westmoreland had not won the war on schedule. He had not lost the war, either. But the United States was running out of time to win (see Table 26–2).

Table 26–2 The Escalating War in Vietnam, 1960–1968

Year	US Troops	US Battle Deaths	S. Vietnamese Battle Deaths	N. Vietnamese and Viet Cong Battle Deaths (estimated)
1961	3,164	11	(three-year total = 13,985)	12,000
1962	11,326	31		21,000
1963	16,263	78		21,000
1964	23,310	147	7,457	17,000
1965	184,000	1,369	11,403	35,382
1966	385,000	5,008	11,953	55,524
1967	486,000	9,378	12,716	88,104
1968	536,000	14,589	27,915	181,149

Sources: Micheal Clodfelter, *Vietnam in Military Statistics*, pp. 46, 57, 209, 258. Clodfelter: Jefferson, NC: McFarland & Co., ©1995; Fox Butterfield, ed., *Vietnam War Almanac*, pp. 50, 54, 57, 64, 102, 132, 158, 192. Butterfield: New York, NY: World Almanac Publications : Distributed in the United States by Ballantine Books, 1985.; Shelby Stanton, ed., *Vietnam Order of Battle*, p. 333. Washington, DC: U.S. News Books, ©1981.

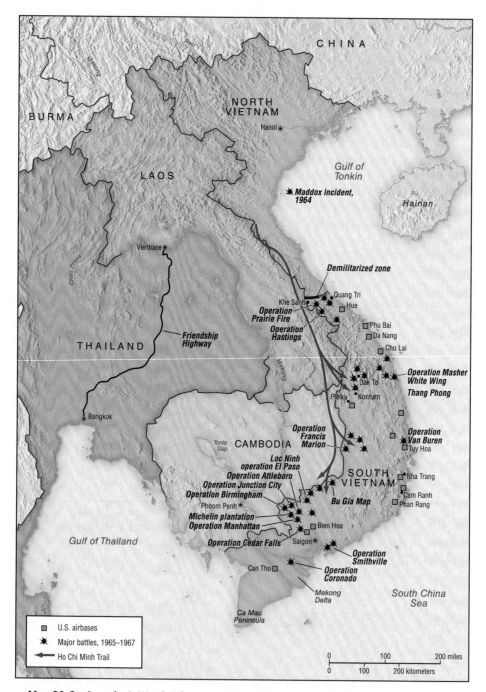

Map 26-2 America's War in Vietnam, 1965–1968 The many military bases suggest how much power the United States had to commit to South Vietnam; the many major battles show how hard American troops had to fight to protect the South Vietnamese regime from the Viet Cong and from the North Vietnamese soldiers who traveled the Ho Chi Minh Trail.

The War at Home

The war in Vietnam had a divisive impact back home. An impassioned antiwar movement, led by SDS and other student radicals, emerged to condemn American policy. Communism in Southeast Asia, they believed, did not pose a real threat to the United States. But the misguided Cold War had led liberals to support an antidemocratic regime. The war also revealed how undemocratic America had become. Johnson, the New Left pointed out, had ignored the Constitution by sending troops into battle without a declaration of war. In addition, the selective service law was forcing a repugnant choice on young men: they could either fight this illegal war or obtain deferments to stay in school and prepare for empty lives as corporate employees in the consumer society.

A growing number of liberals and Democrats shared part of the radicals' analysis. These "doves" acknowledged that the United States was backing an antidemocratic government in a brutal and apparently unnecessary war. The conflict appeared to be a civil war rather than some plot to expand Soviet or Chinese influence. Meanwhile, the war had shattered many liberals' and Democrats' overconfident views of the Great Society. The United States, confessed Senator J. William Fulbright of Arkansas in 1966, was a "sick society" suffering from an "arrogance of power."

Some African Americans viewed the conflict as a painful illustration of American racism. A disproportionate number of poor African Americans, unable to go to college and avoid the draft, were being sent to kill nonwhites abroad on behalf of a racist United States. First the SNCC and then Martin Luther King Jr. condemned the war. Refusing to be drafted, boxer Muhammad Ali was sentenced to jail and stripped of his championship in 1967.

The growing opposition to the war produced large, angry demonstrations. In 1965, students and faculty staged "teach-ins" at college campuses to question American policy in Vietnam. In April, 20,000 people gathered at the Washington Monument to protest the war. Some young men risked jail by returning or burning their draft cards. On campuses, students protested the presence of recruiters for defense contractors. In October 1967, during Stop the Draft Week, radicals in Oakland, California, tried to shut down an army draft induction center, fought with police, and briefly took over a 25-square-block area of the city. Meanwhile, nearly 100,000 people rallied in Washington, DC to protest the war.

Despite the protests, most Americans supported the war. To many people, the demonstrators were unpatriotic. "America—Love It or Leave It," read a popular bumper sticker. "Hawks," mostly conservative Republicans and Democrats, wanted Johnson to fight harder. Nevertheless, by October 1967, support for the war in one public opinion poll had fallen to 58 percent, while only 28 percent approved of Johnson's conduct of the war.

Bad economic news contributed to the public mood. Massive government spending for the war and the Great Society had overstimulated the economy. With jobs plentiful, strong consumer demand drove up prices, which in turn put upward pressure on wages. Anxious about inflation, the Federal Reserve shrank the money supply, making it harder for businesses to get loans. When interest rates reached their highest levels since the 1920s, there were fears of a financial panic.

By the end of 1967 the war had put enormous stress on the Great Society. It undermined liberals' commitment to anti-Communism and their confidence in American power and wisdom. By dividing the nation, the conflict also undermined support for the Great Society. By weakening the economy, furthermore, the Vietnam War made it harder to pay for the Great Society. The United States could not, as Johnson believed, "do it all." The new liberalism had reached its crisis.

THE GREAT SOCIETY COMES APART

Even as Congress enacted the liberals' agenda, many Americans were expressing new dissatisfactions that liberalism could not accommodate. New forms of activism—the Black Power movement, the youth rebellion, and a reborn women's movement—exposed the limits of the liberal vision. In 1968, the strain of new demands, the Vietnam War, and economic realities tore apart the Great Society and destroyed the fortunes of Lyndon Johnson, the Democratic Party, and the new liberalism.

The Emergence of Black Power

For many African Americans, the Great Society's response to racial inequality was too slow and weak. Even as the civil rights movement reached its climax, a wave of more than 300 race riots from 1964 to 1969 dramatized the gap between the promise of the Great Society and the reality of life in Black America. When a white policeman shot a 15-year-old African American in Harlem in July 1964, angry African Americans burned and looted buildings. In August 1965, friction between white police and African American citizens touched off a riot in the poor Watts section of Los Angeles. In five days, more than 1,000 fires burned, and 34 people died. The wave of riots peaked in Detroit in July 1967 when 43 people died (see Map 26–3).

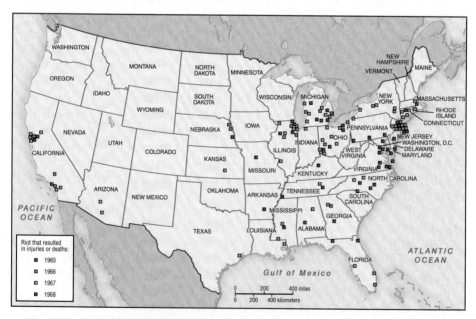

Map 26–3   Race Riots, 1965–1968 The clusters of riots in the Northeast, Midwest, and California emphasize that race was not just a southern issue in the 1960s.
Source: Mark C. Carnes et al., *Mapping America's Past* (New York: Henry Holt and Co., 1996), p. 217.

To many, the riots were, according to an official report on Watts, "senseless," but the disturbances flowed from real frustrations. Despite successful challenges to legalized segregation in the South, African Americans still lived with poverty and discrimination all across the country. Northern cities, the center of the riots, had been largely ignored by Martin Luther King Jr. and other civil rights leaders. The riots signaled that the civil rights movement and the new liberalism, for all their accomplishments, had not addressed some of the most difficult problems of racial inequality.

For years King and other activists had relied on nonviolent demonstrations and ties to white liberals to achieve integration, but that approach proved ineffective in the North. In 1965, King joined marches in Chicago protesting the de facto segregation of the city's schools. King faced the determined opposition of Mayor Richard Daley. Reluctant to challenge the powerful political boss, the Johnson administration did not give King real support. In 1966, King returned to lead the Chicago Freedom movement to wipe out slums and win access to better housing in white neighborhoods. "Go back to Africa," white demonstrators chanted. Daley accepted a compromise on fair housing but repudiated it as soon as King left town. Under the leadership of 24-year-old Jesse Jackson, Operation Breadbasket threatened demonstrations and boycotts against businesses that refused to hire African Americans. The project produced few results; King's nonviolent tactics had failed.

African Americans already had the example of a different approach to the problem of Black–white relations. The Nation of Islam believed that whites were devils and African Americans were God's chosen people. The Black Muslims, as they were known, preached separation of the races and the self-reliance of African Americans. One of the Muslims' most powerful preachers was **Malcolm X**, a former pimp, drug pusher, and convict who angrily rejected integration and nonviolence. Malcolm X moderated his views before being gunned down, apparently by Muslims, in 1965. But he was best known for his militant call "for the freedom of the 22 million Afro-Americans by any means necessary."

By the mid-1960s, many African Americans were willing to follow at least some of Malcolm X's example. Rejecting integration, they now asserted a separate African American identity that declared, "Black is beautiful." Some African Americans wore African robes and dashikis, explored African language and art, and observed the holiday of Kwanzaa, based on an African harvest festival. Instead of working with white liberals and depending on the federal government, some African American activists insisted that Blacks create their own institutions. In 1966, SNCC ousted its white members.

In rejecting nonviolence and integration, a number of African American activists adopted a more militant stance. "What we gonna start saying now is Black Power!" Stokely Carmichael told a rally in Mississippi. The new slogan had different meanings for different people. The most radical interpretation came from the **Black Panthers**, who were first organized in Oakland, California, by Huey P. Newton and Bobby Seale. Dressed in black clothes and black berets, the Panthers armed themselves to protect their neighborhoods from white police. Newton, admiringly described by an associate as "the baddest motherfucker ever to step foot inside of history," went to jail after a shootout with police. The Panthers also founded schools and promoted peaceful community activism, but they were best known in the media for their aura of violent militance.

Particularly because of the violent image of the Panthers, many people, African American and white, were hostile to the new slogan. For King and his allies,

Black Power all too obviously meant repudiation of nonviolent integration. For many whites, Black Power stirred fears of violence. For white leaders such as Richard Daley, Black Power meant giving up political authority to African Americans. For Lyndon Johnson, Black Power obviously meant a rejection of his Great Society.

The Youth Rebellion

The anti–Vietnam War movement was part of a broader rebellion against adult authority and expectations. The battle began at the University of California at Berkeley in 1964. That fall, the university's administration banned political speaking and organizing at the one street corner where it had been allowed. When a civil rights activist was arrested for defying the ban in October, hundreds of students sat down around the police cars, trapping the officers for 32 hours. After the standoff, students created the Free Speech movement (FSM) to pursue greater student involvement in the educational process. When the university refused to accept that demand, students took over the main administration building. Speaking that day, the student leader Mario Savio reflected the ideas of the New Left. "We have an autocracy which runs this university," he exclaimed. "We're a bunch of raw material[s] that. . . don't mean to end up being bought by some clients of the University, be they

A Summer Flower Child Judy Smith, wearing flowers and face paint, joins hippies celebrating the start of summer in San Francisco's Golden Gate Park.

the government, be they industry, be they organized labor, be they anyone! We're human beings!" The administration eventually succumbed to faculty protests and a student boycott of classes and agreed to new rules on free speech.

Americans had never seen anything quite like the Berkeley protests. Here were privileged students condemning society, storming a building, and being dragged off by the police. Many people were infuriated; some younger Americans were inspired.

As campus activism flourished, young people were also creating the rebellious lifestyle that became known as the "**counterculture**." Less politically oriented than the New Left, the counterculture challenged conventional social values. By the mid-1960s, many younger Americans were condemning conformity, careerism, materialism, and sexual repression as they groped toward an alternative lifestyle.

The counterculture rested on the enjoyment of rock music, drugs, and sexual freedom. Beginning in 1964, the sudden popularity of the Beatles, the Rolling Stones, and other British bands brought back a rebellious note to rock and roll. The Beatles' irreverent attitude toward authority, symbolized by their long hair, helped create "Beatlemania" in the United States. Rock also became more socially and politically conscious in the 1960s. Bob Dylan, Simon and Garfunkel, and other musicians rooted in folk music sang about racism, nuclear weapons, and other issues.

Rock music often sang of the virtues of drugs and sex. The use of marijuana, the hallucinogen LSD, and other drugs increased during the 1960s as a way of flouting adult convention and escaping everyday reality for a more liberated consciousness. Sex offered a similar mix of pleasure and defiance. On campuses across the country, students demanded greater freedom, including the repeal of rules that restricted the mixing of male and female students in dorms. By the end of the decade, many students were living together before marriage.

Many young people hoped that the counterculture would weave sex, drugs, and rock into a new lifestyle. Novelist Ken Kesey joined with his followers, the Merry Pranksters, to set up a commune, complete with "Screw Shack," outside San Francisco. By 1965, Kesey had created the "acid test," which fused drugs, rock, and light shows into a multimedia experience and helped establish the popularity of "acid rock," the "San Francisco sound" of the Jefferson Airplane and the Grateful Dead.

The purest form of the countercultural lifestyle was created by the hippies, who appeared in the mid-1960s. Hippie culture centered in the Haight-Ashbury section of San Francisco. Rejecting materialism and consumerism, hippies celebrated free expression and free love. They wanted to replace capitalism, competition, and aggression with cooperation and community. One group of hippies, the Diggers, gave away clothes and food and staged the first "Human Be-In" at Golden Gate Park "to shower the country with waves of ecstasy and purification."

The power of youth rebellion was easy to exaggerate. There were not many full-time hippies. The countercultural lifestyle quickly became conformist consumerism, defined by the right clothes and records.

The counterculture also had roots in the orthodox culture it attacked. By the close of the 1950s, adults themselves had become ambivalent about consumerism, conventional morality, and institutional authority. Sexual freedom for youth was encouraged partly by the greater sexual openness of mainstream culture, the Supreme Court's *Griswold* decision, and the introduction of the oral contraceptive (the "pill") in 1960. Americans chafed at the authority of religious denominations.

Struggles For Democracy
Protest in the Schools

The civil rights movement, college protests, and other grassroots movements set a highly publicized example about the importance of rights and the impact of activism. By the mid-1960s, that example was even influencing students in high schools and middle schools around the country. Like many adults, secondary school pupils began confronting authority to demand more freedom and more democracy. Across the country, school dress codes—written or unwritten rules on clothes, hair, and grooming—became a flashpoint.

Several changes in fashion helped ignite controversy in schools. Long hair, sideburns, and moustaches for males and short "mini" skirts, long "maxi" skirts, pants, and pantsuits for females all conflicted with dress codes. So did blue jeans, untucked shirts, and supposedly excessive makeup. Fashion had come into conflict with dress codes before, but by the mid-1960s, students were more likely to ask teachers, administrators, and school boards to change the rules.

In some cases, those in authority agreed fairly readily to ease dress codes at least a bit and occasionally even eliminated them. But in many cases, the schools refused. Adults, including many parents, feared that students would become rebels unwilling to conform in school and then adapt to the adult world. According to social workers, there was a fear, too, that pants would make girls too masculine and that long hair would make boys too feminine.

The movement to change dress codes often involved more than fashion or comfort: it was about rights and democratic process. Administrators' refusal to listen to students' concerns about dress codes sparked new resentment. "The students. . . are puppets. . . being controlled so tightly by the administration, that they have no freedom of speech without getting in trouble," a female high schooler, calling herself "AN INDIVIDUAL," wrote to her local paper in Wausau, Wisconsin, in the fall of 1968. "We are held to such strict regulations that we are afraid to say what we really

The "pop art" paintings of Andy Warhol and Roy Lichtenstein, the productions of the Living Theater, the essays of Susan Sontag, and the novels of Thomas Pynchon broke with formal, artistic conventions.

Nevertheless, the counterculture was a disruptive force in the 1960s. Like the Black Panthers, hippies deeply influenced young people and adults and encouraged Americans to question conventional values and authority and seek a freer way of life.

The Rebirth of the Women's Movement

By the 1960s, American women were reacting against the difficult social roles enforced on them after World War II. More women than ever went to college, but they were not expected to pursue long-term careers. More women than ever worked feel inside. Is this democratic?" Increasingly, students bristled at the gap between their civics lessons and life in school. "We are taught democracy in class, but when we complain and there is no change we wonder if democracy is working," said Bruce Hollibaugh, a senior at Clinton High School in Decatur, Illinois, in January 1969. "There should be democracy in schools."

That argument didn't persuade many administrators and other adults. Pointing to the school football team and the US Army, Nicholas De Salvo, a vice principal in Dedham, Massachusetts, declared flatly, "This business of democracy in everything just doesn't work. In a training situation, much of democratic procedure must go out the window."

In response, students pressed their demands: they talked to principals and petitioned school boards. Sometimes students used the tactics of grassroots activism. In Lorain, Ohio, in October 1967, high schoolers staged a sit-in on the lawn to protest a ban on blue jeans. Locking them out of school, the principal required the students to bring a parent to gain access the next day. Elsewhere, students occupied administration offices indoors, struck, and marched and picketed outside. Administrators suspended protesters and even had some arrested.

As on college campuses, secondary school protests typically involved a minority of students. Some favored the dress codes; others didn't care enough to take action. Meanwhile, the protests alienated some parents and other adults. "It is sinful," wrote a St. Albans, Vermont, newspaper editor, "when a group of local high school students begin acting like college students in other parts of the nation by plotting out-and-out disobedience just because they don't like the rules and regulations."

Nevertheless, parents and other adults often supported the movement against dress codes. Most important, teachers and administrators, caught in the middle, felt it was not worth the time and upheaval to try and enforce the unpopular regulations. By the early 1970s, public schools had largely eased or eliminated dress codes: long hair for boys, pants for girls were increasingly acceptable. Roman Catholic schools typically kept codes requiring uniforms, but other private schools watered down theirs. Reflecting students' push for democracy, many schools now allowed committees of students to help draw up and enforce dress and other policies.

outside the home, but they were still expected to devote themselves to home and family. Women also had to put up with the continuing double standard of sexual behavior, which granted men more freedom to seek sexual gratification outside marriage. Women began to question their second-class status. In part, they were inspired by the example of the civil rights movement.

Two best-selling books reflected these complaints. In *The Feminine Mystique* (1963), **Betty Friedan** described "the problem that has no name," the growing frustration of educated, middle-class wives and mothers who had subordinated their own aspirations to the needs of men. Meanwhile, Helen Gurley Brown rejected unequal sexual opportunities in *Sex and the Single Girl* (1962). Neither Friedan nor Brown challenged male sexual ethics or male careerism. Instead, both wanted equal opportunity for women, in and out of marriage. Brown explained, coyly, that "nice, single girls do."

Women's complaints received attention but little action from men. In 1961, Kennedy appointed the Presidential Commission on the Status of Women, chaired by Eleanor Roosevelt. The commission's cautious report, *American Women*, documented gender discrimination but reaffirmed women's domestic role. In 1963, Congress passed the Equal Pay Act, which mandated the same pay for men and women

Fighting in Vietnam A wary US soldier at a jungle camp.

TIME LINE

▼**1960**
Greensboro, North Carolina, lunch counter sit-in
Sharon Statement
John F. Kennedy elected president

▼**1961**
First US suborbital space flight by Alan Shepard
Freedom Riders

▼**1962**
Port Huron Statement
Integration of University of Mississippi
Cuban Missile Crisis

▼**1963**
Birmingham, Alabama, civil rights protests

Civil rights march on Washington, DC
Assassination of John F. Kennedy

▼**1964**
Civil Rights Act of 1964
Lyndon Johnson's "War on Poverty"
Free Speech movement

who did the same work, but the measure, full of loopholes, had little impact. A year later, Title VII, a provision of the Civil Rights Act of 1964, prohibited employers from discriminating on the basis of sex in hiring and compensation. Yet the EEOC did little to enforce the law.

In 1966, Betty Friedan and a handful of other women, angry at the inaction of the EEOC, formed the **National Organization for Women** (NOW). Although frustrated with the Great Society, Friedan and the founders of NOW expressed essentially liberal values. They saw NOW as "a civil rights organization" and wrote a women's "Bill of Rights" that focused on government action to provide rights and opportunities. NOW also demanded access to contraception and abortion.

NOW's platform was too radical for many women and not radical enough for others. Some younger women, particularly activists in the civil rights movement and the New Left, wanted more than liberal solutions to their problems. By the fall of 1967, activists were forming new groups dedicated to "women's liberation." Influenced by the New Left, radical feminists blamed the capitalist system for the oppression of women, but a growing number of radicals saw men as the problem. Like African Americans in the Black Power movement, radical women talked less about rights and more about power. Their slogan was "Sisterhood Is Powerful!" Radical feminists also rejected collaboration with male liberal politicians.

Few in number, radical feminists nevertheless commanded public attention. In September 1968, New York Radical Women organized a protest against the annual Miss America pageant in Atlantic City, New Jersey. The pageant, they said, was an act of "thought control" intended "to make women oppressed and men oppressors; to enslave us all the more in high-heeled, low-status roles." The protestors threw bras, girdles, makeup, and other "women-garbage" into a "Freedom Trash Can." Then they crowned a sheep "Miss America." Not surprisingly, men and many women were generally uncomfortable with radical feminism. Onlookers at the Miss America protest called the women "lesbians" and "screwy, frustrated women."

Tonkin Gulf incidents
Lyndon Johnson's landslide election as president

▼1965
US escalation of Vietnam War
Voting Rights Act of 1965
Water Quality Act
Watts race riot

▼1966
National Organization for Women (NOW)

▼1967
Air Quality Act
Stop the Draft Week

▼1968
Tet Offensive in Vietnam
Assassinations of Martin Luther King Jr. and Robert F. Kennedy
Richard Nixon elected president

Conservative Backlash

The rebellions against the Great Society strengthened the conservative movement. Just two years after humiliating defeat in the presidential election of 1964, conservatives won new national prominence. Two politicians became focal points for many Americans' resentment against feminism, civil rights and Black Power, the counterculture and the antiwar movement, and the new liberalism.

George Wallace, former governor of Alabama, increasingly combined his hostility to civil rights and federal power with a populist appeal to working-class and middle-class whites. In 1964, he ran for the Democratic presidential nomination, calling for "law and order." Encouraged by his success in northern primaries that year, Wallace prepared to mount an independent campaign aimed at the "average man—your taxi driver, your steel and textile worker" in 1968. Now he played on anger over the youth rebellion and the antiwar movement, as well as the civil rights movement. "If I ever get to be President and any of these demonstrators lay down in front of my car," Wallace vowed, "it'll be the last car they ever lay down in front of."

Meanwhile, former actor Ronald Reagan became a major conservative force in the Republican Party. A lifelong liberal Democrat, he had moved to the right and supported Goldwater in 1964. Two years later, Reagan ran for governor of California, vowing to "clean up the mess at Berkeley" with all its "Beatniks, radicals and filthy speech advocates" and its "sexual orgies so vile I cannot describe them." He opposed high taxes, Medicaid, and other liberal activism and favored escalation of the war in Vietnam.

1968: A Tumultuous Year

In 1968, the stresses and strains of the Great Society produced the most tumultuous year in the United States since World War II. In January, the Viet Cong and North Vietnamese launched bold, sometimes suicidal attacks all over South Vietnam on the first day of Tet, the Vietnamese New Year. Although US and South Vietnamese forces inflicted punishing losses on the attackers, the Tet Offensive shocked Americans. If the United States was winning the war, how could the North Vietnamese and the Viet Cong have struck so daringly? More Americans now began to believe the war was unwinnable.

The Tet Offensive doomed Johnson's increasingly troubled administration. The president needed to send reinforcements to Vietnam, but he knew public opinion would oppose the move. As it was, he could not even pay for more troops. The economy would no longer support both the war and the Great Society. The political situation was bad, too. On March 12, Senator Eugene McCarthy of Minnesota, a longshot antiwar candidate with little money, nearly beat Johnson in New Hampshire's primary. Four days later, Senator Robert Kennedy of New York, the younger brother of John Kennedy, announced his own candidacy for the nomination. The charismatic Kennedy, opposed to the war, would be a formidable opponent. Besieged by the war, the economy, and the campaign, Johnson went on television the night of March 31. He announced a halt to the bombing of much of North Vietnam and indicated his willingness to talk peace with the North Vietnamese. He then announced that he would not run again for president.

Johnson painfully accepted new limits to the Great Society. Despite liberal pressure, Johnson did not have the money or the clout for new welfare programs, new initiatives to improve race relations, or even much of the space program, that symbol of liberal dreams. The Great Society was coming back down to earth.

Meanwhile, upheaval and violence tore the nation. In the first six months of 1968, students demonstrated at 101 colleges and universities. On April 4, a white man assassinated Martin Luther King Jr. in Memphis, Tennessee, where he had gone to support striking sanitation workers. King's assassination set off riots in more than 100 cities. Forty-one African Americans and five whites died.

The violence soon spread to the presidential campaign. After winning the California Democratic primary on the evening of June 5, Robert Kennedy was shot in a Los Angeles hotel by Sirhan Sirhan, a troubled Palestinian. Kennedy's death the next morning left McCarthy to contest the nomination with Vice President Hubert Humphrey, who still supported the Vietnam War. Humphrey won the nomination at the Democratic convention in Chicago in August, but the party was deeply divided. Outside the convention hall, Mayor Daley's police battled in the streets with antiwar demonstrators.

The Republican Party nominated Richard Nixon, who had lost to John Kennedy in 1960. A critic of the Great Society, Nixon promised to end the war and unify the country. Like the more conservative Reagan and Wallace, Nixon tried to exploit social divisions with promises to speak for "the forgotten Americans, the nonshouters, the nondemonstrators."

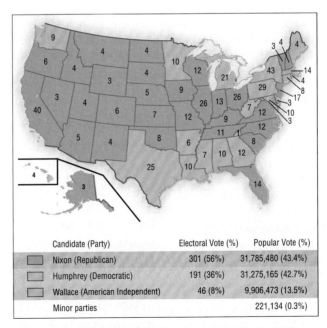

Candidate (Party)	Electoral Vote (%)	Popular Vote (%)
Nixon (Republican)	301 (56%)	31,785,480 (43.4%)
Humphrey (Democratic)	191 (36%)	31,275,165 (42.7%)
Wallace (American Independent)	46 (8%)	9,906,473 (13.5%)
Minor parties		221,134 (0.3%)

Map 26–4   The Presidential Election, 1968 Like the 1960 election, this was a close contest with widespread consequences. But this time, former Vice President Richard M. Nixon was the winner.

Unlike 1960, Nixon won this time. Although Humphrey made it close by repudiating Johnson's Vietnam policy, the vice president could not overcome the troubles of the Great Society. Nixon, running strongly in every region, attracted 43.4 percent of the popular vote to Humphrey's 42.7 percent and Wallace's 13.5 percent (see Map 26–4). Although the Democrats retained control of Congress, the party's eight-year hold on the White House had been broken.

CONCLUSION

The upheavals of 1968 marked the end of illusions about limitless American power. John Kennedy's confident nation—able to "pay any price, bear any burden, meet any hardship, support any friend, oppose any foe"—had vanished. By 1968, the economy could no longer "pay any price." The United States could not support its friends in South Vietnam. The government could not extend the Great Society. Instead, generation, race, and gender deeply divided the nation. The assassinations of King and Robert Kennedy threatened democratic politics.

Nevertheless, the nation had changed in other ways in the 1960s. Americans did not enjoy unlimited power, but across the political spectrum they had found creative ways to change their nation. In critical respects, the United States was more democratic than ever before: African Americans and other Americans had new rights and new power. More people than ever sat, as Ezell Blair put it, at "the table of democracy." The New Frontier and the Great Society had established new protection for the poor, senior citizens, consumers, and the environment, as well as new precedents for supporting health and education.

So the 1960s fostered simultaneously a pessimistic sense of defeat and a triumphal claim to rights and empowerment. The nation would have difficulty coming to terms with these conflicting legacies.

WHO, WHAT, WHERE

REVIEW QUESTIONS

1. What were the tactics of the civil rights movement in the 1960s?

2. What were the key programs of the Great Society?

3. What was the US strategy for winning the Vietnam War?

CRITICAL-THINKING QUESTIONS

1. Why did the Great Society come apart? Was it a success or a failure?

2. Compare liberal and radical feminism. Were these movements incompatible with each other?

3. Did the struggles and changes of the 1960s make the United States more or less democratic?

SUGGESTED READINGS

Asselin, Pierre. *Vietnam's American War: A History*. New York: Cambridge University Press, 2018.

Cohen, Robert, ed. *Rebellion in Black and White: Southern Student Activism in the 1960s*. Baltimore: The Johns Hopkins University Press, 2013.

Rorabaugh, W. J. *American Hippies*. New York: Cambridge University Press, 2015.

For further review materials and resource information, please visit www.oup.com/us/ofthepeople

CHAPTER 26:   "The Table of Democracy," 1960–1968
Primary Sources

26.1   MARTIN LUTHER KING JR., "STATEMENT TO THE PRESS AT THE BEGINNING OF THE YOUTH LEADERSHIP CONFERENCE" (1960) AND STUDENT NONVIOLENT COORDINATING COMMITTEE, STATEMENT OF PURPOSE (1960)

In the spring of 1960, the wave of sit-ins for civil rights dramatically highlighted the power of nonviolent grassroots activism. Consequently, the first issue for the civil rights movement was how to organize that power. In a press release issued in April, Ella Baker and Martin Luther King Jr. laid out the issues for the young activists gathering for a conference at historically Black Shaw University in Raleigh, North Carolina. The result was the formation of the Student Non-Violent Coordinating Committee (SNCC). In its Statement of Purpose, SNCC endorsed the principle of nonviolence rooted in the power of love.

"Statement to the Press at the Beginning of the Youth Leadership Conference": This is an era of offensive on the part of oppressed people. All peoples deprived of dignity and freedom are on the march on every continent throughout the world. The student sit-in movement represents just such an offensive in the history of the Negro peoples' struggle for freedom. The students have taken the struggle for justice into their own strong hands. In less than two months more Negro freedom fighters have revealed to the nation and the world their determination and courage than has occurred in many years. They have embraced a philosophy of mass direct nonviolent action. They are moving away from tactics which are suitable merely for gradual and long term change.

Today the leaders of the sit-in movement are assembled here from ten states and some forty communities to evaluate these recent sit-ins and to chart future goals. They realize that they must now evolve a strategy for victory. Some elements which suggest themselves for discussion are: (1) The need for some type of continuing organization. Those who oppose justice are well organized. To win out the student movement must be organized. (2) The students must consider calling for a nation-wide campaign of "selective buying." Such a program is a moral act. It is a moral necessity to select, to buy from these agencies, these stores, and businesses where one can buy with dignity and self-respect. It is immoral to spend one's money where one cannot be treated with respect. (3) The students must seriously consider training a group of volunteers who will willingly go to jail rather than pay bail or fines. This courageous willingness to go to jail may well be the thing to awaken the dozing conscience of many of our white brothers. We are in an era in which a prison term for a freedom struggle is a badge of honor. (4) The youth must take the freedom struggle into every community in the South without exception. The struggle must be spread into every nook and cranny. Inevitably this broadening of the struggle and the determination which it represents will arouse vocal and vigorous support and place pressures on the federal government that will compel its intervention. (5) The students will certainly want to delve deeper into the philosophy of nonviolence. It must be made palpably clear that resistance and nonviolence are not in themselves good. There is another element that must be present in our struggle that then makes our resistance and nonviolence truly meaningful. That element is reconciliation. Our ultimate end must be the creation of the beloved community. The tactics of nonviolence without the spirit of nonviolence may indeed become a new kind of violence.

SNCC Statement of Purpose: We affirm the philosophical or religious ideal of nonviolence as the foundation of our purpose, the pre-supposition of our faith, and the manner of our action. Nonviolence as it grows from Judaic-Christian traditions seeks a social order of justice permeated by love. Integration of human endeavor represents the crucial first step towards such a society.

Through nonviolence, courage displaces fear; love transforms hate. Acceptance dissipates prejudice; hope ends despair. Peace dominates war; faith reconciles doubt. Mutual regard cancels enmity. Justice for all overthrows injustice. The redemptive community supersedes systems of gross social immorality.

Love is the central motif of nonviolence. Love is the force by which God binds man to himself and man to man. Such love goes to the extreme; it remains loving and forgiving even in the midst of hostility. It matches the capacity of evil to inflict suffering with an even more enduring capacity to absorb evil, all the while persisting in love.

By appealing to conscience and standing on the moral nature of human existence, nonviolence nurtures the atmosphere in which reconciliation and justice become actual possibilities.

Sources: Martin Luther King Jr., "Statement to the Press at the Beginning of the Youth Leadership Conference," April 15, 1960, Student Non-Violent Coordinating Committee, Statement of Purpose, 1960. National Humanities Center.

26.2   JOHN F. KENNEDY, EXCERPTS FROM INAUGURAL ADDRESS (1961)

Taking the oath of office on a clear, cold day in January 1961, John F. Kennedy gave one of the best-known inaugural addresses in US history. The new president spoke squarely and eloquently about the paradox that characterized the United States during the Cold War: Americans felt both a sense of great power and great vulnerability. Kennedy powerfully declared the nation's willingness to "pay any price, bear any burden" for the sake of liberty, but he was silent on many issues, including the African American struggle for civil rights.

. . . The world is very different now. For man holds in his mortal hands the power to abolish all forms of human poverty and all forms of human life. And yet the same revolutionary beliefs for which our forebears fought are still at issue around the globe—the belief that the rights of man come not from the generosity of the state but from the hand of God.

We dare not forget today that we are the heirs of that first revolution. Let the word go forth from this time and place, to friend and foe alike, that the torch has been passed to a new generation of Americans—born in this century, tempered by war, disciplined by a hard and bitter peace, proud of our ancient heritage—and unwilling to witness or permit the slow undoing of those human rights to which this nation has always been committed, and to which we are committed today at home and around the world.

Let every nation know, whether it wishes us well or ill, that we shall pay any price, bear any burden, meet any hardship, support any friend, oppose any foe to assure the survival and the success of liberty.

This much we pledge—and more....

To those peoples in the huts and villages of half the globe struggling to break the bonds of mass misery, we pledge our best efforts to help them help themselves, for whatever period is required—not because the communists may be doing it, not because we seek their votes, but because it is right. If a free society cannot help the many who are poor, it cannot save the few who are rich....

Finally, to those nations who would make themselves our adversary, we offer not a pledge but a request: that both sides begin anew the quest for peace, before the dark powers of destruction unleashed by science engulf all humanity in planned or accidental self-destruction.

We dare not tempt them with weakness. For only when our arms are sufficient beyond doubt can we be certain beyond doubt that they will never be employed.

But neither can two great and powerful groups of nations take comfort from our present course—both sides overburdened by the cost of modern weapons, both rightly alarmed by the steady spread of the deadly atom, yet both racing to alter that uncertain balance of terror that stays the hand of mankind's final war.

So let us begin anew—remembering on both sides that civility is not a sign of weakness, and sincerity is always subject to proof. Let us never negotiate out of fear. But let us never fear to negotiate....

In your hands, my fellow citizens, more than mine, will rest the final success or failure of our course. Since this country was founded, each generation of Americans has been summoned to give testimony to its national loyalty. The graves of young Americans who answered the call to service surround the globe.

Now the trumpet summons us again—not as a call to bear arms, though arms we need—not as a call to battle, though embattled we are—but a call to bear the burden of a long twilight struggle, year in and year out, "rejoicing in hope, patient in tribulation"—a struggle against the common enemies of man: tyranny, poverty, disease and war itself....

In the long history of the world, only a few generations have been granted the role of defending freedom in its hour of maximum danger. I do not shrink from this responsibility—I welcome it. I do not believe that any of us would exchange places with any other people or any other generation. The energy, the faith, the devotion which we bring to this endeavor will light our country and all who serve it—and the glow from that fire can truly light the world.

And so, my fellow Americans: ask not what your country can do for you—ask what you can do for your country.

My fellow citizens of the world: ask not what America will do for you, but what together we can do for the freedom of man....

Source: John F. Kennedy, Inaugural Address, January 20, 1961. https://www.presidency.ucsb.edu/documents/inaugural-address-2

26.3 LYNDON B. JOHNSON, EXCERPTS FROM ADDRESS AT JOHNS HOPKINS UNIVERSITY, "PEACE WITHOUT CONQUEST" (1965)

By the spring of 1965, the US-backed government of South Vietnam was in crisis. Realizing that he would have to increase the American military role in the struggle against North Vietnam and the Viet Cong, President Lyndon Johnson had to justify the war to the American people. In a speech at Johns Hopkins University in April, Johnson laid out a passionate case for American involvement in Vietnam. At the end of July, the president would order 44 more battalions of US troops into combat.

. . . Tonight Americans and Asians are dying for a world where each people may choose its own path to change.

This is the principle for which our ancestors fought in the valleys of Pennsylvania. It is the principle for which our sons fight tonight in the jungles of Viet-Nam.

Viet-Nam is far away from this quiet campus. We have no territory there, nor do we seek any. The war is dirty and brutal and difficult. And some 400 young men, born into an America that is bursting with opportunity and promise, have ended their lives on Viet-Nam's steaming soil.

Why must we take this painful road?

Why must this Nation hazard its ease, and its interest, and its power for the sake of a people so far away?

We fight because we must fight if we are to live in a world where every country can shape its own destiny. And only in such a world will our own freedom be finally secure.

This kind of world will never be built by bombs or bullets. Yet the infirmities of man are such that force must often precede reason, and the waste of war, the works of peace.

We wish that this were not so. But we must deal with the world as it is, if it is ever to be as we wish.

The world as it is in Asia is not a serene or peaceful place.

The first reality is that North Viet-Nam has attacked the independent nation of South Viet-Nam. Its object is total conquest.

Of course, some of the people of South Viet-Nam are participating in attack on their own government. But trained men and supplies, orders and arms, flow in a constant stream from north to south.

This support is the heartbeat of the war.

And it is a war of unparalleled brutality. Simple farmers are the targets of assassination and kidnapping. Women and children are strangled in the night because their men are loyal to their government. And helpless villages are ravaged by sneak attacks. Large-scale raids are conducted on towns, and terror strikes in the heart of cities.

The confused nature of this conflict cannot mask the fact that it is the new face of an old enemy.

Over this war—and all Asia—is another reality: the deepening shadow of Communist China. The rulers in Hanoi are urged on by Peking. This is a regime which has destroyed freedom in Tibet, which has attacked India, and has been condemned by the United Nations for aggression in Korea. It is a nation which is helping the forces of violence in almost every continent. The contest in Viet-Nam is part of a wider pattern of aggressive purposes.

Why are these realities our concern? Why are we in South Viet-Nam?

We are there because we have a promise to keep. Since 1954 every American President has offered support to the people of South Viet-Nam. We have helped to build, and we have helped to defend. Thus, over many years, we have made a national pledge to help South Viet-Nam defend its independence.

And I intend to keep that promise.

To dishonor that pledge, to abandon this small and brave nation to its enemies, and to the terror that must follow, would be an unforgivable wrong.

We are also there to strengthen world order. Around the globe, from Berlin to Thailand, are people whose well-being rests, in part, on the belief that they can count on us if they are attacked. To leave Viet-Nam to its fate would shake the confidence of all these people in the value of an American commitment and in the value of America's word. The result would be increased unrest and instability, and even wider war.

We are also there because there are great stakes in the balance. Let no one think for a moment that retreat from Viet-Nam would bring an end to conflict. The battle would be renewed in one country and then another. The central lesson of our time is that the appetite of aggression is never satisfied. To withdraw from one battlefield means only to prepare for the next. We must say in southeast Asia—as we did in Europe—in the words of the Bible: "Hitherto shalt thou come, but no further."

There are those who say that all our effort there will be futile—that China's power is such that it is bound to dominate all southeast Asia. But there is no end to that argument until all of the nations of Asia are swallowed up.

There are those who wonder why we have a responsibility there. Well, we have it there for the same reason that we have a responsibility for the defense of Europe. World War II was fought in both Europe and Asia, and when it ended we found ourselves with continued responsibility for the defense of freedom.

Our objective is the independence of South Viet-Nam, and its freedom from attack. We want nothing for ourselves—only that the people of South Viet-Nam be allowed to guide their own country in their own way.

We will do everything necessary to reach that objective. And we will do only what is absolutely necessary.

In recent months attacks on South Viet-Nam were stepped up. Thus, it became necessary for us to increase our response and to make attacks by air. This is not a change of purpose. It is a change in what we believe that purpose requires.

We do this in order to slow down aggression.

We do this to increase the confidence of the brave people of South Viet-Nam who have bravely borne this brutal battle for so many years with so many casualties.

And we do this to convince the leaders of North Viet-Nam—and all who seek to share their conquest—of a very simple fact: We will not be defeated. We will not grow tired.

We will not withdraw, either openly or under the cloak of a meaningless agreement.

We know that air attacks alone will not accomplish all of these purposes. But it is our best and prayerful judgment that they are a necessary part of the surest road to peace.

We hope that peace will come swiftly. But that is in the hands of others besides ourselves. And we must be prepared for a long continued conflict. It will require patience as well as bravery, the will to endure as well as the will to resist.

I wish it were possible to convince others with words of what we now find it necessary to say with guns and planes: Armed hostility is futile. Our resources are equal to any challenge. Because we fight for values and we fight for principles, rather than territory or colonies, our patience and our determination are unending.

Once this is clear, then it should also be clear that the only path for reasonable men is the path of peaceful settlement.

Such peace demands an independent South Viet-Nam—securely guaranteed and able to shape its own relationships to all others—free from outside interference—tied to no alliance—a military base for no other country.

These are the essentials of any final settlement.

We will never be second in the search for such a peaceful settlement in Viet-Nam.

There may be many ways to this kind of peace: in discussion or negotiation with the governments concerned; in large groups or in small ones; in the reaffirmation of old agreements or their strengthening with new ones.

We have stated this position over and over again, fifty times and more, to friend and foe alike. And we remain ready, with this purpose, for unconditional discussions.

And until that bright and necessary day of peace we will try to keep conflict from spreading. We have no desire to see thousands die in battle—Asians or Americans. We have no desire to devastate that which the people of North Viet-Nam have built with toil and sacrifice. We will use our power with restraint and with all the wisdom that we can command. But we will use it.

We will always oppose the effort of one nation to conquer another nation.

We will do this because our own security is at stake.

But there is more to it than that. For our generation has a dream. It is a very old dream. But we have the power and now we have the opportunity to make that dream come true.

For centuries nations have struggled among each other. But we dream of a world where disputes are settled by law and reason. And we will try to make it so.

For most of history men have hated and killed one another in battle. But we dream of an end to war. And we will try to make it so.

. . . This generation of the world must choose: destroy or build, kill or aid, hate or understand.

We can do all these things on a scale never dreamed of before.

Well, we will choose life. In so doing we will prevail over the enemies within man, and over the natural enemies of all mankind.

Source: Lyndon B. Johnson, Address at Johns Hopkins University, "Peace Without Conquest," April 7, 1965. https://www.presidency.ucsb.edu/documents/
address-johns-hopkins-university-peace-without-conquest

26.4   DIANE CARLSON EVANS, ORAL HISTORY IN-TERVIEW ON HER SERVICE AS AN ARMY NURSE IN VIETNAM (2012)

Born in Minnesota in 1946, Second Lieutenant Diane Carlson Evans served as a US Army nurse in Vietnam in 1968–69 and later founded the Vietnam Women's Memorial Project. In this oral history interview from 2012, Evans discussed why served and she coped in Vietnam. Compare her understanding of the war with President Johnson's in the preceding source.

I would say that my childhood really shaped who I became. Perhaps all childhoods do. But in my particular experience I had two older brothers, two younger brothers, and a younger sister. And we grew up on a dairy farm where we all worked hard. We all had our chores. We all had our jobs to do. And there was this tremendous work ethic. A tremendous sense of the way our parents raised us [to have] a sense of duty to our community, a sense of duty to our church, and a sense of duty to our country. . . .

I graduated from high school in 1964 . . . I started nurses training in 1964. And be-cause our neighbor boys on the farm, because many of them were not going to college they didn't have draft deferments. This was a war of draft-able young men. And young men who were in college had deferments. And a lot of these farm boys, like my brothers wanted to go back to the farm or stay on the farm. And so all around us we have neighboring boys who had gone to Vietnam. And there were three of my brothers' classmates who were killed in Vietnam. And so my parents were of course naturally concerned.

But it's now 1966 and I'm still studying nursing. And I am very interested in what's happening in Vietnam. I'm very conscious of the protests. I'm very conscious of what's happening in Vietnam because of the six o'clock news. This was an all girl school. There were forty-five of us. And I was pretty much the only one that was interested in watching the six o'clock news in the nursing lounge. So every night at six o'clock I would be down watching the news. And I would be seeing body bags. Up in the fields, I would see the choppers coming in. And I saw all these images of men. I never saw images of women serving. But I knew there must be nurses there. I thought I'm a nurse. I'm going to be a nurse. I want to go to Vietnam. I want to do my part.

I wasn't aware of the Gulf of Tonkin. I didn't know what precipitated the war. I was studying nursing. I wasn't studying history. I wasn't studying geography. I was studying chemistry, biology, and microbiology, a lot of clinical nursing. But what I was sensing from people around me and the news was this war was to prevent the Domino Effect of Communism. So I was hearing about Communism, and I was hearing about the Domino Effect. I was hearing about protecting our American interests. But I was also hearing how the majority of people in the country at this time were opposing the war. So I knew there must be something very—it was very confusing.

I didn't question the validly of the war about I'm going to go off to war because I support the war. I never did support the war before, during, or after. I went because I was a nurse. And I thought they're going to need nurses there. So my whole concept of going off to Vietnam joining the Army was to be a nurse in the Army, not to carry a weapon, and not to be asked to kill people. . . .

So I'm going to college and our academic work is at the University of Minnesota. And my clinical work is at Saint Barnabas Hospital School of Nursing. And the University of Minnesota was a hot bed. Bob Dylan you know the defining music of our era antiwar music. I saw some flags being burned before I left. So I knew the war was very controversial. But inside of me it was not controversial as far as should I go, shouldn't I go. Even though, there wasn't a single person who said to me, I'm so glad you're going to Vietnam, be careful. Everybody was like, Well what do you want to go there for? Instead it was a negative. It wasn't, I'm glad you're serving our country. I'm glad you're going to be a nurse to take care of our boys in Vietnam. It was more like, Well you don't want to go there. So I was questioned about my motives. Why would I go there? But that didn't seem to change the inner, like I said. My childhood I think shaped my life.

The fact that our neighboring boys were going to Vietnam and they were dying there and coming home severely wounded. My sense of duty that was, Well, somebody has to go there. And my mother was a nurse. So my mother was very influential. I watched my mother go to work every day. She worked full time while she raised six children. She put on her white uniform and she was just this wonderful person and wonderful nurse. So yes, before I signed on the dotted line I knew that the war was divisive, controversial, but I knew nothing about Vietnam. . . .

I can't say we were patriotic but yet we were good citizens. So that was sort of a precursor, I guess. But I never looked at it as doing it for my country. I looked at it as doing it for the people. And country is the people. But it really was for the soldiers, someone would need a nurse to take care of them. . . .

.And then I got my orders, for Vung Tau, 36th Evacuation Hospital [in South Vietnam, in 1968] . . . I came to Vietnam with faith. I had gone to a Lutheran church in Minnesota, Swedish Lutheran. I had gone through confirmation. And my pastor had given me this book called, *Prayers for Youth*. And I took that to Vietnam with me. And it became very evident that I needed to do a lot of praying. To just face what I'm facing day in and day out. And I prayed a lot. But the prayers weren't working. . . .

And then I was transferred from the 36th Evacuation Hospital up to the Central Highlands . . .

And it made us medical nurses so upset that it was all based on body count. We're winning the war or losing the war about body count. Well, we've killed this many Viet Cong today. We've killed this many NVA [North Vietnamese Army] today. And that was the benchmark for winning the war? And it just seemed so ludicrous to us. And so yes, we're questioning and now were getting angry. The nurses, the longer we're there we're getting angry at the government because our patients are suffering and dying. Why are they suffering? What is the mission? What's the purpose? And the way I like to describe how I felt was, the government never gave us a purpose that we could believe in, in the politics in Vietnam. And they never did give us a clear mission. But personally, we knew what our mission was as nurses and that was to save lives. And to do everything we could to help the suffering and ease the pain. That was our mission. So that in of itself gave us strength. . . .

I didn't do drugs or alcohol because, maybe it was my upbringing. . . . I lost myself in music. And I loved the music of the times because the music nourished me somehow. Because now I'm just kind of losing faith in our government and why were we there and what is it. The music that I like the most was antiwar music. And I would listen to these songs and it was like, Yes, somebody is paying attention. This music is telling the truth. That would take another hour of an interview to talk about all the different songs that were written and the language and the meaning behind those songs. But the music just gave me inspiration that there's a segment of society back home that really is expressing what we're going through, because they're talking about us in those songs. And that was very I think nourishing for me to hear that. . . .

But how did we get through every day? I think something happens when you're challenged. And that's you forget about yourself. You have all of these patients to think about. And so you don't have time to think about yourself. You don't have time to think about how you're feeling. I know most of us when we first got to Vietnam, we were horrified. I know that some nurses said that they would just go out to the latrine and throw up. That was their way initially. And then they'd say, I got over that in a hurry. Or cry, and crying doesn't help. So, I think we shut down a lot of our feelings emotions. I feel like, I know I shut down. But I don't think most of us did in our ability to still show compassion. We could still be compassionate and caring. But we were kind of shut down in our own selves to just get through every day.

Source: *"Transcript of Interview with Diane Evans,"* Vietnam Era Oral History Project—Utah Valley University Digital Collections.

26.5 JOHN WILCOCK, "THE HUMAN BE-IN" AND "SAN FRANCISCO" (1967)

British-born journalist John Wilcock was a cofounder of New York's *East Village Other*, one of the many "underground" papers including the *Berkeley Barb* and San Francisco's *Oracle* that sprung up as part of the counterculture in the 1960s. Here, he reports on the first Human Be-In at Golden Gate Park in San Francisco in January 1967. After Wilcock conveys the color and excitement of this pivotal countercultural event and its San Francisco context, he describes the nearby hippie enclave Haight-Ashbury and the importance of the music scene. Strikingly, Wilcock details the differences and divisions emerging among the young of the San Francisco Bay area.

HUMAN BE-IN. Single most significant event of my stay in California (early December to late January) has been the "Human Be-In" which took place in Golden Gate Park under the auspices of the San Francisco *Oracle*. A beautiful day in which more than 20,000 hippies—many from L.A., 400 miles away—gathered with no other purpose than to celebrate life and the joy of being together. A fantastic scene: 20,000 young people whose only common link was the fact that they were heads.[1] Many of the current heroes spoke: poets Lenore Kandel (who was facing obscenity charges because of a poem called "To Fuck With Love," only just noticed by SF moral watchdogs after having been freely sold for a year), Allen Ginsberg, Lawrence Ferlinghetti, Gary Snyder, Michael McClure. . . . Most of the Berkeley people, particularly those associated with the militant *Berkeley Barb*, felt that the day's "celebration" was too much of a copout and that the crowd should have been motivated more politically. Undoubtedly the hero of the day was Tim Leary[2] who was treated as befitted the guru he has become for so many young people. Brilliantly planned by a brilliant newspaper (SF *Oracle*, 25¢ from 1542 Haight Street, SF), the celebration included bells, banners, balloons, bubbles, bare-backs, incense, most of SF's best known rock bands and even a parachutist who dropped dramatically out of an empty sky right into the park. Astonishingly enough there were virtually no police present and the smell of pot was everywhere.

SAN FRANCISCO. The kids in the San Francisco Bay area are more or less split into two camps. In Berkeley, most of the action centers around the campus protests at the university, the students having decided that in a university as big as theirs it is becoming necessary for them to help make their own environment and not be treated merely as so much material to be processed through the education machine.

The protests surface in many different ways (the pre-Xmas one centered over the right of Navy recruiters to operate on campus), but what they are basically fighting for is individual students' rights. Socio-political activists such as former student Mario Savio, Jerry Rubin and the editors of the *Berkeley Barb* publicize and encourage the protests as part of a larger battle against the Establishment and, specifically, the Vietnam war.

One of the protestors' problems is that a transient and ever-changing student population is very hard to keep interested in specific action and every semester the whole thing has to be started up all over again. The university has usually acted stupidly enough, however, to provide a new flashpoint for a fresh round of protests.

Over in SF's Haight-Ashbury district, once a semi-ghetto and now blossoming into a hipper North Beach (a similar relationship to NYC's Greenwich Village and East Village), most of the action centers around what can only be described as psychedelia. The long-haired beautiful people only want the right to BE (which includes being left alone). Dozens of stores, coffee houses, etc., provide resting places for the gypsy-like population which drifts in and out, sitting on the floor, studying the notices for parties or roommates on the numerous free signboards, wandering up the street to partake of the free food magically conjured up daily by the Provo-like Diggers.

The common meeting ground, however, for all the kids in the area is the decrepit, old Filmore Ballroom where every Friday and Saturday night SF's top groups (the Grateful Dead, Quicksilver Messenger Service, Country Joe and the Fish, the Jefferson Airplane, Big Brother & the Holding Co.) play at the "light shows." The music is tremendous, as is the geniality of the crowds present (many people sit around on the floor painting words and images in luminous paint, which shines under the black light), but the light shows are not

---

[1] "Heads" was slang for young users, mainly of marijuana, and sometimes of LSD and other drugs.

[2] Timothy Leary was a former Harvard academic famous for his celebration of LSD's mind-altering properties.

too imaginative. Warhol has been doing it so much better, using many more ingredients including film, which strangely is lacking at the Fillmore, and the nearby Avalon Ballroom which runs similar shows.

The main thing to come out of the light shows, in fact, has been an almost totally new art form: the beautiful series of posters, a combination of art nouveau and psychedelic, which are already collectors' items across the world. Each patron is given one free and, promises promoter Bill Graham, will continue to be. But whereas once only 2,000 posters were printed for each show now the press run is 25,000 and these are wholesaled at 60¢ apiece to sell for $1 in local stores and up to three or four bucks in the rest of the country.

Source: John Wilcock, "Human Be-In" and "San Francisco," *Other Scenes*, vol. 1, no. 1 (January 1, 1967), p. 6, from *Independent Voices: An Open Access Collection of an Alternative Press* (https://voices. revealdigital.com/).

Living with Less
1968–1980

< The downfall of Richard Nixon, August 1974

"Fighting Shirley Chisholm"

At the end of the 1960s, Shirley Chisholm, an African American congresswoman from Brooklyn, New York, worried about her country. Amid the upheaval of the Great Society, the United States "sometimes seemed to be poised on the brink of racial and class war." Blacks, women, the poor, and the young demanded change, but the political system resisted. "Our representative democracy is not working," Chisholm declared. "It is ruled by a small group of old men."

It was not in Chisholm's nature to give in. Born to working-class West Indian immigrants, she had pushed her way to a master's degree and a career as an educator. Running as "Fighting Shirley Chisholm," she won election to Congress from a poor, mostly Black and Puerto Rican district in 1968. In January 1972, she became the first Black and first female candidate for the Democratic presidential nomination. "You've never had anyone looking like me running for President," Chisholm declared. "Other kinds of people can steer the ship of state besides white men."

Chisholm's campaign continued the 1960s battle for rights. She wanted to create a coalition of African Americans, women, and the young "to get their share of the American dream and participate in the decision-making process that governs our lives."

Chisholm campaigned hard in several primaries. But with little money and organization, she had little chance. She had to fight to win equal time on television. Black male politicians withheld their support, and Black voters wondered whether an African American could really win. Her female and Black supporters squabbled.

The campaign ended in defeat in California, but it enhanced her reputation. In November, she won reelection to Congress with a huge majority. An exhausted Chisholm did not regret her presidential bid. "I ran for the Presidency in order to crack a little more of the ice which has congealed to nearly immobilize our political system and demoralize people," she explained.

Shirley Chisholm's failed campaign was part of a collision between Americans' aspirations for equality and new political, economic, and cultural realities. As the struggle for rights and opportunities expanded in the 1970s, the nation's economy and global influence continued to weaken. The United States no longer seemed a land of unlimited possibilities. Americans worried whether the nation could afford to meet everyone's needs in an age of dwindling jobs and resources. As a magazine concluded, Americans were "learning to live with less."

The result was not the "racial and class war" that Chisholm feared. But neither did the liberal Great Society give way to a stable new order dominated by one party or ideology. Instead, workers, employers, politicians, and families struggled with the consequences of limited resources and power. While Americans puzzled over the relationship between the economy and government and between the nation and the world, the political system broke down in scandal and failure.

A NEW CRISIS: ECONOMIC DECLINE

During the social, political, and military crises of the 1960s, Americans had largely taken the economy for granted. Prosperous and growing, the United States had seemed destined to remain the world's preeminent economic power. But the economy had faltered as the Great Society came apart. The failings of business, government, and economists, a shortage of oil, intensifying foreign competition, and the multinational strategies of giant corporations combined to weaken the foundations of prosperity. By the end of the 1970s, the United States seemed to be in critical economic decline.

Weakness at Home

Signs of economic weakness were almost everywhere in the 1970s. Although the economy continued to grow, corporate profits and workers' productivity fell off. Unemployment increased; inflation, which usually dropped when unemployment rose, also increased. At best, the economy seemed stagnant. The unprecedented combination of high unemployment and high inflation led to the coining of a new word—**stagflation**—to describe the nation's predicament (see Table 27–1).

Corporations were partially responsible for the weak economy. Corporate leaders had tended to maximize short-term profits at the cost of the long-term health of their companies. Some companies had not put enough of their earnings into research, development, and new equipment. As a result, some American products seemed less innovative and reliable. Detroit's automobiles, so attractive and advanced in the 1950s, now struck consumers as unglamorous, inefficient, and poorly made. Ford's new Pinto sedan had to be recalled because its fuel tank was prone to explode.

Long an emblem of security and stability, corporations now appeared as vulnerable as the Pinto. In 1970, the Penn Central Railroad became the largest corporation in American history to go bankrupt. That year, only federal aid saved Lockheed Aircraft from also going under. The federal government also played a part in the nation's predicament. Massive federal spending had stimulated the economy from the 1940s to the 1960s but did not have the same effect in the 1970s. Some analysts claimed that Washington had diverted too much of the nation's talent and resources from the private sector to military projects during the Cold War. In addition, the government's huge expenditures for the Vietnam War promoted inflation.

Table 27-1 Stagflation in the 1970s

Year	Inflation % Change	Unemployment % Change	Combined* % Change
1970	5.9	4.9	10.8
1971	4.3	5.9	10.2
1972	3.3	5.6	8.9
1973	6.2	4.9	11.1
1974	11.0	5.6	16.6
1975	9.1	8.5	17.6
1976	5.8	7.7	13.5
1977	6.5	7.1	13.6
1978	7.7	6.1	13.8
1979	11.3	5.8	17.1
1980	13.5	7.1	20.6

Source: Statistical Abstract of the United States (1984), pp. 375–376, 463; Tables 624–625, 760; 1971 inflation data from Statistical Abstract (1973), p. 348, Table 569.

* "Combined" means annual percentage changes of inflation and unemployment.

Economists did not give federal policy makers much help. In the 1960s, liberal economists had been sure they understood the secret to prosperity. The new problem of stagflation left them baffled. "The rules of economics," admitted the chairman of the Federal Reserve, "are not working quite the way they used to."

The Energy Crisis

An emerging **energy crisis** intensified economic problems. By 1974, the nation had to import over a third of its oil, particularly from the Middle East. The energy needs of the United States and other western countries empowered the Organization of the Petroleum Exporting Countries (OPEC), a group of third-world nations that had joined together to get higher prices for their oil. In October 1973, war broke out between Israel and a coalition of Arab nations, including Egypt and Syria. Arab members of OPEC refused to send petroleum to the United States and other nations that supported Israel in the conflict. OPEC soon raised oil prices nearly 400 percent.

The effect of the oil shortage spread well beyond gas stations. In some states, truck drivers blockaded highways to protest the high cost of fuel and low speed limits. Lack of fuel grounded some airline flights. Heating oil for homes and businesses was in short supply. Some people could not afford to heat their homes. Although the Arabs ended the oil embargo in March 1974, the underlying energy problem remained.

Competition Abroad

Weakened by trouble at home, the United States was vulnerable to increasingly tough competition from abroad. Thanks to American aid after World War II, Japan and Western European countries rose to create efficient, up-to-date industries. By the 1970s, these nations rivaled the United States, even in the American market.

The Energy Crisis Motorists crowd around an open gas station, New York City, December 1973.

The rise of Japan was the most dramatic. For decades, Americans had derided Japanese goods. By the 1970s, Japan's modern factories turned out high-quality products. Japanese televisions and other electronic goods filled American homes. Japanese cars—small, well-made, and fuel efficient—attracted American buyers worried about the high price of gas.

Because of such competition, the United States fell back in the global economic race. In 1950, the nation had accounted for 40 percent of the value of all the goods and services produced around the world. By 1970, that figure was down to 23 percent. By the end of the 1970s, the United States imported more manufactured goods than it exported.

The Multinationals

Multinational corporations—firms with factories and other operations in several nations—played a key role in the economic crisis. Taking advantage of new technologies and lower trade barriers, US and West European corporations had moved aggressively into global markets after World War II. **Multinationals** accounted for about 15 percent of the world's annual gross product, and the biggest had annual sales larger than the annual product of some countries.

US firms made up the majority of the largest multinationals in the 1970s. As Americans struggled, US multinationals still earned large profits because of their lucrative overseas units. Not surprisingly, these American firms rapidly expanded abroad. In 1957, just 9 percent of American investments went abroad; by 1972, the figure had reached 25 percent.

American Landscape
The South Bronx

Along with the empty factories of the Rustbelt, the empty buildings and rubble-strewn lots of the **South Bronx** epitomized economic and social decline in the deindustrializing United States of the 1970s. In the 1940s and 1950s, the area, part of the borough of the Bronx in New York City, had flourished as a middle-class haven for upwardly mobile white ethnics. But as the city struggled, many of those residents fled to outlying suburbs. Working-class Puerto Ricans and African Americans moved in, but the population of the South Bronx dropped shockingly from 763,326 in 1970 to 459,777 in 1980. As landlords burned down apartment buildings for the insurance money, 30 percent of adult residents were unemployed and 40 percent were on welfare. One-fifth of the population had no running water; one-half had no heat most of the time. Infant mortality, drug use, and crime soared.

Struggling to comprehend the community, residents and observers reached for comparisons. Photographs showed empty stores, burned-out buildings, and debris-covered lots, but no people. "It can only be compared to war," said a local Catholic priest and city councilman. The South Bronx conjured up images of Germany's bombed-out cities and Japan's atomic-incinerated Hiroshima and Nagasaki at the end of World War II.

Those who lived and worked in the South Bronx knew all too well that people lived and died there. For the doctor who founded a local medical center, the area was full of residents struggling and often failing to survive cold weather, malnutrition, drugs, and gang violence. "The South Bronx is a necropolis," he said, "a city of death." City officials feared the South Bronx was a breeding ground, a petri dish for disease. "A prime worry. . . is that the

The multinationals' most controversial foreign investment was the transfer of manufacturing from the United States to nations with lower wages and less restrictive labor laws. As corporations shifted production to plants in Mexico or Asia, American plants closed, with stunning job losses. The combination of overseas production and foreign competition was devastating. In 1954, US companies had made 75 percent of the world's televisions. Twenty years later, they produced less than 25 percent—and almost all of that production took place in Mexico and overseas.

Multinational executives argued that investment abroad increased jobs and prosperity in the United States. Capital invested in Mexico and Asia came back home, they insisted, as dividends to stockholders and tax payments to the government.

The Impact of Decline

Economic decline began to reshape life in the United States in the 1970s. It seemed as if the Industrial Revolution were being reversed. As factories closed, Americans witnessed the **deindustrialization** of their country. Huge steel plants, the symbol of American industrial might, stood empty. In the 1970s, most new jobs were in

Playing in the Rubble The South Bronx, 1979.

the US Cavalry garrison in Arizona during the Apache Wars of the late nineteenth century. "Fort Apache was a racist name," recalled a resident. "It evokes images of savage people, uncontrollable people, people society gives up on."

urban sickness shows signs of spreading to other parts of The Bronx," a reporter wrote in 1973. "If The Bronx goes under. . . there may be little hope for the rest of New York."

For the predominantly white police of the 41st Precinct, engaged in a seemingly constant battle with some of the surrounding nonwhite population, the area was "Fort Apache." The name for the precinct and its bullet-scarred headquarters was an evocation of

Despite its image, the South Bronx, along with the rest of the borough, was a place of extraordinary creativity. In the 1970s, graffiti artists, break dancers, and the first rappers helped create the music and culture of hip-hop. In their 1982 single, "The Message," Grandmaster Flash and the Furious Five offered their own harrowing depiction: "It's like a jungle sometimes it makes me wonder/How I keep from going under."

the sales and retail sectors, intensifying a 20-year trend toward a service-centered economy. America, a union official lamented, was turning into "a nation of hamburger stands."

For workers, the effects of deindustrialization were crushing. Heavy industry had been the stronghold of the labor movement. By the late 1970s, less than one in four workers belonged to a union, and organized labor lost power and influence.

The loss of unionized industrial jobs eroded workers' incomes. After rising from the 1950s into the 1960s, workers' spendable income began to drop. To keep up, more and more women took full-time jobs outside the home: the percentage of women in the workforce, 36 percent in 1960, rose to 50 percent in 1980—the highest level in American history to that time. Many Americans could not find work, however. As the huge baby boom generation came of age, the economy did not produce enough jobs. The unemployment rate, as low as 2.8 percent in 1969, jumped to a high of 9 percent in 1975.

Economic decline accelerated the transformation of America's regions. The energy crisis and deindustrialization sped up the shift of people and power from

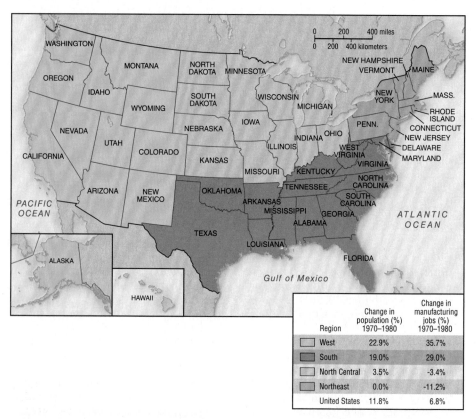

Region	Change in population (%) 1970–1980	Change in manufacturing jobs (%) 1970–1980
West	22.9%	35.7%
South	19.0%	29.0%
North Central	3.5%	-3.4%
Northeast	0.0%	-11.2%
United States	11.8%	6.8%

Map 27–1   Movement from Rustbelt to Sunbelt The percentages track the shift of population (left) and manufacturing jobs (right) from the Northeast and the Midwest to the South and West between 1970 and 1980.
Source: D. K. Adams et al., *An Atlas of North American Affairs*, 2nd ed. (London: Methuen, 1979), p. 85.

north to south and east to west (see Map 27–1). With its cold, snowy winters, the North was especially vulnerable to the oil embargo and higher energy prices. America's Snowbelt now seemed a less attractive place to live and do business. In the 1970s, empty, decaying factories made the Northeast and the Midwest America's **Rustbelt**.

Fleeing deindustrialization and high prices, many northerners moved south to the band of states ranging from Florida to California. As this **Sunbelt** boomed, farms became suburbs, and cities such as Orlando, Houston, Phoenix, and San Diego boomed. Texas and the southwestern states, rich in oil and natural gas reserves, profited from the energy crisis. The Sunbelt was home to new high-technology businesses: aerospace firms, electronics companies, and defense contractors. The Sunbelt was also at the cutting edge of the service economy, which was focused on leisure and consumption. More retirees moved to Florida than to any other state. Tourists flocked to California's Disneyland and Florida's Disney World. They gambled their money in Las Vegas.

CONFRONTING DECLINE: NIXON'S STRATEGY

Richard Nixon was the first president to confront the decline of America's prosperity and power. He recognized that the failed war in Vietnam marked the end of America's Cold War pretensions and that the American economy had weakened. Despite his long opposition to Communism and the New Deal, Nixon was a pragmatist, open to new realities and approaches.

A New Foreign Policy

The president and his national security adviser, **Henry Kissinger**, still regarded Communism as a menace and saw the Cold War rivalry between the United States and the Soviet Union as the defining reality of the modern world. However, Nixon and Kissinger understood that the relative decline of American power dictated a new approach to the Cold War.

The twin pillars of the new foreign policy were the Nixon Doctrine and **détente**. In July 1969, the president announced that the United States "cannot—and will not—conceive all the plans, design all the programs, execute all the decisions and undertake all the defense of the free nations of the world." America would continue to provide a nuclear umbrella, but its allies would have to defend themselves

The Power of the Press In August 1974, a newspaper announces the downfall of Richard Nixon, which had been aided by journalists' reporting on the president's conduct.

against insurgencies and invasions. This Nixon Doctrine was a repudiation of the interventionist Truman Doctrine of 1947 (see Chapter 24).

The United States also pursued a new relationship with the Soviet Union and the People's Republic of China. Nixon and Kissinger wanted to lessen the cost of the rivalry with these two Communist nuclear powers. Separate agreements with the two nations might keep them from combining forces against the United States. Nixon and Kissinger therefore worked to establish détente, the relaxation of tensions.

At the start of Nixon's presidency, the United States had not recognized the legitimacy of the People's Republic of China. Instead, America supported the Communists' bitter foes, the Nationalist Chinese regime on Taiwan. In February 1972, Nixon became the first American president to go to mainland China. He gave the Chinese leaders what they most wanted—a promise that the United States would eventually withdraw its troops from Taiwan. The two sides also made clear they opposed any Soviet attempt to dominate Asia.

Nixon's trip brought American policy in line with the reality of the 1970s and underscored the gradual end of anti-Communist hysteria in America. By design, the trip also left the Soviets with the frightening possibility of a Chinese–American alliance.

Nixon did not want a confrontation with the Soviets, the only power that could destroy America with nuclear weapons. The United States no longer had clear military superiority. Instead, he sought détente. Above all, he wanted the Soviets to agree to limit their long-range or strategic nuclear arsenals. The Soviets also wished to reduce the cost and danger of the Cold War and to counter Nixon's overture to the Chinese. Moreover, the Soviets needed American grain to feed their people.

The two sides began talks on the Strategic Arms Limitation Treaty (SALT I) in 1969. In May 1972, three months after his trip to China, Nixon became the first American president to travel to Moscow, where he signed the SALT treaty, limiting for five years the number of each nation's nuclear missiles. An Anti–Ballistic Missile (ABM) treaty sharply limited the number of defensive missiles the two sides could deploy. Although they did not stop the arms race, the treaties symbolized the American and Soviet agreement that "there is no alternative to. . . peaceful coexistence."

Ending the Vietnam War

Nixon and Kissinger sought better relations with the Soviet Union and the People's Republic of China in part to pressure the North Vietnamese to accept a peace agreement and end the Vietnam War. Nixon knew the United States could not win the war. Meanwhile, the war divided the American people and undermined American prestige and power around the world. But Nixon did not want the United States to look weak.

To appease public opinion, Nixon began to bring American soldiers home in 1969. With US forces reduced, Nixon needed a new strategy to persuade North Vietnam to accept the existence of South Vietnam. He turned to a policy known as "Vietnamization," in which the South Vietnamese were encouraged to defend themselves. But the South Vietnamese military alone could not beat back the Communists.

Accordingly, Nixon turned to US airpower to support South Vietnamese troops and intimidate the North Vietnamese. In March 1969, he authorized B-52 raids on North Vietnamese sanctuaries in Cambodia. Because bombing this neutral country might outrage American and world opinion, the raids were kept secret. Neither raids nor secret negotiations with North Vietnamese diplomats succeeded. Meanwhile, news of the secret bombings leaked out. In October, millions of Americans participated in Moratorium Day, a dramatic break from business as usual, to protest the war. In November, more than 250,000 people staged a "March Against Death" in Washington. That month, Americans learned about one of the most troubling episodes of the war. On March 16, 1968, US soldiers had killed between 200 and 500 unarmed South Vietnamese women, children, and old men in the hamlet of **My Lai**. This atrocity led to the 1970 court martial and eventual conviction of Lieutenant William Calley Jr. for mass murder.

Demonstrations did not stop the president from using violence to force a peace agreement. When General Lon Nol, the new pro-American leader of Cambodia, appealed for aid to stop a Communist insurgency, a joint United States–South Vietnamese force invaded Cambodia to look for North Vietnamese troops in April 1970. The Cambodian invasion sparked demonstrations on campuses across the country. On May 4, National Guard troops fired at unarmed protestors at Kent State University in Ohio. Four students died. Ten days later, state police killed two African American students at Jackson State College in Mississippi. These deaths intensified the outrage over Cambodia. Students went out on strike at about 450 campuses.

Some Americans, angered by these protests, mobilized in support of the president and the war. In New York City, construction workers attacked student demonstrators. "The country is virtually on the edge of a spiritual—and perhaps physical—breakdown," New York's mayor lamented.

As American troop withdrawals continued, the war and the peace negotiations dragged on. Meanwhile, the *New York Times* began publishing the so-called Pentagon Papers, a secret government history of American involvement in Vietnam. The documents, which revealed that the Johnson administration had misled the country, further undermined support for the war. The Nixon administration tried unsuccessfully to persuade the Supreme Court to block publication of the papers.

Nixon Under Pressure Across from the White House, a massive crowd protests the invasion of Cambodia in May 1970.

Unable to secure a peace agreement, Nixon pressed North Vietnam harder for a settlement. When the North Vietnamese army invaded South Vietnam in March 1972, the president ordered Operation Linebacker, an aerial attack on North Vietnam. When negotiations stalled in December, he ordered Linebacker II, the largest bombing mission since World War II, against the North. On January 27, 1973, negotiators signed a peace agreement in Paris. For the United States, at least, the Vietnam War was over.

Nixon had promised "peace with honor," but the agreement did not guarantee the survival of South Vietnam. The cease-fire came at a heavy cost. Twenty thousand Americans and more than 600,000 North and South Vietnamese soldiers had died since Nixon took office in 1969. The number of civilian casualties will never be known. Nixon had ended US participation in the Vietnam War, but his critics asked whether so flawed an agreement had been worth four years of fighting.

Chile and the Middle East

Détente, a practical accommodation with Soviet power, did not mean that the Nixon administration accepted the rise of potentially hostile regimes. To stop the spread of socialism and Communism, Nixon, like the presidents before him, was willing to subvert a democratically elected government and tolerate an authoritarian one. In 1970, he ordered the CIA to block the election of Salvador Allende, a Marxist, as president of Chile. Allende was elected anyway. "I don't see why we need to stand by and watch a country go communist due to the irresponsibility of its own people," Kissinger fumed. The CIA then helped destabilize Allende's regime by aiding right-wing parties, driving up the price of bread, and encouraging demonstrations. When a military coup deposed Allende in 1973, the United States denied responsibility and offered financial aid to the new military dictator, General Augusto Pinochet.

In the Middle East, the Nixon administration also displayed both its hostility to Communism and its inability to shape events decisively. In October 1973, on Yom Kippur, the holiest day of the Jewish calendar, Egypt and Syria attacked Israel in revenge for their defeat in the Six-Day War of 1967, when Israel occupied territory in Egypt, Syria, and Jordan. After the United States sent critical supplies to Israel, Arab countries responded with the oil embargo. Meanwhile, the Soviets supplied the Arabs and pressed for a role in the region. Determined to keep out the Soviet Union, Nixon put American nuclear forces on alert. Kissinger mediated between the combatants, who agreed to pull back their troops in January 1974. The embargo ended, but American weakness was obvious. Supporting Israel, the United States still needed the Arabs' oil. Nixon and Kissinger held back the Soviets but could not bring peace to the Middle East.

Taming Big Government

The problem of decline, addressed in Nixon's foreign policy, proved more difficult to handle at home. Nixon took office with the conventional Republican goals of taming big government. He wanted a balanced budget and a reduction in federal power.

So Nixon cut spending for programs, including defense. The fate of the space program epitomized the new budgetary realities. On July 20, 1969, a landing module touched down on the moon. When astronaut Neil Armstrong set foot on the surface, the United States had beaten the Soviets to the moon, as President John F. Kennedy had vowed. There still seemed no limit to what Americans could do. There were, however, limits to what the space program could do. Congress slashed NASA's budget.

In 1969, Nixon called for a **New Federalism**, which would return "a greater share of control to state and local governments and to the people." Three years later, the administration persuaded Congress to pass a revenue-sharing plan that allowed state and local governments to spend funds collected by the federal government.

Nixon took the same pragmatic approach to domestic problems that he did to foreign affairs. He left popular New Deal and Great Society programs largely intact. Despite his budget cuts, the government kept spending vast amounts of money. By 1971, the cost of big government, combined with the unsettled economy, had produced a huge, un-Republican budget deficit.

The president did try to reform the federal welfare system put in place by the New Deal. Like many Republican conservatives, Nixon believed that welfare made the federal bureaucracy too large and the poor too dependent. His administration tried to replace the largest federal welfare program, Aid to Families with Dependent Children, with a controversial system inspired by presidential aide Daniel Patrick Moynihan, a Harvard sociologist. Moynihan's Family Assistance Plan would have provided poor families a guaranteed minimum annual income, but it also would have required the heads of poor households to accept any jobs available. Opposed by both liberals and conservatives, the program failed to pass Congress.

Meanwhile, the administration went along with several liberal initiatives expanding federal regulatory powers. By the 1970s, many Americans worried that corporations did not protect workers, consumers, or the environment. A grassroots environmental movement grew rapidly, particularly on college campuses, and on April 22, 1970, tens of millions of Americans celebrated the first Earth Day with teach-ins, demonstrations, and cleanup campaigns. Liberals in Congress responded to popular opinion with three new federal regulatory agencies: the Environmental Protection Agency (EPA), the Occupational Safety and Health Administration (OSHA), and the Consumer Product Safety Commission. These agencies enhanced the government's power over corporations, as did laws to safeguard coastlines and endangered species and limit strip-mining of coal, air and water pollution, and pesticide use.

An Uncertain Economic Policy

Nixon believed government should not interfere much in the economy. But high inflation, rising unemployment, and falling corporate profits tested his commitment to Republican orthodoxy. He was unable to persuade business to control price increases and organized labor to limit wage demands.

Meanwhile, the US dollar was in crisis. Since the Bretton Woods Conference (see Chapter 23), many nations had tied the value of their currencies to the dollar. The value of the dollar, in turn, had been supported by the US commitment to give an ounce of gold in return for $35. This commitment to the gold standard had stabilized the international financial system and helped spur global economic development for decades. But by the 1970s, the weakening US economy had undermined the dollar: strong European economies had too many dollars and too little confidence in the United States, and the US government didn't have enough gold. If other countries demanded gold for their dollars, Washington would be unable to pay, and panic would follow.

Confronting inflation, monetary crisis, and economic weakness, Nixon announced his New Economic Policy in August 1971. To prevent the breakdown of the monetary system, the president took the United States off the gold standard by ending the exchange of gold for dollars. To strengthen US producers against foreign competitors, Nixon lowered the value of the dollar and slapped new tariffs on imports; now American goods would sell more cheaply abroad and foreign goods would cost more in the United States. To slow inflation, he authorized a freeze on wages and prices.

The New Economic Policy did strengthen the international monetary system and help US producers. But wage and price controls did not solve the underlying problems that caused inflation. The cost of the Vietnam War and the Arab oil embargo continued to drive up prices. Deindustrialization continued, too.

REFUSING TO SETTLE FOR LESS: STRUGGLES FOR RIGHTS

Despite the troubled economy, many Americans, like Shirley Chisholm, refused to settle for less. In the late 1960s and 1970s, African Americans and women continued their struggles for the rights and opportunities they had long been denied. Their example inspired other disadvantaged groups to demand recognition. Mexican Americans, Native Americans, and gays and lesbians organized and demonstrated for their causes. But other Americans, worried about preserving their own advantages in an era of limited resources, were often unwilling to support these new demands. At times, the result was almost the "racial and class war" that Chisholm dreaded.

African Americans' Struggle for Racial Justice

As the civil rights struggle continued, attention focused on two relatively new and controversial means of promoting racial equality—**affirmative action** and mandatory school **busing**. First ordered by the Johnson administration, affirmative action required businesses, universities, and other institutions receiving federal money to provide opportunities for women and nonwhites. Supporters viewed the policy as a way to make up for past and present discrimination. Opponents argued that affirmative action was itself a form of discrimination that reduced opportunities for whites, particularly white men.

Nixon, despite his commitment to limited government, generally supported affirmative action. His administration developed the Philadelphia Plan, which encouraged the construction industry to meet targets for hiring minority workers. In

1978, the Supreme Court offered qualified support for affirmative action with its decision in *Regents of the University of California v. Allan Bakke*. The justices ruled that the medical school of the University of California at Davis could not deny admission to Bakke, a white applicant with better grades and test scores than some minority applicants accepted by the school. Although the court barred schools from using fixed admissions quotas for different racial groups, it did allow race to be used as an admissions criterion. By the end of the 1970s, affirmative action had become an important means of increasing diversity in schools and other institutions.

School busing was more controversial than affirmative action. By the late 1960s, the Supreme Court had become impatient with delays in integrating the nation's schools. Even in the North, with no de jure, or legal, segregation, there was still extensive de facto segregation. In *Swann v. Charlotte-Mecklenburg Board of Education* in 1971, the court upheld the mandatory busing of thousands of children to desegregate schools in the Charlotte, North Carolina, area. But many Americans opposed busing, because they did not want integration or did not want children taken out of neighborhood schools.

Nixon sided with the opponents of busing. Privately ordering his aides to enforce busing less vigorously, he publicly called for a "moratorium" on new busing plans. Some communities implemented busing peacefully. Others faced protest and turmoil. In 1974, a federal court ordered busing in Boston. When the white-dominated local school committee refused to comply, a federal judge imposed a busing plan on the community. Working-class and lower-middle-class whites formed Restore Our Alienated Rights (ROAR) and other organizations to protest plans to bus students between the predominantly African American neighborhood of Roxbury and the largely Irish American neighborhood of South Boston. In "Southie," whites taunted and injured Black students. Although violence spread through the fall, the busing plan went into effect. With busing and affirmative action, the civil rights movement seemed to have reached its limits: many Americans were unwilling to go any further to ensure racial equality.

Women's Liberation

By the 1970s, the movement for women's liberation was flourishing. Many women came together in "consciousness-raising" groups to discuss a broad range of issues in their lives. To commemorate the 50th anniversary of the women's suffrage amendment to the Constitution, thousands marched in the Women's Strike for Equality on August 26, 1970.

The women's liberation movement, like the struggle for African American equality, was diverse. Liberal feminist groups, such as the National Organization for Women (NOW), concentrated on equal public opportunities for women. Radical feminists focused on a broader range of private and public issues. Oppression, they insisted, took place in the bedroom and the kitchen, as well as the school and the workplace. Some radical feminists, influenced by the New Left, blamed women's plight on capitalism; others traced it to men. Cultural feminists insisted that women's culture was different from and superior to male culture and felt that women should create their own separate institutions. Some lesbian feminists went further to argue that women should avoid heterosexual relationships.

Linking the private and personal with the public and political, the women's movement fought on many fronts. More women who married decided to keep their own names rather than adopt their husbands'. Rather than identifying themselves by marital status, many women abandoned the forms of address "Miss" or "Mrs." for "Ms." Women's liberation made its mark on the media. In 1972, Gloria Steinem began the feminist magazine *Ms.* On television, popular sitcoms portrayed independent women.

In the 1970s, feminists focused especially on three public issues—access to abortion, equal treatment in schools and workplaces, and passage of the **Equal Rights Amendment** (ERA) to the Constitution. Long effectively outlawed, abortions were generally unavailable or unsafe. In *Roe v. Wade* in 1973, the Supreme Court ruled a Texas antiabortion law unconstitutional on the grounds that it violated the "right to privacy" guaranteed by the Ninth and Fourteenth Amendments. With this decision, abortion became legal and widely available.

Like the civil rights movement, the women's movement demanded equal treatment in schools and workplaces. At first reluctant, the Nixon administration opened up federal employment to women and pressed colleges and businesses to end discriminatory practices. In 1972, Congress approved Title IX of the Higher Education Act, which required schools and universities receiving federal funds to give equal opportunities to women and men in admissions, athletics, and other programs.

The women's movement also continued the struggle to enact the ERA. "Equality of rights under the law," the amendment read, "shall not be denied or abridged by the United States or by any State on account of sex." In 1972, Congress passed the ERA. If 38 states ratified the amendment within 7 years, it would become law. But after 28 states ratified within a year, the ERA met heavy opposition. To male critics, feminists were a "small band of braless bubbleheads." Fearing that equal rights would end their femininity and their protected legal status, conservative women, such as activist Phyllis Schlafly, campaigned effectively against the ERA. Although more states ratified the amendment, some rescinded their votes, and the ERA never became law (see Map 27–2).

The ERA's defeat underscored the challenges to the women's movement. Women still did not have full equality, but they had more control over their bodies, more access to education, and more opportunity in the workplace.

Mexican Americans and "Brown Power"

In the 1960s and 1970s, Mexican Americans, the nation's second largest racial minority, developed a new self-consciousness. Proudly identifying themselves as Chicanos, they organized to protest poverty and discrimination.

Despite efforts to keep out Mexican immigrants, the Mexican American population grew rapidly. By 1980, at least 7 million Americans claimed Mexican heritage. The great majority lived in Arizona, California, Colorado, New Mexico, and Texas, most in urban areas and more than 1 million in Los Angeles. Winning more skilled and white-collar jobs, Mexican Americans still earned much less as a group than did Anglos (white Americans of non-Hispanic descent). One in four Mexican American families lived in poverty in the mid-1970s.

Stereotyped as lazy and shiftless, Mexican Americans faced racism and discrimination. Schools in their neighborhoods were underfunded. In some California schools, Mexican American children could not eat with Anglo children. California and Texas prohibited teaching in Spanish.

Gerrymandering diluted the political power of Mexican American voters. Despite its large Mexican American population, Los Angeles had no Hispanic city council member at the end of the 1960s. The justice system often treated Mexican Americans unfairly.

Poverty and discrimination marked Mexican American life. In cities, many Mexican Americans crowded into *barrios*, run-down neighborhoods. In the countryside, many lived without hot water or toilets. Infant mortality was high and life expectancy low. Nationwide, almost half the Mexican American population was functionally illiterate.

Encouraged by the civil rights movement, Mexican Americans protested against poverty and injustice for migrant farm workers. In the fertile San Joaquin Valley of California, the Mexican Americans who labored for powerful fruit growers earned as little as 10 cents an hour and lived in miserable conditions. **César Chávez**, a former migrant worker influenced by Martin Luther King Jr.'s nonviolent creed, helped them organize what became the United Farm Workers of America. In 1965, the union went on strike. The growers, accusing Chávez of Communist ties, called for police, strikebreakers, intimidation, and violence. Chávez's nonviolent tactics, which included a 25-day hunger strike in 1968, gradually appealed to liberals and other Americans. He also led a successful nationwide consumer boycott against grapes. Under this pressure, the growers began to settle with the union.

While King inspired Chávez, the nationalism of the Black Power movement spurred other Mexican Americans. In New Mexico, Reies López "Tiger" Tijerina, a former preacher, created the Alianza Federal de Mercedes (Federal Alliance of Land Grants) to take back land that the United States had supposedly stolen from Mexicans.

Mexican American activism flourished in the late 1960s. In East Los Angeles, the Brown Berets, a paramilitary group, showed the influence of the Black Panthers. In California in 1969, college students began the Movimiento Estudiantil Chicano de Aztlán (Chicano Student Movement of Aztlán, known by its initials, MEChA, or the word for "match" in the Spanish of Mexican Americans). MEChA was meant to kindle social change for Chicanos. In Crystal City, Texas, a boycott of Anglo businesses led to the formation of La Raza Unida ("The Unified Race"), a political party that won control of the local school board in 1970. These protests and organizations reflected a strong sense of pride and a powerful desire to preserve the Mexican American heritage. Activists asserted group identity by referring to Mexican Americans as "Chicanos." "A Chicano," said reporter Rubén Salazar, "is a Mexican-American with a non-Anglo image of himself."

Demanding bilingual education, Mexican American studies, equal opportunity, and affirmative action, activists fought for empowerment, for what some called "Brown Power." On the whole, white Americans paid less attention to Chicano activism than to African Americans' struggles. But Mexican American activists made important gains, including the end of state bans on teaching in Spanish.

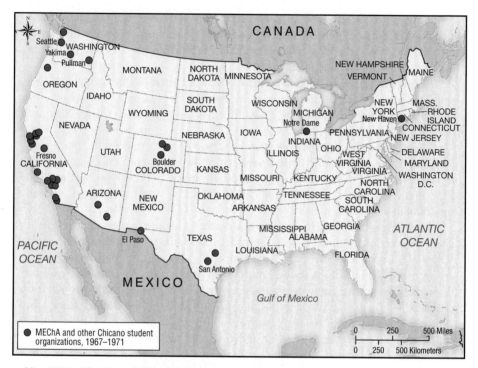

Map 27–2   The Rise of Chicano Campus Activism, 1967–1971 What explains the geographical distribution of MEChA and other student organizations?

Asian American Activism

Asian Americans also pressed for rights and recognition. Like Mexican Americans, they confronted a history of discrimination in the United States and faced denigrating stereotypes and hurtful epithets.

The small size of the Asian American population limited organization and protest, but the Immigration Act of 1965 made possible waves of new Asian immigration. By 1980, America was home to more than 3 million Asian immigrants, including 812,000 Chinese, 781,000 Filipinos, and 716,000 Japanese. Overall, there were 3.7 million Americans of Asian descent, mostly in the Pacific states and in cities.

Asian American activism followed the pattern of other minority movements. By the late 1960s, Asian Americans demonstrated a new ethnic self-consciousness and pride. Many Asian Americans saw themselves not only as Chinese or Japanese but also as members of a broader, pan-Asian group.

In 1968, the Asian American Political Alliance (AAPA) emerged on the campus of the University of California at Berkeley to unite Chinese, Japanese, and Filipino students. In response to demands by Asian American students, colleges and universities established Asian studies courses and programs by the end of the 1970s. Beyond campuses, in 1974 protests forced the hiring of Chinese American workers to help build the Confucius Plaza housing complex in New York City's Chinatown.

In San Francisco, activists brought suit against the public school system on behalf of 1,800 Chinese pupils. In *Lau v. Nichols* in 1974, the Supreme Court declared that school systems had to provide bilingual instruction for non-English-speaking students.

In the 1970s, Japanese groups demanded compensation for the US government's internment of Japanese Americans during World War II. In 1976, Washington rescinded Executive Order 9066, the 1942 directive that led to internment, but it did not make a more comprehensive settlement until 1988.

Asian Americans, like Chicanos, made only limited gains by 1980. However, with a new consciousness and new organizations, Asian Americans had also forced real social change.

The Struggle for Native American Rights

After many years of decline and stagnation, the Indian population had grown rapidly since World War II (see Map 27–3). By 1970, there were nearly 800,000 Native Americans, half of whom lived on reservations. Divided into about 175 tribes and other groups, Native Americans were united by poverty and persistent discrimination. They had the lowest average family income of any ethnic group and faced high unemployment rates and substandard schools.

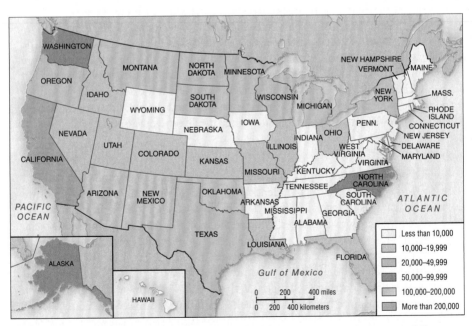

Map 27–3 Native American Population, 1980 After rapid growth in the years following World War II, the Native American population remained largest west of the Mississippi River and, above all, across the Southwest. But there were substantial numbers of Native Americans in every region.
Source: Data from *Statistical Abstract of the United States*, 1973 (Washington, DC: US Bureau of the Census, 1973), p. 348; and *Statistical Abstract of the United States*, 1984 (Washington, DC: US Bureau of the Census, 1984), pp. 375–376, 463, 760.

Native American life was shaped by the unique relationship with the federal government. Many resented the Bureau of Indian Affairs (BIA) for patronizing and exploiting tribes. Like African American and Mexican American separatists, some Native Americans saw themselves as a nation apart. Calling themselves "prisoners of war," they struck an aggressive stance, expressed in such slogans as "Custer Had It Coming" and "Red Power."

Beginning in the 1960s, a Native American movement emerged to protest federal policy, combat stereotypes, unite tribes, and perpetuate their cultures. Native Americans called for an end to employment discrimination and to the sale of Indian lands and resources to corporations. Activists staged "hunt-ins" and "fish-ins" to protest lost hunting and fishing rights. They also condemned the use of Indian symbols by schools and sports teams and demanded Indian-centered school curricula.

Some Native Americans favored more radical action. Copying the Black Panthers, a group of red-beret-clad Native Americans in Minneapolis formed an "Indian Patrol" to defend against the police. The patrol evolved into the American Indian movement (AIM), which spread to other cities. In 1969, AIM activists occupied the abandoned federal prison on Alcatraz Island in San Francisco Bay. They unsuccessfully offered the government "$24 in glass beads and cloth" for the prison, which they planned to convert into a Native American center. In 1972 and 1973, AIM took over BIA headquarters in Washington and the BIA office in Wounded Knee, South Dakota, where federal troops had massacred Indians in 1890.

The Native American rights movement made few gains. The Indian Self-Determination Act of 1975 did allow Native Americans more independence on the reservations, but Native Americans were still divided about their relationship to the government. Many tribal leaders wanted to continue selling off their lands through the BIA but were assailed by AIM for accepting bureau authority. Despite such divisions, the movement had forced Americans to confront the inequitable treatment of Indians more directly than at any time since the Great Depression.

Gay Power

Singled out for persecution in the McCarthy era, most gay men and women had learned to conceal their sexual identity in public. Mainstream American culture ridiculed gays as "faggots," "queers," and "dykes," and the medical profession treated gay identity as an illness. Despite the founding of the activist Mattachine Society in 1950, most gay men and women still maintained closeted identities.

During the 1960s, that began to change. In 1961, Frank Kameny, essentially fired from a federal job for being gay, unsuccessfully took his case to the federal courts. Another catalyst for change was the struggle of women, racial minorities, and students. Inspired by the chant "Black Is Beautiful," Kameny offered the slogan "Gay Is Good" in 1968. A decisive spur to the gay rights movement was a police raid on the **Stonewall Inn**, a gay bar in New York City's Greenwich Village, in June 1969. Such raids were commonplace, but this time gay men resisted. The next night, the police beat and arrested gay protestors, who yelled, "Gay Power!"

Stonewall became a rallying cry for gay activism. The Gay Liberation Front, the Student Homophile League, and other organizations appeared. Activists picketed companies that discriminated against gays, and gays socialized more openly. On the first anniversary of Stonewall, 10,000 gay men and lesbians paraded up New York's Sixth Avenue. "Two, four, six, eight!" marchers chanted. "Gay is just as good as straight!" The gay movement began to have an effect. In 1974, the American Psychiatric Association decided that gay identity was not a "mental disorder" and that gays deserved equal rights.

The emerging gay, Native American, and Chicano movements, along with the ongoing crusades of women and African Americans, made a deep impact on American society. Women, gays, African Americans, Native Americans, and Chicanos did not win full equality, but these groups made important gains despite the troubled economic climate.

BACKLASH: FROM RADICAL ACTION TO CONSERVATIVE REACTION

By the close of the 1960s, American society shook with demands for peace in Vietnam and equal rights at home. Some activists believed the United States would be torn apart and remade by the "racial and class war" that Shirley Chisholm feared, but the revolution never came. Radical movements fell apart. Many Americans abandoned activism for their private concerns; others angrily rejected protest movements. Encouraging this backlash, President Nixon won reelection in 1972.

"The Movement" and the "Me Decade"

By the end of the 1960s, women, minorities, student protestors, and antiwar activists seemed to be creating a single coalition, known simply as "the Movement." In August 1969, a crowd of nearly half a million mostly young people gathered for a music festival on a dairy farm near **Woodstock** in upstate New York. For three days, they created a temporary utopia dedicated to love, equality, and an end to the Vietnam War. What activist Abbie Hoffman called the "Woodstock Nation" briefly symbolized the possibility of a true mass-based coalition for radical change.

Nevertheless, the Movement stalled. "We had the dream and we are losing it," an activist lamented the same year. The different protest groups never merged and were often hostile to each other. Black activists, for instance, criticized white activists for neglecting poverty and other working-class problems.

In addition, Movement groups fell apart. Plagued by internal divisions, SDS held its last convention in 1969. The violent Weathermen called for "Days of Rage" in the "pig city" of Chicago in October 1969, but only a few hundred protestors showed up. Transient radical groups bombed or burned corporate headquarters and other "establishment" targets but succeeded only in giving the New Left and the Movement a bad name. The FBI infiltrated Black Panther chapters to discredit the organization. Panther leaders fled the country, went to jail, or died at the hands of police. Radical feminist groups also declined as women focused on liberal demands, such as the ERA.

Some protest movements lost their targets. After the demonstrations of 1970, the antiwar movement declined as the United States pulled out of Vietnam. The student movement declined as young people lost some of their grievances. In 1971, the voting age was lowered to 18, after ratification of the Twenty-Sixth Amendment.

The revolution also failed because many people turned away from activism and political engagement. Some were disillusioned by the failure of the Great Society and the duplicity of the Johnson and Nixon administrations. Others were disappointed by radicalism's limited victories. Still others joined therapeutic and religious movements concerned with inner needs rather than political change.

To the writer Tom Wolfe, the 1970s were the "Me Decade," a time in which Americans had become self-absorbed and narcissistic. The cause, explained the historian and social critic Christopher Lasch, was the crisis of capitalism in "an age of diminishing expectations." Fears about the self-absorbed Me Decade were as exaggerated as hopes for the revolutionary Movement. People did not stop working for change, but in a time of economic decline and political disappointment, many Americans felt they could not afford the expansive liberal dreams of the 1960s. They had to look out for themselves.

The Plight of the White Ethnics

The "new American revolution" was a victim of anger, as well as apathy. Most lower-middle-class and working-class whites rejected the Movement. They decried radical feminism and resented the students and protestors who had avoided serving in Vietnam. They also rejected the new liberalism of the 1960s. Feeling threatened by urban renewal, welfare, and court-ordered busing, many whites believed the Great Society did too little for them and too much for minorities and young radicals. Most of all, they feared lost jobs and a lower living standard amid deindustrialization. "I work my ass off," said an ironworker. "But I can't make it."

The media painted an unflattering portrait of these Americans as frustrated racists and reactionaries. In reality, they were not all so racist or forlorn. They took renewed pride in the ethnic heritage that set them apart from other Americans. "White ethnics" were self-consciously German American or Irish American, like the opponents of busing in Boston. They were "PIGS"—Poles, Italians, Greeks, and Slavs.

White ethnics tapped their heritage to affirm an alternative set of values—their own counterculture. For them, ethnicity meant a grounding in family, neighborhood, and religion in place of the individualistic American dream and the centralizing federal government. In response, some colleges and universities created ethnic studies programs. In 1972, Congress passed the Ethnic Heritage Studies Act to "legitimize ethnicity" and promote the study of immigrant cultures. Most important, white ethnics formed a large potential voting bloc, attractive to politicians.

The Republican Counterattack

Nixon tried to join white ethnics and white southerners in a Republican counterattack against radicalism, liberalism, and the Democratic Party. The president condemned protestors and demonstrations. "Anarchy," he said, "this is the way civilizations begin to die." Nixon ordered IRS investigations to harass liberal and antiwar figures. He used the FBI to infiltrate and disrupt the Black Power movement, the Brown Berets, and the New Left. He made illegal domestic use of the CIA against the antiwar movement.

Nixon also called for support from "the great silent majority of my fellow Americans." With his "southern strategy," the president reached out to Sunbelt voters by opposing busing, rapid integration, crime, and radicalism. He also tried to create a more conservative, less activist Supreme Court. In 1969, he named the cautious Warren Burger to succeed Earl Warren as chief justice. To fill another vacancy, Nixon nominated first a conservative South Carolina judge, Clement Haynsworth, who had angered civil rights and union leaders, and then Judge G. Harrold Carswell of Florida, a former avowed white supremacist. Both nominations failed, but Nixon had sent an unmistakable message to the "silent majority" and to white southerners.

The counterattack paid off in the 1972 presidential election. The Republican ticket of Nixon and Vice President Spiro Agnew benefited from unforeseen occurrences. Only George Wallace, the segregationist governor of Alabama, rivaled Nixon's appeal to the "silent majority." But Wallace's campaign for the Democratic nomination ended when a would-be assassin's bullet paralyzed him from the waist down. In addition, the Democratic vice-presidential nominee, Senator Thomas Eagleton of Missouri, had to withdraw after revelations about his treatment for depression.

Nixon did not really need good luck in 1972. The Democrats chose a strongly liberal senator, George McGovern of South Dakota, for president. McGovern's running mate was another liberal, Sargent Shriver, a brother-in-law of the Kennedys. The Democratic ticket—which endorsed busing and affirmative action and opposed the Vietnam War—alienated white ethnics, white southerners, and organized labor.

Nixon won 49 out of 50 states and nearly 61 percent of the popular vote, but the victory was deceptive: the Democrats still controlled both houses of Congress.

Nevertheless, the 1972 election was a sign that the traditional Democratic coalition was breaking up. Nixon's triumph, along with the failure of the Movement, the rise of the white ethnics, and the self-absorption of the Me Decade, showed that the glory days of liberalism and radicalism were over.

POLITICAL CRISIS: THREE TROUBLED PRESIDENCIES

Nixon's triumph turned out to be his undoing. The discovery of illegal activities in his campaign led to the revelation of other improprieties and, finally, to his resignation. Nixon's successors, Gerald Ford and Jimmy Carter, could not master the problems of a divided nation discovering the limits of its power. Unable to handle the conflicting issues of rights and economic decline, the three troubled presidencies of the 1970s intensified the sense of national crisis. At the decade's end, Americans wondered whether their democracy still worked.

Watergate: The Fall of Richard Nixon

Nixon's fall began when five men were caught breaking into the offices of the Democratic National Committee in the **Watergate** complex in Washington, DC just before 2:00 a.m. on June 17, 1972. The five burglars had ties to Nixon's campaign organization, the Committee to Re-Elect the President (CREEP). They were attempting to repair an electronic eavesdropping device that had been planted in the Democrats' headquarters.

At first, Watergate had no impact on the president. He won reelection easily, but a disturbing story gradually emerged. Two reporters for the *Washington Post*, Bob Woodward and Carl Bernstein, revealed payments linking the five burglars to CREEP and to Nixon's White House staff. The burglars went on trial with two former CIA agents, who had directed the break-in for CREEP. Facing heavy sentences, the burglars admitted in March 1973 that "higher-ups" had planned the break-in and orchestrated a cover-up. One of those higher-ups, presidential counsel John Dean, revealed his role in the Watergate affair to a grand jury. By the end of April, the president had to accept the resignations of his most trusted aides, H. R. "Bob" Haldeman and John Ehrlichman. To investigate Watergate, Nixon named a special federal prosecutor, Archibald Cox.

In the end, the president was trapped by his own words. A Senate committee, chaired by Sam Ervin of North Carolina, began hearings on Watergate in May 1973. A White House aide told the committee that conversations in the president's Oval Office were routinely recorded on secret tapes. Claiming "executive privilege," Nixon refused to turn over tapes of his conversations after the break-in. When Archibald Cox pressed for the tapes, Nixon ordered him fired on Saturday, October 20, 1973. Attorney General Elliot Richardson and a top aide refused to carry out the order and resigned. A third official finally fired Cox. Nixon's "Saturday Night Massacre" set off a storm of public anger. Nixon had to name a new special prosecutor, Leon Jaworski. The Democratic-controlled House of Representatives began to consider impeachment against the president. "I am not a crook," Nixon insisted.

By 1974, it became clear that the Nixon administration had engaged in a shocking range of improper and illegal behavior. Infuriated by news leaks in 1969, Henry Kissinger had ordered wiretaps on the phones of newspaper reporters and his own staff. Two years later, the White House had created the "Plumbers," an inept group of operatives to combat leaks such as release of the Pentagon Papers. In 1972, Nixon's men had also engaged in dirty tricks to sabotage Democratic presidential aspirants. Nixon's personal lawyer had collected illegal political contributions, "laundered" the money to hide its source, and then transferred it to CREEP.

Nixon himself had ordered the secret and illegal bombing of Cambodia. He had impounded (refused to spend) money appropriated by Congress for programs he disliked. He had secretly approved the use of federal agencies to hurt "political enemies."

As a result of Watergate and other scandals, many of Nixon's associates had to leave office. No fewer than 26, including former attorney general John Mitchell, went to jail. Vice President Spiro Agnew was found to have accepted bribes as the governor of Maryland in the 1960s. In 1973, Agnew accepted a plea bargain deal and resigned. He was replaced by Republican congressman Gerald R. Ford of Michigan.

Under pressure to release his tapes, Nixon tried to get away with publishing edited selections. Revealing a vulgar, rambling, and inarticulate president, the transcripts only fed public disillusionment. In July 1974, the House Judiciary Committee voted to recommend to the full House of Representatives three articles of impeachment—obstruction of justice, abuse of power, and defiance of subpoenas.

Nixon wanted to fight the charges, but the Supreme Court ruled unanimously that he had to give his tapes to the special prosecutor. They showed that Nixon himself had participated in the Watergate cover-up as early as June 23, 1972. The president had conspired to obstruct justice and had lied repeatedly to the American people. Almost certain to be impeached, Nixon agreed to resign rather than face a trial in the Senate. On August 9, 1974, he left office in disgrace. "My fellow Americans, our long national nightmare is over," the new president, Gerald Ford, declared. "Our Constitution works."

Gerald Ford and a Skeptical Nation

At first, Gerald Ford was a welcome relief for a nation stunned by the misdeeds of Richard Nixon. Modest and good-humored, the new president seemed unlikely to abuse authority. But Ford also seemed stumbling and unimaginative in the face of declining prosperity and power. Moreover, he had no popular mandate. Ford was the first unelected vice president to succeed to the presidency. His vice president, former New York governor Nelson Rockefeller, had not been elected, either.

Ford had to govern a nation skeptical about politicians. Johnson's deceitful conduct of the Vietnam War and Nixon's scandals raised fears that the presidency had grown too powerful. To reestablish its authority, Congress passed the War Powers Act of 1973, which allowed the president to send troops to hostilities overseas for no more than 60 days without congressional consent. In 1975, Congress held hearings on CIA secret operations. Amid revelations about the agency's improper roles in domestic spying and the assassination of foreign leaders, Congress created permanent committees to oversee the agency. Ford had to ban the use of assassination in American foreign policy.

Soon after taking office, Ford himself fed the public's skepticism about the presidency by offering Nixon a full pardon for all crimes committed as president. Ford's popularity dropped immediately, and his presidency never fully recovered.

Ford's handling of economic issues did not help his popularity. A moderate Republican, he preferred a less active federal role in managing the economy. But, like Nixon, he could not stop some liberal initiatives, as Congress strengthened the regulatory power of the Federal Trade Commission and extended the 1970 Clean Air Act.

Ford had no solutions for deindustrialization and stagflation. Believing inflation was the most serious problem, he did little to stop rising unemployment, which topped 9 percent. His anti-inflation program, known as WIN for "Whip Inflation Now," mainly encouraged Americans to control price increases voluntarily, but inflation continued.

In foreign affairs, Ford had to accept limits on American power. Despite the 1973 cease-fire, the fighting continued in Vietnam. Ford promised to protect South Vietnam, but Congress cut his requests for monetary aid to Saigon. Sending American troops back to South Vietnam was out of the question. When the North Vietnamese invaded early in 1975, panicked civilians fled southward. As Saigon was overrun, the last Americans evacuated in helicopters. Thousands of loyal South Vietnamese fled with them, but many more were left behind. On April 30, 1975, South Vietnam surrendered. There was nothing Ford could do to prevent the final, ignominious failure of America's 20-year-long Vietnam policy.

The president could also do nothing to save the pro-American government of Cambodia from Communist insurgents, the Khmer Rouge, in April 1975. Ford did act the next month when the Khmer Rouge captured an American merchant ship, the *Mayaguez*, off Cambodia. At the cost of 41 deaths, United States marines rescued the 39-man crew. Despite the rescue, the United States no longer wielded much power in Southeast Asia.

The policy of détente with the Soviet Union, meant to help America cope with its limited power, was also in trouble. The United States and the Soviets failed to agree to a second Strategic Arms Limitation Treaty (SALT II). Critics of détente, including Democratic Senator Henry Jackson of Washington, claimed that the policy sapped American defenses and overlooked human rights violations by the Soviets. In 1974, Jackson added to a trade bill an amendment linking commerce to freedom for Soviet Jews to emigrate. The Jackson-Vanik Amendment helped sour the Soviets on détente. Ford further alienated conservatives when he signed an agreement in Helsinki, Finland, accepting the post–World War II boundaries of European nations.

Ford's troubles affected the polls. The Democrats made large gains in the 1974 congressional elections. Two years later, Ford won the Republican nomination for president, replacing Rockefeller with a more conservative vice-presidential nominee, Senator Robert Dole of Kansas. The Democrats chose former Georgia governor Jimmy Carter, a moderate promising efficiency rather than liberal reform.

With low turnout, Carter took 50.1 percent of the vote to Ford's 48 percent. The Democrat won an Electoral College majority by carrying the Northeast and taking back almost all the South from the Republicans (see Map 27–4). The outcome was less an endorsement of Carter than a rejection of Ford, who became the first sitting president to lose an election since Herbert Hoover during the Great Depression in 1932.

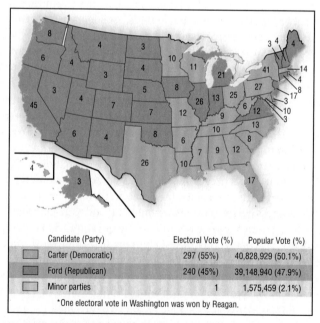

Candidate (Party)	Electoral Vote (%)	Popular Vote (%)
Carter (Democratic)	297 (55%)	40,828,929 (50.1%)
Ford (Republican)	240 (45%)	39,148,940 (47.9%)
Minor parties	1	1,575,459 (2.1%)

*One electoral vote in Washington was won by Reagan.

Map 27–4 The Presidential Election, 1976 Jimmy Carter managed to reestablish the Democratic Party's appeal to white southerners.

"Why Not the Best?": Jimmy Carter

As he took office in 1977, Jimmy Carter seemed capable and efficient. A graduate of the Naval Academy, he had served as an engineer in the nuclear submarine program and successfully managed his family's peanut farm before entering politics. Carter's perfectionism was captured in the title of his autobiography, *Why Not the Best?*

Carter responded more energetically and imaginatively than Ford to the nation's problems. But Carter came to be seen as a weak, uncertain leader. More important, he faced the same intractable problems that had bedeviled Ford.

Like his predecessor, Carter had trouble putting to rest the recent past. He met angry criticism when he pardoned Americans who had resisted the draft during the Vietnam War.

Carter also faced increasing popular resentment of government. Many Americans believed that regulation and taxation had gotten out of hand. When the Endangered Species Act of 1973 forced a halt to the construction of a Tennessee dam because it threatened the survival of the snail darter, a small local fish, it seemed as if the federal government worried more about fish than about people's need for electricity and recreation.

The West was the stronghold of antigovernment sentiment in the 1970s. Assailing Washington bureaucrats, the Sagebrush Rebellion demanded state control over federal lands in the West. Businessmen in the West also wanted more exploitation of oil, forests, and other resources on federal lands. Meanwhile, California became the center of an antitax movement in 1978. Angered by high taxes and local government spending, California voters passed Proposition 13, which sharply reduced property taxes.

As always, antigovernment sentiment was inconsistent. Many of the same people who attacked taxes and regulation expected aid and benefits from Washington. When Chrysler faced bankruptcy in 1979, the government saved the automaker with a $1.5 billion loan guarantee. When Carter moved to cancel federal water projects in the West in 1977, he faced protest from the heart of the Sagebrush Rebellion.

Carter was most successful when he moved to limit government. By the 1970s, some economists were advocating **deregulation** of businesses as a way to lower costs, increase competition, and improve services. In 1978, the government removed price controls on the airline industry. In the short run the move lowered fares, but in the long run it drove some airlines out of business.

Deregulation marked a changing balance of political power. Big business, under attack since the 1960s, now lobbied effectively against regulation, organized labor, and taxes. Liberals, meanwhile, failed to convince Congress to create the Consumer Protection Agency or to make labor organization easier. In 1978, Congress diluted the liberal Humphrey-Hawkins Bill asserting federal responsibility for full employment. When Carter tried to raise business taxes, Congress instead cut taxes on capital gains and added more tax loopholes.

Carter attempted, with mixed results, to adjust the economy to the realities of living with less. His voluntary wage and price controls did not stop soaring inflation. After fuel shortages forced schools and businesses to close in the harsh winter of 1976–1977, Carter addressed the energy crisis. The president told Americans that "the energy shortage is permanent" and urged them to conserve. His energy plan included a new Department of Energy, taxes on gas-guzzling automobiles and large

Struggles For Democracy

The Pollster

As American teenagers went, 18-year-old Patrick Caddell of Jacksonville, Florida had an unusual ambition: he wanted to be a pollster. Although Pat didn't particularly like baseball, he loved the game's statistics. What the high-school senior loved most of all was politics. For a math project in the spring of 1968, Pat produced his own political statistics by conducting a poll during the presidential primary in a working-class area of Jacksonville. He didn't know exactly how professional pollsters worked. Increasingly, they called prospective voters on the phone and asked them precise questions: were they for or against the war in Vietnam? Whom did they favor for president? But Pat, walking from door to door, asked more open-ended questions that turned sometimes into conversations about people's values and beliefs. Without realizing it, the novice pollster was a political innovator.

Enrolling that fall at Harvard College in Cambridge, Massachusetts, Caddell began to work for political campaigns. With two friends, he founded a polling firm. In the fall of 1971, the college senior started polling for the presidential campaign of Senator George McGovern. The 21-year-old's ability stunned McGovern's top aides. "If we wanted to know McGovern's following among divorced women with second homes who also collected rocks," one observed, "Pat Caddell could tell us that." As important, Caddell shared the insight that had grown from his conversations with Jacksonville voters: Americans, upset with the Vietnam war, campus demonstrations, and assassinations, were alienated from politics and government. The best way McGovern could reach those voters, Caddell argued, was to run as an outsider, someone who shared their values and their discontent with Washington. Caddell's strategy helped McGovern win the Democratic nomination. The senator lost to incumbent Richard Nixon, but the campaign had made McGovern's young pollster a star.

Caddell's quick rise came at a transitional time for American democracy. For years, advertising men had dominated political consulting: their television ads seemingly had the power to make presidents. But in the 1960s, careful, detailed, regular polling became more important. Pollsters had the data to guide the advertisers and overall strategy. So, Caddell was the youngest of a new generation of political operatives, pollsters who seemed to shape the workings of democracy at the highest level.

Still focused on alienated voters, Caddell became pollster and strategist for the perfect outsider candidate, Georgia Governor Jimmy Carter, who promised never to lie to the American people. "You know why Jimmy Carter is going to be president?" asked one of Carter's top aides. "Because of Pat Caddell." When his polls and strategy

consumers of oil, tax incentives to stimulate oil and gas production, and development of nuclear power. Conservatives complained that the program expanded government authority, whereas liberals and environmentalists objected to its support for nuclear power and oil-company profits. A weakened plan, passed in 1978, did encourage conservation.

The President and the Pollster In the White House, Jimmy Carter, left, laughs with Pat Caddell, the pollster who helped get him there.

memos helped propel Carter to victory in 1976, Caddell's stardom was assured.

His fame was double-edged. The often temperamental, sometimes immature 26-year-old, who drove a gold Mercedes, provoked jealousy and dislike. Some observers feared his power to warp the democratic will of the people. "He doesn't make predictions," wrote one critic, "he makes events." Other critics charged that Caddell couldn't serve both the president and corporate clients at the same time; the companies would have too much influence. Still others denied Caddell's power and

dismissed him as "a guru still in his 20s" with "half-baked ideas." As the Carter administration foundered, Caddell came in for more criticism, especially when he played a key role in the framing of the president's fateful "malaise" speech. Carter's loss to Ronald Reagan in 1980 was the last straw for Pat Caddell's reputation. At 30, his dark beard already streaked with white, Caddell was worn down. Politics, he said wearily, "takes years off your life. It's like a war."

So pollsters weren't so powerful. Or were they? After all, victorious Ronald Reagan had his own vaunted pollster.

Nuclear power, a key part of Carter's energy plan, lost much of its appeal. In March 1979, a nuclear reactor at **Three Mile Island**, Pennsylvania, nearly suffered a catastrophic meltdown. As 100,000 frightened residents fled their homes, the reactor had to be permanently closed. Around the country, utilities scrapped plans for new nuclear power plants.

Three Mile Island fed broader anxieties about the environmental damage of industrial capitalism. Americans wondered whether their neighborhoods would suffer the fate of Love Canal, near Niagara Falls, New York. There, hazardous waste buried by a chemical company caused so many cases of cancer, miscarriages, and other health problems that residents had to move away. Despite business hostility to regulation, Washington had to create a "Superfund" of $1.6 billion to clean up hazardous-waste sites. The administration also took control of 100 million acres of Alaska to prevent damage from economic development.

At first, Carter had success with foreign policy. Continuing Nixon's de-escalation of the Cold War, Carter announced that "we are now free of the inordinate fear of Communism." Without abandoning détente, he focused on building harmony and supporting human rights and democracy around the world. In 1978, Carter won Senate approval of a treaty yielding ownership of the Panama Canal to Panama at the end of the century, representing a new, more respectful approach to Central and Latin America.

In 1978, Carter also mediated the first peace agreement between Israel and an Arab nation. Bringing together Israeli and Egyptian leaders at the **Camp David** presidential retreat, Carter helped forge a framework for peace that led to Israel's withdrawal from the Sinai Peninsula and the signing of an Israeli-Egyptian treaty. The agreement did not settle the fate of the Israeli-occupied Golan Heights and Gaza Strip or the future of the Palestinian people, but it did create a basis for future negotiations.

Carter viewed a commitment to human rights and democracy as America's way of recapturing the international respect lost during the Vietnam War. In practice, however, Carter supported authoritarian American allies, such as the rulers of Iran and the Philippines, who abused human rights in their own countries.

TIME LINE

▼1968
Assassinations of Martin Luther King Jr. and Robert F. Kennedy
Election of Richard Nixon

▼1969
Secret bombing of Cambodia
Stonewall Riot in New York's Greenwich Village
Apollo 11 moon landing
Nixon Doctrine

▼1970
First Earth Day
Invasion of Cambodia

▼1971
United States off gold standard
Ratification of Twenty-Sixth Amendment, lowering voting age to 18
Supreme Court busing decision, *Swann v. Charlotte-Mecklenburg Board of Education*

▼1972
President Nixon's trips to the People's Republic of China and the Soviet Union

Strategic Arms Limitation Treaty (SALT I) and Anti–Ballistic Missile (ABM) Treaty
Congressional passage of Equal Rights Amendment
Watergate burglary
Reelection of President Nixon

▼1973
Peace agreement to end Vietnam War
Supreme Court ruling to legalize abortion, *Roe v. Wade*

Carter's foreign policy suffered from the collapse of détente. The president did reach an agreement with the Soviets on the SALT II treaty, but the Senate was reluctant to ratify it. Then, in December 1979, the Soviet Union invaded its southern neighbor, Afghanistan. In response, Carter withdrew the SALT II treaty, stopped grain shipments to the Soviet Union, forbade American athletes to compete in the 1980 Olympics in Moscow, and increased military spending. These moves did not affect the Soviets' invasion, but détente was over, and the direction of American foreign policy was unclear.

By 1979, Carter was deeply unpopular. He had not stabilized the economy or forged a coherent foreign policy. After pondering the situation at Camp David for 11 days in July, he told a television audience that the nation was suffering a "crisis of the American spirit." The president offered proposals to deal with the energy crisis but spoke most strongly to the state of the nation. "All the legislation in the world can't fix what's wrong with America," Carter said. "What is lacking is confidence and a sense of community." The speech was popular, but the president failed to turn popular approval into effective legislation.

Carter became still more embattled when the Shah of Iran was overthrown by the followers of an Islamic leader, the Ayatollah Ruholla Khomeini, early in 1979. The Shah had long received lavish aid from the United States. Now, Iranian revolutionaries, eager to restore traditional Islamic values, condemned America for imposing the Shah and modern culture on their nation. In the wake of the revolution, oil prices rose. Americans had to contend again with gas lines and inflation.

The situation worsened when Khomeini condemned the United States for allowing the Shah to receive medical treatment in New York. On November 4, students loyal to Khomeini overran the United States embassy in Teheran, the Iranian capital, and took 60 Americans hostage. Carter froze Iranian assets in the United

▼**1973–1974**
OPEC oil embargo

▼**1974**
Boston busing struggle
Resignation of President
   Nixon

▼**1975**
Surrender of South Viet-
   nam to North Vietnam
Helsinki Agreement

▼**1976**
Announcement of the "Me
   Decade" by Tom Wolfe
Jimmy Carter elected
   president

▼**1977**
Carter's energy plan

▼**1978**
Camp David peace accords
Supreme Court affirmative
   action decision, *Regents
   of the University of California v. Allan Bakke*

▼**1979**
Accident at Three Mile
   Island nuclear power
   plant

▼**1979–1981**
Iranian hostage crisis

▼**1980**
Ronald Reagan elected
   president

Disaster in the Iranian Desert, April 1980 The wreckage of this army helicopter, part of the failed attempt to free American hostages in Iran, symbolizes the weakness of the United States at the start of the 1980s.

States but could not compel the release of the hostages. The United States seemed helpless. In the spring of 1980, a frustrated Carter ordered a secret military mission to rescue the hostages. On April 24, eight American helicopters headed for a desert rendezvous with six transport planes carrying troops and supplies. When two helicopters broke down and another became lost, the mission had to be aborted. An accident left eight soldiers dead. The hostages remained in captivity. And the limits of American power seemed more obvious than ever.

CONCLUSION

As the 1970s ended, Shirley Chisholm was still deeply worried about her nation. The congresswoman feared that "there was a real crisis. . . in this country. . . . Government was being conducted by crisis." The mixture of economic decline with movements for rights and opportunity had proved too much to handle. To Chisholm, even the changes of the liberal 1960s seemed at risk. "Lots happened in the '60s," she noted sadly. "What's happening today? Every gain has been eroded."

As always, Chisholm refused to give in to pessimism. "I will continue to do what I'm doing—fighting, fighting, fighting," she vowed, "because I realize that this country is moving to the right." As the 1980s would reveal, Chisholm was correct. After the political uncertainty of the 1970s, the nation would finally deal with economic decline and the other challenges of the decade by embracing a new conservatism. The future lay to the right.

WHO, WHAT, WHERE

affirmative action   894

busing   894   *bus*

Camp David   910

Chávez, César   897

deindustrialization   886

deregulation   907

détente   889

energy crisis   884

Equal Rights Amendment   896

Kissinger, Henry   889

multinationals   885

My Lai   891

New Federalism   893

Nixon, Richard   889

Roe v. Wade   896   *abort legal*

Rustbelt   888   *doomed pop*

South Bronx   886   *stubble*

stagflation   883

Stonewall Inn   900   *gay bar*

Sunbelt   888   *boomed pop*

Three Mile Island   909

Watergate   903

Woodstock   901

REVIEW QUESTIONS

1. What were the chief causes of American economic decline in the 1970s?

2. What were the main concerns of the white ethnics?

3. What were the key foreign policies of the Nixon administration?

CRITICAL-THINKING QUESTIONS

1. Why did the demands of the African American civil rights movement become more controversial in the 1970s?

2. Did the upheavals of the 1970s strengthen or weaken democracy in America?

3. Analyze the troubled presidencies of Nixon, Ford, and Carter. Did these leaders create their own problems, or did they face impossible situations?

SUGGESTED READINGS

Bailey, Beth, and David Farber, eds. *America in the 1970s*. Lawrence: University Press of Kansas, 2003.

Borstelmann, Thomas. *The 1970s: A New Global History from Civil Rights to Inequality*. Princeton, NJ: Princeton University Press, 2012.

Cowie, Jefferson. *Stayin' Alive: The 1970s and the Last Days of the Working Class*. New York: The New Press, 2010.

For further review materials and resource information, please visit www.oup.com/us/ofthepeople

27.1 TESTIMONY OF GERALD DICKEY, MERGERS AND INDUSTRIAL CONCENTRATION; HEARINGS BEFORE THE SUBCOMMITTEE ON ANTITRUST AND MONOPOLY OF THE COMMITTEE ON THE JUDICIARY (1978)

Deindustrialization was a complex, long-term process. But it also had stark, immediate consequences. On "Black Monday," September 19, 1977, most of the workers at the Ohio steel mill Youngstown Sheet & Tube suddenly lost their jobs. Testifying before a subcommittee of the US Senate, Gerald Dickey, a rigger for the company and an official of the steelworkers' union, traced the closure to a corporate takeover allowed by the federal government nearly a decade earlier. According to Dickey, the new management's ignorance and greed ensured that Youngstown Sheet & Tube failed to modernize and thus compete with efficient foreign rivals.

Youngstown Sheet & Tube was founded in 1900 by Youngstown industrialists. During the twenties the company acquired the Brier Hill Steel Co. in Youngstown, and a steel company in East Chicago, Ind. They bought interest in coal and iron ore mines and some steel finishing mills. Company owners were interested in making and selling steel. They were very successful at it.

Youngstown is a "company town." Years ago, when people migrated to Youngstown, they lived in company houses and bought from the company store. Today the company houses and stores are gone. But recently I heard a top manager say that Youngstown Sheet & Tube controls 1 out of 5 jobs in the Mahoning Valley. So, I guess you could say Youngstown is still a company town.

The people who work at Youngstown Sheet & Tube are second- or third-generation steel workers. Their fathers and grandfathers retired after working all their lives in the mill. To an outsider, a steel mill may not seem like a great place to work. But to us, it means a decent and honorable living. Youngstown steelworkers have always taken pride in their work. They are recognized as the finest labor force in the steel industry.

In 1969 something happened which changed the course of history in Youngstown. A small New Orleans–based shipping company called Lykes Bros. took over Youngstown Sheet & Tube. Lykes had $376 million in assets, while Youngstown Sheet & Tube had $1.026 billion. Something was wrong. Workers knew instinctively that something was wrong. Around the mill the talk was that "Lykes is going to milk this company dry, and let it go." The workers' fears were confirmed when a top Lykes executive. . . said that he would not hesitate to make use of Youngstown Sheet & Tube's $100 million annual cash flow to move into other fields "if our views on the future of steel should change."

Deterioration was slow at first; but before we knew it, we were so far downhill the road back seemed insurmountable. Strange things began to happen. We often had no spare parts to replace worn equipment. Sometimes we had to remove pieces from other machinery just to keep higher priority machines running. I recall an incident when Lyke formed their own trucking company to bring manganese to our open hearth. They replaced a local hauler. After waiting around all day, our supervisors discovered they had only one truck. Our open hearths came close to a standstill from lack of manganese before the supervisor found another trucking outfit.

I remember when hundreds of tons of steel plates were shipped to Lykes for new ship building. We were told that Lykes was taking advantage of our steel company. . . .

Other incidents took place that made us question the actions of our corporate executives. We overheard lower level management complain of irregularities in their purchasing department. Often the company had to purchase parts and equipment from a Lykes subsidiary at a higher price than they had previously paid a local firm. That practice made the subsidiary look good at the expense of the steel operations.

. . . Evidently the corporate leadership from the shipping firm did not understand, or cared to learn, how to maintain and operate a steel mill. . . .

Lower level management could not even purchase spare parts mandatory for operation. When they could get parts and equipment, the price was too high from the supplier, a Lykes subsidiary.

The words of a 40-year veteran of the mill best describe what happened. He said: "It's a crime that the place was allowed to go down so fast without any preventative maintenance."

The end came on September 19, 1977. Lykes Corp. announced they were closing 75 percent of their steelmaking facilities in Youngstown. That was just after workers in the open hearth department set production records during the intense heat of July and August. The months of July and August are, by far, the worst times to be employed in the steel industry because of the intense heat and often unbearable conditions.

In spite of the handicaps, those workers broke records. I suppose it really did not matter, they did not stand a chance. You see, they were competing against themselves and their own past production performance. Their real competitors were the newer, modern mills. Our workers were making steel in mills built before World War I. No matter how talented and dedicated they were, they could not match the performance of basic oxygen furnaces or electric furnaces. We lacked the technology and we did not have control. Lykes had control. By deciding not to invest the capital when it was available, by deciding not to modernize, they doomed our mill, annihilated our jobs and brought havoc to our community.

I'd like to add a special note here. When the shutdown was announced, Lykes blamed part of the reason on foreign imports. Recently we made quite a startling discovery. . . . We learned that the same banks. . . were denying additional credit and at the same time were investing in the Japanese steel industry. That leads us to ask who is really calling the shots?

A crime was committed against the people of Youngstown. Nobody was arrested, indicted, or convicted, or will they ever be. This is a moral crime. There are no laws against it.

If I may, I would like to recommend to this subcommittee that you change the law. Presently, when the U.S. Government makes decisions on mergers between corporations, they decide on the basis of the antitrust laws. As I understand it, they look at competition within the industry to prevent monopoly. Something is missing. What about the workers? What about the communities?

I ask this subcommittee to consider legislation to require the U.S. Government to consider not only antitrust provisions, but also the impact on the workers and communities involved. Something like an "employment impact statement" would work. No merger should be allowed which would be detrimental to a community or the workers.

Source: Testimony of Gerald Dickey, *Mergers and Industrial Concentration. Hearings Before the Subcommittee on Antitrust and Monopoly of the Committee on the Judiciary. United States Senate. Ninety-Fifth Congress. Second Session on Acquisitions and Mergers by Conglomerates of Unrelated Businesses. May 12, July 27, 28, and September 21, 1978* (Washington, DC: US Government Printing Office, 1978), pp. 17–21.

27.2   NIXON DECIDES ON THE CHRISTMAS BOMBING (1972)

Thanks to the taping system he had installed in the Oval Office, Richard Nixon left an unequalled verbatim record of presidential decision making. These excerpts are from a meeting on December 14, 1972 in which Nixon, talking with National Security Advisor Henry Kissinger and Deputy National Security Advisor Alexander Haig Jr., made the controversial choice to intensify the bombing of North Vietnam. As a frustrated Kissinger reports, the North Vietnamese negotiators, representing their government in the city of Hanoi, had a "diabolical" way of avoiding an agreement to end the war. Note how concerned Nixon is about the state of public opinion in the United States, and his desire to avoid the bad publicity of an attack on Christmas. Despite his efforts, the raids, officially codenamed Linebacker II, became known as the Christmas bombings.

Kissinger: So, what they've done is quite diabolical. They've got the issue in a stage where, with one phone call to us, they can settle it in an hour. But they're always going to keep it just out of reach, and. . . . Now, [Secretary of Defense Melvin] Laird thinks we can just yield. We can't yield. . . .

Nixon: What is he suggesting? To yield?

Haig: Yeah. Oh, he called. I told you yesterday. He called me the night before and said, "We can't—we can't take military action. I'm going to send a memo over." Well, the memo got here yesterday morning and it just says we've got to settle. . . .

Nixon: What's new with him?

[laughter]. . .

Kissinger: There's the predominant possibility that there isn't enough pressure on them to make them settle. . . . I—that—what we are seeing now is their normal negotiating habit. They're shits, if I can use a—I mean, they are tawdry, miserable, filthy people. They make the Russians looks good.

Nixon: And the Russians make the Chinese look good, I know. . .

Nixon: All these assholes in the press said we were wrong. Now, at the present time, the press will say. . . ."Peace has escaped da-da-da-da-da," and they're going to be wrong again. . . . My point is, you've got to remember who the enemy are. The enemy has never changed. The election didn't change it. The only friends we've got, Henry, are a few people of rather moderate education out in this country, and thank God, they're about 61 percent of the people, who support us. The left-wingers, most of your friends, and most—and many of mine—

Kissinger: Some friends of mine—

Nixon: —are against us.

. . .

Kissinger: Well, we are now in this position: as of today, we are caught between Hanoi and Saigon, both of them facing us down in a position of total impotence, in which Hanoi is just stringing us along, and Saigon is just ignoring us. Hanoi—I do not see why Hanoi would want to settle three weeks from now when they didn't settle this week. I do not see what additional factors are going to operate. I'm making a cold-blooded analysis. . .

Now, I would recommend that we leave open the possibility of this settlement, if the other side meets the very minimum conditions that we have indicated. I would then recommend that we start bombing the bejeezus out of them within 48 hours of having put the negotiating record out. And I would then recommend that after about two weeks of that, we offer withdrawal for prisoners, about the time that the Congress comes back—

Nixon: Yeah. . . .

Kissinger: I think there's a 50–50 chance if we give them a tremendous wallop, particularly not the sort of shit the Air Force likes to do, if I may use this word—

Nixon: I went over this with them—

Kissinger: —but if we did—

Nixon: It is shit.

Kissinger: If we got all their power plants in one day, so that the civilian population would be without light, knocked out all the docks in Haiphong, so that even if the harbor is cleared, they can't unload there for months to come, then they would know it's. . . We'd have to do it with smart bombs.

Nixon: Well, can then we knock out docks, then, without knocking out the ships?. . .

Kissinger: I'd frankly take my chance on the ships. Your great asset, Mr. President—

Nixon: All right. Take a chance on the ships. All right—

Kissinger: —is your unpredictability—

Nixon: Look, I'm going to do it. . . . Do you think they want to settle?

Kissinger: Mr. President, they are—

Nixon: Do you think they're going to?

Haig: Yes, if they get a good kick in the ass.

Kissinger: They are scared out of their minds that you'll resume bombing. . . .

Nixon: Now, the other point is: what about the [B–]52s? Can't they get in there now?

Kissinger: Yes.

Nixon: Well goddamnit, let's get them in. What's wrong with getting the '52s in—?

Kissinger: Well, we've done—

Nixon: Are we afraid they're going to be shot down?

Kissinger: Well, no. We've got the problem, Mr. President, let's face it: the Chief—the Chairman of the Chiefs [Admiral Thomas Moorer] is a Navy lobbyist; he's not a military commander. . . The Chiefs only give a damn about budget categories. . . . They didn't give one goddamn about the national interest. . . .

Nixon: Well, that's the point. They've got to get it done right, for a change. We cannot make these military decisions and take all the heat, and have them screw it up again. . . .

Kissinger: Thieu's behavior has also been totally unforgivable, Mr. President—

Nixon: Terrible. Never said a goddamn word of thanks for what we've done standing by him, and the rest. . . . I am fed up with him, totally, right up to the [unclear]—

Kissinger: He's been incompetent as a war leader. . .

Nixon: I don't give a goddamn what he accepts. . . . Now, Laird will bitch about the cost of this.

Haig: Right.

Nixon: Now, what is it? Sure, it's a problem. How much is the cost of this?

Kissinger: It's pretty high.

Haig: It—

Nixon: Bombing?

Haig: The real scrub will be about $3 billion, if it had to go through 'til—to June. If it stops short of that, we're talking about 1.5.

Kissinger: I think, Mr. President—

Nixon: You think 1.5—?

Kissinger: —these guys—

Nixon: The Defense Department is going to have to swallow it, anyway. . . .

Nixon: I don't want anybody flying over Christmas Day. People would not understand that. There's always been a truce; World War I, World War II, and so forth. All right, the main thing is for you to get rested and get ready for all this and go out there and just remember that when it's toughest, that's when we're the best. And remember, we're going to be around and outlive our enemies. And also, never forget, the press is the enemy.

Kissinger: On that, there's no question—

Nixon: The press is the enemy. The press is the enemy. The establishment is the enemy. The professors are the enemy. Professors are the enemy. Write that on the blackboard 100 times and never forget it.

Kissinger: I, on the professors—

Nixon: Always—

Kissinger: —I need no instruction at all.

Nixon: Always—

Kissinger: And on the press, I'm in complete agreement with you—

Nixon: It's the enemy. . . Yes, there are still a few patriots, but most of them are—they're very disappointed because we beat 'em in the election. They know they're out of touch with the country. It kills those bastards. They are the enemy, and we're just gonna continue to use them, and never let them think that we think they're the enemy. You see my point? But the press is the enemy. The press is the enemy. That's all.

Kissinger: Mr. President, if you don't do this—

Nixon: [laughs]

Kissinger: —you'll be—

Nixon: I'll do it.

Kissinger: —then you'll really be impotent, and you'll be caught between the liberals and the conservatives. You won't win the liberals. And—and, besides, we'll be totally finished by February. They'll be just be chopping the salami.

Source: Office of the Historian. *Foreign Relations of the United States, 1969–1976*, vol. IX, Vietnam, October 1972–January 1973. Document 175. "Conversation Among President Nixon, the President's Assistant for National Security Affairs (Kissinger), and the President's Deputy Assistant for National Security Affairs (Haig)." National Archives, Nixon Presidential Materials, White House Tapes, Oval Office, Conversation 823-1. No classification marking.

27.3 NEW YORK RADICAL WOMEN, *PRINCIPLES* (1968) AND PAT MAXWELL, "HOMOSEXUALS IN THE MOVEMENT" (1970)

Two documents authored by groups from New York City testify to the rising demands for women's rights and gay rights toward the end of the 1960s. In different ways, the pioneering feminist group, New York Radical Women, and the equally pioneering members of the Gay Liberation Front, convey a common sense of oppression, identity, and pride.

NEW YORK RADICAL WOMEN, *PRINCIPLES* (1968)

We take the woman's side in everything.

We ask not if something is "reformist," "radical," "revolutionary," or "moral." We ask: is it good for women or bad for women?

We ask not if something is "political." We ask: is it effective? Does it get us closest to what we really want in the fastest way?

We define the best interests of women as the best interests of the poorest, most insulted, most despised, most abused woman on earth. Her lot, her suffering and abuse is the threat that men use against all of us to keep us in line. She is what all women fear being called, fear being treated as and yet what we all really are in the eyes of men. She is Everywoman: ugly, dumb (dumb broad, dumb cunt), bitch, nag, hag, whore, fucking and breeding machine, mother of us all. Until Everywoman is free, no woman will be free. When her beauty and knowledge is revealed and seen, the new day will be at hand.

We are critical of all past ideology, literature and philosophy, products as they are of male supremacist culture. We are re-examining even our words, language itself.

We take as our source the hitherto unrecognized culture of women, a culture which from long experience of oppression developed an intense appreciation for life, a sensitivity to unspoken thoughts and the complexity of simple things, a powerful knowledge of human needs and feelings.

We regard our feelings as our most important source of political understanding.

We see the key to our liberation in our collective wisdom and our collective strength.

"HOMOSEXUALS IN THE MOVEMENT" (1970)

Bernard: I see the Gay Liberation Movement as a process which will help liberate gay people by making them fully part of the whole liberation movement. The movement for change in the system that will eventually annihilate any form of oppression. Before GLF I was active in these movements, but anonymously—nobody was conscious of the fact that I was homosexual. I think, the only way we can gain respect for ourselves and any of the help that we need from everyone else in overcoming our oppression is by showing that we participate even though they don't understand why we participate. I think even among a lot of our own people we have to fight for the right to participate as homosexuals.

Bob: I've always been active as a homosexual. Openly, but never publicly. In the past six or seven months I have suddenly found myself living the life of a public homosexual. I find resentment in many parts of the movement. When I find it, I confront it. This is very healthy for me; and it's very healthy for the movement. We can't hold the movement up as being any better or any worse than the rest of us. Gay Liberation to me is seeing 35 or 40 homosexuals marching as homosexuals in a vigil to free political prisoners. We have been political prisoners, and we will be political prisoners. Homosexuals are beginning to see themselves as an oppressed minority. I don't think homosexuality is a magic tie that binds us all but in a sense there is something. It's being proud of ourselves. And I think that's what liberation will help us find—a pride that we can just stand up and be proud of ourselves as human beings.

Bernard: I want to bring up the past in one way. When I was among young people, we had no way of expressing this. I never felt sick, although the attitude then was that we were a sickness. I could only fight this when I talked to individuals. We had no public way of fighting it. And it's exciting to be able to do it now, and the fight must be a very conscious fight.

Bob: Kay, do you have anything to say. Say something, we'll have Women's Liberation after us if you don't.

Kay: I'm very new in GLF and I don't have a great deal to say to people who want to know what it is. I see half of the gay liberation as a sort of attempt to try to change other people outside of ourselves—to try to make them stop oppressing us. But the half that interests me most now, at the beginning of my gay liberation, is self-liberation. I was never open or public. I always felt that I had to be a secret homosexual, and I was terrified. Indeed I am now. This article is the first time I have ever come out in a public way, and I find that a great deal of the oppression is built into myself—is built into us. So I still expect when I come out, people are going to dislike me because I am homosexual. People do dislike homosexuals. On the other hand, I myself have disliked my own homosexuality, so perhaps it's not going to be as bad as I thought.

Bernard: Although I haven't been a public homosexual, among my friends, it was always known. What interests me now is that, although I was completely loved, for me, being a homosexual, I find that now that I'm getting active in GLF there's a resentment. People wonder why I have to work as a homosexual in the movement. Why can't I take it up wherever I am in the movement. I don't think you can take it up wherever you are in the movement. It's only possible when we are working as a homosexual to take it up. I think that we should—those of us who can—be public as well as open.

Bob: I've been in the Village a long time, and I'm well known. There's a lunch room restaurant owned by a homosexual—not an open or public homosexual—but open to homosexuals. Since I've been in GLF, when I've walked into the restaurant, he announces in a very loud voice, "Well, here comes the Gay Liberation Front." I felt, Wow!, and heads turned, There I stood: Capt. Dum Dum, the Gay Liberation Front. I said something like, "Right on!," and sat down and ate. Nothing happened. Nothing at all. Much of our own oppression is in our own minds.

Pat: Well, it seems that as homosexuals in the movement, we have realized that just backing other causes won't liberate us in our particular oppression. Now we have a strange situation setting up where we find oppression in and out of the movement. In terms of homosexuality, the awareness of that oppression isn't anywhere except as that awareness develops in us.

Sources: Robin Morgan, *The Word of a Woman: Feminist Dispatches, 1968–1992* (New York: Norton, 1992). Pat Maxwell, "Homosexuals in the Movement," *Come Out! A Liberation Forum for the Gay Community* 1, no. 3 (April/May 1970): 8–9.

27.4 STATEMENTS BY ROMAN PUCINSKI, ETHNIC HERITAGE STUDIES CENTERS; HEARINGS BEFORE THE GENERAL SUBCOMMITTEE ON EDUCATION OF THE COMMITTEE ON EDUCATION AND LABOR (1970)

In February 1970, a subcommittee of the House of Representatives held hearings over a bill to provide federal support for schoolchildren to learn about "cultural heritages of the major ethnic groups in the nation." In his remarks to witnesses, subcommittee chair Roman Pucinski, a Polish American Democrat from Chicago, revealed the pride and resentment that drove the "white ethnics," German, Irish, Polish, Italian, Greek, and Slavic Americans who took pride in the fact that their ethnic heritage set them apart from other Americans. For them, ethnicity meant a grounding in family, neighborhood, and religion. They rejected such ideas as the individualistic American dream, the new liberalism of the 1960s, and centralized government.

There is a growing sense of sameness permeating our existence—threatening to quiet the creative outpourings of the human soul and the gentle sensitivity of one man to the uniqueness and humanity of another.

Clearly, this sustained melancholia has touched all our lives. Perhaps most seriously afflicted by the deteriorating quality of human life are the young. The Nation's youth are engrossed in a restless, sometimes tumultuous, and often threatening search for identity. Our young people want to know who they are, where they belong, how they can remain distinctive: special individuals amidst the pervasive pressure for conformity.

The basic problem in this country is that we have tried to deny our ethnicity. . . We have engaged in a noble experiment of trying to put 200 million human beings into a melting pot, and trying to make them something that they are not. We have never really tried to tell the American people anything about themselves. I am aware of the influence of the predominant white Anglo-Saxon Protestant ethos that has somewhat been imposed upon every person in this country, whether he wants it or not. . . .

You can go through this whole country and it is amazing how little material you can find about the Italian community, Americans of Italian descent; and, as you know, no group in this country has suffered a greater injustice in terms of outright distortion. You can go into the hustings of America and it is abominable what impressions the people have of an American citizen who happens, by circumstance or happenstance to have an Italian name, simply because of the films that they have seen or late movies on the TV that they have seen, or the kind of press they have seen.

. . . It is an interesting thing now. The Soviet Union is a nation of many states, many nationalities. They have the Georgians and various others, and interestingly enough, in the Soviet Union they encourage the cultural identity of each of these groups. But then, of course, they bring them into their single political structure or governmental structure or whatever you want to call it. They, as a matter of fact, encourage friendly competition among the various ethnic groups of the Soviet Union. This has brought about better understanding, friendly relationships among the various ethnic groups. . . .

We, on the other hand, in this country try to sweep them under the rug and deny it. And I think that a lot of these latent hostilities that we see in people generally, sometimes we think only in terms of problems between the races in America. I think that you have brought up a good point when you talked about the executive suite being closed to all but the chosen few in this country. I think this is a subject that is going to become more and more discussed in America.

Why is it that you can walk through some of the big corporations of this country and you look over the corporate structure and you find a predominance of one category of people? I don't mind telling you I have dinner very often with executives and presidents of the corporations, and they look at my name and they say, "Why, you have a Polish background."

I say, "Yes, I do." They say, "They are hard workers, they are the best workers we have in our plants."

I say, "I am very grateful to you for that, but how many of them are executives?" Then they kind of blush 14 different shades of red and they say, "I don't think we have any."

I say, "Why? If they are good workers, how come?"

Source: Statements by Roman Pucinski, *Ethnic Heritage Studies Centers. Hearings Before the General Subcommittee on Education of the Committee on Education and Labor. House of Representatives. Ninety-First Congress. Second Session on H.R. 14910. Hearings Held in Washington, D.C., February 1, 17, 18, 24, 26; March 4, 5, 19; and May 6, 1970* (Washington, DC: US Government Printing Office, 1970), pp. 1 and 256–259.

27.5   CLYDE WARRIOR, "STATEMENT" (1967)

Clyde Warrior, born in Oklahoma in 1938, was a member of the Ponca tribe who helped found the National Indian Youth Council in 1961. Testifying before a presidential commission in 1967, he linked Native American poverty to the continuing denial of freedom to indigenous people.

Most members of the National Indian Youth Council can remember when we were children and spent many hours at the feet of our grandfathers listening to stories of the time when Indians were a great people, when we were free, when we were rich, when we lived the good life. At the same time we heard stories of droughts, famines, and pestilence. It was only recently that we realized that there was surely great material deprivation in those days, but that our old people felt rich because they were free. They were rich in things of the spirit, but if there is one thing that characterizes Indian life today it is poverty of the spirit. We still have human passions and depth of feeling (which may be something rare in these days), but we are poor in spirit because we are not free—free in the most basic sense of the word. We are not allowed to make those basic human choices and decisions about our personal life and about the destiny of our communities which is the mark of free mature people. We sit on our front porches or in our yards, and the world and our lives in it pass us by without our desires or aspirations having any effect.

We are not free. We do not make choices. Our choices are made for us; we are the poor. For those of us who live on reservations these choices and decisions are made by federal administrators, bureaucrats, and their "yes men," euphemistically called tribal governments. Those of us who live in nonreservation areas have our lives controlled by local white power elites. We have many rulers. They are called social workers, "cops," schoolteachers, churches, etc., and now OEO [federal Office of Economic Opportunity] employees. They call us into meetings to tell us what is good for us and how they've programmed us, or they come into our homes to instruct us and their manners are not always what one would call polite by Indian standards or perhaps by any standards. We are rarely accorded respect as fellow human beings. Our children come home from school to us with shame in their hearts and a sneer on their lips for their home and parents. We are the "poverty problem" and that is true; and perhaps it is also true that our lack of reasonable choices, our lack of freedoms, and our poverty of the spirit is not unconnected with our material poverty.

. . . We know that no one is arguing that the dispossessed, the poor, be given any control over their own destiny. The local white power elites who protest the loudest against federal control are the very ones who would keep us poor in spirit and worldly goods in order to enhance their own personal and economic station in the world.

Nor have those of us on reservations fared any better under the paternalistic control of federal administrations. In fact, we shudder at the specter of what seems to be the forming alliances in Indian areas between federal administrations and local elites. . . .

We are told in the not-so-subtle racist vocabulary of the modern middle class that our children are "deprived." Exactly what they are deprived of seems to be unstated. We give our children love, warmth and respect in our homes and the qualities necessary to be a warm human being. Perhaps many of them get into trouble in their teens because we have given them too much warmth, love, passion, and respect. Perhaps they have a hard time reconciling themselves to being a number on an IBM card. Nevertheless, many educators and politicians seem to assume that we, the poor, the Indians, are not capable of handling our own affairs and even raising our own children and that state institutions must do the job for us and take them away from us as soon as they can. My grandmother said last week, "Train your child well now for soon she will belong to her teacher and the schools."

Fifty years ago the federal government came into our communities and by force carried most of our children away to distant boarding schools. My father and many of my generation lived their childhoods in an almost prison-like atmosphere. Many returned unable even to speak their own language. Some returned to become drunks. Most of them had become white haters or that most pathetic of all modern Indians—Indian haters. Very few ever became more than very confused, ambivalent and immobilized individuals—never able to reconcile the tensions and contradictions built inside themselves by outside institutions. As you can imagine, we have little faith in such kinds of federal programs devised for our betterment nor do we see education as a panacea for all ills. In recent days, however, some of us have been thinking that perhaps the damage done to our communities by forced assimilation and directed acculturative programs was minor compared to the situation in which our children now find themselves. There is a whole generation of Indian children who are growing up in the American school system. They still look to their relatives, my generation, and my father's to see if they are worthy people. But their judgement and definition of what is worthy is now the judgement most Americans make. They judge worthiness as competence and competence as worthiness. And I am afraid me and my fathers do not fare well in the light of this situation and that they individually are not worthy. Even if by some stroke of good fortune prosperity was handed to us "on a platter" that still would not soften the negative judgement our youngsters have of their people and themselves. As you know, people who feel themselves to be unworthy and feel they cannot escape this unworthiness turn to drink and crime and self-destructive acts. Unless there is some way that we as Indian individuals and communities can prove ourselves competent and worthy in the eyes of our youngsters there will be a generation of Indians grow to adulthood whose reaction to their situation will make previous social ills seem like a Sunday School picnic.

For the sake of our children, for the sake of the spiritual and material well-being of our total community we must be able to demonstrate competence to ourselves. For the sake of our psychic stability as well as our physical well-being we must be free men and exercise free choices. We must make decisions about our own destinies. We must be able to learn and profit from our own mistakes. Only then can we become competent and prosperous communities. We must be free in the most literal sense of the word—not sold or coerced into accepting programs for our own good, not of our own making or choice. . . . Community development must be just what the word implies, Community Development. It cannot be packaged programs wheeled into Indian communities by outsiders which Indians can "buy" or once again brand themselves as unprogressive if they do not "cooperate." Even the best of outside programs suffer from one very large defect—if the program falters helpful outsiders too often step in to smooth over the rough spots. At that point any program ceases to belong to the people involved and ceases to be a learning experience for them. Programs must be Indian experiences because only then will Indians understand why a program failed and not blame themselves for some personal inadequacy. A better program built upon the failure of an old program is the path of progress. But to achieve this experience, competence, worthiness, sense of achievement and the resultant material prosperity Indians must have the responsibility in the ultimate sense of the word. Indians must be free in the sense that other more prosperous Americans are free. Freedom and prosperity are different sides of the same coin and there can be no freedom without complete responsibility. And I do not mean the fictional responsibility and democracy of passive consumers of programs; programs which emanate from and whose responsibility for success rests in the hands of outsiders—be they federal administrators or local white elitist groups. . . .

America cannot afford to have whole areas and communities of people in such dire social and economic circumstances. Not only for her economic well-being but for her moral well-being as well. America has given a great social and moral message to the world and demonstrated (perhaps not forcefully enough) that freedom and responsibility as an ethic is inseparable from and, in fact, the "cause" of the fabulous American standard of living. America has not however been diligent enough in promulgating this philosophy within her own borders. American Indians need to be given this freedom and responsibility which most Americans assume as their birth right. Only then will poverty and powerlessness cease to hang like the sword of Damocles over our heads stifling us. Only then can we enjoy the fruits of the American system and become participating citizens—Indian Americans rather than American Indians.

Perhaps, the National Indian Youth Council's real criticism is against a structure created by bureaucratic administrators who are caught in this American myth that all people assimilate into American society, that economics dictates assimilation and integration. From the experience of the National Indian Youth Council, and in reality, we cannot emphasize and recommend strongly enough the fact that no one integrates and disappears into American society. What ethnic groups do is not integrate into American society and economy individually, but enter into the mainstream of American society as a people, and in particular as communities of people. The solution to Indian poverty is not "government programs" but in the competence of the person and his people. The real solution to poverty is encouraging the competence of the community as a whole.

Source: "Statement of Clyde Warrior," *Hearings Before the National Advisory Commission on Rural Poverty, Memphis Tennessee, February 2 and 3, 1967*, pp. 144–52.

The Triumph of Conservatism

1980–1991

< Striking air-traffic controllers, 1981

Linda Chavez

"**O**n Election Day 1980," Linda Chavez re-called, "I did something I had never imagined I could do: I voted for a Republican for president." A lifelong Democrat, she rejected her party's nominee, incumbent Jimmy Carter, and pulled the lever instead for the conservative **Ronald Reagan**. Chavez admitted that she made "an unlikely conservative." The daughter of an Anglo mother and a Mexican American father, Chavez had grown up in the Mexican American neighborhoods of Albuquerque and Denver. Her father, like most Mexican Americans, was a Democrat. Chavez herself was drawn to the party and its causes. As a girl in the early 1960s, she joined the civil rights organization CORE and demonstrated against racial discrimination. Chavez then worked for the Democratic National Committee, a liberal Democratic congressman, two liberal teachers unions, and the Carter administration.

Despite her partisan commitments, Chavez had been changing. As a student at the University of Colorado at Boulder in the late 1960s, Chavez discovered that she did not have to settle for her parents' working-class world. "For the first time," she said, "I realized that I could control my own destiny." Chavez also felt that the university's affirmative action programs shortchanged Mexican Americans by admitting unqualified students, allowing them to founder, teaching them to blame their problems on racism, and then leaving them to drop out.

Those realizations helped Chavez develop a new political outlook in the 1970s. She believed that individuals should take responsibility for their lives. She also rejected affirmative action programs, race-based hiring quotas, busing, and bilingual education as misguided liberal attempts to create equality.

Meanwhile, her stint in the Carter administration left her skeptical about another liberal article of faith. "The federal government was not at all what I expected," Chavez confessed. "Nothing—and almost no one—worked." She was troubled, too, that Carter and the Democrats did not support anti-Communism and a strong defense.

In some ways, Chavez felt that she was not the one who had changed. It was her party that had changed by adopting controversial solutions to racial and gender inequality and by abandoning its pledge to contain Communism. In 1976, Chavez stayed home rather than vote for Carter. By 1980, she was ready to vote for Reagan, another longtime Democrat who felt his party had changed.

Linda Chavez was an unusual figure: there were hardly any prominent Mexican American conservatives, male or female. But her change from liberal Democrat to conservative Republican typified a basic shift in the 1980s. Still dealing with economic and political decline, a new majority of Americans, including businesspeople, evangelical Christians, and "Reagan Democrats" like Chavez, adopted a conservative vision of the country. Rejecting the pessimism of the 1970s, they wanted to believe that individual and national success was still possible. The new conservative majority was open to materialism and to a government that left people free to succeed or fail.

The trend toward conservatism had many consequences. Eager to restore old values, Reagan cut taxes, reduced government regulation, and diminished union power to restore economic growth. The president also embraced a conservative social agenda, including attacks on affirmative action and abortion. His foreign policy was dedicated to confronting Communism. Despite scandals, setbacks, and compromises, Reagan and the new conservatism arrested fears of decline and altered America's politics and culture for a generation.

CREATING A CONSERVATIVE MAJORITY

In the 1970s and 1980s, the conservative movement continued its rise to power. The New Right drew strength from the transformation of the economy, the changing reputation of big business, and the growth of evangelical Christianity. Conservative power became clear in the 1980 presidential election, when voters sent Ronald Reagan to the White House.

The New Economy

Conservatism benefited from the emergence of a **postindustrial**, computer-centered economy. As deindustrialization continued, technological change pointed the way to national economic revival. Along with other innovations, semiconductors—transistorized integrated circuits attached to small silicon crystals—allowed manufacturers to shrink the computer. By the late 1970s, they could put the power of a room-sized mainframe computer into a box that fit on a desktop. In 1981, IBM introduced its first personal computer, or PC. By the end of the 1980s, Americans were buying 7 million PCs a year (see Figure 28–1).

Computers seemed a way out of national economic decline. The microcomputer bolstered older companies such as IBM and created new firms such as Apple and Dell; it enriched new entrepreneurs such as Steve Jobs, a founder of Apple, and Bill Gates, a founder of Microsoft. Asian manufacturers built most consumer-electronics products, but American companies dominated computer hardware and software.

The growth of the computer industry inspired utopian dreams of a high-technology society built on the production of knowledge rather than things. Promoting literacy and education, the computer would lift up the poor and disadvantaged. Unlike the old industrial economy, a computerized economy would cut pollution and the consumption of raw materials. Enabling people to work at home, the microcomputer would eliminate commuting and relieve urban congestion.

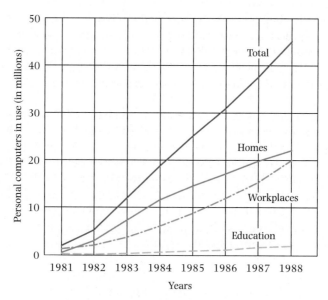

Figure 28–1   The Rise of the Personal Computer The rapid rise in the number of microcomputers in use in homes, workplaces, and schools in the 1980s inspired hopes that the nation's economic decline had ended.
Source: Statistical Abstract of the United States, 1989 (Washington, DC: US Bureau of the Census, 1990), p. 743; *Statistical Abstract, 1993* (Washington, DC: US Bureau of the Census, 1994), p. 761.

The promise of the computer-driven economy helped conservatism. New industries, new companies, and new jobs seemed to confirm conservatives' faith in capitalist free enterprise, unaided by government. The new economy also benefited conservatism by stimulating the flow of people, jobs, and political power from the North and East to the South and West. Computing did revive parts of the Rustbelt. In Massachusetts, computer companies sprang up around Boston along Route 128 to replace long-gone textile mills and shoe factories. But computing most benefited the Sunbelt, birthplace of the new conservatism in the 1950s and 1960s. Dell's headquarters were in Texas. Apple was one of many computer firms clustered in the area called Silicon Valley, outside San Francisco. Rustbelt cities such as Pittsburgh and Detroit lost population, while some Sunbelt counties more than doubled in population. These regional shifts had direct political effects. Reapportionment in 1980 gave more congressional seats and electoral votes to the more conservative states of the Sunbelt.

The Rehabilitation of Business

While the 1980s pointed to a utopian future, the decade also recalled the cutthroat capitalism of the turn of the twentieth century. A wave of corporate takeovers and mergers swept the economy. Aggressive investment bankers and entrepreneurs such as Michael Milken and **Ivan Boesky** used **junk bonds**—high-risk, high-paying securities—and other techniques to finance takeovers. Executives took golden parachutes, huge payments for selling their companies and losing their jobs. Enormous deals merged some of the largest American corporations. In 1985, General Electric bought RCA for $6 billion. In 1986 alone, there were more than 4,000 mergers worth a total of $190 billion. The biggest deal came in 1988 when RJR Nabisco was sold for $25 billion, and the company's president and CEO received a $53 million golden parachute.

The takeover wave and the growth of the computer industry helped rehabilitate business and its values, under attack in the 1960s and 1970s. Although some observers criticized the concentration of so much economic power, others saw the takeovers as a sign of economic vitality. They argued that the mergers created larger, more efficient, more competitive companies, and they praised takeover artists as models of energy and creativity. The media enthusiastically reported on Milken, Boesky, Jobs, and Gates. *Dallas, Dynasty*, and other popular television shows celebrated the fictional sagas of wealthy, freewheeling families. Business was more respectable than at any time since the 1950s.

So were materialism and the pursuit and enjoyment of wealth. "Everybody should be a little greedy," Boesky advised. "Thank goodness it's back," gushed the *New York Times*, "that lovely whipped cream of a word—luxury."

The baby boom generation reflected the new appeal of business. Former 1960s radicals such as Yippie (Youth Independent Party) leader Jerry Rubin took up business careers. By 1983, the media were talking about the emergence of yuppies, young urban professionals in their 20s and 30s. Uninterested in social reform, these optimistic, self-centered baby boomers were supposedly eager to make lots of money and then spend it on BMW cars, Perrier water, and other playthings. Although the transition from Yippies to yuppies was exaggerated, the yuppie stereotype underscored American aspirations to a more conservative, money-centered way of life.

The Rise of the Religious Right

As American culture celebrated materialism, many Americans still turned to spirituality to find meaning in their lives. Their choice of denominations reflected the trend to conservatism. Such mainline Protestant denominations as the United Methodist Church, the Episcopal Church, and the Presbyterian Church, USA, had been losing their share of church members since at least 1940. Meanwhile, evangelical churches boomed (see Map 28–1). By the 1980s, the Southern Baptist Convention was the largest American Protestant denomination. Such smaller evangelical bodies as the Assemblies of God more than doubled in size from the 1960s to the 1980s.

This changing denominational balance had social and political consequences. The mainline churches often took moderate or liberal positions on such issues as civil rights and abortion, but the evangelical churches more often supported conservative positions. Troubled by social change and emboldened by their own growth, **evangelicals** wanted to spread a conservative message across American culture and politics.

The emergence of "televangelists" was the most obvious result of this impulse. From 1978 to 1989, the number of Christian television ministries grew from 25 to 336. The most successful televangelists also had their own networks, colleges, political groups, and even an amusement park. Pat Robertson, a born-again Baptist from Virginia, hosted *The 700 Club* and ran the Christian Broadcast Network.

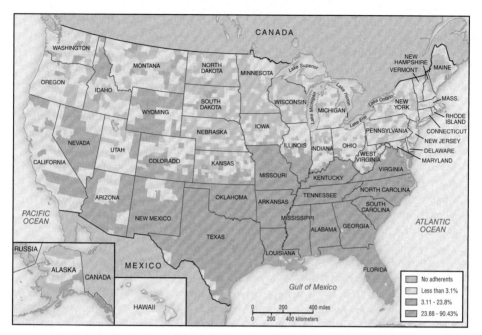

Map 28-1   The Growth of Evangelical Christianity The Southern Baptist Convention's share of the population, by county, reveals a gradual spread beyond its traditional base in the South by 1990.
Source: Peter L. Halvorson and William M. Newman, *Atlas of Religious Change in America, 1952–1990* (Cincinnati, OH: Glenmary Research Center, 1994), p. 120.

Jerry Falwell, a fundamentalist who believed in the literal interpretation of the Bible, hosted the *Old Time Gospel Hour* and founded Liberty Baptist College in Virginia. He also organized the Moral Majority, a political pressure group. Deeply conservative, the televangelists condemned women's liberation, abortion, gay rights, and liberal Great Society programs. They wanted prayer in public schools. Earning millions of dollars, they praised low taxes, limited government, and financial success. Determined to win what Falwell called the "war against sin," the televangelists were the spearheads of a **religious right** ready for politics.

The 1980 Presidential Election

The new conservative majority came together in the presidential election of 1980. Former California governor Ronald Reagan continued his political rise by winning the Republican nomination. Although he chose a moderate running mate, George H. W. Bush of Texas, Reagan ran a conservative campaign. His vision of less government, lower taxes, renewed military might, and traditional social values appealed to business and evangelicals. His genial optimism suggested that the political system could be made to work. As a former Democrat, Reagan reassured Democrats and independents that they too could find a home in the Republican Party.

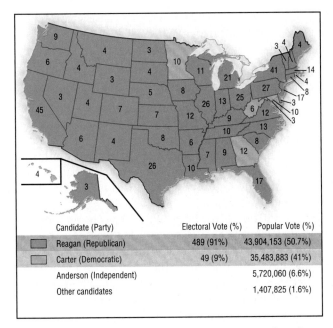

Candidate (Party)	Electoral Vote (%)	Popular Vote (%)
Reagan (Republican)	489 (91%)	43,904,153 (50.7%)
Carter (Democratic)	49 (9%)	35,483,883 (41%)
Anderson (Independent)		5,720,060 (6.6%)
Other candidates		1,407,825 (1.6%)

Map 28–2   The Presidential Election, 1980 As in other elections, a narrow victory in the popular vote translated into a landslide in the electoral college.

Meanwhile, the Democratic nominee, incumbent president Jimmy Carter, struggled with a weak economy and the ongoing hostage crisis in Iran. His moderate, sometimes conservative policies had alienated liberal Democrats. His poor economic record had alienated the party's white ethnics. Moderate Republican congressman John Anderson of Illinois, who ran as an independent, drew voters away from Carter. Meanwhile, Reagan focused relentlessly on America's decline during Carter's presidency. In the last presidential debate before Election Day, Reagan told the audience, "I think. . . it might be well if you would ask yourself, are you better off than you were four years ago?"

Americans answered that question by giving Reagan the presidency. Reagan carried all but four states and the District of Columbia (see Map 28–2). He managed only 50.7 percent of the popular vote, but with Anderson's 6.6 percent, the tally suggested the extent of popular disaffection with Carter and the Democratic Party. The Democrats held on to the House of Representatives, but Republicans won the Senate for the first time since 1962. Sixteen years after the defeat of Barry Goldwater's conservative candidacy, the nation had turned sharply to the right.

THE REAGAN REVOLUTION AT HOME

Ronald Reagan shaped American life more decisively than any president since Franklin Roosevelt. Reagan's folksy optimism made him popular, but the Reagan years were more than a triumph of style. With some justice, his supporters believed that his "Reagan Revolution" spurred a sweeping conservative transformation of American economic and political life.

The Reagan Style

The Reagan Revolution was partly a matter of style. Despite the frustrations of the 1960s and 1970s, Reagan exuded optimism. Rather than ask Americans to live with less, he embraced luxury. Reagan's presidency signaled a confident, even opulent, new era. On Inauguration Day, as if to mark the end of the frustrating 1970s, the Iranian government finally released its American hostages. In his inaugural address, Reagan firmly rejected pessimism. "We are not," the new president declared, "doomed to an inevitable decline." The Reagan inaugural cost five times more than Jimmy Carter's had four years earlier.

Even while Ronald and Nancy Reagan lived lavishly in the White House, the president retained a popular, common touch. After his career in movies and television, he knew how to speak simply and effectively to the American people. He became known as the "Great Communicator."

Reagan also appeared to enjoy and master his job. Although he took office as America's oldest president at the age of 69, he projected vigor and energy. After the troubled presidencies of the 1970s, Reagan made the presidency—and democracy—seem workable again.

The president even managed to survive an assassination attempt. On March 30, 1981, John W. Hinckley, a troubled loner, shot and wounded Reagan, his press secretary, and a policeman. Reagan's chest wound was more serious than his spokesmen admitted, but he met the situation with good humor. "Honey," he told his wife, "I forgot to duck." The president's popularity soared.

Shrinking Government

Reagan offered a clear alternative to the New Deal and the Great Society. Above all, he denied that a large, activist federal government could deal with the challenges of American life in the 1980s. So Reagan vowed to reduce the government's size and power.

The president's efforts to shrink the federal government met with mixed success. In his 1982 State of the Union address, Reagan, like previous Republican president Richard Nixon, endorsed the New Federalism, a plan to transfer federal programs and tax revenues to the states. Reagan insisted the New Federalism would promote efficiency and economic growth, but governors worried that their states would be saddled with expensive responsibilities. In the end, only a few programs were transferred.

Congress also rebuffed administration plans to save money with tighter qualifications for government benefits and with a line-item veto permitting the president to reject specific spending programs.

Reagan had more success when he attacked social welfare programs. Like other conservatives, Reagan condemned antipoverty programs as a waste of federal resources that sapped the work ethic and the morals of the poor. He wanted reductions in food stamps, school meal programs, and aid to cities. In response, Congress cut funding for urban public housing and ended job training for the unemployed.

Reagan found it nearly impossible to touch Medicare and Social Security, two expensive and popular programs that benefited most Americans. By the 1980s, there was concern that workers' Social Security payments would eventually not be enough to cover the cost of benefits to retirees. After a long struggle, Congress produced the Social Security Reform Act of 1983, which raised the minimum age for full benefits from 65 to 67 and taxed some benefits. The measure did little to reduce program costs. By 1984, Reagan promised not to cut Social Security.

Although expenditures for welfare programs continued to rise, the Reagan administration managed to slow the growth of such spending. Benefits did not expand dramatically; there were no costly new programs. Reagan did not reduce the federal government overall, but he did shrink the relative size of some parts of it that he disliked.

Reaganomics

For Reagan and his followers, shrinking the government also meant decreasing Washington's role in the economy. As conservatives, they argued that the nation prospered most when Americans were left free to manage their own businesses and keep their own earnings. The Reagan administration worked to lower taxes, deregulate business, and cut federal support for unions.

Reaganomics drew on a new theory known as supply-side economics. In the 1970s, economist Arthur Laffer had offered an alternative to the liberal, Keynesian economics that had guided federal policy since the New Deal. While Keynesians believed that increased consumer demand would spur economic growth, Laffer contended that an increased supply of goods and services was the key to growth. He rejected the Keynesian idea that more government spending put more money in the hands of consumers. To promote prosperity, he believed government should cut, rather than raise, taxes. Leaving more money in the hands of businesses would allow them to produce more goods and services. The increase in supply would stimulate prosperity and increase, rather than decrease, tax revenues.

Supply-side economics was controversial. Liberal critics called it an excuse to let the rich keep more of their money. Even some Republicans doubted that a tax cut would produce more tax revenues. But the supply-side approach fit neatly with conservative dislike for high taxes and big government.

Following supply-side principles, Reagan asked Congress in 1981 to cut taxes dramatically. Impressed by Reagan's popularity and the electorate's conservatism, the Democratic-controlled House joined the Republican-dominated Senate to pass the Economic Recovery Act of 1981 (the Kemp-Roth Bill). An important victory for Reagan, it cut federal income taxes 5 percent the first year and 10 percent in each of the next two years. It benefited the wealthy by making the tax structure less progressive and by reducing the tax rates on the highest incomes and on large gifts and estates.

Like other conservatives, Reagan believed that federal regulations hamstrung American business and prevented economic growth. Accordingly, his administration stepped up the campaign for deregulation begun by Jimmy Carter. The budgets of such key regulatory agencies as the Environmental Protection Agency and the Occupational Safety and Health Administration were cut. The administration also made sure that officials did not strictly enforce regulatory rules and laws. In addition, the administration deregulated the telephone industry. In 1982, the giant American Telephone and Telegraph Company was broken into smaller regional companies, and new firms such as Sprint and MCI were allowed to compete for AT&T's long-distance business.

Reagan moved to lift environmental restrictions on business. His administration made it easier for timber and mining companies to exploit wilderness areas and for oil companies to drill off the Pacific coast. It also opposed environmentalists' demands for laws to protect against acid rain—industrial air pollution that harmed lakes, forests, and crops. As well, administration members dismissed the importance of the "Ozone Hole," the depletion of the gas that protects life on earth from solar radiation. Reaganomics also weakened organized labor, already suffering from deindustrialization. Ironically, Reagan, once the head of the Screen Actors Guild, was the first former union official to serve as president. Like most conservatives, Reagan believed that unions obstructed business and limited workers' freedom. He believed the federal government had done too much for organized labor since the New Deal.

Reagan took a strong antiunion stance during a strike by the Professional Air Traffic Controllers Organization (PATCO) in 1981. Despite a law banning strikes by federal workers, PATCO walked out to protest unsafe conditions in the air traffic control system. Reagan fired the striking controllers, refused to hire them back, and replaced them with nonunion workers. His action encouraged business to take a hard line with employees. By the end of the 1980s, unions were weaker than at any time since the Great Depression.

Reaganomics did not quite have the effect its supporters anticipated. Reagan's measures did not prevent a sharp recession, which began in the fall of 1981. As the Federal Reserve Bank fought inflation by raising interest rates, the economy slowed and unemployment increased. Reaganomics also increased the federal budget deficit. The supply-side theory that tax cuts would boost tax revenues and balance the budget proved incorrect.

By the spring of 1984, the recession had ended. Thanks largely to the Federal Reserve's monetary policy, "stagflation," the combination of stagnant economic growth and high inflation, was over. As employment increased, Reagan's supporters gave the president credit. His critics charged that the deficit, not Reaganomics, had produced the boom and that the deficit would ultimately hurt the economy. In the mid-1980s, however, Reaganomics seemed to be a success.

The 1984 Presidential Election

The changing impact of Reaganomics affected national politics. In the depths of the recession, the Republicans lost 26 House seats in the midterm elections of 1982. But with the return of prosperity, the president was easily renominated in 1984. Reagan ran against a liberal Democratic nominee, former vice president Walter Mondale of Minnesota. Against a popular incumbent, Mondale made bold moves. He chose the first female vice-presidential nominee of a major party, Representative Geraldine Ferraro of New York. To prove his honesty and openness, Mondale made the politically foolish announcement that he would raise taxes as president. The Democrat was also saddled with the record of the Carter administration and the alienation of white working- and middle-class Democrats.

Reagan ran an optimistic campaign emphasizing national renewal. "It's morning again in America," Reagan commercials announced. "And people have a sense of pride they never felt they'd feel again." Mondale would jeopardize all that, the Reagan campaign charged, with tax increases and favors to such "special interests" as labor unions, feminists, and civil rights groups.

Election Day revealed both the strength and the weakness of the Reagan Revolution. With his conservative message Reagan won 58.8 percent of the popular vote and lost only the District of Columbia and Mondale's home state of Minnesota. But his personal triumph did not translate into one for his party. Holding on to the Senate, the Republicans lost control of the House of Representatives.

THE REAGAN REVOLUTION ABROAD

Reagan's foreign policy, like his domestic policy, rested on old conservative values. The president rejected the main diplomatic approaches of the 1970s—Nixon's détente with the Soviet Union and Carter's support for international human rights. Instead, the Reagan Revolution revived the strident anti-Communism of the 1940s and 1950s. The president moved to restore the nation's military and economic power to challenge the Soviet Union and stop Communism in the Western Hemisphere. Communism, however, had little to do with such difficult international issues as conflict in the Middle East, terrorism, and global economic competition. Nevertheless, the Reagan Revolution refocused American policy on the Cold War confrontation with Communism.

Restoring American Power

After losing the Vietnam War, the United States had reduced both its armed forces and its willingness to risk military confrontations abroad. Reagan set out to restore American power in the 1980s—and the will to use it.

Like most conservatives, the president did not believe that cutting government spending meant cutting the armed forces. Under Reagan, defense spending more than doubled, from $134 billion in 1980 to more than $300 billion by 1989. Reagan also ordered development of controversial weapons systems. Construction of the B-1 strategic bomber, stopped by Carter, resumed, while development of the B-2 Stealth bomber began. Reagan won congressional approval for the MX Peacekeeper, a nuclear missile with multiple warheads, and for work on the neutron bomb, a nuclear weapon. As he built up the military, Reagan faced a growing mass movement against nuclear weapons. In Europe and the United States, millions of people, frightened by nuclear war, called for a halt to new nuclear arms. In June 1982, a crowd of 700,000 in New York's Central Park demanded a nuclear freeze. The National Conference of Catholic Bishops supported the freeze and declared nuclear war immoral. But Reagan rejected the movement as naive and Communist-infiltrated. Peace, he believed, depended on developing more weapons.

The military buildup was also a matter of changing attitudes. In the wake of the Vietnam War, many Americans were reluctant to endorse intervention abroad. They feared becoming entrapped in another costly, losing, possibly immoral battle. This "Vietnam syndrome" threatened Reagan's foreign policy. The president could

"Don't Tread on Me" Striking members of the Professional Air Traffic Controllers Organization march outside John F. Kennedy Airport in New York. The strikers invoked the Revolutionary War flag's motto "Don't Tread on Me," but President Reagan had them all fired.

not afford to let other countries think he would not back up his words with action. Accordingly, Reagan used his speeches to stir up patriotic emotion and to persuade Americans that the Vietnam War had been "a just cause" worth supporting.

By the mid-1980s, Reagan had restored much of America's military power. It remained to be seen, however, whether Americans were willing to use that power abroad.

Confronting the "Evil Empire"

The main purpose of the buildup was to contain the Soviet Union. Suspicion of the Soviets and their Communist ideology was the heart of Reagan's diplomacy. In the early 1980s, Reagan called the USSR the "evil empire" and insisted that failing economies and unpopular regimes doomed the Soviets and their Communist allies. Communism, he predicted, would end up "on the ash heap of history."

Reagan avoided cooperation with the Soviet Union and held no summit meetings during his first term. His administration openly supported the *mujahedeen*, the Afghan rebels who were resisting the Soviets. More important, he avoided arms-control agreements with the Soviets during his first term. Instead, he used the military buildup to pressure the USSR. Reagan refused to submit the second Strategic Arms Limitation Treaty, signed by Jimmy Carter, to the Senate for ratification. In response to the United States' deployment of new nuclear missiles in Western Europe, the Soviets walked out of arms-control talks in 1983.

That year, Reagan put even more pressure on the USSR by announcing plans for the Strategic Defense Initiative (SDI), a space-based defense system of lasers and other advanced technology designed to shoot down enemy missiles. Funded by Congress, SDI was such a long way from reality that critics, sure it was science fiction, called the plan "Star Wars," after the epic space movie.

SDI doubly threatened the Soviets. It seemingly made the USSR vulnerable to attack. Since the 1950s, the Americans and the Soviets had relied on the theory of mutual assured destruction as a deterrent to war: because a nuclear war would destroy both sides, there was no incentive for either to start one. Now SDI raised the possibility that because the United States could survive a nuclear attack, it might be willing to start a war with the Soviets. The Soviets would then need to develop their own SDI. There was the second threat: the USSR would have to divert scarce resources and perhaps weaken their economy in order to compete with the United States.

While the United States pressed the Soviets, Reagan wanted to avoid open confrontation with the major Communist powers. In 1983, a Soviet fighter plane shot down an unarmed Korean airliner, killing all 269 aboard. Although a US congressman was one of the victims, Reagan responded with restraint. A year later, Reagan traded visits with the premier of the People's Republic of China and encouraged stronger relations and a nuclear-weapons agreement.

The Reagan Doctrine in the Third World

The Reagan administration also changed American foreign policy toward the third world. Reagan and other conservatives had been impatient with the Carter administration's attempts to promote human rights abroad. The United States, they believed, needed to back anti-Communist, pro-American governments, whether or not they respected human rights. Jeane J. Kirkpatrick, who became Reagan's ambassador to the United Nations, distinguished between totalitarian regimes hostile to the United States and authoritarian governments friendly to American interests. Critics claimed this distinction was meaningless and insisted the nation not support antidemocratic governments. The administration adopted Kirkpatrick's view, which became known as the **Reagan Doctrine.**

The administration applied the Reagan Doctrine aggressively in Central America and the Caribbean (see Map 28–3). Determined to keep Communism out of the Western Hemisphere, the United States opposed the Marxist Sandinista government of Nicaragua and supported the repressive anti-Communist government of neighboring El Salvador.

Encouraged by the Carter administration, the Sandinistas had come to power in the late 1970s by overthrowing the dictatorship of Anastasio Somoza. The Reagan administration believed the Sandinistas were too friendly to the Soviet Union and to leftist rebels in El Salvador. Reagan halted aid to Nicaragua in April 1981 and directed the CIA to train, arm, and supply the Contra rebels, who opposed the Sandinistas. Many of the Contras had ties to the oppressive Somoza regime, but Reagan praised them as "freedom fighters." Meanwhile, the president strongly backed the right-wing military government of El Salvador, locked in a civil war with pro-Sandinista and pro-Cuban rebels. Employing infamous "death squads,"

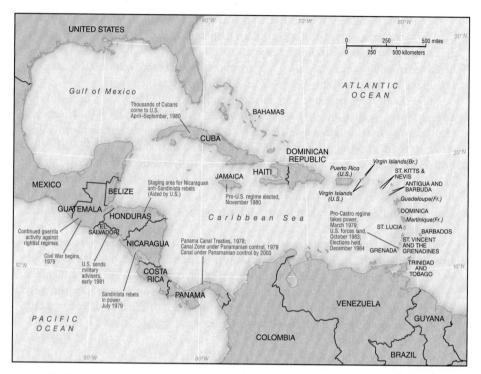

Map 28-3   The Reagan Doctrine in Central America and the Caribbean Events that shaped Reagan's anti-Communist initiative in the Western Hemisphere.

Reagan's Central American Policy The president holds up a T-shirt summing up his approach to the region: "STOP COMMUNISM CENTRAL AMERICA."

the military government engaged in kidnapping, torture, and murder. Some 75,000 people died in the conflict. Still, Reagan did not want this brutal, undemocratic regime to fall. El Salvador, he explained, was "a textbook case of indirect armed aggression by Communist powers."

Despite such rhetoric, the administration could not persuade Congress to support its Central American policy. Congressional Democrats, like many Americans, did not want war in Central America. They were skeptical about the Communist threat and troubled by the antidemocratic character of the Salvadoran regime and the Contra rebels. In 1983, Congress approved Reagan's Caribbean Basin Initiative, an economic development package, but not military aid for the Salvadoran government. Instead, Congress passed the Boland Amendment, which restricted aid to the Contras and banned efforts to topple the Sandinista regime.

Reagan applied the Reagan Doctrine more successfully in the Caribbean. On October 25, 1983, US troops invaded the small island of **Grenada**, supposedly to protect about 1,000 Americans, mostly medical students, from a Marxist regime. Reagan feared Grenada would become a Cuban or Soviet base close to US shores. The invading force quickly secured the island and replaced the government with a pro-American regime. Critics charged that Reagan had violated the sovereignty of another state for an easy military victory. To his supporters, the invasion was a welcome demonstration of the Reagan Doctrine and an antidote to the Vietnam syndrome.

The president also applied the Reagan Doctrine in Africa. The Carter administration had condemned the long-standing policy of *apartheid*—racial separation—pursued by the white government of South Africa. Reagan, despite America's struggle with racial segregation, would not take such a strong stance. Rather than impose economic sanctions on South Africa, he endorsed mild diplomatic discussions known as "constructive engagement" while South Africa suffered violence and near civil war. Reagan held back because the South African regime was an ally against Communism in the region. During the 1980s, the United States supported South African military intervention in Angola, Mozambique, and Namibia against groups aided by Cuba and the Soviet Union. More than a million people died in these conflicts.

The Middle East and Terrorism

The Reagan Doctrine was not much help in dealing with the Middle East and the growing problem of terrorism. Communism and the Soviet Union had little impact on Middle Eastern issues in the 1980s. As before, the United States wanted to ensure its supply of oil and to support its longtime ally, Israel. There was no new Arab oil embargo during the Reagan years, but the administration could not bring peace to the Middle East or end the threat of terrorism.

The United States and the World Economy

Middle Eastern oil was only one economic factor shaping Reagan's foreign policy. The president had to deal with strains on the world economy. Like presidents before him, Reagan believed strongly that free trade would boost national economies. He believed, too, that other nations would benefit from cutting taxes, government spending, and regulation. But after years of economic decline, the United States could not always impose its will on other nations.

Reagan did force his views on weak, debt-ridden, third-world countries. By the end of the 1980s, developing nations owed foreign banks more than $1.2 trillion. Mexico was more than $100 billion in debt. American banks would lose heavily if those nations defaulted on loans. American producers stood to lose if those countries could not afford to buy US goods. The Reagan administration refused to protect American banks from defaults, instead forcing debtor countries to adopt freer trade, deregulation of business, and austerity programs in return for new loans.

America In The World
The Ethiopian Famine

The devastating famine, brought on by drought, complicated by war, and worsened by government policies, began in the African nation of **Ethiopia** in 1983. Although foreshadowed for several years, the crisis in one of the poorest countries on earth evoked a surprisingly slow response from the United States and the rest of the world. The famine starkly illustrated America's diverse, uneven global connections in the age of the Cold War.

As hundreds of thousands of Ethiopians died, most Americans knew little about the unfolding disaster. US television networks showed just over eight minutes' worth of stories on the famine in its first two years. Congressional hearings only briefly stirred public interest in 1983. As a result, American religious organizations, such as Catholic Relief Services, had a hard time raising money for Ethiopia.

The Reagan administration knew much more about the situation but was reluctant to aid a nation aligned with the Soviet Union. Mengistu Haile Mariam, leader of Ethiopia's Communist military junta, had nationalized US businesses and allowed in thousands of Soviet and Cuban military advisers. While the humanitarian crisis intensified, the Reagan administration even eliminated Ethiopian food aid from the budget for 1984. The USSR, federal officials suggested, ought to be providing help to its ally.

Then, a British film crew documented "the closest thing to hell on earth." Shown on more than 400 television stations around the world in October 1984, the film offered a stark, wrenching depiction of emaciated Ethiopians, a dying man, and dead children. In Britain, pop musicians, calling themselves Band Aid, quickly made a hit single, "Do They Know It's Christmas?," that raised money for famine relief. The combination of television coverage and musical celebrity dramatically changed popular awareness and response to the Ethiopian crisis.

In the United States, Americans made a flood of donations to charitable organizations. Church-related groups, including Roman Catholic, mainline and evangelical Protestant denominations, played a particularly important role in the response to the famine. In Fort Myers, Florida, 60 teenagers from two Assembly of God churches fasted for 30 hours to raise money for World Vision International, an evangelical relief organization. The Church of Jesus Christ of Latter-day Saints declared a special one-day fast that raised over $6 million from Mormons around the United States. Criticized for aiding a Communist government, the Mormon president answered "that where there is stark hunger, I will not let political considerations dull my sense of mercy or thwart my responsibility to the sons and daughters of God."

Inspired by their British counterparts, American pop musicians mobilized for the relief effort. Musicians of color, mindful of their African roots, played the lead role. Jamaican American folk musician and civil rights activist Harry Belafonte created United Support of Artists for Africa (USA for Africa). On behalf of the new organization, African American pop stars Michael Jackson and Lionel Richie wrote "We Are the World," which was recorded by a mixed-race group of musicians. "There comes a time when we heed a certain call," the song began. "When the world must come together as one." "We Are the World" quickly became a number-one hit in the United States and other countries.

Popular opinion, religious activism, and musical celebrity put enormous pressure on the Reagan administration to reverse course. The US government began providing hundreds of thousands of tons of food aid to Ethiopia. To make direct food donations legally easier, the administration even designated the Communist Mengistu regime a "friendly government"—a brief break from the Cold War.

"We Are the World" Stars of music and film sing to support Ethiopian famine relief, 1985.

Reagan found it difficult to build on the Camp David Accords between Israel and Egypt, which were supposed to lead to self-government for the Palestinian Arabs living in the Israeli-occupied West Bank and Gaza Strip. Israel and the Palestine Liberation Organization (PLO), the official representative of the Palestinians, remained at odds. The PLO continued to threaten Israel from bases in neighboring Lebanon. In the spring of 1982, the Israelis invaded Lebanon, which was already convulsed by a civil war between Muslims and Christians.

To end the invasion and stabilize Lebanon, the United States sent marines to join an international peacekeeping force. On October 23, 1983, a terrorist bomb killed 241 Americans at marine headquarters in Beirut. The shocking attack marked a low point of Reagan's administration. The president did not retaliate. He did not want to reward terrorism by withdrawing from Lebanon. Nevertheless, he pulled out the soldiers in 1984, even though there was no peace in Lebanon and no agreement between the Israelis and the PLO.

The attack on the marine headquarters illustrated the growing threat of terrorism. Reagan vowed to make terrorists "pay for their actions," but terrorism proved hard to stop. Acts of terrorism by Palestinians and Libyans drew quick American reprisals in the 1980s. After Palestinians murdered an American passenger on a cruise ship in the Mediterranean in 1985, US planes forced down the Egyptian airliner carrying the escaping terrorists. The Reagan administration believed that Muammar Qaddafi, leader of the North African nation of Libya, supported terrorism. In 1982, US Navy fighter planes shot down two Libyan fighters. After American soldiers died in a terrorist bombing in West Germany in 1986, US jets bombed targets in Libya, among them military barracks and Qaddafi's personal residence, killing one of his daughters. Qaddafi seemed to become less critical of the United States, but the threat of terrorism did not go away.

Reagan also acted to safeguard America's oil supply. During a war between Iran and Iraq, the United States sent warships to protect oil tankers in the Persian Gulf. American intervention was costly. In May 1987, Iraqi missiles struck the US destroyer *Stark*, killing 37 of its crew. Unwilling to help Iran, Reagan accepted Iraq's apology. In July 1988, the US missile cruiser *Vincennes* accidentally shot down an Iranian airliner, killing 290 passengers. An American apology did not quell Iranian anger, but the Iran-Iraq war soon ended, and with it the threat to America's oil supply.

The Reagan administration had much less power to dictate trade policy with Japan. As Japanese exports flowed into the United States, Americans increasingly resented Japan's control of its home market. Congress, believing Japan discriminated against American goods, pushed for retaliation. Japan placed voluntary quotas on its export of steel and automobiles to the United States. Although the United States devalued the dollar to make American goods cheaper, the trade imbalance continued. In 1988, the president signed the Omnibus Trade and Competitiveness Act, which allowed the government to place high tariffs on Japanese goods if Japan discriminated against American goods. But as long as Americans wanted Japanese products, retaliation was unlikely. In 1989, a Japanese car, the Honda Accord, was the first international model to become the best-selling automobile in America.

Many Accords had been made in the United States. Even as the administration struggled to open Japanese markets to American goods, Japanese firms increased their direct investment in the United States. Honda built a new factory in Marysville, Ohio, to produce Accords for the American market. As Japanese companies built or took over other facilities, many Americans wondered whether the global expansion of trade really benefited their country after all.

THE BATTLE OVER CONSERVATIVE SOCIAL VALUES

For all of Ronald Reagan's success in the early 1980s, the **new conservatism** met with important opposition. The conservatives' social values were especially controversial. Angered by the changes of the 1960s, many conservatives, like Linda Chavez, wanted to restore supposedly traditional values and practices. The conservative agenda collided head-on with one of the chief legacies of the 1960s—disadvantaged groups' demands for equal rights and opportunities. Many Americans were also unwilling to abandon the social changes of the last generation. Faced with such opposition, conservatives failed to achieve much of their vision.

Attacking the Legacy of the 1960s

The new conservatism was driven by a desire to undo the liberal and radical legacies of the 1960s. Conservatives blamed federal courts for much of the social change over the last generation. In the 1960s and 1970s, liberal, activist justices had supported defendants' rights, civil rights, affirmative action, busing, and abortion while rejecting such conservative causes as school prayer.

Determined to take control of the courts, Reagan appointed many staunch, relatively young conservatives to the federal bench and the Supreme Court. In 1981, **Sandra Day O'Connor**, a fairly conservative judge from Arizona, became the Court's first woman justice. Reagan replaced retiring Chief Justice Warren Burger with conservative William Rehnquist. The appointments of two more conservatives, Antonin Scalia and Anthony Kennedy, seemed to push the Supreme Court away from liberalism.

It did not quite work out that way. In the 1980s, the Court followed conservative views in limiting the rights of defendants. Rulings in *United States v. Leon* and *Nix v. Williams* in 1984 made it easier for prosecutors to use evidence improperly obtained by police. However, on other issues, the Court took a moderate stance. In *Wallace v. Jaffree* in 1985, the Court invalidated an Alabama law that allowed schools to devote a minute each day to voluntary prayer or meditation.

Prayer was part of the conservatives' plan to reform public education. They believed that the federal government had played too large a role in the schools since the 1960s. Parents, meanwhile, had too little say in the education of their children. Preferring to use market forces rather than government to reform the schools, conservatives wanted to abolish the federal Department of Education. They also wanted to let parents choose the best schools—public or private—for their children and cover part of the cost with federally funded vouchers or tax credits.

Because many Americans worried about the quality of the schools, conservatives had a golden opportunity. But Congress refused to adopt vouchers or abolish the Department of Education.

Drug use was another issue conservatives linked to the 1960s. In the early 1980s, drugs again became a major concern with the spread of crack, a cheap, addictive form of cocaine. The sale and use of crack, especially in the cities, led to crime and violence. In 1986, the president and his wife, Nancy, announced a "national crusade" for a "drug-free" America. Their campaign encouraged young people to "Just Say No" to drugs, implemented drug testing for federal employees, and imposed mandatory minimum sentences for some drug use. The "**war on drugs**" was controversial. Critics called its rhetoric naive and ineffective. They also condemned new sentencing laws, which put millions in jail, as unfair to African Americans and expensive to taxpayers. Despite the crusade, drug use did not decrease appreciably.

Women's Rights and Abortion

One of the chief legacies of the 1960s was the women's rights movement. The new conservatism condemned feminism and deplored the changing role of women in America. Many conservatives, especially evangelical leaders, blamed feminists and liberal government for encouraging women to abandon their traditional family role for paid jobs. The conservative movement was especially determined to halt federal initiatives, such as affirmative action programs and the Equal Rights Amendment (ERA), that protected women's rights (see Chapter 27).

The conservative agenda on women's rights met with mixed results. The campaign for the ERA, lagging since the 1970s, ended unsuccessfully, but affirmative action programs to promote the hiring of women continued. So did women's push into the workplace and public life as more families needed two incomes. By 1983, women made up half of the paid workforce. As their economic role expanded, so did their political visibility. Ironically, Reagan gave women new public prominence by choosing Jeane J. Kirkpatrick and Sandra Day O'Connor for important offices.

Women still did not enjoy equality in America. They were generally paid less than men doing the same sort of work, and they had less opportunity to break through the "glass ceiling" and win managerial jobs. Commentators noted the feminization of poverty. Unmarried or divorced women, many with children, made up an increasing percentage of the poor. This unequal suffering, liberals and feminists argued, disproved the conservative claim that women did not need special protection.

Pro-Life Protest Carrying a small coffin, a pro-life march protests the Supreme Court's *Roe v. Wade* decision in Atlanta, Georgia, in 1989.

For many conservatives, the right to abortion, guaranteed by the Supreme Court in *Roe v. Wade* in 1973, was the most troubling change in the status of women. A growing Right to Life movement passionately denounced abortion as the murder of the unborn, practiced by selfish women who rejected motherhood and family.

Conservatives failed to narrow abortion rights significantly in the 1980s (see Map 28–4). Reagan persuaded Congress to stop the use of federal funds to pay for abortions, but a constitutional amendment outlawing abortion stalled in the Senate. Supreme Court rulings in 1983 and 1986 upheld *Roe v. Wade*.

Gays and the AIDS Crisis

The gay rights movement was another legacy of the 1960s that troubled conservatives. Evangelical leaders such as Jerry Falwell condemned gays on religious grounds. Some people believed that equal rights for gay men and women would promote immorality and corrupt children. In 1977, Anita Bryant, a former Miss America, launched a national crusade, Save Our Children, to protest the passage of a gay rights ordinance in Florida. Voters soon repealed the measure. In San Francisco in 1978, Harvey Milk, the first avowedly gay member of the city's board of supervisors, was assassinated, along with the mayor, by a former supervisor. Many were shocked when the assassin received only a short jail sentence.

Despite such opposition, the gay rights movement made progress in the 1980s. In 1982, Wisconsin became the first state to pass a law protecting the rights of gay men and women. By the end of the decade, most states had repealed sodomy laws

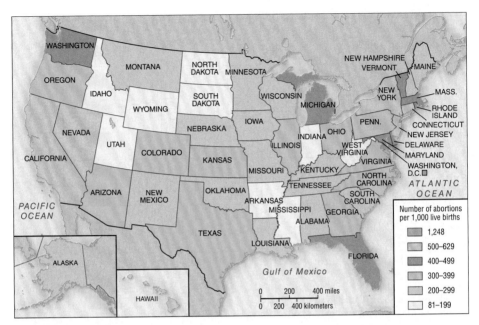

Map 28-4 Abortion in the 1980s The rate of abortions across the United States 14 years after the Supreme Court's decision legalizing abortion in *Roe v. Wade*.
Source: Timothy H. Fast and Cathy Carroll Fast, *The Women's Atlas of the United States*, rev. ed. (New York: Facts on File, 1995), p. 166.

that criminalized gay sex. In *Bowers v. Hardwick* in 1986, however, the US Supreme Court dismissed a gay man's right to sexual privacy as "facetious."

The battle over gay rights took place against a tragic backdrop. In 1981, the Centers for Disease Control began reporting cases of acquired immune deficiency syndrome (**AIDS**), a disease that destroyed the body's immune system and left it unable to fight off infections and rare cancers. By the mid-1980s, researchers had traced AIDS to different forms of the human immunodeficiency virus (HIV) that were transmitted in semen and blood. But no cure had been found. By 1990, there were nearly 100,000 recorded deaths from the AIDS epidemic in the United States (see Figure 28–2).

Because 75 percent of the first victims were gay men, Americans initially considered AIDS a gay disease. Some people, including evangelical leaders, believed this "gay cancer" was God's punishment for the alleged sin of same-sex love. It became clear, however, that AIDS could also be transmitted by heterosexual intercourse, by intravenous drug use with shared needles, and by tainted blood transfusions.

Although understanding of AIDS and HIV increased, the specter of "gay cancer" promoted homophobia and slowed the response to the disease. The AIDS Coalition to Unleash Power (ACT UP) and other organizations staged demonstrations and acts of civil disobedience to call attention to the crisis and push for government action. Nevertheless, the Reagan administration did not fund research on AIDS for several years, and the disease continued to spread.

The AIDS epidemic complicated the struggle over gay rights. For some Americans, the disease reinforced the conservative condemnation of gays. For others, the

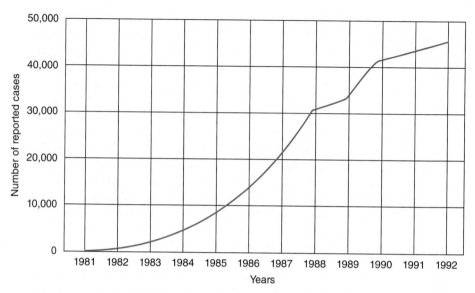

Figure 28–2   The Rapid Rise of AIDS
Source: Statistical Abstract of the United States, 1989, p. 111; *Statistical Abstract, 1993,* p. 203.

suffering of victims evoked sympathy and compassion. As the 1980s ended, the conservative backlash against gay rights had failed, but the epidemic continued.

African Americans and Racial Inequality

Conservatives were uneasy with another legacy of the 1960s, the expansion of African American civil rights and benefits guaranteed by the federal government. They believed that the liberal policies of the Great Society hurt, rather than helped, Black people and argued that individual initiative, not government action, would promote racial equality. Reflecting these ideas, Reagan opposed renewal of the Voting Rights Act and condemned busing and affirmative action. Like many Republicans, he opposed the creation of a national holiday marking the birthday of Martin Luther King Jr.

The conservatives' tough stance came at a difficult time for racial equality. African Americans' crusade for justice and opportunity generally slowed in the 1970s and 1980s. Despite legal equality, African Americans faced persistent racism and discrimination. Disproportionately clustered in manual occupations, they were particularly hurt by deindustrialization and economic decline. After years of improvement, African Americans' economic status relative to whites stagnated or declined during the Reagan era. African Americans still made less money than whites did for comparable work and had much less chance to attain managerial positions. All African Americans were not affected equally. In the 1980s, the African American middle class continued to thrive. Among college-educated Americans, the incomes of Black men rose faster than those of whites into the mid-1980s. Middle-class African Americans could afford to move to better housing, often in suburbs and integrated areas. Meanwhile, working-class African Americans found their wages stagnating or falling compared with those of white workers. In the 1970s and 1980s, poverty rates rose faster among African Americans than among whites. In 1985, 75 percent of poor African American children lived in families headed by a single female. Observers feared there was now a permanent African American underclass segregated in inner-city neighborhoods with poor schools and widespread crime.

As in the past, African American culture, driven by the distinctiveness of the Black experience, was dynamic and controversial. In the poverty of the Bronx in New York City in the 1970s, young African Americans had begun to create a powerful new music, **rap**. Reflecting the city's diversity, pioneering rap artists such as Kool Herc, Afrika Bambaataa, and Grandmaster Flash drew on Caribbean musical styles and the popular dance music disco, as well as on African American expressive traditions. Rap typically featured spoken lyrics over a driving percussive "break" beat, often sampled from other music. Along with graffiti and break dancing, the new sound made up a loose African American cultural movement known as **hip-hop**.

Rap was the first new musical form to rival the impact of jazz in the 1920s and rock and roll in the 1950s. Spreading rapidly, rap crossed boundaries of race, class, and nation to appeal to middle-class, white, and international audiences. Commercially successful, rap was also controversial for its often raw look at ghetto life. The subgenre of gangsta rap, with its celebrations of gang life, violence, and misogyny, was especially provocative to conservatives and other Americans. Rap also deeply influenced other genres of music—another instance of the powerful impact of African Americans on American culture.

African Americans also mobilized to fight for equality and opportunity. Across the nation, the number of African American elected officials increased markedly. The Reverend Jesse Jackson, a protégé of Martin Luther King Jr., won wide attention. Preaching self-esteem and economic self-help for African Americans, Jackson was the leader of Operation PUSH—People United to Save Humanity. In 1984, Jackson challenged Walter Mondale for the Democratic presidential nomination. His campaign suggested how far American society had come in accepting African American political participation.

African American activism and the persistence of inequality made it difficult to undo the civil rights revolution. Most Americans seemed to accept that some federal action was essential to redress the imbalance between races. Despite Reagan's opposition, in 1982 Congress voted to extend the Voting Rights Act for 25 years. In 1983, the Supreme Court ruled that Bob Jones University, an evangelical institution, could not retain its tax-exempt status while it prohibited interracial dating and practiced other forms of discrimination. The Court also rejected the Reagan administration's bid to set aside affirmative action programs.

The battles over the rights of African Americans, gays, and women underscored the limits of conservatism. Many Americans were not ready to undo the social and cultural legacies of the 1960s. New cultural expressions, such as rap, clashed with conservative values. The result was a stalemate. Disadvantaged groups made relatively little political progress in the 1980s, but conservatives also made little progress in their social and cultural agenda.

"The Decade of the Hispanic"

After the changes of the 1960s and 1970s, the Hispanic experience in the United States became quieter and more confident in the 1980s. Hispanics were not a homogeneous group but a diverse population defined by geographical, cultural, and even linguistic differences. In New York City, Puerto Ricans predominated; in South Florida, Cubans; and in the long arc from South Texas to Southern California, Mexican Americans. In 1980, Hispanics were the nation's fastest-growing minority group, with a birthrate 75 percent higher than the national average. Most immigrants to the United States were Hispanic, and demographers predicted that Hispanics would replace African Americans as the nation's largest minority group within a generation.

These growing numbers created a new sense in the 1980s that Hispanics mattered and could not be ignored. "We are," a Hispanic Roman Catholic priest declared, "the future."

In this consumer society, the increasing importance of the Hispanic population could be measured in goods and services. Hispanic culture affected the nation's foodways. From the 1970s into the 1980s, more and more Americans discovered "Tex-Mex," the distinctive cuisine of the Tejanos, the Mexican Americans of South Texas. By the 1990s, salsa had passed ketchup as the best-selling condiment in the United States.

Meanwhile, American business moved to attract Spanish-speaking consumers. The Coors brewery enthusiastically declared the 1980s "The Decade of the Hispanic." By 1983, Coors and other companies could advertise in the expanding Spanish-language media, including newspapers, magazines, and 67 television stations.

For politicians, the 1980s were also "The Decade of the Hispanic." Republicans, long unable to attract a majority of African Americans, hoped that Roman Catholic Hispanic voters, like Linda Chavez, would respond to the new conservatism's emphasis on values, family, and religion. Reagan's anti-Communism did attract Cuban Americans, so many of whom were refugees from the regime of Fidel Castro. However, most Hispanics, including Mexican Americans, emphasized economic issues. They continued to fight poverty and struggle for opportunity. Unlike Linda Chavez, the Hispanic majority preferred the more activist economic and educational policies of the Democrats.

The increasing importance of Hispanic voters also affected the response to the perhaps 3 million illegal immigrants who had crossed the border from Mexico into the United States. The Immigration Reform and Control Act of 1986, known as the Simpson-Mazzoli Act, penalized Americans who knowingly brought illegal aliens into the country and hired them. But the measure also reflected the sentiments of Mexican Americans and other Americans by offering amnesty to illegal aliens who had arrived since 1981.

FROM SCANDAL TO TRIUMPH

The stalemate over social values was not the only sign that there were limits to conservatism in the 1980s. Scandals plagued business and religious figures who had helped create the conservative agenda. Policy setbacks, economic woes, and scandals plagued the Reagan administration. For a time, the conservatives' triumph was in doubt, but then the Cold War began to end.

Business and Religious Scandals

By the mid-1980s, the new conservatism was suffering a series of business and religious scandals. In 1986, Ivan Boesky, the swaggering Wall Street dealmaker, was indicted for insider trading, the illegal use of secret financial information. Rather than go to trial, he agreed to give up stock trading, inform on other lawbreakers, spend two years in jail, and pay a $100 million fine. In 1987, Michael Milken, the junk bond king, was indicted on fraud and racketeering charges. His plea bargain agreement included a 10-year jail sentence and a $600 million fine, the largest judgment against an individual in American history.

Such scandals provoked second thoughts about the celebration of business and materialism. Critics pointed out that Boesky's and Milken's business methods had hurt the economy by saddling corporations with a great deal of debt and little cash to pay for it. Lavish lifestyles no longer seemed so attractive.

Scandal also touched religion. In 1987, Americans learned that televangelist Jim Bakker had defrauded investors in his theme park, Heritage USA, and paid hush money to hide an adulterous liaison with a church secretary. In 1988, Jerry Falwell had to resign from his Moral Majority. That year, televangelist Jimmy Swaggart admitted he "had sinned" with prostitutes.

Political Scandals

The Reagan administration had its own scandals. Before the end of the first term, more than 20 EPA officials resigned or were fired over charges of favoritism toward lobbyists and polluters. In 1985, Secretary of Labor Raymond Donovan resigned after becoming the first cabinet officer ever indicted. In 1988, Reagan's friend and attorney general, Edwin Meese III, resigned amid questions about his role in the corrupt awarding of government contracts. To critics, the administration's "sleaze factor" stemmed from the president's contemptuous attitude toward government and his eagerness to please business.

In his second term, Reagan faced much more damaging accusations. In October 1986, Sandinista soldiers in Nicaragua shot down a plane attempting to supply the Contra rebels. The plane had been part of a secret effort by the administration to violate the Boland Amendment's ban on aid to the Contras. Then, a Lebanese magazine reported that the United States had traded arms to Iran. Despite Reagan's denials, the government had sold arms to win the release of American hostages held by terrorists in Lebanon. The administration had broken the president's pledge not to negotiate with terrorists and had violated a ban on arms sales to Iran. The arms deal and the Nicaraguan plane crash were connected: the government had illegally used proceeds from the arms sale to pay for supplying the Contras.

The scandal that became known as the **Iran-Contra affair** had the potential to drive Reagan from office. If the president had ordered or known about the arms deal and the supply effort, he might have faced impeachment. Three separate investigations made clear the president's probable involvement in the Iran-Contra affair, but none turned up enough evidence to impeach him.

Nevertheless, Reagan's reputation was badly damaged. Several of his associates left office and faced jail sentences. Former national security adviser Robert "Bud" McFarlane pleaded guilty to withholding information from Congress. His successor, Rear Admiral John Poindexter, was allowed to resign. Poindexter's aide, Marine Lieutenant Colonel Oliver North, had to be fired. Meanwhile, the director of the CIA, William Casey, died in 1987, the day after he was implicated in the Contra affair. Much of the country concluded that Reagan must have known about his associates' dealings; his popularity dropped.

American Landscape
Times Beach, Missouri

In the early 1980s, few Americans had any idea what dioxins were. Through volcanos and forest fires, nature had long produced these chemical compounds. But in the twentieth century, dioxins vastly increased as byproducts of human industrial processes, such as insecticide manufacture. Largely ignored and unregulated by government, these chemicals found their way into the air and water, lingered in the ground, entered the food chain, and invaded the human body. Profoundly harmful, some dioxins affected human development and caused illnesses, including cancer.

Dioxins spread in strange, unanticipated ways. In the 1970s, a hauler of industrial waste in Missouri sprayed old, used oil to keep down the annoying dust at horse barns and tracks. He also sprayed the unpaved streets of the small suburban town of Times Beach, southwest of St. Louis. Unknown to his customers, he had allowed dioxins to mix with his oil. Meanwhile, other dioxin waste, so hard to dispose of safely, simply got dumped on the ground or buried in tanks. Despite mysterious illnesses and mounting scientific concerns, no one, including state and US government officials, did anything significant about the dioxin

in Times Beach and across Missouri. Finally, an anonymous phone tip in 1979 led the federal Environmental Protection Agency to court action over a leaking underground dioxin tank. But it wasn't until 1982 that a leaked document revealed that there were perhaps more than 50 dioxin sites in Missouri.

On December 3, white-suited federal workers, looking like "guys from outer space," finished taking soil samples from Times Beach. The next day, before results came back, the Merrimac River overflowed and flooded the town. The more than 2,000 residents evacuated only to find that the local government hadn't renewed federal flood insurance; they would have no financial help repairing and rebuilding their homes and business. At Christmas, things got still worse. The Environmental Protection Agency, assessing the high levels of Dioxin in the soil, told residents not to move back.

Their homes and business worthless, the people of Times Beach were angry and frustrated. Some didn't want to leave. The disaster itself, made worse by the scandalous failures of government, led President Ronald Reagan to push for a solution early in 1983. The EPA official in charge paid

Setbacks for the Conservative Agenda

Amid the scandals, conservatives faced a series of policy setbacks. The Democratic-controlled House of Representatives was less cooperative during Reagan's second term. Democrats became even more combative after winning majorities in the House and Senate in the congressional elections of 1986.

As a result, Reagan had to compromise more with Congress. In 1985, he called for a Second American Revolution, a comprehensive overhaul of the income tax

Welcome to Times Beach In 1991, the former mayor stands next to the sign greeting visitors to the empty, devastated town.

for the neglect of Times Beach with her job. Together, the federal and state governments paid millions for the ruined homes and businesses of Times Beach. The former residents of Times Beach paid in cases of leukemia, liver problems, tumors, seizures, and spina bifida and other birth defects. There was no payment for psychological loss. "We've lost something—we've lost that security, the security of a normal,

healthy life," said a young carpenter and father. "We can never go back."

During the clean-up of the dioxin, Times Beach remained a fenced-in ghost town for years. Bulldozers levelled the buildings and buried them under a huge mound. In 1999, the state turned the former town into a park. A marker proudly declared the cleanup "one of America's greatest triumphs over environmental disaster."

system. But the Tax Reform Act that Congress passed in 1986 did not lower and simplify income taxes nearly as much as the president had wanted.

Reagan also met outright defeat in Congress. In 1988, a coalition of Democrats and Republicans passed a bill compelling large companies to give workers 60 days' notice of plant closings and layoffs. Reagan opposed this liberal measure, but he allowed the bill to become law without his signature.

The president was often defeated on environmental policy at a time of growing concern about environmental hazards. In December 1984, the subsidiary of a

US corporation accidentally allowed toxic gas to escape from a pesticide plant in Bhopal, India. The emission killed more than 2,500 people and injured 200,000. In April 1986, an explosion and fire released radioactive material from a nuclear power plant at Chernobyl in the Soviet Union. The accident killed more than 30 people, injured more than 200, and exposed countless others to radioactivity. Suddenly, Reagan's hostility to environmentalism was no longer so appealing. The president had to accept the 1986 extension of the federal Superfund program to clean up hazardous waste. The next year, Congress overrode his veto of a bill renewing the Water Quality Control Act. Shifting course in 1987, Reagan signed the landmark Montreal Protocol, an international agreement pledging nations to phase out production of substances, including chlorofluorocarbons, that helped produce the Ozone Hole. In 1988, the Reagan administration signed an agreement with Canada setting limits on emissions linked to acid rain.

A Vulnerable Economy

Even the economy, the centerpiece of the Reagan Revolution, became a problem in the president's second term. During the 1980s, the gap between rich and poor widened sharply. From 1977 to 1980, the average family income of the highest-paid tenth of Americans rose 27 percent, whereas that of the poorest tenth fell 11 percent (see Figure 28–3). In the 1980s, only the rich earned more and kept more. Other Americans faced economic stagnation or decline.

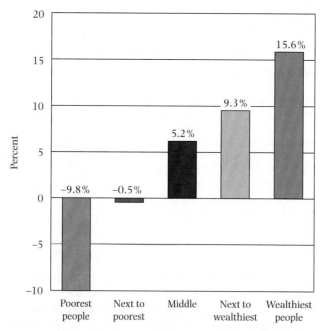

Figure 28-3   Changes in Families' Real Income, 1980–1990
The Reagan Revolution had very different consequences for the rich and the poor.
Source: Copyright © 1989 by the New York Times Co. Reprinted by permission.

In 1980, 29 million Americans lived below the poverty line. Ten years later, that figure had grown to almost 37 million. Despite Reaganomics, the United States had one of the highest poverty rates among industrialized nations.

One of the most visible consequences of poverty was **homelessness**. In the 1980s, the number of homeless Americans increased markedly. The sight of men and women sleeping on sidewalks was common during the Reagan years.

Homelessness, poverty, and inequality produced a spirited debate in the 1980s. Democrats and liberals blamed these problems on Reaganomics. The president, they charged, had done nothing to stop the erosion of high-paying factory jobs. His welfare, housing, and job-training cuts hurt the poor, while his tax cuts and deregulation helped the rich. Conservatives and Republicans maintained that activist, liberal government had hurt manufacturing and weakened the economy. Moreover, welfare programs caused poverty by destroying poor people's work ethic and making them dependent on handouts.

In reality, both liberal and conservative policies had produced flawed economic results. Lyndon Johnson's spending for the Great Society, along with the cost of the Vietnam War, had begun to undermine the economy in the 1960s. His antipoverty programs had been less effective than liberals wanted to admit, but the Reagan Revolution did not end poverty, either. Reaganomics did not reinvigorate manufacturing or boost middle-class incomes.

There were other signs of economic vulnerability by the mid-1980s. Despite Reaganomics, the federal budget deficit did not disappear. Instead, between 1981 and 1986, tax cuts and increased defense spending drove the deficit from $79 billion to $221 billion—a staggering new record.

Like poverty and inequality, the deficit was controversial. Some economists believed the deficit was a sign of great economic weakness; others believed it did not matter. Democrats and liberals blamed Reagan for the red ink. Reagan's supporters blamed Congress for failing to cut the budget.

In fact, both the president and Congress were to blame. Neither Republicans nor Democrats wanted to reduce Medicare and Social Security. Congress enacted the Balanced Budget and Emergency Deficit Control Act of 1985 (the Gramm-Rudman Act), which promised to balance the budget by 1990, but a Supreme Court ruling critically weakened the measure. During Reagan's last years in office, the national debt—the total amount owed by the federal government to its creditors—reached $2.6 trillion.

Along with burgeoning debt, the Reagan years produced a growing international trade deficit. In 1980, the annual value of imports was $25.4 billion greater than the value of the nation's exports. By 1986, that gap had grown to $145.1 billion, as American business lost out to foreign products both at home and abroad. Reaganomics had not solved the problem of America's relative decline in the world economy.

Doubts about Reagan's economic policy increased when the stock market fell unexpectedly on Monday, October 19, 1987, losing 508 points, or 23 percent of its value. It was the biggest one-day decline since "Black Tuesday" in October 1929. The market drop reflected underlying economic problems, including the federal budget deficit, the trade deficit, and deindustrialization, plus lax government regulation of Wall Street. The crash seemed to be a mortal blow to what a journalist called "the

Struggles For Democracy

Reagan at the Berlin Wall

The history of democracy has not only been a tale of elections and legislation. Like other kinds of politics, it has also been a story of theater. American leaders have long tried to capture fundamental political ideas in a vivid moment, a memorable mixture of language and image. President Ronald Reagan, a veteran radio announcer, actor, and television host, was a master of the theater of democracy.

By the spring of 1987, Reagan had largely abandoned the rhetoric of the Cold War as he moved cautiously toward working with Soviet leader Mikhail Gorbachev. Reagan's shift had yet to produce a dramatic easing of the Cold War, but it had already disappointed some of his most ardent, anti-Communist supporters. In June, a trip to West Germany for the 750th anniversary of the city of Berlin offered the president an ideal opportunity to deal with both his domestic and foreign problems.

For four decades, the city—divided between communist, pro-Soviet East and capitalist, pro-American West— had epitomized the divisions of the Cold War. For nearly three decades, the concrete-and-barbed-wire wall separating Berlin's two sections had perfectly symbolized the Cold War's impact on the city, Europe, and the world.

On the drab afternoon of June 12, Reagan, dressed patriotically in a blue suit, white shirt, and red tie, stood on a temporary platform 25 yards in front of the Berlin Wall. His aides had set the stage with care. Looming behind the president and the wall, in East Berlin, was the great Brandenburg Gate. For nearly two centuries, the 12 pillars and crowning arch of the Gate had symbolized peace; now, blocked by the Berlin Wall, the Brandenburg Gate led nowhere. In front of Reagan, an invited crowd of 20,000 waved American and West German flags provided by the president's aides. On the other side of the wall, 200 East Germans could hear Reagan on loudspeakers. Thanks to radio and television, many more East Germans and Soviets, as well as Americans, also heard the president's words.

Those words had been carefully drafted and redrafted by a young speechwriter, Paul Robinson. Inspired by his West German hostess at a dinner party, Robinson had written a line demanding that Gorbachev tear

Reagan Illusion: the idea that there could be a defense buildup and tax cuts without a price, that the country could live beyond its means indefinitely."

Reagan's Comeback

Remarkably able to withstand defeat, Reagan began his comeback from scandals and economic troubles. Opponents dubbed him the "Teflon president" because nothing seemed to stick to him. That was a tribute to his political skills, as well as many Americans' real affection for him. After a series of disappointing presidencies, Americans seemed unwilling to let Reagan fail.

down the Berlin Wall. As Reagan's aides vetted the draft speech, the line had become the subject of a bureaucratic tug-of-war. The State Department and the National Security Council, anxious not to alienate the Soviet Union, had tried repeatedly to have the line removed or diluted. But the line reflected both Reagan's values and his political purposes. "The boys at State are going to kill me," Reagan wryly told an aide, "but it's the right thing to do." The line stayed.

"There is one sign the Soviets can make that would be unmistakable, that would advance dramatically the cause of freedom and peace," Reagan declared that afternoon. "General Secretary Gorbachev, if you seek peace, if you seek prosperity for the Soviet Union and Eastern Europe, if you seek liberalization, come here to this gate!" Then, with practiced, grave assurance, the president delivered Paul Robinson's line. "Mr. Gorbachev, open this gate!" Reagan demanded. "Mr. Gorbachev, tear down this wall!" And then, the president looked ahead to the future. "The wall," he predicted, "cannot withstand freedom."

Gorbachev did not immediately comply, but Reagan's speech served its purpose. Back in the United States, his conservative supporters were pleased by his tough, anti-Communist stance. Meanwhile, both the East Germans

and their Soviet allies complained about Reagan's rhetoric. According to the official Soviet news agency, the speech was an "openly propagandistic speech couched in the spirit of the Cold War times." Nevertheless, Gorbachev continued to pursue diplomatic breakthroughs with the United States. Reagan's speech was almost forgotten.

On November 9, 1989, nearly two-and-a-half years after Reagan's demand, the East German authorities unexpectedly opened the Berlin Wall. Soon, the barrier came down as the Cold War ended. "All of a sudden, within weeks after the wall came down, people were talking about the speech," an American diplomat recalled. "People were saying, 'Look at that. Ronald Reagan foresaw this. He was the one to give it its last push.'"

It was impossible to prove that words brought down the Berlin Wall, just as it was impossible to prove that Reagan ended the Cold War. But the president's appearance in front of the wall suggested the importance of political theater. Mixing language and image, sound and picture, the president, with the help of his aides, had powerfully epitomized the value of freedom and used it as a democratic weapon. Two-and-a-half years later, Berliners who wanted more democracy naturally tore down the wall to make their point.

The economy also helped the president. The stock market crash did not, as feared, lead to depression or recession. The market soon recovered and the economy grew.

Reagan's comeback was probably helped most by the transformation of the Soviet Union. By the mid-1980s, the Soviets suffered from a weakening economy, an unpopular war in Afghanistan, and a costly arms race. **Mikhail Gorbachev**, dynamic and charismatic, became general secretary of the Communist Party and signaled a new era with a series of stunning reforms. At home, he called for restructuring the economy (*perestroika*) and tolerating more open discussion (*glasnost*). Abroad, he sought to ease tensions with the United States and the West.

The Fall of the Berlin Wall Residents celebrate the fall of the Berlin Wall and the collapse of Communist rule in East Berlin and East Germany, November 1989.

TIME LINE

▼**1979–1981**
Iranian hostage crisis

▼**1980**
Ronald Reagan elected
   president

▼**1981**
IBM personal computer
Air traffic controllers' strike

Economic Recovery Act

▼**1982**
Nuclear freeze rally in New
   York City
Boland Amendment

▼**1983**
Strategic Defense Initiative

US invasion of Grenada
Terrorist attack on US Marines in Lebanon

▼**1984**
Reelection of Ronald
   Reagan

Gorbachev's reforms gave the United States an opening to thaw Cold War tensions. Reagan met with the Soviet leader in a series of summits beginning in November 1985. Visiting West Berlin in June 1987, the president challenged Gorbachev to "tear down" the Berlin Wall, which had symbolized the Cold War division of Europe. Meanwhile, it became apparent that the Soviets were changing their foreign policy, as they withdrew their troops from Afghanistan and eased their control over Eastern Europe.

The United States and the Soviets also made real progress on arms control. In December 1987, Reagan and Gorbachev signed the Intermediate-Range Nuclear Forces Treaty (INF), promising to destroy more than 2,500 intermediate-range missiles. For the first time, the two powers had agreed to give up a weapon altogether.

The INF treaty permanently eased tensions. The Cold War suddenly ended. Reagan's presidency ended in 1989; a year later, the United States and the Soviet Union agreed to end production of chemical weapons and reduce existing stockpiles. In 1991, the two nations signed the START (Strategic Arms Reduction Talks) Treaty, which called for each side to reduce its nuclear arsenals as much as 30 percent.

Meanwhile, the Soviet Union weakened. In 1989, Gorbachev could do nothing to stop the collapse of its repressive allies in Eastern Europe, as regimes toppled in Bulgaria, Czechoslovakia, Hungary, Poland, and Rumania. Most dramatically, a new East German government agreed in November to allow travel through the Berlin Wall. As jubilant Berliners dismantled it, the wall's fate epitomized the collapse of Communism. Accepting the transition to democracy, the Soviets withdrew their troops from Eastern Europe.

Powerless to save its allies, the Soviet leadership soon could not save itself. Despite Gorbachev's efforts, the low standard of living, Communist repression, and the unpopular war in Afghanistan made many unhappy. Estonia, Latvia, Lithuania, and other republics chafed under Russia's domination of the USSR. In 1990, Russia chose a charismatic president, Boris Yeltsin, who quit the Communist Party, supported independence for the republics, and challenged Gorbachev. The next year, Gorbachev resigned as party leader and president, and the Soviet parliament suspended the Communist Party. As one republic after another declared its independence, the USSR ceased to exist.

▼**1985**
General Electric purchase of RCA
Gramm-Rudman Act

▼**1986**
US bombing of Libya
Tax Reform Act

Revelation of Iran-Contra affair

▼**1987**
Stock market crash
Intermediate-Range Nuclear Forces Treaty
The Montreal Protocol

▼**1988**
Omnibus Trade and Competitiveness Act

▼**1991**
Collapse of the Soviet Union

With the collapse of the Soviet Union, the United States and its allies had won the Cold War. Conservatives insisted that Reagan's overpowering defense buildup had forced the Soviets to surrender. Democrats maintained that the buildup and the president's harsh rhetoric had actually slowed the thaw in US–Soviet relations and that America won the Cold War because of its long-term strength and strategy. Typically modest, Reagan himself gave credit to American policies reaching back to the 1940s.

Meanwhile, Americans did not celebrate very much as the Berlin Wall came down and the Soviet Union collapsed. The Cold War had cost a great deal in money and lives. Many Americans wondered whether Communism had posed a mortal danger to the United States in the first place.

CONCLUSION

Reagan left office with the highest popularity rating of any president since the beginning of modern polling in the 1930s. His comeback culminated the triumph of the new conservatism, but the nature of that triumph would be debated for years to come. The Reagan Revolution did not solve such basic economic problems as poverty and even worsened some problems, such as inequality and the budget deficit. Much of its conservative social agenda failed to take hold.

Nevertheless, Reagan successfully combated the sense of national decline that had pervaded America in the 1970s. After the troubled presidencies of that decade, Reagan's confident leadership made the democratic system seem viable again. His presidency reinvigorated faith in capitalist innovation, minimal government, and American military power. At the end of the 1980s, business values and evangelical religion claimed a more prominent place in American culture.

The accomplishments of the new conservatism, as Reagan's troubled second term indicated, were fragile. The nation's economic revival was shaky, and Americans were still worried about the future. "I think," a businessman concluded, "the '90s are going to be much trickier than the 1980s."

WHO, WHAT, WHERE

REVIEW QUESTIONS

1. What were the main values and goals of the new conservatism in the 1980s? What role did business and religion play in the conservative movement?

2. What was the Reagan Revolution in domestic policy? How did Reagan's domestic programs reflect conservative values?

3. What were the aims of the Reagan Revolution abroad?

CRITICAL-THINKING QUESTIONS

1. What groups resisted the conservative social agenda in the 1980s? Did the desire for equal rights and opportunities conflict with conservatism?

2. What factors limited the triumph of the new conservatism? Did conservatives really succeed in the 1980s?

3. How did the conservatism of the 1980s differ from earlier forms of conservatism in the twentieth century?

SUGGESTED READINGS

Berlin, Leslie. *Troublemakers: Silicon Valley's Coming of Age.* New York: Simon & Schuster, 2017.

McKevitt, Andrew C. *Consuming Japan: Popular Culture and the Globalizing of 1980s America.* Chapel Hill: North Carolina University Press, 2017.

Rossinow, Doug. *The Reagan Era: A History of the 1980s.* New York: Columbia University Press, 2016.

For further review materials and resource information, please visit www.oup.com/us/ofthepeople

CHAPTER 28: The Triumph of Conservatism, 1980–1991
Primary Sources

28.1 JERRY FALWELL, EXCERPTS FROM *LISTEN, AMERICA!* (1980)

In his 1980 book, *Listen, America!* Reverend Jerry Falwell called on evangelical Protestants to go into politics in order to help solve the nation's problems. The televangelist traced America's decline to a wide variety of sources, including television, secular humanism, liberals, homosexuals, and the federal government. Falwell's brand of evangelical activism played a key role in building the Reagan coalition.

We must reverse the trend America finds herself in today. Young people between the ages of twenty-five and forty have been born and reared in a different world than Americans of years past. The television set has been their primary baby-sitter. From the television set they have learned situation ethics and immorality—they have learned a loss of respect for human life. They have learned to disrespect the family as God has established it. They have been educated in a public-school system that is permeated with secular humanism. They have been taught that the Bible is just another book of literature. They have been taught that there are no absolutes in our world today. They have been introduced to the drug culture. They have been reared by the family and the public school in a society that is greatly void of discipline and character-building. These same young people have been reared under the influence of a government that has taught them socialism and welfarism. They have been taught to believe that the world owes them a living whether they work or not.

I believe that America was built on integrity, on faith in God, and on hard work. I do not believe that anyone has ever been successful in life without being willing to add that last ingredient—diligence or hard work. We now have second- and third-generation welfare recipients. Welfare is not always wrong. There are those who do need welfare, but we have reared a generation that understands neither the dignity nor the importance of work.

Every American who looks at the facts must share a deep concern and burden for our country. We are not unduly concerned when we say that there are some very dark clouds on America's horizon. I am not a pessimist, but it is indeed a time for truth. If Americans will face the truth, our nation can be turned around and can be saved from the evils and the destruction that have fallen upon every other nation that has turned its back on God.

There is no excuse for what is happening in our country. We must, from the highest office in the land right down to the shoeshine boy in the airport, have a return to biblical basics. If the Congress of our United States will take its stand on that which is right and wrong, and if our President, our judiciary system, and our state and local leaders will take their stand on holy living, we can turn this country around.

I personally feel that the home and the family are still held in reverence by the vast majority of the American public. I believe there is still a vast number of Americans who love their country, are patriotic, and are willing to sacrifice for her. I remember the time when it was positive to be patriotic, and as far as I am concerned, it still is. I remember as a boy, when the flag was raised, everyone stood proudly and put his hand upon his heart and pledged allegiance with gratitude. I remember when the band struck up "The Stars and Stripes Forever," we stood and goose pimples would run all over me. I remember when I was in elementary school during World War II, when every report from the other shores meant something to us. We were not out demonstrating against our boys who were dying in Europe and Asia. We were praying for them and thanking God for them and buying war bonds to help pay for the materials and artillery they needed to fight and win and come back. . . .

My responsibility as a preacher of the Gospel is one of influence, not of control, and that is the responsibility of each individual citizen. Through the ballot box Americans must provide for strong moral leadership at every level. If our country will get back on the track in sensibility and moral sanity, the crises that I have herein mentioned will work out in the course of time and with God's blessings.

It is now time to take a stand on certain moral issues, and we can only stand if we have leaders. We must stand against the Equal Rights Amendment, the feminist revolution, and the homosexual revolution. We must have a revival in this country. . . .

As a preacher of the Gospel, I not only believe in prayer and preaching, I also believe in good citizenship. If a labor union in America has the right to organize and improve its working conditions, then I believe that the churches and the pastors, the priests, and the rabbis of America have a responsibility, not just the right, to see to it that the moral climate and conscience of Americans is such that this nation can be healed inwardly. If it is healed inwardly, then it will heal itself outwardly. . . .

We are not a perfect nation, but we are still a free nation because we have the blessing of God upon us. We must continue to follow in a path that will ensure that blessing. . . .

The hope of reversing the trends of decay in our republic now lies with the Christian public in America. We cannot expect help from the liberals. They certainly are not going to call our nation back to righteousness and neither are the pornographers, the smut peddlers, and those who are corrupting our youth. Moral Americans must be willing to put their reputations, their fortunes, and their very lives on the line for this great nation of ours. Would that we had the courage of our forefathers who knew the great responsibility that freedom carries with it. . . .

Our Founding Fathers separated church and state in function, but never intended to establish a government void of God. As is evidenced by our Constitution, good people in America must exert an influence and provide a conscience and climate of morality in which it is difficult to go wrong, not difficult for people to go right in America.

I am positive in my belief regarding the Constitution that God led in the development of that document, and as a result, we here in America have enjoyed 204 years of unparalleled freedom. . . .

Americans must no longer linger in ignorance and apathy. We cannot be silent about the sins that are destroying this nation. The choice is ours. We must turn America around or prepare for inevitable destruction. I am listening to the sounds that threaten to take away our liberties in America. And I have listened to God's admonitions and His direction—the only hopes of saving America. Are you listening too?

Source: Jerry Falwell, *Listen, America!* (Garden City, NY: Doubleday, 1980), pp. 17–23.

28.2 RONALD REAGAN, EXCERPTS FROM "ADDRESS TO THE NATION ON THE ECONOMY" (1981)

On February 5, 1981, President Ronald Reagan gave his first televised national address in which he discussed the troubled US economy. Although he described a difficult situation, Reagan was characteristically optimistic. The answer to the nation's fiscal issues, he insisted, was the set of economic policies, including cuts in federal taxes, spending, and regulation, that would become known as Reaganomics.

I'm speaking to you tonight to give you a report on the state of our Nation's economy. I regret to say that we're in the worst economic mess since the Great Depression.

A few days ago I was presented with a report I'd asked for, a comprehensive audit, if you will, of our economic condition. You won't like it. I didn't like it. But we have to face the truth and then go to work to turn things around. And make no mistake about it, we can turn them around. . . .

The Federal budget is out of control, and we face runaway deficits of almost $80 billion for this budget year that ends September 30th. That deficit is larger than the entire Federal budget in 1957, and so is the almost $80 billion we will pay in interest this year on the national debt.

Twenty years ago, in 1960, our Federal Government payroll was less than $13 billion. Today it is $75 billion. During these 20 years our population has only increased by 23.3 percent. The Federal budget has gone up 528 percent.

Now, we've just had 2 years of back-to-back double-digit inflation—13.3 percent in 1979, 12.4 percent last year. The last time this happened was in World War I.

In 1960 mortgage interest rates averaged about 6 percent. They're 2 times as high now, 15.4 percent.

The percentage of your earnings the Federal Government took in taxes in 1960 has almost doubled.

And finally there are 7 million Americans caught up in the personal indignity and human tragedy of unemployment. If they stood in a line, allowing 3 feet for each person, the line would reach from the coast of Maine to California. . . .

We forgot or just overlooked the fact that government—any government—has a built-in tendency to grow. Now, we all had a hand in looking to government for benefits as if government had some source of revenue other than our earnings. Many if not most of the things we thought of or that government offered to us seemed attractive. . . .

Some government programs seemed so worthwhile that borrowing to fund them didn't bother us. . . .

We know now that inflation results from all that deficit spending. Government has only two ways of getting money other than raising taxes. It can go into the money market and borrow, competing with its own citizens and driving up interest rates, which it has done, or it can print money, and it's done that. Both methods are inflationary. . . .

Now, one way out would be to raise taxes so that government need not borrow or print money. But in all these years of government growth, we've reached, indeed surpassed, the limit of our people's tolerance or ability to bear an increase in the tax burden. Prior to World War II, taxes were such that on the average we only had to work just a little over 1 month each year to pay our total Federal, State, and local tax bill. Today we have to work 4 months to pay that bill.

Some say shift the tax burden to business and industry, but business doesn't pay taxes. Oh, don't get the wrong idea. Business is being taxed, so much so that we're being priced out of the world market. But business must pass its costs of operations—and that includes taxes—on to the customer in the price of the product. Only people pay taxes, all the taxes. Government just uses business in a kind of sneaky way to help collect the taxes. They're hidden in the price; we aren't aware of how much tax we actually pay.

Today this once great industrial giant of ours has the lowest rate of gain in productivity of virtually all the industrial nations with whom we must compete in the world market. We can't even hold our own market here in America against foreign automobiles, steel, and a number of other products. Japanese production of automobiles is almost twice as great per worker as it is in America. . . .

Now, this isn't because they're better workers. I'll match the American working man or woman against anyone in the world. But we have to give them the tools and equipment that workers in the other industrial nations have.

We invented the assembly line and mass production, but punitive tax policies and excessive and unnecessary regulations plus government borrowing have stifled our ability to update plant and equipment. When capital investment is made, it's too often for some unproductive alterations demanded by government to meet various of its regulations. Excessive taxation of individuals has robbed us of incentive and made overtime unprofitable. . . .

Over the past decades we've talked of curtailing government spending so that we can then lower the tax burden. . . . But there were always those who told us that taxes couldn't be cut until spending was reduced. Well, you know, we can lecture our children about extravagance until we run out of voice and breath. Or we can cure their extravagance by simply reducing their allowance. . . .

We must increase productivity. That means making it possible for industry to modernize and make use of the technology which we ourselves invented. That means putting Americans back to work. And that means above all bringing government spending back within government revenues, which is the only way, together with increased productivity, that we can reduce and, yes, eliminate inflation. . . .

We cannot delay in implementing an economic program aimed at both reducing tax rates to stimulate productivity and reducing the growth in government spending to reduce unemployment and inflation. . . .

Source: Ronald Reagan, "Address to the Nation on the Economy," February 5, 1981. https://www.presidency.ucsb.edu/documents/address-the-nation-the-economy-0

28.3   THE DEBATE OVER THE DEFENSE BUILD-UP (1983)

On March 23, President Reagan went on television to rally support for his aggressive build-up of American defenses by offering a frightening report of Soviet military strength and announcing a hopeful plan for his visionary spaced-based Strategic Defense Initiative—"Star Wars." Immediately afterward, Senator Daniel Inouye of Hawaii, gave the Democrats' response. Denying Reagan's account of the Soviet threat, Inouye offered a dramatically different definition of American strength.

. . . We are deeply troubled. Last night, the President attempted to instill fear in the hearts of the American people, to raise the specter of a Soviet armed nuclear attack, and to divert our attention from the dismal failure of his economic policies.

The President spoke of Soviet advances in the development and deployment of missiles armed with nuclear warheads. He left the impression that the United States had stood still while the Soviets accelerated and vastly expanded their nuclear arsenal. Indeed, he left the impression that the United States is at the mercy of the Soviet Union.

Most respectfully, Mr. President, you know that is not true. Our scientists, our engineers, our generals, are not dunces. You could have—but chose not—to mention the superiority of the submarine-based missiles we have developed to counter the Soviets. You could have—but chose not to mention—our superior, indeed our singular development of cruise missiles which can penetrate all known Soviet defenses.

If your urgency is to defend your defense budget, with its huge increases, against the more moderate proposals which have received bipartisan support in the Congress, we believe that you have failed to present an honest picture—here it is—Soviet land-based intercontinental missiles outnumber those of the United States. But the warheads on these missiles are more than offset by our warhead advantage in sea-based submarine missiles, and our bombers and cruise missiles. . . .

The President knows these figures. . . .

Why did he suggest American inferiority? I believe he did so because he is afraid that his excessive defense budget will be trimmed by the Congress and because he wants to take our attention off the economic disasters brought on by his policies. . . .

Our national strength does not depend solely on the number of missiles we have. Of greater significance, is the character and qualifications of our people. We must also weigh in the balance the strength of our economy. If we accept a defense budget which puts a crushing burden on our economy, which drives us closer to the precipice of economic collapse—if we accept a defense budget which dramatically increases to deficit and, in turn, prolongs unemployment, high interest rates, and low productivity, are we a stronger nation? I think not. A gathering majority of the Senate and the House of Representatives feels the same and is preparing to reduce the extraordinary defense expenditures proposed by the President.

President Reagan says he wants a stronger America. So do we Democrats. We differ on how to achieve the goal. In the last three years, defense expenditures have soared. But private investment in factories and machinery has fallen and so has the number of Americans at work. America is getting weaker on the Reagan program.

We are concerned with our national defense. We think it must be strengthened. But, we also believe that our strength is enhanced by programs which strengthen the education and the health of our people. We are concerned that 70 million Americans have difficulty reading and writing well enough to apply for a job.

We were deeply shocked by a recent Department of Education report that indicated that 56 percent of adult Hispanic Americans were functionally illiterate, that 47 percent of adult Black Americans were functionally illiterate, and 17 percent of "White Ameri cans" are functionally illiterate. How can these Americans truly enjoy the fruits of our democracy, if they have difficulty in filling out a job application form?

The President closed his speech last night with a "Star Wars scenario." He spoke of laser technology and other exotic techniques which would be used to destroy incoming missiles. We Democrats would like to suggest that if the United States is to develop, deploy, and man these "Buck Rogers" devices and equipment, we will need an army that is highly trained and knowledgeable in mathematics, sciences, electronics, and computer technology. But what is the picture today? Before the Reagan recession. when unemployment was not too bad, 20 percent of those who volunteered and were accepted into our volunteer army were functionally illiterate. Now, it is true that because of the recession, many high school graduates are seeking employment in our army and the number of functional illiterates has been reduced. But the technology proposed by the President as the answer to our defense requirements would require that more college graduates volunteer to serve in our

Armed Forces. Do you know of any college graduates who have volunteered to serve in the army? Prior to the recession, more than 30 percent of U.S. Navy warships were not ready for combat because there were insufficient trained personnel to make them seaworthy and combat-ready. Don't you believe it is tragic that we have to rely on recession and high unemployment to attract better qualified personnel into our armed services?

Last night, President Reagan spoke of our children in the 21st century—we are concerned about them as well, but we are also concerned about the children of today. Since he has been in office, the President has cut child nutrition programs by 33 per cent—he has cut programs which educate our people by 30 percent. I would submit that this does not make our nation strong.

Mr. President, let us not look for peace in yet another generation of destructive weapons. Let us begin now, with this ·generation of Americans, to destroy weapons. In the long sweep of history, the fundamental lesson is that civilizations do not rise or fall on strength of arms alone.

Democrats have a desire for peace. We recognize that our national defense must be strengthened. We ask only that the needs of our people be equally attended to.

We ask that our leaders bring us together, not huddling together in fear, but in hope for the future. We ask that our leaders attend to the needs of the least fortunate among us. Our strength is that we are "one nation under God, united." Each of us on the foundations of his own joys and suffering builds for all—that is our strength.

Source. *Congressional Record (98th Congress, 1st Session) 129*, no. 6, p. 7100.

28.4   EQUAL PAY FOR WOMEN (1982)

In 1982, hearings in the House of Representatives detailed the complex set of historical circumstances that left women's income far below men's. In her testimony, Eunice Cole, the President of the American Nurses Association, laid out the inequities for women in a female-dominated profession. Why is "the principle of equal pay for work for comparable value" so important to Cole?

. . . Registered nurses, as a group, typify the problems women face seeking equitable compensation for their work. Registered nurses' salaries always have been low relative to other occupations requiring similar-or often, lower-qualifications and skill.

The vast majority of working women are concentrated in occupations predominantly female and which have traditionally paid lower wages. Over half of all women employed full time are in clerical occupations, 78 percent female, or service occupations, 51 percent female. Only 19 percent of full-time women workers are in professional occupations. However, even among professional women, over half are employed as librarians, elementary and secondary school teachers and registered nurses.

It is clear that as long as women continue to be segregated into certain occupations, there can be no economic equality for women without the principle of equal pay for work for comparable value.

Equal pay for work of comparable value directly addresses the reasons women continue to earn far less than men. When women in traditionally female job classifications do work which requires the same or greater skill, effort, and responsibility as the tasks performed by men who work at different jobs, they are denied equal pay. . . .

Nursing is perhaps the only service whose origins belong to nonpaid—that is, voluntary or missionary—work. In its ultimate essence, nursing is a function of caring and compassion and has always been a predominantly female occupation. Because it was voluntary work in the beginning, the true market value has never been established.

The health care service industry has undergone significant change over the past three or four decades. Charity is no longer the major source of financing health care. The outlook of registered nurses in general and their work attitudes have also changed considerably. Old values die hard and slowly, however. Nurses are still experiencing the vestiges of nursing's roots in voluntarism. When they demand equal compensation, they are reminded, not infrequently, and sometimes from people within their own ranks, that nurses should seek their reward in heaven. Heavenly rewards notwithstanding, the American Nurses' Association would like to suggest that nurses' "earthly travail" should not continue to be burdened by job segregation and wage discrimination.

An even more glaring inconsistency between the so-called market forces and the wage rates for registered nurses is demonstrated by the reported nurse shortage, a shortage that has been reported for decades. The American Hospital Association's latest figures estimate the hospital nurse vacancy between 65,000 and 70,000 nationwide.

If the market forces were working to establish wage rates, obviously this shortage would have led to higher wages for nurses. This has not happened. Nurses' salaries have not increased faster than other occupations and have not outpaced the cost of living. Hospitals' response to the nurse shortage has been to substitute less skilled workers and to import nurses from other countries rather than raise wages to alleviate a shortage. Clearly, market forces are not a defense for the low wages paid to registered nurses.

The nursing profession, over 97-percent females, provides the most outstanding example of the systematic discrimination against predominantly female occupations. Society has consistently failed to provide compensation for nurses in accordance with their valuable contribution to the overall welfare of society.

This is evident by looking at wages paid to physicians' assistants and pharmacists, all predominantly male, all requiring similar skill, effort and responsibility, and all paid much higher wages than paid to registered nurses. The undervaluation of registered nurses becomes even more painfully evident when their wages are compared to sign painters and tree trimmers.

Job evaluation studies, without exception, demonstrate that registered nurses are never paid in accordance with their value to an employer. The city of San Jose, Calif.'s 1980 jobs evaluation study, rated the skill, effort and responsibility of the city nurse equal to that of the electrical foreman. City nurses earn, on the average, $839 per month; electrical foremen earn $1,168 per month.

In Minnesota, results of a 1981 job evaluation study showed registered nurses rated equal to vocational education field instructors. The nurses earned, on average, $1,723 per month; the instructors, $2,260 per month. . . .

Source: *Statement of Eunice Cole, President, American Nurses' Association. Pay Equity: Equal Pay for Work of Comparable Value. Joint Hearings Before the Subcommittees on Human Resources Civil Service Compensation and Employee Benefits of the Committee on Post Office and Civil Service.* House of Representatives Ninety-Seventh Congress. Second Session. Part 1. Washington, DC. September 16, 21, 30, and December 2, 1982 (Washington, DC: US Government Printing Office., 1983), pp. 266–268.

28.5 EXCERPTS FROM THE REPUBLICAN AND DEMOCRATIC PARTY PLATFORMS ON THE STATE OF THE AMERICAN FAMILY (1984)

By the 1984 presidential election, the state of the American family had become another battleground for the nation's two major political parties. The Democrats used the words "family" or "families" 27 times in their platform that year; the

Republicans used the words no fewer than 78 times in theirs. As these excerpts from each party's platform make clear, the parties thought about the present and future state of the American family quite differently.

Republican platform:. . . America was built on the institutions of home, family, religion, and neighborhood. From these basic building blocks came self-reliant individuals, prepared to exercise both rights and responsibilities. . . .

Public policy long ignored these foundations of American life. Especially during the two decades preceding Ronald Reagan's election, the federal government eroded their authority, ignored their rights, and attempted to supplant their functions with programs at once intrusive and ineffectual. It thereby disrupted our traditional patterns of caring, sharing, and helping. . . .

Washington's governing elite. . . tried to build their brave new world by assaulting our basic values. They mocked the work ethic. They scorned frugality. They attacked the integrity of the family and parental rights. They ignored traditional morality. And they still do. . . .

Over the past two decades, welfare became a nightmare for the taxpayer and the poor alike. Fraud and abuse were rampant. The costs of public assistance are astronomical, in large part because resources often benefit the welfare industry rather than the poor. . . . This was a fantastic and unsustainable universalization of welfare.

Welfare's indirect effects were equally as bad. . . . Government created a hellish cycle of dependency. Family cohesion was shattered, both by providing economic incentives to set up maternal households and by usurping the breadwinner's economic role in intact families.

The cruelest result was the maternalization of poverty, worsened by the breakdown of the family and accelerated by destructive patterns of conduct too long tolerated by permissive liberals. We endorse programs to assist female-headed households to build self-sufficiency, such as efforts by localities to enable participants to achieve permanent employment.

Many health problems arise within the family and should be dealt with there. We affirm the right and responsibility of parents to participate in decisions about the treatment of children. We will not tolerate the use of federal funds, taxed away from parents, to abrogate their role in family health care. . . .

Republicans affirm the family as the natural and indispensable institution for human development. A society is only as strong as its families, for they nurture those qualities necessary to maintain and advance civilization.

Healthy families inculcate values—integrity, responsibility, concern for others—in our youth and build social cohesion. We give high priority to their well-being. During the 1970s, America's families were ravaged by worsening economic conditions and a Washington elite unconcerned with them.

We support the concept of creating Family Education Accounts which would allow tax-deferred savings for investment in America's most crucial asset, our children, to assist low- and middle-income families in becoming self-reliant in meeting the costs of higher education.

In addition, to further assist the young families of America in securing the dream of homeownership, we would like to review the concept of Family Housing Accounts which would allow tax-exempt savings for a family's first home.

Preventing family dissolution, a leading cause of poverty, is vital. It has had a particularly tragic impact on the elderly, women, and minorities. Welfare programs have devastated low-income families and induced single parenthood among teens. We will review legislation and regulations to examine their impact on families and on parental rights and responsibilities. We seek to eliminate incentives for family break-up and to reverse the alarming rate of pregnancy outside marriage. Meanwhile, the Republican Party believes that society must do all that is possible to guarantee those young parents the opportunity to achieve their full educational and parental potential.

The President's tax program. . . increased tax credits for child care expenses. We will encourage private sector initiatives to expand on-site child care facilities and options for working parents.

The problem of physical and sexual abuse of children and spouses requires careful consideration of its causes. In particular, gratuitous sex and violence in entertainment media contribute to this sad development. . . .

Democratic platform:. . . In Ronald Reagan's vision of America, there are no single parent families, women only stay at home and care for children. Reagan's families do not worry about the effects of unemployment on family stability: they do not worry about decent housing and health care: they do not need child care. But in the real world, most Americans do. Providing adequate child care for the millions of American children who need it, and for their parents, is surely not a responsibility which belongs solely to the federal government. But, like the responsibility for decent housing and health care, it is one where federal leadership and support are essential.

. . . Small businesses have closed: American families are suffering hunger and poor health, as unemployment exceeds depression rates. Women continue to receive less than 60 percent of the wages that men receive, with minority women receiving far less.

. . . Ronald Reagan's tax program gave huge breaks to wealthy individuals and to large corporations while shifting the burden to low and moderate income families. The Democratic Party is pledged to reverse these unsound policies.

. . . There are. . . key goals that a Democratic program for educational excellence must address:. . . ensuring that all American families can send their children on to college or advanced training.

. . . Even in a growing economy, the pressures of competition and the pace of change ensure that while jobs are being created, others are being destroyed. . . . We must make special efforts to help families in economic transition who are faced with loss of homes, health benefits, and pensions.

. . . More than one-third of all female-headed households are below the poverty line, and for non-white families headed by women with more than one child, the figure is 70 percent.

But the numbers tell only part of the story; numbers do not convey the frustration and suffering of women seeking a future for themselves and their children, with no support from anyone; numbers do not recount the pain of growing numbers of homeless men and women with no place to sleep, or of increasing infant mortality rates among children born to poor mothers. Numbers do not convey the human effects of unemployment on a once stable and strong family.

As Democrats, we call upon the American people to join with us in a renewed commitment to combat the feminization of poverty in our nation so that every American can be a productive, contributing member of our society. In that effort, our goal is to strengthen families and to reverse the existing incentives for their destruction. We therefore oppose laws requiring an unemployed parent to leave the family or drop out of the work force in order to qualify for assistance and health care. We recognize the special need to increase the labor force participation of minority males, and we are committed to expanding their opportunities through education and training and to enforcing the laws which guarantee them equal opportunities. The plight of young mothers must be separately addresses as well; they too need education and training and quality child care must be available if they are to participate in such programs. Only through a nation that cares and a government that acts can those Americans trapped in poverty move toward meaningful independence.

. . . Since 1980, however, hunger has returned. High unemployment, coupled with deep cutbacks in food assistance and other basic support programs for poor families have led to conditions not seen in this country for years. Studies in hospitals and health departments document increases in numbers of malnourished children. Increasing numbers of homeless wander our cities streets in search of food and shelter. Religious organizations, charities and other agencies report record numbers of persons standing in line for food at soup kitchens and emergency food pantries.

Sources: "Republican Party Platform of 1984," August 20, 1984. https://www.presidency.ucsb.edu/documents/republican-party-platform-1984 "Democratic Party Platform of 1984," July 16, 1984. https://www.presidency.ucsb.edu/documents/1984-democratic-party-platform

The Globalized, Information Society

1989–2008

< 9:03 a.m., September 11, 2001

951

David Rockefeller

Turning 75 in 1990, David Rockefeller linked two eras of American history. His grandfathers, Standard Oil billionaire John D. Rockefeller and Rhode Island Republican US Senator Nelson Aldrich, had been commanding figures of the industrializing nation. David, inheriting a good chunk of the family fortune, was no industrialist. As Chairman of the Board of the Chase Manhattan Bank, the huge financial institution long associated with his family, David was a pioneer of a new America defined by intricate global connections and information technology.

Rockefeller's global consciousness and commitment were still unusual in 1990, but they were in some ways a predictable result of his experiences. Thanks to his parents, he had toured Europe extensively as a boy. "I am a passionate traveler," he wrote, "and from the time I was a child, travel formed me as much as my formal education. In order to appreciate cultures of another nation, one needs to go there, know the people and mingle with the culture of that country." With a doctorate in economics, he served abroad during World War II. Along with his oldest brother Nelson, David believed in strengthening US commercial, cultural, and political ties with Latin America.

As Rockefeller climbed the ranks of the Chase bank after the war, his global outlook shaped his work. Becoming the leader of the New York City-based company in 1969, David focused Chase on global business by financing international trade and establishing branches around the world. Chase became the first American bank to open in the Soviet Union and People's Republic of China. Rockefeller's ambitious global plans were possible in large part because of new information technologies. Chase made heavy use of computers, satellite communications, and video conferencing to knit together its vast international business.

Rockefeller felt that Americans alone couldn't manage the globalized Chase. "It seemed to me that we needed to get the benefit of the thinking of talented people in places we're operating," he recalled. "It was arrogant on our part to think that we could land in a foreign country without getting feedback from people in the country."

Outwardly affable and modest, David Rockefeller had developed an ambitious global vision that went far beyond economics. In the 1970s, he had helped form the Trilateral Commission, an organization uniting US, European, and Japanese businessmen, politicians, and intellectuals, to promote global connections. Controversial from the start, the commission seemed an extension of traditional Rockefeller family power and a threat to the power of national governments. Rockefeller had no apologies. "The world is ... prepared to march towards a world government," he declared. "The supernational sovereignty of an intellectual elite and world bankers is surely preferable to the national auto determination practiced in past centuries."

Envisioning a unified world without national governments, Rockefeller still saw himself as a loyal American and a proud New Yorker. But David was redefining what America and New York City would be about. With his brother, Nelson had led the push to construct a huge office complex in lower Manhattan with soaring twin towers, nicknamed "David" and "Nelson" by the builders. Opening in 1973, this grand project became the World Trade Center.

By the 1990s, David Rockefeller was no longer so far ahead of his time. During this decade, a complex set of ties clearly bound the United States to the world in fresh ways that became known as globalization. At the same time, an information economy, based on computers, high-speed communication, and other technologies, emerged as the old industrial economy of John D. Rockefeller declined. As the projects of his grandson David suggested, globalization and the **information economy** posed complex challenges for American government and society. Still moving toward conservatism, American democracy struggled with the role of government in the economy, the increasing diversity of the nation's people, and the role of the United States in the post–Cold War world.

THE AGE OF GLOBALIZATION

By the 1990s, Americans increasingly felt enmeshed in global forces. America, of course, had long been defined by its relationship to the world. But this global connection entered a new, more self-conscious phase in the 1980s. During the decade, the term **globalization** first came into use to describe the web of technological, economic, military, political, and cultural developments binding people and nations ever more tightly together. The Cold War's end, technological advances, the spread of multinationals and other organizations, the creation of transnational economic alliances, and a new wave of immigration all drew the United States deeper into globalization.

The Cold War and Globalization

For two generations, the Cold War had both facilitated and hindered globalization. In some ways, the confrontation between the United States and the Soviet Union linked the world more closely together. Each power had a host of ties to other nations. The United States had established regional military alliances around the world and helped rebuild Asian and European economies through lower trade barriers, the World Bank, and the International Monetary Fund.

Still, the Cold War inhibited globalization, too. The United States and the Soviet Union had largely avoided trading with each other. Each power had discouraged its allies from ties with the other side. The collapse of the Soviet Union in 1991 opened the way to further globalization. Now nations and companies could forge new ties more freely across the old Cold War divide.

New Communications Technologies

New communications technologies sped up the global flow of news, ideas, and money. The internet, a product of the Cold War, emerged from a Department of Defense search for a means of maintaining communications in the event of a nuclear attack. Aided by the development of the telephone modem and fiber-optic cable, the internet spread quickly in the 1990s. At first, people used it to send and receive electronic messages, but by the middle of the 1990s, computer users also explored the World Wide Web, a rapidly expanding segment of the internet that blended text, graphics, audio, and video. By 2000, some 304 million people from more than 40 nations already used the global "information superhighway" to do research, create and exhibit art, listen to music, share photographs and films, and buy and sell online.

Communications satellites also played a critical role in globalization. Following the US deployment of Telstar and other satellites in the 1960s, several other nations launched their own. In the 1990s, global satellite communications revolutionized the news business. Cable News Network (CNN), founded in 1979 by the entrepreneur **Ted Turner**, used satellite uplinks to provide live televised coverage of events around the world. Turner wanted CNN to be a "positive force in the world, to tie the world together." Satellite news organizations soon appeared in other countries.

Meanwhile, mobile and cellular telephones spread especially quickly in the United States and many other countries. In 1985, only 340,000 Americans subscribed to cell phone service using bulky phones over a primitive analog network. By 2000, more than half the population owned a cell phone. In relatively impoverished Africa, there were already more than 15 million cell telephone subscribers by the early 2000s.

Multinationals and NGOs

Connecting businesses across national borders, communications advances helped stimulate an astonishing increase in the number of multinational corporations. In 1990, there were 3,000 multinationals worldwide. By 2003, the number mushroomed to 63,000. With some 821,000 subsidiaries, multinationals employed about 90 million people and accounted for perhaps one-fourth of the world's economic output.

Long a leader in creating multinationals, the United States remained home to many of the largest and wealthiest. By the end of the century, Wal-Mart was Mexico's largest private-sector employer, with 100,000 workers. But America now faced intense competition from Japan, China, European nations, and others. In 1962, nearly 60 percent of the top 500 multinationals were American; by 1999, the percentage had declined to 36.

Along with multinational companies, private nongovernmental organizations (**NGOs**) also fostered globalization. Some NGOs, such as the International Red Cross, dated to the nineteenth century. The World Economic Forum, which brought leaders and experts together annually in Davos, Switzerland, was a product of the 1970s. So were the environmentalist Greenpeace and the humanitarian Doctors Without Borders. By the 2000s, there were more than 10,000 NGOs worldwide.

Expanding Trade

Along with peace and communication, the most basic necessity for globalization was the easy movement of goods, services, and capital across national boundaries. After the Cold War, nations, eager to seize their share of the global market, aggressively removed barriers to trade and investment. America established economic relationships with the former republics of the USSR, the European countries of the Soviet bloc, the Socialist Republic of Vietnam, and the People's Republic of China. By 1996, Wal-Mart had a store in Beijing, and McDonald's had restaurants in Russia.

To spur international trade and investment, nations also created regional economic alliances that guaranteed member states trading and investment privileges and lowered or abolished tariffs. In 1991, the member states of the European Economic Community, a pioneering regional trade alliance, signed the Maastricht Treaty to create a single vast unit, the European Union (EU), with its own currency, the euro. With 6.4 percent of the global population, the EU produced a third of the world's goods and more than a third of its trade.

The 1990s also witnessed the transformation of the General Agreement on Tariffs and Trade (GATT). A US Cold War–era creation, GATT had drawn together over 100 nations. Its efforts to increase trade through agreements known as "rounds" culminated in 1993 when the Uruguay Round produced a dramatic victory for free-trade policies. GATT was then reborn as a more powerful global body, the **World Trade Organization (WTO)**, whose decisions would be binding on member nations. The United States joined the WTO in 1995.

Moving People

The movement of human beings as well as goods was critical to globalization. Thanks to regional economic agreements and the end of the Cold War, people could cross national borders more easily. Between 1990 and 1994, 4.5 million immigrants came to the United States. By 2000, the immigrant population had reached 26.3 million, about 11 percent of the national total population, the largest percentage since before World War II.

Travel also facilitated globalization by exposing people to other nations and cultures. Thanks to low-cost jet flights and improved living standards, tourism was possibly the largest single global industry by the 1990s.

Globalization Produced Unexpected Sights
Sewing American flags in the People's Republic of China under the watchful eye of communist leader Mao Zedong.

America In The World
Titanic and the Globalization of Hollywood

In 1998, *Titanic* became the first Hollywood film to earn more than a billion dollars. That feat was the result of globalization: the cinematic tale of doomed, cross-social-class love, set against the tragic sinking of a huge transatlantic ocean liner on its first voyage in 1912, earned nearly twice as much around the world as it did in the United States. *Titanic*'s enormous international success was unexpected but not unintended. From start to finish, the movie project about a failed attempt to connect nations at the beginning of the twentieth century epitomized the emerging web of global connections at the century's end.

Like the United States more broadly, Hollywood—both the place and the industry—had long interacted with the rest of the world. Immigrants, such as Hungarian-born William Fox, founder of Fox Film Corporation, helped create the business in the 1910s and 1920s. After World War I, Hollywood films found a wide audience in Europe. But the Great Depression and World War II hurt Hollywood's exports, just as those upheavals set back the larger processes of globalization. By the 1960s, new global forces transformed Hollywood. Studios were making "runaway films" abroad rather than in California. In the 1980s and 1990s, Hollywood was remade by global corporate takeovers. News Corporation, a foreign firm dominated by

Australian William Rupert Murdoch, took over Twentieth Century Fox, the successor to Fox Film Corporation.

Hollywood rebounded in the 1990s. As prosperity brought new movie screens around the world, the American industry successfully battled for global audiences. The success of films such as *Titanic* reflected old and new national advantages. *Titanic*'s writer, director, and producer was James Cameron, a Canadian immigrant who sold the project to Twentieth Century Fox, which shot much of the film in Mexico. In addition to new digital technologies, Cameron and his colleagues had the benefit of decades of Hollywood experience making films to appeal to the especially diverse US movie audience. *Titanic* "intentionally incorporates universals of human experience and emotions that are timeless—and familiar because they reflect our basic emotional fabric," Cameron explained. "By dealing in archetypes, the film touches people in all cultures and of all ages."

Along with universal emotions and special effects, *Titanic* reached foreign audiences because, paradoxically, it seemed distinctively American. Even moviegoers in nations at odds with the United States found themselves drawn to the film. In Iran, where many people condemned America as the "Great Satan," a 28-year-old electrical engineer admitted that "American culture

Contesting Globalization

Despite differences with one another, political leaders generally agreed with big business that globalization represented a triumph for American institutions and values, including capitalism, free trade, and democracy. Despite tough international economic competition, powerful Americans thought the nation was still better off than in a divided world without free trade.

***Titanic* in China** A woman buys a ticket to the Hollywood blockbuster in Beijing in 1998.

is very dominant." *Titanic* seemed like a "cultural invasion," he said, but he loved it: "I've memorized every line."

In the communist People's Republic of China, the president speculated that *Titanic* might be a "Trojan horse," full of cultural invaders from the capitalist, democratic United States. Even so, the president felt he had to let the film be shown. *Titanic* proved as seductive in China as it did in Iran. "In China today, many people are disillusioned with the past and are searching for new values and new heroes," said a graduate student at Beijing University. "Watching 'Titanic' temporarily injects hope, romance, and fantasy back into some people's lives."

Titanic and the rest of globalized Hollywood seemed to increase the world power of the United States in the 1990s. "The American entertainment complex is one of the strongest forces in the world, and probably has greater global influence than the US military," insisted the dean of an American journalism school.

Other observers argued, however, that globalization had diluted the American-ness of the film business. "Hollywood is not an American industry," a former US ambassador maintained, "but, rather, an entertainment industry that is located in California and belongs to the world." Driven by the capitalist imperative for profit, Hollywood hired foreigners such as Cameron and made films that appealed to "world culture." "This is commerce at its best," the ambassador concluded, "not cultural imperialism."

The argument between the two sides would continue for years to come. In addition, there was a middle ground: because the United States was so diverse, so capitalist, and so open to global forces, the nation took particular advantage of globalization. Precisely because *Titanic* so fully evoked universal hopes, dreams, and fantasies, the film was quintessentially American. Global and American values seemed to merge into a single widely accepted message and a billion-dollar film.

In contrast, many middle- and working-class Americans questioned whether globalization made their lives better. As economists acknowledged, globalization promoted a kind of national economic specialization. Some American industries, such as information technology, agriculture, and entertainment, fared well in global competition, but others, such as steel and traditional manufacturing, did less well. The result was lower wages and lost jobs for many Americans.

The presence of several million illegal immigrants from Mexico angered many American citizens, particularly in Texas and California. Their argument was familiar: illegal aliens drove down wages and took jobs from native-born Americans who paid higher taxes to provide services and benefits to tax-evading immigrants. In 1994, California voters passed Proposition 187, a referendum denying illegal aliens access to public education and other benefits. Two years later, Congress increased efforts to stop the flow of illegal immigrants.

The anti-immigrant movement continued, but business generally welcomed immigration because it provided workers. Calculating the rapid growth of the Hispanic population, political leaders did not wish to antagonize an increasingly powerful group of voters. Many native-born Americans who were descendants of immigrants believed immigration would invigorate the economy and the culture.

International trade also provoked conflict. The US government, faced with the rapid-fire appearance of regional economic alliances, moved to create its own economic bloc. In 1992, the United States joined with Canada and Mexico in the North American Free Trade Agreement (NAFTA), which established the world's largest and richest low-tariff trading zone. Fearing more lost jobs, organized labor opposed the agreement. So did many environmentalists, who believed corporations would get around US environmental laws by moving operations to Mexico. But the leadership of both major parties favored the agreement, and in 1993, the Senate ratified NAFTA.

Opposition to globalization flared again at a meeting of the WTO in Seattle, Washington, in 1999. Labor unions, environmentalists, consumer activists, women's groups, and other organizations staged parades, meetings, and street theater. Demonstrators charged that the WTO favored corporations and developed nations, damaged the environment, allowed AIDS to spread, and destroyed indigenous cultures. Fears of protest and terrorism led to cancelation of the WTO meetings scheduled for 2001.

Globalization was hard to defeat. It would take more than isolated protests to halt the movement of people, ideas, technologies, goods, and capital in the twenty-first century.

A NEW ECONOMY

Globalization combined with technological change to create a new, information-centered American economy. Like the industrial revolution of the nineteenth century, the information economy of the late twentieth century reorganized patterns of work and wealth. But it was unclear whether the new system was quite as revolutionary as the old. Like the Industrial Revolution, the globalized, information economy produced both new insecurity and new prosperity.

From Industry to Information

As global competition closed American factories, the nature of the postindustrial economy clarified. By the 1990s, factories employed fewer production workers than in 1955; meanwhile, the service sector accounted for about 70 percent of America's economic activity. The rise of services using sophisticated communications, computing, and biomedical technology encouraged the belief that information would define the twenty-first-century economy.

From the 1990s into the next century, innovations in electronics continued to transform communications. High-speed fiber-optic cables, cell phone towers, and satellite dishes expanded the power and reach of telephone and television systems. By 1999, more than half of the nation's households had at least one computer. The new information economy spurred the hope that Americans would process data instead of coal and produce knowledge instead of steel.

Advances in genetics and medical technology further sparked hopes for an information-centered economy. At the close of the twentieth century, scientists made rapid advances in understanding animal and human genomes. Corporations began applying this genetic knowledge to agriculture, medicine, and other fields. The result was biomedical technology—the use of organisms and their products to alter health and the environment. By 2000, about one-third of the US corn, cotton, and soybean crops were products of genetic engineering. By then, over 125 genetically engineered drugs had won approval for the treatment of cancer and other diseases.

A Second Economic Revolution?

The information and industrial economies were quite different. Manual, blue-collar labor tended the machines of smokestack America; white-collar, well-educated labor tended the computers of information America. The industrial economy had eaten up fossil fuels, minerals, and other exhaustible resources and produced substantial pollution; the information economy promised less damage to the earth.

In some ways, the rise of the information economy repeated the Industrial Revolution. As in the late 1800s and early 1900s, technological change pushed new corporations to the forefront of American capitalism: e-commerce pioneers such as Amazon.com and eBay, the search engine giant Google, and, in the 2000s, the social-networking leader Facebook. Like the Industrial Revolution, the information revolution spurred a wave of corporate consolidation. In 1989, media company Time, Inc., merged with entertainment conglomerate Warner Communications; in 1995, Time Warner then gobbled Turner Broadcasting. During the 1990s, Microsoft took over 46 companies.

The information revolution also paralleled the Industrial Revolution by producing a wealthy elite. The most famous of the new multibillionaires was Bill Gates, cofounder of Microsoft, who became the richest American since John D. Rockefeller, the cofounder of Standard Oil nearly a century before.

Just as the appearance of trains, planes, and machines stimulated artists and intellectuals in the nineteenth and twentieth centuries, so did the appearance of computers a century later. Digital technology made it easy to copy and manipulate text, images, and sounds, a development that encouraged collage and undermined linear narratives. More broadly, some thinkers believed a new, postmodern culture was replacing the modern culture inspired by industrialism. Hard to define, postmodern culture embraced a more skeptical view of accepted truths and dominant ideologies, and the techniques of hypertext and cut and paste.

Despite parallels to the Industrial Revolution, the information economy was not as potent a revolutionary force in critical ways. Machine tools, railroads, and electricity had greatly boosted workers' productivity in the industrial era.

Computers, the internet, and biotechnology did not do the same. Moreover, factories had generated the need for additional jobs in supporting businesses, such as mining and transportation. Information-centered businesses did not have the same effect. Despite the glamour of information and biotechnology, most service jobs required little education, used limited technology, and paid less than the best blue-collar jobs of the old economy. By the 2000s, the biggest employer in America was not an information company but rather a low-wage retail store, Wal-Mart.

Downsizing America

Like the Industrial Revolution, the information economy and global competition produced upheaval. Millions of American workers found themselves victims of remarkable corporate downsizing. The cutbacks came during a period of prosperity and involved seemingly stable companies, such as computing firm IBM and communications giant AT&T. Large corporations, typically quick to lay off assembly-line and other blue-collar jobs, had traditionally been slow to cut white-collar positions. But now managers and professionals were vulnerable to unemployment as well.

Fundamentally, downsizing reflected corporate managers' imperative to cut costs and increase profits. Despite the general prosperity, management worried about remaining efficient and competitive in the global economy. The end of the Cold War also affected American corporations. As the federal government downsized the military, defense contractors lost business, and they, too, had to downsize.

Downsizing dramatically affected American workers. In the hard search for new employment, many had to settle for lower-paying jobs and cope with a sense of failure and dislocation. Meanwhile, the remaining employees at downsized companies, taking over the responsibilities of laid-off workers, had to work harder than ever. Realizing they could lose their jobs at any moment, employees felt less loyalty to corporations. More broadly, downsizing suggested that the American middle class was not so stable and secure after all.

Not surprisingly, downsizing was controversial. Critics charged that downsizing actually made companies less efficient because the strategy left them short-handed and deprived them of experienced workers' know-how. Downsizing, the critics concluded, was just "dumbsizing." But corporations insisted that downsizing was necessary to restore efficiency, competitiveness, and profits. Rather than threaten the middle class, downsizing would assure its future by paving the way for better, high-paying jobs in new sectors of the globalized, information economy.

Boom and Insecurity

Despite—or because of—downsizing, globalization and the information revolution seemed to benefit the economy for most of the 1990s. Productive American workers and a vital service sector produced economic growth for nearly the entire decade, a record. Because of global competition, corporate cost cutting, and low oil prices, inflation was negligible. Interest rates stayed low; unemployment dropped to record lows. Excitement about information-related companies drove the stock market to one record high after another. After passing 3,000 for the first time ever in 1991, the Dow Jones industrial average soared past 11,000 in 1999. As memories of the 1987 market crash faded, many Americans no longer felt the need to live with less.

Congress repealed the federal 55-mile-per-hour speed limit for interstate highways in 1995, and gas-guzzling sport utility vehicles (SUVs) became popular.

Nevertheless, Americans felt a continuing sense of insecurity about basic features of American life. From 1993 to 2004, the cost of tuition at four-year colleges increased about 50 percent above inflation. As a result, the debt burden on students and their families increased dramatically. The information economy depended on a highly educated workforce, but many Americans worried whether they could afford the education they needed.

The increasing costs of health care also troubled Americans. In the 1990s, the United States spent a greater proportion of its gross domestic product on health care than did other developed nations. Still, 14 percent of Americans had no health insurance in 2000. The United States, almost alone among developed nations, had no national health insurance plan for its citizens. As employers cut costs, they decreased medical benefits for employees. The need for costly medical care would only increase as life expectancy continued to rise and the huge baby boom generation aged.

Americans feared, too, that they could not afford retirement. With the aging of the baby boom generation, there were more Americans over 65 and eligible for Social Security benefits than ever before (see Map 29–1). Many people believed there would not be enough money to pay pensions in the twenty-first century. Private employers, meanwhile, reduced pension benefits for many retirees.

The Social Security, health care, and college issues, along with corporate downsizing, fostered anxiety in the midst of prosperity. Although the economy grew and the stock market flourished, Americans wondered whether the future would be so prosperous. This uneasiness contributed to broader uncertainty about the age of globalization.

DEMOCRACY DEADLOCKED

The economic dynamism of the 1990s was often accompanied by political deadlock. After Ronald Reagan's presidency, his supporters hoped that conservative Republicans would continue to remake American politics. While conservative ideas still influenced policy, Republicans and Democrats shared power in Washington, DC. Generally agreeing about globalization, party leaders differed over taxes, government spending, and many other issues. Many Americans were unhappy with politics as usual and some were angry enough with the government to resort to terrorism. Nevertheless, the political system remained largely unchanged and no party or philosophy molded politics and government.

George H. W. Bush and the End of the Reagan Revolution

The natural choice for Reagan's successor, Vice President George H. W. Bush of Texas, was not a conservative but a moderate willing to make political compromises. Bush, the son of a Wall Street banker and US senator from Connecticut, had attended elite schools and become part of the upper-class "Establishment" that many conservatives distrusted. Nevertheless, Bush had loyally served Reagan through two terms. Bush had a broad background of government service, including stints as a congressman, ambassador to the United Nations, chair of the Republican Party, liaison to China, and director of the CIA.

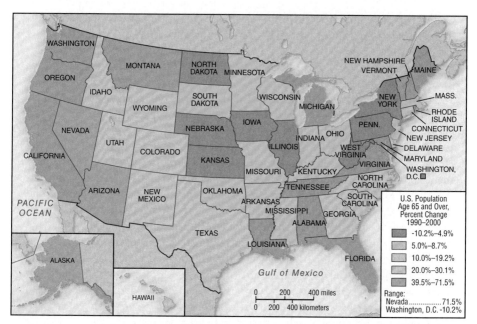

Map 29–1 **Aging in America** The increase in the percentage of the US population age 65 and over from 1980 to 2000 helped fuel worries about health care and Social Security. *Sources*: US Census Bureau, *Population Estimates, July 1, 2000, to July 1*, 2006. He Wan, Manisha Sengupta, Victoria A. Velkoff, and Kimberly A. DeBarros, US Census Bureau, *Current Population Reports, P23-209, 65+ in the United States: 2005* (Washington, DC: US Government Printing Office, 2005).

Committing himself to Reagan's economic policy, Bush easily won the Republican presidential nomination in 1988. "Read my lips," he vowed: "No new taxes." At the same time, Bush softened the image of the new conservatism by emphasizing his support for education and the environment. He easily defeated the Democratic nominee, former Governor Michael Dukakis of Massachusetts, who ran a colorless, ineffective campaign calling for efficient government, civil rights, and little more. On Election Day, Bush polled 53 percent of the popular vote and carried 40 states for a total of 426 electoral votes.

Despite Bush's triumph, the election also revealed the weak electoral impact of the Reagan Revolution. Once again, the Republicans failed to break the Democrats' hold on the House and Senate. Despite Reagan's accomplishments, voters still would not give his party full control in Washington.

The Republicans' limited victory in 1988 reinforced Bush's political moderation. Downplaying conservatism, Bush promised a "kinder and gentler" presidency. He disappointed conservatives by signing the Clean Air Act of 1990, which reduced acid rain by cutting emissions from power plants and automobiles. He disappointed conservatives again by signing increases to federal education funding. Above all, he alienated conservatives by abandoning his no-tax pledge and accepting to a tax increase in 1990 to decrease the federal budget deficit.

Bush's moderation did not ensure his popularity. The abandonment of his no-tax pledge reinforced the sense that he was a weak leader. Then, an economic recession in 1991–1992 intensified Americans' dissatisfaction with the president.

The Rebellion Against Politics as Usual

Americans' unhappiness with George H. W. Bush reflected their broader dissatisfaction with politicians and government. By the 1990s, there were signs of a brewing popular rebellion against politics as usual. Back in 1964, 76 percent of Americans had believed they could trust the government to do what was right always or most of the time. But Lyndon Johnson's "credibility gap" and Richard Nixon's lies and cover-ups had shaken Americans' faith in presidents and politicians. Politics in the 1980s, including the Iran-Contra scandal, had done little to restore that faith. By 1994, only 19 percent of the people trusted government. Politicians, Americans believed, were unethical and out of touch with ordinary citizens.

That belief was reinforced by ethical scandals that compelled the resignation of the Speaker of the House in 1989 and the reprimand of five senators in 1991. Politicians seemed ineffective as well as unethical. By the 1990s, commentators bemoaned the "gridlock" in Washington. Like cars stuck in a massive traffic jam, legislation could not move past squabbling politicians in Congress and the White House. Bush vetoed congressional legislation more than 40 times. Unable to agree on a budget with Congress, the president actually shut down "nonessential" government services over Columbus Day weekend in 1990. That episode epitomized many Americans' sense that the government no longer served their needs.

Moreover, politicians seemed unwilling to reform. By the 1990s, Americans believed that money played too large a role in elections. Politicians spent much of their time raising contributions for expensive campaigns. Huge donations from special interest groups and wealthy individuals, people feared, had corrupted politics. Although Congress and the president talked about the need for reform, attempts to control election spending failed repeatedly.

Americans tried other ways to reform Washington. There was considerable interest in passing laws that would limit the number of terms that officials could serve in Congress. But term limits, which could deny people the right to vote for the candidate of their choice, were too controversial. Instead, Americans settled for a modest but unusual reform, a Constitutional amendment. Known as the "Madison Amendment" for its originator, President James Madison, the measure postponed Congressional pay raises until after members faced voters in the next election. Amid the popular anger at Congress, the Twenty-Seventh Amendment, originally introduced in 1789, was finally ratified in 1992.

For a moment, it seemed as if popular disaffection was about to revolutionize American politics. Running a tired campaign for reelection in 1992, George H. W. Bush faced a sudden challenge from the strongest independent candidate in years, Ross Perot of Texas. A pugnacious, plainspoken billionaire businessman, Perot played to Americans' unhappiness by promising to end gridlock, balance the budget, and reform campaign finances.

As voters wondered whether the quirky Perot could be an effective president, it was the Democratic nominee, Governor Bill Clinton of Arkansas, and not President Bush, who seemed to embody hopes for change. Calling himself a "New Democrat," the charismatic Clinton polled 43 percent of the popular vote to Bush's 37 percent and Perot's surprisingly strong 19 percent. Clinton managed to assemble the kind of voting coalition that had put Franklin Roosevelt and Harry Truman in the White House. Holding on to Black support, the Arkansas governor won back many white southerners and workers, the so-called Reagan Democrats. For the first

The Peaceful Transfer of Power On Inauguration Day, 2001, one two-term president, Democrat Bill Clinton (right) congratulates his successor, another two-term president, Republican George W. Bush.

time in 12 years, a Democrat occupied the White House. With the Democrats in control of the House and Senate as well, gridlock seemed likely to end.

Clinton's Compromise with Conservatism

In some ways, Clinton marked a shift in American politics. The first president born after World War II, Clinton was the first of the baby boom generation to become president. His marriage to fellow lawyer Hillary Rodham was another hint of change. The new first lady was the first presidential wife with her own professional career outside the home.

Clinton did act like a New Democrat by balancing traditional liberal activism with more conservative efforts to shrink government. In 1993, he won congressional approval for a national service plan that provided money for college to young people who performed community service. He signed the Family and Medical Leave Act of 1993, which allowed government workers and employees in most companies with 50 or more workers to take up to 12 weeks of unpaid leave to deal with birth, adoption, or family illness. Clinton was convinced that the federal government could not play an effective social role or maintain prosperity without balancing the budget. As part of a plan to "reinvent government," the president moved to cut the size of the federal workforce.

Nevertheless, Clinton lost his most important legislative battle, an attempt to achieve the longtime liberal goal of federally backed national health insurance. Facing determined opposition from pharmaceutical companies, health insurers, and conservatives, the Health Security Act of 1993, which required employers to provide medical insurance for workers, met defeat.

Meanwhile, a series of scandals, involving allegations about a corrupt real estate deal in Arkansas, the misuse of confidential FBI files, the mistreatment of White House staff, the suicide of a longtime friend, and a lawsuit over an extramarital affair, threatened Clinton's reputation. Although a court-appointed special prosecutor, Kenneth Starr, did not indict Clinton, the president's standing suffered.

As Clinton struggled, power flowed to the Republicans. In 1994, disappointed voters awarded control of the House of Representatives to Republicans for the first time in 40 years. Emboldened, the new majority chose outspoken conservative Newt Gingrich of Georgia as the Speaker of the House. The Republicans vowed to enact a conservative "Contract with America" featuring a balanced budget amendment to the Constitution, term limits, increased defense spending, welfare reform, and tax cuts. The Republicans, however, overplayed their hand. In 1995–1996, Gingrich and congressional Republicans forced two shutdowns of the federal government. Although the Republicans kept control of Congress, the shutdowns hurt the popularity of the party, which failed to enact the balanced budget amendment and term limits.

The Republicans' miscalculation gave Clinton a second chance. To win back the public, the president compromised with conservatism. "The era of big Government is over," he declared in 1996. That year Clinton signed a welfare bill that significantly reduced federal support for the poor, especially children. Reflecting the conservative emphasis on individual responsibility, the measure tried to minimize the role of the federal government in people's lives. The bill replaced Aid to Families with Dependent Children (AFDC), which had long guaranteed federal payments to the poor, with grants to the states for use as they saw fit. To discourage dependence on government handouts, the bill limited welfare recipients to five years of assistance over their lifetime and required household heads on welfare to find work within two years. To discourage extramarital pregnancies that supposedly threatened **family values**, the bill imposed restrictions on unwed teenage mothers receiving benefits and offered bonuses for states with declining rates of illegitimate childbirth. Many Democrats and liberals angrily claimed that the president had betrayed the poor.

Running for reelection in 1996, Clinton benefited from his compromise with conservatism, the strength of the economy, and the weakness of his opponents. Ross Perot's new organization, the Reform Party could not rekindle the enthusiasm of 1992. The Republicans' moderate nominee, Senate Majority Leader Bob Dole of Kansas epitomized the career Washington politician so many Americans distrusted. Never seriously threatened by Dole or Perot, Clinton won a clear victory with 49 percent of the popular vote. Dole attracted 41 percent of the popular vote and Perot only 8 percent.

Domestic Dissent and Terrorism

Beyond Washington, a violent series of confrontations emerged over the role of the federal government in the lives of Americans. By the 1990s, a small number of Americans claimed the right, for religious or political reasons, to live free from governmental authority, which almost inevitably brought them into conflict with the federal government. The result was a series of deadly episodes that raised difficult questions about the way Washington used its power.

In 1992, Randy Weaver, a white separatist who wanted to keep his family away from other races and the government, failed to appear for a trial on weapons charges. When federal agents converged on his remote cabin in **Ruby Ridge**, Idaho, Weaver resisted arrest. An 11-day siege, punctuated by two gun battles, ended with the deaths of Weaver's wife, one of his sons, and a federal marshal. For some Americans, the Ruby Ridge confrontation demonstrated the federal government's arrogance and deceitfulness. They felt vindicated in 1995 when Weaver was acquitted of assault, the US Justice Department agreed to pay him a $3.1 million settlement, five federal agents were suspended for misconduct, and one was convicted of obstruction of justice.

In 1993, another siege provoked more charges about the arrogance of federal power. David Koresh, the leader of the tiny Branch Davidian religious sect, had gathered about a hundred heavily armed followers in a compound outside **Waco**, Texas, to wait for the end of the world. When the federal Bureau of Alcohol, Tobacco, and Firearms (ATF) moved to arrest Koresh on weapons charges, a fierce gun battle killed four agents and at least five Branch Davidians. After an 11-day standoff, federal agents pumped tear gas into the compound, which burned down on April 19. At least 72 Branch Davidians, including Koresh and 17 children, died— some from bullets fired by members of the sect. Many Americans blamed Koresh for the horror, but others blamed the federal government. For critics of the FBI and the Clinton administration, Waco stood as a symbol of Washington's intolerance of personal and religious freedom.

After the Waco and Ruby Ridge incidents, right-wing paramilitary groups, known as "Patriots" and "civil militias," trained with weapons to protect themselves from a government supposedly planning to take Americans' guns and freedom. Other extremists denied that local, state, or national government had the right to tax American citizens.

A handful of antigovernment extremists went further. On April 19, 1995—the second anniversary of the Waco tragedy—a car bomb exploded in front of a federal building in **Oklahoma City**, Oklahoma. Destroying much of the structure, the blast killed 169 people, including children in a day-care center. Americans were stunned that the worst terrorist attack in the nation's history to that time had occurred not in a big coastal city such as New York or Los Angeles, but in the heartland. People were even more surprised when they learned the terrorists were not foreigners but American-born critics of the federal government. In 1997, Timothy McVeigh, an Army veteran with ties to a right-wing militia group, was convicted of murdering the bombing victims. Additionally, one friend of McVeigh's confessed to a role in planning the bombing, and another was convicted of conspiracy and manslaughter for his role.

Fresh incidents intensified fears of domestic terrorism. In July 1996, during the Olympic games in Atlanta, Georgia, a bomb went off in a crowded park, killing one person. That tragedy was followed by the bombings of an abortion clinic in an Atlanta suburb in January 1997, a lesbian bar in Atlanta in February that same year, and a reproductive services clinic in Birmingham, Alabama, in February 1998, which killed two people. The perpetrator in all these incidents was Eric Rudolph, an Army veteran vaguely tied to white supremacists and antigovernment militia, and an opponent of "global socialism" and "the Washington government." Confessing to the bombings, Rudolph was sentenced to two consecutive life sentences.

The sudden spread of domestic terrorism emphasized how much the power of the federal government, along with such changes as legalized abortion and the increased rights of minorities and women since the 1960s, provoked discontent. Almost paradoxically, Americans such as Rudolph, so troubled by the rights of others, wanted the right to live free from government.

Scandal

Despite reelection, Clinton no longer seemed like an agent of change. Then, in 1998, scandal engulfed his presidency. Independent counsel Kenneth Starr and a grand jury explored whether the president had obstructed justice by covering up a sexual relationship with Monica Lewinky, a young White House intern. Initially denying the story, Clinton finally admitted "inappropriate intimate contact" with Lewinsky.

Clinton's presidency hung in the balance. In November 1998, he agreed to pay $500,000 to settle the lawsuit from a former extramarital lover. In December, the Republican-dominated House impeached Clinton for perjury and obstruction of justice in his testimony about Lewinsky. But most Americans, whatever they thought of Clinton's relationship with Lewinsky, separated the private and public lives of the president. Approving his handling of the economy, the majority of Americans did not want him removed from office. Only the second president to go on trial in the Senate, Clinton won acquittal in February 1999.

Holding the presidency, Clinton lost the opportunity to make a major impact on public policy in his second term. Clinton's complicated legacy would rest on his management of the economy and the federal budget, his attempts to chart a course between liberalism and conservatism, and his private scandals. More broadly, the Clinton presidency reinforced the sense that politicians did not serve democracy well enough.

Republicans contributed to that sense, too. In 1999, after a House committee condemned Speaker Gingrich's apparent violations of both House rules on personal finances and federal tax law, he resigned from Congress. Then his designated Republican successor admitted extramarital affairs and quit as well. Neither party seemed able to exploit the politics of gridlock.

CULTURE WARS

While quarrels over the economy and government pushed the nation toward conservatism, issues involving individual rights and social values moved America in the opposite direction. As the experience of African Americans underscored, race and rights remained divisive, explosive matters in the 1990s. Concern about rights spurred a series of "culture wars" over family, sexual values, women, and the gay and lesbian community. Generally speaking, these struggles suggested that Americans were becoming more tolerant of social diversity and more willing to extend rights to disadvantaged groups.

African Americans in the Post–Civil Rights Era

For African Americans, life in the post–civil rights era had become a complex pattern of gains, losses, and continuing inequities. Decades after *Brown v. Board of Education* in 1954, southern schools were largely desegregated, but thanks to white flight from inner cities, northern schools were more segregated than ever. On the plus side, graduation rates for African Americans increased significantly. In 1957, only 18 percent of Black adults had graduated from high school. By 2002, 79 percent had graduated high school, still10 percentage points behind the rate for whites.

Blacks had also made notable economic and political gains. Both the ranks of African American public officials and the Black middle class continued to grow. In public at least, Americans were unwilling to contest the outcomes of the civil rights era. Many whites admired African American athletes such as basketball star Michael Jordan and art such as rap music and the broader hip-hop culture. Yet only about six of every ten Black men and women were in the paid workforce in 2002. Moreover, one of the bipartisan accomplishments of the Clinton era, the Violent Crime Control and Law Enforcement Act of 1994, indirectly but substantially increased the number of imprisoned Black men. The so-called Clinton Crime Bill underscored African Americans' longstanding unequal treatment by the justice system.

During the 1990s, three episodes dramatized the same point. In 1991, Clarence Thomas, George H. W. Bush's conservative African American nominee to the Supreme Court, faced accusations of sexual harassment. Denouncing his Senate hearing as "a high-tech lynching for uppity blacks," Thomas won confirmation. But many Americans wondered whether Thomas had been singled out for embarrassment because of his race.

That year, white police in Los Angeles stopped African American motorist Rodney King for drunk driving and then savagely beat him. Unknown to the officers, an onlooker had videotaped the beating. Despite this evidence, an all-white jury acquitted four policemen of all charges in April 1992. The stunning verdict set off rioting in the predominantly African American community of South Central Los Angeles, including the Watts section, which had been the center of rioting in 1965. Three days of violence left 51 people dead, 1,800 injured, and nearly 3,700 buildings burned. In the aftermath, Americans debated whether the legal system offered justice to African Americans while liberals and conservatives blamed each other for the poverty and despair of many Black communities. Eventually a federal court convicted two officers for depriving King of his civil rights and another court awarded $3.8 million in damages. But no one had concrete solutions to the problems of South Central Los Angeles.

Three years later, difficult questions arose again when Los Angeles authorities charged O. J. Simpson, a popular African American actor, sports announcer, and former football player, with the murders of his white ex-wife and her male friend. Although the mostly African American jury voted to acquit Simpson in 1995, a mostly white jury ordered him to pay millions in damages to the victims' families. The case laid bare deep differences over American justice. Most whites believed Simpson guilty; most African Americans, distrusting police and prosecutors, believed him innocent.

Despite these episodes, governments and police forces took few steps to deal with unequal justice. In 1995. Minister Louis Farrakhan of the Nation of Islam

The Emotional Power of the Rodney King Case As a jury deliberated over the case against King's attackers, a woman prayed in church.

organized the "Million Man March," a demonstration of 800,000 African American men in Washington, DC, to dramatize their commitment to community, family, and personal responsibility. Suggesting the potential mass action, the march did not lead to sustained activism. In an age of popular pessimism about government, relatively few Americans believed new programs could secure equal conditions for African Americans. At the same time, Americans mostly did not want to undo the achievements of the past.

Family Values

The same concern about rights helped drive a cluster of controversies known as "culture wars." At the center of the culture wars was an intense debate over the ongoing transformation of the family. In the 1950s, two out of three families had a parent who stayed at home full time; by 2000, with many mothers in the workforce, fewer than one in four families had a stay-at-home parent. The supposedly "traditional" nuclear family of father, mother, and children no longer predominated American households (see Table 29–1). Married couples with children, 40 percent of all households as late as 1970, made up only 25 percent by 1996. There were

Table 29–1 The Changing American Household, 1960–2000

Year	Households*	Families*	Married-Couple Families % of Total Households	Single-Parent Families % of Total Households	One-Person Households % of Total Households
1960	52,799	44,905	74.3%	10.7%	15.0%
1970	63,401	51,456	70.5%	10.6%	18.8%
1980*	80,776	59,550	60.8%	12.9%	26.3%
1990	93,347	66,090	56.0%	14.8%	29.2%
2000	104,705	72,025	52.8%	16.0%	31.2%

Source: US Census Bureau, *Current Population Survey, March and Annual Social and Economic Supplements, 2011 and Earlier,* https://www.census.gov/data/tables/time-series/demo/families/households.html

*Numbers given in thousands.

**Revised using population controls based on the 1980 census.

proportionally fewer families as the percentage of single-person households rose from 17 percent in 1970 to 25 percent in 1996. Families themselves were also less likely to fit the traditional model romanticized in the situation comedies of 1950s television. By 1996, 27 percent of families with children contained one parent, usually a mother, rather than two.

A number of factors led to these changes in family structure. Americans married later, had fewer children, and had them later in life. The divorce rate had doubled from 1960 to 1990. In the 1990s, about half of all marriages were ending in divorce. As women's wages gradually rose, more women could afford to live alone or head families by themselves.

Many conservatives and Republicans blamed these developments on the nation's alleged moral decline. Supposedly, the 1960s counterculture, liberals, the media, feminists, gays, and others had undermined the nation's family values. "It is a cultural war, as critical to the kind of nation we will one day be as was the Cold War itself," thundered conservative presidential candidate Patrick Buchanan to the Republican national convention in 1992. He urged the delegates to "take back our culture, and take back our country." That year, George H. W. Bush's vice president, Dan Quayle, attacked the TV sitcom *Murphy Brown* for its positive portrayal of the title character's decision to have a child out of wedlock. Some defenders of the family suggested that single mothers should receive fewer welfare benefits and that divorce should be made more difficult.

Liberals denied that conservatives spoke for real family values. The conservatives, they claimed, failed to understand that the family was not dying but simply adapting as it always had. The different forms of the family, like social diversity in general, were supposedly a good thing. Whatever the merits of the liberal argument, conservatives found the battles for family values impossible to win. *Murphy Brown* stayed on TV, but Quayle and George H. W. Bush lost their bid for reelection.

Multiculturalism

Liberals and conservatives also fought over the state of American culture. Since the 1960s, the authority of the Western literary, artistic, and philosophical heritage had been under attack from several directions. Literary critics and other advocates of "deconstruction" argued that cultural products possessed no inherent, objective value, that Western culture was revered not because of any intrinsic merit but because it reflected the interests of powerful Europeans and Americans. Other people, these critics felt, should be free to place a lesser value on Western culture.

Beginning in the 1960s, several groups did just that. As they demanded rights, feminists, African Americans, gays, lesbians, and other groups maintained that white heterosexual European men had not produced all important ideas and art. Society in general and schools in particular needed to recognize the cultural contributions of the disadvantaged and the oppressed. Instead of worshiping one culture, America needed to practice multiculturalism. At Stanford University in 1987, the Reverend Jesse Jackson joined students to protest a Western culture course that excluded the accomplishments of women and minorities. "Hey hey, ho ho," the crowd chanted, "Western culture's got to go!"

That cry horrified conservatives who believed Western cultural values were vital for American society. The multiculturalists, conservatives charged, were destroying the Western heritage. Further, the multiculturalists were destroying free speech by making it impossible for anyone to question their positions. This coercive "political correctness" or "PC" was actually promoting conformity instead of diversity. On some college campuses, the conservatives noted, PC speech codes punished students for using language that might offend others. The conservatives also attacked the National Endowment for the Humanities (NEH) and the National Endowment for the Arts (NEA), created by the liberal Great Society in the 1960s, for unfairly funding politically correct academic and artistic projects flouting Western values.

Liberals, academics, artists, and others responded by defending the NEH, the NEA, campus speech codes, and multiculturalism. It was the conservatives, they asserted, who were trying to censor curricula and wipe out diversity.

In the end, the controversies over culture and the family did little to undermine the new diversity of American life. Although Congress cut the budgets of the NEH and the NEA, these agencies survived the conservative attack, the right to divorce remained, and globalization still confronted Americans with the diversity of world cultures. Meanwhile, the trends toward diverse households and multiculturalism continued.

Women in the Postfeminist Era

As the *Murphy Brown* controversy suggested, women, so often a focal point for fears about social change, were at the center of the culture wars. By the 1990s, women's place in society had changed dramatically since the feminist campaigns of the 1960s and 1970s. The percentage of adult women in the workforce had increased, along with the percentage of women in high-paying white-collar jobs. Women were also more visible in politics. After the 1992 elections, a record 53 women held seats in Congress. In 1993, Janet Reno became the first female attorney general, and Madeleine Albright became the first female secretary of state.

Nevertheless, women faced continuing discrimination. A woman was still likely to make less money than a man and more likely to live in poverty. Like African Americans, women remained underrepresented in Congress and other governmental bodies. Highly publicized incidents of the sexual harassment of women by male US military personnel and politicians, including Bill Clinton, provoked widespread public discussion about the nature of relationships between men and women. As the sexes differed over what constituted harassment, many women complained that men "just don't get it." For these women, Clarence Thomas's confirmation was less about race and more about his alleged harassment of a female subordinate.

Despite such revelations, the organized feminist movement did not grow dramatically at the end of the twentieth century. Many Americans seemingly accepted the expansion of women's rights but rejected feminism as too radical. Feminists often found themselves defending earlier accomplishments, such as affirmative-action programs, rather than pushing for new objectives.

Abortion provided a case in point. From the 1980s into the 1990s, the conservative Right to Life movement continued its passionate campaign against abortion.

At the grassroots level, protestors picketed abortion clinics and tried to discourage pregnant women from having abortions. Some radicals, such as Eric Rudolph (discussed earlier in this chapter), resorted to violence, including the murder of clinic workers. Meanwhile, George H. W. Bush condemned abortion as "murder" and, like Reagan before him, named antiabortion judges to the federal courts.

In spite of this assault, the right and practice of abortion continued. The Supreme Court, declining to overturn *Roe v. Wade*, acknowledged the constitutional right to abortion. In *Planned Parenthood v. Casey* in 1992, the Court narrowly upheld much of a Pennsylvania law limiting access to abortions. But the court declared that a woman's right to choose an abortion was "a component of liberty we cannot renounce." Later that year, the election of Clinton, a strongly pro-choice Democrat, made abortion rights seem more secure. Nevertheless, struggles to shut down clinics and overturn *Roe v. Wade* continued.

Contesting Gay and Lesbian Rights

In a society struggling with diversity, sexuality identity remained perhaps the most controversial difference of all. Like women and African Americans, gay men and lesbian women had made real gains since the 1960s. During the George H. W. Bush administration, the federal government committed more resources to AIDS research. As the disease spread more slowly among the gay population and heterosexuals contracted it, Americans became less likely to consider AIDS the "gay cancer" or God's punishment of gay men. Meanwhile, gays and lesbians became a more accepted social presence. More television shows positively depicted gay identities. Two openly gay men served in Congress. Many businesses, including Disneyland, welcomed gay customers. Leading corporations, including General Motors and Ford, began providing benefits to the partners of gay employees.

Nevertheless, the public understanding of sexual identity lagged. During the 1990s, the term "Lesbian Gay Bisexual and Transgender" (LGBT) emerged as a more inclusive description of the range of identities beyond heterosexual. Even so, many Americans still saw a simple divide between heterosexuals and homosexuals.

Moreover, LGBT calls for equal rights met with substantial opposition. Although most Americans believed businesses should not discriminate on the basis of sexual identity, a majority still considered LGBT identities morally wrong. Every year brought hundreds of documented instances of violence against gays and lesbians. Notoriously in 1998, a gay student at the University of Wyoming in Laramie, Matthew Shepherd, was beaten, robbed, tied to a fence, pistol whipped, and left to die by two homophobic men who were later convicted of murder.

The armed forces especially resisted gay rights. Officially barred from serving, gays and lesbians had long concealed their identities in order to remain in the military. But in the 1990s, more people called on the armed forces to allow openly LGBT officers and enlisted personnel. In 1992 for the first time, a federal court ordered the navy to reinstate an openly gay petty officer who had been discharged. President Clinton, retreating from a campaign promise to lift the ban on gays in the armed services, gave in to military leaders who argued that such tolerance would hurt recruitment and morale. Compromising, Clinton instituted a "don't ask, don't tell" policy. The military would no longer ask recruits about their sexual identity, and gays and lesbians would continue to conceal it.

There was no compromise on legal protection for LGBT rights in civilian life. In communities and states, activists demanded laws that would prevent businesses from discriminating on the basis of sexual identity. In response, conservatives, especially those lamenting the decline of family values, moved to block gay and lesbian rights measures. In 1992, Colorado voters approved a referendum forbidding communities to protect gay rights, but the state's supreme court declared the referendum unconstitutional the next year. The issue did not rest there. In 1996, Congress passed the Defense of Marriage Act, which declared that marriage was the "legal union between one man and one woman," denied federal benefits to same-sex couples living together, and allowed states to refuse to recognize same-sex marriages from other states. In 2000, the United States Supreme Court upheld the right of the Boy Scouts of America to dismiss a gay troop leader in New Jersey, despite the existence of a state gay rights law.

The battles over gay rights, women's rights, family values, and multiculturalism barely altered the direction of social change. Despite the culture wars, Americans seemed willing to balance conservative economic policy with more liberal social attitudes and policies.

REDEFINING FOREIGN POLICY IN THE GLOBAL AGE

Long accustomed to the Cold War, Americans had to rethink foreign policy in the 1990s. Now that the United States no longer had to focus on containing Soviet power, what should the nation's aims be abroad? How much should America promote trade, freedom, and human rights? Could the country afford to spend less on military power? President George H. W. Bush believed the nation should play the role of an active international policeman in a "**New World Order**." However, many Americans were not so sure.

The New World Order

In a changed world, some Republicans called for a new, less internationalist foreign policy. Echoing conservatives of the 1940s and 1950s, they insisted that the United States should no longer provide so much aid and military protection to other countries, especially in Europe. American soldiers, they insisted, should risk their lives to protect the United States, not other countries. In contrast, Democratic and Republican internationalists contended the United States could protect itself and advance its political and economic interests only by participating actively in world affairs. The internationalists insisted America still faced challenges abroad.

The most powerful internationalist was President George H. W. Bush. A naval aviator in World War II, Bush believed that American isolationism had encouraged fascist aggression in the 1930s and 1940s and that American internationalism had won the war, preserved peace, and sustained the nation's economy for decades afterward. In the age of globalization, America should use foreign aid, military strength, NATO, and the United Nations to maintain a stable international system, a "New World Order." Bush wanted "a world in which democracy is the norm, in which private enterprise, free trade, and prosperity enrich every nation—a world in which the rule of law prevails." Much like Woodrow Wilson and Harry Truman before him, Bush blended idealism and self-interest: A free world would be good both for other nations and for the United States.

The New World Order was a broad, vague concept. Critics noted a tension between Bush's call for order and his support for democracy. Was the United States supposed to protect antidemocratic countries in the name of international stability and national prosperity? There was also a tension between Bush's commitment to international cooperation and the long-standing tendency for the United States to act alone in its own hemisphere. While the president spoke of the New World Order, he intervened unilaterally in the Central American nation of **Panama** in 1989 to overthrow General Manuel Noriega, who engaged in drug sales to the United States and other illegal activities.

The Persian Gulf War

A test of the New World Order came soon enough. In August 1990, Iraq, led by President **Saddam Hussein**, overran Kuwait, its wealthy but defenseless neighbor to the south. Entrenched in Kuwait, Iraq now threatened its much larger western neighbor, oil-producing Saudi Arabia. Hussein's actions jeopardized America's oil supply and its Saudi Arabian ally, as well as Bush's ideal of a stable world of free nations.

Comparing Hussein to Adolf Hitler, Bush created an international coalition opposing Iraq. By the end of 1990, over half a million US troops had joined forces from more than 30 nations in Operation Desert Shield to protect Saudi Arabia (see Map 29–2). Convinced that economic sanctions were not enough to drive Hussein's soldiers out of Kuwait, the Bush administration successfully pressed the United Nations to authorize force if the Iraqis did not withdraw by January 15, 1991. The president also obtained congressional approval for the use of force.

When Hussein defied the deadline, Operation Desert Shield became Operation Desert Storm. As television audiences watched around the world on the night of January 17, coalition planes and missiles intensively attacked Iraq. With Iraq's defenses weakened, coalition forces, led by US General Norman Schwarzkopf, began a ground attack against the Iraqi army on February 24. In just 100 hours, Schwarzkopf's solders swept into Kuwait, devastated the Iraqis, and pushed on into Iraq. Impressed by the results, Bush called a halt before the invasion reached the Iraqi capital of Baghdad and toppled Hussein.

At first, the **Persian Gulf** War seemed like a great victory for the United States and the New World Order. Coalition forces suffered only about 220 battle deaths and the United States lost only 148 troops. American technology appeared to work perfectly. Bush's popularity soared.

Americans' euphoria did not last long. US weapons had not worked quite so well after all, and Gulf War veterans began suffering health problems possibly caused by Iraqi chemical weapons. Holding on to power, Saddam Hussein hindered implementation of the agreement ending the war. His aircraft soon encroached on "no-fly" zones over northern and southern Iraq, where they had been forbidden to

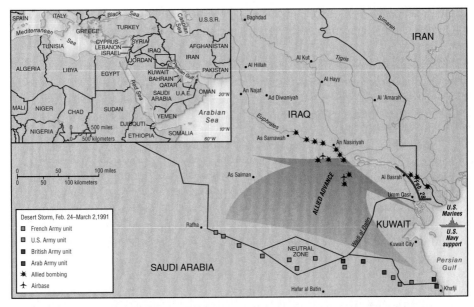

Map 29-2   The Persian Gulf War Operation Desert Storm, the allied attack on the forces of Iraq, tested President George H. W. Bush's vision of a "New World Order" in the oil-rich heart of the Middle East.
Source: Mark C. Carnes et al., *Mapping America's Past* (New York: Henry Holt, 1996), p. 267; *Hammond Atlas of the Twentieth Century* (New York: Times Books, 1996), p. 166.

9:03 a.m., September 11, 2001 As the North Tower of New York City's World Trade Center spews black smoke from a terrorist plane strike, a second hijacked jet blows up in balls of fire in the South Tower. Soon, these twin symbols of American global capitalist might would collapse in rubble and death.

fly, and threatened Kurdish and Muslim minorities. The goals of the New World Order had not been completely achieved after all.

Retreating from the New World Order

In the years after the Persian Gulf War, the United States retreated from Bush's vision of the New World Order. The American people were reluctant to accept the dangers of involvement abroad, especially where there was no obvious military or economic interest for the United States.

That reluctance was apparent when violence followed the collapse of Communist rule in Yugoslavia in 1990. As this Eastern European country broke apart in the early 1990s, three major ethnic groups—Muslim Slavs, Serbs, and Croatians—fought a bitter civil war in the newly independent province of **Bosnia-Herzegovina**. The remnants of the old Yugoslavia, under the harsh leadership of Slobodan Milosevic, aided the Serbs as they carried out "ethnic cleansing," the forcible expulsion of Muslims and Croats from their homes. Faced with the worst mass brutality in Europe since World War II, first Bush and then Clinton were unwilling to risk military involvement. Eventually, in 1994, American planes and missiles, operating in conjunction with NATO, attacked Bosnian Serb forces from the air. The following year, the warring parties accepted a peace agreement brokered by the United States. The Clinton administration committed 20,000 troops to join a peacekeeping force, even though most Americans opposed the move.

Yugoslavia posed a challenge again when the Milosevic regime mistreated and attacked ethnic Albanians in the region of Kosovo. Humiliated by its inability to negotiate an end to the suffering, the Clinton administration finally supported a NATO air offensive against the Yugoslavian government in March 1999. The 78-day war killed between 2,000 and 5,000 people, badly damaged Yugoslavia's infrastructure, and forced Milosevic to accept a multinational peacekeeping force. There were no NATO casualties, in part because Clinton and other NATO leaders were unwilling to risk them. There were other costs for the United States, however. Clinton's unwillingness to commit ground troops to battle made it clear that America was hesitant to pay a human price to intervene around the world.

The New World Order depended on maintaining American power built up during the Cold War, but a reluctance to spend money and make international commitments diminished that power in the 1990s. As budgets declined, leaders cut troops, closed bases, reduced orders for new weapons, and abandoned Ronald Reagan's expensive space-based missile defense system, the Strategic Defensive Initiative. Budgets for intelligence and foreign aid were tight, too.

A New Threat

As the New World Order faded away, no single overarching principle emerged to direct the nation's diplomacy. After the Cold War, anti-Communist passion no longer animated American foreign policy. Eager for trade with an old enemy, the Socialist Republic of Vietnam, President Clinton announced full diplomatic recognition of the Communist nation in 1995. Economic interests, rather than concern for human rights, helped shape policy toward another Asian Communist regime, the People's Republic of China. Both George H.W. Bush and Bill Clinton sought better trade relations with China, even though Chinese leadership violated the human rights of its people, expanded its nuclear arsenal, and apparently spied on US weapons programs.

While America showed little enthusiasm for human rights and the New World Order, the challenge of terrorism proved harder to overlook. In February 1993, a car bomb exploded in an underground garage of the World Trade Center in New York City. Six people were killed and more than a thousand injured in the first major international terrorist incident inside the United States. Investigators traced the attack to followers of a radical Islamic spiritual leader from Egypt, Sheikh Omar Abdel-Rahman, who lived in New Jersey. Rahman and over a dozen associates were convicted for the bombing and other plots. In 1996, another Muslim radical, charged with masterminding the attack, was convicted along with two other Muslims for plotting to blow up US airliners over the Pacific Ocean.

Surprisingly, most Americans paid little attention to terrorism in the aftermath of the attack. US authorities generally ignored the plotters' connections to the terrorist organization, **Al Qaeda**, led by a wealthy Saudi Arabian exile, **Osama bin Laden**. A veteran of the resistance to the Soviet invasion of Afghanistan, bin Laden had gradually made Al Qaeda—Arabic for "base" or "foundation"—into an anti-Western movement dedicated to restoring the supposedly lost glory of Islam. The terrorist financier particularly hated the United States for its support of Israel and its military presence in the Middle East.

Operating out of Sudan and then Afghanistan, Al Qaeda supported Muslim fighters in Bosnia and warlords in Somalia. In 1995 and 1996, the organization was involved in deadly terrorist attacks on US soldiers in Saudi Arabia. In 1996, bin Laden declared jihad—holy war—on the United States. In August 1998, bombs killed at least 190 people and wounded 5,000 at US embassies in the African nations of Kenya and Tanzania. Blaming the embassy attacks on bin Laden, the United States launched missile attacks on targets in Afghanistan and the Sudan linked to bin Laden's organization. Despite these incidents, Americans remained fairly unconcerned about international terrorism.

TWIN CRISES

The approach of the twenty-first century promised the further development of globalization and the information economy in a time of prosperity and relative peace. In 2000, the election of George H. W. Bush's son to the presidency underscored the sense of continuity. But two shocks—a terrorist attack and a severe economic crisis—bookended the administration of George W. Bush and sorely tested the nation.

"Bush 43"

United in their eagerness to reclaim the White House, Republicans nominated Governor George W. Bush of Texas, for president in 2000. His opponent, Vice President Al Gore, seemed unsure whether to embrace the uneven record of the Clinton administration. But a dull campaign became riveting on election night when the crucial state of Florida proved too close to call amid voting irregularities. Both sides turned to the Supreme Court, which risked its credibility in a controversial

5–4 ruling that preserved Bush's narrow margin in Florida. Although Gore won the popular vote by 550,000 nationwide, Florida gave Bush the Electoral College by 271 votes to Gore's 266.

The 43rd president of the United States, George W. Bush was more conservative than his father, the 41st president. The administration of "Bush 43" cut rather than raised taxes, weakened regulation of the financial industry, and limited late-term "partial birth" abortions. Yet Bush also compromised with liberals in Congress to pass the No Child Left Behind Act of 2001, which combined the liberal goal of increased federal funding for public schools with the conservative demand for greater school accountability, including annual standardized testing of students. The president also accepted a classic liberal initiative, an expensive drug benefit program for retired Americans.

In 2004, Bush faced another liberal Democrat, Senator John Kerry of Massachusetts, who tried to capitalize on fears globalization would cost Americans' jobs. Yet Bush prevailed with 50.7 percent of the popular vote and a solid electoral majority. Buoyed by his victory, Bush 43 promised new conservative initiatives, including a reform of the Social Security system. His plans went nowhere, particularly after the Democrats won control of both houses of Congress in 2006. Thanks to Bush's tax cuts, drug plan, and military expenditures, the federal government ran a budget deficit again—another disappointment to conservatives, who yearned for leaner government.

9/11

Despite Bush's accomplishments, two crises ultimately defined Bush's presidency. On the morning of September 11, 2001, Osama bin Laden's Al Qaeda carried out an extraordinary terrorist operation in a clear blue sky. Although Bush had received warning of Al Qaeda's intentions, the nation was unprepared. That day, 19 Al Qaeda members from Saudi Arabia, the United Arab Emirates, Egypt, and Lebanon walked through security at East Coast airports and boarded four passenger jets. In flight, the terrorists, brandishing box cutters and Mace or pepper spray, overwhelmed flight attendants and passengers, killed or wounded pilots, took control, and redirected the planes. At 8:46 a.m., American Airlines Flight 11 sped into the North Tower of the World Trade Center; 17 minutes later, United Airlines Flight 175 hit the World Trade Center's South Tower. At 9:37 a.m., American Airlines Flight 77 struck the west wall of the Pentagon, headquarters of the US Defense Department, outside Washington, DC. Aboard United Airlines Flight 93, there were indications of struggle, a voice shouted, "Allah is the greatest," and the jet crashed into an empty field in Shanksville, Pennsylvania, at 10:03 a.m. instead of hitting Washington, DC. By then, the North Tower of the World Trade Center had collapsed in a cloud of smoke and debris. The South Tower followed at 10:28 a.m.

The tragedy, which became known as "9/11," killed the 19 hijackers, 40 people in the crash at Shanksville, 184 at the Pentagon, and 2,753 at the World Trade Center. More Americans died on 9/11 than had died in the Japanese attack at Pearl Harbor on December 7, 1941. Only the Civil War battles of Antietam and Cold Harbor had been deadlier days.

The Global War on Terror

The catastrophe reshaped American foreign and security policy—and arguably American democracy as well. Vowing privately "to kick some ass," President Bush declared publicly, "We will make no distinction between the terrorists who committed these acts and those who harbor them." When Afghanistan's Islamic fundamentalist movement, the **Taliban**, refused to turn over bin Laden, the United States and other NATO countries responded in October by launching air strikes against Al Qaeda and Taliban targets and sending troops to hunt down bin Laden, destroy his camps, and drive out the Taliban. What the Bush administration called the "global war on terror" had begun.

Afghanistan, weak and impoverished, fell quickly, but bin Laden and many Al Qaeda and Taliban fighters escaped in the remote, mountainous terrain to continue their struggle. US and NATO forces remained to protect the new government and find bin Laden.

Meanwhile, the Bush administration reorganized the federal government to combat terror. Within a month of 9/11, Bush chose the first director of Homeland Security to protect US borders and infrastructure and to respond in the event of a terrorist strike. In 2002, Congress elevated the position to cabinet rank in a new Department of Homeland Security. Two years later, Congress answered harsh criticism of the CIA and FBI for failing to detect the 9/11 plot by transferring oversight of all US intelligence agencies from the head of the CIA to a new position, Director of National Intelligence.

More controversially, the Bush administration worked what Vice President Dick Cheney called "the dark side"—practices traditionally condemned by American law and culture. The government maintained a detention center at Guantánamo Bay, Cuba, where captured "enemy combatants" were denied trials and the protections of the Geneva Convention on prisoners of war and were, in some cases, tortured. In 2006 and 2008, the US Supreme Court asserted the rights of the Guantánamo detainees and reminded Bush that "a state of war is not a blank check for the president."

The government also gathered more information about its own citizens. In October 2001, the hastily passed USA Patriot Act made it easier for the federal government to spy on Americans and allowed the attorney general to imprison indefinitely, without trial, noncitizens considered threats to national security. Opponents condemned the Patriot Act as an unlawful deprivation of civil liberties. In 2004, a federal judge declared part of the measure an unconstitutional infringement on First Amendment rights. But the Bush administration secured the renewal and expansion of the act.

Bush also rethought the use of American military power. Previous presidents had rejected preemptive peacetime attacks on other nations. But Bush believed that terrorism, "a threat without precedent," might require the nation to strike even before a threat emerged. Bush further broke with Cold War presidents, including his father, by calling for the United States to act alone when necessary, rather than through alliances and the United Nations.

The Bush Doctrine of preemption and unilateral action risked isolating the United States and making it seem selfish, dangerous, and illegitimate. Yet Bush, confident of American power and virtue, was willing to go it alone.

The Iraq War

In January 2002, Bush declared that it was not enough to go after terrorist organizations. The United States must also "prevent regimes that sponsor terror from threatening America or our friends and allies with weapons of mass destruction." He identified Iran, Iraq, and North Korea as an "**axis of evil**," potentially able to arm terrorists with nuclear, chemical, or biological weapons that menaced the United States.

Iraq was Bush's primary focus. In his view, Saddam Hussein had plotted to assassinate Bush 41, forced out United Nations weapons inspectors, resumed acquiring weapons of mass destruction (WMDs), and supported Al Qaeda. Bush was also influenced by Vice President Cheney and other advisers who advocated neoconservatism, the idea that the United States should unilaterally promote democracy abroad in order to make a better and more secure world. Replacing Hussein with a democratic regime would, these neoconservatives insisted, encourage the spread of democracy in the Middle East and make US ally Israel safer.

As Bush confronted Iraq, nearly all of America's European allies, as well as Russia, China, and Middle Eastern countries, opposed a unilateral US war. Bush did assemble a "coalition of the willing," but only Great Britain, Australia, and Poland joined the United States in committing troops.

On the night of March 19, 2003, Operation Iraqi Freedom began with a hail of missiles aimed at Baghdad in an unsuccessful attempt to kill Hussein. On March 21, some 1,300 bombs and missiles rained down on Baghdad in a display of "shock and awe" meant to demoralize Iraqis. Sweeping into Iraq, US troops occupied Baghdad and British forces seized a key port to the south. Offering little resistance, much of the Iraqi army disappeared into the civilian population. Hussein disappeared, too.

Swift and short, like the Gulf War 12 years before, the Iraq war seemed everything that Bush had hoped. Only 138 US soldiers had died. Standing before a banner declaring "Mission Accomplished" aboard an aircraft carrier in May, the president jubilantly announced, "Major combat operations in Iraq have ended." The United States seemed well on the way to winning the war on terror and reshaping the Middle East.

Iraq and Afghanistan in Turmoil

It was not that easy. The jubilation of "Mission Accomplished" gave way to sober realities in Iraq during 2003. WMDs, a chief justification of the war, were never found. Unable to prove Hussein's ties to Al Qaeda, the Bush administration faced charges of fighting a needless war in Iraq while bin Laden went free in Afghanistan. Meanwhile, the United States struggled to restart the Iraqi economy, train new police and military, and build a popular, democratic regime.

Soon, a violent insurgency, perhaps orchestrated by Hussein, tried to destabilize Iraq and drive out the United States. Although US forces captured Hussein in December 2003, his brutal execution and revelations of the humiliation and torture of Iraqi prisoners embarrassed the United States. "Al Qaeda in Iraq," a new terrorist group loyal to bin Laden, joined the fight. Although the Bush administration handed over sovereignty to an American-chosen Iraqi government in 2004, over 100,000 US troops remained. Facing failure, Bush ordered a controversial "surge," a temporary troop increase that succeeded, along with changes in Iraqi politics, in decreasing the violence by mid-2008. But American public opinion had turned against the war.

Meanwhile, the Afghanistan conflict worsened. As the United States focused on Iraq, the Taliban, aided by foreign fighters, gradually regained strength and the pro–US government lost power. Osama bin Laden remained at large. By 2008, over 600 US soldiers and uncounted Afghans had died in seven years of fighting.

The wars in Afghanistan and Iraq cost the United States popularity and influence around the globe. Sympathetic to Americans after 9/11, many people no longer supported US military action in the Middle East. Critics argued that war, torture, and civilian casualties helped rather than hurt the terrorist cause. Moreover, the United States no longer seemed an unstoppable superpower able to build democratic nations and reshape the world in its image.

Financial Crisis

Meanwhile, the second great crisis of the Bush years mushroomed. The economic boom of the 1990s and 2000s resembled the boom of the 1920s. In both periods, optimistic American consumers borrowed money to buy houses, cars, and stocks. All that buying spurred the economy and drove the stock market to record heights. But eventually all that borrowing reached its limits: unable to meet their debts, many Americans could not borrow any more. In both periods, business leaders and government officials paid too little attention to dangerous financial practices until it was too late.

In the early 2000s, the housing industry developed a classic "bubble," an unrealistic inflation of prices. Some Americans bought houses they could not afford, and many used houses as collateral for loans. Banks made loans they should not have made, including risky subprime mortgages at high interest rates to people with poor credit. Moreover, financial institutions hid these bad loans by folding them into complex, risky financial instruments known as collateralized debt obligations (CDOs), which were sold around the world. Firms that bought CDOs, vulnerable to trouble in housing, did not understand the danger.

In 2005, US house prices began to fall. As the housing bubble burst, some homeowners, particularly those with subprime loans, had trouble making their payments; foreclosures—banks' repossession of homes for unpaid mortgages—increased. In consequence, the home-construction industry suffered, and consumers had trouble getting loans. Financial institutions suffered, too. In 2008, the federal government had to help firms involved in the mortgage business, and banking giant JPMorgan Chase took over failing investment bank Bear Stearns.

Developments linked to globalization also threatened the United States and other nations. Globalized free trade suffered when the World Trade Organization's round of trade talks in Doha, Qatar, ended without an agreement. Oil prices, driven by demand from the growing economies of China and India, hit record levels. Those prices drove up the cost of other goods and hurt the American auto industry, whose gas-guzzling SUVs became hard to sell. Felt worldwide, these events hit the United States as the global value of the dollar declined and American consumers lost confidence.

As the Dow Jones industrial average fell from a record high, the US financial industry nearly collapsed in November 2008. Investment firm Lehman Brothers

Struggles For Democracy

"Gitmo"

From the camera eye of a satellite miles above, Guantánamo Bay stood out from the rest of eastern Cuba. The inlet was a horseshoe of brown and gray amid the lush green of the island and the bright blue of the Atlantic. To the administration of George W. Bush, Guantánamo Bay was a gray area, too: a place that was American and yet not American, a drab anomaly perfect for one of the most controversial phases of the war on terror.

Guantánamo Bay, 520 miles from Miami, Florida, had been an anomaly for more than a century. After the Spanish-American War of 1898, the US government had taken the spot for a well-protected naval base. The Cuban-American Treaty of 1903 effectively gave America perpetual control over the base. For less than $4,000 a year, the United States could keep the facility until both Washington and Cuba agreed to end the arrangement. Even when Fidel Castro came to power in 1959, the US base remained. So Guantánamo Bay, or "Gitmo," as Americans called it, remained the oldest US

overseas naval base and the only one in a Communist country.

The naval installation at Gitmo became less useful when the Cold War ended. But the war on terror gave the base new life. It was too risky to leave captured Taliban fighters and other "enemy combatants" in unstable Afghanistan or Iraq, but it was also too risky to bring them to the United States, where courts, Congress, and public opinion could interfere with their imprisonment. So the Bush administration, looking for "the least worst place" for prisoners, turned to Guantánamo Bay in 2001. Although the US military controlled the base, US civil law did not apply. Gitmo, with its gray, pebbly beaches, was the perfect gray area for an administration determined to find a way around the law to prosecute the war on terror. By the end of 2008, some 775 people had been incarcerated at Gitmo. To accommodate them, the United States built no fewer than seven separate prison facilities; one of them, known only as "Camp 7," remained secret. Thousands of Americans streamed in to run Gitmo.

became the most valuable American corporation ever to fail. As governments and financial institutions around the world scrambled to save banks and prop up stock markets, Americans feared a repeat of the great crash of 1929. A panicked Congress immediately approved the Emergency Economic Stabilization Act of 2008, a $700 billion financial package creating the Troubled Asset Relief Program (TARP) to bail out the US financial industry, ensure the availability of credit to borrowers, and save the nation from depression.

The near-collapse of the economy, along with the wars in Afghanistan and Iraq, cast a shadow over George W. Bush. Even though, unlike his father, he managed to win two presidential contests, Bush 43 was dogged by the sense that he should have been better prepared for the financial and terrorist threats. Although Bush had managed to rally the country after 9/11, his reputation was tarnished

For a time, the base provided the Bush administration the freedom it wanted and needed. CIA, FBI, and military interrogators, apparently copying Chinese Communist techniques from the 1950s, tortured some prisoners. According to detainees, their captors used sleep deprivation and beatings; they also mocked detainees' religious practices by defacing the Qur'an or flushing it down the toilet. Lacking the protections for captured military prisoners under the Geneva Convention, the detainees lost the right to trial—a feature of justice in the United States. These conditions took a heavy toll on prisoners; an unknown number committed suicide.

As details of Gitmo leaked out, critics of the Bush administration argued that prisoners deserved the protections of the Geneva Convention and US law, including the right to trial. Gitmo seemed proof that the war on terror, like other wars, had eroded due process, human rights, and other features of democracy, all in the name of battling for democracy.

Ruling in 2006 and 2008 on the treatment of prisoners, the US Supreme Court seemed to agree that Gitmo was an assault on democratic values. Even so, the facility remained open—a swath of gray amid all the green and blue.

Gitmo Military police guarding new detainees in orange jumpsuits at one of the prison facilities at the US naval base at Guantánamo Bay, Cuba.

by the belief that his advisers had misrepresented the existence of Iraqi WMDs in order to force a perhaps unnecessary, unwinnable war.

CONCLUSION

Globalization, information, and cultural change inexorably remade the United States in the 1990s and the 2000s. These transformations helped bring prosperity at the end of the old century and then terrorism, war, and financial crisis at the beginning of the new one. Throughout, David Rockefeller observed events impassively from the 56th floor of his family's famed building complex, Rockefeller Center, in midtown Manhattan. On 9/11, the architect of globalization saw the twin towers— "Nelson" and "David"—collapse. "I watched them go up," he said quietly, "and, unfortunately, I also watched them go down." Still, Rockefeller remained optimistic. "I can't believe we won't overcome this," he declared confidently. "We will." But after the financial crisis of 2008, the banker, now in his nineties, feared that frustrated Americans might reject globalization. He had reason to worry.

WHO, WHAT, WHERE

Al Qaeda   977

"axis of evil"   980

bin Laden, Osama   977

Bosnia-Herzegovina   976

family values   965

globalization   953

Hussein, Saddam   974

information economy   953

New World Order   973

NGOs   954

Oklahoma City   966

Panama   974

Persian Gulf   974

Ruby Ridge   966

Taliban   979

Turner, Ted   954

Waco   966

World Trade Organization
   (WTO)   955

REVIEW QUESTIONS

1. What innovations spurred globalization?

2. What were the main features of the information economy?

3. Why were Americans so often frustrated by the political system in the 1990s?

4. What were the causes of the economic recession of 2008?

TIME LINE

▼**1988**
George H. W. Bush elected president

▼**1989**
Collapse of Communist regimes in Eastern Europe
Invasion of Panama

▼**1990**
Partial shutdown of federal government

▼**1991**
Persian Gulf War
Collapse of the Soviet Union

Dow Jones Industrial Average over 3,000 for first time

▼**1992**
Los Angeles riot after first Rodney King verdict
Bill Clinton elected president

▼**1993**
Terrorist truck bombing of World Trade Center, New York City
Ratification of North American Free Trade Agreement (NAFTA)

▼**1995**
Peace treaty in Bosnia-Herzegovina civil war
Opening of World Trade Organization

▼**1995–1996**
Two federal government shutdowns

▼**1996**
Federal welfare reform
First Wal-Mart in People's Republic of China
Reelection of Bill Clinton as president

CRITICAL-THINKING QUESTIONS

1. What made the globalization of the 1990s different from the earlier linkages between the United States and the rest of the world?

2. Considering both the expansion of rights and the rise of gridlock, did the United States become more or less democratic in the 1990s?

3. Did the information revolution affect American society as the Industrial Revolution did?

SUGGESTED READINGS

Engel, Jeffrey A. *When the World Seemed New: George H. W. Bush and the End of the Cold War.* Boston: Houghton, Mifflin, Harcourt, 2017.

Ngai, Mae. *Impossible Subjects: Illegal Aliens and the Making of Modern America, updated ed.* Princeton, NJ: Princeton University Press, 2014.

Troy, Gil. *The Age of Clinton: America in the 1990s.* New York: Thomas Dunne Books, 2015.

Zelizer, Julian, ed., *The Presidency of George W. Bush: A First Historical Assessment.* Princeton, NJ: Princeton University Press, 2010.

For further review materials and resource information, please visit www.oup.com/us/ofthepeople

▼**1998**
Terrorist truck bombings of US embassies in Kenya and Tanzania

▼**1999**
Acquittal of Bill Clinton in Senate impeachment trial
NATO air war against Yugoslavia
Dow Jones Industrial Average over 10,000 for first time

▼**2001**
George W. Bush declared president
9/11 attacks
Invasion of Afghanistan

▼**2002**
Creation of Department of Homeland Security

▼**2003**
US Supreme Court gay rights ruling, *Lawrence v. Texas*

"Operation Iraqi Freedom," coalition invasion of Iraq

▼**2004**
George W. Bush reelected

▼**2007**
US military "surge" in Iraq

▼**2008**
Collapse of Doha world trade talks
US financial crisis

Primary Sources

29.1   KENICHI OHMAE, "DECLARATION OF INTERDEPENDENCE TOWARD THE WORLD—2005" (1990) AND HELENA NORBERG-HODGE, "BREAK UP THE MONOCULTURE" (1996)

The vast, complex process of globalization spawned both optimism and fear. On one hand, Japanese organizational theorist Kenichi Ohmae and his colleagues in a US consulting firm believed that increasing interconnections would make the world better in just about every way. Written in 1990, the "Declaration of Interdependence Toward the World" looked ahead to the year 2005, when a globalized near-utopia would have "no absolute losers" or "winners." On the other hand, Helena Norberg-Hodge, a Swedish-born, American-educated environmental and globalization activist, saw a much bleaker future for a homogenized world. Instead of globalization, the world, she argued, needed "localization."

DECLARATION OF INTERDEPENDENCE TOWARD THE WORLD—2005

In recent decades we have watched the free flow of ideas, individuals, investments, and industries grow into an organic bond among developed economies. Not only are traditionally traded goods and securities freely exchanged in the interlinked economy, but so too are such crucial assets as land, companies, software, commercial rights (patents, memberships, and brands), art objects, and expertise.

Inevitably, the emergence of the interlinked economy brings with it an erosion of national sovereignty as the power of information directly touches local communities; academic, professional, and social institutions; corporations; and individuals. It is this borderless world that will give participating economies the capacity for boundless prosperity.

We avow that the security of humankind's social and economic institutions lies no longer in superpower deterrence but is rather to be found in the weave of economic and intellectual interdependence of nations.

As such, we believe that the interlinked economy

- Enhances the well-being of individuals and institutions.
- Stands open to all who wish to participate in it, mainly through deregulation of trade.
- Creates no absolute losers nor winners, as market mechanisms adjust participating nations' competitiveness rather fairly through currency exchange rates and employment.

Accordingly, the role of central governments must change, so as to

- Allow individuals access to the best and cheapest goods and services from anywhere in the world.
- Help corporations provide stable and rewarding jobs anywhere in the world regardless of the corporation's national identity.

- Coordinate activities with other governments to minimize conflicts arising from narrow interests.
- Avoid abrupt changes in economic and social fundamentals.

The leading nations must be united under this belief, so that they collectively can

- Enhance networking of individuals, institutions, and communities across the borders.
- Develop a new framework to deal collectively with traditionally parochial affairs, such as tax; standards and codes; and laws governing mobility of tradable goods, services, and assets.
- Induce developing, newly industrialized, and developed nations to actively participate in the global economy.
- Address and resolve issues that belong to the global community, such as:
  Enhancement of the earth's environment and conservation of natural resources.
  Underdeveloped nations.
  Human rights and dignity.

BREAK UP THE MONOCULTURE

The president of Nabisco once defined the goal of economic globalization as "a world of homogeneous consumption," in which people everywhere eat the same food, wear the same clothing and live in houses built from the same materials. It is a world in which every society employs the same technologies, depends on the same centrally managed economy, offers the same Western education for its children, speaks the same language, consumes the same media images, holds the same values and even thinks the same thoughts—monoculture. . . .

Although this sameness suits the needs of transnational corporations, which profit from the efficiencies of standardized production and standardized consumption, in the long term a homogenized planet is disastrous for all of us. It is leading to a breakdown of both biological and cultural diversity, erosion of our food security, an increase in conflict and violence, and devastation for the global biosphere. The myth of globalization is that we no longer need to be connected to a place on the earth. Our every need can be supplied by distant institutions and machines. Our contact with other people can be through electronic media. Globalization is creating a way of life that denies our natural instincts by severing our connection to others and to nature. And—because it is erasing both biological and cultural diversity—it is destined to fail.

Human societies have always been embedded in their local ecosystems, modifying and being modified by them. Cultural diversity has come to mirror the biological and geographic diversity of the planet. In arid environments, for example, pastoral or nomadic practices enable people to use more of the sparse resources of their region. . . .

There is still time to shift direction, restore diversity and begin moving toward sustainable, healthy societies and ecosystems. How to begin? In principle, the answer is straightforward: If globalization is the problem, the solution must lie in economic *localization*. This does not mean an end to all trade or intercultural communication, as some have unfairly charged. Nor does it mean that industrialized society must change from a culture of cities to villages.

However, the idea of localization runs counter to today's general belief that fast-paced urban areas are the locus of "real" culture, while small, local communities are isolated backwaters, relics of a past when small-mindedness and prejudice were the norm. The past is assumed to have been brutish, a time when exploitation was fierce, intolerance rampant, violence commonplace—a situation that the modern world has largely risen above.

These assumptions echo the elitist or racist belief that modernized people are superior—more highly evolved—than their underdeveloped rural counterparts. But most Westerners have a highly distorted notion of what life in small communities can be like. . . .

Efforts to rein in the runaway global economy need to be international—linking grassroots social and environmental movements from North and South in order to pressure governments to take back the power that has been handed over to corporations.

But long-term solutions to today's social and environmental problems will also require a range of small, local initiatives that are as diverse as the cultures and environments in which they take place. Promoting "small-scale on a large scale" would allow specific, on-the-ground initiatives to flourish—community banks, local currencies and trading systems, rediscovered traditional knowledge and more. Unlike halting the global economic steamroller, these small-scale steps require a slow pace and a deep and intimate understanding of local contexts, and will best be designed and implemented by local people themselves. Over time, such initiatives would inevitably foster a return to cultural and biological diversity and long-term sustainability.

Sources: Kenichi Ohmae, *The Borderless World: Power and Strategy in the Interlinked Economy* (New York: HarperBusiness, 1990), pp. 216–217.
Helena Norberg-Hodge, "Break Up the Monoculture," *Nation*, July 15/22, 1996, pp. 20–23.

29.2 SOLOMON D. TRUJILLO, "OPPORTUNITY IN THE NEW INFORMATION ECONOMY" (1998)

Like globalization, the information economy simultaneously inspired optimism and fear. In this 1998 speech to the Latin Business Association in Los Angeles, Solomon D. Trujillo, the president of the telecommunications company U.S. West, considered the implications of high technology for the nation's Latinos. Trujillo was confident that the information economy was a democratizing force that would reward the talent of the Hispanic population. Yet he also feared that Latinos, mostly working-class people subject to discrimination and limited opportunity, might be left behind.

… Let's take a look into the future for a moment:

I'd now like to talk about a subject that is near and dear to my heart: what's happening in high-tech industries and around the Internet. I want to focus on it because Information Age industries can overcome traditional barriers that we've faced in the past, such as access to capital. That's why I believe that the greatest opportunity we have is in the emerging, high-tech industries. Indeed, we already have Latino success stories. … We can—and are—succeeding in the economy of the future.

The greatest opportunity in the future for Hispanics is in emerging, information-driven industries. It is the New Economy. And what's exciting about these industries is that "what you know is more important than who you are."

So I want to focus on Information Age industries for a moment, because technology is the great equalizer. It's the great equalizer because new technologies such as the Internet can overcome barriers common to small business such as access to capital, access to markets and access to information. It's the great equalizer because, over the Internet, small businesses can look big. Big businesses can look small or feel small if that's what they want. A business can customize. Or it can mass-market. It can lower the cost of doing business. It can expand to a global scope.

Today's telecommunications technology brings the whole world to anyone with a telephone and a modem. A friend of mine in the high-tech industry described it this way:

"What I do is create products of the mind. I'm not limited by geography or anything else." Brain power is the natural resource of the Information Age. Brain power has no gender, no race, no religion, no ethnicity, no national origin. And brain power is something we have in abundance.

So the Information Age creates great new opportunities for small- to medium-sized businesses.

My last point tonight is that technology has the potential to create a dangerous world of "haves and have nots" in terms of cyberliteracy. Four centuries ago in the novel Don Quixote, Miguel de Cervantes Saavedra warned us of a world of "haves and have nots." Technology has the potential either to enrich everyone's lives or to leave many of us behind. That's our choice.

To participate fully in the New Economy, all Americans—and that includes Latinos—need to acquire the knowledge to use technology to improve our lives. That means we all need to learn a second or third language. Not just English or Spanish, but the cyber language of Internet communications.

A recent study by the Tomas Rivera Policy Institute confirmed that the Internet, which has the potential to remove barriers and raise opportunities, also has the negative potential of becoming the basis of a new elite. How many people here own a home computer? The study found there's a 50 percent gap in home computer ownership between the general population and middle class Hispanics. Let me repeat—a 50 percent gap for middle class Hispanics in computer ownership. The gap grows even wider when we look at the least fortunate among us.

Compounding the computer access problem is the problem of high-speed access. Some companies that offer high-speed Information Age access are deciding to make a bee-line for high-yield business customers or high-income residential customers—in effect redlining the residential and small business markets. These trends are troublesome. ...

Technological literacy is crucial if Hispanics are to avoid becoming the "have nots." And this is an area we can and must do something about. ... If we don't want Hispanic communities to become the "have nots," we must continue to educate our people about technology and ensure that they have equal access.

And, we all need to continue to give back to our community, and to support each other through organizations like the Latin Business Association. There's a *dicho* that seems fitting: *Palabras sin obras, guitarras sin cuerdas*—words without deeds are like guitars without strings.

Source: Solomon D. Trujillo, "Opportunity in the New Information Economy," *Vital Speeches of the Day* 64, no. 16 (June 1998): 490–492.

29.3 THE DEFENSE OF MARRIAGE ACT (1996)

In the 1990s, federal law supported continued discrimination against the LGBT community. The Defense of Marriage Act of 1996 allowed states to refuse to recognize marriages entered into by same-sex couples in other jurisdictions.

AN ACT
TO DEFINE AND PROTECT THE INSTITUTION OF MARRIAGE

Be it enacted by the Senate and House of Representatives of the United States of America in Congress assembled,

Sec. 1. Short Title

This Act may be cited as the "Defense of Marriage Act."

Sec. 2. Powers Reserved to the States

(a) IN GENERAL—Chapter 115 of title 28, United States Code, is amended by adding after section 1738B the following:

Sec. 1738C. Certain acts, records, and proceedings and the effect thereof

No State, territory, or possession of the United States, or Indian tribe, shall be required to give effect to any public act, record, or judicial proceeding of any other State, territory, possession, or tribe respecting a relationship between persons of the same sex that is treated as a marriage under the laws of such other State, territory, possession, or tribe, or a right or claim arising from such relationship. . . .

Sec. 3. Definition of Marriage

(a) IN GENERAL—Chapter 1 of title 1, United States Code, is amended by adding at the end the following:

Sec. 7. Definition of "Marriage" and "Spouse"

In determining the meaning of any Act of Congress, or of any ruling, regulation, or interpretation of the various administrative bureaus and agencies of the United States, the word "marriage" means only a legal union between one man and one woman as husband and wife, and the word "spouse" refers only to a person of the opposite sex who is a husband or a wife.

Sources: National Defense Authorization Act of 1994. H.R. 2401, 103rd Congress (1993). Defense of Marriage Act. H.R. 3396, 104th Congress (1996).

29.4   GEORGE H. W. BUSH, EXCERPTS FROM "ADDRESS BEFORE A JOINT SESSION OF THE CONGRESS ON THE CESSATION OF HOSTILITIES IN THE PERSIAN GULF CONFLICT" (1991)

On March 6, 1991, a week after the end of the Persian Gulf War, President George H. W. Bush addressed a joint session of Congress. Amid jubilation over the quick victory of the United States and its allies, Bush laid down the basic principles of the "New World Order" for the future.

Members of Congress, 5 short weeks ago I came to this House to speak to you about the state of the Union. We met then in time of war. Tonight, we meet in a world blessed by the promise of peace. . . .

This is a victory for every country in the coalition, for the United Nations. A victory for unprecedented international cooperation and diplomacy. . . . It is a victory for the rule of law and for what is right. . . .

Tonight, I come to this House to speak about the world—the world after war. The recent challenge could not have been clearer. Saddam Hussein was the villain; Kuwait, the victim. To the aid of this small country came nations from North America and Europe, from Asia and South America, from Africa and the Arab world, all united against aggression. Our uncommon coalition must now work in common purpose: to forge a future that should never again be held hostage to the darker side of human nature. ...

To all the challenges that confront this region of the world there is no single solution, no solely American answer. But we can make a difference. America will work tirelessly as a catalyst for positive change. ...

The consequences of the conflict in the Gulf reach far beyond the confines of the Middle East. Twice before in this century, an entire world was convulsed by war. Twice this century, out of the horrors of war hope emerged for enduring peace. Twice before, those hopes proved to be a distant dream, beyond the grasp of man. Until now, the world we've known has been a world divided—a world of barbed wire and concrete block, conflict, and cold war.

Now, we can see a new world coming into view. A world in which there is the very real prospect of a new world order. In the words of Winston Churchill, a world order in which "the principles of justice and fair play protect the weak against the strong. ..." A world where the United Nations, freed from cold war stalemate, is poised to fulfill the historic vision of its founders. A world in which freedom and respect for human rights find a home among all nations. The Gulf war put this new world to its first test. And my fellow Americans, we passed that test . ...

Tonight, as our troops begin to come home, let us recognize that the hard work of freedom still calls us forward. We've learned the hard lessons of history. The victory over Iraq was not waged as "a war to end all wars." Even the new world order cannot guarantee an era of perpetual peace. But enduring peace must be our mission. Our success in the Gulf will shape not only the new world order we seek but our mission here at home. ...

I'm sure that many of you saw on the television the unforgettable scene of four terrified Iraqi soldiers surrendering. They emerged from their bunker broken, tears streaming from their eyes, fearing the worst. And then there was an American soldier. Remember what he said? He said: "It's okay. You're all right now. You're all right now." That scene says a lot about America, a lot about who we are. Americans are a caring people. We are a good people, a generous people. Let us always be caring and good and generous in all we do. ...

We went halfway around the world to do what is moral and just and right. We fought hard and, with others, we won the war. We lifted the yoke of aggression and tyranny from a small country that many Americans had never even heard of, and we ask nothing in return . ...

Source: George H. W. Bush, "Address Before a Joint Session of the Congress on the Cessation of Hostilities in the Persian Gulf Conflict," March 6, 1991.

29.5   GEORGE W. BUSH, EXCERPTS FROM "ADDRESS BEFORE A JOINT SESSION OF THE CONGRESS ON THE UNITED STATES RESPONSE TO THE TERRORIST ATTACKS OF SEPTEMBER 11" (2001)

Nine days after the 9/11 attacks, President George W. Bush addressed a joint session of Congress. How does his rationale for war and his view of America's role in the world compare with his father's address in the same chamber ten years earlier?

... On September 11th, enemies of freedom committed an act of war against our country. Americans have known wars, but for the past 136 years, they have been wars on foreign soil, except for one Sunday in 1941. Americans have known the casualties of war, but not at the center of a great city on a peaceful morning. Americans have known surprise attacks, but never before on thousands of civilians. All of this was brought upon us in a single day, and night fell on a different world, a world where freedom itself is under attack. ...

Al Qaida is to terror what the Mafia is to crime. But its goal is not making money. Its goal is remaking the world and imposing its radical beliefs on people everywhere.

The terrorists practice a fringe form of Islamic extremism that has been rejected by Muslim scholars and the vast majority of Muslim clerics, a fringe movement that perverts the peaceful teachings of Islam. The terrorists' directive commands them to kill Christians and Jews, to kill all Americans, and make no distinctions among military and civilians, including women and children. ...

The leadership of Al Qaida has great influence in Afghanistan and supports the Taliban regime in controlling most of that country. ...

The United States respects the people of Afghanistan—after all, we are currently its largest source of humanitarian aid—but we condemn the Taliban regime. It is not only repressing its own people; it is threatening people everywhere by sponsoring and sheltering and supplying terrorists. By aiding and abetting murder, the Taliban regime is committing murder.

And tonight the United States of America makes the following demands on the Taliban:...These demands are not open to negotiation or discussion. The Taliban must act and act immediately. They will hand over the terrorists, or they will share in their fate.

I also want to speak tonight directly to Muslims throughout the world. We respect your faith. It's practiced freely by many millions of Americans and by millions more in countries that America counts as friends. Its teachings are good and peaceful, and those who commit evil in the name of Allah blaspheme the name of Allah. The terrorists are traitors to their own faith, trying, in effect, to hijack Islam itself. The enemy of America is not our many Muslim friends; it is not our many Arab friends. Our enemy is a radical network of terrorists and every government that supports them.

Our war on terror begins with Al Qaida, but it does not end there. It will not end until every terrorist group of global reach has been found, stopped, and defeated. ...

They hate our freedoms—our freedom of religion, our freedom of speech, our freedom to vote and assemble and disagree with each other.

These terrorists kill not merely to end lives but to disrupt and end a way of life. With every atrocity, they hope that America grows fearful, retreating from the world and forsaking our friends. They stand against us, because we stand in their way.

We are not deceived by their pretenses to piety. We have seen their kind before. They are the heirs of all the murderous ideologies of the 20th century. By sacrificing human life to serve their radical visions, by abandoning every value except the will to power, they follow in the path of fascism and Nazism and totalitarianism. And they will follow that path all the way, to where it ends, in history's unmarked grave of discarded lies. ...

Every nation, in every region, now has a decision to make: Either you are with us, or you are with the terrorists. From this day forward, any nation that continues to harbor or support terrorism will be regarded by the United States as a hostile regime . ....

This is not, however, just America's fight, and what is at stake is not just America's freedom. This is the world's fight. This is civilization's fight. This is the fight of all who believe in progress and pluralism, tolerance and freedom.

We ask every nation to join us. ...

After all that has just passed, all the lives taken and all the possibilities and hopes that died with them, it is natural to wonder if America's future is one of fear. Some speak of an age of terror. I know there are struggles ahead and dangers to face. But this country will define our times, not be defined by them. As long as the United States of America is determined and strong, this will not be an age of terror; this will be an age of liberty, here and across the world. . . . .

Source: George W. Bush, "Address Before a Joint Session of the Congress on the United States Response to the Terrorist Attacks of September 11," September 20, 2001. https://www.presidency.ucsb.edu/documents/address-before-joint-session-the-congress-the-united-states-response-the-terrorist-attacks

"The American Dream"
2008–2021

< Protesting the death of George Floyd, New York, May 2020

987

Maria "Bambi" Roaquin

In 2004, Philippine-born Maria Roaquin graduated from community college and went to work as a nurse north of New York City. The 43-year-old, known as "Bambi" to family, friends, and coworkers, embodied the forces of globalization that continually reshaped twenty-first-century America. Bambi, like her mother, was one of a long line of Filipinos who had migrated and nursed in the United States and other wealthy nations since the American takeover of the Philippines at the end of the nineteenth century. Admired for their skills and compassion, Maria and other Filipino nurses were in effect an export product, part of the freer worldwide flow of goods and people in the age of globalization. Raising a son, enjoying travel, fashion, and parties, and volunteering after work, Nurse Roaquin created a fulfilling life. A sister called her "the American Dream."

Sixteen years later, Bambi was a critical care nurse at New York-Presbyterian Hudson Valley Hospital in Westchester County, when another, deadlier result of globalization arrived in the United States from China and Europe. **COVID-19**, the novel infectious coronavirus disease caused by SARS-CoV-2 that emerged late in 2019, posed a severe challenge for the nearly 150,000 Filipino American nurses in the United States, along with all health care workers. As patients overwhelmed hospitals in America and around the world, overworked caregivers often labored without enough protective gear against the still-mysterious disease. Like other nurses and doctors, many Filipino American nurses became ill and began to die. The nurses also faced anger from some Americans who indiscriminately blamed Asians for the pandemic. In early April, a white man shouted a slur and spat at a male Filipino American nurse in San Francisco. Despite a growing shortage of caregivers, the administration of President Donald Trump, opposed to globalization in general and immigration in particular, made it more difficult for Filipino nurses to enter the United States. Meanwhile in the Philippines, a debate emerged over whether the country should keep nurses to fight the pandemic rather than send them abroad.

Against this backdrop, Nurse Roaquin cared for her patients and lamented the fatigue of her colleagues. "Please let it end soon," she posted on Facebook on April 21. The next day, she hoped to be "part of the largest ticker tape parade when this is done!" But five days later, she posted sadly, "It was just a matter of time when I catch this virus. Complete shock to me when I developed body aches and fevers." Now Bambi felt one of the characteristic symptoms of COVID-19—"no taste in my mouth." Despite her condition, she couldn't get an appointment with her doctor or a test for the disease. "After two months of caring for covid patients," she wrote angrily, "I'm being treated like I'm a pariah."

Bambi Roaquin's plight reflected the broader crisis of globalization for the United States by the second decade of the twenty-first century. Gradually, the intertwined global and information revolutions had diversified and divided the United States. The twin crises of war and economic recession at the start of the 2000s gave way to an increasingly bitter politics, remarkable social and cultural stress, two unprecedented presidencies, and then the human and economic catastrophe of the coronavirus pandemic. "We think America is great," another Filipino American nurse lamented, "yet everything that has happened, the fault is from top to bottom. Nothing is working. And we are scared."

OBAMA AND THE PROMISE OF CHANGE

Against the frightening backdrop of military and economic crises, Americans elected the first African American president in the fall of 2008. The groundbreaking choice of Barack Obama offered the promise of change after years of political gridlock. But change came slowly: it proved difficult to end the Iraq and Afghan wars and to get the economy growing strongly again, particularly amid fierce partisan differences.

The Presidential Election of 2008

The presidential election of 2008 featured a major-party candidate different from any of his predecessors. First-term senator Barack Obama of Illinois, the son of a Black Kenyan father and a white American mother, won the Democratic nomination on the promise of "change" for America and the end of the "stupid war" in Iraq. A symbol of the diverse, globalized nation, Obama became the first African American major-party presidential nominee. His Republican opponent, Senator John McCain of Arizona, reinforced a reputation as an independent "maverick" by choosing the second female major-party candidate for the vice presidency, Governor Sarah Palin of Alaska. But the 72-year-old McCain, a generation older than Obama, seemed more like a defender of the status quo, including Bush's policies, and Palin seemed unprepared for higher office. On November 4, 2008, voters did what still appeared unthinkable: they elected an African American to the presidency of the United States. Obama won a clear victory with 52.8 percent of the popular vote, the highest in 20 years, and 365 electoral votes. The Democrat seemed to have his mandate for "change" (see Map 30-1).

Confronting Economic Crisis

Meanwhile, as consumer spending fell and unemployment rose, the nation felt the grip of what became known as the Great Recession. Taking office amid hardship and war in January 2009, Obama optimistically promised a new politics. "We have chosen hope over fear, unity of purpose over conflict and discord," he declared. "We come to proclaim an end to the petty grievances and false

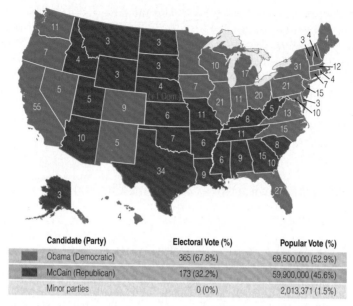

Candidate (Party)	Electoral Vote (%)	Popular Vote (%)
Obama (Democratic)	365 (67.8%)	69,500,000 (52.9%)
McCain (Republican)	173 (32.2%)	59,900,000 (45.6%)
Minor parties	0 (0%)	2,013,371 (1.5%)

Map 30-1 The Presidential Election of 2008 For generations, Democratic presidential victory had depended on carrying the Solid South. Obama's election showed how Democrats could triumph almost without Southern support.

promises, the recriminations and worn-out dogmas that for far too long have strangled our politics."

To restore prosperity, Obama pushed successfully for the deficit spending that liberals had long advocated to stimulate economic growth. The American Recovery and Reinvestment Act of 2009, known as the stimulus package, appropriated three-quarters of a trillion dollars including tax incentives and money for housing, health care, educational programs, food stamps, retirees, scientific research, highways, and other infrastructure. Some liberals believed the stimulus spent too little, while conservatives charged that the act irresponsibly spent far too much increasing federal power and the national debt.

To save Chrysler and General Motors (GM) in 2009, the US government stepped in to support quick bankruptcies for the two manufacturers, which reemerged as new, restructured companies with less debt and new ownership. To Republicans' dismay, the US Treasury temporarily became the majority owner of GM. Despite this controversial "socialism," the bailout worked: the American automakers survived, and the federal government sold off its ownership of GM.

Rather than punish financial leaders for their role in the economic crisis, Obama focused on protecting consumers and regulating banks and insurance companies. In 2009, Congress passed new rules for credit card companies. The next year, the president signed the Wall Street Reform and Consumer Protection Act, known as Dodd-Frank, perhaps the most significant overhaul of federal financial regulation since the 1930s.

As the stock market climbed again and the danger of depression receded, Obama concentrated on winning the longtime liberal goal of national health care. After a lengthy congressional battle, the president signed the **Patient Protection and Affordable Health Care Act of 2010** and the Health Care and Educational Reconciliation Act of 2010. The two measures helped uninsured and self-employed Americans buy health insurance, made more people eligible for Medicaid, allowed parents' health insurance to cover their children for longer, prevented insurance companies from denying coverage because of preexisting conditions, and encouraged large employers to provide health care plans. Finally, a controversial "individual mandate" required all adults to obtain health insurance beginning in 2014 or pay a penalty.

Obama's landmark reform was difficult to explain, passionately attacked by conservatives as "socialism," criticized by some liberals as less than full government-subsidized health care, and limited by a Supreme Court decision. Nevertheless, Obama had achieved the system of national health insurance that Democratic presidents such as Harry Truman and Bill Clinton had failed to win. The measures that became known as "**Obamacare**," like Lyndon Johnson's Medicare in the 1960s and Franklin Roosevelt's Social Security in the 1930s, marked a basic change in the relationship between government and the American people.

Ending the Wars in Afghanistan and Iraq

Like every president since World War II, Obama believed the United States should engage with the world primarily through the United Nations, military alliances such as NATO, and trade agreements such as NAFTA and the WTO. He rejected George W. Bush's experiments in unilateral US action, the threat of preemptive warfare, and neoconservative nation building abroad.

Determined to end the nation's wars, Obama sent 30,000 more troops to battle the Taliban and Al Qaeda in Afghanistan in 2009. Despite the troop increase, American forces couldn't secure the country. As the fighting continued into 2010, Afghanistan surpassed Vietnam as the longest war in American history.

Meanwhile, the Obama administration aggressively used other means to combat terrorists and their supporters. Controversially, the CIA increased the use of unmanned, rocket-firing drones to kill suspected terrorists and their leaders inside Pakistan and Yemen. On May 1, 2011, nearly a decade after 9/11, a daring helicopter raid conducted by Special Forces inside Pakistan killed Osama bin Laden—a turning point in the war on terror.

In the meantime, Obama brought the Iraq War to a close, despite worries that the Iraqi government would prove unable to defend itself. In October 2011, the president announced the departure of US combat troops. The end of the Afghan War proved more elusive. Obama substantially reduced, but did not end, the presence of US troops by 2016.

The Politics of Frustration

As the president struggled to end "stupid" war, his call for a new politics went unheeded. Obama found himself whipsawed by an often nasty debate. On one hand, he disappointed supporters who had expected more aggressive domestic leadership, a better economy, and more "change" generally. Many liberal Democrats and independents, who called themselves "progressives," felt that Obama should have punished Wall Street, expanded federal regulation and spending still further, taxed the rich—the top "one percent" of wealth and income—more heavily, and implemented federally subsidized "single-payer" health care covering all Americans.

On the other hand, conservatives were horrified by Obama's accomplishments, including health care reform and the stimulus. In 2009, the **Tea Party** movement, evoking the spirit of the Boston Tea Party of 1773 before the American Revolution, voiced conservative anger at federal activism and deficits. Composed mostly of white, older Americans, the movement served primarily as a pressure group within the Republican Party pushing more conservative candidates and policies.

Although most Americans endorsed neither Tea Partiers nor progressives, there was considerable disappointment with Obama's presidency. In the 2010 midterm elections, Republicans recaptured the House of Representatives. Once again, the United States had divided partisan control of the federal government, and once again the result was legislative gridlock. Pressured by the Tea Party, Republican leaders wanted to repeal Obamacare, cut taxes, and lower domestic spending; refusing, Obama and the Democrats wanted more economic stimulus. In 2011, the president and the parties finally made a modest bargain to cut the deficit and avoid having the government default on its financial obligations. Many Americans criticized Obama as a weak leader who did not care enough about the nation's financial plight. But they condemned Congress and Republicans even more.

A Second Term

As George W. Bush demonstrated, incumbent presidents were hard to defeat for reelection. Despite the criticism of Obama, Republicans struggled to come up with a strong alternative in 2012. The party, divided by the Tea Party movement, chose Mitt Romney, a wealthy Mormon and moderate former governor of Massachusetts, as its presidential nominee. Obama's supporters, their hopes for change diminished, were not as passionate this time. But Romney suffered from the perception that he was a rich man out of touch with ordinary Americans. The Republican nominee also had trouble explaining his opposition to Obamacare, which borrowed features from the Massachusetts health insurance system that Romney had signed into law as governor. In November, Obama received a smaller percentage of the popular vote (51.1) and a smaller number of electoral votes (332) than four years earlier, but he won reelection.

Once again, Obama faced a divided Congress with a Republican-controlled House and a Democratic-controlled Senate. That combination produced more gridlock. In 2013, the nation endured another temporary shutdown of the federal government when Republicans and Democrats could not agree on budgets, spending, and the funding of Obamacare.

Unable to win legislation from Congress, Obama increasingly relied on the executive power of the presidency. Controversially, his administration issued over 560 major regulations covering health care, financial institutions, industrial pollution, civil rights, and worker and consumer protection—twice as many as the George W. Bush administration. Obama officials raised the value of a human life from $6.6 million to $9.4 million—a key figure used to calculate the impact of regulations and other federal action. Although they had seldom criticized Bush's use of executive power, conservatives and Republicans now condemned the cost and intrusiveness of Obama's regulations.

Climate Change

President Obama used his executive power in response to the problem of **climate change**. As early as the 1950s, scientists had begun to predict and then explore a gradual increase in surface temperatures around the world. By the 2010s, scientific consensus argued that human activity—in particular, the industrial use of coal, oil, and other fossil fuels producing greenhouse gasses such as carbon dioxide—was heavily responsible for long-term global warming. According to scientists, the effects of climate change included melting glaciers, rising sea levels, shifting seasons, spreading deserts, and increasing extreme weather events. In the United States, devastating, deadly hurricanes dramatically underscored the possibilities of climate change. Accordingly, environmental activists urged America to join other nations in seeking solutions and to reduce greenhouse gas emissions by decreasing the use of fossil fuels.

Worried that climate change measures would hurt the fossil fuel industry, George W. Bush had declined to support ratification of a key international treaty, the Kyoto Protocol. In contrast, Barack Obama pushed to develop solar and wind power as alternatives to coal and oil. In 2015, the president implemented his Clean Power Plan, which aimed to reduce carbon dioxide emissions by placing restrictive regulations on coal-burning power plants. That year, the United States joined 195 nations in adopting the path-breaking **Paris Agreement**. To limit global warming, each party to the agreement set its own voluntary targets for reducing greenhouse gases.

Unending War?

The Paris Agreement reflected Obama's strong belief that the United States should engage with other nations to promote its interests and avoid war. Unable to end conflict in Afghanistan and Iraq, his administration also could not unilaterally or collectively stop Russian expansion in Europe. Moreover, events in the Middle East threatened to draw America into new conflicts abroad. Additionally, terrorist acts in the United States made it seem as though the nation was caught in unending war.

In the twenty-first century, Vladimir Putin, serving alternately as president and prime minister, wanted to restore the power Russia had enjoyed as part of the Soviet Union during the Cold War. The Russian leader particularly resented the decision of the United States and its European allies to enlarge the North Atlantic Treaty Organization to include Central and Eastern European nations bordering Russia. In 2008, Putin sent troops across Russia's southern border to ensure that two regions of the neighboring country of Georgia could break free from the Georgian government. In 2014, as troops repeatedly crossed Russia's eastern border into Ukraine, Russia annexed the Ukrainian territory of **Crimea**. In response, the United States and its allies imposed strong economic sanctions against Russian officials and companies. Damaging Russia's economy, the sanctions slowed Putin's aggression in Ukraine but did not stop the annexation of Crimea.

In the Middle East and Africa in 2011, the **Arab Spring** saw popular uprisings against repressive leaders in nations including Tunisia, Egypt, Libya, and Syria. Facing criticism for doing either too little or too much, Obama partnered with NATO and used airpower, without an American military casualty, to help overthrow Libya's Muammar Qaddafi, who had supported terrorism against the United States. In Syria, President Bashar Hafez al-Assad's ruthless repression of the Arab Spring led to civil war. Under pressure to intervene on the side of the anti-Assad rebels, Obama held back. In 2012, the president declared that Assad would cross "a red line" if he used chemical weapons against his own people. But when Assad did just that, Congress refused to authorize retaliatory air strikes.

Meanwhile, one of Assad's opponents created new problems for the United States. The **Islamic State in Iraq and Syria (ISIS)**, a jihadist group that had split from Al Qaeda, aimed to establish a caliphate—an Islamic state—in the Middle East. Amid the chaos of civil war, ISIS fighters took over territory in Syria, and with the aid of former supporters of Saddam Hussein, spread across Iraq. After ISIS murdered Iraqis and beheaded two American hostages, Obama authorized air drops of humanitarian aid to besieged Iraqis and air strikes against ISIS fighters in the summer of 2014. With ISIS rising and Iraq vulnerable, Americans faced the prospect that their nation would remain on a war footing for years to come.

The Obama administration did use collective action to handle challenges in the Middle East and Asia. In 2015, the United States joined European nations, Russia, and the People's Republic of China in a deal to prevent Iran from developing nuclear weapons that would have further destabilized the Middle East. As China grew economically and militarily powerful and as **North Korea** experimented with nuclear weapons, the president tried to contain these developments through diplomacy and alliances. The Obama administration joined negotiations with South Korea, Japan, Vietnam, Australia, Canada, Mexico, Peru, and various Pacific nations that led to the **Trans-Pacific Partnership (TPP)**, a vast new trade agreement, in 2016.

Meanwhile, Obama encountered difficulty scaling back the Bush administration's post-9/11 domestic security measures. Disappointing his supporters, the president could not close the Guantánamo Bay detention center, as he had promised. In 2013, computer specialist and former National Security Agency contractor Edward Snowden leaked classified documents detailing the federal government's extensive surveillance programs around the world and inside the United States. While Americans debated whether the government should be able to collect data about their lives, Snowden found sanctuary in Russia. But the programs, like US involvement in conflicts abroad, continued.

They continued, too, because terrorism endured in the United States. As the fortunes of ISIS declined in the Middle East, the group urged followers to stay home and conduct attacks. In April 2013, two Chechen brothers, seeking revenge for the wars in Afghanistan and Iraq, set off bombs that killed three and injured hundreds at the annual marathon in Boston, Massachusetts. During a subsequent manhunt, a policeman was killed and another mortally wounded, and the brothers were captured: one died from his wounds; the other was sentenced to death. In December 2015, a Chicago-born man and his Pakistan-born wife, inspired by foreign terrorists, shot and killed 14 people at a holiday party in San Bernardino, California. In June 2016, American-born Omar Mateen, who called himself an "Islamic soldier" and apparently pledged allegiance to ISIS, shot and killed 49 people at Pulse, a gay nightclub in Orlando, Florida. The deadliest act of terrorism on US soil since 9/11, the murders were also the bloodiest anti-LGBTQ violence in American history. Meanwhile, a wave of deadly attacks occurred in Australia, Canada, and Europe, as well as the Middle East. The battle with terror seemed far from over.

Against the sobering backdrop of war and terrorism, the US economy gradually improved during Obama's second term. As the stock market reached record heights, the unemployment rate dropped under 5 percent for the first time since the financial crisis. His administration free from scandal, Obama regained public approval.

DIVERSITY AND DIVISION

Along with economic crisis and war, rapid social and cultural change transformed the United States in the twenty-first century. The racial composition of the population, the visibility of LGBTQ people, and the religious beliefs and commitments of Americans shifted dramatically. Sometimes society adjusted surprisingly well to changes in social and cultural diversity; sometimes old and new divisions flared.

A Diverse Society of Color

The racial and ethnic composition of the United States changed rapidly in the twenty-first century. By 2001, Americans of Hispanic origin outnumbered African Americans and became the largest minority group. Thanks to a strong job market, the Hispanic population spread well beyond traditional concentrations in south Florida and the states from Texas to California. Mexican immigrants moved to small midwestern towns and cities, where semiskilled and unskilled jobs paid 10 and 15 times more than jobs in Mexico. By 2010, nonwhites made up more than one-quarter of the population. Americans of Hispanic or Latino origin, both white and nonwhite, numbered more than 50 million—just over 16 percent of the population. Expecting the number of Hispanics and Asians to triple in the next 50 years, the Census Bureau predicted that the United States would become a diverse society of color, with a nonwhite majority. Already in 2014, non-Hispanic whites made up a minority of the children who went to school that fall.

As the population changed, the concept of race became more complicated. To many Americans, race had been largely a divide between Black and white. But the growing Hispanic population, drawn from Cuba and the Caribbean, as well as Central and Latin America, confounded this simple division. So did the growth of the Asian and Pacific Islander population—by 2010, about 6 percent of the population drawn from Chinese, Filipino, Indian, Vietnamese, Korean, Japanese, Pakistani, and other origins. Moreover, many Americans, especially younger ones, felt that mixed racial background was a basic and distinctive part of their identity. In 2000, the Census Bureau let people choose more than one race to describe themselves. Hispanics, epitomizing the complications of race, were allowed to identify themselves both as Hispanic and as members of any race. Naming practices added to the complexity. Although officially labeled Hispanic, many Americans increasingly considered themselves Latinos or Latinas. Some Americans labeled them Latinx.

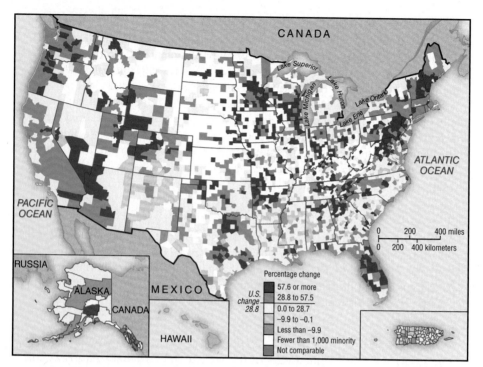

Map 30–2   Percentage Change in Minority Population by County: 2000 to 2010
Minority refers to people who reported their ethnicity and race as something other than non-Hispanic white alone in the decennial census (counties with a minority population of at least 1,000 are included in the map).
Sources: US Census Bureau, *Census 2000 Redistricting Data (Public Law 94—171) Summary File,* Tables PL1 and PL2; and *2010 Census Redistricting Data (Public Law 94—171), Summary File,* Tables P1 and P2.

Tolerance and Intolerance

In some ways, greater diversity brought greater tolerance. In the immediate aftermath of 9/11, American Muslims did not face the discrimination that German Americans confronted during World War I or that Japanese Americans suffered during World War II. As the first Mormon major party candidate for president, Mitt Romney met no significant criticism of his religion.

Nevertheless, social diversity brought division and discrimination. Obama's election occasioned optimism that America was becoming a "postracial" society in which racial differences did not matter. But many Obama supporters believed that racism played a role in the determined opposition to his administration, including unfounded claims by so-called birthers that he was an illegal president who had not actually been born in the United States. Decades after the African American civil rights movement, Black men remained disproportionately likely to be unemployed and imprisoned.

Due in part to new technology, the Obama years saw the raw reemergence of an old racial concern—the justice system's treatment of African Americans. Just as analog videotape footage of the Rodney King beating spurred protest in the 1990s, digital cell phone video of the controversial deaths of unarmed Black men spurred nationwide protests in the 2010s. After a Florida jury acquitted George Zimmerman of murder in the shooting death of Trayvon Martin in 2013, community activists launched an online protest movement with the hashtag "Black Lives Matter." In 2014, the police killings of Eric Garner in New York City and Michael Brown in Ferguson, Missouri, led to nationwide, nonviolent Black Lives Matter protests. In turn, both violence against police and the rise of Black Lives Matter inspired the creation of Blue Lives Matter—a hashtag reflecting the typically blue uniforms of police officers. A White Lives Matter movement also appeared. While Black Lives Matter demanded equal treatment of different races under the law, White Lives Matter often insisted on white supremacy.

The 2010s saw a revival of white supremacist groups and violence that had marked the 1990s. In 2012, a neo-Nazi shot and killed six Sikhs at their temple in Cudahy, Wisconsin. In 2015, a white supremacist obsessed with the Confederacy shot and killed nine African American members of a Bible study group at the Emanuel African Methodist Episcopal Church in Charleston, South Carolina. Afterward, the state government removed the Confederate flag, raised in the 1960s in protest against the civil rights movement, from the statehouse grounds.

Meanwhile, the nation's inability to resolve the status of illegal immigrants from Mexico and Central America indicated continuing uneasiness about the increase of the Latino population. After the Great Recession, about 11 million foreign-born people, around half of them Mexican, lived without legal approval in the United States. While many Americans called for more rigorous enforcement of immigration laws, employers relied on undocumented workers, who made up about 5 percent of the nation's labor force. Public debate focused particularly on the fate of the "Dreamers," brought illegally as children to the United States, typically by their parents. In 2012, the Obama administration's **Deferred Action for Childhood Arrivals program (DACA)** allowed eligible Dreamers to pay a fee to study, work, and postpone deportation. Like other Obama executive actions, DACA met resistance from both anti-immigration activists and opponents of presidential power.

Despite progress toward greater equality, Americans became more pessimistic about racial issues toward the end of Obama's presidency. Majorities of whites, Blacks, and Latinos all believed that race relations were "bad."

LGBTQ Rights

In the twenty-first century, Americans increasingly celebrated or at least accepted sexual diversity. After centuries of hostility and discrimination, the shift in attitudes and policies toward the lesbian, gay, bisexual, transgender, and queer or questioning communities came with stunning speed. Despite conservatives' crusade for family values in the 1990s, Americans' social attitudes became more liberal. To a great extent, the change was the result of activists' courage in beginning to come out in the 1960s as a more visible presence in American society and culture. The change also reflected the rise of a younger generation of Americans for whom sexual equality was as important as racial equality had been for young Americans during the civil rights era. But many older, powerful Americans, including judges, proved open to change, too.

Ruling in *Lawrence v. Texas* in 2003, the US Supreme Court struck down state antisodomy laws and effectively legalized gay sexual behavior. In 2004, the mayor of San Francisco, flouting state law, issued marriage licenses to same-sex couples. Liberal Massachusetts became the first state to legalize same-sex marriages, and couples flocked there to be married. Supported by conservatives and George W. Bush, a constitutional amendment banning gay marriage failed to pass that year. But in 2008, a majority of California voters passed Proposition Eight, a referendum imposing a ban on same-sex marriages.

Despite such setbacks, public opinion increasingly favored LGBTQ rights. In 2010–2011, Obama and Congress ended the military's "don't ask, don't tell" policy. Ruling in *Hollingsworth v. Perry* in June 2013, the US Supreme Court upheld a lower court's decision that California's Proposition Eight was unconstitutional. The same day, in *United States v. Windsor*, the Supreme Court invalidated Section 3 of the Defense of Marriage Act of 1996, which had denied federal recognition of same-sex unions. In 2015, the Supreme Court settled the issue nationwide by ruling same-sex marriage bans unconstitutional in *Obergefell v. Hodges*.

As opinion shifted on LGBTQ rights, Americans became more aware and somewhat more accepting of the transgender population and queer or questioning—as many as 1.4 million by 2016. One sign was the increasing addition of Q to the original term LGBT. In 2016, the Obama administration lifted the formal ban on transgender people serving openly in the military. But that year North Carolina passed the Public Facilities Privacy & Security Act requiring people to use restrooms and changing facilities corresponding to the biological sex on their birth certificates in all government buildings. Intended to keep transgender people from using the facilities of their choice, the "bathroom bill" met opposition, including boycotts, from corporations, musicians, sports leagues, and other states. The US government and North Carolina sued each other. Succumbing to intense pressure, the state legislature repealed the facilities provision in 2017.

Shifting Religious Beliefs and Practices

As the presence of a Sikh temple in Wisconsin suggested, American religious practices became more diverse in the twenty-first century. Non-Christian faith adherents, including Buddhists, Hindus, and Muslims, increased from 5 to 6 percent of the population between 2007 and 2014. Most Americans still considered themselves Christians, but the percentage fell from 78 to 71 percent. Even the largest Christian religious grouping, Evangelical Protestants, saw a slight decline to 25 percent. Most strikingly, the percentage of Americans unaffiliated with any religious denomination jumped from 16 to 23 percent during these years—a larger group than Roman Catholics and mainline Protestants. Like the growth of the nonwhite population, the number of the religiously unaffiliated seemed likely to increase: Americans born after the 1980s were less likely to pray daily, attend religious services, and consider religion very important to their lives than their elders were.

Although the United States still led industrialized nations in the percentage of the population who believed in God and attended Christian churches, some Americans worried that Christianity was under attack. Conservative commentators condemned the "War on Christmas" allegedly led by liberals and progressives.

Too many people and businesses, conservatives argued, said "Happy Holidays" instead of the more Christian "Merry Christmas"; too many local governments were afraid to display Christian symbols such as crosses, Christmas trees, and nativity scenes. In short, the United States was supposedly losing its identity as a Christian nation.

ECONOMIC CHANGE AND A DIVIDED NATION

As so often in American history, anxieties about religion, race, and gender partly reflected anxieties about economic change. In the twenty-first century, the implications of deindustrialization, digitization, and globalization became increasingly clear. Despite the recovery from the Great Recession, the economy divided Americans into unequal groups: the rich and everyone else; men and women; old and young; urban and rural.

Jobs and Growth

By the 2010s, some optimistic forecasts about the information revolution and globalization were not coming true. New technologies and freer trade turned out to be more disruptive than expected. While observers anticipated that globalization would threaten some American manufacturing, they were unprepared for the sharp decline in the twenty-first century. Instead of increasing, jobs in manufacturing dropped 20 percent from 2000 to 2007, dropped again during the Great Recession, and then made only a partial recovery. In 1980, about one in five American workers had labored in factories; in 2016, fewer than one in ten did. Meanwhile, the ranks of coal miners, who had helped power the Industrial Revolution, continued a long-term decline to just 50,000 in 2016. Thanks to new extraction techniques and competitive prices, jobs in the fossil fuel industry—oil and natural gas—grew in the twenty-first century but did not reach the highs of the 1980s.

The service sector, which had grown in the late twentieth century as manufacturing declined, faced upheaval, too. As online shopping became more popular in the twenty-first century, Amazon and other e-commerce companies built new distribution centers and hired more workers. But towns and small cities, which had counted on retail to make up for lost factories, saw local stores shed workers and go out of business.

An intense debate enveloped these changes. As advocates of globalization contended, trade agreements indeed benefited many American workers and offered American consumers a wider selection of goods at lower prices. But freer trade, including the "China Shock"—the admission of the People's Republic of China, with its vast economy of low-wage workers, to the World Trade Organization in 2001—led to the loss of some American factories and jobs. Unexpectedly, technological change proved an even bigger factor in job losses, not only in manufacturing but also in the service sector. Much as the horse gave way to the internal combustion engine, human workers increasingly gave way to robots in factories, warehouses, farms, stories, fast food restaurants, and farms.

All these changes had a dramatic effect on the American economy; some observers believed they added up to a new technological and economic revolution.

American Landscape
The Winter Strawberry Capital of the World

Plant City billed itself as "The Winter Strawberry Capital of the World." Just east of Tampa in west central Florida, the community was a major hub of American strawberry farming. With its humid, subtropical climate and flat sandy soil, the Plant City region was ideal for growing red, sweet strawberries in the winter months when rival California growers had no crop. So, long straight rows of short green plants filled thousands of acres in and around Plant City. Of course, strawberry cultivation, like all kinds of farming, traditionally faced challenges from the weather: delicate berries suffered if it was too cold, too hot, too dry, too wet, or too windy. But in the 2010s, globalization, immigration, and climate change imposed new stresses on the Winter Strawberry Capital of the World. Mexican strawberries, picked by low-wage workers, threatened Plant City's hold on the American market. A lower birth rate and new job opportunities in Mexico, along with tighter US immigration restrictions, threatened Plant City's own crucial supply of seasonal, low-wage immigrant workers, both legal and undocumented. At the same time, strawberry farmers began to realize that more extreme weather conditions threatened their industry now and in the future. "Eat Your Strawberries Now Before Climate Change

Wipes Them Out," ran one alarmist headline.

Gary Wishnatzki, a third-generation strawberry businessman, responded aggressively to the new conditions. At the entrance to his family's Wish Farms, 20-foot-high cardboard cutouts paid tribute to three past and former workers. But Wishnatzki was preparing to do without berry pickers. With fewer and fewer young Mexican workers, he couldn't find American-born workers willing to do the hard work of bending over for hours in the fields. Investing millions of his own money, Wishnatzki formed a company to perfect robots capable of the fast, delicate task of harvesting strawberries more cheaply than even the best pickers could. Harvest Computerized Robotic Optimized Obtainer was attempting an extraordinary coup. It was one thing for industrial robots, working indoors, to do a single repetitive task, such as turning screws, over and over. It was quite another to combine Global Positioning Satellite capability, artificial intelligence, cameras, and fast, delicate, but durable picking claws that could choose just the right strawberries and then pluck them without damage. Nevertheless, Wishnatzki's company was nearing success by the close of the decade. A large, diesel-powered contraption, positioning 16 robots astride four rows of plants,

Politicians, economists, and corporate executives had predicted that new technologies and freer trade would drive the economy to new heights. Instead, national economic growth tapered off. From 1948 to 2000, the United States had grown an average of 2.3 percent per year; from 2001 to 2016, the average growth rate fell to just 1.1 percent.

came close to duplicating the work of 30 pickers. And unlike those workers, Wishnatzki's $300,000 machine could work at night when cooler temperatures meant less damage to the berries.

Awaiting the success of his unconventional robots, Wishnatzki fought back against global competition in a conventional way. Rather than farm more strawberries in Florida, he made arrangements with Mexican growers to supply Wish Farms with cheaper strawberries. In other words, Wishnatzki, like many American companies in the late twentieth and early twenty-first centuries, outsourced production from the United States.

If anything, climate change was an even more difficult problem than globalization, labor, and robot technology. On one hand, it was hard to link any particular weather event to the massive phenomenon. There were consecutive poor growing seasons in the winters of 2015–2016 and 2016–2017, but was that bad luck or a larger pattern? In 2019, the Tampa area saw its warmest months in history. Partly as a result, fungus ruined much of the strawberry crop of 2019–20. More bad luck? On the other hand, some of the direst warnings about climate change applied to the long term, decades after Wishnatzki, a man in his 60s, would be dead. Gradually rising average temperatures would eventually make strawberry cultivation impossible in the Plant City region; strawberry farms would likely move northward to newly friendlier climates. Or perhaps farmers in the United States and around the globe wouldn't be able to grow strawberries at all. At Wish Farms, the complex problem of climate change would fall increasingly to Gary's son, daughter, and son-in-law, the fourth and perhaps the last generation in the business of the Winter Strawberry Capital of the World.

Strawberry Pickers
Migrant and other workers performing the hard, careful labor of picking strawberries at Wish Farms, 2019.

The Rich, the Poor, and the Middle Class

By 2000, the United States, the richest country in the world, also had the largest gap between rich and poor. That gap grew larger in the twenty-first century. On one hand, the bottom 20 percent of American workers received only 3 percent of national income in 2016. On the other, the top 20 percent of American earners received

51 percent of national income that year. In 2012, the top 400 American earners had an average annual income of $336 million, more than four times the inflation-adjusted value of their earnings 30 years before. After the financial crisis of 2008, the stock market soared again to one record level after another—a windfall for the bare majority of Americans who owned corporate shares. The tax cuts of the Reagan and Bush administrations, only partially moderated by Obama-era tax increases, allowed the rich to keep more of their gains. The richest 5 percent of households owned nearly two-thirds of all the nation's wealth. By 2017, the number of American billionaires had grown to 565—more than a quarter of the world's billionaires.

Meanwhile, the middle class—households earning between $35,000 and $100,000 a year—shrank. After decades of downsizing, outsourcing, and deindustrialization, the average weekly earnings of American workers in 2014, allowing for inflation, were less than in 1970. The decline of manufacturing meant the loss of relatively high-paying blue-collar jobs that paid for a middle-class lifestyle. Although workers continued to become more efficient and productive, employers held down the growth of wages and salaries (see Figure 30–1) . For decades, American families

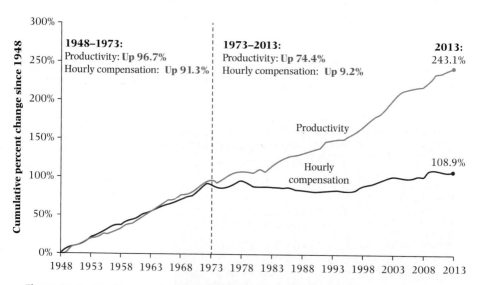

Figure 30–1 Workers' Productivity and Pay, 1948–2013 Why did workers stop benefiting so much from their increasing productivity after 1970?

Note: Data are for compensation (wages and benefits) of production/nonsupervisory workers in the private sector and net productivity of the total economy. "Net productivity" is the growth of output of goods and services less depreciation per hour worked.

Source: Lawrence Mishel, Elise Gould, and Josh Bivens, "Wage Stagnation in Nine Charts," Economic Policy Institute, January 6, 2015, http://www.epi.org/publication/charting-wage-stagnation/.

Data: EPI analysis of unpublished Total Economy Productivity data from Bureau of Labor Statistics (BLS) Labor Productivity and Costs program, wage data from the BLS Current Employment Statistics, BLS Employment Cost Trends, BLS Consumer Price Index, and Bureau of Economic Analysis National Income and Product Accounts. Updated from Figure A in *Raising America's Pay: Why It's Our Central Economic Policy Challenge*, by Josh Bivens, Elise Gould, Lawrence Mishel, and Heidi Shierholz, Economic Policy Institute, 2014.

had made up lost economic ground by having both spouses or partners work. But in the 2010s, that was no longer necessarily enough to maintain a middle-class lifestyle. In the 2000s, 60 percent of adult Americans considered themselves middle class; by 2016, only 51 percent did. Since the 1950s, Americans and their leaders had proudly claimed that the United States was a middle-class country. That claim was harder to maintain in the 2010s.

Official figures hid the extent of some Americans' economic challenges. According to federal statistics, the unemployment rate was a very low 4.3 percent at one point in 2017. However, the government counted among the unemployed only those people actively looking for jobs; in addition to the retired, the statistics omitted discouraged or ill people who had given up looking. Male participation in the labor force had been declining since the mid-1950s to 69 percent in 2017; surprisingly, female labor force participation had peaked at 60 percent in 2000 and only stood at 57 percent in 2017. Among the factors keeping both men and women from work was a stunning increase in physical disability and in opioid addiction. Almost incredibly, for such a rich country, the life expectancy of middle-aged whites, typically rising for decades, began to fall in 2015.

Women and Men

The changing economy reshaped the relative status of women and men. Female workers continued to face discrimination in the twenty-first century. Despite long, slow progress, women earned 85 percent as much as men did in 2015. Just 6 percent of America's 500 largest companies had female chief executive officers. Only about one in three American billionaires was female. Meanwhile, on average, mothers spent about twice as much time per week doing child care and housework as fathers did. These domestic commitments, as well as caring for parents, were reasons why the percentage of women in the labor force fell.

Even so, women fared better than men in important ways. In an economy that demanded well-educated workers, women were more likely to have a college degree than men were for the first time in history. As high-school-educated men found fewer high-paying jobs in heavy industry, the rapidly growing health care sector eagerly sought the social and professional skills of women such as Maria Roaquin. As a result, women, who held about 25 percent of middle-income jobs in 1985, held 44 percent of them in 2015.

Women also dealt with another form of inequality. While the well-publicized examples of male sexual harassment and assault of women had produced little change in the 1990s, more women and gay men spoke out forcefully against these practices in the 2010s. A new openness, demonstrated by the Me Too and Time's Up movements, led to the resignations of powerful men in Hollywood, media, business, and government in 2017–2018.

Baby Boomers and Millennials

Long-term economic change affected generations differently, too. The vast generation of baby boomers, born in the affluent years from 1946 to 1964, lived comparatively well in the twenty-first century. In retirement, they enjoyed Social Security and Medicare benefits, paid partly by the taxes of younger generations. Meanwhile, the Millennials, born from the 1980s to the early 2000s, struggled with student debt, stagnating wages, and a difficult job market. In 2013, the median household headed by people age 65 and older was worth $203,000; the median household headed by people 35 and under was worth $7,000.

Millennials were often negatively stereotyped as thin-skinned, cautious, "entitled whiners" who postponed marriage and adulthood. Supposedly made dependent by constant praise and support from their parents, Millennials were more likely to live at home as young adults than the preceding generation had been. Yet Millennials confronted a genuine decline in generational expectations. "Half of all millennials today think that the American dream is dead," said an observer. "No surprise, when the country's implicit message is: 'Go to school, work hard, and you *might* be able to enter the middle class—but not if you also want to raise a family.'"

Urban and Rural

Economic transformation also helped power an increasing divide between urban and rural areas. Continuing a trend since the end of World War II, the suburban population, part of urban American, increased the largest percentage in the twenty-first century. Particularly in the South and West, less-populated suburbs around large cities—for instance, Kendal and Cosmal Counties, north of San Antonio, Texas—grew especially rapidly. Although the growth of cities slowed, the population of Sunbelt metropolitan areas such as Cape Coral–Fort Myers, Florida, boomed. Some older cities, such as Milwaukee, after decades of deindustrialization, experienced a revival by attracting college-educated Millennials and wealthy, well-educated older people. In turn, corporations, eager for college-educated, tech-savvy workers, moved their headquarters from suburbs to the cities.

In contrast, rural America, made up of small towns and countryside, lost population. By 2016, only 14 percent of Americans lived in the enormous territory outside of metropolitan areas. The rural Midwest and Northeast faced particularly large decreases. In addition to the decline of manufacturing and retail, rural America suffered from the rise of worldwide competition in farming. Brazil, for example, surpassed the United States as the largest producer of soybeans. "You keep pinching and pinching," said a fifth-generation Kansas farmer, "and pretty soon there's nothing left to pinch."

Economic change reinforced social and cultural differences among the regions. In 2017, 40 percent of urban Americans felt rural people had different values while 70 percent of rural people felt urbanites had different values. "It's like two worlds now," said a Virginian.

DEMOCRACY UNDER STRESS

The accumulation of economic, social, and cultural differences fueled intense political division and further strained American democracy. So did massive election spending, changing technology and media, and altered political boundaries and rules. In 2016, a tumultuous, unprecedented presidential election laid bare the strains of the globalized nation. Donald Trump, an unconventional president, faced daunting challenges in living up to his promise to **Make America Great Again.**

Money and Politics

Growing wealth inequality intensified the long-term problem of spending on political campaigns. By the twenty-first century, the 1970s Watergate reforms regulating the role of money in elections had weakened. The Federal Election Commission allowed donors to give unlimited amounts of "soft money"—contributions not directed to specific candidates—to political parties and **political action committees (PACs)**, which could use the funds freely, even for candidate-related advertising. As wealthy donors poured more money into elections, Congress passed the **Bipartisan Campaign Reform Act of 2002**, known as McCain-Feingold after its chief sponsors, Senators John McCain (R-AZ) and Russ Feingold (D-WI) . The measure strictly limited expenditures of soft money and barred corporations, unions, and other groups from funding campaign-related communications 60 days before an election.

Contracting the role of money in politics, McCain-Feingold was inevitably divisive. Critics condemned the law as an unconstitutional interference with freedom and free speech. In a series of decisions, the conservative Supreme Court agreed and effectively gutted McCain-Feingold. The last ruling, *Citizens United v. Federal Election Commission* (2010), invoked free speech rights to invalidate the prohibitions on groups' spending and pre-election campaign communications: the wealthy's money was the same as everyone's speech. The result was still more expenditures on elections, particularly through so-called Super PACs, independent political action committees that could spend unlimited funds on a campaign so long as they had no direct communication with the candidate. The rich now had still more influence over the political system.

Polarized Politics

Twenty-first-century politics became increasingly polarized, much like the intense partisanship of the nineteenth century. For decades after World War II, Americans had mostly gotten their news from the same sources: the three major television networks, officially nonpartisan; and newspapers, either Democratic, Republican, or independent in affiliation, but claiming to offer objective reporting. Arguing that the networks and the press had a liberal bias, new conservative media figures such as the outspoken talk radio host Rush Limbaugh emerged in the 1980s and 1990s. When cable television and the internet destroyed the dominance of the television networks and newspapers in the 1990s and 2000s, Americans increasingly got their news from quite different sources. On cable television, CNN, heir to the ideal of nonpartisan objectivity, competed with right-leaning Fox News and left-leaning MSNBC. With the rise of social media in the 2000s and 2010s, many people got most of their news from feeds specially tailored to their preferences. By then, Americans were less often forced to confront opposing ideas and were increasingly unlikely even to agree about a shared set of facts. Republicans were far more likely than Democrats to believe the birther claim that Obama was born in Kenya, not the United States.

The nation's political geography also became more polarized. State legislatures redrew electoral boundaries to favor one major party or the other. As more state legislative districts and federal congressional districts became safely Republican or Democratic, each party chose candidates who did not have to appeal to the other

Table 30-1 Candidates' Counties Won and Share of GDP in 2016 and 2020

Year	Candidate	Counties won	Total votes	Aggregate share of US GDP
2016	Hillary Clinton	472	65,853,625	64%
	Donald Trump	2,584	62,985,106	36%
2020	Joe Biden	509	79,804,027	71%
	Donald Trump	2,547	73,776,924	29%

Note: 2020 figures reflect unofficial results from 99% of counties.

Sources: Brookings analysis of data from the Bureau of Economic Analysis, Dave Leip's Atlas of U.S. Presidential Elections, the *New York Times,* and Moody's Analytics. https://www.brookings .edu/blog/the-avenue/2020/11/09/biden-voting-counties-equal-70-of-americas-economy-what -does-this-mean-for-the-nations-political-economic-divide/

side. Once in office, they were less likely to compromise, which made gridlock still more likely in state capitals and Washington, DC.

Living in a kind of political isolation, Americans tended to have a more negative view of their partisan opponents. In 1994, 16 percent of Democrats and 17 percent of Republicans had a "very unfavorable" view of the opposition party; by 2014, 38 percent of Democrats and 43 percent of Republicans felt that way. Similarly, growing percentages of Americans wanted their friends to share their own political views.

The intensification of partisanship in turn helped stress the nation's election system. Strongest in less populated areas, the Republican party had a difficult time holding power nationally. In the six presidential elections from 1992 to 2012, the party's nominee won a plurality of the popular vote only once; Republicans typically won the White House because the geographical distribution of their minority vote gave them a majority of the Electoral College vote. Not surprisingly, Democrats discussed eliminating the Electoral College. Similarly, the distribution of the population gave Democrats frequent control of the House of Representatives, but the Constitution's award of two Senate seats to each state, regardless of population, gave Republicans the opportunity to dominate the chamber that voted on nominations to the Supreme Court. Strongest among white voters, Republicans worried about the growing political power of minorities who would eventually make up a majority of the population. Republican state and local officials, claiming widespread voter fraud, instituted laws and policies making it more difficult for Blacks and other people of color to vote. Accurately noting the rarity of fraud, Democrats responded that such "voter suppression" amounted to disfranchisement, to the denial of the right to vote.

The Presidential Election of 2016

Shaped by money, media, and partisanship, the 2016 contest for the presidency became a referendum on America's accumulating social, cultural, and economic strains. The Democrats emphasized comfort with change and continuity with the Obama and Clinton eras. The party nominated Hillary Clinton, the former

First Lady and US senator from New York who had served as Obama's secretary of state.

If the Democratic nomination was unsurprising, the battle for the Republican nomination was shocking. A parade of conservative, mainstream Republicans lost to the brash real estate mogul and reality television star **Donald J. Trump**, of New York, a former Democrat who spoke for a new kind of **populism**. Supposedly a billionaire, Trump shared conventional pro-corporate Republicans' passion for cutting taxes on the wealthy and regulations on business. But unlike the party mainstream, the nominee didn't care about budget deficits and opposed foreign entanglements. Vowing to "Make America Great Again," Trump criticized globalization, immigrants, and liberal elites and promised to "drain the swamp" of lobbyists and corruption in Washington, build a **border wall** between the United States and Mexico, ban Muslim immigration temporarily, renegotiate trade agreements, replace Obamacare with a better health care system, bring back jobs in coal, steel, and other manufacturing, and rebuild America's aging infrastructure of roads and bridges.

Economic Dynamism and Presidential Politics

Although cultural issues often dominated debate, Donald Trump and his Democratic opponents appealed to economically divergent areas of the United States. In both 2016 and 2020, Trump carried the vast majority of counties nationwide, but those counties represented only a minority of America's production of goods and services.

Already remarkable, the presidential contest between Clinton and Trump became a clamorous, rancorous faceoff. Clinton struggled with accusations of mishandling her State Department email by using a private computer server and earning large sums for speeches to Wall Street bankers. Trump faced revelations of discriminating against African American tenants, defrauding contractors and customers, and sexually assaulting women. Unlike all major party presidential candidates since the 1970s, Trump refused to divulge his tax returns. The contest became even more charged with stunning revelations of Russian attempts to influence the outcome of the election. Russian-related groups spread disinformation, placed anti-Clinton ads on social media, and stole and publicized the emails of Clinton's campaign manager and the Democratic National Committee.

Still, Clinton seemed likely to win until the FBI briefly reopened its investigation of her email just before Election Day. Even then, the Democrat won the popular vote, but Trump won the electoral vote and the presidency. Eking out narrow victories in supposedly safe Democratic territory, Trump carried whites, evangelical Christians, and rural and small-town residents. While Clinton ran strongest in the most dynamic and productive economic areas and among minority groups and the poor, Trump's populist message attracted Republicans and just enough Obama voters. "I feel like the American people are at the point where they've had it, and this was the last chance," a steelworker from Indiana explained. With the Republican Party carrying the White House and both houses of Congress, the chance seemed pretty good.

"Make America Great Again"

A controversial nominee, Donald Trump made an even more controversial president. His inaugural address, which painted a dark picture of "American carnage," offered a populist promise: "The forgotten men and women of our country will be forgotten no longer." The day after his inauguration, massive women's marches protested in the nation's capital and around the country. Using Twitter to speak his mind in short bursts, the president freely attacked the media, Obama, Clinton, Democrats, and even fellow Republicans in personal terms and accused them all of misdeeds. Americans differed over whether Trump's behavior was "presidential" or not as he tried to redeem his pledge to Make America Great Again.

Despite controlling both Congress and the White House, Trump and Republicans had a hard time enacting their agenda. Determined to undo Obama's legacy, Trump and his cabinet rescinded his predecessor's executive orders on economic regulation, the environment, DACA, and the status of transgender people in the military. The president withdrew the United States from both the Paris Agreement and TPP. With the enthusiastic support of conservatives, Tea Partiers, and his passionate "base," the Republican congressional majorities enacted and Trump signed the Tax Cuts and Jobs Act of 2017, which drastically lowered taxes on corporations and offered benefits to wealthy Americans. Trump was also able to win the confirmation of no fewer than three Justices of the Supreme Court, along with many appointees to lesser federal courts.

Nevertheless, Trump and his allies faced repeated defeats. Despite the president's promises, they failed to repeal Obama's increasingly popular Affordable Care Act

The 44th and 45th US Presidents Trump and Obama, two charismatic politicians in a rare moment of friendliness, on Inauguration Day, January 2016.

because the measure benefited many of Trump's own voters and the Republicans had no plan of their own. While federal courts slowed Trump's attempts to ban Muslims from the United States and end DACA, Mexico refused to pay for the border wall as Trump had promised and Congress failed to fund it fully. Although Trump touted his skill as a dealmaker, infrastructure legislation never happened. Some of Trump's initiatives seemed to backfire. His "family separation" policy of taking babies and children from asylum-seekers and illegal immigrants at the Mexican border may have helped slow migration, but struck many Americans as inhumane.

Never popular with a majority of Americans, Trump nonetheless held the devotion of his passionate base, some 40 to 45 percent of the population. In 2017, after a neo-Nazi demonstration in Charlottesville, Virginia, left a counterprotester dead, the president seemed unwilling to condemn Nazism and white supremacy. In the following years, Trump similarly failed to reject extremist groups such as the neo-fascist Proud Boys and the followers of QAnon, the unsubstantiated belief that the president was engaged in a secret struggle against an organization of Satan-worshipping child molesters. At the same time, Trump frequently tweeted his belief in the equally unproven **deep state**, an organization of long-term federal employees who supposedly ran the government and opposed him. The deep state in turn had the help of the media—"the enemy of the people"—who conspired against the president with inaccurate "fake news." No American president had ever so openly trafficked in conspiracy theories; no modern one had so openly appealed to white supremacy. But Trump remained popular with his supporters, perhaps because of these views.

Similarly, the specter of Russian involvement in the 2016 election cast a pall over Trump's administration. After the election, US intelligence agencies revealed that Vladimir Putin, who detested Clinton, had tried to elect Trump. As Congress and the Federal Bureau of Investigation explored whether Trump's campaign had illegally colluded with Russians, the president fired FBI Director James Comey. That move triggered the appointment of a special counsel within the Department of Justice to investigate the whole matter, including the president's possible ties to Russia and obstruction of justice. In a matter of months, the special counsel had obtained guilty pleas from Trump's former national security adviser and a campaign member and had indicted two campaign officials. Trump himself refused to speak in person with the special counsel. Meanwhile, a number of Trump appointees to high government positions had to resign because of their own ethics scandals.

Trump certainly paid a price for the Russia investigation, the scandals of his administration, and his unorthodox ideas. In the 2018 elections, the Republicans lost control of the House of Representatives and therefore the chance to enact much more of Trump's agenda. But the stock market continued the boom begun during Obama's term. Unemployment continued to remain low. To the consternation of opponents, Trump endured.

"America First"

Trump summed up the foreign policy of Make America Great Again with another slogan: "**America First**." That proud declaration, echoing the isolationists of the 1930s who didn't want the nation to fight Hitler, dictated a dramatic break with convention. From the destruction of Hitler's Germany and the end of World War

II, American leaders, for all their differences, believed that the United States should take the lead role in maintaining order and furthering globalization worldwide. In contrast, Trump argued that the United States would be stronger and safer if it avoided costly alliances, supposedly bad multilateral trade deals, and—in a rare echo of Obama—"stupid wars."

The president enjoyed success in weakening and even undoing America's global ties. In addition to withdrawing from TPP and the Paris Accords, the United States withdrew from the Iranian nuclear deal. Trump was harshly critical of America's traditional allies, especially the European nations that hadn't yet made their promised contributions to the cost of the North Atlantic Treaty Organization. Leaning away from more democratic nations, Trump cultivated personal relations with autocratic leaders, such as Russia's Putin and North Korea's Kim Jong Un.

Trump's new approach yielded mixed results. His willingness to believe Putin rather than US intelligence agencies about Russian election interference puzzled many who thought America looked weak. In 2020, Trump's refusal to respond to revelations of Russia's massive hacking of American government and corporate computer systems reinforced the image of weakness. The first sitting American president to meet in person with a North Korean leader, Trump got nothing in return: North Korea continued its development of nuclear weapons that threatened the United States and its allies. Despite imposing costly economic sanctions on Iran, the president failed to force a new nuclear deal. After condemning the North American Free Trade Agreement with Canada and Mexico, Trump got only a similar deal under a new name: the United States–Mexico–Canada Agreement (USMCA) of 2018. Rejecting his predecessors' belief in freer trade, Trump tried from 2017 to 2020 to pressure the People's Republic of China into a new trade deal by imposing heavy tariff taxes on the cost of Chinese imports. Trump's trade war hurt many American farmers but did not yield the massive, favorable agreement he sought.

The Trump administration enjoyed its greatest success in the Middle East. To be sure, the president, like his predecessor, found it impossible to withdraw troops as quickly as he wanted. In 2019, his sudden withdrawal of soldiers from war-torn Syria benefited Russia and left US allies, the Kurds, suddenly vulnerable to their Turkish enemies—another sign that America no longer viewed its friends the same way. Meanwhile, the Trump administration benefited from the continued weakening of ISIS, which decreased the threat of war in the Middle East and terrorism in the United States. Moreover, in 2019 and 2020, the administration brokered treaties between Israel and other Arab nations that brought improved relations at the cost of Palestinians' hopes for better treatment and their own state.

America First, with its denigration of alliances and globalization, cost the United States some of its reputation for reliability, friendship, and support for democracy. Late in Trump's term, it was unclear how much power, wealth, and security the nation had gained in return.

THE CRISIS OF 2020

By late 2019, the United States, more deeply divided than ever, seemed likely to confront conflict and disruption in the upcoming presidential election year. Even so, no one anticipated that predictable partisanship and an often unpredictable presidency would collide with a catastrophic pandemic, economic turmoil, and racial reckoning. The year 2020 became a crisis unmatched since at least the upheaval of the 1960s.

Impeachment

The special counsel investigation of Russia ended with neither the indictment nor the absolution of the president. Trump claimed vindication, but the counsel's report contained plentiful evidence that the president had obstructed justice. The result was disappointment for Democrats and enduring bitterness for Donald Trump.

Even as the investigation of the Russian role in the 2016 election came to an end in late 2019, the presidential election of 2020 already began to create controversy. Trump was most concerned that the Democrats would nominate Obama's vice president, Joseph R. Biden of Delaware, a likeable, fairly moderate Democrat hard to attack as a dangerous radical. To undermine Biden, Trump and his allies began looking for evidence that the Democrat had somehow corruptly helped a son obtain undeserved financial opportunity in Ukraine and perhaps China. In the summer of 2019, Trump withheld badly needed military aid in an attempt to get the Ukrainian president's help in disgracing the Bidens.

The revelation of Trump's seemingly illegal effort to force a foreign country to intervene in an American election, so soon after the end of the Russian investigation, created a furor. Unlike the Russian affair, Americans had direct evidence of the president's actions—a transcript of his key phone call with the Ukrainian president. Although Trump declared the call "perfect," the Democratic-controlled House investigated, held hearings, and in December 2019, voted in favor of two articles of impeachment: abuse of power and obstruction of Congress. Only the third president impeached, Trump fared much better in the Republican-controlled Senate. In February 2020, the Republican majority, without hearing evidence, acquitted the president on both counts.

Impeachment did nothing to end partisan division or to curb the president's behavior. As the implications of the episode sank in, Americans were already facing another upheaval.

Pandemic

By the time Americans began learning in January 2020 of the appearance of COVID-19 in Wuhan, China, the disease was beginning to spread in the United States. Briefed about the threat of the highly transmissible virus, President Trump limited travel from China and created a White House Coronavirus Task Force. Although Trump knew the virus was "deadly," he chose not to raise alarm in hopes the disease would disappear. Far from fading away, COVID spread rapidly in parts of the United States, especially in the New York City area. On March 13, Trump declared a national emergency. Within days, governors issued orders to try to limit the spread of the virus. As businesses, schools, and houses of worship closed, much of the nation seemed to shut down. But the virus spread inexorably. Medical worker such as Bambi Roaquin struggled to keep up amid shortages of protective gear and testing. By the end of April, as the virus surged worldwide, the United States had over one million cases and 60,000 deaths.

Struggles For Democracy

#BlackLivesMatter, "Black Twitter," and Smartphones

"**Black Lives Matter**" was at once something old and something new in American activism and politics in the 2010s. It was a slogan and rallying cry like "Black Power" in the 1960s and 1970s. Like the Black Panther Party in the 1960s and 1970s, the Black Lives Matter Global Network Foundation was also the name of a formal, but decentralized, organization of activists in various communities across the United States. In addition, Black Lives Matter, like Black Power, was the name of a broad, informal movement around the country. Indeed, some Black activists spoke of Black Lives Matter as "the movement," just as some student radicals and Black activists spoke of "the movement" in the late 1960s and early 1970s. But "Black Lives Matter" was still something new, a Twitter hashtag. Unlike any previous American activist movement, #BlackLivesMatter grew and drew strength from a microblogging and social networking app and from smartphones more generally.

Because of inequality, smartphones played an especially important role for African Americans in the 2010s. Less likely than whites to own computers and to have broadband access at home, Blacks, along with Latinos, faced a "digital divide" of unequal access to the internet. But African Americans and Latinos were about as likely as whites to own smartphones. There were elements of inequality in smartphone ownership, too: whites were more likely to have more expensive Apple iPhones; people of color, more likely to own less expensive phones with the Android operating system.

In addition to internet access, smartphone technology offered key developments for Black activism. For generations, African Americans had been unable to document their mistreatment at the hands of the police. In the 1980s and 1990s, analog and then digital camcorders offered a new opportunity for justice, as the videotaped recording of part of the beating of Rodney King dramatized in 1991 (see chapter 29). But an unwieldy camcorder wasn't something most people carried around; and there was no readily available internet to spread a recording. The King filming and its aftermath in the streets and in

The pandemic, the greatest national and global health crisis since the influenza pandemic of 1918–1919, had enormous economic consequences. After 113 consecutive months of job growth, over 20 million workers became unemployed in April 2020. From April to June, the nation's GDP suffered its largest quarterly drop—9.1 percent—since the Great Depression. Frightened at the sudden collapse, even conservative Republicans backed the massive Coronavirus Aid, Relief, and Economic Security Act, known as the CARES Act, which appropriated $2.2 trillion to stimulate the economy. The measure's emergency payments and loans helped increase employment, but the economic recovery was slow and uneven. Large corporations, the courts was unique. When smartphones began to offer digital video recording as well as internet access in 2009, opportunities to document police conduct increased dramatically.

Meanwhile, the launch of Twitter in 2006 created a new platform for Black communication and creativity. African Americans were one of the most active groups on the new medium. Indeed, people spoke of "Black Twitter," which was not a distinct platform but rather broad informal interactions about race, entertainment, humor, politics, and the rest of life. After the Florida acquittal of George Zimmerman, Trayvon Martin's killer in 2013, Black activist Alicia Garza of Oakland, California, posted on Facebook. "Black people. I love you. I love us." Picking up the slogan that had been in the air for at least a couple of years, she said, "Our Lives Matter." In turn, Los Angeles activist Patrice Cullors created the Twitter hashtag: "#blacklivesmatter is a movement attempting to visibilize what it means to be black in this country. Provide hope and inspiration for collection action to build collective power to achieve collective transformation, rooted in grief and rage but pointed towards vision and dreams."

As Garza suggested, Twitter wasn't a substitute for organization and action. "It's important to take that hashtag off of social media and into the streets and transform that into organizing." Garza, Cullors, and activist Opal Tometi, drawing on the civil rights, Black Power, and women's movements of the 1960s and 1970s, founded the Black Lives Matter Global Network Foundation.

The police shooting of Michael Brown in Ferguson, Missouri, the next year, both intensified the spread and popularity of #BlackLivesMatter and revealed another dimension of the relationship between the smartphone and Black activism. Spreading the news from Ferguson, phones drew activists from around the country to join the protest. Twitter founder Jack Dorsey, a native of nearby St. Louis, came from California to show support.

Apps and smartphones had minuses as well as plusses for Black activism. Retweets and messages of support didn't necessarily translate into concrete action. White supremacists and other opponents of Black activism used Twitter, too. Social media companies had the power to exclude some voices or to allow untruths and intolerance. Some observers claimed that Dorsey and other corporate leaders used support for #BlackLivesMatter to distract from their failure to address racial injustice in Silicon Valley and other big business. And corporations and governments could use data from smartphones to track and surveil activists and other Americans.

especially those involved in online retail, entertainment, and communication, flourished. Their success kept the stock market soaring to new highs and the richest Americans getting richer still. But many workers struggled with lost jobs, reduced hours, lower incomes, and the demands of caring for children out of school. Working-class Americans, especially Blacks and Latinos, found themselves living and laboring for low wages in the close quarters of meat packing plants and grocery stores, prone to catch and spread COVID-19, without the security of medical benefits.

Just as the pandemic revealed the economic fault lines of America, so to it highlighted the nation's political divide. Unlike most Democrats, the president

Victory over COVID-19 A 78-year-old patient and medical staff cheer as he leaves the hospital in Boston, Massachusetts, in June 2020.

and many Republicans downplayed the severity of the crisis, deemed it largely a Democratic "blue state" problem, denigrated the views of scientists, dismissed the importance of social distancing and mask wearing, demanded the quick reopening of schools and businesses, and sometimes deemed the virus a "hoax." When the virus surged in the South and Midwest during the summer, it became obvious that the pandemic was a national problem for both Democratic- and Republican-dominated states alike. But that reality did little to cool passions and stop the disease. Advocating untested and unsafe treatments, the president used the pandemic to pursue his foreign policy agenda by labeling COVID the "Chinese virus" and the "Kung Flu" and by withdrawing the United States from another global compact, the World Health Organization. The Republican-controlled Senate refused to take up a second House stimulus bill. By the end of September, America led the world with more than seven million COVID cases and over 200,000 deaths.

"I Can't Breathe"

Amid the travail of the pandemic, race relations boiled over. Once again, cell phone video played a key role. In Minneapolis, Minnesota, in May, a Black man, George Floyd Jr., died as a police officer kneeled on his neck for 8 minutes and 46 seconds and ignored his cries of "I can't breathe." Video of Floyd's horrific death, along with revelations of the March police shooting of an African American woman, Breonna Taylor, in her own apartment in Louisville, Kentucky, spurred new protests against law enforcement, the justice system, and Confederate statues across the country.

Protesting the Death of George Floyd A demonstrator confronts a police officer in New York City in May 2020.

Across the country, the vast majority of protests were peaceful, but some devolved into violence, looting, and arson.

Inevitably, the resurgent Black Lives Matter movement provoked division, particularly in a presidential election year. This time, there was more white sympathy for Black Lives Matter and less dismissive insistence that All Lives Matter. But common ground proved elusive. Some activists' calls to "defund" or even abolish police departments provoked a backlash. President Trump, expressing opposition to the killing of Floyd, condemned violence, supported the police and their budgets, assailed the toppling and removal of Confederate statues, and, like President Nixon half a century earlier, called for "law and order." In a controversial episode in June, federal officers forcibly cleared peaceful protesters from outside the White House so that the president could walk to a church, where he posed with a Bible.

The Presidential Election of 2020

Impeachment, the pandemic, the economy, and the Black Lives Matter protests all stoked the already intense campaign for the presidency. Despite the Ukrainian story, Joe Biden defeated more progressive rivals for the Democratic nomination. He then delivered on his promise to choose a woman as his vice-presidential running mate by selecting another of his rivals, Senator Kamala Harris of California. Only the fourth woman on a major party presidential ticket, she was the second Black and the first Asian as well.

Donald Trump topped the Republican ticket once again. But this time, Trump found it harder to bring down his opponent. The 74-year-old president attempted unsuccessfully to portray the 77-year-old Biden as a senile, mask-wearing old man, a tool of socialists who lacked the courage to campaign in person. Even after catching and recovering from COVID-19, the president still downplayed the importance of the disease. Forced to hold smaller rallies because of the pandemic, Trump promised the quick development of a vaccine, a rapid economic recovery, and the defense of Christianity and Confederate monuments. In return, Biden called the election a "battle for the soul of America." His campaign claimed that Trump had divided America, failed to handle the pandemic, run the economy into the ground, exacerbated racial divisions, and weakened US standing in the world. Trump, running behind and unable to lay out a clear agenda for a second term, then tried to discredit the election process and hamstring the US Postal Service's ability to handle citizens' mail-in ballots.

Although the counting of those ballots took days, Biden soon seemed victorious in an election with the highest percentage of voter turnout in more than a century. Like Clinton in 2016, Biden won the most economically productive areas of the country (see Table 30-1). Besting Trump by over 7,000,000 votes, the Democrat took back key states from the Republican, added stunning victories in Georgia and Arizona, and took the Electoral College decisively, 306 to 232. That should have been that. But as he had threatened, President Trump refused to accept results that, he claimed, had been "rigged" by unnamed Democrats. Recounts in closely contested states found no signs of significant fraud. Neither did the Justice Department and the Cybersecurity and Infrastructure Security Agency, both led by Trump's own appointees. Although the Trump campaign mounted over 60 lawsuits to overturn various state results, a series of state and federal judges, including Republicans

TIME LINE

▼**2008**
Collapse of Doha world
   trade talks
US financial crisis
Barack Obama elected
   44th president

▼**2009**
American Recovery and
   Reinvestment Act
   (stimulus package)
Tea Party founded

▼**2010**
Patient Protection and
   Affordable Health
   Care Act

Health Care and Educa-
   tional Reconciliation Act
*Citizens United v. Federal
   Election Commission*

▼**2011**
Death of Osama bin Laden
End of Iraq War

▼**2012**
Barack Obama reelected
   president

▼**2013**
US Supreme Court same-
   sex marriage ruling, *US v.
   Windsor*
Boston marathon bombing

▼**2014**
US air strikes against
   the Islamic State of Iraq
   and Syria

▼**2015**
Paris Agreement

▼**2016**
Trans-Pacific Partnership
   (TPP)
Pulse nightclub attack,
   Orlando, Florida
Donald Trump elected
   45th president

Rioters Do What the Confederacy Could Not Having stormed the US Capitol building, insurrectionists fly Trump and Confederate flags on January 6, 2021.

and Trump appointees, overwhelmingly rebuffed the claims, typically for lack of evidence. Meanwhile, the Democrats not only held control of House by a reduced majority, they also effectively took control of a Senate, split 50–50, because Vice President Harris, presiding over the body, could vote to break ties.

Largely ignoring the raging pandemic and the weakening economic recovery, Trump continued to attack the legitimacy of the election and desperately sought

▼**2017**
US withdrawal from Paris Agreement and TPP
Tax Cuts and Jobs Act of 2017
Special counsel investigation of Russian election interference

▼**2018**
Trump administration family separation policy

United States–Mexico–Canada Agreement (USMCA)

▼**2019**
Trump seeks Ukrainian help in undermining Joseph Biden
COVID-19, the novel infectious coronavirus disease, emerges
House of Representatives votes to impeach President Trump

▼**2020**
Biden defeats Trump to become 46th president

▼**2021**
Pro-Trump insurrectionists overrun US Capitol
House of Representatives votes again to impeach President Trump

some way to stay in the White House in 2021. His hopes came down to stopping Congress from officially accepting the Electoral College tallies and certifying Biden and Harris at the Capitol on January 6. Urging supporters to converge on Washington to "Stop the Steal" in a "wild" protest, the president addressed a crowd of them outdoors that day. "If you don't fight like hell," he declared, "you're not going to have a country anymore." When the president directed his followers to march to the Capitol, many of them, including Proud Boys, QAnon believers, and anti-Semites, did just that. Carrying Confederate, American, and Trump emblems, the rioters overwhelmed the police and stormed the building. The melee forced congresspeople and senators to stop counting and debating the tally and scramble and hide in fear for their lives. By the time law enforcement and National Guard troops restored order hours later, five people were dead, including an officer. For the first time since 1814, during the War of 1812, the Capitol had been overrun.

The nation and the world were stunned by the insurrection—the violent rebellion against government—at the center of American democracy. Later that evening, Congress returned and completed the certification of Biden and Harris's victory. Corporate leaders turned on the president; Twitter and Facebook banned him. A week later, the House impeached the president for an unprecedented second time— on this occasion, for insurrection. He was not in attendance on January 20, when Biden and Harris took the oath of office. By then, more than 24 million Americans had contracted coronavirus; over 400,000 of those Americans had died, more than had died in World War II.

CONCLUSION

Bambi Roaquin was one of those who succumbed to the virus. In May 2020, the nurse passed away in the hospital where she worked. Other nurses, including immigrants and the children of immigrants, took the place of this woman and so many other medical workers who represented the American dream. Across the country, Americans asked hard questions about that dream in the age of globalization and information, in a time of inequality, upheaval, climate change, and pandemic. The country was deeply divided over just how to Make America Great Again and how to put America First, both at home and around the world. But the United States was still more diverse and arguably more inclusive and democratic than at the start of the twenty-first century. For all the strains and stresses, democracy had held in January 2021. The United States remained a government, as Lincoln had declared so long ago, "of the people."

WHO, WHAT, WHERE

REVIEW QUESTIONS

1. What was Obamacare and why was it important?

2. How did the pandemic affect the American economy?

3. Why did Donald Trump lose his campaign for reelection in 2020?

CRITICAL-THINKING QUESTIONS

1. How were Obama and Trump similar in their approach to the presidency?

2. Why did income and wealth inequality matter to the United States?

3. Did Americans become more or less tolerant of one another in the twenty-first century?

SUGGESTED READINGS

Rich, Nathaniel. *Losing Earth: A Recent History*. London: Picador, 2020.

Rucker, Philip, and Carol Leonnig. *A Very Stable Genius: Donald J. Trump's Testing of America*. New York: Penguin Books, 2020.

Sorkin, Andrew Ross. *Too Big to Fail: The Inside Story of How Wall Street and Washington Fought to Save the Financial System—and Themselves*. New York: Penguin Books, 2010.

Vance, J. D. *Hillbilly Elegy: A Memoir of a Family and Culture in Crisis*. New York: HarperCollins, 2016.

For further review materials and resource information, please visit www.oup.com/us/ofthepeople

CHAPTER 30: "The American Dream," 2008–2021

Primary Sources

30.1 BARACK OBAMA, KEYNOTE ADDRESS, DEMOCRATIC PARTY CONVENTION (2004)

In 2004, then-Senator Barack Obama of Illinois emerged as a national figure with this soaring address to the Democratic National Convention in Boston, Massachusetts. Note how the future president invokes the diversity of America while insisting on the nation's fundamental unity.

... Tonight, we gather to affirm the greatness of our nation, not because of the height of our skyscrapers, or the power of our military, or the size of our economy. Our pride is based on a very simple premise, summed up in a declaration made over two hundred years ago, "We hold these truths to be self-evident, that all men are created equal. That they are endowed by their Creator with certain inalienable rights. That among these are life, liberty and the pursuit of happiness."

That is the true genius of America, a faith in the simple dreams of its people, the insistence on small miracles. That we can tuck in our children at night and know they are fed and clothed and safe from harm. That we can say what we think, write what we think, without hearing a sudden knock on the door. That we can have an idea and start our own business without paying a bribe or hiring somebody's son. That we can participate in the political process without fear of retribution, and that our votes will he counted—or at least, most of the time.

This year, in this election, we are called to reaffirm our values and commitments, to hold them against a hard reality and see how we are measuring up, to the legacy of our forbearers, and the promise of future generations. And fellow Americans—Democrats, Republicans, Independents—I say to you tonight: we have more work to do. More to do for the workers I met in Galesburg, Illinois, who are losing their union jobs at the Maytag plant that's moving to Mexico, and now are having to compete with their own children for jobs that pay seven bucks an hour. More to do for the father I met who was losing his job and choking back tears, wondering how he would pay $4,500 a month for the drugs his son needs without the health benefits he counted on. More to do for the young woman in East St. Louis, and thousands more like her, who has the grades, has the drive, has the will, but doesn't have the money to go to college.

Don't get me wrong. The people I meet in small towns and big cities, in diners and office parks, they don't expect government to solve all their problems. They know they have to work hard to get ahead and they want to. . . . But they sense, deep in their bones, that with just a change in priorities, we can make sure that every child in America has a decent shot at life, and that the doors of opportunity remain open to all. They know we can do better. And they want that choice. For alongside our famous individualism, there's another ingredient in the American saga.

A belief that we are connected as one people. If there's a child on the south side of Chicago who can't read, that matters to me, even if it's not my child. If there's a senior citizen somewhere who can't pay for her prescription and has to choose between medicine and the rent, that makes my life poorer, even if it's not my grandmother. If there's an Arab American family being rounded up without benefit of an attorney or due process, that threatens my civil liberties. It's that fundamental belief—I am my brother's keeper, I am my sister's keeper—that makes this country work. It's what allows us to pursue our individual dreams, yet still come together as a single American family. "E pluribus unum." Out of many, one.

Yet even as we speak, there are those who are preparing to divide us, the spin masters and negative ad peddlers who embrace the politics of anything goes. Well, I say to them tonight, there's not a liberal America and a conservative America—there's the United States of America. There's not a black America and white America and Latino America and Asian America; there's the United States of America. The pundits like to slice-and-dice our country into Red States and Blue States; Red States for Republicans, Blue States for Democrats. But I've got news for them, too. We worship an awesome God in the Blue States, and we don't like federal agents poking around our libraries in the Red States. We coach Little League in the Blue States and have gay friends in the Red States. There are patriots who opposed the war in Iraq and patriots who supported it. We are one people, all of us pledging allegiance to the stars and stripes, all of us defending the United States of America.

In the end, that's what this election is about. Do we participate in a politics of cynicism or a politics of hope? . . . I'm not talking about blind optimism here—the almost willful ignorance that thinks unemployment will go away if we just don't talk about it, or the health care crisis will solve itself if we just ignore it. No, I'm talking about something more substantial. It's the hope of slaves sitting around a fire singing freedom songs; the hope of immigrants setting out for distant shores; . . . the hope of a skinny kid with a funny name who believes that America has a place for him, too. The audacity of hope!

In the end, that is God's greatest gift to us, the bedrock of this nation; the belief in things not seen; the belief that there are better days ahead. I believe we can give our middle class relief and provide working families with a road to opportunity. I believe we can provide jobs to the jobless, homes to the homeless, and reclaim young people in cities across America from violence and despair. I believe that as we stand on the crossroads of history, we can make the right choices, and meet the challenges that face us. America!

Source: Barack Obama, "Keynote Address at the 2004 Democratic National Convention," July 27, 2004. https://www.presidency.ucsb.edu/documents/keynote-address-the-2004-democratic-national-convention

30.2 DEBATE IN THE HOUSE OF REPRESENTATIVES ON A RESOLUTION "THAT SYMBOLS AND TRADITIONS OF CHRISTMAS SHOULD BE PROTECTED" (2005)

On December 14, 2005, conservative representative Jo Ann Davis (R-VA), an evangelical Protestant, spoke in favor of House Resolution 579, a statement protesting "attempts to ban references to Christmas" and supporting the "symbols and traditions, for those who celebrate Christmas." How does Davis defend public displays and mentions of Christmas, and whom does she blame for the attacks on the Christian holiday? In reply, two liberal representatives—Gary L. Ackerman (D-NY), a Jew, and Lynn C. Woolsey (D-CA), a mainline Protestant—questioned the purpose of the resolution. The next day, the House adopted the resolution by a vote of 401–22.

Mrs. JO ANN DAVIS of Virginia. This measure simply states congressional support for traditional references to Christmas that I believe are being eradicated from the public dialogue. . . .

Christmas has been declared politically incorrect. Any sign or even mention of Christmas in public can lead to complaints, litigation, protest, and threats. America's favorite holiday is being twisted beyond recognition. The push towards a neutered "holiday" season is stronger than ever so that no one can be even the slightest bit offended. . . .

When did wishing someone a Merry Christmas show insensitivity? According to a recent poll, 96 percent of Americans celebrate Christmas. In an effort to create a generic holiday starting at Thanksgiving and ending at New Year's, what are we exactly celebrating?

The purpose of celebrating the Fourth of July is to celebrate our Nation's independence. Why is it not reasonable to say that celebrating Christmas is a celebration of Christ's birth?

This is a selective assault on religious free speech which is a fundamental right. The Founders did not view celebrating Christmas as an issue of church versus State. It is celebrating a holiday that has for thousands of years been celebrated. The framers intended that the first amendment to the Constitution of the United States would prohibit the establishment of religion, not prohibit any mention of religion or reference to God in civic dialogue.

From Madison Avenue to Wall Street, from activists and lawyers to politicians, educators and the media, a culture is being created that shames people for saying Merry Christmas. . . .

The attack on Christmas, while not new, has now shifted its focus from overtly religious symbols, like the nativity, to symbols regarded by most Americans, including the Supreme Court, to be secular symbols of Christmas, a federally recognized holiday. Now these innocent secular symbols are causing concerns of insensitivity. Santa Claus, Christmas trees, candy canes, Christmas carols, even the colors red and green, they have been place on the endangered list.

They say to boil a frog you have to do it gradually because if you throw it into boiling water, it will jump out; but if you put the frog in cold water and gradually turn up the heat, the frog will never know he is being boiled until it is too late, and I am afraid that is what is happening to us with our Christmas holiday.

The transition to replace Christmas with this vague "holiday season" is a gradual process that over the past few years has reached a new crescendo. Let us protect the symbols and traditions of Christmas for those who celebrate Christmas, or before we know it, we will be looking at a holiday season that represents nothing and celebrates anything.

I for one do not want to surrender and let retailers, overzealous civil liberty lawyers, and the media make me feel guilty for wishing someone a Merry Christmas. For generations, Christmas has been a public expression of the celebration of the birth of Christ. I hope we can say that for many more years to come.

Mr. ACKERMAN. . . . There are people around who need an enemy at all times to try to separate us one from the other as Americans in order to advance their own agenda. I do not think we should be playing into their hands. Nobody is attacking Christmas or its symbols. . . .

I like Christmas. I like the message of Christmas. I like helping the needy and the poor and the least among us. But I did not come here to protect the symbols.

Did something happen when I was not looking? Did somebody mug Santa Claus? Is somebody engaging in elf tossing? . . . What silliness we engage in, protecting symbols.

If you wanted to protect the message of Christmas, come to the floor with real bills with substance. Where is your bill to house the homeless? Where is your bill to feed the needy? Where is your bill to clothe the naked? Where is your bill to protect senior citizens who will not be able to heat their homes this winter? Where is the substance? Why are we engaging, in this terrible time in which we are in, in symbolism?

... I think we could be doing so much more instead of feeding the flames that divide us instead of bringing us together.

I wish the gentlewoman a merry Christmas. I have no compunction about doing that. But I do not want my government to engage in the foolishness of deciding for people what their symbols should or have to be. . . .

Ms. WOOLSEY. Nobody enjoys Christmas more than I. But today we have roughly 160,000 men and women in Iraq putting their lives on the line for an immoral, senseless war. Here at home many of our vulnerable citizens will face a cold, bitter winter because they do not have home energy assistance from the Federal Government. Many others will not get the health care or education they need because of harsh cuts in Medicaid and student loans.

Naturally, the majority does not want to talk about this, and one can always tell when the right wing is in political trouble. They invariably cook up some divisive culture war that has nothing to do with our real challenges in this country.

What American families really want is the ability to afford more gifts for their children this season regardless of whether there is a wreath in the local department store.

Meanwhile, how many casualties have there been in the so-called "war on Christmas"? Here is a hint: several thousand less than in the war on Iraq.

Source: *Congressional Record* (109th Congress, 1st Session) 151, no. 160, p. H11596.

30.3   HARRY M. REID, "THE KOCH BROTHERS" (2015)

For Democrats and left-wing populists, the conservative billionaire brothers Charles and David Koch epitomize the threatening power of the "1 percent" in the age of wealth inequality and *Citizens United*. The Kochs, enriched by their ownership of a huge multinational corporation, spent heavily to create a right-wing network of political action committees (PACs), think tanks, and donors. In this speech from 2015, Harry M. Reid (D-NV), Majority Leader of the US Senate, describes the Kochs' power. What does Reid think the Kochs want, and who does he think can stop them?

Over the last several months, the Koch brothers have been on a public relations campaign. This Koch propaganda campaign has accelerated over the past few weeks. Charles and David Koch have been going to great lengths to convince the American people that they are not just a couple of billionaires who are trying to dismantle Social Security. . . .

The Kochs want everyone to believe they are not the ones rigging the system to benefit themselves and their wealthy friends. The Koch brothers are spending their vast wealth holding newspaper and television interviews on their propaganda campaign. In spite of all their efforts, this Koch media tour has failed to bury the one simple truth: The Koch brothers are trying to buy America.

During an interview yesterday, the scales fell away once again and revealed the Koch brothers' true intentions. In justifying his and his brother's efforts to inject hundreds of millions of dollars into conservative political campaigns, Charles Koch said: "I expect something in return."

The Koch brothers are getting plenty in return. So far they have bought a Republican House, a Republican Senate, a government shutdown, an ousted Speaker of the House, . . .

and a Republican Presidential field where nearly every candidate kowtows to these billionaires. But that is not all. The Kochs have procured a media that is intimidated by their billions—too intimidated to hold them accountable.

Consider yesterday's interview on MSNBC's "Morning Joe" show. This is classic. Here are some of the questions that Joe and Mika asked the Koch brothers.

Joe Scarborough asked: "It's hard to find people in New York, liberals, we were talking about this before, liberals or conservative alike, who haven't been touched by your graciousness, whether it is towards the arts or cancer research. Do you think you got that instinct from your mom?"

Mika asked: "Sitting here in your childhood home"—they were doing this interview in Topeka, KS—"we have the Koch brothers. Which was the good brother?" That was another tough question.

Joe then asked: "You guys both play rugby together, right?"

Sometimes—most of the time—they weren't even questions; they were just compliments.

At one point, here is what he said: "You sound like my dad. That's very diplomatic. That's very good."

Wow. Those were some really tough questions asked by the host of "Morning Joe." . . . Those questions are so easy; they may even qualify them to moderate the next Republican Presidential debate.

It seems that some journalists are determined not to get on the wrong side of the Koch brothers and their billions. After all, we have seen how the Koch empire targets people, cities, and States that do anything that conflicts with the Koch brothers' radical agenda. When the media rolls over for these modern-day robber barons, as it is doing now, our country is in trouble.

As Charles Koch himself said, he and his brother are not spending this money for altruistic reasons; they are doing it for one reason and one reason only—for the profits of themselves and fellow billionaires who have rigged the system against the middle class. They said it themselves. They want something in return, and what they want is profit for their corporations. Their own publicist once explained why the Koch brothers are trying to buy a new government: "It's because we can make more profit, OK?"

That is what this is all about for Charles and David Koch: bigger profits, more money because $100 billion or more isn't enough for them.

By their own admission, the Kochs will spend and spend and spend until they get the government they want—a government—a government that lets Koch Industries do what it wants, a government whose sole goal is to make these billionaires even richer.

Unfortunately for the United States, the Supreme Court has constructed a political system that allows them to do just that. The Citizens United case, decided in January 2010, has effectively put the U.S. Government up for sale to the highest bidder, and right now the Koch brothers are the highest bidder. Right now our country has no real restrictions on how much money a billionaire or a millionaire can spend to buy the government they want. All the power is with the wealthy, and that puts middle-class Americans at a significant disadvantage.

So we can't stand idly by while the government sits on an auction block and neither should any American sit idly by. Instead, we should be working to rid the system of the Koch brothers' dark money, but this cannot and will not happen if reporters and journalists refuse to ask Charles and David Koch questions—maybe even probing questions. Otherwise no one is holding these two oil barons accountable for their nefarious actions.

Source: *Congressional Record* (114th Congress, 1st Session) 161, no. 164, p. S7734.

30.4   DONALD TRUMP, EXTRACT OF REMARKS AT A "MAKE AMERICA GREAT AGAIN" RALLY IN HARRISBURG, PENNSYLVANIA (2017)

After his election as president, Donald Trump continued holding campaign-style rallies for his supporters around the country. Feeding off the energy of the crowd, Trump articulated his right-wing populist message in the Rustbelt community of Harrisburg, Pennsylvania. Whom does he blame for the condition of the country?

THE PRESIDENT: As you may know, there's another big gathering taking place tonight in Washington, D.C. Did you hear about it?

AUDIENCE: Booo—

THE PRESIDENT: A large group of Hollywood actors and Washington media are consoling each other in a hotel ballroom in our nation's capital right now. (Applause.) They are gathered together for the White House Correspondents Dinner—without the President. (Applause.) And I could not possibly be more thrilled than to be more than 100 miles away from Washington Swamp—(applause)—spending my evening with all of you, and with a much, much larger crowd and much better people. Right? (Applause.) Right?

AUDIENCE: U-S-A! U-S-A!

THE PRESIDENT: And look at the media back there. . . .

AUDIENCE: Booo—

THE PRESIDENT: That's right.

AUDIENCE: CNN Sucks! CNN Sucks!

THE PRESIDENT: Media outlets like CNN and MSNBC are fake news. Fake news . . .

The truth is, there is no place I'd rather be than right here in Pennsylvania to celebrate our 100-day milestone to reflect on an incredible journey together, and to get ready for the great, great battles to come, and that we will win in every case, okay? We will win. (Applause.) Because make no mistake, we are just beginning in our fight to make America great again. (Applause.)

Now, before we talk about my first 100 days, which has been very exciting and very productive, let's rate the media's 100 days. Should we do that? Should we do it? Because, as you know, they are a disgrace. . . .

So just as an example of media, take the totally failing New York Times.

AUDIENCE: Booo—

THE PRESIDENT: But that's what we have. They're incompetent, dishonest people. . . . So here's the story. If the media's job is to be honest and tell the truth, then I think we would all agree the media deserves a very, very, big fat failing grade.

AUDIENCE: Booo—

THE PRESIDENT: Very dishonest people. And not all of them. You know, we call it the "fake news." Not all of them. . . . By contrast, for the last 100 days, my administration has been delivering every single day for the great citizens of our country—whether it's putting our coal miners back to work, protecting America's steel and aluminum workers—we love that steel and aluminum—or eliminating job-killing regulations, we are keeping one promise after another. And, frankly, the people are really happy about it. They see what's happening. (Applause.)

But to understand the historic progress that we've made, we must speak honestly about the situation that we and I inherited. Because believe me, the previous administration gave us a mess.

AUDIENCE: Booo—

THE PRESIDENT: For decades, our country has lived through the greatest jobs theft in the history of the world. You people know it better than anybody, in Pennsylvania. Our factories were shuttered, our steel mills closed down, and our jobs were stolen away and shipped far away to other countries, some of which you've never even heard of. Politicians sent troops to protect the borders of foreign nations, but left America's borders wide open for all to violate.

We've spent billions and billions of dollars on one global project after another, and yet, as gangs flooded into our country, we couldn't even provide safety for our own people.

Our government rushed to join international agreements where the United States pays the costs and bears the burdens, while other countries get the benefit and pay nothing.

AUDIENCE: Booo—

THE PRESIDENT: This includes deals like the one-sided Paris Climate Accord, where the United States pays billions of dollars while China, Russia and India have contributed and will contribute nothing.

AUDIENCE: Booo—

THE PRESIDENT: Does that remind you of the Iran deal? How about that beauty, right? . . .

Those are the facts, whether we like them or not. The dishonest media won't print them, won't report them, because the Washington media is part of the problem: their priorities are not my priorities and they're not your priorities, believe me. (Applause.) Their agenda is not your agenda. . . .

But they're all part of a broken system that has profited from this global theft and plunder of American wealth at the expense of the American worker. We are not going to let other countries take advantage of us anymore. Because, from now on, it's going to be America first. (Applause.) . . .

AUDIENCE: U-S-A! U-S-A! . . .

THE PRESIDENT: To protect our jobs and our economic freedom, I immediately withdrew the United States from the horrible, disastrous . . . Trans-Pacific Partnership. (Applause.) . . . That was a total hoax. (Applause.) . . .

Perhaps in no area have past governments sold out to special interests and foreign lobbyists more than on the issue of immigration. Year after year, you pleaded for Washington to enforce our laws as illegal immigration surged, refugees flooded in, and lax vetting threatened your family's safety and security.

Your pleas have finally been—

AUDIENCE MEMBER: Build the wall!

THE PRESIDENT: Oh, don't worry, we're going to have the wall. Don't worry about it. (Applause.)

AUDIENCE: Build the wall! Build the wall! . . .

THE PRESIDENT: We are operating on a very simple principle: that our immigration system should put the needs of American workers, American families, American companies, and American citizens first. (Applause.) . . .

And we are also working around the clock to keep our nation safe from terrorism. (Applause.) My administration has taken historic steps to improve screening and vetting for those seeking visas to enter the United States. We have seen the attacks, from 9/11 to Boston to San Bernardino. We have seen the bloodshed overseas. . . .

We already have enough problems to worry about in the United States, which we love so much. We don't need to be admitting people who want to oppress, hurt or kill innocent Americans. They're not coming in. (Applause.)

So let me state this as clearly as I possibly can: We are going to keep radical Islamic terrorists the hell out of our country. (Applause.)

AUDIENCE: U-S-A! U-S-A!

THE PRESIDENT: So I have a question for you. You've been to a lot of countries, you've seen a lot of rallies. First of all, is there any place like a Trump rally? In all fairness. Right? (Applause.) . . .

Source: Donald J. Trump, Remarks at a "Make America Great Again Rally," Harrisburg, Pennsylvania, April 29, 2017. https://www.presidency.ucsb.edu/documents/remarks-make-america-great-again-rally-harrisburg-pennsylvania

30.5   CHILDREN AND IMMIGRATION POLICY (2018)

Few aspects of the Trump era were more controversial than the administration's willingness to separate children from parents in deterring illegal immigration and legal asylum-seeking. In the first source, at a contentious press conference in 2018, Kirstjen Nilsen, Trump's Secretary of Homeland Security, gives the official justification for the "zero tolerance policy" that allowed "family separation." In the second, Leah, a 12-year-old immigration activist speaking the same year at the "Families Belong Together" march in Washington, D.C., captures the fear that zero tolerance evoked. She singles out ICE—the US Immigration and Customs Enforcement, Homeland Security's law enforcement arm, which oversaw detentions and arrests.

KIRSTJEN NIELSEN: This entire crisis, just to be clear, is not new. It is been occurring and expanded over many decades. But currently it is the exclusive product of loopholes in our federal immigration laws that prevent illegal immigrant minors and family members from being detained and removed to their home countries.

In other words, these loopholes create a functionally open border. Apprehension without detention and removal is not border security. We have repeatedly called on Congress to close the loopholes. . . . We need to reform our asylum laws to end the systemic abuse of our asylum system and stop fraud. . . . We are a country of compassion and heart. . . . We need to . . . allow for family detention during the removal process. And we need Congress to fully fund our ability to hold families together through the immigration process. And until these loopholes are closed by Congress, it is not possible as a matter of law to detain and remove whole family units who arrive illegally in the United States. Congress and the courts created this problem and congress alone can fix it.

Until then, we will enforce every law we have on the books to defend the sovereignty and security of the United States. Those who criticize the enforcement of our laws have offered only one countermeasure: open borders, the quick release of all illegal alien families and the decision not to enforce our laws. This policy would be disastrous. . . . First, this administration did not create a policy of separating families at the border. . . .

We have a long existing policy—multiple administrations have followed—that outline when we may take action to protect children. We will separate those who claim to be a parent and child if we cannot determine a familiar or custodial relationship exists. For example, if there is no documentation to confirm the claimed relationship between an adult and a child. We do so if the parent is a national security, public, or safety risk, including when there are criminal charges at issue and it may not be appropriate to maintain the family in detention together.

We also separate a parent and child if the adult is suspected of human trafficking. There are cases where minors have been used and trafficked by unrelated adults in an effort to avoid detention. . . . And separation can occur when the parent is charged with human smuggling. Under those circumstances, we would detain the parent in an appropriate secure detention facility separate from the child. What has changed is that we no longer exempt entire classes of people who break the law. Everyone is subject to prosecution. When D.H.S. refers a case against a parent or legal guardian for criminal prosecution, the parent or legal guardian will be placed into the U.S. Marshals Service custody for pretrial determination, pursuant to an order by a federal judge, and any accompanied child will be transferred to the Department of Health and Human Services and will be reclassified as an unaccompanied alien child.

Second, children in D.H.S. and H.H.S. custody are being well taken care of. The Department of Health and Human Services Office of Refugee Resettlement provides meals, medical care and educational services to these children. They are provided temporary shelter, and H.H.S. works hard to find a parent, relative or foster home to care for these children. Parents can still communicate with their children through phone calls and video conferencing. . . . Claiming these children and their parents are treated inhumanely is not true, and completely disrespects the hard working men and women at the Office of Refugee Resettlement. . . .

REPORTER: You have seen the photos of children in cages? Have you heard the audio clip of these children wailing that just came out today?

NIELSEN: I have—I have not seen something that came out today but I have been to detention centers and, again, I would reference you to our standards and I would reference you to the care provided not just by the Department of Homeland Security, but by the Department of Health and Human Services when they get to H.H.S.

REPORTER: But is that the image of this country that you want out there, children in cages?

NIELSEN: The image I want of this country is an immigration system that secures our border and upholds our humanitarian ideals. Congress needs to fix it.

. . .

REPORTER: The policy is not by your definition in any way cruel?

NIELSEN: It is not a policy. Our policy at D.H.S. is to do what we're sworn to do which is to enforce the law.

REPORTER: I'm following up on Megan's question there. Former first lady Laura Bush compared this to Japanese internment during World War II, one of the darkest days in the nation's history. Do you believe that the effect of this policy, so not the law, but the effect of it on separating children from families in those specific instances is moral? Is it ethical? Is it American?

NIELSEN: What I believe is that we should exercise our democratic rights as Americans and fix the problem. It is a problem and let's fix it. Yes.

REPORTER: How is this not child abuse?

. . .

NIELSEN We have high standards. We give them meals, we give them education, we give them medical care. There is videos, there is TVs, I visited the detention centers myself . . .

REPORTER: Thank you very much. Are you intending for this to play out as it is playing out? Are you intending for parents to be separated from children? Are you intending to send a message?

NIELSEN: I find that offensive. No. Because why would I ever create a policy that purposely does that.

REPORTER: Perhaps as a deterrence?

NIELSEN: No. . . .

My name is Leah. I am 12 years old and I'm from Miami, Florida. I am the proud daughter of a domestic worker who loves me very much. My mom's job is very important. Unlike our government, she takes care of children as a nanny and makes sure they are healthy and safe. Our government instead harms children and deports parents every day.

I am here today because the government is separating and detaining refugee parents and children at the border, who are looking for safety. Our government also continues to separate US citizen children like me from their parents every day.

This is evil! It needs to stop! It makes me sad to know that children can't be with their parents.

I don't understand why they are being so mean to us children. Don't they know how much we love our families? Don't they have a family, too? Why don't they care about us children? Why do they hurt us like this?

It is unfair that they get to spend time with their families today while there are children in detention centers and in cages all alone missing their parents who are thrown in jail.

I live with the constant fear of losing my mom to deportation. My mom is strong, beautiful, and brave. She is also a person who taught me how to speak up when I see things that aren't fair. ICE wants to take away my mom from me. I don't like to live with this fear.

It's scary. I can't sleep. I can't study. I am stressed. I am afraid that they will take my mom away while she is at work, out driving, or at home. I don't understand why this administration won't support mothers who just want a better life for their children.

This needs to change.

We cannot allow them to keep hurting families, communities, and children. I know that together we can make things better for families and kids.

Sources: "Kirstjen Nielsen Addresses Families Separation at Border: Full Transcript," *New York Times,* June 18, 2018; "This 12-Year-Old Girl Gave An Emotional Speech About Fearing Her Mom's Deportation," Buzzfeednews.com article/remysmidt/girl-immigration-speech.

Appendix A

HISTORICAL DOCUMENTS
The Declaration of Independence

When in the course of human events, it becomes necessary for one people to dissolve the political bands which have connected them with another, and to assume, among the powers of the earth, the separate and equal station to which the Laws of Nature and of Nature's God entitle them, a decent respect to the opinions of mankind requires that they should declare the causes which impel them to the separation.

We hold these truths to be self-evident, that all men are created equal, that they are endowed by their Creator with certain unalienable Rights, that among these are life, liberty and the pursuit of happiness. That to secure these rights, governments are instituted among men, deriving their just powers from the consent of the governed; that whenever any form of government becomes destructive of these ends, it is the right of the people to alter or to abolish it, and to institute new Government, laying its foundation on such principles and organizing its powers in such form, as to them shall seem most likely to effect their safety and happiness. Prudence, indeed, will dictate that Governments long established should not be changed for light and transient causes; and, accordingly, all experience hath shown, that mankind are more disposed to suffer, while evils are sufferable, than to right themselves by abolishing the forms to which they are accustomed. But when a long train of abuses and usurpations, pursuing invariably the same object evinces a design to reduce them under absolute despotism, it is their right, it is their duty, to throw off such government, and to provide new guards for their future security. Such has been the patient sufferance of these colonies; and such is now the necessity which constrains them to alter their former systems of government. The history of the present King of Great Britain is a history of repeated injuries and usurpations, all having in direct object the establishment of an absolute tyranny over these States. To prove this, let facts be submitted to a candid world:

He has refused his assent to laws, the most wholesome and necessary for the public good.

He has forbidden his governors to pass laws of immediate and pressing importance, unless suspended in their operation till his assent should be obtained; and, when so suspended, he has utterly neglected to attend to them.

He has refused to pass other laws for the accommodation of large districts of people, unless those people would relinquish the right of representation in the legislature, a right inestimable to them and formidable to tyrants only.

He has called together legislative bodies at places unusual, uncomfortable, and distant from the depository of their public records, for the sole purpose of fatiguing them into compliance with his measures.

He has dissolved representative houses repeatedly, for opposing with manly firmness his invasions on the rights of the people.

He has refused for a long time, after such dissolutions, to cause others to be elected; whereby the legislative powers, incapable of annihilation, have returned to the People at large for their exercise; the State remaining in the mean time exposed to all the dangers of invasion from without, and convulsions within.

He has endeavored to prevent the population of these States; for that purpose obstructing the laws for naturalization of foreigners; refusing to pass others to encourage their migrations hither, and raising the conditions of new appropriations of lands.

He has obstructed the administration of justice, by refusing his assent to laws for establishing judiciary powers.

He has made judges dependent on his will alone, for the tenure of their offices, and the amount and payment of their salaries.

He has erected a multitude of new offices, and sent hither swarms of officers to harass our people, and eat out their substance.

He has kept among us, in times of peace, standing armies without the consent of our legislatures.

He has affected to render the Military independent of, and superior to, the civil power.

He has combined with others to subject us to a jurisdiction foreign to our constitution and unacknowledged by our laws; giving his assent to their acts of pretended legislation:

For quartering large bodies of armed troops among us;

For protecting them, by a mock trial, from punishment for any murders which they should commit on the inhabitants of these States;

For cutting off our trade with all parts of the world;

For imposing taxes on us without our Consent;

For depriving us, in many cases, of the benefits of Trial by Jury;

For transporting us beyond Seas to be tried for pretended offences;

For abolishing the free System of English Laws in a neighbouring Province, establishing therein an Arbitrary government, and enlarging its Boundaries so as to render it at once an example and fit instrument for introducing the same absolute rule into these colonies;

For taking away our charters, abolishing our most valuable laws, and altering fundamentally the forms of our governments;

For suspending our own legislatures, and declaring themselves invested with power to legislate for us in all cases whatsoever.

He has abdicated government here, by declaring us out of his protection and waging war against us.

He has plundered our seas, ravaged our coasts, burnt our towns, and destroyed the lives of our people.

He is at this time transporting large armies of foreign mercenaries to complete the works of death, desolation and tyranny, already begun with circumstances of cruelty and perfidy scarcely paralleled in the most barbarous ages, and totally unworthy the head of a civilized nation.

He has constrained our fellow citizens taken captive on the high seas to bear arms against their country, to become the executioners of their friends and brethren, or to fall themselves by their hands.

He has excited domestic insurrections amongst us, and has endeavored to bring on the inhabitants of our frontiers, the merciless Indian savages, whose known rule of warfare, is an undistinguished destruction of all ages, sexes and conditions.

In every stage of these oppressions we have petitioned for redress in the most humble terms; our repeated petitions have been answered only by repeated injury. A prince whose character is thus marked by every act which may define a tyrant, is unfit to be the ruler of a free people.

Nor have we been wanting in attentions to our British brethren. We have warned them from time to time of attempts by their legislature to extend an unwarrantable jurisdiction over us. We have reminded them of the circumstances of our emigration and settlement here. We have appealed to their native justice and magnanimity, and we have conjured them by the ties of our common kindred to disavow these usurpations, which, would inevitably interrupt our connections and correspondence. They, too, have been deaf to the voice of justice and of consanguinity. We must, therefore, acquiesce in the necessity, which denounces our separation, and hold them, as we hold the rest of mankind, enemies in war, in peace friends.

We, therefore, the representatives of the United States of America, in general Congress, assembled, appealing to the Supreme Judge of the world for the rectitude of our intentions, do, in the name, and by the authority of the good people of these colonies, solemnly publish and declare, that these united colonies are, and of right ought to be free and independent states; that they are absolved from all allegiance to the British Crown, and that all political connection between them and the state of Great Britain, is and ought to be totally dissolved; and that, as free and independent states, they have full power to levy war, conclude peace, contract alliances, establish commerce, and to do all other acts and things which independent states may of right do. And for the support of this declaration, with a firm reliance on the protection of Divine Providence, we mutually pledge to each other our lives, our fortunes and our sacred honor.

The Constitution of the United States of America

We the People of the United States, in Order to form a more perfect Union, establish Justice, insure domestic Tranquility, provide for the common defence, promote the general Welfare, and secure the Blessings of Liberty to ourselves and our Posterity, do ordain and establish this Constitution for the United States of America.

Article I
Section 1

All legislative Powers herein granted shall be vested in a Congress of the United States, which shall consist of a Senate and House of Representatives.

Section 2

The House of Representatives shall be composed of Members chosen every second Year by the People of the several States, and the Electors in each State shall have the Qualifications requisite for Electors of the most numerous Branch of the State Legislature.

No Person shall be a Representative who shall not have attained to the Age of twenty five Years, and been seven Years a Citizen of the United States, and who shall not, when elected, be an Inhabitant of that State in which he shall be chosen.

Representatives and direct Taxes shall be apportioned among the several States which may be included within this Union, according to their respective Numbers, which shall be determined by adding to the whole Number of free Persons, including those bound to Service for a Term of Years, and excluding Indians not taxed, three fifths of all other Persons. The actual Enumeration shall be made within three Years after the first Meeting of the Congress of the United States, and within every subsequent Term of ten Years, in such Manner as they shall by Law direct. The Number of Representatives shall not exceed one for every thirty Thousand, but each State shall have at Least one Representative; and until such enumeration shall be made, the State of New Hampshire shall be entitled to choose three, Massachusetts eight, Rhode-Island and Providence Plantations one, Connecticut five, New York six, New Jersey four, Pennsylvania eight, Delaware one, Maryland six, Virginia ten, North Carolina five, South Carolina five, and Georgia three.

When vacancies happen in the Representation from any State, the Executive Authority thereof shall issue Writs of Election to fill such Vacancies.

The House of Representatives shall choose their Speaker and other Officers; and shall have the sole Power of Impeachment.

Section 3

The Senate of the United States shall be composed of two Senators from each State, chosen by the Legislature thereof for six Years; and each Senator shall have one Vote.

Immediately after they shall be assembled in Consequence of the first Election, they shall be divided as equally as may be into three Classes. The Seats of the Senators of the first Class shall be vacated at the Expiration of the second Year, of the second Class at the Expiration of the fourth Year, and of the third Class at the Expiration of the sixth Year, so that one third may be chosen every second Year; and if Vacancies happen by Resignation, or otherwise, during the Recess of the Legislature of any State, the Executive thereof may make temporary Appointments until the next Meeting of the Legislature, which shall then fill such Vacancies.

No Person shall be a Senator who shall not have attained to the Age of thirty Years, and been nine Years a Citizen of the United States, and who shall not, when elected, be an Inhabitant of that State for which he shall be chosen.

The Vice President of the United States shall be President of the Senate, but shall have no Vote, unless they be equally divided.

The Senate shall choose their other Officers, and also a President pro tempore, in the Absence of the Vice President, or when he shall exercise the Office of President of the United States.

The Senate shall have the sole Power to try all Impeachments. When sitting for that Purpose, they shall be on Oath or Affirmation. When the President of the United States is tried, the Chief Justice shall preside: And no Person shall be convicted without the Concurrence of two thirds of the Members present.

Judgment in Cases of Impeachment shall not extend further than to removal from Office, and disqualification to hold and enjoy any Office of honor, Trust or

Profit under the United States: but the Party convicted shall nevertheless be liable and subject to Indictment, Trial, Judgment and Punishment, according to Law.

Section 4

The Times, Places and Manner of holding Elections for Senators and Representatives, shall be prescribed in each State by the Legislature thereof; but the Congress may at any time by Law make or alter such Regulations, except as to the Places of chusing Senators.

The Congress shall assemble at least once in every Year, and such Meeting shall be on the first Monday in December, unless they shall by Law appoint a different Day.

Section 5

Each House shall be the Judge of the Elections, Returns and Qualifications of its own Members, and a Majority of each shall constitute a Quorum to do Business; but a smaller Number may adjourn from day to day, and may be authorized to compel the Attendance of absent Members, in such Manner, and under such Penalties as each House may provide.

Each House may determine the Rules of its Proceedings, punish its Members for disorderly Behaviour, and, with the Concurrence of two thirds, expel a Member.

Each House shall keep a Journal of its Proceedings, and from time to time publish the same, excepting such Parts as may in their Judgment require Secrecy; and the Yeas and Nays of the Members of either House on any question shall, at the Desire of one fifth of those Present, be entered on the Journal.

Neither House, during the Session of Congress, shall, without the Consent of the other, adjourn for more than three days, nor to any other Place than that in which the two Houses shall be sitting.

Section 6

The Senators and Representatives shall receive a Compensation for their Services, to be ascertained by Law, and paid out of the Treasury of the United States. They shall in all Cases, except Treason, Felony and Breach of the Peace, be privileged from Arrest during their Attendance at the Session of their respective Houses, and in going to and returning from the same; and for any Speech or Debate in either House, they shall not be questioned in any other Place.

No Senator or Representative shall, during the Time for which he was elected, be appointed to any civil Office under the Authority of the United States, which shall have been created, or the Emoluments whereof shall have been increased during such time; and no Person holding any Office under the United States, shall be a Member of either House during his Continuance in Office.

Section 7

All Bills for raising Revenue shall originate in the House of Representatives; but the Senate may propose or concur with Amendments as on other Bills.

Every Bill which shall have passed the House of Representatives and the Senate, shall, before it become a Law, be presented to the President of the United States:

If he approve he shall sign it, but if not he shall return it, with his Objections to that House in which it shall have originated, who shall enter the Objections at large on their Journal, and proceed to reconsider it. If after such Reconsideration two thirds of that House shall agree to pass the Bill, it shall be sent, together with the Objections, to the other House, by which it shall likewise be reconsidered, and if approved by two thirds of that House, it shall become a Law. But in all such Cases the Votes of both Houses shall be determined by yeas and Nays, and the Names of the Persons voting for and against the Bill shall be entered on the Journal of each House respectively. If any Bill shall not be returned by the President within ten Days (Sundays excepted) after it shall have been presented to him, the Same shall be a Law, in like Manner as if he had signed it, unless the Congress by their Adjournment prevent its Return, in which Case it shall not be a Law.

Every Order, Resolution, or Vote to which the Concurrence of the Senate and House of Representatives may be necessary (except on a question of Adjournment) shall be presented to the President of the United States; and before the Same shall take Effect, shall be approved by him, or being disapproved by him, shall be repassed by two thirds of the Senate and House of Representatives, according to the Rules and Limitations prescribed in the Case of a Bill.

Section 8

The Congress shall have Power

To lay and collect Taxes, Duties, Imposts and Excises, to pay the Debts and provide for the common Defence and general Welfare of the United States; but all Duties, Imposts and Excises shall be uniform throughout the United States;

To borrow Money on the credit of the United States;

To regulate Commerce with foreign Nations, and among the several States, and with the Indian Tribes;

To establish an uniform Rule of Naturalization, and uniform Laws on the subject of Bankruptcies throughout the United States;

To coin Money, regulate the Value thereof, and of foreign Coin, and fix the Standard of Weights and Measures;

To provide for the Punishment of counterfeiting the Securities and current Coin of the United States;

To establish Post Offices and post Roads;

To promote the Progress of Science and useful Arts, by securing for limited Times to Authors and Inventors the exclusive Right to their respective Writings and Discoveries;

To constitute Tribunals inferior to the supreme Court;

To define and punish Piracies and Felonies committed on the high Seas, and Offences against the Law of Nations;

To declare War, grant Letters of Marque and Reprisal, and make Rules concerning Captures on Land and Water;

To raise and support Armies, but no Appropriation of Money to that Use shall be for a longer Term than two Years;

To provide and maintain a Navy;

To make Rules for the Government and Regulation of the land and naval Forces;

To provide for calling forth the Militia to execute the Laws of the Union, suppress Insurrections and repel Invasions;

To provide for organizing, arming, and disciplining the Militia, and for governing such Part of them as may be employed in the Service of the United States, reserving to the States respectively, the Appointment of the Officers, and the Authority of training the Militia according to the discipline prescribed by Congress;

To exercise exclusive Legislation in all Cases whatsoever, over such District (not exceeding ten Miles square) as may, by Cession of particular States, and the Acceptance of Congress, become the Seat of the Government of the United States, and to exercise like Authority over all Places purchased by the Consent of the Legislature of the State in which the Same shall be, for the Erection of Forts, Magazines, Arsenals, dock-Yards, and other needful Buildings;—And

To make all Laws which shall be necessary and proper for carrying into Execution the foregoing Powers, and all other Powers vested by this Constitution in the Government of the United States, or in any Department or Officer thereof.

Section 9

The Migration or Importation of such Persons as any of the States now existing shall think proper to admit, shall not be prohibited by the Congress prior to the Year one thousand eight hundred and eight, but a Tax or duty may be imposed on such Importation, not exceeding ten dollars for each Person.

The Privilege of the Writ of Habeas Corpus shall not be suspended, unless when in Cases of Rebellion or Invasion the public Safety may require it.

No Bill of Attainder or ex post facto Law shall be passed.

No Capitation, or other direct, Tax shall be laid, unless in Proportion to the Census or enumeration herein before directed to be taken.

No Tax or Duty shall be laid on Articles exported from any State.

No Preference shall be given by any Regulation of Commerce or Revenue to the Ports of one State over those of another; nor shall Vessels bound to, or from, one State, be obliged to enter, clear, or pay Duties in another.

No Money shall be drawn from the Treasury, but in Consequence of Appropriations made by Law; and a regular Statement and Account of the Receipts and Expenditures of all public Money shall be published from time to time.

No Title of Nobility shall be granted by the United States: And no Person holding any Office of Profit or Trust under them, shall, without the Consent of the Congress, accept of any present, Emolument, Office, or Title, of any kind whatever, from any King, Prince, or foreign State.

Section 10

No State shall enter into any Treaty, Alliance, or Confederation; grant Letters of Marque and Reprisal; coin Money; emit Bills of Credit; make any Thing but gold and silver Coin a Tender in Payment of Debts; pass any Bill of Attainder, ex post facto Law, or Law impairing the Obligation of Contracts, or grant any Title of Nobility.

No State shall, without the Consent of the Congress, lay any Imposts or Duties on Imports or Exports, except what may be absolutely necessary for executing it's inspection Laws: and the net Produce of all Duties and Imposts, laid by any State on

Imports or Exports, shall be for the Use of the Treasury of the United States; and all such Laws shall be subject to the Revision and Control of the Congress.

No State shall, without the Consent of Congress, lay any Duty of Tonnage, keep Troops, or Ships of War in time of Peace, enter into any Agreement or Compact with another State, or with a foreign Power, or engage in War, unless actually invaded, or in such imminent Danger as will not admit of delay.

Article II
Section 1

The executive Power shall be vested in a President of the United States of America. He shall hold his Office during the Term of four Years, and, together with the Vice President, chosen for the same Term, be elected, as follows:

Each State shall appoint, in such Manner as the Legislature thereof may direct, a Number of Electors, equal to the whole Number of Senators and Representatives to which the State may be entitled in the Congress: but no Senator or Representative, or Person holding an Office of Trust or Profit under the United States, shall be appointed an Elector.

The Electors shall meet in their respective States, and vote by Ballot for two Persons, of whom one at least shall not be an Inhabitant of the same State with themselves. And they shall make a List of all the Persons voted for, and of the Number of Votes for each; which List they shall sign and certify, and transmit sealed to the Seat of the Government of the United States, directed to the President of the Senate. The President of the Senate shall, in the Presence of the Senate and House of Representatives, open all the Certificates, and the Votes shall then be counted. The Person having the greatest Number of Votes shall be the President, if such Number be a Majority of the whole Number of Electors appointed; and if there be more than one who have such Majority, and have an equal Number of Votes, then the House of Representatives shall immediately choose by Ballot one of them for President; and if no Person have a Majority, then from the five highest on the List the said House shall in like Manner choose the President. But in choosing the President, the Votes shall be taken by States, the Representation from each State having one Vote; A quorum for this purpose shall consist of a Member or Members from two thirds of the States, and a Majority of all the States shall be necessary to a Choice. In every Case, after the Choice of the President, the Person having the greatest Number of Votes of the Electors shall be the Vice President. But if there should remain two or more who have equal Votes, the Senate shall choose from them by Ballot the Vice President.

The Congress may determine the Time of choosing the Electors, and the Day on which they shall give their Votes; which Day shall be the same throughout the United States.

No Person except a natural born Citizen, or a Citizen of the United States, at the time of the Adoption of this Constitution, shall be eligible to the Office of President; neither shall any Person be eligible to that Office who shall not have attained to the Age of thirty five Years, and been fourteen Years a Resident within the United States.

In Case of the Removal of the President from Office, or of his Death, Resignation, or Inability to discharge the Powers and Duties of the said Office, the Same shall devolve on the Vice President, and the Congress may by Law provide for the Case of Removal, Death, Resignation or Inability, both of the President and Vice President, declaring what Officer shall then act as President, and such Officer shall act accordingly, until the Disability be removed, or a President shall be elected.

The President shall, at stated Times, receive for his Services, a Compensation, which shall neither be increased nor diminished during the Period for which he shall have been elected, and he shall not receive within that Period any other Emolument from the United States, or any of them.

Before he enter on the Execution of his Office, he shall take the following Oath or Affirmation:—"I do solemnly swear (or affirm) that I will faithfully execute the Office of President of the United States, and will to the best of my Ability, preserve, protect and defend the Constitution of the United States."

Section 2

The President shall be Commander in Chief of the Army and Navy of the United States, and of the Militia of the several States, when called into the actual Service of the United States; he may require the Opinion, in writing, of the principal Officer in each of the executive Departments, upon any Subject relating to the Duties of their respective Offices, and he shall have Power to grant Reprieves and Pardons for Offences against the United States, except in Cases of Impeachment.

He shall have Power, by and with the Advice and Consent of the Senate, to make Treaties, provided two thirds of the Senators present concur; and he shall nominate, and by and with the Advice and Consent of the Senate, shall appoint Ambassadors, other public Ministers and Consuls, Judges of the supreme Court, and all other Officers of the United States, whose Appointments are not herein otherwise provided for, and which shall be established by Law: but the Congress may by Law vest the Appointment of such inferior Officers, as they think proper, in the President alone, in the Courts of Law, or in the Heads of Departments.

The President shall have Power to fill up all Vacancies that may happen during the Recess of the Senate, by granting Commissions which shall expire at the End of their next Session.

Section 3

He shall from time to time give to the Congress Information of the State of the Union, and recommend to their Consideration such Measures as he shall judge necessary and expedient; he may, on extraordinary Occasions, convene both Houses, or either of them, and in Case of Disagreement between them, with Respect to the Time of Adjournment, he may adjourn them to such Time as he shall think proper; he shall receive Ambassadors and other public Ministers; he shall take Care that the Laws be faithfully executed, and shall Commission all the Officers of the United States.

Section 4

The President, Vice President and all civil Officers of the United States, shall be removed from Office on Impeachment for, and Conviction of, Treason, Bribery, or other high Crimes and Misdemeanors.

Article III
Section 1

The judicial Power of the United States shall be vested in one supreme Court, and in such inferior Courts as the Congress may from time to time ordain and establish. The Judges, both of the supreme and inferior Courts, shall hold their Offices during good Behaviour, and shall, at stated Times, receive for their Services a Compensation, which shall not be diminished during their Continuance in Office.

Section 2

The judicial Power shall extend to all Cases, in Law and Equity, arising under this Constitution, the Laws of the United States, and Treaties made, or which shall be made, under their Authority;—to all Cases affecting Ambassadors, other public Ministers and Consuls;—to all Cases of admiralty and maritime Jurisdiction;—to Controversies to which the United States shall be a Party;—to Controversies between two or more States;—between a State and Citizens of another State;—between Citizens of different States;—between Citizens of the same State claiming Lands under Grants of different States, and between a State, or the Citizens thereof, and foreign States, Citizens or Subjects.

In all Cases affecting Ambassadors, other public Ministers and Consuls, and those in which a State shall be Party, the supreme Court shall have original Jurisdiction. In all the other Cases before mentioned, the supreme Court shall have appellate Jurisdiction, both as to Law and Fact, with such Exceptions, and under such Regulations as the Congress shall make.

The Trial of all Crimes, except in Cases of Impeachment, shall be by Jury; and such Trial shall be held in the State where the said Crimes shall have been committed; but when not committed within any State, the Trial shall be at such Place or Places as the Congress may by Law have directed.

Section 3

Treason against the United States, shall consist only in levying War against them, or in adhering to their Enemies, giving them Aid and Comfort. No Person shall be convicted of Treason unless on the Testimony of two Witnesses to the same overt Act, or on Confession in open Court.

The Congress shall have Power to declare the Punishment of Treason, but no Attainder of Treason shall work Corruption of Blood, or Forfeiture except during the Life of the Person attainted.

Article IV
Section 1

Full Faith and Credit shall be given in each State to the public Acts, Records, and judicial Proceedings of every other State. And the Congress may by general Laws prescribe the Manner in which such Acts, Records and Proceedings shall be proved, and the Effect thereof.

Section 2

The Citizens of each State shall be entitled to all Privileges and Immunities of Citizens in the several States.

A Person charged in any State with Treason, Felony, or other Crime, who shall flee from Justice, and be found in another State, shall on Demand of the executive Authority of the State from which he fled, be delivered up, to be removed to the State having Jurisdiction of the Crime.

No Person held to Service or Labour in one State, under the Laws thereof, escaping into another, shall, in Consequence of any Law or Regulation therein, be discharged from such Service or Labour, but shall be delivered up on Claim of the Party to whom such Service or Labour may be due.

Section 3

New States may be admitted by the Congress into this Union; but no new State shall be formed or erected within the Jurisdiction of any other State; nor any State be formed by the Junction of two or more States, or Parts of States, without the Consent of the Legislatures of the States concerned as well as of the Congress.

The Congress shall have Power to dispose of and make all needful Rules and Regulations respecting the Territory or other Property belonging to the United States; and nothing in this Constitution shall be so construed as to Prejudice any Claims of the United States, or of any particular State.

Section 4

The United States shall guarantee to every State in this Union a Republican Form of Government, and shall protect each of them against Invasion; and on Application of the Legislature, or of the Executive (when the Legislature cannot be convened), against domestic Violence.

Article V

The Congress, whenever two thirds of both Houses shall deem it necessary, shall propose Amendments to this Constitution, or, on the Application of the Legislatures of two thirds of the several States, shall call a Convention for proposing Amendments, which, in either Case, shall be valid to all Intents and Purposes, as Part of this Constitution, when ratified by the Legislatures of three fourths of the several States, or by Conventions in three fourths thereof, as the one or the other Mode of Ratification may be proposed by the Congress; Provided that no Amendment which may be made prior to the Year One thousand eight hundred and eight shall in any Manner affect the first and fourth Clauses in the Ninth Section of the first Article; and that no State, without its Consent, shall be deprived of its equal Suffrage in the Senate.

Article VI

All Debts contracted and Engagements entered into, before the Adoption of this Constitution, shall be as valid against the United States under this Constitution, as under the Confederation.

This Constitution, and the Laws of the United States which shall be made in Pursuance thereof; and all Treaties made, or which shall be made, under the Authority of the United States, shall be the supreme Law of the Land; and the Judges in every State shall be bound thereby, any Thing in the Constitution or Laws of any State to the Contrary notwithstanding.

The Senators and Representatives before mentioned, and the Members of the several State Legislatures, and all executive and judicial Officers, both of the United States and of the several States, shall be bound by Oath or Affirmation, to support this Constitution; but no religious Test shall ever be required as a Qualification to any Office or public Trust under the United States.

Article VII

The Ratification of the Conventions of nine States, shall be sufficient for the Establishment of this Constitution between the States so ratifying the Same.

The Word, "the," being interlined between the seventh and eighth Lines of the first Page, the Word "Thirty" being partly written on an Erazure in the fifteenth Line of the first Page, The Words "is tried" being interlined between the thirty second and thirty third Lines of the first Page and the Word "the" being interlined between the forty third and forty fourth Lines of the second Page.

Attest William Jackson Secretary

Done in Convention by the Unanimous Consent of the States present the Seventeenth Day of September in the Year of our Lord one thousand seven hundred and Eighty seven and of the Independence of the United States of America the Twelfth In witness whereof We have hereunto subscribed our Names,

Gᵒ. Washington
Presidt and deputy from Virginia

Delaware
Geo: Read
Gunning Bedford Jr.
John Dickinson
Richard Bassett
Jaco: Broom

Maryland
James McHenry
Dan of St Thos. Jenifer
Danl. Carroll

Virginia
John Blair
James Madison Jr.

North Carolina
Wm. Blount
Richd. Dobbs Spaight
Hu Williamson

South Carolina
J. Rutledge
Charles Cotesworth Pinckney
Charles Pinckney
Pierce Butler

Georgia
William Few
Abr Baldwin

New Hampshire
John Langdon
Nicholas Gilman

Massachusetts
Nathaniel Gorham
Rufus King

Connecticut
Wm. Saml. Johnson
Roger Sherman

New York
Alexander Hamilton

New Jersey
Wil: Livingston
David Brearley
Wm. Paterson
Jona: Dayton

Pennsylvania
B Franklin
Thomas Mifflin
Robt. Morris
Geo. Clymer
Thos. FitzSimons
Jared Ingersoll
James Wilson
Gouv Morris

Articles

In addition to, and Amendment of the Constitution of the United States of America, proposed by Congress, and ratified by the Legislatures of the several States, pursuant to the fifth Article of the original Constitution.

(The first ten amendments to the U.S. Constitution were ratified December 15, 1791, and form what is known as the "Bill of Rights.")

AMENDMENT I

Congress shall make no law respecting an establishment of religion, or prohibiting the free exercise thereof; or abridging the freedom of speech, or of the press; or the right of the people peaceably to assemble, and to petition the Government for a redress of grievances.

AMENDMENT II

A well regulated Militia, being necessary to the security of a free State, the right of the people to keep and bear Arms, shall not be infringed.

AMENDMENT III

No Soldier shall, in time of peace be quartered in any house, without the consent of the Owner, nor in time of war, but in a manner to be prescribed by law.

AMENDMENT IV

The right of the people to be secure in their persons, houses, papers, and effects, against unreasonable searches and seizures, shall not be violated, and no Warrants shall issue, but upon probable cause, supported by Oath or affirmation, and particularly describing the place to be searched, and the persons or things to be seized.

AMENDMENT V

No person shall be held to answer for a capital, or otherwise infamous crime, unless on a presentment or indictment of a Grand Jury, except in cases arising in the land or naval forces, or in the Militia, when in actual service in time of War or public danger; nor shall any person be subject for the same offence to be twice put in jeopardy of life or limb; nor shall be compelled in any criminal case to be a witness against himself, nor be deprived of life, liberty, or property, without due process of law; nor shall private property be taken for public use, without just compensation.

AMENDMENT VI

In all criminal prosecutions, the accused shall enjoy the right to a speedy and public trial, by an impartial jury of the State and district wherein the crime shall have been committed, which district shall have been previously ascertained by law, and to be informed of the nature and cause of the accusation; to be confronted with the witnesses against him; to have compulsory process for obtaining witnesses in his favor, and to have the Assistance of Counsel for his defence.

AMENDMENT VII

In Suits at common law, where the value in controversy shall exceed twenty dollars, the right of trial by jury shall be preserved, and no fact tried by a jury, shall be otherwise re-examined in any Court of the United States, than according to the rules of the common law.

AMENDMENT VIII

Excessive bail shall not be required, nor excessive fines imposed, nor cruel and unusual punishments inflicted.

AMENDMENT IX

The enumeration in the Constitution, of certain rights, shall not be construed to deny or disparage others retained by the people.

AMENDMENT X

The powers not delegated to the United States by the Constitution, nor prohibited by it to the States, are reserved to the States respectively, or to the people.

AMENDMENT XI

Passed by Congress March 4, 1794. Ratified February 7, 1795.

Note: Article III, Section 2, of the Constitution was modified by Amendment XI.

The Judicial power of the United States shall not be construed to extend to any suit in law or equity, commenced or prosecuted against one of the United States by Citizens of another State, or by Citizens or Subjects of any Foreign State.

AMENDMENT XII

Passed by Congress December 9, 1803. Ratified June 15, 1804.

Note: A portion of Article II, Section 1, of the Constitution was superseded by the Twelfth Amendment.

The Electors shall meet in their respective states and vote by ballot for President and Vice-President, one of whom, at least, shall not be an inhabitant of the same state with themselves; they shall name in their ballots the person voted for as President, and in distinct ballots the person voted for as Vice-President, and they shall

make distinct lists of all persons voted for as President, and of all persons voted for as Vice-President, and of the number of votes for each, which lists they shall sign and certify, and transmit sealed to the seat of the government of the United States, directed to the President of the Senate;—the President of the Senate shall, in the presence of the Senate and House of Representatives, open all the certificates and the votes shall then be counted;—The person having the greatest number of votes for President, shall be the President, if such number be a majority of the whole number of Electors appointed; and if no person have such majority, then from the persons having the highest numbers not exceeding three on the list of those voted for as President, the House of Representatives shall choose immediately, by ballot, the President. But in choosing the President, the votes shall be taken by states, the representation from each state having one vote; a quorum for this purpose shall consist of a member or members from two-thirds of the states, and a majority of all the states shall be necessary to a choice. [And if the House of Representatives shall not choose a President whenever the right of choice shall devolve upon them, before the fourth day of March next following, then the Vice-President shall act as President, as in case of the death or other constitutional disability of the President.—]*
The person having the greatest number of votes as Vice-President, shall be the Vice-President, if such number be a majority of the whole number of Electors appointed, and if no person have a majority, then from the two highest numbers on the list, the Senate shall choose the Vice-President; a quorum for the purpose shall consist of two-thirds of the whole number of Senators, and a majority of the whole number shall be necessary to a choice. But no person constitutionally ineligible to the office of President shall be eligible to that of Vice-President of the United States.

AMENDMENT XIII

Passed by Congress January 31, 1865. Ratified December 6, 1865.

Note: A portion of Article IV, Section 2, of the Constitution was superseded by the Thirteenth Amendment.

Section 1

Neither slavery nor involuntary servitude, except as a punishment for crime whereof the party shall have been duly convicted, shall exist within the United States, or any place subject to their jurisdiction.

Section 2

Congress shall have power to enforce this article by appropriate legislation.

AMENDMENT XIV

Passed by Congress June 13, 1866. Ratified July 9, 1868.

Note: Article I, Section 2, of the Constitution was modified by Section 2 of the Fourteenth Amendment.

---

*Superseded by Section 3 of the Twentieth Amendment.

Section 1

All persons born or naturalized in the United States, and subject to the jurisdiction thereof, are citizens of the United States and of the State wherein they reside. No State shall make or enforce any law which shall abridge the privileges or immunities of citizens of the United States; nor shall any State deprive any person of life, liberty, or property, without due process of law; nor deny to any person within its jurisdiction the equal protection of the laws.

Section 2

Representatives shall be apportioned among the several States according to their respective numbers, counting the whole number of persons in each State, excluding Indians not taxed. But when the right to vote at any election for the choice of electors for President and Vice-President of the United States, Representatives in Congress, the Executive and Judicial officers of a State, or the members of the Legislature thereof, is denied to any of the male inhabitants of such State, being twenty-one years of age,* and citizens of the United States, or in any way abridged, except for participation in rebellion, or other crime, the basis of representation therein shall be reduced in the proportion which the number of such male citizens shall bear to the whole number of male citizens twenty-one years of age in such State.

Section 3

No person shall be a Senator or Representative in Congress, or elector of President and Vice-President, or hold any office, civil or military, under the United States, or under any State, who, having previously taken an oath, as a member of Congress, or as an officer of the United States, or as a member of any State legislature, or as an executive or judicial officer of any State, to support the Constitution of the United States, shall have engaged in insurrection or rebellion against the same, or given aid or comfort to the enemies thereof. But Congress may by a vote of two-thirds of each House, remove such disability.

Section 4

The validity of the public debt of the United States, authorized by law, including debts incurred for payment of pensions and bounties for services in suppressing insurrection or rebellion, shall not be questioned. But neither the United States nor any State shall assume or pay any debt or obligation incurred in aid of insurrection or rebellion against the United States, or any claim for the loss or emancipation of any slave; but all such debts, obligations and claims shall be held illegal and void.

Section 5

The Congress shall have the power to enforce, by appropriate legislation, the provisions of this article.

---

*Changed by Section 1 of the Twenty-sixth Amendment.

AMENDMENT XV

Passed by Congress February 26, 1869. Ratified February 3, 1870.

Section 1

The right of citizens of the United States to vote shall not be denied or abridged by the United States or by any State on account of race, color, or previous condition of servitude.

Section 2

The Congress shall have the power to enforce this article by appropriate legislation.

AMENDMENT XVI

Passed by Congress July 2, 1909. Ratified February 3, 1913.

Note: Article I, Section 9, of the Constitution was modified by Amendment XVI.

The Congress shall have power to lay and collect taxes on incomes, from whatever source derived, without apportionment among the several States, and without regard to any census or enumeration.

AMENDMENT XVII

Passed by Congress May 13, 1912. Ratified April 8, 1913.

Note: Article I, Section 3, of the Constitution was modified by the Seventeenth Amendment.

The Senate of the United States shall be composed of two Senators from each State, elected by the people thereof, for six years; and each Senator shall have one vote. The electors in each State shall have the qualifications requisite for electors of the most numerous branch of the State legislatures.

When vacancies happen in the representation of any State in the Senate, the executive authority of such State shall issue writs of election to fill such vacancies: Provided, That the legislature of any State may empower the executive thereof to make temporary appointments until the people fill the vacancies by election as the legislature may direct.

This amendment shall not be so construed as to affect the election or term of any Senator chosen before it becomes valid as part of the Constitution.

AMENDMENT XVIII

Passed by Congress December 18, 1917. Ratified January 16, 1919. Repealed by Amendment XXI.

Section 1

After one year from the ratification of this article the manufacture, sale, or transportation of intoxicating liquors within, the importation thereof into, or the exportation thereof from the United States and all territory subject to the jurisdiction thereof for beverage purposes is hereby prohibited.

Section 2

The Congress and the several States shall have concurrent power to enforce this article by appropriate legislation.

Section 3

This article shall be inoperative unless it shall have been ratified as an amendment to the Constitution by the legislatures of the several States, as provided in the Constitution, within seven years from the date of the submission hereof to the States by the Congress.

AMENDMENT XIX

Passed by Congress June 4, 1919. Ratified August 18, 1920.

The right of citizens of the United States to vote shall not be denied or abridged by the United States or by any State on account of sex.

Congress shall have power to enforce this article by appropriate legislation.

AMENDMENT XX

Passed by Congress March 2, 1932. Ratified January 23, 1933.

Note: Article I, Section 4, of the Constitution was modified by Section 2 of this amendment. In addition, a portion of the Twelfth Amendment was superseded by Section 3.

Section 1

The terms of the President and the Vice President shall end at noon on the 20th day of January, and the terms of Senators and Representatives at noon on the 3d day of January, of the years in which such terms would have ended if this article had not been ratified; and the terms of their successors shall then begin.

Section 2

The Congress shall assemble at least once in every year, and such meeting shall begin at noon on the 3d day of January, unless they shall by law appoint a different day.

Section 3

If, at the time fixed for the beginning of the term of the President, the President elect shall have died, the Vice President elect shall become President. If a President shall not have been chosen before the time fixed for the beginning of his term, or if the President elect shall have failed to qualify, then the Vice President elect shall act as President until a President shall have qualified; and the Congress may by law provide for the case wherein neither a President elect nor a Vice President shall have qualified, declaring who shall then act as President, or the manner in which one who is to act shall be selected, and such person shall act accordingly until a President or Vice President shall have qualified.

Section 4

The Congress may by law provide for the case of the death of any of the persons from whom the House of Representatives may choose a President whenever the right of choice shall have devolved upon them, and for the case of the death of any of the persons from whom the Senate may choose a Vice President whenever the right of choice shall have devolved upon them.

Section 5

Sections 1 and 2 shall take effect on the 15th day of October following the ratification of this article.

Section 6

This article shall be inoperative unless it shall have been ratified as an amendment to the Constitution by the legislatures of three-fourths of the several States within seven years from the date of its submission.

AMENDMENT XXI

Passed by Congress February 20, 1933. Ratified December 5, 1933.

Section 1

The eighteenth article of amendment to the Constitution of the United States is hereby repealed.

Section 2

The transportation or importation into any State, Territory, or Possession of the United States for delivery or use therein of intoxicating liquors, in violation of the laws thereof, is hereby prohibited.

Section 3

This article shall be inoperative unless it shall have been ratified as an amendment to the Constitution by conventions in the several States, as provided in the Constitution, within seven years from the date of the submission hereof to the States by the Congress.

AMENDMENT XXII

Passed by Congress March 21, 1947. Ratified February 27, 1951.

Section 1

No person shall be elected to the office of the President more than twice, and no person who has held the office of President, or acted as President, for more than two years of a term to which some other person was elected President shall be elected to the office of President more than once. But this Article shall not apply to any person holding the office of President when this Article was proposed by Congress, and shall not prevent any person who may be holding the office of President, or acting as President, during the term within which this Article becomes operative from holding the office of President or acting as President during the remainder of such term.

Section 2

This article shall be inoperative unless it shall have been ratified as an amendment to the Constitution by the legislatures of three-fourths of the several States within seven years from the date of its submission to the States by the Congress.

AMENDMENT XXIII

Passed by Congress June 16, 1960. Ratified March 29, 1961.

Section 1

The District constituting the seat of Government of the United States shall appoint in such manner as Congress may direct:

A number of electors of President and Vice President equal to the whole number of Senators and Representatives in Congress to which the District would be entitled if it were a State, but in no event more than the least populous State; they shall be in addition to those appointed by the States, but they shall be considered, for the purposes of the election of President and Vice President, to be electors appointed by a State; and they shall meet in the District and perform such duties as provided by the twelfth article of amendment.

Section 2

The Congress shall have power to enforce this article by appropriate legislation.

AMENDMENT XXIV

Passed by Congress August 27, 1962. Ratified January 23, 1964.

Section 1

The right of citizens of the United States to vote in any primary or other election for President or Vice President, for electors for President or Vice President, or for Senator or Representative in Congress, shall not be denied or abridged by the United States or any State by reason of failure to pay poll tax or other tax.

Section 2

The Congress shall have power to enforce this article by appropriate legislation.

AMENDMENT XXV

Passed by Congress July 6, 1965. Ratified February 10, 1967.

Note: Article II, Section 1, of the Constitution was affected by the Twenty-fifth Amendment.

Section 1

In case of the removal of the President from office or of his death or resignation, the Vice President shall become President.

Section 2

Whenever there is a vacancy in the office of the Vice President, the President shall nominate a Vice President who shall take office upon confirmation by a majority vote of both Houses of Congress.

Section 3

Whenever the President transmits to the President pro tempore of the Senate and the Speaker of the House of Representatives his written declaration that he is unable to discharge the powers and duties of his office, and until he transmits to them a written declaration to the contrary, such powers and duties shall be discharged by the Vice President as Acting President.

Section 4

Whenever the Vice President and a majority of either the principal officers of the executive departments or of such other body as Congress may by law provide, transmit to the President pro tempore of the Senate and the Speaker of the House of Representatives their written declaration that the President is unable to discharge the powers and duties of his office, the Vice President shall immediately assume the powers and duties of the office as Acting President.

Thereafter, when the President transmits to the President pro tempore of the Senate and the Speaker of the House of Representatives his written declaration that no inability exists, he shall resume the powers and duties of his office unless the Vice President and a majority of either the principal officers of the executive department or of such other body as Congress may by law provide, transmit within four days to the President pro tempore of the Senate and the Speaker of the House of Representatives their written declaration that the President is unable to discharge the powers and duties of his office. Thereupon Congress shall decide the issue, assembling within forty-eight hours for that purpose if not in session. If the Congress, within twenty-one days after receipt of the latter written declaration, or, if Congress is not in session, within twenty-one days after Congress is required to assemble, determines by two-thirds vote of both Houses that the President is unable to discharge the powers and duties of his office, the Vice President shall continue to discharge the same as Acting President; otherwise, the President shall resume the powers and duties of his office.

AMENDMENT XXVI

Passed by Congress March 23, 1971. Ratified July 1, 1971.

Note: Amendment XIV, Section 2, of the Constitution was modified by Section 1 of the Twenty-sixth Amendment.

Section 1

The right of citizens of the United States, who are eighteen years of age or older, to vote shall not be denied or abridged by the United States or by any State on account of age.

Section 2

The Congress shall have power to enforce this article by appropriate legislation.

AMENDMENT XXVII

Originally proposed Sept. 25, 1789. Ratified May 7, 1992.

No law, varying the compensation for the services of the Senators and Representatives, shall take effect, until an election of representatives shall have intervened.

Lincoln's Gettysburg Address

Four score and seven years ago our fathers brought forth on this continent, a new nation, conceived in Liberty, and dedicated to the proposition that all men are created equal.

Now we are engaged in a great civil war, testing whether that nation, or any nation so conceived and so dedicated, can long endure. We are met on a great battle-field of that war. We have come to dedicate a portion of that field, as a final resting place for those who here gave their lives that that nation might live. It is altogether fitting and proper that we should do this.

But, in a larger sense, we can not dedicate—we can not consecrate—we can not hallow—this ground. The brave men, living and dead, who struggled here, have consecrated it, far above our poor power to add or detract. The world will little note, nor long remember what we say here, but it can never forget what they did here. It is for us the living, rather, to be dedicated here to the unfinished work which they who fought here have thus far so nobly advanced. It is rather for us to be here dedicated to the great task remaining before us—that from these honored dead we take increased devotion to that cause for which they gave the last full measure of devotion—that we here highly resolve that these dead shall not have died in vain—that this nation, under God, shall have a new birth of freedom—and that government of the people, by the people, for the people, shall not perish from the earth.

Appendix B

HISTORICAL FACTS AND DATA
US Presidents and Vice Presidents

Table App B-1 Presidents and Vice Presidents

	President	Vice President	Political Party	Term
1	George Washington	John Adams	No Party Designation	1789–1797
2	John Adams	Thomas Jefferson	Federalist	1797–1801
3	Thomas Jefferson	Aaron Burr George Clinton	Democratic Republican	1801–1809
4	James Madison	George Clinton Elbridge Gerry	Democratic Republican	1809–1817
5	James Monroe	Daniel D. Tompkins	Democratic Republican	1817–1825
6	John Quincy Adams	John C. Calhoun	Democratic Republican	1825–1829
7	Andrew Jackson	John C. Calhoun Martin Van Buren	Democratic	1829–1837
8	Martin Van Buren	Richard M. Johnson	Democratic	1837–1841
9	William Henry Harrison	John Tyler	Whig	1841
10	John Tyler	None	Whig	1841–1845
11	James Knox Polk	George M. Dallas	Democratic	1845–1849
12	Zachary Taylor	Millard Fillmore	Whig	1849–1850
13	Millard Fillmore	None	Whig	1850–1853
14	Franklin Pierce	William R. King	Democratic	1853–1857
15	James Buchanan	John C. Breckinridge	Democratic	1857–1861
16	Abraham Lincoln	Hannibal Hamlin Andrew Johnson	Union	1861–1865
17	Andrew Johnson	None	Union	1865–1869
18	Ulysses Simpson Grant	Schuyler Colfax Henry Wilson	Republican	1869–1877
19	Rutherford Birchard Hayes	William A. Wheeler	Republican	1877–1881
20	James Abram Garfield	Chester Alan Arthur	Republican	1881
21	Chester Alan Arthur	None	Republican	1881–1885
22	Stephen Grover Cleveland	Thomas Hendricks	Democratic	1885–1889
23	Benjamin Harrison	Levi P. Morton	Republican	1889–1893
24	Stephen Grover Cleveland	Adlai E. Stevenson	Democratic	1893–1897

(continued)

Table App B-1 *continued*

	President	Vice President	Political Party	Term
25	William McKinley	Garret A. Hobart Theodore Roosevelt	Republican	1897–1901
26	Theodore Roosevelt	Charles W. Fairbanks	Republican	1901–1909
27	William Howard Taft	James S. Sherman	Republican	1909–1913
28	Woodrow Wilson	Thomas R. Marshall	Democratic	1913–1921
29	Warren Gamaliel Harding	Calvin Coolidge	Republican	1921–1923
30	Calvin Coolidge	Charles G. Dawes	Republican	1923–1929
31	Herbert Clark Hoover	Charles Curtis	Republican	1929–1933
32	Franklin Delano Roosevelt	John Nance Garner Henry A. Wallace Harry S. Truman	Democratic	1933–1945
33	Harry S. Truman	Alben W. Barkley	Democratic	1945–1953
34	Dwight David Eisenhower	Richard Milhous Nixon	Republican	1953–1961
35	John Fitzgerald Kennedy	Lyndon Baines Johnson	Democratic	1961–1963
36	Lyndon Baines Johnson	Hubert Horatio Humphrey	Democratic	1963–1969
37	Richard Milhous Nixon	Spiro T. Agnew Gerald Rudolph Ford	Republican	1969–1974
38	Gerald Rudolph Ford	Nelson Rockefeller	Republican	1974–1977
39	James Earl Carter Jr.	Walter Mondale	Democratic	1977–1981
40	Ronald Wilson Reagan	George Herbert Walker Bush	Republican	1981–1989
41	George Herbert Walker Bush	J. Danforth Quayle	Republican	1989–1993
42	William Jefferson Clinton	Albert Gore Jr.	Democratic	1993–2001
43	George Walker Bush	Richard Cheney	Republican	2001–2009
44	Barack Hussein Obama	Joseph Biden	Democratic	2009–2016
45	Donald J. Trump	Michael R. Pence	Republican	2017–2021
46	Joseph R. Biden	Kamala D. Harris	Democratic	2021–

Admission of States into the Union

Table App B-2 Admission of States into the Union

	State	Date of Admission		State	Date of Admission
1	Delaware	December 7, 1787	26	Michigan	January 26, 1837
2	Pennsylvania	December 12, 1787	27	Florida	March 3, 1845
3	New Jersey	December 18, 1787	28	Texas	December 29, 1845
4	Georgia	January 2, 1788	29	Iowa	December 28, 1846
5	Connecticut	January 9, 1788	30	Wisconsin	May 29, 1848
6	Massachusetts	February 6, 1788	31	California	September 9, 1850
7	Maryland	April 28, 1788	32	Minnesota	May 11, 1858
8	South Carolina	May 23, 1788	33	Oregon	February 14, 1859
9	New Hampshire	June 21, 1788	34	Kansas	January 29, 1861
10	Virginia	June 25, 1788	35	West Virginia	June 20, 1863
11	New York	July 26, 1788	36	Nevada	October 31, 1864
12	North Carolina	November 21, 1789	37	Nebraska	March 1, 1867
13	Rhode Island	May 29, 1790	38	Colorado	August 1, 1876
14	Vermont	March 4, 1791	39	North Dakota	November 2, 1889
15	Kentucky	June 1, 1792	40	South Dakota	November 2, 1889
16	Tennessee	June 1, 1796	41	Montana	November 8, 1889
17	Ohio	March 1, 1803	42	Washington	November 11, 1889
18	Louisiana	April 30, 1812	43	Idaho	July 3, 1890
19	Indiana	December 11, 1816	44	Wyoming	July 10, 1890
20	Mississippi	December 10, 1817	45	Utah	January 4, 1896
21	Illinois	December 3, 1818	46	Oklahoma	November 16, 1907
22	Alabama	December 14, 1819	47	New Mexico	January 6, 1912
23	Maine	March 15, 1820	48	Arizona	February 14, 1912
24	Missouri	August 10, 1821	49	Alaska	January 3, 1959
25	Arkansas	June 15, 1836	50	Hawaii	August 21, 1959

Glossary

The glossary offers definitions of key concepts and ideas, many of which appear at more than one point in the text. To find individuals, places, and events, you should use the Index.

abolitionist movement   Name for the movement to end slavery. It began in Britain and appeared in the United States after the Revolution. It gained greater power nationwide as the antebellum era progressed.

affirmative action   A federal policy, begun in the Johnson administration in the 1960s, that required businesses, universities, and other recipients of federal funds to provide opportunities for women and people of color. Intended to make up for past and present discrimination, affirmative action remained a controversial practice, subject to political and legal challenge into the twenty-first century.

America First   In 1940-1941, the America First Committee was the leading isolationist group opposed to US involvement in World War II. Opposed to globalization and international alliances, Donald Trump revived "America First" as the slogan of his foreign policy.

antifederalists   A school of thought fighting the idea of strengthening the national government at the expense of local authority.

antinomianism   The belief that moral law was not binding on true Christians. The opposite of Arminianism, antinomianism held that good works would not count in the afterlife. Justification, or entrance to heaven, was by faith alone. *See also* Calvinism.

Arminianism   Religious doctrine developed by the Dutch theologian Jacobus Arminius that argued that men and women had free will and would earn their way into heaven by good works.

armistice   A cessation of hostilities by agreement among the opposing sides; a cease-fire.

associationalism   President Herbert Hoover's preferred method of responding to the Great Depression. Rather than have the government directly involve itself in the economy, Hoover hoped to use the government to encourage associations of businessmen to cooperate voluntarily to meet the crisis.

atomic bomb   A nuclear weapon causing tremendous damage via heat, blast, and radioactivity. The United States, which developed the weapon via the Manhattan Project, dropped the first atomic bomb on Hiroshima on August 6, 1945, and the second on Nagaski on August 9, 1945.

autarky   At the height of the world depression, industrial powers sought to isolate their economies within self-contained spheres, generally governed by national (or imperial) economic planning. Japan's Co-Prosperity Sphere, the Soviet Union, and the British Empire each comprised a more or less closed economic unit.

Benevolent Empire   The loosely affiliated network of charitable reform associations that emerged (especially in urban areas) in response to the widespread revivalism of the early nineteenth century.

Bessemer process   Method invented by Henry Bessemer for removing the impurities from molten pig iron by blasting air through it and readying it to make a stronger steel.

Black Codes   Southern state laws passed just after the Civil War to define the limits of Black freedom, restrict African Americans' right to testify in court, and to mete out distinctive punishments for offenses committed. Their passage helped convince Congress that a federal law protecting civil rights was needed.

blockade   A military tactic used in both land and naval warfare by which a location is sealed off to prevent goods or people from entering or leaving.

budget deficit   The failure of tax revenues to pay for annual federal spending on military, welfare, and other programs. The resulting budget deficits forced Washington to borrow money to cover its costs. The growing budget deficits were controversial, in part because the government's borrowing increased both its long-term debt and the amount of money it had to spend each year to pay for the interest on loans.

busing   The controversial court-ordered practice of sending children by bus to public schools outside their neighborhoods in order to promote racial integration in the schools.

Calvinism   Religious doctrine developed by the theologian John Calvin that argued that God alone determines who will receive salvation, and hence, men and women cannot earn their own salvation or even be certain about their final destinies.

capitalism   The system, characterized by private rather than government ownership of production and by the pursuit of profit, that gradually dominated the US economy and politics. Features included individual property rights, the free exchange of labor, and some resistance to both slavery and governmental regulation.

carpetbagger   A derogatory term referring to northern whites who moved to the South after the Civil War and supported the Republican party. Stereotyped as corrupt and unprincipled, carpetbaggers were in fact a diverse group motivated by a variety of interests and beliefs.

Central Intelligence Agency (CIA)   Federal agency created in 1947 to investigate and advise the president on political and military threats to the United States. The CIA's mission expanded in the 1950s to include clandestine activities abroad.

charter colony   Settlement established by a trading company or other group of private entrepreneurs who received from the king a grant of land and the right to govern it. The charter colonies included Virginia, Plymouth, Massachusetts Bay, Rhode Island, and Connecticut.

Chisholm Trail   Named for Jesse Chisholm, a route blazed after the Civil War to move cattle from Texas to railroad termini in Kansas. Also known as the Abilene Trail.

city busting   As late as the 1930s, President Roosevelt and most Americans regarded attacking civilians from the air as an atrocity, but during World War II cities became a primary target for US warplanes. The inaccuracy of bombing, combined with racism and the belief that Japanese and German actions justified retaliation, led American air commanders to follow a policy of systematically destroying urban areas, particularly in Japan.

city-commission plan   A government overseen by appointed officials who ran a city with an eye to economy and efficiency, as though running a business. Designed as an alternative to the political machines of the late nineteenth century.

Columbian Exchange   The exchange of people, plants, animals, culture, and pathogens between the Americas and the rest of the world that began during the time of Columbus.

common schools   A term for public schools in the 19th century. The common school movement wanted to expand Americans' access to public education.

Common Sense   The title of a well-loved pamphlet written by Thomas Paine at a low point in the American Revolutionary War. The phrase alluded to the idea that human beings have certain natural rights that we all instinctively recognize.

commonwealth   A political community founded for the benefit of its members. The Massachusetts Bay Colony, for instance, was a commonwealth. In the twenty-first century, four states, including Massachusetts, called themselves commonwealths.

communism   The system, characterized by government rather than private control of production and by the abolition of profit, that emerged in the nineteenth century in opposition to capitalism.

communitarians   Individuals who supported and/or took up residence in separate communities created to embody improved plans of social, religious, and/or economic life.

commutation   The controversial policy of allowing potential draftees to pay for a replacement to serve in the army. The policy was adopted by both the Union and Confederate governments during the Civil War, and in both cases opposition to commutation was so intense that the policy was abandoned.

Compromise of 1850   A set of measures proposed by Henry Clay and much revised, to settle all the key issues over slavery: its expansion into the West, the admission of a free state of California, the boundary disputes between Texas and New Mexico, and the slave trade in the District of Columbia.

conformity   Complying with social conventions or other people's behavior and ideas.

conscription   The compulsory drafting of men into the army, imposed by both sides during the Civil War.

consent   One of the key principles of liberalism, which held that people could not be subject to laws to which they had not given their consent. This principle is reflected in both the Declaration of Independence and the preamble to the Constitution, which begins with the famous words "We the people of the United States, in order to form a more perfect union."

conservation   The ideology that public land, and resources on that land, should be managed more efficiently. During the early twentieth century, as a result of the work of figures such as Theodore Roosevelt and Gifford Pinchot, the conservation movement led to an expansion of national parks and the regulation of resource usage inside those parks.

conspiracy theory   A belief that history is shaped intentionally by unseen powers. Conspiracy theory lay behind the McCarthy anti-Communism hearings, which assumed that American society and government had been infiltrated by countless Communist spies.

constitutionalism   A loose body of thought that developed in Britain and the colonies and was used by the colonists to justify the Revolution by claiming that it was in accord with the principles of the British Constitution. Constitutionalism had two main elements. One was the rule of law, and the other the principle of consent, that one cannot be subject to laws or taxation except by duly elected representatives. Both were rights that had been won through struggle with the monarch. Constitutionalism also refers to the tendency in American politics, particularly in the early nineteenth century, to transpose all political questions into constitutional ones.

consumer revolution   A slow and steady increase over the course of the eighteenth century in the demand for, and purchase of, consumer goods. The consumer revolution of the eighteenth century was closely related to the Industrial Revolution.

consumerism   An ideology that defined the purchase of goods and services as both an expression of individual identity and essential to the national economy. Increasingly powerful by the 1920s and dominant by the 1950s, consumerism urged people to find happiness in the pursuit of leisure and pleasure more than in the work ethic.

containment   The basic US strategy for fighting the Cold War. As used by diplomat George Kennan in a 1947 magazine essay, containment referred to the combination of diplomatic, economic, and military programs necessary to hold back Soviet expansionism after World War II.

contraband   In its general sense, contraband of war was property seized from an enemy. But early in the Civil War the term was applied to enslaved people running to Union lines as a way of preventing owners from reclaiming them under fugitive slave laws.

cooperationists   Those southerners who opposed immediate secession after the election of Abraham Lincoln in 1860. Cooperationists argued instead that secessionists should wait to see if the new president was willing to cooperate with the South's demands.

Copperhead   A northerner who sympathized with the South during the Civil War.

cost-plus contract   This style of contract provides manufacturers with a guarantee of costs of research and production and a profit. During World War I, to incentivize wartime industry, the United States government offered cost-plus contracts to industries that switched to production of wartime goods.

coverture   A legal principle according to which a married woman's rights and even identity are subsumed under those of her husband.

crop lien   The first right to the proceeds of a harvested crop, given by farmers to their creditors. At the beginning of the growing season, farmers paid on credit for seeds, supplies, and food to get them through the year. They repaid these debts when the crop was sold.

cultural mediator   A figure able to translate one culture to another, literally and figuratively.

deindustrialization   The reverse of industrialization, as factory shutdowns decreased the size of the manufacturing sector. Plant closings began to plague the American economy in the 1970s, prompting fears that the nation would lose its industrial base.

Democratic Republicans   One of the two parties to make up the first American party system. Following the fiscal and political views of Jefferson and Madison, Democratic Republicans generally advocated a weak federal government and opposed federal intervention in the economy of the nation.

deregulation   Term popularized in the 1970s for the repeal of government controls on business, labor, and the environment.

détente   This French term for the relaxation of tensions was used to describe the central foreign policy innovation of the Nixon administration—a new, less confrontational relationship with Communism. In addition to opening a dialogue with the People's Republic of China, Nixon sought a more stable, less confrontational relationship with the Soviet Union.

disfranchisement   The act of depriving a person or group of voting rights. In the nineteenth century the right to vote was popularly known as the franchise. The Fourteenth Amendment of the Constitution affirmed the right of adult male citizens to vote, but state-imposed restrictions and taxes deprived large numbers of Americans—particularly African Americans—of the vote from the 1890s until the passage of the Voting Rights Act of 1965.

domino theory   The idea that the fall of one country to Communism would lead to the fall of others. The theory was one of the chief justifications for US intervention in Vietnam in the 1950s and 1960s.

downsizing   American corporations' layoffs of both blue- and white-collar workers in an attempt to become more efficient and competitive. Downsizing was one of the factors that made Americans uneasy about the economy in the 1990s, despite the impressive surge in the stock market.

draft riots   Uprisings in New York City, Buffalo, and elsewhere in 1863 in protest of conscription.

Dred Scott decision   An 1857 Supreme Court decision that declared the Missouri Compromise or any Congressional ban on slavery in the territories unconstitutional and denied African Americans from becoming citizens of the United States.

Dust Bowl   Across much of the Great Plains, decades of wasteful farming practices combined with several years of drought in the early 1930s to produce a series of massive dust storms that blew the topsoil across hundreds of miles. The area in Texas and Oklahoma affected by these storms became known as the Dust Bowl.

e-commerce   Short for "electronic commerce," this was the term for the internet-based buying and selling that was one of the key hopes for the computer-driven postindustrial economy. The promise of e-commerce was still unfulfilled by the start of the twenty-first century.

Electoral College Created by the US Constitution as the mechanism for choosing the president and vice president. Voters do not cast votes directly for presidential and vice presidential candidates, but instead for slates of electors pledged to support one presidential ticket or another.

emancipation Literally, the act of freeing someone from slavery. Emancipation movements began in the North shortly after the American Revolution.

encomienda A system of labor developed by the Spanish in the New World in which Spanish settlers (*encomenderos*) compelled groups of Native Americans to work for them. The encomendero did not own the Indians who labored for him, but he had the unlimited right to compel a particular group of Indians to work for him. This system was unique to the New World; nothing precisely like it had existed in Europe or elsewhere.

Enlightenment A shift in thinking that occurred in the eighteenth century valuing the natural rights of individuals over traditional hierarchy, and scientific rationalism over faith. The term is much debated today for a number of reasons, among them the fact that men who considered themselves proponents of the Enlightenment often remained slaveholders.

establishment The elite of mainly Ivy League–educated, Anglo-Saxon, Protestant, male, liberal northeasterners that supposedly dominated Wall Street and Washington after World War II. The Establishment's support for corporations, activist government, and containment engendered hostility from opposite poles of the political spectrum—from conservatives and Republicans like Richard Nixon at one end and from the New Left and the movement at the other. Although many of the post–World War II leaders of the United States did tend to share common origins and ideologies, this elite was never as powerful, self-conscious, or unified as its opponents believed.

eugenics The practice of attempting to solve social problems through the control of human reproduction. Drawing on the authority of evolutionary biology, eugenists enjoyed considerable influence in the United States, especially on issues of corrections and public health, from the turn of the century through World War II. Applications of this pseudoscience included the identification of "born" criminals by physical characteristics and "better baby" contests at county fairs.

family values Rallying cry for conservatives and Republicans in the 1990s and after who believed that gay and women's rights, changing family structures, and popular culture were undermining traditional morality.

Farmers' Alliance A group organized in the late nineteenth century to help farmers pool their knowledge and resources. By 1890, it had entered politics, endorsing candidates and building the political connections in the South and West that would lead to the Populist Party.

Federalists One of the two political parties to make up the first American party system. Following the fiscal and political policies proposed by Alexander Hamilton, Federalists generally advocated the importance of a strong federal government, including federal intervention in the economy of the new nation.

feminism An ideology insisting on the fundamental equality of women and men. The feminists of the 1960s differed over how to achieve that equality: while liberal feminists mostly demanded equal rights for women in the workplace and in politics, radical feminists more thoroughly condemned the capitalist system and male oppression and demanded equality in both private and public life.

feudalism A social and political system that developed in Europe in the Middle Ages under which powerful lords offered less powerful noblemen protection in return for their loyalty. Feudalism also included the economic system of manorialism, under which dependent serfs worked on the manors controlled by those lords.

Fifteenth Amendment An 1870 constitutional amendment forbidding discrimination in voting on the basis of race, color, or previous condition of servitude.

fire-eaters Militant southerners who pushed for secession in the 1850s.

flexible response The defense doctrine of the Kennedy and Johnson administrations. Abandoning the Eisenhower administration's heavy emphasis on nuclear weapons, flexible response stressed the buildup of the nation's conventional and special forces so that the president had a range of military options in response to Communist aggression.

Fordism A system of mass production that relied on mass consumption, pioneered by and named for Henry Ford.

Fourteenth Amendment An 1868 constitutional amendment defining national citizenship, mandating equal justice before the law, guaranteeing essential civil rights, redefining the basis on which seats in the House of Representatives would be apportioned, declaring the national debt inviolate, and disqualifying some Confederate leaders from holding office until Congress had removed their disabilities.

Freedmen's Bureau The Bureau of Refugees, Freedmen, and Abandoned Lands, a government agency formed in 1865 and administered by the army, that afforded aid and protection to former enslaved people, among others.

front Early-twentieth-century mechanized wars were fought along a battle line or "front" separating opposing sides. By World War II, tactical innovations—blitzkrieg, parachute troops, gliders, and amphibious landings—complicated warfare by breaking through, disrupting, or bypassing the front. The front thus became a more fluid boundary than the fortified trench lines of World War I. The term also acquired a political meaning, particularly for labor and the left. A coalition of parties supporting (or opposing) an agreed-upon line could be called a "popular front."

Fugitive Slave Act A widely protested 1850 federal law that increased federal powers to capture people accused of being fugitives from slavery, convict them without a jury trial or the right to testify on their own behalf, and return them to their owners, even in free states.

fundamentalism A conservative Christian doctrine that subscribed to the literal truths of the Bible. Uneasy with the changes of the 1920s, Fundamentalists rejected modern culture and instead advocated a dedication to traditional authority and religious beliefs.

Galveston Plan A system of municipal government by appointed commissioners, each with responsibility for a utility or service. After a hurricane devastated Galveston, Texas, in 1900, unelected commissioners temporarily took charge to oversee relief and rebuilding efforts.

gentility A term without precise meaning that represented all that was polite, civilized, refined, and fashionable. It was everything that vulgarity was not. Because the term had no precise meaning, it was always subject to negotiation, striving, and anxiety as Americans, beginning in the eighteenth century, tried to show others that they were genteel through their manners, their appearance, and their styles of life.

glass ceiling The invisible barrier of discrimination that prevented female white-collar workers from rising to top executive positions in corporations.

globalization This term first came into use during the 1980s to describe the web of technological, economic, military, political, and cultural developments binding people and nations ever more tightly together. America had been defined by its relationship to the world for centuries, but the coining of the term *globalization* reflected the emergence of closer international ties.

gold standard The practice by which gold served as backing for all national currency.

Great Awakening A period in which a large proportion of the populace becomes invested in evangelical revivalism. In American history, there have been a number of such periods, but the term is most often applied to the years of the 1730s through 1750s, and the 1820s and 1830s.

Great Society   President Lyndon Johnson's ambitious legislative program embodying the vision of the activist new liberalism of the 1960s. Enacted from 1965 to 1968, the Great Society sought to wipe out poverty, end segregation, and enhance the quality of life for all Americans.

greenbackers   Those who advocated currency inflation by keeping the type of money printed during the Civil War, known as "greenbacks," in circulation.

gridlock   Term for the political traffic jam that began tying up the federal government in the late 1980s and the 1990s. Gridlock developed from the inability of either major party to control both the presidency and Congress for any extended period of time. More fundamentally, gridlock reflected the inability of any party or president to win a popular mandate for a bold legislative program.

habeas corpus   The right to be released from jail unless you are notified of specific charges against you.

Half-Way Covenant   A policy solution developed by Puritan New England congregations in the second half of the seventeenth century which allowed the children and grandchildren of people who had not had a conversion experience to become partial members of the church.

hard war   A term used to describe the Civil War's transformation into a conflict in which cities and civilians, not just armies, became targets as a means of hastening victory.

headright   The system whereby a white male European settler was offered a certain number of acres of land for every family member or servant he brought with him to the New World.

Hog Island   Site of a shipyard near Philadelphia, which was hindered by the failure of railroads to deliver the materials needed for shipbuilding. The fiasco prompted Wilson to nationalize the railroads and then take a more active role in the economy through the creation of the War Industries Board.

Holocaust   Term for the Nazi murder of about six million European Jews during World War II.

Homestead Act   An 1862 law giving 160 acres of public land without cost to heads of households who would agree to settle and cultivate it for five years.

Hoovervilles   Makeshift settlements created on the outskirts of cities by those left homeless as a result of the Great Depression. Named for President Herbert Hoover, who many Americans believed to be indifferent to their suffering.

horizontal integration   Commonly known as "monopoly." An industry became "horizontally integrated" when a single company absorbed other firms and took control of virtually the entire market for a specific product.

Hudson River school   A movement among mid-nineteenth-century landscape painters. These artists were influenced by romanticism and sought inspiration in the idea of the sublime as embodied in America's natural terrain.

Hull House   After visiting Toynbee Hall in London, Jane Addams opened this settlement house in 1889 with the intent of providing aid to the impoverished population of Chicago's Near West Side.

human equality   The idea that all people are born with the same, unalienable rights.

immediatism   The variant antislavery sentiment that demanded immediate (as opposed to gradual) personal and federal action against the institution of slavery. This approach was most closely associated with William Lloyd.

Immigration Act of 1924   A Federal law that established quotas for immigrants from southern and eastern Europe, and prevented immigration from Asia, dramatically limiting immigration numbers from those regions.

imperialism   A process of extending dominion over territories beyond the national boundaries of a state. In the eighteenth century, Britain extended imperial control over North America through settlement, but in the 1890s, imperial influence was generally exercised through indirect rule. Subject peoples generally retained some local autonomy while the imperial power controlled commerce and defense. Few Americans went to the Philippines as settlers, but many passed through as tourists, missionaries, traders, and soldiers.

indentured servants People who promised to work for a term of years (usually between two and seven) in exchange for passage to the New World.

Indian Territory The portion of land "reserved" for forcibly relocated Native Americans. In 1834, Congress designated land west of the Mississippi as Indian Territory but gradually reduced it until Oklahoma statehood in 1907 marked its disappearance.

individualism The social and political philosophy celebrating the central importance of the individual human being in society. Insisting on the rights of the individual in relationship to the group, individualism was one of the intellectual bases of capitalism and democracy. The resurgent individualism of the 1920s, with its emphasis on each American's freedom and fulfillment, was a critical element of the decade's emergent consumerism and Republican dominance.

industrious revolution Beginning in the late seventeenth century in western Europe and extending to the North American colonies in the eighteenth century, a fundamental change in the way people worked, as they worked harder and organized their households to produce goods that could be sold, so they could have money to pay for the new consumer goods they wanted.

influenza A severe respiratory illness, also known as "flu," that caused the deadly global pandemic of 1918-1919.

information economy The postindustrial economy, gradually emerging in the mid- and late twentieth century, in which sophisticated communications, computing, biomedical technology, and services took the place of manufacturing.

initiative, recall, and referendum First proposed by the People's Party's Omaha Platform (1892), along with the direct election of senators and the secret ballot, as measures to subject corporate capitalism to democratic controls. Progressives, chiefly in western and midwestern states, favored them as a check on the power of state officials. The initiative allows legislation to be proposed by petition. The recall allows voters to remove public officials, and the referendum places new laws or constitutional amendments on the ballot for the direct approval of the voters.

interest group An association whose members organize to exert political pressure on officials or the public. Unlike political parties, whose platforms and slates cover nearly every issue and office, an interest group focuses on a narrower list of concerns reflecting the shared outlook of its members. With the decline of popular politics around the turn of the twentieth century, business, religious, agricultural, women's, professional, neighborhood, and reform associations created a new form of political participation.

internationalists Those Americans opposed to isolationism and supportive of greater US involvement around the world, including trade agreements, international law conventions, and military alliances.

internment Imprisonment, without trial, inspired by political justifications. During World War II, the United States government seized the property of, relocated, and imprisoned both Japanese immigrants and natural-born Japanese Americans based on the presumed threat this population posed to the nation.

isolationist Between World War I and World War II, the United States refused to join the League of Nations, scaled back its military commitments abroad, and sought to maintain its independence of action in foreign affairs. These policies were called isolationist, although some historians prefer the term "independent internationalist," in recognition of the United States' continuing global influence. In the late 1930s, isolationists favored policies aimed at distancing the United States from European affairs and building a national defense based on air power and hemispheric security.

Jacksonian democracy   The style of politics associated with President Andrew Jackson, elimination of property requirements for voting on the state level and the promotion of white male equality, generally at the expense of minority populations.

Jim Crow laws   Statutes discriminating against nonwhite Americans, particularly in the South. The term specifically refers to regulations excluding Blacks from public facilities or compelling them to use ones separate from those allotted to whites.

jingoes   In the Gilded Age, those in favor of an aggressive, expansionist American foreign policy, including war with the Spain in 1898.

joint-stock company   A form of business organization that was a forerunner to the modern corporation. The joint-stock company was used to raise both capital and labor for New World ventures. Shareholders contributed either capital or their labor for a period of years.

Jones Mixer   Developed by Captain William R. Jones, a massive machine used for keeping molten iron hot, until it could be used with other ingredients to make steel.

judicial review   The principle of law that recognizes in the judiciary the power to review and rule on the constitutionality of laws. First established in *Marbury v. Madison* (1803) under Chief Justice John Marshall.

junk bonds   A corporation issues bonds in order to raise investment capital in return for a promise to pay regular interest to purchasers. Junk bonds are particularly risky promises of high interest that may never get paid.

Keynesian economics   The theory, named after the English economist John Maynard Keynes, that advocated the use of "countercyclical" fiscal policy. This meant that during good times the government should pay down the debt, so that during bad times, it could afford to stimulate the economy with deficit spending.

King Cotton diplomacy   Confederate efforts to use European dependence on cotton exports to win recognition as an independent nation.

Knights of Labor   The first national federation of trade unions, led by Terence V. Powderly. The Knights grew to its fullest size in the mid-1880s before a steep decline. The federation was based on the premise of a common interest of all producers (for example, farmers and industrial workers), and it supported reform as well as united action by workers.

liberalism   A body of political thought that traces its origins to John Locke and whose chief principles are consent, freedom of conscience, and property. Liberalism held that people could not be governed except by their own consent and that the purpose of government was to protect people as well as their property. Beginning in the late nineteenth century, liberals, including progressives, favored more government activism to protect rights and regulate the economy.

limited war   In the age of total war in the mid-twentieth century, limited war became a useful term to describe armed conflicts such as the Korean, Vietnam, Iraq, and Afghan wars in which a country did not fully mobilize its population, persistently attack civilians, and use its full arsenal, including nuclear weapons.

linked economic development   A form of economic development that ties together a variety of enterprises so that development in one stimulates development in others, for example, those that provide raw materials, parts, or transportation.

Longhorn cattle   Rangy, tough, resourceful cattle found on the southern Great Plains. They were ideal for long cattle drives like those along the Abilene Trail.

loyalists   Those who remained devoted to the British monarchical government during the Revolutionary War.

lyceum movement   A voluntary adult-education movement that swept New England and the mid-Atlantic states in the early and mid-nineteenth century, credited in large part to the efforts of Josiah Holbrook. Lyceum organizations hosted educational lectures in towns and cities. Lecturers included such prominent speakers as Ralph Waldo Emerson, Mark Twain, and Abraham Lincoln.

manifest destiny   A term first coined in 1845 by journalist John O'Sullivan to express the belief, widespread among antebellum Americans, that the United States was destined to expand across the North American continent to the Pacific and had an irrefutable right to the lands absorbed in this expansion. This belief was frequently justified on the grounds of claims to political and racial superiority.

market revolution   The term used to designate the period of the early nineteenth century, roughly 1815–1830, during which internal dependence on cash markets and wages became widespread.

mass production   A system of efficient, high-volume manufacturing based on division of labor into repetitive tasks, simplification, and standardization of parts, increasing use of specialized machinery, and careful supervision. Emerging since the nineteenth century, mass production reached a critical stage of development with Henry Ford's introduction of the moving assembly line at his Highland Park automobile factory. Mass production drove the prosperity of the 1920s and helped make consumerism possible.

massive resistance   The rallying cry of southern segregationists who pledged to oppose the integration of the schools ordered by the Supreme Court in *Brown v. Board of Education* in 1954. The tactics of massive resistance included legislation, demonstrations, and violence.

massive retaliation   The defense doctrine of the Eisenhower administration which promised instant, massive retaliation with nuclear weapons in response to Soviet aggression.

McCarthyism   The hunt for Communist subversion in the United States in the first years of the Cold War. Democrats, in particular, used the term, a reference to the sometimes disreputable tactics of Republican Senator Joseph R. McCarthy of Wisconsin, in order to question the legitimacy of the conservative anti-Communist crusade.

mercantilism   An economic theory developed in early-modern Europe to explain and guide the growth of European nation-states. Its goal was to strengthen the state by making the economy serve its interests. According to the theory of mercantilism, the world's wealth, measured in gold and silver, was fixed; that is, it could never be increased. As a result, each nation's chief economic objective must be to secure as much of the world's wealth as possible. One nation's gain was necessarily another's loss. Colonies played an important part in the theory of mercantilism. Their role was to serve as sources of raw materials and as markets for manufactured goods for the mother country alone.

Mesoamerica   A region encompassing the land from the Rio Grande to Panama. It is often called "the Cradle of the Americas."

middle ground   A place where two or more groups accommodate each others' cultural practices, the middle ground was central to New France, for instance.

millennialism   A strain of Protestant belief that holds that history will end with the thousand-year reign of Christ (the millennium). Some Americans saw the Great Awakening, the French and Indian War, and the Revolution as signs that the millennium was about to begin in America, and this belief infused Revolutionary thought with an element of optimism. Millennialism was also one aspect of a broad drive for social perfection in nineteenth-century America.

minstrel show   Form of popular theatrical entertainment in the nineteenth century, with Black performers or white ones pretending to be Black.

Modern Republicanism   President Dwight Eisenhower's middle-of-the-road legislative program of the 1950s. Reflecting traditional Republican faith in limited government and balanced budgets, Modern Republicanism still left alone such liberal programs as Social Security and farm subsidies.

modernization   The process by which developing countries in the third world were to become more like the United States—that is, capitalist, independent, and anti-Communist. Confidence about the prospects for modernization was one of the cornerstones of liberal foreign policy in the 1960s.

moral suasion   The strategy of using persuasion (as opposed to legal coercion) to convince individuals to alter their behavior. In the antebellum years, moral suasion generally implied an appeal to religious values.

muckrakers   Journalists whose exposes of social ills, economic malfeasance, and political corruption helped make progressivism popular.

Mugwump   Name applied to liberal reformers in the late nineteenth century. Unattached to either major party, Mugwumps would endorse any candidate supportive of civil service reform, a secret ballot, and honest government.

multinationals   Corporations with factories and other operations in several nations that did not necessarily see themselves as citizens of any one country in particular. Originating in the nineteenth century, multinationals became controversial in the 1970s as the deindustrializing United States lost factory jobs to other countries.

mutual aid societies   Organizations through which people of relatively meager means pooled their resources for emergencies. Usually, individuals paid small amounts in dues and were able to borrow large amounts in times of need. In the early nineteenth century, mutual aid societies were especially common among workers in free African American communities.

National Labor Union   The first federation of trade unions, founded in 1866, and the forerunner of the Knights of Labor and the American Federation of Labor.

National Republicanism   Over the first 20 years of the nineteenth century, the Republican Party gradually abandoned its Jeffersonian animosity toward an activist federal government and industrial development and became a strong proponent of both of these positions. Embodied in the American system, these new views were fully captured in the party's designation of itself as National Republicans by 1824.

Nationalist Clubs   Associations formed in the 1880s to further the social planning ideas of Edward Bellamy.

nativism   A bias against anyone not born in the United States and in favor of native-born Americans. This attitude assumes the superior culture and political virtue of white Americans of Anglo-Saxon descent, or of individuals assumed to have that lineage. During the period 1820–1850, Irish immigrants became the particular targets of nativist attitudes.

Navigation Acts   A series of laws passed by the British Parliament in the seventeenth century to govern trade with the colonies so as to maximize profits for the mother country.

neoconservatism   Form of conservative ideology that advocated the aggressive promotion of democracy abroad by the United States in order to make a better and more secure world. Emerging in the 1970s and 1980s, neoconservative ideas influenced the foreign policy of President George W. Bush.

neutrality   A practice by which a nation remains impartial and refuses to support either side in a conflict. The United States responded to each of the world wars with an initial policy of neutrality.

new conservatism   The resurgent conservative ideology of the 1950s and 1960s reiterated the old conservatism's faith in individual freedom and liberal government and added an aggressive, anti-Communist defense policy.

New Deal   Name for government programs created during Franklin D. Roosevelt's administration intended to end the Great Depression. Shifting in focus across the Depression-era years, the New Deal aimed, at varying times, to regulate, reform, and stimulate the American economy.

New Era   A term, like "the Roaring Twenties," used to describe the social, political, and economic changes of the decade, many of which celebrated the individual.

New Federalism   Conservative policy of President Richard Nixon intended to limit the federal government by returning revenue and control to state and local government.

New France   Term for the French colonies in the New World. An area encompassing trading outposts in Canada, the American Midwest, and Louisiana, New France ceased to exist with the signing of the Treaty of Paris in 1763.

New Left   The radical student movement that emerged in opposition to the new liberalism in the 1960s. The New Left condemned the Cold War and corporate power and called for the creation of a true "participatory democracy" in the United States. Placing its faith in the radical potential of young, middle-class students, the New Left differed from the "old left" of the late nineteenth and early twentieth centuries, which believed workers would lead the way to socialism.

New Negro   A term used to describe African Americans, many of whom had left the rural South during the first decades of the twentieth century, who challenged racial inequality and expressed racial pride.

New Netherland   Term for the Dutch colony in the New World, located in the Hudson River Valley area, until conquest by the British in 1664.

New Right   The conservative movement that swept Ronald Reagan into power in 1980 and sustained his presidency. The New Right was much like the new conservatism of the 1950s and 1960s, but with greater emphasis on social issues such as abortion.

New South   The hope of elite white Southerners that the states of the former Confederacy would attract northern investment, increase industrial production, diversify agriculture, and generally modernize.

New Woman   A term used to describe women of the late nineteenth century who advocated on behalf of their rights to equal educational, economic, and political opportunities. In the 1920s, this figure became increasingly linked to sexual liberation and the culture of fun.

New World Order   With the end of the Cold War, President George H. W. Bush called for the United States to help ensure a world dominated by democracy, free trade, and peace.

nongovernmental organizations (NGOs)   Private, nongovernmental, noncommercial organizations. NGOs such as Greenpeace, the International Red Cross, and the World Economic Forum played key roles in globalization in the late twentieth and early twenty-first centuries.

NSC-68   A secret document issued by President Truman's National Security Council in 1950 that detailed US military strategy, including the development of thermonuclear weapons, to counter the Soviet Union.

nullification   The theory that a state could overturn federal law, which South Carolinians invoked to defy the US "tariff of abominations" beginning in 1828 and set off the nullification crisis.

Omaha Platform   The Populist Party's program endorsed at the party's national convention in Omaha in 1892. Among its planks were government ownership of railroads and telegraph lines, the direct election of senators, a subtreasury system, and an expansion of the money supply.

Open Door   The turn-of-the-twentieth-century American ideal for China, in which the country remained open to international trade. This model would allow the United States to expand its global economic reach without the responsibilities of maintaining an empire.

Oregon or Overland Trail   The route from the Missouri River west to Oregon and California, begun in the early 1840s and eventually replaced by railroads after the Civil War.

Ostend Manifesto   An 1854 declaration justifying the United States' need to buy Cuba, indicating a readiness to take it by force if Spain would not agree to sell it.

Pacifist   Term for someone who opposes war.

Panama Canal   The waterway, constructed between 1903 and 1914, that cuts through Central America and serves as a means of connecting the Atlantic and Pacific Oceans.

participatory democracy Believing that the American political system did not heed the will of the people in the 1960s, Students for a Democratic Society called for a more truly participatory democratic politics that would empower ordinary Americans.

partisanship The strong belief in a particular ideology, often that of a political party.

patent (for land) An early form of land title, through which people could assert their ownership of land.

patriotism Love of country. Ways of declaring and displaying national devotion underwent a change from the nineteenth to the twentieth centuries. Whereas politicians were once unblushingly called patriotic, after World War I the title was appropriated to describe the sacrifices of war veterans. Patriotic spectacle in the form of public oration and electoral rallies gave way to military-style commemorations of Armistice Day and the nation's martial heritage.

patronage Term for the granting of governmental jobs to supporters of a winning candidate. The opposite of a merit-based system, such as that created by the Pendleton Act. *See* spoils system.

Peace Corps Created by John F. Kennedy in 1961, the Peace Corps sent young Americans abroad to promote literacy, public health, and agriculture.

Pendleton Civil Service Act 1883 legislation that set up a merit system for hiring and promoting federal workers, and protecting them from forced political contributions. Covering only a small fraction of all government employees at first, its range expanded with each presidency.

perfectionism The idea, associated with the Second Great Awakening, that people could first perfect themselves and then turn their efforts towards perfecting the world around them on the principles of Protestant Christianity.

political action committee (PAC) Dating to the 1940s, organizations, not part of political parties, that have had greater and lesser freedom from the federal government to accept and spend unlimited donations on issues and candidates.

political economy Traditionally, the study of the connections between economics and politics. In this text, political economy refers to the relationships among the economy, politics, and the daily lives of ordinary people. Use of the term underscores the importance of the economy in shaping American life and the importance of politics in shaping the economy. However, the economy and politics did not simply shape, but were in turn shaped by, the lives and cultural values of ordinary men and women.

political machine An organization controlling a party, usually dominated by a "boss" and held together by loyalty and the distribution of rewards to those who had done the organization service.

popular sovereignty A solution to the slavery controversy espoused by leading northern Democrats in the 1850s. It held that the inhabitants of western territories should be free to decide for themselves whether or not they wanted to have slavery. In principle, popular sovereignty would prevent Congress from either enforcing or restricting slavery's expansion into the western territories.

populism The ideology of the People's (Populist) party in the 1890s, opposing the eastern economic elites and favoring government action to help producers in general and farmers in particular.

postindustrial economy The service- and computer-based economy that was succeeding the industrial economy at the end of the twentieth century.

privateering Piratical ventures authorized by a European government. A colonizing power might provide financial backing to captains who used their ships to attack the galleons or New World settlements belonging to a different colonial power.

producers ideology The belief that all those who lived by producing goods shared a common political identity in opposition to those who lived off financial speculation, rent, or interest.

progressivism   Liberal ideology of late-nineteenth and early-twentieth-century mostly middle-class reformers who wanted to use politics, government, and private initiative to remake industrializing, diverse America in their own image. *See* liberalism.

propaganda   Information used to promote a particular cause or point of view. During the twentieth century, the United States' government attempted to persuade the American people to support various national efforts via text, image, radio, and film.

proprietary colony   Colony established by a royal grant to an individual or family. The proprietary colonies included Maryland, New York, New Jersey, Pennsylvania, and the Carolinas.

public opinion   Not quite democracy or consent, public opinion was a way of understanding the influence of the citizenry on political calculations. It emerged in the eighteenth century, when it was defined as a crucial source of a government's legitimacy. It was associated with the emergence of a press and a literate public free to discuss, and to question, government policy. In the twentieth century, Freudian psychology and the new mass media encouraged a view of the public as both fickle and powerful. Whereas the popular will (a nineteenth-century concept) was steady and rooted in national traditions, public opinion was variable and based on attitudes that could be aroused or manipulated by advertising.

Pueblos   Term for the indigenous group that inhabited New Mexico, the Pueblos were harshly treated by the Spanish and rebelled in in 1680.

Reagan Doctrine   Rejecting the Carter administration's emphasis on promoting human rights around the world in the 1970s, President Ronald Reagan contended in the 1980s that the United States should support authoritarian, antidemocratic regimes friendly to the United States.

Reaganomics   *See* supply-side economics.

Reconquista   Literally "reconquest." Between the eleventh and the fifteenth centuries, Christian nobles in Spain and Portugal fought to eject Muslim conquerors who had come from North Africa in the seventh and eighth centuries. In 1492, Ferdinand and Isabel defeated the last remaining Muslim ruler.

reconversion   The economic and social transition from the war effort to peacetime. Americans feared that reconversion might bring a return to the depression conditions of the 1930s.

Red Scare   The fear of a communist takeover of the United States following the Bolshevik Revolution of 1917. After World War I, the American government attempted to limit radicalism by suppressing the voices of communists, socialists, anarchists, and organized labor.

Redemption   A term used by southern Democrats for the undoing of Radical Reconstruction and the replacement of biracial regimes with conservative, white-dominated ones.

redemptioners   People who sold themselves into indentured servitude. At the end of the voyage to America, they were to be "redeemed" by those who paid the cost of their passage.

Religious Right   Conservative political movement by evangelical Protestants against abortion and for the Republican Party prominent in the 1980s and after.

Republic   A state in which the people, through their elected representatives, hold power. Distinguished in the Federalist Papers from a democracy, which, James Madison argued, would allow factions to gain too much power. In a republic, the people's representatives would guard against factional subversion.

republicanism   A set of doctrines rooted in classical antiquity that held that power is always grasping and dangerous and presents a threat to liberty. Republicanism supplied constitutionalism with a motive by explaining how a balanced constitution could be transformed into a tyranny as grasping men used their power to encroach on the liberty of citizens. In addition, republicanism held that people achieved fulfillment only through participation in public life, as citizens in a republic. Republicanism required the individual to display virtue by sacrificing his (or her) private interest for the good of the republic.

Requerimiento **(the Requirement)**   The statement of the Spanish Crown in 1513 declaring a legal basis for the enslavement of hostile Indians. Each conquistador was required to read a copy of the *Requerimiento* to each group of Indians he encountered. The *Requerimiento* promised friendship to all Indians who accepted Christianity, but threatened war and enslavement for all those who resisted.

reservations   Lands that the federal government reserved for Native American tribes as their homelands, either through limiting the domain that a tribe had claimed originally or through forcible relocation from the place where it already lived.

revivals   Large gatherings of people who come to hear evangelical preachers. Many experience their own Christian conversion and testify before the multitude.

royal colony   A colony owned and managed by the Crown (as opposed to a proprietary colony owned and managed by individual investors).

Rustbelt   Term for the deindustrializing states of Northeast and Midwest that lost jobs, population, and political clout during the 1970s.

safety-valve theory   An argument commonly made in the nineteenth century that the abundance of western land spared the United States from the social upheavals common to capitalist societies in Europe. In theory, as long as eastern workers had the option of migrating west and becoming independent farmers, they could not be subject to European levels of exploitation. Thus, the West was said to provide a "safety valve" against the pressures caused by capitalist development.

scabs   A derogatory term for those hired to take striking workers' places.

scalawag   A derogatory term referring to southern whites who supported the Republican party during Reconstruction.

scientific management   *See* Taylorism.

secession   A state's act in dissolving its allegiance to the United States government, as 11 southern states did in 1860 and 1861. The question of its legality formed the essential issue of the Civil War.

separate but equal   In 1896, *Plessy v. Ferguson* declared segregation was constitutional as long as the different accommodations provided for Blacks and whites were equivalent. The doctrine of "separate but equal" would allow legalized segregation throughout the South until the Supreme Court overturned the edict in 1954 with *Brown v. Board of Education*.

separation of powers   One of the chief innovations of the Constitution and a distinguishing mark of the American form of democracy, in which the executive, legislative, and judicial branches of government are separated so that they can check and balance each other.

sharecropping   The practice of a tenant farming the landlord's ground for a share of the crop, sold when the harvest came in. This became a common form of employment for former enslaved people in the post–Civil War South.

Sherman Anti-Trust Act   An 1890 federal law forbidding business combinations in restraint of trade, which gave the US government power to break up monopolies.

sit-in   An important tactic of grassroots, nonviolent civil disobedience, a sit-in is the occupation of a public place in order to protest and to demand change. The 1960 sit-in by the A&T Four to protest segregation at the Woolworth's lunch counter in Greensboro, North Carolina, popularized the tactic, which spread to the African American freedom struggle and inspired other protest movements for decades to come.

slave power   In the 1850s, northern Republicans explained the continued economic and political strength of slavery by claiming that a "slave power" had taken control of the federal government and used its authority to keep slavery alive artificially.

slave society A society in which slavery is central to the economy and political structure, in contrast to a society with slaves, in which the presence of enslaved people does not alter the fundamental structures of the society.

slavery A system of extreme social inequality distinguished by the definition of a human being as property, or chattel, and thus, in principle, totally subordinated to the slave owner.

Social Darwinism Darwin's theory of natural selection transferred from biological evolution to human history. Social Darwinists argued that some individuals and groups, particularly racial groups, were better able to survive in the "race of life."

Social Security Social insurance plan established in 1935 that required contributions from both employers and employees. The original legislation, though limited, provided Americans with workers' compensation, unemployment insurance, family aid, and old-age pensions.

spoils system The practice of politicians giving offices and contracts on the basis of friendship and loyalty rather than merit.

stagflation The unusual combination of stagnant growth and high inflation that plagued the American economy in the 1970s.

strict constructionism The view that the Constitution has a fixed, explicit meaning which can be altered only through formal amendment. Loose constructionism is the view that the Constitution is a broad framework within which various interpretations and applications are possible without formal amendment.

subtreasury A government-run bank in which farmers could get low-interest loans using their crops as collateral. The creation of subtreasuries formed a key plank in the Populist platform.

suburbanization The spread of suburban housing developments and communities and, more broadly, of the suburban ideal.

suffrage The right to vote in political elections. Women advocated for the right to vote from the mid-nineteenth century on and eventually secured the franchise via the Nineteenth Amendment in 1920.

supply-side economics The controversial theory, associated with economist Arthur Laffer, that drove Reaganomics, the conservative economic policy of the Reagan administration. In contrast to liberal economic theory, supply-side economics emphasized that producers—the "supply side" of the economic equation—drove economic growth, rather than consumers—the "demand side." To encourage producers to invest more in new production, Laffer and other supply-siders called for massive tax cuts.

Tammany Hall A fraternal organization in New York City that developed into a Democratic political machine, electing officials, mobilizing voters, and allotting contracts. Its enemies saw it as a symbol of corrupt, selfish, and incompetent government.

tariff A tax on goods moving across an international boundary. Because the Constitution allows tariffs only on imports, as a political issue the tariff question has chiefly concerned the protection of domestic manufacturing from foreign competition. Industries producing mainly for American consumers have preferred a higher tariff, while farmers and industries aimed at global markets have typically favored reduced tariffs. Prior to the Civil War, the tariff was a symbol of diverging political economies in North and South. The North advocated high tariffs to protect growing domestic manufacturing ("protective tariffs"), and the South opposed high tariffs on the grounds that they increased the cost of imported manufactured goods.

Taylorism A method for maximizing industrial efficiency by systematically reducing the time and motion involved in each step of the production process. The "scientific" system was designed by Frederick Taylor and explained in his book *The Principles of Scientific Management* (1911).

temperance   Moderation, or the use of something with restraint. In the Gilded Age, the temperance movement opposed the use of alcohol.

Ten Percent Plan   Abraham Lincoln's 1863 proposal for reconstructing former Confederate states, based on the creation of governments after 10 percent of the eligible voters had taken an oath of loyalty to the United States.

tenement   A multiapartment building in major cities, generally inhabited by the poor, often under the most squalid conditions.

Tennessee Valley Authority (TVA)   New Deal program that attempted to modernize the rural area along the Tennessee River via environmental control, the introduction of electricity, and the establishment of modern manufacturing.

Tenure of Office Act   Passed by Congress in 1867, the act forbade a president from removing any officer that he had appointed, without the consent of the Senate. Its violation became the central charge in Andrew Johnson's impeachment proceedings.

totalitarianism   An anti-democratic philosophy justifying citizens' submission to dictatorial government.

total war   Armed conflict that involves the complete mobilization of a nation's resources and population and that targets civilians as well as soldiers. A comparatively modern development, total war began in the United States with the Civil War, expanded in World War I with the introduction of bombers, submarines, and poison gas, and grew again in World War II with the strategic bombing of cities, the Holocaust, and the dropping of the first atomic bombs.

trusts   Corporate arrangements to unify action in production and distribution among different firms. Shareholders handed over control of their stock to a board that held the shares in trust and operated the combined concerns.

universalism   Enlightenment belief that all people are by their nature essentially the same.

vertical integration   The practice of taking control of every aspect of the production, distribution, and sale of a commodity. For example, Andrew Carnegie vertically integrated his steel operations by purchasing the mines that produced the ore, the railroads that carried the ore to the steel mills, the mills themselves, and the distribution system that carried the finished steel to consumers.

Victorian era   Literally, the reign of Queen Victoria's over the British empire, from 1837 to 1901. Applied to the United States, the term of dismissively signifies a dominant culture of public propriety, self-control, and starkly different gender roles.

virtual representation   British doctrine that said that all Britons, even those who did not vote, were represented by Parliament, if not "actually," by representatives they had chosen, then "virtually," because each member of parliament was supposed to act on behalf of the entire realm, not only his constituents or even those who had voted for him.

voluntarism   A style of political activism that took place largely outside of electoral politics. Voluntarism emerged in the nineteenth century, particularly among those Americans who were not allowed to vote. Thus, women formed voluntary associations that pressed for social and political reforms, even though women were excluded from electoral politics.

Wagner Act   1935 legislation that guaranteed workers' rights to bargain collectively with their employers, prohibited the firing of workers after a strike, and restricted other antiunion measures.

Waltham system   Named after the system used in early textile mills in Waltham, Massachusetts, the term refers to the practice of bringing all elements of production together in a single factory setting with the application of non-human-powered machinery.

wampum   Shell beads used by Indians of the Eastern Woodlands as jewelry, currency, and memorials of political agreements; later produced as currency in the trade networks established between Europeans and Indians.

War on Poverty   Declared by President Johnson in 1964, the war on poverty became the catch-all term for the Economic Opportunity Act of 1964 and the antipoverty legislation of the Democrats' Great Society.

Watergate   The name of the Washington, DC office and condominium complex where five men with ties to the presidential campaign of Richard Nixon were caught breaking into the headquarters of the Democratic National Committee in June 1972. "Watergate" became the catch-all term for the wide range of illegal practices of Nixon and his followers that were uncovered in the aftermath of the break-in.

The Wealth of Nations   The title of the most famous work of the renowned economist and philosopher, Adam Smith. Today the phrase is often used as shorthand for the core principles of classical economics.

Western Front   The main theater of action during World War I, traveling through France from the North Sea coast of Belgium to the Swiss border. Stretching approximately 440 miles, much of the front was comprised of an intricate system of trenches.

Whig Party   The political party founded by Henry Clay in the mid-1830s. The name derived from the seventeenth- and eighteenth-century British antimonarchical position and was intended to suggest that the Jacksonian Democrats (and Jackson in particular) sought despotic powers. In many ways the heirs of National Republicans, the Whigs supported economic expansion, but they also believed in a strong federal government to control the dynamism of the market. The Whig Party attracted many moral reformers.

Wilmot Proviso   An amendment to a military appropriations bill proposed in 1846 to keep slavery out of all territories taken in the Mexican War. Although it never passed, it excited four years of bitter sectional controversy.

Women's Christian Temperance Union (WCTU)   Women's reform organization founded in 1873 to discourage drinking and close down saloons, if possible, by prohibition of the sale or manufacture of alcohol.

women's rights movement   The antebellum organizing efforts of women on their own behalf, in the attempt to secure a broad range of social, civic, and political rights. This movement is generally dated from the convention of Seneca Falls in 1848. Only after the Civil War would women's rights activism begin to confine its efforts to suffrage.

Women's suffrage   *See* suffrage.

Photo Credits

California Historical Society); ageFotostock; The Granger Collection; Courtesy of the Library of Congress; Courtesy of the Library of Congress; Courtesy of the Library of Congress.

Chapter 17: Bettmann/Getty Images; Nebraska State Historical Society; Puck. New York: Puck Publishing Co., 18771918; The Granger Collection; Bettmann/Getty Images; Image provided by GreatCaricatures.com © 2021; Courtesy of the Ohio History Connection; Art Resource, NY; Kansas State Historical Society; Jacob Riis (1849-1914).

Chapter 18: Courtesy of the Library of Congress; The Granger Collection; North Wind Picture Archives/Alamy Stock Photo; The Granger Collection; Courtesy of the Library of Congress; North Wind Picture Archives/Alamy Stock Photo; Courtesy of the Library of Congress.

Chapter 19: The Granger Collection; Tropical Press Agency/Getty Images; The Kheel Center at Cornell University; Courtesy of the Library of Congress; The University of Chicago Library, Special Collections Research Center, Photographic Archive apf1-08624; The Granger Collection; Chicago History Museum 139070_6f; Courtesy of the Library of Congress; Courtesy of the Library of Congress; Courtesy of the Library of Congress; Courtesy of the Library of Congress.

Chapter 20: "Emergency hospital in the midst of the influenza epidemic, Camp Funston, Kansas, circa 1918," (NCP 1603). OHA 250 New Contributed Photographs. Otis Historical Archives, National Museum of Health and Medicine; Courtesy of the Library of Congress; Courtesy of the Library of Congress; Credit: Courtesy of the Pennsylvania State Archives; The Art Archive/Art Resource; Wikimedia Commons; "Emergency hospital in the midst of the influenza epidemic, Camp Funston, Kansas, circa 1918," (NCP 1603). OHA 250 New Contributed Photographs. Otis Historical Archives, National Museum of Health and Medicine; Photo by NY Daily News Archive via Getty Images.

Chapter 21: Smith Collection/Gado/Getty Images; Courtesy of the Library of Congress; Hulton Archive/Getty Images; Pictorial Press Ltd/Alamy Stock Photo; Photo by Oklahoma Historical Society/Getty Images; Smith Collection/Gado/Getty Images; Duke University Libraries Ad Access, BH0714 Ann Elsner in honor of Allan Todd Sagraves.

Chapter 22: MPI/Stringer/Getty Images; Courtesy of the Library of Congress; Three Lions/Getty Images; Bettmann/Getty Images; MPI/Stringer/Getty Images; AP Photo; Bettman/Getty Images; Courtesy of the Library of Congress; Courtesy of the Library of Congress; Courtesy of the Library of Congress.

Chapter 23: HWRD Photo 136, University Archives & Manuscripts Department, University of Hawaii at Manoa Library; Getty Images; Bettmann/Getty Images; HWRD Photo 136, University Archives & Manuscripts Department, University of Hawaii at Manoa Library; Courtesy National Park Service Museum Management Program and Tuskegee Airmen National Historic Site, TUA131; Getty Images; Bettmann/Getty Images; Bettmann/Getty Images.

Chapter 24: Alamy Stock Photo; Courtesy Turchinetz family; British Cartoon Archive, University of Kent ILW1059; Photo by Galerie Bilderwelt/Getty Images; Bettmann/Getty Images; AP Photo/File; Alamy Stock Photo.

Chapter 25: Guy Gillette/Getty Images; CBS Photo Archive/Getty Images; AP Photos; Guy Gillette/Getty Images; Bettmann/Getty Images; Bettmann; AP Photos; Duke University Libraries Ad Access, T032 Ann Elsner in honor of Allan Todd Sagraves; Photo by Allan Grant/The LIFE Picture Collection via Getty Images; Photo by Grey Villet/The LIFE Picture Collection/Getty Images; A 1957 Herblock Cartoon, © The Herb Block Foundation; Dmitri Kessel/Getty Images.

Chapter 26: AP Photo/Robert W. Klein; GRANGER/GRANGER – All rights reserved; NASA Image and Video Library; Bob Adelman Archive; British Cartoon Archive, University of Kent ILW3584; AP Photo/Robert W. Klein; Bettmann/Getty Images.

Chapter 27: Bettmann/Getty Images; AP Photo/File; Bettmann/Getty Images; Allan Tannenbaum/Getty Images; Bettmann/Getty Images; Fred Ward; U.S. National Archives and Records Administration; Bettmann/Getty Images.

Chapter 28: Bettmann/Getty Images; Linda Chavez; Bettmann/Getty Images; Diana Walker/Getty Images; Bettmann/Getty Images; Getty Images; AP Photo/James A. Finley; AP Photo/Lionel Cironneau.

Figures, maps, and tables are indicated by f, m, and t following the page number. Illustrations and photos are indicated by italic page numbers; (d) and (v) refer to primary source documents and visual materials.

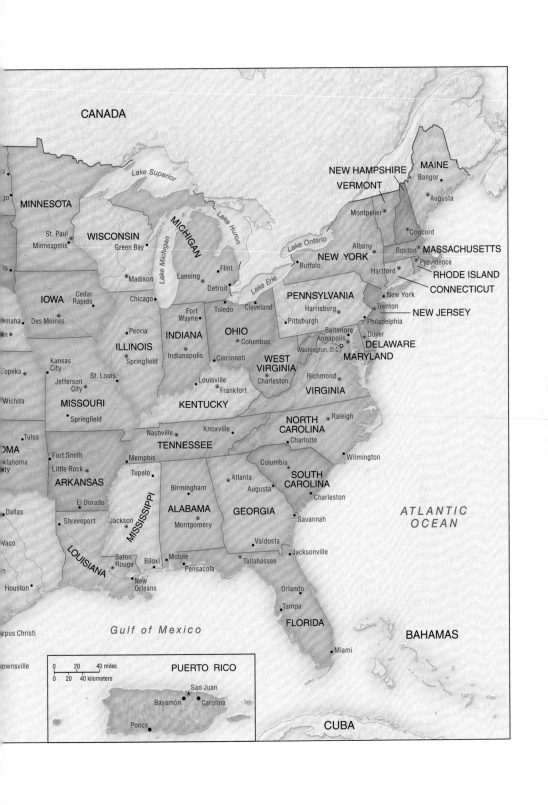

CANADA

MINNESOTA

St. Paul
Minneapolis

WISCONSIN

Green Bay

Madison

Lake Superior

MICHIGAN

Lake Michigan

Lake Huron

IOWA

Cedar
Rapids

Des Moines

Peoria

Chicago

Lansing

Flint

Detroit

Lake Erie

ILLINOIS

INDIANA

Fort
Wayne

OHIO

Toledo

Cleveland

Springfield

Indianapolis

Columbus

Cincinnati

Kansas
City

Jefferson
City

St. Louis

Topeka

Wichita

MISSOURI

Springfield

Louisville

Frankfort

Tulsa

Fort Smith

Oklahoma
City

Little Rock

OMA

Nashville

Memphis

Tupelo

KENTUCKY

Knoxville

TENNESSEE

WEST
VIRGINIA

Charleston

VIRGINIA

Richmond

NORTH
CAROLINA

Raleigh

Charlotte

Columbia

Wilmington

Dallas

Waco

ARKANSAS

El Dorado

Shreveport

Birmingham

Atlanta

SOUTH
CAROLINA

Augusta

Charleston

Jackson

MISSISSIPPI

ALABAMA

Montgomery

GEORGIA

Savannah

LOUISIANA

Baton
Rouge

Biloxi

Mobile

Pensacola

Valdosta

Tallahassee

Jacksonville

Houston

New
Orleans

Corpus Christi

Brownsville

Gulf of Mexico

Orlando

Tampa

FLORIDA

Miami

NEW HAMPSHIRE

VERMONT

Montpelier

MAINE

Bangor

Augusta

Concord

Albany

Boston

MASSACHUSETTS

Providence

RHODE ISLAND

CONNECTICUT

Lake Ontario

NEW YORK

Buffalo

Hartford

New York

PENNSYLVANIA

Harrisburg

Pittsburgh

Trenton

NEW JERSEY

Philadelphia

Baltimore

Dover

Annapolis

Washington, D.C.

MARYLAND

DELAWARE

ATLANTIC
OCEAN

BAHAMAS

0   20   40 miles

0   20   40 kilometers

PUERTO RICO

San Juan

Bayamón

Carolina

Ponce

CUBA

ARCTIC OCEAN

Beaufort
Sea

Baffin
Bay

Greenland
(DENMARK)

Greenland
Sea

Davis Strait

ICELAND

NORW

Bering Sea

Gulf of
Alaska

Hudson
Bay

CANADA

Labrador
Sea

IRELAND

UNITED
KINGDOM

NETH
GER

DENM

BELGIUM
LUX
FRANCE
SWITZ

NORTH PACIFIC
OCEAN

30°N

UNITED STATES

NORTH ATLANTIC
OCEAN

PORTUGAL

SPAIN

MOROCCO

MEXICO

Gulf of
Mexico

BAHAMAS

CUBA

JAMAICA

HAITI

DOMINICAN
REPUBLIC

ANTIGUA & BARBUDA

WESTERN
SAHARA
(Morocco)

ALGERIA

MAURITANIA

MALI

NIG

BELIZE

HONDURAS

ST. KITTS & NEVIS

DOMINICA

ST. LUCIA

CAPE VERDE

SENEGAL

GUATEMALA

Caribbean
Sea

ST. VINCENT &
THE GRENADINES

BARBADOS

GAMBIA

BURKINA
FASO

NIGE

EL SALVADOR

NICARAGUA

GRENADA

TRINIDAD AND TOBAGO

GUINEA BISSAU

GUINEA

BENIN

COSTA RICA

VENEZUELA

GUYANA

SIERRA LEONE

IVORY
COAST

GHANA

PANAMA

SURINAME

LIBERIA

TOGO

COLOMBIA

FRENCH GUIANA (Fr.)

EQUATORIAL
GUINEA

0° Equator

ECUADOR

Gulf of
Guinea

SAO TOME
& PRINCIPE

PERU

BRAZIL

BOLIVIA

PARAGUAY

SOUTH ATLANTIC
OCEAN

30°S

URUGUAY

SOUTH PACIFIC
OCEAN

CHILE

ARGENTINA

60°S

Weddell
Sea

ANTARC

"Mummy, one doesn't just go up to a man, especially a horrible, obstinate, hate-filled man like that, snap her fingers and make him fall in love."

"You've always been a determined flirt, Diana. For heaven's sake, put it to good use for once!"

Diana burst into tears, turned and ran from the room.

"The girl is being an utter fool! Does she not see what will happen to us if she does not do this? She must marry the new earl."

Cal's arrival—and the fear of what he would do—had changed Lady Worthington completely. Julia had never seen her behave cruelly with her daughters. "Diana is just as afraid as you are," Julia said softly. Probably more, she thought. "Please don't be harsh with her."

"I must be harsh, or we're ruined. I suppose she is balking at her duty. She is behaving like a foolish modern girl who wants to marry for love. I suppose she has fallen in love with someone unsuitable, just to spite me."

"How—?"

"Aha! I thought as much." The countess fixed Julia with a penetrating gaze. Julia was astounded at the rapid change in the woman—she had been on the verge of collapse, now she was sharp and angry. This must be what sheer fear did to a person. And it appeared Cal hadn't told her of his plan. Lady Worthington did not know the worst of what Cal wanted to do.

"Who is she in love with?" the countess demanded.

Julia swallowed hard. She believed in honesty but she had to lie for Diana. "You are wrong. She is willing to marry him. For all your sakes."

"Do not sound so disapproving with me, Lady Julia Hazelton. I will protect my family at any cost. Remember that."

"But Cal is in pain, as well," Julia said. "I do not approve

4

Modern Art

Julia knew of one thing that could make a woman forget about marriage and love and all its associated problems.

Well, two things.

She left the house, walking briskly to Brideswell's garage. She had money thanks to Zoe. And a list of women whose lives she was about to change.

That was the first thing that was more important than suitors and marriage.

The second?

Her beloved automobile—a brand-new roadster from America with glossy paint and shiny chrome, leather seats, leather-wrapped steering wheel and an engine that roared with power.

She was driving past the house, toward the front gate, when a young footman ran out and stopped her.

Over the rumble of the idling engine, he shouted, "Lady Diana at Worthington Park asked if you might drive over there right away. She says they are in the midst of a disaster and only you can help, milady."

Julia's heart plunged. The new Earl of Worthington—Cal—must have told them his plans. "Thank you, George." She put her motor into gear and pressed on the accelerator. Trixie, her motorcar, roared down the gravel drive and through the open main gates.

When Julia arrived, Diana met her on the drive. "Goodness, you look pale," Julia gasped. "Are you ill? Is this about Cal's—?"

"Not here." Diana dragged her to the music room. Sunlight flooded in on the grand piano, the harp, the cluster of gilt-and-silk chairs. A maid came in with a tray of coffee and before Julia could ask her question, the countess burst in. Her plucked brows flew up in surprise. "Why are you here, Julia—?"

"To see me, Mother," Diana said. "I asked her to come, since you are so upset. Julia will know what to do."

"Yes, I suppose Julia will." Lady Worthington sank into a chair. "Mrs. Feathers has quit! That man went down to the kitchens and questioned everything she did. Even suggested the servants should eat better and there should be less waste in the dining room. Apparently he cast some aspersion on her character—she believed he accused her of theft. She is packing her bags as we speak. He has done this deliberately to spite us, for where can one find a cook at short notice? He fired his valet, a hall boy and a footman this morning and he has driven away our cook."

Julia stared, dumbfounded. Heavens, Cal had already begun.

"This is wretched," she said. "How can he fire the staff when work is so hard to find?"

"Servants are hard to find," Lady Worthington said, holding out her hand gracefully for coffee.

Julia poured and gave the countess a cup, then handed

one to Diana, who looked everywhere but at her mother and tapped her foot anxiously.

"The earl declared they should find real work and 'do better,'" the countess cried. "Do better than work at Worthington Park? Preposterous!"

Cal simply didn't understand. Many of the servants didn't want to "do better," which often meant long hours in gruesome conditions in factories and offices. They took pride in their work running a great house.

The countess tried to set down her cup, but her hand shook so badly the cup overturned, spilling coffee. "Blast!" the countess gasped. Then she began to sob, burying her face in her hands. Diana stared helplessly, in shock.

Julia quickly put her arm across the countess's shoulders. "I will see about this, I promise. I will stop him."

"Stop him?" The countess lifted her head from her hands. She had turned a terrible shade of light gray and looked deathly ill. "What do you mean?"

Julia swallowed hard. "Did Cal tell you he intended to do this? Did he speak of any plans he has, now that he is the earl?"

"I do not care what he wants—" Lady Worthington broke off, putting her hands to her mouth. Through them, she cried, "I wish we could be rid of him! But we can't." She turned to Diana. "The only way I can see that we might have some protection is to have influence over him. As his wife, you would exert some control. Go and find him."

"Go and find him and do what with him?" Diana protested.

Lady Worthington had been on the verge of collapse. Now she became commanding and strong once more. "We are desperate, Diana. Go at once and make him fall in love with you. It is the only hope we have."

of what he is doing, but it comes from a place of great hurt. Was there a horrible thing that was done to him? If I knew what it was, I could—"

"It is none of your business!" The countess's voice crackled like ice. "Now go. Please."

"I will. I will go to see Cal and try to put a stop to this."

She must do so—just as she had promised Anthony she would look after his family. He couldn't have known such a disaster would strike, and it now seemed so sad and eerie that he had begged her so passionately to take care of them all.

She marched out of the room, but as she reached the hallway, she heard the countess erupt into violent sobs. Julia hesitated. Did the countess need her?

She paused just outside the door, her hand on the door frame.

"I will lose everything," the countess gasped, through choking sobs. "John, you wretched fool. I would have protected you. You didn't have to take your own life."

Julia was stunned. Lady Worthington had lost her eldest son, Anthony, at the Somme. And her youngest son, John, in a motorcar accident. But surely, John's accident had not been deliberate? It had been a foggy night. It was assumed John had taken a wrong turn—the gate to the lane leading to the quarry had been left open. In the poor light, he must have mistakenly gone that way, expecting the gate to be closed, as it usually was. He had gone over the edge—

Julia knew she should not go in now. The countess would be appalled to think her words had been overheard. But if she had kept such a painful secret for years—one Julia wasn't sure how the countess could know—she had suffered greatly in silence. Julia wished to help.

She paused a moment, hoping to cover her eavesdropping, and knocked lightly on the door. Stepping back into the room, she saw Lady Worthington set down her cup. With a frightening calm, the countess said, "The curse is true. There is nothing left for me but tragedy."

"Lady Worthington, please don't say such a thing," Julia began.

"Why should you care about us? You could marry the new earl and become mistress of Worthington after all."

The woman spoke with such bitterness, Julia recoiled. "No. I don't want that at all. I want only the happiness that comes from love—"

"Happiness? What utter madness! Who would aspire to happiness? Who would chase such a fleeting and horrible thing? No one is happy, Julia. Life is about perseverance. I have to protect my girls. That is what is left for me. Protecting them. Settling them. Then nothing can touch them. Nothing."

"Let them find happiness. Please."

But the countess's eyes blazed. "I know what is best for them. Now please go. I wish to be alone."

Julia left, drawing the door closed firmly this time. She was going to leave, but not without confronting Cal over what he was doing.

She knew the countess had spoken the truth in those unhappy moments. The countess believed the crash had been deliberate, not an accident.

But what had driven John to do it?

"Yes, milady," the Worthington maid replied, in answer to Julia's question. "His lordship has gone upstairs, to the attics."

"The attics? Are you sure?"

"Yes, milady." The girl tried to maintain a dutiful expression but then it failed, and her eyes were wide with excitement. "We've all been talking about it downstairs. Lord

Worthington went belowstairs to speak with Mrs. Feathers. Then he wanted to know how to go up to the attics."

"Is it true he has let go his valet, a footman and a hall boy?" Julia asked.

The girl nodded. "It is true, milady. He said they are to find better employment. He told the valet that having a man button his shirt was demeaning to both of them. Mr. Wiggins was right shocked—oh, I didn't mean to be speaking out of turn, milady."

"I will not say a word to the housekeeper, I promise," Julia said.

As soon as she turned away from the maid, her patient smile died. She'd already heard Mrs. Feathers's account of events. To ensure the cook stayed, she needed Cal.

Who was in the attic. For what purpose, she couldn't imagine.

Julia hurried to the stairs that led to the upper story of the house—here were the servants' rooms and the nurseries. Sunlight spilled out into the hallway floor from a room at the end of the corridor and she smelled a strong odor, like potent alcohol.

Was Cal up here drinking?

Julia reached the doorway of the unused nursery—

And stopped in her tracks. A wooden easel stood in the middle of the room, a table set up beside it. A painting stood on the easel, but all Julia could see was Cal's back. He wore a white shirt with sleeves rolled up to bare his forearms. She'd never seen arms tanned to a dark copper on any man but a laborer or farmer. Wide shoulders filled out the linen shirt, and the tails hung out of his trousers. His feet were bare.

He balanced a flat board covered in blobs of oil paint and mixed it with a long, black-handled brush.

The muscles of his broad back moved under his shirt.

She was rooted to the spot—warm, breathless and feeling as if everything had fallen away.

Then Cal moved and she saw the picture.

"But that's me," she gasped.

It was a painting of the terrace where she had stood last night. The picture was only partly finished. It was sketched with lead pencil and her face was filled in, as was some of the background of the night sky.

It was a wild, modernist painting—the sky was rendered in vivid slashes of black and indigo and violet, with gray layered upon it to show moonlit clouds. The sky truly looked as if the clouds were hurtling past the moon. And against all that darkness, she seemed to glow like a candle's flame.

Cal turned. "I don't let anyone look at my unfinished work."

"The door was open," she pointed out.

"I was told nobody comes up here in the daytime."

She looked past him at the intense, vibrant portrait. The woman's face was definitely hers, but more perfect. Her lips even looked as if moisture glistened on them. The blue eyes seemed to burn with inner fire.

"What do you think of it?" he asked.

"You've made me much more vivacious and interesting than I really am."

"I paint what I see, angel—but tempered with my feelings and my soul. I want to put raw emotion on my canvas. And that's what I see in you. Raw emotion. Fire and passion."

No one thought she was fiery or passionate. Everyone thought her cool and controlled. She felt passion, but she almost never showed it. How had he seen that inside her?

"You see something quite different to the person I am, Worthington."

"I don't think so." He mixed colors on his palette, looking at her from under his mussed blond hair. "I think I see the real Lady Julia behind the restrained exterior."

His gaze moved over her in the most shocking way. She should be outraged. Yet it wasn't a bold look. It was a raw, appreciative look, given to her by a stunningly handsome man—

She had better put a stop to it at once.

"I am a lady through and through, Worthington. You won't see anything beyond that."

He grinned. "It's too late, doll. I already do. And it's Cal, remember?"

His soft, deep voice sent a shiver through her. Then she thought of the countess sobbing with shock and terror. Julia crossed her arms over her chest. "Was losing the cook part of your plan to tear Worthington Park to pieces? As well as firing servants who are now out of work, with no place to stay?"

To her shock, he did not respond. He went back to his painting.

"It's rude to not answer," she said.

As he worked he said, "It's true that I would have waited to get rid of the cook. I like to eat. But it made me mad to see so much food thrown away. I know what it's like to be hungry. Have you ever lived a day on some broth and one piece of bread?"

That startled her. "Was that all you had?"

He slashed paint on the canvas and a stone balustrade began to appear. It looked real, as if she could feel the roughness of stone.

"No, I went without food by choice, Lady Julia, what do you think? My mother would feed my brother and me first and if there was nothing left, she didn't eat at all."

"I'm sorry." Of course, she didn't know what it was to be truly starving. Even when they had been in financial dire straits at Brideswell, there was always food. Instead, she had been trained to *not* eat, to do little more than nibble at all the dinner courses to keep her figure. "But I am familiar with hardship. There are many people in the village who are suffering after the War. And surely the food that is not eaten at meals is used."

"Not much of it." His voice was a low growl. "Why shouldn't it go to people who are needy? The dogs get more of the leftover food than people do. The cook didn't see anything wrong with that so I fired her."

For all he growled like a tiger, Julia felt hope. He cared about people who did not have enough. Once he understood the importance of Worthington Park to the tenants, he would never tear it apart.

Surely.

"Well, I have soothed Mrs. Feathers's wounded feelings," she said. "Cooks are accustomed to being the lords of their kitchens. She could be convinced to stay—if you apologize and tell her she may run her kitchen as she has always done—"

"Apologize? Isn't the idea of being the earl that I get to make the rules?"

"Large houses don't run quite that way," she explained patiently. "Servants work for a house for years—often decades. They outlast the peers. The houses run smoothly because servants know their duties and they take charge of them. Zoe—my sister-in-law—says they run like large American offices."

"I could hire another cook."

"A good cook can be difficult to find. All you have to do is tell Mrs. Feathers she can carry on as usual. Charm her. Then a plan must be made to change her to your way of thinking, but cleverly."

"Uh-huh," he said. He crossed his arms over his chest. "Have you ever cooked anything, Lady Julia?"

She felt a blush touch her cheeks. "My presence would not have been appreciated in Brideswell's kitchens. Our cook and kitchen maids would have been thoroughly shocked."

"So shock them," he said. "Or would you just starve to death if you were on your own?"

She would not give him the satisfaction of admitting she would be without a clue if she had to make her own meal. "I am sure I would survive. Can you cook?"

"I can. When my mother was sick, I cooked for all of us. When I paint landscapes, I travel out into the wilderness in a canoe. I camp and paint and cook over a campfire."

"You do?" That sounded so primitive.

He walked over to her. He held out the brush. "Would you like to try your hand at painting?"

"I have painted before in watercolors. And we really should speak to Mrs. Feathers."

"What if I'm not willing to grovel? After all, with all the food in the larders here, I'm capable of feeding myself."

He watched her as he spoke. Obviously, he was looking to get a rise out of her. "The servants must eat, as well as the family."

"I'd be willing to let them look after themselves. Or are you trying to tell me that the countess and her daughters would starve out of pride before they'd condescend to make their own meals?"

"I don't know about them but the servants would."

"The servants would what?"

"Starve before they would cook for themselves."

His brows lifted. "The servants think they're too good to make their own meals?"

"Exactly."

He laughed. "Is snobbery bred into all of you?"

"Everyone is aware of their own position. It's the way we are."

"So I'd have a mutiny on my hands if the cook leaves and I don't replace her." His lazy, sensual grin unfurled. "That could be fun. But I have a better idea. I'll go and make nice with the cook, if you come here and paint."

"What about the footman and the boot boy? And your valet?"

"I'll help the young men find better work. And the valet was glad to leave. He said it was like dressing a performing bear. I told him a bear would be less dangerous, then he ran." Cal crooked his finger at her. "Come and paint with me, Julia. You'll like working with oil paint more than watercolors. It's more sensual."

That word made another shiver rush down her back.

"It's thick and tactile and you can build with it, play with it. I bet you were taught to paint timid little pictures. See what you can do with this." With a palette knife instead of a brush, he scooped up indigo and yellow and layered it thickly on the canvas as if to show her how very much unlike watercolors it was.

"I'm not dressed for painting and you do not have a smock or a coat," she said.

With infinite slowness, his smile lifted the right side of his mouth. That lopsided smile made her tingle deep inside.

He set down his palette, the knife, the brush. He undid the buttons of his shirt and shrugged it off.

Leaving his chest, his torso, completely bare.

Her jaw dropped.

He came toward her and she simply couldn't move. A lady shouldn't look, but she couldn't tear her gaze away from his beautiful, well-muscled form.

"Slide this on."

"Your *shirt*? I can't possibly."

He draped it around her. Staring at the shirt, she realized it was finely made. An expensive shirt. But he was supposed to be a poor, bohemian artist. It was like the beautiful dinner clothes he wore last night. Where had they come from?

She breathed in the scent of him on his warm, luxurious shirt. Heat uncoiled in her, like smoke spiraling from a burning candlewick.

He pressed the paintbrush against her hand and she clasped it. Then her good sense came back. "Cal, I can't wear your shirt. I cannot be in here with you in a state of undress."

"You're a grown woman, Julia." He put his hands on her shoulders, firm and strong. He turned her away from him and toward the canvas. "I've painted women in the nude."

"You were naked? Good heavens."

He laughed. "They were, not me. And I didn't sleep with…all of them."

She knew he was trying to shock her and she calmly said, "That is hardly reassuring."

"I suspect my honor is safe with you, Julia," he teased. He lifted her hand so the brush almost touched the canvas.

"What if I ruin it?"

"You won't. We can paint over anything you don't like."

"You can take your hands off my shoulders." She felt the warmth of his palms through his shirt and her frock.

"Not until you make your mark on your portrait, Julia." He picked up the palette.

"You are infuriating." She dipped the paintbrush into a mound of red paint. Then she made a small dab in the corner of the canvas. "There."

"You're not afraid to paint a canvas, are you? I thought you were going to be a tough adversary."

"Fine." She half turned and took the palette out of his

hand. Using the kind of style he'd done—modernist dabs and slashes of paint—she tried to do the skirt of her dress. Tried to mimic the way it shimmered in the light. She all but threw paint at the picture. Then she stopped, her chest heaving. It was rather exciting—

She saw what she'd created. "It's awful. It isn't anything like what I wanted to do."

"But I got to prove I'm right and you're wrong." He leaned forward. The warmth of his breath caressed her ear. "You are passionate."

He moved, so his lips touched her cheek.

The *whoosh* came again, so startling and swift it almost knocked her back into the picture.

"You want to kiss me," he said huskily.

"I do not." But her heartbeat rushed up and down as if it was playing a piano scale.

She thought of Anthony, who she had loved with all her heart. And Dougal, who was so noble and admirable. She had *loved* those men. She didn't love this man. She barely knew him. And so far she'd learned he was brash and bold and infuriating.

But the temptation to kiss him was so strong she almost wanted him to just kiss her and take all the responsibility for it away.

No, she was *modern*. Modern women didn't act like weak waifs.

She turned, and smacked the paintbrush against his lips. "I do not want to kiss you." She looked straight into his blue eyes. "Now, if you intend to eat anything today, we had better speak to Mrs. Feathers."

She pulled away from him, and grabbed a rag from a small wooden table near the portrait. She tossed it to him so he could wipe the blue paint from his mouth. Then she held out his shirt.

★ ★ ★

Cal rubbed the rag over his lips, taking off the paint in one swipe. Grinning as he did.

If Julia were one of his models, he would put his now-clean mouth to her neck and kiss her until she melted. Until they ended up hot and sweaty in his bed, making love.

After the War, sex had become a hell of a lot more available. Now women weren't willing to deny themselves pleasure until they got married. Everyone had seen that life could be a fleeting thing. One moment you were laughing, deep in love with someone, thinking of the future. The next you were in bits and pieces, strewn across some European field.

Could he coax Julia into his bed?

He threw down the rag, took his shirt from her hands and shrugged it on. After he buttoned it, tucked it into his trousers, he said, "Let's go and see the cook."

"All right." Julia walked ahead of him, her trim-fitting skirt swishing efficiently around her hips. It was a modest length, reaching her midcalves. But he liked the way it clung to the curves of her hips and hinted at the sweet voluptuousness of her backside.

He wanted Lady Julia Hazelton. He wanted to break through her ladylike reserve and release her passion.

Before he left Worthington for good, he was going to do it.

5

The Woman with Shell Shock

Cal followed Lady Julia through a green door. This part of the house looked different. The walls were plain white; the stairs narrow with worn treads. No need for beauty where the servants worked.

"Why you?" he asked. "Why didn't the countess go see the cook? Or Diana, the daughter who's being forced to flirt with me?"

Julia looked startled, but then said, in her cool, ladylike tones, "They are both too upset. The countess is living in terror. Diana is— She isn't well. You have not told them of your plans?"

"Not yet." He leaned against the banister, looking at her. God, she was a beauty. Ivory skin. Full lips lightly colored red with discreet lipstick. Stunning eyes with long, dark lashes.

"You deliberately want to draw it out and be cruel?" she accused.

"I've got my reasons."

Lady Julia had the most impressive poker face. She kept her expression serene but he could feel hot anger inside her under that controlled facade. For a moment, he thought about explaining himself. Telling her why he wanted to hurt the family.

Why should he have to justify himself to her?

"So you're trying to save the house by keeping the cook from walking out because the others don't have the courage."

She gave him a cool stare. "I believed I could convince Mrs. Feathers to stay, so I should try. Whether it is my house or not."

"And you thought I'd thank you for it?"

"You must not take your grievances out on innocent people."

"Her ladyship and the earl did." Cal had to struggle to speak as calmly as she did. "Don't speak to me like I must be scum because I was born poor. I was born to decent and honest parents who helped other people and were charitable, even when they had nothing."

He could see the flash of surprise and shock in her eyes. His heart pounded.

He wanted to kiss her. Wanted to push her back against the plain white plaster wall and devour her with his mouth until she was panting against him.

But that wasn't the way to do it with Lady Julia.

He raised her fingers to his lips. His father used to do this with his mother, and it always made Mam giggle, then melt and sigh and forget worry and despair.

Julia had soft skin. Pretty hands that smelled like flowers. His head told him to be angry that her hands obviously did no work, but lust shot through him at the idea of having such soft, pampered hands gripping his shoulders as he made love to her.

She pulled her hand back. "Stop this, Worthington."

He loved hearing her speak so primly. It entertained him. "I want to make amends."

"Then don't tear Worthington apart. Your father was disowned and that was *wrong*. But what others did to you should not dictate whether you behave nobly or not."

"You people would say a man can never rise above his birth."

"I would never say that." With that, she turned away from him and continued downstairs.

"You know what's funny?" he said. "When I took a tour of the house this morning and came down to the kitchen, the servants assumed I'd gotten lost. Every footman and maid I encountered, the butler, the cook, all thought I must have gotten lost to be down in the servants' basement."

"We refer to it as 'belowstairs.'"

He grabbed her arm, stopping her. "It's a cold, damp, stone basement without enough light. Don't give it a prim name so you people can pretend that the kitchen staff is happy to be trapped down there day and night, scouring pots."

Julia recoiled from his harsh, accusatory words and continued to the bottom of the stairs, but she paused before she opened the door.

"You want to sell Worthington. Whoever buys it will employ a kitchen maid. Count the number of servants next time you're at a house belonging to someone who is 'new money.' They will have more than us."

"New money." He scoffed at the term.

But Julia went on, "Inquire about the working conditions of those servants. Find out what their employers do when they can no longer work or become ill. All too often they are let go and replaced. There is no pension, no care, no compassion. We try to take care of our own. We truly do. You Americans champion capitalism, but it can be a harsh thing."

She pushed open the door and walked out.

He let her get the last word. This time.

Cal followed her through a stone-arched doorway, into a room with a long wooden table. A woman sat at it, sewing. Two footmen where having cups of tea. Two maids sat there, giggling together.

Their happy demeanor startled him. He'd expected to see girls who were exhausted, who looked like they were being crushed. He never dreamed a girl would sparkle when she was working her fingers to the bone as a maid.

Had his mother sparkled and laughed like that? He'd rarely seen her do it while they were struggling to survive.

"Good morning," Julia said. Every person at the table pushed back their chairs and bolted to their feet to stand at attention.

"My lady?" The housekeeper hurried out of a room, keys jangling at her waist. "My lord."

"My lord. My lady." The snobby butler hurried in. "May I help you both?"

"We wish Mrs. Feathers to spare a moment of her time," Julia said. It wasn't a question. It was a command, but a sugarcoated one.

"Of course, my lady." The housekeeper disappeared into the kitchens.

A strident voice cried, "What does 'e want now?" Then it went quiet. A moment later, Mrs. Feathers showed up at the doorway. The pudgy woman wore a coat that strained over her ample figure, and a surprisingly stylish hat with a feather.

Cal was just about to capitulate and agree to a truce with the cook—just to see what would happen if he made nice with Lady Julia and to find out how she would coax Mrs. Feathers to change her way of thinking—when a loud crash sounded in the kitchen and Mrs. Feathers gasped, "Oh Lord, that was the sauce for the duck. Stupid, clumsy girl!"

Cal couldn't see why the cook would care since she was

walking out the door, but then remembered Julia had led the cook to believe he would apologize. Maybe even grovel.

And the crash had interrupted them.

Face reddening with impatience and anger, the cook whirled around and barked into the kitchen, "You daft twit, can't you be careful? That's ruined. And here's his lordship, concerned about waste. Well, we know who's to blame for most of the food that goes in the rubbish bin. You haven't got the wits of a dog."

Mrs. Feathers lunged into the kitchen with her hand raised as if ready to deliver a slap.

Cal had worked on the docks as a young boy. There he'd been hit and abused. No one was going to abuse anyone in his name. He stalked into the kitchen, sensing Lady Julia was close behind.

Mrs. Feathers gripped a young kitchen maid by the shoulders. Her face was contorted and red with fury. The girl, she'd been introduced as Hannah on his previous trip to the kitchens, was thin—skinny arms stuck out of the sleeves of a beige dress, and an apron was tied around a tiny waist. The cook shook Hannah, who had wide, frightened brown eyes and tears on her cheeks. "It was an accident. I was trying to be careful. But then I turned and the dog was there and I fell over him."

His late uncle's dog, a retriever, let out a whimpering sound and dropped to the floor, gazing up with pitiful eyes. The kitchen maid looked more scared than the dog.

Suddenly, Mrs. Feathers shook the girl, her face dark red with fury. She lifted her hand—

He grasped the woman's wrist and hauled her away from Hannah. "So you are responsible for the bruises on this girl," he said, his voice low and cold. He pushed up the girl's sleeve, revealing a row of fading bruises along her forearm. "I noticed them when I was downstairs earlier. But she didn't rat you out. She insisted she got them because she was clumsy. Now I see what's been happening." He dropped his voice lower, so it was nothing more than a growl. "No one hits anyone in my household."

The cook had turned white.

"Apologize to Hannah."

"What?" gasped Mrs. Feathers.

"You had no right to say what you did. No right to touch her. She's a person, not a whipping boy."

"She's not a person, she's a kitchen maid. I know how to keep my staff in line. I know what works with them and what doesn't, my lord—"

"And I know when I see behavior I refuse to condone," he said with lethal cool. "I was told to give you an apology to keep peace in this damn house. But you don't deserve one. I don't want a woman like you working here, taking out your anger on a defenseless girl. I don't care if you've quit or not, because you're fired. Now get out."

The woman's jaw dropped.

Lady Julia's jaw also dropped.

Hannah the kitchen maid stared at him with red-rimmed eyes. She was older than she looked, older than Mam had been when she had to start working as a maid in that Fifth Avenue house.

"Can you cook?" he said to her.

"Y-yes."

"Her? Cook?" cried Mrs. Feathers. "That's a laugh."

"She's going to cook from now on. Congratulations, Hannah. You've been promoted."

He turned to find Julia staring at him, in as much shock as the others. "I've solved the problem," he said. "I have a cook."

★ ★ ★

Julia pursued the infuriating Earl of Worthington along the downstairs corridor. "You simply cannot do that."

The earl stopped and faced her. He looked smug, of course, for he had no idea what he had just done. "It's my house. I can do what I want."

"What you have done is completely unkind to that girl."

His brows shot up. "I gave her a promotion."

"The poor kitchen maid has been just thrust into a terrible position, Worthington. She is too inexperienced, and she must be absolutely terrified."

He glared at her, his eyes a blue blaze. "I wasn't going to stand by and let her be abused. If you think I'm going to let my household be run by bullies, you are wrong, Julia. I don't give a rat's arse if that is the way things have always been done."

She supposed he had a point. "But Hannah has to face tonight's dinner without enough help."

"So she serves a bad dinner, so what?"

"I do not believe she is the sort who can easily ignore a failure. Not to mention she will be teased mercilessly by the other staff, who will not want her to get above herself."

"I'll make someone else help her. There are other kitchen maids. Some of the other staff can help. If they don't like it, they know I am more than willing to fire people who cross me."

"What are you going to do to me because I've crossed you? Forbid me from coming to the house?"

"I'd never do that." That slow, sizzling smile—like the path of a flame on a fuse—lifted his lips again. "I'd never get the chance to bring out your passionate side. When you're angry, you burn. You glow with an energy that crackles like lightning."

A mad thought hit her. "You did not just do all of that to make me angry."

"No, but I'll keep it in mind for the future."

He took two steps toward her. She had to tip her head back to meet his eyes. His arms bracketed the wall on either side of her, making her suck in a sharp breath.

"I figure the cook was stealing from the pantry, too, but I don't much care about that."

"That's a bold accusation to make. Don't Americans believe in a proper trial with evidence, just as the English do?"

"I'm not firing her for the theft, even though I'm sure she's guilty. She was offended right off the mark and I figured all that outrage and indignity was because she was hiding something. Also, she kept glancing at the pantry door. Her guilty conscience revealing itself."

"I—I had no idea this was going on."

"Why should you? It's not your house."

"Anthony—" She broke off.

His fingers gently touched her cheek, turning her to face him. Just the contact of his fingertips made her knees feel wobbly, as if she'd danced to jazz all night.

"What about my cousin Anthony?"

"He asked me to look after his family when he went away to war."

"Why would an earl and countess need you to look after them?"

She couldn't answer that. She'd never really understood why. "I did make him a promise and Lady Worthington needs my help now."

"Well, you'll have to excuse me. I have a painting to finish. I'm hot to get all this fire and fury in you down on canvas. But before I go—"

His lips lowered. They were in a shadowed downstairs

corridor, but only feet away in the kitchens came the voices of the servants—all filled with vehement astonishment over what had just happened.

Anyone could walk in and see.

That thought alone should make her draw back at once.

But his lips seemed to have become the whole of Julia's universe. His lips were full and sensual and she wanted to touch them. The ache that shot through low in her belly made her gasp.

Now she knew what she felt for him. Lust. Pure and simple. And ladies with sense never let themselves be controlled by lust. Even in this modern age.

She had opened her heart twice and had been terribly hurt. She was almost twenty-seven and it was so hard to think she might never touch a man and be touched by him. She might never know passion or make love.

But she wouldn't do it without marriage. She couldn't…

She couldn't do it with this man who wanted only to destroy an estate and people she loved.

She jerked back. "You championed Hannah. What about the other people who live on this estate and who work hard? When you sell to the highest bidder, what will happen to them? You should meet the people who will lose everything when you sell. Or are you afraid to face them?"

He was breathing hard. "You're goading me."

"I'm pointing out the truth," she said sweetly. "I challenge you to take a tour of the estate with me. To meet the people who are now putting their faith and their trust in you. Who are doing so with no idea that you want to destroy everything they've worked for. Some of those families have farmed for generations—"

"All right. I'll go."

"Fine. Why don't we go now? We could ride out from the house? Or do you ride—"

"Of course, I don't ride," he said brusquely. "The closest I'd gotten to a horse before the army were the ones pulling rag-and-bone carts in our neighborhood." His eyes narrowed. "My father did that at one time for the money. He drove a rag-and-bone cart. When do you think I should share that story with the countess?"

"Don't. It would kill her."

She'd spoken without thinking.

It was a mistake. His face tensed. His mouth went hard.

"It would be better to drive," she said quickly. "I have my motorcar."

He leaned closer and she forgot to breathe.

"You are the most beautiful woman I've seen, Julia. That's why I'm painting you. But the portrait can wait for today. I'd much prefer to spend the day having you try to teach me a lesson. Who knows, maybe you will heal my bitter heart and turn me into a changed man."

Oh no. He was mocking the very thing she hoped to do. She hoped to heal his bitterness. She hoped to change him.

He knew it—and was making fun of it.

She gave him the smile all young ladies learned—polite, sweet, the butter-wouldn't-melt smile. "I believe I shall."

"You know," Cal said to Julia from the passenger seat as they rumbled down a country lane, "you're the only woman I've ever let drive me."

"I know my way around the estate and you do not. It is far more sensible for me to drive."

"Yeah, but someday I want to tempt the sensible right out of you." He grinned.

"I doubt that will happen," she said, her tone prim even when shouted over the roar of the engine.

He liked the way she looked while driving. She had put on goggles to keep out the wind and the dust, and they made her look sweetly adventurous. She had pulled on a cloche hat and wound a scarf around her neck that fluttered and snapped behind her like a crisp flag.

She was so determined to change his mind about Worthington. But what he had seen today had cut to his bone. He had felt for the girl Hannah. She was supposed to "know her place." What a load of damn crap.

Cal had returned to the kitchen and told Hannah she could give orders to any of the footmen to help her. The snooty butler, Wiggins, had sputtered, until Cal had told him he could follow Mrs. Feathers out the door if he wanted. Wiggins had drawn himself up and had claimed to have been in service to the family for five decades. "What a hell of a way to waste a life," Cal had said. Then he'd gone out. He'd found Julia in the drawing room with Diana, who looked strained and worried. The thing was—he'd looked at Diana's drawn expression and felt an unexpected jolt of guilt.

"So where did your brother get a beautiful American automobile like this?" he asked. "I'm surprised he lets you drive one of his cars."

"It's *my* motorcar. Not my brother's."

"You bought this fine automobile?" He had to admit he was surprised she knew how to drive and didn't just have a chauffeur take her around.

"It was a birthday present from Zoe, my sister-in-law. She had it sent from New York. She called it a symbol of my freedom. I do love to be able to say 'I shall go here' and I can take myself there. It does make you feel powerful."

"Does it?"

The car was a spiffy roadster. The chrome gleamed and the glossy cream paint shone in the sunlight. Julia was a surprisingly good driver, taking the winding turns with skill. She slowed and accelerated with confidence where she needed to. "I guess a duke's daughter is used to getting what she wants," he said.

"Hardly. I could have never bought a motor on my own. Until I marry, the only money I have comes from my pin money. That was how I was trying to fund my charitable work, at least when I was doing the work that no one approved of. Finally, I made up my mind to sell this car. She would have fetched a tremendous amount of money and I need it for the women I'm helping. It would have utterly broken my heart to do it, but I would have done it."

"Darling, I would never let you sell this car."

She glanced briefly at him. Then looked back to the narrow road. "The only money I can even call mine is my dowry and that is locked up as tight as Fort Knox in America. But my sister-in-law Zoe is going to provide the financial backing and I can use that to help women begin businesses or run their farms so they can feed their families. My brother and his wife take great care of the families on the Brideswell estate, but those on the Worthington estate have needed help."

"The Duke of Bad Manners didn't like the idea of mixing with the poor."

She giggled and it was a lovely sound. "You mustn't call him that. But too many people feel that way. It's rather frustrating."

"You still do it."

She turned, flashing a smile that made his heart stop beating. "I am a duke's daughter."

"You're not what I expected of an aristocrat. Why do you do it, when you have to fight so hard?"

"Once, I would have followed duty and rules, but not now. People lost so much in the War. It is wrong to let children go hungry and women lose their homes! These men gave everything to protect our country, to protect our way of life. I lost Anthony to the Somme and I grieved him for a very long time. Then I realized I needed to find purpose in my life. I didn't want to go back to a life of dinner parties and presentation at court. I wanted to do something of value. It made the pain of losing Anthony go away."

"You're the bee's knees, sweetheart. A dame with a good heart, and a real Sheba."

Her eyes widened. "No one has ever said that to me before. What does it mean?"

"You know what a dame with a good heart is. A Sheba is a girl who oozes sex appeal."

The car jolted in a rut. It was the first time she'd hit anything. Good. It meant he was getting to her. Finding the ways to get under her skin.

Lady Julia turned off onto something that looked like a cart track. Apple trees stretched as far as he could see. "This is part of your orchards," she said.

"We're not on a road, Sheba."

"We are. This is the lane to one of your farms and it also passes several small cottages."

A cottage came into view and she drew off to the edge of the lane. "This is the first family I want you to meet. I was coming here when I received a message to see Diana." She turned off the engine and got out. Then she plucked a basket off the rumble seat behind her—filled with food, he saw—hooked it over her arm and firmly pushed open the small wooden gate in front of the stone building. It was tiny, with a short door flanked by two small windows. Roses budded all over the front.

"These are your tenants," she said. "Your estate encompasses about thirty thousand acres."

"Yeah. That's what the lawyer told me. It's a different thing when you actually see it." But there was something he didn't get. "Why are you looking out for the tenants and not Lady Worthington? Does the countess ignore the lowly peasants? Or is this another promise to my cousin?"

"The countess took very ill after her son John died in the car accident." She hesitated. She wasn't looking at him, which made him curious. "She has experienced so much loss. It was so hard on Lady Worthington. You must consider that—"

"Yeah, but she still hasn't developed an ounce of compassion. Couldn't she have sent her daughters to do what you're doing?"

Julia took a deep breath.

"What is it? What are you hiding from me, Julia?"

"This tenant—Ellen—has had to…to sell herself to men to earn money. That means all respectable women are supposed to shun her. They are not allowed to show kindness."

He knew exactly what she meant. "But not you. You aren't afraid of anything."

"That is not true. But some things are simply more important." She reached up to rap on the door. But it was yanked open.

A kid stood there—a kid in short pants and a cap, who looked as skinny as Cal had been as a boy. The child shouted, "I guessed it would be you, my lady!"

"You are very clever, Ben." Julia smiled.

The little boy looked captivated by her soft, melodic voice. Cal figured, from the boy's blush, he had a crush on Julia. He wasn't surprised.

Julia took something from the hamper. "This is from the village bakery. I bought some yesterday for you." She held out a sweet-looking strawberry tart with a shiny glaze.

The boy devoured it in two bites. "You should savor it!" Julia exclaimed.

Cal grinned. That was just what his mother would have said.

"I *did* sabor it. I could have eaten it in one bite," the boy declared with pride.

Julia shook her head. "That is just what my brother Sebastian would have done. Or my youngest brother, Will. Now, go and fetch your mother, young Ben."

As the boy ran off, Cal saw her brush away a tear. Quickly she smoothed her features into serene, ladylike loveliness, but he asked gently, "What's wrong?"

"He reminds me so much of Will, and we lost Will to the influenza outbreak after the War. He was fifteen."

"I'm sorry." And he was. He'd assumed wealth insulated her from hardship. He could see he'd been wrong. "What about your brother Sebastian? I didn't meet him."

Her whole face glowed when she smiled—even the smallest, gentlest smile. It was sweeter than seeing Paris glitter with light, more breathtaking than dawn in the northern wilds. "He is an artist, like you," she said. "Sebastian went to Capri, but now he lives in Paris. As you did. He is rather like a bohemian, largely impoverished because he wants to support himself with his art, and he is very happy."

"I bet he is. I see the same streak of wildness in you."

She blushed. "Hardly." Then she frowned. "I'm surprised Ellen has not come out to see us." She lowered her voice. "Ben's mother, Ellen Lambert, never married. Ben was born six months after she came back from the War. She had been a VAD and worked as an ambulance driver."

"It was a hell of a job," he said. "A hard, terrifying job. There were a lot of intense romances in the heat of battle."

"You had one?"

"I had several. Only one that really mattered."

Her face shuttered, showing no emotion. "Really? I'm sure the others might have meant a lot to the women involved." Then she left him. She went through the living room to the rear of the cottage. He followed—as if he were tied to Lady Julia Hazelton by an invisible string. He just couldn't let her out of his sight. Every moment with her was proving to be something special.

He stayed behind Julia as she paused in the doorway to a tiny kitchen. A thin woman with short blond hair stood at a metal sink, scrubbing with ferocity at a pot. Her shoulders shook as if she were sobbing.

"Ellen, what's wrong?" Julia asked.

He heard Ellen Lambert take a shaky breath. Then she half looked over her shoulder. "Nothing, my lady. I'm sorry. I didn't hear you."

He figured there were aristocratic women who would be slighted because Ellen hadn't rushed to the door and curtsied. But Julia was not one. "There is something wrong, isn't there?" Julia asked.

"No—"

But Julia hurried forward, grasped Ellen's shoulder, forcing her to turn. The woman's right eye was surrounded by a large blue-and-purple bruise.

"How did that happen?" Julia cried. She urged Ellen to sit in a chair at a tiny, rickety table.

As she did, Ellen's fingers went to the large bruise. "The daftest thing. I woke up in the night and I walked right into the edge of the door."

"I doubt it," Cal said darkly. "That was done by a man's

fist." His mother used to try to help women in their neighborhood who were beaten by their husbands. He knew all
the excuses they'd used.

"What man?" Julia said, her lovely eyes widening. "Was
it one of your—your—" For all she had spoken so derisively
about propriety, Lady Julia was now—sweetly—at a loss for
words.

But Ellen didn't need the word spoken. She paled, but insisted, "It wasn't. It was just a stupid accident."

"Now that I've seen it, why don't we sit down and have
tea? You've nothing to hide anymore," Julia said firmly.
"This is the Earl of Worthington."

Ellen stared at him. She stumbled to her feet. "My lord.
Oh, I'm so sorry—"

"Don't apologize," he said.

The poor woman was white as a sheet. "I shall make tea,"
she said, but Julia insisted she sit down. Hell, Lady Julia went
to the stove and put the kettle on. That stunned Cal.

While the water heated, Julia drew Ellen out of the
kitchen into the small sitting room and gave her the basket
and a small pouch.

Ellen gave it back. "I can't take this, my lady. And I don't
need to, my lady. I've enough for the rent."

"But I don't want you to earn money as you have been
doing," Julia said firmly.

"I would rather earn my money than be given charity."

That sounded just like his mother. Cal knew about a
woman's pride and stubbornness. But then, his mother had
not had any other choice. Just like Ellen.

"You do realize the house is supported by the money
earned off the estate. Why then, should the house not support you?"

Ellen started in shock. "I never thought of it that way."

"Well, it is the correct way. The way it has always been and should be," Julia said.

"There are so many who thought we would go back to happy times after the War," Ellen said sadly. "I knew it wouldn't be so. But I never thought there would be such poverty, such helplessness. I've tried to get work. But with Ben—with everyone knowing my story—no one will give me a decent position."

"Well, you need not worry anymore. I have an idea." Julia outlined her plan to loan money for Ellen to open a business. "You may pay me back over time. First, we will find something for you to do. And Benjamin must go to school."

Cal leaned against the wall, watching Julia at work. Aware he was smiling.

Ellen looked worried though, not relieved. "A good school will look at me and refuse to take Ben." She lowered her voice to a mere whisper. "Perhaps I should give him away. He might have a better chance then. But I—I can't bear to give him up."

There were only two times Cal had seen so much pain on a woman's face. Once was in the War, when a village had been bombed and he had seen a woman who had thought she'd lost her children. He found them in the rubble of a collapsed house and brought them out to her. That moment alone had made his whole damned life worthwhile. The other time had been on his mother's face when he was young—and he hadn't understood back then that she'd feared losing him and David.

"You don't have to. You won't lose your son." Cal hadn't expected to say anything, but the words had just come out. The two women stared at him.

"But how can I have a business? Who would come to be served by the likes of me?"

"Don't say that," Julia admonished. "We can make this into a fresh start."

Lady Julia meant well, Cal knew, but she really did live a cloistered life. She had no idea of the reality—how hard it would be for Ellen.

But Ellen did. Glumly, she whispered, "Your heart is in the right place, my lady. You are so kind. But this won't work—" The kettle let out a sharp whistle. Ellen went to it. Then Ben came into the sitting room. He gazed hopefully at Julia, but she said, "You cannot have another tart, dear. You must save them."

"Ah, give him another one," Cal said. "I'll bring him another treat later."

Julia frowned at him repressively. "Two tarts are rather a lot."

Suddenly Ben said, "Mummy is unhappy, isn't she? I know she's scared and worried. Is that why she doesn't sleep?"

"She does not sleep?" Julia echoed.

"Not very much," Ben said. "I know, because I wake up at night and she is awake. I get in trouble if I won't sleep. Mummy says it's important to sleep. Isn't it important for her, too?"

"Yes, Ben, it is." Cal took a tart from the picnic basket and made a show of sneakily giving it to the boy. Julia looked askance at him, but he asked her softly, "Did you know about this?"

"I had no idea."

When Ellen came back with a teapot and three chipped china cups, Julia asked right away, "Do you not sleep?"

"Of course I do, my lady. If I got no sleep, I'd collapse on the floor."

"Perhaps you only sleep fitfully."

"What woman with a house and a child doesn't sleep in fits? And in a cottage, there are always things that need to be done. The fire needs stoking. More water might be needed.

Often I've forgotten to do things in the day and I remember at night."

"You should try to sleep, Ellen. Exhaustion won't help."

"I will, my lady," Ellen mumbled.

But then Cal understood. "Lady Julia told me you drove an ambulance in the Great War, Ellen," he said. "I went to war in 1917, when America joined the fighting. I saw the women who drove the ambulances. It was terrifying, with shells going off around you. I saw many women killed."

"Don't, my lord," Ellen said sharply. Then she dropped her voice, wringing her hands. "I'm sorry, my lord. But I don't want Ben to hear about it."

"Do you have nightmares?" Cal asked softly.

Ellen hesitated. Shook her head. "'Course not."

"You're not startled by loud noises? You don't always have a feeling of fear?"

"I— Of course not."

"But you do sometimes, Mum," Ben said, startling them all. "Remember when I knocked over the tin bathtub and you screamed so loud?"

"Ben, you have chores to do. Now be off with you." Ellen shooed him out of the room.

Once the boy had gone, Cal grasped Ellen's hand. "Listen to me. You're suffering from shell shock."

She shook her head desperately. "I'm not. That would mean I'm mad. I am perfectly fine. Please—don't take Ben away."

"I won't," Cal said. "I promise I will help you. And I will not let you lose your son."

He felt a stare burning his neck. Julia was looking at him, her mouth open in surprise. Then her eyes softened and she looked at him like he was a hero—looked at him in a way that made him feel damn guilty. "Thank you," she whispered.

6

The Missing Girl at Lilac Farm

This was the most exhilarating and terrifying evening of Hannah's life.

As kitchen maid, she'd made all these dishes before, but tonight she felt like she'd forgotten *everything*. She checked the soup—not a cold soup as it was early June and not stifling hot yet. She'd made mulligatawny because the spice would cover up for any number of evils. The aspic was setting up properly, but it almost slid off the plate when she set it down and her heart just about stopped.

A pot boiled over and Hannah took off at a run, lifting it off the heat. The salmon! How long had it been since she'd last looked at it? She set down the pot, opened the oven. Not burned, thank heavens.

Hannah set to spooning the mustard sauce over the salmon. She looked over. Tansy was halfheartedly stirring the sauce for the Chicken Lyonnaise.

"Why am I running about like a chicken with my head cut off, Tansy?" she demanded. "I'm trying to do everything while you stir a spoon in a pot. You're supposed to be taking care of half of these things I'm doing."

"I *am* doing things. You've shouted at me and ordered me about all day!"

"I'm the cook now! That's what I'm supposed to do. When I was the kitchen maid, I took orders all the time. And I got an earful if I wasn't always rushing at full speed. You didn't finish cleaning the stove after lunch and you forgot to wash half the pots. I would have been sacked for that. You heard his lordship—you're all supposed to help. I am being nice to you."

"Well, thank you, Your Highness," Tansy said, her words dripping with sarcasm.

Hannah sighed. Why couldn't she be commanding? One word from Mrs. Feathers and they all used to quake. But Mrs. Feathers did it with words as sharp and wounding as her cleaving knife and Hannah couldn't do that.

Tansy started to hum a jazz song. She swayed back and forth while she stirred, which made the bowl tip precariously.

"Mind. You'll have it on the floor," Hannah declared. She hurried over and grabbed the bowl. Hannah hated to think badly of anyone, but she feared Tansy was deliberately trying to make her fall flat on her face tonight.

"I'm just happy. Do you want to know why?" Tansy dimpled.

Hannah hated the sour feeling that came over her. She'd never really thought about how she looked until Tansy came. Her mum had always insisted she look "presentable." On her afternoon off once, she'd bought a lipstick and put some on, then forgot about it and had gone home to see her parents with her lips painted red. Mum had scrubbed so hard her lips had stung all day. Of course, now Mum and Father were gone and she had no one.

Hannah brushed back a stray hair with her flour-covered forearm. She had plain brown hair and brown eyes. Tansy's hair was blue-black and she was truly lovely enough to be a film star. Hannah hated the awful feeling of jealousy that now seemed to live in her heart. "Why are you happy then, Tansy?"

"My beau's going to take me out tonight in his motorcar. He's going to wait for me and take me for a quick spin when I'm supposed to go to bed. Says he has to see me tonight. He can't wait any longer. You know what that means?"

"Aye, it means he's going to expect you to give him something in return for these motorcar rides and gifts. You've let him think you're fast."

"I've not let him do anything more than kiss me! I think he's going to marry me."

Hannah's heart sank. "Oh, Tansy, I don't think so."

"He will." Tansy stuck out her lower lip.

"Who is he, anyway? You've never told me his name. Where'd you meet him?"

"Just outside the village. I was waiting for the bus after visiting me family. It was raining something terrible and freezing cold. He offered to give me a ride back here. He's a gentleman, you know. I think he's the younger son of an earl. He doesn't like to talk about it much, but I can tell from his cut-glass accent that he's a toff. Gloriously handsome and he's mad about me."

"What's his name, Tansy?"

"I call him Geoff."

"He didn't tell you the rest, did he? Oh, Tansy, do be careful. An earl's son isn't going to propose marriage to a kitchen maid!"

"These days, gentlemen are a lot more interested in a girl with sex appeal than in marrying some dowdy lady who has a big dowry and a horsey face." Tansy stuck out her tongue. "You're jealous. That's why you're so hard on me."

"I'm hard on you because I know the standards of this house and you have to meet them. And I'm not jealous. I have your best interests at heart." Hannah wagged a spoon at Tansy. "There was a girl I knew. She was the daughter of the people at Lilac Farm. She went out in a car with a handsome gentleman one night. Maybe she ran off with him, or maybe he ruined her and she had to run away for the shame. Either way she disappeared. She was never seen again."

Hell, he found himself looking forward to seeing Julia again.

Rain spattered down as her car pulled up at the front door. Cal ran out so she wouldn't have to get out. He let himself in on the passenger side. Seeing her was like being hit in the gut—and that had happened to him a lot in the Hell's Kitchen neighborhood where he'd grown up.

Her lips were painted a darker red. A gray raincoat covered her, but revealed her stocking-clad legs below the knee. She had gorgeous legs. She smelled…probably the way heaven smelled.

"How was your dinner last night?" she asked.

"Great. Hannah did a good job. We had a dessert that I'll never forget. Fruit and cream and lady fingers soaked in liquor."

"English trifle." She smiled at him. "I'm so glad it was a success."

And off they drove. Along tree-lined lanes that swept up and down hills. Meadows and green fields stretched around them. In the distance he saw a soaring church spire, and buildings nestled among the hills. He had to admit it was pretty.

"This is Lilac Farm." Julia brought the car to a stop beside a low stone wall. Within the wall, a few stone buildings sat in a cluster with a muddy yard between them. The wall continued along a downhill slope, defining small square fields.

Julia pulled up the parking brake. She strode ahead, opening a wooden gate in the stone wall. Cal followed, and as they stepped into the yard, someone inside the largest stone building shouted, "Damn and blast!"

A stream of snorting pigs spilled out of a barn and headed toward them like an unstoppable wave. Pigs moved a hell of a lot faster than Cal expected.

They were going to be crushed against the stone wall. Planting his hands on Julia's small waist, Cal hoisted her up, over the wall. Then he jumped over himself.

The animals scurried everywhere, grunting and squealing. An elderly man stumbled out of the barn. Covered in mud, the white-haired man wheezed, "Stop 'em. They'll get away. Get two of 'em in the front and force 'em back."

Julia scrambled toward the rampaging pigs.

"Go back," Cal shouted. "Let me do this."

He got his hands on one of the pigs but his attention was on Julia. The animal pulled him off his feet. He fell as Julia cried, "Cal!"

Rolling over in the muck, he avoided the hooves and jumped to his feet. Hell, Julia had clambered back over the wall and was waving a scarf at the pigs like a Spanish bullfighter. This time he knew what to expect when he got his arms around one. He held on tight and dug in his heels. Julia flapped frantically and he managed to wrestle the pig so it was facing the barn. Spooked, it ran back toward home. He got a second animal running after the first. Sure enough, the rest began to follow. A splashing sound came as the farmer dumped the contents of a pail into a wooden trough. Grunting, the pigs scrambled over each other for a spot, their desire to escape long gone.

Julia latched the gate, then ran up to him, laughing, gasping for breath. Her shoes sank in the mud. She stumbled forward, hands flailing because her feet were stuck tight. Cal leaped forward and caught her, wrapping his arms around her. It threw him off balance, and he staggered back so they wouldn't fall—

Their faces bumped. "Ow!" she said and he grunted as she dissolved into giggles. Something he never expected Julia to do, but the sound enchanted him. As he helped her stand up, he looked down.

"Your shoes are ruined," he said. "You should've stayed where I put you."

She laughed. Rain ran down her hat and coat. "Shoes can be cleaned. I knew it was more important that we herded the pigs. And you got the worst of it, Cal. It's ruined your rather nice suit."

He looked down. He looked like he used to in the New York slums. Covered in filth. "Damn it." He rubbed hard at the muck on his trousers, trying to brush it off.

Julia touched his arm. "You needn't worry about some mud on your pants. Anyway, I thought you rather liked to look bohemian."

Normally he didn't care what he looked like. But in front of Julia, he suddenly felt like he was a poor kid in the slums again, with a dirty coat, torn breeches and a dirty face. "Maybe I just did that to shock the countess." He turned to the farmer and stuck out his hand for a handshake.

"I would like to introduce you to his lordship, the new earl," Julia said. "This is Mr. Brand, Worthington, and his family has farmed here for almost one hundred and fifty years."

Brand looked guilty. "Begging your pardon, yer lordship. Wouldn't have asked you to help with the pigs, if I'd known who ye were."

"You didn't object to Lady Julia helping," Cal observed. "Does she chase pigs often?"

He felt Julia dig him in his side. "Of course not," she said crisply. "But it is important to pitch in where needed."

"A right good sport is Lady Julia," Brand said. "Comes to see me and the missus all the time, she does."

"Harry!" A panicked woman's voice came from another stone building. An elderly woman hobbled out of what must be their cottage. "Sarah's gone. I don't know where she is."

Cal hoped Sarah was a pet pig who'd just been rescued. Then he saw tears streaking the woman's cheeks. He asked, "Who is Sarah? Are you sure she's missing?"

Julia's hand touched his shoulder. Just one look and he recognized she wanted to take charge. He might be the lord, but Julia knew these people and they knew her. He stepped aside. Julia soothed the woman and led her back to the small stone farmhouse. They had to step down some stone steps and duck to go through the doorway.

As Julia went in with Mrs. Brand, Cal turned to the farmer, who was sucking on his pipe. "Who is Sarah?"

"She were our daughter."

"And she's missing?"

"She went missing in the spring of 1916, before all the lads went to fight at the Somme. The missus gets confused. Some days she thinks Sarah is still here. Or she thinks Sarah has just gone missing. Then she gets upset all over again."

"Did you never find out where Sarah went?"

"I don't know what 'appened to 'er. She wasn't the sort to run off with a man. She was a good girl. Since she never came home, I think she's gone. Gone to a better place."

"You think she was killed?" He hated to be brutal, but it seemed to be what the man was saying.

"Even if she just ran away, she were on her own. Prey to the cutthroats on the roads and the scoundrels who ravish girls. If she were alive, she'd 'ave written to me and the missus. The lass never did. No, in my 'eart, I know my Sarah is gone." The old farmer put his pipe to his lips but tears welled in his bright blue eyes.

Cal pulled out a handkerchief, a fine soft square of linen, handing it to the man. In New York, any woman of the slum neighborhoods knew about Jack the Ripper and the New York murder of a woman in 1891. Cal wouldn't have expected it here, on an English estate. Maybe the girl just ran away. Maybe she was ashamed to write home. She might have gotten pregnant.

"Is there any help I can give you?" he asked.

"We manage just fine, my lord. You may have heard some sorry tales from Mr. Pegg."

The farmer looked defensive, and Cal was thrown off by the shift in conversation. Who in hell was Pegg? Then he remembered the lawyer had told him Pegg was the land agent of Worthington Park. Pegg had left before Cal arrived, taking a job somewhere else. Apparently offended to work for the impoverished American heir.

"Pegg was gone before I got here. Is it just you and your wife on the farm? Do you have other children?"

"Another girl, but she's married. She married a lad from Stonebridge Farm. We lost our boy in the War. At Verdun, my lord."

"I'm sorry. Many good men were lost."

The farmer led him to the house. He ducked his head and went into a rough kitchen. A wooden sideboard held dishes. A teakettle whistled on the stove. Julia plucked it off.

Just as with Ellen Lambert, Lady Julia was making tea for a farmer's wife. No airs and graces. No snobbery. Never once did she behave as if she were too good to make a cup of tea or too good to help these people.

Cal went to Julia and stood behind her as she poured tea in a pot. He had to ask her this privately, so he lowered his lips so they almost touched her ear. This close he could see the skin on her exposed neck looked satin-soft. "What's wrong with Mrs. Brand? Has she lost her mind?"

His warm breath. The closeness of his body. In the Brands' kitchen, Julia felt her knees go weak.

She was very close to crying—seeing the poor Brands always brought her to tears. For some mad reason, she wanted to press tight against Cal's broad chest. She wanted him to hold her.

But she had been raised to always be cool and composed. To never break down, except in private. And to never fling herself into a man's arms. She had never done that. Not even with Anthony or Dougal. She had been kissed but she'd never been comforted by a man.

She turned with the hot kettle of water, which forced Cal to step back.

Thank heaven. She could barely think with his hot breath on her neck. She hoped he thought it was the weight of the kettle that made her tremble.

"I do know the poor thing has been confused ever since her daughter's disappearance," Julia murmured to him as she poured hot water into the teapot.

"Brand told me that some days she believes Sarah is at home. Or she relives the time when Sarah first went missing and she lives through the pain all over again."

"Yes." Julia could understand how such pain could make

you go mad. When she had lost Anthony, it hurt dreadfully. Then there was loss upon loss. All the other young men she knew who never came back from war. Will's death. Her father's passing. Her heart broke and broke.

Oh, she had been strong and stoic. She never let anyone see how much her heart had been shattered. But all that was left of it was bits and pieces inside her.

The only difference between her and Mrs. Brand was that the poor woman's broken heart had broken her mind, too.

"Is there any way to make her understand what happened?" Cal asked.

"I explain it over and over, as gently as I can. But then she forgets what I've told her."

"She just can't face the fact her daughter might be dead. Maybe if she could be snapped into reality—"

"No!" Julia grabbed his arm. "What if that snapped her mind altogether? What if it made her so depressed she did something drastic? That would destroy Brand."

But Cal left her. Frightened, Julia watched him walk to Mrs. Brand.

He dropped to one knee and clasped her hand. "Do you know where Sarah is?"

"Don't do this," Julia hissed at him. "Please don't."

Slowly Cal told the woman who he was. "I'm so sorry to tell you that your daughter is missing. She might have gone away. That's what we hope. I'm going to find out what happened to her. For you. I promise."

He couldn't promise that. How could he find out now, so many years later?

He was gentler with Mrs. Brand than she expected. She had to admit that. He had been that way with Ellen and Ben. Kind. She could see they all liked him.

Of course, they had no idea what he planned.

She bustled forward and gave out cups of tea. "His lordship is worried about you trying to manage the farm," she said to Mr. Brand. "He wonders if you would be happier to leave it. You could be given a cottage—"

"Pensioned off?" Brand exclaimed. His cup rattled, spilling tea. "Nae, I'd not like that at all. This is our home. I won't leave until they carry me out. Brands have farmed this land for over a century. It should have gone on to me son—"

"We can't go." Mrs. Brand looked up suddenly. "We can't! We have to be here for when Sarah comes home! We can't have her come home and we're not here. She'd never find us! If I leave here, she'll never come home to us!"

Julia saw Cal soothe the woman, a look of raw panic on his handsome face. She wanted him to see what it would do to these people to be forced out. Though she hated to make them upset.

"You won't have to leave," Cal said. "Don't worry about it."

Mrs. Brand stared at him, shaking. "Who are you?" she demanded. "I don't know you." The woman looked up helplessly. Then saw her. "Lady Julia! Good afternoon, your ladyship. Is the wedding to Lord Anthony going to be soon? I saw him yesterday. Driving his fancy horseless carriage, he was. All the silver on it shone in the sun. Brilliant red, it was, like a ripe apple. It'll be a lovely wedding, I'm sure."

Julia hated this moment. She didn't want to remind the woman that Anthony died in the War. That would lead Mrs. Brand to remember she'd lost her son, too. But she must be honest.

Then Cal said, "I'm afraid Lord Anthony was killed in the War. He was a brave young man. I am the Earl of Worthington now, Mrs. Brand."

"But you're Lord Anthony. I see it now. You've changed so much, but I do see—"

"No, Mrs. Brand. I'm not Lord Anthony." He gently squeezed her hand. "I'll find someone to help you here, with the farm. How does that sound?"

"We've got our son. And Laura and Sarah. We're just fine."

Cal flashed a helpless look. Julia mouthed: *You can't do anything.*

He stood and reiterated to Mr. Brand, "You need help around here. I'll see that you get it."

He was lying to Brand, surely. And she hated that. As they left, she whirled on Cal. "You aren't going to get them any help. Your plan is to sell their farm out from underneath them. It will probably kill them."

"And it's better to let them die there?"

"I look in on them almost every day. Though, I do agree they need help."

"I will look after them. I gave them my word. And, when I sell this place, I won't leave innocent victims."

"You were kind to Ellen and to the Brands. I can see you really do care about their welfare. You could be a good lord for Worthington Park."

He grimaced, as if in pain. "I couldn't live with myself, angel, if I stayed here and lived like an earl."

Rain came hard that night, slamming against the paned windows of his bedroom. Cal undid his right cuff link and tossed it into a silver dish on the dresser. By rights, he would be undressing Lady Julia right now, exposing her lush, creamy skin, kissing every delicious inch of her. But she kept taking him places where he had no right to be thinking about seduction.

He was going to have to fix that.

Removing his other cuff link, he tossed it, but it bounced out of the dish, landed on the polished floor and skidded beneath one of the wardrobes.

Cal squatted down, reached under the decorative wood skirting and found his cuff link. But his fingers touched something else and he pulled that out, too.

A small photograph, faded and curling.

He looked at it and almost dropped it in shock. Lady Julia gazed back at him with parted lips and enormous innocent eyes, and she was wearing almost nothing at all.

Cal rubbed his eyes. Sure enough, it was not Julia. It was a grainy photo of a black-haired young woman in a corset. The corset gave the woman a generous swell of bosom and the picture showed a stretch of fleshy bare thigh. Her hair was loose and thick. All that dark hair and the huge eyes made the woman look like Julia.

The photograph probably dated from the War, from the look of the corset.

Julia had said John Carstairs was just a boy during the War. So had this naughty photo belonged to Anthony? He flipped it over and there it was—written in careful handwriting. *A, with love.* No initial or name for the woman. Considering he'd sketched and painted dozens of naked women, Cal had to smile. He could imagine a repressed Englishman being titillated by the picture—

"My lord, when do you wish to begin a search for a new valet?"

Cal looked up. He held the photograph in his hand, and Wiggins stood in the doorway. "I told you I don't need one. I'm capable of taking off my own clothes." He held out the picture. "I found this under the wardrobe. Lady friend of Lord Anthony's?" He was teasing, expecting to make the butler blush.

He was surprised when Wiggins turned white. "I apologize, my lord. I did not realize the apartments had not been thoroughly cleaned. I shall have Mrs. Rumpole reprimand the maids for their carelessness." The butler yanked the picture out his hands. "Let me dispose of this, my lord."

Cal didn't want to see a maid getting in trouble. "It's not a problem."

"It is my duty to deal with the matter, my lord. If you will excuse me, I will take my leave."

Wiggins retreated so fast that the door slammed behind him. Lightning forked outside the window, illuminating the room in a flash of silver-blue, then thunder boomed.

It was then he realized that Anthony had never been earl, so had never slept in this room. So why was his picture under the earl's wardrobe?

7

The Gypsy Curse

"I'm to give cooking lessons to the kitchen maid of another house?" Mrs. Creedy, the cook at Brideswell cried, leaning rather fiercely on her rolling pin. Then she suddenly appeared to remember who she'd just barked at. "I mean, if that is what you wish, my lady, of course I would want to do so. But how would I fit it in with the tight schedule of Brideswell? What will Her Grace say?"

Julia smiled, moving back to let the kitchen maid scurry past with pot in hand. "We'll find a way, Mrs. Creedy. And Her Grace has already approved." Zoe was all for the idea, to help Hannah Talbot. "It might not be necessary at all. I shall speak to Mrs. Talbot today. She may not feel she needs help at the moment, but I want us to be there to support her."

"All right, but it seems a strange business to me. A kitchen maid elevated to cook in one afternoon? And I've heard the new earl wants simpler food and less of it."

Julia nodded. "Yes, his lordship is concerned about waste of food, which is quite admirable and noble."

Mrs. Creedy snorted. "His lordship has no idea what needs to be done in a kitchen."

"But he is in charge. And I want to ensure Hannah does not suffer as the new earl endeavors to bring American ways to his kitchens." In the depths of her heart, she did see why waste would appall him. After all, he had been starving. But she would not let him hurt or frighten the poor kitchen-maid-turned-cook, Hannah, even if he believed he was helping her. He had claimed she had produced excellent meals, but rumors had come to Brideswell from the other kitchen maid, Tansy, that poor Hannah was quite out of her depth.

Cal's anger at Mrs. Feathers was justified—Julia had been shocked by the bruises on Hannah's arm—but he had used Hannah as a pawn to score a point on Julia. And she intended to make that right.

"Thank you, Mrs. Creedy," Julia said. But as she walked away, she saw she was as bad as Cal. She was using Brideswell's cook to score her own point on him.

But she would ensure Mrs. Creedy was rewarded for helping, and it would make things much better for Hannah.

She had reached the bottom of the servants' staircase when Bartlet, Brideswell's butler, stepped out of his room and looked at her in surprise. "Lady Julia! I did not expect to see you here. There is a call on the telephone for you. The dowager duchess. I fear she believes she is already speaking to you, my lady. There appears to be sound emanating from the receiver."

Julia couldn't help but smile. "I will take it on one of the upstairs extensions."

Zoe had insisted Brideswell would have more than two telephones—it sported four. Most people were mystified. They all rang at once, for a start. And who needed so many? Their peers dismissed it as American vulgarity.

When Julia lifted up the telephone in the foyer, her grandmother was saying, "That is what I think, Julia. Of course you agree."

Julia rolled her eyes. "Grandmama, I just got to the phone. I haven't heard a word you said. But how are you?"

"Fine, fine, but let's not bother with that. If I shall have to say it all over again, I will."

Julia knew Zoe had given Grandmama a telephone to be cheeky, for the dowager duchess had first approached it as if touching the receiver would mean certain death. Now Grandmama was addicted to the thing. She'd realized its power. On any whim she could make a telephone call and disrupt the entire house.

"You have made a conquest, my dear!"

"A what?"

"A gentleman is smitten. Really, dear, do keep up. I invited the Earl of Summerhay to tea, and he would talk about nothing but you, Julia. All you must do is give a nudge in the right direction—"

"No nudging, Grandmama," Julia broke in. "I do know Summerhay is interested—"

"Then what on earth are you doing about it?"

"I told him I was not ready."

"Not ready? What are you waiting for, dear?"

Julia opened her mouth but the dowager rushed on, "If it's Dr. Campbell, I'm afraid he is out of the picture. If he isn't strong enough to defy all of us to pursue you, he isn't good enough for you."

Julia almost dropped the telephone. For she had not thought of Dougal when her grandmother asked the question. The first face that had come into her head had been Cal's.

But she *wasn't* in love with Cal.

"Grandmama, I must go. I am taking Cal—the new Earl of Worthington—around the estate so he can meet his tenants."

"You call him 'Cal,' do you? And what does he call you? Please tell me it's not 'Julie.'"

"I can safely assure you it is not that."

"Do not be too familiar with that man," the dowager declared, over the wires. "I think he's one who would need no encouragement. And since Nigel was overcome by madness and married an American, I dread to think what folly you might slip into if you are not properly guided."

"I'm rather old to be guided."

"That is often said by people who feel they are capable of living with their mistakes. The problem is that they have no idea how miserable that will be. Now I shall need to speak to Zoe. I think a dinner party is in order and I must convince my granddaughter-in-law to hold one."

Oh, she must stop this. "What of your romance, Grandmama?"

"What romance, dear? At my age, a woman barely remembers what romance was."

"That is not true. You can't deny Sir Raynard is courting you. Did he not invite you to a musical revue in London?"

"He invited me to a jazz club, my dear. Of course I said no. Next thing, he would be wanting me to dance the Black Bottom with him."

Julia had to clap her hand to her mouth. She had to smother the giggles that came from picturing her grandmother dancing a primitive-style dance with her bottom sticking out. "I'm sure he just wanted to introduce you to the new jazz music."

"I fear not. An older gentleman in love can be utterly exhausting. The first thing he wants to do is prove how young he is."

"Please don't discourage him. I think it would be rather lovely for you to have a gentleman in your life."

"I won't discourage Raynard, dear, if you don't discourage Summerhay. Now—to plan a dinner party. Toodle-oo, my dear."

She heard the dial tone. Grandmama was rushing off to scheme. Oh dear.

Julia set down the receiver, and someone cried, "There you are!" right behind her, making her jump. Before her heart slipped down from her throat, her mother grasped her hand and towed her into a drawing room.

Mother carried a letter. Her green eyes sparkled and she looked filled with life. She had not glowed with such happiness for a long time. Not since before Will had died. Losing her youngest son had devastated Mother. A Catholic, Mother prayed every day at the small chapel Father had built for her on the estate. Julia was happy that whatever news Mother had gotten was good.

"Bradstock writes to say how much he enjoyed seeing us again, Julia. Of course he mentions you. Of course he is too much of a gentleman to be blunt, but I know he's wrangling for an invitation. Viscount Yorkville is a disappointment—I heard he became engaged to an earl's daughter. I am going to speak to Zoe and Nigel about throwing a ball. That would be the perfect thing to place you in the path of the duke."

Now she knew why Mother was happy. "Mother, I am not interested in the duke."

Definitely not, after the things he'd said about her charity work. He had apologized but her entire life would be dictated by a man like that.

"Julia, you are almost seven and twenty. You *must* be interested in the duke, whether you like it or not. No woman wants to be a spinster. At this age, you should have an establishment of your own. You are restless—and you can't deny it. That is why you are dabbling in this rather scandalous work. Fallen women indeed!"

For years, after unhappiness in marriage, her mother had withdrawn from the world. For this, she had suddenly found strength. Julia wanted her mother to be strong. To no longer be trapped in mourning Will. But why did it have to be for something they were destined to fight about?

Zoe had confided how her American mama had wanted her to marry Nigel instead of Sebastian from the start. Now Julia found she was saying to her mother exactly what Zoe had said to hers: "Mother, I am not going to marry the duke."

For the first time in forever, Mother set her jaw resolutely. She folded her arms over her gray cashmere cardigan. "Then who will you marry? There were no dowries before, so there were no offers. Now there will not be many, my dear, because of your advanced age. You will never be content as a country doctor's wife. You were raised to be mistress of a grand estate. You would never be happy with anything less."

"As for men attracted by my dowry—what good are gentlemen who assess you only by your money?" Julia asked. "I don't want to be married to one. So many great estates are being sold. I could marry the duke and he could have to sell his home six months later. Nothing is certain in the world anymore."

"Julia, your dowry will be sufficient to keep an estate—"

"Not if he gambles his way through it. Or invests it badly." She spoke on instinct and pain flashed over Mother's face. Father had gambled through the money, and he'd had no sense of investment at all. "I'm sorry, but it is true. I do not want to have to turn over my money to a husband and have no say in how it is spent."

For she realized she didn't blindly trust a man to be cleverer than her. Ten years ago she might have believed it, but not anymore. She now knew marriage was not an achievement, but a beginning—and she didn't want it to be the beginning of a descent into hell.

She had no place in the world. She had been waiting for marriage to define her. She was not supposed to seek a career. And what would she do? Become a secretary? Build engines for locomotives? Take a job from a deserving man with a family to feed?

Her siblings seemed to have found their places. Nigel was the duke and he was a good, responsible one. Sebastian loved to paint. Isobel, her younger sister, wanted to become a doctor.

She needed to find her place.

Her mother touched her arm. "If you make a wise choice, darling, you will have nothing to worry about."

"But that is not true! I do not want to hope and pray I marry a sensible man who doesn't make my life miserable. There must be more for me. Why could I not make money of my own? Buy my own house?"

"You are a duke's daughter. Dukes' daughters marry."

"And those who don't become spinsters. This is the 1920s! There has to be more. More than this constant worry about suitors and titles, dowries and estates."

"Those have been the reasons for marriage in our class for centuries."

"It's not good enough for me. I want love."

"Love and affection can develop."

And she knew that wasn't enough, either. "I want more. I want to be swept away by the person I marry. I want to feel a *whoosh*. I want *passion*."

Her mother's mouth dropped. She went white, then

blushed scarlet. But what was wrong with a woman wanting to go to bed with the man she had married?

She'd had few kisses in her life, but Julia knew what she'd felt when Cal had draped his shirt around her. Hot, trembling, aching—and filled with a dizzying need.

She had seen the way Zoe and Nigel looked at each other. Enough heat to ignite flames. She had seen Nigel sweep Zoe into his arms to carry her to bed—or Zoe lead Nigel by his necktie to his bedroom. Desire and joy had exuded from both of them.

How could a woman think of decades spent with anything less?

But Mother shook her head. "Passion is a terrible reason for marriage. It fades. It ends. And it leads to disaster."

Julia swallowed hard. "Maybe it doesn't have to. If both parties feel it."

"A gentleman is very ready to feel passion for any woman who catches his eye. He may still feel it for you, but I assure you that will extinguish anything you feel for him. You are much better to marry for sensible reasons. If you marry a man like the duke, he can never take away your happiness if you are happy to be a duchess."

"But your happiness was taken away—"

"Because I hoped for more, Julia." Her mother drew herself up, looking almost as fierce as Grandmama. "If I had not had that rather hopeless hope, I would have been happy."

Love would have made Mother happy. But what was the point of saying it?

She couldn't trade an estate for her heart and soul. She simply couldn't. Even if it meant eventually she ended up with nothing. For somehow she would survive. Wouldn't she?

"I must go, Mother. I must visit some families on the Worthington estate. And look in on some of the Brideswell families." She left the room and hurried upstairs. Julia threw on jodhpurs and a hacking jacket, along with her riding hat. The fashions had gone away from the old-fashioned riding habit. She went down to the stables and had a groom saddle Athena. Zoe and Nigel took care of the Brideswell families, but she still liked to visit them. And she had promised Anthony she would look after Worthington. Spurring on her horse, she galloped away to do this work she loved—leaving the problem of marriage behind her.

Being in the house made Cal feel like an animal trapped in a gilded cage.

He was walking down the drive when he saw an elegant white horse canter toward him. A woman was on top, wearing jodhpurs, a trim-fitting black coat, a black riding hat.

Julia. His heart rate accelerated and Cal felt nerves he hadn't felt since he was a boy of fifteen, trying to coax a girl to let him make love to her because he was tired of being the only virgin in the Five Points Juniors Gang.

"I wanted to take you to see more tenants but Athena needed exercise," she called to him. "And the chauffeur was fixing something on my motor. We can take one of your vehicles if you wish. Can I stable Athena here while we go?"

"I haven't been down to see the stables yet."

"You must go. The grooms will be wondering why you have not. I assumed you would have thoroughly explored the house and grounds. If I'd known, I would have taken you myself."

She spoke to him like a disappointed schoolteacher—not that he'd had much experience with one of those. Mam had wanted him to be educated but he didn't see much use for school. But his father bought books and pushed him to read, so they could debate, in the few hours his father was not working at some menial job.

"Worthington's stables are admired throughout the county," she went on. "There are some fierce horses, but there are gentler ones, too, so you could learn to ride."

Julia's smile entranced him, but it reminded him they were from two different worlds.

He had come to Worthington filled with defiance about his humble origins. Now, damn it, when he was with Julia he found himself wishing he had a better past.

Why should he damn well care? He wasn't going to be like the Duke of Bradstock or the Earl of Summerhay. He hadn't been to the right schools and he had the blood of simple, hardworking people in his veins.

He was never going to be good enough for Lady Julia. Not to marry her. But he could be good enough to seduce her.

What he wanted was to see her sparkling eyes filled with desire—for him—as he made love to her. That was all he wanted.

"It would be a good idea for you to learn how to ride. Most gentlemen ride. I would be delighted to teach you."

"I'm not a gentleman," he said, "and I don't have any intention of trying to act like I am one."

Hurt showed in her face.

He needed to remember that she was getting in the way of his plans. She was making him care about the people on the estate. Getting her to leave him alone would be a damn good idea.

But he wanted her. Wanted her badly.

"All right, doll," he said. "Teach me to ride."

Cal may not have ridden before, but he had a way with horses that surprised Julia. He went to the stables with her, dressed in his threadbare clothes, which shocked the grooms at first. But his engaging manner won them over. The head groom, Michaels, found a gentle mare for Cal.

As soon as Michaels gave him the reins, Cal stroked the mare's nose, fed her from the palm of his hand. The horse whinnied happily as he stroked her withers.

Cal could make any female melt, Julia realized.

He spoke in soft murmurs to his mount, Empress, then tried to swing up onto her. The first time, he fell back, landing hard on the ground.

Julia cringed, certain his pride would be hurt.

But Cal laughed. A rich, husky laugh that spoke of joy and wickedness. He tried again, and got into the saddle with stunning grace. He seemed happier, less angry than he had when she and he had herded the pigs.

Within an hour, he'd progressed to trotting around the fenced-in ring. Julia had seen many gentlemen ride and some looked magnificent in the saddle, but compared to Cal they all looked stiff. He had such sensual grace. Watching the loose-limbed movements of his arms and shoulders made her want to snatch off her hat and fan herself.

"You are a natural. Born to it," she called out.

"You're my teacher. The credit is all yours." He grinned. "Where did you intend to take me today? Can we ride there?"

"Lower Dale Farm. It's one of the most productive on your estate. Yes, we can ride."

She led him to a path that wound through the meadow below the stables. Wildflower blooms swayed in the late spring breeze. Bees buzzed around the flowers. The horses flicked their tails. The trail was wide enough for them to ride side by side. She could see Cal's inexperience in the jerky way he handled the reins, but Empress was a patient, placid horse.

"Do you realize everything on this estate needs modernization?" Cal asked. "I've driven around on my own, looking at the farms. I went out early this morning."

"You went to look at them?"

"Yeah. All of these farms would be improved with mechanization. They need tractors instead of horses and plows. They need to adopt some up-to-date methods of farming. New barns. New houses for the farmers. Those stone cottages are damp and cold. How does anyone survive the winter?"

Her heart lifted. For him to show such interest was a good sign. She was getting through to him. These were all the things she and Anthony had planned to do, but she knew she must take a different approach. "We use fires and once there is a good blaze going in the hearth, the houses do warm up. And the people of the estates are hardy. They are accustomed—"

"That's not good enough," he broke in. "What they need are—" He stopped and faced her with a stubborn look on his face. "Don't look so smug, Julia. These are just observations."

Bother. She had hoped to goad him into vowing to do all those improvements because she had "implied" the people did not need them. And it had been working, so it was *impossible* not to look victorious. "Of course. But I think the tenants are very happy as they are."

"And I say they are not." He frowned. Muttered, "Damn it." Then he said, stubbornly, "I have to examine the place before I figure out what it could sell for."

"I hadn't thought of that." She tried to sound disappointed. To sound as if she feared she had lost. But she was *certain* she was winning. So she asked, "What did you mean when you said you couldn't live with yourself if you stayed and lived like an earl?"

He rode in silence for a while. Silence that made her uneasy. She yearned to know the answer. She'd been awake most of last night wondering about it.

Suddenly he said, "I'm obsessed with painting you. I've tried painting you from memory, but I can't capture what I want. I need to have you sitting there so I can study you while I work. I need to paint you, Julia. It's eating at my soul. I need you to pose for me."

The fierce, vehement way he said it shocked her. But she didn't believe he *needed* to paint her. "You are trying to change the subject," she protested.

"I'm not, doll. I'm telling you the truth. For me, painting is like breathing air. I need it to live. And when I get obsessed over painting a woman, it drives me crazy. So will you pose?"

A searing image struck her. Cal in his white shirt with the sleeves rolled up, watching her with this fiery, intense yearning in his eyes. It took her breath away. But a lady would never reveal how unsettled she was. "You paint barely dressed as I remember."

He gave her a scorching look. "I need to be comfortable when I paint. Would it bother you?"

"I don't know," she said. "I don't know about having my portrait painted. I don't think I would like to sit for hours and hours."

"You don't want to spend hours with me?" he asked lightly.

"What if I said yes? Would you explain what you meant?"

He shrugged, holding the reins. "I meant what I said."

"Cal, you are a good man. A kind man. I saw that in the way you leaped to Hannah's defense, in the way you want to help Ellen, and how tender and gentle you were with Mrs. Brand. You don't seem like the kind of man to be vengeful or cruel."

"Every man has his breaking point, Julia," was all he said.

She wished she knew what exactly had happened when the old earl had disowned Cal's father.

"I asked around the village about Sarah Brand, Julia."

She jerked her head toward him. "You did?" He had been concerned about the Brands and that touched her heart.

"I heard she was seen driving with a man in a fancy automobile. How could she never have been found? Wouldn't it have been easy to find a man who drove a car back then? Or didn't they look for her all that hard?"

"What do you mean? I was quite young but I assure you that people scoured the estate in case she'd had an accident, Cal. Even I joined in to search—though my mother was shocked that I did."

He moved at her side, thighs rising and following with the motion of his horse. He seemed lost in thought for a while. Then he said, "People said there were only automobiles at the great houses at the time. Brideswell had a car. So did the earl at Worthington Park. I heard the old earl had bought an up-to-date motorcar for his eldest son."

Her horse reared beneath her. She had jerked abruptly on the reins, startling Athena. With a firm grip of her thighs, firm hands on the reins and soothing words she settled her horse. Was she just leaping to suspicions over what he was implying?

"Mrs. Brand said he had a flashy automobile," he went on. "Which means she must have seen it."

"Anthony loved it and drove it all over Worthington. Of course she would have seen it."

"The man who took Sarah out in his car could have been one of the men at Worthington or Brideswell."

"What are you saying?" she cried. "Brideswell's car at the time was a rather sedate vehicle. And I can assure you that none of my brothers was flirting with Sarah Brand. Nor could it have been Anthony or John."

"Why couldn't it have been one of them?"

"John was young. Only fifteen. And Anthony—Anthony was already courting me."

"You thought he was in love with you by then," Cal said. "I expect he was. But Sarah Brand wasn't a girl like you."

She knew he was implying she might be blind to the behavior of her former fiancé.

"I just wondered if the law believed the man in the car was a toff, a local one, if they really investigated."

"The magistrate did investigate, I assure you," she answered stiffly.

But he had put a horrible thought into her mind. One she had never, ever considered before. Could Anthony—?

What if he'd had his way with Sarah and didn't want to marry her?

No! No—Anthony was not that kind of gentleman. She was sure of it. "You are deliberately trying to poison my mind with awful thoughts so I'll stop fighting you."

She gave Athena a press with her heels and urged her horse ahead as they entered the woods. It was impossible to talk unless they shouted. Once they emerged from the woods into another meadow, Cal caught up to her. "Julia, that wasn't what I was trying to do. I didn't mean to hurt you. But there couldn't have been many men who could afford an automobile. And would Sarah Brand really have gotten justice if an earl's son was involved?"

"Yes," she declared. "She would have done." But in her heart, she feared he was right. About justice, *not* about Anthony.

Cal glanced around, frowning. "I smell smoke."

"Cooking fires," she said. Her hands trembled around the reins.

Strains of music came to them from the other side of a meadow—the jaunty notes of a fiddle, the jingle of a tambourine. And laughter. A group of children exploded out of the tall meadow grass, chasing a young, barefoot girl who ran like wild.

Julia had gathered control of herself, and she turned to Cal. "There are several Roma families who come here to live in the summer and autumn. In return they work to pick fruit and to pick hops later on. Hop picking is grueling work and the hop juice stains your hands terribly."

"I would've thought the earl would have run them off his land."

"Not the old earl—Anthony's father. He appreciated their help with the work. They provided the labor he needed only when it was required, and they were quite content to camp and receive a stipend for their work. Though when John was the earl, briefly, he expressed dislike of the gypsies and did say he should not let them stay. Pegg, the land agent, talked him out of it." She dismounted and smiled at Cal. "Shall we go and say hello?"

Cal watched as the children spotted Julia and ran to her. She laughingly greeted them all and his heart gave a pang. Something he'd never felt. He never wanted to be tied down. Yet he watched Julia and felt yearning.

He also knew he'd frightened her with his speculation. Why else would she have jerked on the reins and made her horse shy?

"You have all grown so much!" she declared. She carried on as if nothing had happened to disturb her. At first, that used to irritate him. He wanted to smash her sangfroid.

Now—hell, now he found he admired it. Lady Julia Hazelton was tough and strong.

She motioned to Cal. "This is the Earl of Worthington."

The girls, all dark-haired and lovely, curtsied to him. The boys bowed.

He dismounted also and tied the reins of his horse to a tree, leaving Empress alongside Julia's mare, and he followed Julia into the camp.

Three caravans—wooden structures with domed roofs, all painted in bright colors—stood around a fire pit. Older men sat and smoked. A young man played a fiddle, all the while watching a young woman who worked with other women, preparing food. Others sat and sewed. The people treated him with deference, though they gave his clothing strange looks. Cal grinned at her. "Even to the gypsies, I guess I make a strange-looking earl."

"Isn't that what you wanted?" she responded teasingly. Then she left him to go and speak to the women of the camp.

Was she really teasing? Disapproving? That was the power of her controlled, ladylike expression. He couldn't tell what she meant. Couldn't see into her heart. And he wanted to know.

He wanted to break through that ladylike armor. Was she a mass of pain, passion and fear inside, and she'd never learned how to let it out? Was that why she'd been locked in grief for so long? That was another thing the villagers told him—that Lady Julia had spent too long grieving.

He stood, watching Julia, then felt someone staring at him and turned.

A woman with a grizzled, tanned face and white-streaked hair was seated in a chair by the fire. She motioned Cal to join her and handed him a drink—strong coffee. The gypsy woman smoked a pipe, and he had the sense she was someone of importance. Brightly patterned skirts spread around her. An embroidered vest and white blouse covered her upper body. Smoke wreathed her.

"I'm Genevra. So ye're the new lordship, are ye?" she asked. "Ye don't look all that happy to be in the role, milord, I would say."

"I never expected to be an earl," he said.

"Aye. I thought not. Ye look like a wild one." Genevra chuckled deeply. "I notice ye've barely taken your eyes off Lady Julia for all the time ye've been here."

His cheeks felt hot. "I like looking at her."

"I can see ye do." She wagged a finger at him. "She's not for you."

It was true, but her nosiness made him angry. "I don't see that's your business."

"Ye've got a hot head, too."

"I'm the earl around here. Did you pass personal observations on my uncle?"

"No. But then, he's not like you." She leaned toward him confidingly. "I'm happy Lady Julia did not marry Lord Anthony, the old earl's son. No good would have come of that. Not when the curse claimed her."

"You're saying there's a curse on Lady Julia?" There were gypsies in America, and they were driven away even there. People were suspicious of them, and many believed they could lay curses. He didn't.

"Does she have to cross your palm with silver to escape it?" he asked mockingly, remembering his dark-haired mother with her long-lashed Irish blue eyes, telling him of pixies, leprechauns, spirits. He had loved the stories as a boy, got impatient with them as a youth. He didn't believe in fortunes and fate.

Genevra shot him a haughty look. He'd offended her.

"There is no curse on her. But if she had married Lord Anthony, there would have been. Have you not heard of it? You being the earl now, I thought someone would have told you. They're all afraid of it, up at the house. Oh, they deny it, but they are. If Lady Julia had married Lord Anthony, the curse would have been on her. That would have been a tragedy. She is good, kind and generous of spirit. Her soul is pure."

The gypsy blew a ring of smoke. It rose above her, lingered like a halo, then blew apart. "It will touch the woman you marry, milord."

"What is this curse?"

"The curse befalls whoever marries Lord Worthington, milord. A century past, the Countess of Worthington ran down one of our children with a carriage. The child's mother cursed whoever became the Worthington Wife. Callous and heartless, that countess was, and she paid the price. She lost six of her eight children to illnesses and accidents. Even the current countess has suffered much loss and much pain."

"I don't believe in curses. You can't say a few words and change someone's fate."

"But someone did with yours, milord, when they told you that you were the new earl."

He lifted his brow at her, and she laughed merrily. The sound was low and husky. "The funny thing about curses, milord, is that we make them come true when we seek hardest to deny them. Or avoid them."

Then the fiddling music grew louder and faster. In the center of the camp, the children danced. Two girls clung to Julia, dancing with her. Julia twirled and laughed, nothing like a cool and austere lady.

And Cal couldn't take his eyes off her.

8

A Birth at Lower Dale Farm

"Do you believe in the Worthington Wife curse?"

Julia looked up, startled. "They told you about that?" They were riding down the lane to Lower Dale Farm. Cal looked magnificent in the saddle.

"The woman called Genevra did," he said.

"She told me not to marry Lord Anthony because of it—she read my palm and gave me a serious warning. She was so intense that I was quite frightened," she admitted. "In fact, I was—I was very angry with her. I thought the whole thing was a joke in poor taste. There was…quite a row over it. Anthony's father went to see her. Her words had made Anthony rethink our engagement. The whole story of the curse is rather terrible."

"Genevra told me that the Countess of Worthington was cursed one hundred years ago, after she ran over a gypsy child."

Julia nodded. "That is the story. Terrible things did happen to that countess, though I suspect that was due to the

lack of medical knowledge and the countess's selfish character and not a curse. I don't believe in curses."

"The current countess has been through a hell of a lot of
trouble," Cal said.

She frowned. "I don't believe the current Lady Worthington has suffered because of angry words spoken by a bereaved
woman who had suffered unimaginable pain. But supersti-
tions run deep in the country. Many tenants of the estate
believe in it, especially with all of the tragedy that had be-
fallen Lady Worthington. It has led to fear for the gypsies.
Terrible, prejudicial fear."

Some villagers had said that the curse had touched her the
minute Anthony proposed to her, the moment he intended
for her to be his wife…

"What's wrong, Julia?" Cal asked gently. "You look so
sad. Have I scared you?"

She could brush him off with a false smile, but she didn't.
"Some said falling in love with me was what killed Anthony.
That the curse took him away from me because I was to be
a Worthington Wife."

"Who said that? Damn, that's a cruel thing to say."

"I knew it couldn't be true. But it did hurt."

"Sure it did. Tell me who said that."

His dark brows were drawn together in anger. Outrage—
over someone saying something to her that hurt. He was
noble. Julia knew she could do what she'd set out to do—
make him care about Worthington. But what had he meant
when he'd said he couldn't live with himself if he lived here
as the earl? That was the key. If she could change his mind
on that, she would win. She would save Worthington. And
give it a master who was obviously worthy of it.

"Cal, it was nine years ago. You aren't intending to be

angry with people over thoughtless words after so long. But I do appreciate you acting the knight in shining armor. For me."

"You don't have to tell me, Julia, but if I find out who hurt you that way, I'll make sure they regret it," he growled.

That was Cal—he was driven by vengeance. "There is a difference between revenge and justice. And I don't need either, Cal."

"There's not a lot of justice in this world, Julia. Sometimes a man has to help it along."

He said it so coolly, and a shiver rushed down her spine.

She slowed her horse to a walk, negotiating the narrow, rough lane that led down to the large, impressive farm. It was time to change the topic of conversation. Brightly, she said, "Lower Dale Farm is the most productive on the estate—the one Anthony was exceedingly proud of, for he and the farmer, Roger Toft, decided to start raising a new and hardier breed of pig and developed better ideas for the rotation of crops."

These had been her ideas, too, and Anthony had agreed, rather than tell her such areas were not for women. Some men would have rejected anything she'd said on principle.

Cal grinned, apparently forgetting his anger. "You're glowing, Lady Julia. I never thought any woman would find crops and pigs sexy."

He let the last word come out in his low, deep voice. She felt a pang of—of something intense that rushed right down to her toes.

He'd said that word to shock her. She lifted a brow at him. "Perhaps they have better sex appeal than some men."

He gave her his cocky grin. When he did, she could see his Irish side in the roguish nature of that smile.

"I have to admit I was impressed at you chasing the Brands' pigs," he said. "I didn't expect that of a duke's daughter."

"I am a rather unusual duke's daughter." She stopped. For a moment, there was silence. Muted baas of sheep. Clucking and honking from the birds. She locked gazes with Cal. "This farm is successful because this is more than the livelihood of this family—it's their life. Mrs. Toft is expecting another child—their fifth. Why should all their hard work be destroyed?"

Cal opened his mouth to answer, but a piercing cry drowned out his words. Julia stared at the house and Cal asked, "What in hell was that?"

It came from the farmhouse—Julia's favorite house on the Worthington estate. But now she looked at it as horror took a twisting grip on her heart. She knew what it was.

With legs trembling, Julia urged her horse to a canter. "It was a woman's scream."

It came again and quivers of terror shot down Julia's spine as she neared the house. She'd heard cries like this before. Mrs. Toft was pregnant and had told Julia, last week, that she was very close to her time—

"I think a woman's in labor," Cal shouted as he caught up behind her.

She reined in and all but flung herself off the horse. Cal followed with a smooth flowing movement. He raced to the door with her—and Julia came to an abrupt halt.

Mary Toft—the oldest girl at age twelve—rushed out of the doorway and hugged Julia. "Me mum is poorly, they say. I'm so afraid."

No. Oh no. "Poorly" was an adult way to hide terrible news. Julia tried to hide the shaking that threatened to overtake her. She crouched down. "I don't know what's happening, my dear. But I think everything will be all right. Where are your brothers and your sister?"

"They're hiding in the kitchen. Father sent us outside, but we didn't want to go."

She must stay strong for the girl. She gently squeezed the child's hand. "Let me go inside and find out what is happening, Mary."

Her heart was in her throat. She remembered Zoe's cries of pain...then Zoe had lost the baby. Julia's strength was failing. Her legs wanted to collapse. But she propelled herself forward.

Cal's hand gripped her wrist before she could go through the door. "Julia, don't go in there."

"I have to. I—I am needed. I must *do* something."

"I'll bring the children out. Stay out here with them."

"No. I can't just sit by and not *help*." Pushing away from him, she ran in, but could feel him close behind her.

The cries and moans led her up the narrow wooden stairs to the largest bedroom. Julia walked into the heat and shouting and frantic activity of childbirth. Oh, heavens.

Mr. Toft was glued back against the wall, horror on his face. On the bed, Elsie Toft was half sitting, with women supporting her. Hair plastered with sweat, her face both white with shock and red with strain. She grunted and scrunched up her face, then screamed. "I can't do it no more."

The women eased Mrs. Toft back and she collapsed limply on the bed, her eyes shut.

"The babe is stuck. Wedged." That was Mrs. Thomas, the local midwife, speaking quietly. A broad, strong woman with a ruddy face. Her sleeves were rolled up, her apron wet and streaked with blood.

Such agony went across Mrs. Toft's face that Julia's heart broke.

"What about the doctor?" she asked. "We must bring him. He would know what to do."

"That fool with the clean sleeves? I doubt—" Turning around, the midwife stopped in midsentence. "My lady, whatever are you doing in here?"

"I've come to help. I could bring the doctor."

"Aye, he should be fetched. But I fear he won't know what to do."

One of the other women said softly, "How long has she got?"

"Not long, the poor thing. She hasn't got the strength anymore."

"And the baby?"

Roger Toft let out a sob. He was a huge, broad-shouldered man with a barrel chest and enormous arms. And it was awful to watch him break. Sobs racked him.

Julia didn't hear Mrs. Thomas's answer. The room seemed to swim around her. It shimmered, the way the air did on a hot day.

"I will get the doctor," she cried. She ran out of the room as if being chased by demons.

If only she had her car. She would have to ride back to Brideswell and drive from there.

But as she spun on her heel to rush to her motor, her legs buckled beneath her. A strong arm slipped around her waist and she was taken down the stairs and outside. She was deposited on an upturned bucket and she looked into concerned, sky blue eyes.

Cal.

"You almost passed out in there. I'll get the doctor."

"I can do it." She had to do something. That funny feeling—that dots were exploding in front of her eyes—was going away. "How can you be so calm?"

"I've done this before."

"You've helped a woman give birth before?"

"I helped my mother when I was a boy. *Her* mother had

been a midwife in Ireland, and she'd learned a few things from her mother. When any woman was giving birth in the tenement, she would ask for my mam."

His mam. The word made her want to cry. This "Mam" might lose her battle—

Standing over her, he shook his head. "You're white as a sheet. You need a drink. Something strong, if they've got it."

"I am fine. I should be useful."

"Fainting won't be of any use."

"I am not going to faint. I wouldn't allow myself to."

"I don't think you'll have a choice, doll. Stay out here until I get back. Don't go back inside. My guess is that your snooty Society wouldn't approve of you helping at a birth."

"I don't care about that!"

"God, you are an amazing woman. You shouldn't have been born a duke's daughter. You're a real person."

That was the strangest thing anyone had ever said to her, yet it touched her heart like no flowery compliment had ever done. But then the worst agonized cry she'd ever heard came from the bedroom. "I must go," she said. When he shook his head again, she cried, "You are hardly in a position to dictate to me. I am tired of being told what I can and cannot do. I am a grown woman, capable of making choices. Capable of doing what is necessary to do! I absolutely must be the one to go. You don't know where the hospital is."

"I'm telling you what to do to protect you."

And she saw then, as she almost screamed with frustration, that she did not *want* to be protected. An English lady's life was all about being supposedly protected, but you were really not protected at all. You still knew loss and pain, heartbreak, desperation and desolation. All you were protected from was taking some control of your life.

"Don't. I refuse to allow anyone to protect me from life

anymore." Courage and determination surged through her. She could do this—ride like the wind to Brideswell. She was going to do it. Julia leaped to her feet.

"I'm riding with you," Cal said. "Back to Worthington, and I'll drive to the hospital."

"You won't be able to gallop as I can. You'll fall."

"I'll take that risk," he said, his jaw set.

That was exactly the kind of person she wanted to be—willing to take risk.

She led Cal out to the road, where they could let their horses gallop. It was too far for a flat-out run. Julia had to admit she was amazed at how Cal stayed in his seat.

They reached Worthington with lathered horses, both coated in perspiration and breathing hard. Cal leaped down from his horse and shouted orders that her car be brought round. Julia wanted to drive, but he jumped into the driver's seat and refused to move, forcing her into the passenger side. Then he stomped the car's accelerator to the floor and took off with a spray of gravel.

Over the roar of the engine, she shouted directions. She couldn't believe Cal could drive so well on a road he barely knew. He slowed as they reached the village—just a moment before she was going to warn him to do so since there were bicycles on the road, and horses, and children.

Even though it was part of Nigel's land holdings, Brideswell's village hospital served much of the area, including the Worthington estate.

Inside the hospital and outside the office of Dr. Hamilton, a nurse tried to insist the doctor could not be disturbed. It was Cal who bellowed, "I am the Earl of Worthington and the doctor had better come with me right now. *Now.*"

She and Cal burst into the doctor's office. The doctor

dropped something very quickly into a drawer of his desk and gazed up at them calmly. "What is all this, my lady? Is there an emergency? Or is this another woman with supposed shell shock?"

Julia gritted her teeth. She remembered the irritating debate she'd had with Dr. Hamilton about Ellen Lambert. He had insisted Ellen could not have shell shock, which only afflicted men. Obviously she had hysteria—it was obvious, he'd said, because her temperament had also *obviously* led her to her scandalous line of work. Julia had wanted to hit him with a bedpan.

Now she cried breathlessly, "You must come at once to Lower Dale Farm. We shall drive you. Hurry—you must hurry!"

She had never thrown away her composure like this with an outsider to her family, with anyone other than Cal.

"You must tell me what is going on," Hamilton said, unruffled. He wore a white coat, his graying hair and mustache elegantly styled with pomade.

"Oh bother! Just come with us," she cried.

But he was not moving, so she threw the story at him. He had a bland face that was somewhat handsome, but also had ferrety attributes. He was no substitute for Dougal Campbell. Not in the least.

He still was not moving. He should leap to his feet—but he did not.

"We must go now, Dr. Hamilton," she cried. Ladylike Lady Julia would never do what she did right then. She stalked around to his side and then she smelled the strong aroma of alcohol. Something snapped in her. "Are you drunk? Is that why you are not getting up? I will have my brother throw you out if you do not get up and come with us at once!"

He had the gall to look offended. "To Lower Dale Farm for a birth, my lady? That is the business of midwives. I'd come at once, of course, if it was a patient of mine at Brideswell. But these people prefer midwives who come from their own social stratum. They have no money to pay for a proper phys—"

"I will pay," Julia bit off. "Do remember my family is the reason this hospital operates. It is by the generosity of the duchy that you can even sit in this office and drink brandy, Dr. Hamilton. If you do not come, you will be removed from your position."

"And as Earl of Worthington, I will destroy your fat arse if you don't listen to Lady Julia," Cal growled. Then Cal made a fist and slammed it so hard on the desk she let out a gasp of shock. The force sent things flying and clattering to the floor. "Get the hell out of that chair and save a woman's life."

She'd never seen such rage on a man's face. Cal's anger wasn't even directed at her and it made her want to whimper. Dr. Hamilton stopped arguing. He did get off his bottom and grabbed his bag. Cal put his hand on the man's shoulder and pushed him all the way to her motorcar. Cal drove with Dr. Hamilton at his side. Against Cal's wishes, Julia chose to perch in the rumble seat.

Cal drove back with such speed the doctor turned green.

But it was all for nothing.

Hamilton examined Mrs. Toft, used forceps to take out the baby. Drenched in sweat, Mrs. Toft could no longer cry out. She sobbed, her breathing coming in small gasps.

The poor infant girl came out and Mrs. Toft gave out a terrible scream. The midwife quickly wrapped up the child. But Julia saw a small bluish face and her stomach churned. The baby was already dead. There had been no hope for the child.

Mr. Toft held his wife's hand. Told her it was all right.

That she was not to worry. That she just had to get strong. He'd look after her. Their children would look after her.

But Mrs. Toft just simply closed her eyes, let out the softest sigh and slipped away.

Julia stood there, staring with horror and not quite believing that something so terrible could have happened. She knew what Zoe had suffered. Now this family had lost a child, and their mother, too.

Mr. Toft collapsed to his knees by the bed at his wife's side. He held his wife's hand. Clung to it. Julia hurried out of the bedroom and downstairs, knowing her own tears were going to come.

Then she saw them—four pale, frightened faces.

The children.

Watching Julia gather up the children to get them outside and away from their mother's room just about broke Cal's heart. Julia had brushed away the tears on her cheeks and she tried to herd them out briskly. But she hadn't told them their mother was gone. To spare them, he figured. But the children were going to find out—he realized he was going to be the one to tell them. He was not going to let Julia go through such a painful thing.

She was trying to urge them out the door that led outside from a surprisingly large kitchen, but he said, "Julia, let me talk to them."

Panic flared in Julia's large blue eyes. She had two little girls by the hand and she was trying to make the boys go outside. "Not yet."

"Now," he said firmly. "They're stronger than you think."

"But there is nothing to be done."

"They have to go in to see her. To say goodbye."

"No. I want to spare them the sight of—"

"Julia, I've been through this," he said softly. "When I was as young as some of them. The children need to see. They need to touch their mother. Give her a last kiss."

Cal got down on one knee in front of the children.

"Don't," Julia protested.

He had to. But suddenly he couldn't find the words. Christ, he just couldn't say it. All he could remember was the gut-destroying pain he'd felt when Mam died. And the anger. The white-hot rage.

The children were sniffling, looking at him. They had to know, but they needed to be told. And Christ, he was failing. "Help me with this, Julia. I need your help to do this."

She touched his shoulder. It was such a tender gesture it gave him a burst of strength. He told the children their mam was called back to heaven. That she loved them, but sometimes love was not enough—a person had to face something they weren't strong enough to battle.

"You have to honor her always," he said to them. "Be strong for her. Look after each other and your father. Your mother will watch you all the time from heaven. If you just think about her, it will be like having her with you."

He told them all the things he'd been told when he lost his mother.

The two girls began to cry and Julia hugged them both to her skirts. The boys sniffled. Cal remembered how he had been told to behave like a man. To hold in tears. But he said to the boys, "People will tell you to be tough. They'll say you have to behave like men. But I'm going to tell you to cry right now if you want to. Do it now, get it out of you. Then you'll be ready to help your father."

One of the boys flung his small body against Cal's chest. Cal embraced the lad. The other bigger boy staunchly held in his tears.

"It's not fair," the older boy said. "It's not fair."

"I know, lad," Cal said. "But even though life doesn't seem fair, we have to survive. You have to keep fighting. You have to get up and kick life in its crotch—"

"Cal!" Julia gasped.

But that was how he'd felt about life. He remembered what had kept him going—knowing he had to care for his brother. "You're the oldest and it's important you look after your siblings. They'll need you."

"Come, we must clean your faces," Julia said. She was using her crisp, lovely, ladylike tones and the children followed her. She herded the children into the kitchen and wiped small faces. She gave them coins for their savings, then she answered all their desperate questions as best as she could.

In that moment, Lady Julia reminded Cal of Alice. He had been deeply in love with Alice. He couldn't show it or act on it—he couldn't hurt his brother, David—but he'd never met another woman who compared to Nurse Alice Hayes.

Julia compared.

He saw her face. How pale she looked. She made tea as she had done before, with a big iron kettle. She poured a cup of tea for each child. Then one more. "Take this for your father. He might not want it now, but leave it close by. He should have something. I've put honey in to make it sweet."

With the tallest girl carrying the cup and saucer, the children went back into the other room to see their father.

Lady Julia leaned against the sink, her head bowed. She kept her back to the doorway, then she put her hands to her face.

She was crying. And she didn't want anyone to see.

His mother used to hide to cry, because she was so worried about where their next dollar would come from. But she always turned a bright and cheery face to him and David, no matter how scared, how hungry, how desperate she felt.

Cal used to wake up and hear her sobs, after his father's death. She would cross herself and touch the one picture she had of Cal's father.

Cal had been too young and too powerless to help his mother. He'd tried—he'd been young but the Five Points Gang had offered a way to make money. A lot of money...

Now he was an adult. An earl. A rich man. He could do anything he wanted.

Including soothe Lady Julia.

He wrapped his arms around her. Her dress was a summer dress, thin and soft. He drew her tight to his chest. She tried to push away, but he wouldn't let her.

"Cry against me," he said.

And she did.

She sobbed and sobbed. Then her crying began to ease. She looked up at him, her lips almost touching his chin.

She was the most beautiful woman he'd ever seen. A nice girl. He didn't know a lot of girls who were truly high-class. But Julia was.

Next thing he knew, he'd bent his head and his mouth touched hers.

"No," she whispered against his lips. "We shouldn't. That family has lost their mother. That tiny baby never had a chance to live. It will never be right...never. If only I could have helped them."

"You did everything you could, Julia. I'll help them. Don't cry and don't worry—the family will be cared for."

Her tongue swept over her lips, and his knees just about buckled. "You will do that?" she whispered.

"Yes."

He lifted her onto her toes to kiss her hard. To kiss her

with his heart so full of longing and need he thought it was going to burst. He couldn't stop remembering his mother's death. How cold and empty he'd felt. He was kissing Julia, struggling to feel warm again.

Her arms wrapped around his neck, holding him tight. She broke away from the kiss. "You are truly an earl," she said, before pushing her lips against his again and kissing him back.

Cal felt a surge of heat like he'd never known.

Not sexual heat. Something deeper. Something more. Something that made him warm right through to his soul.

9

The 9:20 to Paddington

He was *kissing* her.

Cal's large, strong hands skimmed lightly down her back, caressing her. His palms went lower, following the curve of her bottom through her jodhpurs. He cupped one hand there and used it to pull her close. Shock hit her. Shock that his hand felt good there—that she liked the pressure of him holding her tight to his firm, warm body. His tongue traced her lips in a caress that made sparks burst and cascade through her with a hot sizzle.

Then his tongue slipped between her lips.

Panicked, Julia pulled back. Ladies didn't kiss like this. And they didn't do it in the kitchen of someone else's cottage. She'd needed to be held, but she couldn't do this. She gripped Cal's arms, feeling hard muscle through the sleeves of his worn sweater. "No. Don't. Please."

He let her go. "It's okay. We both needed comforting. Nothing more."

Nothing more. Of course, he was a wild artist who had

love affairs with his models. A kiss didn't mean that much to him.

Embarrassment set her cheeks on fire. "I must go and see if I am needed."

He held out his hand for her. "You can't do anything more for them now. Let me take you home."

She wouldn't go until Mrs. Thomas said the same thing. Then she realized—because of her elevated social station, the midwife and the family felt awkward having her help them. She was causing them more distress by being there. When Mrs. Thomas urged her to go home, she finally agreed. Her heart hurt, her stomach hurt, and when she saw Mr. Toft, a most unsentimental man by nature, bend his head into the crook of the neck of his oldest daughter and let his back shake with sobs, she almost dissolved into tears.

Yet there was nothing she could do. Cal drove her home. They didn't speak in the car. Stars began to wink in the darkening sky, and just looking at them made her want to cry. The car rumbled up the gravel drive—a footman was coming out of the door before they had even stopped. As she was getting out, she said, "When you had to force the doctor to come, you used your title to convince him. I won't forget that, Cal."

"I'm sorry, doll. It doesn't mean anything. You aren't going to change my mind."

"I have to," she said. "I can't bear to lose anything more. Not even Worthington Park."

I can't bear to lose anything more.

Dawn light spilled in through the attic windows. It wasn't enough light to paint by, but Cal didn't care. He couldn't sleep. He would drift off, then wake up sweating and tangled in the sheets on his huge bed. He'd stalked up here about

3:00 a.m. First, he'd plundered a few bottles of good red wine out of the wine cellar—he couldn't find the key to the damn lock, so he'd picked it with the end of a kitchen knife.

Despite weaving on his feet from draining the wine to the last drop, he picked up the wooden board he was using as a palette. Squirted paint on it. He painted as hard and fast as he could, working out the frustration inside him.

He wanted to kiss Julia again. The heat she'd sent coursing through his body was like a drug. He wanted more.

His Irish mam had raised him to have a good sense of guilt, and a fear of paying for his sins that he never could quite shake out of his soul.

Both worked on him now, one kicking one side, and one kicking the other, like a couple of gang toughs working him over in an alley.

He'd planned to seduce Julia. Like an artistic challenge. Now he knew he couldn't do it. He couldn't pour on the temptation until she gave herself up to the adventure of sex. He couldn't do it to a woman who transcended the definition of "nice girl."

But that didn't stop him from wanting her. More than food. More than the clean, flower-scented country air that kept going into his lungs.

More than revenge?

Hell.

Voices buzzed downstairs. Cal could smell breakfast, even all the way up here in the attic. His gut growled, making him wonder when he'd last eaten. Not last night. He hadn't come ho— Come back to Worthington for dinner. He'd dropped Julia off at Brideswell, then he had driven down to the local pub.

The Worthington estate was huge, and bordered Brideswell's land. They were neighbors but miles apart. His lands encompassed several towns and villages, like that one of Chipping Worth, called that because it had been a market. The earldom received money from all the tenants and businesses within. Driving into a village and realizing that he was lord of it, that he owned his own tiny town, was crazy to him.

The beer was bitter and no one seemed to have discovered that the stuff tasted good when it was kept on a bed of ice, but he had to admit it wasn't half-bad.

Then, in the pub, he'd met a man whose sister had gone missing...

Cal dabbed green where it shouldn't have gone and stopped. Stepping back from Julia's portrait, he knew he'd done something damn stupid.

He'd destroyed the picture. Lost his focus and ruined it.

It wasn't the blob of green, but how he'd changed her. Her face didn't glow with fiery passion anymore. The portrait was starting to capture her shielded, cool demeanor. It was like she was drawing away from him. There was no spark in her eyes that promised inside there was a lady who would go off like a firecracker.

He'd changed her face with strokes of paint here and there and now he was seeing the women who had pulled away from his kiss yesterday. Who couldn't face losing one more thing.

He put more paint on the palette. He had to fix the damn picture.

He couldn't live with himself if he became part of the family that had left his mother to die. Couldn't face the guilt and pain of giving up this chance to make good on the promise he had made on Mam's deathbed—to make the Worthingtons, as he thought of them, pay.

It meant hurting Julia. Heaping pain on a woman who had known more than her fair share and who had done nothing but care for people and give her heart to them.

He couldn't do that. So how in hell did he get justice for his father, for Mam?

Someone was behind him. Quiet as a mouse, but he knew. Julia? He whirled around, hope, despair, desire, guilt, need and pure joy all fighting through his gut like an army.

Creeping daylight—like it was embarrassed to interject on British gloom—fell in through the window and slanted on a set of spectacles. Clutching a book to her chest, his youngest cousin stood there. Dark-haired, like Julia. Which one? Not the audacious flirt, Diana. Thalia.

"It's a beautiful picture," she breathed.

"It's not," he growled suddenly, hating the picture in front of him. Now he saw the emotion radiating out of Julia's eyes well enough to put a name on it. Sadness. Sadness that he'd put there—and not just with a brush. "It's a piece of damn crap."

He threw the brush, sending a slash of yellow across Julia's bare, color-dappled shoulders and her ethereal white dress. It felt good. Felt good destroying this thing that he'd tried to do and had failed at.

Rage flowed through his arteries and veins, pumped through his heart. He threw the palette at the top of the canvas, watching it slide partway down, covering unhappy Julia with a veil of yellow and ochre, cadmium red and cobalt blue. Halfway, the descent stopped. As if appalled at what it had done, the palette tipped backward and toppled off the painting, landing on the worn plank floor.

Thalia had stepped back, her stance a perfect mimic of a terrified deer. The rage, the act of violence had scared her. A heel—he felt just like that. And had scared himself. He thought he'd gotten the anger—the bitterness, along with the squeezing grip of having failed—under control. He let it fuel his rage but never command it. He could never hurt a woman physically, but Thalia was making little wheezing-sob sounds like she figured he would.

Then she exploded in a gush of tears and just as he said, "I'm sorry," and took a tentative step toward her, she bolted from the room on long colt legs.

In the morning, Julia wanted to hide in bed. Wanted to pretend that the Tofts were not waking up to a day of unimaginable pain.

But she could not hide under her counterpane. There was too much to be done.

It physically hurt to sit up. Her arms ached, feeling heavy as she pushed away the bedcovers. All over, she felt as if bruised. This was the toll of grief.

Imagine how those poor children felt!

Bustling footsteps sounded outside her door. It opened, and Sims glided in, carrying a warming dish and a coffee urn upon a tray. "You are awake, my lady. Her Grace instructed that you would want breakfast in your room this morning."

Zoe had done that. How good of her. But Julia doubted she could manage much food at all—still, she needed to eat something. Then she must get to work.

Sims set the tray across her lap and poured coffee.

"Sims, I will need a black armband." It was what was worn when mourning someone who was not an immediate family member, where the rules were most rigid about wearing black.

Sims arched her plucked brow. Folded her arms over her chest. Sims was rail-thin and managed to look astoundingly haughty when she wished. Even Grandmama had nothing on Sims when it came to pinched lips and disapproving looks. "That would not be appropriate, my lady."

"I wish to mourn a tragic loss. So yes, it is appropriate."

"But this woman was not a member of your family or your class, my lady. Perhaps you could keep a black handkerchief on your person. Where it would not be seen."

"I want an armband. Will you do it?"

"No, my lady, I could not. Your mother——"

"Do not tell me what my mother would want me to do," Julia snapped. She was just…angry and out of sorts today. And she was not going to be bullied by Sims, who acted as lady's maid to her and Isobel. Isobel delighted in irritating Sims, who could be tremendously snobby, by attempting to wear boys' clothing whenever possible and leaving her graphic medical books around her room. Julia had been too polite.

She just couldn't be polite anymore. "I am going to wear an armband even if I must make it myself. I will not be swayed on this. This is important to me."

Sims began to speak, then stopped, as if biting her tongue. "I shall prepare you an armband."

"Thank you. You may go," Julia said firmly.

As Sims left, she set down her coffee and sagged back against her headboard. She was exhausted—she had been awake through most of the night. Sobbing for the Tofts and for a sweet, small baby who would never know life.

Julia lifted the tray off her lap. Instead of summoning Sims again, she pulled on a simple skirt, blouse and cardigan. Thank heaven for modern brassieres—she could put one on herself. Dressed, she went in search of her brother. She could not do much for the Toft family, but she could do one good thing.

She couldn't find Nigel in his usual haunts—the study or the library. The dining room was empty. Frustrated, Julia poured a cup of coffee.

"What's wrong?" It was Zoe, walking in from the salon. "Is it about Mrs. Toft? That is such a tragedy." Zoe hugged her.

"It's also about Dr. Hamilton," Julia said. "He is a hopeless snob. He was going to refuse to help Mrs. Toft because she is not a highborn woman. I threatened him to force him to go."

"You threatened him?"

"I reminded him that our family is the donor for the hospital and Nigel could force him out. Hamilton also drinks while he is working at the hospital."

"I think we must fire him," Zoe said firmly.

Here was her opportunity. "But we need a new doctor. Otherwise people will have no one."

"Better no one than a pickled quack," Zoe said. "You went with the Earl of Worthington, didn't you? You've been spending a lot of time with him. Are you falling in love with him?"

The warm tingle of his kiss sat guiltily on her lips. "Of course not," Julia protested quickly. "He wants to sell Worthington Park and I am fighting to convince him otherwise."

"Why would he do that?"

"He hates the family because they disowned his father. I understand his anger, but I don't want him to make the people of Worthington—the tenants, the servants—suffer."

"And it necessitates that you spend every day with him?"

"Well, yes, it does," she said, rather defensively.

Zoe smiled.

"Anyway," Julia went on, "what we need is a doctor."

"I agree. And I can think of one," Zoe said, casually playing with the long rope of her bead necklace, trying to sound as if this was an obvious, utterly natural decision. "There is Dr. Campbell of course."

"Impossible. He is at the London Hospital, and very happy there. And he is to be married. To someone else."

It was easy to say that now. She no longer felt a stab of pain. When she said those words, she only thought of Cal's mouth coming down over hers and him kissing her slow and coaxingly, and it felt as if the world had tumbled over.

"Yes, he's said that. But is that certain?"

"Zoe, of course it is certain." She hesitated. "Of course, he would be an excellent doctor for the people of Brideswell, but I don't believe we could convince him—"

"We won't even try, Julia. I'm not having you see Dr. Campbell and his new bride here. It would break your heart every single day. For once, you're not going to make a sacrifice for the sake of everyone else. We will find someone else. I must go to London, to Harley Street. Why don't you come with me? You can help in the hunt for a doctor."

"Perhaps I should stay instead. For the Tofts…"

"We could be gone for only a day and a night. Enough time to make inquiries on Harley Street. I'm sure we could find recommendations easily. I'd say we need a new doctor with promise, or an older one looking to escape London's smoke-filled fog." Zoe picked up a plate and loaded it with selections from the warming dishes.

This was something she could do. "I will take up the task, while you go to your appointment." Then she saw, with amazement, the food pile up on Zoe's plate—sausage, roast beef, ham.

Zoe looked up. "I am absolutely starving. I can't seem to eat enough and if I don't eat, I feel sick. No one knows yet but I suppose I have told you now."

"Told me what?"

"You must know, Julia! Why does a woman feel queasy?"

"She's ill?"

"Or she is pregnant," Zoe said, with American bluntness and honesty. An English lady would say "expecting" or "enceinte."

"How wonderful!" Julia cried. Her heart gave a pang. She was so happy, but there was that envy, deep inside. That wish she could have a child of her own. A home of her own. Then the image came again. Mrs. Toft closing her eyes and simply letting go, letting go of the world that her last child never saw—

"I'm sorry," Zoe said suddenly. "I shouldn't have talked about this now. Not after what you went through."

Had she looked so awful? One glance at her face and Zoe leaped to her feet and extended arms in comfort. "Zoe, I am happy you told me. Joyful news is exactly what I need. It gives hope. Little pieces of hope that all join together and become stronger than pain. It was just for a minute that I remembered… I don't want you to walk on eggshells around me. I think I am tough enough—"

"Don't become tough. People call it tough, but it really means they are trying not to feel anything. That never works. Trust me," Zoe said.

Julia hugged her sister by marriage. "You're right. I think—I think I'm going to go to Mother's chapel. I want to say a little prayer for the Tofts. And I shall probably have a good cry. Then I shall prepare for London."

She went out through the terrace doors off the gallery. A cool sting bit the air and clouds rumbled by, driven by a strong breeze that carried more threat of winter than promise of summer. She must go and see her war widows today, check on their progress before she went to London. On the days she hadn't seen Cal, she had begun arranging the loans. She had gone to see Ellen Lambert, urging her to take money and begin some sort of business. But Ellen continued to refuse.

Another figure walked ahead of her, a woman with her head bowed and a scarf fluttering around her head.

Her mother.

She knew where her mother was going—the same place she was. The chapel was a place Julia rarely went. But today she wanted to go there. Julia followed the path that led to the small stone chapel their father had built for their mother when they first married. When Julia was young, she'd thought it was a symbol of her father's devoted love for her mother. Then she'd discovered how unhappy they were. It was strange—one year a girl would have no awareness of her parents' strife, the next year she felt it in every breath she took.

Julia pushed open the low wooden door and stepped into the chapel. The air was almost cold. Her mother knelt at the altar and at the soft hush of the door closing, she turned around. "Julia? Is something wrong?"

She walked to the altar to join Mother. "I was at Lower Dale Farm last night. When Mrs. Toft passed away and her baby was lost."

To her surprise, her mother embraced her. Her mother had not hugged her...in years and years. "What a terrible tragedy," her mother said softly, but Julia didn't care about the words. It was nice to simply be held.

The largest stained glass window, with pride of place behind the altar, depicted the holy infant in the mother's arms.

"Why a baby?" Julia whispered. "A poor child who never knew life? Why?"

"The babe has gone to heaven," her mother said.

"You know as well as I do—any religious man would deny that was true for a baby who wasn't baptized." Tears leaked down.

"I cannot believe that—that an innocent soul would not be saved," Mother whispered.

Julia met her mother's large green eyes. Eyes just like those of her brothers, Sebastian and Will.

"This has broken your heart, my dear," her mother said.

"I want to be strong. I want to be of use. But I'm not sad. Now I understand how I feel. So angry."

"I know, my dear. I was so angry when we lost Will. When Nigel came home to us wounded. I was so afraid to let out that anger that I couldn't let myself feel anything at all."

"It was anger, not sorrow?"

"Grief is many things," Mother said. "Oh, my dear, this has broken my heart, too. We must pray for them both."

Julia knelt at her mother's side. Her mother's soft voice flowed over her as she prayed. She wanted to believe in heaven—that Mrs. Toft could look down over her children and still watch them grow. That perhaps, in heaven, her baby wouldn't be lost and all alone.

After the prayers, Mother and she walked back to the house, their arms linked. Grief and sorrow had driven them apart for years. Yet now, it had brought them together.

"I will not push you to marry, Julia," her mother said.

"Thank you."

And with that, she felt she had put marriage behind her. She must look to a future without it. Once she came back from London—having found a doctor for the Brideswell Hospital—she could move toward the real life she was going to have.

The next morning, as the mist scurried away from Brideswell's lawns, it was a flurry to get to the station for the early train.

Footmen hastened out of the front door with trunks and hatboxes. They stacked the luggage on the back of the Daimler and tied it in place, as the two lady's maids, in their traveling outfits, ensured no box or bag or case was missed.

Julia stood with Nigel, who held Nicholas in his arms, as Zoe came down, drawing on her gloves. Zoe wore a scarlet coat and matching cloche and her heeled black shoes clicked on the tiles. She kissed Nigel farewell—not on his cheek but full on his mouth. Then she lifted her son into her arms and rubbed her nose against his, until he giggled. "I'll miss both my men very much," Zoe whispered, her voice catching.

Julia certainly understood the catch in Zoe's voice, the tears shining in her eyes. Nicholas looked adorable in a blue sailor-style suit. His hair was dark as Nigel's, fine as silk, and his eyes were huge as he said, "Go wif Mama."

"Oh, darling, you can't come with me this time. Just a boring visit to the doctor for me."

"I should go with you," Nigel said.

Zoe gave him a wry, tough smile. "I'll be fine. I'm sure this expensive Harley Street specialist will coddle me since I'm a duchess."

Then Julia was drawn into her brother's embrace. "Look after Zoe," he murmured by her ear. "You know how headstrong she is. I know you'll convince her to be responsible. You understand duty and responsibility."

When she heard it spoken that way, it sounded like a dreaded disease.

Zoe caught her eye and winked. "We will be the most responsible women in the country. I assure you that the prime minister will come calling by the end of our visit, to take notes on how to be properly cautious, responsible and dutiful."

"I know you won't," Nigel said. "But be careful."

"I will take care of her," Julia promised.

"And I'll take very good care of Julia," Zoe added.

When they reached the station, Julia was surprised to see Diana waiting on the platform. She looked lovely in a slim-fitting dress of black crepe with a short skirt, and a jacket of white silk, trimmed in black. Ropes of jet-black beads dangled over the curve of her bosom. Diana linked arms with her. "Do you mind if I go down to London with you?"

"Of course not." Then more quietly. "Why are you going? For shopping?"

"Why do you think? It's to see *him*. This is my last chance—" Diana broke off. "It's Cal."

And it was. The kiss tingled on her lips, as if it were still dancing there. For days, she had thrust herself into Cal's life whether he wanted it or not. Now she didn't know how to stand, or where to look.

He looked stunned to see her. "Julia? What are you doing here?"

She realized she really did not want to see him. She had kissed him. She had never dreamed of kissing a man she wasn't going to marry, even though women did that all the time now. They did just about everything you could do with a husband with men they desired but didn't want to marry. But she could never do that.

"We're going up to London," Diana said.

"So am I," he said.

Diana narrowed her eyes. "What for?" she asked, with bluntness that a lady was never supposed to use.

"To see a lawyer," he answered. "Worthington's man of business."

Julia jerked her head up. She looked at him, but Cal looked innocent, as if butter would not begin to melt on that warm tongue of his.

"Why are you doing that? You're not arranging the sale of anything, are you?" Fear gripped her. Her last words to him had been that she couldn't bear to lose one more thing—including Worthington. But she'd never thought it would change his mind and she supposed it hadn't. But she needed more time!

"Of course not," he answered, after a pause.

But the light way he spoke, with a touch of a lilting Irish accent he must have picked up from his mother, made her certain he was not telling the truth. He was trying too hard to sound innocent. Her heart raced. "You haven't even met all the tenants yet. You can't—"

"Not to worry, doll. I'm not going to pull the rug out from under you."

"Well…well, thank heavens for that at least. For then I would fall on my bottom."

"I would never do that after what you've just been through." He studied her and his voice was caress-soft. "But I'm thinking about making you a deal. If I keep going with you to meet the tenants, you have to sit for me."

"Sit for him? What do you mean?" asked Zoe. She asked it politely, but she watched Cal with a rapier-sharp gaze. Julia wondered if Zoe was worried about her safety with Cal. But she wasn't going to kiss him like that ever again.

"I'd like to paint a portrait of Julia."

"Oh," Zoe said. Then in a softer, but more intense tone, she said. *"Oh."*

"I need to paint you, Julia."

"I thought you already were. I saw the picture."

"I had to scrap it. Without you to model for me, I couldn't get it right. Say yes, Julia. This picture of you—it could be the best thing I ever do."

He'd moved close to her, holding her gaze, his eyes full

of hope and his voice full of urgency. It was as if it meant life and death to him.

She was going to say no—sit in front of him for hours? She'd yearn to kiss him.

Why couldn't she find out about passion with Cal? She couldn't do it without caring too much about him—she already did. And she couldn't lose one more thing—neither Cal, nor the very last unbroken piece of her heart.

"Please, Julia?" His voice was the softest rasp.

But *no* didn't come out. "Would you promise not to do a thing to Worthington while I sit for you?" she asked. She hadn't even consciously thought that.

He cocked his head. A train whistle blew and she heard the clatter of locomotive wheels on the tracks in the distance. "I'm almost willing to do that just to get you into my studio."

"But not willing to go that far?"

He grinned. "That's probably the first time I've said it. I'm not willing to go that far."

"Then what are you willing to do?"

"Keep an open mind. And give you another chance to convince me."

She was about to point out that she was not getting much in return when Diana, who had been standing there, broke in. "Julia, darling, he does paint women naked."

She had forgotten about that. "That's not what you want me to do, is it?"

"I never would have dreamed of asking. Unless you're willing."

She was about to say: *Of course I wouldn't*. Then she saw the wicked grin playing on his lips. He was expecting her to be shocked and outraged. So she gave him a serene smile. "The idea is more intriguing than I expected. I will be in London for three days. I'll give you my answer at the end of the trip."

He made a sputtering sound.

And despite the pain of yesterday, she felt a ray of hope blossom. She might just win the most important battle she'd ever waged.

The train chuffed in and smoke billowed out, wreathing them in its white mist. Julia felt a gaze on her, and turned to see Zoe staring at her with one brow raised.

People disembarked. Porters opened the doors of the first-class carriages. Farther down the platform, Julia saw all their luggage vanishing into the train, then Sims and Zoe's maid climbed the step into their compartment. As they got on board, Julia asked Cal, "Are you opening Worthington House in London for your stay?"

"Wor— What?" he said. He'd been staring at her. She managed to hide a smile of victory.

If he wanted this from her, surely she could use it to save the estate. And to help him heal. She could use the time with him while he was painting to do just that.

"The London house. Worthington House is just a block from our London house. In Mayfair. Near Hyde Park."

Then he said, "I plan to stay at a hotel. I don't think a man needs more than one house that's big enough to house a small village."

"Worthington House is *lovely*," Diana declared. "Of course, you're going to stay there. Once we arrive, I will telephone and have it prepared. It's short notice, but it can be done. I will stay there with you."

"I'd rather stay in a hotel," Cal muttered.

"It is your house," Diana returned. "Get used to it."

Cal murmured something. Julia barely heard it. It sounded like, "Not for long." Her heart plunged. For a moment. Then stubborn determination kicked in as she followed Diana into one of the first-class carriages, and Zoe followed them as Cal held the door.

Maybe she would sit naked for him, if that's what it would take.

But she knew she couldn't. She couldn't do anything so intimate unless it was for a man she loved. And who loved her back.

Diana took a seat by the window and planted her hand on the cushion next to her. "Join me, Cal?"

Julia sat across, so she could sit by the window. A few whistles, much haste on the platform, then the whistle tooted once more and they set off. She pressed close to the window as the wheels began to clack on the rails. She loved to see the steam billowing around them as the train started off, then to watch the scenery stream by.

"You look like a kid on her first train trip, Julia," Cal said. "All excited."

She looked away from the window. Cal was looking at her—only at her—as if they were the only two in the carriage. Zoe was reading a newspaper. Diana looked bored, as only a fashionable woman could, but she was watching Cal from under the fringe of blackened lashes.

"Travel does excite me," Julia admitted. "I love this sense of hurtling somewhere new."

"Hardly new, dearest," Diana drawled. "You've been to London thousands of times."

Diana partly slumped on the seat in a shockingly casual pose, extended one leg so it rested alongside Cal's long legs.

"Have you traveled farther than London?" he asked.

"We go north for shooting," Julia explained. "But that is the absolute farthest."

"Not Paris? Not Monte Carlo?"

She shook her head. "My mother has been very weak and

troubled since after the War, when my youngest brother died. She couldn't travel and I didn't want to leave her. But now she's much better. Time seems to be healing her. And there is Zoe now, who watches out for her, too."

Zoe looked up and smiled, then returned to her newspaper. The *Wall Street Journal*—sent specially to her.

"So you're free now to go wherever you desire," Cal said. "Where would you like to go?"

"I don't know. I've never thought about it." She hadn't traveled very much. If she had married Dougal she wouldn't have traveled. If she married someone like Bradstock, she would be expected to travel to fashionable places—places deemed socially acceptable.

Before she could respond to that further, he said again, "You're free to go anywhere you like. Why don't you travel the world?"

Vivid images flooded her head. Of palm trees and the rippling water of the Nile, where pyramids could be seen from the deck of a steamer. Or the Eiffel Tower in Paris. Or the stunningly tall buildings of New York. Of course, her mental pictures were all from images in advertisements and magazines. "I couldn't afford to do that. Nor can I travel alone. Not as an unmarried woman. It would be much too scandalous and shocking."

"It's a modern world. You can be shocking."

"I'm not shocking at heart."

Zoe was not looking at her newspaper—she was discreetly watching them. But Diana piped up, "Oh no, Julia is not wild and adventurous at all. The most daring thing she's done is go to an underground jazz club. I've tried to coax her to do wild things in London with me. I mix with the most exciting crowd of young artists and bold young peers. They've taken to calling us the Bright Young Things."

Cal pulled out a black-bound book from a satchel and a pencil. He began to sketch. "Where would you like to go, Julia?"

"Paris."

His brow rose. "You're decisive. Why Paris?" Then he smiled. "Your brother lives there. Go visit him."

"I simply...can't. I could hardly get on a ship alone and voyage so far."

"Women do, doll. Or go with a friend. You know, I'd be happy to take you." He had his sketchbook open on his thigh, but his eyes held hers. "I'd be happy to take you to see the world."

She was aware of both Zoe and Diana taking in the whole conversation.

And her heart stuttered. He was gentle and teasing and deeply interested in her. She felt an impossible tug—a yearning to travel with him. To see the lights of Paris, the cafés, the galleries, the parks, and to do it with Cal, who was noble and exciting, naughty and sensitive—

But what did he mean? He must be teasing her.

She sat up in a straight-backed, ladylike way. "That's really not possible," she said briskly. "And I did want to talk to you about how women tenants at Worthington—women like Ellen Lambert—can be helped. I am still trying to push Ellen into starting a business. She is very adept with a needle and thread—and I believe she could readily learn to operate a sewing machine. That would open up many possibilities to her."

Cal looked taken aback. "She's going to struggle if she's suffering from shell shock."

Zoe frowned. "A woman with shell shock? I did not know such a thing was possible."

"It is," Julia said passionately. "Ellen Lambert was an ambulance driver in the War and I believe she is suffering the same symptoms as men. I spoke to Dr. Hamilton of course, but he just dismissed me. What she needs is help. Once she is able to deal with that issue, then she can begin a business."

"Oh, Julia, you are so dreadfully serious," Diana said. She leaned over toward Cal. "What are you doing, darling?" she trilled. "You keep looking at us, then down at your book. Are you sketching *us*? You devilish thing! Let me see."

Laughing, Diana motioned him to show the pictures. But Cal shook his head.

"I shall fight you for that book," Diana teased, batting her lashes.

"You can see them without doing that. But they're rough." He held out the book. Then he leaned back against the seat. His leg stretched along it. Julia realized he always sprawled over chairs in ways that looked defiant, not relaxed.

Propping the book on her skirted lap, Diana leafed through. "Julia...this is a good likeness. Here is Julia again. And—goodness, a figure without her clothing. But I can't see her face. Who *is* she? That isn't one of us, I hope. You aren't sitting there and imagining what we look like without any clothes."

"I hope not," Zoe said. "I'm here as the chaperone."

Cal gave Zoe a charming smile. "I hear you fly airplanes," he said.

"I do. I love it. When Nicholas is older, Nigel and I will take him up. Do you still fly?"

"I haven't done it since the War."

Julia saw the quick look of pain that showed in Cal's eyes. Then she glanced over at the picture. And swallowed hard. The woman was drawn with charcoal. Her hair was short and dark. She couldn't be sure...but the woman's figure looked like hers.

"That's not something a gentleman would do," Cal answered. "I admit I'm not a gentleman, but no, I wouldn't do that. Anyway, Diana, you're my cousin. That wouldn't be right."

Diana's smile vanished. She let the pages fall. "People like us marry cousins all the time."

But Cal just shook his head.

Diana put her hand to her mouth.

Julia realized Diana might be going to visit the married man whom she loved, but she hadn't given up the idea of marrying Cal. Except Cal had just told her he would never do it.

Diana looked at the picture again, then up at Julia, her face sullen. It was as if the woman who had once been her best friend now hated her.

Julia looked at the picture again. Did it mean Cal had been looking at her and picturing what she looked like underneath her dress, her brassiere, her slip? He had said not, but she was not sure.

She felt hot, embarrassed. Uncertain.

Yet she looked at Cal and she remembered what he'd looked like without his shirt. What did *he* look like without any clothes?

"Behave yourselves," Zoe said, glancing over the top of her newspaper.

The first-class compartment suddenly felt too small. Julia stood abruptly. "I have to use the washing compartment."

But when she made her way back, bracing her hand against the swaying of the carriage, Cal stood in the corridor. His broad shoulders almost filled the space wall to wall.

Brilliant blue eyes gazed into hers. "Damn it, I want you, Julia Hazelton."

Julia's heart skipped several beats. Then she managed to

give him a polite, restrained smile. "Cal, please don't. It's quite impossible. We kissed in a moment of intense emotion. But I cannot give myself to you in the way that you want."

His lower lip jutted out slightly, in a sensual pout. "You could. The only thing stopping you is the stupid rules of the aristocracy."

"It's not the only thing stopping me."

She moved to walk past him, but he stopped her. "I thought I could get over it. But I can't. I *dream* about you."

He dreamed about her? A forbidden image rushed in—Cal waking up in his bed, sitting up, sheets tumbling off him, revealing his naked torso. She swallowed hard. Cal made her have unladylike thoughts. Thoughts like she had never had in her whole life.

"I never thought this would happen," he said urgently. "Not with a duke's daughter. But you're different. You're special. I know you'd expect marriage. I know I can't give that to you. I don't know if I could even give you my heart. But I'd love to make you see what I already know—that you're passionate and alive, and you are ready to burst out of your ladylike shell."

"You wouldn't give me your heart," she repeated. She'd never expected him to be so blunt.

"I'd like to lay the world at your feet, Julia. I'd like to take you to Paris to drink wine in Montparnasse and dance to jazz. I'd take you to Santorini, where we could lie naked in the sun and eat figs and olives. I'd take you across a lake surrounded by vibrant autumn leaves in the Canadian north. I'd take you up close to the Arctic Circle, where the northern lights would dance overhead like veils of brilliant color floating through the sky. I'd like to show you the African plains, the South American jungles."

If she never saw the world, and she did good works, and

lived in the country that she knew, she could be content and happy. She was sure she would.

But deep inside, a voice whispered that she should have more. That she had waited and waited for life to begin, yet she had missed the point. She had to set her own life in motion.

What was she thinking? Cal had just told her he would never love her.

He moved toward her, bringing his lips close to hers.

On the brink of melting, she pulled away fast. "No. I can't do it without love, Cal. Without marriage."

"Julia is going to London, and will very likely see a man who was passionately in love with her." Zoe's husky voice startled. He jumped. So did Julia.

Zoe had come out into the corridor and leaned against the wall, smiling innocently.

"Who is it?" he asked. "One of those weak-chinned titled men who were chasing you at dinner? The Duke of Bradstock, a shallow, arrogant idiot who thinks he can rule over you?"

Julia was about to correct what Zoe had said, but her sister-in-law cheekily added, "He's a doctor. A man who saves lives. He was absolutely perfect for Julia—a true hero who passionately believes in helping others, but he left Brideswell because the family objected and he listened, believing he shouldn't marry a duke's daughter."

"Zoe—" Julia began. For Zoe was leaving an impression that was not quite true.

"Of course," Zoe continued, "Julia would be willing to defy all her family...for the right man."

Cal's mouth was harsh, bracketed by lines. "He should have been willing to fight for you."

"He left me for what he thought was my own good." Julia

felt she should leap to Dougal's defense. She had no idea what Zoe was doing, and she felt a bit guilty for leaving the impression that Dougal was still in love with her. But really, did it matter if Cal thought there was someone else? She could never be his mistress. It just felt wrong inside.

Zoe moved on down the corridor. Cal moved closer.

"If I wanted you to be my wife," he said huskily, "I'd fight heaven and earth to have you. I'd fight dirty to have you, Julia."

"But you don't want me to be your wife. And I'm not in love with you, Cal. Just as you are not in love with me. Now I really should return to our compartment. And you are blocking the corridor."

He moved so she could pass him. "If anyone asks, I'm going to the dining car," he growled.

"For lunch? They won't be serving it yet."

"For a stiff drink. Or ten."

10

London

At luncheon, after Zoe's appointment with a Harley Street specialist for pregnancy and "women's concerns," Julia dined with her sister by marriage in the elegant dining room of the Savoy. There had been a huge scandal at the hotel last summer when Ali Fahmy had been shot there by his wife, Marguerite. The trial was sensational, detailing sexual scandals in the style of *The Sheikh*. Despite the notoriety—or because of it—American film actors and royalty still flocked there.

Julia didn't know why that was what she thought of as they swept through the foyer and were escorted to a table, surrounded by London's Bright Young Things. Perhaps it was because it was in all the newspapers, or because she was worried about Diana, or because she was thinking of Sarah Brand—where had she vanished to? They passed a group of laughing women and Zoe murmured, "That one is the Prince of Wales's latest."

Julia recognized her. "She's married," Julia whispered back.

"He appears to like them that way."

Julia thought of Diana, in love and pregnant by a man who was married. Her faith in modernity wobbled a bit. Was the frenetic pace of modern life simply a way to be too busy to be unhappy?

Zoe ordered champagne cocktails, but barely touched hers. "I was told it is not good for the baby. Dr. Haliwell does like to give orders. He also insisted the best man for Brideswell Hospital can be found at the London Hospital. Not Dr. Campbell, but another young, promising surgeon by the name of McLeod. Shall I go and interview him?"

Julia smiled. She knew Zoe was trying to spare her. But she could see Dougal without pain. "I inquired at a few of the other doctors' offices during your appointment. I was also advised to talk to a doctor also at the London Hospital—Dr. Fenwick. So we'll both have to go and compare."

"What if you see Dr. Campbell?"

"Then I shall say hello."

Zoe lifted a brow. "You're remarkable, Julia. You look barely troubled at all."

"It's the breeding. Inside, I feel a mess of nerves."

"The Earl of Worthington said you're obviously very passionate on the inside." Zoe tapped a perfectly manicured nail—clear at the tip and the half-moon at the base, then red for the rest—against her lip. "I wonder how he knew."

Julia felt a blush creep up. "He claims he could tell just by looking at me. I am certain he was making that up. Simply to tease and unsettle me."

Zoe laughed. "The earl unsettles you?"

"We argue and debate constantly, Zoe. Hardly promise of a companionable marriage."

But Zoe's eyes sparkled. "But that isn't what you really want, is it? Nigel used to drive me crazy at first. We seemed to be on the opposite sides of everything. It made it all the more passionate. And the way Worthington looked at you in the corridor of the train, especially when I told him someone else is in love with you—"

"You shouldn't have fibbed. And there will never be anything between Worthington and I. I agree with my mother and grandmother—I think a companionable marriage, where a man and woman's passion hasn't turned to utter hatred, is a much more sensible arrangement."

But she was lying. Completely. Trying not to show that in her expression, she finished her champagne. What was the point in feeling desire for a man who blatantly said he would offer nothing more? Who didn't even bother wooing with pretty words? She admired honesty but she didn't think she could embark on an affair in such a cold-blooded way...

But as Zoe elegantly signed the check—"Zoe, Duchess of Langford"—Julia couldn't help imagining what it would be like to see the world. With Cal. To see all those exotic things he'd whispered about. See them at his side.

"Julia, you're blushing. What are you thinking about?" Zoe asked. She was "Your Graced" by all the staff as they left, all the way to the doorman who opened the door to their car—the Daimler kept at the London house.

"Not a thing," Julia said as she slid into the car, and it took Zoe and her to the London Hospital, a charity hospital on Whitechapel High Street.

They halted on the road outside the front entry. The street was filled with carts pulled by ponies, even oxen. Julia looked up at the long brick facade, the arched entries, the people shuffling up the front steps. Would she see Dougal here? Her heart gave a quick, fast step, as if it was actually trembling with nerves.

With Zoe, she marched up the front steps and walked into the reception room of the hospital, crowded with patients.

A nurse saw them and gaped in surprise. Their clothes and Zoe's announcement she was a duchess got them immediate attention. In moments, she and Zoe were being ushered to the ward where Dr. Fenwick was doing his rounds.

The ward was a large space with a surprisingly tall ceiling. Summer sunlight came in the arched windows and fell across the simple white cots that lined all the walls. Women lay on their beds. One young woman was sitting up and feeding her infant. A nurse in a skirt that swished low on her calves busily made her way from bed to bed with medicine.

Then she saw him as he straightened from the bed of a patient. He wore a white coat with a stethoscope draped around his neck, and carried a chart in his hands.

Not Dr. Fenwick. It was Dougal.

For a moment, she couldn't speak. All she could do was watch him work.

Auburn-haired and handsome, Dougal was so at ease with his patients. He even drew a laugh from a woman who lay on her back and had been groaning in pain. It was as if just hearing his voice had made her feel better. The woman clasped his hand. "Bless ye, Dr. Campbell."

Julia had thought the same herself so many times when she watched him help people at the Brideswell Hospital.

After a few minutes she realized he was happy here. His patients adored him. He was surrounded by people recovering—by people he'd helped. And he discussed their illnesses with the interest of a man driven to find cures. Dougal Campbell's compassion and skill left her awestruck. This was a true modern man. He spent his days pushing his capabilities, his knowledge—the knowledge of medical science.

The hospital, with its nose-tingling scent of carbolic, with the life-and-death drama, was Dougal's place. This was his place in the world. His work here, in London, must be exciting.

He had found his place.

Her heart felt as if it had plummeted to her toes. Watching him work, she realized how much good they could have done together. How she would have been in awe of what he did every day.

What was more important—being with a man you admired or a man who made the whole world stop, but in an unrequited way?

Or maybe the only solution was to have neither man.

She had been raised and trained to be the mistress of a great estate. But that was never going to happen. She could run off to Capri or Paris like Sebastian and become an artist. She was joking—or was she? She remembered the thrill she'd felt when Cal had forced her to put paint on his canvas.

"Lady Julia."

She knew the deep, husky voice, the trace of Scottish burr. She couldn't retreat now, even if she wanted to. Dougal looked startled at first. Then happy. Yes, definitely happy.

Seeing that glow in his dark eyes made her heart twist.

"Good afternoon, Dr. Campbell." She had never faced a man whom she had once loved and now must no longer love. It was an awkward sensation.

"What are you doing here?" he asked quickly. Then he corrected himself. "I mean, I'm surprised to see you at the hospital, Lady Julia. But it's an honor to have you here. A great pleasure." A blush touched his high cheekbones, and as he stumbled over his words, she smiled. But inside, she was remembering that they had kissed once. A polite kiss. At the time, it had been breathtaking. It had been sweet and it had set her heart soaring.

What a thing to think of. She must be serious. Not thinking of his sweet kiss. Or Cal's hot, melting kisses—that Cal gave just because he was bold and he was trying to shock her. Dougal had never tried to shock her. He had always… treated her as an equal. Not as a lady, not as a sexual plaything, but as someone with an intelligent mind.

"We are here to find a new doctor for Brideswell Hospital."

"We?"

"Dr. Campbell," Zoe acknowledged as she stepped forward—rather cautiously for exuberant Zoe.

He bowed to Zoe, fast and startled. "My apologies, Your Grace. I—I didn't see you there."

"No, I could see that," Zoe said, her eyes twinkling. Julia felt Zoe look at Dougal, then at her, and she knew Zoe was appraising them.

But there was nothing between them now. A past, but now only politeness.

"Your replacement at the hospital, Dr. Hamilton, has been a disaster," Julia explained. "He wants to be a fashionable physician. To force him to treat a farmwife on the estate who had trouble in her labor, I had to threaten to have my brother fire him. And he absolutely refused to recognize that women could suffer shell shock. Hysteria, he insisted, and he wouldn't recommend any—" She broke off. She was saying far too much. And not very coherently.

She knew she was blushing.

And Dougal couldn't seem to take his gaze away from her. Probably because she was making a fool of herself.

"We were given recommendations of doctors who work here," Zoe finished. "We were given two names, and assured either man would make an excellent head of the Brideswell Hospital."

Dougal nodded. "I see. You want to interview the men, Your Grace. You need a quiet place for that. Follow me."

That was Dougal—rather blunt in his conversation. Nothing flowery, as if he didn't have time to waste.

He took her and Zoe to the generously sized boardroom used by the directors of the hospital when they met. Portraits of austere gentlemen adorned the paneled walls and leather swiveling chairs were placed the length of a polished oak table. They took seats, Zoe turned things over to her and Julia explained their hope that either Dr. Fenwick or Dr. McLeod would prove to be good for Brideswell.

Dougal leaned back, steepling his fingers. "Both are excellent doctors. My recommendation is McLeod. Young but dedicated. Lives and breathes the work, eager to tackle any case. Good with the patients. He'd appreciate the opportunity to be the head of a hospital. I would be available to consult by telephone, if he needs an outside opinion or finds a problem that stumps him."

"That's very generous of you." Julia met his gaze. She still admired this man and her heart was warm with gratitude toward his offer. Impulsively she said, "You appear to be very happy here."

"Coming to London changed everything for me. My surgical skills and knowledge have expanded threefold. There are surgeries I have done here that I would have never dreamed of attempting at Brideswell Hospital."

"Oh. I am so very glad."

Her heart gave a sharp pang. In that moment, she knew how happy she could have been as Dougal's wife. She would have come to London with him. She would have kept his home for him, and been there to support him when he returned from the hospital, exhausted and carrying worries on his shoulders—

But then she thought of Cal casually draping his shirt around her, then standing behind her and holding her hand as she held the paintbrush. How much she had admired him when he promised to help Ellen Lambert, when he spoke to the Toft children.

Cal knocked her off her feet. He did something to her when she was with him. She felt—even when they were arguing—she felt she crackled with life.

But surely being happy and useful was much better. Companionship, as she'd said to Zoe.

Then Dougal took her and Zoe on a tour of the hospital, explaining the strengths of both men, and also their weaknesses, as they went through the wards. He stressed attributes that he believed would make each man suitable for a small country hospital, and their limitations. Truly, he did make McLeod sound the perfect candidate.

In that afternoon, she was transported into his world again. His world of medicine, and inquiry, and saving lives. She remembered how much she had wanted to be part of that world, to be of use, to do work of importance.

She had never felt so confused—so uncertain.

As he finished, Zoe said, "Dr. McLeod sounds perfect and your recommendation carries a lot of weight, as does your offer. Julia and I will interview both men. If Julia is in agreement, then we will make a decision."

That was Zoe. In matters of business, Zoe knew what to do and she would never simply take a man's advice. She would weigh it.

"Yes, I do agree."

Dougal took them back to the boardroom. "I'll fetch them then."

"Thank you," Zoe said.

"It is the least I can do, Your Grace."

Julia saw how awkward he looked. The only moments he appeared to relax were when he was showing them the wards.

"Congratulations," she added quickly. She didn't want him to be uncomfortable. She didn't want awkwardness to be the last emotion between them. "I should have said before—I am so pleased you are to be married."

"You're very gracious," he said.

It was kind, so why did that word bother her so? Aging queens were gracious. Her *grandmother* could be gracious.

Cal had called her passionate. But he'd done it to tease her.

"I'll summon McLeod," Dougal said. He stood, gave a brief bow and left to find the two doctors.

Within the hour, the business was settled. After speaking with both men, Zoe concurred with Dr. Campbell's opinion. Julia agreed. Dr. Robert McLeod was to be Brideswell's new doctor. Julia felt something good had been accomplished. She and Zoe left, walking briskly down the steps toward the waiting car. Once in the rear seat, she looked back toward the hospital. Would she want that life—or did she want Cal? And did it matter, when she was to have neither man?

She had to decide. What did she want to do—?

She gasped. Dougal had come out onto the top of the steps. He lifted his hand in a brief wave and she waved back, startled he had come to watch her go.

The Earl of Worthington's London house stood on Berkeley Square. A four-story mansion of stone built in the early eighteenth century, it took up half the street. From the drawing room windows, one could see the square—the paths shaded beneath arching branches, the trimmed lawns that stretched within the wrought iron black fences. The park filled in the afternoon with strolling couples, elderly gentlemen taking their constitutional, and a veritable army of nannies and perambulators.

Cal was not in—he had sent word that he wouldn't come back for dinner. But Diana led Julia into the music room. By the window, with sunlight pouring in, Diana exclaimed, "You must come with me tonight. The Black Bottom is London's newest jazz club. It's modeled on a seraglio and most of the women go dressed in Turkish attire. I absolutely have to go."

"I can guess why. Diana, I wish you wouldn't."

"I must! I'm going to force him to make a decision, once and for all. He keeps telling me he yearns to be with me, that he wants to find a way to leave his wife. But then—then nothing happens. The days are ticking by and I know I don't have much longer. Just come with me and let me resolve it. Either I'll know he's going to divorce his wife for me, or I will know it is over."

With a sinking heart, Julia could guess what would happen. Diana would need a friend there for her. "All right. I'll go." Zoe knew Julia was going out to a jazz club, but she'd elected to go to bed early and rest. Pregnancy had made her tired, but she'd urged Julia to enjoy herself.

At the Black Bottom, Julia expected to finally see the heartless wretch who had used Diana so terribly. She didn't expect to see Cal—Cal seated at a table, talking to a black-haired man who dressed just like an American gangster.

She had walked in with Diana, drinking in the smoky atmosphere. The only lighting came from lamps made of metal with decorative cutouts, like those she had seen in pictures of Morocco. The tables were low, surrounded by cushions. The whole place looked like an opium den. Sultry, naughty-sounding jazz music wound silkily through the gloom.

Julia saw several women in embroidered jackets and voluminous harem pants, smoking cigars. She gasped at the sight of two girls, wearing only a strip of fabric over their breasts, along with diaphanous skirts that pooled on the ground. They wore veils, and black kohl rimmed their eyes. Their feet were bare. They looked exotic—except they both spoke with a London accent.

When she saw Cal, her heart gave a leap of surprise. When she looked at Cal, the band ceased to play. The girls serving drinks stopped in midmotion. A stream of champagne stopped in midpour.

The man sitting across from Cal leaned forward and spoke quietly. Cal's expression blackened into one of anger.

A lady shouldn't stare, but at the dramatic change in Cal's face, she did.

The man looked like one of the famed gangsters. She had seen pictures in the newspapers of them. Reputedly Al Capone insisted that there was no excuse not to be well dressed. This man wore clothes just like she had seen in a photograph of Al Capone—a white suit jacket over a black shirt, tie, but a white waistcoat. Gold flashed on his wrist as he lifted a cigar to his lips.

The man leaned close to Cal, muttered something, then straightened with a triumphant smirk. Cal's hand shook as he lit a cigarette—it took him two tries with his silver lighter. Cal's expression was positively thunderous for a moment, while he faced away from the man. Then Cal smoothed his face into a look of jaded boredom, and said something to the man, who didn't like what he heard. He shouted back at Cal. Julia caught two words right at the end. "I'll talk."

Talk about what? Was he threatening Cal?

"See you later, Julia," Diana said.

What? She jerked around, just in time to see Diana disappear behind a diaphanous curtain with a tall man. Damn!

She'd hoped to find out who the gentleman was. Then she was going to tell him to stop stringing Diana along. She feared he had no intention of doing right by Diana—and that would leave Diana with two choices.

Two heart-wrenching choices.

"Care to dance?"

Startled, she looked up—to find Cal beside her. He'd slicked his blond hair back and he wore a gorgeous evening suit that emphasized his broad shoulders. It was black, setting off his tanned face. Sultry music slithered through the smoky interior.

She looked to the table where the American had been sitting, but he was gone.

"All right," she said, and the moment she did, he put his hand to her lower back and drew her close. Right against his hard, lean body. Her head tucked into the space below his jaw, against the wide breadth of his shoulders.

But she felt a jerk of his arm muscles against her, as if his anger hadn't died away.

"Who was that man? And why did he make you angry, before you returned the favor?"

"I thought a lady didn't pry into someone else's business, angel."

"I do when I am concerned about the man doing business," she said, "and the person with whom he's doing that business."

"There's nothing to worry about. Now dance with me, Julia."

He danced divinely, moving her on the parquet floor in a slow, sensuous rhythm. Julia barely felt the floor beneath her feet—she *forgot* there was one beneath her.

Cal had a way of moving his hands that set her skin on fire. It wasn't too scandalous—where a woman might have to resort to a slap. He didn't touch her anywhere naughty. His fingertips stroked in a sensual way, lightly on her back.

He bent to her. His lips grazed the line of her jaw, then moved lower, and on the dance floor of the Black Bottom, Cal kissed her neck.

Sensation shimmered down her spine. She felt hot all over. And that ignited panic. She wanted him to kiss her. She wanted him to keep kissing her until she couldn't think and that would be her ruin. She pushed away from him. "Don't."

She turned, desperately looking for Diana. Yanking her hand free of Cal's grip, she rushed through the dancers, darted around a young waiter who carried a tray of elegant cocktails.

She ran right into her friend who was hurrying from the opposite direction. "Let's go," Diana hissed. "His wretched wife is here."

"Diana, his wife isn't wretched. *He* is."

"He's trapped, Julia. He's trapped in a duty marriage."

"Diana, you must understand he's bad for you."

"But I love him! I love him desperately. I should go to his wife right now and tell her that he—"

"No!" She grasped Diana's arm. Rather harder than she intended. "He won't leave his wife."

"I don't believe that," Diana protested.

But she saw the fear in Diana's blue eyes. "Diana, he should never have put you in this position."

"Then what am I going to do, Julia? What can I possibly do?"

The music pounded and couples danced wildly on the floor. Julia moved close to Diana. She had to speak loudly over the racing jazz beat. "Switzerland." Then she moved Diana to the side of the room, where it was quieter.

Diana desperately shook her head. "No! This is about

love. I don't just want to be hidden away on the Continent, Julia. This is the modern world and I want it all. I want my child, I want love, and I'm willing to go through a little scandal to get it."

"It's not the scandal, Diana—"

"You said you didn't care about scandal when it came to helping your widows. You should know how I feel."

She did. That was the problem—part of her was applauding Diana for wanting more than a ladylike life and a marriage without love. But she knew that Society would judge Diana ruthlessly. "I do. But men do not leave their wives."

"I can't go away anyway. I have no money and Cal won't give me any."

"Perhaps I can—"

"No! Don't tell him. He wants to hurt us all. What do you think he would do to me?"

In truth, Julia didn't know. She had seen him be so good, but he was also filled with anger. Anger that sizzled in him tonight. She felt someone watching her. She turned, expecting it to be Cal.

It was his American companion. Staring at her, and giving her a slow grin. A smile that made her shiver. It wasn't leering, but it looked…mean. She wanted to keep a large distance between her and that man. "We should go, Diana." She hastened Diana to the table, told her she was tired and hurried her to pick up her wrap.

Julia was exhausted, but she could barely sleep. For some reason, that man's smirking smile haunted her all night. So did Cal's kiss.

She lay in bed wondering what it would be like to fall into her bed with Cal. Have him on top of her, kissing her, caressing her, and then—

Oh! What was she doing to herself? Cal wouldn't offer her anything more than Diana's selfish lover had offered her.

Even if she were careful to avoid a disastrous pregnancy, would just sex be enough? Without love? Without a future?

No—because if she went to bed with Cal, it would be because she was in love with him, and was willing to accept that she was, and had stopped trying to fight it.

Right now, she was still fighting it.

But could she really spend the rest of her life as a virgin?

Julia awoke when the sun was streaming around her curtains. She hadn't slept in so late for years. Groggy, she sat up as Sims came in. "There is a telephone call for you, my lady. Lady Diana Carstairs. She insisted you must be woken and brought to the telephone."

Worry gripped Julia's heart.

"I warned it will take quite a while to dress you—"

Of course she had to be dressed as she did not have a telephone extension in her bedroom. "No. It won't." She wore a brassiere and pulled on a blouse and skirt. Sims fussed over her, especially her hair, but the truth was, with modern, simple clothes and bobbed hair, she could dress herself. Then she hurried downstairs and picked up the extension in the hallway. "Hel—"

"Oh, Julia, I can't stand it anymore. Cal knows my secret. I don't know *what* he will do when I return to Worthington Park. I fear he'll throw me out. He hates us, and ruining me would be just sport for him, and—"

"Diana, please calm down." Julia broke in on Diana's desperate, frightened, shrill words. "Let us face this calmly. I don't understand how he could know. I didn't speak a word of it to him. Not to anyone, I promise."

"He insisted you didn't say anything. He just—he just knew! I was having a drink when he returned from the

Black Bottom. He came up to me, took the drink out of my hand. Then he asked me if I am expecting a child. He said he'd just…guessed. How could he do that? I was so shocked I almost passed out. I couldn't say a word, my throat was so tight. But I know—I know he would love to see me ruined. He would love it if I were starving on the street."

"He won't do that." But would he?

In that moment, Julia knew she had learned much about Cal, but she didn't really know him. She couldn't guess what he would do. Could he be kind to Ben and the Toft children, and then hurt Diana and her unborn child?

But Diana was a member of the aristocracy and of the family who had hurt him.

She must protect Diana. How could Cal have guessed? Then she remembered how he'd said his mother would deliver babies. Perhaps he knew the signs of pregnancy and had seen them in Diana. He must be incredibly perceptive—

He was an artist. And he had seen things inside her that she believed she kept completely hidden from the world. He saw things in her that no one else had.

"Julia, I must see *him* again. This will change everything. Now that Cal knows, *he* will know he must look after me. To protect me, he will do something. He wants to be with me. I know it."

Diana's voice rose in desperation.

It was confusing, but Julia knew which man Diana meant by "he" and "him."

"Diana, you must see it won't help to pursue this man—"

"No! He won't leave me at Cal's mercy."

But the man was married. How could he do the right thing? Was a divorce the right thing? It would give Diana marriage—it would save her reputation. But it would hurt another woman.

"I will talk to Cal. I'm sure I can appeal to his better nature."

"You can't."

"Diana, I have seen him be kind. Especially to children—"

"You can't because Cal left this morning. He bought a new motorcar in London and he drove back to Worthington. The butler said he was angry. Very angry. He oozed rage. And I don't know why—but I fear that anger will make him hurt me."

"Diana, no, don't do anything foolish—"

But the line went dead. Oh heavens, this was a disaster. What would Diana do?

"My lady? Is something wrong?"

She was standing, the receiver clutched in her hand. Their London butler wore a look of concern. "Everything is fine," she lied, adopting a bright smile.

"A Dr. Campbell has arrived for you. He is carrying flowers. He is waiting for you in the drawing room."

Dougal—here? And carrying flowers? It would make sense if Dougal had come to discuss Brideswell Hospital, but that didn't explain flowers.

He jumped to his feet as she walked into the south drawing room.

She had never seen Dougal look like this. He wore a simple but attractive suit. His hair was slicked neatly back with pomade. Before she'd managed to say "good morning" in its entirety, he thrust out the bouquet. Pale pink roses.

But she also saw his eyes were red rimmed and somewhat bleary. "Dougal, you look exhausted." She took the bouquet, and took his hand, led him to the brocade settee, then rang for tea.

"Sorry," he said gruffly. "I was up all night in surgery. A man struck by a motorcar."

"Is he all right?"

Dougal's mouth turned grim. "I lost him, Julia."

"I'm so sorry."

He lifted his hand as if to rake it through his hair, then stopped himself. His other hand rested against the sofa arm as if holding up his exhausted-to-the-bone body. "I fought for him. Fought for hours and I thought I was going to win. But in the end—I'm not God apparently. When I begin to think I can outdo our Lord with miracles, then I am brought down and humbled, but at the cost of a man's life."

Tea came, halting their conversation. Efficiently, she poured for him and herself. Dougal's leg was tapping, apparently with pent-up frustration, but it stopped as she handed him the cup.

"You remember exactly how I have it?"

"Of course I do."

"Julia, I have no right to be here when I'm dead tired. No right to be here at all. But I realized, when I lost that patient, that the person I needed to speak to was you. You were the one person I knew I could talk to."

"But your fiancée—"

"I care about Margaret a great deal, but she doesn't have your strength. It made me realize how much I loved being at the Brideswell Hospital."

That surprised her. "I thought you were happier here?"

"The truth is that here I have to answer to a board of governors. There are treatments I want to try but I've been refused. Too expensive. Too controversial. At Brideswell, when I went to the duke—your brother—I found him to be one of the most open-minded gentlemen I have met. He allowed me to do remarkable things. After his marriage, he was an extremely generous patron. He bought much-needed new equipment—gave me free rein in my purchasing and treatment plans—" He broke off, raking his hand through his auburn hair, but he stopped when he realized it was too pomaded to move. She smiled at the sweet gesture, but her heart seemed to have stopped beating.

"I know the duchess offered the job to McLeod, but he would be willing to take my place at the London Hospital, if you would consider allowing me to come back to Brideswell."

"But—but what about your fiancée?"

"I have to establish myself as a doctor before we can marry. I believe I could do that more quickly at Brideswell. Then I can have a house there and make her my wife. If you and the duchess—and the duke, of course—would consider giving me the chance."

Such fervent passion underlay his words.

She thought of the time she'd spent with him. Quiet walks across the village green. Dougal had discussed his cases with her. She'd loved listening to him. She would make suggestions, but he was always lost deep in thought, his brain considering the symptoms, the possible diagnosis, until he came to the right answer. He talked to her like an equal, not like a woman who should be protected from rational thought.

He would come back, but they could not do that anymore.

"Do you believe your family would consider it?"

He would be the perfect doctor for Brideswell. She could live with a little pain—the pain of seeing him, of being so close to him, but so distant.

He was waiting for her answer, hope in his eyes.

Two days after the dance with Julia that Cal couldn't forget, he stepped out of the small police station of Brideswell's village. He'd gone into the village to the local pub to get some information and that had led him to the police station, manned by a sergeant and two young police constables.

He walked out into a downpour. Sheets of gray rain swept in waves through the narrow streets. Cal lifted his collar. It was June, but bone-chilling today in the rain.

Ahead of him, a woman struggled with her black umbrella. She gasped as the wind caught it, turning it inside out and pulling her into the street, just as an automobile roared around the corner, headed toward her.

He ran out, gripped the woman around the waist and pulled her out of the path of the car.

"Goodness!" she gasped.

"Julia." He hadn't seen her since the Black Bottom Club. He hadn't seen her, but he'd thought about her every damn minute. And now he heard his breath hitch as he realized his hand was cupped around her small waist. He moved his hand.

"Thank you." She looked at him awkwardly. He felt damned awkward with her. What would Julia think if she knew the things O'Brien had reminded him about that night in London? He'd heard she had gone to see the doctor she had been engaged to once. Maybe they'd rekindled their romance. Julia deserved a good man and he had to admire her for falling for a doctor, for being willing to marry a man who didn't have a title.

He took the umbrella and held it for her. As they walked together, they struggled to make conversation. She asked, "The gentleman you were speaking with at the Black Bottom, was he a friend from America?"

"Someone I knew in the States. Not a friend." He didn't want to talk about Kerry O'Brien of the Five Points Gang with Julia. He didn't want her to know anything about his past. Or what O'Brien had threatened him with.

"Julia, I have to talk to you," he said.

"I have to talk to you. About Diana."

"We can't talk out here in the rain," he said. "I have my car here. Where can I take you?"

"I'm finished in the village. You could take me home."

He stayed quiet until he got Julia into his automobile, out of the rain. It poured off her hat, dripped off his coat, as he went around to the driver's side, chucked in the umbrella and climbed in. Rain drummed against the windshield, and he couldn't see out.

"Diana hopes the man responsible for her condition will get a divorce from his wife and marry her. She tried to see him again the day after the Black Bottom, but he wouldn't respond. He didn't pick up the telephone, answer her notes. She even went to his house, only to find he and his wife had gone to the Continent. She was devastated. She—"

He heard her take a shuddering breath.

God, she was pale. She hadn't put on any makeup. She was lovely this way, but far too pale. "What did she do?" he asked slowly.

"She broke down into tears in her bedchamber and hammered her fists on her belly. She was trying to make herself miscarry. I stopped her, brought her back here, and promised to talk to you. To plead with you if necessary. She is so afraid, Cal. She fears you will throw her out."

"I wouldn't hurt her. Not when she's expecting a baby."

"What about afterward? If you throw her out because she is ruined, you would be condemning the child to poverty—"

"You mean how could I do that, when I lived through it? You're right. I couldn't. I'd look after Diana. Make sure she always has a roof over her head and enough to eat. I'd make sure the child stayed healthy, grew up happy, went to school. I vow I'd do that. Maybe the hypocrisy galls me. The old earl and countess condemned my mother while their daugh-

ter had an affair with a married man and their son—" He
stopped. "But I wouldn't make the baby suffer. I'm a better
man than that."

"I believed you were," she said softly.

The look on her face—

It made him feel ten feet tall. It made him feel like crap.
He started the automobile.

"Cal, there is something you have to know. Women of
our sort who get into trouble do not keep their babies. It
ends any chance of marriage. Certainly a respectable one.
Girls are taken away. They disappear on an extended holiday,
where they discreetly have the baby. The child is given up for
adoption. The girl comes back and she goes on with her life."

"That's the way it's done." He looked over his shoulder,
through the rain, then pulled away from the curb. "Do you
agree with it?"

"I don't know. If I had a child, I think it would break my
heart to give up the baby. But maybe I would be so terrified,
I would agree. Terrified because I would know I'd lost any
hope of a future. That, as a ruined woman, I couldn't give
my child a life anyway. But I admire the courage of women
who keep their children, who struggle to raise them. I don't
know if I would be so strong."

He was quiet, driving through the narrow High Street.
He accelerated around a plodding horse-drawn cart. "What
does Diana want?" he asked finally. "To keep the child? Or
move on with her life so she can marry some gentleman and
get a fancy title?"

At his side, Julia winced. "She has not thought that far
ahead. She still believes she can have the child's father. She
loves him. And she hasn't accepted yet that he doesn't love
her in return."

"She's not gonna listen to me about that," he said gruffly.

"I know. I simply have to keep trying to make her understand that. At least I can now tell her she will be safe."

"Why you? Why do you have to take care of things?"

"I am her friend."

"And you always take care of everyone."

"You sound as if you don't approve. As if it is wrong for me to do so."

Doubt hit him. Could Julia, who worried about anything, really not have had suspicions about Anthony Carstairs? "There's something I have to know, Julia. Three young women went missing around 1916. Sarah Brand, a woman named Eileen Kilkenny, sister of the local blacksmith, and a maid, Gladys Burrows, who worked for the squire in the next village."

"Three women? All around the same time?" she whispered. "I—I don't understand. We searched for Sarah. We completely scoured the estate in case Sarah had met with an accident. We searched the woods for days. When no trace of her was found, it was assumed she had run away. Then stories came out that she was seen riding with a man in a motorcar. Girls did run off to London. It was thought she might have had a secret love who was going to war and she ran off to London for a hasty marriage."

His hands tightened on the wheel. "I talked to the sergeant at the police station in the village. He confirmed that all three women were seen driving with a man in a flashy red car. They couldn't describe the man—he wore a hat pulled low and a scarf around his face. But I just found out the make of the car. It was a 1914 Rolls-Royce Silver Ghost, painted red. And I saw one this morning in the Worthington garage."

Julia gasped. "What are you saying? You think it was Anthony, don't you? Sarah may have vanished before Anthony went away, but he helped in the search, just before he left because he had enlisted."

"I don't know. All I'm saying is that a bright red Rolls touring car is in the Worthington garage. I'm going to take a better look at it."

"Could I—could I accompany you? I don't want to go to Brideswell now. I want—I want to see."

Her request startled him. Cal didn't want her to see. But he knew she would be able to face anything. She was so strong.

Julia felt sick with fear as Cal drove her to Worthington. It drove all thoughts of Dougal's return to Brideswell from her mind—she had spoken to Nigel and Zoe and they had all agreed to welcome Dougal back. She still did not believe Anthony could have done something to Sarah Brand and two other young women. She simply couldn't.

But as Cal's car turned in at Worthington Park's gates, a small figure rushed out from behind a thick lilac.

"Jesus Christ." Cal slammed on the brakes but the car skidded on the gravel. Right toward Ben Lambert. Julia reached her hand out toward the low windscreen as if she could push the boy out of the way. She shouted, "Run out of the way, Ben."

But the boy was paralyzed, frozen in place, afraid to move.

Cal jerked the wheel hard, cursing with words Julia had never heard before.

The car swerved so abruptly, it lifted onto two wheels and Julia's heart lodged in her throat. She couldn't scream.

As long as Ben wasn't hit, she didn't care what happened to her.

But she didn't want Cal to be killed, either.

The car fell back on all four wheels and skidded onto the lawn. Suddenly it came to a lurching stop and Cal's hand grabbed her shoulder and held her back. He had one hand on the steering wheel and his chest hit hard against it. But with his other hand securing her, she only fell forward a bit.

"Are you okay?" Cal's voice came tightly, and he was short of breath. He must have had all the wind knocked out of him.

"Yes. But what about—"

Cal got out of the car. She followed but he'd sprinted so fast he'd already reached Ben. Cal dropped to one knee in front of him and held Ben's slim shoulders. The boy shook his head then Cal pulled the child into a tight embrace.

Ben must have been telling him he wasn't hurt.

Julia reached them then. "Ben, you aren't hurt? Are you certain?"

"I'm not. But me mum is," the boy sobbed. "She's got hurt bad. I don't know what to do."

"Where is she?"

"At our cottage."

"How bad is she, Ben?" Cal asked, his voice cool and collected. Julia could barely think for the racing of her heart. They needed a doctor. And Dougal had just arrived today— that was why she'd gone into the village. To see him—

"She got knocked out," Ben said. "He hit her so hard she fell down. She won't wake up and she's bleeding. There's all this blood and I don't know what to do."

"Who hit her?" Julia demanded, shocked.

But Ben just mutely shook his head. He was too afraid.

Cal glanced back at the car. Then at the house. "Damn, I need to push the car out. Get behind the wheel, Julia. Put the boy in the car."

With Cal's direction, Julia put the car in gear and pressed gently on the gas while Cal pushed from behind. She turned, watching him. His face grimaced, his arms strained, but he made the car rock. She would let off on the gas and give it more, matching the rhythm he was creating.

Then Cal let out a roar and pushed hard. The car shot ahead and two of the wheels got traction on the drive. "Keep going!" he shouted.

She did. Mud sprayed out from behind her. But she kept going until the car was all the way out of the grass. Cal ran to the passenger side and he vaulted in, beside Ben.

"Drive as fast as you can, doll," he said.

Mud covered his jacket, trousers, shirt. Clumps of it clung to his face. But he obviously didn't care. And she drove as fast as she dared, her heart in her throat. It was only when they reached Ben's cottage that she realized they should have gotten the doctor first.

Cal was out of the car before she'd shut off the engine, running for the front door of the cottage. "Stay there," he shouted at her.

But she didn't. She reached the front door when she heard him curse again. "Ah hell," he muttered. "Who in hell could have done this?"

11

Suspicion

Through the haze of shock and fear, Julia watched Cal crouch beside Ellen and press his fingers to her throat. He bent so his cheek was close to her mouth. Julia knew he was listening for breath.

"Is she breathing?" This was her fault—she had pushed Ellen to stop letting that man hurt her and use her and pimp her, and he had no doubt reacted in pure rage.

Cal looked up. She'd never seen a man look so anguished—except Nigel, when Zoe lost her babies. "Julia, I told you to stay outside."

"What use would I be out there?" But she wanted to be sick and she was fighting to stay on her feet.

"You shouldn't see this. She's been beaten to a pulp." He surged to his feet. "She's breathing but unconscious. I need to stop the blood flow on the wound on her arm. What she needs is to get to a hospital where she can be stitched up properly. Her leg and arm are broken."

Now, without Cal's body blocking her view, she could fully see Ellen. At least, she thought it must be Ellen. Bruises had turned the woman's face into masses of black and blue. The nose—heavens, it was a mess, and there was blood all over her face. There was blood on the floor and on the side of the stove.

Her knees wobbled. *Don't faint and be useless.* Isobel could look at medical illustrations while eating biscuits. She could cope with this. But Julia felt as if her head was full of nothing but air. Spots danced. She feared she would slither to the floor.

But then rage flooded her. Right now was the time to prove she was modern. And strong. She straightened her back; she regained control as Cal asked, "Can we get an ambulance of some kind?"

"There's the local doctor. I can get him and we can get a car from the hospital, Cal."

He looked up at her. His face softened. "Julia." Next thing she knew, he'd led her away, toward the door.

"No," she protested. "If you can face this with strength, I can. I'll fetch Dougal. He's come back to Brideswell and I know he can help her."

"I don't think you're fit to drive—"

"I am!" she cried. "I can do this."

She saw the doubt in his eyes and she wanted to scream. It was because she was a woman. Everyone thought she was so weak—

"Okay. Take the child with you," Cal said, surprising her by showing he believed her capable. "If I could get my hands on who did this, I'd tear him apart."

She nodded numbly, then stumbled to the door. She believed she knew who had done this. But she didn't have his name. The man was a monster, but Cal couldn't tear him apart. The law would make this man pay. She grasped Ben's hand—he was in the hallway, white as a sheet. "Come and help me get the doctor, Ben—"

"I'm not leaving her!" Ben was going to pull away from her hand, but Cal was there, suddenly, at Ben's side.

"We'll get her to the hospital and the doctor will take care of her, Ben. Go with Lady Julia. She needs a strong man at her side."

She was going to protest—then saw, by the way Ben straightened and held her hand firmly, that Cal's words were to help the boy. He had known just the thing to say.

But as Cal turned to go back to Ellen, she heard him mutter, "God, don't let her die. Not like Mam." He stalked to the kitchen.

His mother had died…like this? Julia felt Ben's hand squeeze hers. They had to go. She hurried him outside, helped him into the car, putting him in the front seat next to her.

Having Ben beside her in the car made her aware she must hold herself together. Tears welled, blurring her vision, and she wiped the tears away viciously with her leather-clad hand, then drew her goggles down over her eyes. Ben said not a word.

She feared for Ellen Lambert, and young Ben, and she feared she'd learned an awful truth about Cal's past. She pushed down the accelerator, hurrying to the hospital to fetch Dougal.

Once Julia had driven away—and he'd watched to ensure she wasn't weaving the car because she was about to faint—Cal went back in, ripped up some sheets and made the best tourniquets he could. Mam used to pray. He never did, but he was doing it now. Silently praying for Ellen.

Then Julia's voice called, "Cal, I'm back and I've brought Dougal—Dr. Campbell."

The sound of her voice…it did something to him. It went right to his soul. He couldn't even explain how he reacted. He'd been with a lot of women, but he'd never been through as much as he had with Julia, and he felt so close to her.

A tall, handsome man with auburn hair strode in, with Julia behind him.

Cal realized it was Campbell, the man Julia had intended to marry.

The doctor got on his knees beside Ellen's prostrate body. Nodded approval at the tourniquets Cal had made. Cal got to his feet and got out of the way so the doctor could work.

Dr. Campbell tended to Ellen with Julia at his side. And Cal saw the way Julia looked at the doctor. That look hit Cal right in the gut.

Campbell was a different kind of man to Hamilton. No snobbery, no drunkenness. Campbell got to business and concern for Ellen was obvious on his face. Campbell was different from him, too, Cal realized. The doctor's past included medical school, hard work and saving lives. Not like Cal's past of crimes and violence.

Campbell examined Ellen quickly, checking her heartbeat and for broken bones. He opened his Gladstone bag and gave Ellen an injection. "For the pain," he said in a Scottish burr. "The tourniquets are doing the trick for now. This lass needs to get to the hospital." He frowned. "Assaulted in her own cottage in front of her wee child. What ruffian carried out this misdeed?"

"I don't know," Julia said.

"Shouldn't the police be called in?" Campbell asked.

"I'll do that," Cal said. "But I doubt Ellen will be helpful."

"Surely she will now," Julia cried.

Cal shook his head. "She'll be more afraid. And afraid for Ben." Tires crunched then, and doors slammed.

"That's the car from the hospital," Julia said. "We left Ben there, under the care of nurses. He wanted to come back, but I told him to wait there, to be ready when his mother came."

Cal nodded, seeing how well she handled herself in a crisis. She was perfectly matched to the honorable Dr. Campbell.

The ambulance drove off with the doctor in the back. Julia touched his arm. "I should go to the hospital to watch Ben," she said. "He'll need a familiar face."

"After, he can come and stay with me at Worthington."

She looked startled. "It would be better for him to come with me to Brideswell. The countess may not be welcoming. And Ben knows me."

"They're on my estate. They're my responsibility. That's what you wanted me to learn, wasn't it? I'm taking him to Worthington and the countess can keep her mouth shut."

Julia's eyes widened in surprise. "I will gather some of Ben's things."

She hurried away from him so fast, Cal knew something was wrong. He followed her. She stood in a tiny room by a small cot. She put her hands to her face.

She was crying. And she hadn't wanted him to see.

But he had comforted her after Mrs. Toft died…

Yeah, and he'd kissed her.

"Are you okay?" he asked. Of course she wasn't, but he didn't know what to say.

With her back to him, she wiped her eyes. She faced him looking collected, except for red rims to her eyelids. "I am fine."

She wasn't, but he guessed she didn't need him. He wanted to touch her, put his arm around her to take her to the car, but he didn't. He drove her to the hospital. Along the way, he stayed quiet. His gut was churning. Maybe his actions to-ward Ben made Julia believe he'd accepted his place as earl.

But he hadn't. He was angry about Ellen, but that had nothing to do with being an earl. He didn't need the title, the money, the estate. David, his brother, didn't need it, ei-ther. He'd sent a telegram, telling David he was now the earl. Temporarily. Because he had made a vow when Mam died. Julia didn't know that, but he'd made a promise, and he was going to carry it out—

"You look so angry," Julia said, breaking the silence as he drove on the rough road.

He could have told her exactly what was on his mind. But he just told her part of it. "I am. I guess you did a good job, Julia. You made me care about these people. I'm going to find that thug and make him pay. I'm going to make him suffer."

"What? You cannot. He must be arrested."

"Where I come from, he'd be found dead."

He heard her sharp, shocked gasp. "That is what they do in New York? I thought those stories of gangs and wars were all exaggerated."

"They're not. That's what the poorest neighborhoods are like. A constant war," he said bitterly. "That's the world that the Carstairs family condemned us to."

"Cal—"

"That's why I'm vengeful, Julia. Vengeance made the world go round where I grew up."

He shouldn't be doing this, shocking her when she was hurt. But the old anger was coiling in him. Then the look of horror on her face cut right down to his soul. She wanted to think he could be gentlemanly. But he never could. He'd never be the kind of man who came from her world.

He damn well didn't want to be. At that moment, he actually felt proud of his past. Proud of having survived poverty and fought his way out of the New York slums.

Then he remembered what he'd done to get out and that feeling of pride was replaced with cold, hard anger.

Meeting Kerry O'Brien in London had reminded him that he'd walked away from his past but hadn't escaped it. Most of New York had read about him in the newspapers. The headlines had screamed things like "American Artist Surprise Heir. The Earl of New York—found penniless in Paris." That was how O'Brien had tracked him down. He'd arranged to meet Kerry O'Brien in London to keep him away from Worthington Park. O'Brien wanted money—

"Cal, was your mother attacked like this?"

He hit a hole in the road because her question had stunned him. How had she known?

"I overheard what you said as I was leaving to fetch Dr. Campbell," she said softly.

He was going to say something hard and curt, something to end the conversation, but he opened his mouth and all that came out was a painful sound, like an abbreviated sob of grief.

All he could think of was the last night of his mam's life. How he had found her. The last words she'd said. After, he'd almost killed himself, he'd been so full of drunken rage and guilt. Painting had saved him. Painting and his responsibility to his brother.

He wasn't going to break down in front of Julia.

"Cal, I am so sorry. If that is what your life was like when you were young, I would like to summon the old earl's ghost and give it a damn good slap."

He'd never heard her swear. It made a laugh come up from deep in his chest. And he knew what he was going to do. Tell Julia Hazelton something that no one else knew. David didn't even know what had really happened to their mam. He'd kept the truth from his brother.

"I was fourteen," he said, a blunt beginning.

He'd had money then—nothing like he had now, but something. He'd earned it with the Five Points Juniors Gang. He'd been acting as lookout. Big for his age, he was being recruited to do more. Muscle was needed to threaten people who owed money, to act as protection. His money was supposed to rescue his mother—get her away from what she'd done when she was really desperate for money.

"Mam worked in a factory at a sewing machine in the day, washed dishes in a bar at night. She helped women deliver babies as well, helping those in our neighborhood. She didn't do that for money, but the families would give us food." He took a breath. "I was wild—angry. My father was dead and Mam had written to the Worthingtons, desperate for their help. They wrote a letter back that told her she wasn't good enough to lick their boots. I was so full of fury... I would come home drunk. I'd get into fights—I'd swing my fists at anyone, and half the time I got beaten senseless."

"Oh, Cal." Her voice was a soft, beautiful murmur beside him.

"That helped me learn how to survive the War, at least. But the night Mam died..."

He couldn't bring himself to tell her what else Mam had been forced to do. "I guess a man broke into our room. He must have known Mam kept the money she had wrapped up in her underclothing drawer—" A lie. Mam had let the man into their tenement.

"She had sent David over to a neighbor's house for the night," he went on, "because she...worked so late at the bar. She was so tired, so thin, so worn to the bone, but Mam was still beautiful. Her eyes were pale blue, ice blue, and they looked like they could only have been made by magic."

Julia's fingers rested gently on his forearm as he drove. He knew it was pity for the damn wretch he'd been. He liked himself better as the angry man who'd arrived here determined to get revenge.

"I found her on the floor," he went on. "She was as badly beaten as Ellen. I thought she was dead. I threw up, standing in the doorway." He'd been scared and weak. "I knelt beside her, and she opened her eyes. Then her head rolled to the side and she coughed up blood. I ran for the doctor, clutching a fistful of money so the doc would know I could pay. But after I gave him money and he looked at her, he said nothing could be done. She was too weak to survive. The doctor left—probably to get a drink—and I stayed with her until she died."

Mam had wanted him to be decent and honorable and gentlemanly like his father. He'd sacrificed all of her dreams when he joined the gang. He'd done it for her, and then he'd been too late to save her.

Julia's hand was squeezing his. "I found the man who hurt her," he said coolly.

"What—what did you do?"

"I tried to beat him just as bad but I failed. I was big, but basically still just a fourteen-year-old kid."

"Dear heaven, that's terrible."

Her touch was gone. Startled, Cal looked down and realized she'd released his hand.

Yeah, he wasn't surprised she didn't want to touch him. He looked at her, saw the shock and horror on her face, and the same cold, hard anger that had lived inside him since he was a boy surged up.

"I've done bad things. I know you want to believe I'm a

worthy noble descendent of the earl, but I keep telling you I'm not."

"That was not bad. It was misguided. But understandable."

She had no idea. But the hell of it was, even as he pushed her away, he wanted her. He itched to paint her. Ached to make love to her. He'd planned to seduce her, but now he knew the truth—he could never have Julia.

At the hospital, poor Ben was terrified, but Julia's heart wobbled as Cal lifted the boy into his arms so Ben could see his mother. Ben fought to look stoic and strong. "I'll look after you, Mum. I'm the man of the family."

"You'll need help with that," Cal said. "I'll help you both."

Julia's heart soared as he said that.

The local police constable arrived, a broad, burly man. He asked questions, but it became quickly apparent that the constable knew who Ellen was and what she did to earn money. His attitude was thoroughly unhelpful, until Cal loomed over him. "You will give this case all due attention," Cal growled. "You will find the man who did this. You will arrest him. I don't give a damn what this woman was forced to do to feed herself and her child. I'm the Earl of Worthington and the police had better give Ellen Lambert's attack the attention it deserves."

"The constabulary will give this its due diligence," the policeman promised, chastised.

"See that is does," Cal said.

Julia could have applauded him. Cal truly did care—which meant she had done what she needed to. She had to wipe a tear that tracked down her cheek. A tear of hope.

Cal came to her. "I'm going to take Ben to Worthington. I'll have a warm bath drawn for him and a bedroom made up."

"In the nursery—"

"The hell with the nursery," he growled. "There's a room beside mine."

"Cal, children always sleep—"

"Ben is going to sleep where I say."

"I won't argue," she said softly. "I agree with you." She wanted to embrace him, but of course, she couldn't. She had to restrain her relief over his caring, responsible behavior.

Cal walked her outside. It was almost evening. "I'll take you home to Brideswell, if you like, Julia."

"I think I'll stay longer. With Ellen. I can have a car sent from Brideswell."

But later, when she left, Julia decided to go to Worthington Park to ensure Ben was settling in all right. As the Daimler pulled in front of the house, Julia saw Cal standing outside, drawing on a cigarette.

She got out, told him why she'd come.

He tossed the cigarette away. "Ben's already gone to sleep, Julia. I had to carry him up to bed. I figure he'll be out for a while, so I'm going to look at the car in the Worthington garage."

He hadn't gone yet. She felt exhausted, but she wanted to see it, too. She had to face the truth—whatever it was. "Let me come with you. And don't argue."

Cal shrugged. "Okay."

They reached the garage in silence. At Cal's side, Julia walked in through one of the open double doors. She smelled grease and oil, following him to the very back of the building. A cloth was draped over a car and was gray with dust, except where the corner had been pulled back, exposing the headlight and the red painted fender.

Cal pulled the dustcover completely away.

"This was Anthony's car," she said softly. "He adored it. The only other person who drove it was the earl."

"How old was the earl in 1916?" Cal asked.

Could it really have been Anthony's father who took young women for drives? "He was about forty-two."

"Good-looking? Could he have looked like a younger man?"

"I suppose. He rode religiously and kept himself trim. He was quite a handsome man." She stared at Cal. "Do you really believe he is the one who would meet Sarah and take her driving? And the other girls?"

Cal opened the door and climbed in. "Those girls would be flattered, wouldn't they, by the attentions of a lofty earl?"

Sarcasm made his voice hard. She watched him sit, holding the steering wheel for a moment. Then he bent to the passenger seat and the floor.

"What are you doing?"

"Checking," he said. She had no idea what he meant until he straightened, holding a ball of emerald green cloth. "It's a scarf," he said, and he straightened it out. It was wrinkled and a bit dirty. He looked closely at it. Then showed it to her. "See the dark hairs on it?"

Julia lifted the green silk. She coughed at the musty smell. By the light of the electric bulb, she could see a few long black hairs tangled in the fringe.

"Is it yours?" he asked. "Did you forget it in the car years ago?"

"It's not mine. It's a striking color, but it's a cheaply produced silk. Not the best quality." She frowned. "I doubt Sarah would have had a scarf like this, even so. It would be out of her means."

"But maybe it was a gift. To lower her defenses," he said.

"I don't think—"

"I do. Don't men like that think they can do anything they like to lower-class girls?"

"Not all of them," she said.

"It looks like it was my cousin Anthony or the old earl who picked up the girls in this fancy automobile."

She jerked her head up. "You have no real evidence to say such a thing."

"You just can't believe a gentleman you had dinner with could be a scoundrel."

"No," she said sharply. "I'm very aware of what men do. But I knew both men well. I was in love with Anthony and I was going to marry him. I know what kind of man he was. The earl was very much in love with his wife. She was so much softer and kinder then, before the tragedies happened."

"She wasn't kind to my family."

"I think you just desperately want the earl to have done something scandalous. But we have to know it's true. We need proof."

"That's what I want." Meeting her eyes with a grim gaze, he got out and went to the back of the car.

There was still no explanation for what had happened to the girls. Even if Anthony had flirted with them, where had they gone?

She walked to the boot just as Cal opened it, raising the lid. A spade sat in there, crusted with dried mud, and the floor of the boot was covered in dirt.

A spade? The electric light glittered on something in the corner. Cal lifted up a tiepin, decorated with a sapphire.

"That belonged to Anthony," she whispered.

After Julia left to go home to Brideswell, Cal returned to the house to find Kerry O'Brien waiting for him in his study. Wiggins told him the American *gentleman* had pushed his way in, and had not given his name—had only said to tell Cal that a friend from the Five Points Gang wanted to see him.

Damn O'Brien. "Where are the countess and my cousins?" Cal asked.

"They have retired for the night."

The countess was avoiding him and eighty rooms made that easy to do. She hadn't even come down for dinner in the big dining room for the past few nights. She ate in her room, claiming she had headaches. His cousins ate with him, but they also stayed away from him as much as possible. He'd tried to apologize to Thalia for his outburst over the painting, but she had blinked at him like a baby owl, then scurried away. As if she was afraid that just speaking to him would unleash his rage. He found he felt like an idiot for making a young girl afraid of him.

But tonight, he was glad they weren't here to see O'Brien.

Wiggins cleared his throat. "My lord, if I may be so bold as to make the suggestion… I could return with a strong footman and propel this gentleman out of the house."

Cal tried to imagine the ancient butler trying to get rid of O'Brien, who carried both a gun and a blade. For once he felt a kinship with frosty Wiggins. And grinned. "Not necessary, but I appreciate the thought, Wiggins."

"Very good." The butler withdrew.

He stalked to his study. O'Brien was in his chair, his feet up on the desk. "You really are a goddamned earl," O'Brien said as Cal walked in and shut the door. Kerry waved his hand around at the books, paintings, furnishings. "You could fence this for a fortune."

"Why in hell are you here, O'Brien? We were supposed to meet again in London."

"I figured you might double-cross me." O'Brien took out a cigarette from a gold case. As he did, he let Cal see the butt grip of his pistol stuck in the waistband of his suit trousers. "That old stick-up-the-ass butler looked surprised when I mentioned the Five Points Gang. Just like I figured—your snooty family doesn't know about your past. They don't know what you did. I gave you my price for being quiet. I want to be paid. Now. If you don't got cash, I'll take some of your fancy goods."

"Maybe I don't give a damn if the family does find out."

Obviously that was something O'Brien had never figured. "What in hell do you mean?"

In one fluid motion, Cal ground out his cigarette on the heel of his hand and grabbed O'Brien by the lapels of his shiny pale pink suit jacket. He lifted his former associate off the leather seat. "You can do whatever the hell you want with your story. I'm going to sell this place and take off. And I don't give a flying fuck," he said coarsely, "what Lady Worthington or this family thinks about me."

The truth was he didn't want them to know. He definitely didn't want Julia to know.

"You're bluffing."

"Try me."

O'Brien's face went red—his nose was always red, from a lifetime of hitting the Irish bars. "You owe me, Cal. I saved your life. You remember."

"You did. I've repaid that debt six times already. This time will make seven."

"What do ye mean 'this time'?"

Cal went to the desk drawers, pulled out a key and opened the top one. He pulled out all the ready cash he'd locked up in there—two thousand dollars in American bills. Tossed it on the desk blotter in front of Kerry. "That's all you're gonna get. Two grand."

O'Brien smirked at him, but his blue eyes were still wary.

Watching. Ready to shoot to save his own life. O'Brien stuffed the money in the pocket of his pink jacket. "I need more."

"It's not worth it to me to pay you to keep your mouth shut. That's because I had a debt to you. Now get the hell out."

O'Brien's hand moved toward the gun.

One quick breath later, Cal had O'Brien's arm pinned behind his back and his face shoved hard against the blotter. "Get out, O'Brien. I've got thirty thousand acres here. Easy enough for a body to end up in a shallow grave, never to be found."

As he spoke, he felt his gut churn. For three women, he figured that had already happened. He could be wrong, but his gut instinct told him those women were dead. He had no intention of even getting into a fist fight with O'Brien, so to make sure O'Brien believed his bluff, he leaned over the man and muttered, "I could break your damn neck before you even move. You know that, Kerry."

The War had taken all the brutal skills he'd learned growing up in the gang and perfected them. He eased off on the pressure and when Kerry didn't try to spring up and fight, Cal let go and stepped back completely.

"Let me escort you to the door," he said.

Kerry knew he was beaten, Cal figured. The gangster jerked up, straightened his suit and put his hat back on—it had fallen to the floor as Cal had shoved him down before.

He hauled O'Brien to the large double doors. Wiggins stood there, with a footman who was losing the battle to look like he was made of stone. Wiggins commanded the kid—a lad named Eustace—to open the door. Cal propelled Kerry out to the front step.

"Yeah, I'll go back to London," Kerry growled. "Right to the papers."

"I advise you to go back to the States," Cal said, low and soft. He had no idea what O'Brien was going to do, but he could smell the man's fear. His fear and his anger. Which one was going to win out? "I'm a rich man. I could offer the papers a lot more money to not print that story."

Kerry sneered, but he had a deflated look to him. "I need a drink," he muttered.

"You've got a couple grand on you. Don't spend it all at one bar," Cal said. After O'Brien left, he poured himself a drink. When he'd started painting in Paris, he'd sworn he would never do anything violent again. But to save his arse, he'd done that today.

And—damn it—he was imagining the horrified look that would have been on Julia's face if she'd witnessed it.

By the light of day the next morning, Julia still could not believe it was true. The horrible thing she'd been confronted with last night. That it might have been Anthony who had made Sarah Brand, Eileen Kilkenny and a maid disappear.

Anthony had been a good man. He'd loved Worthington Park with all his soul. If he had been warped, if he had been wrong in the head, surely she would have seen it.

Going down to breakfast was a nightmare. She could not eat. All she could manage was coffee. Black and strong.

"I've had a letter from the Earl of Summerhay," Mother announced. "He has to be in the area—he is purchasing a horse. He wondered, Nigel, if he might be able to stay. I have been corresponding quite regularly with that dear boy."

"The dear boy is almost thirty, Mother," Isobel pointed out. "And you've only been corresponding with him since

Julia said she would never consider marrying the Duke of Bradstock."

Mother ignored that. "He is in need of a place to stay. He intends to stay at a public house, but I told him that is nonsense. He must stay with us. Are you in agreement, Nigel?"

"Mother, you promised not to push me to marry," Julia protested, for this was the last thing she wanted to think about.

"I would never push. But I see no reason why he cannot visit and you could not spend time with him." Mother looked happier than she had in years and Julia's heart twisted.

"Mother, I can't. Invite him if you wish, but don't try to push, or put, us together." She looked at the surprised faces—her mother's lovely pale face, Isobel's curious one, Nigel's startled one.

She couldn't tell them she feared Anthony had committed terrible crimes. "Please. I just can't think of this right now."

"What is wrong?" Nigel asked.

"Nothing. I—I was thinking of Anthony. I'm simply not ready to think of marrying anyone."

She got up. "I must go out—I have things I must do." Julia left the room, the house. It was drizzling, so she threw on a mackintosh from a closet. She got her car and drove as fast as she could to Worthington.

There, she stopped in the drive. Her bare hands clutched the leather-wrapped steering wheel. She hadn't worn gloves. She usually did—Mother had said she could not drive if she didn't, or she would end up with a farm laborer's calluses. How unimportant such concerns were now.

The footman opened the door and Wiggins, walking past the foyer, saw her and hurried to her. "Good morning, Lady Julia."

It wasn't a good morning. It was a terrifying one. "Is the earl at home?"

"The earl has gone to Lilac Farm."

Lilac Farm. Yesterday, Cal had looked down at the shovel in the boot of the car. He had told her about a criminal case in America—a twelve-year-old schoolgirl from the State of New Jersey had been "criminally assaulted" and killed. He had stood there, the light casting the most ominous shadows under his sharp cheekbones, and told her that those three women might be dead. They might be buried somewhere. Even somewhere on the Worthington estate.

"Why has he gone to Lilac Farm?" He couldn't have gone to tell the family what he suspected, could he?

Cal hadn't voiced his thoughts but she'd seen it in the dark anger in his eyes. He thought a man from Worthington Park had done it. It could have been the old earl, or John, or even one of the men who worked on the estate—if he were bold enough to take the car. But she knew Cal was thinking it was Anthony. He'd said: *Likely a man got away with murder because of who he was.*

"My lady, I fear it is his lordship's intent to sell land to an American gentleman."

Wiggins's words broke through her thoughts. Julia felt as if the floor had suddenly tilted and she was going to slide off it. "What? What American?" The man from London, supplied her frantic mind.

"I did not eavesdrop, my lady. The gentleman bluntly asked Lord Worthington if the house was for sale. He also asked if I was for sale."

Her stomach lurched. But she hid her panic. "I am so sorry, Wiggins."

"The earl took this American with him. Should I be concerned for the future of the estate, my lady?"

Wiggins looked utterly composed, except for a twitch to his jaw, but Julia knew the poor man was terrified. Cal had been angry after they had found the shovel. He felt the Carstairs family had gotten away with murder.

She would have known, surely, if Anthony was so bad, so evil. And Cal had no proof. A shovel left in the boot of the car was not definitive evidence. Nor was the scarf.

Cal had been angry. But surely he wouldn't sell the farm away from the Brands because he was angry—without proof—at the Carstairs?

And even if—if Anthony was guilty, poor people like the Brands had suffered enough. Cal's rage must not hurt them, in any attempt to strike the Carstairs family. She had to stop Cal.

"This man was not the only American gentleman who came to the house in the past two days, my lady," Wiggins said. "Late yesterday an unsavory-looking man arrived by motorcar. He wore a suit of a pale pink, shiny material—" Wiggins sniffed "—and he had the mannerisms, accent and air of an American gangster."

That was the man in London. This then was a different man. What did that mean? "I must go. At once." Leaving Wiggins staring in astonishment, she turned from her heel and ran out of the house, as if pursued by hounds.

Was she already too late to save the Brands' farm?

12

The Arrival of Cal's Brother

Julia's shoes crunched on gravel as she rushed toward her car, her mackintosh flapping around her. She would drive like the wind to Lilac Farm—

She stopped abruptly, almost skidding on the drive. Walking away from the house toward the converted stable-garage were two men. One was Cal, wearing his rough sweater and trousers, the sweater spattered with paint. The shorter, portly man walking at his side wore a dapper suit. They hadn't gone yet—or were they returning?

Her heart lodged in her throat. Julia hurried up behind them as the man stuck out his hand to Cal. "If you change your mind about selling, give me a call, my lord. I want that piece of property. Several hundred acres. I could do a lot with that."

Cal shook the short man's large hand. "I'm sorry to have wasted your trip, but things have changed and I'm not planning to sell yet."

"These places can't survive and that's a fact. The future is in men like me," the large man crowed. "The self-made men. It was soap for me. Then locomotives. Love the iron horses and they've made me rich."

"I'm glad I could at least help your wife's charity."

"My Dora is a saint. Your contribution is very generous, my lord. As is your offer to sponsor me at your club. Damned hard to break into those places and my Dora is set on seeing our Annabelle married to a titled man. I don't suppose—"

"Sorry, Mr. Morgan, but I'm already promised to someone."

"Too bad. Annie comes with a dowry big enough to sink a ship." With that, the large man left.

Cal met her gaze. He looked guilty. She felt ready to spit fire. Yet the first thing that came out of her mouth: "I had no idea you're engaged."

"I'm not. I just wanted to make sure he didn't try to sell me Annabelle."

She smiled—just for a moment—then exclaimed, "Were you going to sell Lilac Farm to that man?"

He grimaced. "I'd made the arrangements before we went to London. I forgot to cancel the meeting."

"You changed your mind?" She barely dared to hope.

"Until I find out what happened to those women, until I get justice for them, I don't want to start carving up the estate." His blue eyes held hers. "And I promised you I'd wait if you posed for a portrait. I'm still waiting for your answer."

"I haven't even been able to think about that. A portrait doesn't seem so important now. But you are right to wait until we know the truth. You do agree that we have no proof yet that anyone from Worthington was involved. Not real proof. Americans believe in justice, do they not? That is what you sought when you came here—justice for your parents, especially your mother. Don't condemn without proof. And what of the Brands—haven't they suffered enough? You can't throw them out of their home—"

"I'm not going to do that," he growled. "I'm going to look for evidence, find the truth. If someone on the estate murdered those girls, they must have buried—" He broke off. "Sorry, that's not something you discuss with a lady."

She lifted her chin, fighting to be strong. "I have had to face tragedy. And I'm not afraid of the truth. I would rather have that than have secrets. But how can evidence be found now, so many years later?"

"There are things than can be found. Even years later."

His face hardened as he said that. She knew what he meant—bodies. The spade in the boot of the car, encrusted with dirt. A man with a motorcar could have driven miles to find girls to flirt with, to lure into his vehicle. But why would that spade be left in the boot of Anthony's car?

He could have been helping with planting on the estate. He could have used it when they were searching for the girls. Or perhaps he had some other perfectly innocent reason for it.

Or perhaps someone else had put it there.

"You're pale. Let me take you back to the house, Julia. You don't need to worry about this."

"Cal, I can't just not think about this. I have to know!" She paced in a circle, feeling so tense she might burst. "I should see Ben, see how he is. I should be driving to the hospital to see Ellen. I should ensure the police constable is hunting for the man who hurt Ellen. But all I could do this morning was think of this—of whether Anthony had done this horrible thing."

"The photograph," Cal said suddenly.

She stared at him, confused. She saw the bristle of whiskers along his jaw. He hadn't bothered to shave.

"I found a photograph in my bedroom—it had fallen under the wardrobe. It was of a dark-haired girl wearing a corset. Signed 'to A.'"

"To Anthony? But why would that have been in your bedroom? Anthony never used that room. He was never the earl."

"I know. But the picture was there. And Sarah Brand had dark hair. Her mother confused you for Sarah."

"Sarah had black hair and blue eyes. We were of a similar height. I think her mind wants to believe I'm Sarah, when she sees me."

"Would you know if it was Sarah in the picture?"

"I suppose so."

Cal ran off, suddenly, sprinting to the house. She followed, hurrying as fast as her low heels and trim-fitting tweed skirt would allow. By the time she reached the door, he was already coming back out. Frowning. "He burned the photo," he said.

"Who did?"

"Wiggins," he growled. "Maybe he knew the girl Sarah Brand and he was protecting the family."

"Protecting them?"

"Maybe he knows Anthony Carstairs was driving Sarah around. Or maybe he knows what Anthony did to her—"

"We don't know Anthony did anything!" she cried. "It could have been someone else. Someone else could have used that motorcar and left the spade in it. There could have been some other reason. I want proof before I think of the man I loved as a—a murderer!"

She spun away from Cal, to go to her motorcar.

His hand wrapped firm around her arm—firm but gentle, forcing her to stop. "You aren't driving anywhere. Not upset like this."

"I am going to go to Lilac Farm. You can drive me there if you wish."

They reached the farm to find Brand finally making himself a breakfast of tea and toast after tending to the animals. Julia could see he was exhausted. Mrs. Brand had been awake most of the night, so she was sleeping now, even though it was midmorning.

"I have to watch her," he admitted. "She gets up and she wanders in the night. She tries to go outside. Once she got away and I couldn't find her for hours. I lock the place up now."

The poor man. She had to admit Cal was right—the farm was too much for them.

"I will help," she insisted. And she did, holding her umbrella up as she spread out seed for chickens. Cal helped, too, and when she attempted to carry buckets of water from the pump for the pigs' troughs, he stopped her. Brand looked shocked.

"Nae, ye shouldn't be working, milady," Brand said.

"I cannot stand by idle and not help," she said crisply. "But I wondered if Sarah ever told you she was frightened by a man. A man who might have tried to—to accost her."

She felt guilty as she asked the question. She knew, in her heart, she was trying to prove the man who had been driving Sarah wasn't Anthony.

"She never spoke of any such thing."

"Did Lord Anthony really take her driving in the car?"

"Mrs. Brand thinks Lord Anthony took her in his motorcar, but I don't believe it," Brand said. "Lord Anthony weren't like that. Neither were she. Sarah wanted to be married someday and she had no daft ideas about marrying above her station."

That was hope, at least. "Would you mind if I took a look in Sarah's room?"

Brand allowed it and Julia went to the house. Cal followed. She realized Cal was letting her take charge with this. The tiny room looked as it must have done nine years before. She looked in the one small wardrobe. Sarah's clothes still hung in it, smelling of lavender sachets. She found a diary, but there was no mention of any secret love. But Sarah did record times when she'd watched Anthony drive by in his lovely motorcar.

She had no choice but to let Cal look at it, too. Then she put it away, feeling sick. She left the Brands then. Told Cal, "I must go and see some of the women I'm helping today."

"I'll take you."

"It is not necessary. I am perfectly fine to drive." They argued—to her surprise, he finally relented. He took her back to Worthington, let her go off in her car.

She drove to the cottages and farms of several of the women. It made her feel better to see how they were surviving. One of the women, Mrs. Woddle, was in delight over the success of her sales of preserves. Now, after the War, with girls working in factories, they had to feed themselves and had no facilities to do so. Tea shops were booming.

She went to see the Tofts. Neighbors were helping—and Nigel had been sending baskets of food and treats from Brideswell's kitchens. It was almost heartbreaking, but she put on a brave face. If the family could, so could she. Seeing the eldest daughter, Mary, turned Julia's stomach upside down. The girl had dark hair in pigtails and large blue eyes.

Julia didn't remember any girl going missing after 1916. It seemed the disappearances had stopped then. Why?

Because Anthony went to war.

She did not know that for certain. And it was *not* proof.

Julia drove to see Ellen after that. In Brideswell's hospital ward, she told Ellen, "I will loan you the money to begin a business. A seamstress business, perhaps. Please accept this."

Tucked in her cot, Ellen shook her head. "I would only let you down, my lady. I could never pay you back."

"I believe you can. You must tell me who attacked you. He should be arrested and imprisoned for what he has done."

"I can't tell you his name. He would hurt Ben."

"Ben will be safe. I will ensure this man never comes near him. He almost killed you," Julia said, in a vehement whisper so as not to disturb the other women in the ward. "Help me and we will have him arrested."

But Ellen would not meet her gaze. "I can't do that, my lady."

Cal had been right. So painfully right. Ellen was willing to shield an evil man out of fear.

Julia stood. "I will find out who did this. I am not going to let him get away with it."

Panic flooded Ellen's face, turning her skin white where it wasn't bruised. "Don't, my lady. You have to keep out of it. You'll get yourself in trouble."

"Don't be ridiculous. I will be perfectly fine and I intend to help you."

Julia left, frustrated as she drove through the village. The dark, rainy weather matched her mood. But she was going to protect Ellen in some way—that was one thing she could do. She did not doubt the horrible wretch had taken money from Ellen when he had beaten her. It was the sort of thing a brute would do. And she knew where that money would be spent.

She drove to the village nearest Ellen's cottage, the small village of Worthington. Even in this tiny place, there were three pubs. Then she saw him. A large man leaving the Boar and Castle, the village public house. She was certain this was the man she had seen harassing Ellen on the street weeks ago.

Julia got out of her motor, stalked over to the man. But a few paces away, her courage failed her. But it was too late. He must have sensed her. He turned with surprising speed for such a large man and he strode back toward her.

She lifted her chin. It might be the middle of the day on the main street of the village of Worthington, but the rain meant the street was almost deserted. She had made a terrible, terrible mistake. "Lay a hand on me and I will scream," she threatened, but her voice shook.

"Ye were the one coming after me, milady." His fleshy lips smirked.

"I want your name."

"Ye don't need it. Ye won't have any trouble from me if Ellen keeps doing as she's told." He puffed up his huge chest. "I'm looking after her. She doesn't need meddling from the likes of you, milady. Keep away from her."

"Ellen told me you have threatened her child to force her to—to sell herself and give the money to you. How small and pitiful you are. I will not allow this to continue. I will find out who you are and I will have you arrested."

He laughed cheerfully. "I doubt that. Ellen would be the only one who could back up yer wild tale and she won't grouse on me. Ye can't hurt me. But ye're fragile. I can hurt ye real easy. Ye go to see her one more time, and I'll really make ye pay."

Fury made her stand up to him. "I will have my brother destroy you. I will ensure you never hurt Ellen or her son again. I will move them away, to a place you will not find them. I am a duke's daughter and I have the power to crush you like the worm you are."

"Ye'll regret that," he snarled. "Don't ye dare threaten

me, ye cow." He loomed over her, lifting his fist. She was scared, using every ounce of strength not to melt in panic. But she had a weapon. She lifted her umbrella and poked the pointed end into his stomach.

He let out a howl of pain and doubled over. She spun and raced up the sidewalk.

A car was coming toward her.

It accelerated and as soon as it reached her, it screeched to a stop. The man behind the wheel leaned out to look at her.

Cal.

She wanted to throw her arms around him and hug him so tight he wouldn't be able to breathe. Of course she wouldn't do it.

He jumped out of the car. He ran right past her, down the sidewalk. Shaking, she turned to watch him, but she couldn't see any sign of the man who'd threatened her.

Cal came back to her. "Julia, who was that man?"

"I don't know." That much was the truth. She didn't have his name.

"Don't lie to me, Julia. I couldn't see exactly, but it looked like he was threatening you. I did see you drive your umbrella into his gut and I doubt you'd do that unless he asked for it."

Cal was looking at her as Nigel would. With the same autocratic, protective look.

She swallowed hard. "Perhaps I should return to my motorcar."

"You're trembling and you're pale. You need a drink, Julia. Something for the shock."

He hustled her into the Boar and Castle. He ordered a large brandy for her, an ale for himself. It was warm in the pub—despite being June, it was a cool, cloudy day and she felt cold through to her soul.

"That was the man who hurt Ellen Lambert," Cal said.

"Yes, that was her pimp. How did you know?"

Cal's brows shot up under his blond hair. "Lucky guess. But I'm kind of stunned you know that word."

"Well, I do. I'm not completely naive. But you mustn't tell my brother about this."

"I take it you mean you don't want me to mention some thug threatened to hurt you. If I were your brother, I'd like to know that."

"You can't. *Please.* He would use this as a reason to stop me continuing my work with women like Ellen. And Zoe might agree with him, if she thought I was in danger."

Their drinks came, served by Mr. Grey. As he set down Cal's pint, he asked, "I've been thinking about that business with those missing girls, milord. Did ye talk to old Brown, who used to work at the house? Did he help you?"

"Yeah, he did. Thanks." Cal was attempting to sound off-hand and casual. Then he asked about Ellen's pimp—about the man who had just been drinking in there.

"Aye. Don't know his name. He's only been in here twice for a drink. Usually drinks elsewhere, he said. I banned him for life this time—he wants to brawl and I don't need the trouble."

"If he comes in again, would you find out his name before you toss him out? I'll make it worth your trouble," Cal promised.

The man touched his forehead, a gesture of respect and agreement. "I will, milord."

After Grey left, Julia gasped. "Of course. I remember now. Brown is the former chauffeur at Worthington. When did you speak to him?" She had been hoping to get the name of Ellen's abuser and hadn't really thought about Brown until just now.

"After you left today," Cal said, "I drove over to the village where he lives with his daughter."

"What did you learn from him?"

Cal took a long swallow of beer.

Her heart dipped. He didn't want to tell her.

He set down the glass. "He said that he found Anthony in the garage one night. He was taking something out of the trunk, but when he heard Brown come in, he locked the trunk, then covered up the car with the white sheet. Brown said he looked upset, nervous. It was just the next day that Anthony volunteered and went to war."

"What are you saying? That he went to war to make up for—for taking those women?"

"Maybe."

"Why would he leave those things in the vehicle, where they could be found?"

"Maybe he thought no one would touch his car," Cal said. "Maybe he had no time."

Suddenly she realized the truth. Cal didn't just want justice. He wanted Anthony to be guilty. She believed she knew why—that would prove the Earl of Worthington had been utterly wrong to condemn Cal's family. That the wealthier, titled Carstairs had not been better or nobler people—since they had a criminal strain in their blood.

She wanted Anthony to be innocent. She wanted to believe in the man she had loved deeply.

They could not both get what they wanted.

Cal set down his drink. His hand rested close to hers. She moved hers away. She couldn't touch him.

"You need to go home and forget about all this," he said.

"I won't. I can't let you make Anthony guilty, if he wasn't. What will you do then—use that for justification to destroy Worthington? Hurt more innocent people?"

"I'm not going to say he's guilty if that's not true. But if he's guilty—"

Panic rose. "But if you stop searching for evidence, you can justify calling him guilty." She was sick with fear. "You can't do anything until you have actual evidence. Irrefutable evidence."

He didn't answer.

"What if I agreed to your bargain—that you won't touch Worthington if I let you paint me?"

"You were right, Julia. Portraits don't seem as important now."

Her heart sank. Then she thought of Cal's story. Of his mother dying and of him having to protect his younger brother and raise him—

"This is your brother's birthright also. How can you think of destroying his family home, when he has never even seen it? That is wrong, Cal. He should at least see his father's home. Wouldn't that be fair and just to him?"

"The way I see it, this isn't his father's home. This is where his father grew up, before being disowned by this family."

"But it was still his home when he was a child, and it was a part of him. Your brother should see it," she insisted.

Cal gave her an almost sulky look. She knew she'd scored a point. "Did your father ever talk about Worthington Park?"

"Yeah, he did."

"What did he say about it?"

"Said it was beautiful. That he was sorry we'd never get to see it. I knew we weren't considered good enough for this place—we were the dirt that had to be kept out. But David was younger than me and he didn't understand. He used to dream about seeing it."

"Then no matter what you do to Worthington, you must let your brother, David, see it first."

"You're right. And I did plan to do it. I'll send him a wire. Arrange his passage." He sighed heavily. "I wouldn't have sold the farm today because I know it would have hurt you. I couldn't do that to you now, after you've been through so much. You know I don't want to hurt you, Julia."

She knew the rest—the rest he left unsaid. That he feared he would have to. And inside she was in turmoil. To have a boy think he was dirt that should be kept out of a house… it made her blood boil in anger. But that was the past, and there had to be a way for Worthington and Cal to have a future together.

The day before Cal's brother was to arrive, Mother held a dinner party. Zoe was the duchess, but Mother had actually arranged everything for the party, something she had not done in many years. Not since grief over Will had consumed her. It showed her mother was healing and that was good. Mother insisted it was to help Julia get over her sorrow from the Tofts' losses.

But when she went down for cocktails before dinner, Julia discovered Mother had invited the Duke of Bradstock and the Earl of Summerhay. Nigel had invited Dougal Campbell—he wanted to discuss some business about the hospital.

She wanted to turn and run—she was so worried about what Cal might learn about Anthony she couldn't bear to spend time fending off suitors.

Mother, of course, arranged for her to sit between James—the Duke of Bradstock—and Summerhay.

The electric chandeliers—installed by Zoe—sparkled on crystal and silver. Candlelight flickered on the table.

As they reached the savory after dessert, James leaned toward her. At the exact same moment, the Earl of Summerhay leaned to her also. Both men said, at once, "Would you ride with me tomorrow?"

They stared at each other as she said, "I am afraid I already have plans. But since you both want to ride, why don't you gentlemen go together?"

"We aren't courting each other," James said, lifting his brow in true ducal fashion. "Summerhay is courting you. And I want only to enjoy a ride with you."

But James was courting her, too, she saw. And she didn't want to be courted. Why didn't men listen? But then she felt guilty and softened the blow. "Though of course I am flattered and ordinarily I should love to…" She winced— she did not want to encourage either man, when she knew she couldn't love either one, but she had been trained to be so blasted polite. "But tomorrow I have plans to go to Worthington Park."

She could not wait to meet Cal's brother. He could be a valuable ally and she was going to be there, under any pretext, when he arrived.

"To see the American earl?" James growled. He gripped his wineglass so hard his knuckles went white. "You shouldn't go there. There are rumors—"

"Of an engagement," Summerhay finished.

"Not of an engagement. I knew that was rot," James insisted. "The man's behavior is notorious. I've heard stories about him in Paris, bedding all of his models."

"What is this? Are you speaking of bedding roses?" That was the dowager and Julia was quite sure she'd heard everything, and was stopping James before he said something even more shocking.

"I am going to see Ellen Lambert's son, who is staying there. And my good friend Diana."

"As long as it isn't to see him."

Obviously James did not like Cal, but she couldn't see how he had the right to dictate.

"He's also mentally unhinged," James said. "Apparently he goes around the estate, digging in random places, or so I've been told. Is he looking for buried treasure?"

She swallowed hard—she couldn't say he was looking for the three women, not if there was a chance Anthony had been involved. "This is the first I've heard of that," she hedged.

"He must be looking for something—"

Chairs scraped, interrupting James, signaling it was time to go to the drawing room. Julia sighed with relief. When the men joined the ladies, after having their port, Julia went over to Dougal. "I am concerned about Ellen Lambert."

His sensitive brown eyes showed surprise. "She is recovering well."

"Perhaps physically. I fear she is suffering from shell shock." She did love to be able to speak to Dougal as a partner, to have a meeting of minds.

"Shell shock?" he echoed. "Why do you think this?"

"It was Cal—the Earl of Worthington—who suggested it. She suffers nightmares. She can't sleep. Loud noises make her react in a panic."

"Some women who served at the front proved to be too delicate for the work—"

"It's not delicacy," she protested. "Women witnessed the same horrors as the men. Ellen drove an ambulance, where she saw victims of the worst injuries. According to Cal, the ambulances were shelled and shot at."

"Medical practitioners have diagnosed such women as suffering from hysteria. They proved unsuitable for the work and returned home."

"Unsuitable for the work? Who would be suitable to drive

a vehicle through a battlefield while being shelled?" She stared at him. "It is not hysteria. It's shell shock."

"Shell shock is a different thing entirely. The problems that men experienced were different from those that women did."

"How could they be? They experienced the very same things." She couldn't understand him.

"No male soldier would accept that his condition is like hysteria."

"Oh, that is it! You think the men would be ashamed to have the same problem as women. Well, they had best get over it. She has shell shock. And I fear she will not be able to improve her life until it is dealt with."

Dougal gave an awkward cough. "Julia, I would suspect Ellen Lambert's troubles are due to her current...profession."

She could not believe she had heard such a thing from Dougal. "Her current profession is a result of ignorance on the part of the government and society. We have turned our backs on people like her. I thought you would *champion* her cause. There has been help for men with shell shock. Why shouldn't women be helped? Really, Dougal, I cannot understand you."

"What do you want me to do, Julia? Even if I agreed, a diagnosis of shell shock would not be recognized—and would not help the woman in any way."

"But she could be cured."

"Not necessarily, and the forms of treatment are horrific, Julia. She would certainly be separated from her son."

She fumbled. She hadn't thought of that. And she was startled by the way Dougal smiled slightly, as though he were being patient with her, as though he knew, of course, he should win the argument. "There must be a solution."

"There's nothing more you can do, Julia."

"I thought we could work on this together. I have to

help her—for her sake and for Ben's. She served her country, just as bravely as any man. How can there be no help for her now?" Even as she spoke, she saw from his face that he would not help. She had thought Dougal was a wonderful doctor, a progressive, modern man.

"The officials of her country would never call her condition 'shell shock.' And given what else she has done after the War, they would not help."

"But that's wrong!" she cried.

"What is wrong, Julia?" Grandmama asked, gazing at her with pursed lips.

"Apparently quite a lot with our country," she said. "But of course, nothing is ever solved at a dinner party."

She couldn't explain why—but she felt deeply discouraged that Dougal had turned out to be a different man than she'd believed. Cal had turned out different, too—but in good ways.

Without Dougal's support, what could she do for Ellen?

Julia was still without a solution as she rode over to Worthington Park the next day. The day Cal's brother was to arrive, being driven from the South Hampton docks.

She found Cal pacing outside the front door, a cigarette clenched between his teeth.

"You're waiting for your brother?" She dismounted—it was so deliciously easy to do so in jodhpurs rather than skirts.

Cal nodded, his face grim.

"I thought you would be happy to see him again. He's had a long journey. You will have to smile when he gets here," she teased.

"It's hard," he muttered.

"Why is it hard?" She stood at his side, holding Athena's reins.

"He was wounded badly in the War."

Badly? Heavens, how badly? "I didn't know that. Was the journey hard for him?"

"Yeah, I imagine it was very hard. But he made it—to see this damn house." Cal shook his head. "I told him not to join up. But once I went, there was no one to stop him. He followed me into battle, but I served as a pilot and he served on the ground. I didn't even know he was there until we were in the same hospital together—"

Cal had to stop talking. She saw tears in his eyes. He blinked hard and the tears were gone.

"I am so sorry," she said. "It must have broken your heart to see him wounded."

"It did. He was eighteen. A shell exploded under him after he shoved two men out of the way to save them. They had to take off both of his legs below the knee. At home, when he was a kid, I protected him. Kept him out of—" He broke off. Drew on his cigarette. "Kept him out of trouble," he finished. "But he went to war and destroyed his life."

"He is still alive," she pointed out softly.

"He can't walk and has to spend his life in a wheeled chair."

How hurt Cal looked—he was feeling a huge weight of responsibility. For something that had not been his fault. He believed in protecting people—she knew it meant these wounds went very deep.

He kicked the gravel. "After the War, I hired a staff of nurses and servants to look after him. I went away to Paris. Sometimes I feel I was running away from my guilt. I tried painting it away, but it didn't work. I couldn't forget. So I tried to drink it away with good French wine and brandy. That didn't work, either."

"It is not your fault. He was of age and it was his choice to volunteer."

"But if you have someone you love, you want to protect them," he said.

"I didn't want Anthony to go to War, but I knew I couldn't ask him to stay. His father had not wanted him to go, since he was the heir. His father wanted him to wait until he was conscripted, but Anthony felt it was wrong to stay home when other men were doing their duty."

She expected him to dismiss what Anthony had done, but gently, he said, "You went through what I did. I wrote home and told David it was a living hell, but he ignored my letters. He thought I was trying to scare him away."

Cal's fingers brushed hers. Just that touch made her gasp. Then he moved abruptly away. "He's here." He threw his cigarette away on the drive.

The Worthington Daimler, large and black, drove into view on the drive.

"I shouldn't have brought him here," Cal said suddenly. "He doesn't need any of this. He has a home in America and people to care for him. The countess despises me. How is she going to react to my brother's condition?"

Cal was panicking, she saw. "It will be all right. I will not allow him to be hurt," she vowed.

The car stopped. Two footmen who stood on the front steps sprang forward. But Cal went forward, too, not acting like an earl, not waiting. He went to the boot of the vehicle where a wheeled chair had been folded and attached. After the footman took it off the motorcar, Cal took it from the young servant. With practiced motions he wheeled it to the passenger door on the far side, away from the house.

Wait—she realized what he had said. He had hired a staff

of nurses and servants. She had thought he was an impoverished artist before he became earl. That he had still been poor.

But he could not have been impoverished to have spent so much money to look after his brother.

The front door of the house opened and the countess marched out. Julia saw her mouth held firmly, her eyes blazing. "It is my duty also to greet guests," the countess said to her. "Who is this man?"

Cal hadn't told her? "This is your nephew," Julia said. "He was wounded in the War. You must be kind and welcoming to him."

Julia saw how much Lady Worthington had changed. Once a warm, welcoming smile would have curved her lips. Now she looked tight-lipped, grim. Frightened.

From around the car came the wheeled chair. Cal pushed it smoothly from behind, even over the gravel. A young man—he must be about twenty-five—sat in the chair. He waved cheerfully. Julia had steeled herself to see no legs, or trousers pinned at the knees. But his trousers were filled out and he wore shoes. He must have artificial legs.

"You must be my aunt," said the young man. He held out his hand. His eyes were the same clear, vivid blue as Cal's but a shock of curly black hair framed his handsome face. "Good to meet you. I'm David Carstairs, your younger nephew from the States. I'd get up but you'd be waiting a long time, I'm afraid." He grinned.

His greeting was so warm, so different from Cal's, Julia was stunned. The countess came forward. "I am the Countess of Worthington. Indeed, my husband was brother to your father, Mr. Carstairs."

"Please call me David…Aunt Sophia." He said it with a wistful expression.

Julia's heart tugged.

"You would address me as—"

Julia gave a soft cough, interrupting. The countess was trying to sound austere and Julia had to stop that. And she noticed how the countess's fingers plucked nervously at the beads draped around her neck.

Show kindness, Julia mouthed. *Please do.*

Did the countess read her lips? She didn't know, but the woman's tone softened. "Do call me Aunt Worthington. That is how we do things in this country."

"Aunt Worthington. I think Aunt Sophia sounds prettier but I want to do things right." David Carstairs's winning smile revealed dimples.

Rain spattered down. "I'd better get you inside," Cal said brusquely.

Julia watched Cal negotiate the chair around the house to one of the terrace doors where there was no step, and wheel his brother inside. She followed them in, but the countess went in through the front door.

David whistled as they entered the drawing room. "Whoa. What a beautiful place, Cal," David said. "So what's tea really like? Do they have cakes?"

"All they do here is eat, and have too much food," Cal said. "It's indulgent and disgusting."

"I'd like to have a meal of cakes," David said.

"It should take more than a tray of cakes to win you over, David," Cal muttered darkly.

His brother twisted to look at him. "We haven't got any other family left, Cal."

"David, I'm not here because they wanted to make peace and invited me. I'm here because I inherited the place and they're forced, by their precious English rules, to accept me."

"Yeah, but that doesn't mean things can't work out for

the best," David said. "So have you gone riding? Did you fall off?"

They were very different, the two brothers. And David was on her side, thank heaven.

"I did go riding," Cal said. "Lady Julia taught me."

Julia lifted her head.

"I should have introduced you," Cal said. "David, this is Lady Julia, who lives at Brideswell, which is a neighboring estate."

She smiled brightly. "I am delighted to meet you, Mr. Carstairs."

"Cal me David. Could you stop a minute, Cal, so I can show some manners and shake her hand?"

Looking embarrassed, Cal did. She shook David Carstairs's warm, strong hand. "You taught my brother to ride." He looked down. "I'd like to learn, but I guess that's not possible."

"Perhaps it would be possible for you to sit on a horse and be led?"

"No. Too dangerous," Cal said shortly.

His brother rolled his blue eyes. "I think I've seen worse danger than falling off a horse. I'm game to try."

Julia felt Cal's glare. She thought Cal was wrong—overprotective. But fighting with him now was not sensible. She could arrange for David to ride. That might win him over to convincing Cal to keep Worthington intact. "I am sure we can think of something, together."

David gave her a smile that warmed her heart. "I'm glad to be here," he said. Then to his brother: "Cal, I've been thinking. I want to write a letter to Alice. Maybe we could pay for her to travel here. I'd like to see her. Nothing more, just see her. I know it's hopeless now to dream of more, but it would make my life complete just to see her smile again."

Julia was almost in tears. Alice must have been his sweetheart.

But Cal said abruptly, "No." Then he added, as if he knew he sounded unreasonable, "She's probably married by now. Let it go. It's only going to break your heart."

"Cal, I know there were a hundred soldiers in love with her, and each one had more to offer her than I do. But I'd just like to see her. Maybe she would come, if we invited her to something. Don't the English give fancy parties and balls? Just like they did at Mam's house, when she was a maid?"

Cal's face contorted with pain and Julia's heart contracted with it, too. He was behind his brother, who couldn't see his expression.

She said brightly, "I think it sounds like a very lovely idea."

Cal turned on her. "No, it's not." He whispered it, but so angrily, she was stunned. "I'm not having a ball here, David," he said more loudly.

"Of course you could not hold a ball," Lady Worthington declared as she approached, her heels clicking on the floor. "*You* would hardly know what to do."

It was as if she'd waved a red flag. "I know how to throw a party," Cal said sharply. "Forget what I said. If you want a ball, David, you'll get one."

13

David's Story

Cal carried David up the stairs to show him the bedroom he'd had prepared. He felt guilty and awkward as he put David back into his chair. Guilty because he hadn't been able to protect his younger brother. Awkward because he knew David hated to feel like a burden.

The countess had made him mad and he'd reacted. But having a ball now, when he was trying to find out whether three young women had been killed and whether Anthony Carstairs was responsible? Julia must believe he was a callous monster.

Maybe that was for the best. If Anthony was a killer, had been shielded from punishment, Julia would see Cal when he was full of rage.

"You're lost in thought."

David's voice jerked Cal back. "Do you like the room?" he asked fast. "I can have another fixed up for you, if you'd prefer. I thought you'd like the Oriental look in the place."

One wall was papered in scarlet, decorated with gold. The furnishings all looked like they had come from Japan or

China. A rice-paper screen stood in the corner. This had been John Carstairs's room when John had been just the younger son to the earl. Before he'd become the earl and taken over the earl's bedroom.

Was John maybe the killer? He hadn't been popular with girls, Cal had been told.

"I like it," David said. He added wistfully, "Before the War, I always thought about traveling the world."

Cal's throat tightened. He'd tried to give his younger brother all the opportunity he never had. It was why he'd stayed in a gang. To make money to send David to school. He'd intended to send his younger brother to university. Then America had joined the War—

"I finally made it to England," David said. "I never did during the War."

David should be angry because fate had stolen his chance to travel the world. But his brother looked happy.

Cal stood uneasily beside David's chair. "Where do you want to go—to the window? If you want to rest before dinner, would you like me to put you on the bed?"

It was like he was asking his brother where he wanted to be stored. He'd fired nurses in the States after they just wheeled his brother to a corner and left him there.

"I can wheel myself you know," David said. And he did, taking himself to the window.

Cal went to the table that held a decanter of the best damn brandy they had in this house. He poured two drinks and walked back, giving one to David.

If he'd been in David's position—missing both his legs— he would not be able to be alone with a decanter full of brandy. He likely would have drunk himself to death in despair and anger. Not David.

David sipped it. "Nice. Gosh, it's a beautiful view. Mam would have loved the gardens."

"Yeah, and she was never allowed to see them," Cal said darkly.

"Things can change," David said. "I know about how they can change in a heartbeat. I believe things can change for the better, too."

How did David stay so filled with hope? How did he look on the bright side?

Cal was the one filled with anger. Anger that ran in his blood, oozed through his pores. "There's something you need to know, David…"

His brother looked at him, trusting him. He should tell David about his plans to get rid of the place—but he couldn't do it yet.

"What is it?" David asked. "You look so serious."

"David, I don't want you to talk about my past…in New York."

"Your past?"

"The Five Points Gang. What I did. I don't want them to know. They already think I'm low-class scum."

"You aren't, Cal."

He didn't answer, so David had another sip of his drink. "Cal, I really want to find Alice—"

"No, David. I'm not going to let you do that."

"I'm a grown man. If I had two legs I could do what the hell I want."

For the first time since he got here, David lost his smile. Cal knew he was breaking his brother's heart, but he had to protect him. David was all he had left.

The next morning, Julia went to Worthington Park to talk to David Carstairs. Wiggins answered the door. Goodness, the butler looked as if he'd aged a decade in days. Pale, with dark circles under his eyes, he even appeared thinner than ever. "Is everything all right, Wiggins? You don't look well."

"I am quite all right, my lady," he answered. "If you are seeking his lordship, he has gone down to the kitchens I believe. His lordship tends to be eccentric in his behavior."

"They are his kitchens," Julia said. "And his lordship intends to hold a ball. I expect he wishes to speak to his cook directly about it."

"That should go through myself or Mrs. Rumpole."

"The earl does things in his own way." She realized she had said that with pride—at heart, Cal's independent ideas impressed her. She couldn't deny it.

"Indeed." But Wiggins looked more nervous than affronted.

"I am actually looking for his brother, Mr. David Carstairs."

"The earl's brother had indicated he wished to see the library."

"Thank you, Wiggins. But you do look ill. You should get more rest."

Was the butler really making himself physically ill over having Cal as the earl? What did he fear? Losing his job... or something more?

But as she left the foyer and walked into the wide receiving hall, Diana darted out of a doorway, grasped her hand and towed her into the music room. "Cal is going to help me," she breathed. "He's going to send me to Switzerland to have the baby, then I shall give it up over there and come home. Come home and pretend nothing ever happened."

"Yes. He and I talked about that." But Diana looked despairing and Julia whispered, "Diana, that will *save* you."

"Save my reputation. It won't save me. This will be done

so I can make a discreet marriage—a lonely and cold marriage, because I can't stop my obsession with my baby's father. I know what you'll say—that he used me. But he was so passionate with me. I want that again."

"Diana—"

"He told me that I was the most beautiful woman in the world to him. I don't care if it was lies. Mother always made me believe I wasn't good enough. Not as good as you—she always talked about how accomplished you are, Julia. It's rather a miracle I didn't scratch your eyes out. But when I was with *him*, I felt beautiful and exciting."

"Oh, my dear." Julia embraced her.

Diana nodded. "I was stupid. But I still *want* to love him."

There was so much pain in Diana's face, it scared Julia. "You must go away as Cal says. You do have to think of your future—"

Diana gave a sharp laugh. "An empty, loveless future. And Mother snaps at me all the time. Sometimes I fear she knows about the baby. She's upset and nervy and she finds fault with everything. Cal has told her she can stay here or go and live in the dower house. He has been…surprisingly nice. I guess we have you to thank for that, Julia."

"I think Cal is good by his nature, despite what he says."

"Mother still acts as if she's terrified of him. She keeps saying he is going to ruin us. I don't know what she means, but she says he is working to destroy us."

Julia blinked. She thought of Cal's investigation. Could the countess know about it? Was that what she feared? Cal learning the truth? But what *did* the countess know?

Heavens, could Cal's belief that the servants were covering up be true?

"Cal has been nice to me, but—but I don't want to give up my child." Diana gave a wobbly smile. "I know it's foolish, but I want to keep the baby. Cal has told me he would settle money on me. I would be ruined, but I could live with my child. I would be independent. Mother would disown me, of course. Society would shun me. But I am beginning to think I don't care. I was part of the Bright Young Things and I lived to be popular. I now understand there are more important things in the world." She sighed. "I always thought we would marry titled men and have children and live on grand estates."

"But we can still be happy," Julia said, "even if we don't."

"Yes. I suppose we can."

A sharp, sudden squeak came from the doorway. Julia looked up.

David Carstairs was there, in his chair, a blush coloring his cheeks. "I'm sorry. I was trying to find my way around and I came this way by mistake."

Using his hands to propel the wheels on his chair, he backed out of the room.

Diana was mortified that David had overheard. Julia calmed her—she sensed David would keep a secret as well as Cal. She found David in the library in his chair by the window. The library overlooked the rose gardens, and the woods, which made a dark green counterpoint to the sculpted hedges and the masses of pink, red and yellow roses.

Julia caught her breath. In the rose garden, Anthony had kissed her before he left for France. It felt like a lifetime ago. And was it a good memory now or not?

She pushed those thoughts away. Pasted on a cheery smile. "Good afternoon, David."

He turned in the chair, gave a boyish grin. "Hello, Lady Julia."

"And you must call me Julia." She was suddenly nervous

about begging for his help, launching into such personal matters.

Then he said, "I guess you knew the family really well. Cal says you live at Brideswell Abbey, a big estate next door. What was it like for you, growing up here? I heard you had balls and went on hunts, and got presented at court."

She told him a little about that. He was an enthusiastic listener and appeared fascinated by everything. He wanted to know about the people who lived on the estate. Julia found she was telling him about Ellen—at first trying to avoid revealing Ellen's profession. But he was so concerned and so kind, she spilled out the whole story.

When she was done, he said, "I'm sorry to hear about it. But I'm sure she can be saved. She sounds like a good woman. Cal will help her. I know he will."

"I know he will, too, but she won't listen. She refuses to get any help. I believe—and Cal thinks so, too—that Ellen suffers from shell shock."

She could have bit her tongue—why remind him of the War?

"I'm not surprised it happened to the lass. I'd say what she needs is hope for a future. That's what is the hardest on those that came back. There wasn't hope. I felt sorry for them."

"You did?"

"I had hope."

She stared, realizing David Carstairs was like Cal—a remarkable, unexpected man.

"Cal had made money, you see. After the War, America was poised to succeed and Cal had real smarts when it came to investing money. He got out of the g—" David broke off. He coughed. "I mean, he had enough money to get a house for me and to hire people to look after me. He went to Paris to paint. He said he needed to forget things."

"Do you mean the War?" she asked gently.

"That didn't hit Cal as hard. He's tough. Keeps things inside. That's because it was tough for Cal when we were growing up."

"You were quite poor," she said.

"We were. Our father was a good man and he had an education. But you know that. When Cal and I were small, Da had a good job as overseer at the docks, but one night he was robbed on the way home. Beaten real bad, and it changed him. He couldn't think so well anymore. He got headaches. Lost his job because he couldn't do the work—there was a fire and he evacuated the warehouse. He saved everyone, but the goods inside were burned and destroyed. Father lost his job because the factory owner said he should have tried to put the fire out and save the building."

"That's terrible. Of course he could not have done that!" she gasped.

"I know. But that's the way it was. After he lost that job, Da couldn't get any other work. Mam went to work sewing clothes. Da ended up driving a rag-and-bone cart to earn some money. But he wouldn't pay protection to the local gangs. He was working to shut them down—to get poor people out of their control."

She remembered Cal telling her about the rag-and-bone cart, making it a challenge. Cal had a lot of pride. "Was he able to succeed?"

"He was murdered while he was on his rounds, collecting rags."

Murdered? "Oh—oh my goodness." It was all she could say, struck with horror.

"Two men grabbed him, pulled him down and kicked him to death. I was eight years old then. Cal was eleven. He'd gone out to find Da. He saw the attack."

Julia almost sobbed at the slash of pain that went through her heart. Cal saw his father die after a violent attack. A horrible, horrible thing. Then, three years later, he saw the same thing happen to his mother. "Were—were the men caught?"

David shook his head. "The police never found out who killed our father. Cal was tough. He looked after Mam and me. Said he was the man of the family. I never even saw Cal cry about it. I tried to be as tough as him, but losing Da broke my heart."

"I don't believe Cal was so tough at eleven years of age that he did not cry over his father."

"He's strong. He handled the things we saw in the War better than any man I knew."

Julia twisted her fingers in her lap. She knew Cal had been devastated by what had happened to his mother. Surely he must have felt the same about his father. He'd hid that from David. But he'd let her see it. It came out in his pain, his bitterness. She had been right—Cal needed to heal. How did she help him do that? She could make him care about Worthington, but how did she take away the pain of his past?

She felt a tear drop to her cheek.

"I'm sorry I've upset you," David said. He pulled at his pocket until he got a handkerchief out. He handed it to her. It was silk, of the highest quality.

"I'm glad Cal was able to get out of poverty at least," she said softly.

"He bought stocks in companies. They made money. He taught me to buy, to sell when you made some money and then invest it again. He got good at knowing how a company was run, and when to figure it might get in trouble."

Investing took money, though. "But where did he get the money that he started with?"

"He—uh, he started working. After Da was killed."

"But didn't he need to support you and your mother? Surely he wouldn't have had much money left over."

"I don't know how he did it, Lady Julia. Cal's just a smart man."

David looked embarrassed, and she knew she'd over-stepped her bounds. "I'm sorry. That wasn't tactful at all." She gazed out the window, imagining how Cal felt the first time he saw it. All this wealth when he had lost both his parents…and lost them to the brutality of poverty. No wonder he had seethed with anger.

In retrospect, she realized he had been remarkably re-strained.

"Has Cal told you about his plans for Worthington Park, David?" she asked.

"Plans? No. I hope he wants to stay. Having a home—a real home—will be good for him. He had a lot of pain in his past. And he could do a lot of good as an earl."

"You understand the situation completely," she said. "But do you think—do you think we can change his mind?" But could he ever accept this place? Could he ever heal, with Worthington reminding him constantly of his pain? Was she heartless to demand that of him?

No—she believed he could be happy here. If he healed.

"Change his mind?" David repeated. "What d'you mean?"

"Cal wants to sell Worthington Park, and turn out the countess and her daughters. He says now he'll look after them, but he wants to take their ancestral home away. He wants to put the farmers out of the farms, the tenants from their homes, carve it up and sell it."

David went pale. "I didn't know. I've got to find Cal and talk to him."

"I want to stop him. But he said he could never live with himself if he lived here as earl—"

"That doesn't matter. I've got to make him see that doesn't matter. Would you get him for me, Lady Julia?"

But when she went to the doorway, she saw Cal had found them. He came into the library. He wore his dirty sweater with the sleeves rolled up. Paint spattered his arms and hands. "I've got the food arranged for this swanky ball you want."

"Cal," David said, "I need to talk to you."

"You have to have your fancy tea first. Hannah's been working all day to make cakes, and they're gorgeous. Éclairs and a Victoria sponge—it's a cake but that's what she calls it. She made enough dainty little sandwiches to feed an army." Cal looked up at her. "Would you want to stay for tea, Julia?"

"David wants to talk to you about something important. I should go—" A lady would never say what she was about to. She would use subtlety. But Julia couldn't be bothered with ladylike skill. "David told me what happened to your father. I am so sorry."

For a moment, Cal was expressionless. Then he said, "David, I think your cousins Cassia and Thalia are going to have tea. Would you mind if I took you to the drawing room, then escorted Julia to her car? I need to talk to her."

David agreed. After taking him to the drawing room, she and Cal walked toward the garage.

They'd only gone a few steps when Cal said shortly, "So now you know about my father and my mother. Don't try to tell me I should turn the other cheek. I can't do it, Julia."

"I understand," she said softly. "I don't think I could, either. I think—I think you have been a remarkable man to even allow me to try to convince you. You saw both of your parents' tragic deaths and they were caused by—by the heartlessness of people who did not help you."

★ ★ ★

Cal heard the sympathy in her voice and he bristled.

David had promised he wouldn't tell her about what Cal had done with the Five Points Gang. He knew his brother would keep his vow. Without knowing about that, Julia wouldn't completely understand.

"Don't feel sorry for me, Julia. But I need to talk to you about something else. Something about David."

He wanted to talk about Alice with Julia. He knew he was in the right—but somehow he needed Julia, the woman who cared so much about people, to agree with him. Then he'd know he wasn't being a bastard.

She was waiting for him to speak, all attentive.

"It's about Alice Hayes, the English girl my brother fell in love with. I know you'll understand without me having to draw you a picture." He raked his hand through his hair. "I never thought bringing him to England would mean he'd want to see her."

She looked surprised and confused, but she was Julia. She just said, "Tell me what happened."

"Alice worked as a nurse at the field hospital in France," he said. "After my plane was shot down and, by some miracle, didn't burst into flames, I was loaded on a stretcher and taken there. When I opened my eyes I was looking at the prettiest face I'd ever seen. She had huge blue eyes, and she took good care of me. I fell in love with her, of course. But, as fate would have it, David was brought to the same hospital."

"And you didn't know he had gone to war. It must have been a terrible shock."

"I was walking through the ward when I saw Alice tending to a man. She called him Private Carstairs and my heart stopped right at that moment. The sheets were off him, and I saw the bloody bandages around the stumps of his legs. There he was, my baby brother, lying on the bed. Nurse Alice was helping him eat because his right arm was in a plaster cast. I broke down and cried like a child. Actually, I'd never cried like that before. I learned early on not to cry—"

"I know."

"You know?"

"Your brother told me that you did not even cry when your father was killed."

He shrugged, shaking that off. "I watched how Alice took care of him. She was so gentle with him, and worked to lift his spirits. Some men would've wished they'd died. David is the type of man who felt he'd been blessed to live, even with both his legs gone and his arm hurt. The air force was going to ship me back to the front. I wasn't injured badly enough to go home. But I managed to get a few more days with my brother. He was so doped up for the pain that he didn't recognize me until two days before I was supposed to go back. The day he remembered me is the day I proposed to Nurse Alice. I had no right to do it. I had no money and no prospects and—well, I had no right. But she said yes, and we were going to wait until the end of the War."

"But you didn't marry her and your brother…"

"God, I wanted her. I was still in love with her after the War. She's the kind of woman who makes a man into something worthwhile because he's got to be worthy of her. But I couldn't marry her. David had fallen in love with her while she was taking care of him, too. Loving Alice was what kept him going, what kept him alive. I couldn't take that from him. He lost his legs and he lost his future. I couldn't take his sweetheart from him, too. So I wrote to her and broke off the engagement."

"But if you loved her—"

"It would have been too selfish to break my brother's heart."

"I am sure your brother would want you to be happy."

"No. It would have been impossible. I've come to terms with that." Funny—he hadn't thought of Alice since Julia had started taking him around to the tenants. "But David is still in love with her. Except he can't have her."

"Why not?"

Cal stared in disbelief. "What woman would marry a man who has lost his legs? It would break his heart if she turned him down to his face. I'm scared that he might do something bad if he was hurt like that."

"Do something bad?" Julia repeated.

"Take his life."

"But he isn't that kind of man, Cal. I've only just met him, and I know that. And he wishes to see her. Or is it that you can't face seeing her again?"

She wasn't agreeing with him. Hell, what was she thinking? She was wrong.

"I think he should see her. Perhaps—"

"No," he growled. "I know you believe you can help everyone, Julia. You can't fix this. David is strong and he looks on the bright side, but getting your heart broken is something else entirely."

"I know," she said.

She'd had her heart broken before, but he realized she was also having it broken by his suspicions about Anthony. Damn, he felt like a heel.

"I see no harm in inviting her," she said. "I could find her. They could talk and he would know—"

He stopped her by grasping her wrist. "Leave this alone, Lady Julia. You can rescue any family on the Worthington estate you want—but leave my family alone."

"Cal—"

Suddenly, he kissed her. Not a hard kiss, but a soft one, one that made his heart hurt as he did it.

She pulled back abruptly and he felt worse. She didn't want his kisses. "Promise me you won't do this, Julia. Promise me," he said.

Cadmium red. Vermilion. Cobalt Blue. Sexual frustration made Cal paint harder and faster and wilder than he ever had in his life.

He painted until dawn blushed the sky through the high windows of the attic. He'd done this for three nights in a row, barely sleeping more than two hours. Tonight—or rather, in the early morning—the canvas swum before his eyes.

Yawning, he took his brushes to the table where he kept a basin of water, jars of turps—dirty and clean. He washed out the brush in one of the dirty jars, rinsed it in the clean. Blinking against the fumes, he carefully shaped the brush, wiped the excess solvent on a clean rag. He left the palette to dry. He didn't clean it, just wiped it and let the paint residue harden.

After that, he slugged down the rest of the brandy he'd poured earlier. Then stumbled downstairs to his room on the second floor. Christ, he was tired.

He'd argued with David after dinner. David had told him he loved the house; that he should keep Worthington Park. That it was tradition. *Hell*. Cal had said he wanted to go back to Paris. Give this life a chance, David had said.

He couldn't do that. Talking to Julia the other day about Alice had brought all his memories back.

Cal collapsed on his bed, fully dressed.

He was happy in Paris. It was the only place in the world he'd been happy…

Later that day, he was awoken by his curtains rattling open. Wiggins stood there—Wiggins was acting as his valet, whether Cal liked it or not, because he'd let St. Germaine go.

"My lord, you need a proper valet. Those trousers are creased beyond repair."

"I doubt that," Cal muttered.

"And the state of your shirt. Either you were stabbed with a letter opener while you slept or that is red paint on your shoulder."

"It's paint. I wanted to work on the portrait and I forgot to change my shirt."

"I fear it will never come out."

"Christ, Wiggins, that isn't something to be afraid of. I'll use it when I paint from now on. Don't you English people have more important things to worry about than clothing?"

"While you do not have a valet, it is my job to worry about your clothing, my lord."

Cal's head pounded. "Would you mind bringing me a cup of coffee? My throat feels like it's full of cotton."

"I shall have a footman do that." Wiggins sniffed and left.

Cal swung out of bed. He must have drunk more brandy that he remembered. He wanted to put on his own damn clothes, without someone fussing over him. He pulled open the drawers of his underclothes. Stuff made in Paris—made of silk and fine fabrics.

Something was sitting on top of one of the drawers. A lock of blue-black hair, tied with a pink ribbon.

"I found that in one of my drawers. There was an old Bible in there, and that was pressed between two pages."

Surprised by the voice behind him, Cal jerked around. His brother, seated in his wheeled chair, was at the doorway. "I put it in your room. I thought maybe Lady Julia gave it to you." David grinned.

"It's not Julia's. At least—she didn't give it to me." Cal fingered the hair. The Oriental bedroom had been John Carstairs's bedroom. Why had this been in a drawer, hidden in the Bible?

Then he knew. Sarah Brand, Eileen Kilkenny and the maid, Gladys Burrows, had hair as blue-black as Julia's.

Cal got dressed in his room fast, told David he would be back quick, drove out to the retired chauffeur's cottage. Found out that John Carstairs had gotten lessons from Anthony on how to drive before Anthony had gone away to War. John had been fifteen at the time—too young to enlist. But he'd been tall for his age, as tall as his brother, Anthony. Also awkward, spotty, pudgy and overlooked by girls who'd liked his brother better. For the rest of the day, and the next day, the day of the ball, Cal drove around the estate. After seeing the shovel in the trunk of that car, he knew, in his gut, the women were dead. But he needed to find the truth. Find the bodies. It would hurt their families, but it was better than clinging to false hope for a lifetime.

But Worthington Park had thirty thousand acres of land. How would he find where the bodies were buried? There had to be places on all this land that were pretty isolated.

John and Anthony could be innocent. He had to consider that. Someone else from the estate could have taken the car out secretly.

Either way, both Anthony and John were dead and beyond the grip of the law. So, if he found out one of them had been a killer, what was he going to do?

Smoking a cigarette, Cal looked out over the valley and Lower Dale Farm. Sheep rambled and bleated. A cow mooed from the depths of the stone barn.

He would know that the Countess of Worthington had had a killer for a son.

He thought of that photograph and how sick the butler now looked. How nervy the countess was. He ground his cigarette under his boot heel and got back into the car. He drove back to Worthington and went down to the kitchens to see how Hannah was coping with preparations for a ball and elaborate dinner.

Cal was pleased to find she had everything under control. The girl glowed with excitement—this was her first major event and she was attacking it with all the fervor and drive of a titan of American industry. That was one good thing— he'd made a good decision to promote her.

The housekeeper, Mrs. Rumpole, caught him as he was heading for his study.

She looked like she'd sucked on a toad. "My lord, the countess always attends to the details of balls and dinners. She has always overseen the invitations, the menu, the hiring of musicians, the preparation of the house. But this time, you have done all things traditionally carried out by the countess."

"Yeah, I have."

"It is most unorthodox. Do you intend to do this in the future?"

"I don't know. Maybe I won't be around in the future. Maybe I will."

She looked at him as if he were crazy.

"Delegation and position are the hallmarks of a successful household," she declared. "It is my job to ensure you are not troubled with staff problems, with the myriad decisions involved in running a household."

Position. Hierarchy. Just like a big business. Just as Julia had said. Julia was right—making them afraid for their positions wasn't proving anything, except what a bastard he could be.

"In the future, I'd like this place to run smart," he said.

"I'll talk to you about what the jobs are, how they're done. Maybe I need to learn."

Mrs. Rumpole's brows shot up in surprise. "Very good, my lord." She turned and left.

He kept walking and went into his study. There, through the window, he saw the strangest sight.

David was outside. Diana, her skirts blowing around her legs in the breeze, had wheeled out his chair and she was pointing at things. He'd thought Diana selfish, vain, and he knew she was having an affair with a married man. To him Diana had represented the thing he hated about the aristocracy—they had no damn morals but they were happy to throw stones through their glass windows. They were happy to condemn his mother, who had done desperate things to keep her sons from starving, when they did immoral things just for fun.

But once he knew she was pregnant, he couldn't stand making her feel scared.

David, he saw, was smiling as if he was being given a personal tour of heaven by an angel.

14

The Worthington Ball

Fast-paced jazz music poured out of Worthington Park. Lights glittered in the gardens as if they were filled with fireflies. Silver trays covered in glasses of champagne were whisked by footmen. Julia had never seen this many people for any ball at Worthington before. There were hundreds and hundreds. An orchestra played outside and people laughed and danced wildly on the lawns.

The rest of her family walked up the steps, Nigel escorting their grandmother. Julia hung back, gaping at the scene around her. Zoe had let the others go on ahead, too.

Zoe observed, "It's like a wild American party thrown by a crazy millionaire," Zoe observed.

But would Cal have gone to those? Those parties were for the rich. "Goodness, it's rather stunning, isn't it?" Julia asked. This would be the first time she had seen Cal for days. She'd had to stay away—she'd been carrying out a search. One she didn't want Cal to know about. She hadn't seen him since he'd told her to leave his family alone, then kissed her. She—she was trembling at the thought of seeing him again.

Filled with anticipation, joy, fear. She looked to Zoe. "Is this really what you do in America?"

Zoe laughed. "Julia, I must take you on a tour of America."

Her heart pattered, then she shook her head. "I can't. I have Ellen to protect and people who depend upon my help. My days are busy. I'd have no time to go to America. I have too much to do. So I'll have to enjoy it by proxy tonight."

"We can have your widows looked after while you're gone," Zoe said. "I remember what you said on the train. You want to travel. I'll take you to America. When this little one is born, I want Nicholas to see America, and if I go to America, it means my mother won't stay for months at Brideswell."

"I like your mother."

"But that's because you are just one step away from being saintly, Julia."

"I would like to go to America sometime," Julia said. But strangely, the thought of going rather filled her with panic. This is the life she knew. This was her place in the world. But going away would only be for a visit. Why suddenly feel afraid to even spread her wings a little?

"Julia, I'm still surprised you tried so hard to convince Alice Hayes to come," Zoe said softly. They stood together on the steps, the rest of the family waiting at the door for them.

Alice was who she had searched for. "I thought she would come, but she changed her mind at the last minute. I must thank Nigel again for having the family solicitors locate her so quickly. Cal's brother very much wants to see her again."

"But if Cal is in love with her—"

"I am sure the two men would be able to work this out

between them. It's ridiculous that they both have to give up on love."

"No." Zoe looked at her curiously. "I mean most women don't search for their competition."

"Cal loves Alice Hayes. I could see it in his eyes as he looked at me. That longing. I'm sure of it. And if he marries and is happy, he'll be far more willing to settle at Worthington."

She spoke calmly, but felt a sudden twist of pain inside. Cal loved someone else... Now she understood why he'd said he wouldn't marry.

"Julia, you'd do that to save the estate?" Zoe frowned. "Is your sense of duty more important than love?"

"Cal and I are not in love with each other," she said firmly. "I'm not about to fall in love with anyone in a situation that would be obviously hopeless."

"I know you think a lady must have everything under control, Julia. Love doesn't work that way."

For one foolish moment, she thought of that little kiss, that sweet but snappy touch of Cal's lips to hers. She'd pulled back because of Alice. That was why he'd told her honestly he couldn't marry. He loved Alice. She'd found Alice, but at the last moment Alice had changed her mind, had decided not to come. Julia simply wouldn't breathe a word about it to David so he wouldn't be hurt.

She followed Zoe into the house and gasped in shock. It was impossible to move. People danced everywhere: girls with bobbed hair and short dresses; men in the fashionable baggy trousers and slouching-style jackets.

Julia followed Zoe's example, thrusting aside ladylike behavior to shove through the crowd.

She managed to reach the ballroom just after Zoe. The terrace doors stood open, curtains fluttering in the summer breeze. Another band played jazz in here, with a stylish woman singing with a throaty voice. Her deep brown complexion looked stunning against a gold beaded dress.

Champagne flutes were snatched quickly from the salvers. Crowds filled the stairs, attempting to dance on the steps. A woman tumbled down, but in the crowd, she landed on a dozen other people and didn't hurt herself.

Julia had never seen Worthington like this. A vase fell with a crash. A man shouted, "Watch this," and then slid down the banister. He knocked over a dozen people on his way down.

Julia felt overwhelmed. It was as if an amusement park had been stuffed inside the house.

Where was Cal? With his brother? But she couldn't find either of them as she fought through the crowd. One man grabbed her arm and pulled her into a wild version of a foxtrot. Another grabbed her after him.

"I don't want to dance," she cried, getting free.

The dining room was filled with a buffet—poor Hannah must have worked her fingers to the bone to produce so much food. Even though Cal had hired more kitchen maids, it was still the young cook's duty to oversee everything.

Julia didn't approve of this. It was too wild, too flamboyant, too wrong.

Searching for Cal, she ran into the Duke of Bradstock. "Dance with me?" James shouted.

She shook her head. "No, thank you, James. I must find Cal."

"He's probably having an orgy in a bedroom," James said sourly.

Maybe James was right. But she remembered that look of longing. For all Cal's reputation, she believed he was a man who loved deeply.

It was hard to escape the crowd. She encountered a man

in a drawing room, looking at the items on the mantel-piece. So much like the Klipspringer character in *The Great Gatsby*—Zoe had had a copy sent from New York as soon as it was published—Julia felt she had walked into a fictional world. She expected him to observe that the books on the shelves were real.

"Have you seen the host? The Earl of Worthington?"

"The Earl of Worthington?" He looked blankly at her. "He's here?"

Julia plunged onward. She heard a soft musical sound at the end of the hallway. Another band? This was the study. She knocked on the door and opened it.

Cal sat there, his feet propped on the desk. A gramophone played a soft tune, sounding tinny compared to the vibrant music roaring from the ballroom.

"Do you know it's a madhouse out there? I'm afraid they will tear the house apart—" She broke off. "Was that your plan? To hurt the countess by forcing her to watch a madding crowd destroy things?"

He shrugged. "This is the kind of party I like—a thousand strangers all having a good time."

"That's not an answer."

He swung his legs down, got out of his chair. To Julia's surprise, he came right up to her, then he put her hand on his shoulder, her other at his waist. He waltzed with her, in a tight circle in the middle of his study.

"Stop this. Some of the paintings and porcelain are *price-less*. Something should be done."

He kept twirling her. "I've told the staff to stop the booze at ten o'clock. That will get rid of most of the crowd. And it's just stuff. There are things that matter a hell of a lot more." He stopped dancing. "I like waltzing with you. I like holding you close and moving slowly with you, like we're both suspended in time."

That was how she felt with him.

"No woman has ever gotten under my skin like you. You make me mad, you make me lust, you make me get angry at myself, and you make even the gloomiest day feel like it's radiant and beautiful."

Cal turned her, his feet moving them gracefully across the old Aubusson carpet.

When she looked up into his eyes, she saw so much yearning it took her breath away. But he'd told her he couldn't love her—and she knew why. He'd told her he loved Alice, the woman he couldn't have and he must still love Alice. Perhaps he was dedicated to revenge because he thought he couldn't have love.

"I know you lost your mother and father, and I understand your anger, but is it truly making you happy to turn everything into a battle?" she asked softly. Even the missing women were a fight between them—a fight between her belief in Anthony and Cal's hatred of the family.

He let her go. Backed away. "Don't pity me. I prefer your contempt."

"That's ridiculous. And I don't pity you. I want you to heal. You must make a new life and be happy."

"Some things don't heal, Julia. And what's the point of struggling and fighting to survive if you don't put the things right that hurt you badly?" He took a step away from her. "I should go to my party. Play the host. And remember—don't pity me. I'd rather have you hate me."

Then he was gone.

Julia's heart trembled, like a large rose bloom on a slender stalk. "It's not pity," she said softly, because he couldn't hear. "It's love."

It was true. Zoe had known—Zoe had seen it. But Julia was like Cal with David…she only wanted his happiness. She had to remember he'd told her he loved Alice Hayes.

She hurried out, with no idea where to go or what to do, wanting to escape the raucous party. She spied David sitting in his wheeled chair along the wall, near an open door. He grinned at her. "When I said I wanted a ball, I didn't expect this. It's like Grand Central Terminal in here."

"Yes, but unfortunately nobody leaves," she muttered.

"Pardon me?" David shouted.

"David Carstairs? Is that you, David?" A rich and clear voice struggled to be heard over the crowd. Julia looked up at the same moment David did, and she heard him say, "Oh Lord. It's Alice."

Julia straightened. "She came after all."

The crowd had one of those moments where it parted, revealing the woman who stood there. A young woman who seemed to glow because her hair was pure gold, and her dress was a soft shade of pink that spoke of summer gardens. She was older than her midtwenties, beautiful with an oval face, high cheekbones, a small nose and large eyes.

David gulped. "God, I didn't really think… What's she going to think…? What am I gonna do?"

Julia touched David's shoulder. "Don't worry. You are going to talk to her, that's what you are going to do."

Then Cal would, of course. Julia would probably love Cal forever—but he would be happy with Alice.

Cal looked out the window. Hanging lights gave the garden a surreal glow. He saw a rotating glint that caught his eye. It was David's wheeled chair, the wheel spokes reflecting the lights. Someone was pushing him. Someone with light blond hair.

Then he saw *her.*

He stalked out, confronting Julia who was walking back up the stone steps to the terrace. "That's Alice Hayes pushing David's chair."

"I know," Julia said softly. "I found her, wrote to her, and she came tonight to see David after all. I've offered to let her stay at Brideswell for a few days."

"You brought Alice here? I told you I didn't want that. You had no right."

"Your brother wished to see her, and in her letter answering mine, she expressed a strong desire to see him."

"Goddamn it," he snapped, "he's going to get hurt."

Julia flinched. But insisted, "She seems genuinely happy to see David."

"That doesn't mean she can find it in her heart to love a man who can't provide for her, who needs her protection rather than the other way around."

"But she came here, knowing that he did not have legs. That has to mean something, Cal. Perhaps you should give Alice more credit. Cal, you told me how much you love her. It's obvious why you are notorious for love affairs with models and such scandalous things. You believe you can't have the woman you love. But I think you would be happy if—"

"I don't want to be damn well happy. I want to protect my brother. Look at them," he snapped.

Alice and his brother were talking. David held Alice's hand, but she was shaking her head. He could read her sadness in the way her head was bowed, and he saw pain on his brother's face.

"I'm watching my brother get his heart broken. Why couldn't you have left it alone? Neither David nor I belong here. I'm not going to fight to belong in a world that doesn't want me. I'm not going to put my brother through it, either."

"But Alice—"

"I could never damn well have Alice. Not without telling her a bunch of lies. I want you to keep away, Julia. Keep away from David. Stay at Brideswell. I'll help the families on this estate from now on. Not you."

The pain on her face made him feel like crap. But she'd pushed too hard. She wanted too much. She was never going to make him happy—she was the thing making him crazy.

"I won't stop doing that, Cal. Not for anyone."

"There's someone who can stop you. I'm going to tell your brother that Ellen's pimp almost attacked you, and that I'm forbidding you from dealing with my estate to keep you safe. He won't let you out of his sight."

She recoiled, white as meringue frosting. "How could you do that? This is so important to me—it is the only thing that I have."

And he knew this was his chance to push her away completely. To take the thing that mattered most away from her. Then she'd leave him the hell alone. Leave him to his revenge, and stop tempting him with what he couldn't have.

15

Attack on Julia

For days after the party, Julia's heart was in turmoil. She had wanted to give David Carstairs his chance to see his beloved Alice again. She had hoped to save Worthington by giving Cal the chance to be happy. How much of his anger was driven by having to walk away from the woman he loved for his brother's sake?

Finally, Cal had admitted to her he wouldn't "rat out" to her brother as he'd put it. But he was hurt, angry, protective as a bear. He'd cut off the liquor and shut down the party after that. David had coerced him to let Alice Hayes stay at Worthington. Would Cal surrender to love with Alice so close?

Ellen had been sent home from the hospital yesterday, having improved a great deal. She'd only just learned Cal had taken Ellen back to the cottage, and had taken Ben, too. Ellen's pimp was still at large and Ellen still refused to give his name. She had admitted the man had beaten her badly because she had refused to prostitute herself anymore.

What had happened to Ellen—and Cal's anger—made Julia

question herself. Was she making things better for people—
was she truly helping, or making things worse?

Now, carrying her umbrella—it had proved invaluable—
she knocked on the door of Ellen's cottage, rather startled
when a burly-looking man answered it. "Who are you?" she
asked. This was not the man who she had confronted in the
village about Ellen. This specimen stood even larger.

Off went his cap and he bowed. "Makepeace Jones, my
lady," he answered. "Hired by his lordship to keep watch
over Miss Lambert and her lad."

So Cal had thought of that. "I have food for Miss Lambert." She saw Ellen, and shared the special sticky buns between Ben and Makepeace. She did not launch into a plea for
Ellen to give the name of her attacker. Instead she ensured
Ellen was eating well, and she took a look at the bandages—
Dougal had shown her how. It had been awkward dealing
with Dougal. Julia could not forget how he had dismissed
the possibility Ellen had shell shock. His stubborn acceptance
of the prevailing *male* point of view had shocked her. And
even now, she could see Ellen tremble. She had seen Nigel
do that, even though he used to hide it well.

But when she left the cottage, at least she knew Ellen
would be safe, with Makepeace to watch over her.

Julia walked back to her car. She'd had to leave it down
the lane as there was an enormous muddy hole between her
motorcar and Ellen's gate. After the hot night of the ball, the
weather had been stormy. Many places had flooded, creeks
had spilled over their banks, and it made for a wet, mucky
trudge on the lane. At least the rain had stopped today.

Ahead of her sat her car, the cream-painted sides and
chrome spattered with mud. She had to turn it around. But
that put her at risk of getting stuck in the quagmire of mud
in front of her car.

"I'm going to have to reverse," she murmured aloud.

She did, twisting around and moving slowly to ensure she didn't drive off the track and get stuck. Then, as she put her foot on the accelerator, a large figure jumped out from a laurel bush behind her. Julia slammed down on the brake. In her shock, she jerked the wheel and the car shot sideways, off the track. She lurched to a stop and had to swallow hard for her heart was in her throat.

"Are you all right?" she cried, her hand on the door handle.

Suddenly the man was at the side of her car. Her door was ripped open. He grabbed her wrist and jerked her toward him—fast enough to pull her right off the seat—and she went down on her knees on the muddy track. Stones bit into her knees. She cried out in pain.

Julia saw mud-encrusted, battered brown boots, then looked upward. His face—it was covered by a black mask from his hairline to his lips. "Who are you?" she demanded. "What are you doing?"

Was it Ellen's pimp? He towered over her as that man had done. He wore the same clothing as most laboring men of the village—checked cap, heavy brown coat, worn trousers.

Why was he wearing the mask?

So she couldn't bear witness against him? So no one else could?

Fear swamped her, running through her veins like ice water. She must fight. She thought of what Ellen had been through. She lashed out with her leg, trying to kick him.

The slap he gave her sent her head snapping to the side.

"Who are you?" she demanded again, trying to sound like the angry daughter of a duke and not a terrified woman, while her face throbbed with pain. "You would be a fool to hurt me. You will end up in prison."

Apparently he didn't fear her threat for he pulled her to her feet as if she had the weight of a pillow. He started down the lane away from her motor, dragging her with him. Without saying a word. She tried to dig in her heels, grabbed at branches. Desperately, she screamed, hoping sound would travel past the bushes to the cottage. He jerked her to him and slammed his gloved hand over her mouth.

She bit his hand and he pulled it away. "You let me go or you will suffer the consequences. My brother is a duke. Hurt me and he will see you—"

He put his hand back to silence her, cursing low under his breath. And he raised his other hand to hit her again.

She kicked at his legs and her shoe connected with his shin. He stumbled. In rage, his other hand shot forward and wrapped around her neck He was throttling her. All she could see was the triumph in his dark eyes in the eyeholes.

His fingers tightened and she tried in vain to pull them away from her throat.

Julia struggled. Her lungs oddly felt like exploding when nothing was going into them. Like the sound of a hundred mocking crows, his laughter filled her ear.

Wildly she swung her arm and tried to drive her finger into the eyehole on the right side. At the same moment she drove her knee up and hit as hard as she could into the front of his trousers.

She missed his eyes. He gave a grunt of pain, but it wasn't enough. It was like poking a bull with a sewing needle. She'd only provoked him.

He pulled out a knife. A horrible, wicked-looking dagger-type thing.

Was this what had happened to Sarah, Eileen, Gladys? It wasn't Anthony or John, but some brute who had surprised them and dragged them away? She had no weapon. She had nothing but her *social* position and that was hardly going to stop this man—

A large shape suddenly appeared behind the fiend and she cried out before she realized who it was. Her attacker jerked, started to turn, but before he could, Cal grabbed the knife out of the man's hand and pressed the blade to her assailant's neck.

"I would suggest you let Lady Julia go. Let her go gently and I won't be forced to draw this blade in a quick slice across your throat."

He said it in a ruthless tone that made even her blood run cold—and he was saving her.

Pressing the blade harder against the man's throat, Cal forced the man to release her. Then Cal gripped the man's muscular arm, twisted it, bent it behind the man's back. She was stunned at his strength and the way the simple maneuver immobilized the brute. Her attacker stood about the same height as Cal.

"What's your name?" Cal snapped. But he didn't say it quite like that—he spoke in a low, ruthless tone that made her shudder. And he threw in a very shocking, naughty word.

Then Cal's gaze met hers and he jerked. It was as if he'd forgotten she was there.

The man didn't answer.

Cal twisted the man's arm and the cry of pain made her wince. "Oh, don't—" she began.

"Julia, he was going to hurt you. Don't waste your good heart on this scum. We have to get him to the local jail," Cal said. "I'm going to get some rope to tie up his hands." To the man, he growled, "Get walking."

She followed. This all seemed so unreal. Cal shoved the brute along the lane back toward the cottage. Her neck was so tender. She touched it. Then the full miracle of her escape hit her. "You saved my life. If you hadn't come— But what are you doing here?"

"I was keeping an eye on you. I didn't like the idea of you going around alone after Ellen was attacked."

"You were protecting me. Even after you were so angry with me at the ball."

"I was mad, but I'd never forgive myself if anything happened to you."

Cal's prisoner made a grunting sound of disgust. Julia stumbled on the rough track in her heeled shoes. She regained her balance, but Cal turned to her. His attention was on her, not on her attacker. In that moment the man jerked around and he managed to pull the knife from Cal's grip. Snarling in rage, he slashed it at Cal.

"Look out!" she cried.

Off balance, Cal stumbled as he avoided the slicing arc. The man took off running. He left the lane and sprinted down a slope into a valley.

Cal ran after him, his tweed jacket open and flapping. He almost lost his balance on the ground. He threw himself forward and grabbed the man by the legs. They both went down, rolling over and over. They slapped into the stream, which was a bubbling rush of water after the rain. And the attacker had a knife.

Oh God. Julia couldn't breathe—her heart pounded in her throat. She had to run to the cottage and fetch Makepeace and a weapon of some kind.

But at that moment, Cal slammed his fist into the man's jaw, water spraying around him. She heard him shout. "That's for hurting Lady Julia."

He hit the man again and again. Violence had erupted in him. If the attacker still held the knife, he was given no chance to use it.

The man slammed his fist into the side of Cal's face. The knife must have been dropped when they fell. Huge, heavy, the man managed to shove Cal over and Cal landed with a splash. He kicked Cal with his heavy boots.

She shouted, "Help! Help us!" and she ran for the cottage. Alerted by her cries, tall, powerful Makepeace Jones was coming out of the cottage. "Have you got a weapon?" she cried. "A shotgun? A man is attacking Worthington!"

"I do!" Ellen cried. "I'll fetch it."

That took precious moments and Julia shouted for Ellen to stay with Ben. She dragged Jones up the lane. They reached the place where the man and Cal had run down, just as Cal was making his way back up, panting hard. His clothes and hair were soaked. Blood tinted the water that streamed down his face. "You're hurt," she gasped.

"Flesh wound," he said. "But the bastard got away. Damn—beg your pardon, Julia." Then he asked, "Who was he?"

"I don't know. With the mask, I have no idea."

"Are ye all right, milord?" Makepeace asked.

"Yes. I'm going to get you back to Brideswell, Julia, then do a sketch of the bas— The man," Cal said.

"But I didn't see him."

"It has to be the man who attacked Ellen and you've seen him before. He must have been waiting for you to come here, to get revenge. I'll take the sketch around the village. Someone has to know who he is. Maybe the sketch is what will make the difference and someone will finally be able to identify him. And you are not to come out alone again. Do you understand?"

Julia nodded. The insulation of shock was wearing off. She felt sick and cold. "I won't. I promise I won't."

"He's frightened you a hell of a lot."

She winced again at his harsh words. "He threatened to kill me."

"Hell, he tried to do it," Cal said. His voice was half growl, half thunder.

Ellen joined them, her face white.

"He didn't seem to care that such a thing was against the law," Julia said primly. "This might be the modern world where there are laws, rights and civilization, but there are still men who believe violence can get them what they want."

"That, sweetheart, is the brutal truth. And something I don't think you understood."

"I do now," she whispered.

"I'm sorry," Cal said. "I'm being too harsh."

"You're bleeding," she pointed out. "Are you all right?"

"No, I'm not all right, because for a damned moment there, I thought I was going to lose you. But I'm going to find him. I'm going to hunt him down."

"You absolutely cannot! It's too dangerous."

"Hunt down a goon like him? That isn't dangerous. I've done worse."

Ellen said suddenly, "No. I'll tell you who he is. I'll tell you, my lord. I don't want Lady Julia hurt again. I didn't mean to cause this. I'm so sorry."

Ellen hurried to Cal, whispered something, then Cal told Makepeace to take her back to the cottage, warning the man to keep the weapon on hand and to watch over Ellen and Ben.

With that, Cal carried Julia down the lane to his car. "What did Ellen tell you?"

"Precious little," he growled. "She only had his first name—Jack. Doesn't know his surname. She doesn't even know where he lives. Unless she's still lying—"

"I don't think she would now. Cal, what did you mean you've done worse? In war?"

Cal set her on her feet at his vehicle. "I'll get men from the local garage to get your car out, Julia." He didn't answer her question or say another word as he drove her to Brideswell. There, he carried her to the front door.

"Cal, I am fine. I am capable of walking."

His hand lingered at her waist as he set her on her feet. Then he took her inside and told Nigel and Zoe what had happened to her—even though she begged him not to.

"Not this time, Sheba," was all he said. And she knew—everything she loved to do would be over now.

Zoe put her arm around Julia's shoulders. Next thing Julia knew, she was in her dressing room and Sims had drawn a steaming bath for her.

The warm water was lovely—she hadn't realized her teeth were chattering until she sank into the steamy water in the deep tub. Plumbing was a marvelous thing. She was glad Zoe had insisted on it. But even the warmth didn't melt fear—she knew what was to come.

After she'd dried, put on fresh clothes, a knock sounded and Nigel called out, "May I talk to you, Julia?"

"Of course." She swallowed hard.

Her brother closed the door behind him. He was pale, his mouth tight with fear. He looked a dozen years older suddenly. "I'm so sorry," she whispered. "You look terrible, Nigel."

"I'm just thanking God you are all right." He bent and hugged her. And Nigel was not a demonstrative man. He was very much a cool, aloof Englishman. But he bent and kissed the top of her head.

Then it began, of course.

"Julia, I will not allow you to do this work anymore," he

stated. "It's too dangerous. It is putting you in the path of dangerous, ruthless people."

Panic flared. "I'm twenty-seven. You can't forbid me."

"You live in my house and you are dependent on me. So that does give me the ability—and I believe the right—to tell you what you can do."

Her heart sank. "Nigel, I need to help these women."

"No, Julia. This has become too dangerous. You are not to continue. *That* is the final word on the matter."

She tried to make him see how important this was. It was who she was! The thing of value she could do in the world. But Nigel was unmoved.

All the rest of the day, Mother fussed over her. And urged her to consider marriage as a much safer and happier thing to do. Grandmama arrived and laid down the law with Nigel. Julia could hear them in the drawing room. "She is your sister—how could you condone this behavior? Rough laborers. Women of the night. You are to protect her until she is married!"

Julia hurried into the room to protest. "Nigel is not my jailer."

"No, he is your guardian. And you must obey him."

"Grandmama, this is 1925!"

"And a woman is still vulnerable and at risk, Julia."

It was true—she knew that so very well now—but it made her so thoroughly angry.

She'd frightened them all. It made her feel guilty, but she couldn't simply be packed away in a closet until she decided to marry.

By the next morning, Julia couldn't cope with being treated like an invalid for another moment. When her sister-in-law came to her room, she cried, "Zoe, I'm going to go mad. Nigel insists that I continue to rest. It has been a whole day. I am quite recovered. And nothing really terrible happened to me. Cal got there in time."

"He did. But it was still a frightening experience," Zoe said. "And you know Nigel—perhaps you've recovered, but he hasn't."

In her vanity mirror, Julia glimpsed her reflection. She had covered the bruises on her neck with foundation powder, but she could see them faintly. The imprint of the man's fingers. But what was worse was she was realizing what Nigel said was true. She lived under his roof. She was dependent on him. In that circumstance, she was expected to obey him.

"Dr. Campbell has come to see you," Zoe said.

"Dougal? Heavens, I'm not wounded, I assure you. Just bruised."

Zoe waved her hand. "Nigel didn't send for him. He came himself."

Sunlight spilled through the drawing room windows onto Dougal's auburn hair as he paced, making it glint like copper. She assumed he'd come in a professional capacity. The moment he saw her, he blushed and he hurried to her. He grasped her hands. She'd never seen him so…passionate. "Julia, I heard you were badly hurt. Of all people, I do understand your desire to help people, especially the less fortunate. You know, as I do, how those people can end up ignored. But, Julia, you must not do this any longer."

She blinked. "Dougal?"

"This woman consorted with dangerous men and brought you into danger. You say she has resisted your every attempt to help her. You must leave this alone."

"How can you say that? You save lives—you know how important this is. I can't just give up, Dougal. This is not like you," she said desperately. "I don't understand. And you certainly can't tell me what to do."

"I haven't done this well. I haven't expressed it properly. I mean to say, that I will help her, Julia. I will study her condition, determine if she has shell shock and treat her."

"Thank you. What has changed your mind?"

To her surprise, Dougal dropped to one knee. "Julia, being here has made me realize I need you at my side."

He couldn't be…that was impossible. "But you are engaged—"

"It's not a formal engagement yet. I tried to throw myself into work, into research, but I can no longer focus, no longer think. All I can think of is you, Julia. I knew I couldn't have you, and I knew Margaret, as a doctor's daughter, would make me a good wife. I care very deeply for her. But being here, with you again… I was a damn fool to ever leave Brideswell. Julia, would you ever consider marrying me? I know I have no right to ask, but I knew, after I saw you in London, that I could not live without you."

"You would end your…not formal engagement?"

"How can I make Margaret happy when I am in love with you?"

In love with her. She had longed for this moment before— to find out Dougal loved her deeply and would surmount the obstacles for her, overcome the bridge of their class difference. But—

He was waiting for her answer, hope in his eyes. This man who fought to save lives every day had told her he needed her. "Julia, I know there is no other woman in the world for me but you."

She could be a doctor's wife, and have a family of her own. She would have purpose. She could do good things. But—

"Dougal, I can't. I admire you. I did love you very much. But I—I can't marry you now."

"Because of my engagement?"

"Because I fear I have fallen in love with someone else."

"Are you engaged?"

"No and I won't be, because he has no intention of marrying, and even if he did, I think he would marry someone else. I believed I wouldn't marry and I thought I had found my place—helping women like Ellen. Now, all the men in my life insist I can't do it. So I no longer have a purpose and I am supposed to…do nothing but wait for marriage. But I can't do that. Not anymore. And I can't make you happy if I'm not deeply in love with you. I want you to find happiness with your fiancée. If you believe you can't, you shouldn't marry her. Don't marry her to simply have a wife."

The pain on his face sliced to her heart. "Julia, are you certain?" he begged.

She could change her mind. She could embrace everything she'd always wanted… No, she could not. "I'm so sorry, Dougal. I hope I haven't hurt you."

"And I am sorry if I ever hurt you," he said gruffly. He bowed stiffly, then took his leave. From the doorway, she watched him walk away through Brideswell's salon, out through the front door, holding his hat in his hand.

She never dreamed Dougal would propose. Two years ago, she would have happily accepted. But that was before she'd met Cal.

She glanced up to find Bartlet, Brideswell's butler, standing in the doorway. "Mr. David Carstairs to see you, my lady. I have taken him to the south drawing room. The doors are open, the breeze is pleasant today and Mr. Carstairs should be able to maneuver in the room as it is more spacious."

"Thank you. That should be perfect."

She was tremendously worried about why David Carstairs had come—until she reached the drawing room and he smiled at her. He reached out. Warmed by the gesture, she went to him and clasped his hands.

"I had to come—forcing a lot of footmen to carry me downstairs and put me in my chair," he said, wearing that endearing, self-effacing smile. "I had to come and thank you. I heard Cal was angry with you at the ball. He was afraid I was going to be hurt when Alice told me she is in love with someone else. I'm actually happy. When you really love someone, you just want them to be happy."

Her heart stuttered. Was Cal the person Alice loved? "I was afraid I had meddled and hurt both you and Cal," she admitted.

"I know Cal told you not to do it. I'm really glad you didn't listen. It was good to see her again."

"But didn't it hurt?"

"Yeah, there was some pain. But that's how I know I'm alive—because I can still feel some pain in my heart. Cal was trying to spare me pain. But he's wrong. I can take it." He squeezed her hand gently. "I know you understand. You survived losing your fiancé."

"I managed to get through it. *Survived* is probably too generous a word."

"I told Cal he has to apologize to you, Julia. For his outburst. When he returns, he will come and tell you."

"Returns? Where is he?"

"He's found the man who beat up Miss Lambert. I guess that's the same man who attacked you."

16

Fight at the Sawmill

"Who is this man?" Julia gasped.

"A gypsy woman named Genevra came to the house," David explained. "Wiggins tried to tell her to run off, but Cal saw her and insisted she come in. She read my palm, told me I had a long life line, and that I would find great love. Then she talked to Cal and he took off in his automobile. I thought he should go to the police, but he said he wanted to take care of things himself."

David looked satisfied about that, not in the least worried. And she was pleased Genevra had read such a wonderful future for David, but her heart slammed against her chest. What had Cal been thinking? What did he plan to do? "Where did he go?"

At her frantic tone, David's blue eyes stared at her in shock. "Genevra told him that the man he was looking for works for the Worthington sawmill. She told him to beware, but Cal thought that was funny. I didn't know the estate owned a sawmill."

"The estate owns everything upon it," she said distractedly. Cal was going to confront that brute of a man. She stood abruptly. "I must go to the police station in the village, to tell them where Cal has gone. They can arrest him."

David touched her arm. "Cal doesn't want the police involved."

"Cal will have to have the police involved." She couldn't imagine why he would not. That simply made no sense. "I must go." Her heartbeat, hard and frantic, filled her head. "It's impolite, but I must leave you here. I'll tell Zoe—the duchess—she'll look after you."

"Lady Julia, wait!"

She hesitated at the door.

"Cal can take care of himself," David promised.

"That's what I fear."

Leaving the house caused a flurry of panic. Zoe agreed to stay with David, to play hostess after Julia was racing off rudely, but Nigel stepped in front of her and refused to let her go. "He'll be killed because of me if I do nothing." Or worse, he would kill. And then what? Cal might think earls were above the law but they really weren't. His American belief that titled men could do whatever they wanted might get him in terrible trouble.

Nigel tried to take charge. "I'll take care of this, Julia. You stay—"

"No! We must get the police constable. You can do that, and I shall try to stop Cal." She raced out through the front door, not caring about a coat, or gloves.

Nigel took the front steps in one leap, which gave him the advantage and he caught her. "I don't want you going anywhere alone, Julia."

He insisted they go together to the police. She was about to go mad but Nigel drove faster than she'd ever seen him. He drove rather like Zoe for once—like a race car driver. At the tiny stone building used as the police station, complete with small cells in the basement, he pulled ducal privilege when the police sergeant refused to see why he should rush to the sawmill. If a duke demanded the sergeant go, the man was not going to refuse, and the balding, craggy-faced sergeant traveled with them in the Daimler. The constable followed on his bicycle.

Dust and a smoky, sweet smell filled the air as Nigel raced down the lane to the large stone building used as the Worthington sawmill. Lumber was stacked all around and carts stood, carrying logs. The air was filled with the screech of saws.

Julia had the door open before the motor stopped and Nigel stomped on the brake, halting them with a lurch.

Men milled about, forming a circular crowd, catcalling and shouting, and she knew at once Cal must be in the middle of it.

"Julia, wait," Nigel called, but she tried to push her way between two of the men—bulky, barrel-chested specimens with bulging biceps, who smelled of sweat. One lifted his huge arm, yelling something, and she was almost knocked back, but she ducked in time.

Her slender size was an advantage—she slipped between the men, stopping on the inside of the rough circle. Ellen's pimp stood there, his pockmarked face red with fury, his fists doubled up. His cap was gone, revealing thinning brown hair, and his biceps strained at his sleeves. He was even bigger than she remembered.

Then she saw Cal. Blood ran down from his temple. Sweat soaked his hair to amber. The pimp lunged and threw his fists with intense speed. Cal ducked the blow to his head but took a punch in the gut that made her want to be sick. The brute was fast and powerful. Cal landed blows, but the pimp's fists were hard, as huge rocks, and were damaging Cal in a horrible way.

But Cal bounced lightly on his feet, seeming able to take the horrifying punishment. Truly, he should be unconscious.

Ellen's pimp—the men were shouting, calling him "Lowry"—grinned. The smug grin of confidence. He lunged again, ready to fell Cal.

Fists flew, but they were Cal's fists. Cal moved so fast, she could barely tell what was happening. She was almost swaying from lack of breath, from her heart forgetting to beat, when Cal slammed his fist into the man's gut, and as the fiend doubled over, Cal's blow to his jaw sent him sprawling.

Cal towered over the fallen man. His mouth twisted into a snarl. His eyes blazed. Pure rage flashed across his face—the heat and rage seemed to glow from him, so hot and different than the cool, controlled anger she'd seen before.

She remembered how he said he'd done far worse than fighting a goon like this man. She could believe it. He looked…lethal.

Cal lunged down and clamped his hand around the man's throat. For all the man had a huge neck, Cal's powerful hand spanned it. "I've broken men's necks before. Hand to hand. In battle."

Lowry blubbered. He was pleading for his life. This vicious man who hadn't listened to any of Ellen's pleas or screams…

"No! Stop!" She hurried forward, into the center of the circle on the muddy ground, aware of murmurs halting, men staring.

"Break this up now. Move out," commanded the police sergeant. He pushed the men aside with aplomb.

"This man, Jack Lowry, attacked Ellen Lambert in her

cottage and almost beat her to death. He also assaulted Lady Julia Hazleton," Cal declared.

"It was an attempt at an assault," Julia said to the sergeant, "thwarted by the earl. But this man has been abusing Miss Lambert. He's stolen money from her, forced her into prostitution."

The sergeant's eyes bulged in shock as she declared that. Lowry snarled, "I didn't force her into nothin'."

"You did, and you took money from her. Then you almost beat her to death," Julia cried, glaring down at the fallen brute. She realized she'd drawn back her shoe. She wanted to kick him, and she had to stop herself.

The constable, a young, strong lad, came up, puffing. Between the constable and sergeant, they got Lowry to his feet. "I'm innocent," he growled. "Never touched 'er ladyship."

"You assaulted her outside Ellen Lambert's cottage and tried to drag her away with you. What was your damned intent?" Cal stalked up, glaring down at the man, even though Lowry was two inches taller.

"What're you talking about? You're trying to pin somethin' on me. I never touched her."

"You touched her outside the Boar and Castle in the village," Cal barked. "Then, because Lady Julia stood up to you, you went after her again."

"I talked to her at the village, but she came up to me. I never saw her near the cottage. That's a lie. I swear."

"There are other women missing from this estate," Cal said. "Maybe you know something about that."

Lowry stared with panic.

The sergeant pulled Lowry's thick arms behind his back and snapped on metal shackles with a swift, careful motion. "You're coming back to the station. You're going to be charged with assault, Lowry, likely attempted murder."

"You can take him in my car," Cal said.

As they hauled Lowry away, she stepped toward Cal. There was blood all over his face, but he held up his hand. "Listen up," he shouted to the workers. "I want you to see I don't allow this kind of behavior. No one working for me beats up a woman, hurts his wife, hits his kids. No one bullies or hits anyone weaker than he. You want to work off some anger, we'll set up a ring and you can do it with some boxing. As for the conditions in that mill—things are going to be changing around here. Starting with the fact I need a new foreman. I'd appreciate applications dropped off with— Who's in charge of keeping the accounts here?"

The smallest man, a slim one in an old suit, lifted his hand. "Stevens, my lord."

"Give them to Stevens."

"There are good men who cannot write," Stevens pointed out.

"Hell," said Cal. "Then you take down the information about who they are and what qualities they've got for the job. Can you take charge for today, step in for Lowry?"

"Yes, my lord."

"Now go back to work, all of you. Stevens is acting as foreman until I hire a new one."

The men began moving back to the mill, all murmuring, realizing any of them could apply to be foreman. From the lighter expressions she saw on faces, she had no doubt Lowry bullied men here, too. Pleased, she fished out a handkerchief and briskly went to Cal. "We must clean you up. Thank you—thank you for capturing the man who hurt Ellen. But still, you shouldn't have put yourself in such danger."

"Julia, you shouldn't have come forward. You could have gotten hurt," Cal said.

"I was afraid—" She broke off. How did she politely say what she'd feared?

Cal's expression darkened. "I saw it in your face. You thought I would kill him. You thought the wild, violent American would murder a man in cold blood."

"I've never seen you angry like that."

"I thought you've always seen me angry."

"Not like *that*. That was hot and wild and for a moment, I thought it was out of your control. All the other times, your anger has been cold and obviously controlled. I don't understand why you were fighting. You should have telephoned the police. You are the earl. You had no need—"

"This isn't entirely for Ellen Lambert. Lowry, as foreman of this mill, was cutting corners on safety, endangering men. When I told him things would be run differently, he thought he could scare me with the threat of physical violence. I gave him the chance to show me what he could do."

Cal tried to make his blue eyes look guileless, but he failed.

"So you let him beat you up, then you took control and pounded him into the ground—" She broke off. She saw respect in the eyes of the other men around, and they were all large, muscled specimens. They all respected Cal, the Earl of Worthington. He wasn't a weak man given power by the accident of birth. He was a man who believed in their rights and safety, and who could fight as rough as any of them. He had shown them he was an honorable man and a tough one.

"I'm going to clean this place up," Cal said. "Improve conditions. Then I guess I'd better take a look at the other industries on this estate— Stop smiling, Julia. This doesn't mean anything."

But it did.

"But if Lowry was the foreman of the mill," Julia mused, "why did no one identify him?"

"I guess he hasn't lived here long. Came from Yorkshire originally. Most people were afraid to get on his bad side."

"And you have stopped his reign of terror."

He grinned at her, one of those slow grins that made her ache, and melt, and yearn.

Nigel came forward. She realized he had been unable to get through the crowd and stop her, and she'd never seen him look so worried over her. "Don't do that again," he said, as he escorted her back to their car.

"I had to ensure Cal didn't hurt that man badly," she said softly, trying to recover from—and hide—the devastating desire Cal's smile had evoked. "I had to ensure there could be no charges against him. We must take Cal back with us."

Nigel frowned, then nodded. The three of them traveled back to Worthington Park.

"How did you know I was there?" Cal asked.

"David told me. He told me Genevra had looked at the sketch, told you the man worked at the sawmill." She shivered as she thought of Lowry fighting Cal. Lowry might have hit her like that, if Cal had not rescued her.

Her stomach felt rather strange. Oddly weightless and funny.

"I asked Genevra if she thought he was responsible for the other girls' disappearances," Cal said.

He had done that. He had looked into a different possibility than Anthony.

"Disappearances?" Nigel asked, at the wheel.

Cal explained. But he did not tell Nigel what they had found in the car, what he suspected.

"Genevra pointed out the women must have been laid to rest somewhere or else they would have been found. I've been searching the estate. Driving around where the women were likely taken from. Now I'm expanding the search."

"I could—" Julia began.

"No." Both men said it at once.

"Genevra suggested I ask you," Cal said. "She said there is no one who knows Worthington Park as well as you. I told her no. I'm not putting you through that."

"I want to help. And both of you cannot dictate to me." Her head did feel oddly dizzy. It must be from seeing the force and violence in that fight and fearing Cal might lose control.

"Genevra said that Lady Worthington is suffering, just as the curse decreed. But this has nothing to do with a curse. This is human evil. And for that reason, I'm not asking you to help, Julia. I asked Genevra why she thought it stopped. She told me a hunter might search for prey farther away. Or he might have a reason to stop. She told me to look farther away to see if any girls with black hair and blue eyes had disappeared. Genevra has more brains than the police sergeant—"

"Those women look like you, Julia," Nigel said suddenly. His hands gripped the wheel. His face went white. "And you were attacked outside Ellen Lambert's cottage. Julia, you will have to stop your work. You cannot be putting yourself in danger."

"But that must have been Lowry and he has been arrested."

"No, Julia, I'm putting my foot down," Nigel said, in his ducal tones. "You are to stay close to home."

"No—" she began.

"You are under my roof and this time you will listen to me."

She knew he was scared, but he was going beyond unreasonable. "But there is no danger now." Even as she said that, she had to admit, she didn't feel completely sure. There was something wrong. She remembered her attacker gripping her throat. He'd been so strong—

But had he really been that big? She struggled to remember. Thought of the horror. Thought of how Cal had been covered in blood and now in cuts and bruises. She had thought the attacker was the same height as Cal, but that was when Cal had his arm captured behind his back. Could that have made him seem shorter?

Her attacker hadn't spoken. He had dragged her, struck her in terrifying, creepy silence. If he had spoken she would have known for certain if Lowry had been that man. Still, she wasn't going to point out that her memory of her attacker didn't quite match Lowry. Instead, she protested, "You can't forbid me from doing the one thing I can do." But they'd arrived at Worthington.

Cal got out. Julia wanted to move to the front seat to argue with Nigel all the way back to Brideswell. But as she stepped out of the car, her legs seemed to disappear and the ground rushed up toward her.

She opened her eyes to a darkened room, the flutter of pale ivory drapes and a gentle breeze that eased the too-hot feeling of the air.

"Are you all right? I've never seen you faint, Julia. Not even when— I mean, you have always been so remarkably strong."

Julia recognized Diana's voice. Wearing a loose dress with many layers of tulle, Diana sat down on the edge of the settee Julia lay on. She also recognized the pale pink decor— this was the most feminine drawing room at Worthington.

Julia sat up. "What happened? Did I really faint?"

"You did. Cal fears it was his fault, because you saw him

fight. He fears you have been through so much. Both he and your brother feel you need rest."

"Oh no. That means I'll be essentially locked up at Brideswell. They'll never let me out."

"Between men and mothers, we women never get to have any lives at all." Diana smiled, but then Julia saw there was sadness in Diana's eyes.

"What's wrong?" she asked. "It's not something with— I mean, all is all right, isn't it?"

Diana let out a deep sigh. "I really shouldn't trouble you now—"

"Diana, you can tell me. I'm not a piece of porcelain. I imagine it was just the heat that felled me. The sun was scorching and of course there were no shade trees around the sawmill. So tell me!"

"I've made my decision. I've realized I can't keep my baby. I have been thinking of how much Ellen Lambert has suffered. It would be condemning the baby and me to hardship. I don't think I'm that strong."

"Diana, you are strong."

"Julia, don't lie. I am too used to being an earl's daughter, one with position, privilege and very few real cares in the world. Even if Cal sells Worthington, the one thing protected is my dowry. I could marry."

"Cal promised to help you."

"He can't help me if everyone is judging me for being a fallen woman."

Which was wrong. So wrong. Julia was getting more and more fed up with societal rules. "There must be a way."

"This is the best way. And I'd probably make a wretched mother. Too selfish." Diana tried to smile.

Julia didn't believe Diana was. She had changed—she was

more thoughtful, less wild. But to protest that Diana would make a good mother would make this hurt more.

"This week I'll leave for Switzerland," Diana declared. "I didn't think I would show yet, but in the past few days, I've suddenly developed a little bulge. Cal will take me to Paris. He knows a widow there that he wants to hire as my companion in Switzerland. She's Parisian but speaks excellent English. She's titled and respectable, but in need of money. He'll turn me over to her. We'll claim she's a distant relative of his, so it makes it look like I'm just traveling to Switzerland to see the sights. I'm sure there will be gossip but no one will be able to prove anything. So after it's all over, I can marry." She sighed. "I wish I'd have a friend with me, not a stranger."

"I could go with you."

It came out impulsively. But Julia saw she could go. She was forbidden from working with her widows. What she could do was go away, give Nigel instructions on all the work to be done for the women—and he would have to do it since he was pigheadedly stopping her. By the time she returned, Nigel would beg her to take over. And by then, surely he would see sense about the risk of danger. She would also be able to see Sebastian in Paris.

"Will you come? Are you certain?" Diana bit her lip. "I would so love to have you with me. It's going to be hard, when I have to give my child away," she whispered.

"I'll be there," Julia promised, "to support you."

"You are the very best friend in the world, Julia."

Julia stood. "I should go back to Brideswell. I have to prepare for going away."

"Pack?"

"Well, that. But I must send a telegram to Sebastian in

Paris, telling him I'm coming. Then I have to write a very large list of instructions for my other brother."

Diana looked mystified, but stood and hugged her. Diana then went to fetch Nigel. Julia went to the terrace and looked out over the lawns. Soon she would see Paris, a lifelong dream—

"We could marry now."

Julia started. She heard the voice from around the corner of the house. It sounded like Alice Hayes.

"I know why you broke it off all those years ago. I did marry after the War, but my husband had wounds—he died of them."

"I'm sorry, Alice."

Cal's voice. When Alice had told David she loved someone else…she must have meant Cal. Cal said huskily, "I can't marry you, Alice. Even if David had never been in love with you, I couldn't do it."

"Because you are an earl now?"

"No. You think I'm turning you down because of social position? God, no. I don't deserve a woman like you, Alice. Being an earl doesn't change who I was. What I was."

A lady would not listen in. A lady— Oh, forget being a lady. Her heart ached. Of course she could never have him, but she hated to know how much this must hurt him.

Alice said, "I know how you grew up in New York—"

"No, you don't. David would never tell you the full story."

"It doesn't matter. I've always loved you, Cal Brody."

"My name is actually Carstairs. I loved you, too, Alice. I'm sorry to hurt you."

"I do think your brother would accept your marriage. David is a good man. And I would be happy to help take care of him."

"There can't be anything between us, Alice. I'm not planning to marry anyone. I'm going back to Paris. I could turn this place over to David. He'd make a better earl than me."

Julia's heart plunged. It thrilled her to think Worthington Park wouldn't be destroyed, but she realized how little that mattered, if Cal never healed, never found happiness.

"Cal, I think you will be a smashing earl," Alice said. "It was so good to see you again. I don't regret coming. And I wanted to see David. But I guess this is goodbye."

"My lady?" Wiggins stood in the terrace doorway and Julia almost leaped out of her shoes with guilt. "His Grace is out on the drive with the motor."

"Th-thank you." She hurried out. No doubt Wiggins knew she'd listened in, and there was no way she could gracefully explain that.

All the way home, she bit her lip and fought tears. Cal had been in love. Cal, who deserved love more than anyone, could not have the person he adored. Because he loved his brother so much.

And he might leave Worthington forever.

She arrived at Brideswell to find her maid, Sims, standing in the foyer, with a carpetbag beside her. Zoe was there, holding Nicholas. "Sims has found a new position with Grandmama. Apparently, Grandmama's maid has left her and—well, you know the dowager. She wanted someone at once."

"I can work my notice, my lady, if that's what you want."

"Oh, Sims, that is fine," Julia said. "I can brush my own hair, and I don't need anyone putting me in a corset anymore. I wish you the best of luck with Her Grace. This will be a great step up for you and I am happy."

"Are you certain you will be all right without a lady's maid?" Zoe asked. "I can have my maid help you and Isobel as needed."

Julia watched Sims get into the Daimler and drive away. "I'm going to Paris, Zoe. And I intend to pack my own trunk."

"Paris?"

Julia hastily explained as they walked back to the drawing room, the one used in the late afternoon.

"I will help Nigel with the widows," Zoe said. "I think it's a rather good idea to let him take charge for a while. You've dreamed of seeing Paris—you should see it. It will be a wonderful adventure."

"Yes. It's been my lifelong dream. Perhaps I'll find my heart's desire there. I'll stay in Paris with Sebastian and become an artist."

"Why not?" said Zoe. "It's time you did something just for you—to make you happy."

17

Paris

Paris had been the first big city outside of New York that Cal had ever seen, when he'd arrived there in 1917. It had been wild in the War. When you could die any day, you fit in a lot of living.

In Paris, he drank a lot of red wine. He gambled. He seduced a few bold French girls. They liked the Americans—their money, the treats they brought, their bravado and their bold, cocksure attitude.

Cal had gone back to Paris after the War, after he made money bootlegging and in other...illegal enterprises. Paris always made him feel like he could be something more. Made him forget what he'd done. When he argued about art in the cafés, he felt like he was more than a rough kid from the slums.

He wanted to show Paris to Julia—Julia who had never traveled but always dreamed of it. Maybe he wanted to do it so badly because it was a gift he could give her before he left.

Once he'd started talking about changes for the sawmill he'd seen the hope in Julia's eyes. She thought she'd won. And for a moment, she almost had. When he was talking to

Alice, he'd got a crazy idea. He'd looked out over the green lawns of Worthington and he'd thought about getting married, having a family, staying there. Julia had almost made him forget the promise he'd made to Mam.

He would take care of Diana—he would never turn his back on an innocent child. And he would lay Paris at Julia's feet.

From Brideswell's station, he traveled with Julia, Diana and David by train to London's Victoria Station. They took a ferry to cross the Channel to Calais, and were now on a train steaming across the French countryside to Paris.

Cal knew Julia was worried about her brother Sebastian. Something about a telegram she'd received just before she left Brideswell—days after she'd telegrammed her brother to let him know she was coming. But when Cal asked what was wrong, she told him she didn't know. He could tell she was hiding something. Why?

Right now, the troubled look had left her eyes. She glowed with excitement. The train to Paris clacked along the tracks. Following Julia's gaze, Cal looked out at the blur of scenery. It was strange to see leaves on the trees and fertile fields following the tracks. He remembered blackened trees, bombed villages, fields that were wet, muddy mires. Or frozen with ice.

"Are you remembering the War?" Julia asked gently. She sat across from him.

He glanced up. "How did you know?"

Her hand brushed his wrist. He forgot all his memories and got hard at once. The more he was with her, the less of her touch it took to arouse him. But he knew he couldn't have her.

"I can see it in your face."

He'd been a flyer. There was no need to tell her what it had felt like to look at the charred remains of men pulled from wrecked planes—fuel consumed those bits of wood, paint, cable and fabric and burned the men down into wizened statues of charcoal.

She touched his knee as if soothing him.

But her light touch was like a jolt of lightning.

"Are the memories troubling?" she asked.

He met her large, concerned blue eyes, and—and hell, he wanted to be alone with her. He wanted to lay her back on the velvet first-class seat and make her scream with ecstasy. He wanted to be thinking about nothing but pleasuring Julia.

"They do trouble you, don't they?"

"They aren't sunshine and roses, but I don't have shell shock, Julia. I'm fine." He sounded abrupt, fighting to hide the raw need coursing through him. Anyway, war memories weren't the ones that haunted him. It was the memories of what he'd done before that.

"I learned you are hiring a special doctor to come from London to heal Ellen's shell shock. Dougal told me, before we left. Thank you." She smiled.

And he knew that was why he'd done it. Not just for Ellen, but to see Julia glow. "You're welcome. Tell me, what's the first thing you're going to do when you reach Paris?"

"I'd like to go to a dressmaker," Diana said. Then bit her lip. "If I have a clothing allowance."

"You do. Get the bills sent to me," Cal said. "What about you, Julia? Are you going straight to the House of Worth and Coco Chanel's establishment?"

She looked surprised he would know fashion designers. Then an adorable frown puckered her brow. One day he would paint her like that. He loved her expressions when she forgot the rules about ladies hiding emotion and let the real woman peek out.

Hell, he wasn't going to paint her. He should leave before that.

"I should like to see the Eiffel Tower. But I would love to visit a café. Or go to one of the clubs. Seeing Josephine Baker perform would be thrilling. I would also love to see the Left Bank and see where you would paint." Words bubbled out of her, like she was made of champagne. "Paris is filled with painters, writers, dancers, musicians. I'm so excited to see that world. Since I'm going to give up on marriage, perhaps I could become an artist or novelist. Though I fear that artistic talent begins and ends with my brother."

"You'll never know unless you try. I never thought I could really paint until I came to Paris," he admitted. But her words had hit him hard. She was giving up on marriage.

This was Paris, where he'd reveled in a bohemian artist's life. He'd get drunk and engage in wild sexual activity—love affairs with married women, multiple partners in one bed. But he didn't want that now.

He wanted Julia.

When he desired a woman, he would paint her, make love to her, and once the painting was finished, his ardor was spent. He always chose experienced women who wanted no more of him than a wild affair.

Damn it, he couldn't have Julia.

Alice had told him she was in love with him and he'd pictured marriage. But it had been Julia's laughter he'd heard in his imagination. Julia playing with their children on the Worthington lawn. It was a fantasy he would never have—not with his past. He couldn't marry a lady like Julia without lying to her about his past, or keeping it hidden. And he couldn't seduce her.

The train chuffed into the station. "I'm here. I'm finally here," Julia breathed, and her delight almost broke his heart.

Cal summoned a cab. The car made its way through the ancient streets and took them to their hotel—the Hotel Le Meurice. Julia's sister-in-law, Zoe, had suggested it. Old and beautiful, it had majestic rooms. The largest suite had a terrace that gave a complete circular view of Paris.

He hadn't wanted to spoil Julia's chance to stay in Paris's most beautiful hotel, or his brother's chance to savor the luxury and the views. So Cal had agreed. It had been a long time since he'd been at Le Meurice and he figured no one would remember him.

"Do you like it?" he asked Julia as they drew up in front of the classic stone facade, the archways decorated with ivy, and the French flags snapping in the wind.

"It's beautiful."

Then he saw the surprise in Julia's eyes as the doorman's face lit up in recognition.

He was wrong. They remembered him.

Julia received a message from the concierge, left by Sebastian, to meet her brother at a Parisian café at two o'clock that day. Just before they moved from the desk, Julia heard the concierge say to Cal, "So delightful to have you with us again, Monsieur—Monsieur Le Comte."

She turned to Cal to ask him about it, but he put his hand on her lower back and led her through the lobby.

Her heels clicked on tiles polished to a mirror finish. Cal was recognized here and the Hotel Le Meurice was one of the most fashionable hotels in Paris. The cream of Parisian society dined at the beautiful Roof Garden. Picasso and his wife had selected the hotel to host their wedding dinner.

"You've stayed here before," she said as he took her to the lift. She spoke casually, but she *ached* with curiosity about his past.

Cal shrugged. "When I sold a few paintings I brought a model here to celebrate. We dined on the rooftop. That's how I know the hotel. And that's where I would like to have dinner tonight. All four of us. Surrounded by the lights of Paris."

But the staff wouldn't remember him from that. No, he had been important to them. But a lady couldn't pry. "It sounds lovely."

"It is. And I want to see you, silhouetted by Paris."

Her heart pattered. But Cal loved Alice Hayes—and she wanted him to find happiness with Alice. She had no right to be dazzled by the idea of dining with him with the lights of Paris spread around them.

Cal helped David roll his chair into the lift, while a porter brought the luggage and trunks. She and Diana followed and when she stepped into the suite she was sharing with Diana, Julia ran across the thick carpet, pulled open the glass doors and stepped out onto the balcony.

Paris spread out around her, trees rich with foliage, the streets in the complex circular pattern of an ancient city. The Eiffel Tower rose against the sky. Boat and traffic horns blared, and out there, all around her, adventure waited.

Behind her, Diana laughed. "Julia, I've never seen you like this. Bouncing like a child."

Julia spun. "I'm being thoughtless. This isn't such a happy time for you."

"No, I don't think I shall enjoy the wildness of Paris this time," Diana said ruefully. "But I should be relieved—that's a good enough substitute for happy, isn't it? And at least my mother never found out I'm pregnant."

Julia knew relieved wasn't as good as happy, but someone rapped on their door and she went to answer it. Cal lounged there, looking gorgeous in a summer-weight suit of pale gray.

It made his hair look utterly gold. "I'll escort you to meet your brother," he said. "Since I know my way around."

She hesitated. Sebastian had warned her something devastating had happened. He could be awfully dramatic, but his terse words in the telegram made her realize this was the truth. Sebastian had secrets he wouldn't want a stranger—Cal—to know. "I don't know—"

"I'll leave you to meet him alone. But I don't want you getting lost in Paris."

She agreed and Diana offered to stay with David. As they exited the hotel, Cal commanded a car—a gleaming blue four-seater Citroën. The driver wound his way through streets crowded with cars, motorized streetcars and horse carts. Everything was thrilling to see.

Cal smiled at her excitement. Then he pointed out the window. "Here's the café from your brother's message."

Heavenly yeasty scents of bread wrapped around Julia, along with another rich scent of coffee roasting. Small tables sat on a cobblestone terrace. Across the road from them, a railing followed the Seine, and beyond the railing the water rippled.

Julia looked in the café. Inside sat old men and young women with lipsticked mouths. But no Sebastian. "He's not yet here. I am early, of course."

"Have some coffee. I'll sit with you and leave when he comes." Cal pulled out a seat for her.

A waiter wearing a long white apron came to them and took orders. Her café au lait arrived in an enormous bowl-like cup. Frothy milk defied gravity to sit upon her cup, already melting away into the hot drink. She cradled the cup and sipped.

She was here. In Paris with Cal. Except there could be no romance in it. She had to make him see he should be with Alice. "Cal, you should bring someone special to Paris," she began.

He set down his coffee. Slowly, gently, he drawled, "Sheba, I already have—"

"Julia!"

She looked up and saw golden hair beneath a white hat—brilliant and gleaming in the sunlight. "Sebastian!"

Her brother looked utterly stylish in a white boater, white trousers and a white jacket over a shirt of pale pink and a tie of the same color. As she stood, he embraced her, kissing her cheek. "Julia, my angel. My savior. My dearest one."

She lifted her brow. "I know you too well. When you slather on compliments like marmalade on toast, you are up to something." For example, there was his engagement to Zoe, when he needed a marriage and had tried to make Zoe believe he loved her. But then Julia saw the shadows under her brother's eyes and knew he was truly troubled.

Sebastian looked toward Cal, then leaned close to her ear. "This one looks wilder and more interesting than Dr. Campbell."

"Behave," she whispered.

"If that is what you wish, then behaving is all that I will do, my dear."

"This is the Earl of Worthington." She inclined her head toward her brother. "My brother, Lord Sebastian Hazelton."

Cal held out his hand. Sebastian took it and they shook hands as Cal said, "Call me Cal. I don't believe in titles. I'm an American."

Sebastian cocked his handsome head. "I recognize you. I think I've met you before. At Bricktop's place. Don't think we had a formal introduction." And under his breath, to her, "More intriguing all the time."

"Cal lived in Paris to paint," Julia explained.

Sebastian murmured by her ear, "A wild, artistic American. Have you brought him here—" He broke off. He coughed. "Wait. You are my sister. No love affairs for you."

"*Sebastian*," she whispered fiercely. Of course she couldn't have a love affair with Cal. But deep inside, she felt an astonishing pang of regret.

And despite Sebastian's lightheartedness, his eyes bore sadness.

Cal stood. "I should leave the two of you to speak of your private business. I think I'll go to my favorite bookstore. Shakespeare and Company. A gathering spot of Americans in Paris. When should I return for you, Julia?"

"I know the store. I'll bring her to you," Sebastian said.

As soon as they were alone, she asked, "What is wrong, Sebastian?"

Coffee arrived for Sebastian—the waiter didn't even have to ask his order. Sebastian took it with thanks. He swirled it. "Just seeing you, having you here, is a blessing for me, beloved sister."

"You look so thin and pale, Sebastian. I am terribly worried about you."

She had always admired Sebastian's courage. He had fallen in love with a handsome young man, Captain Ransome. It was still forbidden in England. She knew of the trial of Oscar Wilde. She knew Sebastian could be arrested and imprisoned. Yet she knew Sebastian was a good man who was only seeking love. He truly cared for John Ransome. And to be together, both men had left England to live in Capri, and now in Paris.

"John left me," he said bluntly.

Her heart broke at the pain on her brother's handsome face. He looked a lot like Nigel except his hair was gold and his eyes a stunning green. "I thought you were both happy."

"We were," he said darkly. "But John's family issued him an ultimatum. He had to return or he'll be dead to them forever. I told him there's nothing for him there. How can he be happy trying to live a lie, living a life without love? I didn't see how he could go back, after we'd been living together in Capri, then Paris, but his parents have told their friends he went on a tour of Europe with me—that we are friends from school. They believe that if he 'quells his disgusting proclivities' as they put it, he can return to the army. They actually want him to marry 'for appearances.'"

"You were considering marriage for appearances, once," she reminded him. "It was Zoe who realized that was a foolish idea. You can't condemn Captain Ransome if he does the same things you thought you must do."

He grimaced. "I know. I didn't feel like getting beaten to a pulp by English louts trying to prove their manliness. It's why I came here. But did John leave for his family, or did he leave because he no longer cares for me?"

"Didn't he give you his reasons?"

"We fought, I got roaring drunk, and when I woke, he was gone and only a note remained."

He drew a folded paper out of his pocket. "You want too much from me," it read.

"Do I chase him, Julia, or do I accept defeat? I'm happy to live in exile as long as I have John. Yes, once I was engaged to Zoe, but only because she needed a hasty wedding herself. I've changed. Love is too important to toy with, too important to cast aside. John is willing to give me up to return to England and live a lie, rather than accept exile. Perhaps there's no hope for us."

"I think—I think you should fight for love."

"What if I fail? Having a broken heart hurts."

"I know. But you do heal."

"As you have. Admirably, Julia. But why are you with the wild American?"

She explained about Cal and Worthington Park. She could

not reveal Diana's secret—Diana had not given her permission, but Sebastian believed she'd come to Paris only for him, and she couldn't bring herself to disabuse him of that.

"So you're going to marry the wild American?"

"No! He has no interest in marriage. And neither do I. I've decided that instead I should grasp life on my own terms. I won't marry without love. And I won't marry a man who wishes to put me in a box or a gilded cage."

"Julia, there will eventually be a man who loves you enough, who does not see your desire for freedom and autonomy, your desire to be equal to him, as a price to pay but rather an asset."

Her heart ached, but she smiled to hide it. "That is rather lovely."

"I agree. I surprise myself. Perhaps I should have taken to writing prose instead of painting." He winked at her. "Do you want me to take you to the most shocking Parisian clubs?"

She knew he was teasing. But she called his bluff. "I came to Paris to experience adventure." And to see what she really wanted in her life. "Tonight I am definitely going to wild clubs."

She finished her coffee with a flourish. It was lush and strong and gave her a jolt that shot to her fingertips and toes. "I have spent twenty-seven years being dutiful and ladylike. It hasn't brought me anything I wanted—love, a home, a family. Now I am going to begin my life all over again. I am going to try being wild. Then, I am going to help you heal your rift with John Ransome. You deserve to have love, Sebastian."

Julia quickly saw Paris was a place one must go with someone one loved.

With Sebastian, she met Cal at the bookstore, Shakespeare

and Company, where she bought a travel guide to Paris and met sparrowlike Sylvia Beach. Then the two men together took her everywhere. On a boat on the Seine. To view the monuments—L'Arc de Triomphe, the Eiffel Tower. Her day was a whirl of cafés and flowers and many glasses of wine. Then they returned to the hotel, having dinner with Diana and David on the rooftop of Le Meurice.

At night, lights glittered all around, reflecting on the Seine to make the river appear to be full of diamonds. Julia changed into a sheath of a dress, pale blue with silver beads. Her dress glittered and sparkled every time she drew breath, but it was nowhere near as brilliant as the lights of Paris.

She had been to jazz clubs. Before Nigel married Zoe, she and Zoe had gone to a secret downstairs club in London where—to Julia's shock—a dancer had taken her clothes off.

She was rather nervous. Paris must be even wilder than London. She had boldly told Sebastian she wanted an adventure. But did she?

The five of them made their way to the neighborhood of Montparnasse, past cafés with lights that gleamed on cobblestones and wrought iron fencing and on the faces of chic women. Cal pushed David's chair and she had linked arms with Sebastian. Diana walked at David's side.

As they reached the famous Café de la Rotonde, Cal clasped her hand. Threaded his fingers through hers and she felt it. A *whoosh*. All of Paris stopped in its tracks—and if a man could stop Paris, that man had to be truly something.

She had to release his hand so he could steer David inside, into a room filled with cigarette smoke, crammed with people—women in brief dresses or plain trousers, men dressed in either immaculate dinner jackets or threadbare sweaters. There appeared to be an understanding that the young man in the chair must have been wounded in war, because a path was cleared for them all.

"Cal!" someone called. Cal sat her at a table, and greeted many friends, introducing her.

As Cal fell into conversation with fellow artists, a young gentleman smiled at her from another table. He asked if he could break off the end of the baguette in the basket on their table.

She handed him the whole thing. He waved his hands. "Not all that. I'd be asked to pay."

Another man joined him. "Still nursing that one cup of coffee?"

The first man smiled. He was young, tanned, with curling black hair. "Ten centimes for the cup and I can sit for the day and sketch."

The other man laughed. "I would like to sketch that lovely one."

Julia blushed and looked up as Cal returned with a bottle of red wine and five glasses that he held adroitly by their stems.

The noise grew louder—she could hear the debate of the two men beside her better than she could the conversation at her table. The man with the black hair insisted the new art would be found in the objects used by the masses—automobiles, the newfangled toaster, furniture. "Mass production allows us to bring great art—to bring beautiful but practical form—to all people," he declared. "We must educate people so they learn to throw off Victorian fuss and frippery. And see the beauty of simple form—of a form that follows from its function."

They argued vehemently. Then the second man left and the black-haired man leaned to her and pointed to the walls. "Those sketches are mine." He grinned. "People come to

Montparnasse to sin disgracefully. How unfortunate I didn't get to do it with you. Unless you wish to come to my studio and I will paint you. Then make love to you."

"The lady is with me," Cal growled.

"Actually I am not…exactly. But as delightful as your offer is, I must decline. My time in Paris is limited and my schedule is already thoroughly booked," she said politely.

That was how it would be done in the drawing room. But the man put his hand on her knee, bent to her and kissed her neck. She was shocked into immobility.

Until Cal hauled the man off. He helped her to her feet. "We're going. There's a fight about to break out."

"Between you and he?" she inquired. The dark-haired man was cursing eloquently in French.

"It might, but that wasn't the one I was thinking about. That intellectual debate in the corner over there is about to erupt into a brawl."

And it did, just as Cal whisked her out, followed by Diana and Sebastian, pushing David's chair.

Julia tried not to look shocked. "Did you paint in places like that? That man wouldn't accept bread from me in case he had to pay for it. Are they really so impoverished?"

Cal grinned. "We all were. The proprietor, Libion, would let me stay there and drink his coffee if I gave him a picture or two to keep up until I could pay."

That didn't make sense. She was certain he had done more than have one dinner at the exclusive Le Meurice, so how could he not have afforded to pay for coffee? But ladylike training would not allow her to say he was lying—questioning him would imply that. David had told her Cal had made money, but she had thought it was enough to care for David.

"What would you like to do with all of Paris here for your pleasure?" Cal teased.

"Sebastian has promised to take me to a jazz club," she said. "Let's go together."

Sebastian and Cal then traded names of clubs back and forth—names that didn't mean anything to her. Cal suggested one that made Sebastian's brow shoot up and Julia said quickly, "That one. I want to try that one."

David and Diana decided to return to the hotel, and Cal acquired a taxicab to take them, helping David out of his chair.

It was strange—she was eager to be shocked, and terrified of it at the same time. It made for a rather intoxicating mix of emotions as they made their way through the steamy streets of Montparnasse. Finally, Cal led her beneath an awning that read Dingo American Bar and Restaurant. He held the door for her and murmured, "One of the favorite bars of the ex-pat American painters and writers. A lot of my friends are here."

A long wooden bar stretched before her, crowded with patrons. Simple stools of bent wood gathered around small tables. Here was more hazy smoke. Sensuous music drifted out, much more mournful and aching than any jazz she'd yet heard. It called to her. The whole night felt like a surge of electricity—and she was thrilled by the glow but also afraid of the shock. It was so crowded, noisy, wild. She was used to crushes at balls, but this was a world she didn't know.

However, everyone seemed to know Cal. Especially the women. Women wanted to talk to him, touch him, slip away into a dark, quiet corner of the bar with him.

Cal was invited to a table. A good-looking man with dark hair and a bourbon in front of him pulled out a chair for her. Julia sat as Cal made introductions. On her left, the handsome man who had pulled out her chair was named Ernest

Hemingway. "The writer," Cal added. "And his wife, Hadley Richardson."

On her other side sat Zelda Fitzgerald, famous in America, the embodiment of the "flapper." And wife to F. Scott,
who had written the rather stunning novel *The Great Gatsby*.
Julia felt awed to be there—she had never run with the artistic set or the Bright Young Things.

Zelda had bobbed blond hair and compelling, emotive
eyes. Mrs. Fitzgerald burst out with the most intriguing
and unusual comments. "Why do they call you 'ladies'?"
she asked pointedly. "Isn't it rather obvious that is what you
are? And for those who aren't called ladies, what is that supposed to imply?"

Julia was taken aback. "Do you know," she answered finally. "I truly don't know. It was really a way of distinguishing those who wanted an elevated position. It goes back
centuries."

"Are you slavishly devoted to having a title?" Zelda demanded.

Julia knew how to be polite in awkward situations. "I've
never thought about it, since I keep mine no matter what."

"Do you?" Zelda drank the rest of her cocktail. "How
positively open-minded of your country. Marriage is the
ruin of any woman, you know. I haven't any idea why we
rush to do it. It's all we girls are brought up to hope for, isn't
it? You build your whole life on the idea of landing a man
who's worthwhile. Then, once you've done it, it doesn't take
long before you realize there's not much to it. It can stifle a
woman. Once you're married, you're not interesting. Unless
you are really good at something."

Julia managed to follow the swift, dramatic speed of her
words. She asked, "Do you write?"

"A little. I was trained as a dancer. I'm quite good. If I were dedicated, I could really be something, you know. Something really dazzling."

"Well, you are, aren't you?" Julia's heart panged. There was something a little desperate about Mrs. Fitzgerald. Beneath the beauty, the perfect brazen flapper loveliness, she looked haunted. "You are both quite famous in America. The predominant couple of the Jazz Age."

Zelda shrugged. As if it was of no consequence. As if it wasn't enough. Then her gaze went to her husband and became a little wilder. "You see the woman he's talking to? That creature in the man's tuxedo? She's the kind of woman who entices a man until he just can't look away."

Julia saw a kind of anguish in Zelda's eyes. She, like Zelda, had been raised to plan for marriage. Now she was going to have to build an entirely different future. And she could see Zelda was searching as she was—and maybe was as lost, for all she was lovely and famous.

Hemingway was talking to Cal. Leaning over to hear Zelda, Julia couldn't hear much of the men's conversation. She heard the term "bullfighting," then talk of Italy and Spain. She gathered Hemingway admired Cal for having been a pilot in the War.

Zelda leaned close.

"I have a daughter, you know," she said. "Just the most precious thing. When she was born, I was coming out from the ether and I said the most unrelated things. He wrote them down, you know. Scott. And he used them. The words that came right out of my mouth when I didn't even know where I was. It would be so much easier to be a beautiful fool, wouldn't it?"

Zelda liked to say shocking things, Julia felt. She answered thoughtfully, "I don't know. I was raised to expect to marry, manage a house, and let my life be directed and shaped by my family and by circumstances. And yes, it would have been best if I had been nothing more than a beautiful fool. Now I realize it's frightening to want more. But I'm ready to face being afraid."

"The Lost Generation," Hemingway said then, his voice carrying over the table. "It's a name for us all. Gertrude gave it to me. She had work done on her car. The young mechanic didn't impress her. She asked the garage owner where the man had been trained. The owner said the man had been through the War and they were all *une génération perdue*."

"The Lost Generation. It suits us, doesn't it?" said Fitzgerald.

They looked at her.

Julia said, "It does. I feel quite lost sometimes. As though there is something of great importance I could do, but I don't quite know what it is."

She felt Zelda Fitzgerald staring at her.

Couples got up to dance then. Not wives with husbands—the couples split apart and paired up with others. Julia was left at the table with Cal, Hadley Richardson and a female author—the woman in the man's tuxedo.

"What do you do?" The question came from the author. She smoked a cigarette in a long holder. Her dark hair was cropped short and slicked back with pomade. "You must do something."

What did she do? She thought of Ellen. Of the Brands. Of the people on the estate like Mrs. Billings, who had lost all her sons to the War. "The work that I do that truly inspires me is my charity work. Though I have rather shocked Society with what I do."

"Darling, you look as if butter wouldn't melt in your mouth. How could you shock anyone?"

"I work with women who lost their husbands and have

to turn to drastic measures to support their families. Fallen women."

"You, darling? Work with prostitutes?" The woman's hand stroked down her arm.

The woman blew a smoke ring. Julia found the woman's kohl-ringed eyes rather magnetic. They were huge and pale blue. She had a strong nose and high cheekbones. Almost masculine features, but she was strikingly beautiful.

"You're really lovely, Lady Julia. I've been on a man kick for the last few months. About every six months, I change my mind. My last really serious love affair was with a woman. She was married, but I adored her. Then, I decided it was time for men. But you've tempted me to change my mind tonight."

The woman's hand settled on her leg. And squeezed.

And in that moment, Julia knew she hadn't wanted quite this much adventure. Paris was wild and she wasn't. Not desperately, determinedly wild, anyway. She loved art and literature and beauty—but she loved her work at Brideswell, her home, country life.

But suddenly, a strong hand gripped hers and she was lifted to her feet. "Julia isn't available." To her, Cal said, "We should get you back to the hotel. We'll tell your brother that you're leaving."

They were almost at the door—the crowd had magically parted for Cal. She gripped the door frame to stop him. "I don't want to run away. I know I'm not wild. I wasn't going to slip off with her into a corner and do—do Sapphic things, you know."

Cal groaned loudly. "That is an image I didn't need right now, Julia."

"Well, I don't need a man rushing me away from something a little scandalous." In truth, she was rather glad to get away—but she didn't want to be hastened away as if she were a young virgin who mustn't see anything.

"That's not what I'm doing. I'm rushing you to the hotel because I need to paint you."

"Paint me?"

"I've watched you all night, falling more and more under your spell. The only thing that's going to save me is to paint you. I thought I wasn't going to do it. But I have to."

"You mean our bargain. The one we hadn't actually made yet." She was confused. She thought that hadn't mattered anymore. And she thought it didn't need to matter—not after he'd talked about future changes for the estate. Not after he'd chosen to take care of Diana and Ellen. "Where you said you'd be willing to leave Worthington untouched while you painted me?"

"I'm willing to give you anything you want for it, Julia."

18

Painting in Paris

A lady should not be alone with a man in a hotel room.

Julia stood in the middle of the living area, on the elegant Turkish carpet. She was surrounded by furnishings of royal blue silk and gilt in the style of Louis XIV. A canvas was set up near the window. The deep blue and gold curtains were tied back, and Paris glittered below them. Cal was pouring champagne.

Julia could just imagine Mother falling into a swoon at the thought of her doing such a scandalous thing. In England, if a rumor began to spread that she had been in Cal's room her reputation would be in shreds.

Of course, nothing would happen. This was for her to sit for a portrait. She knew he loved Alice and she believed Cal would not try to seduce her. He'd teased her with that before, but he'd proven himself honorable.

"You aren't going to want me to take off my clothes, are you?" She had wanted adventure in Paris. And for art, why would she be so nervous about doing that? Could she do it?

The champagne bottle jerked in his hand and the stream flew clear of the glass.

"I'm not sure if I can do it," she admitted. "Tonight, I met the most exciting, artistic people of our times and—and I was shocked. By what they said, how they live, the fact some of them take both men and women as lovers." She sighed rue-fully. "I'm simply not modern. I don't belong in this world. Even if you asked me to pose naked to save Worthington, I now know I couldn't do it. I'm not daring and brave. I'm dull and boring. A true English lady."

Champagne dripped off his hand and Cal grabbed one of his painting rags to clean up. "You are anything but dull and boring. Just because you were shocked doesn't mean you don't belong here. I'm not going to ask you to take off your clothes. You're something special, Julia. Something remark-able and unique. You are really the perfect lady."

Strangely, she wasn't so sure she liked that. She didn't know quite what he meant. She thought Cal disliked per-fect ladies.

He handed her the flute of champagne. She sipped and the bubbles tickled her nose.

"I'll show you how I want you to pose. Fully clothed." He pulled a stool over so it stood in front of the window and the view of Paris. "First, I want you to sit there. Talk to me."

As she settled down delicately, Cal took off his dress jacket and his tie. Watching his shoulders and back move and his muscles bunch made her feel giddy. He kicked off shoes and socks so he was barefoot. Even in his fine shirt and tailored trousers, he looked bohemian. Wild.

But his heart was Alice's.

He began to squirt paint onto his palette.

"Why do you need to paint me?"

"Because you're the most beautiful thing I've ever seen in

my life and an artist gets an obsession to record something like that," he said.

The champagne was loosening her inhibitions—on top of the cocktails she'd drunk. He gave instructions and she sat as he wanted. As he sketched on the canvas, he kept looking at her so intensely. With a hot, penetrating gaze. She knew it was just to get the detail, but she felt her cheeks grow warm.

Giggling a little, she said, "You told me that the staff of the hotel knew you because you came here to celebrate after you sold a painting. I don't believe that. They know you too well."

"What I told you was true. Whenever I sold a painting, I always came here. I tipped well, which guarantees they'll look after you and remember you." He shrugged. "I always took the viewpoint that money would come from somewhere, so I spent it when I had it."

"Truly? Even though you had been poor?" The English aristocracy used to take it for granted they would be the upper tier of society, with grand houses and grand lives. They feared losing everything now. Brideswell was safe, but she remembered how terrifying it was to fear losing her home and having the tenants lose theirs. That was why she sympathized with Lady Worthington, Diana and her sisters.

"Having been poor once meant I wasn't scared of being poor again," he said. "After the War, everything felt like heaven. Even camping out and sleeping beneath the stars felt like luxury after catching a few minutes' sleep standing up in a trench that was ankle-deep in sloppy, stinking cold water."

"You camped under the stars?" Goodness, had he not been able to afford a roof over his head?

He laughed. "*That* shocks you, doll? I went to paint the north—the wilds in the north of Canada, just below the Arctic Circle. There are artists painting landscapes not as dainty places tamed by men, but as wild and untamed land. I joined them, canoeing into the north, then camping and sketching."

"But didn't you get wet and cold?"

"I set up a canvas tent. I had to fit what I took in a canoe." He grinned. "I had a sleeping sack made of waterproof cloth and sheep's wool. I cooked food over a campfire. I learned I could live with very few belongings."

She stared at him, amazed. He was so intriguing—he knew so much, had done so much.

He sketched, looking at her, then at the easel.

She loved to watch him draw, with all his focus on the picture. He brushed his hair back as he worked, as the pencil flew over the canvas. He frowned, smiled, grimaced, as if experiencing all the emotions possible in the minutes while he sketched.

She couldn't stop watching him. She wanted to touch him. *All* of him.

Suddenly the room felt hotter than even on the most baking summer's day. But she couldn't touch him. She couldn't have a love affair with a man who truly loved someone else.

"I would be scared of being poor," she admitted. "I don't have that much courage."

"I think you have a lot of courage," he said.

She was about to shake her head, then remembered models were not supposed to move. "I don't really. I just hide things very well. Ladies do. For a long time, we had no money and we thought we would have to lose Brideswell. But the aristocracy wants to 'keep up appearances.' We threw dinner parties we could not afford and ate tiny meals as a family. We burned fewer fires and shivered more in the winters. We shut up much of the house."

"What would you have done if you'd lost the house?"

"I guess we would have found somewhere smaller to live.

We would have had much less, but we would have still tried to carry on as if nothing changed. That is what people like us do."

He shook his head. "You come from a world I'm never going to understand."

"It doesn't make sense to me anymore, either. Our world has value and meaning but it needs new ideas—it needs men like you. You truly were born to be an earl," she insisted. "To be a true self-made man, you are obviously quite brilliant at business. And you truly care about people. You are probably more qualified to be an earl than most men who have the title."

He didn't answer.

She went on, in a voluble rush, "You could make Worthington into a great place. You could marry Alice Hayes and have a family. You could be happy."

"Marry Alice?"

"I—I overheard her tell you that she is in love with you. I am sorry. That was most unladylike of me. I know you don't want to hurt your brother—"

"Julia, there are a hell of a lot of reasons I wouldn't marry Alice. David is only one of them."

He looked past her at the city beyond, and she was sure he was drawing in the background. She knew she mustn't stop now. "I understand why you hate Worthington. How could you ever forgive the old earl and the countess? But it was *their* mistake and it's wrong for innocent people to suffer—"

"They forced my mother into committing a sin—at least she believed it was a sin. Mam apologized to me. She said she was already damned forever. She said she was better dead than alive to poison us. Don't you see I can't forgive that? *Goddamn* them. I hope there is a damn curse."

Julia jumped at his rage. She almost fell off the stool. "A sin? I don't understand—"

"It was my fault, don't you see? My fault... Christ." He threw the palette to the floor.

She was shocked. His head was bowed. His shoulders were tense, his hands fisted. She got off the stool. "Whatever it was, whatever this sin was, it was not your fault."

"It was. It— Damn, you don't know."

She kept trying to reassure him.

Tears glittered in his eyes and she thought of a fourteen-year-old, too late to save his mother, blaming himself for her death. It was so wrong.

"Maybe you are right," she whispered. "Maybe Worthington has been poisoned by pride and arrogance. If there was a way to ensure the people who live on the estate are safe, I guess I would say—destroy it."

"Julia—"

She jumped off the stool, hurried to him. She kissed him. A passionate kiss.

He pulled away, cupping her face. Then he groaned with such frustration and pain, she felt it shiver down her spine.

Cal braced his hand against the top of the canvas. He tossed the pencil to the small ornate table beside him. "I'm going crazy, Julia. Crazy with wanting you." His blue eyes blazed at her. "You're the real reason I wouldn't marry Alice. I thought I loved her—until I met you." He kissed her again, trailed kisses down her neck and she was turning to steam.

She should stop him. She was still a lady. Years of training told her that she must not do this. She had been taught five words: *wait until your wedding night.*

But she wanted Cal.

His arms went around her and he swept her up off her

feet. He lifted her so high that an instinct kicked in and she wrapped her legs around his hips so she didn't fall.

She didn't want him to stop and she knew, with a lady's intuition, that they were perilously close to the point she *must* stop him.

His lips trailed over her jawline. Teasing sensations made her whimper.

His mouth skimmed down, and he eased the straps down her shoulder—the straps of her dress and her brassiere.

She knew he would kiss her nipple. He couldn't—he mustn't—but she ached for it. Her nipple puckered and poked against the firm fabric of her lingerie. Her back arched, lifting her bosom toward him. His lips trailed over her skin, above the lacy trimming of her undergarment.

Julia never dreamed she would physically hurt with the wanting.

His hand cupped the top of her thigh and she gasped. She'd never had anyone touch her so close to her private place. His rough palm slid up her bare thigh, above her rolled-down stockings. Oh, the touch of fingers on her skin—

He pulled something out of the back waistband of his trousers. His paintbrush. A clean one. He brushed the soft bristles across her lower lip. Then down, across her collarbones, into the low neckline of her dress to caress the swells of her breasts held up by her brassiere.

With his paintbrush he teased her all over. He drew up the skirt of her dress, revealing her girdle and her panties. Up went the brush, making her tremble. The soft bristles tickled her inner thighs.

She moaned with the sheer need.

Cal got onto his knees in front of her. He took hold of her girdle, unfastened it and drew it down. She stared at him, but she didn't want to stop. Then she stood in front of him

SHARON PAGE

in her filmy underpants. He leaned forward and kissed her. There, right between her legs, against her silk undies.

She almost died of shock.

He swept her up into his arms and carried her easily to the bedroom. Julia gasped as she saw the huge ornate bed, festooned with silk and gilt, and large enough to fit the entire court of Louis XIV on top of it.

She wanted Cal. But this was disaster. Every lady knew that. Panic took her. Panic she couldn't stop or control. "No!"

He set her down on her feet.

"I *can't*. I want to, but I don't dare. I know you have no intention of marrying me. I desire you like I have never desired any other man. But I can't have a love affair."

Cal panted hard, his brain full of hot desire. One promise would be all it took. One question.

He'd come to Worthington full of rage. Being in Paris with Julia had been the sweetest time of his life. He'd loved seeing her delight, her shock. She made him laugh, made his heart glow. She made him want something more than anger and revenge.

He wanted to laugh with her, make love to her. Wanted to watch her eyes go wide and flash with pleasure when she came beneath him. Or on top of him. He was more than happy to bow to a woman's desire for equal control in sex.

He wanted it so much his every breath hurt.

"I won't ruin you, Julia. I wouldn't do that to you."

Yet even as he made that promise, he knew he needed her. "I was thinking of asking you to marry me."

"Just so you could sleep with me? Cal, that's a terrible reason."

He laughed; a raw, hoarse laugh from deep inside him. She had no idea what a damn hellish thing he was doing—

proposing to her when she didn't know the truth about him. "A better reason than an aristocratic one like marrying you to get your dowry or a tract of land. At least marrying you for lust would be all about you, doll."

"That is rid—" She broke off. "I suppose it is true. But it's not a very wise reason."

He stroked her hair "Marrying me would be a dangerous thing for you. I wouldn't accept separate bedrooms and discreet visits for the purpose of making an heir." He didn't know what he was doing—trying to scare her into saying no? To ease his conscience. When he ached for her.

"I don't believe that is what I want."

He took her hand, led her to the bed. He sat on the end of it, pulling her with him. He pulled her onto his lap. Felt her rounded bottom settle on him, smelled her light rosy perfume, gazed at her perfect profile. And something happened to him. He threw aside any noble part of him.

"I'd want to take you around the world while I paint," he said, keeping his voice low and seductive. "I'd want to sleep under a lean-to with you in the north, cuddled tight together against the cold of frost."

She caught her breath. And he was holding his. Expecting her to turn him down flat. Giving her every reason why she shouldn't want him—except the real one.

"I wouldn't mind that," she breathed. "Being with you—every moment I've spent with you—has made me see there's something I couldn't live without in marriage."

"What's that?" he asked, all innocence, even as he trailed his lips down her neck, then nipped the very base of it.

She moaned and he felt a jolt of lust and pain. "What can't you live without?" he asked again.

"Passion," she squeaked.

The way she said it, all wrapped up in ladylike nerves,

only served to make him want her more. Wanting her was a feeling more powerful than the beat of his heart.

"You could marry me," he said, "if you were willing to live a nomadic life with me."

"But I want you to find a home. To build a family and be happy. What if there are children? They can't live in a tent or be taken all over the world."

"Worthington will never be my home."

"I haven't changed you at all, have I?" she asked softly. "It's not you selling Worthington that frightens me now. Doing so will not give you peace from the past or change anything that happened. It won't make your past go away. It won't heal your pain."

"If I gave you the choice, Julia, would you choose Worthington over me?"

"It doesn't have to be a choice."

"Yes." His voice was cool and low. "It does."

"No, it doesn't." She moved away from him.

"If you don't marry me, I'd sell the damn place in a heart-beat."

Her eyes went wide. "You can't blackmail me into mar-riage."

"I can."

"No, you cannot. This is a mistake. A terrible mistake." She jumped off the bed to her feet. "I'm going back to my room." She pushed her skirt back down so it covered her thighs. Hiking up her straps, she hurried to the door. Cal followed her and saw her snatch up her girdle. He almost smiled as she clutched it to her chest and ran out into the hall.

He stalked over to the champagne bottle in the bucket. The hell with a glass. He lifted it to his lips and drank straight from the fancy bottle.

He knew loss and he knew pain. He'd lost his father and

mother. Both deaths—in a way—had been his fault. He had witnessed hell in the War. He'd seen David wounded. He knew what it was like to have your heart broken by grief and pain.

But right now, it felt like his heart had shattered. Into pieces too small to ever fix.

He couldn't lose Julia.

Every moment he'd spent with her flashed before his eyes, like a moving picture. The first night he saw her on the terrace, sparkling as if all the stars in the world surrounded her. Her determined vow to make him love Worthington. Her glowing smiles for young Ben. Her strength when she helped Ellen. How she'd gamely herded the pigs.

He loved her. More deeply, more intensely than he'd loved anyone.

He shouldn't marry her. Not a girl like Julia. He had no right to her, but he was going to make her his. And he would sell his soul to do it—that's what Mam would say, wasn't it? That keeping the truth from Julia was as good as lying to her. Marrying her that way had to be a sin.

Julia knew a lady should probably throw herself on the bed and cry. But she jumped on her bed and pummeled it with her fists.

Inside, she was all wound up. And all mixed-up. Had he seriously offered marriage—or was it a joke? Or was he just trying to get her into his bed?

A knock sounded at her door. "Julia, it's Cal. I want to ask you to marry me. Seriously this time. Honest."

His words answered her unspoken question so clearly, it stunned her. Sometimes she'd imagined a proposal from Cal—imaginings she wouldn't even admit to herself. She never dreamed she would feel as if walking across clouds to receive it. As if she could fly, as if she were lighter than air, but tentative and full of nerves, too.

The instant she opened her door, Cal dropped down on one knee and took her hand. "You've changed me, Julia. I know Worthington means so much to you. You don't know how much it touched me to have you say you agreed with me—that maybe the place is poisoned and should be destroyed."

She was about to speak, but he rushed on. "Julia, I'd rather live with you at Worthington than live in pain and anger for the rest of my life. I need you. A life without you would be too empty for me to bear. I love you. You've changed me because I love you. Would you do me the honor of marrying me?"

"I *didn't* change you," she whispered. Her throat was so tight. "You've always been a loyal, loving, good man. I know that from everything you have done for your brother, for Ellen and the Brands."

Cal got to his feet. What did it mean when a man got off his knee during a proposal, before she'd answered? Had she ruined the moment? Julia struggled to find a rule of polite behavior to deal with such a thing—

He drew her out to the terrace, holding her hand. He walked with her to the railing. Lights sparkled all around her, streamed up the Eiffel Tower and shimmered at the dizzying top.

"In front of all Paris, Julia, tell me—do you care for me enough to marry me?"

She sucked in a breath. She saw the vulnerability in his eyes. The hope.

"You're the most wonderful woman I've ever met," he said softly. "You're ladylike and elegant—"

"I thought you didn't like such things."

"I adore them about you. But you also have all the kindness my mother always had. You truly care about people. You are too good for me. I've no right to ask you to become my wife—"

"Stop that. I love you—" She hesitated. "And you are really willing to keep Worthington?"

"Yes, Julia."

"Then, yes, I will marry you. Yes! Very much yes! But we should be modern about this. Are you, Cal Carstairs, willing to become my husband?"

He grinned, dazzling her. "With all my heart, Julia."

19

Wedding at Worthington

"Silly twit. I'm right worried about her," Hannah muttered as she worked on the preparations for the wedding feast. Tansy had vanished again, just when Hannah desperately needed her help. The food for the earl's wedding must be perfect.

"Worried about whom?" Eustace the footman asked. He was clearing the luncheon dishes, bringing them down from upstairs.

"I'm just wondering where Tansy has got herself to."

"Maybe she's lying down. She's kind of delicate," Eustace said.

"She's kind of lazy," Hannah said sourly. "I expect she's snuck out to see that man."

At first Eustace had looked affronted by her comment, then he looked panicked. "What man?" He was in love with Tansy—that was written all over his face. But Tansy didn't even know the poor lad was alive.

If it were Hannah that he admired, she'd be thrilled. And she hated the way flighty Tansy was making her growl and snap—everyone thought it was her new position going to her head. But she had so much responsibility, and no one seemed to understand.

She hated to break Eustace's heart. And she knew he wouldn't thank her for giving him the truth, but she was tired of covering up. She was also scared. "Tansy is chasing after a toff who takes her for rides in his motorcar. It will end badly. I just know it."

"What do you mean?"

"He'll seduce her, use her and then leave her hanging."

"But Tansy's lovely and any man could fall in love with her."

Hannah wished it would all work out for the best. But she had a country-bred mother—the sort who always saw disasters and dangers looming. She sighed. "Anyway, I have bigger problems to worry about. I have to make a wedding cake and I have no idea what to do!"

"Don't you just bake it?"

Hannah shook her head. "Wedding cakes are fashionable, so I must make something grand and dazzling. I tried one already and—" She went to the larder and took out her first attempt. She'd found some little decorative columns stored away in the kitchen and she'd used them to stack two layers of cake. The upper one had crushed the columns right through the lower one.

Eustace frowned. "You can't stack something on a cake. Of course it won't hold it up."

"Then how do they do it?"

"I don't know. You're the cook. Can't you read a book?"

Hannah bit her lip. She could read a little, but she hadn't found any recipes for wedding cakes. And she couldn't really read most of the recipe books that Mrs. Feathers had kept.

If she failed at this, she would be out on her rump. What was she going to do?

"Mrs. Talbot? May I speak to you for a moment?"

Hannah jerked her head up. She gazed into concerned blue eyes and gasped, "My lady, I didn't see you there. Of course you can speak with me." She bobbed a quick curtsy to lovely Lady Julia of Brideswell Abbey, the woman about to become Countess of Worthington.

"I wished to speak to you about the menu for the wedding reception, Mrs. Talbot. I wish to know if you can cope. Do you need extra help?"

Oh God, her soon-to-be mistress doubted she could do it. "Of course I can, my lady," Hannah said defensively. "You've nothing to worry about." She thought of the horrible squashed cake. Her cheeks got hot. She swallowed hard.

"How many kitchen maids do you have?"

Hannah saw Lady Julia was not going to be easily bamboozled. "There's two." Did she defend Tansy? Did she reveal the truth—that she was trying to do most of the work herself? She hated to admit that she couldn't control Tansy. That she gave orders and Tansy did whatever she wanted. She might get the sack for Tansy's disobedience.

Lady Julia looked over to Pru, the new kitchen maid, who was scrubbing the breakfast pots. "You seem to have only one helper today. Where is the other maid?"

Hannah gulped. Why risk her job for Tansy? But she couldn't bring herself to tattle. Tansy would be fired without a character. She wouldn't do that to her worst enemy.

"I think she's under the weather," Hannah began.

Then they all heard feminine squealing and Tansy rushed into the kitchen. She called over her shoulder, "You can be a naughty thing, can't you, Stephen?"

The first footman came in, grinning. He saw Lady Julia and froze. Eustace glowered at Stephen.

"Hurry up and get to work, Tansy," Hannah snapped.

"There's to be no fooling around in my kitchen." She tried to sound as forceful as Mrs. Feathers. Especially in front of her future mistress. She just wasn't good at it and she feared Lady Julia would think her inadequate. "You don't want her ladyship to think we will let her down over the wedding meal," she said briskly.

Tansy gushed over Lady Julia, giving all kinds of promises. Tansy could lay it on thicker and gooier than treacle when she wanted. Then, Hannah almost fainted in shock when Tansy said, "Everything will be just perfect, my lady. Except for the wedding cake. Hannah has no idea how to make a wedding cake."

"That's not true," Hannah declared, panicking.

Lady Julia lifted a brow. "Could we speak privately, Mrs. Talbot?"

Hannah saw Tansy's tiny smirk as she followed her ladyship. And she knew—Tansy wanted to become cook.

They went into the housekeeper's sitting room, which was empty. Hannah was impressed—her ladyship was sparing her embarrassment—but also terrified.

Lady Julia closed the door quietly, then said, "A wedding cake is a very difficult thing. We could have it made in London."

And she'd look like a failure. "I can do it, my lady."

"Have you ever made one before?"

"I—" She could lie, but she'd be caught. She shook her head. "No. I have no idea how to make a wedding cake." She winced. "Are you going to tell his lordship to let me go?"

"Of course not." Lady Julia tapped her finger against her chin. "What we must do is find someone to teach you. We have a few days yet. Perhaps we can find a chef in London to assist you. That way, you will learn how to do it."

"But, my lady—" She broke off. No doubt she would lose her place—to the chef!

"What is it, Mrs. Talbot?"

"I feel I've failed you."

"You have not. But I will be disappointed if you do not take this opportunity."

"You'd be disappointed if I don't let him help me?" She didn't understand.

"I want you to learn. I don't expect you to magically know how to do things."

"I will learn, my lady," Hannah said quickly. If she wasn't so afraid, she'd be over the moon to be getting lessons. But she was a simple girl from a simple family. What if she couldn't learn how to make a fancy cake? What then?

It was the morning of her wedding and she was in her wedding gown.

Julia took a deep breath and turned in front of her mirror. The white silk dress skimmed over her breasts and hips to a dropped waist accented with a band of pearls. The skirt flowed to midcalf, so it showed off quite a bit of her legs in silk stockings. An overskirt of tulle billowed behind her, tumbling over her train of satin. Light and airy, the dress seemed to float on its own and she felt as though if she lifted her arms, she'd take flight.

After all, she was floating on air. Though trembling with anticipation.

"There, my lady."

Zoe's maid, Callie, sat back on her heels, and let out a big puff of breath. She'd had to fix a small tear in the hem and she'd done it quickly but admitted, "It's not as well done as I'd like, my lady. But it will last for today."

"It's wonderful." Julia was grateful and did think it was wonderful. "You've done miracles."

"Thank you, milady," Callie said.

After all, with help from one of the upstairs maids, Callie had managed to dress Isobel and Zoe, and then she had tackled Julia's wedding gown. It had been made in London, rushed to be prepared in days because Cal had wanted to marry quickly.

She didn't understand why, but after they'd returned from Paris, she'd barely seen Cal. He went out all day in his motorcar, touring around the estate. He had been invited for several dinners at Brideswell and she saw him then, but in the crowded dining room and drawing rooms. He had never tried to get her alone. He had spent more time with Nigel than with her—he'd gone to Nigel not to ask permission but to say they were getting married.

If Cal was trying to build anticipation...well, she was ready to explode.

But strangely it was as if he was avoiding her. Nerves? What was he doing? She was going to marry him. She should trust him. She knew it was wrong to doubt, to wonder: Was he breaking apart Worthington and not telling her?

Julia took a deep breath. She would not think of things like that.

Callie fussed a bit with her hair. Then said, worriedly, "But we don't yet have something old, something new, something borrowed and something blue."

Zoe breezed into her bedroom. She wore a beautiful dress of white and blue that set off her golden hair. "Oh my gosh, you look beautiful." Zoe laughed, brushed a tear and embraced her.

"Oh dear." Julia broke from the hug, laughing too and waving her hands. "You'll make me cry."

Callie held a mass of tulle. "It's time for your veil, my lady."

Zoe stepped back. Julia turned to face the mirror and stood utterly still as Callie secured the veil and diamond-encrusted circlet in place. Grandmama had worn it for her wedding and while it was old-fashioned and Victorian, Julia had been touched when her grandmother gave it to her to use. It was her borrowed item.

Grandmama had done nothing more than raise a brow and say, "Oh, you're marrying the *American*. I can't say I'm surprised. But I can't say I approve, my dear. You barely know him—and while I grew up in a time when it was best to know as little as possible about one's husband when marrying him, I fear it will cause trouble between you."

Julia had smiled. "I intend to find out everything about him now, Grandmama."

"You'll only learn as much as he wants you to know," the dowager had replied. "At least until you fight. Then you'll learn everything."

"There, my lady," Callie said, bringing her back to the present as she smoothed the tulle.

Zoe sat on the edge of the bed. "Now that you're leaving Brideswell, you'll need a lady's maid."

Julia jerked up her head. "I hadn't thought of that."

"You hadn't? Julia, you always think of everything when it comes to running a household."

"I know, but since coming back from Paris, all I could think of was Cal. Being in b— I mean, marrying him. I suppose I will have to advertise. And quickly."

"It is a shame there is no one local who could do it. That makes it so much faster. You'll need someone responsible, someone with excellent sewing skills, someone you can trust."

Julia's heart soared. "Of course. Ellen Lambert."

"The woman with the small boy? The one who—"

"That one."

"Do you really see her working as a lady's maid at Worthington?"

"Zoe, you are an American. You can't turn snobbish on me now."

Zoe waved her hand. "Lots of Americans are terrible snobs. We're worse than the English because we don't have our social structure all laid out." Then Zoe winked. "But I agree with you—it would be perfect. I just wanted you to know you'll have to fight prejudice to do this. Not from me—from other people."

"I'm willing to fight. Ellen needs a second chance. This would give her references. And Ben loves Worthington," Julia said. "It's perfect."

This whole day would be perfect. Diana was to be her maid of honor and would go to Switzerland after the wedding. Cal had wanted her to go on from Paris with the companion, but Diana had pleaded to come back for the wedding. Cal relented to make Diana happy. Sebastian had come home to England to pursue Captain Ransome.

Julia smoothed down her skirts, aware of Zoe gazing at her thoughtfully.

"What?" she asked.

"You left for Paris determined to strike out on your own. You came back engaged to Cal—and ready to be mistress of Worthington Park. How did he convince you to give up your plan?"

Julia frowned. She hadn't really thought about "giving up" anything. "He proposed—and I realized I wanted to marry him. I realized this is where I belong."

"Callie, would you check on Lady Isobel?" Zoe said. Then

when they were alone, Zoe stood and clasped her hands. "You went with him to Paris and came back engaged. You aren't marrying him because you think you have to, are you? Because something happened in Paris?"

"Something came very close to happening in Paris, but didn't quite."

Zoe looked grave. "You don't have to marry him just because you want to make love with him. He's bold, wild, and he's angry—and brooding anger is gosh-darn sexy in some men."

"There's more to Cal than just that," Julia declared. "That's why I love him. And why I'm marrying him."

"That's good enough for me." Zoe pulled out a handkerchief. "Now I'm going to cry. Because when I first came to Brideswell, I wanted to see you become happy. And here you are—about to be happy for the rest of your life."

Julia hugged Zoe and together they left her room. She took one last look—this was not to be her room any longer. Then she walked down the hall.

Did all brides feel this strange mixture of emotion—half anticipation and half poignant sorrow at leaving their homes?

Here was the little niche in the wall where she used to hide and jump out at Nigel to scare him. Here was the landing where she and Sebastian had dropped peas onto the heads of guests—they'd gotten in enormous trouble for that.

She was going to Worthington, which was full of memories, too. But she was going to make new memories. New and happy ones with Cal.

She'd reached the top of the stairs when her mother caught up to her. Zoe was ahead on the stairs.

Mother looked nervy and pale and Julia worried, until mother said, "Now I must tell you what you must expect for your wifely duties."

"Oh no," she said hastily. "Don't worry. I know what to expect."

"You know?" Mother gasped. "Has the earl compromised you? He seemed so gentlemanly."

Julia was rather delighted Mother thought so. And Cal, for all his insistence he wasn't a gentleman, had always been one with her. He had kissed her with her skirt up…but he'd still been quite a gentleman. "I haven't done anything. But I have an idea what is involved."

"Well…it is the most intimate you will ever be with another person," her mother said.

"It's not necessary for you to explain, Mother—"

"It can be the most wonderful thing—shocking but special," her mother continued, regardless. "Or it can be the most dreadful thing. I shall not say more. I just want you to be happy, but I have no advice to give you about a happy marriage, I fear."

"I will be happy. I don't need advice. It is just wonderful to know you want me to be happy and that you are here."

"I am always here for you. I was so sad for such a long time. Your husband-to-be said you feel you failed me because I was grieving for so long."

"Cal told you that?" Julia was shocked. She'd never said that to him.

"He came to my little chapel to introduce himself. I had no idea, Julia. My unhappiness was not your fault. I am sorry my pain pushed you away."

Julia felt her mother kiss her forehead and her heart wanted to break. Tears came, but they were happy ones. "I love you, Mother," she whispered.

"Now we must get to the church or your groom will think you're not coming."

She hadn't heard Mother be joking and firm for ages. It

made her so happy, even as she scrambled to gather up her train and hurry downstairs to where Nigel waited in the foyer. Her mother was going to follow in a second car with Zoe and Isobel.

Nigel smiled. "You are so beautiful." But he scrubbed his hand over his jaw. "You are marrying Cal for love, aren't you, Julia? I wouldn't accept this union for any other reason."

"Nigel, only you could drive me mad and touch my heart in one statement. It would not matter if I had your acceptance or not. But I am moved that you want me to marry for love. It shows that marriage to Zoe has been the making of you."

He cleared his throat. "I can see many good traits in Worthington. But I cannot see what you have in common with him. People are often attracted to opposites, but it might not be the strongest foundation for a marriage—"

"I think we have many things in common—he cares about people as I do. I also love him for all the things about him that are different. Cal put a paintbrush in my hand and showed me how thrilling it is to paint. He showed me Paris. Each time I am with him, I feel like I am having a whole new world unfurled for me."

"I was worried you were marrying him for Worthington Park."

"That's ridiculous. Nigel, I am marrying him for love."

"Julia!" Sebastian waved from the top of the stairs, ran down and jumped the last four steps.

His jaw dropped as he saw her. "You look like a star plucked from the heavens and brought to earth. That Earl of Worthington is an attractive man. Full of sex appeal, I have to say. But will he make you happy?"

"Not you, too! Nigel has already been through this with me. I *know* Cal will make me happy"

Sebastian pouted. "We love you and are doing our protective brotherly duty."

"And I love both of you for it," she said, and hugged them both.

Cal stood at the altar. How had he got here—to a four-hundred-year-old church in the English countryside, a title attached to his damn name and a beautiful English lady about to marry him innocently, without knowing the truth about him?

He could give her the whole world—could give her anything she wanted.

But without Worthington Park, he knew he wouldn't be enough for her.

A week ago, he'd been in the study of the Duke of Langford, telling the man he intended to marry Julia. Langford had asked about his past and Cal had said bluntly, "I grew up in a seedy tenement in Hell's Kitchen. My father was working as a rag-and-bone man and was murdered on the street, likely by members of a gang. My mother was beaten to death. And if that hadn't killed her, she would have worked herself to death, because she worked so hard to support my brother and me. So that's my inglorious past. I've got an earl's blood in me, but you would never know it."

He'd said it carelessly, casually, making it sound like the whole truth. But he'd left out a few important things.

Langford had studied him. "Julia told me that you had devised a plan of revenge when you learned you had inherited Worthington Park. She told me what she has done to make you change your mind."

And Cal knew, then, he'd carried off the bluff. "She tried to make me love Worthington Park with the same passion and fire as she does," he'd said.

"She believes you intend to keep the estate intact and live there. But I understood that you agreed because if you'd said no, she wouldn't have married you," the duke had said. "I want you to understand something, Cal. Worthington was a second home to her when she was growing up. A refuge from our parents' unhappy marriage. It represents her first great love in Anthony Carstairs. It would destroy Julia to watch it go, especially if she was mistress of it."

"I know how much it means to her."

"It would destroy her if you went back on your word. It would destroy your marriage. I'd be damn tempted to destroy you," Langford had said.

Cal respected a man who was direct. "I love her and would never hurt her. I know what the estate means to her."

"Good. Then you have my blessing."

He knew he didn't need approval. He and Julia were both adults. But what surprised him—scared him—was that he wanted Langford's approval. Langford, he'd learned, was a man who helped his tenants. Who, since his marriage, embraced new technologies and industries. Langford was a duke born and bred, but one who apparently enjoyed tinkering on airplane engines with his wife. For a moment, Cal had thought: *I'd like to be worthy of the approval...*

But if Langford knew the truth, he wouldn't have let Julia within a mile of Cal.

"You okay, Cal?" David's voice, at his side, brought him back to the present—to the interior of the church, filled with women wearing fancy hats, and men in funny coats with tails. Morning coats, they were called. Like the one Langford had insisted Cal had to wear.

David was his best man. To Cal's surprise, his cousins had thought that idea brilliant. Thalia had added flowers to his brother's chair, and David had been happy to let her do it.

He couldn't tell David why he was so damn nervous. That guilt had kept him away from Julia for the past few days. But before he could give his brother a lie for an answer, the wedding march burst out, soaring in the church. Sunlight filled the arched doorway like a curtain of gold. Into all that gold stepped Julia, her arm linked with her brother's. Right then, Cal didn't give a damn about their differences. Or that he'd lied to her. It was worth it for this moment. To know she was coming down the aisle to him.

Even down the length of the aisle, she glowed with happiness. Her lips parted and her tongue swept them.

His knees almost buckled.

Love didn't conquer all. He knew that. His parents had loved each other but poverty, fear and violence had destroyed them. But he was still going into this marriage hoping that he could make love—and lust—work for him. Hoping he could keep Julia happy and keep her from learning the truth about him.

Then she was there, at his side, and her brilliant smile was for him. Her radiance almost knocked him on his heels. Flowers and people filled the church, but the only thing that existed for him was Julia.

He was supposed to take her hand. He did it gently. The significance of it almost floored him. They were to go through life hand-in-hand now.

They'd practiced the vows but now he couldn't remember a word. Somehow he managed to repeat the words after the reverend, so dazzled by Julia that he forgot each one as it came out.

"I do," he said. In his head, he thought, guiltily: *I do agree to lie to you, to keep my past hidden from you because I want you so much.*

Clearing his throat, the reverend read Julia's vows. She

got through his name—Calvin Urqhart Patrick Carstairs—
without even a look of surprise. She recited each word with
clear precision.

Then the reverend reached the words "to love, honor
and…" and the man hesitated. Cal heard a hushed gasp ripple
over the assembly. There was something going on.

Or maybe the reverend could see Julia had changed her
mind… Maybe she'd found out the truth and she'd let him
cling to a dream until this point, when she'd confront him
over his past, over what he'd done, tell him she didn't love
him…she hated him—

No, the man kept going.

Then they got to the question that really mattered. Cal
couldn't breathe. No man, he realized, knew for sure what
his bride was going to say until those two words came out.

"I do," Julia said, her lovely voice rising in the sunlight-
filled church.

The usual stuff came next. About any man who knew of a
reason why they should not be joined, etc. He was the only
one who knew of a reason and he kept his peace.

"You may now kiss the bride."

One kiss and it was official. Lady Julia Hazelton was his.

She gasped as he lifted her off her feet into his kiss. His lips
caressed hers. A surge of desire—the most damned inappropriate thing—swelled in him. He almost let her go in case
a bolt of heaven-sent lightning fried him to a crisp because
he was lusting in church. Mam would have been shocked.
But after all, he was bad.

He broke away from the kiss. He wanted to paint Julia
at this moment and capture the flush of her ivory cheeks,
the sheer radiance of her. He had two unfinished paintings
of her. Now he had a lifetime with her to complete them.

But first, he wanted to carry her off to bed.

"Now, we have to sign the marriage registry. Then we are to go outside," she reminded him. She tightened the link of their hands. "I want to make you happy, Cal."

He wanted to believe it. But in his gut, he knew what she meant: *I want to make you happy to be an earl, to be a gentleman, to have Worthington Park.*

A slow grin lifted his mouth. "Remember I want to make you happy, too."

He swept her into his arms and he kissed her again, even though they were supposed to be leaving the church. His desire felt like what happened when you tossed airplane fuel on a bonfire.

Minutes later, he was signing the names he'd hated—Carstairs and Worthington—to a paper that was intended to represent the happiest moment of his life.

It stunned him to realize those names didn't represent the old earl to him anymore. It felt like they represented him. He was so stunned Julia had to lead him out of the church.

Rice showered them. People rushed forward with hugs, kisses, congratulations. Flashbulbs popped. A photographer with a camera mounted on a tripod took photos of Julia and him, then commanded, cheerfully, "Now the family of the Earl of Worthington. All together."

Cal grasped the handles of David's chair and wheeled him. Diana and her sisters took their places. Then, Cal offered his arm to the countess. In a low voice he said, "The dower house is ready for you to move, whenever you want, like I promised."

"Thank you," she whispered. "I shall go this afternoon. I am ready to go."

He caught Julia looking at him with surprise. Then she smiled again and he saw the hope in her eyes.

When he'd told the countess he was marrying Julia, he'd

asked her about her sons and the three missing women. She had insisted Anthony had looked at no one but Julia, and that John was too young for driving motorcars and flirting with women. Then she'd apologized, profusely, for not helping his mother. She'd broken down in tears. He'd tried to harden his heart, but Julia had gotten to him.

He was tired of hatred, tired of anger. That fantasy of a happy home—it had wrapped around his heart, and that afternoon, he'd made peace with the countess.

Glowing, Julia brought her brothers, her sister and Zoe over for photographs. Then she fetched her frail-looking mother and her autocratic, tough-looking grandmother.

After the photos were done, Julia tossed the bouquet. A chubby girl tried to push Isobel aside, but his new sister-in-law caught the flowers. Then tossed them quickly away, where young women jumped for them like cats on a mouse.

Ignoring the melee, Isobel came up to him. "I am happy to have you as my brother by marriage."

"I'm happy to have you as a new sister."

Together they looked over to Julia, who stood with her mother and grandmother and chatted with guests.

"Did you like her dress?" Isobel asked. "It's all anyone has talked about since she got back from Paris. What she would wear and how long it should be."

"She was wearing a dress?"

"Of course! She would have looked pretty shocking in the church without one." Then she grinned. "You were teasing."

"Sure I was."

"Did you hear Reverend Wesley pause? He looked at me as if he was going to smite me."

"The reverend can't smite you, Isobel. Only God can do that—and he's not going to do it to innocent young girls."

"You don't know what happened last time, when Nigel got

married. I scratched out the word *obey* in his sermon book. Zoe didn't want to say it, and the reverend wouldn't omit it to please her. So I took it out."

Cal had to laugh.

"I got caught out at the ceremony. Anyway, if a woman has to obey her husband, why shouldn't he also agree to obey her?"

"Maybe because two people can't be masters in one house. It's better if they're equals." But he and Julia could never be that. They were from different worlds.

"I suppose that is true." Isobel frowned. "There's a man standing there, smoking a cigar. I've never seen him before. He looks like one of the pictures in the newspapers of Al Capone."

Cal turned. The man, standing beneath an oak, had his hat pulled low. It was like the feeling of having his fighter plane engine cut out on him. Kerry O'Brien was here. At Worthington. On his wedding day. What the hell—?

"Is he a friend of yours?" Isobel asked. She must have seen the recognition on his face.

His blood felt colder than ice coating a northern lake. "Not exactly. Why don't you go and see how Julia is feeling? Would you do that for me?"

It took some coaxing, but Isobel left him and he went over to O'Brien.

The bastard grinned. "Congratulations, Cal. But I bet your new wife doesn't know where you come from."

Cal didn't answer. Julia knew—but not the things O'Brien could tell her. But he knew to never show fear.

"I need more cash, Cal."

"Or you tell my wife?"

"I figured you might care what she knows about you."

"We had this discussion before. You were supposed to go back to New York."

"I hung around. Then heard you were getting hitched to a real fancy lady. That means things have changed, Cal. You've got something to lose now."

He did. But coolly he said, "I need time to think about it."

"Two days. Or I tell your precious wife everything about you."

"A week, damn it." His heart thundered. If O'Brien did it, he'd lose Julia forever. His hands shook and he fisted them by his side.

The man shrugged. "Okay. But I ain't going nowhere. And don't think you're gonna get me bumped off quietly and buried somewhere. I'm too careful."

O'Brien walked away then, toward the woods and the path that led down to the village.

Cal looked up toward the church. Only Zoe, Nigel and Julia were left, waiting to leave. Julia was going to wonder where in hell he was, why he was not with her. He started walking toward his new wife, when a hand touched his arm. He swung around, ready to slam his fist into O'Brien's mug—

He was face-to-face with piercing black eyes. It was the older woman from the gypsy's encampment. He forced himself to calm down. "Morning, Genevra. Are you coming to our wedding reception?"

Genevra cackled. "'Course not, yer lordship. I wouldn't be welcome at the big house."

"Why not?" he said stubbornly. "You live on the estate like anyone else."

When she laughed again, he said, awkwardly, "If you'd like to take some food, there will be plenty. I could have the cook put together a basket for you to take back to the camp."

"Ye're kind, milord." She was swathed in a black shawl and her eyes were unblinking, like a crow's. "You shouldn't have married her ladyship. You've condemned her to the curse."

"I told you I don't believe in curses. I'm going to take care of Lady Julia."

"It might be your life that's in danger, milord. For what would be a greater tragedy to the new countess than to lose the husband she loves?"

"If you've come to spread fear, you can leave my family alone."

Genevra backed away.

Then he felt like a heel for scaring her. It was O'Brien he was mad at, not Genevra. Suddenly Cal realized when he'd said *family* he hadn't only meant Julia and him. He'd meant his cousins and even the countess. Julia really had gotten under his skin.

"I'm sorry, Genevra," he said. "But I don't like threats."

"There's something you should know, milord. I were out walking yesterday and a fancy motorcar drove past me. Driving it was a man with a fedora pulled low. The girl beside him had blue-black hair."

"Who was the man?"

Genevra shook her head. "I don't know either of them and the man was driving fast. But it was near the road by Miss Lambert's cottage, where a man attacked Lady Julia. And now you've married her." With that, the gypsy turned and ran off.

He scowled, his mind racing at the possibility of the brute still out there, targeting young women.

"Cal?" Julia was walking toward him, puzzlement on her face.

He pushed aside the threats from O'Brien, his own lies and Genevra's warning. This was his first day married to Julia, the only nice girl he'd known. If O'Brien talked, she would be gone, but this day was precious—he wanted this day, and he was committing a sin to have it. He tried to push aside the threats from O'Brien, his own lies and Genevra's warning. But he couldn't help looking at Julia's neatly bobbed, shining blue-black hair.

In the center of a long table, the wedding cake stood.

Hannah had slipped up the servants' stairs. She peeked through the rear doorway into the ballroom. No guests were inside, but footmen rushed in and out and Mr. Wiggins was overseeing.

Biting her lip, she studied the cake.

It was made of octagonal shapes. The wine-soaked fruitcake had been carefully measured, then shaved with a knife to make the shape even. Dowels had been used within to support the structure. Pure white royal icing covered each layer, decorated with fanciful icing shapes that were tinted rose, pale blue and mint green. Edible silver balls reflected the sunlight pouring into the room. The cake stood elevated on pillars, and real white- and cream-colored roses were heaped at the base.

Hannah felt a glow of pride. Mrs. Feathers had always accused her of being clumsy. Obviously she wasn't. She truly had the skill to be a fine cook. She was glad she had made something beautiful for the earl and Lady Julia.

She no longer felt terrible jealousy for Tansy, who was so much prettier than she would ever be and who had Eustace wrapped around her—

A flurry of noise startled Hannah and she stepped back, closing the door until it was open just an inch. She peeped through. The earl's family came in, the young ladies elegant in their hats with feathers and their flowing summer dresses.

Lady Julia's family also walked in, the gentlemen startlingly handsome in tailcoats. Then the earl came in himself with his new bride.

Holding her breath, Hannah watched the new Lady Worthington approach the cake. "Cal, look! It's exquisite."

"It's a work of art, that's for sure," he agreed.

Then, in front of them all, the earl swept his wife into a kiss. A kiss that could have melted all the ice in the icehouse, it was so wonderfully romantic.

20

Wedding Night at Worthington

With Cal at her side, Julia cut into the beautiful wedding cake. Laughter surrounded them, and cheers rang up as she made the first slice. Wishes flowed for their happiness, for a fruitful marriage. A string orchestra played and Cal put his hand on her lower back and led her into a waltz.

She was gloriously in love. It made her heart ache with the sheer joy of it.

Cal danced with her toward the terrace windows. They slipped outside—where they were alone. Cal led her into the shade. He held her hand, fingers entwined with hers. "Suddenly I have good memories of this place."

"I'm so glad." Worthington had been filled with poignant memories for her. The joy of having been in love with Anthony; the sorrow of losing him to the War. For her, those memories were as imbued into the estate as wax was worked into the woodwork. But now this would be the house where she had married. Where she built a future with Cal.

She had saved Worthington. But that mattered far less than the fact Cal must be healing. "I always loved it here."

Her voice wobbled. "But now it seems so much more precious—because I am here with you."

"Julia—no one's ever said anything like that to me before. And I feel like you mean it."

"Of course I do." He was the confident man who painted naked models, yet sometimes he was so vulnerable.

He grinned—more shyly than she'd ever seen. "I can't wait for tonight," he said softly.

Tonight. Their wedding night.

He drew her into his arms. Cal kissed her neck, right at the join with her shoulders. The day was warm, but this set her on fire. She was ready to dissolve...

"We should go back," she said briskly. At least she tried to sound brisk. It came out rather croaky. "The guests will think we've slipped away...to do things."

"We can do things now, Sheba. Any wicked thing you want. I bet you've fantasized but made sure no one ever found out about it. Or do ladies not allow themselves to have erotic fantasies?"

She blushed fiercely. "Don't tease me."

"I'm sorry. Just don't ever forget how much I love you."

"Of course, I won't," she promised. "And Paris opened my eyes to naughty ideas."

He drew in a sharp breath. "We'll go back to the crowd for now," he said, his voice more hoarse. "But tonight I'm going to make you mine."

"I already am yours."

"I want to make sure I can never lose you."

Julia caught her breath. Why would he fear losing her? Because he had lost people he loved? His smile had faded and he led her back to the glass terrace doors.

Later, as she was preparing for bed—for her wedding night!—Julia gazed in her mirror and she hurt for him as she remembered how nervous he'd sounded about losing her. She wanted this night to be special. Perfect. Ellen was behind her, brushing out her hair. "You do not need to do one hundred strokes tonight." Cal, being sweet, had arranged for Ellen and Ben to move into the house that afternoon. His specialist was already helping Ellen, who had told Julia she was having fewer nightmares.

"It's my wedding night. My husband will be here any minute," she added.

Ellen smiled. "And you'll bowl him over, I'm sure. You look lovely, my lady."

Julia gazed at her reflection. Did she? She wore a new nightgown from her trousseau. There was barely anything to it. It looked like what a moving picture star would wear. Silk with tiny straps, a bodice of lace shaped to curve around each breast, so it was almost like having them bare. Although it was pure, pale white, she knew it certainly did not look virginal.

Cal was going to see her in this. And he might want to see her in much less.

"I will go, my lady."

"Wait—"

Ellen stopped. "Yes, my lady?"

She'd realized that once Ellen left her, Cal could come in. Nerves gripped her. But this was the 1920s, not Victorian England. She was supposed to be brave about this.

But that was also what scared her. People talked about sex all the time—women and men. Everyone wanted passion and if it wasn't to be had in marriage, they got it elsewhere. The women in the Parisian nightclub talked openly about sex, but she—she didn't really know anything about it. For all she'd told Mother she did.

"What's wrong, my lady?"

Really, she couldn't stall all night. Or night after night. "Nothing at all. Thank you."

"Yes, my lady," Ellen said, and left.

Once she was alone, Julia got up from the vanity, pulled on her robe and tied it tight. She started to pace. She was in the countess's room. Cal had vowed to hire an army of decorators to change it however she wished. The countess had gone to the dower house on the estate. And now the wedding was over, Diana must soon go to Switzerland to have her baby.

At the wedding reception, the Earl of Summerhay had been a true gentleman about losing her to Cal, wishing them happiness. The Duke of Bradstock, however, had said, "Julia, I am afraid he's going to make you unhappy. He's not one of us. But I will be there for you. I promise. I won't let him break your heart."

"How considerate of you to worry about me," she had said, secretly rolling her eyes.

What was taking Cal so long?

On the other hand, was she ready for him? How did one go from being too ladylike, embarrassed and restrained to even address the subject, to actually doing it in a way that would please a man?

What if this part of their marriage didn't work? Would he stray?

"Stop," she said to her reflection. It was crazy to worry about losing him before they'd even started. She ached for his touch. Didn't that promise it would be wonderful?

The door opened and Cal stepped into her room.

"Oh, er," she said. Eloquently.

He wore a robe of indigo silk, belted at the waist. His feet were bare. His tousled blond hair fell over his brow.

A lady took charge of all situations—she greeted visitors,

knew how to engage in polite conversation, knew how to address the myriad details that went into running a house.

How on earth did one greet a man before getting into bed with him? Julia tried what any social hostess would do—bright and innocuous remarks. "The wedding was lovely, wasn't it?"

"All I needed was to hear you say, 'I do,' doll. The rest of it just got in the way."

"In the way of what?"

"Making love to you."

The intense way he looked at her—all blue eyes and heat—made her feel she was melting. There was such naughtiness in his gaze. She focused on his wrists, of all things. Bare under the sleeves of his robe. He had elegant, long fingers.

"Perhaps we should slip into the bed. Which side would you prefer?" she asked politely.

That ignited one of his naughtiest grins.

He came to her, tipped up her chin, slanted his mouth over hers. His tongue teased hers. He tasted of brandy, but mostly of Cal—the warm, sensuous flavor she knew from kissing him.

He slipped his hand in her robe, cupped her breast through the filmy bodice of her scandalous nightdress.

"Oh," she gasped.

His palm caressed her nipple, then his fingers lightly closed around it. He gently pinched.

"Oh!" It came out much louder.

His fingers did wicked things to her nipple and, through the satin of her nightdress, to the private place between her legs.

She felt the familiar flare of nerves over doing something naughty. But she could now be as wicked with Cal as she wanted to be.

"I want to watch you come, Julia. I want to see you in ecstasy, hear you scream my name."

She stared, not comprehending a thing.

"You're the most beautiful woman in the world, Julia. I used to dream I could escape New York's slums and touch the stars. Holding you in my arms is as magical as touching all the stars in the universe."

Hands trembling, she undid his robe. He murmured, "Yes, Julia," as the dark blue silk parted, revealing his lean body. She'd never seen a whole naked male body. Statues always had fig leaves; illustrations in books had some kind of demure covering added.

She giggled.

Cal stopped kissing her and his hands stopped caressing. "I look funny?"

Oh goodness, he was pouting. "No. You're just so lean and firm. And then there's that part that sticks out. Like a baton. I just didn't know it looked like that." Her cheeks burned.

Cal grinned. "You're more than lovely. You're like a drug I can't get enough of." He opened her robe. She knew it was going to happen but she felt nervous, standing before him in her skimpy gown. His eyes went wide, met hers, glowing a fiery blue. "Julia—you aren't just as lovely as a star, you're the sexiest Sheba I've ever seen."

She blushed. A lady should be shocked to be described so, but she felt a thrill. She moved to close the robe again, but he pushed it off her shoulders. It fell to the floor. Cal lifted her up, her silk skirts spilling over his arms. He carried her to her bed. Then he whisked up the skirt of her nightgown and—to her absolute shock—buried his face between her bare legs, kissing her in that most intimate place.

"Cal! What are you doing?"

He couldn't answer, of course—

Oooh. His tongue moved over her private place, caressing her. This was stunningly wonderful. Julia closed her eyes, too ladylike to look as he did things to her. He tasted her in such an intimate way that she was blushing. He didn't seem to mind. Or be shocked.

Oh!

She'd never dreamed Cal would put his mouth to her sex and would caress her, nibble her. Or that it would feel so good. Julia stretched her arms over her head. Pleasure made her want to moan. She felt so sensuous. So thoroughly feminine.

His hands pressed to her naked bottom, making her gasp as he lifted her.

She opened her eyes and saw Cal's heavy-lidded blue eyes watching her. A bit of blond stubble graced his jaw and cheeks. She couldn't resist—she reached out and rubbed her palm against it. It tickled and the light stab sent a shot of desire right between her legs.

"Oh!"

He was hers now. She could touch him in any way she liked. She couldn't quite believe it.

He bent to her sex again and caressed with his tongue. He flicked a place that sent a bolt of lightning through her.

Pleasure grew and grew. She rocked her hips, driven to satisfy this need building in her. A need that made her hands curl into the bed. That made her moan his name. She'd never known anything like it.

"Ooooah!"

The most unladylike things happened. Her hips launched up and smacked him. Her arms flailed on the bed. She cried out. She was in a maelstrom of pulsing muscles and pleasure.

She reached a peak, almost flying off the bed. It began to loosen its grip and she flopped back to the mattress feeling as if she was floating, as if she weighed nothing at all.

Cal moved up and kissed her. She tasted ripeness and blushed. Perspiration prickled on her and she was panting for breath.

"Good?" he asked.

"The bee's knees. I had no idea. I mean—I've felt desire for you that is so strong it made me rather desperate. But I had no idea it made one feel *this* wonderful."

His grin would have melted icebergs. "Once you've had an explosive climax, Julia, you're driven to seek it again. Now, let me give you another."

Julia looked down and saw he was still erect. "Oh yes. Of course. That is my duty—"

"The hell with duty," he said roughly. He moved over her, naked. His legs were spread to rest on either side of hers. "I just want to make you feel good."

He kissed her and she ached inside. She felt empty and wanted—needed—him to fill her. Was this what she'd been missing all her life? She'd thought dancing wildly to jazz was thrilling, but this was the most special dance of all.

Then he touched the tip of his erection to her most private place. She held her breath. Held his gaze—his vivid blue gaze. The way he looked at her…it was the most intimate thing. She'd never had any man look so deeply into her eyes.

He touched her down there, opening her. Something thick and warm pressed against her. She had never dreamed it would be like this. Primitive. Hot. Sweaty. Earthy and real.

Daringly, she let her hands move over his back. She shivered at the flex of his big, powerful muscles. He was so different than her—broad back and narrow hips. Her hands went down low enough to feel the hard curves of his naked buttocks.

Beautiful. He was so beautiful.

She let her hand drift around his hip. Her fingers brushed

the hair that grew thickly between his legs. It tickled her fingertips.

Then she touched it. The thick shaft of his erection. Her fingers skimmed over velvet skin, the ridges of veins, and touched a soft full shape at the end. Wetness stuck to her fingertips.

Cal groaned. "I like that, Julia." His eyes glowed. "I knew you would be like this. Here, in bed, I knew you wouldn't be ladylike at all."

His fingers touched her as she stroked him. He opened her and she gasped at the flood of wetness he released.

"Do you want me?" he asked.

"So much it hurts." She giggled shyly, but it was true.

The world hadn't stopped this time. It still raced on all around them. But nothing else mattered other than this moment. Nothing except showing Cal how much she truly loved him.

She arched her hips against him. Gasped as his hardness slipped inside a little.

"Let me do it," he murmured. "I'll be gentle."

He was. Slow, gentle, moving himself into her with restrained power. She felt a twinge of pain, dug her fingernails into his bare arms.

He stopped. "Are you okay?"

The pain eased. "I am now."

Then he was inside her. Completely. Deeply. His body lay along hers, touching hers, though he supported his weight on his arms.

"You're so lovely. So hot. Like silk." His words came out jerky. "I can't hold on."

"Hold on to what?" she breathed.

"Sanity," he muttered. He moved inside her, drawing

back. Slowly, he thrust forward again. Sensation exploded in her brain like a band bursting into frantic jazz music.

Over and over, he thrust. She—she liked it. Moans escaped her. She made all kinds of funny little sounds because she had to let them out or she'd explode.

He shifted, so his shaft rubbed the place he'd touched with his mouth—

She squealed. A wave of sheer joy hit her. Her whole body erupted all at once. All her muscles pulsed. Pleasure rushed all over her again.

She clung to him. Felt him go stiff against her. He shuddered. "Julia."

She'd never had her name said like that. As though she was the most powerful thing in the whole world.

His hips moved against her. He was having his pleasure, too. She held him, loving that she could share this with him.

After, Cal rolled off her and wrapped his arms around her. He covered them both with the sheets and counterpane. He kissed the top of her head. "I love you so much. I'm a lucky man."

She closed her eyes. "Not half as lucky as me," she breathed.

He gave a soft laugh. "Oh, Julia. God—" He broke off and kissed her passionately.

Sapped of strength, still delirious with pleasure, she cuddled in his arms.

Just before she fell asleep, she knew she'd found her place in the world.

Julia woke in the morning, cradled by Cal's muscular arm. It was the second most thrilling moment she'd ever known. Most aristocratic couples did not share a bed. After last night, she would not accept anything less.

He stirred at her side. She gazed up at him, and he kissed her forehead gently. "Good morning, my lovely wife."

She giggled. "Good morning, my gorgeous husband." Wild ideas filled her head. She wanted to make love again—but it wasn't nighttime, of course.

"I knew when I broke through that ladylike shell I'd find a woman inside who was all fire and passion. I want you like this always, Julia. I don't want you hiding who you really are anymore. Promise me you'll never hide the fire inside you again."

"Cal, I can't be like this at dinner parties and in the drawing room."

"Sheba, you're not going to have time for dinner parties and drawing rooms. I'm going to keep you in here." Then he looked serious. "Except for today. I have to go out this morning. I have some business to attend to."

That startled her. "You do? What sort of business?"

"Some private business."

She realized he was not going to say any more than that.

"I don't want you to worry your pretty head about things," he said. "That's what I do as your husband. I take care of you. I have to leave right after breakfast. I don't know how long I'll be."

"Pretty head!" She frowned teasingly. "Cal, I expect to share burdens with you as your wife. But you don't know when you will return?"

"No." He hesitated. "I might be out tonight."

"Tonight? But it is the night after our wedding."

"Sorry, Julia. I have to do this. I'll make it up to you. And, Julia, you can't go anywhere on your own. Genevra saw a man in a fancy automobile driving a dark-haired girl on the estate."

She wanted to ask him more, but he was gone then, out of

their shared bed. He wrapped his robe around him, but left his belt untied, as if he didn't want to linger long enough to do it up. He went through the connecting door to his room with the parting words, "See you later."

She didn't quite understand. She thought they were beginning their lives together. Being alone wasn't what she'd planned for the first day after their marriage.

Minutes later, her door opened and her heart leaped with hope he'd changed his mind—

Ellen came in with a tray. She placed it across Julia's hips. A married woman had breakfast in her bed. "His lordship said you were ready for your tray." Ellen poured her a cup of tea. "What will you be doing today, my lady? What clothing should I put out?"

"I will do what I always do. Put out my light tweeds. I suppose I will go and see the various women who have accounts with me. But first I have work to do—review the menus, arrange to meet with the housekeeper."

She knew what it was to be mistress of a great house. This was what her mother and grandmother had groomed her to do. It would not worry them in the least to have their husbands disappear. They would have expected it. She had thought, long ago, she would be mistress of Worthington. And now she was here, in the house she loved, that had been so special to her.

But Julia felt empty. She felt as if a huge part of her would be missing, if Cal was not here.

That was nonsense. She drank her tea. There was so much to be done. She could now fulfill all the plans she and Anthony had made for Worthington.

She should be happy. She had purpose. And much to do.

21

An Automobile Accident

After breakfast, the lady of the house always took care of the business of the house in the morning room. At Worthington Park, the morning room was painted pale lavender, the furnishings in the same pale purple and gilt. A walled garden lay outside its windows, with small paths and fountains and statues of slender Grecian ladies.

Julia took her seat at the desk. For years, she had been prepared for this day. She drew out the day's menu. She telephoned the housekeeper on the house telephone and relayed changes she'd made to the menu. "I have to go out this morning," she said, "but this afternoon we shall review the rooms, the linens and the household accounts."

"Very good, my lady." The housekeeper rang off.

After that, Julia set out in her motorcar. Cal was not here to go with her, but this was her place, her work, and she would not be kept from it.

Her morning spent with the various women of Brideswell and Worthington, the woman who had accounts with her, cheered her immensely. Her loans had started a tea shop in the village and a millinery, had sent a woman for medical training and saved a widow's farm, allowing two war veterans to be employed as farmhands. Julia drove to Lower Dale Farm with treats and books for the children. Everyone congratulated her on her marriage, wished her well.

But as she was walking back to her car at Lower Dale Farm she spotted Genevra.

The elder woman wagged a finger at her. "You be careful, my lady. Now that you're wed, you'll be in danger."

"From the curse? Genevra, I don't believe in such things."

"You'd best heed my warning," the gypsy woman said. "Look out for yourself." With that, she retreated into the woods and disappeared between the fluttering leaves.

Julia did drive back to Worthington very carefully. Foolish to be even a little superstitious, but she was. She left her car outside the garage and started up toward the house.

She was halfway, passing a large grove of leafy laurels, when a branch snapped behind her. She heard a sharp breath drawn from someone who was close to her. She fought panic and turned—

The Duke of Bradstock stood on the path behind her. He wore breeches and a riding jacket of black. His hat was tucked beneath his arm.

"You startled me." But she smiled in great relief. It was no mystery man here to attack her.

"I apologize. I came down from London. Just bought a horse from your brother's stables today. Took my new gelding for a run. I decided to ride over and see you, Julia. I was riding up from the path through the woods when I saw your car. I left my mount at the stables. I wondered if you would care to come for a ride with me this afternoon."

She had not been riding in a long time—since she had ridden with Cal. Athena had been brought to the Worthington stables. "I would love to, James. Just allow me a moment to change."

She did so quickly, eager to ride. Soon, hooves clopped as their horses trotted along a dirt track that wound through a meadow and led to fields. Then James sent his horse racing off. She did the same. He soared over a stone wall. She followed. After taking the jump, she leaned against her horse's extended neck, laughing.

James reined in, brought his horse to a walk, patting the animal's lathered withers. She joined him. His dark eyes glittered. "I guess you do not do this with your American husband."

"Cal does ride, though he is just learning."

"If you yearn for a good gallop, Julia, you need only make a telephone call to me. I'll be more than happy to join you. In fact, I see it as my duty."

"And why would it be your duty to accompany me when I'm riding?" she asked.

"It is my duty to ensure you are not denied the activities an English lady enjoys. I should be more than happy to join you on a ride, take you to London, escort you to the opera. I've heard your husband regularly travels to the wilds of Canada to paint. I assume he will still do it. I think it's a crime for him to leave you alone while he lives in the bush like a savage. It would be a privilege to ensure you are never lonely, my dear."

"James, perhaps I am misinterpreting but I thought this was to be a ride of two friends. You aren't flirting with me, are you?"

"Of course I am."

"But I'm married."

"Married women have love affairs, Julia. I would be an escape from your uncouth husband."

"I love my husband," she protested.

"Rubbish. Your father hoped to marry you to the Earl of Worthington years ago. I can only assume your brother continued the family ambition and pushed you into the marriage."

"He certainly did not. I made my own choice."

"You chose a man who dresses in rags and possesses no manners?"

"He dressed that way deliberately to shock people. In truth, Cal is very gentlemanly."

James scowled. "His ignorance of our rules will frustrate you and his cocky attitude will grow tiresome."

"James, I would never betray my husband. The fact you believe I'm that sort of woman hurts me deeply. I am going to return to the house." She turned Athena around.

But Bradstock had his horse canter beside her, and positioned himself to block her path.

"What about when he's unfaithful to you? Are you going to allow him to paint nude women? He's been notorious for love affairs. Men don't change."

She'd struggled not to blush at the word *nude*. Now she felt her blood turn to ice. "I believe people can change. I've seen evidence of it again and again." Cal *had* changed.

"I'm not giving up, Julia. At some point you will despise that rough diamond you married. And I will be there for you."

"Forget about me, James. Marry someone for love and devote yourself to them."

He reached out and grasped her reins, startling her. Suddenly, his arrogant mask had dropped. She'd never seen him look so vulnerable. "I'm in love with you, Julia. I've been in love with you for a long time. That has never changed. I'm hoping, someday, you might finally see what you've over-looked all these years."

"James—"

"I paid one of those private investigators in New York, a former policeman, to find out something of your husband's past."

"You didn't—"

"I did it for *your* sake. Some of the things I learned about your husband would shock you. He associated with those mobsters involved in prohibition. He's a thug, Julia."

"I don't believe that."

"Ask him about it. I can give you evidence if you want it. The investigator has photographs, statements. Your husband is a rich man, Julia, and he made his fortune illegally in the trade of selling bootleg liquor. Men who crossed him were beaten up. There were men who accused him of being in-volved with murders. He is a ruthless criminal, Julia."

Murders? Assaulting people? How could Cal do that—after what he'd seen happen to his father? Her heart raced, but she hid the cold fear in her veins. "I will talk to Cal about this, James. For now, I think I had better return to the house. Good afternoon." She skirted Athena around him and took off at a gallop. She arrived at the Worthington stable alone— James had not followed her. She supposed she had offended him, but she refused to worry about that.

Cal did not return for dinner.

Julia ate with David and her new cousins by marriage, but she couldn't get James's words out of her mind. David asked where Cal was—so she knew he hadn't confided his plans with his brother. She retired early, her heart pounding. Was Cal really a criminal in America? Had he behaved with vio-lence? Had James made up the awful story?

For her whole life, she'd slept alone in a bed. Now it felt

strange to do it. After just one night sleeping with Cal, she found her bed empty and cold. She turned off the light, rolled on her side.

Her door opened with a soft whisper and Cal walked in. Light spilled in through the connecting door. He wasn't changed for bed—he wore trousers, suspenders and a white undershirt that molded to the muscles in his arms and stretched over his broad chest. "Sorry I had to miss dinner, doll. Let me make it up to you."

She sat up. "Where were you? What was it you had to do?"

She should ask: *Did you really do criminal things in America?* But she couldn't.

Cal didn't answer. Instead, he casually stripped naked. The sight stole any further words out of her mouth. He got on the bed, sitting beside her. He leaned over and kissed her.

Cal didn't just kiss. His hands did the naughtiest things. Caressing her breasts through her nightdress and hiking up the skirt to stroke between her legs.

She should talk to him—but she wanted him too much.

"I've been thinking about this all day," he rasped. "I'm going to make love to you all night."

And he did. She had no idea she could reach her peak so many times. Finally, she was an exhausted puddle on her bed, but he took her one last time, giving her a long, languorous wave of pleasure.

She cried out in sheer joy. Then Cal arched against her, driving his hips tight to hers. He shuddered and gasped her name. "Julia, my love. My beautiful love."

She thought of James's words as Cal slumped against her, but carefully so he didn't press his weight on her. She stroked his damp back, dizzy with pleasure.

And she knew what she was doing. She was afraid to find out the truth.

He rolled off her and she stiffened, expecting him to leave her bed. But he snuggled against her, caressing her shoulder. "What did you do today, love?"

"I went to see the women who have business with me." She wished she could relax under his touch. But she kept *thinking*. The illegal things—that must have been where he'd made the money to stay at Le Meurice.

Cal sat up. Moonlight outlined his wide shoulders and his strong muscled arms with silver. "Alone? Julia, it's not safe."

"I had no other choice."

"Julia, this house is crawling with servants. Take some of them with you. Do that or you can't go."

She blinked. "Cal, this is important to me." It was her place in the world.

"There's something you have to know, Julia. The police sergeant telephoned for me—that's why I missed dinner. I had to go back out, down to the station. Lowry has an alibi for the time you were attacked. He's charged with assaulting Ellen Lambert, but he couldn't have been the man who attacked you."

She stared in shock, but then Cal's strong arms went around her. His lips closed over hers and she couldn't be afraid. Not with him kissing her. Not with him making love to her. And she went to sleep in his arms.

After breakfast, Cal left again. Julia watched him go out to his motorcar from the drawing room window. She'd promised Cal she wouldn't leave the house alone. His words had chilled her. If Lowry hadn't been the man who attacked her, then who was it?

How could it be possible there was a man who had once lured and killed women with dark hair back in 1916, and now, nine years later, was doing it again? She had asked Cal that very question and Cal had given her terrifying answers.

That maybe the man had gone to the War, and had only just returned here. Or maybe innocent women had disappeared in other places over the years and no one knew it was the same man behind them all.

As a new bride, Julia had correspondence to attend to. But she sat, pen in hand, unable to do the duty she'd been trained for. The housekeeper had to telephone her to ask about the menu. Flustered, she made no changes and as she set down the receiver, Wiggins came in.

"There is a—a gentleman caller to see you, your ladyship."

From the sour face on Wiggins, Julia knew the man was not what the butler considered a gentleman. "Did he give his name?"

"His name is O'Brien, my lady. He visited his lordship before. He is an American. I believe they exchanged heated words." Wiggins sniffed. "This gentleman was also seen on the grounds two mornings ago, at the wedding reception, but he did not enter the house as a guest. However, he has insisted on speaking to you. He claims he has something to tell you that you would wish to hear about his lordship."

She frowned. Curiosity ate at her.

"I put him in the library until I could speak to you, my lady. Not one of the finer drawing rooms, however there are still objects that may take his fancy and thus disappear."

"Wiggins, that is most prejudiced."

"He has the look about him of an American criminal, my lady. A 'mobster,' as they are termed in colloquial American. I obtained the impression his lordship is not pleased with this man."

A mobster? Could it be the man arguing with Cal in London? She was even more curious, but pointed out, "Americans speak English."

"Not by my definition, my lady."

She had to smile. But she asked, "Wiggins, before you go—his lordship mentioned a photograph that he found. I believe you destroyed it. Why did you do that?" She watched Wiggins's face carefully. Saw the flicker of fear behind the correct facade.

"I believed it would spare her ladyship—the dowager, now—a great deal of pain, my lady." He bowed. "I must return to the wine cellar, my lady. The delivery will soon arrive."

She watched him go. What did that mean? But if she'd been attacked by the same man, Anthony and John were innocent. There was no reason for Wiggins to protect them, then.

She wanted to speak to this man, find out why Cal had been angry with him. Cal had been mysterious—keeping quiet about where he went, about the business he had to do. Was this man involved? What was going on with Cal?

Cal slowly walked along the lane behind Lilac Farm. Above him, a bird cawed, and a breeze sent tree branches shivering.

He crept along, moving as stealthily as he would have when he'd had to land his plane behind German lines. War had taught him a lot of things about killing and survival— he never expected to use any of that knowledge in the rarified world of the aristocracy.

But he had to use every skill he had to keep Julia safe. Julia had been attacked here. This was where Genevra had seen a man and a dark-haired woman in a car.

If he hadn't been here that morning, that bastard would have pulled Julia into a waiting car—

Christ, he couldn't think about that. He couldn't think about what would have happened if he'd been too late.

He scanned the ground for some kind of clue. Desperate and crazy, likely enough, but he knew a lot of the criminal element wasn't all that smart in covering tracks.

But he kept thinking of Julia. Couldn't stop his thoughts from going to their wedding night. Which got him hot under the collar. He'd had to leave her the day after their wedding. Gone to see O'Brien and warned the gangster not to reveal the truth of his past to Julia. Warned Kerry that he'd get hurt if he did it. But he saw the smirking appraisal in O'Brien's eyes and knew the bastard wouldn't give up so easily. He must figure he had a plum mark in Cal now. He had to know Cal was desperate to keep his wife in the dark about his past. That was the "private business" he'd had to take care of.

He'd intended to keep Julia happy in bed. Never dreamed it would feel like…like he'd gotten a chance to have real heavenly bliss. Making love to Julia had seared him to his soul. It wasn't just sex, it was like a special painting that was more than just a canvas—it was a revelation.

Ahead, Cal spotted the pattern of automobile tires in the dried mud. On the edge, branches were broken down. He walked up to the spot. Someone had parked a car there, hiding it from sight. Why?

Had it been to spy on Julia? Sunlight reflected off something that glinted. Stooping, he picked it up. A button of onyx rimmed in silver. Not likely from the clothing of the laborer who'd grabbed Julia. Nor had a man like that likely had a car.

So who had been there?

Julia hurried to the library, her skirts swishing around her calves, her heels clicking. Cigar smoke floated from the open door. From the doorway, all she could see was the back of the man's head. He lounged on the settee, his arm stretched along the back of it. The electric light gleamed on his hair, slicked down and neatly parted in the middle.

Julia walked in, saying briskly, "Good morning, Mr. O'Brien. I am Julia, Lady Worthington."

The man clamped the cigar between his teeth and held out his hand to her. She recognized him—he was indeed the man Cal had been speaking to in the Black Bottom Club in London.

He shook her hand firmly, startling her. He definitely did have the look of an American mobster. The newssheets carried pictures of famed American criminals such as Al Capone and Charles Luciano. This man was dressed in the same manner—a pinstripe suit, with matching waistcoat, a white hat on the seat beside him.

"Hello, Julia." He grinned, a smug, arrogant grin.

"I would prefer Lady Worthington," she said. That smile had put her back up. "Would you care for tea?"

"Don't mind if I do, Julia."

She could reprimand him over the use of her name again, but she didn't. He exuded edgy nervousness. His gaze flicked all around the library, and he kept grinning until tea came. Then he pulled out a flask and took a long swallow before taking his cup of tea. She noticed the scar running from his ear to his throat. A war wound, perhaps?

"I have to say, Julia, sitting down to tea with you is a lot more pleasant than looking at Cal's mug."

"You are a friend of my husband's, from America?"

"Cal and I go way back." He leaned back. "Grew up together. There ain't nothing I don't know about Cal. I hear he didn't tell you much about his past. There are a lot of stories I could tell you...but Cal wouldn't like that. He wouldn't want me talking about that stuff with his pretty new bride."

She thought of James's words, but she said politely, "I am sure Cal has just not had time to tell me many stories about his youth."

"I don't think he'd like to talk about that to a nice girl like you."

"Mr. O'Brien, I feel you have something you want to say to me."

"I could be willing to give away some of Cal's secrets. For the right price. Wouldn't you want to know all about Cal's dirty past?"

He smirked. A look that made her shiver in apprehension. She was so curious, but she wouldn't give this man the satisfaction of letting him talk. "I am afraid you have made a wasted trip. Cal has been nothing but honest with me." She stood.

"Wouldn't you wanna hear about what he did as a bootlegger? Wouldn't you wanna hear about the Five Points Gang?"

"Mr. O'Brien, I suggest you leave. I shall summon my butler, Wiggins, to escort you to the door. This house can be quite confusing, when one is in a hurry to depart."

She hadn't even reached the bell when two of the Worthington footmen walked in. "Mr. Wiggins sent us to help the gentleman out."

Mr. O'Brien's expression was livid. "There's other people who'd be interested in knowing the real truth about the Earl of Worthington. You tell Cal I said that, Julia. How about that? And tell him I'm staying at the Boar and Castle hotel in the little hick village."

"The public house," she corrected automatically.

He stood, straightened his tie and plopped his hat on his head. "I'll follow the penguins outside. But you give my message to Cal."

She watched him exit the room. After he left, Julia sank

to the chair, shaking. What James had told her—it must be true. It explained why Cal had money. It explained...why he was ashamed of that money.

But Cal had needed money to take care of David. Cal would have been desperate to protect his brother, desperate because of what the earl and countess had done.

She was still in the library, staring out the window, when footsteps stormed into the room. "I've torn a strip off Wiggins. He should have thrown O'Brien out. He should never have let you speak to him—"

"Why not?" She turned around to confront a white-faced, angry Cal. Then she saw dirt was streaked over his face and his hands were covered in mud. She wanted to tackle Cal about his past, but horror filled his eyes. "What have you been doing?"

"Doing my lordly duty and traveling around my estate, greeting my tenants."

She didn't believe him. It was the way he kept his blue-eyed gaze right on her as he said it. "You look exhausted," she said crisply. "I shall ring for tea."

"Julia, what did O'Brien say to you?"

"Very little, since I was not willing to pay him."

"Did he frighten you? Threaten you?"

"Do your friends always behave like that?"

"He's not a friend, Julia. And I need you to tell me the truth."

"He told me he would be willing to give away some of your secrets for the right price. He asked if I would like to know about what he termed your dirty past. Cal, were you a bootlegger? Did you commit...crimes to make money... to support David?"

"O'Brien was trying to con money out of you. I was never arrested for doing anything illegal. He probably figured you'd be shocked to know I was poor. But you know all about that."

She did. They were married and the future was what mattered now. Impetuously, she said, "Cal, whatever was in the past is behind us. We have both had sorrow in the past and I believe we must focus on the future. We'll have tea, then I must go out. I want to bring food for the Tofts."

"Forget tea, Julia. There's something I need to do. Upstairs."

Mystified, she followed Cal up the sweeping stairs to their connecting bedrooms. He closed his bedroom door behind them and turned the key.

"Cal—" She broke off as he lifted her off her feet and into his arms.

"Wrap your legs around my waist, doll."

"Around your waist?"

He set her back on her feet, skimmed her skirt up to bare her legs. She squealed—then prayed it wasn't loud enough to startle the upstairs maids. He lifted her up, put his hand under her round bottom to carry her.

She gasped as her husband balanced her on the marble surface of the vanity table on her bottom. Sensually he kissed her neck, his tongue running along her sensitive skin.

She clung to his shoulders. "Cal, it isn't nighttime."

He laughed, low and gruff. Deeply, he made love to her, rocking her with him as pleasure built. Her nails dug into his broad, strong shoulders. Heavens, she could see them in her mirror, doing this intimate thing.

"I'd like to paint you like this. The way you look when I'm making love to you. You're the most beautiful creation on earth, Julia."

She gasped at the glorious peak. She cried his name, which ended on a moan. Then he cried out her name.

He held her in his powerful arms and she pressed her cheek over his heart. She loved hearing the fast beat, knowing she'd done that to him.

"I'd like to keep you in bed day and night."

She flushed. "Cal, I have things I must do." Then she regretted the prim words.

"I'll go with you." He nibbled her ear as he said it, and she almost melted. "Cal, I have pies for their dinner. I simply can't wait or I'll be too late."

He smoothed down her skirt, held out his hand.

Cal's automobile was still sitting in Worthington's front drive. He walked around to the right-hand side of the car without thinking. Then growled, "Forgot again."

"Could I drive?" she asked, as she went to the driver's door. "I've never driven your motor."

He winked at her, and she blushed. But he tossed her the keys. "Sure," he said.

It was almost as delightful a vehicle as her Trixie. The engine purred and the car clung to every turn, rumbling with the promise of decadent power—if she dared. But on the winding road, she just didn't dare.

They'd crested a hill and were heading down toward the road that led to Lilac Farm. From there, she would turn off to Lower Dale Farm. Like the other roads, this was narrow, winding around rocks, trees, following stone walls that bordered fields.

She pressed the brake pedal but nothing seemed to happen. The car was going fast—too fast.

Cal's hand braced against the mother-of-pearl inlay on the dashboard. "Julia, doll, you have to slow down on this road. You don't have to prove to me you're a fast driver."

She pushed desperately down on the brake pedal. But it simply sank to the floor, with all the resistance of a dry sponge. She released her foot and tried again, pushing it down. Nothing happened. "Cal, I'm not trying to prove anything. The brakes don't work!"

Zoe had taught her how to drive, but she didn't really know how one of these automobiles worked, and right now, she rather wished she did. "I will try again. Harder. So this motorcar knows I mean business."

"Try it, doll. Push down hard."

She did, but the brake simply refused to work.

A stone wall was coming up—one that bordered a farm. The rutted road made a sharp turn in front of it. What if she couldn't make the turn? They'd crash. Cal, in the passenger seat, would be plowed into the stone wall. The motorcar was filled with fuel. Could it explode?

She had to make this corner.

Julia held her breath and stiffened like a board. She thought she'd known fear before. It was nothing like this. She couldn't even feel her heartbeat—which might mean it had stopped.

Cal reached over her and planted his hand on the wheel. "Hang on to it. I'll help you steer."

Even from the passenger side, he was steering with aplomb.

But they were hurtling toward the wall at the bottom of this hill.

"Stay calm, Julia. We can stop this car. I want you to downshift to a lower gear. But do it slowly. I'm going to steer to the side here and use the rougher grass to slow us down."

He moved the wheel firmly and the car rattled toward the edge of the track. She felt the jerk as the wheels left the firm track of the lane.

"Now gear down."

"What will that do?"

"It slows the engine. We're going to put on the hand-brake."

But with the hill they just seemed to go faster. Cal said a very rude word. She didn't blame him. She was thinking it herself.

"We're going to have to do a controlled crash."

"*Controlled* and *crash* are two words that can't possibly belong together."

He grinned—a wild, confident grin in the face of danger. "See that bunch of bushes over there? I'm going to steer us into them. I want you to duck down. Cover your face."

"Those are *laurels*. You can't mean you deliberately intend to—"

Cal put his hand on her shoulder and pushed her down. She had one last view of leafy branches coming at the windscreen at high speed. Snapping sounds came from all around her. Something scratched her cheek and she made sure her hands covered as much of her face as possible. The car lurched and there came more sickening breaking and grinding sounds.

The car stopped. The sound of the engine ceased.

Julia parted her gloved fingers and looked between them. Leaves seemed to fill the car. Cal was no longer forcing her down so she straightened. He grabbed broken branches and threw them away. The car and a scrawny laurel brush seemed to have merged in some kind of unholy alliance.

"Are you okay, Julia?"

"Yes. Much better than your motorcar." The glossy front end was crumpled inward. The car had mown over the shrubs with smaller trunks, leaving a trail of destruction.

Cal was fighting with a branch that jutted into the car on the passenger side and prevented him from opening the door.

"Goodness, this is my very first motorcar crash."

Cal broke the branch with a loud crack and threw it out of the car. "I'd like to think it's going to be your only car crash."

She looked back toward the road. If he hadn't forced them

to crash, they would have gone hurtling down the treacherous hill with the right-angle turn at the end and the stone wall at the bottom. If he hadn't forced a crash, they would have been...killed.

"Well, thanks to you, I survived it. I think you deserve a reward."

To Cal's surprise, Julia flung her arms around his neck. Her mouth met his in a searing kiss and knocked him back against his seat. At once, he felt the rush of blood to his groin, hardening and thickening him.

They could have been killed. Julia should have been terrified and fainting. But she was talking with toughness. And all he wanted to do was open his trousers and pull her on top of him and take advantage of all this hot passion she was giving him.

So he did that.

With laurel branches tangled in the car, he held Julia on his lap. And he pushed her short skirt out of the way. With his fingers, he teased her, gazing deep into her eyes. He could have lost her. The thought speared him.

She moaned. "Oh yes."

He pulled open his trousers and she wrapped her hand around his shaft, making him groan in sensual agony. To his shock, Julia took him inside and began moving on him. He grasped her hips and met her thrust for thrust. He was driving to take her to her peak when he heard a loud bleating. A voice called, "Hello there? Are you all right?"

"We're okay," Cal called casually, as if he wasn't making love to his wife in a crashed car.

A flock of sheep wandered up to inspect the car. Then Cal saw a gnarled man with a walking stick making his way toward them. The farmer, Brand. He quickly lifted Julia off him and set her back beside him. He heard her giggle behind her palm.

"I can bring me plow horses and pull the car back to the big house for ye, if it will roll," Brand said as he approached.

"I'd appreciate it, Brand," Cal said, fighting to discreetly fasten his trousers. "The brakes failed and we had to crash."

"Newfangled things." Brand shook his head and went to get the horses.

"What happened to the brakes?" Julia asked. "When I put my foot on the pedal, it sank to the floor without doing a thing."

"There was no hydraulic pressure in the line."

"What does that mean?"

He explained quickly how brakes worked. "There's got to be a break in the line." He would be able to figure out what happened if he could get under the car and check the line. But there were too many broken branches snagged beneath the car, and the rutted ground was too high for him to crawl underneath.

Then he saw Julia was shaking. Cal swung out of the vehicle, lifted her out and led her to the farmhouse. Mrs. Brand was upstairs, asleep. Cal made tea.

After a few sips, Brand said, "You'd best be careful. We don't want any harm to fall upon her ladyship, my lord. She's most beloved around here."

"I know she is. And I won't let anything hurt her."

"There's the curse, you know."

"There's no such thing as curses," Cal muttered.

"The curse came true for the dowager countess. Old Lady Worthington has known nothing but pain. Her eldest lad was killed at the Somme and the youngest died in a motorcar accident."

Cal's mam was Irish and believed in pixies, fairies and evil sprites. But he had grown up in a world where he'd fought to get out—and he'd won. Airplanes and motorcars were possible, and they were based on the principles of physics, on chemical reactions and combustion and gears.

"I don't believe it, Brand. No one can utter a few words and cause accidents to happen, or create illness, or cause people to die. A man can cause harm to other men—but he's got to use something physical to do it. Like a machine gun or an artillery shell."

But when he got the car back to Worthington, after giving Brand some money for his trouble and sending the chauffeur to deliver the pies for the Tofts—which had survived the accident—he took a look under the automobile to see what had gone wrong with the brakes. What he saw gave him the shock of his life.

Cal went to Julia's bedroom. He didn't knock. Julia was his wife, and he didn't see that a husband and wife should be asking permission to see each other. But when he opened the door, Ellen Lambert stood there, arms crossed over her chest.

"Her ladyship is not well tonight."

"What's wrong?" Fear gripped him.

"Your automobile crashed into a tree. My poor lady was shaking. She certainly does not need...attentions from a husband tonight."

"I crashed the car to save her life. Is she all right? Does she need a doctor?"

"She needs her rest."

He was going to push past, but then Ellen added, "Her ladyship has not looked well since the day after the wedding, when you went away."

Guilt hit him. He couldn't admit he'd gone to tell O'Brien

to get the hell away from his family. And his anger had only made O'Brien realize he was afraid of Julia learning the truth.

Retreating to his room, Cal undid his robe. He was naked underneath, hadn't bothered to put on pajamas. It almost physically hurt not to be with Julia.

He was stepping into trousers when his door opened.

Julia stood there. "Ellen told me she sent you away. But I wanted you to come to me tonight." She shut the door. "Then I realized I could come to you."

"Then I should be a good host. Do you want a drink?" Cal pulled out a flask. He was tired of brandy and cognac, snooty drinks consumed by pompous men. He needed a stiff drink right now.

"What is it?"

"A drink I would have drunk at home."

"Moonshine?"

He laughed. "I've never had moonshine. Some of it could make you blind. So could bathtub gin, but I admit I've drank that. But this I bought in London. Good Irish whiskey."

"I've never had whiskey. Women don't."

He poured a finger of the liquor in a tumbler. Handed it to her where she sat on the edge of the bed. "But you aren't controlled by rules and tradition, Julia." He held his glass in the air as if toasting her, and took a drink.

She took a swallow. Pulled the glass from her lips. Coughed. "It's like fire in a glass—if fire tasted bitter and awful."

He grinned, though he was troubled. "That is fine ten-year-old whiskey."

"Then I think it has gone bad. Unlike wine, aging didn't seem to help."

He swung away from the bedpost and sat down beside her.

She looked a bit shocked, then, to his delight, she pressed against him.

"I know you looked at the motorcar. What had gone wrong?" she asked. "It wasn't the chauffeur's fault, was it?"

"No, it wasn't his fault."

"What is it?" He didn't answer and she pressed, "There's something wrong, isn't there?"

"The brake line had been cut. Deliberately." Had he been too blunt?

"I don't know a lot about automobiles," she said, looking direct and determined. "But if someone cut the brake, doesn't that mean that person meant us to have a car accident?"

God, he admired her. She had incredible strength. "Yeah, I think so."

"That means someone wishes us ill."

"It was my car. It looks like it was intended for me. There have to be a lot of people who'd like me dead," he said. O'Brien, possibly. The dowager countess—maybe her apology had been false.

"Why do you think that?" she protested. "All the tenants believe they have no better champion."

The idea of someone wanting him dead didn't surprise him. He'd run the risk of getting killed in a gang. At war, he'd escaped death more times than he could remember. In the prohibition world, he'd almost been snuffed several times. Death had been a part of his life for as long as he could remember.

What made him angry this time was that Julia had been in danger.

"What about Lowry?" she asked. "He might have friends getting revenge for him."

Cal nodded. She was a smart woman. "Maybe the dowager countess did it."

Her mouth turned down. "I thought you two were growing to accept each other. And can you really imagine the dowager countess getting on the ground beneath your vehicle to cut a brake line?" Suddenly she giggled. But then she quickly sobered. "What of the man who attacked me?" she asked. "Could it be him—whoever he is?"

"It could be. I'm going to find out who was responsible—and make them pay."

He saw her shiver. "I overheard the maids talking about the curse on the Worthington Wife." She lifted her chin. "A brake line isn't a curse. It's a deliberate act of malice."

"That's true." He took the glass out of her hand, put them both on the bedside table. "Don't think about this anymore. You don't have to worry about anything with me around.

"Tomorrow, I want you to pack, Julia. I want to take you to Italy, to Nice, to wherever you want to go. We'll get away from here." He fell back on his bed, pulling her with him. "Now let me make you forget about all this with a sweet roll in the hay."

And he was pretty sure he did.

22

The Dowager Countess

When Julia went to sleep, Cal got out of bed quietly, got dressed and went out. He drove the Worthington Daimler to the Boar and Castle, parked outside.

Maybe O'Brien had cut the brake line to give Cal a warning.

The publican was still up, serving the last round. Cal found O'Brien with a glass of whiskey. "I wondered when you would show up after I met your wife. Do I tell the newspapers about your past or do I get my dough?"

"I gave you money to get the hell out of England. You're not getting another penny from me."

"Do you really want your pretty wife to read about you in the headlines?"

Cal was aware of the other few men in the bar staring at them, at O'Brien's pale pink suit. In a low voice, he asked, "Did you cut the brake lines of my car?"

Kerry shrugged. "What if I did?"

Cal got up. He grabbed the bastard's arm, twisted it behind him. "I'll break your damned arm if you don't promise to leave Julia and me alone. I'm willing to take care of you like we used to do it back in the Five Points Gang. Understand?"

"You wouldn't. You'd be arrested—"

"I don't give a damn. You almost killed my wife."

He hauled O'Brien to his feet. Dragged him outside and sure enough, people looked at them, but no one said a word. Outside of the pub, he growled, "If you keep pushing me, you ain't gonna live long enough to enjoy Jolly Old England."

Once it wouldn't have been an empty threat. But it was now. He prayed O'Brien didn't figure that out.

O'Brien pulled out a knife, but Cal took care of that with a twist of the man's wrist. "You sell the story to the newspapers, I'll come for you. You do anything to hurt my wife, my family, or me, and I'll get you. You know what I am capable of, O'Brien."

His foe lost his bravado. "All right, damn it."

Cal dragged Kerry O'Brien back into the public house and ordered him another drink. He paid for it. He was walking toward the door when O'Brien said, "I didn't do it. Those brakes—that wasn't me."

He turned. "What?"

"I took credit for someone else's work. I wouldn't want to see you dead. Someone else wants that." Sniggering, he tossed back his whiskey.

Cal went out the door, almost staggering. He'd thought that O'Brien had done it, which would mean it had nothing to do with the missing women or the attack on Julia. Damn. He drove back from the village to Worthington. The shortest route took him past Lilac Farm. It was faster, even though it was a rougher, windier road.

Something jumped in front of him. He slammed on the brake. The car screeched to a stop and his headlights illuminated a small hunched-over person. A woman, and she put her hands up to shield her eyes and let out a shriek.

Cal jumped out of the car. In the streams of light, Mrs.

Brand huddled in a ball. He crouched beside her, trying to soothe her. He knew he hadn't hit her, but she was terrified.

"Are you all right, Mrs. Brand?" Nothing looked broken, but as he tried to lift her to her feet, she struggled to scramble away, getting covered in mud. More forcefully than he wanted, he lifted her and drew her toward the car.

She took one look at his vehicle and screamed again. "The motorcar... You!" Frantic she shouted, "Sarah! I remember. The motor. It were here. What did you do with Sarah? I saw you!"

"I'm not the man who took Sarah," he said, in a gentle voice. But she still screamed. He caught her and wrapped one arm around her shoulders. "I'm Cal Carstairs. The earl. I want to *find* your daughter, Sarah."

"I can't find Sarah. It's too late. I told her to go away if she couldn't behave. What have I done?"

"It's not your fault." Gently he got Mrs. Brand to the door. "This isn't the car that Sarah got into," he said. "That was a dark red car. This one is dark blue." Then, he gambled. "It was John Carstairs who took Sarah. Or was it Anthony?"

"That night..." She stared helplessly ahead. "The lights were so bright. I followed Sarah to the road. Sarah got into the car and I shouted at her not to go. That she was being wicked. That she would have a terrible reputation. They drove away. But I knew the shortcuts through the woods. I found the car. It was going slow up the lane. It had its lights off. I saw it turn. I followed, trudging and out of breath. But I found the car. I saw Sarah—she were asleep. I heard— It was a spade I heard. And I saw—"

She started to scream again.

Cal pulled out the small flask he kept in his pocket. "Irish whiskey. Like medicine." He forced her to take two swallows. She couldn't cry out while swallowing and he took care to make certain she didn't choke. "Who took Sarah?"

"He were all in black. Like a demon. Then the car went away. I ran down to the farm, but when I got there…when I got into the kitchen I felt all dizzy. I don't remember…"

"It's okay. I'm going to take you back to the farm. I'm going to find Sarah."

He got Mrs. Brand to sit in the car. Pulling a rug out of the back rumble seat, he wrapped it around her. That gave her lucidity long enough for her to look at him in shock. "My lord? Whatever am I doing here?"

"You don't remember?"

The question made her panic.

"You were out walking," he said. "I'll drive you back to the farm."

"Thank ye, milord," she whispered.

When he reached Lilac Farm he found Brand holding a lantern, calling out in panic for his wife. The man almost fainted with relief as Cal drove up and helped her out. He helped Brand get her to her bed. "Brand, I believe she saw the man who took Sarah. I found her on the road—"

"She always chases after cars, thinking Sarah's in one of them."

"I think she saw something, up one of the lanes. She saw the car there that night."

"She never told me. I didn't know she'd gone out that night. I found her in the kitchen."

Mrs. Brand must have collapsed because her mind had been unable to cope with the truth. Perhaps seeing his vehicle had made her remember. Which meant they might have been near where Sarah had been taken by a man who'd used a shovel.

Julia was still sleeping when Cal got back to Worthington. He left her alone, crawling into his own bed. At about three, he dozed off. When he woke, the sky had lightened to the color of steel. It was daylight, but the day was cloudy. Cal got up, got dressed. He got his car—the brake line was now fixed—and was driving past the house when a figure rushed toward him. He hit the brake.

This time it was Julia. She wore a skirt and blouse and held a shawl that flapped in the wind. "I saw your light go on. Where are you going so early?"

"I think I know where to find Sarah Brand. I'm going now so I can be there when it's light."

"I am coming, too."

"No, you're not, Julia."

"Yes, I am." She pulled open the passenger door.

"All right. But you will have to stay in the car."

As they drove he told her what Mrs. Brand had said. "I think she saw Sarah's killer."

"But why didn't she ever say anything?" she asked.

"Maybe it was too much for her and the shock of it made her mind snap. I think seeing my automobile made her remember. You'd have to get a headshrinker like Sigmund Freud to figure it out." He drove to the lane that led to Lilac Farm.

"It's so awful to think she saw it," Julia murmured.

"You don't have to do this."

"I do—I have to."

He admired her courage. He drove slowly, looking for—looking for anywhere that might make a good place for a grave. Or graves. It had to be secluded enough that the killer had felt he could carry a body and dig a grave and not be seen. It had to be close enough to the farm that Mrs. Brand had been able to catch up to him. Obviously the killer didn't know Mrs. Brand had seen him.

On his left was a lane that crawled up a hill. Tall grass filled in the track and tree branches hung over it. The grass had been knocked down recently. Some of the branches had been snapped. Someone had driven up this relatively unused path in the past few days.

I saw it turn. I followed, trudging and out of breath.

If Mrs. Brand had followed the car up the hill, she would have been out of breath. Cal crept up the track. He saw the fear on Julia's face.

The track ran out on the top of a hill. There was an outcropping of rocks.

Julia pointed at them. "There were legends that those were used for sacrifices. It is supposed to be haunted. All nonsense, of course."

"But it could explain lights being seen here. Headlights," Cal murmured.

He stopped the car as close to the large rocks as he could get. He got out, opened up the trunk and got out his shovel. He started walking around. Smaller stones were piled up—obviously by human hands. Behind those piles he scraped fallen leaves aside and discovered the ground was lumpier. The area had been dug up before.

He started to dig. Julia was getting out of the car. He called, "Don't come over here, Julia. I don't want you to see this. If I find what I'm looking for—it's going to haunt you forever."

The summer morning was cool, with gray clouds overhead—but he was digging hard and started to sweat. In the War, he'd dug graves for bodies—especially the bodies of pilots, if there was anything left to bury. He stopped digging, wiped his face. He was actually wiping his eyes, because he damn well felt like he could cry.

"Are you all right?" Julia called. "Oh, I'm sorry—what a foolish thing to ask."

"I appreciate you asking. I thought I'd learned to be tough

when I was growing up. But when I think about what it is that I'm doing right now, I want to be sick. Stay by the car."

The earth was compacted, which made it hard to shovel with care. He pushed the shovel in and went deeper than he'd expected. And hit something.

He uncovered more and his gut clenched. He was looking down at the head that had almost decomposed to a skeleton, still with some black hair. He dropped down on one knee. Around the skeletal neck was a tiny silver locket. "Sarah" was engraved on the front. With initials upon the back. "J.C."

John Carstairs? Cal carefully prized open the locket. A lock of black hair was inside.

He found another two piles of pebbles and figured that they probably marked the graves of the other girls who had vanished—Eileen Kilkenny and Gladys Burrows.

Julia walked toward him but he stopped her. "I'm taking you back home."

"I saw your face, Cal. I saw the horror and torment in your eyes. You found one of them."

He let the shovel fall. He went to Julia, wrapped his arms around her, burying his face in her hair. The wave of grief was staggering. "I found Sarah."

"Oh—oh no. Poor, poor girl." She let out a sob, then took a deep breath. "Is there any clue to who did it? Don't spare me if you believe you know."

"I don't know yet, angel. But there's a locket around Sarah's neck with some black hair in it, and the initials J.C. It must be John Carstairs. God, there's been so much tragedy here. Maybe they're right and this place was cursed."

"What do we do now?"

"Go to the police."

"But we— I would like to go to the dowager countess first. I would like her to know, before the police come."

"Why?" he asked, confused.

She touched his arm with that gentle, elegant way she had. "Plans must be made, because once the police constables know, there will be gossip. It can't be stemmed." She stroked down his arm, clasped his dirt-covered hand. "This has been awful for you. We will see the dowager and we will get you a cup of tea. That is the best thing for a bad shock."

He couldn't understand how Julia could be so cool and collected. His heart hammered and his eyes burned with tears of grief—even though he'd never met these girls—and his blood burned with outrage. John Carstairs would have thought of him as nothing—Cal knew that—and all along, he'd been a sick, vicious killer.

Then he looked at Julia and saw the tears streaking down her cheeks.

She wiped them away. "Falling apart does nothing. But I—" Tears came and he held her until they stopped. Then he took her back to the car. He drove to the dower house, a two-story brick building that looked huge for one woman. The countess was the only one who had gone to live there—he'd found it odd, but the countess told him the girls were to stay in the mansion until they married. They weren't to go with their mother. Cal found this world strange.

He walked up to the front door and knocked on it, Julia following him. Upstairs, a curtain moved. He saw the countess's frightened white face through the panes of glass. She let the curtain drop hurriedly.

He knocked on the door. Kept knocking. Finally it was pulled open. An elderly butler blinked at him. Cal didn't know the man—he'd let the countess hire whatever servants she'd wanted. "My lord?"

"I have to talk to the dowager countess."

"My lord, her ladyship attended a late party last night. I do not believe the dowager is awake."

"She is. I saw her at her window."

"I do not believe she is receiving. If you will kindly wait one moment, my lord…" The butler drifted away up the stairs, like a disembodied spirit. When the man returned, Cal could tell what he was going to say. "The countess is not well. She is not—"

"She had better see me. If she doesn't, I'm driving right to the police station. I think she'll know why."

"Cal, what are you talking about?" Julia breathed.

When the butler hesitated, Cal pushed past him. He stalked up the stairs. Felt that graceful touch—Julia's hand on his arm. "Cal, stop."

"She saw me coming and she looked terrified. Why else would she be scared of me?" The burned picture. The car under wraps, the shovel, the scarf hidden there. She knew he was looking for the killer of Sarah Brand. "I think she knew, Julia. That's why she's been afraid of me." He didn't have proof of that, but instinct had kept him alive in New York and in the skies over France.

"She couldn't—"

"I think she knew and she kept the truth hidden."

"But—" Julia gasped. "Once I overheard her say that John had taken his own life. She believed—or knew—it wasn't an accident. Oh, heavens, perhaps it meant…a guilty conscience."

He doubted it. A man like Carstairs likely believed he could do anything he wanted. What it meant was that the former Countess of Worthington had left Cal's parents to die and David and him to starve, while she knew one of her sons was a rapist and a killer.

He ran up the stairs.

Heavy footsteps followed him. Cal jerked around at the

top of the stairs. Julia was behind him and the dowager's butler was behind her, already wheezing.

"I'm not going to hurt her," Cal said coldly. "Don't give yourself a heart attack trying to stop me. I just want the truth. Finally, after all these years. I want her to admit that it's her family that's rotten to the core. And that she denied justice to innocent families."

Julia touched him in her gentle way. "Cal, we don't know this for certain yet."

"We will soon." It didn't take long to figure out which room was the dowager's. A door slammed down the hallway. He heard the click.

Reaching the paneled door, he ran his hand over the doorknob. Locked. He took a step back, lifted his foot and kicked the door open. With a splintering shriek, it flew open.

The dowager screamed. "Don't kill me! You've come to destroy me!"

When he'd come here weeks ago, this was what he'd wanted. The dowager cowering from him. But now, all his rage just kind of ran out. He felt like a sputtering engine, trying to keep going, but failing.

She just looked like a terrified old woman. Not the devil he used to imagine in his head as a young starving boy. "Sit down," he said gruffly. "I came here to talk about John. And Sarah Brand."

She seemed to get older in front of his eyes. "I see. What is it that you think you know about John?" She lifted her chin and her blue eyes glittered with defiance.

For all the countess was no spring chicken, she dressed to the nines, even for bed. Her hair was bobbed, all silver waves. Her nightdress was embroidered silk, festooned with feathers and pearls. It screamed wealth. And she'd known her son had killed innocent women. He was sure of it now—sure she had known.

"My lady, should I summon help?" It was the butler, staring from the shattered door at his mistress.

"If you want to call the coppers, go ahead," Cal said.

"We do not have coppers. We have the police, but we do not need to bring them here. Please leave us."

"My lady, the American—I mean the earl—"

"Leave us now, Montrose. I do not see how I have not made myself clear."

Montrose, the butler, left. The dowager gazed haughtily. "I should prefer we speak in my dressing room. The door there is intact. I do not want this spread as gossip."

"All right." He would give her that. She swept on ahead of him.

Julia clasped his arm. "Cal, you must calm down. You broke the door. You are rather terrifying."

He'd scared Julia. But what did she want of him? He couldn't behave like an emotionless English earl. If the dowager had known the truth, she'd let three women's deaths go unavenged. She'd subverted justice. Three families had lived a hell for years, with no idea whether their daughters were alive or dead. All to save the lily-white arse of her precious, evil son.

Even now, what the dowager countess really cared about was the gossip. The scandal. The damn family.

And that made him mad.

She seated herself gracefully in a white chair in her dressing room. He took the one opposite.

"What do you wish to tell me about John? I presume you have unearthed a pack of lies?"

"I've found the truth. From your reaction, I'd say you know what he did. And you said nothing."

"What do you believe my son is responsible for?"

"The rapes and murders of three young women."

She flinched. She paled even more. In her eyes was the terror of self-preservation. But she said, "What evidence do you have to support such a vile accusation?"

"We both know it's true," he said softly. "In 1916, Sarah Brand disappeared. I found evidence she'd been in one of the older cars in the Worthington garage. I learned that a woman named Eileen Kilkenny also disappeared. And a maid named Gladys Burrows. Today I found Sarah's body."

She gasped.

"According to your former chauffeur, there weren't many automobiles around here in 1916—but there was a red one at Worthington. Sarah had a crush on John's older brother, and I figure John pursued her, taking his brother's car. Maybe she was willing to go driving with John but I don't think she was willing to sleep with him. So he drove her to a reasonably remote place, attacked her, killed her and buried the body."

The countess shuddered. "Stop…stop."

"Having an automobile made it easy for him, except he was careless. He left evidence in the car. Left the shovel in the trunk that he used to bury them. Left a woman's scarf."

"How can you know it is John?"

"I found evidence on Sarah's body."

"Where is this evidence?"

Her blunt, calculating question surprised him. "I've kept it somewhere safe."

"So you have not gone to the police yet?" she asked.

"Not yet." He leaned close, aware of Julia standing by the fireplace. "How did you know the truth? And how in hell could you keep such a secret? You let those families continue to suffer. Mrs. Brand wanders at night in her confused state, still searching for her daughter. She walked right in front of my car and I almost hit her."

Tears dripped to the countess's cheeks. "What was I to do? He came to me and he confessed," she whispered. "It was just before his accident."

"You could have spared those innocent families. You could have told the truth."

"And my son would have been hanged! He didn't mean to do it. He was always...not quite right. And the girls—they should have known better than to go out alone in a motorcar with a man. One of them gave him photographs of herself wearing nothing but her undergarments. They were no better than—"

"Don't," Julia said fiercely. "Do not blame the girls."

"Your son was to blame, not them," Cal snapped "I don't care if Sarah paraded in front of him naked—he had no right to force himself on her. No right to kill her. Your son had every advantage—money, education, your precious bloodlines— and look what he was. He should have paid for what he did."

He spoke low, fighting to keep his voice controlled, but she had drawn back into the chair. "Now that he is dead," the dowager whispered, "he's answered for everything he did. He paid with his life."

"The families need to know—"

The dowager jerked in the chair. "No! People cannot know!"

"I don't give a damn about protecting you from scandal. Not now."

"It's not me," she cried. "Think of my daughters. They are innocents in this, but they will be punished. What gentleman would marry them after such a scandal?"

"Of course they're innocent, so why shouldn't someone marry them?"

She sneered. "You have no idea how Society works."

"No. I can't say I do. And I'm glad of it. It's made me a hell of a better man."

"She is right, Cal," Julia said. "Cassia, Diana, Thalia will all be hurt by this. It will ruin their lives. They will be ostracized."

"No man would want to tie himself to a family that is notorious," the dowager countess cried. "The girls would be ruined by association. Spare them, at least. John is beyond punishment on this earth. He pays now in eternal damnation. I believe he took his own life. He deliberately drove off the ridge into the quarry."

"Cal, there is nothing to be served by destroying the family. It will even hurt us—and it will touch David, also. Everyone will be ruined," Julia whispered.

"There needs to be justice," he growled. Then he realized...the countess had known he was looking for the truth. "Did you cut the brake lines of my car?"

"What are those? What are you talking about?"

He explained about the crash and she gasped. "I would never do such a thing."

He now had the ultimate power to hurt the dowager. To do the worst thing that she could imagine: making her the object of scandal. When his mother had died, he had promised to hurt them all. But now he kept thinking of the dowager's daughters, who were innocent. How could he let them be hurt by his actions?

"You won't tell anyone about this," the countess said quickly. "Or I'll tell the world the truth about your mother."

"What?" he growled.

"Do you know why I objected to your arrival so strongly?" she demanded.

"Why don't you tell me?" He spoke smoothly. But inside his gut churned.

"We knew what your mother was. We had reports sent to us. She entertained men in her rooms—"

"That's a damned lie." Cal rose from his seat.

"You know it is quite true. Your mother was a prostitute. And she behaved scandalously before the marriage, having relations with your father and becoming preg—"

"Goddamn you," he barked. "Goddamn you to hell. You paid for an investigator and had him spy on us, but you wouldn't send any money when she was sick. Money that would have paid for a doctor and medicine. Money that would have saved her life. She sold herself for money to feed David and I. You forced her to do it. I've got the power now. I could destroy you. I could let you watch while Worthington Park is sold around you—"

He stopped, chest heaving. Julia had gone very, very white.

"Then what—you'll tell the world about John?" the countess said. "And I'll make sure no one believes you. I know all about your past, Worthington. I have been told about all of it. I am sure Julia knows nothing about—"

"You can tell her whatever you want. I'm going to lose her anyway when I destroy this place. And I'm damn well going to the police. I couldn't live with myself if I didn't get justice. Maybe nothing can be proved now, after nine years, but I want them to damn well try."

Slowly, he met Julia's eyes. He expected anger. Shock. She now knew one of the things he had been most ashamed of— that he hadn't been able to prevent his mother from selling her body, doing something that tormented her to her soul.

But Julia whirled on the dowager countess. "How could you threaten such a thing?" she demanded of the dowager. "It is true that if the truth about John gets out, the girls will suffer in the stead of their brother. I understand your fear and I don't want my friends—my family now—to suffer. But you cannot be so heartless. You were never like this. You were always kind."

"I must protect the family I have left," the dowager

croaked. "Julia, this will touch you. If you have children, a scandal would hurt them. Is that what you want?"

Cal felt Julia look to him. He said, "We could leave this place, get rid of this cursed estate, travel the world. Live anywhere we want, keeping our children away from here, so they'd never be hurt by it. We could go to South America. Santorini. Venice—"

"I don't want to run away, Cal, and leave everyone else to suffer. I won't."

With Cal she went to the police station. To Julia's surprise, he did not tell them of John Carstairs's confession to his mother. He told them he suspected John because of the car in the garage, the spade, the locket. After, as he drove them to Worthington, with rain pattering the windshield, she asked, "Why did you keep his confession a secret?"

"He didn't confess to me. I don't know what exactly he said to his mother. If there's evidence, they'll find it. Maybe, if they can't prove anything, I'll tell them. But even then, it's not cold, hard, irrefutable proof. I know this is going to hurt my cousins. But you understand, Julia, that I couldn't keep the deaths secret?"

"I understand," she whispered. "I do want to go with you when you show the police sergeant the—the place." Scotland Yard was to be called in, too.

"No. I don't want you to see any more of that. I'm taking you home, then showing the police the graves."

"Cal, are you really going to destroy Worthington now— because of what the dowager threatened? It was wrong. Unconscionable. But—"

"I don't know. I— Hell, I want you to come away with me and I want to forget about Worthington Park."

His heart was raw and she understood. But she had to fight

for Worthington. Not for the estate—for Cal. He needed to finally escape the pain of his past.

At Worthington, Cal left her there, then returned to the police station. She went to the morning room. She didn't tell the servants any of what had happened. She began a letter beseeching the dowager countess not to reveal a word about Cal's mother.

"My lady?" A maid bobbed a curtsy, holding out a folded page. "This note was delivered for you. A young lad brought it to the kitchen door. Said it was dreadful important."

Julia hurried to the maid, took the note.

The writing was shaky, terribly so. Julia struggled to read it. But when she did, an icy, sick feeling washed over her. It was from Lower Dale Farm. Their father was ill.

"I must go and fetch Dr. Campbell. Is the boy still here?"

"He ran off, milady."

And Cal was gone—with the police. She must deal with this herself. She needed her vehicle. She would drive directly to the hospital to fetch Dr. Campbell. She would test the brakes. The garage was always locked now, and the chauffeur took great care, checking the vehicles each day. Surely she would be safe enough if she traveled directly to the hospital to get Dougal.

At the front door, she put on her coat. But as she stepped outside to go to the garage, the Duke of Bradstock drove up. He leaned out the open window. "Julia, I was coming to see you. I want to apologize for upsetting you." His car purred as he shifted it into Neutral.

Then she had the perfect idea. "Would you be willing to do me a favor, James?"

"Anything, dear Julia. Ask me anything."

Should she involve him? She must. "I need you to take

me to the hospital and collect Dr. Campbell, then take us to Lower Dale Farm. We must make haste."

Belowstairs, Tansy ran into the kitchen and burst into tears. Hannah almost knocked her bowl to the floor in her surprise. "Tansy, you must stop being so dramatic."

"You were right all along," the girl cried. "Oh, I've been so stupid."

"Tansy, what on earth—" Then Hannah knew and she touched Tansy's shoulder. "He had his way with you, didn't he? I know you saw him last night. You gave in and he broke it off with you."

Tansy shook her head. "I didn't see him last night. I snuck out to meet him but he never came. I wouldn't let him have his way—and I was afraid that's why he didn't come. And now I just saw him! With her! She's so hoity-toity, and there's her husband so much in love with her, but I saw her get into his motorcar just now. I saw the look in his eyes as he drove off. He's in love with her. He looked right at me, because I was standing there, and it was as if he didn't even see me."

Hannah was all mixed-up. "Who do you mean? Who is 'she'?"

"He came, and Lady Worthington got into his car. And the way he looked at her—well, he never looked at me that way. Never."

"He's probably a friend of Lady Worthington."

Tansy moaned. "She's his lover, more like. And I found out he didn't give me his real name. She called him James."

23

Disappearance in a Motorcar

James's motorcar rumbled along the road toward the village. Julia shivered in the seat beside him. Cold air had swept in and fog was settling on the countryside. They drove through it in valleys and it swirled alongside the road like ghostly apparitions.

This wasn't the main road, but it was a lane Julia knew well. A shortcut to Brideswell village. It would come out very close to the hospital.

There were few motorcars in the village—no one passed them. James was driving quite quickly, as she'd asked, turning the wheel with skill to avoid holes in the road.

He slowed a bit, then pushed down on the pedal and the car went perilously fast. With a rapid movement, he turned the steering wheel. The car seemed to skid onto two wheels and she shut her eyes out of instinct.

When she opened them, they were on a different lane—a rougher one that was just two tracks cutting through a field. "Shouldn't we be going the other way to the village?"

He kept his focus on staying on the tracks. "Shortcut."

Men. And they complained about women behind the steering wheel. Julia's heart thudded. She didn't want to waste precious time. "The *other* road is a shortcut. I think it would be fast enough. This looks like the kind of track you can get stuck on." It couldn't be much used. She, who knew the estate well, did not know where it led.

"Be quiet. Leave the driving to me."

"Women are no longer seen and not heard, James. This track seems to be going away from the village. I don't think this is a good idea."

"It's a perfect idea." Then he added, "I learned your husband is taking you on a long trip. A tour through the Mediterranean, then on to Egypt, where you will explore the archeological digs and travel up the Nile. It appears I wouldn't be seeing you for a very long time."

"What? We didn't decide on a trip." She had said she did not want to run away from Worthington Park. "How did you know about it?"

"Your husband told your butler and a footman overheard."

She peered ahead. Fog swirled and it looked milky white in front of them, the headlights picking out trees that seemed to fly at them out of nowhere. What he'd said didn't quite make sense. "But how did *you* know?"

"I paid the footman to give me information."

"You paid a footman to spy? Why?"

"I wanted to know what your husband was doing to you."

She was stunned. How could James have thought such a thing was right? He was truly far too arrogant. "We should have been at the hospital by now." He must have gone the wrong way after all.

"Don't fret, Julia."

"James, Mr. Toft is ill. It could be very serious."

She gasped as the stream of light from the lamps on the

car picked out looming trees in the mist. James slowed the car, picking his way along the track. He must know where it was; Julia could see nothing that looked like a road.

They passed through a wooded area. James stopped the car. Here, it was utterly gray, but for the two pinpoints of the headlights, which illuminated nothing but bracken and tall grass. She stared at him, shocked and confused. "What are you doing?"

"We've run out of road."

His wretched shortcut had turned out to be useless. She'd told him not to do this. And they'd wasted so much precious time. Panic rose and she struggled to fight it. "You have to turn around. We must go back—"

"Calm yourself, Julia. The bugger at Lower Dale Farm is not in any danger."

She flinched at his harsh description. "You don't know that—"

"But I do. I know it because I wrote the note and paid some village boy to deliver it."

"Why would you do that? Was this intended as a joke?"

"I needed to get you into my car, Julia. You should have seen your face when I drove up. You looked as if your knight errant had arrived."

"I don't understand."

"I've waited a long time for this. I didn't want to have to hurt you. I thought you might come to me willingly, become my mistress, once you found out the truth about that American thug you married. But then I learned I was running out of time."

"What are you talking about?"

"He is going to take you away. He would not bring you back here. I'd waited too long already. I paid a man to cut the brakes of his damn car, but that failed to kill him. I am not going to let him take you from me forever."

Shock had made her wits freeze, made it hard to think. James wanted her. Learning Cal wanted to take her away had made him determined to act.

Three women with dark hair and blue eyes. But that had been John Carstairs. What was Bradstock going to do—try to seduce her? "What do you want from me?"

"I want to be intimate with you. I've wanted it for so long. When I was going to propose marriage to your father—"

"Propose marriage to Father?"

"I had a proposition for him," he said impatiently. "It was common knowledge he'd frittered through his fortune. His debts couldn't be covered, and the income was dissolving because of his poor management. I was going to cover his debts, if he gave me you."

"This is not the eighteenth century. I wouldn't have allowed myself to be sold, no matter what Father said," she declared.

"Then your engagement with bloody Anthony Carstairs was announced," he said, ignoring her. "I'd waited too long. I was going to get your father to demand you break the engagement. He would have done anything to get his hands on money to cover his debts. I could have ruined him."

She sucked in a cold, sharp breath. Bradstock was mad.

"Before I could do that, Anthony volunteered for battle. All I had to do was wait. Reports were coming back—thousands of men were being blown to bits. Anthony was so stupidly brave I was sure he'd get killed."

"He was *truly* brave. How dare you mock him?" But even as she threw those words at him, she looked around. She could get out of the car and run. She was going to have to do that. She hadn't paid a lot of attention to where they had turned exactly, because she'd been so fearful for the Tofts of Lower Dale Farm. The fog made it confusing, but she thought she recognized where she was. On the other side of the hill from where Cal had found the bodies.

He had wanted her—and three dark-haired women had died. "Did you— Were you the man in the motorcar with Sarah Brand? What of John Carstairs? Did he—he kill Sarah or did you?"

The moment she asked the question, she knew she could not turn back.

He smiled. "I did. I met him and we both had our way with her. She looked so much like you. John loved you so much, Julia. I found out about how much John loved you, Julia, when I came to visit Anthony and Nigel. I came to see you, even knowing I couldn't have you. Once I learned about John's lust for you, I knew he was going to be the perfect scapegoat. I tempted him with photographs I got of Gladys, the maid."

Julia felt frozen. Of course. J.C. Not John Carstairs. But James. And he was heir to the dukedom then, known by his courtesy title, the Earl of Cavendish. "The photograph was signed to 'A.' I told the daft girl my name was Anthony." His smile widened. "John enjoyed our game, having women who looked like you, the woman who loved his precious brother. I knew I could lay the blame at his door if things went wrong. Then the War came. I managed to avoid conscription—my father ensured that. I returned from university, and wanted to play the game again, with Anthony gone. But John had an attack of conscience and killed himself, the bloody fool. That's why I had to stop for so long. But seeing you made it so painful that I needed another girl…"

While he was talking happily, she grasped the door handle to the car. With a swift motion, she shoved open the door and she jumped out of the car as fast as she could. She skidded on the ground—the misty rain made it slippery.

Something grabbed the sleeve of her coat and she screamed. Using all her might, she pulled free and she began running down the track back the way they had come. Behind her, she heard Bradstock curse. "Bollocks. Don't be a damn fool. There's nowhere to run."

But she kept going. She plunged off the track, into tall damp grass. She could see nothing, and that must mean he couldn't see her. But he could hear her crunching through the grass, couldn't he? Julia dropped to her knees. She was going to move quietly, and low, below the height of the grass.

A car door slammed, echoing eerily in the vast silence.

He was coming after her.

"Stupid cow," he said, his words partly muffled by the mist. But now that she wasn't running, she could hear him much better. "We can be together now," he growled. "I won't let that American scum have you. I won't let him take you from me. I found out all about him. Told Lady Worthington what he was—everything I'd found out."

Julia bit her lip so she wouldn't shout at this evil, awful man. She was too scared to move, in case she made a sound.

"I'm going to keep you," he said, his voice filled with triumph. "Only I will know where you are. It will be my secret forever."

The police constable worked at uncovering Sarah's body, with the sergeant watching the procedure. The young constable had gone behind bushes to throw up once. Cal had helped him for a while. Then something had caught his eye. He bent down. Crisp footprints had dried into formerly wet mud. They had to be fresh—these couldn't have lasted years. He hadn't walked over here. Neither had Julia.

Someone had been here recently. Obviously not John Carstairs.

Julia had been attacked and not by Ellen's pimp, Lowry. Julia, with blue-black hair and stunning blue eyes...

He had to see her. Had to know she was safe. He would get her trunks packed today—they could be gone tomorrow, leaving Worthington Park behind. David could stay if he wanted, as long as he wanted. They could take Diana with them, head to Paris, send her on her way safely to Switzerland with the chaperone.

He told the policemen he needed to check on his new bride, needed to see her. He drove fast to get back to Julia. The wind whipped back his hair. Grit flew against his driving goggles. Despite the conditions of the road, he drove like a bat out of hell. His car springs screeched with each bang and jolt. His headlamps tried—and failed—to cut through a veil of swirling mist. He crunched a headlamp against a stone wall that appeared out of nowhere.

Still, he didn't ease up. Who could have been there? A farmer? One of the gypsies? But Cal doubted it—it was off a narrow track, behind a grove of trees.

He hit the brakes as he roared into the drive, skidding to a stop right in front of Worthington. Within minutes, he learned Julia was gone. She had received a note that Toft was ill. But the chauffeur told him Julia hadn't taken a car.

"His lordship's going mad upstairs. He thinks Lady Worthington has gone missing." Eustace had come into the kitchen to impart the latest and most exciting gossip.

Hannah lifted her head from her rolling pin just as Tansy gave a little cry and dropped her bowl. It shattered with such a loud sound that Tansy shrieked. Batter flew everywhere.

Hannah sighed. "Tansy, clean up that mess." To Eustace

she said, "Lady Worthington went out for a drive with a friend."

"Don't tell him," Tansy urged. "Don't."

"Why not? She was driven away by a gentleman that she knew. She called him James. Go tell him that. I guess she didn't leave a note or anything."

Eustace went up to relay the message.

Moments later, Hannah and Tansy were shocked to hear heavy, fast footsteps pound down the stairs and the Earl of Worthington burst into the kitchen.

"Eustace told me you saw my wife get into a car," he said abruptly.

"I didn't—" Hannah saw Tansy make eyes at her and shake her head. Then she realized Tansy feared the earl would find out she had been slipping out to meet this man. "One of the maids did and she told me."

The earl frowned. "Why didn't this maid come forward upstairs when I asked if anyone had seen my wife?"

Hannah had to think quickly—because of course, it hadn't been an upstairs maid. "She was outside when she shouldn't have been. She was scared she would get into trouble."

"Who was driving the car?"

"I don't know. She didn't know, either. But Lady Worthington called him James."

"What did he look like?"

Hannah had no idea. She looked desperately at Tansy.

"This is very serious."

"My lord, will you promise you won't get the maid into trouble? You won't dismiss her?"

"If someone knows something, I need to hear it now," he said angrily.

Hannah shuddered. She was going to lose her place for Tansy. But the earl wasn't only angry, he was frightened.

She could tell. "Don't get her in trouble. It was my job to discipline her, and I failed. She wanted me to keep her confidence. I'm going to break it, so I should pay."

He looked at her in surprise. Then said, "I won't fire the girl. Who was it?"

"Tansy, my lord." Hannah pointed at the cowering, white-faced kitchen maid.

The earl went over to her. "You're not in trouble, Tansy. Just tell me what the man looked like. Where were they going?"

Tansy looked down more demurely than Hannah had ever seen. "He said he'd take her to the farm. She wanted to fetch Dr. Campbell first. He has black hair and he's a gentleman. I never knew his real name. But he drives a beautiful car. Dark red and all covered in shiny chrome. And she called him James."

Hannah swallowed hard. "This man—he's been showing attentions to a girl when he shouldn't have done."

Tansy made a strangled sound, but Hannah knew she had to go on. His lordship had looked concerned about this man, and Hannah knew he was a bad sort. "He lied to the girl about who he was. Made her false promises. I thought maybe her ladyship should know about this gentleman."

The earl stared at Tansy—at her lovely blue-black hair. "Tansy, were you the girl? You aren't in trouble—you won't lose your job. I need your help. Desperately."

"Yes. I didn't do anything really naughty, I swear. He used to take me driving."

"Where did he used to take you?"

Tansy tried to explain it, but she didn't know the surrounding land. Hannah did and she could guess where it was from Tansy's confused description. When she told the earl, he lifted her hand and kissed it!

"Thank you. Both of you." With that, the earl ran to the stairs. He grabbed the banister and took the steps three at a time.

Tansy tried to stir again, but began to cry. Hannah told her to sit down. As she brewed tea, Eustace came by her. "That was bally good of you, Han—Mrs. Talbot. Protecting Tansy when she was doing something so daft."

Hannah looked up in surprise to see Eustace regarding her with a soft, caring look in his eyes. The way he used to look at Tansy. But she was a cook now, happy with her career, and she knew Eustace had been wounded by Tansy's interest in another man. His attentions to her might be coming from his hurt pride. Anyway, she was quite happy with her future as a cook. She wasn't ready for a romance. But she prayed everything was all right with the new ladyship. Why was the earl so afraid?

Cal almost crashed into David, who was wheeling his chair down the hall, hands pushing on the rubber wheels.

"Cal, what's wrong?" David asked.

"Julia's gone. She's been taken." It had to be the Duke of Bradstock. Julia had called him James. And Bradstock had wanted Julia. Was that why he took black-haired women? Fear beat like a pulse in Cal's head.

David stopped rolling. "Julia got a note—"

"I know. I saw it. She went with the Duke of Bradstock in his car." Had Bradstock and Lord John Carstairs been abducting and murdering young women together? "I think he has killed women who looked…" God, his legs went weak with fear. "Like Julia."

David's face whitened. "We've got to find her—" He looked down at his artificial legs. "What can I do?"

"Stay here. I think I know where he's taken her." He was

praying he was right. If he wasn't, what else was he going to do? Combing the countryside would take forever. There weren't many roads, but they covered a hell of a lot of land.

"I'll send everyone else out looking that I can, Cal. I'll call the village police station. That I can do," David said.

"Thank you," Cal said. He gripped his brother's forearm. There were a lot of things he'd always wanted to say to David. For some reason, he needed to say them. Fast. "I'm sorry I couldn't get enough money to save our mother. I'm sorry I was too late to save Father. I'm sorry I didn't keep you out of danger in battle—"

"None of that is your fault so shut the hell up, Cal. Go and get your wife."

Cal ran out to his car. Maybe he wanted to say those things because it was likely he wouldn't see David again. If he couldn't save Julia, he was going to kill Bradstock. Or die trying.

Christ, he had to save her. But his gut was like lead, his heart like ice. He had been too late to save his father. Too late to protect his mother.

He couldn't be too late now.

The fields stretched around her. Julia was on her hands and knees, hidden by the wet grass, terrified to make a sound. She heard Bradstock stomp through the grass. Moving away from her.

What was she going to do? She could double back to the car.

Cal had told her she was brave. She thought of Ellen Lambert being completely vulnerable, driving an ambulance through shelling. She owed it to all modern women not to be a coward.

Staying low, Julia ran back to the car. Wincing at the

sound, she opened the door and climbed in. He would know where she was as soon as she started the car. As soon as the engine caught, she shoved the pedal to the floor. The engine screamed and the car lurched forward. Almost giddy with hope, she went a few feet, clinging to the wheel with hands that were frozen with fear.

A sound, sharp and explosive as a gunshot, made her scream. It came from the front of the car. The wheel moved funny. The steering wheel jerked in her hand. She'd hit a hole and buggered up the front of the car. She was moving downhill. The tire was flat, but still turning.

The lights picked up Bradstock as he reached the edge of the track. Showed the vicious fury on his face as he ran out into the track in front of her.

To escape she was going to have to run him down.

If she didn't, he'd kill her.

She had to do it. She couldn't leave him alive to kill anyone else.

She accelerated—

No, she couldn't do it. She took her foot off the accelerator, slammed on the brake. The engine stalled. The car stopped.

Oh God. She was a fool. She thought of Zelda Fitzgerald's words. She *was* an utter fool—a softhearted one. Strangely, she still heard the rumble of an engine. It sounded far away, lost in the rising fog. It couldn't be her engine.

Then the sound disappeared. Her imagination?

Bradstock slammed his hand on the hood of the car. He didn't seem aware of the low, soft sound of a motorcar—so she must have dreamed it. Rage emanated from him. Slapping his hand along the hood of his car, he prowled toward her.

She had no weapon. She was more scared than when Ellen's attacker had come after her. Her hand was still clutched around the key.

The key—

Julia pushed the car door open. It was a barricade between her and him as she scrambled out of the car. She ran several feet, then he grabbed her arm and jerked her back. He pulled her with him back to the car. Flung her against the hood. She cried out as she slammed into the metal.

He was on top of her, trying to force her arms back. She drove her knee at his vulnerable place. He howled. He didn't let her go, but his grip slackened. She broke her hand free and scratched his face with the key.

He roared. "Bitch!" His palm cracked against her face.

"You were the one. The one who tried to take me outside Ellen's cottage."

"You were spending so much time with Worthington. I was so angry with you," Bradstock snapped. He wrestled to get the key out of her hand. She hung on like a hunting dog. His hand wrapped around her wrist, forced it back. The key fell out of her hand. She looked desperately down the lane—

There was something there.

The beams of light illuminated a silver motorcar coming up the track toward them. She yelled, "Help me! He wants to kill me!"

Bradstock swung around, just at the moment the other car stopped and a large male shape jumped out. The lights picked up golden hair. Then Cal's face, contorted with a viciousness she'd never seen on it. He lunged for Bradstock. His fist sliced across Bradstock's face. He punched again, right into the duke's face. Bone crunched.

Bradstock hit back. She saw, in the light, silver in the villain's hand. The blade of a knife. "Cal, look out."

Bradstock stabbed wildly at Cal, but Cal blocked his every

attempt. Cal fought like a man possessed. Better than a prize-fighter.

She looked for a weapon. Something to use on Bradstock to protect Cal... Heavens, Bradstock would have a shovel in the boot. She could threaten him with that.

But as she slid along the side of the motor toward the boot, Bradstock let out a roar as Cal snapped his wrist back. The breaking sound echoed across the empty field. The knife glinted as it fell to the ground.

One more punch to Bradstock's face sent the fiend reeling back. His huge, broad-shouldered body slumped bonelessly over the hood of his motorcar.

"Julia."

Cal's arms went around her, engulfing her in warmth, in safety.

"How did you get here?" she whispered. "I thought— I was certain I—"

"Hannah convinced Tansy to tell me she saw you get into Bradstock's car and where he used to take her. Bradstock used to take her out in his car. I guess because she looks like you."

Hannah. Tansy. The women in the kitchen had helped save her life.

"I was scared I was too late," he said gruffly. "When I saw the car headlights coming toward me, my heart just about stopped. But when I saw him outlined in them, I knew you'd gotten behind the wheel. You almost saved yourself, you smart, smart girl. But you couldn't run him down, could you?"

"No. I simply couldn't bring myself to do it. It wouldn't have been right. It wouldn't have been cricket."

Cal laughed huskily, with a catch in his voice. His arms tightened. He laid his cheek against her head. "You even tried to escape a killer in a ladylike manner. What am I going to do with you?"

"I wasn't all that ladylike. I scratched his face with his key."

He kissed her. His mouth took hers in such a fast, overwhelming passion, she was literally lifted off her feet. When he set her down he said, "You should have gone for his eyes."

She shuddered. "Cal, I'm sorry. I'm just not that ruthless."

"You don't have to be. You're perfect, Julia. Perfect in every way. God, I love you. I love you with all my soul. And thank God, you're safe." He hugged her to him. "David telephoned for the police. They should arrive soon. Then I'll take you home."

She could hear the sounds of cars roaring up the path. "Home to Worthington? It is our home, Cal. Truly, it is."

24

America

For the next month, Julia was treated like a Hollywood movie star. Cal pampered her in every way. He brought her champagne, and asked for the most delectable dishes and desserts for dinner. He took her out riding in the mornings and she loved showing him how the mist rose from the fields and sunlight glistened on dew. They had tea on the lawns under the spreading branches of an oak, while the lawn mowers clacked. In the evenings, they walked through the woods with the estate's dogs following them. They would return and sit with the terrace doors open to the breeze, drink cocktails, then go up to bed…where the most decadent and naughty things happened. Day by day, Cal healed her from the shock of Bradstock's attack.

After all the fear and pain that had come before, it filled her with joy to be building this life with Cal at Worthington.

Diana wanted to stay longer at Worthington and she fussed over Julia, and seemed happy with her more sedate life and spending time with David. Julia knew they must take Diana away soon. They did not tell Diana, Cassia and Thalia about

John. The Duke of Bradstock never went to trial—he hanged himself, taking his own life, and Cal had not told the police about John's involvement. In the end, he decided justice had been served by John's death and he didn't want to hurt his cousins' futures.

But the dowager and Cal did not speak to each other. Julia believed the dowager would not hurt Cal by exposing what his mother had done, since Cal had protected John.

A week after the attack, on a morning Cal went out, knowing she was now safe, Julia visited the ladies she was helping. She saw Mrs. Billings, who lived in a cottage alone, now that Mr. Billings had passed on. They had lost all their sons in the Great War and Julia had suggested that one of her widows, a young woman with three children, share Mrs. Billings's cottage. Mrs. Billings was delighted to have children around her. Julia had also introduced Mr. Toft to a widow of another farm. They were working their farms together. She hoped that in time a romance might take root.

She drove to Lilac Farm, knowing that soon the Brands would be leaving it. They now knew what had happened to Sarah. It had broken their hearts, but Brand had insisted there was peace in knowing the truth. They were to move into a cottage on the estate.

But as she reached the farm, Julia heard a great deal of banging. She followed the sound, and stopped her car on a rise. Below her, men scurried everywhere around all kinds of newfangled equipment. Wood from the sawmill lay in huge stacks. Houses were being built on land that had once been the fields of Lilac Farm.

She quickly drove home. Heart in her throat, she found Cal in his study. "You are building houses? But what about Lilac Farm? The land is needed for the farm."

He shoved back his golden hair. "It's sold, Julia. It was the best land to begin building and I received a damn good offer for it. For the Brands, the farm is wrapped up in sad memories. I'm going to take care of them."

"But…but you never talked to me about this." She felt numb with shock. "Have you sold more?"

"Yes."

Then he told her what he had sold. Three farms belonging to families no longer able to farm. Nausea rose in her belly. "How could you?"

He paced on the Aubusson rug in front of the fireplace. "With the money I've made on the land, the families are living rent-free in new homes. The children of those families will be sent to school. I've seen the squalor of slums. It's the same here. People live on top of each other while I have acres of underused land."

She could see the benefit, but still felt fear over such abrupt change. "But you did not talk to me about it."

"You would have said no. The truth is, Julia, I can't stay here. The dowager can destroy my mother's name if she wants and I've realized I can live with that. What matters is that I can still hear the condescending sneer in the dowager's voice. It cost my mother her soul to do what she did. It cost her life. Do you look at me now and see only a man with a mother who whored herself because her boy was too late to protect his father, too late to protect her?"

His words went through her like a blade of ice. The pain in them broke her heart. "I see a man who loved his parents and who would have risked his own life to help them."

He looked away from her. She saw that—but he didn't. How could she make him see?

"This place will never be a home to me, Julia," he said harshly. "What matters is us and not Worthington Park. We can be together anywhere. It doesn't have to be here."

Leave and never come back? Then she saw the truth. "Cal, you have to stop running away. You cannot run from your past. You have to heal from it."

"We could be happy if we were away from here. I want to build a future for us. Don't you want that?" His golden brows drew down.

"Yes, but I feel we do belong here. You're angry and you are doing rash things—"

"These changes aren't rash. My desire to leave here isn't rash."

"But when you proposed, you told me you wouldn't destroy Worthington."

"So it was the damn estate all along. Julia, do you even love me?"

"Of course I love you."

"But if I'd been honest, if I told you that Worthington wasn't part of the deal, you never would have said yes."

"Honest? Do you mean you lied to me?" Shock hit her.

"Yeah, I lied to you. I made a vow to my mother as she was dying that I would make the Carstairs family pay. How in hell could I ever be lord of this when she had to condemn her soul?" He raked back his hair. "Julia, which do you choose—Worthington or me?"

"This is ridiculous. It should not have to be a choice." They were echoing the night he had proposed in Paris and she had only the same answer to give.

"It is. For me."

"Cal, I can't accept this." She wanted Cal to find happiness in the same life that she did. And it hurt that he'd lied. Her father had lied to her mother. Mother had found out about all his affairs. His lies had made her desperately unhappy.

"Julia, damn it, tell me which you choose." He stalked

toward the window, his shoulders stiff and tense. "It's Worthington, isn't it? You'll always love it more than me."

How could she trust anything he told her now? She would always worry about what was unsaid. "Why couldn't you have been honest?"

He turned. "That night in Paris, would you have said yes if I told you I still wanted to sell Worthington?"

"I—" She wouldn't have done.

"You would have said no. I can see it in your eyes."

"I am not to blame for this!" she cried. "Cal, Worthington is my place in the world. It is where I belong. I once thought love was all that mattered in marriage. But you've shown me I was wrong. Love is meaningless without one thing—honesty."

"Hell—" He broke off. "Julia, I've never been honest with you. What Bradstock told you about me was true. He may have been a vicious killer, but he was right about that. That's what Kerry O'Brien was going to give you. All the rotten details of my past. You're right—you deserved honesty. And you deserve better than a man like me."

Then he was gone. He walked right out of the room, walking past her.

She shook with pain. He'd lied to her from the very beginning. She didn't know how to fix this. She didn't know how to stop feeling sick with betrayal. Or how to stop what he was doing to Worthington.

For all her training to be a lady and to handle any situation, she felt powerless. Brokenhearted. Afraid.

Cal did not come down for dinner. Nor did he come to her room that night. The next morning, she marched upstairs and pushed open the door to his room. A modern woman would sort this out.

But the bed was smooth and a sheaf of white paper sat in the middle of it. Her heart stuttered when she saw her name at the top. It was a letter written from Cal.

I don't even know how to write this. I'm no good at putting things into words.

I made a vow, a promise, when my mother died. Mam told me to forgive the old earl. I told her she was worthy of justice. When the dowager looked down on Mam, it made me almost choke in my guilt, so I think I was lying to myself when I thought I sold the land for good reasons. I did it in anger.

I saw your face when I admitted that most of the things Bradstock told you were true. I did run with the Five Points Gang. It was work with them or be targeted by them. My mother told me to stand up for what I believed in, but in the end, I wanted the money. That was a lot easier to live with when I was a young, arrogant thug than it is now. I never expected that.

I'm sorry I lied to you about Worthington. I'm sorry I didn't tell you about my past. I knew I would lose you if you knew the truth about me.

So I'm gone. As my aunt said, I'm not fit for decent society.

I said I don't believe in curses, but my mam did. If there's a curse on you, Julia, it's me.

I'm going to London first to meet with the solicitors. Worthington Park will be yours. The title is entailed, so is the estate, but I could sell it for debts. So I'm taking out a big loan in your name, then I'll have the lawyers draw up the papers for you to foreclose.

The estate is yours. You are the sole owner.

I guess you changed me because I want Worthington

to survive. You can make that happen. There's no one else I would trust with the estate. You called it "your place in the world." I would never take that away from you, Sheba.

I love you with all my heart, Julia. I'll come back in a few months and if you want me gone, I'll give you a divorce. I'm sorry if I caused you pain.

That's what I'm good at. The only thing I've done well, except for painting, is hurting people. And I can't paint now. It's all garbage, what I'm putting on the canvas. Now that I don't have your love, I can't seem to paint right.

You were my muse. I was right about that. It's killing me to leave, but it's the right thing.

Yours regretfully,

Cal

For a long while, she held the note, staring blankly at it. Then, out of the small cupboard in the bedside table, she took out Cal's bottle of fiery whiskey. She poured some into a tumbler and walked back into her bedroom as Zoe walked in.

"What is that?" Zoe asked.

Julia took the tiniest sip. "Gah!"

Zoe's brows rose. "Julia, what on earth are you drinking?"

"Irish whiskey." She had literally just touched her tongue to the stuff and shuddered. Yet the burning sensation after was rather pleasant. "Cal says this drink relaxes him. I was hoping to discover that was true for me, as well. Would you like some?"

"No, thank you, I shouldn't. Besides, I much prefer cocktails. That's the only way hard liquor is palatable. But why are you drinking?"

Julia lifted the glass to take another sip, but her eyes watered. Perhaps the promise of feeling less upset wasn't worth the price of drinking this. "My husband has left me."

"What?"

She gave Zoe the letter. She adored her sister-in-law, and Zoe's business acumen had made her wise in other ways, as well.

Suddenly, the urge to cry overwhelmed her. Julia set down the glass and sobbed. Zoe embraced her. She cried and cried. Then sucked in a deep breath in an unladylike way. "I'm sorry. Falling into disarray is not something I do lightly."

"Disarray? Julia, your silly husband has gone away. You have the right to be upset." Zoe sighed. "Marriage can be so annoying. That was why I wanted to be independent. Fortunately I discovered the blessings of marriage outweigh the times when you'd like to bean your husband over the head."

Julia laughed—Zoe had taught her to not restrict herself to ladylike smiles—but almost as quickly she felt like crying again. "It's so complicated. He lied to me and he didn't tell me about his past. He was a mobster, apparently. I don't know what he did, but it sounds as if it was terrible. I wish he would have talked to me instead of leaving."

"I went through the same problems with your brother, Julia. He wouldn't tell me what caused his shell shock."

"But you convinced him to tell you. And you both worked together to heal him. Cal has just…left. I should be angry with him for doing that. But I know he did it because he believes he is doing it for me. He gave Worthington to me."

She had made him see how important Worthington was. But this was not the outcome she'd hoped for. "He asked me if I chose Worthington or him. I couldn't answer then—I was too shocked and angry that he was asking me to choose. But I choose him. And now it's too late."

And just like that, the tears began again.

She'd cried buckets for Anthony when she'd learned he'd been killed. She had not cried when Ellen had been hurt—she'd been too outraged. She had cried when Mrs. Toft had died in childbirth. "I'm sorry. I don't know why I am crying so much. I feel rather sick—"

Zoe plucked the glass of whiskey out of Julia's hand. "I know why it is. You are pregnant, dear."

Could it be true? Could she be…enceinte? She'd been married just over a month.

"You're a married woman, and nausea and tears are two signs that you might be having a baby, Julia. We must go to London to see a specialist. But first, you must go for breakfast. Now is not the time to not eat. I'm sure Cal will come back."

"In months, he has said." She wanted him there, to share her news with him. But she went down for breakfast with Zoe as their guest—where David, Diana, Cassia and Thalia were in the dining room. They did not need to know Cal had gone. But Cassia asked if it was true that he had left for America.

"Wiggins told our lady's maid that Cal ordered his trunk be brought down from the attic," Diana said. "And he saw the tickets for the *Olympic*, lying out on Cal's bedside table. He is sailing for New York. But there was only one ticket."

"He has gone to New York City. For a visit," she lied. "He left me in charge of the estate."

Diana's eyebrows lifted. "Is more of the estate going to be sold?"

"No. Worthington Park is safe now. I promise." And in a soft voice, she said to Diana, "I will take you to Paris as soon as I can."

But Diana shook her head. "I— No— Julia, it's so complicated." Diana got up and left and Julia understood the rush of painful emotions she must be feeling.

After breakfast, Zoe left and Julia walked through the corridors. She was supposed to run Worthington but all she could think of was Cal. She saw David in the library, gazing at a shelf out of his reach. She hurried in, fetched the book he wanted, handing it to him.

"Thank you," he said shyly. Then, "Julia, there's something I need to ask you. Maybe you'll think I'm crazy, too. Cal would. But I want to do it."

"What is it?"

"I know Diana is expecting. I know her beau let her down—Cal told me. I want to ask Diana to marry me. Cal settled a lot of money on me when he made his fortune. I can't give her a title, but I can give her a nice house. I know I'm not a catch without my legs—"

"David, you are a true gentleman, a hero and a good man." Julia's heart wobbled. She was so touched. But then, practicality set in. "But Diana...may still be in love with this man, even though he is utterly useless. I don't know what she will say."

"I can hear 'no.' But I want to try."

"Then I do hope, with all my heart, that she says yes."

After she left him, she found Diana. A lady would never leave such a thing to chance. "Could I speak to you for a moment? In the morning room, perhaps?"

Diana's loose dress floated around her as they went into the morning room and Julia carefully closed the door. A lady got to the point when it was necessary. "Diana, David has fallen in love with you and he intends to ask for your hand in marriage."

"David—marriage?"

"Yes. He adores you. He has accepted that you will be reluctant to marry him because he has lost his legs in the War. It happened in the most heroic way possible—he was saving the lives of other men. Be gentle when you refuse him. Be as kind as you can. He is a very good man."

"Julia, I'm not going to gently refuse David Carstairs."

"Diana, please—"

"I'm going to accept him. Could you tell him that, so he will get the courage to ask me?"

"Diana, please don't do it just because you need a marriage. He deserves much more—"

"Julia, sometimes you are terrible. You are completely insulting me. You really think I'm not capable of loving him, don't you? Why—because he was wounded in battle? I do love him. He knows about my child and offered to help me with money. I said I couldn't ask that of him. He is a good man. He knows the worst about me—all my horrible sins—and he doesn't condemn me for them. David says that when he sees me in the morning, it is as if he has awoken to a perfect day. He made me see there is more to life than a title, than being mistress of a large house that is really an empty home."

Julia jerked. That was what she was—mistress of a vast house that now felt empty, when what she had wanted more than anything was happiness.

"I will tell him. I will tell him right away." Julia clasped Diana's hands. "I would love to know you two are going to be married, before I go away."

"Where are you going?"

"America."

New, sleek, renowned for its speed, the *Athena* was like no ship Julia had ever seen. Everything was clean glass, polished silver metal, smooth lines. Her stateroom was done in white and black, crisp and striking. There were no frilled velvets, no Italianate smoking rooms and staterooms designed to look like fussy Victorian rooms in an English manor. Here the lines were streamlined, promising a voyage to a new, thrilling world.

Julia had been startled that even Nigel approved of her pursuing Cal. Cassia had taken command of her work with the widows while she traveled with Zoe and Nigel, along with Nicholas and his nurse They intended to visit Zoe's mother in New York, as Mrs. Gifford was thrilled to see her grandson and to know Zoe was expecting again.

Over dinner in the dining room with a modern silver-and-white ceiling, she said, "Cal gave me Worthington to keep it safe. I've realized *this* is my place in the world—to fight for important things that I believe in. And I believe in Cal. More than he believes in himself. But can I convince him to come back with me? He said he is not worthy of me. I don't know how to make him see that isn't true."

"Go to him. And you will find a way," Zoe said, with all her modern confidence.

"You're right, Julia. This is where you belong," Nigel said. "Taking charge suits you."

Julia was nervous until the day they docked. She stood at the railing, breathless. The city rose out of the water like something magical, with buildings that scraped the sky.

Once they disembarked, they hired a car. Zoe drove, as she knew the city well. David had given Julia the address of the house they used in New York. It was outside the city, in a place called "Great Neck" on Long Island Sound. Where wealthy people went to summer.

It felt like they had plunged into the country. Green trees shimmered lushly against the blue sky. Fields stretched around her and in the middle sat quaint clapboard farmhouses with large porches.

The roads became narrower and they got lost. Stumbling upon a house, Julia got directions from the butler who answered the door, who was quite stunned when she introduced herself as the Countess of Worthington. She learned that the roads and railways were kept deliberately in disrepair to discourage the city people from flocking to the area in the spring and summer.

Following the directions, their Chrysler motorcar pulled into a long drive. Julia put her hands over her mouth as the mansion came into view.

"This belongs to Cal?" Nigel stared.

The large mansion followed the curving drive, giving views of the grounds from all directions. It was white as snow, striking with black shutters and a large black front door. Two large wings branched off the main portion of the house. From the drive, as they neared the house, they could see the gray crashing waves of the ocean beyond. The house stood at the end of a spit of land that bravely pushed out into the sea.

"I had no idea Cal had the money to buy this," Julia whispered. Coming to Worthington Park had not been so much of a shock to him. He hadn't told her the whole truth about his wealth.

Nigel stopped the car and Julia didn't wait for any servants to appear. She got out and rapped on the front door. The door opened, and she got to shock another butler with the announcement of her title.

"Is my husband in?" she asked. Her heart hammered—she didn't know for certain he'd come here. He could have traveled anywhere. Even left America by now.

She could have laughed with joy and relief when the butler bowed. "The master is in his study, madam."

"My lady," Zoe corrected cheekily.

Then Zoe squeezed Julia's hands. "Go and see Cal." To the butler, she said, "My husband and I would like to wait in another room."

"Allow me to show you the drawing room that overlooks the Sound, madam."

"That is the Duchess of Langford," Julia pointed out. "I'm afraid you address her as 'Your Grace.' It is rather complicated, but I know you'll get the hang of it."

His jaw dropped so fast he almost had to catch it in his hands. Julia had him point her toward Cal's study. At first, she walked there like a lady. Then she couldn't wait and she ran.

Her shoes clicked on the gleaming marble tile and skimmed across beautiful carpet. She knocked on the white paneled door to the study.

"Come in."

She felt a sharp jolt of delight at the sound of his voice. She gently pushed open the door. He stood by his window, looking out at the lawns and the white-capped gray waves of the sea.

"What is it?" he asked brusquely.

"Hi, Cal," she said, as casually and jauntily as she could.

He spun around and he staggered backward as he saw her. A tumbler with a small amount of dark gold liquid fell out of his hand. "Julia?"

"You've dropped your—"

She broke off as he gripped her around the waist and lifted her in his arms. His mouth covered hers, in a hot kiss that could have made the cold ocean water boil.

Julia had feared he might not want to see her or he might be determined to keep distance between them even when they were in the same room. But he pulled her so close there wasn't any space between her breasts and belly and his hard body.

"Julia, why are you here? Here in America?"

"I've come after you, Cal. I'm chasing you in a bold, brash, modern way. And you've dropped your drink."

His blue eyes went large with disbelief. "You came across an ocean for me? You shouldn't have done. If you wanted to see me, Sheba, all you had to do was telephone and I would have swum the ocean for you. You shouldn't have gone to so much trouble. The truth is, I'm not worth it."

"Cal, I know you are. And I enjoyed taking charge and traveling across the ocean for my very first time."

He set her down, cupped her cheek. "Before you say I'm worth it, you need to know the truth about me, my muse. You need to know where I've come from and what I've done."

With the fabric top up on his 1924 Rolls, Cal drove into the city, making his way to the area where he'd grown up. He drove through streets that still cried of squalor, where the stink of industry and the smell of sewage rolled up the streets from the river.

He didn't look at Julia. Didn't need to see her to know what she must be thinking.

"This is where you grew up?"

"Yes," he said abruptly. "The neighborhood is known as Hell's Kitchen."

"Hell's Kitchen. That's a curious name. Was it because of the heat in the summer?"

He gave a hard laugh. "No one agrees on where the name came from. A reporter from the *New York Times* called one of the tenements 'Hell's Kitchen,' back in the 1880s. It's at 39th Street and Tenth Avenue. The reporter went there to write a story on a multiple murder and called it the lowest and filthiest place in the city. Or some say the name came from a veteran police officer who was watching a riot with a rookie copper. The rookie calls the place 'hell itself,' and the veteran says, 'Hell's a mild climate. This is Hell's Kitchen.'"

Cal stole a glance, expecting to see her look disgusted. "I should have known," he muttered.

"What?"

"You're too much of a lady to show your shock on your face." It came out angrier than he'd intended. "I want to see it—don't hide it. Hiding it means you pity me."

He stopped the car on the road outside the sagging, worn, mean-looking walk-up tenement in which he'd lived as a boy.

Julia, her lips perfectly slicked in dark red lipstick, her skin glowing like the sheen of silk, looked up beneath the brim of her hat. "I do not pity you. You survived poverty I cannot even imagine and you got out. I admire you and respect you—how could I not respect a self-made man? As someone who inherited her position, her place in her home, I have nothing but intense respect, Cal."

"Julia, you earned your place in the world, as you call it. I'm a self-made man, but it's how I made it that you should hate me for. You know, it killed me to leave you—"

She had her hand on the door handle, ready to push the door open. He stopped her. "You aren't getting out here."

"I want to look inside. To see your old home."

"It's not a home," he said bitterly. "It was a small, dirty apartment, filled with stink, disease and violence." He put the car in gear—he hadn't turned it off in case they had to leave in a hurry. Before he started moving, a boy ran out of the shadows and stroked the smooth, curved fender.

"She's a beaut, mister," the boy said.

Cal's throat tightened. In the boy's low whistle, he heard himself twenty years ago. In the boy's look of longing and desire as he cooed over the car, Cal saw his own hunger, when he'd been a boy, to get money and go places.

"What's your name?" he asked.

"I'm Tom."

On a whim, Cal motioned Tom to come over to his window. He talked to the lad, found out the boy's father had been a mechanic, but was out of work after the War. "Pa lost his leg, and can't get any work," Tom said.

"How terrible," Julia breathed. "Even here, there isn't the kindness and care given to the war heroes that should be given."

"No," Cal said. "Which is why boys ended up in gangs, fighting for money, fighting to move up in the world." To Tom, he said, "Tell me where you live. I need a man to fix my engines. I keep a few cars out of the city, and my chauffeur's leaving me to get married and move out to California. I need a new man. Give me your address, and I'll come back and talk to your pa. If I think he's right for the job, there's a cottage out at my place on Long Island Sound."

Tom grinned, gave him the address, then took off. He ran up the steps into the open front door of the building.

Cal shook his head. "What are the odds?" he said thoughtfully. "He lives in the apartment I lived in."

"Will you give his father a job?"

"A missing leg won't make it impossible for him to tend an engine. That takes a man's hands and his head. The boy can help him and learn a few things when he's not in school."

"This is very good of you."

"I learned it from you, Julia. The pure, sweet pleasure that comes from helping someone. From changing even one life."

"Cal...that's so sweet. Thank you."

He saw her smile, a smile more radiant than any sunrise, or autumn-leaved forest, or stunning wilderness scene he'd tried to capture on a canvas.

As much as he wanted to turn around and drive away

and have Julia, keep her, make sure he never lost her, he knew he had to be honest with her.

Cal drove away from the sidewalk. Julia reached out and touched his shoulder. More sad apartment buildings flashed by them. She smelled the river, heard a mournful horn.

They were driving toward the tall buildings of the center of Manhattan.

"When I was a kid," Cal said, "I wanted to make money for my family. I told you my father worked at the docks. He hated the brutality, the intimidating, the thieving. He stood up to the gangs and that got him beaten up. I ended up working for them. First I was running messages and acting as a lookout when they broke into warehouses."

"But you were just a boy—"

"I knew it was against the law. And I knew it would break my mam's heart if she knew I'd been helping the gangs. But I needed the money. After Father was killed, I swore I'd never be vulnerable like that. Mam worked as a seamstress in the daytime. Twelve hours a day, every day, she worked in a warehouse with bars over the windows and poor light, worked until she was losing her eyesight. And after she'd slaved all day making clothes, she spent the nights washing dishes at pubs. She worked so hard she got sick. That's when she got desperate. She feared David and I wouldn't be able to survive if she couldn't earn, so she swallowed her pride and wrote to the Carstairs family. She hated that they felt she was nothing. But she kept muttering that they were right and she was nothing because she wasn't strong enough to look after her boys. She was weak, thin as a tiny bird, because she let David and I have almost all the food. I wouldn't eat all of mine so she could have some.

"She got sicker, and she lost her jobs. Then she—she sold

herself to men for money. I used to hear her cry at night. Some of the men were like the one that beat up Ellen Lambert. They didn't want sex unless they could use the woman as a punching bag."

Julia wanted to say something, but saw he needed to talk. So she let him.

"Having to prostitute herself finished her. It ate away at her inside. I wrote to Lady Worthington myself, begging her to help my mother. I hoped for some pity, some shred of kindness. But I didn't get any. I went back to the Five Points Gang. Then America entered the War and I signed up along with a man I knew, Wild Bill Lovett. When I got out, he was heading up the Jay Street Gang. Prohibition started and I got involved with them and with bootlegging. In war, I'd learned how to kill—"

"Did you—did you do that in the gang?"

"No. I was muscle. I threatened people, collected debts. I never took an innocent life." They were moving into the tall buildings. "I'm taking you to the Plaza for luncheon. There's something I've got to tell you there."

"Cal, you don't have to tell me anything more. I love you, you know."

They drove down Park Avenue to the Plaza Hotel. Cal stopped there. Cars zipped past them. A cacophony of horns rose around them. Girls strode past on clicking heels.

"I'll drive you back to Nigel and Zoe if you want, after I tell you this," Cal said. "I left the Jay Street Gang and started my own enterprise. Bootlegging and fake bonds." He hung his head. "A member of one of the gangs tried to kill me, to move into my position and get my turf. I had to fight for my life. He stabbed me and I beat him badly. Then he went and got drunk and got hit by a car."

"That wasn't your fault," she said.

"I'd almost beaten him to death, Julia. Rumors started that it was one of my men who ran him down. I don't think that's true and I didn't order it, if it was. Stories grew that I killed people. I didn't, but that night I had come close to becoming the kind of thug my father hated, the kind of thug who had killed him. I was afraid that next time I might cross the line. I had to fight to succeed without hurting anyone. I got out of crime and spent day and night studying companies so I could invest my money and make enough to look after David."

"Looking after David is what drove you. You never took anyone's life. And you got away from crime."

"That man's death is on my soul. I pounded him and he likely got drunk to ease the pain. I was sure Mam was turning in her grave over what I was doing. So I went to Paris and tried painting. My dad had taught me how to draw, and he'd brought some paints and pencils from England when he left for good. I found I loved painting, and I guess I could have let it completely heal my soul, but I didn't. I didn't want to give up on my desire to get revenge."

"Do you still want that? I understand if you do—"

"Julia, you crossed an ocean for me. I have to make myself worthy of you. I'm not going to hurt the family. Or destroy the estate. It's yours, angel, so I can't do that."

"You're helping that young boy. That's what we should do together. Help people."

Cal said softly to her, "I used to dream of having a rich man come up and offer me work. Give me a way to escape this place. So maybe I've made someone's dreams come true."

"You made most of mine come true," she whispered. "My heart was in bits and pieces and you've given me the strength to make it whole. I understand that you can't see Worthington as a home. Cal, maybe I am too late, but I choose you over Worthington."

He shook his head. "You were right, Julia. I was always running away. But you can never outrun yourself. I don't want to run away from the life you want. I know now that I can't live without you. And, you know, I guess I actually miss Worthington Park."

She smiled. "Now, let's go inside, shall we? I have something to tell you."

"I think we should take a room in there."

"Really? Whatever for?"

"I want to spend the rest of the day making love to you, Sheba."

Her heart glowed with joy. "There is something I must tell you, Cal. I believe I am expecting our child. If all goes well, you are going to become a father. And I know you will be the most wonderful father."

"Julia!" He kissed her senseless. "Then we should go home. Back to Worthington."

He'd called Worthington home. Her heart soared.

"I don't want to go home just yet," she said. "I have a few months—and you promised to show me adventure. I want to travel with you and paint."

Cal looked stunned. But two months later, Julia drew the paddle of a canoe through crystal-clear water. Liquid dripped with each stroke, forming rings and ripples. The morning sun was rising over the mountains, sending warm light over the lake.

"You're a great paddler," Cal said, behind her.

Julia half turned, but carefully—she was still concerned she might tip the canoe. "I feel I'm doing it completely out of synchronization with you."

"It's perfect," he said.

"It is." She gazed over the water. Yellow and red leaves blazed around the lake. They had traveled by train into Canada, then up into the north of the province of Ontario. For weeks, they had traveled, as summer became fall, and had spent days here in a tent. At night they snuggled together in a sleeping sack.

"You know, you look damn sexy in trousers," Cal said.

Julia blushed. "I don't know how women ever did this in skirts."

"Are you really enjoying this, or is this too rough for you?"

They glided toward a rocky point. A huge fir tree towered there. Julia paused, resting her paddle. "I love this," she said. "I wasn't certain I'd love sleeping beneath the stars, but I do."

Cal steered them to the rocky shoreline and Julia got out, her leather boots balancing on the uneven rock. She loved the crispness of the morning air and the pure scent of it. It was wilder than the English countryside, but it spoke to her soul.

With Cal, she unpacked the canoe. He always wanted to do most of the work, but she helped him set up the tent and lay out the sacks and blankets they used for sleeping. Cal set up a fire. That night, they sat beside the fire and watched the stars. And she saw the glorious northern lights—stunning displays of dancing green, purple and yellow.

The next day, they worked together at the edge of the rock, sketching on small canvases. Cal painted the landscape and she tried to paint him. Much to her chagrin, he took the picture from her at the end of the day and looked at it. His eyes widened. "It's incredible. You have real talent, my beautiful muse. More talent than me."

She laughed. "I don't."

"You've made me more handsome than I really am."

"That is exactly how you look to me. Even here, in the wilds, I think you are the perfect Earl of Worthington."

He kissed her. "You know, Sheba, I think it's time to travel home. Since you're in a delicate condition."

She nodded. "If I get very large, I'll probably tip the canoe." And she laughed as Cal pulled her back into his arms.

In April, when snowdrops blossomed over the lawns of Worthington, Julia gave birth to two beautiful babies—twins! Cal was there, helping her through the birth. Dr. Campbell and a London specialist attended. She had just sent Cal home from the hospital for some sleep, Nigel and Zoe had come and left. Isobel had come, fascinated by the medical practicalities of birthing twins. Although many medical schools had closed their doors to women now that the War was behind them, there were still some places and Isobel was determined to leave that year to study.

Then Julia heard a nurse giggling outside her room, and she knew who had come. Seconds later, her charming brother Sebastian peeked around the door. "Only you would have one of each rather than having to choose. It's more perfect this way," he said, grinning.

She held both babies in her arms, which she felt rather nervous about doing. She asked her brother about John Ransome.

"Alas, I've realized I can't change John's mind. He won't turn his back on his family—and their expectations—for me," Sebastian said.

"As you said to me, he should be willing to fight for you. Perhaps if I bring you together—arrange dinner parties—"

"You will be too busy being a mother. I'm philosophical about this, Julia. Love will come for me eventually. I plan to return to Paris and paint. But I'm going to stay in England for the summer, to see my adorable nephews and niece."

"It will be wonderful to have you here," she said.

She sensed Cal just as he came in her room, carrying a bouquet of roses. He stopped in the doorway and just looked at her. She had never seen him look so happy. Diana had given birth to her daughter a few months before, after her marriage to David. David had even ridden a horse just before that, as Julia had vowed he would. It had been a delightful time. This was even more wonderful. "You are supposed to be resting," she said.

"I couldn't stay away. You look radiant, Julia. Perfect."

"You mean they are perfect."

"All of you are perfect," he said softly. "There is no curse now. There can't be. Your blend of modern compassion and old-world elegance and honor has broken the curse forever. You've brought happiness to Worthington. And brought the most wonderful miracles of all to me. Two beautiful babies, the perfect wife and love."

"Amen," Sebastian said.

Julia looked up. She saw the dowager countess in the corridor, afraid to come in. "Would you take our daughter?" Julia asked him.

He looked confused, then embarrassed, and she smiled. "Our daughter has the curls."

As he scooped their little girl into his arms, she said, "You could introduce her to the dowager. I've had to think long and hard about it, but I think we should give her a second chance."

Cal nodded. "She wrote me a letter telling me that she would never breathe a word about my mother. I admit, I haven't answered it." He made a beckoning motion. As the dowager Lady Worthington came in, she whispered, "I'm sorry. So very sorry. For everything."

Julia looked to Cal. He said gently, "It's accepted. And

thank you for your decision. Now, come here and meet the future Earl of Worthington and his perfect sister."

The dowager did, wiping a tear from her cheek.

Then her mother and grandmother came into the room. Julia saw the joy in her mother's eyes, and she had Cal help her mother hold each baby, one at a time. "They are beautiful," her mother cooed, her eyes bright with happy tears. "It is so miraculous. Two wonderful babies. And speaking of something miraculous, your grandmother has allowed Sir Raynard to court her more seriously."

"Court me? Rubbish," Grandmama declared. "But perhaps I have realized I have been blessed with everything—a home, a family, delightful grandchildren. So perhaps I could risk allowing a gentleman into my life once more."

"I highly approve," Julia said teasingly. And she knew she would be a Worthington Wife who had perfect happiness.

★ ★ ★ ★ ★

Acknowledgments

Many, many thanks to Allison Carroll, my editor for *The Worthington Wife*. Your enthusiasm for this story from the very beginning has inspired me and pushed me to make this book the very best it could be. From working back and forth with me on revisions when my life took a turn to brainstorming titles, you've been wonderful.

A huge thank-you to everyone at Harlequin and HQN. You have all put so much care and attention into this book. The lovely cover made me almost swoon with joy.

Also, thanks to my agent, Evan Marshall, for your support and for being there whenever needed.

I have to thank my family for putting up with a writer on deadline—and there are quite a few deadlines along the way to getting a book out in the world. Their faith and support have made me feel blessed.

And of course, thank you to all who read this story. It was always my dream to write about the Roaring Twenties, and I hope you enjoy the ride as much as I have.